CULTURES

of the

JEWS

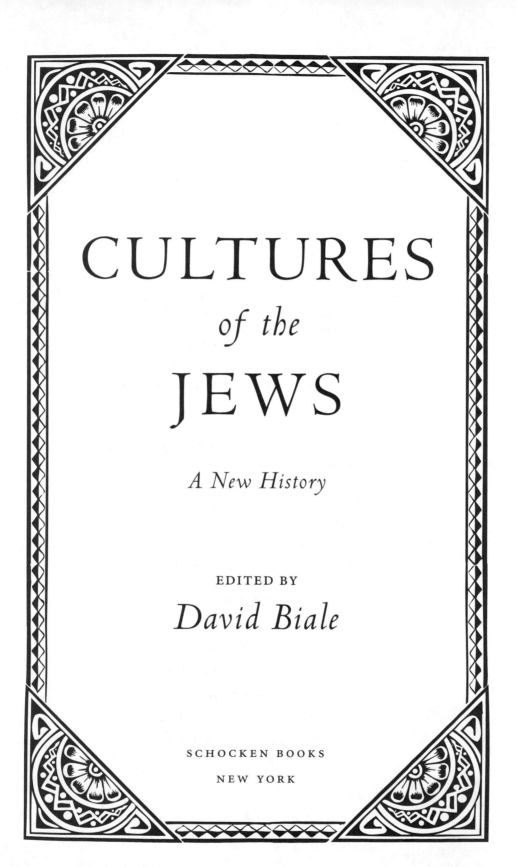

CULTURES

of the

JEWS

A New History

EDITED BY

David Biale

SCHOCKEN BOOKS

NEW YORK

All rights reserved under International and Pan-American Copyright
Conventions. Published in the United States by Schocken Books,
a division of Random House, Inc., New York, and simultaneously in
Canada by Random House of Canada Limited, Toronto. Distributed by
Pantheon Books, a division of Random House, Inc., New York.

Schocken and colophon are registered trademarks of Random House, Inc.

Grateful acknowledgment is made to the following for permission to reprint
previously published material:

The Sheep Meadow Press: Poem "Tefillin" from *Wild Light: Selected Poems of
Yona Wallach*, translated by Linda Zisquit. Reprinted by permission of Sheep
Meadow Press, Riverdale-on-Hudson, New York.

Steerforth Press: Excerpt from *Infiltration* by Yehoshua Kenaz. Reprinted by
permission of Steerforth Press, S. Royalton, VT., www.steerforth.com.

Library of Congress Cataloging-in-Publication Data

Cultures of the Jews : a new history / edited by David Biale.
p. cm.
Includes bibliographical references (p.).
ISBN 0-8052-4131-0
1. Jews—History.   2. Jews—Civilization.   3. Judaism—History.
I. Biale, David, 1949–

DS102.95 .C85 2002   909'.04924—dc21   2002023008

www.schocken.com

Book design by M. Kristen Bearse

Printed in the United States of America
First Edition
2   4   6   8   9   7   5   3   1

In memoriam

CONTENTS

Part Three
MODERN ENCOUNTERS

LIST OF CONTRIBUTORS

DAVID BIALE is Emanuel Ringelblum Professor of Jewish History and Director of the Program in Jewish Studies at the University of California, Davis.

RICHARD I. COHEN holds the Paulette and Claude Kelman Chair in French Jewry Studies, Department of Jewish History, The Hebrew University of Jerusalem.

REUVEN FIRESTONE is Professor of Medieval Judaism and Islam and director of the Graduate School of Judaic Studies at Hebrew Union College–Jewish Institute of Religion in Los Angeles.

ISAIAH GAFNI is Sol Rosenbloom Professor of Jewish History at The Hebrew University of Jerusalem.

BENJAMIN R. GAMPEL is Associate Professor of Jewish History at the Jewish Theological Seminary of America.

ERICH S. GRUEN is Gladys Rehard Wood Professor of History and Classics at the University of California, Berkeley.

RONALD HENDEL is the Norma and Sam Dabby Professor of Hebrew Bible and Jewish Studies at the University of California, Berkeley.

ARIEL HIRSCHFELD is Professor of Hebrew Literature at The Hebrew University of Jerusalem.

ELLIOTT HOROWITZ is Associate Professor of Jewish History at Bar-Ilan University.

ODED IRSHAI is Senior Lecturer in Jewish History at The Hebrew University of Jerusalem.

YOSEF KAPLAN is Professor of Jewish History at The Hebrew University of Jerusalem.

IVAN G. MARCUS is Frederick P. Rose Professor of Jewish History and Professor of History and Religious Studies at Yale University.

ERIC M. MEYERS is Bernice and Morton Lerner Professor of Judaic Studies and Director of the Graduate Program in Religion at Duke University.

ILANA PARDES teaches Comparative Literature at The Hebrew University of Jerusalem.

ARON RODRIGUE is Eva Chernov Lokey Professor in Jewish Studies and Professor of History at Stanford University.

MOSHE ROSMAN is Professor of Jewish History at Bar-Ilan University.

SHALOM SABAR is Professor of Art History at The Hebrew University of Jerusalem.

HAGAR SALAMON is Senior Lecturer at the Department of Jewish and Comparative Folklore and Research Fellow at the Harry S Truman Institute for the Advancement of Peace at The Hebrew University of Jerusalem.

RAYMOND P. SCHEINDLIN is Professor of Medieval Hebrew Literature at the Jewish Theological Seminary of America.

YOSEF TOBI is Professor of Hebrew Literature at the University of Haifa.

LUCETTE VALENSI is Directrice d'études and Directrice de l'Institut d'étude de l'Islam et des Sociétés du Monde Musulman at the École des Hautes Études en Sciences Sociales in Paris.

STEPHEN J. WHITFIELD is the Max Richter Professor of American Civilization at Brandeis University.

ELI YASSIF is professor and chair of the Department of Hebrew Literature at Tel Aviv University, where he teaches Jewish folklore and Hebrew literature of the Middle Ages.

ACKNOWLEDGMENTS

The contributors to this work deserve the greatest thanks, not only for their own contributions but also for serving as equal partners with the editor, assisting in the selection of other contributors, and making invaluable suggestions to improve the work as a whole. Meeting twice as the project evolved—once in Berkeley at an early stage and later in Jerusalem—the authors read and criticized one another's chapters in a quest to find common ground without stifling individual voices. Rare it is in the humanistic disciplines that scholars, instead of working in isolation, come together for a shared purpose.

A special session at the 2001 World Congress of Jewish Studies in Jerusalem, organized at the initiative of Moshe Rosman, produced a lively debate over the work's governing hypotheses about Jewish culture. In the context of that session, Moshe's perceptive and critical reading of my general introduction contributed greatly toward refining that portion of the manuscript.

The origins of this work go back to a telephone conversation in 1995 with Arthur Samuelson, then the editor-in-chief of Schocken Books. Together, we developed the basic outlines of the project. Arthur participated as a full equal in the first conference of contributors and made a signal contribution by encouraging the authors to envision an audience beyond the academy. Arthur was succeeded some years later by Susan Ralston, who played no less important an editorial role. Susan entered the scene as the contributors submitted their chapters and her razor-sharp editor's pencil turned academic prose into much more accessible writing. Her advice, support, and good humor were indispensable in producing a coherent book from what had been piles of pages.

The members of the Editorial Advisory Board, whose names are listed elsewhere in this book, made many useful suggestions at different stages of the project's development. Two of them, William Brinner and Steven Zipperstein, deserve to be singled out for contributions beyond the call of duty, including reading and commenting on some of the chapters.

Abe Socher served as the project's editorial assistant and made many valuable comments on early drafts of chapters. Joe Socher did yeoman's duty as source checker. Julia Johnson Zafferano's careful copyediting assured consistency in spelling and style throughout the manuscript. Dassi Zeidel, at Schocken, coordinated much of the project, including the collection of illustrations. Susan Smith and Kathleen van Sickle deserve special thanks for their assistance in preparing the manuscripts. Carol Cosman translated Lucette Valensi's chapter from French, Murray Rosovsky translated Yosef Tobi's from Hebrew, and Azzan Yadin translated Ariel Hirschfeld's chapter, also from Hebrew.

Two foundations supported this work. The Koret Foundation of San Francisco helped underwrite the conferences that brought the contributors together. The Maurice Amado Foundation of Los Angeles subsidized the chapters on Sephardic, North African, and Middle Eastern Jewish cultures.

—DAVID BIALE
January 2002

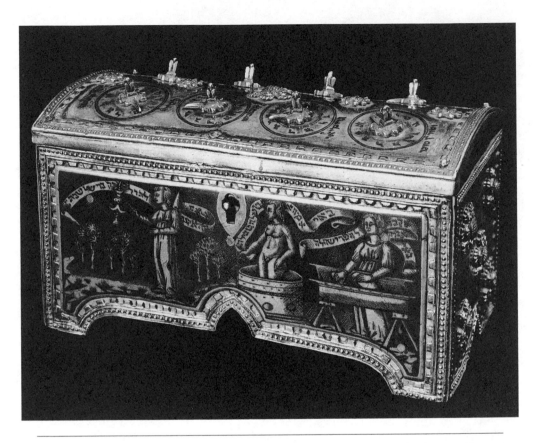

Cofanetto (small casket or box), Ferrara (?), second half of the fifteenth century. Silver. (The Israel Museum, Jerusalem)

PREFACE: TOWARD A CULTURAL HISTORY OF THE JEWS

DAVID BIALE

Sometime in the fifteenth century, a small silver casket was fashioned by an Italian Jewish craftsman known to us from his embossed signature on the lid as Jeshurun Tovar. The casket was intended as a wedding gift for a bride in northern Italy, probably to hold the keys to her linen closets.[1] On the lid of the casket are small dials indicating, in Hebrew numerals, quantities of different kinds of linen and clothing noted by their Italian names written in Hebrew characters: tablecloths, towels, men's shirts, women's chemises, handkerchiefs, knickers, and aprons or cloths for menstruation. It has been suggested that the purpose of this accounting system was to keep track of the items in characters unknown to the woman's Christian servants, although the Hebrew alphabet may also have been the only one that the woman or her Jewish servants could read. The nielloed front panel of the casket depicts three scenes of a Jewish wife fulfilling her cardinal religious duties: separating the ḥallah from the dough, lighting the Sabbath candles, and immersing herself in the ritual bath, which symbolized the separation of husband and wife during her menstrual period.[2]

What meaning does this intricate piece of craftwork have for understanding Jewish culture? Culture is an elastic term that can be stretched in many directions: indeed, the authors of the chapters in these volumes have each followed his or her own definitions. One way to define culture is as the manifold expressions—written or oral, visual or textual, material or spiritual—with which human beings represent their lived experiences in order to give them meaning.[3] But culture is more than just the literary or aesthetic products of a society. As one witty adage goes: "Culture is how we do things around here." From this point of view, culture is the practice of everyday life.[4] It is what people do, what they *say* about what they do, and, finally, how they understand both of these activities. If Jewish culture is broadly conceived along these lines, objects like the silver casket are as precious repositories of meaning as learned texts: the keys contained in it may unlock more doors than just those of linen closets. For example, the dresses worn by the three female figures on the casket are clearly similar to those worn in a somewhat earlier period in Italy by Christians as well as Jews. Yet the artistic themes themselves suggest a specifically Jewish culture. What, then, was the relationship between Jewish culture in that particular epoch and the culture of the non-Jews among whom the Jews lived? What can we learn from the casket about Jewish culture internally—especially, in this case, about the lives of Jewish women? Finally, can we speak of one Jewish culture across the ages or only Jewish cultures in the plural, each unique to its time and place? These are some of the questions that *Cultures of the Jews* will raise and attempt to answer.

The *Mekhilta,* one of the oldest rabbinic midrashim, tells us that the ancient Israelites were preserved as a distinct people in Egypt for four reasons: they kept their names; they maintained their language; they resisted violating the biblical sexual prohibitions (by which the midrash means that they did not intermarry); and they did not engage in "idle gossip" (*leshon ha-ra,* which the midrash understands as collaborating with the gentile government).[5] The *Mekhilta* nostalgically portrays the biblical Jews in Egypt as an "ideal" nation in exile. But from what we know of biblical times (and the Bible says nothing about the 430-year period in Egypt to which the midrash refers), this is an unhistorical portrait. Did the biblical Jews—or, more precisely, the Israelites, as they called themselves— resist foreign names, languages, and intermarriages? Quite the opposite. The name Moses itself is almost certainly of Egyptian origin; the Hebrew language borrowed its alphabet from the Phoenicians and is closely related to Ugaritic, the language of an earlier Canaanite culture (perhaps the earliest Hebrew ought to be called—tongue-in-cheek—"Judeo-Canaanite"); and the Bible is replete with intermarriages, from Joseph's marriage to the Egyptian Asnat to Bathsheba's marriage to Uriah the Hittite (not to speak of Solomon's many foreign wives). All the earmarks of "assimilation" can be found in the Bible itself.

Although it is not possible to date this rabbinic midrash precisely—it is probably from the late second or third century C.E.—the *Mekhilta's* cultural context was the Greco-Roman period, a period when all of these "prohibitions" were manifestly violated: Jews did adopt Greek names and the Greek language, intermarriage was not unknown, and some Jews did act as agents of or informers to the non-Jewish authorities. A stunning example of such interaction between Jewish and Greek culture was revealed in the excavations at Bet She'arim in the lower Galilee. An enormous third-century C.E. Jewish burial chamber at the site contains many sarcophagi decorated with a variety of mythological motifs, such as Leda and the swan, a favorite artistic theme from Greek mythology. Inscriptions in Greek are mixed with those in Hebrew. The Bet She'arim necropolis also contains the graves of rabbis contemporary with Judah the Prince, the compiler of the Mishnah, demonstrating that the cultural syncretism of the site was not alien to the rabbis themselves, despite the statements to the contrary in the *Mekhilta*. Did these Jews who shared a burial space—rabbis and others clearly of a wealthy class—believe in some fashion in the Greek myths portrayed on their tombs? Or, as seems more likely, were they adopting Greek motifs for their own purposes? What meaning did such images have for them, if not what they meant in Greek culture? Were they purely ornamental, or did the Jews graft onto them symbolic meanings consonant with their understanding of Jewish tradition?[6]

In the light of such findings as Bet She'arim, it is impossible to maintain the popular conception of rabbinic Judaism flourishing in splendid isolation from its Greco-Roman surroundings. We now know that the development of rabbinic culture involved the adaptation of legal principles and language from the Hellenistic and Roman worlds.[7] Although concerned with inoculating the Jews against contamination by pagan idolatry, the rabbis also made a clear distinction between images and idols. An image such as a statue of Aphrodite might be acceptable in a bathhouse but not in a pagan temple, where it functioned as an idol and was thus forbidden.[8] Similarly, Greek images might be incorporated into Jewish funerary practices, as at Bet She'arim, without this necessarily constituting adoption of their Greek meaning.

How should we label such adoption of non-Jewish culture? Does it suggest "assimilation" or, to use a less loaded term, "acculturation"? The Italian Jewish culture that produced our casket has frequently been described as one of the most assimilated or acculturated in all of pre-modern Jewish history. But perhaps the contemporary model of assimilation is misleading when applied to the Jews of Renaissance Italy.[9] Here was a traditional community intent on drawing boundaries between itself and its Christian neighbors but also able to adopt and adapt motifs from the surrounding culture for its own purposes. Indeed, the Jews should not be seen as outsiders who borrowed from Italian culture but rather as full participants in the shaping of that culture, albeit with their own concerns and mores. The Jews were not so much "influenced" by the Italians as they were one organ in a larger cultural organism, a subculture that established its identity in a complex process of adaptation and resistance. Jewish "difference" was an integral part of the larger mosaic of Renaissance Italy. Expanding beyond Renaissance Italy to Jewish history as a whole, we may find it more productive to use this organic model of culture than to chase after who influenced whom.

The findings at Bet She'arim—as well as our richly decorated silver casket—challenge another common misconception: that Jewish culture was hostile to the visual arts. The Jewish religion has traditionally been understood as a textual or written tradition in which visual images played a minor role at best. According to some interpretations, the second of the Ten Commandments, which prohibits all images of God, also prohibits, by extension, human images. But it is questionable whether such a prohibition ever really existed.[10] In the Middle Ages, illuminators of Jewish manuscripts were not shy about depicting human beings; the famous *Bird's Head Haggadah* and other Ashkenazic manuscripts from that period, in which people are portrayed with the heads of birds or other animals, are exceptions that prove the rule, and their meaning is still hotly debated.[11] Even within the textual tradition, there developed a particularly Jewish form of art, called micrography, in which the letters of a text were written in tiny characters that formed visual images.[12] In most cases, such as that of the casket, Jewish art involved an interaction between Jewish and non-Jewish motifs and artistic techniques. This interaction demonstrates how the culture of a minority group like the Jews can never be separated from that of the majority surrounding it.

Even in the earliest phases of Jewish history, the ancient Israelites were probably most often a minority among the Canaanite and other Near Eastern peoples who inhabited what the Bible itself calls "the Land of Canaan." In fact, the archaeological evidence suggests that many, if not most, of the Israelites were culturally and perhaps even ethnically descended from the Canaanites. As much as the authors of biblical monotheism tried to isolate the Israelite religion from the practices of their neighbors, it is now generally accepted among scholars of the biblical period that ancient Israel's cult, especially in its popular manifestations, was bound up with Canaanite polytheism.[13] The theological segregation of "Israelite" and "Canaanite" religions is just as mythic as the social and cultural segregation of the two peoples called "Israelite" and "Canaanite." The correct question may therefore not be the difference between "polytheism" and "monotheism" but rather how a theology that claims one, transcendent God nevertheless surreptitiously incorporated and transformed many of the elements of polytheism.

What was true for cult is true for culture. For every period of history, interaction with the non-Jewish majority has been critical in the formation of Jewish culture. Even those Jewish cultures thought to be the most insular adapted ideas and practices from their surroundings. A case in point are the medieval Ashkenazic Jews, whose culture is often considered to have been far more closed than the culture of the contemporaneous Sephardic Jews. Yet their spoken language was essentially that of their Christian neighbors. And, consider how the thirteenth-century German *Hasidim* (Pietists), whose ideals included segregation not only from Christians but also from nonpietistic Jews, adopted ascetic and penitential practices strikingly similar to those of the Franciscan Order from the same period.[14]

Rather than the *Mekhilta*'s explanation for why the Jews survived in exile—as well as in their own land—perhaps our supposition ought to be just the reverse: that it was precisely in their profound engagement with the cultures of their environment that the Jews constructed their distinctive identities. But this engagement involved two seeming paradoxes. On the one hand, the tendency to acculturate into the non-Jewish culture typically produced a distinctive Jewish subculture. On the other hand, the effort to maintain a separate identity was often achieved by borrowing and even subverting motifs from the surrounding culture.[15]

Language was one arena in which this complex process took place. Jews were remarkably adept at adopting the languages of their neighbors but also in reshaping those languages as Jewish dialects by adding Hebrew expressions: language was at once a sign of acculturation *and* cultural segregation. Yiddish, Ladino, and Judeo-Arabic (the latter is actually vernacular Arabic written in Hebrew characters) are the best known of these dialects, but there were many others. In the Greco-Roman world, Jews did not develop a Judeo-Greek, but they incorporated so many Greek words into both Hebrew and Aramaic that those languages, in Late Antiquity, must be considered "fusion" or "acculturated" languages (that is, languages strongly reflecting Greco-Roman culture).

The cases of Yiddish and Ladino are more complicated. Both started out as Jewish dialects of the local non-Jewish language: Middle High German (with some medieval French) for Yiddish, and Castilian Spanish for Ladino. But both took on a much more segregated quality when the Jews who spoke them migrated elsewhere. So, when the Ashkenazic or German Jews moved to Poland in the late Middle Ages, they did not develop a Judeo-Polish but rather absorbed some Slavic words into the Judeo-German that would come to be known as Yiddish. In Germany itself, the Jews continued to speak *ma'arav Yiddish* (Western Yiddish) into the early nineteenth century, long after the Germans themselves no longer spoke the German of the Middle Ages. Ladino was spoken by the Jews of the Iberian Peninsula, but it remained their language for half a millennium after the Expulsion in the Balkans, Greece, Turkey, and other areas of the Ottoman Empire; in these countries of "double exile," the Sephardim never developed Judeo-Greek or Judeo-Turkish. So, two processes were at work: first, intense linguistic acculturation in the early and high Middle Ages, and then, later, a kind of linguistic conservatism—the preservation of these earlier dialects as ever-more distinctive markers of difference from the surrounding cultures, at times even regarded as the "secret" languages of the Jews.

Only in modern times did the Diaspora Jewish languages begin to die out, replaced by the languages of the countries in which the Jews became citizens or by Hebrew, revived by the Zionist movement as a spoken language. Yet even in the

modern process of linguistic acculturation, one can discern Jewish inflections in
the way Jews wrote and spoke languages like German and English. In describing
the translation of the Bible into German that they published in the 1920s, Franz
Rosenzweig and Martin Buber used the word *Verdeutschung* rather than the
standard German word for translation *(Übersetzung)*.[16] *Verdeutschung* obviously
means "a rendering into German," but it is also the Yiddish word for both translation into Yiddish and commentary (*teitsh ḥumesh* means something like "the
Bible translated and explained in Yiddish"). It is doubly ironic that Yiddish refers
to itself as *teitsh*—that is, German—and to translation into Yiddish as "to render
into German." By using this rare German word with its Yiddish reverberations,
Rosenzweig and Buber were hinting that one goal of the Bible translation was
not so much to translate the Bible into "pure" German, as Martin Luther had,
but to infuse German with the intonations of the original Hebrew and thus
make it a "Jewish language." And they performed this linguistic magic with the
very word they chose to describe their project.

Linguistic adaptation was part of a larger strategy of resistance in which the
Jews asserted their identity in intimate interaction with the majority culture.
The study of indigenous groups living under colonialism has enriched our
understanding of how a politically subjugated people shapes its culture and
identity.[17] This process involves both defending one's native traditions *and* incorporating and transforming the culture imposed by the colonial power. Both
parties to these negotiations end up defining themselves through and against
the other. Although the situation of the Jews as a minority was not precisely
analogous to that of non-Western colonized peoples under Western imperialism, there is a similarity in the way Jewish identity developed in a rich dialectic
with the identities of the non-Jewish majority: the category of "Jew" assumed
and, indeed, produced the category *goy*.[18] The production of Jewish culture and
identity in such circumstances can never be separated from the power relations
between Jews and their neighbors.

A fascinating visual example of this process can be found in numerous Jewish
medieval illuminated manuscripts. In 1215, the Fourth Lateran Council required
that Jews wear identifying insignia, a piece of legislation purportedly motivated
by fears of sexual relations between Jews and Christians. Among the distinctive
forms of Jewish dress that one finds in the later Middle Ages is the hat, which assumed a variety of different shapes. In many Hebrew illuminated manuscripts,
the Jews are depicted wearing these hats as a matter of course.[19] If the intention
of the Christian rulers was to degrade the Jews, it seems evident from these pictures that the Jews did not feel degraded, for otherwise it is hard to imagine
why they portrayed themselves—or commissioned Christian artists to portray
them—wearing the distinctive hat in scenes of private or synagogue life. In a

later period, the age of emancipation, the Jewish hat came to be seen as humiliating. Yet, for the Jews of the Middle Ages, the way Christians commanded them to dress became badges of their own identity, as much a part of their culture depicted in these manuscripts as the sacred words on their pages.

The Jewish minority often adopted non-Jewish beliefs or practices but infused them with traditional Jewish symbols. For instance, the ritual—practiced widely in many different communities—of the first day of school, during which a young boy would eat honey in the shape of Hebrew letters, may have been enacted by the medieval Ashkenazic Jews in a way that responded to the new Christian dogma and rituals of the Eucharist.[20] And when the same Jews confronted the Crusaders in 1096 with a messianic theology of blood vengeance—a theology that led some to slaughter their own children and commit suicide in order to bring down the divine wrath on their persecutors—much of the language of blood, sacrifice, and atonement, although rooted in earlier Jewish sources, resonates with similar Christian concepts from the time.[21]

The example of the Crusades suggests that the Jews did not interact with the cultures of their non-Jewish neighbors only during peaceful times but also in times of conflict. While much of this violence flowed from the majority toward the minority, the street was not exclusively one-way. In the Middle Ages, Jews also utilized violence, sometimes real and sometimes symbolic, to enforce the boundaries that they, no less than Christians and Muslims, wished to maintain. A particular instance of such ritualized violence was the custom of hanging an effigy of Haman on a cross during Purim, thus demonstrating the Jews' contempt for Christianity.[22] Moreover, great cultural interchange, such as occurred during the so-called Golden Age of Spain (roughly 1000–1400), did not preclude such acts of real or symbolic violence.[23] Relations between the minority and the majority cultures cannot, therefore, be so easily categorized as either peaceful "symbiosis" or unrelieved antagonism, or, more broadly, as "golden ages" versus "dark ages."

Jewish self-definition was, then, bound up in a tangled web with the non-Jewish environment in which the Jews lived, at once conditioned by how non-Jews saw the Jews and by how the Jews adopted and resisted the majority culture's definition of them. For all that Jews had their own autonomous traditions, their very identities throughout their history were inseparable from that of their Canaanite, Persian, Greek, Roman, Christian, and Muslim neighbors. An old Arabic proverb claims that "Men resemble their own times more than the times of their fathers." Viewed in this light, Jewish identity cannot be considered immutable, the fixed product of either ancient ethnic or religious origins, but rather to have changed as the cultural context changed.

But if Jewish identity changed according to differing historical contexts, can we speak at all of *a* Jewish history, a common narrative stretching from the Bible, through the Hellenistic and rabbinic periods, the Muslim and Christian Middle Ages, and into the modern period? Is there or was there *one* Jewish people with one history? Is there or has there ever been one Jewish religion called Judaism? Both high literary culture and material culture, from the way Jews dressed to the way they looked and behaved, from their natural landscapes to the architecture of their homes and communal institutions, differed radically from period to period and place to place. Culture would appear to be the domain of the plural: we might speak of Jewish *cultures* instead of culture in the singular.

And, yet, such a definition would be missing a crucial aspect of Jewish culture: the continuity of both textual and folk traditions throughout Jewish history and throughout the many lands inhabited by the Jews. The multiplicity of Jewish cultures always rested on the Bible and—with the exception of the Karaites and the Ethiopian Jews—on the Talmud and other rabbinic literature. In the Middle Ages, philosophical, legal, exegetical, and mystical traditions added to the edifice built on earlier textual foundations. This extraordinary library became the cultural legacy not only of the legal authorities and intellectuals who produced it but also of the people as a whole, as defining of Jewish identity as the diverse cultural interactions of which we have already spoken. To be sure, the Jewish library cannot be reduced to a single "essence." As the work of the great historian of Jewish mysticism, Gershom Scholem (1897–1981), taught us, myth and magic occupy as much room on its shelves as law and philosophy: Jewish religion—and, more broadly, Jewish culture—contain the rational *and* the irrational.

As the *Mekhilta*'s ideal of national isolation and purity demonstrates, the Jews throughout the ages *believed* themselves to have a common national biography and a common culture.[24] These beliefs are also an integral part of the history of Jewish culture because their very existence made them as true as the historical "facts" that seem to contradict them. The history of other national groups suggests how complicated the relationship is between the belief in the unity of the nation and historical reality. The Germans and the French, for example, only really became united peoples with a common language in the nineteenth century (although the French had a much older unified state, whereas the Germans did not). Yet the *idea* of a common French or German identity long preceded the historical reality and, indeed, contributed toward creating this reality. In a similar way, we can speak of a dialectic between, on the one hand, the *idea* of one Jewish people and of a unified Jewish culture, and, on the other, the history of multiple communities and cultures.

The role of rabbinic law in Jewish history demonstrates how this dialectic worked. The development of rabbinic law often appears to follow its own inter-

nal logic, with a sixteenth-century authority debating a twelfth-century predecessor as if both were in the same room. The legal innovations of a particular authority, often couched to appear as if they were really present in an earlier text,
might seem to be utterly divorced from the culture, both Jewish and non-Jewish,
in which the authority lived. Yet between the lines of this ethereal discourse, one
often finds echoes of the external world, intruding and shaping the rulings of
judges and scholars. In addition, the rigid fences of the law typically bent to include local customs *(minhagim)*, unique to particular communities, which also
reflected historical developments. And if rabbinic law can be considered the
product of "elite" culture, "popular" culture exhibited the same dialectic: Jews
throughout the world shared common beliefs—as well as actual books—about
demons and how to ward them off. Yet these folk customs varied in their details
from place to place, often reflecting the practices of the surrounding non-Jewish
folk cultures. On both the elite and popular levels, then, the Jewish people were,
at once, one *and* diverse.

Let us return to our silver casket as a case in point. A particular detail in
the center of the frontal panel attracts our attention: the woman standing in the
barrel-shaped ritual bath is naked. Does the presence of a nude woman on this
object suggest that, following the predominant cultural values of the Italian Renaissance, the Jews of the time did not regard depiction of the unclothed human
body as immodest, religiously unacceptable, or, perhaps, even erotic? Or, perhaps it *was* considered erotic, since the bed linens indicated by the dials on top of
the box are connected with an act that Jewish law considered a suggestion of intimate marital relations: a wife making the bed for her husband (because during
her menstrual period she was not allowed to make the bed).[25] Might, then, this
image, appearing on a casket holding keys to the linen closet, serve to arouse her
(or her husband) sexually? What does the casket teach us about attitudes toward
the body among Italian Renaissance Jews? Was the woman who owned the casket aware of the discrepancy between rabbinic prohibitions of nudity and this
particular image? Was her understanding of the images on the casket the same as
that of her husband or of the casket's maker? What did the rabbinic authorities
of the day think of such depictions? Do we have evidence here of divisions
among the Italian Jews between a "secular" class and rabbinic authority or, perhaps, among the rabbis themselves?

Whatever the answers may be to these questions—and some will be found in
the chapter on Jewish culture in the Italian Renaissance—it would be a mistake
to assume that the maker and users of the casket necessarily intended to contradict the dictates of Jewish law. After all, the images were designed to remind the
woman of the house of the primary commandments of her religious life. Rather,

the cultural means by which people chose to represent and express rabbinic law changed from period to period and from context to context. Culture acted as a kind of expansive interpretation of the law, or, to put it differently, law was only one aspect of a wider culture that as much shaped the law after its own values as it was shaped by it. Instead of imagining an elite rabbinic culture coexisting perhaps uneasily with an opposing popular or nonlearned culture, we might see the two as much more tightly entangled with each other, for rabbis and other authorities often shared many of the cultural practices of the common folk, just as those who were not authorities incorporated "elite" culture into their own. The Talmud, for example, though the product of an elite class of rabbis in Palestine and Babylonia, contains much folklore, both Jewish and non-Jewish, suggesting that these rabbis were not walled off from the larger culture in which they lived. And in the Middle Ages the Talmud, while remaining a book studied by a small, male elect, came to shape popular Jewish culture, not only through its laws but also through its maxims and legends. While the terms "elite" and "popular" may still be useful in thinking about Jewish culture, it is equally important not to be seduced by such polar opposites and to recognize the common ground that existed between the two.

For the cultural historian, the intellectual elite does not exist in isolation, just as daily life does not remain in its own mute universe, unencumbered by intellectual reflection. Cultural history is an effort to see the connections between them. Those who produce cultural objects, whether written, visual, or material, can never be isolated from the larger social context, the everyday world, in which they live, just as those who belong to this larger world are not immune to the ideas and symbolic meanings that may be articulated by intellectuals. The relationship between text and context ought rather to be seen as the relationship between different types of texts, rather than between the "ideas" of elites versus the "material" reality of the wider society.[26] At times, those among the uneducated mobilized ideas, perhaps derived from old, subterranean traditions, to subvert the dominant discourse.[27] In the Jewish sphere, one might turn to folklore for such traditions or to the rabbinic responsa literature, which can provide not only a history of legal precedents and case law but also evidence of the actual beliefs and practices of Jews who lived their lives outside the *bet midrash* (the study hall) and the *bet din* (the rabbinic court), perhaps even in opposition to these venerable institutions.

An example of such subversion and of the complex relations between rabbinic and nonrabbinic culture for the same period as our silver casket are two prayer books copied by one of the leading rabbis of the day, Abraham Farissol. The first was commissioned by a man for his wife in Ferrara in 1478, and the second was ordered by a married woman in Mantua in 1480. In both cases, the morning blessings—when men traditionally thank God for "not making me a woman" and women thank God for making them "according to His will"— contain a radical revision: the prayer thanks God "for making me a woman and not a man."[28] Whose decision was it in the first case to change the blessings: the man who commissioned the work, or his wife? How did the woman in the second case decide to make this revision, and did she have the approval of her husband? We know nothing about the negotiations between the wealthy patrons and the learned rabbi who copied the books. Did Farissol resist the revision or, alternatively, did he perhaps suggest it? What more do these objects tell us about attitudes toward Jewish women in Renaissance Italy among the wealthy classes and among the rabbis? And, what meaning—if any—ought we assign to the fact that someone at a later point erased the names of the patrons from the title pages of the books?

Both the silver casket and these prayer books were objects intended for use by women. Introducing gender into the study of Jewish history is one way of including alternative voices and extending the scope of our inquiry from high or learned culture to the culture of everyday life. These objects suggest a cultural matrix for Italian Jewish women in the Renaissance that may have differed significantly from that of men of the time, but also from that of Jewish women in other periods and places. The woman who commissioned the prayer book was clearly educated enough to read Hebrew, as was the woman who owned the casket. Such details allow us to reconstruct at least some aspects of Jewish women's lives and thus to portray Jewish culture as much more diverse and heterogeneous than one might conclude from a study of rabbis or other learned men. Another example is the rich body of literature, written in Yiddish, that provided women with private prayers (tehines) about issues, such as the three cardinal commandments or conception and childbirth, specifically germane to their lives.[29]

Cultures of the Jews is therefore shaped by a broad definition of culture. As we have seen, this approach challenges such conventional distinctions as "unity" versus "diversity," "textual continuity" versus "cultural ruptures," "monotheism" versus "polytheism," "isolation" versus "assimilation," "golden ages" versus "dark ages," and "elite" versus "popular." Jewish history consisted of all these centripetal and centrifugal forces, and each coexisted with its opposite, to the point where the very opposition between them appears artificial and overly simplistic. More than just expanding our story to include what has been neglected, we will question these very dichotomies.

There is yet one more dichotomy that we need to examine: the opposition between "Homeland" and "Exile." The belief in a "Promised Land," the Land of Israel, lies at the core of the biblical narrative and subsequent Jewish thought; it is this belief, in barely secularized form, that animated the Zionist movement in its reestablishment of the Jewish state. Yet the Bible itself oscillates between the two. The Book of Genesis starts with exile from the Garden of Eden, and Abraham, almost immediately after arriving in the Land of Israel, goes "down" to Egypt. Exile and Return are the recurring motifs of the biblical text.[30] And, as we shall see repeatedly in this work, the Jews of many Diaspora communities, while holding onto the messianic vision of return to the Land, often saw in their own countries a remembrance of an ideal past and a taste of that messianic future: so it was that the Lithuanian Jews referred to Vilna as "the Jerusalem of Lithuania." So, too, the Jews of the Greco-Roman Diaspora, Sassanian Babylonia, Muslim al-Andalus, Christian Spain, and contemporary America seemed to feel at home in exile.

Even the modern return of the Jews to their historic homeland and the restoration of Jewish political sovereignty have not definitively resolved this dialectic between Land and Exile. The "national poet" of the Zionist movement, Ḥayyim Naḥman Bialik, perhaps the last person we might expect to endorse life in exile, described in an essay written in 1922 what he called the "Jewish dualism" of expansion and contraction, wandering and returning. He concludes with a startling prophecy:

> After wandering for thousands of years and after endless changes and re-evaluations . . . after influencing the whole world and being influenced by it, we are now, for the third or fourth time, once again returning to our land. And here we are destined to fashion a culture sevenfold greater and richer than any we have heretofore created or absorbed. And who knows? Perhaps after hundreds of years we will be emboldened to make another exodus that will lead to the spreading of our spirit over the world and an assiduous striving towards glory.[31]

Rather than an end to Jewish wandering, the new nation of Israel may be only the latest phase in an eternal cycle of leaving and returning, Homeland and Diaspora. This, too, is an enduring theme in the cultural history of the Jews.

The ambiguous relationship today between Homeland and Exile, foreshadowed by Bialik, finds concrete expression in this work. For the first time, a collaborative history of the Jews includes an equal number of scholars from Israel and the Diaspora. Moreover, the lines between the two seem increasingly fuzzy. Many of the Israeli scholars were born and educated in the Diaspora (particularly the United States and Canada), while others born in Israel received their training in universities abroad. And, virtually all of the scholars currently based in the Diaspora have spent considerable periods in Israel, studying, teaching, or doing research. Jewish Studies as a field has become "globalized" and, though differences surely remain, the categories of Israel and Diaspora no longer occupy the central place in scholarly agendas they once held.

In the chapters that follow, scholars from many disciplines—archaeology, art history, ancient Near Eastern studies, cultural history, literary studies, and folklore—offer their answers to the questions raised in this introduction. Just as culture itself consists of many dimensions and facets, so there are many windows through which scholars may try to view this imprecise object of study. Instead of following one ironclad set of guidelines, each has been free to approach the subject with his or her own particular tools. The sum total of their diverse efforts constitutes a better or more approximate definition of Jewish cultures than does any one chapter.

This enterprise certainly does not exhaust its subject. For every major cultural formation discussed in these pages, a multitude of other approaches and other sources would be equally legitimate. Similarly, the reader should not expect to find an encyclopedia, with entries for every Jewish culture. We have attempted to identify the most significant and original cultures, often by subsuming regional variations under broader headings. The authors were also encouraged to frame their chapters with specific examples—a text, an artifact, or an anecdote—and undertake a "thick description" of them, as with our example of the Italian silver casket.

The questions we have posed in this study of Jewish culture are hardly new, and, indeed, every generation of scholars has asked them in one form or another. But the answers have not always been the same, because every generation weaves its image of the past out of the cloth of its present. In the past half-century, there have been two great, multivolume collaborative histories of the Jews, each a product of its own time and place. In the late 1940s, Louis Finkelstein of the Jewish Theological Seminary edited *The Jews: Their History, Religion and Contribution to Civilization.* The third volume of Finkelstein on the contribution of Jews to civilization takes an expansive view of culture, but it is primarily concerned with what its title suggests—the Jewish *contribution*—rather than with the mutual interaction between Jewish and non-Jewish cultures. Finkelstein makes it clear that he believes that the primary Jewish contribution to civilization was in religion, a view that dominates his understanding of Jewish culture and reflects rather accurately the self-definition of American Jewry in the late 1940s.

In the late 1960s, Haim Hillel Ben-Sasson edited *A History of the Jewish People*, three volumes written exclusively by scholars from the Hebrew University, published first in Hebrew and subsequently in English. The Ben-Sasson volumes are characterized by a distinct, if muted, nationalist teleology, reflecting the post-1967 atmosphere in Israel. Thus, Shmuel Ettinger, who wrote the chapter on modern Jewish history, concludes with the State of Israel. The authors emphasize the historical continuity of Jewish identity. In Ettinger's words: "One cannot overemphasize the tremendous force of historical continuity and of enduring conscious historical existence.... The Holocaust and the State of Israel are indisputable testimony to the fact that ... the communal and national uniqueness [of the Jews] has never ceased to be significant." Although some of the authors, notably Ben-Sasson in his medieval chapter, investigate cultural interaction, the work as a whole conveys a sense of Jewish difference and isolation.

Both of these collaborative histories were notably deficient in their treatment of the Ladino-speaking Diaspora and, especially in the modern period, of the Jewish communities of North Africa and the Middle East. Despite chapters on the Jews of Arab lands in the Middle Ages, these works were highly Eurocentric, reflecting the dominant intellectual tendencies of their times. This is a deficiency we have taken pains to correct. For the first time, these Jewish communities receive their due, a corrective that is particularly important given the growing influence of North African and Middle Eastern Jews on the politics and culture of the State of Israel.

The present work is also the product of a particular time. Ours is a self-conscious age, when we raise questions about old ideologies and "master" narratives and no longer assume as unchanging or monolithic categories like "nation" and "religion." Teleologies, whether national or religious, are harder to sustain, just as categories that were foundational for previous generations, such as Homeland and Exile, have lost their ideological edge. We have become acutely aware—and critical—of how we use these categories to construct the past; instead of accepting them as immutable and given, we try to see them too as products of historical contexts. We are conscious, perhaps more than any earlier generation, of how our contemporary culture and commitments influence the ways we view our historical subjects.

Our silver casket may once again demonstrate this point. As cultural historians, we are aware that we are viewing an object not intended for public display, which is its fate today in the Israel Museum. Perhaps the nudity of the woman portrayed in her ritual bath excited no curiosity or controversy when it was made precisely because the casket was intended for private, female use. Just as the Hebrew lettering on the lid may have been used to hide the number and type of the woman's linens from her Christian servants, so the casket itself, despite its revealing nakedness, is a kind of repository of secrets. We are like voyeurs peering into a world not our own and asking questions that are peculiarly modern. The cultural historian cannot ignore the gap that separates his or her investigations from the lived reality of those people—educated and uneducated, rich and poor, male and female—who have left us such artifacts. Our concerns may not have been theirs.

The task of the contemporary historian of Jewish culture is, then, paradoxical: to find commonalties between the past and present, but also to preserve all that is different and strange in that past. The singularly modern questions of Jewish identity—what is it that defines a Jew and where are the borders between what is and is not Jewish—preoccupy each of us as we reconstruct the variety of Jewish cultures. What it meant to be a Jew in biblical Canaan, Hellenistic Alexandria, sixteenth-century Poland, or nineteenth-century Morocco was certainly not the same as what it is today, nor were the questions we pose necessarily their questions. But by refracting our study of cultures past through such modern questions, those cultures appear at once more familiar *and* more alien. And by looking in the mirrors of the many and diverse Jewish cultures over the centuries, we may hope to see reflections of who the Jews were, what they are now, and, perhaps, some shards that they may use in fashioning what they will become.

NOTES

1. For a description of the casket, see Mordecai Narkis, "An Italian Silver Casket of the Fifteenth Century," *Journal of the Warburg and Courtland Institutes* 21 (1958): 288–95. See also Vivian Mann, *Gardens and Ghettos: The Art of Jewish Life in Italy* (Berkeley, 1989), 309–10; Elias Bickerman, "Symbolism in the Dura Synagogue," *Harvard Theological Review* 58, no. 1 (1965): 131–32; and Shalom Sabar, "Bride, Heroine and Courtesan: Images of the Jewish Woman in Hebrew Manuscripts of the Renaissance in Italy," *Proceedings of the Tenth World Congress of Jewish Studies*, Division D, vol. 2 (1990): 67.

2. The source for these commandments is m. Shabbat 2.6, which presents them negatively by stating that women die in childbirth for transgressions of these three laws. It should be noted that men are also subject to these laws. See Rachel Biale, *Women and Jewish Law* (New York, 1984), 40.

3. See Clifford Geertz, *The Interpretation of Cultures* (New York, 1973). For some critiques and expansions of Geertz, see Sherry B. Ortner, ed., *The Fate of Culture: Geertz and Beyond* (Berkeley, 1999), and James Clifford, *The Predicament of Culture: Twentieth-Century Ethnography, Literature, and Art* (Cambridge, Mass., 1988).

4. See Michel de Certeau, *The Practice of Everyday Life,* trans. Steven Rendall (Berkeley, 1984), and Michel de Certeau, *Culture in the Plural,* trans. Tom Conley (Minneapolis, 1997).

5. *Mekhilta,* Bo, parasha 5. The saying appears in a number of places in various forms in rabbinic literature: e.g., *Leviticus Rabba* 32.5; *Numbers Rabba* 13.19 and 20.22; Song of Songs Rabba 24.25, and *Tanhuma,* Balak 16.

6. For one view emphasizing a kind of mystical Judaism, see Erwin Goodenough, *Jewish Symbols in the Greco-Roman Period,* vols. 1–13 (New York, 1953–68). For a critique of Goodenough, see Bickerman, "Symbolism."

7. See Saul Lieberman, *Greek in Jewish Palestine,* 2d ed. (New York, 1965).

8. M. Avodah Zara 3.4. See the discussion of this problem in the chapter by Eric Meyers in Part I.

9. Roberto Bonfil has made a cogent case for this position in his *Jewish Life in Renaissance Italy,* trans. Anthony Oldcorn (Berkeley, 1994).

10. See Cecil Roth, *Jewish Art: An Illustrated History,* rev. ed. (London, 1971); Therese and Mendel Metzger, *Jewish Life in the Middle Ages: Illuminated Jewish Manuscripts of the Thirteenth to the Sixteenth Centuries* (New York, 1982); and Kalman Bland, *The Artless Jew: Medieval and Modern Affirmations and Denials of the Visual* (Princeton, 2000).

11. Ruth Mellinkoff has argued recently that such depictions of Jews were inserted by anti-Jewish Christian illuminators. See her *Antisemitic Hate Signs in Hebrew Illuminated Manuscripts from Medieval Germany* (Jerusalem, 1999). It seems hard to believe that the Jewish patrons who commissioned such works would have accepted these depictions if they were truly antisemitic. Nevertheless, Mellinkoff is convincing, following other Jewish art historians, in showing that there was no rabbinic prohibition on portraying the human face that might have led to the use of animal heads. The mystery remains unsolved.

12. See Stanley Ferber, "Micrography: A Jewish Art Form," *Journal of Jewish Art* 3–4 (1977): 12–24.

13. For a recent example, see Susan Ackerman, *Under Every Green Tree: Popular Religion in Sixth Century Judah* (Atlanta, 1992).

14. F. Y. Baer, "The Religious-Social Tendency of 'Sepher Hasidim' " (Hebrew), *Zion* 3, no. 1 (1938): 1–50.

15. See Marc Michael Epstein's fascinating study, *Dreams of Subversion in Medieval Jewish Art and Literature* (University Park, Pa., 1997).

16. See Martin Buber, *Die Schrift und ihre Verdeutschung* (Berlin, 1936), which contains essays by both Buber and Rosenzweig on the Bible translation.

17. See the collection of essays edited by Bill Ashcroft, Gareth Griffiths, and Helen Tiffin, *The Post-Colonial Studies Reader* (London, 1995).

18. See my "Confessions of an Historian of Jewish Culture," *Jewish Social Studies,* n.s. 1, no. 1 (Fall 1994): 40–51.

19. See an especially striking case in the *Bird's Head Haggadah:* one of the pages illustrating the "Dayanu" shows the Israelites in the desert collecting manna and receiving the law.

All have birds' heads on which are perched typical "Jew's hats." See the reproduction in Bazalel Narkis, *Hebrew Illuminated Manuscripts* (Jerusalem, 1969), 96–97. Another example in which human faces are shown with at least one figure wearing a "Jew's hat" at a Passover Seder is the *Darmstadt Haggadah* in ibid., 126–27. For a pictorial collection of such headgear, see "Head, Covering of the" in the *Encyclopaedia Judaica*. See also Raphael Straus, "The Jewish Hat as Cultural History," *Jewish Social Studies* 4 (1942): 59.

20. See Ivan G. Marcus, *Rituals of Childhood: Jewish Culture and Acculturation in the Middle Ages* (New Haven, Conn., 1996), as well as his chapter in Part II of this work.

21. See Yisrael Yuval, "Vengeance and Damnation, Blood and Defamation: From Jewish Martyrdom to Blood Libel Accusations" (Hebrew), *Zion* 58, no. 1 (1993): 33–90.

22. See Elliott Horowitz, "The Rite to Be Reckless: On the Perpetration and Interpretation of Purim Violence," *Poetics Today* 15, no. 1 (Spring 1994): 9–54. See also his *Reckless Rites* (Princeton, 2001).

23. See David Nirenberg, *Communities of Violence: Persecution of Minorities in the Middle Ages* (Princeton, 1996).

24. See Ilana Pardes, *The Biography of Ancient Israel: National Narratives in the Bible* (Berkeley, 2000), and her chapter in Part I of this volume.

25. See the discussion in b. Ketubot 61a.

26. See Dominick LaCapra, *Rethinking Intellectual History: Texts, Contexts, Language* (Ithaca, N.Y., 1983), 116–17. LaCapra suggests that the relationship between ideas and context ought to be drawn using theories of intertextuality, since even the context is itself composed of texts.

27. Carlo Ginzburg, *The Cheese and the Worms: The Cosmos of a Sixteenth-Century Miller,* trans. John and Ann Tedeschi (Baltimore, Md., 1980).

28. The manuscripts are, respectively, 1478=JTSA MIC. 8255 (ms. JMC 16), 5b and 1480=JNUL 8°5492, 7a. See David Ruderman, *The World of a Renaissance Jew: The Life and Thought of Abraham Ben Mordecai Farissol* (Cincinnati, 1981), appendix, and Shalom Sabar, "Bride, Heroine and Courtesan," 68. I thank Sabar for drawing the text from the Jewish Theological Seminary Library to my attention. My student Yoel Kahn will be publishing his own study of these manuscripts in a work on the history of the morning blessings. Based on his examination of the manuscripts, he has concluded that the one from 1478 was written by Farissol, whereas the new version of the words in the one from 1480 was written in a different hand.

29. See Chava Weissler, *Voices of the Matriarchs* (Boston, 1998).

30. See Arnold Eisen, *Galut* (Bloomington, Ind., 1986).

31. Translation in Ḥayyim Naḥman Bialik, *Revealment and Concealment: Five Essays* (Jerusalem, 2000), 43–44. See also the afterword by Zali Gurevitch in which he describes Bialik as "the poet of exile."

Part One

MEDITERRANEAN

ORIGINS

INTRODUCTION TO PART ONE:
MEDITERRANEAN ORIGINS

DAVID BIALE

When and where does the first Jewish culture begin? Two deceptively simple questions whose answers remain shrouded in the mists of ancient Near Eastern history. Our sources are the Hebrew Bible and archaeological evidence, but these sources raise as many questions as they answer. The earliest mention of ancient Israel appears on a stele or victory monument of the Pharaoh Merneptah in the second half of the thirteenth century B.C.E. There the pharaoh boasts: "Israel is laid waste, his seed is no more." An inauspicious beginning for a people that was to last over three millennia after their proclaimed extermination! From this point on, the archaeological record becomes murky: we possess no external evidence of the Exodus from Egypt and ambiguous evidence for the subsequent conquest of Canaan. The archaeologists tell us that the material culture of ancient Israel differed little, if at all, from that of the Canaanites who inhabited the coastal plain; some have concluded that the Israelites *were* Canaanites who lived in the hill country between the Jordan River and the Mediterranean. According to this hotly contested opinion, the Exodus was a myth, because the Israelites never left the Land of Canaan.

And what of the Bible, which tells the familiar story of Abraham, whom God commands to leave Ur of the Chaldeans and go to the land of the Canaanites, whose possession he is promised? Does this mean that the "children of Israel," as they would later call themselves after the second name of Abraham's grandson, Jacob, originated in the fertile plains of Mesopotamia? The stories of the three patriarchs and their four wives certainly suggest such a connection. But then the Bible offers contradictory evidence. A gap of 400 (or, in another tradition, 430) years separates the Genesis stories from the emergence of the Israelite nation from slavery in Egypt. Why does the book that the Israelites themselves wrote— based, no doubt, on ancient traditions—contain no trace of memory for such a long period? Could it be that the stories of the patriarchs and matriarchs were independent tales added later to give a new and, even worse, a "slave" nation some venerable antiquity? The Exodus story itself admits that the nation left

Egypt as a "mixed multitude" (Exodus 12:38), the very opposite of an ethnic or tribal group with a common lineage. Much later, the prophet Ezekiel would thunder: "By origin and birth you are from the land of the Canaanites—your father was an Amorite and you're a Hittite" (Ezekiel 16:3).

These texts raise as many questions as do the archaeologists. Why would a nation preserve as canonical admissions of such a tainted genealogy? If the Exodus was a myth, why would a nation invent such a disreputable story of slave origins? If all nations are "imagined communities," ancient Israel has left us evidence of a very conflicted imagination. Certain real historical events may well underlie what some dismiss as literary myth. History and literature cannot be so easily separated.

If, additionally, a culture is determined by the borders between "us" and "them," the culture of biblical Israel was very poorly defended, because, even as the nation was commanded to eradicate its neighbors ("you must doom them to destruction: grant them no terms and give them no quarter"—Deuteronomy 7:2), both persons and ideas from those neighbors persistently appear and reappear in the Bible. An example is Uriah the Hittite, David's general and the first husband of Bathsheba, who, once David had Uriah killed in battle, became David's wife and was the mother of King Solomon. What was a Hittite doing as a general in David's army if, as Deuteronomy 7 prescribes, the Hittites should have been exterminated? Why does he have a name that suggests that he worships the God of Israel? And David himself, the great-grandson of a Moabite woman, would also, according to a Deuteronomic law, have been forbidden to enter "the assembly of God." These examples suggest that the boundaries between Israelites and non-Israelites in the Land of Canaan were evidently much fuzzier than we have traditionally believed. Categories of "ethnicity" and "religion" may have meant something very different then than they mean to us now.

To compound our difficulties, the biblical text itself—or, better, the disparate and manifold collection of texts that we call the Bible—was not edited into the form we have it until much later than the events it narrates. Even if, as seems very likely, it was based on much older sources, it was not until after the destruction of the First Temple in 586 B.C.E., the Babylonian Exile, and the building of the Second Temple (probably mid-fifth century B.C.E.) that the texts were compiled and canonized. The Bible as we know it is a document of the Second Temple period, but exactly when it was redacted remains a mystery. So, to speak of the culture of ancient or biblical Israel immediately raises the question of whether we are talking about the *actual* culture of those Israelites described in the Bible, or, conversely, about how their culture was *imagined* by later generations.

Since no single answer to this question will suffice, the first two chapters of Part I approach the task with different sets of tools. Ilana Pardes takes the first six books of the Bible (the Torah plus Joshua) as the narrative expression of ancient Israel's history, regardless of when it was written or of how many sources it was composed. It is this collective biography that defines the Israelite nation— as well as the later Jewish people—but it is filled with conflict and contradiction. Ronald Hendel comes to a similar conclusion but from a consideration of ancient Israel in its Near Eastern context, at once an organic part of its neighborhood but also insistent on its uniqueness. Israelite and Canaanite cultures overlapped greatly, which was perhaps the reason that the Bible insisted so strongly on separating them.

The redaction of the Bible took place during the period when the Israelites became known as Jews, the inhabitants of *Yahud,* or Judaea. Who exactly were these Judaeans? The Second Temple period begins with Ezra the Scribe, who proclaims a ban on intermarriage between those who returned from the Babylonian Exile and the "peoples of the land." Some of these peoples were undoubtedly non-Israelites, but others, such as the Samaritans, believed themselves to be descendants of ancient Israel and worshipped, as their few surviving members do even today, the God of Israel. For Ezra, however, a Jew was a descendant of those who had gone into exile and returned, and he permitted none of the easy boundary crossing that evidently had taken place in the period of the First Temple. Ezra proclaimed an ethnic or even biological definition of the Jews, as a "holy seed" *(zera kodesh)*. Yet his attempt at ethnic "purity" was honored more in the breach, because many who remained in exile or Diaspora, whether in Babylonia or Egypt, also considered themselves to be Jews. And a few centuries later, the Hasmonaean or Maccabean kingdom conquered and converted various peoples to the Jewish religion/nation. In fact, the evolution of a strict procedure of conversion probably began at this time and was finally codified by the rabbis in the second century C.E.

Thus, to be a Jew in antiquity involved elaborate juggling of religious, ethnic, and political affirmations. It meant that one worshipped the God who, unlike all the other gods, had no visual representation (which led some ancient "antisemites" to hold that the Jews were atheists, since their god could not be seen). It meant that one considered oneself an ethnic descendant of the ancient tribes of Israel even if, like King Herod, one's real ancestors were Edomites. And it meant one was a subject of a Jewish government in Jerusalem, though not if one lived outside of the Land of Israel (whose very borders, then no less than today, were never stable). The complexity of Jewish identity in the Second Temple period, and even later, rivals that of the modern age.

It was the encounter with the powerful culture of Hellenism that challenged the Jews to define themselves culturally. Unlike other imperialistic powers in the ancient world, the Greeks created a truly cosmopolitan or, in today's terms, a globalized culture: it was not necessary to be an ethnic Greek to partake of and identify with this culture. The process by which the Jews met this challenge was no less complex than the way they interacted with the earlier Canaanite cultures. Despite their own professions and the views of some outsiders, the Jews did not isolate themselves from this world culture but rather used its very riches to cultivate their singularity. Greece and Rome were, to be sure, at times the Jews' political and military enemies, but, culturally, there were startling similarities between them. Like the Romans, the Jews nourished a story of their origins that involved a lengthy journey, led by a hero, that eventually brought them to a new land that was also their ancestral patrimony. Like the Greeks, the Jews considered themselves an ethnic group, clearly distinguishable from the *barbaroi* (barbarians). But like the Greeks after Alexander's conquest of the Near East, and like the Romans later, they did not believe that their culture could only flourish on its native soil. Just as Hellenism and Roman culture might be transplanted to the far reaches of those empires, so the Jews, without an empire, scattered the seeds of their religion and culture throughout the Mediterranean basin, in part as they themselves migrated but also in part (the extent of which remains contested) by proselytism.

Once again, two chapters take up these themes: Erich Gruen considers the vast literature that the Jews produced primarily in Greek, and Eric Meyers weaves archaeological evidence from Palestine in the Persian to the Greco-Roman periods with the Hebrew and Aramaic literature produced by priests, rabbis, and other literati. In both material and literary culture, the confrontation with Hellenism produced new forms of Jewish culture and identity. The emphasis here is on the plural—*forms*—since the period was one of great pluralism, even factionalism, as dissident groups, such as the Dead Sea or Qumran communities, challenged the priestly establishment in Jerusalem, and as Diaspora communities, though still tied religiously to Jerusalem, experimented with their own interpretations of tradition. These new interpretations were not so much *influenced* by Greco-Roman culture as they were *part and parcel* of that culture.

It is frequently assumed that, with the destruction of the Second Temple by the Romans during the Great Jewish Revolt of 66–70 C.E., the fragmentation and diversity of the earlier period came to an end as the rabbis consolidated their hold on the definition of Jewishness. Although the destruction of the Temple was an event of enormous religious and political consequence, its cultural significance is less clear. The culture of the "rabbinic" period in Palestine continued to be dominated by Hellenism, and it did not lose its contentious diversity. The very term "rabbinic period" must be set in quotation marks, for it is only in historical hindsight that the rabbis loom so large. For many centuries, first under pagan Rome and then under Byzantine Christianity, the culture of the Jews reflected active interaction with both of these cultures. As in the Second Temple period, the question of what it meant to be a Jew might be answered in a variety of ways, despite the attempts by the rabbis to standardize identity.

Three chapters take up the diversity of Jewish culture in the period of Late Antiquity. Oded Irshai considers how the Jews of Palestine, still a sizable population, especially in the Galilee, responded to living for the first time under Christian rule, and how the boundaries between Judaism and Christianity continued to be quite porous. Isaiah Gafni takes up the culture of the Jews of Babylonia, an ancient community, as we have already noted, but one that began to feel a sense of its own intellectual and religious authority as the Palestinian Jewish community declined under Roman and Byzantine domination. It was these two communities that produced the two versions of the Talmud, the Babylonian and Jerusalem (or Palestinian). But a full understanding of the culture of these Jews requires going beyond the views of the rabbinic elite to consider other cultural centers, such as the synagogue, or the voices of the folk, preserved in rabbinic literature, and for whom rabbinic teachings may not yet have been normative. As an example of such an "alternative" Jewish culture that flourished far from the orbit of the Babylonian and Palestinian rabbis, Reuven Firestone treats the Jews of Arabia, the first to come into contact and confrontation with emerging Islam in the seventh century. Here, too, Jewish identity turns out to have been an intricate mixture of tribalism and religion, and Jewish culture was influenced by and also influenced that of the new Muslim religion.

A certain thematic unity therefore links the earliest with the latest Jewish cultures discussed in this volume, as the Jews in various contexts defined how they were different by using the very language and practices of their surroundings. Yet, unlike other ancient ethnic groups, the Jews had some singular qualities: although many others combined national and religious components in their identities, only the Jews—like Christians and Muslims—eventually came to worship a God who negated the existence of other gods. And the Jews developed a unique procedure for conversion to the Jewish *ethnos,* a possibility unknown to the ancient pagans, for whom an ethnic identity could not be adopted, even if one paid obeisance to a foreign god. "Jewishness" (an ethnic identity) came increasingly to be identified with "Judaism" (a religious credo), the latter probably developing in dialogue with nascent Christianity and leaving its mark on early Islam. Jewish culture at the end of our period thus made major contributions to the politics of ancient identity as Christians and Muslims came to dominate the Mediterranean basin, a domination that concludes Part I and becomes central to Part II.

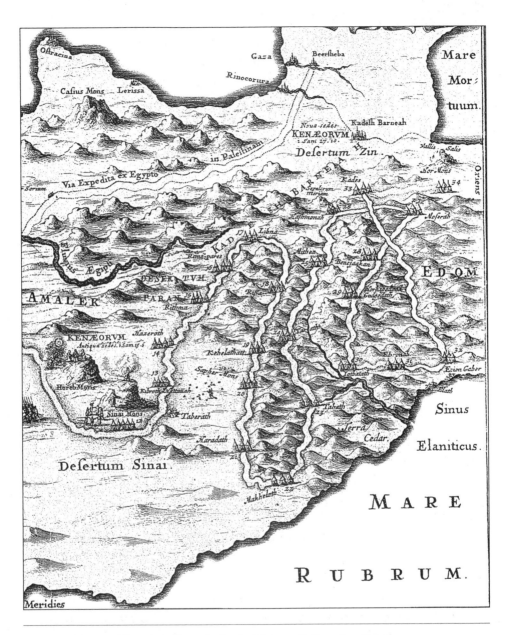

The map of wandering by Thomas Fuller, 1650. Detail.
(Courtesy Ilana Pardes)

ONE

IMAGINING THE BIRTH OF ANCIENT ISRAEL:

National Metaphors in the Bible

ILANA PARDES

The Bible begins not with the culture of the Hebrews but with the origins of culture as such. The initial concern with the origin of civilization is already evident in the story of the Garden of Eden, where Eve and Adam acquire the first taste of "knowledge," but it is only in the account of the bold building of the Tower of Babel, East of Eden, that we get a fuller consideration of human culture. Humankind was once one, we are told, and "everyone on earth had the same language and the same words" (Genesis 11:1). But this era of cultural unity does not last for long. One day the people say to each other "Come, let us build us a city, and a tower with its top in the sky, to make a name for ourselves; else we shall be scattered all over the world" (11:4). In response to this challenge against heaven, God shatters the builders' dream of grandeur, confounds their language, and scatters them in all directions. Culture, however, is not destroyed. Rather, it assumes a different form. From now on its distinguishing mark is diversity and dispersion. From now on, its distinct site becomes the nation.

Of the many nations that "branch out" in the vast expanses of the earth, Israel is singled out. In the episode following the Tower of Babel, God demands that Abraham leave his birthplace (Ur of the Chaldeans) and go forth *(lekh lekha)* to the land shown to him. There, God assures him, "I will make of you a great nation, and I will bless you; I will make your name great" (Genesis 12:2). Abraham's migration to Canaan offers a new departure. Whereas the sinful homogeneous community of Babel failed, Abraham's descendants, the people God has chosen from a multitude of peoples, seem to hold much promise, destined as they are (unlike the builders of the Tower) to acquire a "great name."[1] The primary exile of the first patriarch, his capacity to part from his cultural origins, is construed as an essential rift, a prerequisite for the rise of the nation. Later, in Exodus, the people as a whole will follow a similar route, moving out of Egypt, wandering in the desert, and fashioning the cultural contours of the nation on their way to the Promised Land.

Dispersion and exile, however, do not lead to clear-cut borders between cultures. Languages intersect in unexpected ways. The very name "Babel," which commemorates the primary linguistic splitting, is also a cross-cultural product. Its meaning in Akkadian is presumably "the gate to the gods" *(bab iley)*, but in the course of the biblical story it is Hebraized via a pun when it is linked to the Hebrew root *blbl* (to confuse). Perhaps this interpretation of "Babel" is an attempt to mock the pretentious temples of Mesopotamia: the tower that was meant to lead to the gods leads only to confusion.[2]

But what turns out to be far more confusing is the lack of clear demarcation between the chosen and the non-chosen. As the history of the children of Israel unfolds, we discover that the rebellious quality of primeval culture does not dissipate once we move into the realm of the chosen ones. Quite the contrary: rebellion is one of the salient features of the chosen nation. The Israelites do not venture to construct brick temples whose tops reach heaven, but their idolatrous cravings betray a similar tendency to transgress sacred boundaries.

The question of national identity—the attempt to fathom the entangled relations between Israel and God, between Israel and other nations—is one of the most resonant and unresolvable questions in the Bible. In tackling it, the biblical text relies not on philosophical contemplation but rather on narrative. More specifically, it offers a narrative in which the nation is personified extensively. Any attempt to understand the history of the children of Israel, to fashion a conception of national identity, to grasp communal motives and fantasies, collective memories and oblivions, the Bible seems to suggest, requires a plunge into the intricate twists and turns of the individual life.

The nation—particularly in Exodus and Numbers—is not an abstract detached concept but rather a grand character with a distinct voice (represented at times in a singular mode) who moans and groans, is euphoric at times, complains frequently, and rebels against Moses and God time and again. Israel has a life story, a biography of sorts.[3] It was conceived in the days of Abraham; its miraculous birth took place with the Exodus, the parting of the Red Sea; then came a long period of childhood and restless adolescence in the wilderness; and finally adulthood was approached with the conquest of Canaan.

To be sure, a collective character is necessarily more heterogeneous and less predictable. The Pentateuch's account of national formation resists fixed definitions of the various phases in the nation's life cycle. Roughly speaking, chronology is maintained, and yet images of birth, youth, initiation, and suckling intermingle throughout. Thus, the distinct manifestation of national suckling appears only in Numbers 11, where Moses likens the people to a suckling infant in the wilderness, long after the grand-scale initiation at Sinai. But, after all, such boundaries are never that clear in individual biographies either. Infantile dreams may linger on and initiation is rarely exhausted in one rite.

National literatures were not common in the ancient world. Israel's preoccupation with its reason for being is exceptional in the ancient Near East.[4] In Greece and particularly in Rome, however, narratives concerning national origins are equally important.[5] Israel's history bears resemblance to the Roman one. It too involves a divine promise, individuation from a major civilization, a quest for lost roots, a long journey to what is construed as the land of the forefathers, and a gory conquest.[6] What makes the Bible unique is the extent to which the nation is dramatized. In the *Aeneid*, by way of comparison, the plot revolves round Aeneas. The wanderings between Troy and the promised new land are primarily Aeneas's wanderings: the people remain a rather pale foil. They engage in no conflict—either with Aeneas or the gods—that would grant them access to the central stage. The biblical text is significantly different in its rendering of national drama. Israel is a protagonist whose moves and struggles determine the map—so much so that 40 years of wanderings in the desert are added to the itinerary as a result of the people's protest against the official preference of Canaan over Egypt.

The fashioning of Israel as a character is a forceful unifying strategy, but the metaphor does not yield a homogeneous account of national formation. The biblical text reveals points of tension between different traditions regarding the nation's history and character. Even the nation's sexual identity is not stable. Although the Pentateuch shapes a male character, referring to the people as *am* (singular masculine noun), the Prophets, more often than not, represent Israel as female, using "Jerusalem" or "Zion" (feminine nouns) as alternative designations.

This essay focuses on the intricacies of national imagination in the Pentateuch, and as such it is concerned with the fashioning of a male character who is marked as God's firstborn son.[7] Double personification is at stake—of God and the nation—creating a familial link between the two.[8] If Rome's sacred origin is assured through the divine blood of its founding fathers—Aeneas is Venus's son, and Romulus and Remus are the offspring of Mars—in the case of Israel, the nation as a whole, metaphorically speaking, is God's son.[9] On sending Moses to Pharaoh to deliver the people, God proclaims: "Israel is My first-born son. I have said to you [Pharaoh], 'Let My son go' " (Exodus 4:22–23). The priority given to Israel by the Father represents a translation into national terms of the reversal of the primogeniture law—a phenomenon so central in the lives of the patriarchs. The late-born nation that came to the stage after all its neighbors had assumed their historical roles is elevated by God to the position of the chosen firstborn.[10]

Israel is a chosen nation, God's nation, but the reason for its chosen-ness remains obscure. It does not succeed in following traditional norms of male heroism, nor does it become an exemplary nation with high moral and religious
standards. The more mature Israel, in the plains of Moab, on the threshold of
Canaan, is far more established a community than the nascent nation on the way
out of Egypt, but this by no means suggests that biblical historiography relies on
the principle of progress. Whereas in the initial stages of the journey the children of Israel worship a Golden Calf in a carnivalesque feast, at the last station,
just before crossing the Jordan river, they "cling" to Baal Peor (under the influence of Moabite women), adopting Canaanite religious practices with much enthusiasm. The Song of Moses, with its synoptic presentation of Israel's history,
regards the nation as an ungrateful son whose conduct fails to improve over
time: "Do you thus requite the Lord, O dull and witless people? Is not He the Father who created you, fashioned you and made you endure!" (Deuteronomy
32:6). Instead of appreciating God's vigilance, Moses claims, once the nation
"grew fat" it used its new powers to "kick" (Deuteronomy 32:15).

What is most fascinating in the primary biography of ancient Israel is the
ambivalence that lies at its very base, an ambivalence that is expressed so poignantly through the intense struggles between the Father (or Moses) and His
people. The nation is both the chosen son and the rebel son, and accordingly its
relationship with the Father is at once intimate and strained.

The fictional quality of the struggle between God and the nation does not
preclude the historicity of the text. Israel's beginning is situated in historical
times—in the days of the Exodus—rather than in a mythical "in illo tempore."[11]
Similarly, God defines Himself, at Sinai and elsewhere, as the one who brought
Israel out of Egypt—not as the Creator of primeval times. Even at moments
when the biography of ancient Israel relies on mythical materials—primarily,
on the myth of the birth of the hero and the myth of the hero's return—these
are inextricably connected with a historiographical drive to record memorable
past events and question their meaning. In the Bible, history and literature go
hand in hand, more explicitly than in modern historiography, which is why it
serves as a paradigmatic case for the examination of the narrative base of national constructions.[12]

NATIONAL BIRTH

The metaphor of birth is probably the most resonant anthropomorphic image
in national narratives from antiquity to modern times. In fact, it is so resonant
one tends to forget that nations are not born literally but are, rather, imagined in

these terms. Every nation, however, has its own birth story, or birth stories. The book of Exodus provides an intriguingly complex representation of Israel's birth in keeping with the preliminary imaginings of the nation in Genesis. The opening verses of Exodus 1 make clear that God's reiterated promises to Abraham, Isaac, and Jacob—the grand national annunciation scenes of Genesis—are finally realized. The descendants of Jacob, whose names are listed solemnly, multiply at an uncanny pace and turn into a "mighty" nation: the nation of the "children of Israel."[13] "Israel" for the first time is not merely Jacob's second, elevated, name but rather a collective designation of a burgeoning community that "fills" the land. But then we discover that God's darker prophecy, in the covenant of the parts (Genesis 15:13), is equally fulfilled: Israel is born in a prolonged exile, against Pharaonic bondage.

Representing the birth of a nation is not a simple task. The imagining of this dramatic event in Exodus is facilitated by the interweaving of two biographies: the story of the birth of Moses, and that of the nation.[14] The fashioning of Israel as character, here as elsewhere, is inseparable from a complementary narrative strategy: the marking of individuals whose histories are paradigmatic. The nation's life story, in other words, is modeled in relation to the biographies of select characters.[15] Abraham, whose departure from Ur serves as prefiguration of the nation's exodus, is only the first exemplary figure. The heterogeneity of national imagination in the Bible depends on a variety of representatives. Fragments of the biographies of Isaac, of Jacob, the eponymous father, and even of Hagar, the Egyptian handmaid, whose affliction foreshadows the nation's enslavement in Egypt, are also linked in different ways to the nation's biography and take part in its construction.[16]

On the question of birth, Moses' story is of special importance. The analogy between the one and the multitude in this case is more immediate. Unlike the patriarchal biographies that pertain to a distant past and flicker over the chasm of time, Moses' birth occurs within the same historical setting. Moses is a national leader whose history blends with the history of the nation. He is one of many Hebrew babies persecuted by Pharaoh. His story, however, is marked as the exemplary account that sheds light on the collective birth story as it prefigures the deliverance of the nation as a whole from bondage.

Moses' birth story shares much in common with mythical birth stories. What characterizes the birth of a hero? The conception of the hero is usually impeded by difficulties such as abstinence or prolonged barrenness. During or before pregnancy there is a prophecy, or an oracle cautioning the father against the hero's birth; the father tries to shape a different future and gives orders to kill his new-born son; the babe is then placed in a basket or a box and delivered to the waves. Against all odds, however, the hero is saved by animals, or by lowly people, and is suckled by a female animal or by a humble woman. When full grown, he discovers his royal parents, takes revenge on his father, and, recognized by his people, finally achieves rank and honors.[17]

Moses' story is indeed compatible in many ways with this model: a threatened child, the exposure in the basket, the miraculous deliverance of the foundling, the two sets of parents, and the final acknowledgment of the hero's power.[18] But there is a significant difference: Moses' true parents are not the royal ones but rather the poor Hebrew slaves. At a moment of national birth, the inversion of the two sets of parents is not without significance. Moses' "true" parents are higher in rank despite their lowly position precisely because they are members of the chosen nation-to-be.

THE POLITICS OF BIRTH

The juxtaposition of Moses' story and that of the nation entails an adaptation of the myth of the birth of the hero on a national plane. Put differently, it enables the construction of a myth of the birth of the nation. Israel's birth, much like that of Moses, takes place against Pharaoh's will.

But the Israelites were fertile and prolific; they multiplied and increased greatly, so that the land was filled with them. A new king arose over Egypt who did not know Joseph. And he said to his people, "Look, the Israelite people are much too numerous for us. Let us deal shrewdly with them, so that they may not increase" (Exodus 1:9–10).

Interestingly, the expression *am beney yisrael* (the nation of the children of Israel) is first used by none other than Pharaoh. Pharaoh's anxieties over the safety of his rule enable him to perceive the rise of Israel long before the Hebrews themselves can. Intimidated by the growth of the Hebrews, Pharaoh orders that every son born shall be cast into the Nile "but let every girl live" (Exodus 1:22). Much has been written about his curious choice to get rid of the male babies alone, but with no consideration of the mythical background.[19] What is at stake here is an application of the exposure motif (a male motif to begin with) to a community of sons. Pharaoh, the ruler of the parent-nation, fears the power of a budding nation of rivals growing within Egypt. Parental anxieties—what will emerge from the teeming womb?—thus conflate with racist anxieties—will the others overbear?

Shiphrah and Puah, the two midwives whose names are associated with "beauty" (the former) and "birth sighs" (the latter), are the national correlate of Moses' female deliverers in Exodus 2.[20] Here too a curious detail in the text—the fact that two midwives are considered sufficient for a national massacre—can be explained in terms of the mythical context and the interrelations of the two biographies. The midwives, much like humble rescuers of heroes, choose to violate the king's decree and save the threatened newborns. They trick Pharaoh by telling him midwives' tales:

> So the king of Egypt summoned the midwives and said to them, "Why have you done this thing, letting the boys live?" The midwives said to Pharaoh, "Because the Hebrew women are not like the Egyptian women: they are vigorous. Before the midwife can come to them, they have given birth." (Exodus 1:18–19)

Shiphrah and Puah outwit Pharaoh by confirming his racist anxieties concerning the proliferation of the Hebrew slaves. Relying on a common racist notion, according to which the other is closer to nature, they claim that the Hebrew women need no midwives, for unlike Egyptian women, they are animal-like *(ki ḥayot hena)* and can give birth without professional help. There is an outburst of vitality out there, they seem to suggest, that cannot be yoked to the legal apparatus of the Pharaonic court. The recurrence of the term "midwife" in this brief episode—it appears seven times—highlights the power and courage of the two women.

Myth and history, however, are inseparable in this scene. The nation's birth story does not merely offer a mythical account of the rise of the nation but also a historical consideration of the concrete horrors of bondage.[21] Regulation and distortion of the process of reproduction is a mode of dehumanization that is all too well known from testimonies regarding other instances of slavery.

To reclaim birth in the context of slavery is a revolutionary act. It discloses hope for the newborn and the power to imagine a different future, one without bondage and tyranny; it means to reclaim subjecthood, to turn the birth of the oppressed into a meaningful historical event that needs to be recorded and narrated. The story of Israel's origins is one of trauma and recovery. The founding trauma in the nation's biography is bondage, the repression of birth. But then a process of recovery begins that entails the inversion of exposure from an antinatal act to a means of rescue. Yocheved casts her son into the Nile, but Moses' exposure is not meant to comply with Pharaoh's decree but rather to undo it. Similarly, the nation as a whole multiplies despite Pharaoh's tireless attempts to restrict its growth. "But the more they were oppressed, the more they increased and spread out" (1:12). The relation between affliction and growth is provocatively inverted. Pharaoh expected a reduction in the birthrate, but his harsh treatment of the Hebrews led to the opposite, to a mysterious increase.

"IN THY BLOOD LIVE"

In his explicit and rather graphic use of the metaphor of birth vis-à-vis the nation, Ezekiel sheds much light on the representation of national formation in Exodus. In a famous passage in Ezekiel 16, which relates the story of national birth, Jerusalem stands for the nation:

> As for your birth, when you were born your navel cord was not cut, and you were not bathed in water to smooth you; you were not rubbed with salt, nor were you swaddled. No one pitied you enough to do any one of these things for you out of compassion for you; on the day you were born, you were left lying, rejected, in the open field. When I passed by you and saw you wallowing in your blood, I said to you: "Live in spite of your blood." Yea, I said to you: "Live in spite of your blood." I let you grow like the plants of the field; and you continued to grow up until you attained to womanhood, until your breasts became firm and your hair sprouted. You were still naked and bare when I passed by you [again] and saw that your time for love had arrived. So I spread My robe over you and covered your nakedness. (4–8)

Israel was ruthlessly deserted by its parents at birth, soaking in blood helplessly without even receiving elementary postpartum care. The horrifying aspects of parental neglect are depicted in vivid detail. The newborn was not washed in water, her umbilical cord was not cut, her body was not salted (a practice that was apparently perceived as essential for the newborn's skin), nor was she swaddled. Then God passed by and adopted the neglected nation, adjuring Israel to live in her blood, to regard the marks of blood on her body as a source of life. What is more, He raised the nation and enabled its multiplication and growth. He provided her with the much-needed care and compassion that she lacked, washing the blood off her skin and furnishing her with excellent ornaments. Being a foundling nation is a traumatic experience but it ultimately turns out to be beneficial: it leads (as is the case in the myth of the birth of the hero) to the discovery of/by more distinguished parents and ensures the transition from rags to riches, or rather from nakedness to royal garments.

The story of the Exodus is indeed the story of Israel's rescue and adoption by a more distinguished Father who is not merely royal but divine as well. It is a Father who has the force to wash off the signs of a collective trauma, to turn a helpless late-born nation into a powerful chosen one. In Ezekiel, the adoption is construed as a marital bond between God and the nation, whereas in Exodus it entails a bond between the Father and His firstborn son.[22] In both cases the chosen-ness of Israel is defined in familial terms. The change in the representation of the nation's gender allows for a multifaceted treatment of the complex relation of Israel and God. Suffice it to say within the limited scope of this discussion that, whereas the representation of the nation as female accentuates the erotic aspect of the relationship, the father-son dyad is far more concerned with pedagogic issues as well as with the question of heroism.

REVENGE

Birth and revenge—or, rather, revenge fantasies—go hand in hand in birth myths. The hero's triumph over the "evil" father who tried to prevent his birth is a sign of utmost valor. A similar triumph may be traced in Exodus. Pharaoh, the anti-natal force with respect to both Moses and the nation, is defeated, at first by the ongoing multiplication of the Hebrews and then in a direct confrontation: the 10 plagues. Early commentators noted the gradual escalation of severity in the plagues, beginning with nuisances and pests, continuing with destruction of livestock and crops, and ending with the gravest of all—the death of human beings.

This last plague seems to represent the final push in Israel's delivery. It is the night of Passover. Pharaoh, who has refused to set the Israelites free, suffers from a symmetrical punishment. The Egyptian firstborn die while God's firstborn, Israel, is saved. The differentiation between the Egyptians and the Hebrews is now enhanced by means of blood. God demands that the children of Israel take the blood of the Paschal sacrifice and put it on the two door-posts and the lintel, where it will serve as "a sign for you: when I see the blood I will pass over you, so that no plague will destroy you when I strike the land of Egypt" (12:13).

The blood that marks the Israelites is not only apotropaic. Its location on the two side posts of the door evokes natal imagery.[23] The Israelites are delivered collectively out of the womb of Egypt. National birth, much like individual births (and all the more so in ancient times), takes place on a delicate border between life and death. It involves the transformation of blood from a signifier of death to a signifier of life. It also involves the successful opening of the womb, the prevention of the womb's turning into a grave. The term "opener of the womb" *(peter reḥem)* is introduced in Exodus 13:2 as a synonym for "firstborn." It appears in the depiction of the law regarding the firstborn, a law that is construed as a commemoration of the last plague: "Consecrate to Me every first-born; man and beast, the first issue of every womb among the Israelites is Mine." Although the term is not used explicitly with respect to the nation as a whole, this is precisely what is at stake in the context of the Exodus. The first opening of the womb (an act that is reminiscent of deflowering) is a unique and dangerous occurrence that requires divine vigilance. Those who do not deserve divine protection—namely, the Egyptians—find their death in the process, but Israel, God's firstborn, is consecrated as it opens the matrix.

Then comes the climactic moment of the delivery, which includes the ultimate revenge: the scene by the Red Sea.[24] Moses parts the waters at God's command. The Israelites walk upon land in the midst of the sea, and the Egyptian soldiers, who are pursuing them, drown as the waters return. The downfall of the parent nation seems total. Pharaoh, who wished to cast the Hebrew babies into the Nile, now finds his soldiers and fancy chariots sinking "like a stone" in the waters of the Red Sea.

"Did not old Pharaoh get lost, get lost, get lost in the Red Sea" marvels a famous African-American slave song. The song promises that power relations may change and conveys confidence in the possibilities of redemption. Even if the scene by the Red Sea is something of a slave fantasy—there is no evidence in Egyptian sources regarding such a defeat, nor did the great Egypt disappear from the map at this time—the importance of the moment lies in its carnivalesque spirit, in the reversal of hierarchies. The master falls and the oppressed spring to life.

From here on, time will be perceived differently. Everything will be measured in relation to the moment in which God delivered Israel from Egypt. "This month shall mark for you the beginning of the months; it shall be the first of the months of the year for you" (12:2). A new calendar is established with the birth of the nation as its point of departure. It is a revolutionary moment, a wondrous new beginning.[25] Slavery is left behind, and the intoxicating smell of freedom is in the air.

WONDER

God performs a variety of wonders in Egypt (the 10 plagues in fact are perceived as such), but the parting of the Red Sea seems to surpass them all. It marks the nation's first breath—out in the open air—and serves as a distinct reminder of the miraculous character of birth. Where there was nothing, a living creature emerges all of a sudden. If the myth of the birth of the hero accentuates the wonder of birth on an individual level, here the miracle is collective. Much like Moses, the nation is drawn out of the water against all odds. It is an intensified miracle: a wonder on a great scale. The two enormous walls of water, the ultimate breaking of the waters, and the exciting appearance of dry land all seem to represent a gigantic birth, a birth that is analogous to the creation of the world.

The parting of the waters evokes Genesis 1, and the "blast" of God's "nostrils" on the waters (Exodus 15:8) calls to mind the creation of Adam in Genesis 2:7: "The Lord God formed man from the dust of the earth. He blew into his nostrils the breath of life." Accordingly, God is defined as the "maker" of the nation *(am zu kanita),* a term that otherwise is used only in the context of the creation (Exodus 15:16).

On witnessing this great wonder, the people as a whole burst out singing. The Song of the Sea, with its fast tempo, celebrates the singularity of the nation's miraculous delivery:

> Who is like You, O Lord, among the celestials; Who is like You, majestic in holiness, Awesome in splendor, working wonders! . . . For the horses of Pharaoh, with his chariots and horsemen, went into the sea; and the Lord turned back on them the waters of the sea; but the Israelites marched on dry ground in the midst of the sea. (15:11–19)

It is at once a breathtaking and breath-giving moment. All doubts and fears dissolve. Everything seems possible. Crossing the Red Sea is a leap of faith, a leap into life.

The birth of the nation involves a bewildering blurring of the boundaries between nature and history.[26] Nature participates in the shaping of this grand historical event, which is why the Song of the Sea is the Song of the Birth of the Nation. The sudden break in the rhythm of natural phenomena is used here to express the intense excitement of a nascent people.[27]

DIVINE MIDWIVES

Much has been written on the image of God as Warrior in the Song of the Sea in relation to other divine wars that hover in the background—above all, the crushing of the revolt of the sea by the Creator in the cosmic beginning (see Isaiah 51:9–10).[28] The image of the Warrior is indeed a central image in this song, but not the only one. God has feminine facets as well, though partially hidden.[29] Behind and against the "right hand" of the Warrior, one can detect a feminine hand: the strong magical hand of a grand Midwife drawing the newborn nation out of the depths of the sea, "the heart of the sea" (Exodus 15:8), into the world of the living, beyond the engulfing flood. God, as it were, follows in the footsteps of the two midwives who loom so large in the opening chapter of Exodus, though here the Israelites need to be rescued from the "mighty waters" of the Red Sea rather than the Nile.[30]

Ezekiel's depiction of the postpartum care that God bestows on the foundling nation reinforces the impression that the Father is something of a Midwife. The washing of the baby and the cutting of the umbilical cord were tasks usually performed by the midwife.[31] More important, they were at times, at least in Egyptian mythology, performed by divine midwives. A Middle Kingdom story records the miraculous birth of the first three kings of the Fifth Dynasty. The mother, Rudjedet, is attended at birth by four goddesses: Isis, Nephthys, Meskhenet, and Hekat. Each birth is represented in a similar manner:

> Isis placed herself before her [Rudjedet], Nephthys behind her, Hekat hastened the birth. Isis said: "Don't be so mighty in her womb, you whose name is 'Mighty.' " The child slid into her arms. . . . They washed him, having cut his navel cord, and laid him on a pillow cloth. Then Meskhenet approached him and said: "A king who will assume the kingship in this whole land."[32]

In the Bible, however, the mythical delivery is not merely that of a king but of an entire nation that is treated as if it were royal.

The fact that the Song of the Sea is sung by the women alone in the concluding lines of the scene adds yet another feminine touch to this miraculous birth. "Then Miriam the prophetess, Aaron's sister, took a timbrel in her hand, and all the women went out after her in dance with timbrels. And Miriam chanted for them: Sing to the Lord" (Exodus 15:20–21). Miriam, who stood between the reeds by the Nile watching over Moses' ark, orchestrating his deliverance, now dances by a Sea of Reeds (*yam suf*), with a timbrel in her hand, celebrating the redemption of the nation with an entire community of women.[33]

THE QUESTION OF NATIONAL IDENTITY

Nations may try to fashion a coherent conception of identity, or origin, to seek unity at points of clear disjunction, but their success can be only partial. The intertwined biographies of Moses and Israel poignantly disclose the difficulties in defining national identity for both the individual and the community. Moses' birth story differs from that of his heroic counterparts at another point as well. He is transferred back and forth between his Hebrew and Egyptian mothers. Yocheved places him in a basket at the Nile; he is found by Pharaoh's daughter, who then hands him back to Yocheved (believing her to be a wet nurse). Later Moses is brought back to the palace, where the princess adopts him and endows him with a name. He is raised in the palace but ultimately returns to his family and people.

The very fact that there are two sets of parents in the myth of the birth of the hero already intimates the difficulties involved in fashioning an identity. The myth addresses primary questions: Who am I? Who are my parents? Where do I come from? But the questions of origin become all the more complex when the two sets of parents pertain to two different nations. Moses' split national identity at birth will follow him for the rest of his life. When his first son is born in Midian, he chooses to name him "Gershom," saying, "I have been a stranger in a foreign land" (Exodus 2:22). His naming-speech relies on a pun that links the name "Gershom" with the word "stranger" *(ger)*. But in what sense is Moses a stranger at this point—in relation to Midian (where Jethro's daughters regard him as an Egyptian), or Egypt (his words echo the oracular announcement of Israel's troubling future as "strangers *[ger]* in a land not theirs" in Genesis 15:13)?[34] Moses will devote the bulk of his life to constructing the concept of Canaan as homeland and will lead his people persistently toward the land of "milk and honey," but ultimately he will die in the wilderness, between Egypt and the Promised Land.

And the nation? Israel's lineage is far more complicated than Moses' family tree, but here too the multiple parental figures point to diverse national origins. The conflict between God and Pharaoh is but one expression of the issue. The nebulous identity of the two midwives is another case in point. Are the two midwives who deliver the Hebrew babies Egyptian or Hebrew? The problem stems from the indefinite use of the word "Hebrew" *(ivriyot)* in Exodus 1:16. If it is read as an adjective, then Shiphrah and Puah are Hebrew midwives. But the verse may mean that these are Egyptian midwives who specialize in delivering Hebrew women. Numerous commentators have tried to solve the problem. Thus, Josephus suggests that the king chose Egyptian midwives, assuming that they "were not likely to transgress his will." Similarly, Abarbanel claims that "they were not Hebrews but Egyptians, for how could he trust Hebrew women to put their own children to death." The midrash, on the other hand, perceived them as Hebrews and identified the two midwives with Yocheved and Miriam.[35] What these commentaries neglect to take into account is the significance of the indeterminate origin of the midwives, the extent to which the nation's story repeats the confusion about identity embedded in Moses' biography.

The children of Israel are torn between the two lands, between their deep ties to Egypt and their desire to seek another land. They were not raised in the Egyptian court, as Moses was, but nonetheless Egypt is more than just a site of trauma for them: it served, however partially, as a nurturing motherland, especially the luscious land of Goshen.

The birth of Israel entails a painful process of individuation from Egypt that is never fully resolved. Just before the parting of the Red Sea, God promises the children of Israel that they shall see the Egyptians no more (14:13). But the drowning of their pursuers does not lead to the effacement of Israel's strong longings for the land of Egypt. National identity is thus poised on the brink of a loss of identity.[36]

THE EMERGENCE OF THE NATIONAL VOICE: INTERNAL ANTI-NATAL FORCES

The nation's first words are delivered on the way out of Egypt. On seeing the Egyptian chariots pursuing them, the children of Israel cry out unto the Lord:

> And they said to Moses, "Was it for want of graves in Egypt that you brought us to die in the wilderness? What have you done to us, taking us out of Egypt? Is this not the very thing we told you in Egypt, saying, 'Let us be, and we will serve the Egyptians, for it is better for us to serve the Egyptians than to die in the wilderness'?" (Exodus 14:11–12)

National birth means gaining consciousness and the power of verbal expression. During their bondage in Egypt, the Israelites could only moan and groan. They were in a pre-verbal and pre-conscious state, unaware of God's providence. Or else their discourse was silenced (as they now claim), not deemed worthy of attention. Something changes with the Exodus. They acquire the capacity to verbalize their needs and cry out to the Lord through Moses. And yet the emergence of the voice of the nation is accompanied by anti-natal cravings. They use their new power of expression to convey their discontent, their desire to return to Egypt, to undo the birth of the nation. In a fascinating way they question the official biography. God here turns out to be not the Deliverer of the nation but rather the bearer of death, an abusive Father who seeks to kill His children in the wilderness. God now seems to be just as bad as, or even worse than, Pharaoh.

The children of Israel are masters of complaint. This is just their first complaint, but it initiates a long series of murmurings in the desert. It has the characteristic rhetorical questions, much anguish, and anger. The people evoke the land they left behind, obsessively ("Egypt" is mentioned five times in their grumbling), like an infant craving for a lost breast.[37] Egypt seems to have far more to offer than the desert—even its graves (and Egypt does indeed excel in its death culture) are more attractive than those available in the wilderness. The primary national biography is far from linear. Birth does not necessarily move the children of Israel unambiguously forward. Another forceful desire compels them to look back toward Egypt.

Pharaoh, then, is not alone in wishing to stop the birth of the nation. Anti-natal forces erupt from within as well. The Bible highlights the complexity of national formation in revealing counter-trends that challenge the very notion that the nation is an urgent, vital project. The people oscillate between a euphoric celebration of their deliverance—as after the parting of the Red Sea—and a continual questioning of the official consecration of national birth.

Before the Israelites actually leave Egypt, Moses turns the Exodus into a ritual to be cherished now and in days to come. He demands that they commemorate the event and pass the story on from one generation to another:

And Moses said to the people, "Remember this day, on which you went free from Egypt, the house of bondage, how the Lord freed you from it with a mighty hand: no leavened bread shall be eaten. . . . And you shall explain to your son on that day, 'It is because of what the Lord did for me when I went free from Egypt.' " (13:3–8)[38]

But the children of Israel choose to revere other memories. Against the recurrent injunction to remember the Exodus, they set up a counter-memory: a benevolent Egypt. Relentless, they persist in recalling life by the Nile, where they took pleasure in fleshpots and other Egyptian delights. Individuation from Egypt does not seem to be the only route. Memory can be shaped in a variety of ways.

Such counter-trends would seem to deflate national pride. Israel's heroism does not follow traditional perceptions of male courage. There is a good deal of fear of life in the nation's nascent voice and an acute horror of what lies ahead. God Himself often regrets having delivered the nation. The children of Israel do not succeed in fulfilling His expectations, and He never hesitates to express His disappointment in them. The people are blamed for being ungrateful, for forgetting even the unforgettable—the God who miraculously begot them (Deuteronomy 32:18). Of the numerous unflattering national designations God provides, the most resonant is His definition of Israel as "a stiff-necked people" (Exodus 32:9). The nation withholds its body from God and in doing so reveals a sinful lack of faith and an unwillingness to open up to the divine Word.

But then Israel's challenge to the national plans of Moses and God is not merely a sign of weakness. There is something about the stiff neck of the nation and the refusal to take national imaginings for granted that reveals an unmistakable force. The nation's very name, "Israel," means to struggle with God, and in a sense this is the nation's raison d'être. In this respect, the biography of the eponymous father, Jacob, is also relevant to the understanding of national birth. In the womb, Jacob struggles forcefully, trying to gain priority over his elder brother, Esau. Rebekah, who asks the Lord to explain the significance of the turmoil in her womb, is told: "Two nations are in your womb, Two separate peoples shall issue from your body; One people shall be mightier than the other; And the older shall serve the younger" (Genesis 25:23). We have seen the significance of the reversal of the primogeniture law on the national level, but what this primal scene equally emphasizes is the importance of the struggle for national formation. Not only the struggle with the other (Esau or Edom in this case) but also a struggle from within, a struggle with the Ultimate Precursor: God.[39] The uterine struggle between Jacob and Esau prefigures the momentous struggle with the angel. It is through wrestling in the night with a divine being that Jacob acquires the nation's name. "Your name shall no longer be Jacob, but Israel," says the divine opponent, "for you have striven with beings divine and human, and have prevailed" (32:29). Jacob does not become angelic as a result of this nocturnal encounter, but the struggle reveals a certain kind of intimacy with God that is unparalleled.

In its rendition of the ambivalence that characterizes the Father-son relationship, the primary biography of ancient Israel offers a penetrating representation of national ambivalence, making clear from the outset that the story of the nation is not a story without fissures and lapses. The nation, like the eponymous father, is the chosen yet unyielding son, and as such the history of its relationship with God is punctuated by moments of unfathomable violence and overwhelming intimacy. From the time of Israel's birth, mutual adoration and disappointment mark the bond of the nation and God, and this is true of later stages in the nation's life as well. The tension between God and the nation only increases as the nation becomes a restless adolescent in the wilderness.

THE SPIES IN THE LAND OF GIANTS

On the threshold of Canaan, in the wilderness of Paran, Moses sends 12 representatives, one from each tribe, to explore the Promised Land. "See what kind of country it is," Moses instructs them. "Is the soil rich or poor? Is it wooded or not?" (Numbers 13:18–20). After 40 days, the men—better known as the 12 spies—return with pomegranates, figs, and an enormous cluster of grapes borne by two men. Presenting the fruits to the people, they unanimously praise the fertility of the land: "We came to the land you sent us to," they say to Moses, "it does indeed flow with milk and honey, and this is its fruit" (13:27). The Mosaic image of the Promised Land as a land of milk and honey seems to be confirmed. But then a fissure opens up as 10 of the spies swerve from the official line and depict a land that has little to do with what had been promised. Canaan is more perplexing than anticipated: it is *both* good and bad, "fat" yet inhospitable. Despite the milk and the honey, they claim, it is a land "that devours its settlers. All the people that we saw in it are men of great size; we saw the Nephilim there . . . and we looked like grasshoppers to ourselves, and so we must have looked to them" (13:32–33). The home of the fathers, of Abraham, Isaac, and Jacob, turns out to be a strange land, a land of menacing giants, a land of others.

Of the 12 men only 2, Joshua and Caleb, are in favor of attempting the conquest of the land. The others advise against it, maintaining that the Israelites are incapable of overcoming the formidable Canaanites with their huge fortified cities. The people find the "evil report" of the 10 spies more convincing. They cry and protest, ready to stone their leaders yet again. The promise that lured them out of Egypt now seems a sham. "Let us head back for Egypt," they say to one another and turn their backs on Canaan (Numbers 14:4). God's wrath is kindled. The 10 spies die in a plague, and the desert generation as a whole is punished for its rebellious conduct. They do not deserve to enter the land, God declares, and condemns them to wander in the wilderness for 40 years—based on the number of the days in which the spies searched the land—until their carcasses fall down.

The map of the wanderings is drastically changed. Forty years of desert life are added, which means many more stations along the road. The voyage has a vertical dimension as well, with unmistakable symbolic implications. The Promised Land is set up high, the very opposite of Egypt. Egypt is a land one always "descends" to: Abraham and Sarah went down to Egypt (Genesis 12:10) when famine struck Canaan; Jacob and his sons, in their turn, did the same, settling down in Goshen with the help of Joseph. On hearing that Joseph has been devoured by a wild beast, Jacob, whose grief is immense, wishes to go down to *Sheol*, to the realm of the dead, with his beloved son (37:35), but ends up instead following him down to Egypt, the land of the monumental worship of the dead.[40] Egypt is not an underworld, strictly speaking, but it comes close to being one when it is seen as a house of bondage at the bottom of the world. The Exodus, for this very reason, entails a magnificent ascent: out of Egypt and up to Sinai, the mountain of God, and then to the Promised Land, home of the living and the free. Canaan is predominantly a mountainous land, far closer to God, as it were, than Egypt. The question the spies quarrel over is whether or not "to go up" to the Promised Land. While Joshua and Caleb insist that such a move is within their powers—"Let us by all means go up *[alo na'ale]*, and we shall gain possession of it" (Numbers 13:30)—the others refuse to climb up impossible mountains in quest of a home that is possessed by others. Such heights seem to them more deadly than Egypt's lows.

The spies' story is a strange tale of no return, no homecoming. The hero's last trial—the final mark of his maturation—is to return home (older and wiser) after many years of wars and wanderings (which include, at times, a voyage to the underworld) and establish himself as a glorious leader, worthy of assuming the father's position. The *Odyssey* reminds us how difficult such homecoming may be. Agamemnon, who triumphed in the war against Troy, is murdered by his wife, Clytemnestra, on entering his palace, and Odysseus undergoes many hardships before and after he lands on the shores of Ithaca.

Biblical heroes are expected to return as well. Abraham and Sarah come back to Canaan after their sojourn in Egypt. The story of Jacob's homecoming to Canaan, however, is the most elaborate one. After 20 years of exile spent in Aram at the household of Laban, he sets out to return to his homeland at God's command. Jacob has a big family and much property by now—2 wives, 11 sons, many servants, and much cattle. He is no longer the helpless youth who ran away after stealing his elder brother's blessing, but nonetheless fear envelops him on the bank of the Jabbok, just before he crosses the border into Canaan:

> Then Jacob said, "O God of my father Abraham and God of my father Isaac, O Lord, who said to me, 'Return to your native land and I will deal bountifully with you'! . . . Deliver me, I pray, from the hand of my brother, from the hand of Esau; else, I fear, he may come and strike me down, mothers and children alike." (Genesis 32:10–12)

The blessing may be his, but the patrimony, that is, the power to hold it, is in the hands of Esau—or so it seems to Jacob on the eve of his return. The underlying fear is that the return will entail a regression to earlier times, when Jacob was indeed weaker than Esau, incapable of defending himself against the wrath of his elder sibling. Jacob, much like Odysseus, must refashion his identity in order to come back home safely. A mysterious "man" helps him do so. Wrestling in the night with the divine being, he acquires a new name, "Israel," which marks a break with the trickster that he was in the past and designates his new role as the nation's father.

The desert generation is even more confused and fearful about homecoming than was the eponymous patriarch. The discontinuities, or the fissures of identity, that characterize the return of the individual hero are far more pronounced in the case of collective identity, a construct whose unity is far more difficult to maintain. The wandering Israelites are skeptical about the very premise that Canaan is their homeland. The only land they wish to return to is Egypt. But they end their days in the wilderness, between Egypt and the Promised Land, returning to neither. They remain, in other words, in an in-between zone, between infancy and adulthood, in a prolonged phase of unsettling youth. Jeremiah depicts the desert years as a golden age, in which the nation followed God with the "devotion of youth" (*ḥesed ne'urim,* 2:2). Such "devotion," however, is shattered by moments in which the Israelites refuse to follow the Father and seek other routes.

The desire to return to Egypt is evident from the outset, but in Numbers 13 the people are ready to act on it. It is a moment of intense controversy that calls into question the official construction of Canaan as national home. To better understand the fracture, Moses' vision of the Promised Land needs to be explored further.

IMAGES OF THE LAND

Moses attempts to create what is so central to the formation of national belonging: a sense of home. He relies on two concepts: "the land of milk and honey," and "the land of the fathers." Home, for Moses, is a site where the mother—who is revealed solely via figurative language—provides space, and where the fathers provide the temporal dimension.

Let us begin with the fathers. The children of Israel spend 400 years (or 430, according to another tradition) in Egypt, oblivious of their past. It is left for Moses to evoke—or fashion—those long-buried memories of the three founding patriarchs, the divine promise, and the ancient patrimony far away. Just before the Exodus, Moses addresses the children of Israel in God's name, saying: "I will free you from the labors of the Egyptians and deliver you from their bondage. . . . I will bring you into the land that I swore to give to Abraham, Isaac, and Jacob, and I will give it to you for a possession" (Exodus 6:6–8). From the depths of misery, from "under the burdens" of bondage, God will lift them up to the land of promise, the land he swore (literally, "raised His hand") to give to their ancestors, to Abraham, Isaac, and Jacob. Moses offers the children of Israel a respectable lineage, the necessary cultural capital: three fathers who had the privileged position of the chosen, who won the favor of God and were deemed worthy of a promise and a heritage. They are models to be cherished and imitated for those who wish to be counted among the chosen.[41] To return to Canaan is thus defined as a return back home, as a quest for lost roots, a continuation of the glorious lives of the three founding patriarchs.

Moses creates continuity with a most suitable historical past. The promise that is given in the past is meant for the future, for the "seed" of the founding fathers, the nation-to-be. Much like the Trojan refugees in the *Aeneid* who discover (after a few mis-discoveries) that Italy, where they end up founding a new nation, is their ancestral home, so the Israelites discover that Canaan is their land from time immemorial.[42] Whether or not the "true origins" of the Israelites lie in Canaan, there is a significant breach of time between the patriarchs and the liberated Hebrew slaves, a breach that Moses denies as he sends spies to follow the route of their ancestors and explore the land that the latter possessed.

The plenitude conveyed by the image of a "land that flows with milk and honey" has been often noted, but little attention has been given to the choice of milk and honey in particular—that is, to the implied maternal facets of the representation of the land. The word "flow" *(zavat)* is usually used in the context of bodily fluids, reinforcing the notion that the land is a maternal body, with admirable flowing breasts. What Moses promises the children of Israel resembles an infantile dream of wish fulfillment, an image of a benevolent motherland whose milk is always available, flowing in abundance, intermingled with honey. The Promised Land, in other words, is imagined as a perfect mother with a perfect nature who can satisfy all the desires of the young nation: plenitude, pleasure, love, and security.

One needs to bear in mind, however, that in a sense the mother is a beloved as well, something that becomes all the more evident the closer the Israelites get to Canaan. The sexual dimension of milk and honey is revealed in the Song of Songs. "Sweetness drops From your lips, O bride; Honey and milk Are under your tongue" (4:11), says the lover to his beloved, while seducing her to open up her locked garden with its sealed fountain *(gan na'ul, ma'ayan ḥatum)*. To reach the Promised Land thus means to find the best of all feminine gardens: maternal nurturing coupled with erotic delights.

Joel's prophecy regarding the end of days illuminates the utopian connotations of the metaphor: "And in that day, The mountains shall drip with wine [the Hebrew word *asis* also stands for fruit juice], The hills shall flow with milk" (3:18; compare with Isaiah 66:9–13). Canaan is surely a concrete territory, but the historicity of the site does not preclude its mythical qualities. Much like the nation that calls it "home," the Promised Land has an imaginary dimension.

At first sight, however, Canaan does not seem like home sweet home. It definitely does not radiate the kind of warmth and familiarity one would expect. What the spies—the 10 rebellious ones—seem to claim is that the mother/bride who was to welcome them home turned out to be a great disappointment. Instead of supplying her sons and lovers with the goods, with the promised milk and honey, she threatens "to devour the inhabitants of the land" *(eretz okhelet yoshveha)*. Instead of being a source of nourishment, an object of desire, she is a perverse mother with cannibalistic impulses and an appetite of her own.

On the paternal front, the picture is not brighter. The fathers, or their traces, are simply absent. Their absence is all the more threatening in light of the fact that the land is packed with other nations. "Amalekites dwell in the Negeb region," say the spies. "Hittites, Jebusites, and Amorites inhabit the hill country;

and Canaanites dwell by the Sea and along the Jordan" (Numbers 13:29). There is no empty place in any direction. Neither God nor Moses conceals the fact that the land of the fathers is in the possession of others, but the promise includes divine intervention against the natives. "I will send an angel before you, and I will drive out the Canaanites, the Amorites, the Hittites, the Perizzites, the Hivites, and the Jebusites" (Exodus 33:2). And yet, upon seeing the inhabitants of the land, the possibility that they might vanish into thin air seems far less plausible. The land is truly theirs. No glimpse of continuity with the patriarchal tradition is to be seen on the horizon. The only past the spies evoke is pre-patriarchal. They depict the tall inhabitants of Canaan as *nefilim,* the legendary gigantic heroes of the antediluvian period who were considered to be the curious product of the couplings between the sons of God and the daughters of Adam (Genesis 6:2–4). The history of the patriarchs is provocatively eclipsed as another continuity between the *nefilim* and the inhabitants of Canaan is established. For the spies, the Promised Land is not merely an Old World awaiting their return. It resembles a threatening—though marvelous—New World whose relation to Israelite historiography is questionable.

NEW WORLDS

Travel accounts regarding the "discovery" of the New World can teach us much about the first encounter of the spies with the Promised Land. The relevance of the comparison did not escape William Bradford. In his report on the Pilgrims' first explorations of New England, he alludes to the story of the spies' expedition to Canaan. He writes of 16 armed men, under the conduct of Captain Standish, who ventured to explore the shore of Cape Cod. To their delight, they discovered buried Indian baskets full of corn, which they hastened to bring back to the ship. "And so like the men of Eshcol [the cluster of grapes], carried with them of the fruits of the land and showed their brethren, of which, and their return, they were marvelously glad and their hearts encouraged."[43]

One of the characteristic features of the discoverers' accounts is their emphasis on the wonder experienced on seeing the new landscapes. Such wonder was so great at times that it generated narratives of a superlative mode in which the immeasurability of the sights was celebrated. An exemplary case is Columbus's account of Española: "It is very fertile to a limitless degree, . . . it has many good and large rivers which is marvelous; and its mountains are most beautiful of a thousand shapes, and all are accessible and filled with trees of a thousand kinds and tall, and they seem to touch the sky."[44]

Just such wonder is evident in the spies' depiction of the exceptional fertility of Canaan, with its big lush fruits, samples of a different agriculture and a different climate, unknown back in the irrigated flatlands of Egypt.[45] Here too, nature is beyond measure, and particularly the grapes, not to mention the interminable flow of milk and honey. The surpassing of measure includes the inhabitants of the land as well. Three different terms are used to underline the unusual stature of the men they encountered: *anshey midot* (men of great stature), *beney anak* (sons of giants), and *nefilim* (the primordial gigantic heroes). And as if all these synonyms were not enough, they go on to explain that "we looked like grasshoppers to ourselves, and so we must have looked to them."

The spies' words disclose the projection at work. They move swiftly from their own perspective to that of the giants, never considering the possibility that the latter may have a different worldview. The midrash already noted the phenomenon when conjecturing God's response to the spies: "I take no objection to your saying 'We looked like grasshoppers to ourselves' but I take offense when you say 'so we must have looked to them.' How do you know how I made you look to them? Perhaps you appeared to them as angels?"[46]

The shock at the sight of the other and the fantasies and projections created as a result are a familiar feature in European descriptions of the natives of the New World. The natives were often depicted as utterly strange in their appearance and customs. The most powerful fantasy, however, operative in all early encounters in the New World, was cannibalism. In part, it was a matter of misinterpreting different eating habits and unfamiliar non-Christian religious rituals, but it also had to do with a more deep-seated anxiety about losing one's identity in the other.[47]

The fear of cannibalism hovers over the travel account of the spies as well. The land as a whole is described as a cannibalistic (m)other who swallows up her children. And even the representation of the giants is colored in similar hues insofar as grasshoppers are known as the smallest edible animal, according to biblical law (see Leviticus 11:22).

There are, however, significant differences between the biblical explorers and the "discoverers" of the New World. In the account of the spies, unlike Columbus's *Diario*, there is more fear than wonder, although in both cases one finds an intriguing mixture of the two. Whereas Columbus, Cortés, and the American Pilgrims seize the lands they explore ravenously, the spies—who perceive themselves as inferior in size and power to the natives—recommend avoiding the conquest of Canaan. Bradford surely smooths out the subversive aspect of the tale in contriving a "happy ending" to the story. According to his narrative, Captain Standish and his men return from the shore with the fruits of the land (the corn) and all were "marvelously glad" and much "encouraged." But the biblical spies are neither encouraged nor encouraging. They come to uncover the secrets of the land, to uncover "her nakedness," to use Joseph's definition of spying (on accusing his brothers of spying on Egypt), but are overwhelmed by the giants who possess her.[48]

The giants, strangely enough, seem to represent not only the indigenous Canaanite population but also a distorted image of the patriarchs. The fathers and the others blend at points. The fact that the giants turn up, of all places, in the area of Hebron, the burial site of Abraham, Isaac, and Jacob (see Genesis 23), reinforces this notion, as if they were tall ghosts of the distant forefathers who have risen from their grave in the cave of Machpela to haunt their descendants.[49] Note that the term *refa'im,* associated with the giants of Hebron in Deuteronomy 2:11, makes an analogous connection: it stands both for a legendary pre-Israelite community in Canaan and for the ghosts of the underworld.[50] Canaan, far more than Egypt, seems from the spies' point of view a shadowy frightful realm, dominated by the dead. Voyages to the underworld to speak with the dead (of the kind found in *The Epic of Gilgamesh* or in the *Odyssey*) are impossible within the biblical framework, where *Sheol* remains a secluded realm below, beyond narrative, but at times mythical overtones seep into the text, hinting at a more dramatic underworld behind the scenes.

On seeing the giants, the spies sense their powerlessness. They seem to shudder at the thought that they will never "grow up" or reach such stature.[51] The tradition Moses had invented for them has a dark side. If they really had such glorious ancestors, how could they follow in their footsteps? Canaan is the land of the "grown-ups," which means that there is no room in it for them. But then their reluctance to enter the world of adults is also a challenge to the underlying presuppositions of adulthood. Adulthood entails conquest and a mode of heroism they find hard to accept.

THE QUESTION OF HEROISM

The desert generation is not a generation of warriors. On hearing the spies' report, the people lift up their voice and cry:

> The whole community broke into loud cries, and the people wept that night. All the Israelites railed against Moses and Aaron. "If only we had died in the land of Egypt," the whole community shouted at them, "or if only we might die in this wilderness! Why is the Lord taking us to that land to fall by the sword? Our wives and children will be carried off! It would be better for us to go back to Egypt!" (Numbers 14:1–3)

Fighting with giants is the dream of every warrior. (David, who managed to triumph over the giant Goliath, is exemplary in this connection.) But the wandering Israelites do not find such dreams attractive. They worry about the horrifying outcome of war, the possibility that their wives will be captured and their children will be as prey in the hands of the enemy. They refuse to endanger their lives. Although Moses insists that there is no other home but Canaan, the desert generation wonders about the validity and value of the newly discovered memories of the Promised Land. And wondering means wandering—being in exile.

CARCASSES IN THE WILDERNESS

God's response is harsh. "Ten times" they have "tried" Him, and He is tired of their complaints (Numbers 14:22). First they rejected His laws, then His manna, and now the land He had designated for them. Once again, as in the episode of the Golden Calf, God is ready to annihilate the nation on the spot and fashion another via Moses, but Moses manages to dissuade Him. And yet the pardon is only partial. The people are by no means exempt from punishment. In His wrath, God chooses to take their request literally:

> Say to them: "As I live," says the Lord, "I will do to you just as you have urged Me. In this very wilderness shall your carcasses drop. Of all of you who were recorded in your various lists from the age of twenty years up, you who have muttered against Me, not one shall enter the land in which I swore to settle you—save Caleb son of Jephunneh and Joshua son of Nun. Your children who, you said, would be carried off—these will I allow to enter; they shall know the land that you have rejected. But your carcasses shall drop in this wilderness, while your children roam in the wilderness for forty years, suffering for your faithlessness, until the last of your carcasses is down in the wilderness." (Numbers 14:28–33)

Given that dying in the wilderness seemed preferable to them than waging war on the Canaanites, He'll grant them their wish. They will die in the wilderness, not immediately, but within 40 years of wanderings. The depiction of their death is blunt and gruesome. It sounds like an elaborate sonorous curse, voiced repeatedly. They will not simply die in the desert but rather "drop dead," or, in biblical idiom, their "carcasses will drop," with nothing to soften the blow, without, one suspects, the elementary right of the dead: burial.[52] Instead of going up to Canaan, they will fall as low as one can get. Their death will be total, their bodies will be wasted completely *(ad tom pigrekhem)* in the arid desert, leaving no room to hope for a change of fate. The Promised Land will remain forever beyond their reach.

The children of the desert generation, however, the very children they feared would fall prey, will ultimately enter Canaan and settle there. Whereas the parents are doomed to "know" what it means to thwart God (Numbers 14:34), their offspring will have the privilege of "knowing" the Promised Land.[53] Their only suffering will be caused not by God but rather by the burden of their parents' "whoredoms," which they will need to bear for many years until the carcasses of the desert generation fall apart, setting them free.

THE CLUSTER OF GRAPES:
NEW SITES ON AN OLD MAP

Greek mythology tells of Persephone, Demeter's daughter, who yielded to Hades' offer and took a few seeds of pomegranate on leaving him. As a result, she was doomed to return every year to the underworld for four months. Something similar happens to the spies. In picking the fruit of the Promised Land, they become part of it, regardless of their fears and reservations. According to a parenthetical comment of the narrator, we learn that the place where they had found the fruit, "That place was named the wadi Eshcol [cluster] because of the cluster that the Israelites cut down there" (Numbers 13:24).

Naming is a mode of discursive appropriation that is an integral part of every conquest.[54] The spies are not the agents of naming; it is not they who call the brook Eshcol. And yet their story participates in the appropriation of Canaan. In taking the fruit, they commit themselves to the land of milk and honey and disclose their underlying desire to conquer it, to taste its fruits, to make new marks on the ancestral map: to imprint the name "Eshcol" alongside "Hebron," the burial site of the patriarchs.

The desert generation, despite itself, craves for a home of its own, free of oppression and shame. They yearn for it to the extent that, right after the conflict over the spies' report, they regret having rejected Canaan and decide to wage war with the Amalekites and the Canaanites: "Early next morning they set out toward the crest of the hill country, saying, 'We are prepared to go up [hinenu ve'alinu] to the place that the Lord has spoken of, for we were wrong' " (Numbers 14:40). Now they finally want to go up the mountain and seek the promise, but it is too late. Moses warns them that, because of their sin, God will not stand by them in battle. They insist on trying. As expected, they lose. The Amalekites and the Canaanites who dwell in that hill come down and smite them (45). It is an aborted attempt to climb up the mountain that marks their ongoing ambivalence with respect to Canaan.

The spirit of the desert generation unsettles future generations as well. Even when the Israelites finally invade Canaan, the wandering does not fully stop. Exile piles up on exile. The Promised Land continues to be regarded throughout biblical times with some ambivalence, never to be seen as a truly stable home, nor as the only center of holiness.[55] "I accounted to your favor the devotion of your youth, Your love as a bride—How you followed Me in the wilderness, In a land not sown," says Jeremiah in the name of God to Israel (2:2). In this verse, Jeremiah ventures to claim that the desert offers a youthful passion the Promised Land lacks. He realizes, with his wandering precursors, that a land that is not "sown" leaves more room for dreaming than a tilled land.

In Numbers 16, Moses is challenged once again, this time by Dathan and Aviram who ask: "Is it not enough that you brought us from a land flowing with milk and honey to have us die in the wilderness, that you would also lord it over us?" (16:13). They provocatively turn *Egypt* into the land that flows with milk and honey, calling into question Moses' authority and national vision. Their punishment is not without significance: the earth of the desert "opens" her "mouth" and swallows them up. They "go down alive into Sheol," the realm of the dead (16:30). Canaan is not inherently a land of milk and honey, nor is it the only land with cannibalistic tendencies. Any land can be both. Any land can be both the home of the living and the home of the dead. It all depends on the eye of the spy.

JOSHUA: THE REVISED VERSION

In Joshua 2, we are given a revision of Numbers 13 that accentuates the antithetical character of the first expedition to Canaan. Joshua sends two spies to explore Jericho before approaching his first target in Canaan. Joshua, as one recalls, supported the official line already in Numbers. It was he and Caleb who inverted the claim of the other 10 spies in describing the inhabitants of Canaan as "bread" (Numbers 14:9) that could be eaten up easily. And indeed, 40 years later, Joshua sets out to "devour" the Promised Land and force the cannibalistic mother back to her position as an object of desire, whose only role is to provide her hungry children with the milk and honey they long for.

Joshua's spies reach Jericho and lodge in the house of the prostitute Rahab. The King of Jericho tries to catch them, but Rahab hides them in the roof of the house, explaining her motives to the men at length:

> I know that the Lord has given the country to you, because dread of you has fallen upon us, and all the inhabitants of the land are quaking before you. For we have heard how the Lord dried up the waters of the Sea of Reeds for you when you left Egypt. (Joshua 2:9–10)

She goes on to request that, once they conquer the city, they will not harm her family. The giants have disappeared and so has the mythical aroma. This time it is not the spies whose hearts fall at the sight of the inhabitants but rather the natives who "quake" at the prospect of an Israelite invasion: a significant departure from the previous tale.

Rahab is a key figure in the drama. Her theophoric name, which means "God has broadened" or "will broaden" (like the name "Rehavia"), intimates that she serves as an opening of sorts, a gate to the Promised Land.[56] Put differently, Rahab, who resides at the city wall, points to the way in which the "fortified cities" of Canaan may be penetrated. With the scarlet rope that she ties as a sign on her window (the same rope with which she helped the two spies escape), she makes clear that Jericho, like the other cities of Canaan, is not as impenetrable as it may seem at first sight: There is a breach in the wall and a hopeful red rope in the window.[57]

The conquest of the land goes hand in hand with sexual conquest. Rahab offers her body in addition to strategic suggestions. There is no detailed description of the affair; it is simply intimated via the word "lie," which means both "to lodge" and "to have sexual relations." Whereas the spies in Numbers merely pluck the fruit but do not eat it (and the sexual connotations of fruit-eating are all too well known from the days of Eden), in Joshua 2 the spies "lie" with an inhabitant of the new land while hiding in her protective home. The nation is "mature" enough, as it were, to conquer. The people do not shy away from sexuality or from possessing the land; they are willing to break through the fortified walls of Jericho and demand their patrimony.

CROSSING THE JORDAN

The history of ancient Israel is replete with meaningful repetitions, intimating that nothing is random: every event is connected to a whole gamut of other incidents. Some links are explicit, others less so, but all point to a divine hand above that shapes the course of events below, however incomprehensible the nation's route may be. When the children of Israel finally cross the Jordan River, their crossing is modeled—most conspicuously—on the wondrous parting of the Red Sea. Here too they walk on dry land in the midst of water, here too the waters return to their place as the crossing ends. And as if these recurrent motifs were not clear enough, an explicit statement by Joshua follows:

> For the Lord your God dried up the waters of the Jordan before you until you crossed, just as the Lord your God did to the Sea of Reeds, which he dried up

before us until we crossed. Thus all the peoples of the earth shall know how mighty is the hand of the Lord, and you shall fear the Lord your God always. (Joshua 4:23–24)

It is a moment of rebirth, an initiation rite that marks Israel's coming of age. Much as Jacob's initiatory crossing of the Jabbok (after struggling with the divine being) recapitulates his uterine struggle with his elder brother Esau, so the nation's crossing of the Jordan evokes the natal imagery of the primary parting as it fashions a new birth, a transition into another phase. The rite of passage by the Jordan River may not be as exhilarating as the one by the Red Sea (we do not hear the people singing), but it clearly reveals a tremendous change in the nation's position: no longer a multitude of runaway slaves, a nascent nation, but an established community, with the Ark of the Covenant at its midst, with priests who lead the ceremonial crossing, and with 40,000 soldiers ready to wage war on Jericho, the first city to be conquered.

The final note of this initiatory ceremony takes place on the other side of the Jordan, after the crossing has been completed. Twelve stones are taken from the river and placed together to commemorate the occasion of the passage of the 12 tribes into Canaan. At this liminal site, all the men are circumcised together (circumcision is a very common practice in initiation rites) by means of sharp knives made of flint. Joshua chooses to call the place Gilgal, and God provides the explanation: "Today I have rolled away *[galoti]* from you the disgrace of Egypt" (Joshua 5:9). The pun on which this naming-speech relies associates the name Gilgal with the root *glh*. The cutting of the foreskin, on the threshold of Canaan, is seen as God's rolling off the disgrace of Egypt, the turning of a new national page, far away from the humiliation of bondage.

But this national rite of passage is not a magical coming of age in which the foundling nation suddenly matures into an invincible upright hero and acquires cultural individuation and dominance. The yielding of the Israelites to the seduction of the daughters of Moab just before the crossing, much like the inclusion of Rahab's household within the Israelite camp right after the crossing, indicates that Israel is not that successful in "dwelling apart," not even on entering a land of its own.

The shadow of exile hovers on the threshold of Canaan. If Israel fails to erase the traces of previous cultures from the Promised Land, Moses warns, and defiles its home with idolatrous rites of the sort adopted in the plains of Moab, that which God planned to do to the Canaanites will be enacted upon them (Numbers 33:56). The Israelites will be dispossessed at once.

Biblical historiography points to the complexity of national imagination. It offers penetrating renditions of national ambivalence, resisting the temptation of endorsing idealized epic narratives of devoted ancestors who had no qualms. It offers a daring representation of national formation, where conflicting views of the nation are placed side by side, where exhilarating moments of collective creativity are juxtaposed with moments of immense despair and appalling violence, where the fragility of concepts such as "chosen-ness" and "promise" is an ongoing concern. The nation is the privileged site of cultural production in the Bible, but its privileged position by no means exempts it from critique.

NOTES

1. For more on the relation between the stories of the Tower of Babel and Abraham, see Martin Buber, *On the Bible* (New York, 1982), 30–31.

2. See Umberto Cassuto, *Commentary on Genesis I: From Adam to Noah* (1944; reprint, Jerusalem, 1961).

3. I take the concept of "national biography" from the inspiring study by Benedict Anderson, *Imagined Communities: Reflections on the Origin and Spread of Nationalism* (London, 1981), 204–6.

4. For an extensive discussion of the question of national literature in the ancient Near East, see Moshe Greenberg, *Understanding Exodus* (New York, 1969), 12–13.

5. For more on Greek foundation stories, see Irad Malkin, *Religion and Colonization in Ancient Greece* (Leiden, 1987). On Roman national identity, see Erich Gruen, *Culture and National Identity in Republican Rome* (Ithaca, N.Y., 1992).

6. On the comparison between the Bible and the *Aeneid*, see Moshe Weinfeld, *The Promise of the Land: The Inheritance of the Land of Canaan by the Israelites* (Berkeley, 1993), 1–21, and Yaakov Licht, *Ta'anat ha-kinun ha-mikra'it: Shenaton lemikra u-lecheker ha-mizrach ha-kadum* (Jerusalem, 1980), 98–125.

7. It is only in the Prophetic texts that the nation is construed as God's wife. For a cogent analysis of the husband-wife metaphor, see Moshe Halbertal and Avishai Margalit, *Idolatry* (Cambridge, Mass., 1992), 9–36.

8. Much has been written on the anthropomorphic character of God by scholars as diverse as Yehezkel Kaufmann, *The Religion of Israel* (New York, 1972); Phyllis Trible, *God and the Rhetoric of Sexuality* (Philadelphia, 1978); and Jack Miles, *God: A Biography* (New York, 1995). In most of these cases, however, the concomitant personification of the nation has not received much attention.

9. This is an interesting monotheistic revision of the divine lineage attributed to heroes in polytheistic traditions. No biblical hero could be defined as God's son (that would make Him far too anthropomorphic), but the nation as a whole may acquire such a status precisely because it is more clearly a metaphoric affiliation.

10. Greenberg, *Understanding Exodus.* For more on the biblical treatment of Israel as a "young" nation, see Amos Funkenstein, *Perceptions of Jewish History* (Berkeley, 1993), 50–53.

11. Funkenstein, *Perceptions,* 51. See also Yosef Haim Yerushalmi, *Zachor: Jewish History and Jewish Memory* (Seattle, 1982).

12. Much has been written on the intricate interrelations of literature and history in biblical narrative. See the insightful studies of Robert Alter, *The Art of Biblical Narrative* (New York, 1981), and David Damrosch, *The Narrative Covenant: Transformations of Genre in the Growth of Biblical Literature* (San Francisco, 1987).

13. For more on the link between the opening of Exodus and the promises and blessings of Genesis, see Umberto Cassuto, *A Commentary on the Book of Exodus* (Jerusalem, 1967), 7–9.

14. My analysis of the interrelations between the birth story of Moses and that of the nation is indebted to the insightful observations of James Nohrnberg, "Moses," in *Images of Man and God: Old Testament Short Stories in Literary Focus,* B. O. Long, ed. (Sheffield, Engl., 1981), 35–57. Nohrnberg, however, focuses on the representation of Moses rather than that of Israel.

15. The midrash noticed this structuring and defined it as *ma'aseh avot siman lebanim* (the deeds of the fathers are a sign for their children).

16. For more on the intertextual links between the story of Hagar and that of the nation, see Phyllis Trible, *Texts of Terror: Literary Feminist Readings of Biblical Narratives* (Philadelphia, 1984), 9–36, and Yair Zakovitch, *And You Shall Tell Your Son: The Concept of the Exodus in the Bible* (Jerusalem, 1991).

17. I rely on Otto Rank's list of recurrent motifs in *The Myth of the Birth of the Hero* (New York, 1932). Rank refers to a variety of myths—from the birth legend of Saragon, the third-millennium B.C.E. king of Akkad, to the renowned story of Oedipus's exposure, and the tale of Remus and Romulus, the legendary founders of Rome. Biblical scholarship mostly focused on the Mesopotamian version of the "Legend of Saragon," regarding it as a possible source of influence on the biblical writers. The relevant section of the text reads as follows, as quoted in Nahum Sarna, *Exploring Exodus: The Origins of Biblical Israel* (New York, 1986), 30: "Saragon, the mighty king, king of Agade, am I. / My mother was a high priestess, my father I knew not . . . / My mother, the high priestess, conceived; in secret she bore me. / She set me in a basket of rushes, with bitumen she sealed my lid. / She cast me into the river which rose not over me. / The river bore me up and carried me to Akki, the drawer of water. / Akki, the drawer of water, lifted me out as he dipped his ewer. / Akki, the drawer of water, took me as his son and reared me." One could add another story of Egyptian mythology to the list: that of Horus among the bulrushes. See my discussion on the interrelations of the birth stories of Moses and Horus in *Countertraditions in the Bible: A Feminist Approach* (Cambridge, Mass., 1992).

18. See Sigmund Freud, *Moses and Monotheism,* trans. Katherine Jones (1939; reprint, New York, 1967), 3–15.

19. See D. Zeligs, *Moses: A Psychodynamic Study* (New York, 1986).

20. For more on the names of the two midwives, see Cassuto, *Commentary on the Book of Exodus*, 13–14.

21. For more on the political aspects of enslavement in Exodus, see Michael Walzer, *Exodus and Revolution* (New York, 1985).

22. It is noteworthy that Ezekiel provides a different account not only of the nation's gender but also of its place of birth and primary lineage. "Thy birth and thy nativity is of the land of Canaan," he claims, "thy father was an Amorite and thy mother an Hittite" (16:3). He regards the Amorites and Hittites (closely connected with the Canaanites according to biblical ethnography) as parent-nations (rather than Egypt) because he is interested in raising a more immediate concern—Israel's distinctiveness (or lack thereof) vis-à-vis the neighboring nations of Canaan. The Exodus tradition, however, is still present in the scene, because God's second passing by seems to take place in Egypt. See Moshe Greenberg, *Ezekiel 1–20* (Garden City, N.Y., 1983).

23. See Nohrnberg, "Moses," 46.

24. "Red Sea" is a well-established mistranslation. *Yam suf* actually means "Reed Sea."

25. For more on calendars and revolutions, see Walter Benjamin, *Illuminations* (New York, 1969), 261.

26. See Martin Buber, *Moses: The Revelation and the Covenant* (Atlantic Highlands, N.J., 1988), 75–76.

27. See Robert Alter, *The Art of Biblical Poetry* (New York, 1985), for a fascinating analysis of the literary aspects of the Song of the Sea.

28. See Cassuto, *Commentary on the Book of Exodus*, 177–79.

29. For more on the feminine metaphors of God, see Trible, *God and the Rhetoric of Sexuality.* Trible, however, does not consider the Song of the Sea in this connection.

30. Perhaps God is a cross between the midwives and Pharaoh's daughter.

31. Sarna, *Exploring Exodus*, 24.

32. Quoted in G. Robins, *Women in Ancient Egypt* (Cambridge, Mass., 1993), 82.

33. For more on Miriam's role in this scene, see the essays by F. Dijk-Hemmes and by Carol Meyers in *Feminist Companion to Exodus-Deuteronomy*, A. Brenner, ed. (New York, 1994), 200–206, 207–30.

34. For an extensive consideration of the etymology of the name "Gershom," see Sarna, *Exploring Exodus*, 37.

35. Nehama Leibowitz offers an insightful analysis of the various traditions regarding the two midwives in *Studies in Shemot*, trans. Aryeh Newman (Jerusalem, 1981), 31–38.

36. Julia Kristeva, *The Kristeva Reader* (New York, 1986), 304.

37. Leibowitz, *Studies*, 245.

38. On the injunction to remember the Exodus, see the illuminating discussion in Yerushalmi, *Zachor.*

39. Esau is the eponymous father of Edom. "Edom," in fact, is another name for Esau, at-

tributed to him (according to Gen. 25:30) for gulping down the red *[adom]* stew Jacob prepared for him.

40. Alter, *The Art of Biblical Narrative*, 170–71. For more on Egypt as an underworld of sorts, see J. Ackerman, "Joseph, Judah, and Jacob," in *Literary Interpretations of Biblical Narratives*, K. R. Gros Louis, ed., with J. S. Ackerman (Nashville, Tenn., 1982), 92. Thomas Mann provides an elaborate reading of Joseph's descent to Egypt as a descent to the underworld in *Joseph and His Brothers*, trans. H. T. Lowe-Porter (New York, 1934).

41. On ancestors and the nation, see Ernst Renan, "What Is a Nation?" in *Nation and Narration*, H. Bhabha, ed. (London, 1992), 19.

42. For more on the conflicting traditions regarding the origins of Rome, see Gruen, *Culture and National Identity in Republican Rome*.

43. William Bradford, *Of Plymouth Plantation* (New York, 1967), 65–66.

44. On the representations of the New World, see Stephen Greenblatt, *Marvelous Possessions: The Wonder of the New World* (Chicago, 1991).

45. In Deuteronomy, one finds an interesting comparison between Egyptian and Canaanite agriculture: "For the land that you are about to enter and possess is not like the land of Egypt from which you have come. There the grain you sowed had to be watered by your own labors, like a vegetable garden; but the land you are about to cross into and possess, a land of hills and valleys, soaks up its water from the rains of heaven" (11:10–11).

46. *Numbers Rabbah* 16:2, *Tanhuma B. Numbers* 66.

47. Greenblatt, *Marvelous Possessions*, 136.

48. Interestingly, in the texts of the New World one finds a similar notion of the nakedness of the land. By the 1570s, as Louise Montrose shows, "allegorical personifications of America as a female nude with feathered headdress had begun to appear in engravings and paintings, on maps, and title pages, throughout Europe." In *New World Encounters*, S. Greenblatt, ed. (Berkeley, 1993), 179.

49. The notion that the choice of Hebron had something to do with the burial site of the fathers is evident in BT Sota 34. According to this tradition, Caleb visited the fathers' graves during the expedition and asked the deceased to help him in his struggle against the other spies.

50. See Shamaryahu Talmon, *Literary Studies in the Hebrew Bible: Form and Content* (Jerusalem, 1993), 76–90.

51. See Bruno Bettelheim, *The Uses of Enchantment: The Meaning and Importance of Fairy Tales* (New York, 1977).

52. See Jacob Milgrom, *Commentary on Numbers* (Philadelphia, 1990), 114.

53. Ibid., 115.

54. See Tzvetam Todorov, *The Conquest of America: The Question of the Other*, trans. R. Howard (New York, 1984), and Greenblatt, *Marvelous Possessions*, for extensive discussions on naming and the New World.

55. On the ongoing ambivalence vis-à-vis the Promised Land, see the thought-provoking

discussion in Zali Gurevitch and Gideon Aran, "Never in Place: Eliade and Judaic Sacred Space," *Archives de Sciences Sociales des Religions* 87 (Sept. 1994): 135–52.

56. See G. Boling and E. Wright, *Joshua* (Garden City, N.Y., 1982), 145.

57. In Hebrew one can discern wordplay between "rope" and "hope," given the double meaning of *tikvah, tikvat chut hashani.*

SELECTED BIBLIOGRAPHY

Alter, Robert. *The Art of Biblical Narrative.* New York, 1981.

Bal, Mieke. *Death and Dissymmetry: The Politics of Coherence in the Book of Judges.* Chicago, 1988.

Buber, Martin. *Moses: The Revelation and the Covenant.* Atlantic Highlands, N.J., 1988.

———. *On the Bible.* New York, 1982.

Damrosch, David. *The Narrative Covenant: Transformations of Genre in the Growth of Biblical Literature.* San Francisco, 1987.

Douglas, Mary. *In the Wilderness: The Doctrine of Defilement in the Book of Numbers.* Sheffield, Engl., 1993.

Freud, Sigmund. *Moses and Monotheism.* Trans. Katherine Jones. 1939. Reprint, New York, 1967.

Greenberg, Moshe. *Understanding Exodus.* New York, 1969.

Halbertal, Moshe, and Avishai Margalit. *Idolatry.* Cambridge, Mass., 1992.

Josipovici, Gabriel. *The Book of God: A Response to the Bible.* New Haven, Conn., 1988.

Nohrnberg, James. *Like unto Moses: The Constituting of an Interruption.* Bloomington, Ind., 1995.

Pardes, Ilana. *The Biography of Ancient Israel: National Narratives in the Bible.* Berkeley, 2000.

———. *Countertraditions in the Bible: A Feminist Approach.* Cambridge, Mass., 1992.

Sarna, Nahum. *Exploring Exodus: The Origins of Biblical Israel.* New York, 1986.

Schwartz, Regina. *The Curse of Cain: The Violent Legacy of Monotheism.* Chicago, 1997.

Trible, Phyllis. *God and the Rhetoric of Sexuality.* Philadelphia, 1978.

———. *Texts of Terror: Literary Feminist Readings of Biblical Narratives.* Philadelphia, 1984.

Walzer, Michael. *Exodus and Revolution.* New York, 1985.

Weinfeld, Moshe. *The Promise of the Land: The Inheritance of the Land of Canaan by the Israelites.* Berkeley, 1993.

Yerushalmi, Yosef Haim. *Zachor: Jewish History and Jewish Memory.* Seattle, 1982.

Gold pendant representing the great Syrian goddess Kadesh,
Ugarit (Ras Shamra), thirteenth century B.C.E.
(Louvre Museum, Paris. Photo: Chuzeville.
© Réunion des Musées Nationaux / Art Resource, New York)

ISRAEL AMONG THE NATIONS:

Biblical Culture in the Ancient Near East

RONALD S. HENDEL

". . . Yahweh, the God of all the earth"
—Hebrew inscription from Khirbet Beit Lei
(SIXTH CENTURY B.C.E.)[1]

After defeating King Og of Bashan, whom biblical tradition remembers as a giant,[2] Moses and the Israelites camp in the plains of Moab, east of the Jordan River. Frightened at their numbers, the king of Moab summons the foreign seer Balaam to curse this people, but instead of a curse, Balaam pronounces God's blessing. As Balaam tells the story:

From Aram has Balak summoned me,
the king of Moab from the eastern mountains.
"Come, curse Jacob for me,
come, condemn Israel!"
But how can I curse what God has not cursed,
how can I condemn what Yahweh has not condemned?
For I see them from the top of the mountains,
from the hills I gaze upon them.
Behold, it is a people dwelling apart,
not counting itself among the nations.
Who can count the dust of Jacob,
who can number the dust-cloud of Israel? (Numbers 23:7–10)[3]

Balaam perceives that Israel is a unique people whom God has blessed, a people set apart from the usual run of ancient Near Eastern nations.

My theme is taken from Balaam's description of Israel as "a people dwelling apart, not counting itself among the nations." Israel was a nation and a culture of the ancient Near East, yet it saw itself as different and somehow incommensurate with the other nations. On one level, this sense of uniqueness is far from unique: it is the root of nationalism and ethnicity in its many forms.[4] The Greeks denoted non-Greeks as barbarians *(barbaroi)* because they did not speak Greek, the language of civilized people. The Egyptians referred to themselves as "people" *(rmt),* implicitly—and sometimes explicitly—evoking the nonpeoplehood of others. But, on another level, the ancient Israelite claim to uniqueness was more forceful than most peoples' and more central to its self-definition.[5] Indeed, it is arguable that this claim to uniqueness was in some measure self-fulfilling, enabling the Jewish people to outlive all the other cultures of the ancient Near East. By persisting in its claim to uniqueness, and by routinizing this claim in its cultural habits, the Jewish people made that uniqueness a historical reality. The fact of its being alive today, roughly three millennia later, seems to ratify Balaam's perception that this is a people apart.

The boundaries that biblical culture set about itself were in a sense more permanent and decisive than those of its ancient peers. Elsewhere in the ancient Near East, one could identify one's own gods and religious practices with those of other nations.[6] For example, the Egyptians could adopt Canaanite gods and their mythology into the Egyptian religious system simply by equating them with native gods (Baal = Seth; El = Ptah; etc.). The standard formula of international treaties required that both parties' gods participate as witnesses, acknowledging a degree of communication and mutual recognition among the gods of different cultures. Although the names, languages, and local practices might differ, there was a consciousness of a basic cultural translatability in the ancient Near East. Ancient Israel seems to have been the exception to this rule.[7] Israelite writings from the earliest period repeatedly sound the theme of nontranslatability, of the birth of something new and different.

The choice of the seer Balaam to announce this basic difference reveals some interesting aspects of Israel's claim to uniqueness. Balaam is a foreigner—he is identified as an Aramean from the eastern mountains—and we now know that he was a figure of some repute in other neighboring cultures. In 1967 a Dutch excavation at Tell Deir Alla, not far from the plains of Moab, discovered an inscription from the eighth century B.C.E. that relates "the account of Balaam, son of Beor, the man who was a seer of the gods."[8] The language of this inscription is a Northwest Semitic dialect not hitherto known, sharing some distinctive features with Ammonite and Aramaic. This is an inscription of one of Israel's neighbors, showing us the continuity of religious and literary traditions—and their dramatis personae—in the West Semitic cultural sphere. Balaam, it seems, was an exemplar of the virtuous foreign seer. His dual status as a true seer and a foreigner makes him an apt figure to proclaim the uniqueness of Israel in the biblical narrative. As a foreigner, he is not prone to Israelite partisanship, and as an inspired seer, he speaks only the truth. But the fame of Balaam in West Semitic traditions shows that Israelite traditions were not unique—that is, they shared a common root and repertoire with Israel's neighbors. The voice of Balaam subtly proclaims that Israel was not wholly a nation apart.

In contrast to this early portrait of Balaam, later biblical traditions had trouble assimilating the idea of him as a virtuous foreign seer. The doctrine of cultural and religious uniqueness, which Balaam announces, led perhaps inevitably to a reevaluation of his character. In later biblical writings, this righteous gentile is recast in the common stereotype of the dangerous and/or stupid foreign Other. In the Priestly source—dating from roughly the sixth century B.C.E.[9]—Moses blames Balaam for inciting Israelite men to have sex with foreign women, a grievous sin in God's eyes, and Balaam dies in battle as his just punishment (Numbers 31:8, 16). In a later postexilic supplement to the story, Balaam is derided as more stupid than his donkey, since even the donkey can see the angel of God (Numbers 22:22–35).[10] The foreign seer who sees truly has been transformed into an agent of sin and a blindly blundering fool. These are typical biblical tropes for the foreign Other: obtuse, seductive, and/or evil. The bitter side of Israel's claim to uniqueness is revealed by its inability to preserve Balaam's virtue in its narrative traditions. The righteousness of the foreign seer was lost in translation.

Interestingly, the chief exceptions to the disparagement of foreigners in the Bible are foreign women. Tamar in Genesis 38, Rahab in Joshua 2, Jael in Judges 4–5, and Ruth in the book of her name are the paradigm examples of the righteous foreigner, and all are women. This situation turns the table on Balaam's sin of inciting Jewish men to have sex with foreign women, because in at least two out of these four instances, the virtuous act of the foreign women involves having sex with Jewish men. (The Rahab story is ambiguous on this issue, though she is a prostitute by profession.) Tamar's seduction of Judah and Ruth's seduction of Boaz result in the restoration of an Israelite lineage that would otherwise have been lost—the lineage that produces King David. Without their exceptional actions, the line of Judah would have been forfeit, and David would have never been born. The virtues of these foreign women have to do with their preservation of the tribal patriline. Because they are foreigners, their virtues are extraordinary, and their seduction of Jewish men is, in these cases, a moral good. Tamar and Ruth are the antitheses to the late portrayal of Balaam.

The Bible presents many ways of defining and negotiating the boundaries between Israel and the foreign nations. In this chapter, I will address some of the ways that biblical culture approached the differences between Israel and its Others. The questions involved (Who is an Israelite? What are the distinctive structures of Israelite religion? What are the implicit boundaries of Israelite culture?) are both historical and hermeneutical: they touch upon what really happened in the history of ancient Israel *and* how these events and circumstances were interpreted in the biblical writings. But first a caveat—history does not come neat or plain in these writings; the Hebrew Bible consists in large part of interpretations and reflections on history—more a midrash on the times than the times themselves. But, of course, this is part of what makes the Bible a timeless book. Interpretation or commentary is, as Gershom Scholem observed, part of the essence of Judaism.[11] This process of making sense of texts begins in the interpretations and contested meanings within the Hebrew Bible.

One of these conflicts of interpretation, we shall see, concerns the nature of Israel's relations with its foreign Others. Balaam's statement is not the last word on Israel's distinctiveness in the Hebrew Bible. A dialectic of sharing and distancing, of inclusion and estrangement, characterizes biblical culture from its earliest sources to its most recent.

THE EXODUS AND THE CULTURAL CONSTRUCTION OF ISRAEL

The origins of Israel in history are obscure. In the year 1207 B.C.E., the Egyptian pharaoh Merneptah stated in a royal inscription that he had conquered Israel (among other peoples) in a military campaign through Canaan. The key line reads in Egyptian: "Israel is laid waste, his seed is no more."[12] Merneptah overstated the case, as was conventional in royal inscriptions, since Israel continued to exist. In spite of its pharaonic hyperbole, the Merneptah stele provides the earliest textual evidence outside of the Bible for Israel's existence as a people in the Near East.

The archaeological evidence shows that, beginning in the late thirteenth century B.C.E.—around the time of this inscription—there was significant population expansion in the central highlands of the land of the Canaanites.[13] This new group of highland settlers was presumably the people Merneptah called Israel—or possibly Israel was one of several groups in the highlands at this time. The settlements excavated by archaeologists share a number of similar cultural features. They are small, unwalled villages, some probably no more than the dwellings of extended families. There are no signs of social stratification or permanent military establishments. The material culture in general is a local, rural development of Canaanite culture.

This evidence indicates that early Israel was largely a local culture, a variant of regional Canaanite or West Semitic cultural traditions. If this was so—if Israel was a frontier society in the now habitable highlands—then how did being an Israelite differ from being a rural Canaanite or an Ammonite or a Moabite? (Ammon and Moab were neighboring cultures coming into being at roughly the same time as Israel.) This essential question concerns the construction of ethnic identities and cultural boundaries in this period.

Recent research has demonstrated that culture and ethnicity are more matters of belief and custom than they are proof of common descent. In the memorable title of one such study, nations or ethnic groups are "imagined communities,"[14] imagined into existence by those who believe in the group and participate in its social interactions. In the case of ancient Israel, the imagination that flows into the construction of a cultural identity is, at least in part, preserved for us in the biblical portrayal of Israel's origins. The most important of these imaginative constructs are the stories of the Exodus-Sinai-Wanderings period, related in the books of Exodus through Deuteronomy.

These stories can be regarded not only as a national biography, in Ilana Pardes' evocative phrase,[15] but also as a historical engine for the construction of cultural identity. That is, the stories not only narrate the life of a nation but also functioned in historical time as a key agent in the formation of the nation they narrate. Early Israel included, in the words of the biblical story, "a mixed multitude" (Exodus 12:38). Many of the people who settled in the early highlands community would have fit this description; they probably included peasant farmers and pastoralists, fugitives and bandits, and escaped slaves. How did they become incorporated into a cohesive social community? In no small part this transformation of identity was created by shared belief in a common story: the Exodus from Egypt, the revelation at Sinai, the wanderings in the wilderness, and the passage as a unified people into the Promised Land. These stories, in their aggregate, constitute a collective rite of passage for the people of Israel, transforming a mixed multitude from their former identity as slaves in a foreign land into a new identity as a free people—God's people—in a land of promise and plenty.[16]

Even if some or many of these formative events did not really happen in the way that they are told, they were—and still are—felt and understood to be a shared memory of a collective past. Such stories of an epic past function as a symbolic shaper of community, joining people together around a common ethnic, cultural, and religious identity. The celebrations and tales of the Exodus create and periodically reaffirm this common identity. The most obvious example is the Passover meal, the Seder, which includes the retelling of the Exodus story as an expression of the continued collective significance of the deliverance from Egypt. Jewish identity, from its beginnings to the present day, is formed in no small part by the recitation of these stories.

The function of ethnic identity-formation bound up with these stories is at

times directly indicated in the biblical writings. In the midst of the plague narratives, God tells Moses that he is performing these deeds "so that you will tell your
children and your children's children how I dealt with Egypt and how I brought
my signs upon them, so that you [plural] will know that I am Yahweh" (Exodus
10:2). Knowing God's power and identity seems to be the point of these deeds
and the point of preserving their memory in stories. But knowing God's identity
also has a social correlate—knowing that Israel is God's people. This is emphasized in God's repeated promise: "I will be your God and you will be my people."
In his command that the Israelites recount the story to their children and grandchildren, God seems to acknowledge that the stories of his great deeds on behalf
of his people are a narrative that binds the people together as a cohesive religious
community (12:24–27, 13:8). The command to tell these stories in each generation is, in a sense, a self-fulfilling command that constructs the cultural identity
of its primary audience.

The cultural boundaries of early Israel were, at least in part, constructed
by the dissemination of stories about the deliverance of Israel from Egyptian
bondage and the birth of a free people in the Promised Land. It is important to
note that even Israelite settlers who had never been slaves in Egypt could easily
participate in this narrative memory, because Egypt had been the overlord of
Canaan for several centuries previously (ca. 1500–1200 B.C.E.). Egyptian rule during this period had often been harsh, including the regular export of Canaanites
to Egypt to serve as slaves.[17] With the waning of the Egyptian empire in Canaan,
the memory of oppression and slavery and the concomitant memory of deliverance to freedom would have resonated in the drama of the Exodus story.[18] By
adopting this story as their own, the villagers in the highlands became Israelites,
and a mixed multitude crystallized its collective identity as the people of Yahweh.

GENEALOGY AND DIFFERENCES

One of the ways that the ancient Israelites joined together was by forming
genealogical alliances. In so doing, they defined who was an Israelite and who
was an outsider. The difference between inside and outside inevitably became
charged with moral difference, with the insiders superior to the outsiders. This is
a universal human trait, egoism on a national scale.

Sigmund Freud once commented, somewhat diffidently, on the reasons that
closely related peoples disparage one another:

I once interested myself in the peculiar fact that peoples whose territories are
adjacent, and are otherwise closely related, are always at feud with and ridicul-

ing each other. . . . I gave it the name of "narcissism in respect of minor differences," which does not do much to explain it.[19]

This trait of cultural narcissism is strongly at work in the genealogical stories in the Bible, primarily in Genesis, in which the relations between Israel's ancestors and the ancestors of other nations are recounted. In these stories, the cultural boundaries of Israel are continually endangered by the presence of the ancestors of other peoples, and the Israelites survive the slings of fortune by varying means—including virtue, guile, and divine intervention. Before we turn to these stories, let us examine more closely the importance of genealogies and genealogical narratives in the construction of cultural identity.

A genealogy shows, in a memorable way, who is related to whom. In many small-scale societies, including early Israel, genealogical relations are the internal boundaries of society. That is, person X and person Y are both members of the same society because, at some level of the national or tribal genealogy, they descend from a common ancestor. The degree of distance from the common ancestor determines the particular status of the relationship between the two persons. For example, in a patrilineal society such as ancient Israel (where descent is measured on the male side), two siblings are related because of a common father, two cousins by a common grandfather, two members of the same clan by a common ancestor of the clan, two tribesmen by a common ancestor of the tribe, and two Israelites by common descent from the ancestor Israel, father of the twelve tribes. The closer the common ancestor to the generation of X and Y, the closer their relationship to each other. The degree of closeness determines their mutual obligations and responsibilities.

The idiom of descent or genealogy is itself a cultural construction; that is, one does not need to be related by blood to be genealogically related. It is a regular rule in patrilineal societies that women enter into their husband's lineage at marriage. At times in the Bible, we can see whole clans or villages changing their places in the genealogy because of a change of historical circumstances. For example, the clans or villages of Hetzron and Carmi are both sons of Reuben in some texts (Genesis 46:9; Exodus 6:14; cf. 1 Chronicles 5:3) but are elsewhere listed as sons of Judah (1 Chronicles 4:1). This shift in genealogical affiliation probably provides a glimpse of tribal history, as Reubenite clans were absorbed into Judah. Even foreign villages and clans can become Israelite and enter the genealogy. The foreign clan of Jerahmeel later became a clan of Judah, again reflecting the tribal expansion of Judah and the absorption of foreign clans into its lineage (cf. 1 Samuel 27:10 and 1 Chronicles 2:9, 25). A group can change its status from outsider to insider by assuming a new social identity and entering the genealogy. One's place in the genealogy is a sign of cultural self-definition more than it is a sign of biological descent.

With the social function and historical fluidity of genealogies in mind, let us see how they are used in the Bible to mark the boundary between inside and outside, between Israel and the nations. In Genesis, these boundaries are fragile and contentious. The legal status of the firstborn son to carry the main line of the genealogy is highly contested, most obviously between Jacob and Esau but also between Sarah and Hagar (on behalf of their sons, Isaac and Ishmael), Perez and Zerah, Joseph and his brothers, and even Cain and Abel. Usually the younger son prevails and the older son is denigrated in some way, as if the firstborn were unworthy of carrying the lineage that issues in the people Israel. In these lineage conflicts, the Israelite ancestors are extolled and the ancestors of its cultural neighbors disparaged. Although the genealogical stories acknowledge Israel's relatedness to its neighbors, the relationship is colored by various stereotypes of the Other. Through a dialectic of structural opposition, Israel asserts in its genealogical stories that it is a righteous and civilized people, in contrast to the foreigners who more often than not are seen as creatures of nature: wild, stupid, sexually licentious, or violent.

In the primeval narratives of Genesis 1–11, three peoples are singled out for genealogical derision: the Kenites, the Canaanites, and the Babylonians. Cain (originally *Qayn*) is clearly, by his distinctive name, the eponymous ancestor of the tribe of Kenites (originally *Qayni*).[20] Cain, of course, is a fratricide whom God curses to wander without home or refuge (Genesis 4:12). This is an attribution of a shameful, violent ancestral origin. The Israelites, in contrast, are descended from Adam and Eve's third and youngest son, Seth. The next people disparaged are the Canaanites, whose ancestor is Canaan. He is cursed for his father's sexual transgression—"Ham, Canaan's father, saw his father's nakedness"— and is consigned to servitude (9:20–27). Canaan's curse in this story is, as Rashi noted, a justification for God's decision to reassign the land of Canaan to the children of Israel. This, too, is a shameful origin for this foreign people and a warrant for Israelite domination. The third people disparaged in the primeval narratives is Babylon, whose city becomes a watchword of cultural arrogance and disaster (11:1–9). The Tower of Babel story deflates the cultural pretensions of Babylonian civilization. In all three of these ethnographic tales, a foreign people is colored with shameful origins.

In the patriarchal narratives of Genesis 12–50, the genealogical contrast of wild foreigners with the civilized precursors of Israel is both heightened and complicated. The three generations of the patriarchs—Abraham, Isaac, and Jacob—each portray a different set of genealogical oppositions. In the first,

Abraham's righteousness is contrasted with his nephew Lot's flaws. Lot's most egregious fault occurs in Genesis 19, when he offers his daughters to the lustful townsmen of Sodom in an attempt to protect his guests. In an apt and shameful turnabout, his daughters later seduce Lot, and they become pregnant and bear the ancestors of Moab and Ammon (19:30–38). Lot's incest with his daughters is a grievous sin, which stains the ancestry of the peoples of Moab and Ammon. Although Israel is related to its Transjordanian neighbors and is at times on good terms with them, these peoples are denigrated by their ancestors' shameful sexual origins.

The next generation juxtaposes Ishmael, the son born of the slave woman Hagar, and Isaac, the son born of Abraham's wife, Sarah. Ishmael, who is cast out at Sarah's insistence, becomes the ancestor of the Arab peoples. Although an angel of God gives him the promise of a great nation, the angel also promises that "he will be a wild ass of a man, his hand against everyone, and everyone's hand against him" (Genesis 16:12). Later, Ishmael prospers as a hunter in the wilderness and marries an Egyptian woman (21:20–21). The story of Ishmael gives a mixed portrait: he is blessed by God, but he ends up as a predator on the outskirts of civilization, violent as a wild ass and marrying a foreign woman. In terms of the story, Ishmael—and, by implication, his descendants—are less civilized than the line of his younger half-brother, Isaac.

It is illuminating to note how Islamic and Christian traditions later revise the structural opposition of Abraham's two sons in accord with their cultural and genealogical preferences. In post-koranic Islamic tradition, Ishmael is exalted as the beloved son whom Abraham almost sacrifices, and Ishmael and Abraham together build the holy shrine of the Kaaba in Mecca.[21] In the New Testament, Paul identifies the child of the promise, Isaac, as the symbolic precursor of the Christians, and the slave's child, Ishmael, as the symbolic precursor of the Jews (Galatians 4:22–31). In all three Abrahamic religions, the genealogical process of cultural self-definition is at work in the portrayal of Abraham's sons.

The third generation of the patriarchal lineage in Genesis contrasts Jacob, the younger son, with Esau, the firstborn. Whereas Jacob is a smooth man—a term that applies both to his body and to his deceptive stratagems[22]—his brother Esau is hairy, a wild man like Ishmael, more at home in the wilderness than in human settlements. "When the boys grew up, Esau was a man skilled in hunting game, a man of the open country; but Jacob was a civilized [literally, 'pure, whole'] man, dwelling in the tents" (Genesis 25:27). Esau is a man of nature, in contrast to Jacob, the man of culture.[23] Esau's brutish simplicity makes him an easy mark for Jacob's wiles when he sells his birthright for a bowl of lentil soup (25:29–34). At the end of this tale, Esau does not even seem to realize what he has done: "He ate and he drank and he rose up and he walked away"—he is a man who thinks with his belly.[24] Because Jacob is the intelligent one—and is favored by his intelligent mother—he also tricks his father and obtains the patriarchal blessing and promise (27). Later he resourcefully wins from God the name Israel (32:29), sealing his identity as Israel's ancestor. By contrast, Esau is identified as the ancestor of Edom because he is unable to think of the correct name for the lentil soup, referring to it stupidly as "this red red stuff" (*ha'adom ha'adom ha-zeh* [25:30]). In these stories, the Edomites are collectively stereotyped by their simple and brutish ancestor.

In the processes of genealogical self-definition expressed in these stories, the foreign Other is generally described as, to varying degrees, uncivilized or immoral. One would expect that the hero of the Israelite patriline is, in contrast, civilized and just. Such is the case with Abraham versus Lot and, perhaps, Isaac versus Ishmael (though Isaac is not a major character). But the case of Jacob versus Esau is more complicated, because Jacob, while clearly civilized, is not wholly moral. There is a slippage in the case of Israel's eponymous ancestor.

Jacob is morally challenging—a man of culture, but not a man consistently presenting the best face of human culture. His wiles (and his mother's) win him the birthright and patriarchal blessing. But he pays for his trickery when Laban substitutes his firstborn daughter Leah for the younger daughter Rachel on Jacob's wedding night (Genesis 29:23). In this turnabout, the father tricks the son-in-law in a manner that mirrors the son's earlier trick of his own father. The older child is now substituted for the younger, and Laban justifies the deception in words heavy with irony: "It is not done in our place to give the younger before the firstborn" (29:26). Later, in Genesis 37, Jacob's sons avenge themselves on their precocious younger brother, Joseph, and deceive their father by cleverly manipulating Joseph's special cloak. This trick also echoes Jacob's deception of his father, which involved wearing his brother's best clothes. Jacob pays the price for his tricks several times over, though he retains his status as the eponymous ancestor, Israel. Even Esau seems to grow in maturity by the end of the story (see Genesis 33), while Jacob is still a trickster in old age (see his deception of Joseph in Genesis 48), in spite of having grown wiser.

In the stories of Jacob/Israel, the cultural narcissism of genealogical self-definition is turned, at least in part, into a self-representation of impropriety and guilt. The complexities of the Jewish soul are foreshadowed by this ambiguous characterization. On the one hand, Jacob/Israel is the man of the promise and blessing, who has "striven with God and with men and has prevailed" (Genesis 32:29). On the other hand, he suffers for his triumphs and pays a price for taking the name "Israel." Though he prevails, he also limps (32:32).

THE CANAANITE MATRIX

The prophet Ezekiel, in a message of divine wrath against Israel, castigates its genealogical origins: "Your origins and birth are from the land of the Canaanites. Your father was an Amorite, and your mother was a Hittite" (Ezekiel 16:3). Formulated in the same idiom as the genealogical stories discussed above, this is an attribution of shameful origins, leading to the application of the proverb "Like mother, like daughter" to Israel's infidelity (16:44). Although this genealogical insult is intended to inspire shame and guilt, it also seems to be a fairly accurate portrayal of Israel's origins. There is a deep ambivalence in Ezekiel's angry speech—even though there were marked continuities between Canaanite and Israelite culture, the principle of nontranslatability applies. Anything Canaanite is foreign and abominable in the prophet's eyes.

The extent of the Canaanite matrix of Israelite culture has become clearer over the past several decades. The twin turning points have been the archaeological finds about Israel's origins discussed above, and the discovery of religious texts from the ancient city of Ugarit on the coast of modern Syria, beginning in the 1930s and continuing to the present day.[25] Ugarit was a flourishing Canaanite city-state in the Late Bronze Age (1500–1200 B.C.E.), and most of the texts come from this period, which was immediately prior to the rise of Israelite civilization farther to the south.

The texts from Ugarit are in a language (called Ugaritic) closely related to Hebrew. They tell stories whose themes, diction, and characters are often familiar from the Bible. For example, the following passage from the Ugaritic myth of Baal stands in close relation to a passage from the book of Isaiah written over half a millennium later:

When you killed Litan, the fleeing serpent,
finished off the twisting serpent,
the mighty one with seven heads,
the heavens withered and drooped.[26]

On that day, Yahweh will punish
with his fierce, great, and mighty sword
Leviathan, the fleeing serpent,
Leviathan, the twisting serpent,
he will slay the dragon of the sea. (Isaiah 27:1)

In this instance, as in many others, the Ugaritic and biblical texts draw on a common West Semitic cultural tradition. The monster Litan/Leviathan (variants of the same name) is destined to die at the hand of the great Divine Warrior, Baal at Ugarit and Yahweh in Israel. In Isaiah 27, this myth is projected into the future, when all the forces of chaos will be defeated, and God's rule will be established forever. The defeat of chaos at the dawn of time will recur at the dawn of the hoped-for new era.[27] In the comparison of these two passages, we can see plainly the continuities and the transformations of tradition in Canaan and Israel.

Israelite culture inherits and transforms not only the mythology of the Divine Warrior but also the stories and traits of other figures of the Canaanite pantheon. Perhaps the most surprising survivals and transformations belong to the mythologies of El and Asherah, the father and mother of the Canaanite gods. In the Bible and in several recently discovered Hebrew inscriptions, we can see how aspects of these deities were woven deeply into Israelite conceptions of the divine.

El is the high god of the Canaanite pantheon at Ugarit. His name simply means "God."[28] El is described as wise and gracious; he is called "El, the kind and compassionate one." He is an elderly god with a gray beard and is depicted in reliefs and statuary seated on a royal throne. His image is comparable to the description of the God of Israel in Daniel 7:9: "As I looked, thrones were set up, and the Ancient of Days sat down. His garment was white as snow, and the hair of his head was [white as] pure wool." In other Canaanite and Phoenician texts, El is called "creator of earth," just as the God of Israel is called "El most high, creator of heaven and earth" by Abraham (Genesis 14:22).[29] El is the father of the gods, who are appropriately called the "Children of El" *(banu ili)*, just as the subordinate deities or angels in the Bible are called the "Children [or Sons] of God [El]" *(beney el, beney elohim,* and similarly). El lives on a mountain or, alternately, at the "source of the two seas." Similarly, the God of Israel dwells on a mountain (Sinai or Zion), and his divine garden ("Eden, the garden of God" on "the holy mountain of God" in Ezekiel 28:13–14) is the source of the four rivers (Genesis 2:10). In name, character, and locale, Canaanite El and the God of Israel are closely affiliated.

El is also the "Father of Humans" and "Creator of Creatures," and he blesses his favored worshipers by granting them sons when they lack heirs. The similarities to the biblical stories of the creation of Adam and the granting of sons to Abraham and the other patriarchs are apparent. The decrees of El, promulgated from his mountain home, also remind us of the laws that the God of Israel grants from His holy mountain. The Law at Sinai, in some respects, echoes old cultural memories of the wise decrees of El. Even the name "Israel" *(yisra'el)* seems originally to mean "El rules." The fact that Israel's God is often simply

called "El," as for example in the titles *el olam*, "El
the Ancient One" (Genesis 21:33), or *el shaday*, "El the
One of the Mountain" (17:1, etc.), underscores the
continuity of divine traits shared by Canaanite El
and the God of Israel.[30]

The mother of the gods in the Ugaritic texts is
Asherah, whose name derives from the word for
"trace, path, or place."[31] She is the "Creatress of the
Gods" and is probably referred to as the "Holy One."
As El's wife, she effectively appeals for his blessing
on behalf of other gods. In the Baal myth, she approaches El for his permission to grant Baal a palace,
using sweet and well-balanced words:

Coin depicting sacred place
of Tyre with incense, altar,
standing stones, and tree.
The inscription below reads
"ambrosial stones."
(British Museum, London)

> *Lady Asherah of the sea replied:*
> *"Your decree, O El, is wise,*
> *your wisdom is eternal,*
> *a fortunate life is your decree."*[32]

With such elegant poetic diction—including the interwoven sounds and sense
of *taḥ muka* (your decree), *ḥakamu* (wise), and *ḥakamuka* (your wisdom)—El
easily accedes to her request.

Asherah is also a beneficent goddess for her earthly worshipers. The wise King
Kirta makes an oath to Asherah at one of her temples, promising great tribute if
Asherah grants success to his quest for a wife.

> *They arrived at the holy shrine of Asherah of Tyre,*
> *and of the goddess of Sidon.*
> *There the noble Kirta made a vow:*
> *"As Asherah of Tyre lives,*
> *and the goddess of Sidon,*
> *if I take Hurraya into my house*
> *if I bring the maiden to my court,*
> *I will give double her [weight?] in silver,*
> *triple her [weight?] in gold."*[33]

This passage shows that Asherah had local shrines and worshipers, and that she
was appealed to for her blessings, including matters of marriage and the accompanying expectation of offspring. Such matters seem appropriate for the wife of
El and mother of the gods.

In the Bible, Asherah is known as a goddess who was imported into Israel from Phoenician culture. (Phoenicia was a direct descendant of old Canaanite culture.) The dread Queen Jezebel seems to have brought the "prophets of Asherah" into Israel from her Phoenician homeland (1 Kings 18:19). The evil king Manasseh is said to have erected some sort of statue to Asherah in the Jerusalem Temple (2 Kings 21:7), and there were special rooms in the Temple where women wove embroidered garments for this statue (2 Kings 23:7).[34] The Queen Mother Maacah is also said to have made an "abominable thing" for Asherah (1 Kings 15:13), which suggests some sort of statue or image. It is interesting that these references to the worship of Asherah are restricted to royal families, who are thereby marked as wicked and corrupt.[35]

Elsewhere in the Bible, Asherah (or asherah, with small "a") is used as a word referring to a wooden pole or tree that is part of the cultic furniture of the local shrines in Israel.[36] This "asherah" is a common noun, not a personal name, and, perhaps curiously, has a masculine plural ending. It is not clear whether this asherah-object was conceived as a symbol of the goddess Asherah or whether it had become somehow denatured as a holy symbol of the God of Israel. The prominence of holy trees in various foundation stories of local shrines—including Shechem ("the oak of the Teacher" in Genesis 12:6, probably the same as "the oak in the sanctuary of Yahweh" in Joshua 24:26), Beersheba ("a tamarisk tree," Genesis 21:33), and Ophrah ("a terebinth tree," Judges 6:11)—suggests a diversity of Israelite interpretations of the symbolism of trees at shrines. In these texts, the sacred trees are an unproblematic part of ordinary Israelite worship. In Deuteronomy and other related texts (discussed below), the holy trees, asherahs, and related cultic objects are castigated as foreign abominations, along with the local shrines themselves.

The discovery of several Hebrew inscriptions from the eighth century B.C.E. that mention Asherah—or asherah—has highlighted the prominence of this goddess and/or holy object in ancient Israelite religion.[37] From a local shrine at Kuntillet Ajrud, a stop on an ancient trade route in the northern Sinai, come the following inscriptions on pots and plaster, some quite fragmentary:[38]

    1. "I bless you by Yahweh of Samaria and by his asherah."

    2. ". . . by Yahweh of Teman and by his asherah."

    3. "I bless you by Yahweh of Teman and by his asherah. May he bless you, protect you, and be with my lord forever."

    4. ". . . let them say, 'By Yahweh of Teman and by his asherah . . . May Yahweh do good'. . . ."

Another inscription from the same general period, from a rock tomb at Khirbet el-Qom, also mentions Asherah:[39]

> 5. "May Uriah be blessed by Yahweh, my protector, and by his asherah. Deliver him. . . ."

These inscriptions share the same general blessing formulas that we find in the Bible and other Hebrew inscriptions, with the notable addition of the appeal to "his asherah" (*šrth,* which can be vocalized in biblical style as *asherato*). But who or what is "his asherah"? There are several possible ways to read this reference, and none is entirely satisfactory.

The simplest way to construe "his asherah" is as a reference to the wooden pole or tree that was part of a shrine. This would cohere with the references to the local cults of Yahweh: "Yahweh of Samaria" (the capital city of the northern kingdom), and "Yahweh of Teman" (probably a reference to the region of Kuntillet Ajrud—*teman* means "south"). Each of these local shrines plausibly had an asherah-object or sacred tree beside its altar. This object is perhaps called upon here as an aspect of the sacred presence of Yahweh that is manifested in these places. The "asherah," in this reading, is a symbol of Yahweh's presence, not a separate deity. This coheres with the requests that follow in three of the blessings, in which it is Yahweh alone who acts: (3) "May he bless you, protect you, and be with my lord forever"; (4) "May Yahweh do good . . ."; and (5) "Deliver him. . . ." All of these verbs are in the masculine singular, clearly referring to Yahweh.

A slightly more difficult construction is to read "his asherah" as the goddess Asherah, appealed to in these blessings as a distinctive deity and object of worship. In this reading, Asherah is Yahweh's wife, just as she was El's wife in Canaanite religion. The chief problem for this reading is that the pronominal suffix, "his," is not used for proper names in classical Hebrew. To see the goddess clearly in these blessings requires that the blessing formula be ungrammatical, which seems unlikely. A way around this grammatical objection is to read "asherah" as a generic word for "goddess," which is plausible but not elsewhere attested.

A third way to read this reference combines the meanings of the asherah-object and the goddess Asherah. The reference may be to the asherah-object, but the object may have been generally understood to be a symbol of the goddess. In this reading, the goddess is implicit in the object. There can be no grammatical objection to this reading, but it still encounters some difficulty in the absence of the goddess in the invocations following, which are limited to the masculine singular, "may *he* bless you, protect you," etc. One way out of this difficulty would be to see Asherah as a mediating deity between the worshiper and Yahweh, who is the effective bestower of blessing.

We still do not possess a conclusive understanding of these blessings "by Yahweh and his asherah." One way or another, however, it seems to shed further light on the Canaanite matrix of Israelite religion. Matrix literally means "womb," from the Latin word for "mother." Perhaps in the legacy of Asherah in Israelite religion, we see the trace of the Mother of the Gods in the worship of Yahweh, who, though male, is the one who grants the "blessing of breasts and womb" (Genesis 49:25). Asherah's blessing persists in some measure in the character of this God and his A/asherah.

RITUAL BOUNDARIES: THE BODY, FOOD, TIME

Israelite religion and culture were not monolithic. There were, to borrow William James's phrase, varieties of religious experience in ancient Israel.[40] Recent scholarship has brought to light regional, chronological, and sociological differences in religious practices and beliefs. One of the primary sociological differences is that between family religion and state religion, which at times clashed in the turmoil and social upheavals of Israelite history.[41] Family religion centered on marriage, offspring, and good fortune—as exemplified in the family stories of the patriarchs and others. State religion often centered on national wars and the ideologies of kings—as exemplified in many of the narratives of Judges, Samuel, and Kings.

In the differences between the one religion and the other, we find the natural locations of the legacies of El, the gracious god of the fathers, and Baal, the Divine Warrior. In the patriarchal stories, God is a beneficent divine patriarch; in the national battles of the Exodus and Conquest, he is a warrior and king. For example, the patriarch Jacob blesses his son Joseph by "the God of your fathers, who helps you, the God of the mountain [literally, 'El, the One of the Mountain'], who blesses you" (Genesis 49:25).[42] This is the god of family religion. But in the context of great national events, such as after God's victory at the Red Sea, the divine portrayal is in a different register: "Yahweh is a warrior" and "Yahweh will rule forever and ever" (Exodus 15:3, 18). The two divine "types" emerge in these differing social contexts.

Although the varying internal boundaries in Israelite religion and culture suggest a real cultural pluralism,[43] there were also external boundaries that demarcated, more or less clearly, where Israelite culture began and ended. These external boundaries determined whether or not one was an Israelite. One such common cultural ground was, of course, language, though there is evidence of dialectal variation within Hebrew.[44] Another source of shared identity was the recitation of traditional stories of the past, such as the Exodus story discussed above. A third source was the web of genealogies, in which one's family and clan were explicitly related to everyone else in the lineages of Israel. And fourth was the body of shared rituals. In the practices of everyday life, Israelites enacted their cultural identity in symbolic actions, whether offering animal sacrifice at local shrines, making pilgrimages on the major festivals, or undergoing rites of healing or passage.

A range of ritual practices served to mark the implicit boundaries of cultural identity. Some of these were identical in origin to the practices of neighboring peoples, but over time they came to be understood, by insiders and outsiders, as distinctively Israelite. Among these many acts, three that were—and still are—singled out as distinctive are circumcision, food laws, and observance of the Sabbath. The domains of these practices—the body, food, and time—are exemplary for showing the effective symbolism of rituals as markers of cultural boundaries.

The Body   In ancient Israel, a patrilineal society, the male body was ritually marked by circumcision, called a "sign of the covenant" (Genesis 17:11).[45] By so marking the male organ of procreation, each Israelite family was covered with a sacred sign. Various kinds of symbolism—patrilineal descent, sexual fertility, male initiation, cleansing of birth impurity, and dedication to God—are intermingled in this mark. It has been elegantly described as "the fruitful cut."[46]

For this bodily mark to serve as a cultural boundary, there must be contrasting male bodies that lack it—the uncircumcised. Curiously, the evidence indicates that most of the males in Israel's immediate vicinity were also marked by circumcision. The prophet Jeremiah informs us that many of the peoples of the ancient Near East practiced circumcision, including "Egypt, Judah, Edom, the Ammonites, Moab, and all the desert dwellers who clip the corners of their hair" (Jeremiah 9:25). Textual and pictorial evidence from outside the Bible also indicate that the practice went back thousands of years.[47] The only males among Israel's immediate neighbors who lacked this mark were newcomers—the Philistines.

The Philistines were peoples from the Greek Aegean region who invaded and settled in the eastern Mediterranean shortly after 1200 B.C.E., precisely the period of the cultural formation of Israel in the highlands of southern Canaan.[48] The Philistines, with their superior technology, became the dominant political and military force of the region, as recalled in the stories of Samson, Saul, and David. This was probably the major impetus in the transformation of Israel from a tribal society to a unified kingship, with a permanent standing army. The Philistines were the dominant foreign Other in this crucial period, and their male bodies were uncircumcised.

In the biblical stories about this period, the term "uncircumcised" is often used as a synonym for "Philistine" (e.g., Judges 15:18; 1 Samuel 14:6, 31:4). In David's lament over Saul and Jonathan, killed in battle against the Philistine army, he cries:

> *Do not tell it in Gath*
> *Do not recount it in the streets of Ashkelon,*
> *Lest the daughters of the Philistines rejoice,*
> *Lest the daughters of the uncircumcised exult. (2 Samuel 1:20)*

It is interesting to note in this regard that the bride-price Saul had earlier requested of David was a hundred Philistine foreskins (1 Samuel 18:25). By this means, Saul managed not only to endanger David's life but also potentially to refashion the Philistines, reconstituting them as circumcised men.

It appears that the origin of circumcision as a cultural boundary of the Jews was facilitated by the dangerous presence of the uncircumcised Philistines.[49] Uncircumcision as a sign of the dangerous and dominant Other was later associated with the Assyrians and Babylonians, and later still the Greeks. Perhaps in response to the hegemony of these foreign powers, ancient Israel developed the belief that the uncircumcised had a particularly gloomy place reserved for them in Sheol, the underworld, alongside the unburied (Ezekiel 28:10, 31:18, 32:19–31). To have a foreskin was to be barbarous, cruel, and doomed to the "death of the uncircumcised."[50]

Curiously, the cultural boundaries drawn by this opposition between circumcised and uncircumcised—involving the contrast of civilization versus barbarism—are in tension with those constructed in the genealogical stories discussed above. Circumcision was a shared cultural trait of other neighboring peoples (Ammonites, Moabites, Edomites, Phoenicians, Arameans, etc.), who were thus grouped on the inside of this boundary. A kinship with these people as similarly circumcised and therefore civilized is implicit.

By this logic, a foreign people could become kin of the Israelites on the condition of their being circumcised. So Jacob's sons say to the Hivites of Shechem: "Only on this condition will we agree with you (to marry our sister), if you become like us, to have every male among you circumcised" (Genesis 34:15). Jacob's sons don't intend to go through with the bargain, but their pledge seems to show how the rite worked as a cultural boundary in matters of kinship. To be circumcised—or to be a daughter of a circumcised father—is to be a potential Israelite. Thus, David can marry an Aramean princess (2 Samuel 3:3); Solomon can wed an Egyptian princess (1 Kings 3:1) along with Moabite, Ammonite, Edomite, Phoenician, and Hittite women (1 Kings 11:1); Ahab marries the Phoenician Jezebel (1 Kings 16:31); and Chilion marries the Moabite Ruth (Ruth 1:4)—they are all eligible brides on account of their male kin's circumcision. This ritual logic was apparently later overruled by the postexilic ban on inter-marriage with "the peoples of the land" (Ezra 9–10; Nehemiah 10:31, 13:23–27). In this revision of custom, national boundaries replaced the older ritual bounda-ries. Or, to be more precise, the nation or ethnos replaced the tribal system as the locus for kinship relations.[51]

The expansive cultural boundaries of circumcision seem to be restricted to the children of Abraham in God's covenant with Abraham in Genesis 17, in which circumcision is a sign of the covenant. This is a Priestly text, probably written around the sixth century B.C.E. This mark, which previously was a gen-eral sign of West Semitic culture, crystallized into one of the most prominent boundary markers of Jewish identity. At some time during the Second Temple period, the rite became obsolete in other West Semitic cultures.[52] By this fruitful cut, the identity of the Jewish male body—and the Jewish social body—came to be distinguished from the bodies of other cultures.

Food   Another daily reminder of cultural identity is food. Ethnic foodways de-velop in varying degrees in different cultures, but food is always a sign of home—certainly in Judaism. What one eats and with whom one shares food are visible expressions of social bonds and boundaries. The biblical food laws are, like circumcision, reminders of God's covenant with Israel. The theological issue is holiness, as God commands in the conclusion to the food laws in Leviticus: "You shall be holy, for I am holy" (11:45). To be holy with respect to food means to eat what is allowed and to abstain from what is prohibited. As the anthropolo-gist Mary Douglas demonstrated in her classic essay "The Abominations of Leviticus," the biblical food laws have to do with boundaries—cultural, theo-logical, and conceptual.[53]

The earliest trace of these food laws in Israelite material culture comes from the era of Philistine hegemony, the same period when circumcision seems to have become an ethnic boundary marker. Recent archaeological excavations of early Israelite and Philistine sites show a remarkable contrast in the presence and absence of pig bones. The archaeologist Lawrence Stager reports that "In the highland villages [of early Israel] of the Iron I period, the bones of pigs are rare or completely absent, but in Philistia they constitute a significant proportion of excavated faunal remains."[54] This contrast is not explicable on ecological grounds; it rests, rather, on cultural ones. The archaeological evidence indicates that pig production was scarce in West Semitic culture,[55] but in Mycenaean Greek culture pigs were a valued source of meat. The Philistine preference for pork was apparently imported from their Aegean homeland. It was arguably the catalyst for the explicit avoidance of this food in early Israelite culture.[56]

With this dietary law, as with the rite of circumcision, a general West Semitic practice crystallized into a mark of Israelite cultural identity. The dangerous presence of the Philistines was the foil for the formation of a "counter-identity" in Israel; a traditional foodway became transformed into a theological and cultural affirmation. Holiness was endangered by taking pork into the Israelite body, just as Philistine culture was a threat to the wholeness of the Israelite social body. The ritual boundaries of the Israelite meal celebrated and maintained the boundaries of society.

Time   The way that time is measured is another mark of cultural boundaries and group authority. Judaism, Christianity, and Islam each have different religious calendars, counting time from different foundational events (creation, the birth of Christ, the exodus from Mecca). In biblical writings, time is marked according to key moments such as the Exodus or the reigns of Israelite kings. In the later era of the Second Temple, the Essenes proclaimed their cultural boundaries by advocating a calendar based on the solar year, in contrast to the traditional lunar (or lunisolar) calendar.[57] The high priest of Jerusalem even seems to have journeyed to Qumran to discipline the wayward community for deviating from the official calendar. Since then, Jewish groups and authorities have continued to vie over calendrical issues, such as the beginning of the day, the times and durations of festivals, and intercalation.

One of the distinctive ritual marks in biblical time is the Sabbath. It is, like circumcision, a "sign of the covenant" (Exodus 31:12–17), and, like the food laws, it is a matter of holiness. God commands: "You shall keep the Sabbath, for it is holy to you" (31:14, similarly 20:8–11). Just as God rested on the seventh day of creation, Israel shall rest every seventh day. Time becomes sacred, periodically, in this fruitful temporal cut.

The institution of the Sabbath is an Israelite innovation, as is the division of time into weeks.[58] It is impossible to tell when this system was invented, but a Hebrew inscription of the seventh century B.C.E. mentions the Sabbath,[59] and it is prominent in writings of the eighth-century prophets.[60] It is plausible that such a mark of temporal distinctiveness—involving cultural and religious difference—derived from an early era of Israelite culture, perhaps the same formative period when circumcision and food laws began to be ritual identity-markers. At minimum we can say that the Sabbath was an important pre-exilic institution.[61]

The divisions of time, along with demarcations in foodways and the body, have long marked the external boundaries of the Jewish body politic. In ancient Israel, these were part of the growing system of ritual practices that served to display the inclusions and exclusions of Israelite cultural identity. Such clear external boundaries have long provided a protective cover for the plurality of religious experience within Judaism.

REVISIONISM AND TRADITION

Ancient Israel shared many cultural features with its neighbors in the Near East. In matters of ethics, law, architecture, medicine, poetry, theology, and ritual, Israel belonged to a family of West Semitic cultures.[62] Differences certainly existed, and these were made emblematic of a perception of cultural uniqueness, of a people dwelling apart. Yet, as we have seen, differences also existed within Israelite culture. Over time, some of these internal differences were felt by some to be problematic. Certain biblical authors came to reject some of the ancient customary features of Israelite religion, labeling them as foreign and therefore corrupt and irreligious. Native practice was reinterpreted as a foreign assault on Israel's cultural boundaries, following the idiom of the dangerous and seductive Other.

During the eighth to sixth centuries B.C.E., a powerful revisionist movement developed among various prophets, priests, and sages. The result was a far-reaching upheaval in the boundaries and structures of Jewish identity. An argument began that has not yet ceased on what Judaism is, and who is an authentic Jew.

The first such critic known to us is Hosea, who prophesied in the Northern Kingdom in the mid-eighth century B.C.E. He abhorred many of the religious practices, institutions, and beliefs of his day. Prominent among these were the major northern shrines at Gilgal and Bethel (which he mockingly called Beth-Aven, "house of wickedness"):

Do not come to Gilgal,
and do not go up to Beth-Aven,
and do not swear: "As Yahweh lives." (Hosea 4:15)

These shrines and their cultic practices—including sacrifices[63] and oaths—were illegitimate in Hosea's eyes. He also objected to the multiplicity of local religious shrines, which typically featured sacrificial altars, standing stones, and holy trees or asherah-objects. He associates the worship at these shrines with illicit sex and promiscuity:

> *On the mountaintops they make sacrifices,*
> *and on the hills they burn offerings;*
> *Beneath oaks, poplars, and terebinths*
> *whose shade is good.*
> *That is why their daughters have illicit sex,*
> *and their daughters-in-law commit adultery. . . .*
> *And they too turn aside with prostitutes,*
> *and sacrifice with sacred whores.*[64] *(Hosea 4:13–14)*

The equation of religious and sexual misconduct provides the background for the cautionary story of Hosea's marriage to a prostitute (Hosea 1 and 3) and the metaphor of Yahweh's marriage to promiscuous Israel (Hosea 2).[65] The language of sexual misconduct—whether historically accurate or not—gives Hosea a broad brush to paint Israel's depravity.[66]

But when we look at earlier portraits of Israelite religious practice, the local shrines are depicted as perfectly orthodox and innocuous. For example, Abram's first act when he enters the Promised Land is to build such a shrine:

Abram traveled across the land to the site of Shechem, to the Oak of the Teacher. The Canaanites were then in the land. And Yahweh appeared to Abram and said, "To your descendants I will give this land." And he built there an altar to Yahweh, who had appeared to him there. (Genesis 12:6–7)

Abram next builds an altar on a hill between Bethel and Ai, and he prays to Yahweh there (Genesis 12:8). Later Yahweh appears to Jacob at Bethel, and Jacob makes a vow and erects a standing stone to mark it as a holy site: "And this rock, which I have set up as a standing stone, will be a temple [lit. "house"] of God *[beth elohim]*" (Genesis 28:21). From these and many other examples, we can see that these were normal shrines in the Yahwistic cult. Why should Hosea disparage them with such a blanket denunciation?

There were probably many factors at play in the prophet's rejection of the legitimacy of the local shrines, but one was likely the fact that these were cultic features shared with Israel's neighbors. Local shrines with altars, standing stones, and trees were a common phenomenon in West Semitic culture, probably going back to the Stone Age.[67] Phoenician coins clearly depict the iconography of such shrines (Figure 1). One of Hosea's objections is that the shrines were devoted to

"Baal" (or "the Baals"), even though he admits that the sacrifices and oaths were offered to Yahweh.[68] The repudiation of the local shrines with "the Baals" seems, at least in part, to follow the same logic of nontranslatability that we saw above in the castigation of the seer Balaam. A trait that is shared with non-Israelites is damned as foreign and illicit, and it is redescribed as conducing to illicit sex.

Baruch Halpern has described this phenomenon, which Hosea begins and which bears fruit in Deuteronomy and other biblical books, as "the elite redefinition of traditional culture."[69] The old religious practices and ideas—which shared features with neighboring cultures—were derided as alien, foreign, and corrupting. The new religious elite developed a critique that at times extended to all traditional forms of religious ritual, setting in its place the primacy of individual ethics and interior piety. This critique, when implemented following the reforms of Kings Hezekiah and Josiah, transformed the local aspect of Israelite religion from family religion to personal, interior devotion.[70] Hosea captures the direction of this movement by posing ritual and ethics as antithetical, a contrast that would have seemed strange and radical to most Israelites:[71] "For I desire love, not sacrifices, / knowledge of God rather than burnt offerings" (Hosea 6:6).

The old practices are empty, and inner religion becomes ascendant. This gives rise to Jeremiah's later formulation of the "new covenant," which is purely interior: "I will put my teaching within them, and I will write it in their hearts, so that I will be their God, and they will be my people" (Jeremiah 31:32).

According to the biblical accounts, the elimination of the local shrines was adopted as public policy by Kings Hezekiah and Josiah (2 Kings 18 and 23).[72] Among the circumstances that made possible the rejection of these shrines and the uprooting of traditional religious practice was the devastation wrought by the Assyrians in the Judaean countryside in the campaign of 701 B.C.E.[73] With only Jerusalem left, the decision to abolish local shrines and transform kin-based religion was perhaps inevitable: the Assyrian armies had already done the work of demolition. In the wake of this calamity, Jerusalem and its Temple became the primary locus of Israelite religion.

More than any other biblical book, Deuteronomy (composed in the seventh–sixth centuries B.C.E.) defines the new course of Judaism as a religion of interior choice and commitment.[74] The object is to love God and to obey the law that God has planted in our hearts. Priests, prophets, and other religious intermediaries are rarely mentioned; rituals are mere reminders of God's gracious laws. God is transcendent and One, not a multiplicity of local phenomena, as might be gathered by the multiplicity of shrines. (Note the local divine titles "Yahweh of Samaria" and "Yahweh of Teman" discussed above.)[75] These emphases of Deuteronomy are aptly captured by the Shema:

Hear, O Israel, Yahweh our God, Yahweh is One. You shall love Yahweh, your God, with all your heart, with all your soul, and with all your might. These things that I command you today shall be upon your hearts. You shall repeat them to your children, and you shall speak of them when you sit in your house, when you walk on the way, when you lie down, and when you rise up. (Deuteronomy 6:4–7)

This is classic Jewish spirituality, nurtured by Deuteronomy and transmitted through the centuries.

The obverse side of this interior spirituality is the condemnation of the old shrines as foreign and corrupting, inevitably leading to sex with foreigners.[76] Rather than be seduced by foreign culture, Moses in Deuteronomy commands the Israelites to destroy it:

This is what you shall do to them: pull down their altars, break their standing stones, cut up their wooden pillars [asherahs], and burn their idols in fire. For you are a holy people to Yahweh your God. Yahweh your God has chosen you to be His precious people, over all the peoples on the face of the earth. (Deuteronomy 7:5–6)

The language of cultural distinctiveness is here joined to the alienation of native tradition. The local shrines are now defined as foreign Canaanite snares, on the far side of Israelite identity. Because Israel is different, it must spurn the practices of the nations. Thus, the old-time religion became stigmatized as the foreign Other. Only Jerusalem, "the site that Yahweh your God will choose" (Deuteronomy 12:5, cf. 1 Kings 8:16), is hallowed as the place of God's true name.

Deuteronomy's revisionism ushers in a new Jewish theology and identity. God is transcendent, uncontained by heaven and earth, having no shape or form, "for you saw no form when Yahweh spoke to you on Horeb out of the fire" (4:15). He demands that Israel love and obey him, each by his or her free choice: "Choose life . . . by loving Yahweh your God" (30:19–20). Wherever one is—whether in Jerusalem or not—God is there: "If you look there for Yahweh your God, you will find Him, if you seek with all your heart and soul" (4:29). Yahweh's law, which is wise and perfect, exists within the individual: "It is not too wonderful for you or too distant . . . but the word is very close to you, it is in your mouth and your heart, to do it" (30:14). And as God is wise and profound, so is His people, as the nations—obtuse no more—proclaim: "This great nation is indeed a wise and profound people" (4:6). Thus do the nations add their assent to the revision of the traditional structures of Judaism. For a brief moment, the foreign nations, like the early portrayal of Balaam, are truthful seers of Israel's wisdom.

The *way* that Deuteronomy revises Jewish tradition is also fraught with significance. The book is presented as Moses' farewell discourse to Israel, in which he recounts the instructions that God gave to him at Mount Horeb.[77] Moses recalls that God said to him: "As for you, stand here before Me so that I may tell you all the commands, the laws, and the statutes that you will teach them" (Deuteronomy 5:28). Forty years later, on the threshold of the Promised Land, Moses finally teaches the Israelites "all that Yahweh had commanded him concerning them" (Deuteronomy 1:3) at the holy mountain. By means of this narrative frame, the book of Deuteronomy authorizes its version of Israelite laws and traditions as *torah misinay,* "Torah from Sinai," to use the later rabbinic term (though it is "Torah from Horeb" in this case). Deuteronomy begins a process that will become central in rabbinic Judaism: attributing all revisions and interpretations of biblical law and religion to the original revelation at Sinai.[78]

Deuteronomy makes interpretation of the law a fundamental way of constructing Jewish culture, and it does so by placing its interpretation in the foundational setting of God's revelation at the holy mountain. In this process, the Torah becomes an interpreted artifact, with the chain of Mosaically authorized interpretations stretching to the horizon. A later rabbi drew out some of the more extravagant consequences of this idea: "Torah, Mishnah, Talmud, and Aggadah—indeed, even the comments some bright student will one day make to his teacher—were already given to Moses on Mount Sinai."[79] All interpretation is always already there in the initial revelation at Sinai. From the precedent of Deuteronomy, interpretation has become both essential and interminable in Jewish culture. Every new boundary or relationship, every freshly redrawn inclusion or exclusion, are already implicit in God's original discourse, according to this ancient hermeneutical key. As a fascinating text from the Talmud puts it: "What is Torah? The interpretation [lit. "midrash"] of Torah" (BT Kiddushin 49a–b). Revision has come home to roost.

CONCLUSION: NEIGHBORS AND FENCES

Robert Frost famously observed that "good fences make good neighbors." A clear sense of the differences between oneself and others can conduce to a true neighborly relationship. But fences are often barbed, and a moral difference tends to inhere in the separation of inside from outside. Such is the case in many of the instances of genealogical, ritual, narrative, and revisionist self-definition in ancient Israel. Moral claims are often asserted in the differentiation of the collective self from the Other, of Israel from the nations.

Some biblical writings protested against this process of drawing the boundaries so that Israel is, by definition, on the side of the good and the nations on the side of evil. They pointedly confused and problematized these simple moral boundaries, providing a legacy of cultural self-critique within Judaism. I have mentioned above the stories of foreign women—Tamar, Rahab, Jael, and Ruth—who are, as Judah says, "more righteous than I" (Genesis 38:26). The book of Job presents a uniquely righteous man who is a foreigner (from "the land of Uz").[80] Job, like Abraham, argues with God about issues of morality, though the outcome is more ambiguous than in Abraham's case. Most important, the classical prophets also tended to criticize the ethnocentric claims of Israel. Amos warns: "Are you not like the children of the Cushites to me, O children of Israel, declares Yahweh? Did I not bring Israel out of the land of Egypt, and the Philistines from Caphtor, and Aram from Kir?" (Amos 9:7). This universalizing tendency offset the ethnocentrism implicit in a "chosen people" and created the potential for a powerful cultural critique, one of the great legacies of the biblical prophets.[81] The prophetic writings are not fond of the cultural fences that divide neighbor against neighbor.

The moral problem of nationalism and ethnic boundaries is most directly addressed in the book of Jonah, in which the reluctant prophet is angry and despondent when Yahweh forgives the people of Nineveh:

> This seemed like a great evil to Jonah, and he was very angry. He prayed to Yahweh, saying, "O Yahweh, isn't this what I said when I was in my own land, and why I earlier fled to Tarshish? For I know that you are a gracious and compassionate God, slow to anger, abundant in kindness, and renouncing evil. Now, Yahweh, take my life from me, for I would rather die than live." (Jonah 4:1–2)

In the end, Yahweh teaches Jonah his lesson, that the nations are precious in God's eyes and that cultural narcissism is irrational and immoral. Notably, in view of the prominence of humor in later Jewish self-critique, God accomplishes this with a dash of humor. God's final comment—and the last word in the book—refers to the "many cattle" (4:11) who too had fasted and worn sackcloth alongside the Ninevites (3:7–8).[82] The comic image of penitent cows drives home the point that Israel has no intrinsically superior claim to God's love than the other nations. Or even their cows.

Biblical Israel shows many faces in its relations with its neighbors and fences in the ancient Near East. It is a member of a larger cultural family but a self-consciously unique member of that family. It constructed its self-image out of the rich traditions of prior ideologies, narratives, and rituals, but it made something new out of the old worlds.[83] One of the leitmotifs in modern biblical scholarship has been the recovery of the cultural context of ancient Israel, allowing us the opportunity to read the biblical writings anew. When read in the context of the ancient Near East, the Bible shows itself to be more complex, variegated, and even self-contradictory than we knew before. Moral and philosophical issues are debated in this book, and often they are not settled. Cultural identities are constructed in one part, only to be deconstructed in another. A culturally and historically alive Bible may be unsettling to some, for whom its meanings require the stable sediment of tradition. But tradition is itself unstable, and interpretation goes on, without end.

NOTES

1. R. Hestrin et al., eds., *Ketovot Mesaprot* (Jerusalem, 1973), 94. On the difficulties of this text, see P. D. Miller, Jr., "Psalms and Inscriptions," *Supplements to Vetus Testamentum* 32 (1981): 320–22.

2. According to Deuteronomy 3:11, Og was the last of the *rephaim,* the aboriginal giants of Canaan, and his huge iron bed (or iron coffin) was on display at Rabbah, the capital city of Ammon. Its dimensions were 13½ feet (9 cubits) long by 6 feet (4 cubits) wide. It is possible that the tradition of the giant stature of the aboriginal Canaanites was inferred from the huge ruined walls of Middle Bronze Age (2200–1500 B.C.E.) tells, combined with old traditions of the quasi-divine Rephaim; see H. Rouillard, "Rephaim," in *Dictionary of Deities and Demons in the Bible,* K. van der Toorn, B. Becking, and P. W. van der Horst, eds., 2d ed. (Leiden, 1999), 692–700.

3. This passage belongs to the oldest stratum of biblical poetry; see S. Morag, "Layers of Antiquity: Some Linguistic Observations on the Oracles of Balaam" (Hebrew), in S. Morag, *Meḥkarim bi-leshon ha-Mikra* (Jerusalem, 1995), 45–69.

4. See A. D. Smith, *The Ethnic Origins of Nations* (Oxford, 1986); B. Anderson, *Imagined Communities: Reflections on the Origin and Spread of Nationalism,* rev. ed. (London, 1991).

5. P. Machinist, "The Question of Distinctiveness in Ancient Israel: An Essay," in *Ah, Assyria . . . Studies in Assyrian History and Ancient Near Eastern Historiography Presented to Hayim Tadmor,* M. Cogan and I. Ephal, eds. (Jerusalem, 1991), 196–212; P. Machinist, "Outsiders or Insiders: The Biblical View of Emergent Israel and Its Contexts," in *The Other in Jewish Thought and History: Constructions of Jewish Culture and Identity,* L. J. Silberstein and R. L. Cohn, eds. (New York, 1994), 35–60.

6. J. Assmann, *Moses the Egyptian: The Memory of Egypt in Western Monotheism* (Cambridge, Mass., 1997), 44–47.

7. Ibid., 2–3.

8. Deir Alla I.1. See J. A. Hackett, *The Balaam Text from Deir Alla* (Chico, Calif., 1984), and S. Ahituv, *Asupat Ketovot Ivriyot* (Jerusalem, 1992), 265–86.

9. On the methods involved in dating the biblical sources, see R. E. Friedman, *Who Wrote the Bible?* (San Francisco, 1997), and D. M. Carr, *Reading the Fractures of Genesis: Historical and Literary Approaches* (Louisville, Ky., 1996).

10. A. Rofé, *Introduction to the Composition of the Pentateuch* (Sheffield, Engl., 1999), 93–94; A. Rofé, *Sefer Bilam* (Jerusalem, 1979), 49–57.

11. Gershom Scholem, "Revelation and Tradition as Religious Categories in Judaism," in Gershom Scholem, *The Messianic Idea in Judaism and Other Essays on Jewish Spirituality* (New York, 1971), 289–90: "Not system but *commentary* is the legitimate form though which truth is approached. . . . Commentary thus became the characteristic expression of Jewish thinking about truth."

12. P. K. McCarter, Jr., *Ancient Inscriptions: Voices from the Biblical World* (Washington, D.C., 1996), 48–50. For the whole text, see M. Lichtheim, *Ancient Egyptian Literature, Vol. II: The New Kingdom* (Berkeley, 1976), 73–77. For a recent discussion, see J. R. Huddlestun, "Merneptah's Revenge: The 'Israel Stela' and Its Modern Interpreters" (forthcoming).

13. See the recent syntheses of L. E. Stager, "Forging an Identity: The Emergence of Ancient Israel," in *The Oxford History of the Biblical World*, M. D. Coogan, ed. (New York, 1998), 123–75; I. Finkelstein, "The Great Transformation: The 'Conquest' of the Highlands Frontiers and the Rise of the Territorial States," in *The Archaeology of Society in the Holy Land*, 2d ed., T. E. Levy, ed. (London, 1998), 349–65; and W. G. Dever, "The Late Bronze–Early Iron I Horizon in Syria-Palestine: Egyptians, Canaanites, 'Sea Peoples,' and Proto-Israelites," in *The Crisis Years: The 12th Century B.C. from Beyond the Danube to the Tigris*, W. A. Ward and M. S. Joukowsky, eds. (Dubuque, Iowa, 1992), 99–110.

14. Anderson, *Imagined Communities*.

15. See chapter 1 in this volume and Ilana Pardes, *The Biography of Ancient Israel: National Narratives in the Bible* (Berkeley, 2000).

16. On the Exodus stories as a symbolic rite of passage, see R. L. Cohn, *The Shape of Sacred Space* (Chico, Calif., 1981), 7–23; R. S. Hendel, "Sacrifice as a Cultural System: The Ritual Symbolism of Exodus 24:3–8," *Zeitschrift für die Alttestamentliche Wissenschaft* 101 (1989): 375–79; and W. H. C. Propp, *Exodus 1–18* (New York, 1999), 35–36.

17. D. B. Redford, *Egypt, Canaan, and Israel in Ancient Times* (Princeton, 1992), 221–27.

18. For further details, see B. Halpern, "The Exodus from Egypt: Myth or Reality?" in *The Rise of Ancient Israel*, H. Shanks, ed. (Washington, D.C., 1992), 86–113, and R. S. Hendel, "The Exodus in Biblical Memory," *Journal of Biblical Literature* 120 (2001): 601–22.

19. Sigmund Freud, *Civilization and Its Discontents*, trans. J. Riviere (New York, 1958), 64.

20. The Kenites are mentioned in only a handful of biblical passages: Joshua 15:57; Judges 4–5; Judges 1:16; 1 Samuel 15:6, 27:10, 30:29; and 1 Chronicles 2:55. See B. Halpern, "Kenites," in *The Anchor Bible Dictionary*, D. N. Freedman, ed. (New York, 1992), 4: 17–22.

21. R. Firestone, *Journeys in Holy Lands: The Evolution of the Abraham-Ishmael Legends in Islamic Exegesis* (Albany, N.Y., 1990).

22. R. S. Hendel, *Epic of the Patriarch: The Jacob Cycle and the Narrative Traditions of Canaan and Israel* (Atlanta, Ga., 1987), 84, 128.

23. Ibid., 128–31.

24. See R. Alter, *The Art of Biblical Narrative* (New York, 1981), 42–45.

25. The major studies are F. M. Cross, *Canaanite Myth and Hebrew Epic: Essays in the History of the Religion of Israel* (Cambridge, Mass., 1973), and M. S. Smith, *The Early History of God: Yahweh and the Other Deities in Ancient Israel* (San Francisco, 1990). Translations of the major religious texts are available in S. Parker, ed., *Ugaritic Narrative Poetry* (Atlanta, Ga., 1997); W. W. Hallo, ed., *The Context of Scripture: Vol. I: Canonical Compositions from the Biblical World* (Leiden, 1997), 239–375; M. D. Coogan, *Stories from Ancient Canaan* (Philadelphia, 1978); and J. B. Pritchard, ed., *Ancient Near Eastern Texts Relating to the Old Testament*, 3d ed. (Princeton, 1969), 129–55.

26. M. Dietrich, O. Loretz, and J. Sanmartín, eds., *The Cuneiform Alphabetic Texts from Ugarit, Ras Ibn Hani and Other Places* (Münster, 1995), 1.5.1–4.

27. Biblical allusions to the defeat of chaos monsters in primeval times include Psalms 74:13–14 (the vanquished monsters are Sea, Dragons, Leviathan), Isaiah 51:9–10 (Rahab, Dragon, Sea), and Job 40–41 (Leviathan and Behemoth). See J. Day, *God's Conflict with the Dragon and the Sea: Echoes of a Canaanite Myth in the Old Testament* (Cambridge, Engl., 1985).

28. On El in Canaan and Israel, see Cross, *Canaanite Myth*, 13–75; Smith, *Early History of God*, 7–12; and W. Herrmann, "El," in van der Toorn et al., eds., *Dictionary of Deities*, 274–80.

29. A Hebrew inscription from the eighth or seventh century B.C.E. reads "[El], creator of earth" (a trace of the *lamed* is readable). See P. D. Miller, "El, The Creator of Earth," *Bulletin of the American Schools of Oriental Research* 239 (1980): 43–46, and Ahituv, *Asupat Ketovot*, 22–23.

30. The term *shadday* is also used, in the plural, to denote the gods of the Deir Alla inscription (see n. 8 above). These gods are the *shaddayin*, the "mountain ones."

31. On Asherah in Canaan and Israel, see Smith, *Early History of God*, 80–114; J. Day, "Asherah in the Hebrew Bible and Northwest Semitic Literature," *Journal of Biblical Literature* 105 (1986): 385–408; S. M. Olyan, *Asherah and the Cult of Yahweh in Israel* (Atlanta, Ga., 1988), 1–37; and N. Wyatt, "Asherah," in van der Toorn et al., eds., *Dictionary of Deities*, 99–105, and references.

32. Dietrich et al., eds., *Cuneiform Alphabetic Texts*, 1.4.4.40–43.

33. Ibid., 1.14.197–206.

34. On the *battim* woven for Asherah, cf. Akkadian *betatu,* "a decoration used on garments and leather objects" (*Chicago Assyrian Dictionary* [Chicago, 1956–92], s.v.), and note the comparable function of the *bet pirishti,* "a room in the Babylonian temple complex which was used to house the vestments of priests and the garments used to clothe the statues of deities" (L. T. Doty, "Akkadian bet piriŝti," in *The Tablet and the Scroll: Near Eastern Studies in Honor of William W. Hallo*, M. E. Cohen, D. C. Snell, and D. B. Weisberg, eds. [Bethesda, Md., 1993], 87–89).

35. On the theme of cultic purity and impurity among Israel's monarchs in the books of Kings, see B. Halpern, *The First Historians: The Hebrew Bible and History* (San Francisco, 1988), 220–28.

36. On the biblical passages, see especially Olyan, *Asherah*, 3–22.

37. The literature on these inscriptions is vast; see, e.g., the thorough treatments and reviews of literature in O. Keel and C. Uehlinger, *Gods, Goddesses, and Images of God in Ancient Israel* (Minneapolis, 1998), 210–48; S. Wiggins, *A Reassessment of 'Asherah': A Study According to the Textual Sources of the First Two Millennia* B.C.E. (Neukirchen, Germany, 1993); and W. Dietrich and M. A. Klopfenstein, eds., *Ein Gott allein? JHWH-Verehrung und biblischer Monotheismus im Kontext der israelitischen und altorientalischen Religionsgeschichte* (Göttingen, 1994). See also n. 31 above.

38. Ahituv, *Asupat Ketovot*, 152–60.

39. Ibid., 111–13. Some of the words are indistinct or overwritten, and there are other possible readings.

40. W. James, *The Varieties of Religious Experience: A Study in Human Nature* (New York, 1902).

41. See K. van der Toorn, *Family Religion in Babylonia, Syria and Israel: Continuity and Change in the Forms of Religious Life* (Leiden, 1996), and R. Albertz, *A History of Israelite Religion in the Old Testament Period* (Louisville, Ky., 1994), 1: 25–39, 94–103, 186–95.

42. Reading *el shadday*, "God (El), the One of the Mountain," with the Samaritan Pentateuch and the Syriac Peshitta (the Septuagint also reads *el*); the Masoretic text reads *et shadday*, "with the One of the Mountain." The poetic parallelism of this line strongly supports reading *el* here rather than the preposition *et* (which is found predominantly in prose); the Masoretic text has apparently suffered a small scribal error.

43. See, e.g., M. Weippert, *Jahwe und die anderen Götter: Studien zur Religionsgeschichte des antiken Israel in ihrem syrisch-palästinischen Kontext* (Tübingen, 1997), 1–24, and S. Ackerman, *Under Every Green Tree: Popular Religion in Sixth-Century Judah* (Atlanta, Ga., 1989).

44. For one such dialectal variation, see R. S. Hendel, "Sibilants and šibbolet (Judges 12:6)," *Bulletin of the American Schools of Oriental Research* 301 (1996): 69–75.

45. M. Fox, "Sign of the Covenant: Circumcision in the Light of the Priestly *ôt* Etiologies," *Revue biblique* 81 (1974): 557–96.

46. H. Eilberg Schwartz, *The Savage in Judaism: An Anthropology of Israelite Religion and Ancient Judaism* (Bloomington, Ind., 1990), 141–76.

47. The earliest evidence is from ca. 2800 B.C.E. in Syria; see J. Sasson, "Circumcision in the Ancient Near East," *Journal of Biblical Literature* 85 (1966): 473–76; W. H. C. Propp, "The Origins of Infant Circumcision in Israel," *Hebrew Annual Review* 11 (1987): 355; and R. de Vaux, *Ancient Israel: Its Life and Institutions* (New York, 1961), 46–48.

48. L. E. Stager, "The Impact of the Sea Peoples in Canaan (1185–1050 BCE)," in *The Archaeology of Society in the Holy Land*, T. E. Levy, ed. (London, 1995), 332–48.

49. This is suggested in passing by Stager in ibid., 344.

50. Propp, "Origins of Infant Circumcision," 363–66.

51. On this transformation, see S. J. D. Cohen, *The Beginnings of Jewishness: Boundaries, Varieties, Uncertainties* (Berkeley, 1999), 241–62.

52. Josephus, *Antiquities,* 13.257–58 (Edom), 318 (Ituria/Yeter); Judith 14:10 (Ammon). On the significance of circumcision in the Hellenistic and Roman periods, see Cohen, *Beginnings of Jewishness,* 39–49, 120–25, and J. J. Collins, "A Symbol of Otherness: Circumcision and Salvation in the First Century," in J. J. Collins, *Seers, Sybils and Sages in Hellenistic-Roman Judaism* (Leiden, 1997), 211–35.

53. Mary Douglas, "The Abominations of Leviticus," in Mary Douglas, *Purity and Danger: An Analysis of the Concepts of Pollution and Taboo* (London, 1966), 41–57. See also Mary Douglas, "Deciphering a Meal," in Mary Douglas, *Implicit Meanings: Essays in Anthropology* (London, 1975), 249–75, and Mary Douglas, *Leviticus as Literature* (Oxford, 1999), 134–75.

54. Stager, "Forging an Identity," 165; see also Stager, "Impact of the Sea Peoples," 344.

55. On the general rarity of pork production in the Levant in the second and first millennia B.C.E., see B. Hesse, "Pig Lovers and Pig Haters: Patterns of Palestinian Pork Production," *Journal of Ethnobiology* 10 (1990): 195–225.

56. Stager, "Impact of the Sea Peoples," 344.

57. See S. Talmon, "The Calendar of the Covenanters of the Judean Desert," in S. Talmon, *The World of Qumran from Within: Collected Studies* (Jerusalem, 1989), 147–85, and J. C. VanderKam, *Calendars in the Dead Sea Scrolls: Measuring Time* (London, 1998).

58. W. W. Hallo, *Origins: The Ancient Near Eastern Background of Some Modern Western Institutions* (Leiden, 1996), 127–35 and references.

59. Ahituv, *Asupat Ketovot,* 98–99 (the Yavneh Yam letter).

60. E.g., Amos 8:5, Hosea 2:13, and Isaiah 1:13, each in the context of a critique of public injustice or immorality, implying that the Sabbath was a well-entrenched religious tradition by this time.

61. M. Z. Brettler offers cogent counterarguments to the view—originally rooted in religious apologetics—that circumcision and the Sabbath only became signs of Israelite identity after the exile (Brettler, "Judaism in the Hebrew Bible? The Transition from Ancient Israelite Religion to Judaism," *Catholic Biblical Quarterly* 61 [1999]: 436–38).

62. See the excellent survey in J. J. M. Roberts, "The Ancient Near Eastern Environment," in *The Hebrew Bible and Its Modern Interpreters,* D. A. Knight and G. M. Tucker, eds. (Chico, Calif., 1985), 75–121.

63. The prohibition, "do not go up" *(al-taʿalu)* in the second line is also a wordplay on "do not sacrifice."

64. The sense of *kedeshot,* lit. "sacred women," in parallel with "prostitutes," is uncertain; see K. van der Toorn, "Cultic Prostitution," in Freedman, ed., *Anchor Bible Dictionary,* 5: 510–13, and the next note.

65. M. J. W. Leith, "Verse and Reverse: The Transformation of the Woman, Israel, in Hosea 1–3," in *Gender and Difference in Ancient Israel,* P. L. Day, ed. (Minneapolis, 1989), 95–108; P. A. Bird, " 'To Play the Harlot': An Inquiry into an Old Testament Metaphor," in P. A. Bird, *Missing Persons and Mistaken Identities: Women and Gender in Ancient Israel* (Minneapolis, 1997), 219–36.

66. On adultery and nymphomania as metaphors for idolatry, see M. Halbertal and A. Margalit, *Idolatry* (Cambridge, Mass., 1992), 9–20.

67. T. N. D. Mettinger, *No Graven Image? Israelite Aniconism in Its Ancient Near Eastern Context* (Stockholm, 1995), 168–91.

68. See B. Halpern, "The Baal (and the Asherah) in Seventh-Century Judah: Yhwh's Retainers Retired," in *Konsequente Traditiongeschichte: Festschrift für Klaus Baltzer zum 65. Geburtstag,* R. Bartelmus et al., eds. (Fribourg, 1993), 115–54. Halpern argues that the "baals" in such denunciations often refer to the "heavenly host," i.e., the angels. On the denigration of the angels in biblical writings of this period, see also A. Rofé, *Ha-Emunah bi-Melakhim be-Yisrael* (Jerusalem, 1979).

69. B. Halpern, "Sybil, or the Two Nations? Archaism, Kinship, Alienation, and the Elite Redefinition of Traditional Culture in Judah in the 8th–7th Centuries B.C.E.," in *The Study of the Ancient Near East in the Twenty-First Century,* J. S. Cooper and G. M. Schwartz, eds. (Winona Lake, Ind., 1996), 291–338.

70. Van der Toorn, *Family Religion,* 375.

71. R. S. Hendel, "Prophets, Priests, and the Efficacy of Ritual," in *Pomegranates and Golden Bells: Studies in Biblical, Jewish, and Near Eastern Ritual, Law, and Literature in Honor of Jacob Milgrom,* D. P. Wright, D. N. Freedman, and A. Hurvitz, eds. (Winona Lake, Ind., 1995), 185–98.

72. P. K. McCarter, Jr., "The Religious Reforms of Hezekiah and Josiah," in *Aspects of Monotheism: How God Is One,* H. Shanks and J. Meinhardt, eds. (Washington, D.C., 1997), 57–80.

73. B. Halpern, "Jerusalem and the Lineages in the Seventh Century B.C.E.: Kinship and the Rise of Individual Moral Liability," in *Law and Ideology in Monarchic Israel,* B. Halpern and D. W. Hobson, eds. (Sheffield, Engl., 1991), 41–49; Halpern, "Sybil," 311–21.

74. On the date of Deuteronomy and its religious innovations, see M. Weinfeld, *Deuteronomy and the Deuteronomic School* (Oxford, 1972), esp. 191–243; Halpern, "Sybil," 327–37; and B. M. Levinson, *Deuteronomy and the Hermeneutics of Legal Innovation* (New York, 1997).

75. On the issue of multiple manifestations of Yahweh, see McCarter, "Religious Reforms," 57–80.

76. On the key texts, see G. N. Knoppers, "Sex, Religion, and Politics: The Deuteronomist on Intermarriage," *Hebrew Annual Review* 14 (1994): 121–41.

77. The name of God's mountain fluctuates between Sinai (in J and P sources of the Pentateuch) and Horeb (in the E source and Deuteronomy). On these sources, see R. E. Friedman, *Who Wrote the Bible?* (New York, 1987).

78. On the exegetical issues raised by Deuteronomy, see M. Fishbane, *Biblical Interpretation in Ancient Israel* (Oxford, 1985), 435–40, and Levinson, *Deuteronomy,* 15–17.

79. Midrash Tanḥuma 2.58b; trans. Scholem, "Revelation and Tradition," 289.

80. The land of Uz (Job 1:1) is probably to be located on the Arabian peninsula; see E. A. Knauf, "Uz," in Freedman, ed., *Anchor Bible Dictionary,* 6: 770–71.

81. See the illuminating discussion of M. Walzer, *Interpretation and Social Criticism* (Cambridge, Mass., 1987), 67–94.

82. Note that the object of the command "let them pray" (Jonah 3:8) can also be construed as including the cows; see J. M. Sasson, *Jonah* (New York, 1990), 257.

83. R. S. Hendel, "Worldmaking in Ancient Israel," *Journal for the Study of the Old Testament* 56 (1992): 3–18.

SELECTED BIBLIOGRAPHY

Albertz, R. *A History of Israelite Religion in the Old Testament Period.* 2 vols. Louisville, Ky., 1994.

Coogan, M., ed. *The Oxford History of the Biblical World.* New York, 1998.

Cross, F. M. *Canaanite Myth and Hebrew Epic: Essays in the History of the Religion of Israel.* Cambridge, Mass., 1973.

Day, P. L., ed. *Gender and Difference in Ancient Israel.* Minneapolis, 1989.

King, Philip J., and Lawrence E. Stager. *Life in Biblical Israel.* Louisville, Ky., 2001.

Miller, P. D. *The Religion of Ancient Israel.* Louisville, Ky., 2000.

Pedersen, J. *Israel: Its Life and Culture.* 2 vols. London, 1926–40.

Shanks, H., ed. *Ancient Israel: From Abraham to the Roman Destruction of the Temple.* 2d ed. Washington, D.C., 1999.

Smith, M. S. *The Early History of God: Yahweh and the Other Deities in Ancient Israel.* San Francisco, 1990.

van der Toorn, K. *Family Religion in Babylonia, Syria and Israel: Continuity and Change in the Forms of Religious Life.* Leiden, 1996.

Greek motifs decorating the cave walls of a Jewish burial chamber in Tell Maresha,
in southern Judaea, illustrate the adaptation of Hellenic symbols in Second Temple Judaism.
(Israel Antiquities Authority, Jerusalem)

THREE

HELLENISTIC JUDAISM

ERICH S. GRUEN

Alexander the Great burst like a thunderbolt upon the history of the Near East. Within a dozen years in the late fourth century B.C.E., he humbled the mighty Persian Empire, marching its length and breadth, defeating its armies, toppling its satraps, terminating its monarchy, and installing a Greek hegemony from the Hellespont to the Indus. It was a breathtaking achievement—and on more than just the military front. The conquests of Alexander provided a springboard for the expansion of Greek culture in the lands of the eastern Mediterranean. That world would never be quite the same again.

No direct confrontation occurred between the great Macedonian conqueror and the Jews of Palestine. Fanciful tales sprang up later in which Alexander paid homage to the high priest in Jerusalem and Yahweh sanctioned his subjugation of Persia. None of them has a basis in fact. Palestine was of small interest to the king who captured the great fortress of Tyre, then marched straight to Egypt and subsequently to Mesopotamia, on the way to the heartland of the Persian Empire. Judaea was spared—and largely ignored.

The long-term impact on Jewish culture, however, was momentous. Jews had hitherto lived under a Persian yoke, a light one and a relatively benign one. The centers of royal power lay at a great distance, in Susa and Persepolis, with little direct effect upon the society of the Jews. A major change occurred with the coming of the Greeks. Alexander's vast holdings splintered after his death, as his powerful marshals divided and fought fiercely over the territories he had claimed. In the new configurations of the Hellenistic kingdoms, Greco-Macedonian dynasts held sway, and Hellenism became the culture of the ruling class in the major cities and states, both old and new, of the Near East—in places like Sardis and Ephesus, Alexandria and Antioch, in Babylon, Tyre, and Sidon, and in the coastal communities of Palestine.

The political constellation affected Jews everywhere. Palestine itself came under the control of the Ptolemies of Egypt for about a century after Alexander's death, and, when power shifted in the region, the land entered the hegemony of the Seleucid monarchs of Syria from the beginning of the second century B.C.E. The Maccabean rebellion ushered in a Jewish dynasty, the Hasmonaeans, followed by the house of Herod, who provided ostensibly indigenous rule. But the Hasmonaeans, in fact, governed only under the shadow of the Seleucids, and the Herodians under the shadow (sometimes more than the shadow) of Rome. The Hellenistic monarchies continued to reckon Palestine within their sphere of influence, and Rome later undertook to supply its own governors of the region. In the Diaspora, Jews everywhere lived in circumstances where pagan power held sway. Through most of the third and second centuries B.C.E., the Ptolemies exercised authority in Egypt and usually in Cyprus and Cyrene; the Seleucids held power in Syria, Phoenicia, and at least nominally in the lands across the Euphrates; the Attalids ruled in Pergamum and extended their influence elsewhere in Asia Minor where a diversity of dynasts struggled for control; and in Greece itself contending forces from Macedon and various states and federations kept the Jews of their region in a politically subordinate position. The subsequent dominance of Rome in the eastern Mediterranean, beginning in the late second century B.C.E., brought Jews, among others, into direct contact with Roman governors, officialdom, and imperial power.

The Jewish Diaspora, to be sure, did not await Alexander. Jews had certainly found their way to Syria, to Egypt, and to the lands of the Tigris and Euphrates well before. But the arrival of the Greeks proved to be an irresistible magnet. Jews migrated to the new settlements and expanded communities in substantial numbers. A Greek diaspora had brought the Jewish one in its wake. Within a few generations, Jews had installed themselves in an astonishing array of places all around the Mediterranean and beyond. If one can believe the author of 1 Maccabees, composed in the late second century B.C.E., they could be found not only in Syria, Egypt, the Parthian empire, and throughout the cities and principalities of Asia Minor, but even in Greece itself, in various islands of the Aegean, and in Crete, Cyprus, and Cyrene.[1] This remarkable dispersal impressed itself even upon pagan writers like Strabo, who commented that the Jewish people by his day (late first century B.C.E.) had moved into almost every city and that hardly a place remained where they had not made their presence felt.[2]

The consequences are readily discernible. Jews became exposed to and thoroughly engaged with the Greek culture that prevailed in the various communities in which they settled. And not only in the Diaspora. Greek towns sprang up in Palestine itself, from Akko to Gaza on the Mediterranean coast, in the Lower Galilee, and in various sites on both sides of the Jordan.[3] Hence, even the Jews of Judaea could not and did not isolate themselves altogether from the pervasive aura of Hellenism. For many Jews, especially in the Diaspora, the close contact with the institutions, language, literature, art, and traditions of Hellas reached the point where they lost touch with Hebrew itself. The translation of the Hebrew Bible into Greek, probably in Alexandria sometime in the third or second century B.C.E., reflects the needs of Jews settled abroad for several generations for whom Greek was the primary, perhaps sole, language and for some of whom education gave greater familiarity with Plato than with Moses. The Jewish involvement with Hellenism in the period from Alexander the Great to the destruction of the Second Temple in 70 C.E. was a central, even a defining, characteristic.

But the involvement is rife with ambiguities. Indeed, ambiguity adheres to the term "Hellenism" itself. No pure strain of Greek culture, whatever that might be even in principle, confronted the Jews of Palestine or the Diaspora. Transplanted Greek communities mingled with ancient Phoenician traditions on the Levantine coast, with powerful Egyptian elements in Alexandria, with enduring Mesopotamian institutions in Babylon, and with a complex mixture of societies in Anatolia. The Greek culture with which Jews came into contact comprised a mongrel entity—or rather entities, with a different blend in each location of the Mediterranean. The convenient term "Hellenistic" signifies complex amalgamations in the Near East in which the Greek ingredient was a conspicuous presence rather than a monopoly.

The tombs of Bnei Hezir (on left) and Zechariah (in center) in Jerusalem's Qidron Valley (probably first century C.E.) exhibit the appropriation by the Jewish elite of Greek architectural forms. (Israel Antiquities Authority, Jerusalem)

"Judaism," it need hardly be said, is at least as complex and elastic a term. The institution defies uniform definition. And changes over time, as in all religions, render any effort to capture its essence at a particular moment highly problematic. "Hellenistic Judaism" must have experienced considerable diversity, quite distinct in Alexandria, Antioch, Babylon, Ephesus, Cyrene, and Jerusalem. Simplistic formulations once in favor are now obsolete. We can no longer contrast "Palestinian Judaism" as the unadulterated form of the ancestral faith with "Hellenistic Judaism" as the Diaspora variety that diluted antique practices with alien imports. Hellenism existed in Palestine—and the Jews of the Diaspora still held to their heritage. Each individual area struck its balance differently and experienced its own peculiar level of mixture. It is essential to emphasize that Jews were not obliged to choose between succumbing to or resisting Hellenism. Nor should one imagine a conscious dilemma whereby they had to decide how far to lean in one direction or another, how much Hellenism was acceptable before they compromised the faith, or at what point on the spectrum between apostasy and piety they could comfortably locate themselves.

A different conception is called for. Many Diaspora Jews and even some dwelling in Hellenistic cities of Palestine after a generation or two were already confirmed Greek speakers and integrated members of communities governed by pagan practices and institutions. They did not confront daily decisions on the degree of assimilation or acculturation. They had long since become part of a Hellenic environment that they could take as a given. But their Judaism remained intact. What they needed was a means of defining and expressing their singularity within that milieu, the special characteristics that made them both integral to the community and true to their heritage.

JEWISH CREATIONS IN GREEK GENRES

How does one locate the boundaries between the cultures? The issue put in that form is itself problematic. The very metaphor of boundaries, even permeable boundaries, begs the question. The Jews, it might better be said, redefined their heritage in the terms of Hellenistic culture itself. They engaged actively with the traditions of Hellas, adapting genres and transforming legends to articulate their own legacy in modes congenial to a Hellenistic setting. At the same time, they recreated their past, retold stories in different shapes, and amplified the scriptural corpus itself through the medium of the Greek language and Greek literary forms. The challenge for the Jews was not how to surmount barriers or cross boundaries. In a world where Hellenic culture held an ascendant position, they strove to present Judaic traditions and express their own self-definition through the media of the Greeks—and to make those media their own.

This refashioning can be illustrated in a number of ways. Tragic drama is perhaps the quintessential Greek medium. This did not render it off-limits to the Jews. Quite the contrary. In one instance at least (and it can hardly be the only one), a Jewish writer named Ezekiel tried his hand in that genre, probably in the second century B.C.E. Working within the tradition of classical tragedy, influenced particularly by the plays of Aeschylus and Euripides, Ezekiel produced his own dramas, one of which—or at least a substantial portion of one—survives. The theme, however, is not drawn from Greek mythology or from the titanic clashes within Greek royal houses of distant and legendary antiquity. Ezekiel turned instead to material from his own people's legacy. The extant text, the *Exagoge,* is based on the story of Moses leading the Israelites out of Egypt. The choice of that tale clearly indicates an appeal to pride in national history and tradition produced in the most characteristically Hellenic mode.[4]

Ezekiel hewed closely to the narrative line contained in the Book of Exodus. He cast it in different form, of course, employing the conventions of the Greek theater, writing monologues and dialogues, keeping the battle scenes and the gore offstage, even bringing on the trusty messenger's speech to summarize events that transpired between dramatic episodes. But his tale diverges little from the biblical version. It was not Ezekiel's purpose to raise any doubts about the authority or adequacy of the Scriptures. The Septuagint, the Greek version of the Hebrew Bible, served as his text, and he conveyed its narrative faithfully. But Ezekiel was not wedded to it irrevocably. In a few key instances, he added new material to the mix. And they supply important clues to the tragedian's intent.

One item in particular merits special notice. Ezekiel inserted a remarkable scene that has no biblical prototype. Moses, in dialogue with his father-in-law, reports a puzzling dream in which he had a vision of a great throne high upon a summit extending to the cleft of heaven. There a noble man sat with diadem and a great scepter, summoned Moses to him, handed him the scepter and diadem, and departed from the throne. From that spot Moses had a view of the whole earth, both below it and above the sky, and a multitude of stars fell on their knees. Moses' father-in-law provides a most heartening interpretation of the dream: it is a sign from God that Moses will lift up a great throne, will issue judgments, and will serve as guide to mortals; the vision of the whole world, things both below and beyond God's firmament, signifies that Moses will perceive what is, what has been, and what will be.[5] This striking passage corresponds to nothing in the Book of Exodus. Indeed, no other tale anywhere in literature ascribes a dream vision to Moses. Furthermore, the very idea of a dream by a Hebrew figure rendered intelligible by a non-Hebrew figure is unparalleled. Ezekiel plainly aimed to capture his readers' attention here.

Greek tragedy could supply precedents of a sort. Certainly Attic plays include dream visions in sufficient quantity. And some approximations can be found in the Bible: a few fortunate figures received visions of God in their dreams, and still fewer actually glimpsed a throne. But nothing is quite like the sight seen by Moses in *Exagoge*. Nowhere does God relinquish his seat to anyone else.

The creativity of Ezekiel should receive its due. In the Book of Numbers, God announces that, though he reveals himself to others in visions and dreams, he speaks to Moses directly, face to face, without enigmatic messages.[6] Ezekiel chose to ignore or sidestep that message. It seemed a small price to pay. The playwright had a powerful scene in mind: the forecast of Moses' future through a dramatic dream that gave him access to divinity. Ezekiel employed forms and material drawn both from Greek literature and from Jewish traditions, but he shaped them to convey an original conception. The dramatist not only intensifies the grandeur of Moses but also reconceives Moses' relationship with God.

Moses encounters a "noble man" with scepter and diadem on the great throne that extends to Heaven. The image here plainly presents God as sovereign power, ruler of the universe. The celestial realm appears as analogous to royal governance on earth. God beckons to Moses to approach the throne, then bids him sit upon it, hands over the scepter and diadem, and departs. The meaning can hardly be that God has relinquished universal dominion. Rather, Ezekiel directs attention to the analogy. Moses' ascension to the throne and acquisition of royal emblems signals his appointment as the Lord's surrogate in governing the affairs of men. That meaning is reinforced when Moses' father-in-law interprets the dream. His reference to the great throne, to the exercise of jurisdiction, and to the leadership of men had clear resonance to the contemporaries of Ezekiel. Moses' role as executor of God's will on earth, with absolute authority, is modeled on royal rule in the Hellenistic realms.

Ezekiel deftly combined familiar conventions with striking novelty to create a complex portrait. He nowhere disputes or denies the biblical account. But the admixture of the dream episode both magnifies the Moses figure and renders it more accessible to the dramatist's own society. He expressed the powers of the Hebrew prophets in terms that applied to Greek seers. And he draped Moses in the emblems of royal power that would carry direct relevance to those who lived in the era of the great monarchies. The author reinvents the position of Moses on the model of Hellenistic kingship while making him the model and precursor of Hellenistic kingship itself. God places Moses upon his own throne, a symbolic assignment of universal authority, to sit in judgment and be a guide for all mortals. Those lines have telling significance: they betoken the application of the Law as a pattern for all nations. The Israelite hero thus becomes a beacon for humankind, a representative of the divinity on earth, described in phraseology that struck responsive chords among Ezekiel's Hellenic or Hellenized compatriots.

The tragic poet held scriptural authority in awe. But that did not prevent him from occasionally improving upon it. His most inventive scenes gave heightened force to Jewish traditions by commingling them with features arising from Greek culture and society. God's elevation of Moses to glory signified a royal dominion familiar to Hellenistic readers and a universal message that Jews could claim as their own. Ezekiel had effectively commandeered a preeminent Greek genre and deployed it as a source of esteem for his Jewish readership.

Jewish writers also adapted another and even more venerable Greek medium: epic poetry. Extant fragments are scanty and tantalizing—but also informative and illuminating. Record survives of a second-century-B.C.E. epic poet named Theodotus, whose remaining verses treated the tale of the rape of Dinah by Shechem and the consequent destruction of the Shechemite city by Dinah's brothers Levi and Simeon, the sons of Jacob.[7] The poet had obviously imbibed Hellenic culture and enjoyed thorough familiarity with Homeric language and epic technique. But he took as his text, at least in the surviving lines, an episode recorded in Genesis 34.

The biblical account has Jacob return to Canaan, after his lengthy absence in the land of Laban, and reach the city of Shechem. His daughter Dinah wanders into the city, only to be seized and ravished by the like-named Shechem, son of the ruler, Hamor. The event sets matters rapidly in motion. Shechem may have been initially overcome by lust, but he soon aims to make an honest man of himself. He obtains the intercession of his father, who speaks to Jacob about arranging a wedding. Hamor indeed goes well beyond that initial request. He generously proposes a host of marriage alliances between Jacob's people and his own, and makes his land and possessions available to the newcomers. The sons of Jacob, however, outraged at the defilement of Dinah, plot deception and revenge. They consent to the uniting of the peoples but only on condition that the Shechemites circumcise themselves, because intermarriage with the uncircumcised would be intolerable. Hamor and Shechem readily agree, and their example is swiftly followed; within a short time all the males in Shechem are circumcised. That provides the opportunity for Dinah's brothers. While the Shechemites still suffer the effects of the surgery, Levi and Simeon swoop down upon them, murder every male, loot the city, and carry off the women and children. The underhanded scheme and the ruthless butchering of a compliant people sits ill with Jacob. He rebukes his sons for making him vulnerable to the hostility of his neighbors. And he never forgives them. On his deathbed, he curses Levi and Simeon for their resort to the sword and their reckless yielding to animus and anger.[8] The tale hardly casts the Israelites' actions in the best possible light.

Theodotus's version adheres to the basic narrative but turns it in quite a different direction.[9] Both his elaborations and his omissions set the events in contrasting colors. Theodotus kept his eye on the Genesis narrative throughout. Nothing in his account stands in flagrant contradiction to it. But he felt free to embroider or suppress matters, thus giving a distinctive slant and allowing for an alternative meaning.

The epic poet blended Greek elements with the Hebrew legend. Theodotus identified Shechem's founder with the son of Hermes, a feature that linked the city's story to *ktisis* (colonial foundation) tales and Greek mythology.[10] And he has the divine impetus for the attack on Shechem delivered through an oracular forecast, in Hellenic fashion.[11] The pagan trimmings were plainly congenial to the auditors of Theodotus's epic rendition of the Scriptures.

More important divergences, however, lay elsewhere. The biblical tale casts a cloud on the Israelites. Shechem's act of rape, to be sure, is hardly exemplary conduct, nor is it condoned in Genesis. But the young man hastens to make amends; his father is magnanimous toward Jacob's people; and the Shechemite males unhesitatingly subject themselves to circumcision—a stunning display of neighborliness. Yet it earns them only massacre, pillage, and captivity, the result of deception and a sneak attack. Theodotus puts a different twist on the tale. God implants the thought of revenge in the minds of Simeon and Levi. And the Shechemites get what they deserve, because they are a godless and disreputable people, maimed by God to set them up for the slaughter by Jacob's sons. Theodotus leaves out any calculated ruse on the part of the Hebrews. Nor does he suggest that the Shechemites had circumcised themselves and were still recuperating when attacked—although Hamor did encourage them to do so. The poet also omits any reproach or dissent from Jacob. The retaliation for Dinah's disgrace goes unquestioned.

What significance do these changes bear? Theodotus's revisions of Genesis do not so much excoriate the Samaritans as exculpate the Hebrew forefathers. The alterations are subtle rather than radical. Theodotus forbears from demonizing the Shechemites. In the poem, Hamor receives Jacob in welcoming fashion and provides him with land—thus going one better than the biblical version, which has Jacob purchase the lot.[12] Hamor further graciously meets Jacob's conditions and undertakes to persuade his people to circumcise themselves. Theodotus holds close to the biblical text here.[13] He avoids contradiction or challenge, let alone any suggestion of undermining the authority of the Bible. The selective omission had greater effect. No hint of duplicity on the Israelites' part, no actual circumcision by the Shechemites, no attacks while they were disabled, and no censure by Jacob of his sons. This rendition smoothed out some rough spots in the Genesis narrative. Theodotus's tale nowhere contravened the Scriptures; it left the Shechemites' behavior ambiguous but cleared the Hebrew leaders of acting deceptively, passed over their internal friction, and set the outcome as the execution of the divine will. Even though the fragments are few, they exhibit the skill of a Jewish poet employing a Hellenic genre to refashion his own people's history.

Epic poetry evidently had an audience among Hellenistic Jews. At least one other writer composed in that mode: the poet Philo, of uncertain date, a few of whose verses have reached us, produced a poem of substantial size with the title "On Jerusalem."[14] What survives may constitute no more than a tiny fraction of the whole. The few extant lines treat only Abraham, Joseph, and the waters of Jerusalem. And even they are expressed in tortured language enveloped in studied obscurity, with a variety of arcane allusions.[15] But a number of the preserved verses suggest that Philo, like Theodotus, may have endeavored to enhance the luster of the patriarchs.

Philo's inflated vocabulary, however pompous and pretentious, could serve that purpose. He hails Abraham in words either invented or refashioned as "widely famed," "resplendent," and "abounding in lofty counsels." He applies to the patriarch some striking terms to arrest the attention even of highly cultivated Jews conversant with the epic language of Hellenic literature.[16] Joseph receives comparable elevation. Philo depicts him not only as prophetic interpreter of dreams but also as holder of the scepter on the thrones of Egypt, a man who discloses the secrets of fate in the stream of time.[17] His extravagant language was more than mere bombast. Like Theodotus, Philo employed the genre to expand upon Scripture.

The re-inscription of biblical legend in Hellenic form had multiple manifestations. Perhaps the most extraordinary, however, came in the romantic story *Joseph and Aseneth*. This tale moves in a realm quite distinct from those discussed above, that of novelistic fantasy. Genesis provides barely a pretext for this invention. The Scriptures report only that Pharaoh gave to Joseph as his wife Aseneth, daughter of Potiphar the priest of On, and that she subsequently bore him two children.[18] All else is embellishment. And *Joseph and Aseneth* embellishes in style.

The genre of the work has evoked discussion and controversy. Noteworthy affinities exist with Greek romances like those of Chariton, Heliodorus, Achilles Tatius, or Xenophon of Ephesus. One can, to be sure, find differences and contrasts. The erotic features usually prominent in Greek novels are subordinated in the first part of *Joseph and Aseneth* and altogether absent in the second. Parallels can also be found in Jewish fiction of contemporary or near-contemporary eras, like Judith, Esther, and Tobit. The mutual interactions and influences cannot be traced. But there is little doubt that *Joseph and Aseneth* emerged in the literary climate that also produced and encompassed the Hellenic novel.[19]

A summary of the yarn would be apposite. Joseph, gathering grain in the course of his duties as Pharaoh's agricultural minister at the outset of seven plenteous years, reaches the territory of Heliopolis. There he encounters the eminent priest Pentephres and his beautiful 18-year-old daughter Aseneth. The maiden, however, like Puccini's Turandot, scorns all men and rudely rejects suitors from noble houses in Egypt and royal families elsewhere. Pentephres immediately proposes to betroth Aseneth to the righteous, powerful, and pious Joseph. But Aseneth recoils in anger: she will have nothing to do with one who is a stranger in the land, a shepherd's son from Canaan, sold as a slave and imprisoned as an adulterer. The arrogant girl will accept marriage only with the son of Pharaoh. When she spies Joseph from her bedroom window, however, Aseneth is smitten—and overcome with self-reproach. Joseph in turn has his own reasons for reluctance. He first fears that Aseneth is yet another predatory female determined to bed him, like Potiphar's wife and a host of others. And then he recoils from Pentephres' arrangement on other grounds. The purist devotee of a sole deity will have no congress of any kind with an idolatress. Aseneth will have to mend her ways and acknowledge the true god.[20]

The maiden turns her religious life around at a stroke. Much weeping and wailing ensue as she repents of former heresies, removes all the idols from her home, and falls to fasting and mourning, self-flagellation and humiliation, uttering desperate prayers to her newly found god, seeking forgiveness for past sins and rescue from the fury of spurned divinities. Aseneth's prayers are answered. An angel of the Lord materializes, offers her absolution, and bids her prepare for a wedding. Pharaoh himself presides over the ceremonies, places crowns on the heads of the couple, and sponsors a spectacular banquet that lasts for seven days. The marriage is consummated, and Aseneth subsequently produces two sons as Joseph's legacy.[21]

The happy ending, however, has not yet come. A second part of the tale, quite different from the love story, moves the narrative in a new direction. Internal friction shows itself both in the Hebrew patriarch's household and in that of Pharaoh. Joseph's brothers Simeon and Levi take joy in the company of Aseneth, while other brothers feel only envy and hostility. Further, Pharaoh's son determines to take her by foul means, enlisting certain of the brothers in his nefarious enterprise. They lead Egyptian armed men in an ambush of Aseneth and her entourage, and plots are hatched to murder Joseph and his sons, while the heir to the Egyptian throne prepares to assassinate his own father. All the schemes, of course, are foiled. Benjamin, now a strapping lad of 18, protects Aseneth and launches 50 stones, each of which fells an Egyptian, including Pharaoh's offspring. His brothers wipe out the remaining foes. And when the wicked brothers make a final effort to slay Benjamin and Aseneth, their swords fall miraculously to the ground and dissolve into ashes. Aseneth then intervenes to urge forgiveness and concord. The peace-loving Levi stays Benjamin's hand when he attempts to finish off Pharaoh's helpless son. In gratitude, Pharaoh prostrates himself before Levi. The aging, ailing ruler subsequently turns his kingdom over to Joseph, bestowing upon him the diadem that signals royal authority. And Joseph goes on to reign as monarch of Egypt for 48 years.[22]

So ends the narrative, an agreeable and entertaining one. In fact, it consists of two narratives, a love story followed by an adventure tale, the two only loosely connected. The work has generated immense discussion, most of it concerned with language, date, provenance, genre, and audience of the text.[23] We focus here on a different matter of broader consequence: the relation between Jew and gentile in the Diaspora. An initial impression might suggest that the tale pits the two cultures against one another. Joseph's insistence upon the purity of the faith and the pollution of idolatry, Aseneth's abject debasement and thorough break with her past to achieve absolution, the rigorous separation of Hebrews and Egyptians, and the favor of God supporting the faithful against the idol worshippers all seem to suggest a stark dichotomy between the forces of good and evil. But the breakdown is not so simple and the polarity not so sharp. Friction exists after all *within* each of the two communities. Joseph's brothers engage in potentially murderous activities against one another, and Pharaoh's son plots the assassination of the king. The fact that the wedding of Joseph and Aseneth takes place under the auspices of Pharaoh, who had not himself become a convert, holds central symbolic significance. The enemies of the faithful were forgiven, harmony and reconciliation followed, and the gentile ruler presided over the union of the Hebrew patriarch and the daughter of an Egyptian priest. The fable plainly promotes concord between the communities. Equally important, it asserts the superiority of Jewish traditions and morality—even against some Jews themselves.

Joseph exudes power and authority, more strikingly in this work than in Genesis or any other Hellenistic elaboration. The author of *Joseph and Aseneth* introduces Pentephres as chief of all satraps and grandees in the realm.[24] Yet, when he learns of Joseph's imminent visit, he is beside himself with excitement and goes to every length in preparing his household to receive so eminent a guest—one to whom he refers as "powerful man of God." Pentephres breath-lessly describes Joseph to his daughter as ruler of all the land of Egypt and Pharaoh's appointee as all-powerful governor.[25] Joseph then enters the gates of his host's estate in a royal chariot, resplendent in purple robes and a gold crown with precious stones. Pentephres and his entire family hasten to prostrate them-selves. The text could not make plainer the fact that, no matter how lofty was the position of Pentephres in the court and in the realm, he was far below the station of Joseph the Jew.[26] His crown radiated with 12 golden rays, emblematic of a sun god.[27] Aseneth's prayer to the Lord describes Joseph as beautiful, wise—and powerful.[28] Joseph himself emphasizes his stature by dismissing Pentephres' offer to provide a wedding banquet. He would have none other than Pharaoh perform that task.[29] At the conclusion of the narrative, the dying Pharaoh pre-sents him with the diadem, and Joseph reigns as king of Egypt for five decades.[30] This goes well beyond the biblical tale and probably beyond any subsequent Hellenistic version of it.

The superiority of the Hebrews, their character, faith, and traditions, consti-tutes a central theme of the work. Joseph's contemptuous refusal to have a meal with Egyptians deliberately reverses the biblical passage that has the Egyptians shun any table occupied by Hebrews.[31] Aseneth's smashing of idols and her ab-ject submission to the Lord accentuate the inferiority of her native religion. Pharaoh makes obeisance to Joseph's god when he conducts the wedding cere-mony.[32] The second segment of the narrative demonstrates that the authority of the Hebrews is physical as well as spiritual. Pharaoh's son acknowledges that they are powerful men, beyond all others on the face of the earth.[33] And, in a climactic scene, Pharaoh descends from the throne to prostrate himself be-fore Levi, who had spared his defeated son.[34] The harmonious relationship be-tween Jews and gentiles stands at the core of the tale, but it is achieved only through the Egyptians' affirmation of the Hebrews' distinctiveness. This novel, therefore, fits a pattern that can be discerned again and again. Jews appropriated a genre familiar in the Hellenic cultural world, crossed conventional boundaries, underscored commonalties, but reiterated the special eminence they claimed for themselves.

Jewish writers in Greek entered still another realm preeminently associated with the Hellenic achievement: historiography. Here again, as in other modes, they utilized the conventions to present or to expand upon biblical material. They had no desire to compete with Greeks in recording the exploits of other peoples—let alone of the Greeks themselves. But they saw the virtue of borrow-ing the methodology to reproduce their own past.

A certain Demetrius saw the advantages. He is one of the first Hellenistic

Jews, perhaps *the* first (around the late third century B.C.E.), to venture into the arena of the historians. He is frequently called "Demetrius the Chronographer," a somewhat unfair label. His interest in chronological matters is clear enough. But the extant fragments of his work evince broader concerns.[35]

Demetrius composed an account, historical in form, that treated material in Genesis and Exodus. Three fragments at least, perhaps as many as five, attest to it. A sixth is ascribed to a work entitled *On the Kings in Judaea* and concerns subjects deriving from 2 Kings. Demetrius's attention was captured by problems and puzzles for which he could offer solutions. So, for instance, he addresses the issue of how Jacob managed to father 12 children in just seven years. The schedule is tight, but Demetrius works out a timetable that includes all 12, produced by four different mothers.[36] Similarly, he confronts the question of why Joseph fed Benjamin five times what he offered his other brothers and bestowed four times the amount of clothing upon him. He supplies an answer: Leah had seven sons, Rachel but two; hence Benjamin's five portions plus Joseph's two evened the balance. The disproportion appears in Genesis, but the explanation is Demetrius's.[37] When the historian moves on to Moses, he grapples with another puzzle: how is it that Moses could marry Zipporah, who like him traced her descent from Abraham, if Moses was six generations distant from the patriarch and Zipporah was seven? Demetrius's reconstruction answers the question: Isaac was already married when Abraham married Keturah and had a second son, who was thus of the same generation as the son of Isaac from whom Zipporah descended—a solution Demetrius evidently developed from a piecing together of biblical testimonies and some shrewd calculations.[38] And he also tackles a very different issue in the Exodus story: how did the Israelites, who left Egypt unarmed, manage to secure weapons in the desert? An easy answer: they appropriated the arms of Egyptians who drowned in the sea. The conclusion plainly depends upon historical hypothesis, not any textual testimony.[39]

What ends were served by such exegesis? Demetrius's agenda surely had Jewish ends in view. That he was himself a Jew can hardly be questioned. Gentiles with an interest in the minutiae of biblical chronology or a concern about the disproportionate share meted out by Joseph to Benjamin would be rare birds indeed. But it is hard to detect any apologetic purposes here. The narrative is sober, dry, and colorless. No hint of polemic exists in Demetrius's austere renditions, no embellishments of character, no syncretistic transformation of biblical personages into figures of universal significance. The exercise has a starkly academic quality. Demetrius may well have imbibed the exacting principles of Alexandrian scholarship and put the techniques of Greek learning to the service of Jewish hermeneutics. Yet the extant fragments breathe hardly a hint of texts or traditions outside the Septuagint. Demetrius's narrative appears to be a rigor-ously internal one.

It does not follow that Demetrius provided exegesis for its own sake. His read-ership plainly consisted of Jews; why rewrite a historical narrative for those already familiar with it? In fact, Demetrius, as even the scanty fragments show, avoided a mere reproduction of Scripture. He abbreviated, streamlined, and modified the text—to the detriment of vividness and drama. He had other ob-jectives. For Jews who read and spoke Greek, especially those attracted by Hel-lenic rationalism and critical inquiry, the Bible presented some vexing questions: inconsistencies, chronological disparities, and historical perplexities. Demetrius took up the tangles, reduced narrative to bare bones, assembled chronological data, straightened out genealogies, and supplied explanations for peculiar deeds and events. His work or works, therefore, offered reassurance on the reliability of the Scriptures. Demetrius engaged in ratiocination, not apologia. Nor did he offer an alternative to the biblical narrative. The authority of that narrative was taken for granted by the historian for whom it was the sole source of his recon-struction. He appealed to a sophisticated Jewish readership that posed tough questions but also sought edification. Demetrius's rewriting may have come at the cost of aesthetic quality and dramatic power. But it reinforced confidence in the tradition. Demetrius adapted the mode of Hellenic historiography to cor-roborate the record of his nation's past.

A more venturesome effort came from the pen of another Jewish historical writer, Eupolemus, who in the second century B.C.E. also composed a work enti-tled *On the Kings in Judaea*. Its scope extended beyond the limits suggested by the title, because even the scanty fragments include comments on Moses. The principal focus, however, evidently rested upon the era of the monarchy, at least to the inception of the Exile.[40]

Eupolemus took some interesting liberties in his narrative of David and Solomon. He records, for instance, a surprising string of military successes for King David. In his compressed account, David subdues Syrians dwelling along the Euphrates and the area of Commagene, Assyrians in Galadene, and Phoeni-cians; he further campaigns against Idumaeans, Ammonites, Moabites, Ituraeans, Nabataeans, and Nabdaeans. He then takes up arms once more against Souron the king of Tyre and Phoenicia, makes the people tributary to the Jews, and frames a pact of friendship with Vaphres, the ruler of Egypt.[41] Questions arise about virtually every name in the text—not to mention a glaring omission: David's renowned conquest of the Philistines. Eupolemus departs drastically from the biblical narrative. The king's exploits in 2 Samuel include only a small portion of these victories. The Hellenistic historian extends David's territorial advance well beyond the scriptural testimony.[42] His conquests extend to the Taurus range in the north, the Euphrates in the east, and the Gulf of Aqaba in the south. Eupolemus takes a marked departure also in his treatment of Solomon. An exchange of correspondence between Solomon and Vaphres of Egypt appears in the text—a sheer invention. Solomon requests that Vaphres supply men to assist in the completion of his new temple, and the pharaoh responds with deference. He addresses Solomon as "great king," reports his joy at Solomon's accession, and expresses readiness to send workers from various parts of his realm.[43] The mutual messages are polite and cordial, drawing upon the Hellenistic conventions of royal correspondence. But, although Eupolemus takes care to affirm the independence and pride of the pharaoh, Solomon's ascendancy is clear and unequivocal.

Eupolemus's vision pierced beyond partisan politics and current events. The exaltation of Solomon through an ascendant relationship to pharaonic Egypt had wider significance. Vaphres not only acknowledges Solomon's superiority but even pays homage to the Israelite god.[44] The historian unhesitatingly "improved upon" the biblical account, depicting the ancient kingdom, at the time in which its sacred shrine was created, exercising widespread authority accepted even by the ruler of Egypt. Eupolemus may not have expected his Jewish readers to take the account literally, but it gave them the sense of a grand heritage, of a nation whose impressive history both reflected divine favor and earned the approbation of the great powers. For the Jews of Palestine and the Diaspora, that pride in their past buoyed the spirit and uplifted perceptions of national identity.

The fragment of Eupolemus on Solomon concludes in remarkable fashion. After the completion of the Temple, the king magnanimously restores the Egyptian and Phoenician craftsmen to their native lands with enormous severance pay, dispatches lavish gifts to Vaphres, and to Souron of Phoenicia he sends a golden column, set up at Tyre in the temple of Zeus.[45] Here once more Eupolemus supplies details for which no scriptural authority exists, employing the occasion to embellish the wealth, power, and generosity of Solomon. The final item, however, deserves special notice. Would the devout Solomon, having just completed the most monumental act of piety, actually send a pillar of gold to stand in a pagan temple? No need for tortured explanations here. The Bible itself records Solomon's penchant for foreign wives and for foreign gods. Among the divinities whom he honored was Astarte, the goddess of the Sidonians.[46] Eupolemus simply pursued the point a step further: Solomon enabled the Phoenician king to honor Zeus with a handsome offering. The implications of this notice deserve emphasis. Eupolemus saw no inconsistency in presenting Solomon both as a dedicated devotee of the Lord and as a patron of foreign princes who honored alien cults. This is not "syncretism," as some have characterized it. Rather, it highlights Jewish superiority in the spiritual and material spheres. Solomon requisitioned the manpower of other kingdoms to erect his magnificent structure to the supreme deity; he could in turn take responsibility for subsidizing the worship of his compliant neighbors.[47] That theme supplies a leitmotif for Jewish depiction of ancestral achievements that extended even to the enhancement of foreign cultures. The Jews had successfully enlisted the craft of historiography to augment the accomplishments of their past.

Another form of Greek learning comes in for modification and manipulation by a very different Jewish text. The *Letter of Aristeas,* composed probably in the second century B.C.E., may be the most famous surviving product of Hellenistic Judaism apart from the Septuagint—its fame due in no small part to the fact that it recounts the creation of the Septuagint itself. The text describes the decision of Ptolemy II to have the Hebrew Bible rendered into Greek and added to the shelves of the library in Alexandria, the negotiations with the high priest in Jerusalem to send the most learned sages to Egypt to produce the translation, their collaborative work, and the end product that was so warmly received by Ptolemy and the Alexandrian Jews.[48] The tale, of course, should not be confused with history. It is hardly likely that Ptolemy II marshaled the resources, commissioned the scholars, and financed the elaborate translation of the Books of Moses just to add some volumes to the royal library. That Hellenistic Alexandria was the site for a rendition of the Torah in Greek we may well believe. As late as the time of Philo, in the first century C.E., Egyptian Jews still celebrated an annual festival on the island of Pharos to mark the completion of that task.[49] The needs of Greek-speaking Jews who had lost command of or even contact with Hebrew surely motivated the project to provide a Greek version for liturgical or instructional purposes or even for private worship. But little else in the *Letter of Aristeas* commands confidence as history. The yarn spun by its author is largely creative fiction.

The story of the translation, however, though central to the narrative, actually forms only a small part of it. For our purposes, another portion of the text, indeed a healthy chunk of it, holds special interest. When the Jewish elders, selected for their profound learning in both Hebrew and Greek literature, arrive in Alexandria, Ptolemy orders an elaborate welcome: an extended symposium, seven full days of formal banquets—all served with kosher food. In the course of this drawn-out entertainment, the king puts a different question to each of his guests, most of the questions concerning how best to govern a kingdom and to conduct one's life. Each of the sages responds promptly, includes a reference to God as principal ingredient in the answer, and receives warm compliments from Ptolemy, who is awestruck by their acumen.[50]

What is one to make of this? Ptolemy II, as portrayed by "Aristeas," is in control throughout: his power and authority go unquestioned. He issues the orders to write to the high priest and get the project under way.[51] It is his decision to have the Hebrew Scriptures translated into Greek, that he might add them to his library.[52] He even orders the kosher meal for his guests and partakes of it as well, a gesture of his good nature, but also of his authority, the entire banquet orchestrated at his behest.[53] The dependence of the Jews upon royal power is unequivocally acknowledged. This is not a subversive document.

The Letter of Aristeas is thoroughly Hellenic in character, a fact of which the reader is repeatedly reminded. Greek men of learning and culture make an appearance or are referred to in the treatise. Even the Jewish high priest is described in terms that evoke a cultivated Hellenic aristocrat.[54] The scholars whom he sends to Alexandria not only command Greek as well as Jewish learning but express the noblest Hellenic ideal of striving for the "middle way."[55] The symposium in which the Jerusalemite sages are interrogated, of course, constitutes a fully Greek setting. And most of the sages respond with answers familiar from Greek philosophy or political theory—for example, they speak of the duty of the king to exercise restraint and honor justice; the definition of philosophy as reasoning well for every contingency, resisting impulses, and controlling the passions; and the designation of injustice as the greatest evil.[56] "Aristeas" has the high priest himself speak like a Greek philosopher.[57] The treatise plainly portrays Jews as comfortable in a Hellenic setting, attuned to Greek customs and modes of thought, and content under the protection of a Hellenistic monarch.

But to leave it at that is to miss the main message. The table talk of the symposium has a clear and unmistakable point: the superior wisdom of the Jews. Their representatives answer every question unhesitatingly, exhibiting their mastery of precepts familiar to the Greeks but incorporating in each response a reference to God as ultimate authority. The replies offer little that is distinctively Jewish—or even very specific. The sages never mention Moses, the Law, the Scriptures, or any practices peculiarly linked to Judaism. Indeed, God often appears in mechanical, even irrelevant fashion. The intellectual context is strictly philosophical, not at all theological—and rather superficial philosophy at that.[58] What matters is that the Jewish elders impress the king, over and over again. He commends every statement made, never moving from one interlocutor to the next without complimenting the speaker. The point of the episode, of course, is that the biblical scholars display an insight eclipsing anything that could be mustered by Greek philosophers. Ptolemy acknowledges it explicitly: the Jewish elders stand out in virtue and discernment, because the foundation of their reasoning lies in God.[59] More tellingly, the Greek philosophers themselves admit that they cannot equal the Jews' sagacity. The whole presentation has more than a touch of tongue-in-cheek. The narrator concludes his account of the seven banquets with a final dig at the Hellenic philosophers. In his own voice he observes that the scholars from Jerusalem were obviously worthy of the highest admiration from him, from those present, and especially from the philosophers.[60] That was no innocent remark.

The treatise of "Aristeas" is a complex, multilayered, and occasionally entertaining piece of work. No single purpose drove its composition. The idea, prevalent in modern scholarship, that it promoted a synthesis between Judaism and Hellenism is inadequate. The narrative implies that Jews are fully at home in the world of Hellenic culture. The use of a fictive Greek as narrator and admirer of Judaism carries that implication clearly enough. But the message has a sharper point: not only have Jews digested Hellenic culture but they have also surmounted it. Just as other Jewish writers displayed mastery of the tragic or epic art form, of romantic fiction, and of historiography, employing those Hellenic genres to embellish Israelite exploits, so the author of *The Letter* exhibits his familiarity with philosophic precepts and conventions while concocting a scenario in which all the advantage goes to the Jews.

Whether the texts discussed above typify Jewish attitudes cannot be said with certainty. But they (and other instances that could readily be cited) do represent a significant segment thereof. And the message rings loud and clear. The notion of a barrier that had to be overcome between Jewish and Hellenistic cultures casts precisely the wrong image. The Jewish intellectuals who sought to rewrite their past and redefine their traditions grew up in Diaspora or even Palestinian communities suffused with Hellenism. For them it *was* their culture. Their ideas and concepts expressed themselves quite naturally in Greek forms. But this in no way compromised, diminished, or undermined their sense of Jewish identity. On the contrary. Jewish thinkers and writers showed little interest in the Trojan War, the house of Atreus, the labors of Heracles, the customs of the Scythians, or the love of Cupid and Psyche. They mobilized the Hellenic crafts of epic, tragedy, philosophy, romance, and historiography to reproduce the record of their own people, to convey their conventions, and to enhance their achievements.

THE JEWISH CONSTRUCTION
OF GREEK CULTURE AND ETHNICITY

The embrace of Hellenic culture, as we have seen, served to reinforce rather than to dilute a sense of Jewish identity. But the broader the embrace, the more urgent it became to foreground those characteristics that distinguished Jews from the gentiles in whose lands they lived and with whose world they needed to come to terms. The Jews, in short, needed to establish their own secure place within a Hellenistic framework and to make it clear that they were not swallowed up by that prevailing cultural environment. The construct of Jewish identity, an ongoing, complex, and shifting process, was tightly bound up with the construct of Greek ethnicity—that is, the character, values, and beliefs of the Greek *ethnos* in Jewish eyes.

That these were constructs is inescapable. Although Jewish intellectuals could draw distinctions among Greek peoples, communities, and conventions, they frequently lapsed into broad characterizations and stereotypes. The reasons are obvious enough. They had a definite agenda. In some form or other, Jews had to confront—or to formulate—those Hellenic traits from which they wished to disassociate themselves and, at the same time, to account for those characteristics that they had themselves adopted.

Greeks regularly reckoned other people, including Jews, as *barbaroi* (barbarians): they did not speak Greek and hence were unintelligible. But the Jews could turn the tables. The author of the Second Book of Maccabees was a Hellenized Jew of the late second century B.C.E., a writer thoroughly steeped in the traditions of Greek historiography, who composed his work in Greek.[61] His topic, however, was the background, circumstances, and consequences of the brutal persecution of Jews by the Hellenistic monarch Antiochus IV Epiphanes. The Jews resisted and retaliated under Judas Maccabaeus. According to 2 Maccabees, they fought nobly on behalf of Judaism and, though few in number, ravaged the entire land and drove out the "barbarian hordes."[62] So the author, well versed in the conventions of the genre, employed the standard Hellenic designation for the alien—but applied it to the Hellenes themselves. And it was not the only such occasion.[63]

A whole range of texts discloses the drive of Hellenistic Jews to brand the Greeks as villainous or ignorant aliens, thus to distinguish more dramatically the advantages of being a Jew. Apocalyptic literature served this purpose. The visions of Daniel, which received their current shape in the very era of the persecutions, speak in cryptic but unmistakable tones of the catastrophic evils brought by the rule of the Hellenic kingdom. The terrifying dream that paraded four huge beasts in succession represented the sequence of empires, the fourth the most fearsome of all, a dreadful monster with iron teeth and bronze claws that devoured and trampled all in its path. That portent signified the coming of the Greeks. The forecasts given to Daniel, however, promised a happy ending: triumph over the wicked, a divine intervention to sweep aside the brutal Hellenic empire and bring about an eternal kingdom under the sovereignty of the

Most High.[64] The Greeks here embody the mightiest of empires—and the one destined for the mightiest fall.

That theme is picked up in the prophecies of the Third Sibylline Oracle. The Sibyl had venerable roots in pagan antiquity, but the surviving collection of pronouncements stems from Jewish and Christian compilers who recast them for their own ends. The contents represent the earliest portion, which is almost entirely the product of Jewish invention, and some parts of which at least date to the era of the Maccabees.[65] The text repeats in varied form the sequence of empires: representing the Greeks as impious and arrogant; forecasting internal rot; condemning the Greeks for overbearing behavior, the fostering of tyrannies, and moral failings; and predicting that Hellenic cities all over the Mediterranean would be crushed by a terrible divine wrath.[66]

The portrait is hardly less severe in the First Book of Maccabees. That work, extant now only in Greek, appeared first in Hebrew, the product of a strong supporter of the Hasmonaean dynasty; it was composed probably in the late second century B.C.E.[67] The book opens with a harsh assessment of Alexander the Great, an arrogant conqueror whose campaigns brought slaughter and devastation in their wake, and whose successors over the years delivered multiple miseries upon the earth.[68]

The stark contrast between Jew and Greek receives dramatic elaboration in the martyrologies recorded in 2 Maccabees. Under Antiochus Epiphanes, the elderly sage Eleazer resists to the death any compromise of Jewish practice, calmly accepting his agonizing torture. The same courage is exhibited by the devout mother who witnessed proudly the savage execution of her seven sons and joins them herself in death—memorable testimony to Jewish faith and Hellenic barbarity.[69] The stories were retold many generations later, in a text preserved in some manuscripts of the Septuagint under the title of 4 Maccabees, but at a time when the fierce emotions of the Maccabean era were a distant memory. The torments inflicted upon Eleazer and the unnamed mother with her seven sons were described in exquisite detail. The work was composed in Greek, probably in the first century C.E., by a Jew trained not in history but in Greek philosophy. He employed the martyrologies to illustrate Stoic doctrines of the command of reason over the passions. The author, therefore, ironically appropriated the Hellenic medium to express commitment to the Torah by contrast with the irrationality and atrocities of the Greeks themselves.[70] The schema that pits Jews against Greeks, the latter standing outside the bounds of morality and humane behavior, persists in all these texts.

A comparably sharp contrast surfaces in a most unexpected place. The *Letter of Aristeas* generally exudes harmony and common objectives between the cultures. Yet all is not sweetness and light even here. Eleazer the High Priest, when he responds to queries by Greeks about the peculiar habits of the Jews, affirms in no uncertain terms that those who worship many gods engage in foolishness and self-deception. Eleazer declares that Moses, in his wisdom, fenced the Jews off with unbreakable barriers and iron walls to prevent any mingling with other nations, to keep them pure in body and soul, and to rid them of empty beliefs.[71] So, even the veritable document of intercultural concord, the *Letter of Aristeas,* contains a pivotal pronouncement by the chief spokesman for Judaism, who sets his creed decisively apart from the ignorant and misguided beliefs of the Greeks.

The contrast is elaborated at some length by Josephus. The Jewish historian of the late first century C.E. distinguishes unequivocally between the steadfastness of Jews and the inferiority of Hellenic practices and institutions. He records repeated interference by Greeks with the ancestral practices of the Jews and outright atrocities in Cyrenaica, Asia Minor, Alexandria, Damascus, Caesarea, and other cities of Palestine.[72] Josephus pulls no punches: the disposition of the Greeks is labeled "inhumanity."[73]

Elsewhere Josephus conceives the contrast on a broader front. He singles out Moses as the most venerable of lawgivers and speaks with scorn of Greeks who take pride in such comparable figures as Lycurgus, Solon, and Zaleucus. He disparages Hellenic philosophy and education: the philosophers directed their precepts only to the elite, whereas Moses' teaching encompassed all. The study of Jewish traditions exposes the deficiencies and one-sidedness that inhere in both the Spartan and Athenian systems.[74] More important, he places particular weight upon the Jews' faithful and consistent adherence to their own laws. To the Greeks, such unswerving fidelity can hardly be imagined. Their history is riddled with inversions and deviations. Greek authors heap praise on the longevity of the Spartan system; for Josephus, that is preposterous. The endurance of that system was a mere trifle, not comparable to the 2,000 years that had elapsed since the time of Moses.[75] Josephus exploits Hellenic writings themselves to make a point about the foolishness and absurdity of their religious beliefs. The myths multiply deities without number, portray them in a variety of human forms, and have them engage in every type of licentiousness, misdemeanor, folly, and internecine warfare with one another. And, as if that were not enough, the Greeks grow weary of their traditional divinities and import foreign gods by the score, stimulating poets and painters to invent new and even more bizarre images of worship.[76] There could be no stronger contrast with the tenacity and constancy of Jewish practice.

The celebrated lines of the apostle Paul allude directly to the antithesis between the peoples: "there is neither Jew nor Greek, slave nor free, male nor fe-

male, for you are all one in Jesus Christ."[77] The string of antinomies makes it
clear that the two nations represented conventionally opposite poles. The distinction held firm in Jewish circles.

The evidence to this point seems clear and consistent. Jewish compositions
constructed the Hellenes as foils, as aliens, as "the Other," the better to set off
the virtues and qualities of their own *ethnos*. But those constructs do not tell the
whole story. The Jews' perceptions (or at least expressed perceptions) of the
Greeks were more complex, varied, and subtle. In other texts, Greek character
and culture acquire a more positive aspect, because they are conceived as owing
those qualities to the Jews themselves.

Aristobulus, a second-century-B.C.E. Jew of philosophic education and pretensions, played with what became a favored Jewish fiction: that Hellenic ideas
derived from Hebraic roots. A mere handful of fragments survive, and the identification of Aristobulus himself is disputed. But the emphasis on Jewish priority
in concepts later conveyed by Greeks is plain enough.[78]

In Aristobulus's imaginative construct, Moses provided a stimulus for Hellenic philosophers and poets. The Torah inspired the loftiest achievements of
the Greek intellectuals. Aristobulus asserts that Plato's ideas followed the path
laid out by the legislation of Moses, indeed that he was assiduous in working
through every particular contained in it. And he cites an earlier case still, an
equally distinguished name, the sixth-century philosopher Pythagoras, who also
found much in the Hebrew teachings that he could adapt for his own doctrines.[79] For any discerning reader, those pronouncements create some serious
chronological problems. How would the Greek sages have had access to the Hebrew Scriptures generations or centuries before the Septuagint? Aristobulus has
no qualms about fabricating one fiction to save another. He reassures potential
skeptics by maintaining that translations of the Israelite escape from Egypt, conquest and settlement of the new land, and all the details of the law code were
available long before the composition of the Septuagint.[80] Aristobulus com-
pounds his creative fabrications.

That accomplished, Aristobulus proceeds with flights of fancy. He includes
Socrates with Pythagoras and Plato among those whose reference to a divine
voice in contemplating the creation of the cosmos derives from the words of
Moses. And he goes well beyond. Aristobulus offers a broadly embracing doctrine that sweeps all of Greek philosophy within the Jewish orbit. He affirms
universal agreement among the philosophers that only pious opinions must be
held about God. And, since that view is embedded in Mosaic law, it follows that
Jewish conceptualizing supplied the wellspring for Hellenic philosophizing.[81]

If Jewish inspiration could be claimed for Greek philosophy, why not for poetry? Aristobulus and others had no hesitation in extending the Jewish reach

into that realm. References to the number seven in Greek poetry were seized upon as evidence that the institution of the Sabbath had seeped into Hellenic consciousness. Aristobulus goes back to the beginning. He summons up the verses of Greece's premier epic poets, Homer and Hesiod, to affirm that they endorsed the biblical sanctification of the holy day. This requires some fancy footwork. Aristobulus or his Jewish source exercise special liberties in twisting the texts to his will. Hesiod's reference to a seventh day of the month becomes the seventh day of the week, and a Homeric allusion to the "fourth day" is transformed through emendation to the "seventh day." Other lines quoted by Aristobulus but not attested in the extant texts of Homer and Hesiod may also have been tampered with or simply invented.[82] The subtle—or not so subtle—reworking had Homer and Hesiod acknowledge the consecration of the Sabbath. From the vantage point of Aristobulus, it is all for a good cause: to demonstrate the dependence of Greece's most ancient bards upon the teachings of the Torah. Observance of the Sabbath, in this conception, is no mere idiosyncrasy of an alien and self-segregated sect but a principle cherished in Hellenic song. Aristobulus thereby harnessed some of the most celebrated Greek thinkers and artists, real or legendary, to the antique traditions of the Jews.

In this venture Aristobulus was by no means alone. Jewish intellectuals ransacked the texts of Greek drama, chasing after verses that might suggest Hellenic borrowings from Hebraic ideas. And when they did not find appropriate lines, they simply manufactured them. Concepts with Jewish resonance were ascribed to the great fifth-century-B.C.E. tragedians Aeschylus, Sophocles, and Euripides, and to the comic poets Menander, Philemon, and Diphilus.[83]

Thunderous verses allegedly composed by Aeschylus exalt the authority of God. The eminent tragedian warns mortals to acknowledge his splendor and to recognize his presence in every manifestation of nature, an omnipotence that can shake the earth, the mountains, and the depths of the sea: "The glory of the highest god is all-powerful."[84] Such sentiments, whether authentic Aeschylus or not, would certainly play into Jewish hands. Sophocles too was exploited, for similar purposes. He trumpeted the unity and uniqueness of the Lord, rebuking mortals who installed graven images of bronze, stone, gold, or ivory.[85] He even supplied an eschatological text that forecast the destruction of the universe in an all-consuming flame to issue in the salvation of the righteous.[86] Euripides also served to advance the cause. A passage attributed to him asserts that no dwelling fashioned by mortal hands can contain the spirit of God, and another characterizes God as one who sees all but who is himself invisible.[87] These concocted lines—and doubtless many others no longer extant—conscripted the Attic tragedians in the service of Hellenistic Judaism.

A similar process enlisted Greek comic poets. Passages ascribed to one or another of them disclose the objectives of those who preserved (or forged) them. They include admonitions to the wicked, assertions that God punishes the unjust, insistence that upright conduct is more important than sacrificial offerings, and exhortation to honor the one God who is Father for all time, the Inventor and Creator of every good.[88]

Hellenistic Jews were evidently tireless in rummaging through the Greek classics to find opinions and sentiments that evoked scriptural teachings. The assiduous efforts gave forceful reminders to their countrymen of Jewish priority in the thinking of great thoughts. More striking still, they imply that the Hellenic achievement, far from alien to the Hebraic, simply restated its principles.

A famous story, but not one usually cited in this connection, underscores the point. Paul's celebrated visit to Athens in the mid-first century C.E. can exemplify this form of appropriation. The tale is told in the Acts of the Apostles.[89] Paul proselytizes among the Jews and "God-fearers" in the synagogue—and with any person who passes by in the *agora* (central market place). This upsets certain Stoics and Epicureans, who haul him before the high tribunal of the Areopagus and question him about the new doctrine. Paul is quick to turn the situation to his own advantage—and in a most interesting way. He remarks to the Athenians that they are an uncommonly religious people. He has wandered through many of their shrines and has found one altar inscribed to an "unknown god." Of course, he is there to tell them precisely who that "unknown god" happens to be. Paul then speaks of the sole Divinity, Creator of the world and all that is in it, a God who dwells in no temples and can be captured in no images.[90] The description plainly applies to the God of the Hebrew Bible, with no Christian admixture. Paul, like other inventive Jews, quotes Greek poetry to underpin his claims. So, he remarks to the Athenians, "as some of your own poets have said, 'We too are His [God's] children.' "[91] The poet in question is, in fact, Aratus of Soli, no Athenian. But that detail can be comfortably ignored. The parallels with other texts cited above are quite striking. Paul deploys Greek poetic utterances as certification for Jewish precepts, and he cites a Greek dedicatory inscription as evidence for Hellenic worship of the right deity—even if the Greeks themselves do not know who he is.

This heartening construct of Hellenic dependence on Jewish precedents appears notably, and perhaps surprisingly, even in the work of Josephus. As we have seen, he took pains to underscore differences between the Jews and the Greeks, to stress the stability of Jewish institutions and the durability of faith as against the multiple inadequacies of Hellenic practices. Yet Josephus also follows the line that many Greeks have embraced Jewish laws—though some have been more consistent in maintaining them than others. Indeed, he acknowledges,

Jews are more divided from Greeks by geography than by institutions.[92] Like Aristobulus and others, he finds Greek philosophers hewing closely to the concept of God that they obtained from acquaintance with the Books of Moses—noting in particular Pythagoras, Anaxagoras, Plato, and the Stoics.[93] And he makes still larger claims. Greek philosophers were only the first of those drawn to the laws of the Torah, adopting similar views about God, teaching abstinence from extravagance, and harmony with one another. The masses followed suit. Their zeal for Jewish religious piety has now spread around the world so that there is hardly a single community, whether Greek or barbarian, unaffected by observance of the Sabbath, various Jewish practices, and even dietary restrictions. Indeed, they labor to emulate the concord, philanthropy, industry, and undeviating steadfastness characteristic of the Jews.[94] The hyperbole is obviously excessive. But Josephus's insistence on the Greek quest to duplicate Jewish ethics, religion, institutions, and customs is noteworthy—and quite different from his drive elsewhere to underscore the distance that separated Jew from Greek.

An ostensible tension thus exists in Jewish perspectives on Hellas. A strong strain emphasized the differences in culture and behavior between the peoples, categorized the Greeks as aliens, inferiors, even savage antagonists. Other voices, however, embraced and absorbed Hellenic teachings, reinterpreting them as shaped by acquaintance with the Hebraic tradition and as offshoots of the Torah. From that vantage point, the Hellenic character becomes, through emulation and imitation, molded to the model.

Is there an explanation for these discordant voices? The discrepancies that we discern or construct may not have had comparable significance in antiquity. It is especially striking that the supposedly different voices coexist in the same texts. The matter is obviously complex and involved.

The author of 2 Maccabees, as we have seen, writing in Greek and in the genre of Hellenistic historiography, reversed convention and labeled the Greeks themselves as *barbaroi*. That was ironic and pointed—but it did not set a style. Other Jewish writers adopted the very antithesis long current in the classical world, contrasting Greek with barbarian. It can be found, for instance, in the philosopher Philo of Alexandria, who boasts of the widespread attraction of Jewish customs, embraced in various parts of the world by both Greeks and barbarians.[95] Josephus employs the contrast regularly as a means of dividing the non-Jewish world.[96] It appears also in Paul, who proclaims his message to "Greeks and Barbarians, the wise and the ignorant"—no pagan could have said it better.[97] Philo, in fact, can even adopt the Hellenic perspective wholesale and count the Jews among the *barbaroi*![98] Here is inversion indeed. Contrast between the nations need not betoken irreconcilability.

Nor, however, do the texts that signal cultural conjunction negate the force of pronouncements that differentiate the peoples. In various formulations, Greek poetic inspiration came from a Hebrew bard; Hellenic philosophers, dramatists, and poets who recognized the sole divinity, expressed lofty ethical precepts and honored the Sabbath took their cue from the Torah; and even the Athenians un-wittingly paid homage to the god of the Scriptures. These fictive inventions hardly dissolved the distinctions between Hebrews and Hellenes. Instead, they elevated the best in Hellenism by providing it with Hebrew precedents. The rest, by definition, fell short.

The Jews' reconception of the Hellenic achievement turned it to their own benefit. They simultaneously differentiated their nation from that of the Greeks and justified their own immersion in a world of Hellenic civilization.

INVENTIVE TALES FOR POPULACE AND ELITE

A critical question must now be addressed, a troubling but inescapable compli-cation. To what degree do the Jewish texts that survive from this era give access only to a small, elite segment of society? Do they seal us off from anything that might be considered "popular culture"?

A difficult matter. Indeed, it raises further and even more formidable ques-tions: how are these texts to be understood, to whom were they directed, by whom were they composed, and what were their objectives?

The limitations under which we labor have to be acknowledged at once. We normally do not know the author, the date, the place of composition, or the his-torical context of these works—let alone the motivations or intentions of the composer. Much scholarly energy has been devoted to reconstructing (or, better, to conjecturing and speculating about) when, where, and under what circum-stances a text was produced. Much of it is an exercise in futility. More important, however, the very questions of who, what, when, and why are not only often unanswerable but are probably the wrong questions. It is crucial to remember that we are dealing with texts that, for the most part, have gone through many versions, revisions, recasting, and redaction, and have passed through many hands, indeed perhaps circulated orally over an extended period of time before reaching the stage in which we finally possess them. Hence, to puzzle out the his-torical circumstances of the original composition, the Ur-text, the audience to which it was directed, and the society it reflects, even if we could do so, might not be very helpful.

The texts as we have them are the ones with which we must grapple. If they appear to have different layers of meaning and more than one level of understanding, that should not surprise us. Indeed, it makes them all the more valuable—especially for the complex issue of elite vs. popular culture. That dichotomy itself misleads and deceives. The texts can work on several planes, and they appeal to a diverse readership. The same stories ostensibly designed for "popular" consumption, such as folktales, romances, and fantasies, and plainly enjoyed on that level, can also carry deeper meaning and greater nuance directed to a sophisticated audience.

Joseph and Aseneth serves as an example. The entertainment value of the novel is high. The dramatic transformation of the two chief figures from bristling antagonists to a loving couple certainly has that quality. So does the adventure story that has the "good" brothers of Joseph prevail over the wicked sons of Leah and the nefarious plots of Pharaoh's son. The work can happily be read for diversion and amusement, and in that sense it is attractive to what is customarily considered a "popular" constituency.

But more serious, complex, and even baffling elements lurk within. As we have seen, the text raises pointed issues about Jewish/gentile relations in the circumstances of the Diaspora. Recurrent tension, animosity, and open conflict have as counterpoint union and harmony, reconciliation and communal concord. The meaning is not easy to ferret out. Further, the balance between royal authority and Joseph's extraordinary powers possesses political implications not readily explicable to readers content with the surface narrative.

Still more difficult matters confront interpreters of the text. Aseneth's adoption of Joseph's faith (nowhere identified as "Judaism" in the narrative) has stirred widespread discussion of what "conversion" might mean, whether the tract encourages missionary activity, what message is delivered about mixed marriages, and how gentile converts were viewed from a Jewish perspective.[99] All of this may be a red herring. An author engaged in missionary efforts would not likely feature a story in which the impulse to conversion came from sexual passion! But the ambiguities at least prompt deeper probing.

Even better examples occur in the Greek additions to the Book of Daniel. The author or authors, probably in the late second century B.C.E., fiddled freely with the received text, inserting folktales of independent provenance and applying some acid drollery to refashion the Jewish image. These include two quite amusing pieces of folklore: "Bel and the Dragon" and "Susanna."

"Bel and the Dragon" actually consists of two tales cobbled together and placed at the conclusion of what became the canonical text of Daniel. The first features Cyrus, king of Persia, as a devoted disciple of the Babylonian god Bel, on whom is lavished vast quantities of sheep, flour, and wine every day. Cyrus wonders why his chief adviser Daniel does not share his enthusiasm for this divinity.

Daniel retorts that he worships only the God who created heaven and earth, not some fabricated idol, and offers to prove that Bel is the invention of conniving Babylonian priests. He devises a clever scheme whereby ashes are scattered around the floor of the sealed temple one night, after offerings are made to the idol. Telltale footprints the next morning showed that the priests and their families used a trapdoor to steal off with the provisions themselves. The somewhat dull-witted Cyrus now sees the light, orders the execution of the priests and their families, and turns the statue of Bel over to Daniel, who promptly destroys it and its temple.[100]

The narrator proceeds directly to the next legend, that of the dragon or the snake. Here the king, still looking for a tangible deity to revere, points to the large snake that the Babylonians worship and bids Daniel to pay it homage as well. The Jewish counselor, of course, remains faithful to his own God, and he offers to expose the snake's impotence by killing it without recourse to a weapon. Cyrus grants permission. Daniel then mixes a concoction of pitch, fat, and hair and feeds it to the snake, which bursts open on the spot, allowing Daniel to crow, "Now look at your object of worship!" The Babylonians strike back, pressuring the king to turn Daniel over to them and cast him into the lions' den. But Daniel is undeterred. The prophet Habbakuk, sent flying through the air by an angel who tugs him by the hair, brings food to Daniel that sustains him in the pit. And when the king finds him miraculously unharmed after seven days among the beasts, he heaps praise upon Daniel's god, rescues his counselor, and tosses his enemies to the lions.[101]

These tales amuse and instruct. Most readers would delight in the triumph of virtue over evil, of monotheism over the practitioners of idol worship, a dominant theme in biblical and post-biblical literature, an easy and obvious moral to grasp. But that does not exhaust the implications of the fables. In fact, theology hardly gets much emphasis in the narrative. Daniel makes only passing references to his God and says nothing about his beliefs. The emphasis throughout rests not on divine intervention but on Daniel's own sagacity and resourcefulness.

Different undercurrents would appeal to those, whether elite or common, who read more closely. Cyrus holds a high place in Jewish memory as the monarch responsible for the return of the Jews from the Babylonian Exile. But in these tales, the king, far from being a magnanimous benefactor of the humble Jews, is represented as something of a dullard, manipulated and even mocked by those around him—including the shrewd Jew. Daniel more than once laughs at Cyrus's folly. The Persian ruler is as gullible about the snake as about the idol, is brow-beaten and intimidated by his Babylonian subjects, and has little influence on the course of events. The narrator misses no chance to expose his naiveté and deride his vacillation. There is subtle irony here, not mere playfulness. If this is the ruler under whom the Jews returned to their homeland, one must infer that a Jew pulled the strings on this hapless puppet. The story has deeper meaning for a Diaspora existence. Daniel's people may have to live under the rule of alien kings, but the rewritten fables reassure them of how far they surpass those kings in mental agility and insight. The irony reflects a shared perspective of author and reader, a joint scorning of the inadequacies of the political authority. That element takes the stories out of the realm of mere diversion.

More revealing still is the celebrated tale of Susanna and the elders in the Greek text of Daniel. Is it "highbrow" or "lowbrow" literature? Is it a pleasant yarn conceived to amuse or does it have a deeper structure to provoke reflection upon Jewish conditions in the Diaspora? Is it aimed at a select group of intellectuals or the "common man"? Is it imaginative fiction or an authentic evocation of Jewish experience? In fact, one can argue, it is all of the above.

According to the narrative, Susanna, the beautiful and devout wife of a prominent Jew in Babylon, is lusted after by two elders of the people. They hide in the garden, spy upon her in the bath, and confront her with an intimidating proposition: either have intercourse with them or face (fraudulent) charges of adultery with a young man. Susanna, coerced into an unwelcome decision, chooses the latter. The lecherous elders then deliver their indictment before a gathering of the people and persuade the congregation to condemn Susanna to death. Young Daniel, however, emerges as God's answer to Susanna's prayer, roundly rebukes the people, and denounces them for exercising peremptory judgment even without interrogating the elders. He denies the validity of their statements and offers to grill them himself. Daniel wisely takes the precaution of separating the two men and questioning each independently. In this fashion, he brings to light discrepancies in their claims, exposes their perjury, and draws cheers from the congregation. The elders are executed, the virtuous Susanna is vindicated, and Daniel gains great esteem among the people from that day on.[102]

To what audience would such a work be addressed? It contains obvious folktale elements. The story of the wise youth outsmarting the wicked elders has many parallels. So does the motif of the innocent woman as victim but vindicated in the end. Analogous tales can be found in the *Arabian Nights,* Grimm's fairy tales, and a variety of Eastern and Near Eastern literary texts.[103] It has been widely popular across the ages and was doubtless popular in antiquity. The engaging character of the tale guarantees that. Daniel's outwitting of the two bungling, dirty old men and the confirmation of the matron's virtue would have wide appeal. For many readers or auditors, no more was needed: good yarn, happy ending, virtue rewarded, villains punished. It was also reassuring to have flawed leaders exposed and flawed procedures denounced. Such might be a "popular" reading—and a perfectly legitimate and meaningful one.

It need not, however, be the only one. The tale takes place in Babylon; the Jews are presumably in exile or, at least, in an alien land. But they are represented as an autonomous community, with its own leaders, its own process of governance. The malefactors are Jews, not gentiles. And not only does the text depict the elders as corrupt and immoral, but it portrays the populace that rendered judgment as compliant, easily swayed—and not very bright. It requires a noble youth to bring them to their senses and rescue the maligned but blameless Susanna. Indeed, the noble youth himself is far from flawless. Daniel succeeds not as a devout adherent of the faith but as a crafty prosecuting attorney. He convicts the elders even before questioning them, and he declares the first to be a lascivious perjurer although his story has yet to be contradicted.[104] The lawyerly techniques hardly embody exemplary justice. A clear strain of Jewish self-criticism exists in this text. It offers a subtle reminder that Jews need to look to their own shortcomings, especially in a Diaspora setting. The legend, in short, carried import at more than one level and could have resonance with more than one stratum of society.

Does this narrative actually describe life in the Jewish community of Babylon at a particular point of history? That is more than dubious. The text mentions Babylon at the beginning to supply an ostensible context, but the remainder of the work gives no concrete details about location. The story could take place anywhere; the setting is imaginary, and the events, of course, are fictitious. But the message is meaningful, more than mere entertainment. The exposure of arrogance in the leadership and gullibility in the rank and file delivered a pointed lesson to the nation. It recalled to mind basic principles of justice and morality that needed to be observed—especially in Jewish communities that governed their own activities but whose internal divisions could make them vulnerable to greater powers. The message did not apply to a particular geographic locale or to a specific time period. Indeed, the significance of the story is precisely that it transcends time and place. Nor does it speak only to an elite or only at a popular level. It holds a place in the cultural legacy for Jews across the generations, across geographical boundaries, and across intellectual strata.

An altogether different text can offer comparable conclusions. In 2 Maccabees one finds a peculiar and puzzling work that continues to intrigue scholars and students. It is a work of history, but one punctuated by miracles, marvels, and martyrologies. It celebrates the deliverance of Jerusalem, its Temple, and its inhabitants from the terrors wrought by a Hellenistic king, but it was composed, at least in its fuller form, by a Hellenized Diaspora Jew from Cyrene. It bears notice here for certain arresting stories that it preserves and that certainly cater to what is conventionally categorized as popular taste.

An engaging tale occurs near the beginning of the main narrative. Heliodorus, the agent of the Seleucid king, arrives in Jerusalem to check on reports that the Temple treasury possesses incalculable riches. When told by the high priest that there are indeed deposits held in trust for widows and orphans as well as the savings of a prominent and wealthy Jewish leader, Heliodorus insists that the monies belong to the king and should be handed over to him. He heads for the Temple to make an inventory, alarming the priests and people. Heliodorus, however, presses on. He is about to enter the Temple with his bodyguards when a fearsome rider on a mighty horse, splendidly attired, attacks him. Two strapping youths, magnificent in beauty and strength, then appear and pummel him further. The minister is carried off in a litter, now obliged to acknowledge the sovereignty of God. Indeed it looks as if he will not recover. But the merciful high priest Onias III sacrifices to God for Heliodorus's recovery, and he is spared. He goes back to the king and extols the power and majesty of the Jewish God.[105]

The popular appeal of such a story is obvious. The greedy minister of the king gets his comeuppance, the sacred Temple is spared, and divine intervention saves the day. But subtle thrusts exist in this text that go beyond the surface reading. The author has a wry sense of humor that seems aimed at a discriminating reader. One might note, for instance, the prayer uttered by the priests and the people when Heliodorus is about to violate the Temple treasury. It was not a plea to God to protect the sanctity of his house; rather, it calls upon the Lord Almighty to keep the deposits safe and secure for those who have placed their cash there![106] The author composed this with a wink and a nod. And Heliodorus receives no conventional punishment. He gets a double dose. It is not enough that a horse charges him and kicks him. There are also two powerful young men who beat him to a pulp.[107] That seems a bit of overkill—and another example of some whimsy on the author's part. The penchant for irony can hardly be missed in the finale of this episode. Heliodorus, though practically breathing his last, is spared by the high priest and returned to Antioch. When asked by his king who should next be sent to Jerusalem in order to recover the money, Heliodorus replies, in effect, "If you want to send somebody, send your worst enemy; he will get thoroughly thrashed." And still another concealed barb can be discerned. Heliodorus remarks, "If you have an enemy or a plotter against the government, send him to Jerusalem."[108] As it happens, it was Heliodorus himself, not long thereafter, who plotted against the king and was responsible for his death. The anticipated audience here had to know its contemporary history—and to appreciate the irony.

In a different mode, it is instructive to look at the treatment in 2 Maccabees of the villainous Antiochus IV. The scene of his agonizing death is justly famous. The gory details, including the worms swarming about him and flesh rotting off, can be paralleled by various Greek texts. It appears to be a motif for the deaths of cruel tyrants. But the author of 2 Maccabees added an extra touch of his own when he had the persecutor repent in the end, declare Jerusalem a free city, grant prerogatives to the Jews, and promise to adorn the temple with lavish gifts and finance all its sacrifices.[109] The characterization of one of these promises is especially noteworthy. Antiochus vows that he will give privileges to the Jews equal to those enjoyed by the citizens of Athens. This would seem to be an allusion to the golden age of democratic Athens. Such an age, however, had long since passed— contemporary Athens was hardly a model of autonomy and privilege. The insertion here is yet another instance of the author's sardonic streak. Only a few select readers would detect that allusion.

The Book of Judith, composed perhaps in the early first century B.C.E., provides an edifying and uplifting tale. One need not have intellectual credentials to appreciate it. The setting (wholly imaginary) is a putative military campaign ordered by Nebuchadnezzar, here identified as an Assyrian monarch, against various peoples of the Near East, including those dwelling in Judaea and Samaria. The military man Holofernes is appointed commander-in-chief of the armies that sweep through the lands, looting, sacking, and destroying sacred shrines. When the forces threaten Judaea, the Israelites, their high priest, and their officials are terrified, block the mountain passes, put on sackcloth and ashes, and pray to the Lord for rescue. The Ammonite chieftain Achior, whose people have already surrendered to the invaders, warn Holofernes that the Israelites are invincible if their God favors them, but vulnerable if they have sinned against Him. Holofernes scorns the advice, mocks Achior, and delivers him to the Israelites themselves. The army then undertakes the siege of the (unlocatable) Israelite town of Bethulia. Its inhabitants swiftly become desperate, the people pressing their leaders to surrender before they are annihilated. The city's most prominent figure, Uzziah, proposes a five-day wait, in hopes that God might intervene, but promises surrender if there is no sign of such intervention.[110]

At this point Judith enters the scene. A respected and wealthy widow, renowned for her piety and wisdom, Judith denounces the city's elders for giving a deadline to God and promises that she will take action to deliver Israel with the aid of the Lord. Uzziah and the magistrates give her free rein. Judith first prays to God, then takes matters into her own hands. A beautiful as well as wise woman, she bedecks herself alluringly and, with a single maidservant, goes straight to the camp of Holofernes. Judith dazzles the general not only with her beauty but also with beguiling and manipulative language, leading him to believe that, with her aid, he can subdue the Israelites without difficulty. A few days later comes the inevitable invitation to spend the night in Holofernes' tent. Judith arouses his desire, then plies him with wine. When the intoxicated Holofernes passes out, Judith, armed with prayer and a sword, lops off his head. She slips from the camp with the head in a sack and has the elders display it proudly on the battlements. The people are in awe of the deed, and Achior the Ammonite faints dead away. Upon recovery he praises Judith to the skies, has himself circumcised, and converts to the Israelite religion. The Assyrians, stunned and crestfallen, are easy prey for the Israelites. The city is saved, the enemy routed and despoiled. Judith, much lauded not only by the citizenry of Bethulia but also by the high priest and his council in Jerusalem, retires to her own estate, emancipates her loyal attendant, declines all offers of marriage, and lives out her days in serenity, dying at the age of 105.[111]

As a tale of Jewish success against heavy odds, this narrative has immense appeal. It was often retold over the ages and has been represented many times in European art. The image of Judith holding Holofernes' head can be found in museums throughout the world. Its hold on popular imagination is clear and readily comprehensible.

But, here again, currents of a less distinct and more subterranean character come into play. The tale upsets expectations, inverts the norm, and invites thoughtful interpretation.

Judith herself is an ambivalent, often surprising figure. Her story can be correspondingly perplexing. She is an adherent of law and ritual but has no hesitation in practicing deceit. She roundly rebukes Uzziah and the elders, but, far from feeling aggrieved, they give her full authority. She exhibits greater devoutness than the males in her society but also exercises greater ruthlessness. She uses sexual wiles on Holofernes but remains a chaste widow to the end of her days. She plays the most central public role, and then retreats to an innocuous private life. She utters repeated prayers to the Lord but, in fact, accomplishes all through her own wits and guile.

Holofernes is a no less surprising, indeed implausible character. He rampages through most of the Near East and is then content with a long and leisurely siege of a small Judaean town. He swallows wholesale Judith's line about the Israelites and their God, although he has just rejected the same line when uttered by Achior. He waits patiently for four days before trying to seduce Judith—and then falls into a stupor when the opportunity arrives.

Minor personalities also behave in peculiar ways. Achior, gentile though he be, has a clearer vision of Jewish principles than Uzziah, the Judaean magistrate. Achior, warrior though he be, keels over at the sight of a severed head. And

Uzziah, chief magistrate though he be, allows Judith to proceed with her plan—despite the fact that he has no idea what it is.

Reversals and surprises abound. Just what they signify cannot be determined with any certainty. But they subvert a simplistic reading. The text plays with chronology and geography, turns history into fantasy, casts doubt upon Jewish leaders' grasp of their own precepts and traditions, both asserts and questions religious values, and confuses gender roles. The Book of Judith blurs boundaries throughout. The straightforward triumph of pious Jews over gentile aggressors, exemplified by the image of Judith brandishing the head of Holofernes, dissolves upon closer scrutiny. Reception of the tale for its entertaining quality constitutes but one mode of understanding. Like all the works discussed here, the Book of Judith operates at several levels. Therein lies its strength and its enticement.

As is clear, these texts undermine any lowbrow/highbrow dichotomy. The idea that creations of this sort could only be appreciated either by a "popular" mentality or by a sophisticated elite breaks down upon examination. Such a boundary eludes sharp definition. Folktales and romances are regularly transformed through retelling over time, with a range of readers or auditors. Populace and intelligentsia alike could take pleasure both in their narrative charm and in their subversive character. The richness of the texts signals a multitude of voices and the complex process of reshaping wrought by the interests and concerns of many generations.

WOMEN IN FICTION AND FACT

The tale of Judith draws attention to yet another complication: the constructs of gender. Narrative texts that engaged Jews with gentiles or probed Jewish self-perception in a broader culture frequently centered upon the demeanor, actions, and place of women. The frequency of such constructs by (presumably) male authors betrays a need to confront the tensions produced in gender roles by the pressures of a wider society.

The subordinate position of Jewish women in this period (as in most others) is marked and clear. Hellenistic writers make no bones about it. A purveyor of proverbs, hymns, and doctrinal advice called Ben Sira, writing in the early second century B.C.E., deemed the birth of a daughter to be a major burden for her father, who would have to supervise her behavior and protect her chastity. Daughters are a constant source of anxiety, prone to be wayward, keeping fathers awake with concern lest they be unmarried or childless or, worse, unwed mothers. Given the slightest chance, they will leap into the embrace of strangers. Without surveillance, they are liable to humiliate their parents, bring disgrace on their families, and make their fathers a laughingstock to their foes and a disgrace in public. Not that wives are any better. Ben Sira claims that he would rather share a house with a lion or a snake than an evil woman. Husbands can expect nagging, tantrums, and misery. Indeed, he goes so far as to assert that a man's wickedness is preferable to a woman's goodness![112] Comparable statements can be found in other Jewish-Hellenistic texts.[113] The expressions are rhetorical and extreme. Ben Sira acknowledges that a virtuous woman can bring benefits. But the characterization of that virtue is still more revealing: a man can count himself happy in having a sensible and devoted wife.[114] That translates into a wife who is chaste and beautiful, honors her husband—and keeps quiet.[115]

Ben Sira's attitude corresponds, in no small measure, to the position of women in Second Temple society. They were expected to maintain a chaste and modest demeanor, remain for the most part at home, stay out of the sight of strangers, and hold as first priority the reputation of the household. Marriages, at least among the middle and upper classes, were arranged by parents. And wedlock was far from an equal partnership. Men had the option of polygamy; women did not. Adultery was punishable as a crime, but only for women; men were exempt—unless they dallied with a married woman. A man could initiate a divorce at any time; a woman had no comparable privilege. Women were not even qualified to serve as witnesses in a legal proceeding. They could inherit, own, and bequeath property, but the instances of such activity are few in the era of the Second Temple. Insofar as they engaged in occupations and professions, these were largely confined to supporting their husbands and grew out of household tasks or areas appropriate to women such as weaving, spinning, cooking, baking, and midwifery.[116] In such circumstances, women could hardly expect to exercise leadership or achieve positions of authority.

Literature, however, seems to tell a different story. Women are conspicuous, active, and pivotal in the narratives. Memorable heroines stand out: Judith, Esther, Susanna, Aseneth. Did this represent a critique of gender hierarchy, a subversive treatment of societal norms? A closer reading of the texts may suggest more conformity than censure.

Judith is unquestionably the most potent female figure in Jewish-Hellenistic literature. She rescues a nation driven to despair and on the point of catastrophe. She rallies sagging spirits, seizes initiative from a languid leadership, devises a bold plan, and executes it remorselessly. Her resolute actions destroy the enemy and restore her nation to its glory. No male had been up to the task.

Yet even this dramatic narrative, with all its role reversal, does not challenge conventional social expectations. The dynamic and resourceful character of Judith serves primarily as a means to discredit the timid leaders of the community at a moment of crisis. The fact that Holofernes has to be dispatched by a woman, underscored more than once in the text, has less to do with female emancipation than with the acute humiliation of the men whose trust in the Lord has eroded.[117] Judith's rebuke of the elders is pointed and piercing.[118] Her own successes, even when achieved through guile and audacity, are always accompanied by prayers to Yahweh and humble obeisance to His presumed will, which is ultimately responsible for the outcome. Judith's piety is her most conspicuous characteristic.[119] And the outcome of her exploit is to restore an order and stability to the realm that allow it to settle back into its conformist mode. Appropriate gifts are offered to Yahweh, not only the customary sacrifices but also all the spoils from the camp of Holofernes. The Jews withdraw, each to his own inherited property, signifying the return of routine existence. Judith herself repairs to her estate, her public appearance brief and now concluded for good. She retired to private life and widowhood, a status she maintained throughout the many decades that remained to her. Fittingly enough, she chose to be buried with her husband. Her spectacular deed has saved the nation. But, lest there be any anxiety over a reversal of social and gender hierarchy, Judith's withdrawal to quiet piety puts it to rest.[120]

The figure of Esther also upsets certain expectations—but reinforces most.[121] Her famous tale opens at the court of Ahasuerus, master of the Persian Empire, whose domain reaches from India to Ethiopia. The king hosts a lavish banquet for all the officialdom of the realm, thus to put his great wealth on display. The festivities are to be culminated by a visit from the ravishing Queen Vashti, summoned by the ruler to exhibit her beauty for his guests. Vashti, however, refuses to parade herself before the assemblage. Ahasuerus swiftly consults his counselors and then banishes Vashti from his presence forever. He subsequently warns all women in his kingdom to be deferential to their husbands.

Ahasuerus decrees a competition—a beauty contest for the realm's young virgins—to find a new queen. Among those who answer the call is the beautiful Jewess Esther, an orphan raised by her cousin Mordekhai. After each of the maidens has undergone elaborate cosmetic treatments and spent a night with Ahasuerus, he selects Esther as his favorite (she had concealed her Jewish identity, on Mordekhai's advice) and sets the regal crown on her head. The event is celebrated by yet another extravagant banquet.

Ahasuerus's principal vizier is the ambitious Haman, promoted and honored by the king but ever grasping for more. The minister's demand for obeisance has been flouted by Mordekhai, who declined to bend a knee, thus prompting Haman to seek revenge on Mordekhai and the entire Jewish people. The compliant Ahasuerus authorizes the slaughter of Jews everywhere, man, woman, and child.

Mordekhai greets the news with sackcloth and ashes. But he also communicates with Esther, reminding her of her origins, and prodding her to intervene with the king. Esther overcomes her initial reluctance and takes the grave risk of an unsummoned appearance before Ahasuerus. Fortunately for Esther and for the Jews, he is still smitten with his young consort, promising her anything, up to half his kingdom. Esther plays her cards carefully, inviting the king and Haman to dinner on two consecutive evenings, piquing the interest of the former and deftly misleading the latter.

Ahasuerus, in the meantime, learns that Mordekhai had once saved his life by warning him of an assassination plot. He therefore plans to honor the Jewish courtier. Haman, assuming at first that such favor will be his, learns with dismay of Mordekhai's elevation. The humiliations multiply. Not only must Haman humble himself before Mordekhai; he has to hear from his own wife that he cannot succeed against the Jew.

Esther's plan can now come to fruition. She unveils her request at last: a plea that she and her people be spared destruction. And she dramatically points to Haman as the villain who had plotted the genocide. Ahasuerus directs that his minister be hanged on the very gibbet he had prepared for Mordekhai.

The king's about-face is complete. He awards Haman's estate to Esther and gives carte blanche to Mordekhai and Esther to compose a decree that will be sent to every province of the empire, not only rescinding Haman's instructions but also authorizing the Jews to take up arms against their enemies, kill them all, and confiscate their property. The Jews implement those orders unhesitatingly and ruthlessly. Mordekhai took his place as the most trusted and powerful of the king's ministers as well as chief advocate for the welfare of Jews throughout the realm.

What implications does this story possess for the expectations and aspirations of women? The opening scene sets the conventions within which society operates. Vashti defies her husband and is banished. An imperial edict demands that wives respect the authority of their husbands and that men be masters in their own homes.[122] The setting, of course, is Persian, not Jewish, and the satiric quality of the account is transparent, but the restrictions on female behavior would not be altogether unfamiliar to a Jewish readership.

Esther is a complex and changing character, but she does not stray far beyond the boundaries. Mordekhai pushes her into the contest; Esther meekly complies. She continues to obey Mordekhai, who checks up on her daily.[123] When he learns of the palace plot to assassinate Ahasuerus, he directs Esther to disclose it, and she does.[124] When Mordekhai dons the garb of mourning, Esther, concerned but clueless, sends him some new clothes.[125] He has to instruct her on how to dis-

suade the king from the slaughter of the Jews. And his suggestion that she might
have been made queen precisely to rescue her people gives her courage.[126]

Esther matures swiftly and suddenly. From this point on she acts with resolution and resourcefulness. She will face Ahasuerus no matter what the risk. Now
it is she who gives Mordekhai instructions—which he obeys. She appears before
the king, ensnares Haman, and persuades Ahasuerus to reverse his homicidal
decree.[127]

Has Esther been transformed from obedient ward to formidable potentate, a
model for subordinate Jewish women aspiring to burst the bonds of convention?
Not exactly. Ahasuerus may be putty in her hands, but the lines of authority are
not breached. The king awards Haman's estate to Esther, appropriately enough,
for women could own property in the Persian system. Esther, however, immediately turns it over to Mordekhai. A magnanimous gesture by a queen? Perhaps.
But more likely a dutiful gesture by a foster-daughter. This restores the proper
gender relationship. Ahasuerus notably gives his signet ring—and with it the authority to issue decrees in the king's name—to Mordekhai. Esther gets her way,
but only by falling at the feet of Ahasuerus, bursting into tears, and pleading
with him to avert the calamity that Haman had planned for the Jewish people.[128]
It is Mordekhai who, clad in royal purple and sporting a golden crown, wields
power in the palace and directs the celebration of the festival of Purim.[129] The
Book of Esther concludes with a reference to the royal chronicles, in which were
inscribed the authority of the king and next to him, as second in command, his
grand vizier Mordekhai, most powerful of the Jews and spokesman for their welfare. No mention of Esther.[130]

As in the Book of Judith, the traditional order, in the end, is reinforced. Esther, demure and docile at the outset, placed in the palace through Mordekhai's
machinations, spurred into action by his instructions, evolves into a clever and
designing woman, even a vindictive one—but never usurps the role occupied by
ascendant males.

The date of composition for the canonical Book of Esther cannot be fixed
with precision. In all probability it came sometime in the late Persian or early
Hellenistic period (between the mid-fifth and mid-third centuries B.C.E.). But
supplements were added in Greek, which must be Hellenistic in date, and these
include a striking revision of the character of Esther.

Additions C and D, so labeled by scholars, were inserted in the story right
after Mordekhai's appeal to Esther to intercede with Ahasuerus. The first invented prayers by both Mordekhai and Esther; the second supplied the actual
encounter between Esther and the king. Esther's plea in Addition C is unlike
anything in the Hebrew text. She strips off her splendid garments, covers herself

with ashes and dung, and makes herself as unattractive as before she had been comely. She concedes that she slept with the uncircumcised king—but she hated every minute of it. Yes, she wears a crown, but only in public and only because she must. She twice proclaims her loathing of the crown and compares it to a polluted rag. She insists even that she never took food at Haman's table, thus to declare her adherence to dietary laws—though the canonical account betrays no concern on the matter.[131] The queen protests too much. The author of the addition, by stressing her strained denials, calls attention to her weaknesses.

Addition D buttresses this conclusion. It describes the audience of Esther before the king. Unlike the Hebrew text, she is here depicted as terrified. She has dressed herself once more in resplendent robes, she has summoned her God and savior, and she glows at the peak of her beauty, but inside she is racked with fear. When she sees the king, magnificent and awesome on his throne and flashing an angry glance at her, she passes out on the spot, not once but twice.[132] This is hardly the stuff of a heroine. The interpolator evidently augmented the tale at Esther's expense. Lest anyone think that Esther comes off too well in the Hebrew version, the Hellenistic Jewish author decided to fix that.

As for the striking figure of Aseneth: the chaste and haughty virgin who defies her parents and heaps scorn upon the noble Joseph, only to shift suddenly into reverse, shattering idols and abasing herself, cuts a memorable figure. With what meaning? One cannot argue that her saga, set in the milieu of the Egyptian elite in the legendary era of Jacob and Joseph, reflects in any significant way the ordinary lives of Hellenistic Jews. But it may well resonate with ideological presuppositions about women's appropriate role in Jewish society.[133]

Aseneth's arrogance, disdain, disobedience of her parents, and virginal superiority represent all that Jews (and not they alone) found threatening and repugnant in women. She even boasts of a bed in which she sleeps alone and which has never been sat upon by man or woman.[134] The fiery Aseneth breaches every convention, and her actions, for the author of the text, naturally go hand in hand with ignorance of the true God and reckless idolatry. Aseneth has few redeeming features.

With the arrival of Joseph, however, Aseneth's hard exterior, cockiness, and contemptuousness vanish. Once the embodiment of all that is undesirable in a woman, she is now submissive, subservient, and self-abasing. And her rescuer from the abyss of despair is, appropriately, a male, the angelic figure whose ministrations restore her former beauty and make her a fitting bride—though only after she has made a fool of herself yet again.[135] Aseneth humbly and gratefully welcomes her marriage, accepting her role as handmaiden to her bridegroom and insisting on washing his feet.[136] Her gratitude, expressed in a prayer to the

Lord, consists of further self-denigration, confession of sins and offenses, and a declaration that her previous arrogance has been recast as humility.[137] Her former assertiveness could only be undone by degradation. *Joseph and Aseneth* reaffirms the suitable demeanor of women: deference to parents and submissiveness to husbands. Aseneth, who violates all the norms at the outset, spends much of the remainder of the tale reproaching herself, *ad nauseam.*

The story of Susanna sustains the theme. No need for remorse or transformation here: Susanna is virtue itself from the outset. The prim, modest, faithful matron was brought up properly by her parents: they instructed her in the Law of Moses. And she has been wed to a pillar of the Jewish community. Susanna epitomizes the figure of the pious and demure wife.[138] Her very innocence, however, renders her vulnerable to the wicked elders who present her with a grievous choice. The unhappy woman chooses the lesser evil: an unfair trial rather than the loss of her virtue. But her decision only underscores her helplessness. This is not so much steadfastness as resignation.

Susanna suffers further humiliation at the hearing: she is stripped naked (so the Septuagint version indicates), a prejudgment of her crime and public mortification. She does not utter a word in self-defense; only after being condemned does she release a plaintive wail, asking the Lord why an innocent victim must perish.[139] She is, of course, rescued and vindicated, but not through any actions of her own. Daniel materializes, as God's agent, to foil the elders' scheme.

The heroine of this tale, in short, is hardly heroic—an admirable, but a purely passive, figure. Susanna lacks the weight to resist the mighty and lets her fate be decided by others. At the conclusion, her reputation restored, she returns meekly to the household of her husband—who, so far as we can tell, had not even been present at her trial. The public credit for this success goes to Daniel.[140]

Women, in sum, figure prominently in the fictional compositions of Hellenistic Jews. But these creations do not serve to challenge the conventions of society; they manage, in fact, to reinforce and confirm them. The uppity Aseneth becomes a penitent, and arrogance is turned into abject submissiveness. Esther's position gives her access to power and a means to save her people, but she needs to be prodded, gives way to stereotypically female faintheartedness, and defers to male authority. The innocent and docile Susanna, the ideal wife, is helpless in the face of injustice but is rescued by a male hero and restored to the bosom of her presumed protectors. Even Judith, the respected widow, who bursts from her privacy to eclipse inept male leadership, reverts to private life and public invisibility. The inventive constructs of fertile writers largely reasserted the values of their society and the place of women within it.

DIASPORA AND HOMELAND

A firm sense of Jewish identity required more than the definition of a relationship with other cultures and peoples. A matter internal to the nation demanded repeated reappraisal: the issue of Diaspora and the homeland.

The destruction of the Second Temple in 70 C.E. constitutes, in most analyses, a watershed event for the Jews of antiquity. The elimination of the center, source of spiritual nourishment and preeminent symbol of the nation's identity, compelled Jews to reinvent themselves, to find other means of religious sustenance, and to adjust their lives to an indefinite period of displacement. That trauma has pervasive and enduring resonance. But it tends to obscure a striking fact. Jews faced a still more puzzling and problematic situation *prior* to the loss of the Temple. Diaspora did not await the fall of Jerusalem. Very large numbers of Jews dwelt outside Palestine in the roughly four centuries from the time of Alexander the Great to that of Titus.[141] The era of the Second Temple in fact brought the issue into sharp focus, inescapably so. The Temple still stood, a reminder of the hallowed past, and a Jewish regime had authority in Palestine. Yet the Jews of the Diaspora, from Italy to Iran, far outnumbered those in the homeland. Although Jerusalem loomed large in their self-perception as a nation, only a few of them had seen it, and few were likely to. How then did Diaspora Jews conceive their association with Jerusalem, the emblem of ancient tradition?

A dark picture prevails. Diaspora appears as something to be *overcome.* Thunderous biblical pronouncements present it as the terrible penalty exacted by God for the sins of the Israelites. They will be scattered among the nations and pursued by divine wrath. Spread among the lands, they will worship false gods and idols and enjoy no repose from the anger of the Lord. If the children of Israel abandon the ancestral precepts, they will have to enter the servitude of foreign lords in foreign parts. They will be dispersed among peoples unknown to them or to their fathers and will suffer God's vengeance until their destruction.[142] Through much of the Scriptures, only a single goal keeps flickering hopes alive: the expectation, however distant, of returning from exile and regaining a place in the Promised Land. Obedience to the Lord and repentance for past errors will induce Him to regather the lost souls spread across the world and restore them to the land of their fathers. He will raise a banner among the nations and assemble the people of Judah from the four corners of the earth.[143] It should be no surprise that a negative verdict on Diaspora life and a correspondingly gloomy attitude are conventionally ascribed to the Jews of the Second Temple period.[144]

Yet that convention ignores a grave implausibility. It is not easy to imagine that millions of Jews in the Diaspora were obsessed with a longing for Jerusalem that had little chance of fulfillment. It seems only logical that they sought means whereby to legitimize the existence that most of them inherited from their parents and would bequeath to their descendants.[145] Large and thriving Jewish communities existed in numerous areas of the Mediterranean, with opportunities for economic advancement, social status, and even political responsibilities.[146] Did their members, as some have claimed, take recourse in the thesis that the nation is defined by its texts rather than by its location?[147]

The dualism is deceptive. The Jews of antiquity, in fact, never developed a systematic theory or philosophy of Diaspora. The whole idea of valuing homeland over Diaspora or Diaspora over homeland may be off the mark. Second Temple Jews need not have faced so stark a choice.

The characterization of Diaspora as exile occurs with some frequency in the works of Hellenistic Jewish writers. But close scrutiny discloses an important and neglected fact. The majority of these grim pronouncements refer to the *biblical* misfortunes of the Israelites: expulsion by Assyrians, the destruction of the Temple, and the Babylonian captivity. Were they all metaphors for the Hellenistic Diaspora? The inference would be hasty, and it begs the question.

Ben Sira, for instance, laments the sins of his forefathers and records the fierce retaliation of the Lord that uprooted them from their land and dispersed them into every other land.[148] The reference, however, is to the era of Elijah and Elisha, to the ills of the Northern Kingdom, and to the Assyrian conquest that scattered the Israelites. It may have carried a warning to Ben Sira's contemporaries, whose shortcomings paralleled those of his ancestors—but it did not condemn the current Diaspora. The Book of Tobit tells a tale that ostensibly transpires in the Assyrian captivity as well. Tobit bewails his own fate, prompted by the sins of his forefathers, and the fate of his countrymen, an object of scorn and a vulnerable prey to those in the nations whence they have been dispersed.[149] But Tobit also forecasts the recovery of the Temple and portrays the outcome as the culmination of Israelite dreams, a happy ending to endure indefinitely.[150] This hardly suggests that the Hellenistic Diaspora is a vale of tears.

One text, to be sure, with explicit reference to Hellenistic Jews, does suggest that they were in dire straits in the Diaspora. The inventive tale of 3 Maccabees, composed probably in the second or first century B.C.E., places the Jews of Egypt in the gravest peril. Thrice they are almost annihilated by the wicked schemes of the mad monarch Ptolemy IV. The fantasy implies a precarious existence at the mercy of their enemies. They are to perish unjustly, a foreign people in a foreign land.[151] But the dire foreboding does not come to pass. The Jews triumph, their enemies are thwarted, and their apostates are punished. More significantly, the

victory will be celebrated by an annual festival—in Egypt.[152] The Diaspora existence can go on indefinitely and contentedly.

Satisfactory circumstances in the Diaspora, however, did not diminish the
sanctity and centrality of Jerusalem. Its aura retained a hold on the consciousness of Hellenistic Jews, wherever they happened to reside. Jerusalem is referred
to on several occasions as "the holy city." The Jews' devotion to their sacred
"acropolis" is observed even by the pagan geographer Strabo.[153] Numerous other
texts characterize Palestine as the "holy land." The designation appears in works
as different as 2 Maccabees, the Wisdom of Solomon, the Testament of Job, the
Sibylline Oracles, and Philo.[154] Most, if not all, of these texts stem from the Diaspora. They underscore the reverence with which Jews around the Mediterranean
continued to regard Jerusalem and the land of their fathers. But the authors who
speak of reverence do not demand the "Return."

How compelling was the notion of a "homeland" to Jews dwelling in Mediterranean communities? In principle, the concept held firm. Loyalty to one's native
land was a deep commitment in the rhetoric of the Hellenistic world.[155] Philo
more than once endorses the idea that adherence to one's *patris* has singular
power. He speaks of the charms of kinsmen and homeland; trips abroad are
good for widening one's horizons, but nothing better than coming home. Failure to worship God is put on a level with neglecting to honor parents, benefactors, and patris. Defending one's country is a prime virtue. And, as Philo has
Agrippa say to Caligula, love of one's native land and compliance with its precepts is deeply ingrained in all men.[156] It does not follow, however, that Diaspora
Jews set their hearts upon a return to the fatherland. Broad pronouncements
about love of one's country accord with general Hellenistic attitudes and expressions. They do not require that those native environs be reinhabited for life to be
complete.

Did Jewish settlement abroad carry a stigma? Jews in fact formed stable communities in the Diaspora, entered into the social, economic, and political life
of the nations they joined, and aspired to and obtained civic privileges in the
cities of the Hellenistic world. Josephus maintains that Jews have every right to
call themselves Alexandrians, Antiochenes, or Ephesians. And Philo refers to his
home as "our Alexandria."[157] That form of identification surfaces more poignantly in the petition of an Alexandrian Jew threatened with the loss of his
privileges. He labels himself an "Alexandrian" at the head of the document, alluding to his father, also an Alexandrian, and the proper education he had received, and expresses his fear of being deprived of his patris.[158] Whatever legal
meaning this terminology might have carried, it signals the petitioner's clear affirmation of his roots in the community. A comparable sentiment might be

inferred from an inscription of the Phrygian city of Acmonia, alluding to fulfillment of a vow made to the "whole patris." A Jew or a group of Jews must have
commissioned it, because a menorah appears beneath the text. Here again the
"native city" is honored, presumably through a gift for civic purposes. The donor
pronounces his local loyalty in a conspicuous public manner.[159] Philo confirms
the sentiment in striking fashion: Jews consider the holy city as their "metropolis," but the states in which they were born and raised and which they acquired
from their fathers, grandfathers, and distant forefathers they adjudge their *pa-
trides.*[160] That fervent expression eradicates any idea of the "doctrine of return."
Diaspora Jews, in Philo's formulation at least, held a fierce attachment to the
adopted lands of their ancestors.

Commitment to one's local and regional community in no way diminished
one's devotion to Jerusalem. That the two were mutually exclusive alternatives is
plainly false. Reverence for Jerusalem was indeed publicly and conspicuously
demonstrated every year by the payment of a tithe to the Temple by Jews all over
the Mediterranean.[161] The ritualistic offering carried deep significance as a bond-
ing device.

In the mid-sixties B.C.E., economic circumstances in Rome and abroad
prompted a series of decrees forbidding the export of gold. In accord with this
policy, the Roman governor of Asia, L. Valerius Flaccus, banned the sending of
gold by the Jews of Asia Minor to Jerusalem. The action not only provoked resentment in Flaccus's province but also stirred a hornet's nest of opposition in
Rome itself. Cicero, who conducted Flaccus's defense at his trial for extortion
in 59, comments bitterly about the horde of Jews crowding around the tribunal,
exercising undue pressure upon the proceedings, and passionately exhibiting
their "barbaric superstition."[162] The account, of course, is partisan, rhetorical,
and exaggerated—but Cicero conveys some precious information. First, he indicates the Jews' earnest commitment to provide funds annually to the Temple
from Italy and from all the provinces of the Roman empire. Next, his record of
Flaccus's activities indicates that Jewish communities collected the tribute, city
by city, wherever they possessed sufficient numbers in Asia Minor. And, most revealing, his speech, however embellished and overblown, shows that the plight
of the Asian Jews who were prevented from making their contributions stirred
the passions of their compatriots far off in Rome and generated impressively
noisy demonstrations on their behalf.

References to the importance of the tithe abound. Josephus proudly observes
that the donations came from Jews all over Asia and Europe, indeed from everywhere in the world, for countless years. And when local authorities interfered
with that activity, the Jews would send up a howl to Rome.[163] The emperor Au-

gustus himself, and Roman officials acting in his name, intervened to ensure the untroubled exercise of Jewish practices in the province of Asia and elsewhere.[164] And the Jews in areas beyond the reach of Roman power also tithed with rigor and consistency. Communities in Babylon and other satrapies under Parthian dominion sent representatives every year over difficult terrain and dangerous highways to deposit their contributions in the Temple.[165] The issue of paying homage to Jerusalem was paramount. Indeed the Romans, even after they destroyed the Temple, did not destroy that institution—an ironic acknowledgment of its power. They simply altered its recipient. The tithe would no longer go to the demolished shrine; it would metamorphose into a Roman tax. The money would now subsidize the cult of Jupiter Capitolinus.[166]

The stark symbolism of the tithe had a potent hold upon Jewish sentiment. That annual act of obeisance was a repeated reminder, or rather display, of affection and allegiance, visible evidence of the unbroken attachment of the Diaspora to the center. How to interpret its implications? Did the remittance imply that the Diaspora was only a temporary exile?

In fact, the reverse conclusion holds. The yearly contribution proclaimed that the Diaspora could endure indefinitely and quite satisfactorily. The communities abroad were entrenched and successful, even mainstays of the center. Diaspora Jews did not and would not turn their backs on Jerusalem, which remained the principal emblem of their faith. Their fierce commitment to the tithe delivered that message unequivocally. But the gesture did not signify a desire for the "Return." It rendered the Return unnecessary.

A comparable phenomenon reinforces that proposition: the pilgrimage of Diaspora Jews to Jerusalem. Major festivals could attract them with some frequency and in quantity. According to Philo, myriads came from countless cities for every feast, over land and sea, from all points of the compass, to enjoy the Temple as a serene refuge from the hurly-burly of everyday life abroad.[167] The most celebrated occasion occurred after the death of Jesus. The feast of Pentecost brought throngs of people into the city from far-flung and diverse locations: from Parthia, Media, and Elam, from Mesopotamia and Cappadocia, from Pontus and Asia, from Phrygia and Pamphylia, from Egypt and Cyrene, from Crete and Arabia, and, indeed, even from Rome, all witness to the miracle of the disciples speaking in tongues.[168] The women's court at the Temple was large enough to accommodate those who resided in the land and those who came from abroad—a clear sign that female pilgrims in some numbers were expected visitors.[169]

The holy city was a forceful magnet, but the demonstration of devotion did not entail a desire for migration. Pilgrimage, in fact, by its very nature, signified a temporary payment of respect. Jerusalem had an irresistible and undiminished claim on the emotions of Diaspora Jews; it was indeed a critical piece of their identity. But home was elsewhere.

The self-perception of Second Temple Jews projected a tight solidarity between Center and Diaspora. Images of exile and separation did not haunt them. What affected the dwellers in Jerusalem affected Jews everywhere. The theme of intertwined experience and identity is reiterated with impressive frequency and variety.

The Letter of Aristeas, for instance, makes an unequivocal connection between Jerusalemites and other Jews. King Ptolemy's letter to the high priest in Judaea asserts that his motive in having the Hebrew Bible rendered into Greek is to benefit not only the Jews of Egypt but all Jews throughout the world—even those not yet born. And it is fitting that, when the scholars from Jerusalem complete their translation and it is read out to the Jews of Egypt, the large assemblage burst into applause, a dramatic expression of the unity of purpose.[170]

The narrative of 3 Maccabees depends on that same unity of purpose. It presupposes and never questions the proposition that the actions of Jerusalemites represent the sentiments of Jews anywhere in the Diaspora. When Ptolemy IV is thwarted in his design to enter the Holy of Holies in Jerusalem, he resolves to punish the Jews of Egypt. The king is determined to bring public shame upon the *ethnos* of the Jews generally. Egyptian Jews are "fellow-tribesmen" of those who dwelled in Judaea.[171]

The affiliations emerge most dramatically and drastically in the grave crises that marked the reign of the emperor Caligula (37–41 C.E.). Harsh conflict erupted in Alexandria, bringing dislocation, persecution, and death upon the Jewish community. And a still worse menace loomed over Jerusalem when the erratic emperor proposed to have a statue of himself installed in the Temple. When Alexandrian Jews were attacked, says Philo, the word spread like wildfire. As the synagogues were destroyed in Alexandria, reports swept not only through all the districts of Egypt but from there to the nations of the east and from the borders of Libya to the lands of the west. Jews had settled all over Europe and Asia, and the news of a pogrom anywhere would race through the entire network.[172] Philo's claim of such speedy communications may stretch a point, but the concept of tight interrelationships among Jews of the Diaspora is plain and potent.

Philo himself headed the delegation to the emperor that would plead the cause of the Alexandrian Jews. Their objective, however, was swiftly eclipsed by word of Caligula's decision to install his statue in the Temple at Jerusalem. Philo's words are arresting: the most grievous calamity fell unexpectedly and brought peril not to one part of the Jewish people but to the entire nation at once.[173] The letter of Agrippa I, a friend of the emperor and recently awarded a kingdom among the Jews, urgently alerted Caligula to the gravity of the situation. Agrippa maintained that an affront to Jerusalem would have vast repercussions: the holy city was not merely metropolis of Judaea but of most nations in the world since Jewish colonies thrived all over the Near East, Asia Minor, Greece, Macedon, Africa, and the lands beyond the Euphrates.[174] The image of Jerusalem as binding together Jews everywhere in the world held a prominent place in the self-perception of the Diaspora.

A moving passage elsewhere in Philo encapsulates this theme. Although he thrived in the Diaspora, enjoyed its advantages, and broadcast its virtues, Philo nevertheless found even deeper meaning in the land of Israel. He interprets the Shavuot festival as a celebration of the Jews' possession of their own land, a heritage now of long standing, and a means whereby they could cease their wandering.[175] Philo saw no inconsistency or contradiction. Diaspora Jews might find fulfillment and reward in their communities abroad, but they honored Judaea as a refuge for those who were once displaced and unsettled—and the prime legacy of all.

Josephus makes the point in a quite different context but with equal force. In his rewriting of Numbers, he places a sweeping prognostication in the mouth of the Midianite priest Balaam. The priest projects a glorious future for the Israelites: they will not only occupy and hold forever the land of Canaan, a chief signal of God's favor, but their multitudes will fill all the world, islands and continents, outnumbering even the stars in the heavens.[176] That is a notable declaration. Palestine, as ever, merits a special place. But the Diaspora, far from being a source of shame to be overcome, represents a resplendent achievement.

The respect and awe one paid to the Holy Land stood in full harmony with a commitment to the local community and allegiance to gentile governance. Diaspora Jews did not bewail their fate and pine away for the homeland. Nor, by contrast, did they shrug off the homeland and reckon the Book as surrogate for the Temple. The postulated alternatives are reductive and simplistic. Palestine mattered, and it mattered in a territorial sense—but not as a required residence. A gift to the temple and a pilgrimage to Jerusalem announced simultaneously one's devotion to the symbolic heart of Judaism and a singular pride in the accomplishments of the Diaspora.

The Jews forever refashioned their identity and adjusted their self-perception with an eye to the cultural milieu in which they found themselves. The age when Hellenic culture held sway in the Near East was no exception. Jews adopted a range of strategies that allowed them to negotiate their presence within that milieu. I have endeavored in this chapter to break down the usual dichotomies and question the customary boundaries. The image of confrontation, tension, and antagonism between Judaism and Hellenism needs to be reassessed. This was no zero-sum game in which every move toward Hellenism meant a loss for Jewish tradition. A complex process of adjustment took place whereby Jews found expression for their own heritage in the language and conventions of the larger community. The process, to be sure, sometimes involved struggle, dissension, and occasional catastrophe, but it did not reduce itself to mere conflict between the cultures.

Jewish perspectives on the Greeks (or gentiles generally) in this era show variety, overlapping, and nuance, rather than the simplistic alternatives of sharp differentiation or a striving for accommodation. The internal boundaries were as fluid as the external ones. The divide between elite and popular Jewish culture is elided by the nature of our texts and their history. The process of transmission and rewriting over the course of many generations produced cultural artifacts that spoke in a variety of voices and at several levels of meaning across conventional social and intellectual barriers. Women were reconceived by Jewish fiction as figures of prominence and high visibility, in ostensible contradistinction to the realities of social life. Yet fiction and fact had more convergence than divergence: the imaginative tales largely endorsed the gender hierarchy. And even the familiar duality of homeland and exile requires reconsideration. Jews thoroughly embraced the Diaspora communities in which they could lead full and rewarding lives—without compromising their allegiance to the symbol of their faith in Jerusalem. They successfully negotiated their own place within the world of Greco-Roman society: they were appropriationists rather than assimilationists. And they shunned the melting pot.

NOTES

1. 1 Maccabees 15:22–23.

2. Strabo, in Josephus, *Ant.*, 14:115.

3. See, e.g., V. Tcherikover, *Hellenistic Civilization and the Jews* (New York, 1970), 90–116.

4. The surviving fragments of the play were preserved by the first-century-B.C.E. pagan writer Alexander Polyhistor and transmitted by the Church fathers Clement and Eusebius. Ezekiel wrote a number of tragedies on Jewish themes, as we know from Clement, *Stromata* 1.155.1. One may conveniently consult the fragments in the fine studies by H. Jacobson, *The Exagoge of Ezekiel* (Cambridge, Engl., 1983), 50–67, and C. Holladay, *Fragments from Hellenistic Jewish Authors: Vol. II: The Poets* (Atlanta, Ga., 1989), 344–405. The date and prove-

nance of the work can be determined only within broad limits. Ezekiel employed the Septuagint version of the Pentateuch, as his language makes clear, and he must precede Alexander Polyhistor—thus sometime between the later third and early first centuries. The subject matter of the *Exagoge* does not suffice to fix the place of composition in Alexandria or elsewhere in Egypt. On these issues, see Holladay, *Fragments*, 2: 308–13, with references to earlier literature.

5. Ezekiel, in Eusebius, *Praeparatio Evangelica* [hereafter *PE*], 9.29.4–6.

6. Numbers 12:6–8.

7. The text is contained in Euseb. *PE*, 9.22.1–11. It can be conveniently consulted in A.-M. Denis, *Fragmenta Pseudepigraphorum Quae Supersunt Graeca* (Leiden, 1970), 204–7; H. Lloyd-Jones and P. Parsons, *Supplementum Hellenisticum* (Berlin, 1983), 360–65; and Holladay, *Fragments*, 2:106–27, with translation. Theodotus's date and provenance remain uncertain. For a survey of modern opinions, see Holladay, *Fragments*, 2:68–72, with notes.

8. Genesis 33:18–34:31, 49:5–7.

9. Euseb. *PE*, 9.22.1–11.

10. Ibid. 9.22.1.

11. Ibid. 9.22.8.

12. Gen. 33:18–20; Euseb. *PE*, 9.22.4.

13. Gen. 34:18–23; Euseb. *PE*, 9.22.5, 8.

14. Text in Denis, *Fragmenta*, 203–4; Lloyd-Jones and Parsons, *Supplementum Hellenisticum*, 328–31; and Holladay, *Fragments*, 2: 234–45. A single reference survives to one other Jewish presumed practitioner of epic poetry: a certain Sosates described as the "Jewish Homer in Alexandria" (C. Frick, *Chronica Minora* [Leipzig, 1892], 278).

15. The most valuable treatments of Philo may be found in Y. Gutman, "Philo the Epic Poet," *Scripta Hierosolymitana* 1 (1954): 36–63, and the exhaustive notes of Holladay, *Fragments*, 2: 205–99.

16. Euseb. *PE*, 9.20.1.

17. Ibid., 9.24.1.

18. Gen. 41:45, 50–52, 46:20.

19. On *Joseph and Aseneth* as a Hellenistic romance, see M. Philonenko, *Joseph et Aséneth* (Leiden, 1968), 43–47; S. West, "Joseph and Aseneth: A Neglected Greek Romance" (1974): 71–77; and C. Burchard, "*Joseph et Aséneth: Questions actuelles*," in W.C. van Unnik, ed., *La littérature juive entre Tenach et Mischna* (Leiden, 1974), 84–96. For parallels with Jewish fiction, see C. Burchard, *Untersuchungen zur Joseph und Aseneth* (Tübingen, 1965), 106–7. See also L. M. Wills, *The Jewish Novel in the Ancient World* (Ithaca, N.Y., 1995), 170–84.

20. *Joseph and Aseneth*, 1–8.

21. Ibid., 9–21.

22. Ibid., 22–29.

23. See the thorough and analytic review of the scholarship by R. D. Chesnutt, *From Death to Life: Conversion in Joseph and Aseneth* (Sheffield, Engl., 1995), 20–93.

24. *Joseph and Aseneth*, 1:4.

25. Ibid., 3:1–6, 4:8; cf. 20:7.

26. Ibid., 5:4–10.

27. Ibid., 6:2; cf. 5:6.

28. Ibid., 13:11, 18:1–2, 21:21.

29. Ibid., 20:6–21:5.

30. Ibid., 29:10–11.

31. Ibid., 7:1; Gen. 43:32.

32. *Joseph and Aseneth*, 21:4.

33. Ibid., 23:3; cf. 24:7.

34. Ibid., 29:5–7.

35. The most fundamental and thorough study of Demetrius is in J. Freudenthal, *Alexander Polyhistor* (Breslau, 1875), 35–82. The fragments can be usefully consulted in C. R. Holladay, *Fragments from Hellenistic Jewish Authors: Vol. I: Historians* (Chico, Calif., 1983), 51–91, with Holladay's valuable introduction and notes. More recently, see the discussion by G. E. Sterling, *Historiography and Self-Definition: Josephos, Luke-Acts, and Apologetic Historiography* (Leiden, 1992), 153–67, with excellent bibliography.

36. Euseb. *PE*, 9.21.3–5.

37. Ibid., 9.21.14–15; Gen. 43:34, 45:22.

38. Euseb. *PE*, 9.21.1–3.

39. Ibid., 9.29.16; cf. Exodus 13:18.

40. Among recent treatments of Eupolemus, see B. Z. Wacholder, *Eupolemus: A Study of Judaeo-Greek Literature* (Cincinnati, 1974); Holladay, *Fragments*, 1: 93–156; Sterling, *Historiography and Self-Definition*, 207–22.

41. Euseb. *PE*, 9.30.3–4.

42. The narratives of David's victories and annexations appear in 2 Samuel 5:17–25. 8:1–14, 10:6–19. Souron the king of Tyre, represented as a victim of David, is obviously equivalent to the biblical Hiram with whom David enjoyed a positive and productive association (2 Sam. 5:11). The Egyptian Vaphres has a place in the pharaonic royal genealogy but long after any putative date for David.

43. Euseb. *PE*, 9.31.1, 9.32.1.

44. Ibid., 9.32.1.

45. Ibid., 9.34.18.

46. 1 Kings 11:1–6.

47. A similar posture was taken later by King Herod, both rebuilder of the Temple and subsidizer of pagan shrines.

48. Among the more useful editions or commentaries, see R. Tramontano, *La Lettera di Aristea a Filocrate* (Naples, 1931); M. Hadas, *Aristeas to Philocrates* (New York, 1951); A. Pelletier, *Lettre d'Aristée à Philocrate* (Paris, 1962); and N. Meisner, *Jüdische Schriften aus hellenistisch-römischer Zeit*, vol. 2 (Gütersloh, Germany, 1973), 1, 35–87. A general bibliogra-

phy is in E. Schürer, *The History of the Jewish People in the Age of Jesus Christ,* rev. ed. by G. Vermes, F. Millar, and M. Goodman (Edinburgh, 1986), vol. 3.1, 685–87.

49. Philo, *Moses,* 2:41.

50. *Letter of Aristeas,* 187–294.

51. Ibid., 11.

52. Ibid., 38.

53. Ibid., 181.

54. Ibid., 3.

55. Ibid., 122.

56. Ibid., 209, 211, 222–23, 256, 292.

57. Ibid., 128–70.

58. On the banquet and the dialogue, see O. Murray, "Aristeas and Ptolemaic Kingship," *Journal of Theological Studies* 18 (1967): 344–61. Cf. P. M. Fraser, *Ptolemaic Alexandria* (Oxford, 1972), 701–3, and F. Parente, "La lettera di Aristea come Fonte per la storia del Giudaismo Alessandrino durante la prima metà del I secolo a. C.," *Annali della Scuola Normale Superiore di Pisa,* 2, no. 2 (1972): 546–63.

59. *Letter of Aristeas,* 200.

60. Ibid., 200–201, 235, 296.

61. The work itself is an epitome of the now lost five-volume history of the Maccabees by Jason of Cyrene, plainly also a Hellenized Jew (2 Macc. 2:19–31). For a recent register of scholarship on 2 Maccabees, see Schürer, *History of the Jewish People,* vol. 3.1, 536–37.

62. 2 Macc. 2:21.

63. 2 Macc. 10:4; cf. 5:22.

64. Daniel 2:31–45, 7:1–27, 8:1–26, 11:21–45, 12:1–3.

65. The chronology is complex and contested. A valuable recent treatment may be found in J. M. G. Barclay, *The Jews in the Mediterranean Diaspora* (Edinburgh, 1996), 216–25.

66. 3 Sibylline 166–90, 202–4, 341–49, 381–400, 545–55, 638–45.

67. On the date, see Schürer, *History of the Jewish People,* vol. 3.1, 181, and J. Sievers, *The Hasmoneans and Their Supporters* (Atlanta, Ga., 1990), 3.

68. 1 Macc. 1:1–4, 9, 43–44.

69. 2 Macc. 6:18–7:41.

70. 4 Macc. 4–18. For recent discussions of the text, with bibliography, see H. Anderson, "4 Maccabees," in J. Charlesworth, ed., *The Old Testament Pseudepigrapha,* vol. 2 (Garden City, N.Y., 1985), 531–43, and Schürer, *History of the Jewish People,* vol. 3.1, 588–93.

71. *Letter of Aristeas,* 134–39.

72. See, e.g., Josephus, *Ant.,* 16:160–61, 18:257–60, 19:300–312, 20:173–84.

73. Ibid. 16:161.

74. Josephus, *C. Apionem,* 2:154–56, 168–74.

75. Ibid., 2:220–31, 279.

76. Ibid., 2:239–54.

77. Galatians 3:28; cf. 1 Corinthians 12:13.

78. An up-to-date edition of the fragments, with translation, thorough notes, and comprehensive bibliography has been produced by C. Holladay, *Fragments from Hellenistic Jewish Authors: Vol. III: Aristobulus* (Atlanta, Ga., 1995).

79. Aristobulus, in Euseb. *PE*, 13.12.1; Clement, *Strom.* 1.22.150.1–3.

80. Aristobulus, in Euseb. *PE*, 13.12.1; Clement, *Strom.* 1.22.150.2.

81. Aristobulus, in Euseb. *PE*, 13.12.3–4, 8; Clement, *Strom.* 5.14.99.3.

82. Aristobulus, in Euseb. *PE*, 13.12.13–15; Clement, *Strom.* 5.14.107.1–3. See the careful discussion in N. Walter, *Der Thoraausleger Aristobulos* (Berlin, 1964), 150–58, with reference to the relevant Homeric and Hesiodic lines; cf. Y. Gutman, *ha-Siprut ha-Yehudit-ha-Helenistit*, vol. 1 (Jerusalem, 1958) 210–12, and Holladay, *Fragments*, 3:234–37.

83. The fragments can be found in A.-M. Denis, *Fragmenta*, 161–74. A translation by H. Attridge is in J. Charlesworth, ed., *Old Testament Pseudepigrapha*, 2: 824–30. And see the valuable treatment by M. Goodman in Schürer, *History of the Jewish People*, vol. 3.1, 656–61, 667–71, with bibliographies.

84. The lines appear in Pseudo-Justin, *De Monarchia* 2; Clement, *Strom.* 5.14.131.2–3; Euseb. *PE*, 13.13.60.

85. Ps. Justin, *De Monarch.* 2; Clement, *Strom.* 5.14.113.2; Euseb. *PE*, 13.13.40.

86. Ps. Justin, *De Monarch.* 3; Clement, *Strom.* 5.14.121.4–122.1; Euseb. *PE*, 13.13.48.

87. Clement, *Strom.* 5.11.75.1; *Protrepticus* 6.68.3; cf. Ps. Justin, *De Monarch.* 2.

88. Clement, *Strom.* 5.14.119.2, 5.14.121.1–3, 5.14.133.3; Euseb. *PE*, 13.13.45–47, 13.13.62, 13.36.2; Ps. Justin, *De Monarch.* 2–5.

89. Acts of the Apostles 17:16–33.

90. Acts 17:24–26.

91. Acts 17:28.

92. Josephus, *C. Apionem*, 2:121–23.

93. Ibid., 2:168; cf. 1:162.

94. Ibid., 2:280–84.

95. Philo, *Moses* 2:18–20.

96. See, e.g., Josephus, *BJ*, 5:17; *Ant.*, 4:12; *C. Apionem*, 2:282.

97. Romans 1:14.

98. Philo, *Moses* 2:27; *Quod Omnis Probus Liber Sit*, 73–75.

99. For a sampling of divergent views, see Philonenko, *Joseph et Aséneth*, 53–61; Chesnutt, *From Death to Life*, 153–84; and Barclay, *Jews in the Mediterranean Diaspora*, 204–16.

100. Daniel 14:1–22. On the texts that convey this tale, see C. A. Moore, *Daniel, Esther, and Jeremiah: The Additions* (Garden City, N.Y., 1977), 23–34. The date of composition, perhaps later second century B.C.E., remains uncertain; cf. M. J. Steussy, *Gardens in Babylon: Narrative and Faith in the Greek Legends of Daniel* (Atlanta, Ga., 1993), 28–32.

101. Dan. 14:23–42.

102. Dan. 13:1–64.

103. Cf. Moore, *Daniel, Esther, and Jeremiah,* 88–89, and L. M. Wills, *The Jew in the Court of the Foreign King: Ancient Jewish Court Legends* (Minneapolis, 1990), 76–79.

104. Dan. 13:49, 54–55.

105. 2 Macc. 3:1–40.

106. Ibid. 3:15, 22.

107. Ibid. 3:25–27.

108. Ibid. 3:37–38.

109. Ibid. 9:13–16.

110. Judith 1–7. See the valuable editions and commentaries in M. S. Enslin, *The Book of Judith* (Leiden, 1972), and C. A. Moore, *Judith* (Garden City, N.Y., 1985).

111. Jth. 8–16.

112. Ben Sira 7:24, 22:3–5, 25:16–26, 26:6–12, 42:9–14. A useful translation and full commentary may be found in P. W. Skehan, *The Wisdom of Ben Sira* (New York, 1987).

113. See, e.g., Testament of Reuben, 5:1–3, and Josephus, *Ant.,* 5:294.

114. Ben Sira 25:8, 40:19.

115. Ibid. 26:13–26, 36:27–29.

116. On all this, see the fine study of T. Ilan, *Jewish Women in Greco-Roman Palestine* (Tübingen, 1995), esp. 79–88, 122–47, 163–72, 184–90.

117. See Jth. 13:15, 14:18, 16:5.

118. Jth. 8:12–15.

119. Jth. 8:6–8, 25, 9:1–14, 10:9, 12:8, 13:4–7, 14–16, 16:1–5, 13–17, 19.

120. Jth. 16:18–25. See the cogent comments of A. -J. Levine "Sacrifice and Salvation: Otherness and Domestication in the Book of Judith," in J. C. VanderKam, ed., *"No One Spoke Ill of Her": Essays on Judith* (Atlanta, Ga., 1992), 17–30.

121. Valuable analyses of the narrative may be found in S. B. Berg, *The Book of Esther: Motifs, Themes, and Structures* (Missoula, Mt., 1979); M. V. Fox, *Character and Ideology in the Book of Esther* (Columbia, S.C., 1991); and J. Levenson, *Esther* (Louisville, Ky., 1997).

122. Esther 1:12–22.

123. Ibid. 2:5–20.

124. Ibid. 2:21–22.

125. Ibid. 4:1–4.

126. Ibid. 4:5–16.

127. Ibid. 4:17–5:8, 7:1–10.

128. Ibid. 8:1–6.

129. Ibid. 8:15 9:3–4, 20–23, 29–32.

130. Ibid. 10:2–3.

131. Ibid., Addition C, 12–13, 26–28.

132. Ibid., Addition D, 1–15.

133. See the provocative suggestions in R. S. Kraemer, *When Aseneth Met Joseph* (Oxford, 1998), 191–221.

134. *Joseph and Aseneth,* 2:8–9.

135. Ibid., 14–17; see, esp., 17:7–10.

136. Ibid., 19:4–5, 20:4–5.

137. Ibid., 21:11–21.

138. Dan. 13:1–4.

139. Dan. 13:32–35, 41–43.

140. Dan. 13:63–64; cf. 13:30.

141. For population estimates, see *Encyclopaedia Judaica,* 13: 866–903, and L. H. Feldman, *Jew and Gentile in the Ancient World* (Princeton, 1993), 23, 468–69, 555–56.

142. Leviticus 26:33; Deuteronomy 4:26–28, 28:63–65; Jeremiah 5:19, 9:15.

143. Deut. 30:2–5; Isaiah 11:12.

144. See, e.g., Y. F. Baer, *Galut* (New York, 1947), 9–13, and A. Eisen, *Galut* (Bloomington, Ind., 1986), 3–34. The most sweeping argument on melancholy Jewish attitudes toward the Diaspora in the Second Temple era is made in W. C. van Unnik, *Das Selbstverständnis der jüdischen Diaspora in der hellenistisch-römischen Zeit* (Leiden, 1993), *passim.* See also the very useful survey by W. D. Davies, *The Territorial Dimension of Judaism* (Berkeley, 1981), 28–34, 61–100.

145. See I. M. Gafni, *Land, Center, and Diaspora* (Sheffield, Engl., 1997), 19–40.

146. The classic study is J. Juster, *Les juifs dans l'empire romain,* 2 vols. (Paris, 1914). Among recent treatments, see Schürer, *History of the Jewish People,* vol. 3.1, 1–176; Barclay, *Jews in the Mediterranean Diaspora,* 19–81, 231–319; and I. Levinskaya, *The Book of Acts in Its Diaspora Setting* (Grand Rapids, Mich., 1996), 127–93.

147. See, esp., G. Steiner, "Our Homeland, The Text," *Salmagundi* 66 (1985): 4–25. On the ambivalence of exile and homecoming in recent Jewish conceptions, see the comments of S. D. Ezrahi, "Our Homeland, the Text . . . Our Text, the Homeland: Exile and Homecoming in the Modern Jewish Imagination," *Michigan Quarterly Review* 31 (1992): 463–97.

148. Ben Sira 48:15.

149. Tobit 3:3–4, 13:3–6, 14:4.

150. Tob. 13:10–11, 14:5–6.

151. 2 Macc. 6:3; cf. 6:10.

152. 3 Macc. 6:36, 7:15, 19.

153. 2 Macc. 1:12; Philo, *Legatio ad Gaium* 225, 281, 288, 299, 346; Strabo, 16.2.37.

154. 2 Macc. 1:7; Wisdom of Solomon 12:3; Testament of Job 33:5; 3 Sib. 267, 732–35; 5 Sib. 281; Philo, *Heres* 293; *In Flaccum* 46; *Leg.* 202, 205, 330. Cf. Zechariah 2:16.

155. Cf. Polybius 1.14.4.

156. Philo, *De Abrahamo* 63, 65, 197; *Mos.* 2:198; *De Mutatione Nominum* 40; *De Cherubim* 15; *Leg.* 277, 328.

157. Josephus, *C. Apionem,* 2:38–39; Philo, *Leg.* 150.

158. *Corpus Papyrorum Iudaicarum,* II, #151.

159. *Corpus Inscriptionum Iudaicarum,* #771.

160. Philo, *Flacc.* 46.

161. See the useful summary of testimony and the discussion in S. Safrai and M. Stern, *The Jewish People in the First Century* (Philadelphia, 1974), 1:186–91.

162. Cicero, *Pro Flacco,* 66–68.

163. Josephus, *Ant.,* 14:110, 16:28, 45–50; cf. 18:312–13; *BJ,* 7:45.

164. Philo, *Leg.* 291, 312; Josephus, *Ant.,* 16:163, 166–71.

165. Philo, *Leg.* 216.

166. Josephus, *BJ,* 7:218; Dio Cassius, 66.7.2.

167. Philo, *Spec. Leg.* 1:69; cf. Safrai and Stern, *Jewish People,* 1:191–94.

168. Acts 2:1–11; cf. 6:9.

169. Josephus, *BJ,* 5:199.

170. *Letter of Aristeas,* 38, 307–11.

171. 3 Macc. 2:21–27, 3:21.

172. Philo, *Flacc.* 45–46.

173. Philo, *Leg.* 184; cf. 178, 351, 373.

174. Philo, *Leg.* 277–83; cf. 330.

175. Philo, *Spec. Leg.* 2:168.

176. Josephus, *Ant.,* 4:115–16. Josephus departs here quite substantially from the corresponding text in Numbers 23:6–10. Cf. also Josephus, *Ant.,* 1:282, 2:213.

SELECTED BIBLIOGRAPHY

Barclay, J. M. G. *The Jews in the Mediterranean Diaspora.* Edinburgh, 1996.

Bickermann, E. *The Jews in the Greek Age.* Cambridge, Mass., 1988.

Braun, M. *History and Romance in Graeco-Oriental Literature.* Oxford, 1938.

Brenner, A. *A Feminist Companion to Esther, Judith, and Susanna.* Sheffield, Engl., 1995.

Charlesworth, J., ed. *The Old Testament Pseudepigraphy.* Vol. 2. Garden City, N.Y., 1985.

Cohen, S. J. D. *The Beginnings of Jewishness.* Berkeley, 1999.

———. *From the Maccabees to Mishnah.* Philadelphia, 1987.

Collins, J. J. *Between Athens and Jerusalem.* 2d ed. Grand Rapids, Mich., 2000.

Feldman, L. H. *Jew and Gentile in the Ancient World.* Princeton, 1993.

Gafni, I. M. *Land, Center, and Diaspora.* Sheffield, Engl., 1997.

Grabbe, L. L. *Judaism from Cyrus to Hadrian.* 2 vols. Minneapolis, 1992.

Gruen, E. S. *Heritage and Hellenism: The Reinvention of Jewish Tradition.* Berkeley, 1998.

———. *Diaspora: Jews amidst Greeks and Romans.* Cambridge, Mass., 2002.

Hayes, J. H., and S. R. Mandell. *The Jewish People in Classical Antiquity.* Louisville, Ky., 1998.

Hengel, M. *Judaism and Hellenism.* 2 vols. London, 1974.

Ilan, T. *Jewish Women in Greco-Roman Palestine.* Tübingen, 1995.

Levine, L. I. *Judaism and Hellenism in Antiquity.* Seattle, 1998.

Modrzejewski, J. *The Jews of Egypt.* Princeton, 1995.

Momigliano, A. *Alien Wisdom: The Limits of Hellenization.* Cambridge, Engl., 1975.

Nickelsburg, G. *Jewish Literature Between the Bible and Mishnah.* Philadelphia, 1981.

Safrai, S., and M. Stern. *The Jewish People in the First Century.* 2 vols. Philadelphia, 1974.

Schürer, E. *The History of the Jewish People in the Age of Jesus Christ.* Vol. 3.1. Rev. ed. by G. Vermes, F. Millar, and M. Goodman. Edinburgh, 1986.

Sterling, G. E. *Historiography and Self-Definition: Josephos, Luke-Acts, and Apologetic Historiography.* Leiden, 1992.

Tcherikover, V. *Hellenistic Civilization and the Jews.* New York, 1970.

VanderKam, J. *An Introduction to Early Judaism.* Grand Rapids, Mich., 2001.

Wills, L. M. *The Jewish Novel in the Ancient World.* Ithaca, N.Y., 1995.

Ancient synagogue at Khirbet Shema', near Meiron, looking southwest.
The building dates to the third and fourth centuries c.e. and is the only broadhouse
synagogue with internal columnation in ancient Palestine.
(Courtesy Eric Meyers)

FOUR

JEWISH CULTURE IN GRECO-ROMAN PALESTINE

ERIC M. MEYERS

In the early third century c.e., the Mishnah (the first edited body of rabbinic writings) tells the following story about Gamaliel, the *nasi,* or patriarch, of the Palestinian Jewish community in the previous century:

> Proklus the son of Philosophus asked Rabban Gamaliel who was bathing in Acco in the Bath of Aphrodite. He said to him: "It is written in your Torah, 'And nothing of the devoted (forbidden) thing should cling to your hand' (Deuteronomy 13:17). Why are you bathing in the Bath of Aphrodite?" He answered him: 'One ought not respond in a bath." When he came out he [Rabban Gamaliel] said to him: "I did not come into her borders, she came into mine! People do not say, 'Let us make a bath for Aphrodite,' but rather, 'Let us make Aphrodite an ornament for the bath.' Moreover, even if they would give you a large sum of money, you would not approach your idol naked and suffering pollutions, and urinate before it; yet, this goddess stands at the mouth of a gutter and all the people urinate before her. [Lastly] it is written 'Their gods' (12:3), that which they refer to as a god is forbidden and that which is not referred to as a god is permitted."[1]

The Greek philosopher accuses Gamaliel of hypocrisy: how can he bathe in a bathhouse dedicated to Aphrodite when the Torah clearly forbids benefiting from idolatry? Gamaliel responds by denying that the statue of Aphrodite, especially one placed above the public urinal, is anything more than ornamentation. Bathing is not worship and statues are not necessarily idols! Yet, by going to the public bath in the first place, Gamaliel, the titular leader of the rabbinical caste, engaged in behavior that clearly reflects the influence of Greco-Roman culture. For Gamaliel, though, the bath is not a foreign institution: "I did not come into her borders, she came into mine!" The very exchange between the rabbi and the Greek philosopher, fictional though it may have been, also attests to the sense the Jews had of participation in the discourses of the wider culture.

In this pregnant text, we find precious evidence of the complex cultural interchange between the Jews and the Greeks and Romans in whose empires they lived. They absorbed many elements of Greco-Roman culture but at the same time transformed them into something indigenous. Yet they were equally preoccupied with maintaining firmly the boundaries between their own identity and religion and that of their non-Jewish neighbors. The ancient biblical struggle against Canaanite idolatry took new forms as the Jews confronted the religions of the Greeks and Romans. As we shall see, these complex processes took place in Jewish Palestine on a variety of levels and in a variety of genres: from the elite, rabbinic culture represented by Rabban Gamaliel to the popular, material culture of cities like Sepphoris in the lower Galilee, from literary texts to engravings on sarcophagi. I will argue that it was Hellenism, as both a challenge and an inspiration, that produced the most creative expressions of Jewish culture in Palestine, expressions that greatly enriched the Jewish tradition without sacrificing its own indigenous, semitic core.

The period of this chapter—from the return from the Babylonian Exile in the sixth and fifth centuries B.C.E. to roughly the third century C.E.—was a time when the Jews of Palestine lived under great world empires: the Persian Empire established by Cyrus the Great, the Hellenistic empires that came after the conquests of Alexander the Great, and the Roman Empire. Although the biblical kingdoms of Israel and Judah were occasionally dominated by imperial powers—Assyria and Babylonia—the Second Temple state (and its immediate successor) was primarily a vassal of the great world empires. This political fact had major cultural consequences, especially when the Jews confronted, for the first time, a world culture, Hellenism. In many ways, the manner in which the Jews accommodated to living in such a world culture, or were acculturated to it, became the paradigm for future accommodation to other major world civilizations, such as Rome, Byzantium, Islam, and Christianity.

As a result of this confrontation with a world culture, the Jews developed new identities that were also to become paradigms for Jewish identity in the coming millennia. During the First Temple period, the ethnic group referred to typically by others as "Hebrews" called itself the "Children of Israel," thus designating its descent from the founder Israel, or Jacob. But those who went into exile in Babylonia were known to others, as to themselves, as "Judaeans," for they came from the southern kingdom of Judah. With the early Persian period, "Judaeans" took the place of "Israelites." But what was a Judaean? Clearly it meant someone descended from an ethnic group connected to a particular geographical location, Judaea or Palestine (to use the later Latin terms) or *Yehud* (Judah—as it is known from archaeological inscriptions). But it also came to designate a fol-lower of a particular religion that was not geographically or even ethnically limited. As we shall see, when the Hasmonaean kings conquered other ethnic groups, such as the Edomites, and forced them to convert to Judaism, they broadened the definition of a Judaean beyond an ethnic category: this was one stage in the transformation of "Judaeans" to "Jews." These Jews followed a religion that a few Greek texts came to call "Judaism," a term that was, nonetheless, relatively rare in antiquity. By the time of the Mishnah, the rabbis had evolved a legal procedure for conversion from other religions to Judaism: one could become a Jew, even if one were not born one.[2] This was a revolutionary development, with implications not only for Judaism but for other ancient identities as well.

THE PERSIAN PERIOD

When the Judaeans or Jews returned from the Babylonian Exile, these events would still lie far in the future. Indeed, if the text with which we began from the end of our period attests to broad cultural interchange between rabbis and Greeks, the period opens with a far more xenophobic expression: the ban on intermarriage by Ezra the Scribe in the middle of the fifth century B.C.E. Defining his people as *zera kodesh* (a holy seed), Ezra sought to erect high walls between the returnees and the "people of the land," who may have been a mixture of remnants of the indigenous Canaanites and of Judaeans and Israelites who had not gone into exile. Ezra represents the opposite pole to the figure of Gamaliel in our opening story: the voice of ethnic and religious segregation in the face of outer pressures for accommodation and acculturation. Indeed, throughout our period, these two poles, the forces of separation and assimilation, struggled with each other in ways that are more complex than is commonly believed.

The response of the Judaeans in exile to the Persian offer to return to Palestine was underwhelming at first, and even after the Second Temple was rededicated (515 B.C.E.) the number of returnees to Yehud was very small. Such a modest return perhaps meant that Jews in the Diaspora, mainly Egypt and Babylonia, were so successful and assimilated that they viewed Zion more as their ancestral homeland than as a place to which they and their extended families would return. The extent of assimilation of the Egyptian-Jewish community situated at Elephantine is well documented, especially in the onomasticon of the papyri from there; a similar case may be made for some of the Jewish communities in Babylonia. When Ezra reestablished the Torah in Israel in the second half of the fifth century B.C.E., there were 18,000–20,000 Jews in all of Yehud—the majority of Jews remained in the Diaspora. By about 400 B.C.E., the reforms of Ezra and

Reconstruction of the Second Temple after L. Ritmeyer.
(Israel Exploration Society)

Nehemiah were in place as Yehud became a theocracy based on the Hebrew Bible and run primarily by priests. In addition to the priests, there were probably also nonpriestly "elders" who shared in the governance of the province (the Mishnah refers to the "men of the Great Assembly," a body whose historicity cannot be definitively established). Nehemiah, the Persian-appointed governor *(pehah)*, took the place of the earlier kings and foreshadowed the later role of the patriarch. This political system may have survived into the Greek period.

That the Jewish community survived both Persian and early Greek rule was a direct result of their flexible attitude, which would justify a Judaean leadership without a king but with a governor. The reestablishment of the Jewish community in Palestine and the rebuilding of the Temple in Jerusalem ensured a certain measure of continuity between the First and Second Temple periods. The Temple priesthood and its hierarchy would assume an even greater role in society than before. They would even take on a new role in explaining biblical law to the people, a development that would presage the era of the sages.[3]

Said the Book of Haggai:

> Seek a ruling from the priests, as follows: If a man is carrying sacrificial flesh in a fold of his garment and with that fold touches bread, stew, wine, oil, or any other food, will any of these become sanctified? In reply, the priests said, "No."[4]

Although the priestly leadership no doubt took a major role in editing and promulgating the earliest forms of the Bible, the Pentateuch *(Humash)* and the books of the Prophets, other individuals, perhaps wisdom teachers as well as some teaching priests, and a new cadre of translators or interpreters (Nehe-miah 8) assumed an entirely new role in communicating the interpreted word of God's scriptures. This is quite clear from the report of Ezra's reading the law at the Feast of Tabernacles when Nehemiah was governor. Ezra, who was both priest and scribe, read from a wooden platform or *bema* as in the later syna-gogue with the help of many others: "They read from the scroll of the Teaching of God, translating it and giving the sense; so they understood the reading."[5]

It was thus during the Persian and early Greek periods that the process of or-ganizing, editing, and promulgating large portions of the Hebrew Bible took place. These portions probably included the Pentateuch, the historical writings (Judges, Joshua, Samuel, and Kings), the major and minor Prophets, and some of the Writings, such as the Psalms and Proverbs. The impulse toward this first stage of canonization may have been partly the result of similar efforts initiated by the Persians in Egypt, Babylonia, and other satrapies.[6] If this was the case, then the Hebrew Bible, the literary record in which the Jews asserted their singu-larity, was, ironically, in part the product of an international process. But it was also during this period that other books of the Bible were actually composed. These included the postexilic prophets Haggai, Zechariah, and Malachi, the book of Daniel, the books of Ezra and Nehemiah, and the books of Chronicles, in ad-dition to certain priestly writings that were incorporated into the Pentateuch.

Scholars have also speculated that some of the so-called Wisdom literature—as well as other less easily categorized literature, such as Job, Ecclesiastes, and perhaps Jonah and Ruth—was written during this period. Although it is difficult to speculate about the settings in which these books were written, we can iden-tify some common themes that suggest the cultural mentality of the age. As opposed to pre-exilic biblical books, God does not speak directly and unprob-lematically to human beings. In Job, for instance, God's silence is the central concern of the book and God's speech out of the whirlwind at the end is less a prophetic message than a show of divine power. In Job, we find a new sensibility about God's justice, quite different from the earlier prophetic idea of divine punishment for sin; here, God's ways are mysterious and the righteous suffer de-spite their virtues.

In Ecclesiastes, God is equally mysterious. Whether or not it was influenced by Greek philosophy, as some have claimed, Ecclesiastes confronts an intellec-tual world at odds with biblical religion and betrays a sense of cynicism and frustration: "Utter futility!—said Kohelet—Utter futility! All is futile! What real value is there for a man in all the gains he makes beneath the sun? One genera-tion goes, another comes, but the earth remains the same forever."[7]

The word "futility" *(hebel)* appears 38 times in the work and is applied to all manner of human activity and pursuits. The futility of life or even the pursuit of wisdom in this age evokes the memorable statement: "For in much wisdom is much vexation, and those who increase knowledge increase sorrow."[8] And at the end: "The making of many books is without limit and much study is wearying of the flesh."[9] If this is wisdom literature, it is wisdom turned against itself! Is it possible that, in denouncing the writing of books, the author may be reflecting a struggle within the culture over the editing and canonization of the Book of Books? Or, alternatively, might this comment reflect the proliferation of many books composed in this era and competing to enter the developing canon? If so, then we are in possession of only a small fragment of what must have been a large and vibrant literature.

Many of these works seem deliberately archaic—that is, they are set in earlier, even mythological periods of Israel's history: Job in the time of the biblical patriarchs, Ecclesiastes in the time of Solomon, Jonah rather vaguely in the period of the Assyrian Empire, and Ruth in the period of the Judges. In the persistent tendency of this literature to situate itself in the distant past, we sense a nostalgia for a golden age that has irrevocably disappeared. With the substance of God's revelation a thing of the past, it was a time of small men and small deeds. Perhaps this is the reason also for the fact that, after Ezra and Nehemiah, we cannot identify any author by name—until Ben Sira at the end of the third century B.C.E. Not without reason have some labeled the late Persian and early Hellenistic period, the 200-year period from the end of the fifth century, an "age of silence."

EARLY PALESTINIAN HELLENISM

Alexander the Great conquered the Near East at the end of the fourth century B.C.E., but, as opposed to what many have assumed, Hellenistic culture did not follow suit in quite as rapid a way. The process was more complex. Archaeology teaches us that the influence of the Greeks predated even Alexander. Already in the fifth century B.C.E., the first clear signs of the appeal of Greek culture began to appear in Yehud: the adoption of coinage as a medium of exchange along with the use as the standard of the Attic tetradrachm with Greek symbols, such as the Athenian owl; the establishment of Greek trading emporia along the coastal plain; the importation of Attic black-glazed ceramic wares as luxury items; and the opening of new trade routes connecting the Persian Gulf with the Aegean as well as others that would bring Egypt in closer touch with both the Levant and the Aegean. Numerous Palestinian sites both on the coast and inland, moreover, have yielded statues of Greek figures. All of these developments occurred when Persia held sway in the region.

After Alexander's death, his generals established two successor Hellenistic empires in the east: the Seleucids in Syria and the Ptolemies in Egypt. Now Greek culture became more prominent in Yehud: in the orthogonal plan adopted in some cities, the layout of some walls, the introduction of round towers for additional protection, forms of dress, and some types of ceramic fineware. The coins of the Judaean capital, minted in Jerusalem, show a strong continuity with the Persian era. The few coins of the Ptolemaic era that we do have date to Ptolemy I (301–282 B.C.E.) and depict Ptolemy, his wife Berenice, and the Ptolemaic eagle. These coins lack the identification of the "secular" Jewish authority, *pehah,* and hence seem to suggest a shift in authority to the high priesthood, signaling a major trend that was to influence the course of events, namely, the increasing involvement of the Temple officers and establishment in the affairs of state. The Yehud coins of this era with their secondary Hebrew inscriptions were of very small denominations, ⅛ to ⅟₉₆ of a tetradrachm, and reflect the limited means of the constituency being served. That the Ptolemies allowed the Jews to mint coins, albeit in standards adopted from them, shows how they intended to control and exploit the local constituency at least until the time of Ptolemy II (282–246 B.C.E.), but such limited privileges by no means indicated autonomy for the Jewish community.

But Hellenistic culture encroached only gradually and unevenly in Palestine. The archaeological record from monumental remains suggests strong Greek influence at coastal sites such as Dor, where a Greek-style fortification was introduced in the time of Ptolemy II. Dor has also produced the earliest examples of indigenous pottery stamped with Greek letters. But we should not infer from Dor too much about Palestine as a whole, since many of the towns and villages were completely unaffected by Hellenism. Especially in the Judaean heartland, with Jerusalem at its center, there is little evidence for the encroachment of Greek culture, while just 40 kilometers to the southwest a Sidonian colony was established by the Ptolemies at Marissa in a purely Greek layout. Ptolemaic and Greek influence tended to be focused around the cities that had military or strategic importance or cities or sites that were important economically but had only small Jewish minority communities.

There is another small corpus of stamped jar handles from Yehud that should be mentioned in this connection; both are dated to the mid-third century B.C.E. and shed light on the administrative structure that operated in Palestine before the Maccabean uprising. Many of them are stamped with YHD in paleo-Hebrew letters and bear a variety of symbols that appear to be a government seal. Another large group bears the letters YRŠLM (Jerusalem) between the axes of a five-pointed star, the symbol of the high priest. These jar handles point to a very traditional repertoire of symbols in a time when many scholars assumed Hellenism to be making great inroads. This relatively small group of stamps with a limited symbolic vocabulary demonstrates quite clearly that Hellenistic culture had not yet affected the heart of Judaean culture. That these stamps point to a centralized system of taxation, however, cannot be doubted.[10] The corpus of stamped jar handles testifies to the rather complex system of taxation that was introduced by the priests. It is quite clear too from this evidence that not all of the priesthood shared in the new wealth; it was the Jerusalem priesthood and establishment that benefited the most.

The economic upgrading of the Levant as a result of Ptolemaic rule and its mercantile practices had an enormous effect on Judaean life. The emergence of a Jewish middle class, merchants and bureaucrats, transformed society. While the Greek ethnic population remained in the strong military bases among the coastal cities, some settled in Idumea to the southeast and Samaria to the north, thus promoting increased mercantile activity. As a result of this new international commerce, there emerged in Ammon (or Transjordan) one of the most prominent Jewish families, probably descended from the Tobiads mentioned in the prophets Isaiah and Zechariah. Although they were well established before the Ptolemies, they became involved with the new Ptolemaic infrastructure for tax collection. By the end of the third century or beginning of the second century B.C.E., the Tobiads had built a huge administrative center and trading emporium just south of Amman at Arak el-Emir.

In short, during the Ptolemaic era Palestine underwent enormous change, albeit at an uneven pace. The culture of Palestinian Jewry slowly began to be transformed by new political and social circumstances, but not all segments of society were pleased by these developments. In addition to the effect of the new economy on social stratification, the new intellectual world appeared to be at odds with biblical religion and nascent Judaism. Among the most serious philosophical challenges that came from the Greeks was the Orphic view that the individual is dualistic in nature and that the "soul" is immaterial, encased in a physical body. The dominant semitic view, however, was that the human being is a unitary entity and the "soul," or *nefesh,* is the totality of all the physical parts along with the deeds and accomplishments of the individual. A name or reputation would symbolize the "corporate" personality of the individual, and mortal or physical remains had to be buried and cared for in very special ways. (Biblical and rabbinic law forbid both cremation and embalming, such laws arising out of the biblical view of the unitary nature of the individual.)

In another important area, too, the world of Greek philosophy began to make its influence felt—that is, the world of critical or empirical thinking. The preexilic Israelite religion challenged the Near Eastern myths in which divinity and nature were often seen as synonymous. The Israelites articulated a new idea of God, removed from nature and history, yet able to control the world from beside or above it. Here was the origin of the idea of "the will of God." In serving God, human beings could help the divine will prevail in history. Such a conception was at odds not only with Near Eastern mythology but also with Greek philosophy, which viewed the world as an entity made intelligible by the use of reason. Just how much Greek philosophy penetrated the intellectual world of Yehud remains a mystery. Even though Greek material and political culture was having an increasing influence, it seems less likely to be true of more rarefied ideas. Yet it is possible that the Book of Ben Sira, written between 198 and 175 B.C.E., may reflect explicit knowledge of and rejection of philosophical Hellenism. A wisdom teacher who brought the fundamentals of Jewish life to the communities he visited, Ben Sira describes Wisdom in strictly biblical terms: "All this [Wisdom] is in the book of the covenant of the most High God, the law which Moses commanded us as an inheritance for the congregation of Jacob" (24:23).

Ben Sira wrote in Hebrew but his words were translated into Greek by his grandson for the Egyptian Jewish community. Some have seen in the work echoes of Stoic thought, but, even if one can trace some Hellenistic influences, it is clear that Ben Sira wanted his audience to find Wisdom in the biblical tradition and not in the works of the Greek philosophers.

THE HASMONAEAN ERA

At the beginning of the second century B.C.E., the Seleucid Empire in Syria succeeded the Ptolemies as the landlords of Palestine. In the 160s, a bitter revolt, led by the Maccabee family of the clan of Hashman (Hasmonaeans), broke out against the Seleucids, ultimately resulting in a period of Jewish sovereignty in the Land of Israel from 142 to 63 B.C.E., when the Romans entered the scene. The Maccabean Revolt is usually associated with the struggle against Hellenization of Jewish culture and with the will to fight foreign intervention. Both of these considerations figure into the reasons for the bitter war between the Judaeans and the Seleucids, but the story, as we shall see, was more complex. A new class of well-to-do Jewish citizens emerged in the Ptolemaic era, many of them attached to or even related to the influential priestly families. It is not difficult to imagine how such circles became easily enamored with the new Greek lifestyle that embraced clothing, language, education, and a willingness to cooperate with foreign rule, first the Ptolemies and subsequently the Seleucids. This new constituency may be described as pro-Hellenizing, although it has been argued that their main interest was not Hellenistic culture but rather the political and economic benefits that might be obtained by converting Jerusalem into a Greek *polis* (city-state). In an effort to secure these benefits, they turned the office of the high priest into a political pawn to be bought or sold. The attempt to transform Jerusalem into a polis challenged the traditional political order, since the Jews were no longer governed according to "the traditions of their fathers." The resistance to this new state of affairs may have involved less rejection of Hellenism per se, than class rivalry over control of the city. Cultural factors may have played a smaller role than later Hasmonaean propaganda claimed, for, as we shall see, the Maccabees themselves were not immune to Hellenistic influences.

Considerable debate continues among historians about the sequence of events that precipitated the revolt: whether the ban by Antiochus IV on the Sabbath, circumcision, and other rituals of traditional Judaism were the cause or, perhaps, constituted some kind of punishment for a prior civil war within Jewish society. But in addition to banning Judaism, Antiochus, or his soldiers, erected "an abomination of desolation upon the altar of burnt offerings" in the Temple.[11] This "abomination" seems to have been a statue of the Syrian Baal, which was probably identified with the Greek god Zeus. Other deities worshiped there included Dionysus and Anath, the consort of Baal, who is associated with prostitution in the Temple.[12] This evidence suggests that, although the biblical Canaanites had long disappeared from the scene, elements of their religion remained and were now combined syncretistically with Greek religion.

Resistance to the Seleucids came from several sources. Those who remained committed to the more conservative way of life were called "pious ones," or *Hasidim*. But, as is often the case with conservatives, this faction may have itself represented something new. The Book of Maccabees claims that these pietists would not fight on the Sabbath, a prohibition unknown in the Bible. The awakening of resistance to the Greeks may have thus created new forms of piety. Indeed, the Hasidim's resistance to change and suspicion of the foreigner foreshadow the more xenophobic monastics of the Dead Sea community at Qumran.

The main resistance was led by the Hasmonaean family, of whom Judah "the Maccabee," or "hammer," was the leading figure. The Hasmonaeans were rural priests, and their role in the revolt may have had something to do with rejection of the more cosmopolitan urban priesthood of Jerusalem. The Hasmonaean Revolt was, in some measure, an uprising of the countryside against the city. The highly partisan accounts in 1 and 2 Maccabees emphasize the popular resistance and the courage of the martyrs, but it is likely that only a small minority chose resistance, at least initially. Nevertheless, from 167 to 164 B.C.E., the resistance movement led by Judah and his brothers Jonathan and Simon achieved remarkable success in a brief time. And on 25 Kislev (December 164 B.C.E.), Judah retook the Temple, which was purified and rededicated to the worship of Yahweh, the sole God of the Jewish people:

> At the very season and on the very day that the gentiles had profaned [the altar], it was dedicated with songs and harps and lutes and cymbals. All the people fell on their faces and worshiped and blessed Heaven, who had prospered them. So they celebrated the dedication of the altar for eight days and offered burnt offerings with gladness; they offered a sacrifice of deliverance and praise.[13]

The festival of rededication was based on the festival of Tabernacles, which the Maccabees claimed they had not been able to celebrate since the Temple had been desecrated. Like Tabernacles and Passover, it lasted eight days (1 Maccabees 4:36–61; 2 Maccabees 10:1–8). But the festival, which soon became known as Hanukkah ("Dedication"), was intended to be a new holiday to celebrate the Maccabees' victory, and it was, in fact, the only festival, with the exception of Qumran, added to Jewish practice in the Second Temple period that is not mentioned in the canonical Bible. In creating a new holiday commemorating the restoration of traditional Judaism, the Maccabeans departed from Jewish practice and imitated their Hellenistic enemies.

The Hasmonaean family subsequently provided the accepted leadership of Judaea, and during the next 20 years or so they successfully repulsed Seleucid political interference, exploiting weaknesses in their empire. Jonathan was the first Hasmonaean to become high priest of the Jewish people, in 152 B.C.E. By 142, his brother Simon declared independence; he too was recognized as high priest, in 140 B.C.E. By declaring himself *hegemenos* (leader), *strategos* (general), and high priest (1 Maccabees 14:41–47), Simon revolutionized the priestly state and signaled his clear intention to restore Judaea to the glories of the past kingdoms of David and Solomon. It was not until Aristobulus I (r. 104–3 B.C.E.) and Alexander Jannaeus (r. 103–76 B.C.E.), however, that the Hasmonaeans took the title of "king" to be used alongside that of high priest. Although the Hasmonaeans did not claim to be descendants of King David, a number of their actions, such as adopting the paleo-Hebrew script on coins and seals, were designed to give their regimes a sense of antiquity and legitimacy. At the same time, as the above titles make clear, their political vocabulary was drawn from the Hellenistic world and their rule resembled that of other Near Eastern states in this period. They took Greek names and adopted foreign symbols such as the sun, anchor, caduceus, and cornucopia in imitation of other regimes, seeking to combine the old with the new, the religious with the political. Despite their ideology of ethnic and religious nationalism, the Hasmonaeans had no qualms about conforming to the conventions of the Hellenistic world.

It was the assumption of the office of the high priesthood by the Hasmonaean family that occasioned the most opposition from among those who had so successfully fought beside them to oppose the Syrians. The high priesthood by ancient custom was the ancestral inheritance of the family of Zadok; the Hasmonaeans, however, did not descend from Zadok. The usurpation of this office, more than that of the royal crown, occasioned open hostility, resentment, and ultimately sectarian opposition that would not go away. Thus, less than a century after the Maccabean wars began, a permanent rift between the leaders of the revolt and their sometime followers and comrades had opened. No more inauspicious way could have been conceived for the reestablishment of Judaean independence and religious freedom. In the hundred years or so of Hasmonaean control, this egregious affront to biblical tradition, the combining of royal and priestly powers, could not be overcome, leading ultimately to enervating divisiveness. Yet it does not appear that the Hellenistic elements of Hasmonaean rule were a major cause of dissension. There is enormous irony in the fact that the reestablishment of Judaean independence and religious freedom by the Hasmonaeans became the setting in which new sectarian opposition would emerge from the very ranks of individuals who years before had been their chief supporters.

The Hasmonaean kings enlarged the orbit of Jewish culture by forcibly converting inhabitants of the biblical lands of Ammon and Edom, east of the Jordan. Some of these areas—Ammon, with its tradition of the Tobiads, and large parts of Peraea—were successfully absorbed into the new kingdom and remained Jewish at least until the Great Revolt (66–70 C.E.). In Galilee, mainly depopulated since the Assyrian conquest in the eighth century B.C.E., excavations and surveys indicate that there were a significant number of new settlements by the time of Jannaeus, whose coins appear nearly everywhere. At Sepphoris, in the lower Galilee, an *ostrakon* (a pottery shard bearing an inscription) from about 100 B.C.E. suggests the complicated relationship that emerged between the Hasmonaean state and Hellenistic culture. The letters are Hebrew but the language is Greek: *epimeles* (or *epimeletes*), the designation for an official of the Jewish community or perhaps a quartermaster in the Hasmonaean army. In establishing political independence from a Hellenistic empire, the Hasmonaeans became the new sponsors of Hellenistic culture.

HEROD THE GREAT TO THE FIRST CENTURY C.E.

Hasmonaean rule and full Jewish sovereignty in the Land of Israel came to an abrupt end with Pompey's annexation in 63 B.C.E. With two descendants of the Hasmonaeans engaged in civil war over the dynastic succession, some Jews welcomed Rome as an alternative to the excesses and divisions perpetrated by the Hasmonaeans, their erstwhile liberators. For others, however, Roman rule quickly became as odious as anything they had endured earlier. An apocryphal Psalm of Solomon alludes to Pompey's invasion and prophesies the coming of the Davidic messiah who would reverse the status of Judah as a client kingdom to Rome and reestablish the Davidic kingdom. Pompey's annexation signaled politically the end of the Hellenistic age in Jewish history and the beginning of the Roman period, but because the dominant culture in the Eastern Mediterranean (and, indeed, to some degree, in Rome itself) remained Greek, the Roman period is aptly designated "Greco-Roman."

The Romans preferred to rule their empire through local authorities, and, failing to find a reliable agent from within the Jewish elite, they elevated Herod (37–4 B.C.E.), whose grandfather was an Edomite converted by the Hasmonaeans and whose father, Antipater, was already a high official under Roman rule. Herod the Great is one of the most controversial figures in Jewish history, a tyrant who massacred members of his own family, a calculating ally of Rome, and a builder on a monumental scale. Herod's shrewd and prescient shift to support Mark Anthony along with Octavian and Lepidus in the Second Triumvirate was a major factor in his rise, as he had come to power with the assistance of Roman soldiers.[14] His strategy, to serve Rome's larger interests in the region through cooperation, was not that different from earlier attempts in the Second Temple period to assuage the dominant superpower. Herod exercised control over the Judaean state and over his enemies by maintaining a first-rate army of Edomites and Jews. He was free to indulge himself at home as long as Rome was happy. That meant paying tribute, keeping the borders of the state free of unwanted foreign intrusions such as the Nabataeans or Parthians, maintaining order and peace within his own territory, and being ready to serve Rome's larger military needs at a moment's notice.

Herod's most important cultural legacy was the magnificent architectural monuments he left behind: the rebuilt Temple with its magisterial scale and classical style; his theaters; his resorts and refuges at Masada and Herodium; and his glorious harbor at Caesarea. Jerusalem and its environs were alive with artists and architects from abroad, and the harbor at Caesarea teemed with boats brim-

Caesarea Maritima: Theater from the time of Herod the Great
(Courtesy Eric Meyers)

ming over with new supplies and wares from the Mediterranean Basin. Herod's remodeled Jerusalem Temple came to be considered one of the wonders of the Roman world and attracted tourists, both Jewish and non-Jewish, from far and wide.

In all these activities, Herod was meticulous in not offending Jewish sensibilities. His palaces in places like Jericho contain numerous ritual baths, which suggests that he was meticulous in making the Jewish purity laws available to his staff and family. He was also careful to build institutions of Hellenistic culture primarily in areas not dominated by Jews. Only in Acco/Ptolemais, or Tripolis, or in Damascus, for example, did Herod venture to build a *gymnasion,* where youths were educated in Greek language and culture. Only in Caesarea Maritima did he organize the quinquennial games. And in Samaria/Sebastia he built a new city for gentiles. Near Jerusalem, possibly outside the city, Herod added a few items of Greco-Roman culture that could have aroused the concerns of some of the Jewish population: a theater, amphitheater, and hippodrome, probably because (like his Roman sponsors) he enjoyed sports and spectacles. Thus, he attempted to shrewdly solve the inherent conflict between Jewish and Hellenistic culture by a policy of geographical separation between predominantly Jewish and non-Jewish areas.

In so doing, Herod demonstrated that he was acutely cognizant of one of the persistent features of Palestine throughout our period: the Jews' sharing of the land with other peoples, including Greek descendants of Alexander's armies, Syrians, and other Near Eastern ethnic groups. Jewish culture could never remain pure and traditional in such a multiethnic and multicultural atmosphere. Whereas the Hasmonaeans had sought, at least in some areas, to create or impose ethnic and religious homogeneity by converting other groups to Judaism, Herod's tactic was less coercive. But this mixture of populations, starting with biblical times and continuing long after our period (indeed, even to the present day), remained a central and unsolvable political and cultural issue for the Land of Israel.

A CULTURE OF SECTARIANISM

Herod's rule was despotic, and he destroyed many members of his family as well as other potential challengers from the Judaean elite. When he died in 4 B.C.E., he left a political vacuum, soon to be filled by Roman procurators. Jewish self-government in the first century C.E. was severely weakened, and a variety of groups competed for political power and cultural and religious authority. Some of these groups originated in Herod's time and perhaps even earlier, during the Hasmonaean period, reflecting the tensions and divisiveness of these regimes. These were the Sadducees, Pharisees, and Essenes as well as the revolutionary Zealots. The Sadducees, the party of priests, enjoyed particular power and enhanced status in Herod's remodeled Temple. In order to undermine the Hasmonaean priests and co-opt the priesthood for his regime, Herod brought in priestly families from Egypt and Babylonia.[15] The Sadducean party was therefore, at least in part, a foreign import.

The Pharisees, the forerunners of the rabbis, evidently suffered from persecution from the Herodians, but it was in this period that some of their "founding fathers" flourished: Shemaiah and Abtalion, Hillel and Shammai. Their alienation from the government is captured in a saying from the Mishnah, which, though compiled 200 years later, may reflect the atmosphere of the Herodian period and its immediate aftermath: "Shemaiah and Abtalion who received the tradition from Simeon ben Shetach and Judah ben Tabbai. Shemaiah said: 'Love labor and hate the government, and seek not intimacy with the ruling powers.' "[16]

The Qumran Sect reached its height during the Herodian period, although it continued to the Great Revolt. This monastic community by the Dead Sea reflected the separatism of certain pietists, called Essenes, perhaps spiritual descendants of the Hasidim of the Hasmonaean age. Some of these Essenes were located in cities such as Jerusalem, while others, such as the "covenanters" of Qumran, left society for the desert. It is probable that the term "Essene," used by

Josephus in his histories written at the end of the first century C.E., refers not to one specific group but to a wide variety of pietistic rebel sects. Indeed, Josephus cast his description of the various Jewish parties, including the Essenes, as philosophical schools to make them comprehensible to his Roman audience. But who they really were and how they related to each other may have been considerably different from Josephus's overly stylized portrait.

With the discovery of the Dead Sea Scrolls and the excavations of Qumran, where the library of the scrolls was located, it is possible to obtain a window onto Second Temple sectarian culture independent of Josephus. Many members of the Dead Sea community were men of priestly descent who rejected the practices of the Jerusalem priesthood; their story therefore belongs to the internal history of the priesthood. It is possible that they opted out of Jerusalem society as a result of the Hasmonaean usurpation of the office of high priest. Although the Essenes as described by Josephus were not all necessarily priests, I believe that the Qumran covenanters belong to this general category of pietists.

On the basis of coins and pottery, we can say that the community at the Dead Sea was established around the time of Simon Maccabee, circa 140 B.C.E., plus or minus a decade. Paleographic evidence for some of the scrolls recovered from the nearby caves predates this by more than a century, meaning that sectarian

Aerial view of Khirbet Qumran, ruin of the Dead Sea sect.
(Courtesy Richard Cleave, Pictorial Archive)

ideas did not originate wholly after or as a result of the Maccabean rebellion. Also, many of the earlier scrolls are not sectarian but merely noncanonical. The *floruit*, or heyday, of the community at Qumran thus occurred during the years of Alexander Jannaeus and Herod the Great, though there may have been a short hiatus in connection with a violent destruction around 9–8 B.C.E. The resettlement of the community, after a very brief abandonment, survived until the first Roman War.

The Dead Sea community's separatism was expressed in the sense of their election as the "True Israel" and their apocalyptic mentality, the idea that they were living in the "end time." They were the first group to explicitly deny that other Jews were true Jews and, in their messianic doctrine of a "New Covenant," paved the way for later Christian supersessionism, the belief that the Church was the true Israel. Although such exclusivism may be traced back to Ezra the Scribe, who, we recall, called the returnees from Babylonia the "holy seed" and banned intermarriage, it is by no means certain whether those Ezra opposed were in fact Jews or foreigners. The Qumran sectarians, however, labeled the Jerusalem establishment the "children of darkness," in part because of their violation of the sect's ideas of purity and in part because of their alliance with the Romans (referred to in some of the scrolls as *Kitti'im*). The sect believed that Roman rule presaged a final apocalyptic war and that those on the side of the imperial authorities would be destroyed along with them. The "holy ones" were the forces of light in whom the gifts of the holy spirit were manifest. Those contradictory forces would face each other in a final end-of-time battle that is described in the famous War Scroll. Not only did the Essenes adopt an apocalyptic view of the end of time, but they also believed that God had predetermined everything.

In light of their belief in predetermination, the Dead Sea community's calendar was of great importance. They followed a 364-day solar calendar at Qumran that was at variance with the 354-day lunar-solar calendar of the Jerusalem community. At Qumran the day was reckoned from sunrise to sunrise. In Jerusalem the day was reckoned from sundown to sundown. Holidays could never be celebrated together. In fact, the Habakkuk Scroll relates that the "Wicked Priest" (possibly a Hasmonaean or Herodian high priest?) attacked the sect on Yom Kippur, the Day of Atonement, when a high priest (not to speak of any other Jew) would be fasting and sacrificing in the Temple. The calendar dispute was understandably a central bone of contention between the communities. The Jerusalem Temple establishment was therefore deemed to be corrupt and, because it was perpetually in violation of the calendar, thoroughly impure.

Because time was conceived to be at the edge of a momentous event about to happen, the Dead Sea Sect applied certain biblical laws with much greater severity than was the case for the priestly establishment. For example, in wartime the laws of ritual purity operated in a very strict way, especially as they related to sexual activity, which was prohibited. The so-called Temple Scroll prescribes much stricter standards of purity not just for the Temple but for the city of Jerusalem as a whole. The sectarians thus lived as if they were at the time of that final battle, in a state of ritual purity. They held all goods in common, practiced ritual immersion regularly, would not eliminate bodily fluids or wastes within the camp, studied and worshiped much of the day, and believed in two messiahs, one priestly and one Davidic.

In their material culture, though, the sectarians were quite normal in respect to purity laws, utilizing stone vessels for hand-washing just as did the pious in Jerusalem or Sepphoris. Although some of their pottery exhibits new shapes, especially the jars containing their scrolls, most of the pottery and glass reflect the early Roman-period culture of Palestine at large. The architecture at the Dead Sea community is familiar as well, though the communitarian aspect of the sect is reflected in the organization of the tiny hamlet, large enough for only around 120 souls. The number of ritual baths discovered suggests the special emphasis on purity.

COMMON JUDAISM

The sectarian nature of the Dead Sea community should not, however, mislead us. Despite the tensions and conflicts between Sadducees, Essenes, Pharisees, and other groups, this period of factionalism was also a period in which what might be called "common Judaism" began to emerge. Indeed, a true portrait of the Jewish culture of the period needs to emphasize not only the culture of sectarianism but also the way in which certain common ideas and practices, based on biblical sources, pointed ahead toward later rabbinic Judaism.

The historian Josephus is our primary ancient source for Jewish sectarianism in the prerabbinic period. In both the *Jewish Antiquities* and the *Jewish Wars*, he describes the various sects, which he calls, in Greek, *philosophiai* or *haireseis*. These passages not only cover Pharisees, Sadducees, and "Essenes" but also include the controversial discussions of Jesus, James the brother of Jesus, and John the Baptist and his followers. It is remarkable, therefore, that in another book, his *Contra Apionem*, Josephus describes the Jews in the following terms:

To this cause above all we owe our remarkable harmony. Unity and identity of religious belief, perfect uniformity in habits and customs, produce a very beautiful concord in human character. Among us alone will be heard no contradictory statements about God, such as are common among other nations, not only on the lips of ordinary individuals under the impulse of some passing mood, but even boldly propounded by philosophers; some putting forward crushing arguments against the very existence of God, others depriving Him of His providential care for mankind. Among us alone will be seen no difference in the conduct of our lives. With us all act alike, all profess the same doctrine about God, one which is in harmony with our Law and affirms that all things are under His eye.[17]

This statement stands in seeming contradiction to Josephus's careful accounts of Judaism as divided into three "philosophiai" or "haireseis." Unless we assume that, in our text, Josephus is simply obfuscating for the purposes of apologetics, we must conclude that he did not perceive the "haireseis" of his time as equivalent to its later meaning of "heresy" or *minut,* its Hebrew equivalent.[18] These schools in no way disturbed the essential religious and communal unity of the Jewish people, certainly no more than did the divisions among the Greeks between Cynics, Epicureans, and Pythagoreans. Indeed, for Josephus, the differences between these Greek sects or philosophies was much more fundamental than that between Pharisees, Sadducees, and Essenes, who, for all their divisions, were still committed to observance of God's Torah around questions of Sabbath, *kashrut,* circumcision, and confession of the Shema. In short, the "sectarianism" of the Second Temple period did not preclude inclusiveness or a sense of a "pluralistic" Israel.

The discoveries at Qumran can shed light not only on sectarian differences but also on commonalities. From texts such as the Temple Scroll and the MMT Scroll ("Some of the Works of the Torah"), a letter probably intended for the priests in Jerusalem delineating the differences between the two groups, we can observe the development of later rabbinic law at an early stage. In the MMT Scroll, in particular, it becomes evident that the sect's *halakhah* (law) shared certain key ideas with what must have been Pharisaic legal arguments of the time. The complex biblical hermeneutics utilized by the sectarians, including their extensive use of biblical intertextuality, also suggest real similarities to the methods used by the later rabbis.

The vast library at Qumran also sheds light on literary activity in the last few centuries of the Second Temple period. Eleven caves in the immediate vicinity of Qumran produced fragments of nearly 800 manuscripts. A number of them have been dated paleographically to the third or early second centuries B.C.E., before the establishment of the Qumran settlement. These scrolls were almost certainly brought from elsewhere, though this does not mean that all other scrolls were brought to Qumran from elsewhere, as a small group of scholars still maintains. The sectarian documents all date to the period of settlement at Qumran and no doubt relate to the unique history and ideology of the community that made its home in the monastery located below the caves.

Many of the scrolls contain books or fragments of books of the Hebrew Bible. It is no surprise that the Pentateuch is so well represented in the corpus. The Book of Deuteronomy is first among the five, found in 29 manuscripts; only Psalms is found more frequently, in 36 manuscripts. The third most attested book in the Qumran library is the Book of Isaiah, which is found in 21 manuscripts. Not unexpected is the fact that the only other books represented in double digits are those in the rest of the Pentateuch, namely Genesis, Exodus, Leviticus, and Numbers. In all, 202 copies or fragments of biblical books are represented, or around 25 percent of the total trove. Although the statistics surely inform us about the importance of biblical books in the lives of the people who lived in Qumran, the sum total of all the manuscripts demonstrate the richness of literature that was available, mainly in Hebrew and Aramaic, outside of what was to become the Hebrew canon of Scripture in the later centuries C.E. In this connection, the absence of any copies or fragments of the Book of Esther is noteworthy. Though it may be the result of happenstance, Esther is the only book in the Hebrew Bible that does not mention the name of God; nor does it mention the city of Jerusalem, the festivals, and many Jewish laws and practices. The feast of Purim that is associated with the book, likewise, is never mentioned in any Qumran text. Although its absence could be due to sheer chance, perhaps it was its lack of piety or its celebration of a victory of the Diaspora Jews that caused the Essenes to reject it.

Among the remainder of the manuscripts are many of the apocrypha and a new corpus of Jewish pseudepigrapha, and the rewritten Torah. Other texts deal with the cycle of Jewish worship and holidays, especially the Sabbath, within the framework of the distinctive solar calendar of the sect. All of these materials testify to the centrality of biblical texts and biblical figures in the Jewish literature of the turn of the common era, to the rich variety of genres found in the sectarian library, and to the belletristic character of the entire corpus, both sectarian and nonsectarian. All of this compositional activity occurred well in advance of the finalization of the Jewish canon of Scripture in the first centuries C.E. Moreover, the great variety of types of writing reflected in the Qumran corpus shows that the sectarians as well as most other Jewish groups were more or less in accord about the Pentateuch and Prophets, although the Kethubim or Writings were still in a state of some flux in the first centuries C.E. The copious use of quotations from the Hebrew Bible in the New Testament (especially the Gospel of

Matthew) further confirms that even sectarian groups like the early Christians relied on the same scriptures as the elite establishment. The common Judaism that was emerging at this time was based on what was developing into a commonly held library of texts, but the sense that Scripture was still unfulfilled and incomplete, in both a canonical sense and an eschatological sense, allowed openings to apocalyptic groups such as the Qumran community and the early Christians to base their visions of the future on the biblical text.

The figure of Hillel, elevated to leader *(nasi)* of the Pharisaic legislative body around 30 B.C.E., affords a helpful example of the similarities among the early Jewish sects. Whereas our sources for Hillel stem from several centuries later, many of the sayings attributed to him resonate with other sources that are demonstrably from his time. His use of intertextuality or midrash exegesis, or citing Scripture to support his views, was not unlike the Essene hermeneutic or the exegesis attributed to Jesus; this method doubtless developed long before in Palestine and can even be found in the Bible itself.

Hillel's preoccupation with social concerns echoed the prophets and demonstrated the persistence of these subjects at the turn of the era. His successful campaign for banking reform and the adoption of the *prosbul* placed him clearly on the side of the poor.[19] The prosbul was a legal device for securing the repayment of loans in the sabbatical year. Without this legal enactment, moneylenders were hesitant to make loans in the sixth year of the seven-year cycle, because debts could not be collected in the seventh year. That the prosbul was practiced is clear from a text found in the Judaean desert and dated to the second year of Nero (Oct. 55–Oct. 56 C.E.), in which a borrower promises to repay a loan plus interest of one-fifth "even if it is a year of rest."[20] In his defense of the poor, Hillel's teachings bear a striking resemblance to those of the Jesus of the Gospels. Most famous of all is his summary of the whole of the Torah "while standing on one foot": "What is hateful to you do not do to your neighbor—this is the Torah; the rest is commentary."[21] But his advocacy of love and humility as the core teachings of Torah can be found equally in the sectarian literature of the time, as well, of course, as in the Christian Gospels.[22] Like Qumran and the early Christians, the Pharisees formed "table fellowships," pietistic circles who ate together, preserving a special sense of their own purity. Unlike the sects, however, the Pharisees appear to have sought reforms within society. In the words attributed to Hillel: "Do not separate yourself from the community."[23]

Another unifying element was the Temple. All the competing groups of the Second Temple period recognized the Temple as the central institution of the Jewish religion. Although the Dead Sea community was at war with the contemporary custodians of the Temple, their vision of an eschatological future included a purified Temple. The early Christians, too, although they later came to reject Temple sacrifices, at least initially made the Temple their place of regular prayer and the breaking of bread.[24] And Jesus himself was reported to have prophesied that, following the destruction of the Temple, a new Temple would take its place, but not one built by human hands.[25] Finally, all these groups appear to have believed in the coming of a messianic age, even if they differed on the details. Apocalyptic groups, like the Dead Sea community, the Zealots, and the early Christian Church, were all radical offshoots of a common belief.

All these common principles—the Bible and its interpretation, the Temple, and the Messiah—compensated for the differences between Sadducees, Pharisees, Essenes, Zealots, and early Christians. In fact, close examination often reveals surprising similarities. According to Josephus as well as later Jewish tradition, the Sadducees rejected the Oral Law and belief in the afterlife, whereas the Pharisees affirmed these two principles as core beliefs.[26] Yet the Sadducees did have their own "oral" traditions, especially, as one might expect from priests, related to ways of performing sacrifices, purity laws, criminal law, and aspects of civil law as well. At times, their interpretations of these issues were more remote from the literal meaning of the Bible than those of the Pharisees.[27]

Similar blurring of boundaries becomes evident over the question of resurrection of the dead. Here, one of the most vexed questions in Palestinian archaeology may shed some light: the custom of *ossilegium* (collecting the bones of the deceased around a year after death and reburying them in a container in a subterranean tomb chamber or catacomb). Ossuary reburial is not prescribed in the Pentateuch and clearly puts at risk of defilement the person involved in the act of reburial. By the time of the Mishnah, it had become a well-established custom, because the Mishnah regards the reburial of a parent as a paramount obligation that overrides all else, "for on that day (the day of reburial), it is an occasion for rejoicing."[28] It seems likely that expending considerable effort on a second burial would signify some sort of belief in postmortem existence, which would, in turn, justify incurring the ritual impurity associated with corpses. For this reason, both ancient sources and modern interpreters have identified the custom with the Pharisees. But there is considerable evidence that the practice extended beyond the Pharisees to include Jews from different strata of society.

Where did this practice come from? There is substantial evidence that it was very ancient, even if it seems to contradict biblical custom. We know from archaeological finds that there was a 3,000-year history in Palestine of what is called "secondary burial," in which the disarticulated remains are transported to a charnel house or family chamber without housing them in a container.[29] The Romans, however, buried incinerated remains in ossuaries or urns. The wealthy classes in our period may have borrowed the practice of reburial into ossuaries from the Romans, but I believe that the custom was taken over from the Parthians, who practiced decarnation by vultures and subsequent reburial into ossuaries called *astodans;* such a practice was only reinforced by Roman custom. Whatever the case, we have here an interesting amalgamation of an old Palestinian custom—Jewish and non-Jewish—of secondary reburial with a custom imported from abroad of reburial in a receptacle.

The recent discovery in Jerusalem of the tomb and ossuary of Caiaphas, the high priest who presided over the trial of Jesus, reinforces the view that a common Jewish burial practice undergirded many and diverse forms of Jewish life and culture in the first century C.E.[30] A coin of Herod Agrippa I, dated to 42–43 C.E., was found in the skull, a Greek custom (also found in a Jericho tomb) signifying payment to the Greek deity Charon for carrying the deceased's spirit across the river Styx. However, the remains of Caiaphas were deposited in an ossuary in a very traditional Jewish loculus tomb located south of the Hinnom Valley and Abu Tor, well beyond the city limits and away from the busy pathways of shoppers, pilgrims, and other visitors. Once again, we are witness to cultural syncretism in burial practices in which Greek, Jewish, and possibly Roman or Parthian customs all played a role. Moreover, because Caiaphas was unquestionably a Sadducee, his reburial strongly suggests that even the Sadducees may have held some belief in what Josephus calls "renewed existence."[31] This fact urges us to be cautious in taking the Sadducean belief system too literally, especially on the matter of life after death. Actual cultural practices, as revealed by the archaeologist's spade, once again complicate the neat ideological divisions of the literary texts. And we must be equally cautious in assuming that the Sadducees knew nothing of the Oral Law, later codified in the Mishnah.

The belief that one was released from judgment at a second burial also left an echo in the New Testament, in Matthew 8:21–22 and Luke 9:59–60. When a would-be disciple expresses his readiness to follow Jesus after he has (re)buried his father, Jesus refuses to accept the delay: "Let the dead bury their own dead," he responds.[32] The passage is often taken to refer to Jesus' demand for an absolute commitment to leave family ties behind and follow him. Assuming the common practice of secondary burial, we may conclude that the disciple is asking for time to fulfill his familial obligation. In their burial practices, as in so much else, the early Christians were as much a part of the larger Jewish culture as the Pharisees and Sadducees.

PRIVATE LIFE AND POPULAR CULTURE

Most of the literary texts of our period were products either of elite groups, like the Qumran sect or the historian Josephus, or of the later rabbinic elite. Although archaeology can help illuminate private life, we are fortunate in possessing another body of literature that offers us a unique window onto the culture of the folk in the first century C.E.: the library of the early Christians. The historicity of the Gospel documents remains hotly contested, but regardless of whether or not Jesus actually said and did the things attributed to him, the New Testament texts can be used for another purpose altogether: to gain some insight into the rural culture of first-century Palestine.

Whereas the early Church was primarily an urban movement, the Jesus movement itself came from the countryside of Galilee. Jesus was from Nazareth, in the lower Galilee, and although the New Testament does not mention his having set foot in nearby Sepphoris, which was the major urban center in Galilee at the time, he could hardly have avoided going there on occasion. As we shall see, by the late second and early third centuries C.E., Sepphoris was to become a highly Hellenized city, but we do not have evidence that this was the case in the time of Jesus. So, despite efforts by some to see in Jesus a preacher of a popular form of Greek Cynic philosophy, there is little evidence that he could read Greek philosophy, although he probably knew enough Greek to get along in the marketplace. His language was Galilean Aramaic, and he probably also knew some Hebrew. In short, it is doubtful that Jesus was exposed to the kind of urban Hellenistic culture that might be found in Jerusalem or Caesarea.

Each of the three villages near the Sea of Galilee mentioned in the New Testament—Bethsaida, Capernaum, and Chorazin—probably consisted of fewer than 2,000 souls and was agricultural in character. This kind of settlement was the focal point of Jesus' ministry. But he did not avoid all cities, because he was, in fact, active in some where there were Jewish minorities and audiences of gentiles to address. His visit to Caesarea Philippi (Baneas), where there was an active shrine to Pan, included the "villages" that were part of the municipal territory of the city.[33] In places with mixed populations like Tyre or Bet Shean (Scythopolis), Jesus might have found a more tolerant audience than in Sepphoris, where the population was overwhelmingly Jewish and the Jewish authorities dominated.

The synoptic Gospels are filled with parables based on agricultural metaphors, as one might expect from a primarily agrarian society: "The kingdom of heaven is like a landowner going out at daybreak to hire workers for his vineyard."[34] The parable goes on to ground its message—"the last will be first and the first, last"—in what must have been a common wage dispute between itinerant field hands and their employer. Or, the eschatological teaching might be based on the experience of farmers whose fields were vulnerable to sabotage by their enemies: "The kingdom of heaven may be compared to a man who sowed good seed in his field. While everybody was asleep his enemy came and sowed darnel all among the wheat."[35]

The Jesus of the Gospels is also heavily engaged in faith healing and exorcism, magical practices that must have been crucial to his rural society. The Talmud contains stories of charismatic magicians, such as Honi the Circle Maker, who were also active around the same time in the Galilee.[36] Men like Jesus and Honi were not, however, the only magicians at work in popular culture. The Talmud also regularly associates women with magic, some of which it pejoratively labels "witchcraft."[37] Amulets from the later rabbinic period show that both men and women engaged in various forms of magic. The use of amulets was so widespread that we must question whether the rabbis, who generally condemned such magic when practiced by those outside their own caste, really controlled this aspect of popular culture.

Much of Jesus' preaching took place in Galilean synagogues.[38] Although there are presently only architectural remains of few synagogues from first-century Palestine—Masada, Herodium, Qiryat Sefer, and Gamala—there can be no doubt that the synagogue was already well established in Second Temple times as a site for local religion. The Temple remained the primary cultic destination on the major pilgrimage holidays, but everyday worship and teaching of the Torah took place in the synagogue. In addition to these ritual and study functions, synagogues might serve as hostels for pilgrims, as the Theodotus inscription from Jerusalem makes clear:

> Theodotus, son of Vettenos the priest and archisynagogos [synagogue leader], son of an archisynagogos and grandson of an archisynagogos, built the synagogue for reading the Law and studying the commandments, and as a hostel with chambers and water installations to provide for the needs of itinerants from abroad, which his fathers, the elders and Simonides founded.[39]

Three generations of priests were involved in building and maintaining this particular Jerusalem synagogue, whose existence near the Temple suggests that many of the functions the synagogue would fulfill after the Temple's destruction in 70 C.E. were already in place while the Temple still stood.

Surprisingly enough, the title "archisynagogos" was not limited only to men. On a marble plaque from Smyrna (Izmir), we find the following: "Rufina, a Jewess, head of synagogue, built this tomb for her freed slaves and the slaves raised in her house. No one else has the right to bury anyone here."[40] Inscriptions found in Diaspora synagogues contain the names of women who evidently served in similar roles. Moreover, it appears that women and men may have sat together in the synagogue, because excavations of synagogues from both the Diaspora and Palestine do not seem to include separate women's galleries. Contemporary practices from Qumran and later rabbinic strictures against women's participation in worship may not reflect the most common customs of the earlier period. Although women were excluded from the Inner Court of the Temple, they were not as segregated from men in public worship elsewhere, nor were they excluded from the study of Torah to the extent that at least some rabbinic authorities desired. The fact that women were active in the Jesus movement and in the early Church may have been more a reflection of contemporary Jewish popular culture than a radical departure from it.

Similarly, the layout of private houses, as revealed by archaeological excavations, challenges the assumption, derived from rabbinic texts, that men and women were regularly separated at home for moral, purity, or legal reasons.[41] Women had their own defined sphere, to be sure: following common practice in the ancient Mediterranean, spinning and weaving were ritualized occupations for them.[42] But in both their private and their public roles, women were less excluded and segregated than is commonly believed.

If life in the Galilean countryside remained largely insulated from Hellenistic influence during the first century C.E., the same cannot be said for a major urban center like Jerusalem or, perhaps to a lesser extent, Judaea as a whole. The homes that have been uncovered in Jerusalem illustrate a lifestyle and degree of wealth previously thought unlikely. The homes are huge in size and functional within. Excavations reveal mosaics, decorated stucco or frescoes in houses, expensive glassware, imported eastern *terra sigillata,* impressed fineware typically from North Africa, amphorae from Italy, and jars of wine from Rhodes. The upper classes, especially the priestly families, were able to purchase such items and decorate their houses with them. The Jerusalem elite was tied into the global material culture of the time, and their everyday life reflects a largely Hellenistic lifestyle.

In addition to Hellenistic material comforts, the residents of Jerusalem seem to have been quite familiar with the Greek language. Greek inscriptions number about one-third of all known inscriptions from the city, and 37 percent of Jewish ossuaries bear Greek inscriptions. In the Bar Kokhba letters from the 130's C.E., which were discovered in caves overlooking the Dead Sea, the rebels against Rome wrote not only in Hebrew and Aramaic but also in Greek. (The Greek documents appear to be primarily related to business matters.) The culture of Judaea appears therefore to have been trilingual—Hebrew, Aramaic, and Greek—and we shall have occasion to see how this linguistic fact would find echoes in later rabbinic culture.

Many, if not most, of the Jerusalem houses had internal ritual baths. Individual families would go to great lengths to install these *mikva'ot,* for the common Judaism of the day made purity of the body a central element of everyday life, especially for priests. It took great ingenuity and considerable technology to accommodate the law for ritual immersion. A fresh water source had to be brought from a considerable distance via aqueducts and underground channels. In Jerusalem, at least part of the year, rainwater could be saved on the roof and then used for ritual purposes. However it was stored, it had to be transported to the bath in such a way that there was always a proper mixture of pure or running water and stored or standing water. The dramatic remains of these installations provide striking, visual corroboration of the halakhic orientation of Judaism as practiced at the highest level of government and in private life. It also reinforces the thesis that the leadership saw no inherent contradiction between a Hellenized lifestyle and Jewish practice.

The poor of the city enjoyed the material benefits of Hellenistic culture far less than the wealthy, but we are hard pressed to say a great deal about their lives. That harmony scarcely reigned between the upper and lower classes becomes evident from a talmudic text that sounds very much like an authentic popular chant against the families of high priests:

Woe is me because of the House of Boethus, woe is me because of their denunciations.

Woe is me because of the House of Elisha, woe is me because of their fist.

Woe is me because of the House of Ishmael ben Phiabi who are high priests and their sons-in-law are trustees and their servants come and beat us with sticks.[43]

Despite the violence to which this text bears witness, it is notable that popular discontent is not focused on the Hellenized lifestyle of the priests. While it may be difficult to speculate from silence, it appears that the inner social tensions that were to burst forth in revolt against the Romans in 66 C.E. had little to do with the influence in Jerusalem of Greco-Roman culture as such. Whatever the political and religious causes of the Great Revolt, it was not primarily an attempt to eradicate the culture that had struck such deep roots in Judaea since Alexander the Great, if not earlier.

THE EMERGENCE OF "RABBINIC JUDAISM"

Whether the Great Revolt of 66–70 C.E. was the product of sectarian forces, such as the Zealots, or reflected a common resistance to Roman oppression remains a hotly debated issue among historians. Josephus, whose history is our main source, is clearly biased, because he was a general in the early stages of the revolt and subsequently switched sides. It was in Josephus's interest to portray the first part of the revolt as united and the later period as riven by extreme factions. Similarly biased are the later talmudic accounts, which portray Yoḥanan ben Zakkai, the subsequent rabbinical patriarch, as an opponent of the revolt who was smuggled out of the besieged Jerusalem in a coffin. By the time these texts were written—possibly hundreds of years later—the rabbis, like Josephus, had an interest in distancing themselves from rebellion against the Roman Empire.

The trauma of defeat and the sacking of Jerusalem meant tremendous dislocation for the great masses of people in Judaea, many of whom sought to resettle in the Galilee, which had remained largely Jewish during the first century. This process of depopulation of Judaea and shift of the center to the Galilee was to accelerate dramatically after the Bar Kokhba Revolt in 132–35 C.E. Still others left for faraway places in the Diaspora where they knew Jews were living or welcome. The Essenes and Qumran covenanters were swept away into the dustbin of history, the apocalypse of the Roman War having produced the wrong outcome, although some have argued that their ideology was an important component of the nascent Jesus movements. There is increasing evidence that groups of priests continued to function as organized bodies and leaders for quite a few centuries in Palestine, even perhaps retaining sufficient vitality to enable a recovery of leadership with the demise of the patriarchate in the early Byzantine period. Sadduceeism, however, as a separate religious identity, seems to have receded gradually during the early centuries of the Christian era in the face of increasing rabbinic dominance. The more extremist elements of Judaism, the Zealots and their followers, either went underground or changed their views on war as a vehicle for bringing about change. The first Christians, the earliest Jewish Christian community in Judaea, in part fled perhaps to Transjordan, to Pella, and in part fled to the north with their fellow Jews. In both these regions they sank their roots, while their gentile counterpart was absorbed in the West and Asia Minor and Greece.

The destruction of the Temple necessarily had cataclysmic political and religious consequences. Because the Temple had functioned as a political as well as cultic center, its loss left a vacuum into which the rabbis would move, eventually becoming, with the confirmation of the Romans, the primary legal and governmental authorities. According to talmudic legends appropriated as history by many historians, following Yoḥanan ben Zakkai, Gamaliel II, whom legend claims to have been descended from Hillel, established the patriarchate as the Jewish self-government and received the imprimatur of the Romans. Other scholars, reading the talmudic record more critically, assume that the narratives of both Yoḥanan's and Gamaliel's patriarchates are virtual foundation legends of the house of Rabbi Judah the Prince, the first named patriarch, appointed by the Romans in the late second century C.E. to govern the Jews in a manner that would be productive for the *Pax Romana*. By the late second century, in any case, the patriarch had become a quasi-prince, with mercenary guards and significant powers bestowed by the Romans. The political history of this period demonstrates real tensions between the patriarchs, descendants of the House of Gamaliel, and the first group of rabbis, the early *tanna'im*, who were formed primarily of the disciples (and *their* disciples) of Rabbi Yoḥanan ben Zakkai.[44] It was, however, the power of the patriarch, as well as his relative closeness to the various groups of scribes and Pharisees remaining vibrant after the two revolts, that enabled the rabbinic movement to consolidate itself out of the joining of these various groups and the gradually successful imposition of their religious views as a virtual orthodoxy on the Jews of Palestine, Babylonia, and eventually—after several centuries—the Diaspora as well.[45]

The loss of the Jerusalem Temple also meant that the Jewish religion had to transform itself from a Temple-based, sacrificial cult to a culture rooted in domestic and local practices: prayer; celebration of the annual cycle of agriculturally based holidays; and transferal of the purity laws to the home and to the house of study. This work of transformation was undertaken in the years after 70 C.E. by Yoḥanan ben Zakkai and his successors. Although the stories about the court at Yavneh, which Yohanan established either during or immediately after the war, may have been fictions projected back into history by later generations of rabbis, there can be little doubt that he and his disciples began the process of turning priestly Judaism into the rabbinic culture that developed in subsequent years. The house of study *(bet midrash)* and the synagogue, both of which were institutions long in existence during the late Second Temple period, now became primary; indeed, most of the synagogue sites excavated in Palestine stem from the third century and later. The synagogue liturgy developed beyond its Second Temple origins and became the basis for all Jewish liturgy in subsequent centuries. The rabbis were not, however, to control the synagogue institution and its traditional religious forms for centuries.[46]

The transformation of Pharisaism from a sect into a hegemonic orthodoxy took place over the course of the second and third centuries, during which time it dropped the name Pharisee (which means "Separatist" and ran, therefore,

counter to the new ideology of a common, catholic Judaism). The statement attributed to Gamaliel III (mid-third century; Avot 2:4), "Do not 'separate' from
the public," is a reflection of the new status of the erstwhile sect of the Pharisees.[47] To the extent that we know anything about them—a very limited extent
indeed—it would seem that the leaders at Yavneh had fairly modest and limited
aims: it fell to the next generation of tanna'im to expand the purview of rabbinic
law and practices. Some scholars have held that the canon of Scripture was established at Yavneh, but this view has been largely discredited in recent scholarship.[48] Some have held that events at Yavneh precipitated the final split between
Judaism and Christianity,[49] the so-called parting of the ways, but this view is
even more discredited than the previous one.[50] The following example apparently exemplifies the very limited scope of any Yavnean adjustment in Jewish
law. Before the destruction of the Temple, when a New Year fell on the Sabbath,
the shofar would only be sounded in Jerusalem. The amended law allows for the
shofar to be blown wherever the Jewish court or Sanhedrin would sit (Mishnah
Rosh Hashana 4:1). In such a revision, the sages declared their courts the lawful
successor to the priestly court of Jerusalem. Their preoccupation with such matters was not unlike that of the exiles in Babylonia in the sixth century B.C.E., who
sought ways for the community to stay together without a Temple and in a foreign land.

Just as the Primary History, consisting of the Pentateuch and Former Prophets,
most noticeably influenced by Deuteronomic theology, had interpreted the destruction of the First Temple as having been occasioned by sin and idolatry or
covenant disobedience, so too did some of the contemporaries of Yavneh see the
destruction in 70 as arising out of sin—God acted righteously in punishing Israel (2 Baruch 10:6–7, 9–15, 17–18)—though, with repentance, redemption would
ultimately come about (44:12–15). In the end the Temple will be reinstituted
along with its sacrificial system, God will redeem humankind, and the Messiah
will come to transform the world.

The tanna'im, however, took a more cautious position on messianism. According to later tradition, Yoḥanan ben Zakkai taught that, if one is engaged in
planting a vineyard and someone announces the coming of the Messiah, then
one should finish planting.[51] However, other traditions claim that significant
members of a later generation of rabbis, especially the great Rabbi Akiva, supported the Bar Kokhba Revolt and considered its leader, Simon Bar Kokhba, to
have been the Messiah. The fact that many rabbis were martyred by the Romans
for their support of this revolt seems to corroborate this tradition. It is somewhat hard to believe that the disciples of Yoḥanan's school would have taken
such a strong eschatological stance less than 60 years after their teacher had eschewed messianism. It is more likely that the Yoḥanan tradition was created by a

later generation of post–Bar Kokhba rabbis who drew the lesson from that disastrous revolt that messianism exacted too high a price. Their compromise was to preserve the messianic idea but to relegate it to the future.

Although Rome remained their historic enemy, some of the rabbis made pragmatic accommodation with the empire their guiding principle:

> Our [ancient] Rabbis have taught: When Rabbi Yose the son of Kisma became ill, Rabbi Hanina the son of Teradion went to visit him. He said to him: "Hanina, my brother, don't you know that this nation was set to rule over us by Heaven, and it has destroyed His house, and burned His temple, and killed His saints, and destroyed His goodly things, and still it exists, and I have heard that you gather crowds together in public, with a Scroll of the Torah in your lap, and you sit and teach!" He [Hanina] said to him, "From Heaven they will have mercy." He [Yose] said to him, "I say logical things to you, and you answer me: 'From Heaven they will have mercy!' I will be surprised if they do not burn you and the Scroll of the Torah with you."[52]

Rabbi Hanina is one of the prototypical martyrs in the talmudic literature.[53] This text thus eloquently reflects the critique that much of post–Bar Kokhba rabbinic culture produced against any open resistance to Roman rule, arguing instead that Jewish law and the study of Torah should be maintained in private, while, in public, attempts would be made to accommodate to the empire. Any open resistance, according to the position attributed to Rabbi Yose, will result in Hanina's needless death.

An exchange attributed to two other rabbis of the post–Bar Kokhba era captures the duality of the rabbis' view of Rome. Rabbi Judah ben Ilai is quoted as saying: "How beautiful are the deeds of that nation [the Romans]. They set up marketplaces, build bridges, construct baths." Rabbi Simon bar Yohai is said to have retorted: "Everything they do for their own good. They set up marketplaces to place their harlots there, baths for their pleasures, bridges to levy tolls."[54] But, as the story with which we began this chapter—of Gamaliel in the Roman bath—makes clear, the Jews themselves, including the rabbis, took advantage of the many benefits of the empire.

Following the devastating defeat of the Second Revolt under Bar Kokhba in 135, the Jews virtually abandoned Judaea, and the Galilee became the center of Jewish life and culture for the next 400 or 500 years. This shift to the north coincided with Rome's general policy of urbanization of the eastern part of the empire, which resulted in an even greater concentration of wealthy landowners in Sepphoris and Tiberias. The localization of such considerable wealth in cities no doubt led to the increase in civic building projects that included colonnaded streets, market buildings, shops, and public buildings, which in turn led to a greater acceptance of a Hellenistic lifestyle, at least from an external point of view.

The reconfiguration of Jewish life took place in several locations in the north. Judging from the amount of new settlements in the Upper Galilee, considerable numbers of Jews chose the rugged and isolated mountain terrain of the Meiron Massif over the gentle rolling hills of the Lower Galilee. The Upper Galilee had remained more or less untouched by the massive urbanization policies of the Romans, who administered this region through a small confederation of four medium-sized villages. The culture of Tetracomia, or "Four Villages," was distinctive in significant ways: it was purely rural; its dominant language was Aramaic, with almost no Greek; and it lacked almost totally high Hellenistic art or architecture. Yet, numismatic evidence demonstrates that the Upper Galilee engaged in active trade with the city of Tyre, providing it with workmen, agricultural goods, and ceramics. While this remote region was therefore economically tied into city life, it remained culturally isolated.

Adjacent to and east of the Upper Galilee, in the high, elevated plateau of Transjordan, is the Golan Heights, ancient Gaulanitis. In many ways the Golan resembles the culture of the Upper Galilee, though the farther north one goes in the Golan the closer one comes to the cities of Damascus or Baneas (Caesarea Philippi). Toward the southern end of the plateau, one approaches the city of Gadara. The relative isolation of the Golan, however, and its contiguity with a large portion of Galilee, suggest that many Jews of Roman Palestine sought isolation from the mainstream out of fear or choice, and they chose a rather conservative cultural lifestyle over one more intensely involved with Roman culture and Greek language and mores. Yet Roman-style baths are known in the Golan (at Hamath Gadera) as well as other aspects of Greco-Roman culture, so the area was not completely immune to outside influence. But, in general, the villages of this large region correspond more to the Upper Galilee than to the more urban and Hellenized Lower Galilee.

It was, however, in the Lower Galilee that the bulk of the Jewish population settled, and there, from a cultural point of view, the greatest creativity was manifested. In the cities of Usha, Tiberias, and Sepphoris, the Sanhedrin, transplanted from Yavneh, flourished. In these cities the tanna'im and their successors, the amora'im, compiled their great literary and legal works. As we shall see, rabbinic culture took form precisely in those areas in which Hellenism was most prominent, rather than in the more conservative Upper Galilee.

Before turning to the Hellenistic context in which the rabbis operated, I will describe briefly the major features of the nascent culture of the tanna'im. As we have seen, traditions of legal exegesis reached back into the Second Temple period and included many Jewish groups, including the Qumran sect and the

Sadducees as well as the Pharisees. There was undoubtedly a fund of popular religious practice as well. With the rabbis now establishing themselves as the sole legal authorities, they sought to ground their traditions, which they called the "Oral Law," in Divine Authority. In sharp contrast to earlier groups, however, such as the Qumran covenanters and authors of the Book of Jubilees, the rabbis did not seek to add to Scripture itself. Although there is reason to believe that the canon of Scripture had essentially been established and closed before the end of the Second Temple period, later talmudic tradition insists that it was at Yavneh and later that these decisions were taken. The sacred status of certain books of the Bible, including the Song of Songs, Ecclesiastes, Esther, Ezekiel, and Proverbs, is represented to have been debated at Yavneh.[55] The possibility that certain books might not be included in the canon and the institution of a category of "external books" (sefarim hitzonim) were the product of the rabbinic belief that prophecy had ceased with the destruction of the Temple. Taken together, these rabbinic legends constitute a powerful technique for the transfer of power from traditional modes of authority, whether prophetic or popular, to the newly constituted institution, the House of Study, and its denizens, the rabbis themselves.

God no longer revealed Himself to His followers, so the Palestinian rabbis could not rely on direct revelation as their source of legitimacy. Instead, in a development closely related to the Hellenistic philosophical schools that traced their lineage back to Plato himself, they created a "chain of tradition" that stretched back to Moses.[56] According to this chain, the process of ordination of rabbis by their teachers had started with Moses. The earliest such chain of tradition appears in a Mishnaic book, the "Sayings of the Fathers" (Pirkei Avot).[57] Here the rabbis trace the lineage of their authority back through the Prophets and elders who had inherited the chain of ordination from Joshua and Moses. In an innovation roughly parallel in time to the second-century invention of the "apostolic succession" among Catholic Christians (and indeed among some of their opponents as well), this chain became transformed from the succession list of a particular school of rabbinic thought and practice, that of Yoḥanan ben Zakkai, to the guarantor of the sole legitimacy of the "universal" rabbinic leadership. It also served as a foundation myth for the political leadership of the patriarch.

Astonishingly, this fictitious political history leaves out the kings and priests who, of course, were the primary authorities in the First and Second Temple states. Moses is called "our rabbi" (Moshe rabenu), thus turning him into the source of rabbinic legitimacy. In addition to a chain of authority, the rabbis also claimed that their legislation was not new but was, rather, an "Oral Law" revealed to Moses at Sinai. In a kind of circular argument, they held that possession of this Oral Law was proof of their divine appointment: the chain of tradition and the Oral Law mutually reinforced each other's antiquity and authenticity.

By claiming that revelation and prophecy had ceased, the rabbis implicitly banished God from the stage of history and arrogated to themselves exclusive power to interpret the revealed law. An extraordinary talmudic legend summarizes this theory of rabbinic autonomy. A majority of rabbis take a certain position and are opposed by Rabbi Eliezer, who calls upon a series of divine miracles to prove that God Himself is on his side. The majority rejects this procedure out of hand: "It [the Torah] is not in the heavens" and "We do not pay attention to a heavenly voice *[bat kol]*." The story ends with God laughing and exclaiming: "My sons have defeated Me, my sons have defeated Me."[58] Here, then, is a legend that paradoxically invokes a heavenly voice at the end for the rejection of heavenly voices. And it is no accident that it is God's "sons" who have defeated Him, for the rabbinic consolidation of all religious authority in their own hands involved displacement of women's religious traditions, which, as we have seen, had left traces of their vitality in the synagogue and elsewhere. Women were sometimes thought to have charismatic authority, so the rabbis were clearly interested in rejecting such prophetic activity.

This legend also highlights the singular culture of disputation that we find in rabbinic literature. The rabbis grounded their laws in the Bible by hermeneutic or exegetical arguments, but they never promulgated one authoritative or dogmatic procedure. Thus, different schools, such as that of Rabbi Ishmael versus that of Rabbi Akiva, disagreed not only over substantive legal matters but also over the correct exegetical methods to derive these laws. And the proof that neither substance nor method ever became dogmatic is that minority opinions, such as that of Rabbi Eliezer, are preserved in the later edited texts. The definition, however, of who constituted a legitimate voice within the chorus of dissent was sharply constrained. Indeed, it could be argued that the very possibility of a multivocal, elastic understanding of the truth of Oral Torah was contingent on the rabbis legitimating themselves as the sole and unchallenged arbiters of Jewish life. As opposed to orthodox Christianity, as it began to develop by the end of the second century C.E., rabbinic Judaism never developed a set of dogmas, but neither was it quite as open as it seems or as some have claimed it to be. Those whom the rabbis included within their circles were allowed extraordinary freedom of expression and interpretation. Those who were excluded were suppressed, notably the groups called *minim* ("kinds" or "sects"), those Jews who did not accept universal rabbinic hegemony.

Many of the minim or heretics appear to have been Jewish Christians, and there are echoes in tannaitic literature of actual discussions or debates that were carried on between these Christians and the rabbis. These early Palestinian Christians may have been much closer to the rabbis than the later tradition wishes us to remember. They had their own halakhic interpretations that were of interest to certain rabbis. Indeed, the same Rabbi Eliezer is said to have listened favorably to a piece of law from the mouth of a min—which was perhaps one reason that he himself was suspected of heresy.[59] In fact, the story of Eliezer, as well as other rabbinic stories of dealings with Jewish Christians, demonstrate that the split between Judaism and Christianity did not occur as early and as definitively as is often believed. Christians continued to frequent synagogues throughout the second century (and undoubtedly much later as well). The "curse on the minim," which appears in the Palestinian liturgy, probably comes from the late second century, rather than from the first, as has often been assumed, as both rabbis and Church fathers tried to disentangle the two traditions.

The existence of active groups of Jewish Christians throughout the tannaitic period suggests that the Palestinian Jewish community was by no means monolithic in the generations following the destruction of the Temple. The sects of the Second Temple period were no longer on the scene, to be sure, but the fact that political power came to be concentrated in the hands of the patriarchate and the rabbis did not mean that all Jews followed their traditions. Rabbinic literature from the period testifies to many practices, including magic and astrology, with which the rabbis disagreed but which were nevertheless common among the folk.

The Jewish Christians are proof that identity was not entirely stable. We also know of groups of pagans—referred to as "fearers of heaven"—who followed certain aspects of Jewish law or worshiped the Jewish God, without converting fully to Judaism. In many of the cities of second-century Palestine, such as Caesarea, Bet She'an (Scythopolis), Acco (Ptolemais), Samaria (Sebaste), Neapolis, and Tyre, Jews lived in close proximity with non-Jews. At the beginning of the Great Revolt, tensions between Jews and non-Jews in some of these places broke out into full-fledged warfare, which was one of the causes of the Jewish rebellion against the Roman occupiers. But there was another side to these mixed cities, and that was the more positive cultural and religious discourse between the Jews and their neighbors. It is no surprise, therefore, that some of these pagans might find aspects of Judaism attractive, just as the Jews would incorporate features of pagan culture into their own.

HOW MUCH GREEK IN JEWISH PALESTINE?

We now return to the subject with which this chapter began: the degree to which the Jews adopted Greco-Roman culture in the century or two after the destruction of the Second Temple. Was Rabban Gamaliel's willingness to enter a bath boasting a statue of Aphrodite a flagrant violation of Judaism or perhaps a symptom of a much more complex relationship between Jewish and Hellenistic culture? The answer to this question is itself complicated. For instance, the rabbis were acutely aware of the idolatrous rituals of their pagan neighbors; the tractate Avodah Zara of the Talmud catalogues these practices in minute detail. One has the sense that in order to build high fences against pagan cults, it became necessary to do extensive anthropological fieldwork to describe them. Yet the general rabbinic attitude toward the pagans themselves was, on the whole, quite tolerant.

Greco-Roman culture often glorified the body, and sports such as wrestling were a prominent part of everyday life.[60] The rabbis rejected sports as an occupation and even criticized someone who acted during ritual immersion as if he were engaged in water-sports.[61] However, they did not forbid physical exercise outright, as long as it did not contradict the law. The gymnasium had evidently become far less threatening than it was prior to the Maccabean Revolt, when those opposed to Hellenism regarded as a flagrant provocation the sight of Jewish men concealing their circumcisions to participate naked in sports. Moreover, the case of Gamaliel in the bath demonstrates that care of the body, beyond the requirements of ritual purity, was acceptable to the rabbis, as long as the ritual bath *(mikveh)* was not confused with the Roman bath.

The Greek language became the *lingua franca* of many urban Jews by the second century. An educated person was expected to know Greek, and even the lower classes knew some as well. Rabbi Simon, the son of Gamaliel, claimed, "There were a thousand young men in my father's house, five hundred of whom studied the Law, while the other five hundred studied Greek wisdom."[62] His son, Rabbi Judah the Prince (the editor of the Mishnah), reinforced this view: "Why speak Syriac [Aramaic] in Palestine? Talk either Hebrew or Greek."[63] Rabbinic literature from this period contains thousands of Greek words, testifying to the prevalence of the Greek language at all levels of the culture, from the legal and political to mundane matters of the marketplace and even to prostitutes and criminals. Rather than seeing these as "loan words," it would be more useful to think of the presence of so much Greek as the sign of a new amalgam or fusion language, containing Hebrew, Aramaic, and Greek. The culture was indeed trilingual but was also in the process of forging a new language out of all three.

The influence of Greek culture can be seen in many spheres of Jewish life. The rabbinic school of Rabbi Ishmael is said to have used 13 methods of legal exegesis. It has been shown that these methods as well as other related forms of talmudic literature have their precise parallels in Greek legal hermeneutics.[64] Similarly, the Jews took over Greek artistic forms. As the Jerusalem Talmud relates about the synagogues of the third and fourth centuries: "In the days of R. Yoḥanan [third century c.e.], they began depicting [figural representations] on walls, and he did not protest; in the days of R. Abun [fourth century c.e.], they began depicting [such figures] on mosaic floors, and he did not protest."[65]

The fact that the text considers it noteworthy that the rabbis did not protest such decoration, of course, suggests that a significant change had occurred. The coins of the Hasmonaean and Herodian periods lack figural representations, which may mean that such art was considered to violate the Second Commandment prohibiting graven images. But, by the middle-late Roman period, this understanding of the commandment, if that is what it was, no longer pertained. Virtually every archaeological site from this period contains some representational art, whether it is a figurine, a statue, or something else. Zodiac themes on mosaics only appear from the fourth century on, but earlier mosaics and decorated architectural fragments often bear such figures as an eagle (Gush Halav), a sheep, or a rabbit (Nabratein).

The decorated sarcophagi from the Roman-period catacombs at Bet She'arim provide the most stunning and irrefutable evidence that the rabbis were at home with pagan art and its mythological scenes, such as Leda and the Swan. At Bet She'arim some of the most important rabbis of the time, including Judah the Prince, chose to be buried. Some scholars have suggested that pagan scenes appear because the artisans were gentile or that they are merely ornamental, without intrinsic meaning. But whatever the reason for it, the presence of mythological Greek images on the sarcophagi of the sages suggests that burial in such containers did not contradict rabbinical Judaism.

Let us conclude this discussion of the synthesis between Greek and rabbinic culture by examining one city of Lower Galilee, Sepphoris, which was the seat of the patriarchate under Judah the Prince. It was here that the Mishnah was codified in the early third century. What did this city, the seat of what we might anachronistically today call "orthodox Judaism," look like when Rabbi Judah held court there? Sepphoris dates back to the Hasmonaean period, from which time, we recall, an ostrakon with a Greek word written in Hebrew characters was found. Herod Antipas, the son of Herod the Great, had ambitious plans in the early first century for converting Sepphoris into a great oriental city, "the ornament of all Galilee," but he was not able in his lifetime to complete those objectives. The main north-south roadway of the Lower City, the cardo, may well be attributed to his activities, but the main buildings alongside the cardo come from a slightly later period, probably the second century. When Jesus was active in the Galilee, Sepphoris was probably one of the major urban centers, but, as we have observed, Jesus is not mentioned in any literary sources as having been there, though no doubt he may have visited from time to time. Moreover, the evidence for spoken Greek at Sepphoris at so early a time is almost nonexistent.

It was not until the late first or early second century that Sepphoris began to expand and become what Antipas had wished it to be. The great theater, with its 4,500 seats, though thought at one time to be from the period of Antipas, most likely dates from this period. Indeed, it is possible to suggest that the urban expansion of Sepphoris is attributable to its unique position vis-à-vis Rome during the Great Revolt. Though it was fortified and Roman troops were even stationed there for a while, sometime in the year 67 or 68 C.E. the city decided to adopt a pro-Roman stance and not be part of the larger Jewish war effort.

As a consequence of these actions, Emperor Nero granted Sepphoris the unusual privilege of minting its own coins. These coins, struck in 68 C.E., bear the legend "Irenopolis" or "City of Peace." (Apparently an influential group of Sepphoreans had been so inclined when a delegation of them welcomed Vespasian and his army into the country.) The coins also bear the legend "Neronias," in honor of the emperor Nero, but it is significant to note that they bear no image or any pagan elements that might offend more traditional elements of the city. By the time of Trajan, however (98–117 C.E.), the Sepphoris coins do in fact bear the image of the bust of the emperor, and the city is renamed "Diocaesarea." On the other side, however, are Jewish or neutral symbols: two ears of barleycorn. The coins also record the special privilege given the *boulē*, or council, of Sepphoris to mint them. A medallion with a bust of Caracalla is on the obverse of one, and a very special inscription on its reverse reads: "Diocaesarea the Holy City of Shelter, Autonomous. / Loyal [a treaty of] Friendship and Alliance with the Romans." This alliance between Sepphoris and the Roman government lends some credibility to the later talmudic legends that say Rabbi Judah had a special relationship with the emperor.

It is no wonder that the city blossomed as an urban center with an overwhelmingly Jewish majority after 68 C.E. The multiethnic character of much of the site during the Byzantine period has been confirmed by extensive analysis of animal remains. The areas presumed to be Jewish have yielded no pig bones whatsoever, and more public areas from later periods have produced only 18–20 percent pig bones, a percentage that would be quite a bit higher for one of the mixed cities.[66] All the houses had immersion pools that were most probably ritual baths, so it is reasonable to infer that they were Jewish. The Jewish demographic dominance at Sepphoris culminated when Judah moved the Sanhedrin there and undertook to edit and redact the Mishnah with the other sages who assisted in this task at the beginning of the third century C.E.

Given the heavily Jewish population of the city and the presence of Judah and his court, it is particularly striking how Hellenistic the material culture of Sepphoris was. The Dionysos mansion near the theater stems from the period of Rabbi Judah's life. This building, which was probably an inn or guesthouse for distinguished visitors, contains 15 scenes from the legends of the god Dionysos, with explanatory labels in Greek. Of all the gentile gods, Dionysos was perhaps the most popular, due no doubt to his association with wine, revelry, the theater, and the afterlife.[67] His popularity at such a nearby city as Bet She'an may have influenced the decision to depict him in the mansion in a drinking contest with Heracles.

Panel of so-called Mona Lisa from the Dionysos mosaic at Sepphoris.
The level of artistry in the mosaic is unparalleled in the ancient Near East.
(Courtesy Joint Sepphoris Project)

It is therefore clear that the rabbinic leadership saw no conflict between the Greco-Roman culture of the day and their own. Judging from Sepphoris and Bet She'arim, most of the leadership viewed that culture and its art, including mythological scenes, as a means of participating in a larger cultural identity. An inscription or menorah might identify such individuals as Jewish, and they often appeared alongside a pagan symbol. The urban environment that produced so great and productive a mixture as that which emerged in third century Sepphoris, when the Mishnah was published or promulgated, was certainly a fertile setting for a constructive symbiosis between Jewish and Hellenistic cultures. If the whole history we have discussed of Palestine under Persians, Greeks, and Romans bears witness to an extended experiment in negotiating between Jewish identity and cosmopolitan cultures, it was the tannaitic rabbis who seem to have found the most stable resolution of this dilemma. Far from attempting to preserve some archaic "biblical" culture in the face of foreign temptations, they forged a new culture out of old traditions, their own innovations, and the language, art, and law of the Greco-Roman world of which they were an active and integral part.

NOTES

1. M. Avodah Zara 3.4.

2. See Shaye J. D. Cohen, *The Beginnings of Jewishness: Boundaries, Varieties, Uncertainties* (Berkeley, 1999), 25–69.

3. See C. L. Meyers and E. M. Meyers, *Haggai, Zechariah 1–8. Anchor Bible 25B* (Garden City, N.Y., 1987), 76–82, where Haggai's priestly ruling on a very complicated matter of biblical law concerning purity is discussed. The prophet mediates the discussion between the priests and God and utilizes the answer to make his own points about the priests and biblical law. The language is very stylized and suggests a kind of proto-rabbinic discourse.

4. Haggai 2:11–12.

5. Nehemiah 8:8; see further vv. 4, 7.

6. See J. Cook, *The Persian Empire* (New York, 1983).

7. Ecclesiastes 1:2–4.

8. Ibid. 1:18.

9. Ibid. 12:12.

10. Paul Lapp argued that the two groups of stamped handles pointed to a division of power between the civil and religious authorities, a separation he argues that went back to the Persian era in the pattern of a dyarchy, governor and high priest. But there is no evidence other than this small corpus, and the Yehud coins to make a compelling case that Judaea was autonomous in the time when the Ptolemies were in charge of taxation. Indeed,

the testimony of the Zenon Papyri shows how very intimately the Ptolemies were—the papyri are from Ptolemy II Philadelphus (261–229 B.C.E.)—involved in tax collecting. Judaea was administered in the same way as Egypt, which was a royal estate, to the degree that the local population cooperated with their Ptolemaic/Egyptian administrators. There is no recognition among the papyri that deal with Egypt and Palestine that Judaea had a governor. See Paul Lapp, "Ptolemaic Stamped Handles from Judah," *Bulletin of the American Schools of Oriental Research* 172 (1963): 22–35, and R. Harrison, "Hellenization in Syria-Palestine: The Case of Judea in the Third Century B.C.E.," *The Biblical Archaeologist* 57 (1994): 98–108.

11. 1 Maccabees 1:54. See also Daniel 11:31, 12:11, and 2 Maccabees 6:2.

12. See 2 Macc. 6:4, 7.

13. 1 Macc. 4:54–56. See also 2 Macc. 10:1–8.

14. Herod's political savvy is central to understanding his life's accomplishments at home and abroad. Peter Richardson's biography, *Herod: King of the Jews and Friend of the Romans* (Columbia, S.C., 1996), examines and expands on this theme in a most compelling way.

15. Hananel was a Babylonian of "high priestly" ancestry (Ant. 15:40–41), but in m. Parah 3.5a one Hanamel *(sic)* is referred to as an Egyptian. For a full discussion of this problem, see Richardson, *Herod*, 242–44.

16. M. Avot 1:10.

17. Josephus, *Contra Apionem*, 2:179–81. Compare *Antiquities*, 18:11–24. The term "common Judaism" is based on E. P. Sanders' use in *Judaism: Practice and Belief, 63 B.C.E.–66 C.E.* (Philadelphia and London, 1992), 47–303.

18. See Martin Goodman, "The Function of Minim in Early Rabbinic Judaism," in H. Cancik, H. Lichtenberger, and P. Schäfer, eds., *Geschichte—Tradition—Reflexion: Festschrift für Martin Hengel zom 70. Geburtstag* (Tübingen, 1996) 1: 501–10.

19. The prosbul is attributed to Hillel in Sifre Deut. 113 (cf. Shebiith 10:3–4).

20. See P. Benoit, J. T. Milik, and R. de Vaux, eds., *Discoveries in the Judaean Desert II: Les grottes de Murabba'at* (Oxford, 1961), 100–104, no. 18.

21. BT Shabbat 31a.

22. For Qumran, see 1 QS 10:17–21; see also the Testament of Benjamin 4:2–34 and Matthew 5:43–44.

23. M. Avot 2:4.

24. Acts 2:42.

25. Mark 14:58, Matt. 26:61.

26. See M. Sanhedrin 11:1.

27. See Lawrence Schiffman, *Reclaiming the Dead Sea Scrolls* (Philadelphia, 1991), 73–75.

28. Moed Qatan 1:5.

29. I have discussed this topic at length in my book, *Jewish Ossuaries: Reburial and Rebirth* (Rome, 1971). My views are opposed to those of L. I. Levine in *Judaism and Hellenism in Antiquity: Conflict or Confluence?* (Seattle, 1998), 65–71.

30. See D. Flusser, *Jesus* (Jerusalem, 1997), esp. 195–206.

31. Josephus, *Contra Apionem* 2:218 (cf. fn. 17 where Josephus text is *Contra Apionem*).

32. See B. McCane, "Let the Dead Bury Their Own Dead: Secondary Burial and Mt. 8:21–22," *Harvard Theological Review* 83 (1990): 31–43.

33. Mark 8:27. Jesus appears in some places to reject overtures from non-Jews, but the geographical evidence from the New Testament suggests that he must have had gentile audiences.

34. Matthew 20:1–16.

35. Ibid. 13:24–25.

36. M. Ta'anit 3.8. for a discussion of Jewish charismatics in relation to Jesus, see G. Vermes, *Jesus the Jew* (London, 1973), 58–82.

37. Y. Sanh. 7, 19, 25d. On this subject, see M. Aubin, "Gendering Magic in Late Antique Judaism" (Ph.D. diss., Duke University, 1998).

38. See, e.g., Luke 4:15–30, 33, 38, 44.

39. This translation is taken from L. I. Levine, ed., *The Synagogue in Late Antiquity* (Philadelphia; 1987), 17. Levine has an excellent discussion of the evidence of the synagogue in the Second Temple period in his new book, *The Ancient Synagogue* (New Haven, Conn., 2000), 42–73.

40. See Bernadette Brooten, *Women Leaders in the Ancient Synagogue* (Chico, Calif., 1982), 35 (for quote), 103–35 (for discussion about a women's gallery).

41. See Cynthia Baker, "Bodies, Boundaries, and Domestic Politics in a Late Ancient Marketplace," *Journal of Medieval and Early Modern Studies* 26 (1996): 391–418, and her "Rebuilding the House of Israel: Gendered Bodies and Domestic Politics in Roman Jewish Galilee c. 135–300 C.E." (Ph.D. diss., Duke University, 1997).

42. Miriam Peskowitz, *Spinning Fantasies: Rabbis, Gender, and History* (Berkeley, 1997), offers a new perspective on rabbinic Judaism by examining everyday tasks and artifacts. She demonstrates how issues of gender were inextricably tied up with the emergence of post-Temple Judaism.

43. T. Menahot 13.20, BT Gittin 55b–56a, and B. Shabbat 119b.

44. Albert I. Baumgarten, "The Akivan Opposition," *Hebrew Union College Annual* 50 (1979): 179–97.

45. Jacob Neusner, "The Formation of Rabbinic Judaism: Yavneh (Jamnia) from A.D. 70 to 100," in Wolfgang Haase, ed., *Principat: Religion (Judentum)* (Berlin, 1979), 3–42; Daniel Boyarin, "The *Diadoche* of the Rabbis; or Tractate Avot and the Patriarchal Presumption" (forthcoming).

46. Cynthia Baker, "Neighbor at the Door or Enemy at the Gate? Notes Toward a Rabbinic Topography of Self and Other" (paper presented at the American Academy of Religion, New Orleans, 1996). But see also Levine, *The Ancient Synagogue*, 501–60.

47. Boyarin, "The *Diadoche* of the Rabbis."

48. David Aune, "On the Origins of the 'Council of Yavneh' Myth," *Journal of Biblical*

Literature 110, no. 3 (1991): 18–33; Günther Stemberger, "Die sogennante 'Synode von Jabne' und das frühe Christentum," *Kairos* 19 (1977): 14–21.

49. W. D. Davies, *The Setting of the Sermon on the Mount* (Cambridge, Engl., 1966), 256–351.

50. Reuven Kimelman, "Birkat Ha-Minim and the Lack of Evidence for an Anti-Christian Jewish Prayer in Late Antiquity," in E. P. Sanders, A. I. Baumgarten, and A. Mendelson, eds., *Aspects of Judaism in the Greco-Roman Period* (Philadelphia, 1981), 226–44; 391–403.

51. Aboth d.R. Nathan B XXXI. N. N. Glatzer translates the text in *The Judaic Tradition* (Boston, 1969), 239: "Rabban Jochanan ben Zakkai used to say: If there be a plant in your hand when they say to you: Behold the Messiah!—Go and plant the plant, and afterward go out to greet him."

52. BT Avodah Zara 18b.

53. See Daniel Boyarin, "Martyrdom and the Making of Christianity and Judaism," *Journal of Early Christian Studies* 6, no. 4 (1998): 577–627.

54. BT Shabbat 33b.

55. BT Shabbat 13b, 30b, and Hagigah 13a. See also J. T. Barrera, *The Jewish Bible and the Christian Bible: An Introduction to the History of the Bible* (Grand Rapids, Mich., 1998), 165–67, and S. Leiman, *The Canonization of Hebrew Scripture: The Talmudic and Midrashic Evidence* (Hamden, Conn. 1976). Aboth d'Rabbi Nathan A. ch. 1 reports: "Originally it is said, Proverbs, Song of Songs, and Kohelet were suppressed: for since they were held to be mere parables and not part of the Holy Writings (the religious authorities) arose and suppressed them."

56. On the Hellenistic schools, see John Glucker, *Antiochus and the Late Academy* (Göttingen, 1978). On the rabbinic chain of tradition, see Elias Bickerman, "La chaine de la tradition pharisienne," *Revue biblique* 59, no. 1 (1952): 44–54, and Boyarin, "The *Diadoche* of the Rabbis."

57. M. Avot 1:1.

58. BT Baba Metzia 59b.

59. T. Hullin 2:24.

60. For a general discussion of games and athletics in Palestine in Roman times, see Z. Weiss, "Buildings for Entertainment," in D. Sperber, *The City in Roman Palestine* (New York, 1998), 77–91.

61. See Saul Lieberman, *Greek in Jewish Palestine* (New York, 1942), 92–93.

62. BT Sotah 49b.

63. Ibid.

64. D. Daube, "Alexandrian Methods of Interpretation and the Rabbis," in *Festschrift Hans Lewald* (Basel, 1953), 27–44. See also the essays in H. Fischel, ed., *Essays in Greco-Roman and Related Talmudic Literature* (New York, 1977).

65. JT Avodah Zara 3.3 42d.

66. See Billy J. Grantham, "A Zooarchaeological Model for the Study of Ethnic Complexity at Sepphoris" (Ph.D. diss., Northwestern University, 1996).

67. See M. Smith, "On the Wine God in Palestine (Gen 18, Jn 2, and Achilles Tatius)," in *Salo W. Baron Jubilee,* vol. 2 (Jerusalem, 1975), 815–29.

SELECTED BIBLIOGRAPHY

Aubin, M. "Gendering Magic in Late Antique Judaism." Ph.D. diss., Duke University, 1998.

Aune, D. "On the Origins of the 'Council to Yavneh' Myth." *Journal of Biblical Literature* 110, no. 3 (1991): 18–33.

Baker, C. M. "Bodies, Boundaries, and Domestic Politics in a Late Ancient Marketplace." *Journal of Medieval and Early Modern Studies* 26 (1996): 319–418.

———. "Neighbor at the Door or Enemy at the Gate? Notes Toward a Rabbinic Topography of Self and Other." Paper presented at the American Academy of Religion, New Orleans, 1996.

———. "Rebuilding the House of Israel: Gendered Bodies and Domestic Politics in Roman Jewish Galilee c. 135–300 C.E." Ph.D. diss., Duke University, 1997.

Barrera, J. T. *The Jewish Bible and the Christian Bible: An Introduction to the History of the Bible.* Grand Rapids, Mich., 1998.

Baumgarten, A. I. "The Akivan Opposition." *Hebrew Union College Annual* 50 (1979): 179–97.

Bickerman, E. "La chaine de la tradition pharisienne." *Revue biblique* 59 (1953): 44–54.

Boyarin, D. "The *Diadoche* of the Rabbis; or Tractate Avot and the Patriarchal Presumption." Forthcoming.

———. "Martyrdom and the Making of Christianity and Judaism." *Journal of Early Christian Studies* 6, no. 4 (1998): 577–627.

Brooten, B. *Women Leaders in the Ancient Synagogue.* Chico, Calif., 1982.

Chancey, M., and E. M. Meyers. "How Jewish Was Sepphoris in Jesus' Time?" *Biblical Archaeological Review* 26 (2000): 18–33.

Cohen, S. J. D. *The Beginnings of Jewishness: Boundaries, Varieties, Uncertainties.* Berkeley, 1999.

Cook, J. *The Persian Empire.* New York, 1983.

Daube, D. "Alexandrian Methods of Interpretation and the Rabbis." In *Festschrift Hans Lewald.* Basel, 1953.

Davies, W. D. *The Setting of the Sermon on the Mount.* Cambridge, Engl., 1966.

Fischel, H., ed. *Essays in Greco-Roman and Related Talmudic Literature.* New York, 1977.

Flusser, D. *Jesus.* Jerusalem, 1997.

Glucker, J. *Antiochus and the Late Academy.* Göttingen, 1978.

Grantham, B. J. "A Zooarchaeological Model for the Study of Ethnic Complexity at Sepphoris." Ph.D. diss., Northwestern University, 1996.

Kimelman, R. "Birkat Ha-Minim and the Lack of Evidence for an Anti-Christian Jewish Prayer in Late Antiquity." In E. P. Sanders, A. I. Baumgarten, and A. Mendelson, eds., *Aspects of Judaism in the Greco-Roman Period.* Philadelphia, 1981.

Levine, L. I. *Judaism and Hellenism in Antiquity: Conflict or Confluence?* Seattle, 1998.

———. *The Ancient Synagogue: The First Thousand Years.* New Haven, Conn., 2000.

———, ed. *The Synagogue in Late Antiquity.* Philadelphia, 1987.

Lieberman, S. *Greek in Jewish Palestine.* New York, 1942.

McCane, B. "Jews, Christians, and Burial in Roman Palestine." Ph.D. diss., Duke University, 1992.

———. "Let the Dead Bury Their Own Dead: Secondary Burial and Mt. 8:21–22." *Harvard Theological Review* 83 (1990): 31–43.

Meyers, C. L., and E. M. Meyers. *Haggai, Zechariah 1–8.* Anchor Bible 25B. Garden City, N.Y., 1987.

Meyers, E. M. "Jesus and His Galilean Context." In D. R. Edwards and C. T. McCullough, eds., *Archaeology and Contexts in the Greco-Roman and Byzantine Periods.* Atlanta, Ga., 1997.

———. *Jewish Ossuaries: Reburial and Rebirth.* Rome, 1971.

———. "The Pools of Sepphoris: Ritual Baths or Bathtubs?" *Biblical Archaeology Review* 26 (2000): 46–48, 60–61.

———, ed. *Galilee Through the Centuries: Confluence of Cultures.* Winona Lake, Ind., 1999.

Neusner, J. "The Formation of Rabbinic Judaism: Yavneh (Jamnia) from A.D. 70 to 100." In W. Haase, ed., *Principat: Religion (Judentum).* Berlin, 1979.

Peskowitz, M. *Spinning Fantasies: Rabbis, Gender, and History.* Berkeley, 1997.

Sanders, E. P. *Judaism: Practice and Belief, 63 B.C.E.–66 C.E.* Philadelphia and London, 1992.

Schiffman, L. *Reclaiming the Dead Sea Scrolls.* Philadelphia, 1991.

Sperber, D., *The City in Roman Palestine.* New York, 1998.

Weiss, Z. "Buildings for Entertainment." In Sperber, ed., *The City in Roman Palestine,* 77–91.

The figure of Helios (Sol Invictus) on the floor of the Hammath-Tiberias synagogue. (Israel Antiquities Authority, Jerusalem)

CONFRONTING
A CHRISTIAN EMPIRE:

Jewish Culture in the World of Byzantium

ODED IRSHAI

On an early spring morning in the fourth century C.E., the Palestinian sage Hanina attended the service in the new and small but elaborately decorated synagogue of Hammat Tiberias. On his way out he was intercepted by a certain Pinehas, a wood merchant from the nearby village of Kifrah, who asked Rabbi Hanina how he could have set foot in a House of God whose floor was adorned with a figure clad like an emperor, holding a scepter and a bronze globe, with seven rays coming out of his head. Hanina was not entirely surprised by this query, for he had been perplexed when he discovered, some months earlier, this iconographical ornament. Now he replied to Pinehas that, in his judgment, the figure, though resembling the usual representation of the pagan sun god Helios, might be interpreted simply as a personification of the sun. On second thought, Hanina added, the imperial figure could be read as the personification of the Messiah, whom the liturgical poets of the day described as the "Light of Israel," "the Eternal Sun." And, he went on, he had heard that some of the Jews' most bitter opponents, the Christian preachers, faced the same dilemma concerning the adoration of the sun among their own flocks—and had come up with similar interpretations.

This dialogue (which I have invented) expresses the sentiments of the Jews who encountered this and similar icons on the floors of some half-dozen synagogues in Byzantine Palestine. It reflects both the internal cultural concerns of a society living with growing apocalyptic anxieties and the cultural encounters and tensions between that society and the surrounding pagan and Christian world of Late Antiquity.[1]

The period between the fourth and seventh centuries C.E. was one of momentous change for the inhabitants of Palestine. Gradually, Palestine ceased to be predominantly Jewish. Most of the Jews were still concentrated in the Galilee (though not all of it) and the Golan, but much of the country's non-Jewish population had been won over by Christianity, which ruled the land under the aegis of the Roman emperors. The Jews had lost their central leadership, the institution of the patriarchate; their copious literary legacy was redacted and completed; and the centers of their spiritual creativity, the academies *(yeshivot)*, were in decline. A strong trend to decentralization augmented the status of the local communities whose public life centered on the synagogues, in which liturgical poets, preachers, and interpreters from Hebrew into Aramaic were active. In the words of the midrash, "A small city, that is a synagogue, and the few people there—that is a community" (Ecclesiastes Rabbah 9:21). In short, the cultural center of gravity shifted over time from the intellectual elite of the academy to the "masses" in the synagogues. The void created among Diaspora Jews, who had previously been under the sway of the Palestinian patriarchate,[2] was increasingly filled by the leadership in Babylon, which by the early days of the Muslim conquest established itself as the dominant cultural and political center of Jewry. But the saga of Palestine and its Jewish inhabitants in this period is of utmost relevance to our understanding of the transformation of Jewish life, institutions, and culture from the nascent rabbinic period during the early centuries of the Common Era to the Middle Ages.[3]

For the most part, these alterations occurred as a result not of internal Jewish needs or pressures but of the strife caused by the growing presence and power of Christianity in Palestine. From the fourth century on, Palestine became a focus of interest for Christians who, with the help of the emperors and other powerful figures, transformed their utopian religious vision into reality.[4] The barren country's historical sites became holy places and shrines, and the idea of *Terra Sancta* (the Holy Land) was thus formed. This annexation of the local collective (though primarily Jewish) memory and topography had a major impact on the Jews' sense of identity. The encounter with victorious Christianity and some of its most zealous representatives was aptly recorded by a contemporary liturgical poet: "We do not have the splendid attire of the *kohen* [priest], and the wearers of sackcloth [monks] rule over us."[5]

Apart from this and a few other scanty references in fragmentary collections of rabbinic legal rulings, midrashic texts, liturgical poetry, and apocalyptic treatises, our main source of information on the life and culture of the Jews of this period is Christian: the writings of the Church fathers and Church historians, plus travel guides, pilgrims' itineraries, and polemical disputations.

THE THIRD-CENTURY "CRISIS"
AND THE TRANSFORMATION OF THE EMPIRE

From the early fourth century, the Roman Empire, under the rule of the enigmatic Constantine the Great,[6] was transformed into a Christian society. What exactly precipitated the "crisis" that led to this political and cultural transition is still debated, but there is hardly any doubt that its early stages were already visible during the third century, when Rome witnessed immense internal political instability—an eclipse of the Senate and a corresponding rise in the influence and power of the army—exacerbated by economic hardships (debased currency, agricultural failure) and mounting military pressures from barbarian tribes to the north and west and the assertive Persian-Sassanian kingdom in the East.[7]

The repeated and devastating Persian invasions during the middle of the century must have had some impact on the Jews residing on either side of the Euphrates in Mesopotamia and Syria, and in Palestine. Roman rule in the East was frail, and though some of the soldier-emperors managed to negotiate settlements with the mighty Persian emperor Shapur I, the region was far from secure. In some intellectual circles (among which we find the rabbis), the political situation and the attendant anxiety were seen as signs that the ailing Roman Empire was on its last legs. However, when Rome was rescued (during the 260s) from a Persian military victory and humiliation by its client princedom Palmyra in the Syrian desert, sentiments of deep disappointment were voiced. In both instances rabbinic utterances disclose a sense of what could be easily regarded as apocalyptic frustration.[8]

A dialogue of the period, recorded in the rabbinic commentary on Genesis, illustrates the Jews' intense expectation that Rome would fall:

> A *hegemon* [Roman military officer] asked a man of the House of Silani [a respected Jewish family in Tiberias]: "Who will seize [power] after us?" He [of the House of Silani] brought a piece of paper, took a quill, and wrote on it: "Then his brother emerged, holding onto the heel of Esau; they said: See old things from a new old man." (Genesis Rabbah 63:9)

Toward the end of the century, it seemed that conditions had ripened for Rome's complete collapse. When a Dalmatian cavalry officer named Diocletian seized power in 284 under somewhat suspicious circumstances,[9] people thought that he, like his predecessors, would not last long. In a Palestinian midrash, he is portrayed as the "one heralding the last king of Edom."[10]

However, much to the chagrin of the sages, this emperor succeeded in holding onto his throne for some two decades, finally relinquishing it of his own free will. Diocletian demanded that his subjects receive him with rituals of quasi-divine adoration, but he set the empire on a new path by presenting a model of orderly, planned succession that would give the empire political, defensive, and economic stability. In the Roman Orient, he redivided some of the provinces, among them the Provincia Palestina, to which he annexed territories from Arabia. This made Palestine the largest and most important of the provinces that bordered on Sassanian territory.[11]

Far more significant for our discussion here were Diocletian's religious reforms. He created a unifying religio-political mechanism through which he led the entire empire toward a monarchy under the exclusive aegis of Jupiter and Hercules, whom the Romans also venerated as a god. At the core of this new imperial theology was a system of divine cooperation with the temporal monarch, which in essence resembled Christian theological constructs.[12] These far-reaching steps, taken by Diocletian with the objective of stabilizing the government and renewing the ancient Hellenistic ideal of a monarch who represents a god, prepared the ground for the revolutionary measures of the first Christian emperor, Constantine the Great, who joined the imperial leadership cadre in 306, at the height of the great persecutions of the Church and its believers. The growing affinity of ideas between pagans and Christians exacerbated the tension, for the closer the two religious camps came to each other, the greater was the pagans' need to create effective symbols of political allegiance to the empire and the emperor.[13]

Animosity toward the Christians broke out in full force throughout the empire when decrees were issued between 303 and 312 that imposed public cultic sacrifice on all. Eusebius, bishop of Caesarea, recorded at length (in a volume called *Martyrs of Palestine*) the lives, and especially the trials, of Christians who were executed, banished, or sentenced to hard labor. This Christian ordeal, which according to Eusebius surpassed any similar event elsewhere in the empire, can be said with hindsight to have been a kind of sacrificial altar on which the land was presented to the Christians.[14] For the Jews, the internal tension that accompanied the persecutions may have added another dimension to the wobbly image of the state and to their sense of its approaching end, but they were to be disappointed. Rome did not collapse; it merely changed its appearance. Constantine, who during the years of the "Great Persecutions" was ruler of the western regions of the empire, quite dramatically issued an edict of toleration of the Christians under his control following the end of the persecutions (in 313).[15]

The embracing of Christianity by Constantine, who would 10 years later become the sole, unchallenged ruler of the empire, was to have a decisive influence on the political and religious character and culture of Palestine. The local rabbis, whose explicit reactions to this great transformation have not come down to us,[16] found some consolation in the change, and the form of their expectations of the approaching salvation adjusted to the new reality. The support of an official as important as Constantine foreshadowed the Christianization of the whole empire. Deep down, this was the historical and theological dilemma with which the rabbis contended: as Rome converted from paganism to Christianity, should they consider the Christian Empire a new entity, or simply a mutation of the old? If the latter, faithful to their own contention that redemption would come once the "empire shall fall into heresy" (Mishnah, Sotah 9, 15), then salvation was around the corner.[17] Therefore, this item in the description of the eschatological scheme of the "End of Days" was reformulated by a contemporary sage: "Rabbi Isaac said: Until the whole Empire is converted to the heresy" (BT Sanhedrin, 97a). By this textual emendation, not only was the estimated time of the End of Days postponed but, paradoxically, the Jews joined with the Christians in seeking to hasten the transformation, though from opposing motives. After all, prominent Church fathers (such as the Caesarean Origen) also believed that salvation would come about only as a consequence of the spread of the Christian faith among all the nations of the world.[18]

The Christianization of the empire presented Constantine with an extraordinary opportunity to harness the imperial system, which had already undergone some changes, in the service of a universal religion possessing a heritage, authority, and a well-established missionary apparatus. In the eyes of the Jews, this radical change apparently symbolized the transition of Rome from a nation and a rule that, though it placed a heavy yoke on the Jews, nevertheless tolerated them as a nation, to one that was the utterly polar opposite to Judaism.[19] The new situation also altered the dimensions and fundamental assumptions of contemporary Christian apologetics and polemics. For instance, Bishop Eusebius went to great lengths, utilizing much theological ingenuity, to define the Church's attitude toward the Jewish nation.[20] The rabbis must have seen the hostile relations between Caesarea (the seat of the Roman governor and thus a symbol of Rome itself) and Jerusalem as beyond reconciliation. They described both centers as though they could not endure under one roof: "That Caesarea is laid waste and Jerusalem flourishing, or that Jerusalem is laid waste and Caesarea flourishing, believe it" (BT Megillah, 6a).

A quick deliverance from the yoke of Christian Rome was, as we have seen from Rabbi Isaac's saying, an aspiration for the future. A similar sentiment was voiced by the renowned fourth-century Babylonian sage Rava, who adopted the terminology of the biblical laws concerning leprosy and applied it, metaphorically and suggestively, to the current state of affairs: "That is the meaning of the verse, He has turned all white" (Leviticus 13:13; BT Sanhedrin, 97a). Rava compared heresy to leprosy this way: just as when leprosy has completed its spread throughout the body, then—quite paradoxically—it is healed and is ready to be purified, so too when heresy (i.e., Christianity) has completed its takeover of the empire, then the time of Redemption will finally come.

It was apparently no coincidence that this simile was used in another rabbinical tradition. Famous among the stories that sprouted up around the figure of Constantine, this one described the legendary circumstances of his conversion: While the Christians were being hounded to death and Sylvester, Bishop of Rome, had gone into exile, Constantine became severely afflicted with leprosy. His physicians and other savants having failed to find a cure for his illness, priests of the Capitoline temple in Rome proposed that he come to them and immerse his body in the blood of infants. Constantine, horrified by this notion, stopped his chariot on the way to the temple and addressed the masses, resolutely declaring that it was unfitting for a warrior such as himself to be healed by such means. He immediately commanded that the babies that had already been brought to the temple be returned to their mothers. That very night the patron saints of Rome, Peter and Paul, appeared to Constantine in his dream and promised him salvation and healing by means of the immersion (i.e., baptism) that the exiled Sylvester would conduct for him; and so it happened. Cured of leprosy, Constantine tied his destiny to that of the Church and promulgated decrees for its benefit.[21] The following midrash seems to allude to the same story:

> For this reason it was said, When a person has on the skin of his body a swelling, a rash, or a discoloration, and it develops into a scaly infection on the skin of his body; and so forth (Leviticus 13:2). The text speaks of [four] kingdoms. A swelling is Babylon . . . a rash is the kingdom of the Medes . . . a discoloration is the kingdom of Greece . . . a scaly infection is the kingdom of evil, Edom [Rome], that the Holy One Blessed Be He afflicts with leprosy, and likewise its prince [the emperor]. (Midrash Tanhuma, Tazri'a, 11)

Shortly after Constantine gained control over the whole empire in 324, he began to put into practice his plan to appropriate Palestine for the Christians. From that time on, relations between the Jews and Christian Rome and its official Church were much determined by their opposing eschatologies. This was nowhere more apparent than in Palestine, the land that harbored their mutual collective memories of their formative history, and yet was to be the venue of their contradictory scenarios of the "End of Days."

GALILEE AND JUDAEA: CENTER AND PERIPHERY

By the 320s, when Constantine began to implement his plan to make the "Holy Land" Christian, the Galilee was densely inhabited by those Jews who rejected the Gospel. Eusebius and his contemporaries, who were the driving force behind the changes taking place in Palestine, were probably quite disappointed that they were, so to speak, "effectively expelled from the Galilee, the homeland of their Lord."[22] By the late third century, the Galilee had been well established as the "new Judaea," and its inhabitants began to form what seems to have been a regional Jewish identity. By weaving expressions concerning place and time into an extensive fabric, the Galilean Jews created their own local, mythic-historic past, importing many biblical narrative traditions from other parts of the land. For instance, they identified the spot where the Children of Israel crossed the Jordan not near Jericho but in a place not far from the Lake of Genesereth, and they transferred the tomb of Joshua from the region of Samaria to a location in the Lower Galilee. Through such transferals of personages, tombs, and events, the Galilean Jews sought to challenge the new, unwelcome inheritors of the land.[23] Hence it is not surprising that those who molded the sacred traditions of Christianity transferred narratives connected to Jesus from the Galilee to the terrain of Judaea and Jerusalem and downplayed the importance of other Galilean sites. Nor is it surprising that in some Jewish polemics of the same period we find the Passion of Jesus set not in Jerusalem but in Tiberias,[24] or that in Jewish apocalyptic literature we are told that the early signs and initial activities of the coming messiah will also take place in the Galilee.[25] The Christians who successfully appropriated Judaea and other areas still found it difficult, through most of the Byzantine era, to penetrate the region that had been the site of their Savior's initial success. Each side, in drawing a sort of demarcation line between them, essentially sought to claim that its own share of the land represented the whole—*pars pro toto.*

This kind of historical revisionism tells us much about the psychological framework in which Palestinian Jewish culture evolved between the fourth and seventh centuries. But this evolution did not occur in an environment dominated solely by the Christian-Jewish encounter. Rather, it bears the marks of a wider interaction with late Hellenistic culture. As Eric Meyers shows in the preceding chapter, the elaborate mosaics discovered in Sepphoris—one showing Dionysus[26] and another depicting the pagan Nile festival—are significant signs of this interaction, although the houses in which these mosaics were found have not been identified as having belonged to Jews. Other evidence is even more definitive of cross-cultural influence between Hellenistic and Jewish culture. Archaeologists have found the portrait of Siren tempting Odysseus in the house of a Jew named Leontius who lived in Scythopolis (Bet She'an). And the representation of the sun god Helios that we encountered at the beginning of this chapter, in the central panel of a Tiberias synagogue, shows that such influences were not limited to the private sphere. The meaning and significance of these mosaics have been evaluated in several ways[27] as evidence of an internalization of influences with various degrees of compromise, or as a sign of a diffused "realm of culture."[28] But in either case, Jews, like Christians of the time, were part of a wider Greco-Roman culture.

The Galilean cultural matrix was exceptional only in its intensity and duration, for there were similar encounters between Jews and other religious and ethnic groups elsewhere in Palestine in towns such as Lydda (Diospolis), as well as in the metropolis of Caesarea. In these centers the Jews were considerably outnumbered, though the surrounding areas were studded with small and medium-sized Jewish communities.[29] In Caesarea, the city with the most mixed population in Palestine, Samaritans, pagans, Christians, and an ever-increasing number of Jews lived side by side in relations that fluctuated between reserved neighborliness and frequent friction. The city's cosmopolitan character had been shaped by its position as an administrative and military center of Roman (and, later, Byzantine) rule and as an important international port.[30] It was in Caesarea that an almost unique social and religious fabric of life was woven among the different religions. Thus, in fourth-century Caesarea one could hear Jews—possibly immigrants from the Diaspora—recite the *Shema* in Greek.[31] (This astonished the sages; nevertheless, they accepted it.) And there one might come upon a Jew who was a stagehand and maintenance man in the local theater.

The Christian intellectual elite of Palestine had established itself in Caesarea, led by the Church father, preacher, and exegete Origen (d. ca. 253) and his successor Eusebius (d. 339), the most prominent bishop of his day. Rabbi Abbahu of Caesarea (d. ca. 300), who was acquainted with the Greek culture and language (and may even have been fluent in it), provided his daughters with a Greek education, and was a constant visitor to the home of the Roman governor, was extremely well suited to serve as the main Jewish spokesman in the developing conflict between Judaism and Christianity. Like Origen, Abbahu understood that at the heart of the conflict lay what was also the most important element linking the two camps: the Bible. Abbahu declared to the *minim* (heretics; that is, Judeo-Christians or gentile Christians) of his city that their neighbors, the Jews, had the responsibility of studying the Bible in order to respond to their arguments—just as, a few decades earlier, Origen had advised a friend to study

the Bible diligently so that he would be able to combat Jewish claims and interpretations.[32] Caesarea thus became an important outpost on the frontline of the
Jewish-Christian encounter.

Although the importance of Caesarea in Roman Palestine cannot be exaggerated, the fourth century saw a diminution of its status when the province was
subdivided into several smaller regions, each with its own administrative center.
Nonetheless, Caesarea continued to have an influential status in Palestine, and it
strove forcefully to preserve its primacy in Church administration against the
rising power of the bishopric of Jerusalem, which in the first half of the fifth century was declared a Christian patriarchate.[33]

Although Caesarea and Diospolis were outstanding centers of Torah study in
their own right, the threads of spiritual creativity woven in them were drawn to
and from the Galilee, where most of the religious literature—Talmud, midrash,
and apparently the wealth of early liturgical poetry too—took their final shape.
These works, most of which were compilations of earlier material (though some
were composed in this period) tell us nothing about their authors, and only
careful reading between the lines teaches us something about the circumstances
of their creation. Thus, without ignoring the important contribution of Caesarea and Diospolis, one can state that the Galilean intellectual elite was the driving force shaping Jewish culture in this period.

THE SON OF DAVID AND THE SONS OF AARON: A TRANSITION IN LEADERSHIP

An important ingredient in the cultural identity of the Palestinian Jews was the
hereditary office of the patriarch. Perceived by Christians and, to a certain extent, by the Jews as something like a client king, he nevertheless was a respected
political figure with substantial communal functions and power, his authority
having been ratified in fourth-century imperial legislation.[34] We possess reports
that the patriarch was involved in administrative appointments made by the
secular authorities, and that he intervened in the affairs of the Diaspora communities. For a while his political influence was so great that at least once,
toward the end of the fourth century, a conflict between a patriarch named
Gamaliel VI and a senior Roman official led to the latter's execution.[35]

The patriarchs also served as religious and cultural figures, as is apparent
from the wide-ranging correspondence between Gamaliel V and the famous
fourth-century Antiochean orator Libanius.[36] However, by this period we witness signs of decline in the patriarchate.[37] At the beginning of the third century,
Rabbi Judah the Prince had been the uncontested leader of the laity as well as

of the intellectual elite (the sages), but during the fourth century the emperor himself had to forbid public displays of contempt of the patriarch.[38] The third-century patriarchs are known to us by their names and their deeds (which were not always approved of by some of the contemporary sages), but with those of the fourth century we are much less familiar. In fact, much of our information about them emanates from Christian sources that tended to denigrate them. But it has been suggested that the later patriarchs lacked the spiritual stature and the level of learning of their forerunners and gradually became alienated from the community, which they treated aloofly and haughtily.[39] As early as the beginning of the fourth century, matters had reached such a point that a prominent sage, Rabbi Jeremiah, sent a letter to the patriarch containing an especially insulting phrase: "To hate those who love you and to love those who hate you" (JT Megillah, 3:2b). Lurking in the background of this local contest of authority and prestige was another, between the head of the Babylonian Jewish center, the *Rosh Gola*, and the Palestinian patriarchate. As Isaiah Gafni argues in the next chapter, in the second half of the third century the rising center of Judaism in the East was claiming superiority over the Land of Israel in more than one sense. The Babylonian community's antique roots and its long and stable history—only a small portion of which has been preserved in the records—became a source of deep cultural "local patriotism." And when its leadership, too, claimed a Davidic pedigree, this thriving cultural and spiritual center asserted itself vigorously as an alternative to the one in Palestine.[40]

However, the more immediate interests of the patriarchate, especially during the fourth and early fifth centuries, concerned the Jews and their Christian opponents. The patriarch did serve his people as a sort of perpetual symbol of Jewish "sovereignty," especially in the Diaspora communities,[41] but this image, based on the notion that the patriarch was a descendant of the House of David, irritated Christians who could not tolerate another claimant to Christ's royal, messianic pedigree. A long stream of polemical statements defamed the image of the patriarchs and the patriarchal family, a wave of criticism that intensified during the fourth century.

Here is a story that illustrates this dispute and the methods adopted by the Christians to win it. About the year 375, the fanatical Church father Epiphanius of Salamis (in Cyprus), who had been raised in the vicinity of Eleutheropolis (Beth Govrin, in the southwestern area of Judaea), recorded a testimony that he had heard some two decades earlier from a Jew named Joseph, a confidant of the Jewish patriarch. Joseph, who subsequently converted to Christianity and became close with Emperor Constantine, was actually relating the story of his own life and the circumstances of his conversion, but he spun his tale around his intimate acquaintance with the patriarch. Among other things, he recounted the ailing patriarch's concealed conversion to Christianity, when he supposedly had secretly received the sign of Jesus (i.e., baptism) from the bishop of Tiberias. As if this were not enough, Joseph supplied Epiphanius with tales about the decadent lifestyle in the household of the patriarch, elaborating on the wretchedness of his sons "who acted like reckless good-for-nothings."[42] Epiphanius emphasized the patriarch's role in the leadership of the Jewish community (corroborated by other Christian and pagan writers), which only made more poignant his underlying message that those who accepted this tarnished leadership really deserved a new patron, the Church.

Although it is doubtful whether any of the Jews actively wanted to do away with the patriarchate, it is difficult to overlook the simultaneous eruption of criticism from within the community and the attack from without. Even given the meager historical value of the tales recounted by Epiphanius,[43] his "message" must have played a role in the battle of disinformation that was an attempt to abolish the institution. The portrayal of the patriarch's sons as unworthy to inherit the office, and the attempt by some other Church fathers to disprove the family's genealogical claim to it,[44] made a fitting backdrop to Joseph's libelous tale of the patriarch's alleged conversion.

However, from a literary point of view, the episode narrated by Epiphanius can be seen as a cultural duel, full of symbolism, between the "doomed" Jewish nation and the victorious Christian power.[45] Against the "inheritance of the flesh" that passed from father to son in the patriarchal family, the Christians proposed an "inheritance of the spirit."[46] The patriarchs symbolized the leadership of the vanishing past, and the Church symbolized that of the felicitous present and future. Not everyone, however, shared these polemical sentiments, because they led to a conflict of interest between the Church and the imperial authorities who desired to preserve the power and dignity of the patriarchate in order to monitor and control their relations with the Jewish community. But, though official policy lagged behind the wishes of the Church, it was not by much. The mounting pressure of venomous Christian propaganda, coupled with what the authorities deemed unlawful behavior by Patriarch Gamaliel VI, led in the autumn of 415 to the stripping of his honor and the curbing of his power.[47] (Ironically and perhaps as a sign of collapse of patriarchal power, this was the very Gamaliel who only a few years earlier had been able to orchestrate the execution of a Roman official.) By 429, the Roman authorities were alluding to the patriarchate as a thing of the past.

Nothing is known of the methods, composition, and character of the new leadership. However, if we may judge from contemporary inscriptions and later evidence, some vestige of the patriarchate was preserved, especially in matters having to do with the ties between the community in Palestine and those in the Diaspora. For example, the funerary inscription of the daughter of a sixth-century Jewish municipal leader in Venosa in southern Italy mentions the presence and eulogies of two emissaries and two sages ("Apostoles and Rebbites") from the Land of Israel.[48] As in the days of the patriarchs, these emissaries may have been sent to collect contributions (despite the legal limitations imposed by the authorities on fundraising at the end of the fourth century), but their primary objective was probably to guide the Diaspora communities in spiritual matters.

The demise of the patriarchate occurred around the time when Jewish literary activity in Palestine was in decline. The Jerusalem Talmud and the classical *Midrashei aggadah* (a compendium of exegetical and homiletic material on the Bible that also incorporated other legendary and folkloristic tales) were being redacted. Indeed, most of the canon of Jewish lore was completed at this time,[49] a development that led to a loss of status and prestige for the Palestinian centers of learning and their leaders. Thus, by the mid-fifth century, the historical role of the two leading elements of Jewish cultural and political life in Palestine seems to have come to an end. The creation of halakhic works did not entirely cease, but the format changed to compendia of rabbinical dicta such as the treatise known as *Sefer ha-Ma'asim* (The Book of Rulings).[50] This compilation, extensive sections of which have survived in the Cairo Genizah, reflects everyday life in Palestine during the sixth and seventh centuries. The tone of these dicta, which may have originated in the registers of the rabbinic court in Tiberias, is that of late Hellenistic culture, and they are suffused with the legal and economic terminology of their surroundings.

What we learn about the lives of women is especially fascinating; for example, "And it is forbidden for a woman to adorn her daughter and take her out to the marketplace because she is risking her life, and a woman who has perfumed herself and goes to [houses] of idol worship is to be flogged and her hair shaved off."[51] The rabbis' objective, the preservation of female modesty, was compatible with the demands Church leaders made of the Christians.[52] The Jews sought to adopt some of the practices of the surrounding society, because they were fearful of the social proximity between the groups. Indeed, questions that emerged in the wake of instances of conversion make up much of this collection of rabbinical rulings. It is tempting to envisage the compilation of this practical compendium and the earlier redaction of the Talmud as being something of a rabbinical equivalent of the codification of Church canonical and Byzantine imperial laws that was achieved during the fifth and sixth centuries.[53]

Thus, by the middle of the fifth century, the Jewish cultural elite was facing a substantial transformation. There are strong grounds to assume that the vacuum created by the decline of the patriarchal dynasty, and in some sense also of the rabbinical leadership, was being filled by another element that claimed an aristocratic lineage: the priestly caste. Although the priests' status had diminished since (and because of) the destruction of the Temple, they nonetheless represented the most significant era of the Jewish past, its cultic age, which every Jew prayed would return. As early as the Yavneh generation (ca. 100 C.E.) and for hundreds of years afterward, the priests sought to maintain their special status and influential position, at times in conflict with the sages, but more often with their homologous leaders, the patriarchs as well as with the Babylonian exilarchs. When the Palestinian patriarchate no longer existed, they were, it seems, presented with an opportunity to reenter the public sphere. Explicit hints of this major change have been preserved, surprisingly enough, in Christian writings. Time and again, fifth- and sixth-century Christian authors supply information about the leading priests in Tiberias. Thus, we learn that a man named Pinhas (a priestly appellation) from that city participated in a Christian assembly that convened in Alexandria in 552, as an expert on the calendar.[54] Elsewhere we read that priests sent by the Jewish authorities in Tiberias were involved in agitation against the Christians by the Judaizing Himyarite kingdom in southern Arabia (which will be discussed later in this chapter).[55] However, the most significant attestation comes from a series of anecdotes in a treatise composed in Carthage (ca. 634) by two Jewish converts to Christianity. The two, Jacob and Justin, who lived in Acare and Sycamina (near Haifa) and converted during the days of the Byzantine emperor Heraclius, describe priests as leading communal figures in places like Tiberias and Acco.[56] It is unlikely that such recent converts made faulty use of the term "priests" or were anachronistically reviving a concept from the biblical or post-biblical past. What sort of leadership did this priestly caste represent? Was it perceived by the community as a substitute for the patriarchate? Most probably not; however, our sources do not provide a clear answer.

PRIESTS, PREACHERS, AND SAGES: THE SYNAGOGUE VS. THE HOUSE OF STUDY

Although the reemergence of the priests was probably facilitated by the leadership void, it was more an effect of the relocation of the public center of gravity from the house of learning to the synagogue. The priests stood at the core of this transformation of Jewish communal life. With the disintegration of the traditional leadership, the synagogue remained the last element that could still serve the Jews as a focus of attraction. A set of three imperial laws promulgated between the years 415 and 438 prohibited them from building or establishing new synagogues. But a short while later, around 442, in Constantinople, the imperial center of Christian rule, the Jewish community procured permission from the local governor to build a synagogue in the copper market, not far from Hagia Sophia. And though this building was confiscated a few years later by Pulcheria, the sister of Emperor Theodosius II, who dedicated the edifice to Mary, this instance demonstrates just how strictly the law was obeyed.[57] However, archaeological research has revealed that, at least in Palestine, and especially in the Galilee, these laws were defied and the construction of new synagogues actually increased.[58]

In a flourishing synagogue culture, the priests played a major role, especially in the formulation of the liturgy. It is in this period that a list of "priestly courses" was drawn up which included the names of the various watches (divisions) that had served in rotation in the Temple, and their places of residence (mostly in the Galilee). Though historicity of this document is subject to doubt, its importance is more symbolic than historical. The many early liturgical poems *(piyyutim)* dealing with the list, the references to it in synagogue inscriptions in Palestine and the Diaspora (in Yemen), and the custom of publicly recalling the watches and their service every Sabbath in the synagogues reinforced the prestige of the contemporary priests' lineage and antiquity.[59] The priests understood that, in order to sustain the Jewish community and its spiritual assets in a hostile world, they must mold that community's identity and foster it by forging a link to the synagogue. They revived the saga of the priestly lineage of the Hasmonaean kings. Synagogue ritual and liturgy reflected increasing messianic themes in prayers that envisioned the approach of a new age in which the Temple would be rebuilt and its cult reinstated.[60] Only the priests, who were historically the custodians of this cult, could lead this new liturgical synagogue ritual.

The description "A small city, that is a synagogue" (Ecclesiastes Rabbah 9:14) signifies precisely the social and cultural atmosphere of this period. Synagogue inscriptions that include the terms *kehillah* (community) and *kehillah* or *karta kadishah* (holy community or village) illustrate this dictum.[61] In this new context, the influence of the communal leaders, the congregational leaders *(archisynagogoi)*, the attendants (here called *ḥazanim*), and the priests increased greatly, whereas the status of the sages, traditionally connected with halakhic teachings and rulings, somewhat declined.[62] How did this transformation come about?

Earlier we described the decline of the regional centers of learning and national institutions, and the decentralization of Jewish cultural and public life that shifted the center of gravity from the cities (Tiberias, Sepphoris, Caesarea, and others) to the smaller towns and the rural areas.[63] The decentralization of communal life has registered, however faintly, in one of the most central elements of congregational life: the yearly calendar. In some communities, the local calendar was at variance with the one supervised by the rabbis.[64]

The flowering of the local communities centered on the synagogues. Despite the imperial ban mentioned earlier, the Jews were able to build and embellish their synagogues and make them centers of communal and cultural activity as well as worship.[65] For example, on the floor of the Ein Gedi synagogue (western shore of the Dead Sea), an Aramaic inscription cautioned the congregants against dissension and slanderous speech, and above all against the revelation of communal secrets to the gentiles.[66] Although synagogue premises were also used as houses of learning, they were, for the most part, not a locus of this traditional function of the rabbinical class. Christian sources describing synagogue activity do not mention the rabbis, and no rabbi known to us from the literary corpus is mentioned in any of the numerous synagogue inscriptions.[67] On the contrary, some rabbis seem to have disapproved of synagogue practices, and others stated

A votive inscription commemorating a certain R. Isi, a priest, for donating
a mosaic floor for the Hurvat-Susiya (south of Hebron) synagogue.
(From *Qadmoniot*, Vol. 5, 1972, Israel Exploration Society, Jerusalem)

openly that they held the academy in higher regard. Thus, in the social and cultural matrix of Late Antiquity, the academy and the synagogue seem to have been distinct, even contradictory institutions, serving different social strata.[68] The vast repertory of synagogue inscriptions in the everyday languages of the people—Hebrew, Greek, and most frequently Aramaic—reflects a social world that is quite diverse and stratified, with great involvement of the prosperous and the influential. In one inscription we encounter Severianos Ephros, the highly praised archisynagogos of Tyre who settled in Sepphoris. In another, among the worshipers at the famous synagogue at Sardis in Asia Minor we find city councilors and procurators. Still other inscriptions disclose the trades and professions of members of the congregation—wood merchants in Gaza, *scholastikoi* (lawyers) in Sepphoris—and their financial means, revealed by their contributions to the synagogues.[69] As Eric Meyers has suggested in his chapter, there is even evidence in the inscriptions that women served as leaders of the synagogues. Scholars are still debating whether they held true leadership functions or were merely wealthy benefactors; it is also doubtful whether such women had any liturgical functions.

However, the growth of the synagogues may well have further weakened the social cohesion and solidarity between the different communities, especially those of the Babylonians, Alexandrians, Tyrians, and others who had returned to Palestine with a sense of common origin, established their own synagogues, and made little effort to integrate with the larger community.[70] It is possible that rudeness and arrogance directed at these immigrants (for example, the harsh statements of the rabbis concerning the Babylonians) contributed to their alienation.[71]

Communal worship in Palestine (particularly in the Galilee and its periphery) inspired great intellectual and spiritual works—the piyyutim (a term derived from the Greek word for poetry) and the homilies. Whatever the origin of the piyyut, or the historical circumstances surrounding the birth of this novel facet of Jewish spiritual culture,[72] these liturgical hymns were composed to accompany sections of the service and the order of reading the Pentateuch and accompanying chapters from the prophets,[73] and they shaped the nature of the synagogue ritual for generations to come.

Among the *paytanim* (liturgical poets) were quite a few priests, such as Yose ben Yose (perhaps the earliest of them all, though whether he actually was a priest has been questioned), Simeon ha-Kohen be-Rabi Megas, Yoḥanan ha-Kohen, and Pinḥas ha-Kohen son of Jacob from Kifra (a suburb of Tiberias), nearly all of them Galileans.

The return of the priests to the cultural arena revived an old, esoteric, but la-

A Cairo Genizah fragment of a Jewish Palestinian Mahzor (a festival prayer book)
from c. early tenth century C.E. This particular text is a liturgical poem lamenting
the contemporary status of the priesthood due to the ruination of the Temple.
(Bodleian Library, University of Oxford; MS Heb. d.41 fol. 1-42714/1)

tent trend in Jewish thought: the mystical speculations expressed in the Hekhalot literature.[74] This priestly mystical literature has strong echoes of the Dead
Sea scrolls from nearly half a millennium earlier.[75] The paytanim lamented that
the status of the priesthood was lowly because the Temple was still in ruins, and
they expressed profound yearning for its reconstruction. Long works were com-

posed on the high priest's rite in the Temple on Yom Kippur. Indeed, the poets'interest in such subjects did not derive only from their need to remind the public of the prestige of the priesthood. Rather, it seems that they intended to arouse and express intense messianic expectations that were reinforced by the increase in apocalyptic predictions among their contemporaries, most notably from the fifth century on.

Preoccupation with the oppressive subjugation of the Christian world and concern with the approaching redemption were not limited to a few individuals. The poets expressed the deepest, most existential aspirations of the entire community of worshipers; moreover, the rise of Jewish liturgical poetry and the significant role of salvationist themes within it were paralleled in time, and perhaps even in content, by a similar process among Christians. From the second half of the fourth century, major transformations were wrought in the Christian religious rites, changes in which the Jerusalem Church played a decisive role. During the fifth century, especially in its latter years, anxious Christians aroused by millennial anxiety were also awaiting the approaching Salvation. There are signs that these phenomena, occurring within both the Jewish and the Christian folds, were connected in some way, inspiring mutual agitation; however, such a conclusion necessitates further study.[76]

The fact that piyyutim were accepted and integrated into the established liturgy with little opposition indicates that we are dealing with works suitable for all. These works were certainly complex, embracing various cultural tastes, but apparently they were also accessible to the general public's level of knowledge and understanding. However, this body of work, composed in a variety of languages (Hebrew for liturgical purposes, Aramaic for joyous occasions and eulogies, with touches of Greek), doubtless reflected to some extent the gap between the lofty style of the elite and the more common taste and proficiency of the populace.[77]

The liturgical poets had important partners in the process of transforming the synagogue into a central institution of Jewish society in Palestine as well as in the Diaspora. These were the translators (from Hebrew to Aramaic) and the preachers. Both accompanied the three-year cycle of readings from the Torah. (Some scholars contend that a one-year cycle also existed in Palestine, and consider it to be a more ancient one that for some reason has become fixed in people's minds as a Babylonian custom.) Translations into the Aramaic vernacular, which was first used in services during the Second Temple period (as is demonstrated in both the New Testament and rabbinic writings),[78] accompanied the public readings from the Torah, a verse or two or three at a time, and provided explanation and clarification by incorporating midrashic material as well as popular lore and customs.[79] The rabbis established the manner in which the translator was to carry out his task, seeking to prevent his art from overshadowing the reading itself; but he became part of the regular, paid staff of the synagogue. The narrator mediated between the biblical text and its "consumers," the congregants, who came from many social strata.

However, the full integration of the biblical text with the public celebration of the holidays (Sabbaths, festivals, days of atonement and mourning) was achieved by means of the public sermon. This custom, too, was an ancient one, going back to the Second Temple period.[80] At the end of the third century, there was an about-face in the sages' attitude toward synagogue sermons and those who prepared and delivered them. It is difficult to know what caused this turnabout and whether or not it was connected to the decline in creativity in the academy. According to at least one tradition, the growing stature of the sermon was an outcome of the unique, social needs of the public as it experienced increasing distress. Thus, for example, Rabbi Isaac said: "Formerly, when a man possessed a *prutah* [small coin], he yearned to hear passages from the Mishnah and the Talmud, and now when he does not have a prutah, and especially when we are sick of [being oppressed by] the government, a man longs to hear words from the Bible and the Aggadah."[81] However, we must distinguish between scholarly sermons and addresses whose place was in the house of study[82] and the homilies that were delivered in the synagogue in the presence of tanners, filigree makers, women, and infants, a distinction that has some bearing on the dissimilarity we have described between the synagogue and the House of Study *(bet midrash).*[83] Scholars have recently concluded that, though many anecdotes are scattered through the Talmud and the aggadic literature concerning the delivery of sermons in public (that is, to the community), these sermons were in fact expounded to students in the houses of study.[84] They were learned and elitist in content and vocabulary, and were generally not understood by the ordinary public, although there is some evidence that at times members of the multitude did also flock to the houses of study.[85] It stands to reason, however, that the sages fostered an exalted image of the lessons taught in the bet midrash while they disparaged the synagogue preachers for being able to attract a larger audience. The popular sermons were delivered in the synagogue as an exposition of and elaboration upon the cycle of biblical recitations (along with their rendering into Aramaic) as part of the liturgical rite. The topics discussed in the sermons addressed the immediate issues that weighed upon the community, and, as in the liturgical poems, the vocabulary was adapted to suit the hearers. When matters of Jewish law were part of the sermons, they were presented clearly so as not to mislead the listeners.[86]

Enjoyment of the sermon and adherence to its message depended on the preacher's merits, the content of his address, and the manner in which it was delivered. His strength lay in his ability to fascinate his audience and give it not only a moral lesson but entertainment and aesthetic pleasure as well. Allegories, tales, expositions, and narratives done up in a wealth of rhetorical devices imbued his talk with beauty and helped to draw the public's attention, to the point that the rabbis compared these sermons to the Roman theater or circus, praising the Jews who attended the former and avoided the latter.[87] These rhetorical devices did fall short of the perfected art of classical civilization, and it is doubtful whether even those aggadic scholars who were exposed to Greek culture were familiar with the rhetorical manuals compiled by Menander of Laodicea or Quintilianus.[88] However, the public sermon served to bind and sustain the community and was a tool of the first order for persuasion, or illustrating a point. If we are to judge by the sarcastic comments of the Church Father Jerome, the preachers did their work well, since "they succeed through theatrical means in causing their listeners to believe in the fictions that they invent."[89]

The third element in the public liturgical framework was the work of the artists who decorated the synagogues with wall paintings or mosaics. These decorative elements first appeared in synagogues during the third and fourth centuries and, as Eric Meyers has shown in his chapter, even enjoyed the sanction of the sages, or at least a tacit approval that may have stemmed from a growing acceptance of the importance of such ornamentation as a liturgical tool. Synagogue architecture also changed at this time, especially in the Galilee, where some of the later edifices (fifth to seventh centuries)—such as Beit Alpha and Sepphoris and others noted for their elaborate internal decorations—showed the influence of the Byzantine basilica style.[90] Forerunners of the embellished interior were also to be found in Diaspora communities, such as in the third-century synagogue in Dura Europos, on the Euphrates.

The decoration of the synagogue was intended to be a visual narration of the biblical stories and at times to represent the thoughts and allusions of the preachers. A comment by the Church Father Gregory of Nyssa (second half of the fourth century) can well be applied to synagogue floor mosaics. Referring to the Church of Theodore the Martyr, Gregory wrote: "The hues of the ornamentation in the church are veritably like a book that speaks, for painting even if silent knows how to speak from the wall."[91] The biblical scenes, the complex symbols, and their interrelationship required from the observer a considerable intellectual effort, though here too we are dealing not with an elitist work but with one that, like the piyyut and the sermon, was adapted to the taste and ability of the observer.

Indeed, a great deal of effort went into the decoration of the synagogues. The stunning mosaic floors offered an abundance of decorations and symbols, some of them clearly Jewish (candelabra, shovels for incense burning, the four species of plants shown on Sukkot to represent the harvest in the Land of Israel, and the ram's horn) and biblical (especially the Binding of Isaac), and others distinctly non-Jewish (the zodiac, Helios, and representations of the four seasons). Scholars may differ on the nature and interpretation of this amalgamation of motifs; nonetheless, the synagogue was a faithful reflection of the cultural world in which it stood. It is no wonder that, in an atmosphere so redolent of syncretism, the Jews did not hesitate to adopt, for instance, the symbol of Helios, nor to turn toward it in prayer, as we see in the fourth-century *Sefer ha-Razim* (The Book of Secrets, a treatise on magic).[92]

The mosaic floor recently discovered at Sepphoris contains a wealth of biblical scenes and symbols, some unknown heretofore. Analysis of the individual panels and of the mosaic as a whole suggests that the unifying motif is God's promise to Abraham (in the Binding of Isaac) and the expected Redemption. This connection was made clear to those frequenting the synagogue by depicting the consecration of Aaron the Priest and the daily sacrificial offerings, the latter symbolizing the continuity of the ritual even in a time when actual sacrifices could not be carried out. Many sermons and piyyutim were heard in that synagogue on those very topics. By integrating what was heard and what was seen, the expectation of Redemption was instilled in those who entered the synagogue to pray.[93]

Salvation was linked, no doubt, to another motif: that of undisguised hostility toward the Sons of Esau, that is, Edom, the Empire of Heresy (i.e., Christianity) that ruled over the Jews. In the world of the sages, the polemic with the Church was conducted on an intellectual plane in a cultured manner, but in the emotionally charged atmosphere of the synagogue the dispute became rancorous. The poets set the tone, filling their work with expressions of scorn toward the Christian Savior, as in the words of the paytan Yannai: "Those who praise the *kilai sho'a*" ("generous miser"; also a play on the Hebrew name for Jesus and on the word for "salvation," *yeshu'a*). And they demanded of God, "Uproot the Empire of Dumah" (*Piyyutey Yannai* 11; again a play on words: Dumah = Edom, and perhaps also an allusion to Roma = Rome). (A Byzantine melody called "On Earthquakes and Fires," written by one Romanos, who lived in Constantinople, may have been a Christian reply to those aspirations. It mocked the ruins of the Temple of Solomon by contrasting them with the splendor of the Church of Hagia Sophia, which had also been damaged by Heaven with fire and earthquake, followed by local political upheaval known as the Nika ("victory")

revolt in 532 C.E., but had immediately been reconstructed.)[94] Despite these insults, the synagogues, especially during the festivals, seem to have attracted not
only Jews but also Christians with Judaizing tendencies. In the late fourth century, the Church Father John Chrysostom bitterly attacked members of his congregation who attended synagogue services on Sabbath and other festivals.[95]

The similarities between the Jewish and Christian cultures in Palestine
extended even further. As the focal point of Jewish life shifted from the scholarly
elitism of the academy to the public arena of the synagogue, a parallel development occurred among the Christians, albeit in a different manner. Hesi-
tantly, and despite the open hostility of the zealots, the Christians adorned their
churches with handsome mosaic floors and frescoed walls.[96] By the fourth century, the churches echoed to orderly, well-executed liturgical ceremonies that
were based on selected readings from Holy Scripture and accompanied by sermons. Christian liturgy attained a significant level of refinement and was shaped
by the hallowed space in which the services were held, both inside the edifice and
outside it (in nearby holy sites). The Church authorities attempted to create a
nexus and harmony between the two kinds of space and to make the worshiper-
pilgrim feel as close as possible to the event being celebrated. Indeed, the Christian world was engaged increasingly in the sanctification of space,[97] a concept
made especially tangible in the Jerusalem liturgy that was developed in this pe-

A fresco from sixth-century Caesarea, depicting three Christian holy men
in a posture of prayer. (Israel Antiquities Authority, Jerusalem; no. 2000-803)

riod and was to influence decisively the liturgies of other Christian centers such as Antioch and Constantinople.[98]

While there was considerable innovation in ritual and ornamentation in the churches, when it came to sermons the Christian preachers had recourse to the traditional world of classical rhetoric. Although they would never admit it, their writings demonstrate that they internalized the devices but avoided the pomposity, because the public welfare required that the sermon suit the audience. Origen, the famous third-century presbyter of Caesarea, saw the high priest's service in the Temple—slaughtering the sacrificial animal, flaying it, separating its organs, and sacrificing them—as a kind of paradigm of the task of the preacher, who stripped the text of its attire and divided it into its several meanings (from the plain and simple to the allegorical).[99] If the preachers took care to follow this procedure, the worshippers who heard his sermon would be able to savor the scriptural texts. Fourth-century Church fathers such as Jerome and John Chrysostom repeatedly advised the preachers to take into account the narrow minds and shallow knowledge of their listeners, and to deliver their sermons calmly and logically, not loudly or hastily.[100]

The centrality of the rules of rhetoric to Christian public discourse was clearly expressed in pictorial art, both in choice of subject matter and in the location of works of art within the church space. In this place of public assembly, it was especially important to combine all the components of the discourse described above into a unified setting. Thus, in Christian society too the house of worship became the religious center of attention,[101] part of a remarkable trend toward the democratization of public and religious life. John Chrysostom asked: "Did you know of such a burning desire to hear sermons among our Christian contemporaries?"[102]—one more indication of the increasing involvement of the simple masses in shaping the spiritual environment. In church, Christian men and women absorbed the principles of their faith and fostered and refined their emotional world. But they were also exposed in sermons and prayers to propaganda and vicious attacks on the enemies of the Church, among whom the Jews occupied a special place.

Thus, the Church and the Synagogue faced one another, each struggling to preserve its identity, each rejecting the other. From the early fourth century the Church had enjoyed the advantage of imperial sponsorship, and by the middle of the sixth century the authorities were intervening harshly in synagogue affairs. In 553 Emperor Justinian issued a decree that was intended to redirect the contents of study and ritual activity. Study of the Mishnah *(Deuterosis)* was forbidden, and readers of the Bible in Greek were specifically obliged to use the Septuagint or the Aquila translation. This was part of the emperor's campaign to bring the Jews "to the prophecies contained in [the Holy Books] through which they will announce the great God and the Savior of the human race, Jesus the Christ."[103] If further proof were needed of the vitality of the synagogue and its centrality to Jewish culture in this period, this blunt attack on the institution would convince us. The monitoring of the synagogues is emblematic of the disintegration of the Jewish community, whose other traditional institutions and authority systems were, as we have seen, in decline. The end of the Palestinian hegemony approached while the Babylonian center arose that was to govern Jewish society for centuries to come.[104]

The author of an early-ninth-century pamphlet known as "The Epistle of Pirkoi ben Baboi" describes from a Babylonian perspective the cultural and spiritual bankruptcy of the Palestinian Jewish community in the period under Christian rule:

> Thus, said Mar Yehudai [one of the most important of the early *geonim*] of blessed memory: religious persecution was decreed upon the Jews of the Land of Israel—that they should not recite the *Shema* and should not pray, because the practice of renouncing religion is what evil Edom [Rome, Byzantium] decreed, religious persecution against the Land of Israel that they should not read the Torah, and they hid away all the Torah scrolls because they would burn them and when the Ishmaelites [Muslims] came they had no Torah scrolls and they had no scribes [to copy scrolls] who knew the pertinent laws for doing [this]. . . and up till now they carry on like this. . . . But in Babylon Torah [study] has not ceased among Israel . . . and the Evil Empire [i.e. Rome] did not rule over Babylon . . . and two *yeshivot* have not forgotten the Oral Law nor the law to be practiced from ages ago until now.[105]

Was Pirkoi referring, among other things, to Justinian's draconian law? We cannot know. However, if what he wrote had any basis in reality, it reflected a very grim picture of Torah study or the forms of halakhic decision making in Palestine, and more so of the faulty customs surrounding the liturgy and prayer in its synagogues. Pirkoi's categorical assertions regarding the wretched spiritual condition of the Palestinian Jews were part of the long-standing rejection of the ancient center of Jewish culture in the Land of Israel by the young, proud Babylonian center. Pirkoi's readers were highly receptive to such remarks, which signify the transition from one cultural center to another and the passage into a new age in the history of the nation.

BABYLON'S ASCENDANCE TO DOMINANCE, AND OTHER COMMUNITIES OF THE DIASPORA

As Gafni discusses in the next chapter, everything that the Jews of Palestine wished for was already enjoyed by their brethren in Babylon: benevolent treatment, on the whole, by the Sassanian state; a recognized leadership, centralized and vigorous, in the form of the exilarchate; a diverse and creative world of Torah study; and economic security. All they lacked was a unique status and prestige in the network of Jewish centers in the Diaspora. The Babylonian was the earliest of the Diaspora centers and had long existed in a truly stable manner. But this did not suffice as long as the center in Palestine survived.

The Babylonian Jews' struggle to achieve political and cultural ascendancy constituted only one part of the Jewish cultural scene of this period. While the Babylonians were promoting their own interests and image, the influence of the Palestinian center was still strong in other Mediterranean communities such as Antioch, Constantinople, and those in Egypt (mainly the one in Alexandria) and Rome.

The level of cultural and religious contact between Egypt and Palestine is indicated by a marriage contract from Antonopolis dated 417, in Aramaic and Greek (written in Hebrew letters and according to the Palestinian marriage ordinances), and by a series of questions posed to the Palestinian center by the Alexandrian Jews. The appearance of Hebrew on other papyri of this period is surprising; however, it does not mean that a full-scale retreat from the Greek language and culture in favor of Hebrew was under way. It is safer to postulate the existence of a lively cultural diversity among the Egyptian communities.

The Christian onslaught on the pagans (toward the end of the fourth century) left the Jews as the only strong oppositional minority in Alexandria. The tension between Jews and Christians reached its peak during the riots of 414–15, in the course of which the synagogues were destroyed and the Jews were, for a limited time, expelled from the city, which was followed by a wave of conversions. The ongoing animosity led to the compilation of a set of treatises, *Contra Judeos*, formatted as dialogues between representatives of the two faiths. Although it is difficult to know to what extent these dialogues represent "face-to-face" confrontations, they do on the whole reflect contemporary notions and anxieties in both camps. Notwithstanding the tense atmosphere in Alexandria, in general the Jews of Egypt maintained social and cultural contacts with their surroundings.[106] Indeed, such inter-religious and communal relations, together with the links with the Palestinian center, determined the culture of most of the Jewish communities of the Mediterranean basin.

The extent to which the Palestinian center influenced the Italian Jews is unknown, though evocative funerary and synagogue inscriptions have been found in several locations. Few and scattered though they are, apart from attesting to the strict observation of the Jewish calendar and the occasional visit of "apostoloi" (emissaries from Palestine), these inscriptions "tend to confirm the importance of the study of the Law, the gradual revival of Hebrew, and the coming into currency of the term 'rabbi.' "[107] Yet the Jews of Rome, like those of Alexandria, exhibit a clear pattern of interaction with non-Jews. In the remnants of artifacts and catacombs from third- to fifth-century Rome, we see ornamentation and iconography that display a shared workshop identity with the local pagan and Christian cultures as well as distinct, unmistakable expressions of Jewish identity. Indeed, the *Collatio Legum Moisacarum et Romanarum,* a systematic comparison of Mosaic and Roman law probably produced by a Roman Jew toward the end of the fourth century, has the same characteristics. Its author intended it "to stress the great age of the Mosaic Law and emphasize its essential conformity to the legal system of other, non-Jewish peoples."[108]

During the early Middle Ages, Italian Jews remained on the receiving end of the spiritual and cultural heritage of the Palestinian Jewish center. The surviving works of the gaonic period indicate that this influence was most apparent in the areas of liturgical poetry and synagogue ritual. But the Italian link with Palestine was not exclusive, for ties with the Babylonian center were formed as well.[109]

AN AGE OF TRANSITION: EMPIRES IN CONFLICT

In the year when the King-Messiah is revealed, all the kings of the
nations of the world will challenge each other.
—PESIKTA RABBATI, QUMI ORI, 36

Although the splendor of the Land of Israel had faded somewhat for the Jews, the gentiles now turned their attention to it. The sixth and early seventh centuries were a stormy period for the Jews of Palestine, an age imbued with apocalyptic expectations, when ruling empires changed position and the people heard tidings of Redemption.

Did the Jews take advantage of this volatile situation? They seem to have been quite proactive, taking part in bloody skirmishes with the Byzantine authorities that had been initiated by the Samaritans, and getting involved in or perhaps (as some Christian sources would have us believe) themselves initiating a political-religious conflict far from the borders of Palestine, in the land of the Himyarites in the southern Arabian peninsula. Were these actions merely the attempts of an oppressed people to avenge itself against the ruling power, or was there more to them? Let us look more closely at the events in Himyar.

Although the focus of the conflict was Himyar, its reverberations were felt far away, in the capitals of Persia and Byzantium. At that time, in the 520s, the influence of the Jewish presence around the southern shores of the Red Sea and along its important trade routes was felt—according to Christian sources—in the conversion to Judaism of the Himyarite king, Joseph Dhū Nuwās. Contemporary documents ascribe to emissaries of the priests of Tiberias a significant role in the affair. Were it not for the important location of Himyar, on the southern shores of the Red Sea very near the trade routes to the kingdom of Axum (Abyssinia, which had only recently been Christianized), and if Dhū Nuwās had not begun to persecute the Christian communities in his kingdom and in the area to the north, in the city of Najran, it is doubtful whether this episode would have attracted so much attention. One Christian author even claimed that Joseph's pretext in instigating this persecution against the local Christians was to alleviate the empire's pressure on its Jews. But the conflict in Himyar ended with the defeat of King Joseph by a unified Byzantine camp consisting of the joint forces of Justin I and the Axumite king.[110] According to a later, perhaps legendary tale, at this very time a sage from Babylon named Mar Zutra was appointed head of the local academy in Palestine. This Mar Zutra was the only son of the exilarch, also named Mar Zutra, who had been executed by the Persians toward the end of the fifth century, after an uprising that reached its climax with the creation of an autonomous Jewish territory.[111] Did the appearance of a new scion of the House of David in Palestine infuse the events in Babylon and Himyar with messianic overtones? Did the Jews of Palestine seek to restore past glory by replanting an offshoot of the stock of Jesse in their midst? At first sight this seems very doubtful, until we recall the cultural climate in the synagogues of Palestine, an atmosphere of mounting enmity toward Rome and Christianity. Political unrest and other signs of the empire's coming collapse fanned messianic hopes among the Jews. These lines by Yannai, a poet whom we have already encountered, are a sample of the vigor with which this "public campaign" was conducted:

> *May it be reported of Edom [Rome] as it was reported of Egypt*
> *The vision of Dumah like the vision of Egypt*
> *Receiving retribution from Pathros [Upper Egypt], at the end of a tenth plague*
> *And a tenth horn shall utterly settle accounts with Edom.*[112]

Apocalyptic expectations, which would later emerge in a form of "End of Days" literature, were thus to color much of the Jewish culture of this region until the Arab conquest in the seventh century.

The death of Emperor Justinian in 565 foretold the approaching end of
Byzantine rule in Palestine. The ticking of the apocalyptic clock became much
louder. Growing tensions between the Sassanian kingdom and Byzantium gave
new meaning to the rabbinic saying that Rome would be brought down by the
hands of the Persians, because it was the Persians who initiated the building of
the Second Temple, which the Romans had destroyed.[113] This ancient belief was
to be realized in the early decades of the seventh century.

Messianic fervor intensifies in times of political, social, and religious instability, of which violence is an important ingredient. One of the characteristics of
this age was increasing violence, in which the Jews had a share. Jewish people enjoyed going to the theater and to gladiatorial fights, circuses, and chariot races,
activities that were criticized by both the rabbis and the Church fathers. The
races inspired riotous factional rivalries between the charioteers' ardent partisans, *iuvenes* (youngsters) with "Hunnic" hairstyles, beards, mustaches, and
special garments. This tumultuous atmosphere did not deter the Jews. In Alexandria, Antioch, and Constantinople, they not only attended the spectacles but
on many occasions also joined the melee. The riots had religious and political
overtones, and more than once they resulted in the looting and the burning
down of a synagogue or the destruction of a church.[114] At the turn of the sixth
century, factional rivalry was an important factor in the strife that swept the East
and contributed to the downfall of two successive Byzantine emperors, Maurice
and Phocas, and to the accession of a third, Heraclius. We may plausibly tie some
of this spell of violence to the growing apocalyptic fervor among the Jews.

A converted Jew named Jacob attested to these hopes. While describing an encounter in Acre that he witnessed in his youth during the reign of Emperor
Maurice (582–602), Jacob told of "a priest from Tiberias" who had a vision that
the Messiah, King of Israel, would come at the end of eight years.[115] If the Tiber-
ian indeed saw this vision toward the end of Maurice's reign, then its "fulfillment" would have begun in 611 with the conquest of Antioch by the Sassanian
army. We may assume from this story that messianic fervor had not waned
among the Galilean Jews, who played an important role during the Persian invasion of Palestine. According to Christian sources, the Jews joined forces with the
Persians who invaded the country through eastern Galilee. The line of advance
passed through lower Galilee to Caesarea and Jerusalem, where the Persians
slaughtered many Christians, apparently with the Jews' help. The taking of Jerusalem, the crowning achievement of the campaign, was viewed by the Jews in
redemptionist terms. The many apocalyptic treatises compiled at this time reflected, no doubt, contemporary anxieties and widely held expectations.[116] This
literature had much to do with the writings known as the Hekhalot and Merka-

vah, which describe mystical journeys to the heavenly palaces and give esoteric explanations of the divine chariot in the biblical Book of Ezekiel, and which some scholars maintain was contemporaneous.[117] The author of the apocalyptic Book of Zerubbabel wrote: "All the children of Israel will see the Lord like a man of war with a helmet of salvation on His head. . . . He will do battle against the forces of Armilus [an epithet for the king of Rome, the Antichrist] and they will all fall dead in the Valley of Arbael."[118] Here again we see the array of mythic traditions that the Galileans had formed about their region.

The reconquest of Palestine by the Byzantine emperor Heraclius in 630, a conquest that had messianic connotations for the Christians (restoration of the True Cross to Jerusalem from its Persian captivity, and a campaign of persecution against the Jews), intensified the Jews' sense of the approach of the End of Days. And when the Muslims appeared in Palestine four years later, a liturgical poet recalled the apocalyptic vision of Zerubbabel:

> *[The kings from the land of] Edom will be no more*
> *And the people of Antioch will rebel and make peace*
> *And Ma'uziya [Tiberias] and Samaria will be consoled*
> *And Acre and the Galilee will be shown mercy*
> *Edomites and Ishmael will fight in the Valley of Acre.*[119]

The Arab conquest, which at first was deemed by the Jews to be a stage in the divinely determined redemption, soon appeared to be yet another yoke.[120] In these dismaying circumstances, the words of this anonymous poet may have been of some comfort: "The Messiah will emerge in dignity like the sun rising in strength." In this light, when a worshiper entered a synagogue and encountered the seemingly pagan image of *Sol Invictus* (the Sun Triumphant), exemplifying the figure of the Redeemer, it must have served as the ultimate consolation and promise for the victory of the Jews over their opponents.

NOTES

1. One ought obviously to place some limitations on the interpretation of Jewish art from that period. On the considerations involved in this process, see the most comprehensive study yet of the Jewish synagogue: Lee I. Levine, *The Ancient Synagogue: The First Thousand Years* (New Haven, Conn., 2000), 569–79.

2. The patriarch's influence and control was apparent mostly among the Diaspora Jews; see S. Shwartz, "The Patriarchs and the Diaspora," *Journal of Jewish Studies* 50 (1999): 208–22.

3. For a comprehensive survey on the history of the Jews in Palestine during the period under discussion, see M. Avi-Yonah, *The Jews of Palestine: A Political History from the Bar Kokhba War to the Arab Conquest* (Oxford, 1976). However, see also G. Stemberger, *Jews and Christians in the Holy Land: Palestine in the Fourth Century* (Edinburgh, 2000). Stemberger's study, though covering only the initial part of the period, offers many new insights.

4. See Robert L. Wilken, *The Land Called Holy: Palestine in Christian History and Thought* (New Haven, Conn., 1992).

5. Cairo Genizah fragment, *Cambridge, Taylor-Schechter,* H 6.38.

6. A recent treatment of Constantine's political policies and cultural endeavors has been offered by H. A. Drake, *Constantine and the Bishops: The Politics of Intolerance* (Baltimore, Md., 2000).

7. On the third-century "crisis" and its different dimensions, see David S. Potter, *Prophecy and History in the Crisis of the Roman Empire: A Historical Commentary on the Thirteenth Book of the Sibylline Oracle* (Oxford, 1990), 3–69. For a more toned-down view, see A. Watson, *Aurelian and the Third Century* (London, 1999), 1–38.

8. See O. Irshai, "Dating the Eschaton: Jewish and Christian Apocalyptic Calculations in Late Antiquity," in Albert I. Baumgarten, ed., *Apocalyptic Time* (Leiden, 2000), 113 ff., esp. 135–39.

9. See *Historia Augusta, Carus, Carinus and Numerian,* 13 ff.

10. *Genesis Rabbah* 83:4: "A vision appeared to R. Ammi in a dream. Today Magdiel has become king, said he [R. Ammi]: Yet one more king is required for Edom [i.e., Rome]." On this midrash, see D. Sperber's attractive interpretation, "Aluf Magdiel: Diocletian," in his *Magic and Folklore in Rabbinic Literature* (Ramat Gan, 1994), 127–30. Compare this to a contradictory, extremely confident mood concerning Diocletian's achievements reflected in a Latin dedicatory inscription from Heliopolis in Syria, describing him as "the liberator of the Roman World, the bravest and most dutiful and most unconquered," *Inscriptions grecques et latines de La Syrie* 6, no. 2771.

11. See T. D. Barnes, *The New Empire of Diocletian and Constantine* (Cambridge, Mass., 1982), 213–15.

12. See J. H. W. G. Liebeschuetz, *Continuity and Change in Roman Religion* (Oxford, 1979), 242–44, and G. Fowden, *Empire to Commonwealth: Consequences of Monotheism in Late Antiquity* (Princeton, N.J., 1993), 53–54.

13. In recent years, scholars have made it quite clear that the path leading to the success of Christianity in the fourth century was laid by third-century Roman emperors who reformed state religion, unified it, and granted it a "monotheistic" aura. Such was the case in Aurelian's cult of Sol, the Sun, a decade prior to Diocletian's accession, and was most probably the case already in Decius's day, when persecution of the Christians was conducted under the notion that Roman religion was evolving into a universal organism; thus, compliance with decrees relating to it was a declaration of membership in the Roman Empire and adherence to the imperial religion. See, e.g., J. B. Rives, "The Decree of Decius and the Reli-

gion of Empire," *Journal of Roman Studies* 89 (1999): 135–54. If accepted, this reconstruction alters significantly the prevailing theory dating the cultural change to Constantine's day and attributing it much to his own efforts. According to the new evaluation, Christianity's triumph had begun as early as circa 250 C.E. See, e.g., T. D. Barnes, "Constantine and Christianity: Ancient Evidence and Modern Interpretations," *Zeitschrift für Antike und Christentum* 2 (1998): 274–94.

14. The driving force behind the creation of the matrix of sacred space in the new Christian world was the developing cult of saints and martyrs. For one exemplary instance describing the path between martyrdom and cultic reverence, see Eusebius, *Martyrs of Palestine*, 11, 28. Cf. R. A. Markus, "How on Earth Could Places Become Holy," *Journal of Early Christian Studies* 2 (1994): 257–71. For a more comprehensive and up-to-date view of this aspect of Christian culture, see B. Caseau, "Sacred Landscape," in G. Bowersock, P. Brown, and O. Grabar, eds., *Late Antiquity: A Guide to the Postclassical World* (Cambridge, Mass., 1999), 21–59.

15. For Constantine's portrayal by the contemporary historian and the emperor's panegyrist, the above-mentioned Eusebius of Caesarea, see A. Cameron and Stuart G. Hall, eds. and trans., *Eusebius: Life of Constantine* (Oxford, 1999).

16. This in itself is quite puzzling. However, in light of T. D. Barnes's recent contention (see n. 13 above), it is not entirely surprising. Another view arguing that the rabbis simply ignored the transformation that took place in the empire has been recently put forward by M. Goodman, "Palestinian Rabbis and the Conversion of Constantine," in P. Schaefer and C. Hezer, eds., *The Talmud Yezushalmi and Graeco-Roman Culture*, vol. 2 (Tübingen, 2000), pp. 1–9.

17. The Christian thinkers who basically accepted the biblical eschatological blueprint were faced with similar dilemmas. When Christianity arose under pagan Roman rule, they had to come to terms with the prospects of salvation under this rule, a matter most probably referred to by Paul in his Second Epistle to the Thessalonians, 2:7: "For the power of wickedness is at work, secretly for the present until the Restrainer disappears from the scene." Cf. Tertullian's explanation in his *De resurrectione mortuorum*, 24. However, once Rome became Christian, the question became even knottier: were conditions ripe for the Second Coming of Jesus?

18. On the opposing views of historical destination and eschatological redemption in both camps as they evolved in the fourth and fifth centuries, see Irshai, "Dating the Eschaton," 139–53.

19. It must be emphasized that recent studies have convincingly demonstrated that the fourth century presents a watershed in the relations between Christianity and Judaism from without as well as toward the heretical sects (Arians, Neo-Arians, and others) within. On this, see D. Boyarin, *Dying for God: Martyrdom and the Making of Christianity and Judaism* (Stanford, 1999), 18.

20. This runs in many of Eusebius's works, though it is most apparent in his apologetic

treatise *The Proof of the Gospel,* especially in books 2 and 3. On Eusebius's theological attitude toward Jews and Judaism, see J. Ulrich, *Euseb von Caesarea und die Juden: Studien zur
Rolle der Juden in der Theologie des Eusebius von Caesarea* (Berlin, 1999).

21. This legend appeared in the *Actus beati Silvestri,* and though its earliest attested written form dates from the sixth century, most probably oral versions circulated as early as the
latter part of the fourth century. On that stage of the legend and its impact on Christian-
polytheist relations, see G. Foweden, "The Last Days of Constantine: Oppositional Versions
and Their Influence," *Journal of Roman Studies* 84 (1994): 146–70. On the Jewish angle of this
tradition, see Israel J. Yuval, "Jews and Christians in the Middle Ages: Shared Myths, Common Language. Donatio Constantini and Donatio Vespasiani," in R. S. Wistrich, ed., *Demonizing the "Other": Anti-Semitism, Racism and Xenophobia* (Amsterdam, 1999), 88–107.

22. See Eusebius, *Demonstratio Evangelica,* IX, 8, on the important role of the Galilee in
the initial dissemination of the Gospel. For more on Eusebius's complex attitude toward the
Galilee, see P. W. L. Walker, *Holy City, Holy Places? Christian Attitudes to Jerusalem and the
Holy Land in the Fourth Century* (Oxford, 1990), 133–70.

23. This phenomenon (which admittedly became full-fledged during the high Middle
Ages) and the process by which it evolved has been demonstrated in the most fascinating
manner by E. Reiner, "From Joshua to Jesus: The Transformation of a Biblical Story to a
Local Myth—A Chapter in the Religious Life of the Galilean Jew," in A. Kofsky and Guy G.
Stroumsa, eds., *Sharing the Sacred: Religious Contacts and Conflicts in the Holy Land—First
to Fifteenth Centuries C.E.* (Jerusalem, 1998), 223–71.

24. This tradition is found in various versions of the "Toldoth Yeshu" (The Life of Jesus)
that had circulated widely since its early formation, most probably during the later talmudic period. See S. Krauss, *Das Leben Jesu nach jüdischen Quellen* (Berlin, 1902), 43–45,
146–47, and W. Horbury, "The Trial of Jesus in Jewish Tradition," in E. Bammel, ed., *The
Trial of Jesus: Cambridge studies in honour of C.F.D. Moule* (London, 1970), 108–9.

25. See, e.g., in the Book of Zerubbabel, trans. M. Himmelfarb, in D. Stern and Mark J.
Mirsky, eds., *Rabbinic Fantasies: Imaginary Narratives from Classical Hebrew Literature*
(Philadelphia, 1990), 74, 77.

26. On the place of Dionysus in late antique culture, see G. W. Bowersock, *Hellenism in
Late Antiquity* (Ann Arbor, Mich., 1990), 41–53.

27. See, e.g., Lee I. Levine, *Judaism and Hellenism in Antiquity: Conflict or Confluence*
(Seattle, 1998), 3–32, 96–179 (discussing the earlier rabbinic period too).

28. Y. Tsafrir and G. Foerester, "From Scythopolis to Bysān: Changing Concepts of Urbanism," in G. R. D. King and A. Cameron, eds., *The Byzantine and Early Islamic Near East,*
vol. 2 (Princeton, 1994), 102.

29. For an up-to-date survey of archaeological findings in Byzantine Palestine, see
S. Thomas Parker, "An Empire's New Holy Land: The Byzantine Period," *Near Eastern Archaeology* 62, no. 3 (1999): 134–80 (with extensive bibliography).

30. See Lee I. Levine, *Caesarea Under Roman Rule* (Leiden, 1975). Since the publication of
Levine's important monograph, much more of Caesarea's architectural structure and, with

it, more of its unique cultural setup have been revealed, on which see the recent collection of studies, Kenneth G. Holum, ed., *Caesarea Maritima—Retrospective After Two Millennia* (Leiden, 1996).

31. JT *Sotah*, 7:1 (21b). S. Lieberman's classic studies concerning the knowledge and usage of Greek in rabbinic circles, *Greek in Jewish Palestine* (New York, 1942) and *Hellenism in Jewish Palestine* (New York, 1950), have so far not been surpassed. However, some of his basic premises and conclusions have been recently challenged by A. Wasserstein, begging for more caution in the examination of the sources and suggesting that the presence of a large number of Greek words in rabbinical traditions should be attributed to the apparent dependence of the rabbis on the Aramaic dialect in which many of the Greek loanwords had been absorbed earlier. See A. Wasserstein, "Non-Hellenized Jews in the Semi-Hellenized East," *Scripta Classica Israelica* 14 (1995): 111–37, esp. 119–30.

32. BT *Avodah Zara*, 4a. Compare Origen's *Epistle to Julius Africanus*, 5, and see also Mark G. Hirshman, *A Rivalry of Genius: Jewish and Christian Biblical Interpretation in Late Antiquity* (Albany, N.Y., 1996), and W. Horbury, "Jews and Christians on the Bible: Demarcation and Convergence," in his *Jews and Christians in Contact and Controversy* (Edinburgh, 1998), 200–25.

33. E. Honigmann, "Juvenal of Jerusalem" *Dumbarton Oaks Papers* 5 (1950): 212–16 (on the background leading to Juvenal's acclamation as the patriarch of Jerusalem). For an up-to-date survey of the struggle between the sees, see Z. Rubin, "The See of Caesarea in Conflict Against Jerusalem from Nicaea (325) to Chalcedon (451)," in Holum, ed., *Caesarea Maritima*, 559–74.

34. Theodosian Code, 16:8:8, 16:8:11. Over the past decade or so, much has been written about this institution. There are varied views concerning its origins and period of consolidation; see, e.g., D. Goodblatt, *The Monarchic Principle* (Tübingen, 1994) and M. Jacobs, *Die Institution des jüdischen Patriarchen* (Tübingen, 1995).

35. Jerome, *Epistle 57* (to Pammachius).

36. See M. Stern, *Greek and Latin Authors on Jews and Judaism*, vol. 2 (Jerusalem, 1980), fragments 496–504, pp. 589–99.

37. Lee I. Levine, "The Status of the Patriarch in the Third and Fourth Centuries: Sources and Methodology," *Journal of Jewish Studies* 47 (1996): 1–32.

38. Theodosian Code, 16:8:11. See Levine, "Status of the Patriarch, 2, n. 6.

39. The status of the patriarch in imperial law is somewhat enigmatic. The Theodosian Code acknowledges the preeminence of the institution for the first time as late as the days of Theodosius the First (392 C.E., though the patriarch is mentioned previously in an epistle of Julian the "apostate" from the spring of 363), and from there in a somewhat strange manner in a set of laws and decrees stretching to the year 415. Studied more closely, it seems that the constant changes for the worse in the imperial legislation toward the patriarchate might have come as a result of what was perceived by the authorities as the patriarch's misconduct, as well as a result of the mounting pressure within clerical circles to annul this institution.

40. For a detailed account of this most important transformation in late antique Jewish

history, see I. M. Gafni, *Land, Center and Diaspora: Jewish Constructs in Late Antiquity* (Sheffield, Engl., 1997), esp. 96–117.

41. See Schwartz, "The Patriarchs and the Diaspora."

42. Epiphanius, *Panarion,* 30, 4–12.

43. For instance, the mentioning of a Bishop of Tiberias, when in all probability the earliest period one could imagine the presence of a Christian bishop in that predominantly Jewish town was during the second half of the fifth century.

44. See Cyril of Jerusalem (ca. 350), *Catechetical Lectures,* 12, 17.

45. The Epiphanian story has been interpreted in this way only recently in a fascinating study by E. Reiner, "Joseph the Comes from Tiberias and the Jewish-Christian Dialogue in Fourth-century Galilee" (Hebrew), (forthcoming).

46. See, e.g., the new model of the monastic bishop advanced by the Cappadocian Church fathers: A. Sterk, "On Basil, Moses and the Model Bishop: The Cappadocian Legacy of Leadership," *Church History* 67 (1998): 227–53.

47. *Theodosian Code,* 16:8:22.

48. See D. Noy, *Jewish Inscriptions of Western Europe,* vol. 1 (Cambridge, Engl., 1993–95): 114–19. For more on the Jewish community of Venosa (southern Italy), see M. Williams, "The Jews of Early Byzantine Venusia: The Family of Faustinus," *Journal of Jewish Studies* 50 (1999): 38–52.

49. See G. Stemberger, *Introduction to the Talmud and Midrash,* 2d ed. (Edinburgh, 1996).

50. A critical edition of this most important register of halakhic rulings accompanied by a historical analysis is currently being prepared by Dr. Hillel Newman.

51. J. Mann, "Book of the Palestinian Halachic Practice" (Hebrew), *Tarbiz* 3 (1930): 12.

52. On women's lifestyle in that period and the ideals of domesticity and asceticism required of them, see G. Clark, *Women in Late Antiquity: Pagan and Christian Lifestyles* (Oxford, 1993), esp. 94–118.

53. Although this novel construct requires a more thorough exposition, see for now the interesting comparisons demonstrated by C. Hezser, "The Codification of Legal Knowledge in Late Antiquity: The Talmud Yerushalmi and the Roman Law Codes," in P. Schäfer, ed., *The Talmud Yerushalmi and the Graeco-Roman Culture* (Tübingen, 1998), 581–641.

54. The anecdote originating from a Christian tradition is cited by S. Lieberman, "Neglected Sources" (Hebrew), *Tarbiz* 42 (1973): 54.

55. On this episode as reflected in the contemporary Christian sources, see I. Shahid, *The Martyrs of Najran—New Documents* (Brussels, 1971), 11–117. For a more up-to-date historical survey on the princedom of Himyar, see Walter W. Müller, under "Himyar" in the *Reallexicon Für Antika und Christentum,* vol. 15 (Bonn, 1991), col. 303–31. (German).

56. The treatise was a polemical work addressed to their ex-brethren, the Jews. For a critical edition of this unique text, see G. Dagron and V. Déroche, eds., *Doctrina Jacobi nuper baptizati, Travaux et Mémoire* 11 (1991), pp. 17–43 (historical introduction), 47–219 (Greek text and French translation). The anecdotes on the priests appear in ibid., III, 12 (171–73); V, 6 (193).

57. Concerning the laws, see Theodosian Code, 16:8:22 (415 C.E.); 16:8:25 (423 C.E.); Theodosius II, Novella, 3 (438 C.E.). According to the legislation, existing synagogues were to remain intact and protected from Christian violence. On Pulcheria's action against the Jewish synagogue, see Theophanes, *The Chronicle of Theophanes Confessor: Byzantine and Near Eastern History, A.D. 284–813*, ed. and trans. C. Mango and R. Scott (Oxford, 1997), 159.

58. See R. Hachlili, ed., *Ancient Synagogues in Israel: Third–Seventh Century C.E.* (Oxford, 1989), 1–6, and, more recently, J. Magnes, "Synagogue Typology and Earthquake Chronology at Khirbet Shema, Israel," *Journal of Field Archaeology* 24 (1997): 211–20.

59. E. Reiner, *Mishmarot Ha-Kehunah: Mythos Byzanti Glili* (in preparation).

60. The Hasmonaean priests' saga, especially their zealous and heroic struggle with the Greeks, resurfaces in the liturgical poetry of the sixth century. See, e.g., J. Yahalom, *Poetry and Society in Jewish Galilee of Late Antiquity* (Tel Aviv, 1999), 113–14. It is interesting to note that this phenomenon had its parallel in the Christian Maccabean martyr's cult that evolved in Antioch during the second half of the fourth century, in part as a result of the strained relations between Christians and Jews in that city. See M. Vinson, "Gregory Nazianzen's Homily 15 and the Genesis of the Christian Cult of the Maccabean Martyrs," *Byzantion* 64 (1994): 166–92. As to the messianic tone in contemporary synagogue liturgy, see W. Horbury, "Suffering and Messianism in Yose ben Yose," in W. Horbury and B. McNeil, eds., *Suffering and Martyrdom in the New Testament: Studies Presented to G. M. Styler* (Cambridge, Engl., 1981), 143–82. Concerning synagogal ornament, see my opening paragraph concerning the presence of Helios, the sun god, on synagogue mosaics and its possible context and meaning.

61. On the synagogue as a communal center in Late Antiquity, see Levine, *Ancient Synagogue*, 357–86. Generally speaking, epigraphy as well as rabbinical sources have demonstrated the synagogues were products of local communal enterprises. A similar phenomenon can be detected in Christian communities, where churches were being founded by the local residents rather than by central government; see L. Di Segni, "The Involvement of Local, Municipal and Provincial Authorities in Urban Building in Late Antiquity," *Journal of Roman Archaeology* 14 (1995): 317 ff. The centrality of the synagogue, at least (and this is not entirely surprising) in the institutional and cultural dimensions of Diaspora Jewry, is reflected in the great interest the Church fathers took in it; see Epiphanius, *Panarion*, 30:11.

62. On the *archisynagogos*, see T. Rajak and D. Noy, "*Archisynagogoi*: Office, Title and Social Status in the Greco-Jewish Synagogue," *Journal of Roman Studies* 83 (1993): 75–93. It seems that the rabbis changed their public function and increasingly assumed the role of deliverers of sermons. On Late Antiquity rabbis as homilists and public rhetoricians, see the anecdote on Rabbi Samuel the son of Yossi son of Bun (late fourth century), JT Horayot, 3:8 (48c).

63. The centers of learning were mostly concentrated in the cities. See H. Lapin, "Rabbis and Cities in Later Roman Palestine: The Literary Evidence," *Journal of Jewish Studies* 50 (1999): 187–207. It could have also been the case that the process described here occurred within the cities themselves, where their communal cohesion, led by a central or dominant

center or synagogue, simply disintegrated into smaller fractions of communities. Nonetheless, archaeological surveys of recent years, especially in the Galilee and on the Golan, have pointed out the great upsurge in synagogue as well as church building in rural areas.

64. This striking phenomenon seems to emerge from a set of dated funerary inscriptions found in the town of Zoar (south of the Dead Sea); see S. Stern, *Calendar and Community: A History of the Jewish Calendar Second Century BCE–Tenth Century CE* (Oxford, 2001), 87–98, 146–54.

65. On imperial restrictions and the significance of their ineffectiveness, see G. Stemberger, *Jews and Christians in the Holy Land,* 121–60. However, for a description of a much more relaxed interreligious atmosphere in Late Antiquity Palestine, consult G. W. Bowersock, "Polytheism and Monotheism in Arabia and the Three Palestines," *Dumbarton Oaks Papers* 50 (1997): 1–10.

66. See Levine, *Ancient Synagogue,* 362.

67. This assessment is based on the strange phenomenon that none of the rabbis mentioned in the epigraphical findings can be identified by our rabbinic literary sources; see S. J. D. Cohen, "Epigraphical Rabbis," *Jewish Quarterly Review* 72 (1981–82): 1–17.

68. See Levine, *Ancient Synagogue,* 440–51. For a different view on the matters discussed here, at least in regard to Palestine, see C. Hezser, *The Social Structure of the Rabbinic Movement in Roman Palestine* (Tübingen, 1997), 119–23, 214–25.

69. Several collections and surveys of synagogue inscriptions have been carried out in recent decades. See J. Naveh, *Al Pesefas ve-Even: ha-Ketovot ha-Aramiyot ve-ha-Ivriyot mi-Batei ha-Keneset ha-Atikim* (Jerusalem, 1978) (mainly on the Palestinian synagogues); L. Roth-Gerson, *The Greek Inscriptions from the Synagogues in Eretz-Israel* (Jerusalem, 1987); W. Horbury and D. Noy, *Jewish Inscriptions of Greco-Roman Egypt* (Cambridge, Engl., 1992) (covering the entire corpus of inscriptions, but mainly relating to an earlier period than the one discussed here); and D. Noy, *Jewish Inscriptions from Western Europe,* 2 vols. (Cambridge, Engl., 1993–95).

70. Although this phenomenon goes back to the decades preceding the destruction of the Second Temple, we encounter it later in, among other places, Tiberias, Sepphoris, and Lydda.

71. Rabbi Shimon son of Lakhish (late third century) once said to the Babylonian sage Rabbah bar Hannah that God hated them (the Babylonian Jews) for not returning to the Land of Israel as a whole during the days of Ezra (see BT *Yoma* 9b). In fact, the Babylonian Jews were blamed for the harsh fate of the entire nation (see Song of Songs Rabbah, 8, 9). In one case, immigrants in Sepphoris complained that the locals refrained even from greeting them (JT Sheviit, 9, 5). On this phenomenon, see S. Lieberman, " 'That Is How It Was and That Is How It Shall Be': The Jews of Eretz Israel and World Jewry During Mishnah and Talmudic Period" (Hebrew), *Cathedra* 17 (1981): 3–10.

72. Varying and at times contradictory views have been voiced concerning this rather difficult problem; see Levine's summary in *The Ancient Synagogue,* 552–53.

73. On the latter custom, see the early attestations found in the Gospels, Luke 4, 16–20.

74. The Hekhalot (literally, "halls" or "palaces") literature is a set of mystical speculations and visions centering around the heavenly halls through which the mystic travels in order to reach the divine throne. The term *hekhal* is based on the concept and modeled on the architecture of the halls in the earthly Jerusalem Temple. This and the Merkavah (literally, "chariot") literature—a complex of mystical speculations and visions about the *divine chariot* described in Ezekiel chap. 1—were most probably redacted and written during the period of the fifth to sixth centuries.

75. See R. Elior, "From Earthly Temple to Heavenly Shrines: Prayer and Sacred Song in the Hekhalot Literature and Its Relation to Temple Traditions," *Jewish Studies Quarterly* 4 (1997): 217–67.

76. On millennial calculations in Christian circles at that period, see R. Landes, "Lest the Millennium be Fulfilled: Apocalyptic Expectations and the Pattern of Western Chronography 100–800," in W. Verbeke et al., ed., *The Use and Abuse of Eschatology in the Middle Ages* (Leuven, Belgium, 1988), 137–211. On a possible correlation between Jewish and Christian calculations, see Irshai, "Dating the Eschaton," 139–53.

77. See Yahalom, *Poetry and Society,* 46–63.

78. See the anecdote in the Tosefta, Shabbat, 14, 2. The rabbis regarded the Targum as an oral form of the Bible; see JT, *Megillah,* 4, 1 (74a). On the links between the New Testament and the Targum, see B. D. Chilton, *Targumic Approaches to the Gospels: Essays in Mutual Definition of Judaism and Christianity* (Lanham, Md., 1986).

79. A. Shinan, "The Aramaic Targum as a Mirror of Galilean Jewry," in Lee I. Levine, ed., *The Galilee in Late Antiquity* (New York, 1992), 241–51.

80. Performed by Jesus, Luke 4:20–21, and described by Philo, *Hypothetica,* 7, 13; see Levine, *Ancient Synagogue,* 145–47.

81. Pesikta de-Rav Kahana, 12:3.

82. For the different views on this term and the reality reflected by it, see C. Hezser's summary, *The Social Structure of the Rabbinic Movement in Roman Palestine* (Tubingen, 1997), 195 to 214.

83. See Levine, *Ancient Synagogue,* 449–51. The assertion at hand also concerns the physical layout; that is, are we dealing with different locations altogether or with different spaces under the same roof?

84. J. Fraenkel, Darkhê ha-Aggadah we-ha-Midrash, vol. 1, Giv'ataim (1991), 17–26, and M. Hirshman, "The Preacher and His Public in Third-Century Palestine," *Journal of Jewish Studies* 42 (1991): 108–14.

85. See JT *Baba Mezia,* 2:11 (8d).

86. The formula, consisting of a homiletic midrash coupled with a halakhic poem, is best seen in the Midrash Tanhuma-Yelamdenu, on which see G. Stemberger's recent survey in *Introduction to the Talmud and Midrash,* 302–6.

87. See Lamentations Rabbah, Petichta, 17. In this context it is interesting to note the entirely opposite impression reported by the fifth-century Church historian Socrates

Scholastikos, who described the conduct of the Alexandrian Jews of his day thusly: "the Jews being disengaged from business on Sabbath, and spending their time not in hearing the Law, but in theatrical amusements" (*Church History*, 7, 13).

88. On rabbinic acquaintance with Greek lore, see notes 27; 31 above. Concerning rabbinical acquaintance with rhetoric, some scholars have recently insinuated that this might have well been the case; see J. Yahalom's interpretation of the Akedah (the sacrifice of Isaac) scene on the Sepphoris synagogue floor, *Et Ha'Daat* 3 (2000), Hebrew University, Jerusalem, 40–41.

89. Commentary on Ezekiel 34:3.

90. On the ongoing debate surrounding the architectural typology of Palestinian synagogues, see Levine, *Ancient Synagogues*, 296–302.

91. On this and other links between art and homiletic expression in early and late Byzantium, see H. Maguire, *Art and Eloquence in Byzantium* (Princeton, N.J., 1981), p. 9 ff.

92. The supplicant entreats "the adored Helios, the radiant leader" (*Sefer ha-Razim*, ed. M. Margalioth [Jerusalem, 1967], 99). On magic among the Jews in Late Antiquity, see, e.g., J. Naveh and S. Shaked, *Amulets and Magic Bowls: Aramaic Incantations of Late Antiquity* (Jerusalem, 1985). On magic and its function in the ancient world, see, e.g., the celebrated monograph of F. Graf, *Magic in the Ancient World,* trans. Philip Franklin (Cambridge, Mass., 1997).

93. See Z. Weiss and E. Netzer, *Promise and Redemption: The Synagogue Mosaic from Sepphoris* (Jerusalem, 1996).

94. Romanus Melodus, "On Earthquakes and Fires," 21; see R. J. Schork, trans. and ed., *Sacred Song: From the Byzantine Pulpit to Romanus the Melodist* (Gainesville, Fla., 1995), 193.

95. John Chrysostom, *Against Judaizing Christians*, 1.5, 8.4, 8.8; see also Robert L. Wilken, *John Chrysostom and the Jews: Rhetoric and Reality in the Late Fourth Century* (Berkeley, 1983), 73–79. On the Jewish community of Antioch in late antiquity, see Bernadette J. Brooten, "The Jews of Ancient Antioch," in Ch. Kondoleon, ed., *Antioch: The Lost Ancient City* (Princeton, 2000), 29–37.

96. For a succinct and well-presented description of the transformation of art and its links with religion in Late Antiquity, see J. Elsner, *Imperial Rome and Christian Triumph* (Oxford, 1998), 199–235.

97. See Caseau, "Sacred Landscape," esp. 38–45.

98. The earliest account of the institutionalized Jerusalem liturgy has been preserved in the late-fourth-century diary written by the pilgrim Egeria; see J. Wilkinson, *Egeria's Travels to the Holy Land,* rev. ed. (Warminster, Engl., 1981). On the underlying concepts of that local liturgical scheme, see Jonathan Z. Smith, *To Take Place: Toward Theory in Ritual* (Chicago, 1987), 74–95.

99. Origen, *Sermons on Leviticus,* 1:4.

100. See, e.g., Jerome, Epistle 52 (to Nepotianus). An unfriendly witness, the pagan histo-

rian Zosimos noted how John Chrysostom managed to control the masses during his sermons; see his *History,* 5, 23, 4. For more on the Christian styles and methods of preaching with a wide array of examples, see Mary B. Cunningham and P. Allen, eds., *Preacher and Audience: Studies in Early Christian and Byzantine Homiletics* (Leiden, 1998).

101. On different aspects of Church architecture, art, and liturgy as a center of spiritual guidance, as well as cultural and social cohesion in Byzantine society, see L. Safran, ed., *Heaven on Earth: Art and the Church in Byzantium* (University Park, Pa., 2000).

102. John Chrysostom, *On the Priesthood,* 5, 8.

103. Justinian, *Novellae,* no. 146.

104. One of the signs of the diminishing authoritarian power of the Palestinian center was the cessation (during the second half of the fifth century) of the "life line" of disciples traveling between Palestine and Babylon and transmitting to the latter the traditions and teachings of the Palestinian academies. See B. M. Levin, ed., *Iggeret Sherira Gaon* (Haifa, 1921), 61.

105. L. Ginzberg, *Ginze Schechter: Genizah Studies in Memory of Dr. Solomon Schecter,* vol. 2 (rpt., New York, 1969), 552, 561–62.

106. On Jews in Egypt in general, see Roger S. Bagnall, *Egypt in Late Antiquity* (Princeton, 1993), 275–78. For a more detailed account of the Jewish Alexandrian community of Late Antiquity, see Ch. Haas, *Alexandria in Late Antiquity: Topography and Social Conflict* (Baltimore, Md., 1997), 119–27 (with extensive bibliography).

107. See the careful survey of the evidence (which includes inscriptions from Spain and Asia Minor) by F. Millar, "The Jews of the Graeco-Roman Diaspora Between Paganism and Christianity, AD 312–438," in J. Lieu et al., eds., *The Jews Among Pagans and Christians in the Roman Empire* (London, 1992), 97–123, esp. 110–11.

108. On these issues, see the comprehensive study of Leonard V. Rutgers, *The Jews in Late Ancient Rome: Evidence of Cultural Interaction in the Roman Diaspora* (Leiden, 1995).

109. It has been postulated that, during the tenth and eleventh centuries, Palestinian traditions and lore were channeled via Italy to the newly forged German (Ashkenazic) community, which explains their strong presence in the local tradition. On Italy as a bastion of Palestinian Jewish traditions in the early medieval period, see A. Grossman, "The Yeshiva of Eretz Israel: Its Literary Output and Relationship with the Diaspora" (Hebrew), in J. Prawer and H. Ben-Shammai, eds., *The History of Jerusalem: The Early Moslem Period 638–1099* (Jerusalem, 1996), 243–56.

110. On this conflict, see M. Avi-Yona, *The Jews of Palestine: A Political History from the Bar Kokhba War to the Arab Conquest* (Oxford, 1976), 251–53; for more on this episode, see the studies cited above in n. 55. On the Byzantine campaign, see A. A. Vasiliev, *Justin the First* (Cambridge, Mass., 1950), 274–302, and I. Shahid, *The Martyrs of Najran* (Brussels, 1971).

111. Seder Olam Zutah; A. Neubauer, ed., *Medieval Jewish Chronicles, II* (Oxford, 1895), 72–73, 76. On the background of this tradition and its possible messianic connotations, see Irshai, "Dating the Eschaton," 152–53.

112. M. Zulai, ed., *Piyyutei Yannai* (Berlin, 1939), 90.

113. BT Yoma 10a.

114. See A. Cameron, *Circus Factions: Blues and Greens at Rome and Byzantium* (Oxford, 1976), 74–80, 149–52, 271–96.

115. Dagron and Déroche, eds., *Doctrina Jacobi nuper baptizati*, 5, 6, p. 193. Jacob reports at least two other similar episodes. Compare the apocalyptic visions reported by the contemporary Byzantine historian Theophylact Simocatta, in M. and M. Whitby, *The History of Theophylact Simocatta* (Oxford, 1986), 222–35.

116. Apart from the Book of Zerubbabel, we have the Book of Elijah and a few other smaller treatises; see Y. Even-Shmuel, *Midrashei Geulah* (Jerusalem, 1954), 15–64. *Sefer Zerubbabel* received a translation and commentary by M. Himmelfarb in Stern and Mirsky, eds., *Rabbinic Fantasies*, 67–90. It is important to note that earlier signs of Jewish-Sassanian collaboration against the Christian overlords had occurred in Southern Arabia already during the second half of the sixth century; see Ch. Robin, *L'Arabie antique de Karib'il à Mahomet* (Aix-en-Provence, 1993), 144–50.

117. See, e.g., J. D. Halperin, *The Merkabah in Rabbinic Literature* (Leiden, 1980), and P. Schaefer, *The Hidden and Manifested God: Some Major Themes in Early Jewish Mysticism* (Albany, N.Y., 1992). See also R. Eliot's study, n. 75 above.

118. Himmelfarb, *Sefer Zerbabel*, 78.

119. The text (in my own translation) is taken from the poem "In Those Days and In That Time"; see Even-Shmuel, *Midreshei Geula*, 114.

120. On the change of sentiment among the Jews, see J. Yahalom, "The Transition of Kingdoms in Eretz Israel as Conceived by Poets and Homelists" in *Shalem: Studies in the History of the Jews in Eretz Israel* 6 (Jerusalem, 1992), 1–22. It ought to be noted that the Arab conquest of the East posed a grave problem to the Christian concept of history as well, resulting in new waves of apocalyptic anxiety. For an overview of the Byzantine tick and chime of the eschatological clock, see P. Magdalino, "The History of the Future and Its Uses: Prophecy, Policy and Propaganda," in R. Beaton and Ch. Rouche, eds., *The Making of Byzantine History: Studies Dedicated to Donald M. Nicol on His Seventieth Birthday* (Aldershot, Engl., 1993), 3–34. One of the earliest and most influential attempts to address the historical transformation in apocalyptic terms was that known as the *Ps.-Methodius*, which was written in northern Syria circa 692 C.E. See G. J. Reinink, "Ps.-Methodius: A Concept of History in Response to the Rise of Islam," in A. Cameron and Lawrence I. Conrad, eds., *The Byzantine and Early Islamic Near East, Vol. 1: Problems in the Literary Source Material* (Princeton, 1992), 149–87.

SELECTED BIBLIOGRAPHY

Avi-Yona, M. *The Jews of Palestine: A Political History from the Bar Kokhba War to the Arab Conquest.* Oxford, 1976.

Cameron, A., and P. Garnsey, eds. *The Cambridge Ancient History.* Vol. XIII: *The Late Empire, AD 337–425.* Cambridge, Engl., 1997.

Cameron, A., B. Ward-Perkins, and M. Whitby, eds. *The Cambridge Ancient History.* Vol. XIV: *Late Antiquity: Empire and Successors, AD 425–600.* Cambridge, Engl., 2000. (Both volumes are the most comprehensive and up-to-date general introductions to a wide array of topics in the history of the Byzantine period.)

Elsner, J. *Oxford History of Art: Imperial Rome and Christian Triumph—The Art of the Roman Empire AD 100–450.* Oxford, 1998.

Levine, Lee I. *The Ancient Synagogue: The First Thousand Years.* New Haven, Conn., 2000.

Safran, L., ed., *Heaven on Earth: Art and the Church in Byzantium.* University Park, Pa., 2000.

Wilken, Robert L. *The Land Called Holy: Palestine in Christian History and Thought.* New Haven, Conn., 1992.

Two views of two incantation bowls.
(British Museum, London)

BABYLONIAN RABBINIC CULTURE

ISAIAH GAFNI

In the context of a lengthy discussion on the nature, merits, and handicaps associated with the ongoing scattering of the Jewish people, a dispersion for which no imminent conclusion was visible on the horizon, the Babylonian Talmud offers an ingenious observation on its own community's unique predicament. More than a millennium prior to the redaction of the Babylonian rabbinic corpus, vast numbers of Judaeans had been transplanted to lands east of the Euphrates River. The majority of these were captives, a consequence of the initial Babylonian capture of Jerusalem in 597 B.C.E. and the deportation to Babylonia[1] at that time of the Judaean king Yehoyakhin. Another wave of captives arrived shortly afterward, following the second conquest and final destruction of Jerusalem and its Temple by King Nebuchadnezzar in 586 B.C.E.[2] Why, the Talmud innocently asks, were the Israelites exiled to Babylonia rather than to any other land? Of course, the modern historian's response to such a question would simply be to point to precisely those events just cited. But in the context of rabbinic theodicy and an interpretation of history as the stage upon which a saga of providential causality was being played out, it made all the sense in the world to inquire as to the implications of a Babylonian setting for Jewish captivity and communal rebuilding. And thus the Talmud proceeds to explain why, in fact, it was Babylonia that was chosen: "Because He [God] sent them [back] to their mother's[3] house. To what might this be likened? To a man angered at his wife. To where does he send her—to her mother's house!" (BT Pesahim 87b).

The Jewish people, we are thus informed, were not merely removed to a random land of captivity but were benevolently transferred to what might be considered their original homeland, inasmuch as their patriarch, Abraham, had his roots in those very same lands east of the Euphrates. Implicit in this statement is not merely the theodicic observation that God did not randomly exile the nation for its sins, but also that they were granted haven in the one territory uniquely qualified to receive them in light of their ancient roots therein, thereby affording them, even while uprooted, a sense of comfort and familiarity rather than the expected alienation of captivity.

Familiarity with an ancient "homeland," however, need not presuppose an assimilatory process resulting from an identification with the local culture or civilization. Ironically, it would be precisely in this land of ancient roots, albeit imagined ones, that the Jewish community would evince the greatest degree of cultural autonomy, certainly when compared with parallel processes played out in communities west of the Euphrates, namely those situated within the political and cultural boundaries of the Hellenistic-Roman world. In time the sages of Babylonia would come to be recognized as the outstanding Jewish intellectuals of their day, vying with and ultimately surpassing their colleagues in Palestine. The achievements of this community would determine for almost a millennium central elements of a Jewish self-identity and religious expression, as well as the basic literary curriculum and legal code embraced by Jews throughout the world. If ever there were a communal success story in the annals of Jewish history, it was the meteoric ascendancy of the Babylonian rabbinic community in Late Antiquity and the early Middle Ages to a position of primacy within the Jewish world. It is to this story that the present chapter addresses itself.

A good place to begin our tale—and certainly one that the sages of Babylonia themselves would have recommended—is an event that took place some 800 years prior to the first appearance of a "rabbinic community" there. In the fourth year of the reign of the last king of Judah, Zedekiah (i.e., 594 B.C.E.), and just a few years before the final Babylonian onslaught and destruction of First-Temple Jerusalem, the prophet Jeremiah wrote a letter to those of his countrymen who had already been exiled to Babylon some years earlier.[4] In that letter, God, through the prophet, beseeches them:

> Build houses and settle down. Plant gardens and eat their produce. Marry and beget sons and daughters, in order that you may increase in number there rather than decrease. Seek the welfare of the country to which I have deported you, and pray on its behalf to God, for on its welfare your own depends. (Jeremiah 29:5–7)

One would be hard pressed to find another example in ancient Israelite history in which a community heeded the words of the prophet so scrupulously and in such detail. Not only were Jews destined to thrive demographically and economically in this new land of captivity,[5] but ultimately even the latter part of Jeremiah's exhortation, bearing a decidedly political significance, would achieve a fruition of sorts with the formulation by Samuel, a third-century Babylonian sage, of the well-known statement that "the law of the kingdom is law" (*dina demalkhuta dina*).[6] Although that principle appears in the Babylonian Talmud within a more narrowly defined legal context, recognizing the government's legitimate right to enforce the collection of taxes and customs and to determine legal frameworks for establishing land-ownership, the fact is that it ultimately attained a sweeping political significance for the totality of Jewish Diaspora life. In rabbinic eyes, however, past and present tend to coalesce, and thus in time the rabbinic community of Babylonia would point to those earliest biblical days of captivity as the first links in an unbroken chain of enhanced Jewish existence "by the rivers of Babylon," claiming that all the requisite trappings of a vital and self-sufficient community were transported from Jerusalem to Babylon even prior to the destruction of the First Temple.

And yet, if the great success story begins at that earliest of stages, one cannot ignore the fact that the very same story also represents one of the great riddles of Jewish history. To be sure, only a small portion of the Babylonian Jewish community participated in the "return to Zion" during the sixth and fifth centuries B.C.E., while the vast majority remained in the eastern Diaspora and ultimately grew to become second in size only to Palestinian Jewry among all the other concentrations of Jews throughout the world. But though they grew into a community of "countless myriads whose number cannot be ascertained,"[7] the Jews of Babylonia would at the same time recede into a shadowy background, with practically nothing to be heard from them for almost 750 years. Throughout the Second Temple period (516 B.C.E.–70 C.E.), and indeed for the entire tannaitic era of post-Temple Palestine as well (70–220 C.E.), this community provides us with no meaningful information on its inner development, nor do we possess any significant literary product from its midst. Inasmuch as Jewish historiography in Second Temple times focuses almost exclusively on the affairs of Jews situated within the Hellenistic-Roman spheres of influence (primarily in Judaea, but also in major Jewish centers such as Ptolemaic and Roman Egypt), allusions to Jews beyond the Euphrates are almost always linked to events in the west: thus, for example, we hear only fleetingly of the reception granted the captured high priest of Jerusalem, Hyrcanus II, by the Jews of Babylonia in the wake of the Parthian invasion of Judaea in 40 B.C.E.[8] Expressions of the commitment of Babylonian Jewry to the Temple of Jerusalem, exemplified by their annual monetary contributions as well as by their potential for armed intervention in the face of any perceived Roman tampering with the nature of the Jewish cultic center (as evinced in the days of Gaius Caligula), all find their way into the writings of Josephus and Philo, but even this information does not really shed any light on the communal structures and cultural character of the Babylonian community.

Nor does the appearance on the Judaean scene, beginning with the reign of King Herod (37–4 B.C.E.), of various Babylonian personalities such as Hillel the

Elder, really inform us about the nature of contemporaneous Babylonian Jewry, notwithstanding the claims of numerous Jewish historians of the nineteenth and twentieth centuries. The historical Hillel, it appears, is just one of the casualties of the vigorous controversy between liberal and traditional representatives of nineteenth-century Jewish *Wissenschaft,* many of whom frequently rendered ancient Jewish history a battleground for their own contemporary disputes. In the case of Babylonia, the paucity of any hard information from Second Temple times enabled liberal opponents of Jewish Orthodoxy to claim that the Babylonian Talmud—the ultimate legal authority in traditionalist eyes—was in fact conceived in a land at first devoid of ancient Jewish tradition and instead caught up in the "superstitions" of the Persian East.[9] Orthodox Jewish historiography would respond by projecting a "Torah-oriented" society among Babylonian Jews as far back as the earliest days of captivity.

In similar fashion, Hillel was cited by nineteenth-century writers as proof either of Babylonia's deep-rooted Torah orientation or of the total lack of Torah-knowledge in that land, which therefore required that Hillel "come up" to Palestine if he wished to engage in the study of Torah. In truth, nothing on the nature of Second Temple Babylonian Jewry can really be gleaned from the Hillel stories. It was precisely this lack of any real information that enabled both sides to play fast and loose with it. All this, then, tends to enhance the riddle. What were the objective political and social conditions that contributed to the fashioning of the Babylonian Jewish community, even as it remained out of close touch with the rest of world Jewry, and what were the factors that rendered the community so special in its own eyes, affording it a self-assuredness that determined its behavior toward surrounding cultures, on the one hand, and a distinct assertiveness in its relations with other Jewish communities—most notably that of Palestine—on the other?

In strictly political terms, the Jews of Babylonia were ruled over and influenced by a succession of kingdoms, each of which cultivated its own unique cultural environment. The Babylonian kingdom that originally transported the Judaean captives to their new surroundings was conquered shortly afterward by the Persian Achaemenid monarchy, under whose rule those Judaeans who so desired were allowed to return to the areas around Jerusalem and rebuild the Temple. We have, however, no substantial information on the nature of Jewish life under the Persians, and the same holds true for the subsequent period, when the bulk of Alexander the Great's eastern conquests came under Hellenistic-Seleucid rule (ca. 323–140 B.C.E.). What is noteworthy, however, is that this Seleucid rule over Babylonia marks the last chapter in ancient history during which the Jews of Palestine and their brethren east of the Euphrates were ruled by the same monarchy, a political reality to be reestablished only in the wake of the Islamic conquests of the East. The prolonged disintegration of the Seleucid Empire, beginning in the mid-second century B.C.E., would ultimately find the two Jewish centers separated again: Babylonian Jewry found itself under Parthian rule for over 300 years,[10] until the fall of the Parthian kingdom to the Sassanian rulers in the early third century C.E.—that is, precisely at the dawn of the Babylonian rabbinic era. The Jews of Palestine, meanwhile, would experience two generations of political independence under the Hasmonaean priests (141–63 B.C.E.), to be followed by the Roman conquest of the land and the establishment therein of successive regimes, all ultimately controlled by the Roman state.

It was arguably in this prolonged state of communal separation that much of the self-image of Babylonian Jewry may have been determined. The Parthian Empire differed both from its Achaemenid and Seleucid predecessors, and even more so from its Sassanian successor, in that it never constituted a unified empire under strong central rule. Instead it functioned as a weak confederation of vassal states whose loyalty to the Parthian sovereign was put to the test only during major confrontations with external threats, primarily in the form of Roman legions. But though usually successful in amassing great military force to thwart Roman designs, the Parthians evinced no zeal for the establishment of a unified social and political order, based on foundations that might have served to create a more homogeneous society. Particularly noteworthy is the lack of a formal state religion under the Parthians. While they did recognize Iranian deities and also fostered Zoroastrianism, this was never cultivated to the extent and with the dedication shown by their Sassanian successors. In fact, Hellenistic culture also served as a counter-influence in the Parthian court,[11] and although this may have been a superficial legacy from the Seleucid period, it nevertheless testifies to the lack of any predominant political or cultural enterprise on the part of the Parthian monarchy. What emerged was a loosely knit confederation with a decidedly feudal nature, and although this tended to weaken the kingdom as a whole, it also served as a unifying and strengthening factor for the individual ethnic groups within the empire, allowing them to cultivate a sort of tribal autonomy as long as the sovereignty of the Parthian ruler was officially recognized.[12]

Moreover, if the various ethnic communities managed to achieve a significant degree of political and military potency, they were in the advantageous position of being able to offer their services to the king should these be required for purposes of subduing rebellious elements within the empire. Josephus provides us with two stories relating to Jews or the Jewish community in first-century Parthia.[13] In both cases, the king was willing to grant elements within the community—be they renegade Jewish brothers who set up a short-lived pirate state, or recent converts to Judaism from among a local royal dynasty—an enhanced degree of regional autonomy in exchange for their support against all sorts of local satraps and strongmen who might be harboring mutinous aspirations. Although the novelistic and fictionalized elements in both narratives are apparent, they nevertheless represent an accurate picture of a decentralized environment, in which Jews were free to run their own lives unhindered by external political pressures and, even more important, were not engulfed by a pervasive, attractive, and assimilatory cultural presence so familiar to the Jews of the Hellenistic world. Given such an atmosphere, we can appreciate the concern expressed by representatives of the early rabbinic community with the fall of the Parthian kingdom and the ascendancy of the Sassanians. Upon the death of the last Parthian king, Artabanus V (ca. 224 C.E.), we are told that the renowned sage Rav proclaimed: "The bond is snapped" (BT Avodah Zara 10b).

RABBINIC BABYLONIA:
THE INTERSECTION OF PAST AND PRESENT

It was upon this extended period of communal autonomy that the rabbis of talmudic Babylonia would graft their own unique contribution to the social and cultural self-image of Babylonian Jewry. On the most basic level, Babylonian Jews even mildly conversant with biblical tradition would be aware that they dwelt not only in one of the ancient lands of the Bible but literally in the cradle of earliest biblical civilization. For instance, they were able to identify in their midst two of the four tributaries of the river that flowed out of Eden, namely the Tigris "which flows east of Assyria" (Genesis 2:14) and the Euphrates. It is hardly surprising that rabbis residing in the very setting of the opening chapters of Genesis identified sites mentioned in that book with Babylonian or Persian cities of their own day. Thus Genesis 10:11 tells us: "From that land [Bavel] he [Nimrod] went into Assyria [Ashur] and built Nineveh and Rehovoth-Ir and Kalah," and the Talmud records: "Rav Joseph taught: 'Ashur is Sileq [Seleucia]. . . . Nineveh is what it says, Rehovoth-Ir is Perat de-Meshan, Kalah is Perat de-Borsif' " (BT Yoma 10a).[14] Another example relates, " 'And the mainstays of his [Nimrod's] kingdom were Babylon, Erek, Akkad and Kalneh' (Genesis 10:10)—[they are] Edessa and Nisibis and Ktesiphon."[15]

In similar fashion, even though the giants Ahiman, Sheshai, and Talmai lived, according to Numbers 13:22, in the vicinity of Hebron, this did not prevent the sages in Babylonia from pointing to three islands in the Euphrates as having been built by them: "Ahiman built Anat, Sheshai built Alush, Talmai built Talbush" (BT Yoma 10a).[16]

The game of identifying ancient biblical cities with nearby and familiar sites thus transcended a simple form of geographical exegesis, because it effectively put the exegete himself—together with his audience—on the biblical map as well. But this was not just a process of biblical "immersion"; the intersecting of past and present took on a far greater significance when the past was not merely "biblical" but related to ancient Israelite (i.e., "Jewish") history as well. If, as we noted in the opening to this chapter, Abraham was perceived as being not just the first Hebrew but also a "Babylonian," how much more meaningful were those attempts at identifying sites connected with King Nimrod—inasmuch as rabbinic lore described how that ruler was responsible for the incarceration of "our patriarch" Abraham. A heightened sense of continuity with the biblical narrative, as well as an immediate link to the historical arena of that narrative, was the natural consequence. Nothing could now prevent the rabbis from identifying the very location of our patriarch's incarceration: "Rav said: 'Our father Abraham was imprisoned ten years, three in Kuta and seven in Kartu.' . . . Rav Hisda said: 'Ibra ze'ira [the small crossing] de Kuta—that is the Ur of the Chaldeans.' "[17]

Once these ancient biblical sites became "known" to the rabbis, this information could be introduced into their halakhic discourse as well: "Rav Hamnuna said: He who sees the lion's den or the furnace should say: Blessed is the one who performed miracles to our fathers on this spot" (BT Berakhot 57b).

Of course, the sages were well aware of the events that introduced the descendants of Abraham into the lands east of the Euphrates. Here, too, the attempt would be made to juxtapose past and present:

> R. Abba b. Kahana said: What is meant by "and the King of Assyria exiled Israel to Assyria and he settled them in Halah and along the Havor, and the River Gozan and the towns of Media" (2 Kings 18:11)? Halah is Helwan, Havor is Hadyab [Adiabene], the River Gozan is Ginzak, the towns of Media—this is Hamadan and its neighbors, and some say Nehavand and its neighbors. (BT Kiddushin 72a; BT Yevamot 16b–17a)

The focus of all this exegetical activity, if our analysis is correct, was not the Bible and a need for up-to-date knowledge of its geography but rather the self-image of the Jewish community of Babylonia in Late Antiquity. What we have seen up to now suggests yet another way for Jews to understand their position and status in a "foreign" land, where they are engulfed by an alien society and culture. Erich Gruen in his chapter in this volume has described the unique coming to terms of Hellenistic Judaism with the various strains of Greek culture. The nature of that environment, however, was totally different from what we have encountered in the East. The role of Hellenistic culture was so overpowering in countries such as Egypt that Jews—even if they were to preserve and perpetuate their culture—would have to do this through the media and the methods of that pervasive culture. A Jewish author in Egypt such as Artapanus (second century B.C.E.) would attempt to straddle both worlds—that of his Jewish roots alongside his Egyptian cultural environment—by evincing what the eminent classical historian Arnaldo Momigliano has referred to as "something like Egyptian patriotism."[18] Artapanus could thus recognize that the land of Egypt is the cradle of civilization but would claim that much of that culture was brought there by his Hebraic progenitors: Abraham taught astrology to the Egyptian king, Joseph introduced order into the country's economy, and Moses "the teacher of Orpheus . . . invented boats and bricklaying machines, weapons for Egypt and tools for irrigation and war, philosophy, and also divided the land into thirty-six districts, assigning to each its own deity[!] . . . and thus Moses came to be loved by the masses and respected by the priests, and came to be known by the name of Hermes."[19]

The rabbis of Babylonia seem to have taken a different approach. For them, "belonging" did not so much require a cultural accommodation, and certainly this was not the legacy they received from the Parthian period and its decidedly amenable atmosphere of cultural and ethnic diversity. To be sure, that atmosphere would undergo definite changes during the Sassanian period, and we will address these shortly. But the first order of business seems to have been affording the local Jewish community a sense of "home while abroad," and this was achieved at least in part by creating a sense of familiarity with the physical environment. Jews have roots there that go back to their ultimate patriarch, and possess a literary tradition in which the surrounding geography plays a major role. In total contradistinction to the path taken by Hellenistic Judaism in Egypt, this sort of "belonging" does not require an accommodation with the surrounding culture or a meaningful social interaction, and it might even encourage a certain insularity. With such impeccable documentation of their inherent links to their surroundings, the urgency of evincing cutural ties toward that same end was significantly reduced.

ANTIQUITY AND CONTINUITY: INTERCOMMUNAL RABBINIC IMPLICATIONS

Creating a sense of local antiquity for Babylonian Jews may have been only part of the rabbinic agenda, because the Babylonian rabbis were involved in a different confrontation with their contemporaries in Palestine. The stakes here were particularly high: of all the Diaspora communities in Late Antiquity, only the Babylonian one embraced the new (post-70 C.E.) Jewish devotion to Torah-study as a religious value and personal calling, a process frequently attributed to the sages at Yavneh following the destruction of the Second Temple and considered by some to be their singular greatest achievement. By the third century C.E., a parallel movement appears in Babylonia, probably drawing at first on the emigration of central rabbinic figures from Palestine but ultimately claiming to be on a par with their colleagues in the Holy Land. But that of course was precisely the problem: Babylonia was not "the Holy Land," and would that fact alone not automatically relegate its spiritual leadership to a secondary or subservient role within the rabbinic world?

It was precisely in this context that the Babylonian Jews' links with antiquity would come to play a second major role. To be sure, this process did not take place overnight, and the vigor with which the Babylonian rabbis asserted themselves vis-à-vis their Palestinian counterparts hinged to no small degree on political and religious developments over which the sages had no control whatsoever.

The earliest roots of the community, we have been told, were to be found not only in the patriarchal biblical narrative but, more immediately, in the mass removal of the Judaean population just prior to, and in the direct aftermath of, the destruction of the First Temple. These two waves of captives, we have already seen, were the recipients of Jeremiah's instructions regarding proper behavior while abroad, but just prior to the text of that communication the author of Jeremiah 29 actually spells out precisely the addressees of his letter: "To the *priests*, the *prophets*, the rest of the *elders* of the exile community, and to all the people whom Nebuchadnezzar had exiled from Jerusalem to Babylon— after *King Yekhoniah*, the queen mother, the eunuchs, the *officials* of Judah and Jerusalem, and the *craftsmen and the smiths* had left Jerusalem" (29:1–2). This, then, was no rabble or riffraff that set up shop in Babylonia but rather the most cultivated and esteemed strata of Judaean society. Centuries later, this fact was crucial, for it suggested that the captivity was the ancient repository of Judaean tradition as well. To the rabbinic ear, the term "elders" (*zekenim*) implied sagacity, and in similar fashion the "craftsmen and the smiths" of Jerusalem would be taken as an allusion to Torah scholars who were deported with providential care that a foundation for learning be established in Babylonia at the earliest stages of captivity.[20]

Indeed, this projection of the present into the past went even beyond the world of Torah and came to encompass all the communal institutions of Babylonian Jewry. The most prominent beneficiary of this process would be the Babylonian exilarch (*resh galuta*). Although we possess no hard evidence for the existence of this office prior to the late second or early third century C.E.,[21] the exilarchate could now claim that its Davidic pedigree went all the way back to the exiled House of Yehoyakhin (Yekhoniah). Even the synagogues of Babylonia would benefit from this bestowal of antiquity on communal institutions. Having established that the captives found solace in the fact that they were accompanied into exile by the *shekhinah* (divine spirit), the rabbis naturally inquired as to the precise location of God's presence: "Abaye said: In the synagogue of Huzal and in the synagogue of Shaf ve-Yatib in Nehardea" (BT Megillah 29a). By post-talmudic times, claims for such continuity were enhanced even more, and Rav Sherira Gaon (tenth century) informs us that the synagogue of Shaf ve-Yatib in Nehardea was actually built from the rubble of the destroyed First Temple, brought to Babylonia by the earliest wave of captives.[22]

It should be apparent, by now, how different the cultivation in Babylonia of this perception of "belonging" to the local environment was from that employed by the Jews of the Hellenistic world. But these same processes could be adapted by the rabbis of Babylonia in their contest over spiritual and legal authority with the sages of Palestine. The Babylonian position would be enhanced even more by claims to a purity of national pedigree that exceeded even that of Palestinian Jewry (the rest of world Jewry was of course a distant third).[23] The most blatant statement to this effect was the claim that Ezra rendered Babylonia "like pure sifted flour" by taking with him to the Land of Israel all the doubtful or not-quite-pure elements of the Jewish population.[24] It is for this reason, we are told, that "all countries are an admixture (with impure lineage) in comparison to Eretz Israel, and Eretz Israel is an admixture (in comparison) to Babylonia."[25] Indeed, to be sure one was marrying a "pure" Babylonian Jew, a person would have to make inquiries on the geographical background of a potential spouse, and this procedure actually led to the talmudic demarcation of boundaries for "Jewish Babylonia."[26] What ensued was an enhanced reverence for the physical "land" of Babylonia, a thinly disguised replication of the very attitude maintained by the Jews of Palestine toward their "Holy Land." Indeed, if burial in the Land of Israel had become by the third century yet another expression of devotion and religious piety,[27] can we be surprised at finding those who claim that even burial in Babylonia is equivalent to burial in the Land of Israel?[28]

What was being played out here was not only an exercise in ethnic and religious survival abroad but also a reimaging of the Babylonian community into something radically removed from any other communal context in the Jewish world. The ultimate conclusion—if not the original goal—of this exercise would be the Babylonian rabbinic statement, attributed already to a late-third-century sage, to the effect that "we have made ourselves in Babylonia the equivalent of Eretz Israel" (BT Gitin 6a; BT Bava Kamma 80a).

"IN THE SHADOW OF GOD":
JEWISH PROSPERITY IN A NON-ROMAN WORLD

We have yet to address the question of whether the reimaging of their community and its history for internal (i.e., local and inter-Jewish) purposes had a direct impact on the Babylonian rabbis' attitudes toward the political and cultural behavior of the gentile world in whose midst they also functioned.

Notwithstanding all the advantages of an unequaled communal antiquity, whether based on fact or fancy, the Jews of Babylonia were absolutely certain of one critical political and cultural reality: unlike their brethren in Palestine and the entire Hellenistic-Roman world, they were able to function beyond the political reach of the Roman state. For the sages, this was an object of considerable reflection: it touched directly not only on the degree of practical autonomy enjoyed by their community but, even more important, on the significance of Jewish removal beyond the all-embracing influence of Hellenistic culture. With the acceptance of Christianity by the Roman Empire in the fourth century, a major new component was added to this equation, because it now also placed the Jews of Babylonia and their spiritual leadership beyond the constant need to respond to theological confrontations with the Church, a new reality that would become increasingly apparent in the statements—to say nothing of the biblical exegesis—of the sages of Byzantine Palestine.

The following anecdote[29] expresses in no uncertain terms the Babylonian rabbis' awareness that their position was radically different from that of the Palestinians:

> Rabbah bar bar Hanna was ill, and Rav Judah and the disciples entered to inquire about him. . . . meanwhile one of the *habarim* [Persian priests][30] came and took the candle from them. [Rabbah bar bar Hanna] said: "Merciful One [God]! [Let us live] either in your shade or the shade of the son of Esau [Rome]!" Does this imply that the Romans are preferable to the Persians? Did not R. Hiyya teach: "What is the inference of the scripture 'God understands the way to it, He knows its source' (Job 28:23)—God knew that Israel could not survive the decrees of the Romans and so he exiled them to Babylonia." This [seeming contradiction between the two rabbis] does not pose a difficulty: The [teaching of Rav Hiyya preferring Babylonia] was before the *habarim* came to Babylonia, the [statement of Rabbah bar bar Hanna]—after they came to Babylonia.[31]

All of the political acumen, as well as the doubts and fears, of the Babylonian rabbinic movement appear to be wrapped up in this anecdote. Indeed, we could not ask for a keener appreciation of the historical vicissitudes that transpired precisely as the leadership of that movement began to emerge and to compete for communal control with their counterparts in Roman Palestine.

Rabbi Hiyya's pronouncement seems to reflect the reality of his day (the late second and early third centuries C.E.). With the attractive possibilities for communal autonomy still available under a feudal Parthian regime, on the one hand, and, on the other, harsh memories of the aftermath of the Bar Kokhba rebellion and the ensuing religious persecution[32] still fresh in the mind, a preference for Parthian Babylonia was only to be expected. Moreover, Jews throughout the world could never forget that it was the Roman army that was responsible for the destruction of Jerusalem and its Temple. Although the political situation in late-second-century Palestine was about to undergo a temporary improvement, with the appearance on the scene of Judah the Patriarch and the improved relationship between Jews and the new Severan imperial dynasty, Hiyya (a Babylonian by birth who immigrated to Palestine) seems to reflect the established political wisdom born of decades of strained relations with Rome. The third decade of the third century, however, presented the Jews of Babylonia with a new and threatening political reality of their own: the Parthian Arsacid rulers had just been defeated by the armies of a family of Mazdean priests from the district of Fars in southeastern Persia. The new Sassanian dynasty that succeeded the Arsacids would be characterized by a more centralized political regime, imagining itself as the new coming of the ancient Achaemenids, and even more important by a new commitment to the old Zoroastrian religion.[33] This zeal manifested itself in the appearance of an assertive and revitalized state church, and the removal of a flame from among the rabbis in the talmudic anecdote is one of numerous allusions to the fire-priests *(ḥabarim)* who at first seem to pose a threat to the established freedoms of the local Jewish community.[34] These same priests are cited in the Babylonian Talmud as the reason that rabbis granted permission to move Hanukkah candles on the Sabbath; keeping the candles out of sight would, they hoped, preclude any hostile action by the fire-priests (BT Shabbat 45a).

The dilemma for the Babylonian sages was acute and somewhat ironic. If, indeed, their community had taken comfort in its relatively favorable political situation, compared to that of the Jews under Roman rule, now it too was confronted with a new situation that threatened to undermine those advantages. The fears related to political as well as religious winds of change. A frequently examined story in the Babylonian Talmud (Bava Kamma 117a) reports that Rav—

a Babylonian sage who spent part of his youth in Palestine but returned to Babylonia to witness the changing of the guard in his homeland—advised his disciple Kahana to flee Babylonia after the latter had apparently taken the law into his hands and executed a potential informer: "Until now [ruled] the Greeks [an allusion to the Hellenistic influences manifest at the Parthian court][35] who were not strict about bloodshed, now there are the Persians [a clear reference to the neo-Persian self-image of the Sassanian dynasty][36] who are strict about bloodshed—go up to the Land of Israel."

Ultimately these fears of forceful interference in the communal life of the Jews would be proven exaggerated, and the modus vivendi formulated by Samuel— the law of the kingdom is law—seems to be reflected in the amicable relationship between a number of Sassanian Kings and Jewish sages, at least according to stories recorded in the Babylonian Talmud. Samuel is described in four talmudic traditions as having maintained a decidedly courteous relationship with King Shapur I.[37] Thus we are told that

> King Shapur once said to Samuel: "You [Jews] profess to be very clever; tell me what I shall see in my dream." He [Samuel] said to him: "You will see the Romans coming and taking you captive, and making you grind date-stones in a golden mill." He [Shapur] thought about it all day, and in the night saw it in his dream.[38]

Another anecdote describes Samuel juggling eight glasses of wine before the king.[39] A century later, we encounter a certain Ifra Hormiz,[40] mother of Shapur II (309–79 C.E.) according to talmudic accounts, not only befriending some of the sages but actually intervening on their behalf with her son. When a rabbi (Rava) was suspected of having overstepped the bounds of recognized legal authority granted the Jews, she declared: "Have no dealings with [i.e., do not punish] the Jews, for whatever they ask of their master He gives to them."[41] Another anecdote describes three fifth-century sages at the court of King Yazdagird I (399–420 C.E.) and again suggests a friendly context.[42] A number of factors might have contributed to this atmosphere, not the least being the fact that Jews under Persian rule would hardly be suspected of harboring loyalties toward the mutually despised Roman Empire. With the embracing of Christianity by Rome in the fourth century, any such suspicion would have been further alleviated; if any elements of society were suspected of constituting a potential fifth column in Sassanian Persia, these would more likely have been adherents of the Christian faith. The very fact that the Sassanian dynasty conjured up memories of a "Persian" monarchy might have made it even easier for the sages to attach to them the favorable memories of an earlier "Persia," and thus we encounter a uniquely rabbinic approach to the laws that govern the unfolding of historical processes:

> Rabbah bar bar Hanna, in the name of R. Yohanan, following a tradition from R. Yehuda b. Ilai, said: "Rome is destined to fall to Persia, *kal va-homer* [even more so]: If the First Temple, built by the sons of Shem [Israel] was destroyed by the Chaldeans [Babylonians], and the Chaldeans were defeated by the Persians, [and] the Persians built the Second Temple [through permission granted by Cyrus] [only to have it] destroyed by the Romans—is it not fitting that the Romans should fall to the Persians?"[43]

In another source, the Talmud actually appears to go out of its way to absolve the Persian king Shapur I of complicity, or at least of intentional malice, in the deaths of 12,000 Jews in Mazaca of Cappadocia during the wars of the mid-third century between the Sassanian Empire and Rome.[44] Nor do we hear of masses of Jews beyond the Euphrates rising up in support of the invading armies of Emperor Julian in the mid-fourth century, notwithstanding that ruler's promises regarding the rebuilding of the Jewish Temple. Politically, it would appear, the Jews of Babylonia did not suffer inordinately under the new Sassanian regime and probably fared significantly better under the new rulers than did their Christian contemporaries. In a total reversal of roles when compared to Palestine, it is striking to encounter the fourth-century Christian Father Aphraates, living in close proximity to the Jews of Ktesiphon, describe how the Jews mock the Christians in their midst for their lowly status and for the fact that God does not come to their aid![45]

Even more striking than the absence of any significant deterioration of the political status of Jews under the Sassanian monarchy was the lack of a systematic religious persecution at the hands of the new state church. Although the Talmud alludes to pressures felt as a result of action taken by the Zoroastrian clergy, a closer examination suggests that this was not a product of a coordinated persecution of Jews, nor even of any missionary zeal on the part of the local priests. Robert Brody has conclusively shown that, inasmuch as Zoroastrianism maintained a position of indifference toward conversion, there is no reason to believe that the actions described in the Babylonian Talmud, such as limiting certain Jewish practices, were the result of a concerted attempt at bringing over to the Persian religion—by force, if necessary—large numbers of Jews.[46] If, as we have seen, fire-priests intervened in Jewish life when they discovered the latter producing flames, this was a result of the clergy's wish to preserve the sanctity of fire, one of the central tenets of the Zoroastrian religion. Being Jewish or adhering to Jewish tradition was not the issue here; maintaining the purity of fire was. The same holds true for another Babylonian talmudic tradition that has been interpreted as referring to "persecution":

> They [the Zoroastrian clergy] decreed three because of three: they decreed concerning meat because of the [priestly] gifts, they decreed concerning bathhouses because of ritual immersion, they exhume the dead because of [Jewish] rejoicing on their [Zoroastrian] holidays. (BT Yevamot 63b)[47]

The source here appears to be saying that Jewish neglect of their religious ordinances (not granting the requisite portions of slaughtered animals to priests, laxity in the laws of purity and immersion, etc.) was the cause of their mistreatment at the hands of the Zoroastrian priesthood. The question is, does all this fall under the heading of religious persecution?

To be sure, the terminology—"they decreed" *(gazru)*—is the common talmudic allusion to religious persecution, more frequently found in the context of Roman Palestine. What we apparently have here, however, is a reference to those areas of daily Jewish life that might be affected by the more activist Zoroastrian clergy that appeared on the scene with the rise of the Sassanians. The source indeed alludes to three areas in which a uniquely Zoroastrian religious sensitivity would have caused new difficulties for ongoing Jewish behavior. Thus, for example, the exhuming of the dead by Zoroastrians is a clear consequence of that religion's unique concept of the earth's sanctity, which required that the dead be exposed rather than buried:[48] "Where then shall we carry the body of a dead man, where lay it down? Then said Ahuara Mazda: 'On the highest places, so that corpse-eating beasts and birds will most readily perceive it.' "[49] It is precisely in light of such beliefs that the following talmudic tale conforms so naturally with the surrounding religious environment:

> A *magus* used to exhume corpses. When he came to the [burial] cave of Rav Tuvi bar Matna, [the latter] seized him by his [the priest's] beard.[50] Abaye happened by and said to him [Rav Tuvi]: I beg you, release him. The following year he [the priest] returned. He [Rav Tuvi] seized him by his beard; Abaye came— but [Rav Tuvi] would not release him, until they brought scissors and cut off his beard. (BT Bava Bathra 58a)

In a similar manner, the immersion of menstruant women in waters deemed pure would be equally offensive to Zoroastrian believers.[51] And yet, all this

notwithstanding, one fails to sense an *ongoing* confrontation in rabbinic literature between Jews and representatives of the government or officials of the state
church. To be sure, gaonic chronicles such as Iggeret Rav Sherira Gaon describe
a series of anti-Jewish persecutions during the fifth century, beginning with
the reign of Yazdagird II (438–57 C.E.) and continuing under his son Peroz (459–
84 C.E.). Sabbath observance was forbidden, synagogues were closed, and Jewish
children were seized to become servants in fire-temples. All sorts of explanations
have been offered for this radical departure from the earlier atmosphere of relative tolerance; some point to the religious zeal evinced by Yazdagird II in his relations with Christians as well as Jews, whereas others have searched for factors that
may have weakened the central government and thereby enabled the more extreme elements within the church to consolidate their power through the use of
terror and persecution.[52] In truth, no single explanation has proven totally convincing, and the very need to provide some sort of rationale for an abrupt change
of policy points to the predominantly favorable relationship between the Jewish
and Iranian communities.

CROSSCURRENTS OF INFLUENCE:
CULTURAL CONTACTS BETWEEN JEWS AND PERSIANS

Charting the twisted and circular paths of cultural dissemination among communities of the ancient world is one of the more speculative undertakings of
historians. Attempts at uncovering ancient Iranian influences on the formative
stages of Judaism are no exception, and the question of the degree—and indeed
the very existence—of a significant Zoroastrian impact on Judaism dating back
hundreds of years prior to the rabbinic era finds scholars divided into diametrically opposed camps: "One of these [camps] emphatically denies the actual existence or possibility of Persian cultural influence on Judaism as a factor affecting
Jewish thought. . . . [T]he other position is the one which would explain almost
everything in the development of post-biblical Judaism as stemming directly
from Iran."[53] To be sure, the Iranian and Jewish worlds of religious thought contain similar notions relating to a wide variety of themes. These include aspects of
dualism, angelology and demonology, the destiny of the world and the duration
of its existence, as well as various eschatological images and beliefs. What is
striking, however, is that almost none of these expressions can be found in any
extant pre-talmudic Babylonian Jewish literature, but instead they survived almost exclusively in the Palestinian Jewish writings of the Second Temple period.
Given the known policies of the Persian government in Achaemenid times, it
would be difficult to attribute such influences to a concerted effort on the part of

the Persian administrators of Palestine during the first centuries of the Second Temple period. A more likely scenario would be to assume an initial Jewish exposure to Iranian ideas within the boundaries of Persia and Mesopotamia, where Jews lived among a predominantly Persian population, and thus "the most likely carriers of this new set of ideas may have been Jews from that Diaspora who had constant communication with their brethren in Palestine through pilgrimage and immigration."[54]

Though addressing an earlier stage of Persian-Jewish contacts within Iran, this proposal might nevertheless contribute to our understanding of the nature and degree of cross-cultural influences in rabbinic Babylonia as well. To begin, it is doubtful to what degree the feudalization within Iran, in Parthian as well as Sassanian times, effected—as claimed by Salo Baron—a "mutual segregation of all corporate groups, and particularly the ethnic-religious communities."[55] If anything, the feudalization of the Persian Empire, which contributed toward the maintenance of distinct tribal and ethnic identities, probably also produced a sense of self-assuredness that would have allowed rabbis to loosen their reins and enabled them to permit a significant degree of interaction with the surrounding society. If we nevertheless encounter numerous Babylonian talmudic discussions that, in the context of attitudes toward idolatry, seek to erect barriers between Jews and non-Jews by prohibiting access, among other things, to gentile bread, wine, and other foods, we should note that almost all these "Babylonian" discussions are based directly on the Palestinian Mishnah and the ensuing halakhic traditions that are also of Palestinian provenance. And so, just as certain Persian concepts and attitudes might have been introduced into Palestinian Jewish society through the mediation of Jews traveling from Iran to western lands, we may note in rabbinic times a reverse phenomenon: the rabbis of Babylonia were almost certainly the recipients of certain religious and social attitudes that were spawned in a decidedly Hellenistic-Roman and ultimately Christian environment, one that demanded a heightened degree of caution in light of constant and even conscious efforts at cultural and religious assimilation. Morever, even in certain spheres of "popular" cultural activity, such as magical incantations so frequently attributed to a Persian environment, we may in fact be confronted by behavior with decidedly Palestinian roots that found its way to Babylonia through some sort of internal Jewish pipeline:

A comparison of the metal amulets from Palestine and surrounding countries to the magic bowls from Mesopotamia shows in several cases clear Palestinian influences and only rarely if ever can one detect influences in the other direction. . . . When formulae from the two geographical areas converge, it may be invariably established that the origin of the theme is Palestinian, rather than Babylonian.[56]

All this notwithstanding, the Jews of Babylonia lived in proximity to non-Jewish centers of population and maintained ties on a daily basis with those communities. Indeed, we find gentiles living in the same courtyards with Jews (BT Eruvin 63b), and we even encounter a Jew and a gentile living in the same house: "the Israelite in the upper story and the gentile in the lower" (BT Avodah Zara 70a). Jews and non-Jews would greet one another in passing (BT Gitin 62a) and would even offer a hand to the elderly of the other community (Kiddushin 33a). To be sure, our information on such matters is incidental and appears primarily within the context of some legal issue. Thus, for example, we find Samuel in the house of a gentile on Shabbat, wondering whether he may make personal use of a flame lit by the owner on the Sabbath—if the fire was not lit for Samuel's benefit.[57]

We also encounter a reverse reality, in which gentiles can be found in the houses of Jews on Jewish holidays (BT Bezah 21b). We even hear of Jews and gentiles exchanging gifts on the respective holidays of the two communities: a non-Jew dedicated a candle to the synagogue of the third-century leader Rav Judah (BT Arakhin 6b), and the same rabbi is supposed to have sent a gift to a gentile on that person's holiday (BT Avodah Zara 64b–65a).[58] In fact, Rav Judah actually permitted the sages to conduct business with gentiles on their holidays (BT Avodah Zara 11b). In sum, one senses, at least in this respect, a far more flexible and cordial stance toward the surrounding community than the rigid and indeed at times suspicious attitude evinced by the Palestinian rabbis. The same holds true for a significant amount of commercial cooperation between the communities.[59] Jews and gentiles worked the same fields and even took each other's place as watchmen on the respective holidays of their partner (BT Avodah Zara 22a). We find Jews and gentiles pressing grapes together in the city of Nehardea (BT Avodah Zara 56b) and a Jew renting his boat to a gentile for the purpose of shipping wine (BT Avodah Zara 26b). What is striking is that the rabbis of Babylonia are frequently named as maintaining a variety of business relations with gentiles; they buy and sell fields from them, and one story even has Rav Ashi selling trees to "a house of fire"—which to the Talmud sounds suspiciously close to indirectly lending a hand to some sort of idolatrous enterprise (BT Avodah Zara 62b). Clearly the segregation of ethnic communities is not the dominant reality emerging from a wealth of talmudic anecdotes.

Even the most casual mingling of Jews and gentiles in Babylonia required a common language of discourse, and such a tool most certainly existed. The daily language of almost all the local Jews was undoubtedly Babylonian Aramaic, a dialect of eastern Aramaic[60] that served the Jewish community at least until the end of the gaonic period in the eleventh century. Rav Hai Gaon, head of the Pumbedita rabbinic academy at the beginning of the eleventh century, declares that "from long ago Babylonia was the locus for the Aramaic and Chaldean language, and until our time all [local] towns speak in the Aramaic and Chaldean tongue, both Jews and gentiles."[61] The Babylonian *geonim* (heads of the academies) refer to Aramaic as "our language," the one to be found "even in the mouths of women and youngsters."[62] By this statement the Babylonians did not wish to deny or ignore their obvious knowledge and literary use of the Hebrew language, but in all fairness it must be noted that, by talmudic times, Hebrew had reverted even in Palestine more into a literary vehicle within the Jewish community rather than a means of daily communication.[63]

Babylonian Jews were clearly aware that other languages were also in use in their immediate vicinity, most significantly the Parthian and Pahlavi dialects of what is commonly called "Middle Persian." Although the literary heritage of this dialect was preserved primarily in Zoroastrian writings rooted in the Sassanian period but surviving primarily in products of the ninth and tenth centuries,[64] it did serve as the vernacular of the Sassanians and would probably have been identified by the Babylonian rabbis as the language of the Iranian government and clergy. As such, the rabbis apparently attained some degree of familiarity with Middle Persian and even introduced it into their exegetical activity:

> Rava said: "On what basis [i.e., what is the biblical analogy] do the Persians call a scribe '*debir*'? From this [scripture]: 'Now the name of [the city] *Devir* was originally Kiriath-*Sefer*.' " (BT Avodah Zara 24b)

The exegesis here is based on the Hebrew letters SPR, which can be read as either "book" *(sefer)* or "scribe" *(sofer)*. The fact that the biblical city of Kiriath-*SPR* was originally called "debir," which is also the Persian word for "scribe," facilitated the rabbinic etymological link—tenuous as it may be—of a familiar contemporary Persian word with a statement in biblical Hebrew.[65]

In the continuation of the same portion of the Babylonian Talmud, we find Rav Ashi explaining the Pahlavi word for menstrual blood—*dashtan*—on the basis of a contraction of Rachel's words in Genesis 31:35, "For the manner of women *[derekh nashim]* is upon me."

Such explicit allusions to "Persian," however, are sporadic at best and hardly represent an indication of the nature and extent of cultural ties or influence. The number of Persian loanwords found in the Babylonian Talmud, while considerable, is dramatically less than the thousands of Greek and Latin words found throughout the parallel rabbinic corpus of Palestine.[66] Moreover, the study or knowledge of "Persian" never assumed the ideological significance that accompanied a parallel pursuit of Greek in Palestine and that caused fathers to address rabbis with questions regarding the permissibility of teaching their sons (and daughters) Greek.[67] Nor were the qualities of the Persian language extolled in the manner that Palestinian sources refer to the Greek language, such as its being the only language into which the Torah might be accurately translated.[68] Indeed, the statement by Rav Joseph—"Why [speak] the Aramaic language in Babylonia, [better] either the Sacred Tongue [Hebrew] or the Persian language" (BT Sotah 49b)—can hardly be taken as a serious attempt at abandoning Aramaic in favor of a Persian dialect. The statement is no more than an artificial replication of a declaration attributed to the Palestinian patriarch Judah (180–220 C.E.): "Why speak Syriac [i.e., Aramaic] in Palestine? Talk either Hebrew or Greek" (BT Sotah 49b). Both statements recognize that Jews in Late Antiquity were interacting with three languages: the sacred Hebrew language of Scripture and synagogue liturgical activity; the vernacular (Aramaic); and the "official" language of the government and surrounding elements of the indigenous aristocracy or clergy. But the comparison ends here, and Persian among Babylonian Jews never assumed the position evinced by Greek among the Jewish populations of Palestine and the Roman Empire. The latter were surrounded by broad sections of a gentile society for whom the Greek language was not just a vehicle for daily discourse but the ultimate underpinning of an all-embracing culture. This was not the case in Babylonia; here no such equation between the "official" language of government and the vernacular of the cultured masses existed. Persian was far more limited to government and the Iranian church, whereas Aramaic served as the vernacular—both for Jews and for the indigenous non-Jewish population.

If, however, Middle Persian was perceived by the rabbis as primarily a language of the Iranian government and clergy,[69] the use—or at least passive knowledge—of words in that dialect by Babylonian Jews might nevertheless serve to indicate the areas of cultural interaction between the latter and certain representative elements of Iranian society. Sure enough, of those Persian words that found their way into the Babylonian Talmud, a significant number relate precisely to those spheres of public behavior where Jews and Persian officials came into actual contact. These include state administration, official titles of office, the administration of justice and forms of punishment, and military terms.[70]

Similarly, it is not at all surprising to find rabbinic allusions to the festivals of "the Persians." The main reference in the Babylonian Talmud (Avodah Zara 11b)

lists four "Persian ones" alongside "four Babylonian ones," and this distinction—
to say nothing of the actual names of the festivals cited for each group by the
Talmud—is far from clear.[71] The parallel discussion in the Palestinian Talmud
(Avodah Zara 1:1 39c) quotes Rav as saying that "three holidays are in Babylonia
and three holidays are in Media." In both cases the names of the holidays were
corrupted by copyists over the generations and thus prove nothing regarding the
original familiarity of the talmudic rabbis with Iranian festivals.[72] But the vast
scholarship on these lists[73] has succeeded at least in identifying two well-known
Iranian holidays in both versions. They are "Noruz" ("Musardi" in manuscript
versions of the BT; Noroz in the PT), which signified the coming of the spring or
the summer,[74] and "Mihragan" ("Muharnekai" in the BT), which designated the
onset of the rainy season. The halakhic context for the preservation of these lists
was the Palestinian rabbinic prohibition on conducting business transactions
with the heathen on their festivals (Mishnah Avodah Zara 1:1–2). Whereas the
Mishnah proscribed such transactions "on the three days preceding the festivities," the Babylonian sage Samuel declared that "in the diaspora [Babylonia] it is
only forbidden on the actual festival day" (BT Avodah Zara 11b), possibly hinting
at a diminished fear in Babylonia that Jews might somehow become involved in
local cultic worship.

The underlying assumption in all cases was that the Jew had sufficient knowledge of the surrounding calendar so that he might refrain from business on
those days. It could be, however, that—as in the case of Iranian loanwords—here
too the rabbis referred precisely to those days on the Persian calendar that directly affected their own lives. The two festivals noted above were apparently
also days of tax collection in the Sassanian Empire, and indeed we hear elsewhere that Jews were accused of attempting to avoid payment of "the king's poll-
tax" twice during the year, "a month in the summer and a month in the winter"
(BT Bava Metzia 86a).[75] This would tend to dovetail with those sources cited already, relating to the interference of the Persian priests in the daily life of Jews,
such as by the removal of fire from their midst. This sort of activity apparently
also took place on specific days of the Persian calendar,[76] and so—as in the case
of tax collection—rabbinic awareness of particular components of Iranian culture need not necessarily reflect an internalizing process of acculturation but instead might point at times to a more prosaic reality of Jewish life being affected
by the proclivities of the surrounding—and ruling—local administration.

Yet when all is said and done, it would be impossible to deny some obvious
similarities between certain Iranian and Babylonian rabbinic aspects of theology
that manifest themselves not only in parallel terminology but also in actual expressions of popular belief and concomitant behavior. To be sure, not all "simi-

larities" necessarily point to an Iranian influence upon Babylonian Jewry,[77] but the fact that we possess the literary product of two parallel rabbinic communities, those of Babylonia and Palestine, affords us with at least some degree of control. Consequently, when we encounter fairly obvious affinities of expression or behavior between Babylonian Jews and their Persian neighbors, with no parallel expression anywhere in Palestinian rabbinic literature, the likelihood of an internal Iranian process of acculturation is at least partially enhanced.

One seemingly obvious example of contact between popular Iranian culture and statements recorded in the Babylonian Talmud relates to the realm of demons and demonology.[78] To be sure, a belief in the existence of vast armies of demons and spirits existing alongside human beings and constantly interacting with them was shared by all the peoples of the Ancient Near East. Among the biblical sins of ancient Israel was their recurrent sacrificing to *shedim,* a Hebrew term translated in the Septuagint as *daimones* (demons).[79] Second Temple Jewish literature is replete with allusions to a variety of such forces of evil, and Josephus even claims that King Solomon was trained in the ways of fighting evil spirits, and that he "composed incantations . . . and left behind forms of exorcisms with which those possessed by demons drive them out, never to return."[80] Josephus himself testifies to witnessing the activity of an exorciser in the presence of Vespasian and his soldiers,[81] and of course the New Testament is replete with stories of people possessed by a variety of evil spirits.[82] Scholars have even noted distinct similarities in the import assigned to some terms that refer to a variety of spiritual forces in Palestinian sectarian literature with those found in Iranian terminology,[83] suggesting some sort of Iranian cultural impact on the religious thought and imagery embraced by certain Palestinian Jewish circles.[84]

It is hardly surprising, then, that the Palestinian rabbis were also party to this widespread belief in spirits; according to one opinion in the Mishnah, "the harmful spirits" *(mazikin)* were among the 10 things created on Sabbath eve at twilight.[85] Rabbi Shimon b. Yohai interpreted the word "all" in a particular scripture ("And *all* people of the earth shall see that thou art called by the name of the Lord"—Deuteronomy 28:10) to refer "even to spirits and even to demons."[86] Such beliefs found their way into halakhic discourse as well, and thus, for example, the Tosefta addresses the permissibility of whispering an incantation "about demons" on the Sabbath.[87]

The universality of belief in demons and spirits notwithstanding, it is nevertheless in the Babylonian rabbinic corpus that we sense a true affinity to specific demonological images prominent in Iranian religious thought. The pervasiveness of demons so common in Pahlavi literature[88] resonates clearly in the Babylonian Talmud:[89]

It has been taught: Abba Benjamin says: "If the eye had the power to see them, no creature could endure the demons." Abaye said: "They are more numerous than we are and they surround us like the ridge around a field." Rav Huna says: "Every one among us has a thousand on his left hand and ten thousand on his right hand." Rabba says: "The crushing in the Kallah [i.e., the gatherings for public learning among the Babylonian rabbis] is from them. The wearing out of the clothes of scholars is due to their rubbing against them. . . . If one wants to discover them, let him take sifted ashes and sprinkle them around his bed, and in the morning he will see something like the footprints of a cock."[90]

Another talmudic tradition describes the queen of demons—Igrath, the daughter of Mahalath—at the head of 180,000 "destructive angels." Originally, we are told, these forces had unbridled permission to wreak destruction, but their powers were curtailed following the decree of one of the rabbis[91] ordering her never to pass through settled regions. " 'I beg you'—she pleaded—'leave me a little room,' so he left her the nights of Sabbath and of Wednesdays." It is for this reason, the Babylonian Talmud warns, that "one should not go out alone . . . on the nights of either Wednesday or Sabbath" (BT Pesahim 112b). Yet another sage—Abaye—succeeded in limiting the activities of these angels to isolated areas, removing them by his decree from settled regions (BT Pesahim 112b). Not only are these allusions to such demonic forces introduced into the talmudic discourse without any sign of skepticism or inferred disbelief, but they actually suggest that the most noted legal scholars of the rabbinic world accepted the existence of such forces; however, the scholars were able to overcome their destructive powers either by some specific knowledge they possessed or by virtue of their own pious behavior. Prayer, we can assume, would be a particularly potent weapon in this confrontation, and thus we read the following story about "a demon" that haunted the schoolhouse of Abaye, so that whenever two disciples would enter the premises, even during daytime, they would be harmed. Upon the arrival of another sage—Rabbi Aha b. Jacob—in town, Abaye saw to it that none of the townsmen offered him hospitality, thereby requiring the rabbi to spend the night in the schoolhouse:

The demon appeared to him in the guise of a seven-headed dragon. Every time he [Aha] fell on his knees [in prayer] one head fell off. The next day he reproached [the men of the schoolhouse]: "Had not a miracle occurred, you would have endangered my life." (BT Kiddushin 29b)

Legal discussions and allusions to demons seem to merge effortlessly in the Babylonian Talmud, hardly leaving an impression that the world of halakhah—

rather than that of devils and spirits—is the "real" and exclusive environment in which rabbis function. The long discussion of demons, magic, and the like found in the Babylonian Talmud (Pesahim 109b–112b) is introduced through a question relating to the mishnaic stipulation that at the Passover seder one must drink four cups of wine: "How could our Rabbis enact something whereby one is led into danger? Surely it was taught: A man must not eat in pairs [i.e., eat an even-numbered amount of dishes] nor drink in pairs nor cleanse himself twice nor perform his requirements [a euphemism for intimacy] twice." All this, we are ultimately informed, is because—as the demon Joseph once told Rabbi Joseph—"Ashmedai[92] the king of the demons is appointed over all pairs" (BT Pesahim 110a).

What is striking, however, is not merely the credulity evinced by the Babylonian rabbis toward these phenomena but also their knowledge that such beliefs were not always shared by their Palestinian counterparts: "In the West [Palestine] they are not particular about 'pairs' " (BT Pesahim 110b).[93] Moreover, it appears that all sorts of Babylonian rabbinic customs are related to fears well established in Iranian demonology. For example, the care that the rabbis demand in not randomly discarding the parings of human fingernails—"One who buries them is righteous, one who burns them is pious, and one who throws them away is a villain"[94]—derives directly from Iranian fears about the powerful potential, for good as well as evil, found in nail-parings. According to the Vendidad (17.9), nail-parings should be dedicated to a particularly fabulous bird (known as "Asho.zushta" and identified as the owl) renowned for uttering holy words in its own unique tongue, thereby causing devils to flee. This bird was charged with guarding the parings, lest they fall into the hands of the devils who then turn them into hostile weapons.[95]

The rabbis of Babylonia were aware of potential danger lurking wherever the demons and their kind might be found, which was just about everywhere. Particularly susceptible moments were during the various functions connected with eating and drinking:

Abaye said: "At first I thought the reason why the last washing [of the hands after a meal] may not be performed over the ground [but only over a vessel] was that it made a mess, but now my master [Rabbah bar Nahmani] has told me it is because an evil spirit rests upon it [i.e., the water]." (BT Hullin 105b)

Abaye was also advised by his mentor not to drink water from the mouth of a jug but to pour off some water first and then drink, "because of evil waters"— that is, the fear that demons may have drunk from the water at the top of the jug

(BT Hullin 105b).[96] In general, demons rendered the drinking of water a potentially dangerous activity, and one had to know precisely when and where it was advisable to refrain from drinking: "A man should not drink water from rivers and pools at night, and if he drinks, his blood is on his own head, because of the danger."

What is the danger?—the Talmud asks, and responds by citing the name "Shaberiri," apparently the demon that causes blindness. Fortunately, the rabbis were also privy to the effective incantation that might ward off this particular spirit: "O So-and-so, my mother told me: 'Beware of Shaberire, berire, rire, ire, re; I am thirsty for water in a white glass' " (BT Pesahim 112a).[97]

Here too it was Zoroastrian literature that also warned against drinking water at night. In a collection of Zoroastrian traditions known as *Sad Dar* (lit. "The Hundred Subjects"),[98] we read that "it is not proper to swallow water at night, because it is a sin."[99] A Pahlavi fragment alludes to the contamination of well-water at night,[100] and yet another text[101] explicitly relates to the presence of demons and fiends who seize upon the wisdom of one who eats or drinks in the dark.

For Zoroastrians, however, demons did not only lurk in various locations and wait to pounce on some hapless innocent. Just as one's physical being might be assaulted by these forces, so others might lay siege to a person's moral nature and behavior.[102] Pahlavi texts describe various spirits taking over a man's personality: "A man whose body is inhabited by Akoman [Evil Mind], this is his mark: He is cool as regards good works, has bad relationships with the good, is difficult [in] making peace, is an advocate of the destitute good and is himself [miserly].[103] The same text goes on to describe a man "whose body is inhabited by Xesm [Anger]" and the negative impact on his behavior: "It is impossible to talk to him, when people talk to him he does not listen.... [H]e tells many lies to people and inflicts much chastisement on an innocent person."

This being the case, we can understand how all sorts of actions might be attributed to such demons who take control of a man's faculties, thereby controlling his deeds as well. Not only was this sort of compulsion known to the Babylonian rabbis, but they even attempted to define the legal ramifications of such behavior. In this context the Talmud cites the following halakhah: "If a man is compelled by force to eat unleavened bread [on Passover], he thereby performs his religious duty." The nature of this compulsion, however, is immediately addressed: "Compelled by whom? Shall I say by an evil spirit?" (BT Rosh Hashanah 28a). The conclusion, of course, might be to consider "sin" as well the result of various powers that have taken control of one's being, thereby possibly alleviating any moral culpability for such action. Although this was not addressed directly by the Babylonian rabbis, they nevertheless appear to have been familiar with the image of one whose actions seem to be directed, and indeed coerced, by some sort of invading demon. When asked why her children are so beautiful, a woman ascribes it to her husband's modesty, describing how her husband cohabits with her only at midnight, and even then "uncovers a handbreadth and covers a handbreadth, and is as though he were *compelled by a demon*" (BT Nedarim 20b).[104]

The belief in demons and spirits demanded a powerful arsenal of protective measures to ward off potential dangers, and the ancient world produced an enormous variety of them. The Jews of Babylonia were no different in this respect from their brethren in Palestine and elsewhere, nor from the non-Jewish environment in which they lived. Amulets, incantations, and other measures were employed universally, but certain discoveries relating to this community would appear to shed some interesting light on one particular aspect of the relationship between Jews and gentiles east of the Euphrates River.

During the past 150 years, hundreds of earthenware bowls, containing incantations primarily in Jewish Aramaic but also in Syriac and Mandaic, have been discovered in Mesopotamia and Iran, the areas that in Late Antiquity and the early Middle Ages constituted the regions of talmudic and gaonic Babylonia.[105] These bowls are usually dated between the fourth and seventh centuries C.E.—that is, the second half of the talmudic era and the immediate post-talmudic period. The vessels are inscribed in ink, usually on the concave side in spiral concentric circles, but there are various exceptions to this pattern.[106] (See p. 250.) A large number of such bowls were found in 1888–89 at excavations at Nippur, where they were discovered *in situ* in private dwellings, usually in what is assumed to be their original position, upside down. Scholars have assumed that, positioned in such a manner, and given their contents, the bowls were intended to trap and imprison various demons. Although this interpretation is reinforced by the language frequently found in the bowls ("bound and sealed are all demons and evil spirits"),[107] other such vessels were intended to rid a person or a house of some evil spirit ("now flee and go forth and do not trouble Komes b. Mahlaphta in her house and her dwelling").[108] The removal of the spirit or demon was effected in a manner very similar to the dispatching of a writ of divorce, and indeed some of the bowls actually use the terminology of a Jewish *get,* except that in place of a woman being divorced, we encounter Lilith or some other demon as the object of the process:

I, Komes bat Mahlaphta, have divorced, separated, missed thee, thou Lilith, Lilith of the Desert. . . .[I]t is announced to you, whose mother is Palhan and whose father [Pe]lahdad, ye Liliths: Hear and go forth and do not trouble

Komes bat Mahlaphta in her house. Go ye forth altogether from her house and her dwelling and from Kaletha and Artasria her children . . . for so has spoken to thee Joshua ben Perahya: A divorce has come to thee from across the sea.[109]

Even more striking is the fact that these "deeds of divorce" frequently adhere not only to the terminology of a *get* but to legal stipulations as well, such as the requirement that the document cite explicitly the full name of the intended divorcee, as well as the person charging the particular spirit with removal. Indeed, one bowl actually alludes to a previous case where the banned spirit was not named, thus rendering that earlier document invalid: "Just as there was a Lilith who strangled human beings, and Rabbi Yehoshu'a bar Perahya sent a ban against her, but she did not accept it because he did not know her name."[110]

The numerous references in the bowls to Yehoshua ben Perahya, the "rabbi" we encountered in a talmudic confrontation with "the queen of demons," is just one of many factors that support the widely—albeit not universally[111]—accepted theory that these bowls were inscribed not only by Jews but indeed by those Jews who had at least some access to rabbinic legal formulae. The language in many of the bowls has been definitively identified as Babylonian Jewish Aramaic, and the frequent quotation of biblical scripture in Hebrew lends further support for assuming that before us are the products of Jewish practitioners of magic.

But if the language and content all point to Jewish magicians, one factor in many of the bowls almost certainly suggests a non-Jewish involvement as well: the clients on whose behalf the bowls were produced very frequently go by decidedly Persian names, at times even Zoroastrian theophoric ones.[112] Some Jews may have adopted Persian names, but the preponderance of otherwise Jewish components in the vast majority of magic bowls found to date, alongside a decidedly non-Jewish nomenclature for the beneficiaries of the bowls, seems to point to a fascinating social and cultural reality in talmudic Babylonia. As a minority group, however self-assured, the Jews may have been considered by the indigenous population of Babylonia not only as "different" and even "outsiders" but, more important, as "others" who nevertheless have access to certain knowledge, or powers, that "we" locals are not privy to. In fact, societies frequently attribute such extraordinary talents precisely to groups living outside the mainstream, or on the fringes of society. It may very well be that the Jews of Babylonia were willing to offer their services in connecting with certain forces or spirits not readily accessible to the masses. And while this activity might have been frowned upon—at least in principle—by the rabbis themselves, they could not prevent their coreligionists from providing a service in great demand by neighboring groups who were not party to the same misgivings.

This last observation deserves some further explication. On the one hand, the

An example of Aramaic magic bowls, written by Jews but
possibly intended to heal non-Jews in Sassanian Babylonia.
(The Israel Museum, Jerusalem)

rabbis evinced enormous discomfort with all sorts of magical activities,[113] considering them an attempt at circumventing proper channels of prayer and behavior in the process of seeking certain benefits, and thereby constituting a
denial of the exclusive role of "the heavenly *familia*" in the granting of such rewards.[114] Yet, on the other hand, it is clear from what we have seen that the belief
in an army of demons and spirits was deeply embedded in the rabbinic mind
and that the rabbis did not shy away from addressing this "reality" with their
own unique recourse to a wide array of incantations and other activities, all
aimed directly at the threatening entity and forgoing supplication to the divine
protector or benefactor.

This seeming inconsistency characterizes the rabbinic position vis-à-vis
all sorts of popular beliefs and their attendant behavior. Among the most obvious examples of such fence straddling are the numerous rabbinic statements
addressing astrology. Here, of course, the barriers between Babylonia and the
rest of the Jewish world had long ago been removed. While the very phrase

"Chaldean" served in ancient times to link the land of Babylonia with a propensity for astrological activity,[115] astrology had become so popular by the Greco-Roman period that "scarcely anybody made a distinction between astronomy and its illegitimate sister."[116] For the rabbis, however, recognition of the efficacy of astrology placed in question not only man's freedom of choice but also the whole concept of Divine providence and its critical link with the principle of free will.[117] Recourse to astrological divination was tantamount to recognition that events were predetermined in the stars and not dependent on God's will, which properly should be influenced by man's behavior. Consequently the third-century sage Rav, in the name of one of the few second-century rabbinic authorities also of Babylonian origins (Rabbi Yosi of Huzal), declared: "How do we know that you must not consult Chaldeans [astrologers]? Because it says: 'Thou shalt be whole-hearted with the Lord thy God' (Deuteronomy 18:13)."[118]

But neither in Babylonia nor in Palestine could the rabbis bring themselves to deny outright the "science" of their day, "a science recognized and acknowledged by all the civilized ancient world."[119] Moreover, just as Jewish authors of the Second Temple period had already identified Abraham as one who "sought and obtained the knowledge of astrology and the Chaldean craft,"[120] so too did the Babylonian sages attribute to Abraham a belief in planetary influence. When he is promised by God that he will have an heir, he replies:

> Sovereign of the Universe, I have looked at my constellation and find that I am not fated to beget a child. He [God] told him: "Leave your astrological calculation, for Israel is not subject to planetary influence [lit. 'there is no planet—*mazal*—for Israel']."[121]

God's response does not deny the power of the stars but claims that Israel— unlike the rest of humankind—has been removed from planetary control. Though clearly striving to maintain the theological purity of Israel's relationship with Divine providence, this somewhat contrived rabbinic compromise never really convinced the Babylonian sages that there was nothing in the stars for them. A passage in the Babylonian Talmud elaborates precisely what characteristics will adhere to people born on each of the seven days of the week (BT Shabbat 156a). The continuation of that same text notes how being born under the various planets also determines one's behavior:

> He who was born under Venus will be wealthy and an adulterer.... He who was born under Mercury will be of a retentive memory and wise. . . . He who was born under Mars will be a shedder of blood. Rav Ashi said: "Either a surgeon, a thief, a slaughterer or a circumciser."

Elsewhere, Rava declares that "life, children, and livelihood" are not the consequence of one's merits but are "dependent on the planet" (BT Mo'ed Katan 28a). Yet another sage, Rav Papa, suggests that one should plan various activities in accordance with the planetary constellation. Thus, for example, a person should avoid litigation during the month of Av, "whose planet is pernicious," and prefer instead the month of Adar, "whose planet is favorable" (BT Ta'anit 29b).

Even more telling is the foresight that the rabbis attribute to the various "Chaldeans" that they themselves solicited for advice. Rav Joseph turned down an offer to serve as head of the rabbinical academy "because the astrologers had told him that he would be head for only two years." And so his colleague Rabbah filled the position for 22 years, ultimately to be succeeded by Rav Joseph who indeed served for only two and a half years (BT Berakhot 64a).[122] Interestingly, a later (tenth-century) version of this same story claims that it was Rav Joseph's mother who had contact with the astrologers,[123] and we can only wonder if this latter rendition is not something of a cleansed version intended to distance the sage himself from behavior that does not quite conform to the standards set by the rabbis themselves. Elsewhere in the Babylonian Talmud we do, in fact, find a story describing contacts between the mother of a sage and Chaldeans, and there, too, the prophesies of the astrologer are proven correct:

> Rav Nahman b. Isaac's mother was told by Chaldeans [astrologers]: "Your son will be a thief." She did not permit him to go bareheaded, telling him: "Cover your head so that the fear of heaven may be upon you, and pray [for mercy]." He did not know why she said this.
>
> One day when he was sitting and studying under a palm tree, his garment fell from over his head, he raised his eyes, saw the palm tree, and temptation overcame him. He climbed up and bit off a cluster [of dates] with his teeth. (BT Shabbat 156b)

The Talmud cites this story to prove that Israel is *not* given to the influence of planets, but, inasmuch as Rav Nahman's behavior until his "fall" overcame the Chaldeans' prophesy, the bottom line of the story would appear to prove just the opposite. Moreover, this is not an isolated case of a sage interacting with an astrologer, and in those other cases as well the pronouncements of the "Chaldeans" invariably prove to be accurate.[124]

In sum, all of these sources seem to suggest a unique social and cultural reality. The Babylonian sages knew quite well what a "perfect" Jewish world ought to look like, and we would do well to interpret many of their programmatic declarations as just that: idyllic guidelines for a world that could not possibly exist given the cultural milieu in which these rabbis functioned. And so, theoretical declarations notwithstanding, in practice both the rabbis and their flock functioned as part of their social and cultural environment. Did these beliefs and their consequential behavior render the rabbis themselves "non-rabbinic"? Not really, if we accept the multiplicity of cultural influences all contributing to the uniquely Babylonian version of rabbinic society. In Jewish terms, much of their learning was nothing if not a continuation and intensification of Palestinian rabbinic teaching. Even here, however, they almost certainly grafted at least some aspects of the local Sassanian legal process to the mass of Palestinian material that they succeeded in co-opting and making their own.[125] As for popular culture, here too they forged an amalgam between ideas passed on from Palestine through the same rabbinic pipeline that transmitted legal materials and the surrounding Iranian environment that supplied them with a wealth of religious and spiritual imagery.

The genius of Babylonian rabbinic leadership, however, was not so much in the melding of such variegated influences into a broad cultural mosaic but rather in the creation and propagation of a self-image that would project this culture as being the embodiment of the one unique and ancient model of true, unadulterated Israelite tradition, with uncontaminated roots going back to First-Temple Jerusalem and the days of the prophets. Given all that we know about the diverse influences that left their mark on Babylonian Jewish culture prior to their establishment as a literary corpus, one undeniable fact remains. By post-talmudic times, the sages of Babylonia would not only assume the upper hand within the rabbinic world of their day but also ultimately succeed in securing a near-universal acceptance of their Talmud as the definitive expression of rabbinic Judaism. Having emerged out of almost total obscurity only a few centuries earlier, the communal success story of Babylonian Jewry would now be complete.

NOTES

1. The import of the names "Babylon" and "Babylonia" is far from consistent. Whereas the former is commonly employed as a designation of the ancient city, it (as well as "Babylonia") frequently refers to the vast territories between the Tigris and Euphrates rivers, south of Baghdad and constituting much of the southeastern areas of modern-day Iraq. In "Jewish geography," however, talmudic "Babylonia" usually includes all the Jewish communities east of the Euphrates, i.e., not only southeastern Iraq but also Mesopotamia to the northwest, as well as the Iranian territories east of the Tigris, such as Assyria, Media, and Elymais (Khusistan).

2. For surveys of the early Jewish captive community in Babylonia, see R. Zadok, *The Jews in Babylonia During the Chaldean and Achaemenian Periods According to the Babylo-*

nian Sources (Haifa, 1979), and E. J. Bickerman, "The Babylonian Captivity," in W. D. Davies and L. Finkelstein, eds. *The Cambridge History of Judaism*, vol. 1 (Cambridge, Engl., 1984), 342–58.

3. The Munich manuscript of the Babylonian Talmud reads "to her father's home," probably influenced by the allusion to the patriarch Abraham.

4. The date of the letter does not appear in chapter 29 of Jeremiah, but the passage seems to belong to the same historical context as the two previous chapters; see J. Bright, *Jeremiah*, 2d ed. (New York, 1984) 210–11.

5. The earliest successes of the Judaean captives in adjusting to their new land, while maintaining some degree of unique ethnic identity, are documented in the Murashu archives, discovered in 1893 at Nippur. See M. D. Coogan, "Life in the Diaspora: Jews at Nippur in the 5th Century B.C.," *Biblical Archaeologist* 37 (1974): 6–12, and S. Daiches, *The Jews in Babylonia in the Time of Ezra and Nehemiah According to Babylonian Inscriptions* (London, 1910).

6. BT Bava Bathra 55a and parallels; see J. Neusner, *A History of the Jews in Babylonia*, 5 vols. (Leiden, 1965–70), 2: 69. For the subsequent implications and various interpretations of the principle, see S. Shiloh, *Dina de-Malkhuta Dina* (Jerusalem, 1975). For a brief discussion of the principle's impact on Jewish communal development, see D. Biale, *Power and Powerlessness in Jewish History* (New York, 1986), 54–57.

7. This statement by Josephus (*Antiquities*, 11:133) seems to reflect a common general impression shared by other Jews in the west (see, e.g., Philo, *Legatio ad Gaium*, 216, 282) of vast numbers of Jews populating the lands beyond the Euphrates; in a way it also seems to highlight a shared ignorance of any real internal communal structures and cultural activities among those Jews.

8. Josephus, *Antiquities*, 15:14–15; here again Josephus relates that Hyrcanus II settled in Babylonia "where there was a great number of Jews."

9. For the role of Babylonian Jewry and Judaism in early modern Jewish scholarship, see I. Gafni, "Talmudic Research in Modern Times: Between Scholarship and Ideology," in A. Oppenheimer, ed., *Jüdische Geschichte in hellenistisch-römischer Zeit* (Munich, 1999), 134–48. For the place of Hillel in this dispute, see ibid., 145.

10. The formal reckoning of Parthian history begins with the uprising of Arsaces I and his brother Thiridates against the Seleucid Empire, circa 247 B.C.E. In effect, the beginning of Parthian rule in portions of Babylonia overlaps with the Seleucid era, but the main thrust of Parthian expansion at the expense of the Seleucid Empire, under King Mithridates I (171–138 B.C.E.) coincides with the Hasmonaean brother's rebellion against those very same Hellenistic rulers.

11. Parthian kings frequently attached titles such as "Philhellene," "Epiphanes," or "Euergetes" to their names, and Plutarch (Crassus 33) describes how one of Euripides' plays was being presented at the Parthian court when word was received there about the victory over Crassus at Charrae. Interestingly, the Babylonian Talmud (Bava Kamma 117a, according to most manuscripts) has the third-century sage Rav describe the Parthians—who had just

been defeated by the "Persians" (Sassanians)—as "Greeks." On Parthian attitudes toward Hellenism, see R. Ghirshman, *Iran* (Harmondsworth, 1954) 266–68, and R. Ghirshman, *Iran, Parthians and Sassanians* (London, 1962), 1–12, 257–81. Note also the title "The Adaptable Arsacids" for the Parthians, in R. N. Frye, *The Heritage of Persia* (Cleveland, 1963).

12. For general surveys of the Parthian Empire, see N. Debevoise, *A Political History of Parthia* (Chicago, 1938); A. D. H. Bivar, "The Political History of Iran Under the Arsacids," in E. Yarshater, ed., *Cambridge History of Iran*, vol. 3(1) (Cambridge, Engl. 1983), 21–99; and J. Neusner, "Parthian Political Ideology," *Iranica Antiqua* 3 (1963): 40–59.

13. *Antiquities*, 18:310–79 (the story of the brothers Asinaeus and Anilaeus); *Antiquities* 20:17–69 (the conversion of the royal family of Adiabene). Here, too, various nineteenth-century Jewish writers thought they might derive from these narratives solid information on the cultural and religious fabric of the Babylonian Jewish community in pre-talmudic times; however, see Gafni, "Talmudic Research," 144–45, esp. n. 59.

14. These identifications are in fact untenable. Borsif has been identified with the Burs mentioned by Yaqut and other Arabic sources (present-day Birs Nimrud) and is situated southwest of Babylonia, whereas the biblical text clearly refers to cities in Assyria; see A. Oppenheimer, *Babylonia Judaica in the Talmudic Period* (Wiesbaden, 1983), 104. The same is true for Perat de-Meshan, clearly in the vicinity of the Shatt al-Arab and consequently far removed from any Assyrian locality (ibid., 348).

15. BT Yoma 10a; Gen. Rabbah 37:4.

16. Yaqut and other Arab geographers have identified the three as islands in the Euphrates; see Oppenheimer, *Babylonia Judaica*, 28, 446.

17. BT Bava Bathra 91a; Kuta, or Kuta Rabbah, is the present-day Tall Ibrahim on the Habl Ibrahim canal, 30 kilometers northeast of Babylon; see Oppenheimer, *Babylonia Judaica*, 175, who notes that Arab sources also connect Kuta with Abraham.

18. A. Momigliano, *Alien Wisdom* (Cambridge, Engl., 1975), 116.

19. Apud Eusebius, *Praeparatio Evangelica*, 9.27.4.

20. BT Gitin 88a; see also Tanhuma Noah 3: "He [God] acted righteously with Israel in that He had the exile of Yekhoniah precede the exile of Zedekiah, in order that the Oral Torah not be forgotten by them."

21. All the attempts at identifying an exilarch in Babylonia prior to the third century C.E. are based on late and insufficient evidence; see J. Liver, *Toldot bet David mi-Ḥurban Mamlekhet Yehudah ve-ad le-aḥar Ḥurban ha-Bayit ha-Sheni* (Jerusalem, 1959), 41–46, and other literature cited in I. Gafni, *Land, Center and Diaspora: Jewish Constructs in Late Antiquity* (Sheffield, Engl., 1997), 55 n. 37. To be sure, given the overall paucity of information on the Babylonian Jewish community prior to the talmudic era, the existence of an early exilarchate cannot be dismissed out of hand and may actually have made sense within the political and social frameworks of the Parthian Empire.

22. *Iggeret Rav Sherira Gaon*, ed. B. M. Lewin (Haifa, 1921), 72–73. The antiquity of synagogues played a major role in Babylonian historical consciousness; see A. Oppen-

heimer, "Babylonian Synagogues with Historical Associations," in D. Urman and P. V. M. Flesher, eds., *Ancient Synagogues: Historical Analysis and Archaeological Discovery,* vol. 1 (Leiden, 1995), 40–48.

23. BT Kiddushin 69b, 71a; BT Ketubot 111a.

24. BT Kiddushin 69b.

25. Ibid.

26. BT Kiddushin 71b, and BT Gitin 6a; see also A. Oppenheimer and M. Lecker, "Lineage Boundaries of Babylonia," *Zion* 50 (1985): 173–87, and A. Oppenheimer and M. Lecker, "Burial Beyond the Euphrates," in S. Ettinger et al., eds., *Milet,* vol. 1 (Tel Aviv, 1983), 157–63.

27. See I. Gafni, "Reinterment in the Land of Israel: Notes on the Origin and Development of the Custom," *The Jerusalem Cathedra* 1 (1981): 96–104, and Gafni, *Land, Center and Diaspora,* 79–95.

28. *Avot de-Rabbi Nathan,* ed. S. Schechter, version A, chap. 26, p. 82.

29. Of course, the historicity of the story itself is not the issue here, but rather the self-image and political awareness that it reflects.

30. A frequent talmudic rendition of "herbad" or "erbad," one of several Persian titles for priests of the Zoroastrian church.

31. BT Gitin 16b–17a. For an exhaustive study of the talmudic source, its textual variants, and the wider religious realities and implications of the Zoroastrian priestly attempts at safeguarding the purity of fire and removing it from nonreligious contexts, see E. S. Rosenthal, "For the Talmudic Dictionary—Talmudica Iranica," in S. Shaked, ed., *Irano-Judaica,* vol. 1 (Jerusalem, 1982), Hebrew sec. 38–134, esp. 38–42, 58–64, and the notes on 75–84, 128–31.

32. For the nature of the Roman persecution of Jews during and following the Bar Kokhba uprising, see M. D. Herr, "Persecutions and Martyrdom in Hadrian's Days," *Scripta Hierosolymitana* 23 (1972): 85–125.

33. See J. Duchesne-Guillemin, "Religion and Politics Under the Sasanians," in E. Yarshater, ed., *The Cambridge History of Iran,* 3(2): 874–97.

34. BT Yevamot 63b.

35. See n. 11 above.

36. The text is quoted here according to almost all the important manuscripts of BT Bava Kamma and has undergone extensive scrutiny because of its obvious reference to the major political changes of the day. See Rosenthal, "For the Talmudic Dictionary," 54–58, 87, and D. Sperber, "On the Unfortunate Adventures of Rav Kahana: A Passage of Saboraic Polemic from Sasanian Persia," in Shaked, ed., *Irano-Judaica,* 1: 83–100.

37. BT Berakhot 56a; BT Sukkah 53a; BT Mo'ed Katan 26a; BT Sanhedrin 98a.

38. BT Berakhot 56a.

39. BT Sukkah 53a.

40. See D. Goodblatt, "A Note on the name 'ypr' / 'pr' hwrmyz," *Journal of the American Oriental Society* 96, 1 (1976): 135–36.

41. BT Ta'anit 24b; for the other stories, see J. Neusner, *Jews in Babylonia*, 4: 35–39.

42. BT Ketubot 61a–b.

43. BT Yoma 10a. Not all the Babylonians concurred with this prognosis, and in the continuation of this same source Rav predicts the opposite: Rome will defeat Persia. When asked how the destroyers will emerge victorious, the Talmud—anonymously—suggests that the latter were also guilty of destroying synagogues. (Rav himself is simply quoted as stating that this was God's wish—without elaborating.) This vague allusion to religious pressure on the part of the Sassanians might reflect the harsh reactions to some of the behavior attributed to the Zoroastrian priests, or possibly it was formulated during the few periods of outright persecution in Persia of minorities in general, not only Jews. These occurred in the late third century and again in the tumultuous days of the fifth century. For brief surveys of the attitude toward Jews under the Sassanians, see G. Widengren, "The Status of the Jews in the Sassanian Empire," *Iranica Antiqua* 1 (1961): 117–62; J. Neusner, "Jews in Iran," in Yarshater, ed., *The Cambridge History of Iran*, 3(2): 909–23.

44. BT Mo'ed Katan 26a.

45. See W. Wright, *The Homilies of Aphraates: The Persian Sage*, vol. 1: *Syriac Text* (London, 1869), 394. For literature on this relationship, see J. Neusner, *Aphrahat and Judaism* (Leiden, 1971), 7–12. The confidence of the Jews in their confrontation with Iranian Christianity may also be the result of superior numbers; see F. Gavin, *Aphraates and the Jews* (Toronto, 1923), 17. See also G. F. Moore, "Christian Writers on Judaism," *Harvard Theological Review* 14 (1921): 199.

46. See R. Brody, "Judaism in the Sasanian Empire: A Case Study in Religious Coexistence," in S. Shaked and A. Netzer, eds., *Irano-Judaica*, vol. 2 (Jerusalem, 1990), 52–61.

47. On this source, see M. Beer, "Notes on Three Edicts Against the Jews of Babylonia in the Third Century," in Shaked, ed., *Irano-Judaica*, 1: 25–37, and Brody, "Judaism in the Sasanian Empire."

48. For the rite of Zoroastrian exposure, see M. Boyce, *Zoroastrians, Their Religious Beliefs and Practices* (London, 1979), 14–15, 44–45, 120–21.

49. From Vendidad 6. The Vendidad, consisting of 22 sections, was most probably compiled in the Parthian period. It deals with a variety of legal topics and contains elaborate laws relating to purity. The translation here is from M. Boyce, ed. and trans., *Textual Sources for the Study of Zoroastrianism* (Manchester, 1984), 65.

50. The "Persians," in rabbinic imagery, "grow hair like bears" (BT Megillah 11a; BT Kiddushin 72a; BT Avodah Zara 2b), and in fact Sassanian art (coins and rock-carvings) almost always portray Persian rulers with grown beards, frequently in contradistinction to the Roman rulers shown in those same depictions.

51. It is not absolutely clear what aroused Zoroastrians to prohibit the slaughtering of animals by Jews; see Beer, "Notes on Three Edicts," 29–31. S. Shaked, "Zoroastrian Polemics Against Jews in the Sasanian and Early Islamic Period," in Shaked and Netzer, eds., *Irano-Judaica*, 2: 93, quotes certain Zoroastrian texts that advise "not to kill cattle before they reach

maturity" and claim that "Dahag"—the mythical representative of the negative views that oppose the true faith—"taught to kill cattle freely, according to the custom of the Jews."

52. See Brody, "Judaism in the Sasanian Empire," 61, and the literature cited in I. Gafni, *Yehudei Bavel bi-Tekufat ha-Talmud: Ḥaye ha-Ḥevrah ve-ha Ruaḥ* (Jerusalem, 1990), 49–51, 251.

53. S. Shaked, "Iranian Influence on Judaism: First Century B.C.E. to Second Century C.E.," in Davies and Finkelstein, eds., *The Cambridge History of Judaism*, 1: 308–25, esp. 309. A copious literature exists on the possible bilateral influences of the Jewish and Persian religions and cultures, alongside an equally elaborate bibliography denying the "influence" aspect and arguing for a more independent, albeit at times chronologically concurrent, development of similar ideas. See G. W. Carter, *Zoroastrianism and Judaism* (Boston, 1918); J. Barr, "The Question of Religious Influence: The Case of Zoroastrianism, Judaism and Christianity," *Journal of the American Academy of Religion* 53, no. 2 (1985): 201–35; J. Neusner, *Judaism, Christianity and Zoroastrianism in Talmudic Babylonia* (Lanham, Md., 1986); and M. Boyce and F. Grenet, *A History of Zoroastrianism*, vol. 3: *Zoroastrianism Under Macedonian and Roman Rule* (Leiden, 1991), 366–67, 392–440.

54. Shaked, "Iranian Influence on Judaism," 324–25.

55. S. Baron, *A Social and Religious History of the Jews*, vol. 2 (New York, 1952), 191.

56. J. Naveh and S. Shaked, *Magic Spells and Formulae—Aramaic Incantations of Late Antiquity* (Jerusalem, 1993), 21.

57. BT Shabbat 122b; Palestinian Talmud (henceforth: PT) Shabbat 16:15d. It is interesting to note that the gentile is referred to in the PT as "a Persian," whereas in the BT simply as "nokhri"—a gentile. It appears that the PT uses "Persian" as a generic term for gentiles in Babylonia, whereas the BT reserves the use of "Persian" to government or church officials (see Gafni, *Yehudei Bavel bi-Tekufat ha-Talmud* 153 and n. 18).

58. See also BT Avodah Zara 65a: Rabah sent a gift to one bar Sheshak.

59. Most of the relevant information has been gathered by M. Beer, *Amora'ei Bavel: Perakim be-Ḥaye ha-Kalkalah* (Ramat Gan, 1974), 207–11.

60. For the various Aramaic dialects found in Iran from the Achaemenid period and down to the talmudic era, see *Encyclopaedia Iranica*, vol. 2 (London, 1987), 251–56. On the use of Aramaic by Jews, from late biblical times and down to the present, see the concise overview by J. C. Greenfield, "Aramaic and the Jews," in M. J. Geller et al., eds., *"Studia Aramaica," New Sources and Approaches* (Oxford, 1995), 1–18.

61. From a responsa of Rav Hai, published by A. E. Harkavy in *Hakedem* vol. 2 (St. Petersburg, 1908), 82.

62. See the sources cited in J. N. Epstein, *Dikdut Aramit Bavlit* (Jerusalem, 1960), 17.

63. The question of Hebrew as a commonly spoken vernacular even in Second Temple Palestine, as well as the first centuries of the Common Era, has been heatedly debated for over 150 years, with accusations of "Zionistically inclined" Hebraism and tendentious romanticism frequently introduced into the polemic. See, for a brief discussion, E. Y. Kutscher,

A History of the Hebrew Language (Jerusalem, 1982), 115–19; much of the relevant research has been cited by S. D. Fraade, "Rabbinic Views on the Practice of Targum, and Multilingualism in the Jewish Galilee of the Third–Sixth Centuries," in L. I. Levine, *The Galilee in Late Antiquity* (New York, 1992), 253–86. For one historian's perspective of the debate, see S. Schwartz, "Language, Power and Identity in Ancient Palestine," *Past and Present* 148 (1995): 3–47. Whatever the reality might have been in Palestine, few would argue for any widespread use of Hebrew as a vernacular among Jews of the Babylonian Diaspora in Late Antiquity.

64. See E. Yarshater, "Zoroastrian Pahlavi Writings," in Yarshater, ed., *The Cambridge History of Iran*, 3(2): 1166–69.

65. This tendency to provide biblical etymologies for Persian words fits nicely with the rabbinic propensity in the Babylonian Talmud of linking biblical place-names with contemporary cities in the Iranian countryside.

66. Only 130 examples of Iranian loanwords were noted by S. Telegdi, "Essai sur la phonétique des emprunts iraniens en araméen Talmudique," *Journal Asiatique* 226 (1935): 177–256; see also S. Shaked, "Iranian Loanwords in Middle Aramaic," *Encyclopaedia Iranica*, 2: 259–61. Shaked notes that many of the Iranian loanwards that appear in Middle Aramaic (i.e., the Aramaic of the Babylonian Talmud) may have entered that language over a protracted period of time and would thus not necessarily attest to contacts between Jews and Iranians during the talmudic period alone. In contradistinction to the Babylonian Talmud, over 3,000 Greek and Latin loanwords were cited by S. Krauss, *Griechische und lateinische Lehnwörter im Talmud, Midrasch und Targum*, vols. 1–3 (Berlin, 1898–99). Notwithstanding the problems involved in portions of Krauss's lists (see D. Sperber, "Greek and Latin Words in Rabbinic Literature," *Bar Ilan* 14–15 [1977]: 9–20 [English sec.]), the discrepancy between the scope and nature of the influence of surrounding "official" languages on the literary production of the Jews of Palestine and Babylonia is undeniable.

67. See S. Lieberman, *Hellenism in Jewish Palestine* (New York, 1950), 100–114.

68. PT Megillah 1:2, 71c; see S. Lieberman, *Greek in Jewish Palestine* (New York, 1942), 17.

69. See A. Christensen, *L'Iran sous les Sassanides* (Copenhagen, 1944), 45.

70. See Shaked, "Iranian Loanwords," 260–61.

71. See B. M. Bokser, "Talmudic Names of the Iranian Festivals," *Journal of the American Oriental Society* 95 (1975): 261–62.

72. See Neusner, *Jews in Babylonia*, 2: 88, and J. Neusner, *Talmudic Judaism in Sasanian Babylonia* (Leiden, 1976), 142.

73. See Gafni, *Yehudei Bavel bi-Tekufat ha-Talmud* 157 n. 33.

74. In Achaemenian times, Noruz (lit. "new day") was celebrated in spring (March/April); in the early Sassanian period it was also celebrated in autumn, thus leading to a dual celebration. However, with the establishment by the first Sassanian king, Ardashir I, of a 365-day year with no intercalation, Noruz crept backward every year by one quarter of a day, and thus the autumn festival of Noruz was actually being celebrated by the fifth cen-

tury in July. Subsequent calendar reform resulted in multiple celebrations of the holiday during the year. See M. Boyce, *Zoroastrians, Their Religious Beliefs and Practices* (London, 1979), 72, 105–6, 124, 128–30. To this day, various Zoroastrian factions celebrate Noruz at different times of the year; see S. A. Nigosian, *The Zoroastrian Faith* (Montreal, 1993), 115.

75. See Neusner, *Jews in Babylonia*, 2: 88, and D. Goodblatt, "The Poll Tax in Sasanian Babylonia," *Journal of the Eonomic and Social History of the Orient* 22 (1979): 275–76, and nn. 111–14.

76. See Rosenthal, "For the Talmudic Dictionary," 39–42.

77. The most comprehensive argument for such influence was put forward by J. Scheftelowitz, *Die Alpersiche Religion und das Judendum* (Giessen, 1920); some criteria for identifying apparent influences, albeit not necessarily for Babylonian Jewry alone, have been presented by S. Shaked, "Qumran and Iran: Further Considerations," *Israel Oriental Studies* 2 (1972): 433–46. See also D. Winston, "The Iranian Component in the Bible, Apocrypha and Qumran: A Review of the Evidence," *History of Religions* 5 (1966): 183–216, and E. Spicehandler, " 'Be Duar' and 'Dina de-Magistha,' " Hebrew Union College Annual 26 (1955): 333–54.

78. For a general comparison of demonology in Judaism and the Iranian religion, see Scheftelowitz, *Die Alpersiche Religion*, 25–61. On Iranian demonology, see A. Christensen, *Essai sur la démonologie iranienne* (Copenhagen, 1941), and M. Boyce, *A History of Zoroastrianism*, vol. 1, 2d ed. (Leiden, 1989), 85–108.

79. See Deut. 32:17; Ps. 106:37.

80. *Antiquities*, 8:45; compare the Wisdom of Solomon 7:20 as well as rabbinic statements linked to Solomon in connection with Ecclesiastes 2:8. See also L. Ginzberg, *Legends of the Jews*, vol. 6 (Philadelphia, 1956), 291 and nn. 488–89.

81. *Antiquities*, 8:46; Josephus describes in great detail how a demon was removed "through the nostrils" of a man possessed, who proceeded to "speak Solomon's name and recite the incantations he had composed."

82. Matthew 8:28–34, 12:43–45; Mark 1:23, 5:1–20; Luke 8:26–38.

83. The various Palestinian uses of the Hebrew term *ruah* (spirit), especially those found at Qumran, dovetail with parallel meanings applied to the Iranian term *menog;* see Shaked, "Qumran and Iran," 434–37.

84. Scholars long ago recognized the similar use of the word "heaven" as a reference to the deity in both Iranian and rabbinic literature; see E. E. Urbach, *The Sages*, vol. 1 (Jerusalem, 1975), 70 and n. 11. Yet another parallel has been noted between the Pahlavi concept of "wrath" and the the rabbinic concept of *midat ha-din* (the attribute of justice), whereby a concept well established in Zoroastrian dualism was adapted by the rabbis as a means of attributing man's suffering to the omnipotent God; see S. Pines, "Wrath and Creatures of Wrath in Pahlavi, Jewish and New Testament Sources," in Shaked, ed., *Irano-Judaica*, 1: 76–82, and Urbach, *The Sages*, 1: 451, 460–61.

85. Avot 5:6.

86. PT Berakhot 5:9a.

87. Tosefta Shabbat 7:23; see BT Sanhedrin 101a.

88. See Boyce, *A History of Zoroastrianism,* 1: 85.

89. For some of the relevant sources and a brief discussion, see Neusner, *Jews in Babylonia,* 4: 334–38, and 5: 183–86.

90. BT Berakhot 6a. Iranian demonology in fact assigned the form of various birds to a number of fabulous creatures that composed the vast army of supernatural forces existing alongside human beings and playing destructive as well as beneficial roles in this world; see Boyce, *A History of Zoroastrianism,* 88–90.

91. The Babylonian Talmud identifies him as R. Hanina b. Dosa, actually a first-century quasi-rabbinic figure in Palestine, known for his wonder-working activity rather than for any halakhic teaching; see B. M. Bokser, "Wonder-working and the Rabbinic Tradition: The Case of Hanina ben Dosa," *Journal for the Study of Judaism* 16 (1985): 42–92 (esp. 42 n. 1, which provides a list of earlier studies on Hanina ben Dosa).

92. This particular demonic figure never appears by name in Iranian sources, although it is apparently a derivation of the Zoroastrian *Aeshma Daeva* (the demon of wrath); the Greek form—Asmodaeus—appears in the Book of Tobit (3:8), a Second Temple apocryphal work likely to have been written in Babylonia and in an obvious Iranian environment. See R. N. Frey, "Qumran and Iran," in J. Neusner, ed., *Christianity, Judaism and Other Greco-Roman Cults (Studies for Morton Smith at Sixty),* vol. 3 (Leiden, 1975), 170. "Ashmedai King of Demons" is known only to the Babylonian Talmud, most notably in a highly detailed account of his relationship with King Solomon (BT Gitin 68a–b); parallel traditions in Palestinian rabbinic sources (PT Sanhedrin 2:20c) talk only about "an angel" who appeared in the image of King Solomon.

93. Scholars have in fact noted an Iranian propensity for considering odd numbers favorable and even numbers dangerous; see Scheftelowitz, *Die Alpersiche Religion,* 88–91. See also BT Gitin 68a for another example where the Babylonian Talmud admits to a demon-connected interpretation of scripture (Eccles. 2:8) while acknowledging that the Palestinian exegetes understood the same text differently.

94. BT Mo'ed Katan 18a.

95. Boyce, *A History of Zoroastrianism,* 1: 90. Boyce notes that the practice of dedicating nail-parings to this bird while uttering appropriate words from the Vendidad is still observed by strictly orthodox Zoroastrians.

96. Rabbis not only knew how to limit the danger from demons but at times even knew how to get them to do one's bidding. A demon employed by Rav Papa "once went to fetch water from the river but was away a long time. When he returned he was asked: 'Why were you so long?' He replied: '[I waited] until the evil waters [i.e., the water from which demons had drunk] had passed.' But when he saw them [R. Papa and friends] pouring off [some water] from the mouth of the jug, he exclaimed: 'Had I known you were in the habit of doing this I would not have taken so long'" (BT Hullin 105b–106a).

97. The demon is apparently overcome by hearing his name diminish letter by letter.

98. On the nature of this book, see E. W. West, introduction to *The Sacred Books of the East—Pahlavi Texts,* vol. 24, part III, ed. F. Max Mueller, 3d ed. (Delhi, 1970), xxxvi–xlv.

99. Ibid., 292. In another tradition on the same page we are told that "it is not proper to pour away water at night, especially from the northern side which would be the worst"; the reason for this is that demons are supposed to come from the north, and anything thrown out northward might be of use to them.

100. See *Sacred Books of the East,* vol. 37, part IV, 3d ed. (Delhi, 1969), 471.

101. *Shayast ne-Shayast,* ix, 8; *Sacred Books of the East,* vol. 5, part I, ed. F. Mueller (Oxford, 1901), 310; on this collection, see Yarshater, ed., *The Cambridge History of Iran,* 3(2): 1177–78.

102. Boyce, *A History of Zoroastrianism,* 87.

103. Denkard, Book VI, 78; quoted in Shaked, "Qumran and Iran," 437.

104. Although the woman referred to is Imma Shalom, wife of the late-first-century Palestinian sage Rabbi Eliezer b. Hyrcanus, the story and language are definitely of Babylonian rabbinic provenance. The Baylonian Talmud frequently tells stories using well-known Palestinian figures as its heroes, but these are frequently couched in local Babylonian reality as well as terminology and have no parallels in Palestinian rabbinic literature.

105. There is extensive literature on the ongoing publication of these texts; see, e.g., Neusner, *Jews in Babylonia,* 5: 217 n. 1; J. Naveh and S. Shaked, *Amulets and Magic Bowls—Aramaic Incantations of Late Antiquity,* rev. ed. (Jerusalem, 1998), 19–21; L. H. Schiffman and M. D. Swartz, *Hebrew and Aramaic Incantation Texts from the Cairo Genizah* (Sheffield, Engl., 1982), 17–18 and notes; and P. S. Alexander, "Incantation Bowls and Amulets in Hebrew and Aramaic," in E. Schuerer, *The History of the Jewish People in the Age of Jesus Christ (175 B.C.–A.D. 135),* a new English edition revised and edited by G. Vermes, F. Millar, and M. Goodman, vol. III, part I (Edinburgh, 1986), 352–57. For a recent publication of one major collection, see J. B. Segal, *Catalogue of the Aramaic and Mandaic Incantation Bowls in the British Museum* (London, 2000). Yet another study is D. Levene, *A Corpus of Magic Bowls* (New York, 2001).

106. See Naveh and Shaked, *Amulets and Magic Bowls,* 13 n. 1.

107. Ibid., 135.

108. J. A. Montgomery, *Aramaic Incantation Texts from Nippur* (Philadelphia, 1913), 191.

109. Ibid., 190–91 (quoted in Neusner, *Jews in Babylonia,* 5: 223).

110. Naveh and Shaked, *Amulets and Magic Bowls,* 159; see also Alexander, "Incantation Bowls," 354 n. 24, for an attempt at recreating the halakhic context for the situation described on the bowl.

111. The major doubt was cast by Montgomery, *Aramaic Incantation Texts,* 112–13, who claimed that the use of names such as "Moses" and "Yehoshua ben Perahya" had already found its way into an eclectic magical environment, thereby removing the certainty of a Jewish connection. Many of Montgomery's readings, as well as conclusions regarding the Jewish origins of the bowls, were challenged in a brilliant review essay by J. N. Epstein,

"Gloses Babylo-araméennes," *Revue des Etudes Juives* 73 (1921): 40–72. Montgomery's contention is further weakened not only by the quoting of Hebrew scripture in some of the bowls but also by the references to uniquely Jewish legal conventions in the production of divorce writs; see Naveh and Shaked, *Amulets and Magic Bowls*, 17–18. See also J. C. Greenfield, "Notes on some Aramaic and Mandaic Magic-Bowls," *The Journal of the Ancient Near Eastern Society of Columbia University* 5 (1973): 149–56; B. A. Levine, "The Language of the Magic Bowls," appended in Neusner, *Jews in Babylonia*, 5: 343–73; and Alexander, "Incantation Bowls," 353 n. 23.

112. Naveh and Shaked, *Amulets and Magic Bowls*, 18.

113. For an overview of rabbinic attitudes toward all manifestations of magical activity, see G. Veltri, *Magie und Halakha*, (Tübingen, 1997), 295–326 (containing a comprehensive bibliography on the subject and related issues). See also G. Veltri, "Defining Forbidden Foreign Customs: Some Remarks on the Rabbinic Halakhah of Magic," in *Proceedings of the Eleventh Congress of Jewish Studies*, Div. C, vol. 1: *Rabbinic and Talmudic Literature* (Jerusalem, 1994), 25–32. Veltri's work addresses primarily the rabbinic attitudes toward phenomena of the Greco-Roman world.

114. BT Sanhedrin 67b; for a brief overview of rabbinic attitudes toward magic, see Urbach, *The Sages*, 97–101. Urbach senses the fuzzy demarcation in rabbinic tradition between those statements that appear to prohibit any recourse to magic and others that clearly suggest the sages' own involvement in a variety of such magical practices (see 101–2). Note the statement by L. H. Schiffman, "A Forty-two Letter Divine Name in the Aramaic Magic Bowls," *Bulletin of the Institute of Jewish Studies* 1 (1973): 97: "It is also clear that these incantations and the attendant magical practices could not have had the approval of the rabbinic authorities." To this, Greenfield ("Notes on Some Aramaic and Mandaic Magic-Bowls," 150 n. 10) responded—accurately, to my mind—"But even if there was no approval, these practices were condoned and tolerated." For a brief survey on the growing scholarly recognition of "the extent to which magic was ingrained in the rabbinic milieu," see M. D. Swartz, *Scholastic Magic* (Princeton, 1996), 18–22 and the bibliography in nn. 58 and 63. See also the comments and literature cited in Y. Harari, "If You Wish to Kill a Person: Harmful Magic and Protection from It in Early Jewish Magic" (Hebrew), *Jewish Studies* 37 (1997): 111–42.

115. And thus Cicero felt required to point out that "Chaldaei" was not the designation for practitioners of a specific training, but rather the name of a tribe (*De Divinatione* I, 1, 2). Indeed, the Third Sybilline Oracle (227; see also J. H. Charlesworth, ed., *The Old Testament Pseudepigraphy*, 2 vols. (Garden City, N.Y., 1983–85), 1: 367) praises Israel as a race of righteous men who "do not practice the astrological predictions of the Chaldeans nor astronomy" (cited in S. Lieberman, *Greek in Jewish Palestine* [New York, 1942], 97–98).

116. F. Cumont, *The Oriental Religions in Roman Paganism* (New York, 1956), 146.

117. See Urbach, *The Sages*, 277.

118. BT Pesahim 113b.

119. Lieberman, *Greek*, 98.

120. Pseudo-Eupolemos, apud Eusebius, *Praeparatio Evangelica* 9.17.3 (Charlesworth, *Old Testament Pseudepigrapha*, 2: 880). The Egyptian-Jewish author Artapanus (third–second centuries B.C.E.) claims that Abraham actually taught Parethothes, the King of Egypt, astrology (ibid., 2: 897).

121. BT Shabbat 156a and parallels; later midrashim leave even less to the imagination: "You are Jews, the words of the astrologers do not apply to you, for you are Jews" (Tanhuma, Shofetim 10).

122. The reference to "Chaldeans" is missing in some manuscript versions and also in the parallel version in BT Horayot 14a.

123. *Iggeret Rav Sherira Gaon,* ed. Lewin, 85–86.

124. BT Yevamot 21b; BT Sanhedrin 95a.

125. The degree of Iranian legal knowledge possessed by the rabbis, and their willingness to apply this knowledge to their own deliberations, is still open to debate, but for one recent attempt to prove the feasibility of such a process, see M. Macuch, "Iranian Legal Terminology in the Babylonian Talmud in the Light of Sasanian Jurisprudence," in S. Shaked and A. Netzer, eds., Irano-Judaica, vol. 4 (Jerusalem, 1999), 91–101.

SELECTED BIBLIOGRAPHY

Barr, J. "The Question of Religious Influence: The Case of Zoroastrianism, Judaism and Christianity." *Journal of the American Academy of Religion* 53, no. 2 (1985): 201–35.

Beer, M. *Amora'ei Bavel: Perakim be-Ḥaye ha-Kalkalah.* Ramat Gan, 1974.

———. *Rashut ha-Golah bi-Yeme ha-Mishna ve-ha-Talmud.* Tel Aviv, 1970.

Brody, R. "Judaism in the Sasanian Empire: A Case Study in Religious Coexistence." In S. Shaked and A. Netzer, eds., *Irano-Judaica.* Vol. 2. Jerusalem, 1990.

Gafni, I. "Expressions and Types of 'Local-Patriotism' Among the Jews of Sasanian Babylonia." In S. Shaked and A. Netzer, eds., *Irano-Judaica.* Vol. 2. Jerusalem, 1990.

———. *Yehudei Bavel bi-Tekufat ha-Talmud: Ḥaye ha-Ḥevrah ve-ha-Ruaḥ.* Jerusalem, 1990.

———. *Land, Center and Diaspora: Jewish Constructs in Late Antiquity.* Sheffield, Engl., 1997.

———. "Talmudic Research in Modern Times: Between Scholarship and Ideology." In A. Oppenheimer, ed., *Jüdische Geschichte in hellenistisch-römischer Zeit.* Munich, 1999.

Goodblatt, D. "The Poll Tax in Sasanian Babylonia," *Journal of the Economic and Social History of the Orient* 22 (1979): 233–94.

———. *Rabbinic Instruction in Sasanian Babylonia.* Leiden, 1975.

Naveh, J., and S. Shaked. *Amulets and Magic Bowls—Aramaic Incantations of Late Antiquity.* Rev. ed. Jerusalem, 1998.

———. *Magic Spells and Formulae—Aramaic Incantations of Late Antiquity.* Jerusalem, 1993.

Neusner, J. *A History of the Jews in Babylonia.* 5 vols. Leiden, 1965–70.

———. *Judaism, Christianity and Zoroastrianism in Talmudic Babylonia.* Lanham, Md., 1986.

———. *Talmudic Judaism in Sasanian Babylonia.* Leiden, 1976.

Oppenheimer, A. *Babylonia Judaica in the Talmudic Period.* Wiesbaden, 1983.

———. "Babylonian Synagogues with Historical Associations." In D. Urman and P. V. M. Flesher, eds., *Ancient Synagogues: Historical Analysis and Archaeological Discovery.* Vol. 1. Leiden, 1995.

Shaked, S. "Iranian Influence on Judaism: First Century B.C.E. to Second Century C.E." In W. D. Davies and L. Finkelstein, eds., *The Cambridge History of Judaism.* Vol. 1. Cambridge, Engl., 1984.

———. "Zoroastrian Polemics Against Jews in the Sasanian and Early Islamic Period." In S. Shaked and A. Netzer, eds., *Irano-Judaica.* Vol. 2. Jerusalem, 1990.

Abraham about to sacrifice his son Ishmael
(the Muslim version of the biblical "binding of Isaac").
(New York Public Library, Spencer Collection, Persian ms. 46)

SEVEN

JEWISH CULTURE IN THE FORMATIVE PERIOD OF ISLAM

REUVEN FIRESTONE

The prophet Muhammad lived to witness the success of Islam in Arabia by the time of his death in 632 C.E. Initially, however, he failed to win his fellow Arabs to Islam in Mecca, the pagan city of his birth. In fact, Muhammad's prophetic activities and behavior made him persona non grata in his native city; he was forced out of town in 622 and found success only after having made his great *hijra* (emigration) from Mecca to Medina, a large agricultural settlement populated by many Jews as well as other inhabitants who practiced the indigenous religious traditions of Arabia. It would be Medina where Islam would take hold. Medina would also serve as the crucible wherein the complex relations between Jews and Muslims and between Judaism and Islam would be forged.

THE CONVERSION OF RABBI ABDULLAH

A story is told by Muhammad ibn Isḥāq, the eighth century biographer of the prophet Muhammad, of the latter's coming to Medina:[1]

> This is the story of Abdullah ibn Salām, the learned rabbi,[2] that one of his kinsmen told me about his conversion to Islam. [Abdullah] said: When I heard about the Apostle of God, I knew from his description, name, and time [of his appearance] that he was the one we were expecting. I was overjoyed about this but kept it to myself until the Apostle of God arrived in Medina. While he was staying in [the Medinan neighborhood of] Qubā' among the Banū 'Amr b. 'Awf, a man came with the news of his arrival while I was working at the top of a date tree with my aunt Khālida bint al-Ḥārith sitting below. When I heard the news of his arrival I called out: *"Allahu Akbar!"* When my aunt heard this she said to me: "My goodness! If Moses ibn 'Imrān [that is, the Moses of the Bible—see Exodus 6:20] had come you would not have become more excited." I replied: "O aunt! By God, he is the brother of Moses ibn 'Imrān and of the same religion, having been sent on the same mission." She exclaimed: "O ne-

phew! Is he the prophet whom we have been told will be sent at this hour?" I answered: "Yes!" and she responded: "Then this is it!" I immediately went to the Apostle of God and became a Muslim. Then I returned to my family and ordered them to become Muslims as well.

I kept my conversion hidden from the Jews and went to the Apostle of God and said: "O Apostle of God, the Jews are a people of lies. Will you take me into your house and hide me from them? Then ask them about me and they will tell you what they think of me before they know I have become Muslim, because if they know [that I converted], they will falsely denounce me." So the Apostle of God put me in a room. [Some Jews] entered and began chatting. He asked them: "In your opinion, what kind of a person is al-Ḥuṣayn ibn Salām?" They answered: "[He is] our master and prince, our learned rabbi." When they had finished I came out to them and said: "O Jews, be reverent to God and accept what has come from Him, for by God, you know that this is the Apostle of God. You have found his description and his name written in the Torah. I bear witness that he is the Apostle of God. I believe in him, pronounce him true, and acknowledge him." They said: "You are lying!" and slandered me. So I said to the Apostle of God: "Did I not tell you that they are a people of lies, deceit and perfidy?" I then publicly revealed my conversion and the conversion of my family, and my aunt Khālida also became a good Muslim.

Although this apocryphal story cannot be accepted without corroboration as an accurate witness to the particular event it describes,[3] it contains within it important incidental data about Jews living in the environs and period of emerging Islam. We learn that the Jews had scholarly religious leaders to whom they referred as *ḥaver* and who worked in the local economy. Jews were involved in the date agriculture of the region and worked alongside their extended family kin, including women. Our story, like many others about Arabian Jews of this period, teaches us that both Jewish men and women had Arabic names. It is likely that al-Ḥuṣayn was Abdullah's "Jewish" name before he became a Muslim and took on the epithet, "servant of Allah" *(Abdullah)*, a common Islamic "conversion name." Although Abdullah's expression of amazement, "Allah is most great!" *(Allahu akbar)* is most likely a later Islamic interpolation, it is possible that Arabic-speaking Jews in this early period as well as in later centuries referred to their God as *Allah*. (The famous Saadiah Gaon [d. 942], for example, the most brilliant scholar of the gaonic period, regularly referred to God in his Arabic commentary as Allah.) And perhaps of greatest interest here, as will become clearer below, is that Arabian Jews spoke of the coming of a "prophet," some even predicting the hour of his coming based on biblical interpretation.

This famous story of Abdullah ibn Salām's conversion to Islam, like many other stories about Muhammad and his interaction with Jews found in the earliest Islamic sources, is not an objective historical report but, rather, in the form we have it, a literary composition—a tale or legend. Despite its unreliability as a factual report of the specific event it purportedly describes, however, it and other such tales contain fine and often detailed historical and cultural information that is repeated with subtle and nuanced variations in a great many other early Arabic sources and references. This quality of the early Arabic sources allows, therefore, for a guarded confidence in the historicity of certain of the data contained within them.

Our tale, along with many others, depicts the Jews living in Arabia during Islam's emergence as veteran inhabitants of the peninsula and deeply integrated into Arabian culture and civilization. The Jews are described both as Jews and as Arabs, and they are depicted as having been organized and acting according to indigenous Arabian paradigms of social organization and behavior. It is not easy to define the boundaries of identification that separated Jews from other inhabitants of Arabia, because they not only lived among their own in "Jewish" tribes but were also members of tribes not referred to in the sources as being specifically Jewish. Moreover, the Jews of Arabia appear not to have been physically distinguishable from the indigenous Arabs, many of whom consider themselves to have derived originally from the biblical Ishmael.[4] Arabian Jews spoke Arabic even among themselves, although there is evidence that at least some of them spoke a particular Jewish dialect referred to in Arabic sources as "Jewish" (yahudiyya), perhaps a Jewish dialect of Arabic similar in role to Yiddish as a Jewish dialect of Medieval German. Jewish professions mirrored those of the larger civilization in which they lived, with Jewish farmers, craftsmen, and even Bedouin, and the Jews could arm and protect themselves just as other tribal groups in the region. In fact, the Jews of sixth- and seventh-century Arabia appear so highly integrated economically, ethnically, and geographically into the local culture that they must be considered culturally or ethnically Arab, just as the Jews of Babylonia, speaking Babylonian Aramaic, were so deeply integrated into their local culture that they would refer to themselves as Babylonians.

At the same time that the Jewish communities that penetrated Arabia became "Arabized" through language, customs, and even personal names, so too did indigenous Arabian civilization come under the influence of Judaism. One pre-Islamic term for a high god in the old Arabian pantheon, for example, was al-Raḥmān, "the Merciful One," exactly equivalent to the Jewish Aramaic Raḥmānā that occurs in the Babylonian Talmud more than 250 times. Christian communities also made their way into Arabia, and many religious or cultic terms that became a part of Islam derive from Aramaic Jewish or Christian religious terminology that was applied to pre-Islamic Arabian religion.[5]

As these and other examples to follow will make clear, the cultural and even religious influence between Jews and Arabs and Jews and Muslims flowed in both directions, but, despite this bi-directionality during the pre-Islamic period, the Jews were known as monotheists in an overwhelmingly polytheistic region. Whether or not these Jews practiced one or more expressions of Judaism found also in the Land of Israel, in Babylonia, or in highly Hellenized areas has not yet been determined. The sources do clearly differentiate Jewish Arabs from other pre-Islamic Arabs when concerned with religious beliefs and practice. Nevertheless, the relationship between Arabian Jewry and the still-mysterious and possibly monotheistic religion of the pre-Islamic Arabian *ḥanīfs* remains unclear.

Muhammad himself fully expected the Jews of Arabia to become Muslims as well—to be "submitters" (the meaning of the term, "Muslim") to the will of God as articulated in the qur'ānic revelations that he heard and recited. That most Arabian Jews did not submit was a shock to Muhammad, because he believed during his initial period in Medina that the religion he preached, in opposition to the indigenous Arabian polytheisms of his generation, was virtually synonymous with the monotheism of the Jews. In fact, the story of earliest Islam is, in large part, a story of an emerging identity constantly being tested by the tension between God's word and the reality of a world, including the world of Arabian Jews, not easily willing to accept it. The ambiguous cultural and religious boundaries between Arabian Jews and other Arabs in pre-Islamic and early Islamic Arabia, therefore, established a series of tensions that would epitomize the foundational relationship between Jews and Muslims. These tensions are the center point around which the cultural history of the Jews in Islamic lands must be written.

ARAB CONQUESTS FIRST, ISLAMIZATION AFTERWARD

As mentioned above, Muhammad was initially unsuccessful in Mecca, but he succeeded brilliantly in Medina, and his success eventually spread back to his hometown and to much of Arabia before his death in 632. This was followed in the century after his death by a series of brilliant and extraordinary military conquests that took the world by surprise. Rising up out of an obscure desert region—physically near to the world empires of Byzantium and Persia but light-years distant from their level of civilization—the Arabs overwhelmed both within a decade. From the first Byzantine defeat at Ajnadayn in 634 to the fall of Alexandria in 643 and the last of the great Persian cities in 644, the Arabs found themselves in control of the center of world civilization. They pushed through Damascus, Jerusalem, Caesarea, Edessa, Ctesiphon (the capital of Persia), and then to the east toward India, from Alexandria and Old Cairo (called Babylon of Egypt) westward across North Africa and, eventually, Spain, and north from Arabia to the very gates of Constantinople itself.

These were conquests by Arabs. Because Islam as a religious civilization was still in formation, it is uncertain what the first conquerors knew and believed of Islam. It would soon become clear to the world that the triumphant Arabs also represented a new religion that would forever change the entire world constellation of religious civilizations, but in the early conquests Arab believers, other followers of Muhammad, pagans, and even Arab Jews and Christians took part.[6] Islam was one of the powerful motivators of the huge movement of peoples and energy that would come to dominate much of world history for the next millennium, but it was still in the process of formation during the great Arab expansion. The Qur'an itself, for example, was not "collected" or canonized until the caliphate of Uthman (644–56), who rose to his position 12 years after Muhammad's death and only after the Arab conquest of most of the Middle East.[7] Nor had the great compendia of Islamic law and tradition been formulated or the theologies systematized during the first century or more after the death of Muhammad. Islam was in the process of emerging, and like the butterfly that emerges in glory from its cramped chrysalis, it would take time for the life-sustaining fluids to flow through the expanding arteries of the empire and bring the necessary energy and sustenance to allow it to take off.

This was the formative age of Islam, when Islam was busy not only managing an empire but also defining itself. During the two centuries following the death of the Prophet in 632, its major literatures, theologies, and institutions would be established. During this period, and especially during the early decades, Jews would have a profound impact on the emergence of Islam. Soon afterward, Islam would stamp its own legacy on the evolution of Judaism.

ANCIENT JEWS ENTER ARABIA

Exactly when Jews had penetrated the peninsula remains a mystery, but Arab legend suggests as early as the Exodus from Egypt when Moses sent a contingent of soldiers deep into Arabia to fight the Amalekites living there. According to the tenth-century *Kitāb al-Aghānī*, the Israelite soldiers destroyed their enemy and eventually settled in the west-central area known as the Hijaz, the very region in which the towns of Mecca and Medina are situated. Other legends place the migration of Jews to the region in the wake of Roman persecution, a far more likely scenario. Jewish communities were established not only in the oasis towns of the Hijaz but also in the southern region that is now within the borders of the modern state of Yemen. Yemenite Jews credit their origins to the famous story of King Solomon and the Queen of Sheba. According to this tradition, the queen returned to her native land, a region of Yemen that to this day is called Saba, with a son fathered by Solomon. The King, in turn, sent Jews to settle in Yemen so that his son might be properly educated.

The true origin of the Jewish communities of Arabia may never be determined, but we have noted from the story of Abdullah ibn Salām that they were a significant part of the Arabian landscape by the time Muhammad was born, in 570. The Jews of Medina, for example (which was called Yathrib prior to Islam), were the dominant community of the town until shortly before Muhammad's birth. In the town of Taymā', about halfway between Medina and the great Nabatean center of Petra in today's Jordan, the Jews are said to have been powerful enough to insist that non-Jewish Arab tribes interested in settling in the town adopt Judaism.

The Jews of sixth- and seventh-century Arabia were highly integrated into Arabian culture—so much so, in fact, that it is often difficult to determine whether a person referred to in the sources is Jewish or not unless this is specifically noted. Jews tended to take on Arab names and adopt Arabian cultural practices. The renowned poet al-Samaw'al b. 'Ādiyā, who lived in the mid-sixth century, is a classic example. His own name, Samaw'al, is an Arabized form of Samuel, but the name of his father is purely Arabian. It is assumed by some scholars, therefore, that only his mother was Jewish, although many other Jews in the period seem to have taken on equally Arabian names. Al-Samaw'al's fame as a pre-Islamic Arabian poet denotes his deep integration into Arabian civilization, because this ancient art form is considered the most sublime form of indigenous Arabian culture. Unfortunately, considerable controversy remains regarding the poems attributed to him. Some contain material reflecting Jewish ideas, but these have not been considered genuine by many scholars. Other poems that seem more likely to have been composed by Samaw'al himself contain no indication of Jewish background. Yet tradition associates him quite strongly with Judaism, along with the tradition that his grandson converted to Islam after the rise of Muhammad as Prophet.

Al-Samaw'al's greatest fame, however, derives from his celebrated loyalty rather than his poetry. The legend of his absolute fidelity has become proverbial in Arabic: "more loyal than al-Samaw'al." According to the story, Imru' al-Qays, one of pre-Islamic Arabia's greatest poets and the youngest son of the last king of the Kinda, led an unsettled life as an adventurer. Among his exploits was the attempt to avenge the assassination of his father. He eventually lost his allies and sought refuge from his pursuers by appealing to the hospitality of al-Samaw'al, who lived in a famous and impenetrable castle called Ablaq (one legend claims that it was built by Solomon himself). Al-Samaw'al recommended Imru' al-Qays to an Arab client king of the Byzantine emperor, who received him. Imru' al-Qays asked al-Samaw'al to guard his daughter, his paternal inheritance, and his valuable and famous family armor for the duration of his journey, to which al-Samaw'al agreed. When Imru' al-Qays' enemies learned that his armor was under al-Samaw'al's protection, they besieged the castle with a great army. Al-Samaw'al refused to release anything of Imru' al-Qays to his enemies, even after they managed to capture al-Samaw'al's son and threatened to kill him. Al-Samaw'al persisted in refusing to betray his trust, though he witnessed the death of his own son before his very eyes. The besiegers eventually withdrew without achieving their purpose, and al-Samaw'al's fidelity became legendary.

Although the historicity of this legend must be regarded with skepticism, it provides interesting cultural information relevant to the period just prior to the emergence of Islam. Such traits as hospitality, loyalty, and betrayal, use of armor and fortified castles, political alliances, and expectations of vengeance all correspond quite well with other information representing the period. That a Jew should be located in the midst of such a legend is not surprising considering the Jews' level of integration into the pre-Islamic Arabian world.

Just as the Jews absorbed and assimilated Arabian culture prior to the emergence of Islam, so too did they infuse Jewish or biblical culture into the indigenous cultures. The nebulous boundaries between "Jewishness" and "Arabness" did not interfere with the transmission of culture in both directions. Perhaps the most profound example of Jewish cultural infusion is that of the many biblical legends, ideas, and personages that had penetrated deeply into Arabia already in pre-Islamic times. Biblical stories circulated among Jews and Christians living in the region and were naturally and unselfconsciously shared with neighbors who were unfamiliar with the Bible. Many of these stories, which themselves originated as oral midrashic interpretations of biblical texts, were told and retold as part of normal human interaction at trading fairs and tribal or regional gatherings and celebrations. They naturally evolved to fit the specific contexts of individual recitations as they were passed from person to person and place to place, thereby unfolding into forms that conformed to local traditions. Many of these stories, therefore, like their Jewish or Christian bearers, became "Arabized" as they blended into the local topography and folklore traditions. As a result, uniquely Arabian legends began to emerge that reflected both the biblical and the indigenous heritages. Some of these would be absorbed into the religious civilization of Islam, and some of the "Islamized" legends would eventually be reabsorbed into the literary corpus of Judaism.

THE LEGEND OF ABRAHAM VISITING ISHMAEL

One classic example of "Arabization" is the story of Abraham's visits to Ishmael, found in both Jewish and Islamic literature. In Genesis 21, Hagar and Ishmael are banished from the tribe of Abraham and left alone and defenseless in the desert. Such behavior, hardly befitting a Jewish patriarch known for his hospitality and care for the stranger, inspired a series of midrashim, narrative interpretations that tried to make sense of the difficult biblical passage. One reading suggests that Abraham did not really abandon his son but visited him regularly in order to ensure his viability and well-being:[8]

"And [Ishmael] lived in the wilderness of Paran" [Genesis 21:21]. Ishmael took a wife from Arvot Mo'av whose name was 'Ayefa.[9] After three years, Abraham went to see his son Ishmael and swore to Sarah that he would not dismount from his camel at Ishmael's abode. When he arrived there at midday, he found Ishmael's wife. He asked: "Where is Ishmael?" She answered: "He and his mother went to bring the fruit of date trees from the desert." He said: "Give me a little bread and water, for my soul is faint from the desert journey."[10] She answered: "There is no bread and no water." He then said to her: "When Ishmael comes [home], tell him this. Say that an old man came from the Land of Canaan to see you, and that the threshold of the house is not good." When Ishmael came [home], his wife told him what he said. [Ishmael then] sent her out, and his mother sent for a wife from her father's house, whose name was Fatumah.[11]

Again, after three years, Abraham went to see his son Ishmael and swore to Sarah as the first time that he would not dismount from his camel at Ishmael's abode. When he arrived there at midday, he found Ishmael's [new] wife. He asked: "Where is Ishmael?" She answered: "He and his mother went to tend the camels in the desert." He said to her: "Give me a little bread and water, for my soul is faint from the journey," so she brought it out and gave it to him. Abraham stood and prayed before the Holy One for his son, and Ishmael's home was filled with all good things and blessings. When Ishmael came [home], his wife told him what he said, and Ishmael knew that his father's compassion was still extended to him, as it is said: "As a father has compassion for his children" [Psalm 103].[12]

This legend depicts a compassionate Abraham who, unwilling to abandon his own flesh and blood to the vicissitudes of the desert (see Genesis 21), personally ensures the viability of his son and progeny. The threshold to Ishmael's home symbolizes Ishmael's wife, the mother of his offspring. Abraham, the father of many nations (Genesis 17:5–6), ensures through this story that Ishmael's wife is a fitting matriarch of the Arab line. The names of the wives clearly indicate Islamic influence because they each duplicate the name of one of Muhammad's wives or daughters. The Muslim names do not, however, prove an Islamic origin for this story; the nature of the tale indicates a Jewish concern, quite well represented in the midrash, to preserve the status of Abraham in the face of criticism for seemingly abandoning his own family in the desert.

Because of Ishmael's biblical as well as rabbinic association with Arabs, the context for the narrative extension naturally incorporated such motifs associated with Bedouin life as date agriculture and camel herding. It thus serves as a Jewish story of intersection with classic Arab life by acknowledging the proximity between the Genesis Abraham character and classical Bedouin life depicted by Ishmael. Such proximity was not lost on the Jews living throughout the Fertile Crescent: from ancient antiquity into the period of the Arab conquests, migrations and raids of camel-herding nomads regularly brought Arabs into the settled agricultural areas that surrounded the Arabian Peninsula.

Given the continual interaction between Jews and Arabs from biblical days to the present, it is not surprising that Arabic versions of this foundation story follow the basic Jewish narrative quite closely. Before examining them, however, it should be noted here that no pre-Islamic Arabian literature has been preserved in its pristine form. No manuscripts, for example, exist such as we have for ancient Judaism and Christianity with the Dead Sea Scrolls and early Christian papyri. We can only extrapolate, therefore, from our knowledge of literary history and methods to arrive at a theoretical pre-Islamic literary form. Everything we do have describing or reflecting pre-Islamic Arabia, from ancient legends to poetry and genealogies, can be found only in the form that was recorded by later Muslims, and these texts therefore strongly reflect the influence of Islam. The Arabic renderings of Abraham's visits to Ishmael are no exception. They epitomize the continued fusion of cultures.

In the Arabic versions found in many Islamic sources,[13] Abraham feels the need to visit his son but promises Sarah that he will not dismount. He arrives at Ishmael's home, meets the inhospitable wife, and delivers through her the coded message to change the threshold of the house. Ishmael understands, divorces her, and marries a woman who hospitably offers Abraham a feast on his subsequent visit. Certain aspects of the story, however, are now particular to an Arabian environment. The names and genealogy of Ishmael's wives derive from local tribal traditions, for example, and they are not the names of Muhammad's wife or daughter. When the good wife feeds Abraham, the food is the diet of the Bedouin, which Abraham blesses. This, it explains, is why agriculture is impossible in the desolate mountainous settlement of Mecca, because Abraham specifically blessed the food of pastoral nomads rather then oasis dwellers. It is assumed in the Arabic tellings that Ishmael is living in Mecca; medieval Arab geographers recorded the tradition that the Arabic equivalent to the Hebrew *paran* mentioned in Genesis 21:21 is *faran,* a reference to the mountains of Mecca.[14]

Ishmael's association with Mecca leads us to the Arabic extension of the story, not found in any Jewish sources, which brings Abraham there on a third and final visit to his beloved son. The following translation is from Muhammad b. Isma'il al-Bukhārī (d. 869), *al-Ṣaḥīḥ.*[15]

[Abraham] stayed away from them for a while, but then came while Ishmael was sharpening some arrows he had under a tree near the Zam-zam well.[16] When [Ishmael] saw him [approach], he arose and they greeted each other as a father would his son and as a son would his father. [Abraham] said: "O Ishmael, God has given me a command." [Ishmael] replied: "Then do as your Lord has commanded you." [Abraham] asked: "Will you help me?" He answered: "I will help you." So he said: "God has commanded me to build a house [*bayt*] here," and he pointed to a small hill raised up above what was around it. And with that, they raised the foundations of the Ka'ba [*al-Bayt*]. Ishmael would bring the stones and Abraham would build it. When the building was raised up high [so that Abraham had difficulty reaching up to place the stones, Ishmael] brought a certain stone and set it down for him. [Abraham] stood upon it and built as Ishmael would hand him the stones, both of them saying "O Lord, accept this from us, for You are the All-hearing, the All-knowing" [Qur'an 2:127].

The journey of this story of Abraham is striking. A biblically centered Jewish story evolves into an Arabian one as it journeys through the medium of oral tellings. It may have continued to be considered a "Jewish" legend as successive narrators began to incorporate local motifs, but it eventually moved across the boundary of Jewish particularity into generic Arabian culture. It became a legend that, for Arabian Jews, Christians, and pagans, provided meaning to local traditions.

Abraham is known in the Bible as a wanderer and founder of sacred places. From Ur of the Chaldeans he moves to Haran in northern Mesopotamia, and from Haran to the Land of Canaan. He sojourns in Egypt and returns to Canaan to build an altar at Beth El and another at the oaks of Mamre in Hebron. He plants a sacred tree in Beersheba and offers sacrifices in other places where God speaks with him directly. Such an important founder of sacred places would easily be associated with local Arabian sites as well. Why should he not have made his way into Arabia to found the Ka'ba in Mecca, an ancient religious shrine and place of sacrifice? Even before Islam, he was known to pagan Arabs. Ancient traditions recall that pictures of Abraham, Ishmael, and Mary, the mother of Jesus, were kept among the figurines and effigies of the pre-Islamic Ka'ba.[17]

Abraham, then, had become a generic hero known to all the pre-Islamic inhabitants of the peninsula. His name and image were shared, but his essence was not identical: to the Jews he was the originator of God's covenant with their people; to the Christians he was the first to acknowledge the truth of faith and spirit over the law;[18] and to the pagans he was the founder of the sacred shrines and cult places in Mecca. In the seventh century, however, as Islam came to dominate the peninsula, the Ka'ba and the sacred shrines in and around Mecca were shed of their idols and incorporated into Islamic tradition. The Islamizing process included an increasing association with the ancient and original monotheist Abraham, who naturally provided the proof of monotheistic authenticity as the *original* intent of the sacred sites. The Islamic Abraham cycle thus depicts the patriarch, with the help of his son, establishing Mecca as a purely monotheistic site. Only generations later did Ishmael's descendants gradually abandon the strict monotheism of their ancestors and degenerate into the state of religious anarchy known as pre-Islamic polytheism. The purpose of Muhammad's prophethood was to correct this error and reestablish Abraham's pristine monotheism. As the Abraham narrative journeyed through its Arabian environment from the pre-Islamic period into that of Islam, therefore, the *generic* or multiple Arabian associations with Abraham coalesced into an Islamic particularity. Abraham himself became Islamized.

The Qur'an, the very divine revelation of Islam, would claim Abraham as its own:

And when We made the House[19] a refuge and safe for humankind [We said]: Take as your place of worship the Place of Abraham [*maqam ibrahim*]. We made a covenant with Abraham and Ishmael [saying]: Purify My house for those who circumambulate, are engaged [with it], and bow and prostrate themselves. So Abraham prayed: Lord, Make this area safe, and bestow its people with fruits—those among them who believe in God and the Last Day.

[God] answered: As for the unbeliever, I will grant him a little happiness. Then I will force him to the punishment of the Fire and a horrible end. And when Abraham and Ishmael were raising up the foundations of the House [they prayed]: Our Lord, Accept [this] from us, for You are the Hearer, the Knower. Our Lord, Make us submitters [*muslimayn*] to You and our progeny a submissive people to You [*umma muslima laka*]. Show us the ritual places and turn toward us, for You are the One who causes to turn in repentance, the Merciful. (Qur'an 2:125–28)

Ironically, rather than serving as a unifying motif to bring the "Abrahamic religions" together in dialogue as is attempted in our day, the person of Abraham served at times as the center of polemic between them in Late Antiquity and the Middle Ages. The Qur'an itself bears witness to the controversy over Abraham:

O People of Scripture! Why do you argue about Abraham, when the Torah and the Gospel were not revealed until after him? Have you no sense? Do you not argue about things of which you have knowledge? Why, then, argue about things of which you have no knowledge! God knows, but you know not! Abraham was not a Jew nor a Christian, but was an early monotheist [*ḥanīf*], a muslim [i.e. one who submits to God's will], not an idolater. (3:65–67)

Our story of Abraham's visits to Ishmael thus turns full circle. A Jewish midrashic tradition became part of the pre-Islamic "public domain" as it was woven into the very fabric of generic Arabian culture. As Islam then absorbed relevant Arabian lore into its emerging ethos, the story became part of the legacy that would be Islam. What began, then, as a narrative interpretation of a biblical passage among Jews, ended as a narrative interpretation of a qur'anic passage among Muslims.

Is this Islamic "borrowing" from Judaism? Did Judaism provide the source for the qur'anic verses and the Islamic concepts? This is a classic question that has influenced the nature of research on Islam and its relationship with Judaism and Christianity. Classic Orientalist studies of Islam tended to assume *a priori* that Islam "borrowed" its ideas from the "original" ideas or beliefs of "Judeo-Christianity." They then set out to trace that history through textual analysis. As we have seen above, it is true that parallels may be found between Islamic and Jewish or biblical ideas and texts, and the parallels are many. But no religion is created *ex nihilo*. On the contrary, all scriptures and all religions combine *inspiration* (pure creativity), with *influence* (absorbing outside ideas). This includes the Bible. The many striking parallels between biblical *realia* and those of Canaanite culture and literatures demonstrate the heavy influence of Canaanite civilization. But because no human creation is absolutely without precedent, must every creation be assumed to be, at core, unoriginal and merely a result of borrowing? The answer is, of course, no, because the essence of creativity is inspiration within a context composed of preexisting realia—that is, influence. The question of borrowing, therefore, becomes beside the point, because no creation can consist only of inspiration without influence. Jews and Judaism indeed had a profound impact on emerging Islam, as did Christians and Christianity, pagan Arabs and pre-Islamic Arabian culture, and Persians and Zoroastrian traditions as well as those of Abyssinia, Greece, and so forth. But so, too, would Islam strongly affect those very evolving traditions that influenced it in its formative stages. Such fluidity might be considered "reciprocal influence": the commerce of cultures naturally ensures that they interact, absorb, discharge, and recombine as they contact one another through the ever-permeable boundaries of interethnic human contact and communication.

WHAT KIND OF ARABIAN JUDAISM?

A second classic question affecting Western students of Islam is why Islamic expressions of some themes that have parallels in Judaism and Christianity seem at times to be so contrary to Jewish or Christian expressions. Some Islamic parallels and references to Jewish tradition seem so odd that they are generally assumed by Westerners to have been misunderstandings or outright errors. The Qur'an, for example, claims: "The Jews say: Ezra [*'uzayr*] is the son of God, and the Christians say: The messiah is the son of God. This is what they say from their [own] mouths, resembling the speech of unbelievers of old. God fight them, for they lie!" (9:30). In another passage, the Qur'an asserts: "The Jews say: the hand of God is fettered. [But] their hands are fettered! And they are cursed for what they say!" (5:64).

From the perspective of Judaism in all of its extant forms, these verses seem to exhibit an extraordinary misunderstanding of Jewish belief. It is also possible that these qur'anic verses are polemical statements meant to discredit Judaism, because it is quite clear that the Qur'an, like other scriptures, is in part a polemical text. Rather than taking either of these approaches, we shall undertake to examine such Islamic records of Arabian Judaism from the hypothesis that they might in fact be accurate representations of Jewish ideas or practice.

The Qur'an represents itself as the word of God spoken through the prophet Muhammad to the people of seventh-century Arabia. However, because the Qur'an appears as if it were revealed in serial form during the 22 years of Muhammad's prophetic mission, it seems on many occasions to describe or respond to actual historical phenomena or situations that he encountered. Muslim Qur'an scholars have attempted to reconstruct the occasions of revelation based on their impression of Muhammad's biography, but little consensus has been reached among them. This, in part, has led some Western scholars to suggest that the Qur'an represents the thinking or history of an entirely different period and geography ranging from pre-Islamic Arabian tradition to heterodox Babylonian Jewish traditions of the eighth or ninth centuries. These views are interesting but not compelling, and they have not garnered enough support to merit abandoning the traditional chronographic and geographic setting for the contents of the Qur'an. The verses cited above therefore seem to reflect an observation of seventh-century Medinan Jewish belief.

It is clear that sixth- and seventh-century Judaisms were still in a state of flux as rabbinic Judaism was establishing itself as the dominant and soon to be virtual monopolistic expression of the religion of Israel. It would be a grave error to assume, *a priori*, that the kind (or kinds) of Judaism believed and practiced by seventh-century Arabian Jews was the same as that of Maimonides in twelfth-century Egypt. Despite its relative proximity to the Land of Israel, Babylon, and Egypt, the largely desolate Arabian Peninsula was not a regular stop for travelers moving within the "Fertile Crescent," and it cannot be assumed to have fallen under the influence of distant schools. In fact, the isolated peninsula served regularly as a refuge for people seeking freedom from outside influence. We know, for example, that early Christian communities found asylum from Roman persecution in various desert regions, and later groups of non-Orthodox Christians, to escape the theological compulsion of the Orthodox Byzantine Empire, sought sanctuary in Arabia. It is quite likely, although we have less documentation for Jews of this period than for Christians, that some nonrabbinic or marginal groups did the same when rabbinic proselytizing to them became more forceful.

Although perhaps surprising, some of the ideas attributed to the Jews by the qur'anic passages cited above are very much within the parameters of Jewish thinking in Late Antiquity, although they may not necessarily reflect what we would today call rabbinic Judaism. In relation to the passage suggesting that the Jews deify Ezra, for example, the originally Jewish books known as 4 Ezra (14:9, 50,[20] also known as 2 Esdras) and 2 Enoch (22:11) attribute a near-divine or angelic status to the biblical personages of Ezra and Enoch that could have been construed by early Muslims as compromising an austere and absolute conception of monotheism. The second qur'anic citation may in fact reflect a Jewish interpretive midrash on Lamentations 2:3: "He has withdrawn his right hand in the presence of the foe."[21] The text of 3 Enoch 48a actually reads, "R. Ishmael said to me: Come and I will show you the right hand of the Omnipresent One, which has been banished behind him because of the destruction of the Temple."[22]

If some Jews of the seventh-century Hijaz were familiar with these noncanonical compositions, it is likely that they were not all rabbinic Jews. The Qur'an itself seems to refer to different categories among those who accept the Torah as Scripture: "We have sent down the Torah [al-tawrāt] containing guidance and light, by which the prophets who surrendered [to God] judged the Jews [al-ladhīna hādū], the rabbāniyūn, and the aḥbār" (5:44). The latter two terms are generally identified in traditional Islamic scholarship as "rabbis" and "scholars," and there is indeed support for the singular form, rabbānī, deriving from the Hebrew rav, rabbi, or rabbān, and for the Arabic ḥabr or ḥibr, deriving from the Rabbinic title ḥaver. Yet this verse seems to posit three related but different groups who were judged by God through the Torah and the prophets. Another translation might read: "We have sent down the Torah containing guidance and light, by which the prophets who surrendered [to God] judged the Jews, the Rabbanites and those of the havurot."[23]

In another qur'anic passage, the same rabbāniyūn are described specifically as being very closely engaged in the study and teaching of Scripture: "Be rabbāniyūn by virtue of your teaching/knowing the Book, and in virtue of your studying it" (3:79). Might this be a reference to a distinctively rabbinic, text-centered Judaism, as opposed to other Judaisms—perhaps even a form that may have survived from the period before the destruction of the Temple? It is still impossible to arrive at any firm conclusions, but the evidence suggests that the Jews of Arabia at the birth of Islam were not all rabbinic and that a range of Jewish expression existed.

There is certainly evidence that at least some seventh-century Jews of the Hijaz went into trances and engaged in other mantic activities, perhaps even engaging in mystic journeys that parallel those of the Merkavah mystics of the Land of Israel. In one case, which appears to reflect at least an element of historical reality, Muhammad himself attempted to observe a Jewish practitioner engaged in mantic activity in Medina.[24] Muhammad, in fact, had a great deal of contact with a large and diverse Jewish community in Medina, and the relationship that ensued between them would have a tremendous impact on the future of world Jewry. But in order to make sense of this important period, we must first backtrack to the origins of Islam as understood by Islam itself.

EARLY ISLAM CONFRONTS MEDINAN JUDAISM

Muhammad received his first divine revelation in about 610 C.E. while meditating in a cave on the outskirts of his native town, Mecca. He shared his experience with his wife, Khadīja, and with his family and close friends, but according to the collective memory of Islam he refrained from preaching publicly until about three years later.

Islamic tradition describes Muhammad's prophetic mission in great detail, from the first words of revelation he received at that terrifying moment in the cave at Mt. Hira to the last words he uttered at the moment of his death. The general chronicle of his mission unfolds as a single narrative in the great biography of the Prophet known as the *Sīra,* but that composition is a result of the collecting and editing of thousands of brief, independent oral tellings, called *ḥadīth,* which depict discrete parts of his life. These ḥadīth are literary building blocks in the form of short, eye-witness reports describing various aspects of Muhammad's life, his habits, and his utterances. They existed in oral form for generations before being systematically collected and reduced to writing in a genre of literature called the Ḥadīth. Only after their collection into the large compendia, organized first by the names of those who told them and then by topics, were they rearranged into the linear narrative of the *Sīra.* Often consisting of only a dozen or so words, each ḥadīth focuses on one small item, ranging from how Muhammad cleaned his teeth to his very words describing his experience of God. As might be expected of such data, the ḥadīth often contradict one another. The ancient collectors of these traditions therefore faced a daunting task: evaluating and organizing the material into forms that would lend insight and provide spiritual and intellectual guidance to the community of believers.

The *Sīra,* composed by Muhammad ibn Isḥāq in the mid-eighth century, is the earliest and best-respected biography of Muhammad. However, it does not always agree with the parallel material found in such early historical works as al-Wāqidī's *al-Maghāzī,* Ibn Saʿd's *al-Ṭabaqāt,* or other early collections, and no corroborative record may be found outside the religious literature. The available narrative of Muhammad's prophetic career therefore represents the collective memory of Islam, and this memory includes a great amount of information about the Jewish communities and individuals among whom Muhammad lived. In fact, the *Sīra,* the Qur'an, and other early sources all openly acknowledge the major impact of Jews and Judaism on early Islamic history. Muhammad recited the divine revelations to Jews and expected them to join his religious fellowship. He spoke, argued, and fought with them, and he warmly accepted them as converts. But this period of intense interaction with Jews occurred only after he left Mecca.

After receiving the divine call, Muhammad preached openly in his native town and gained followers, but he also created enemies when he disparaged the old gods. For generations before the birth of Muhammad, Mecca had been a cultic center, a major place of pilgrimage for the idolatrous Arabs. Perhaps because of this idolatrous quality of Meccan life, there is no record of Jewish or Christian communities in the town, though biblical ideas were known in Arabia by the early seventh century and, as we have seen, biblical motifs had penetrated even into pre-Islamic cultic practices. While still in Mecca, according to an Islamic tradition accepted by most Western scholars, Muhammad recited revelations containing references to personages, occasions, and concepts found in the Hebrew Bible and New Testament. For example, Noah, the Flood, Abraham, Moses, Jesus, a day of judgment, and concepts of heaven and hell may all be found in what are generally considered the "Meccan" verses.

According to the Islamic sources, powerful Meccans had much at stake in the local religious tourism industry. Pilgrims needed food, lodging, and guides to take them to the shrines and direct them as to the most efficacious activities and offerings required at each sacred site, and these services were provided, for a fee, by families and coalitions in the town. When Muhammad denounced the idolatry that was at the base of this economy, he gained serious enemies. He was protected by powerful members of his extended family for a time, but his two most stalwart protectors died in the same year, leaving him in a position of great weakness. It was shortly thereafter that he received an invitation from Medina to arbitrate an intractable feud that had developed between the major tribal clans of that settlement. Muhammad made his hijra with his followers in 622, which marks the year zero of the Islamic or hijri calendar. It was in Medina that Muhammad would come into regular and ongoing contact with a substantial Jewish community.

Muhammad knew that he was a prophet of God sent to the Arab people. The Qur'an itself, narrated in God's words, proclaims that the divine revelations he received were sent to enlighten the Arabs: "By the Book that makes clear, We have made it an Arabic Qur'an, so perhaps you will all understand. It is [from] the Mother of Books,[25] in Our presence, exalted, wise. Shall We deny you the Word because you are a people of excess?" (43:2–5). He had been opposed by most of the Arabs in Mecca, but in Medina, he believed, the large Jewish Arab community, which had a long history of prophets and Scripture, would naturally flock to his divine revelations and prophecies. We have already learned the story of Abdullah ibn Salām, but he was not the only Jew to have awaited a messianic figure. Others seem to have expected a redeemer to arise from the south, which from the perspective of Medina was the direction of Mecca. The *Sīra* records the statement of Salama b. Salāma b. Waqsh:

> We had a Jewish neighbor among the [clan of the] Banu ʿAbd al-Ashhal who came out to us one day from his home. . . . He spoke of the resurrection, the [divine] reckoning, the [heavenly] scales, the Garden and the Fire. . . . [They asked] "What would be a sign of this?" He said, pointing with his hand to Mecca and the Yemen [i.e., southward]: "A prophet will be sent from the direction of this land." They asked: "When will he appear?" He looked at me, the youngest person, and said: "This boy, if he lives his natural term, will see him." And by God, a night and a day did not pass before God sent Muhammad, His messenger, and he was living among us. We believed in him, but [the Jewish neighbor] denied him. . . . When we asked him, "Aren't you the man who said these things?" He said, "Certainly, but this is not the man."[26]

The expectation of a messiah arising from Arabia was widespread enough to have attracted some Jews to the area from the Land of Israel and its environs. The following statement is cited on the authority of a leader *(shaykh)* of the Jewish tribe in Medina known as the Banū Qurayẓa:

> A Syrian Jew[27] named ibn al-Hayyabān came to us a few years before Islam and lived with us. . . . When he was about to die, he said: "O Jews, what do you think made me leave a land of bread and wine to come to a land of hardship and hunger?" We answered: "You know best." He said: "I came to this town to see the emergence of a prophet whose time had come. This is the town to which he will migrate."[28]

Such traditions are clearly made to prove, from the Islamic perspective, the authenticity of Muhammad's prophethood, but they correspond with Jewish ideas and are found so frequently that they seem to reflect a genuine expectation among at least some Jews. The irony of this is clear from another tradition found later in the *Sīra:*

> ʿĀṣim b. ʿUmar b. Qatāda said on the authority of some elders of his tribe, who said: When the Messenger of God met them he said: "Who are you?" They answered: "From the Khazraj [tribe of Medina]." "Are you allies of the Jews?" "Yes," they answered. So he said: "Will you not sit with me so I can talk with you?" "Of course," they replied. So they sat with him, and he called them to

God, expounded to them Islam, and recited for them the Qur'an. Now God had prepared them for Islam in that the Jews, who were People of the Book and knowledge while they themselves were polytheists and idolaters, lived with them in their towns. They used to raid [the Jews] in their settlements, and when [bad feelings] arose between them the Jews would say: "A prophet is being sent soon. His time has come. We will follow him and kill you with his help [just as] 'Ad and Iram were destroyed."[29] So when the Messenger of God spoke with this group and called them to God, some of them said to the others: "By God, this is the very prophet about which the Jews had threatened us. Do not let them get to him before us!" So they responded to his call, believed him, and accepted his teaching of Islam.[30]

Given the messianic expectations of at least some Jews in Medina, it may seem surprising that, with few exceptions, the Jews did not flock to Muhammad's teachings despite the general acceptance of his leadership among many non-Jews within a few years of his arrival. With the highly Arabized nature of the Jewish community of Medina and at least a certain amount of common Arabized biblical culture shared between Jews and pagans, one might expect a more equal response to the option of joining the Arabian monotheism being introduced by Muhammad. But he seems not to have fit the specifically Jewish cultural paradigm of the Expected One closely enough, and the revelations and prophecies he recited in the squares of Medina, though parallel to many in the Hebrew Bible, seem not to have satisfied Jewish expectations. The community chose not to follow him, and it eventually suffered exile, slavery, and destruction as a result.

The Qur'an innocently provides some specific information about the way Jews responded to Muhammad's teachings in Medina. It expresses bitterness and disappointment at their refusal to accept the new divine dispensation. Yet it notes with some consolation that this behavior was not new, because the Israelites were a stiff-necked people who did not fully follow Moses, nor were they true to their own covenant. "Remember: We made a covenant with you and raised up the mountain over you [saying]: 'Take hold firmly of what We have given you and remember what is in it. Perhaps you will be pious.' But you turned away after that. If it were not for God's grace and mercy toward you, you would have been among the losers" [2:63–64, directed as if to Jews].[31] This image of God threatening the Israelites with death under a mountain if they will not accept the Torah finds a parallel in pre-Islamic rabbinic tradition,[32] demonstrating the Qur'an's intertextual relationship not only with biblical lore but with rabbinic tradition as well.

Most Medinan Jews did not accept Muhammad's revelations as accurate statements of Scripture. The Qur'an observes that they would note the discrepancies between his renderings of biblical themes and those with which they were already familiar. It therefore accuses them of distorting their own scriptural record from the original revelation they received at Sinai. The pure and undistorted Sinaitic revelation would have been consistent with that of the new revelation given to Muhammad, and indeed, according to later Islamic tradition, it even included prophecies of the coming of the Arabian prophet. "There are some among [the People of the Book] who distort Scripture with their tongues so that you would think it is from Scripture, but it is not from Scripture. They say: 'This is from God' though it is not from God. They knowingly speak falsehood about God" (3:78). Because the Hebrew Bible, like the Christian, is considered to have been tampered with, neither are accepted by Islam as dependable sources of divine revelation. Yet the Qur'an also notes that some Jews did indeed believe Muhammad's words of prophecy: "There are some among the People of the Book who believe in God and in what He revealed to you and what has been revealed to them, humbling themselves to God." (3:199).

Jews also challenged Muhammad to demonstrate the truth of his prophethood according to biblical precedents such as that of Elijah, who in 1 Kings 18 had his sacrifice consumed by a heavenly fire. "[There are] those [Jews] who say: 'God has obligated us not to believe in a messenger until he offers a sacrifice that the fire will consume' " (3:183).

The Qur'an remained an unwritten oral text throughout Muhammad's lifetime, which proved a difficulty for him, because he was challenged by the Jews to confirm his prophecy by showing them that he was in possession of a physical book of Scripture: "The People of the Book ask you to bring down to them a Book from heaven" (4:153). It is quite clear that the Jewish rejection of Muhammad was not a polite refusal to accept his authority and program but rather a serious and proactive resistance. "Many of the People of the Book want to make you unbelievers again after your having believed" (2:109). Why, we might ask, would the Jews take such an active stand against Muhammad and his community?

The answer to this question lies both in the distinct nature of the Jews' cultural identity and in their particular political and religious standing in Medina. The Jewish community had recently lost its absolute political dominance in the town but remained a powerful force, and the three major Jewish tribes were allied with the now dominant non-Jewish factions in a complex set of political and kinship relationships. That is, not only did Jewish tribes have alliances and pacts of nonaggression with non-Jewish tribes, but there were also Jewish clans or factions that were members of tribes not identified specifically as Jewish. It was therefore not uncommon for Jews and non-Jews to belong to identical kinship groups, suggesting that intermarriage between kinship groups probably also occurred.

Medina suffered from a great deal of tension and violence between competing tribes and kinship groups just prior to Muhammad's immigration there; he was actually invited to Medina to arbitrate and resolve the rampant factionalism of the town. His main strategy to this end was to create a trans-tribal organization of believers whose loyalty to God (and God's religious community) would transcend loyalty to tribe. The traditional tribal system of relationships upon which the Jewish community depended was therefore beginning to give way to Muhammad's super-tribe, which threatened the Jews in three ways. First, their protective alliances began to unravel and become meaningless as the Muslim community grew. Second, by claiming to be God's prophet and spokesman, Muhammad threatened the important and prestigious standing of the Jews as representatives of ancient monotheism in a region dominated by pagan idolaters. And third, as more and more Medinans were influenced by Muhammad and his message, the very essence of the Jews' distinct Jewish-Arab identity was threatened by the likelihood that there would be no role for them in a Muslim Medina. In their opposition to Muhammad, therefore, the Jews were guarding their political position, their religious tradition, and their identity within the larger fabric of Arabian culture.

The Jews therefore sought to prevent Muhammad's rise to dominance in the city, and in doing so they engaged in tactics that fully reflect Arab cultural norms and expectations. The composition and public recitation of poetry, for example, was used to discredit or humiliate enemies as well as enhance the status and pride of one's own community in pre-Islamic Arabia, and poetic satire was used in Muhammad's day as well in order to demean or humiliate one's enemy. Medinan Jews such as Abu 'Afak, Ka'b b. al-Ashraf, and 'Asmā' bt. Marwān are cited in Islamic sources as having written poems criticizing Muhammad and his followers and even inciting people against him. Women as well as men engaged in this activity on both sides. The Muslim poetess Maymūna bt. 'Abdallah, for example, is said to have answered Ka'b al-Ashraf's negative verse in kind. And 'Asmā' bt. Marwān, who may have been a convert to Judaism, was considered such a threat that Muhammad asked for a volunteer to silence her. The great Ḥassān b. Thābit, sometimes referred to as the "poet laureate" of the Prophet, threatened her with death in a poetic retort to her poem discrediting Muhammad's leadership and calling on her fellow Medinans to attack him. As the conflict intensified, the stakes grew higher. Some of the incendiary poems and their responses are reproduced in the *Sīra,* and all three Jewish poets mentioned here were eventually assassinated by Muhammad's followers.[33]

The Qur'an and *Sīra* bear witness to this war of words and its effect on the people of Medina. One difficult and somewhat obscure qur'anic verse, for example, seems to allude to an attempt by Jews to humiliate Muhammad in public. It reads,

> There are some Jews who change the words from their places by saying: "We hear and disobey" [*sami'nā wa'aṣaynā*] and "Listen, you who are not listened to," and "Look at us," twisting their tongues and speaking evil of religion. If they had only said, "We hear and obey" [*sami'nā wa'aṭa'nā*]... it would be better for them and more upright. But God cursed them for their unbelief, and they do not believe, except for a few. (4:46)

Three incendiary remarks are made by the Jews in relation to Islam and the Prophet, and the Qur'an corrects them by stating what they *should* have said.

It is impossible to reconstruct the original context of any ancient text with confidence, and this certainly includes the Qur'an. Nonetheless, we can imagine the satirical power of such gibes if we sketch a context for this particular passage given other information we have regarding the cultural history of seventh-century Medina. The Qur'an depicts Muhammad publicly reciting and interpreting the divine revelations to his followers and other interested onlookers. One of the Jews in the crowd publicly calls out to Muhammad *"Sami'nā wa'ṣaynā, ya Muhammad! Sami'nā wa'aṣaynā!"* The phrase is immediately recognizable to a Jew familiar with biblical recitation in Hebrew, because, although it is Arabic, it *sounds* virtually like a quote of Deuteronomy 5:24: *"Shamā'nū ve'asīnū* [We hear and we obey]." In the Arabic, however, it means the opposite: "We hear and disobey." To the Jewish bystander, the phrase would be understood according to its bilingual meaning with the full force of the double entendre: "We hear and obey *our* religious tradition, O Muhammad [Hebrew meaning] but we hear and publicly acclaim our *disobedience* to *your* religious preaching [Arabic meaning]!" This clever taunt would undoubtedly elicit a laugh among the Jews, whereas the Muslims and other non-Jews would simply fail to understand the humor. Muhammad and his followers would be confused, and embarrassment and humiliation would attend their confusion and the mockery of their opponents—always the goal of effective public satire.

This passage portrays the Jews of Medina as being familiar with Arabian linguistic, literary, and cultural norms yet loyal to their particular identity as Jews. Despite their deep and successful acculturation, their Jewishness seems not to have been determined only by religious beliefs. They are sometimes described in the sources as a *jummā'* (meaning "aggregate" or "collective"). This could be a reference to a certain range of religious expressions within a collective identity of Jewishness, or it could refer to a trans-tribal "ethnic" Jewish subculture, not based on a genetic or biological distinction but rather on a transcendent sense of peoplehood that could include a variety of subsumed expressions of practice or beliefs within it. Either of these possibilities might seem to contradict the earlier observation that Medinan Jews were not above the tribal factionalism that plagued the city. In fact, however, the two trajectories of identity may have lived quite intimately together. Highly integrated into the tribal system of Arabian society, Jews naturally identified closely with their kinship groups though they still retained a super-tribal sense of Jewish identity, even if they did not always share every detail of religious belief. The Islamic sources are certainly not consistent in their descriptions of Medinan Jews, suggesting that the community was layered— that it was not monolithic politically, economically, socially, or religiously. Although the Medinan Jews are identified as a "collective," they are described as speaking, looking, dressing, and acting like other Arabs. Sometimes they are portrayed as identifying themselves as Jews and being identified by others as such. At other times, they are portrayed acting exactly like any other Medinan Arab and without any hint of their Jewish identity.

The Medinan Jews failed to prevent Muhammad's rise in influence and power. Instead, they were successfully divided and conquered by the Prophet and his followers. Two of the three powerful Medinan Jewish tribes were exiled, and, of the third, the Banū Qurayẓa, the women and children were taken as booty and the adult males were killed. This important episode of Jewish and early Muslim history has been of some interest to Western scholars, which has in turn stimulated a reexamination by Muslims, and the entire issue has become controversial.[34] Western scholars have tended to condemn the Muslims' treatment of the Jewish tribes, and particularly that of the Banū Qurayẓa, as cruel, unnecessary, and unethical. Muslims in turn condemn the Jews as treacherous in aiding the enemies of Muhammad, conniving against him, and murderous, thereby deserving of such draconian measures. What both viewpoints omit is the observation that both Muhammad and the Jews were acting according to the cultural expectations of their time and place. It should only be expected that the nature of politics is informed by culture. The two sides were both working under the same basic "rules of engagement," according to which factions at the time jockeyed for dominance when the stakes were high. The competition between Muhammad and the Medinan Jews was a "zero-sum game" in which there could be only one winner—and both sides seem to have known that.

By the time of Muhammad's death in 632, there were only a few Jews still living in what had by then become known as *Madīnat al-Nabī*, the "City of the

Prophet." The conflict was immortalized in the Qur'an as well as the Ḥadīth, and anti-Jewish sentiment based on this conflict has become canonized as Scripture. However, some (though far fewer) qur'anic passages demonstrate a sense of openness and toleration of Jews and other Peoples of the Book: "Those who believe [in Islam], the Jews, Christians, and Sabians—whoever believes in God and the Last Day, and has acted uprightly, have their reward with their Lord. They shall not fear nor grieve" (2:62).

In the aftermath of the great Arab Conquest, the many Jewish communities that suddenly came under the hegemony of Islam did not fare any worse than they had under the Christians and Zoroastrians, and in most cases it appears that they fared significantly better. It should be remembered that, during the first century or more, Islam was continuing to define itself, so its influence and pressure was negligent in the immediate wake of the conquests and then increased over the years. It must also be remembered that the official Muslim policy toward "Peoples of the Book"—that is, Jews, Christians, and other religious groups that could claim a divine Scripture—was quite different than it was toward polytheists. According to the Qur'an: "[T]hen kill the polytheists wherever you find them, and seize them, beleaguer them, and lie in wait for them everywhere; but if they repent, and establish prayers and pay *zakāt* [a required tax distributed to the needy], then open the way for them: for God is forgiving, compassionate" (9:5). This verse became the authoritative source for the absolute outlawing of idolatry within the Islamic world. Polytheists were to be given the choice of conversion or death.

The policy toward peoples of Scripture was based on Qur'an 9:29: "Fight against those who do not believe in God or in the Last Day, and do not forbid what God and His messenger have forbidden, and do not practice the religion of truth among those who have been given the Book, until they pay the *jizya*, off hand, humbled." Scriptuaries were to be fought until they accepted the hegemony of Islam but were then free to practice their religions without interference on the condition that they pay a special tax (jizya) and submit to a secondary societal status.

Eventually, most Jews living in the Islamic world did become Muslim, and an even higher percentage of Christians converted.[35] The debate over the reason for this has also raised controversy, with one view claiming that Muslims forced conversion either outright or through "cultural imperialism," whereas the other suggests that conversion is a natural, voluntary response of subdominant groups to the attraction of a dominant one, allowing for relatively porous boundaries between the cultures of the rulers and the ruled.

It would take at least three centuries for the majority population of the Islamic Middle East to become Muslim. Certainly in the earliest period, most Jews seem to have remained faithful to their ancestral traditions. A few key converts, however, had a profound effect on emerging Islam. The first, as noted above, was Abdullah ibn Salām, who became an exemplar in Islamic tradition of the few Jewish scholars who would admit that Muhammad was indeed referred to in the Torah as the final prophet of God. Another early convert, who was extremely influential in the developing methodologies and contents of Islamic exegesis and tradition, was a Yemenite Jew named Abū Ishāq Kaʿb b. Matīʿ, but known more commonly as Kaʿb al-Aḥbār, meaning roughly, "Kaʿb, the religious scholar."[36]

KAʿB AL-AḤBĀR: FROM FAME TO NOTORIETY

Kaʿb and the tale of his conversion and subsequent influence on the early caliphs and other Muslim leaders are enveloped in legend. Nevertheless, we shall observe how his story, even with its marbled layers of fact and fiction, sheds important light on aspects of the complex relationship between Jews and early Muslims and between early Medieval Judaism and the emergence of Islam.

Kaʿb was from southern Arabia, which, in the sixth and seventh centuries, had a large Jewish and Christian population. Very little is known of his life before he converted, but the sources suggest that he derived from a well-known tribe, perhaps even from the great one of Ḥimyar, which produced kings that ruled much of southern Arabia for centuries and may have converted as a collective to Judaism in the early fifth century. Kaʿb was greatly revered by his Muslim contemporaries for his wisdom and scholarship. He counted among his students two of the most important early Muslim scholars and traditionists: Abdullah ibn ʿAbbās, who is known as the originator of Islamic exegesis; and Abdullah Abū Hurayra, one of the most prolific sources of ḥadīth on the behavior and sayings of Muhammad.

Like other Yemenite Jews and non-Jews, Kaʿb did not become a Muslim during Muhammad's lifetime or even during the reign of the first caliph, Abū Bakr. He was born before Muhammad, and it is curious that he seems to have changed his mind about Islam only when he was in his seventies or perhaps older. What exactly inspired him to convert is unknown, but he made his way as a Jew to Medina during the reign of the second caliph, ʿUmar ibn al-Khaṭṭāb. When he arrived there in 636, he found few Jews remaining in the town; most had been exiled or had converted to Islam. Kaʿb became close to the caliph and attracted pious Muslims to him because of his knowledge of the Bible and its midrashic interpretation. This period in Medina is quite interesting because, according to the histories, Kaʿb lived there as a Jew for some two years before becoming a Muslim.

Kaʿb is described as teaching from a Torah scroll in the mosque, according to the Muslim traditionist Ḥusayn b. Abī al-Ḥurr al-Anbārī, and famous scholars are described as asking him to interpret difficult verses from the Qur'an, which, typically, he would interpret from the context of biblical stories. In a tradition found in the famous Ḥadīth collection of Mālik b. Anās, Ka'b is said to have observed a man who took off his shoes in a mosque. Ka'b turned to the man and said: "Why did you remove your shoes? Was it because you were interpreting the [Qur'an] verse: 'Take off your shoes, for you are in the holy valley, Tuwa?' [20:12]."[37]

This scriptural verse is part of a qur'anic narrative parallel to Exodus 3, in which Moses sees a burning fire out of the midst of which his name is called. Ka'b then asks the man who had removed his shoes: "And do you know of what Moses' shoes were made? They were made from the leather of a dead donkey." It is clear from both Exodus 3:5 and Qur'an 20:12 that God demanded of Moses that he remove his shoes. Both scriptural texts associate the removing of shoes with Moses being in a sacred place, but neither explains exactly what the reason was for removing shoes in such circumstances. Ka'b fills in the gap with the explanation that Moses' shoes were made from the skin of a dead donkey (jild ḥimār mayyit). The exact significance of this fact has been lost to us, but it was obvious enough in Ka'b's day that the listener did not need further explanation. Could the issue have been that shoes made of donkey leather were considered defiling and therefore must be removed when one is in a sanctified place?[38] Was his point that any clothing made of animal skin was forbidden in such a place, or was he simply suggesting a reason for an old local custom?

Because Ka'b's explanation is found in Islamic literature, he is portrayed as making his point about the Islamic custom of removing one's shoes when entering a place of prayer, and he does so by anchoring it to a scriptural text in typical exegetical fashion, Muslim or Jewish. In doing so, however, he refers to a reason that is no longer remembered, perhaps reflecting an old Jewish Arabian custom no longer practiced today in a Jewish context but now standard practice in Islam. Ka'b cites the Qur'an, but he may well be citing it as a parallel to the Exodus text, subsequently applying a Jewish explanation to the qur'anic verse in order to make his point. The comment that Moses' shoes were made of the skin of a donkey cannot be found in extant Jewish sources, but, given Ka'b's acknowledged Jewish background, he may have been articulating an old interpretation that has since been lost from Jewish tradition.

Ka'b is typically portrayed as using biblical and midrashic literature as the basis for his views on Islamic doctrine and tradition. His Jewish knowledge seems to have served him well, and he was well respected by his Muslim peers, who often consulted him. One tradition, found also in Malik's collection,[39] has the famous Muslim scholar Abū Hurayra recount his meeting with Ka'b:

I sat with him. He told me about the Torah and I told him about the Apostle of God. One of the things I told him was that the Apostle of God said: "The best of days upon which the sun ever arose is Friday. Adam was created on that day, was brought down from the Garden on that day, was pardoned on that day, and died on that day. The [final] Hour will occur on that day . . . and there is a time during that day when a Muslim does not pray [formally, but if] he asks something of God, he is granted it." Ka'b said: "This is [but] one day of the year." I answered: "No, every Friday." So Ka'b consulted the Torah [*tawrāh*] and said: "The Apostle of God is correct."

Later, Abu Hurayra related this conversation to Abdullah ibn Salām.

I told [Abdullah] that Ka'b said: "This is [but] one day of the year." Abdullah ibn Salām replied: "Ka'b is lying!" I then told him that Ka'b consulted the Torah and agreed that it was every Friday. So Abdullah said: "Ka'b is correct." Abdullah then said: "I know which time it is [that a Muslim will receive anything he requests from God]." [Abu Hurayra] said to him: "So tell me and do not hold back." So Abdullah ibn Salām said to him: "It is the last hour of Friday."

This exchange raises a number of issues related to the intersection of customs and traditions between Judaism and early Islam. Ka'b's "one day of the year" may have referred to Yom Kippur, but he later revises his statement after "consulting the Torah," thereby agreeing with Muhammad's teaching. Abdullah becomes quite angry when hearing Ka'b's initial statement of what would appear to be the normative Jewish view, but he is satisfied when learning that Ka'b revised his position, perhaps drawing on the Jewish tradition that many extraordinary things were created at the last hour of the Friday of creation.[40] Because of the divine wonders associated with that hour, it could have been considered a particularly auspicious time for personal supplication.

This story of Ka'b, Abū Hurayra, and Abdullah, with Muhammad's statement about the merits of Friday a constant referent, serves as an important foundation story to justify the Islamic day of religious congregation on Friday, in juxtaposition to the Jewish Saturday or Christian Sunday. It is impossible to reconstruct what Ka'b was thinking or reading when he gave his view on Muhammad's wisdom as told him by Abu Hurayra, but the "Torah" that he consulted was certainly not the Five Books of Moses. It was, rather, the extended Jewish meaning of Torah as "Jewish learning," because the legend of the special creations on Friday afternoon are found only in the Midrash and Talmud. We also observe in this story about Ka'b al-Aḥbār that he had the temerity to question a statement of the Prophet and, after consulting his Jewish sources, was bold enough to say, "The Apostle of God is correct."

This story again raises the question whether it reflects a true historical occasion. We know that many Islamic traditions of this nature were fabricated, and it is possible that this one was, too. A number of factors, however, strongly suggest that its core indeed reflects history. The most striking is that the story depicts Ka'b as unwilling to accept the word of the prophet Muhammad without corroboration, and that he consults the Torah to confirm a prophetic statement. Such behavior would probably not have been fabricated by Muslims, who would strongly criticize Ka'b for this in later generations.

According to the tradition, Ka'b accompanied the caliph Umar northward into Palestine and Syria during the Arab conquests, and was with him upon his first visit to Jerusalem. Ka'b, who is quite moved by Jerusalem, tells the caliph about a Jewish prophecy that Arabs would conquer the city from the Romans (which in Arabic parlance includes the Byzantine Roman Empire). His particular reverence for Jerusalem seems to have landed him in a bit of trouble, however.

When the Arabs capture the city, they discover that the site of the ancient Temple had been turned into a garbage dump. This was fully in keeping with Byzantine Christian doctrine, which sought to demonstrate through its imperial policies that the old divine covenant with the Jews was no longer valid after the appearance of Jesus. Henceforth, the only valid covenant would obtain with those who believe in the saving grace of Christ. As the primary symbol of ancient Judaism, the Temple and its environs were purposefully desecrated by the Byzantine authorities. Both Muslim and Jewish versions of the story depict the Arab conquerors proceeding directly to the Temple Mount, which they thoroughly cleanse. Umar himself is often featured in these accounts as the leader of the clean-up.

Umar wanted to build a mosque on the Temple Mount, and he asked Ka'b's advice. According to an early version in the great universal history of Muhammad ibn Jarīr al-Ṭabarī (d. 923),[41] Umar asked him:

"Where do you think we should put the mosque?" "By the rock," answered Ka'b. "By God, Ka'b," said Umar, "you are following after Judaism. I saw you take off your sandals." "I wanted to feel the touch of it with my bare feet," said Ka'b. "I saw you," said Umar. "But no. We will make the forepart the *qibla* [the direction of prayer], as the Prophet of God made the forepart of the mosques their *qibla*. Go along! We were not commanded concerning the rock, but we were commanded concerning the Ka'ba!"

The rock here is the portion of bedrock that protrudes slightly from the surface of the level of the Temple Mount, known in the Mishnah (Yoma 5:2) as the "Foundation Stone" *(sh'tīyāh)* upon which the Holy of Holies, the most sacred part of the Temple, stood. When Ka'b came to the Temple Mount, he immediately removed his shoes, clearly in response to entering a holy place. As in the previous narrative, we must ask if removing his shoes was a Jewish act or a Muslim act. Whichever it was, he was criticized by the caliph for doing it *there,* which clearly indicates a Jewish response to entering into the sacred area of the Temple.

The last part of the story is a bit confusing in this version. To clarify: the *qibla* is the direction of Islamic prayer. It always faces toward the Ka'ba in Mecca, the most sacred and central religious shrine of Islam, and from Jerusalem and its environs, Mecca is due south. There is evidence in the Qur'an and early Islamic tradition that the qibla, like the direction of Jewish prayer, was toward Jerusalem for a brief period when Muhammad first came to Medina. Shortly after his arrival, however, the qibla was turned toward Mecca. The controversy becomes clear in another version of the story:[42]

> [T]he caliph himself went there, and Ka'b with him. Umar said to Ka'b: "O Abū Ishāq, do you know the position of the Rock?" Ka'b answered: "Measure from the well which is in the Valley of Gehenna so and so many ells; there dig and you will discover it," adding, "at this present day it is a dungheap." So they dug there and the rock was laid bare. Then Umar said to Ka'b: "Where do you say we should place the sanctuary, or rather, the *qibla*?" Ka'b replied: "Lay out a place for it behind [that is, to the north of] the Rock and so you will make two qiblas: that, namely, of Moses and that of Muhammad." And Umar answered him: "You still lean toward the Jews, O Abū Ishāq. The sanctuary will be in front [that is, to the south of] the Rock." Thus was the Mosque [of al-Aqsa] erected in the front part of the *Haram* [Temple Mount] area.

Ka'b is accused here of trying to insert Jewish religious ideas into Islam. Yet in the previous story, he was not criticized for confirming a statement of Muhammad by consulting the Torah, an act that could have been considered just as egregious as regarding the Temple Mount a sacred site. Ka'b even refers to the Torah as the Book of God, despite the fact that Islam does not consider the Torah an accurate divine revelation. He is depicted elsewhere as counseling Umar to refer to Jerusalem not as Aelia, the name applied to it by Hadrian in the second century in order to dissociate the holy city from its Jewish heritage, but as Bayt al-Maqdis, the exact Arabic equivalent to the Hebrew "Beyt Hamiqdash," the Jerusalem Temple.

In a story told by Ibn ʿAbbās's student ʿIkrima,[43] a man says to the great scholar and exegete,

> "O Ibn ʿAbbās, I heard something remarkable from Kaʿb the *ḥabr* about the sun and the moon." [Ibn ʿAbbās] had been reclining, but he sat upright and said, "What is it?" [The man went on], "He claims that the sun and the moon will be brought on the Day of Resurrection as if they were castrated bulls and thrown into hell."[44] One of Ibn ʿAbbās's lips flew up in anger and the other dropped. Then he said three times, "Kaʿb lies! Kaʿb lies! Kaʿb lies! This is Judaism that he wants to insert into Islam! God is too great and honorable to punish the obedient. Have you not heard God's word: "He has made the sun and the moon work for you diligently?" [Qurʾan 14:33].

Ibn ʿAbbās, agitated and upset, finally cites traditions on the authority of Muhammad himself that contradict Kaʿb's teaching. ʿIkrima then decides to tell Kaʿb what has been said.[45]

> I got up with those who had been told [the story]. We came to Kaʿb and told him Ibn ʿAbbās's reaction upon hearing [Kaʿb's] statement and what he reported [in response] on the authority of the Apostle of God. So Kaʿb arose and accompanied us to Ibn ʿAbbās. [Kaʿb] said: "I heard your reaction to my statement. I ask God's forgiveness and repent. I simply reported from a book of midrash that was in circulation.[46] I did not know that there were Jewish changes [*tabdīl al-yahūd*] in it."

Kaʿb was actually citing a midrash containing material that would be considered outside the parameters of normative rabbinic tradition. His final comment suggests, interestingly enough, that he may have ultimately realized this. From the standpoint of Islam, however, such distinctions were irrelevant (nor is it clear how fixed was the midrashic canon at this time). In this story, Kaʿb is condemned for attempting to insert "Jewish teachings" into Islam, yet we noted previously that he was not condemned in other tales for doing exactly that. On the contrary, he was sought out by early Muslims exactly because he had access to ancient monotheistic lore that could lend insight into God's word and will as expressed in Islamic Scripture and tradition. Why was he so harshly condemned here and so welcomed in other contexts?

The definitive answer may never be known, but two aspects of Kaʿb's situation provide significant clues. Although it was known to all that Kaʿb was knowledgeable, the Jewish nature of his knowledge seemed to matter little if at all. What was important was that he had access to ancient monotheistic wisdom. Because Islam was only in formation during Ka'b's lifetime, it was not yet clear exactly where it fit in relation to Judaism and Christianity. Most of what would become Islamic dogma simply had not been established at this point. Ka'b, for example, could question and then find Jewish confirmation of Muhammad's statement about the status of Friday. Later, however, the belief developed that the word of the Prophet was infallible, after which Ka'b's behavior could no longer be considered acceptable. While he lived, however, Ka'b was regularly consulted both for his access to divine wisdom and, like other scholars of Holy Scriptures either Jewish or Christian, for his ability to predict future events based on his knowledge of divine revelation.

More significant than this, however, is the fact that Ka'b's reputation declined in subsequent generations as Islam began increasingly to view itself as an independent religious civilization. Material attributed to Ka'b was tainted by his unabashed association with Judaism. Islam provided the ideological basis of the largest and most successful empire of the age, and any hint of dependence or subordination to another tradition would have been considered at the least impolitic. By the end of the eighth century, it became improper to consult Jews about problems of religion and belief. In later texts Ka'b was occasionally accused even of surreptitiously attempting to corrupt Islam from within while masquerading as a convert.

One may detect the change in Ka'b's status by examining the sources of tradition in which he is cited by name. In the canonical collections of Ḥadīth, the most highly respected sources, his name cannot be found at all. Many of the traditions attributed to him in extra-canonical literature, however, can be found also in the Ḥadīth collections, although there they are attributed not to him but to his students. He himself was too tainted to be included in the Ḥadīth by the time of its assembly in the ninth century. Some of the information he brought was too important to be excluded from it, however, so it is found attributed to students of his such as Ibn 'Abbās, who is not suspected of being too closely associated with Judaism or other foreign religious traditions. Ka'b's stories and teachings may be found in his own name, however, in the popular literature of the story-tellers, or quṣṣāṣ, who told tales of ancient prophets and patriarchs. Reflecting popular culture that transcended religious affiliation, these "Stories of the Prophets" (qiṣaṣ al-anbiyā') preserve much of the aggadic material for which Ka'b was famous.[47]

The story of Ka'b al-Aḥbār reflects aspects of Jewish culture and civilization of seventh-century Arabia just as it reflects aspects of emerging Islam. The midrashic traditions Ka'b cites sometimes lie outside of the canon of rabbinic

Judaism that we know today, suggesting that the religious ideas and practices of ancient Arabian Jews may have been somewhat different from what we know from the Talmuds of Babylon and the Land of Israel. Ka'b partially judaized the very religion into which he assimilated. He is not unique, of course; proselytes often contribute something of their prior religious ideas and practices as they integrate into the systems of new religions.

In fact, the Islam that Ka'b knew must have looked quite different from later forms. It was most certainly less distinct from Judaism than it is today. As Muhammad's expectations that the Jews of Medina would follow him suggest, the boundaries between the two systems were simply not so clear. One tradition even states that a group of Jews who had embraced Islam asked (but did not receive) Muhammad's permission to observe the Jewish Sabbath and to study the Torah at night.[48] Early Muslims came to Jews like Ka'b and to Christians for monotheistic wisdom and lore that would help them understand their own revelation and the acts of Muhammad. But as Islam developed, as its tenets and practices became more standardized and unified, its adherents came to see themselves as distinct, unique, and different from other religious civilizations.

During Ka'b's lifetime, rabbinic Judaism itself was still emerging and its boundaries were still permeable. Some of Ka'b's teachings may have since fallen out of Judaism because they became irrelevant and were forgotten, or because they were rejected. In a fascinating reversal, however, some of Ka'b's and other Jews' traditions, preserved in Islamic literature, would reappear in Jewish literature when, by the tenth century, Jews began to absorb and appropriate aspects of the powerful and attractive Islamic religious, intellectual, and cultural civilization.

NOTES

1. *Al-Sīra al-Nabawiyya* (Beirut, n.d.), 1: 516–17; translated by Alfred Guillaume as *The Life of Muhammad: A Translation of Ibn Ishaq's Sirat Rasul Allah* (Karachi, 1955), 241–42.

2. Ḥabr 'ālim. The Arabic term, ḥabr, is simply the Arabic pronunciation of the talmudic title, ḥaver, or learned scholar (Bava Batra 75a: "ḥaverim are none other than talmidey ḥakamim").

3. Its strongly polemical nature should immediately raise caution regarding its historicity. See A. J. Wensinck, *Muhammad and the Jews of Medina* (Berlin, 1982); R. Firestone, "The Failure of a Jewish Program of Public Satire in the Squares of Medina," *Judaism* (Winter 1997): 438–52; W. M. Watt, "The Condemnation of the Jews of Banū Qurayẓah," *Muslim World* 42 (1952): 160–71; and G. Newby, "The Sīrah as a Source for Arabian Jewish History: Problems and Perspectives," *Jerusalem Studies in Arabic and Islam* 7 (1986): 121–38.

4. According to classical Arabian genealogies, the "original Arabs" (*al-'arab al-'āriba*)

have died out, whereas the "arabized Arabs" (*al-'arab al-musta'riba*) derive from nonindigenous tribes who assimilated Arabian culture and language after migrating into the Arabian Peninsula; see G. Rentz, "Djazirat al-'Arab," in *Encyclopaedia of Islam,* 2d ed. (Leiden, 1: 543–46. 1983), Many contemporary Arabian tribes, including the Quraysh tribe from which Muhammad derived, trace their ancestry to Ishmael, whom Abraham brought to Arabia (see Gen. 21).

5. Many of these terms were absorbed into Islam. For a listing of foreign religious vocabulary found in the Qur'an, see Arthur Jeffery, *The Foreign Vocabulary of the Qur'ān* (Baroda, India, 1938). Christian communities also lived in Arabia during this period, and they too contributed cultic and religious terminology to what would emerge as Islam. See Spencer Trimingham, *Christianity Among the Arabs in Pre-Islamic Times* (London, 1979).

6. S. D. Goitein, "Jewish Issues in *Kitab Ansāb al-Ashrāf* of al-Balādhurī" (Hebrew), *Zion* 1 (1936): 76.

7. Earlier attempts at establishing an authoritative text may have occurred, such as the "collection" under the first caliph, Abu Bakr, but even that under Uthman was not conclusive. The primitive nature of Arabic orthography and various "readings" or different ways of pronouncing the words continued to plague the Muslims, and some modern scholars question the traditional account of the collection and canonization of the Qur'an altogether. For a synopsis of the traditional Islamic view with minor criticisms, see Richard Bell and W. Montgomery Watt, *Introduction to the Qur'ān* (Edinburgh, 1970).

8. The earliest complete narrative, reproduced here, is found in *Pirqē Rabbi Eli'ezer* (Warsaw edition with commentary of David Luria), chap. 30, a work that was redacted in its present form after the emergence of Islam and that contains Islamic influence but is made up mostly of pre-Islamic material. An English translation (of a different manuscript) of *PRE* was made by Gerald Friedlander, *Pirkē De Rabbi Eliezer* (London, 1916; reprint, New York, 1981), 218–19. A more embellished rendering may be found in the later *Sefer HaYashar* (Tel Aviv, 1980), 55–56.

9. The *Targum Pseudo-Yonatan* (Gen. 21:21) has " 'Adisha." Most likely added to an earlier narrative core, these allusions to the name of Muhammad's beloved wife, 'Ayyishah, date its final redaction to after the emergence of Islam.

10. Note the double entendre in the words, *'ayefā nafshī* ("my soul is faint") in relation to the name 'Ayefa.

11. *Targum Pseudo-Yonatan* (Gen. 21:21) has Fatima, which was the name of Muhammad's daughter.

12. In the continuation of this story, Abraham also demonstrates his continuing love for Hagar by taking her back after Sarah's death. Traditional commentaries from the targums to Rashi suggest that Abraham's wife, Qeturah, named in Genesis 25:1, was none other than Hagar.

13. For a synopsis of 17 versions of this story in Arab sources, see Reuven Firestone, *Journeys in Holy Lands: The Evolution of the Abraham-Ishmael Legends in Islamic Exegesis* (Al-

bany, N.Y., 1990), 76–82. See also Aviva Schussman, "Abraham's Visits to Ishmael—The Jewish Origin and Orientation" (Hebrew), *Tarbiz* 49 (1980): 325–45.

14. Yaqūt b. 'Abdallah al-Rūmī (d. 1229), *Mu'jam al-buldān*, 7 vols. (Beirut, 1990), 4: 255.

15. *Al-Anbiyā'*, #583. This work is one of the two most highly revered Islamic religious books after the Qur'an, so such a narrative remains of great importance in contemporary Islam.

16. The Zam-zam well is the sacred well in Mecca, only a few steps away from the Ka'ba, from which Muslim pilgrims still drink.

17. See, e.g., Bukhārī, *Ṣaḥīḥ, anbiyā'* 9:23, 24.

18. See, e.g., Romans 4:9–25 and Galatians 4:21–31.

19. The qur'anic term for the Kaaba in Mecca. In qur'anic discourse, capitalized "We" refers to God, who is the divine narrator of the Qur'an.

20. This verse is found only in the Oriental (Syriac, Ethiopic, Armenian, and Arabic) recensions, not in the Latin.

21. Lamentations Rabbah 2:6, as suggested by David Halperin and cited indirectly in Gordon Newby, *A History of the Jews of Arabia* (Columbia, S.C., 1989), 59.

22. Cited in Newby, *History,* 59. See also David Halperin, *The Faces of the Chariot* (Tübingen, 1988), 467–68.

23. Or, "those of the *ḥaverīm.*" See, however, Qur'an 5:63.

24. David J. Halperin, "The Ibn Sayyad Traditions and the Legend of al-Dajjal," *Journal of the American Oriental Society* 96 (1976): 213–25.

25. This common idiom means, in essence, the "essential divine word" or divine source from which all revelation comes.

26. *Al-Sīra al-Nabawiyya* (Beirut, n.d.), 1:212/Guillaume 93–94.

27. The common designation for the Land of Israel in medieval Arabic texts is (greater) Syria (*al-shā'm*).

28. *Sīra* 1:213–14/Guillaume 94.

29. 'Ād and Iram are names of ancient Arabian tribal groups that had disappeared long before the emergence of Islam but that still lived in the memories and oral traditions of the Arabs.

30. *Sīra* 1:428–29/Guillaume 197–98.

31. The theme of the Israelites breaking their own covenant is repeated in the Qur'an: 2:84, 93, 100; 3:187; 5:12–13.

32. See, e.g., BT *Shabbat* 88a, Avodah Zara 2b. *Tanḥuma, Bereshit* 58:3. The motif is also repeated in the Qur'an: 2:93; 4:154.

33. *Sīra* 2:51–58, 635–38/Guillaume 364–69, 675–76; Wensinck, *Muhammad and the Jews of Medina,* 110–12; Michael Lecker, *Muslims, Jews and Pagans: Studies on Early Islamic Medina* (Leiden, 1995), 38–48; W. Montgomery Watt, *Muhammad at Medina* (Oxford, 1956), 15, 18, 178–79, 210.

34. See, e.g., Wensinck, *Muhammad and the Jews of Medina;* Watt, *Muhammad at Me-*

dina; W. F. Arafat, "New Light on the Story of Banu Qurayza and the Jews of Medina," *Journal of the Royal Asiatic Society* (1976): 100–107; and Barakat Ahmad, *Muhammad and the Jews: A Re-examination* (New Delhi, 1979). M. J. Kister summarizes the various views in his "The Massacre of the Banu Qurayza: A Re-examination of a Tradition," *Jerusalem Studies in Arabic and Islam* 8 (1986): 61–96.

35. Richard Bulliet, *Conversion to Islam in the Medieval Period* (Cambridge, Mass., 1979).

36. Literally, "Ka'b of the *haverim.*" *Al-ahbār* is a plural form of *hibr,* the Arabic equivalent of the talmudic title, *haver.* Although in early Islam the term is usually applied to a few pious and learned Jewish converts, it was sometimes also associated with exceptional Muslims lacking any known Jewish lineage.

37. *Al-Muwatta', K. al-libās* 16 (Cairo, n.d), 916.

38. See Exodus 13:13 and the extended discussion in BT *Bekhorot* 1.

39. *Al-Muwatta', K. al-Jum'a* 16 (p. 108).

40. BT *Pesahim* 54a. See Louis Ginzberg, *The Legends of the Jews,* trans. from German by Henrietta Szold, 7 vols. (Philadelphia, 1968), 1: 83, 5: 103.

41. Muhammad ibn Jarir al-Tabarī, *Ta'rīkh al-rusul wal-mulūk,* ed. M. J. De Goeje (Leiden, 1964), 1: 2408–9, translation in Bernard Lewis, *Islam from the Prophet Muhammad to the Capture of Constantinople,* vol. 2 (New York, 1974), 3.

42. F. E. Peters, *Jerusalem: The Holy City in the Eyes of Chroniclers, Visitors, Pilgrims, and Prophets* (Princeton, 1985), 189.

43. Al-Tabarī, *Ta'rīkh,* 1: 62–63, and translated in *The History of al-Tabarī,* vol. 1 (Albany, N.Y., 1989), 233. Translated and annotated by Franz Rosenthal; editor, Ehsan Yar-Shater.

44. *Thawrān 'aqīrān.* See D. Halperin and G. Newby, "Two Castrated Bulls: A Study in the Haggadah of Ka'b al-Ahbār," *Journal of the American Oriental Society* 102, no. 4 (1982): 631–37.

45. Al-Tabarī, *Ta'rīkh,* 1:74, translation in *History of al-Tabarī,* 1: 243.

46. *Kitāb dāris,* which is generally translated as "well-worn book." Halperin and Newby ("Two Castrated Bulls," 632–33) correctly translate *dāris* through its meaning as study or reading, equal to the Hebrew *midrash.*

47. One of these collections has been translated into English by Wheeler Thackston, *The Tales of the Prophets of al-Kisā'ī* (Boston, 1978). A great deal of this material may also be found in the first few volumes of the recently translated *History of al-Tabarī* (variable dates as volumes are translated).

48. Kister, "*Haddithū 'an banī isrā'īla wa-lā haraja:* A study of an early tradition," *Israel Oriental Studies* I (Tel Aviv University, 1972), 238.

SELECTED BIBLIOGRAPHY

ARABIC SOURCES IN TRANSLATION

Guillaume, Alfred. *The Life of Muhammad: A Translation of Ibn Ishaq's Sirat Rasul Allah.* Karachi, 1955.

Ṭabarī, Muhammad ibn Jarir al-. *The History of al-Ṭabarī.* Vol. 1. Albany, N.Y., 1989. Translated and annotated by Franz Rosenthal; ed., Ehsan Yar-Shater

Thackston, Wheeler. *The Tales of the Prophets of al-Kisā'ī.* Boston, 1978.

SECONDARY STUDIES

Firestone, Reuven. "The Failure of a Jewish Program of Public Satire in the Squares of Medina." *Judaism* (Winter 1997): 438–52.

———. *Journeys in Holy Lands: The Evolution of the Abraham-Ishmael Legends in Islamic Exegesis.* Albany, N.Y., 1990.

Halperin, David. *The Faces of the Chariot.* Tübingen, 1988.

Lecker, Michael. *Muslims, Jews and Pagans: Studies on Early Islamic Medina.* Leiden, 1995.

Newby, Gordon. *A History of the Jews of Arabia.* Columbia, S.C., 1989.

Peters, F. E., ed., *Arabs and Arabia on the Eve of Islam.* London. 1998.

Trimingham, Spencer. *Christianity Among the Arabs in Pre-Islamic Times.* London, 1979.

Watt, W. Montgomery. *Muhammad at Medina.* Oxford, 1956.

Wensinck, A. J. *Muhammad and the Jews of Medina.* Berlin, 1982.

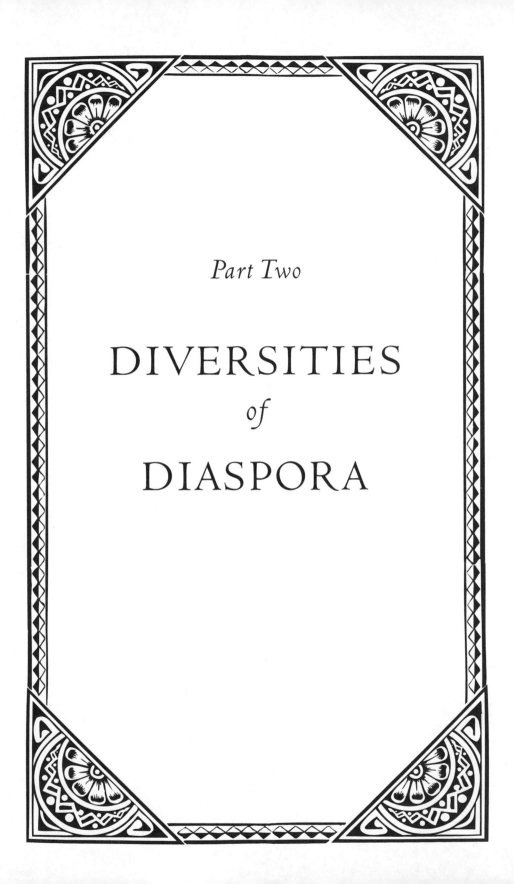

Part Two

DIVERSITIES

of

DIASPORA

INTRODUCTION TO PART TWO: DIVERSITIES OF DIASPORA

DAVID BIALE

Christianity bequeathed to us the term "Middle Ages," by which it meant the period—no matter how long—between the first and second coming of its Messiah. For Islam, which began its career in what became for the Christians the "early" Middle Ages, the term has little meaning. For the Jews, as well—and especially for the vast majority who lived in this period under Muslim rule—the "Middle Ages" was a misnomer. From a purely religious point of view, the destruction of the Second Temple marked the beginning of a new era without Temple sacrifices, an era that continues to this day. We might define the "Jewish Middle Ages" as the period when rabbinical Judaism, as expressed in the talmudic literature produced in Palestine and Babylonia, became the dominant practice for the majority of Jews. But this was a process that happened gradually, and the editing of the two Talmuds did not coincide with the rabbis becoming the hegemonic authorities. On the contrary, as we shall see, rabbinic law, for all that it came to govern the Jews throughout the Diaspora, did not do so without opposition and persistent local reinterpretation. Moreover, despite the great authority the rabbis came to enjoy in most Jewish communities, they were not the only creators of culture.

The cultural life of the Jews in the long period covered in this volume—from roughly the seventh to the eighteenth centuries—developed first in Islamic and later in Christian environments. These two "daughter" monotheistic religions (although given the fact that rabbinic Judaism coincided with early Christianity and Islam, "sibling" religions might be better) treated the Jews differently. For the Muslims, the Jews (like Christians and Zoroastrians) were a "people of the book," that is, a people who had received a divine revelation—partial and misunderstood, to be sure, but still a venerable precursor to the revelation of Islam. As such, they were tolerated but subjected to what we would today call "second class" status. The Christian attitude toward the Jews was more ambivalent though also motivated by theology. The Jews were bearers of God's First Testament, but they had rejected the messianic message of their own erstwhile son. In the formulation of Augustine, which became canonical for the later Middle Ages, the Jews were to be tolerated as witnesses of the veracity of biblical prophecy but, until they converted to Christianity, they had to be kept in a degraded state. In practice, though, the Hellenistic and Roman laws that gave the Jews considerable communal autonomy as a "legal religion" (*religio licita*) continued in new forms under Islam and Christianity. Self-government meant that the Jewish communities could control—or attempt to control—the cultural practices of their members and could police the borders between Jewish and non-Jewish cultures.

Not that these borders were any higher or stronger than in antiquity. As Raymond P. Scheindlin demonstrates in his chapter on Jews in the Muslim Mediterranean basin from the seventh to the sixteenth centuries, all Jews—rabbinic as well as dissenters—enthusiastically adopted Arabic language and culture as they had earlier embraced the Greek, making it their own and transforming it in the process. "Judeo-Arabic culture" may be the best term for this unique linguistic, philosophical, religious, and folkloristic synthesis that was to persist into the twentieth century. To be sure, this cultural "symbiosis" was not without its tensions and conflicts—Jews as a group were a tolerated minority at best—but whatever political and social struggles they underwent with their Muslim neighbors, their culture (both elite and popular) was tightly bound to their surroundings.

Just as the earlier periods of Jewish history were characterized by fissures and factions, so, too, were the Jewish Middle Ages anything but homogeneous. The formation of Judeo-Arabic culture was marked by the schism between Karaites and Rabbanites, the first a group that rejected the Judaism of the second. Although Karaites still exist in a number of tiny communities today, it is easy to forget that, in the Byzantine and Islamic empires, the Karaites were a major force competing with the rabbis. The emergence of Jewish philosophy, which owed much to Arabic philosophy, was in part also motivated by the desire to systematize arguments against the Karaites.

Yet another division began to emerge as small colonies of Jews migrated, starting perhaps as early as the ninth century, from Italy to France and Germany. From these minute seedlings grew the powerful Ashkenazic Jewish culture of Northern and, eventually, Eastern Europe. This was a culture that cultivated its own indigenous traditions (*minhagim*) together with equally strong enterprises of biblical and talmudic interpretation. These communities were established as Christianity itself began to become slowly entrenched in Northern Europe. As Ivan G. Marcus argues in his chapter on Ashkenazic culture in the High Middle Ages, these Jews developed their particular beliefs and practices in intense interaction with their Christian neighbors, a process that involved both borrowing and polemics. Among other innovations, the Ashkenazic Jews responded to the

Crusader pogroms of 1096 and later persecutions by developing a cult of martyrdom and rituals to memorialize the dead, elements of which they adapted
from Christian imagery.

The customs and scholarly pursuits of the Ashkenazic Jews were markedly
different from those of their coreligionists in the Mediterranean, especially the
Sephardim, the Jews of the Iberian Peninsula. The Jews of al-Andalus, as it was
known in its Islamic period, had created a flourishing culture that, as Scheindlin
shows in his chapter, was really the western branch of a much larger Judeo-
Arabic culture extending as far to the east as Iraq and Iran. Under Muslim and,
later, Christian rulers, the Jews of Iberia developed their own traditions of biblical exegesis, law, and custom. Heirs to Arabic thought, they also cultivated the
study of philosophy; indeed, the greatest Jewish philosopher of the Middle Ages,
Moses Maimonides, was a product of al-Andalus, even though he spent much of
his life in Egypt. But in addition to religious philosophy and literature, Jewish
literati in Spain also produced great works of "secular" poetry. The Sephardic
Jews (including Jews of southern France) were the ones who, starting in the late
twelfth and early thirteenth centuries, developed the medieval mystical doctrines of Kabbalah, the greatest book of which, the *Zohar*, was the pseudonymous work of a late-thirteenth-century mystic, Moses de Leon.

Spain was the only major area of the "sphere of Islam" that fell to a Christian
"reconquest," beginning in the twelfth century and reaching completion at the
end of the fifteenth. Because this process took many centuries, Jewish culture on
the Iberian Peninsula evolved in a unique and complex borderland between
Christian and Muslim cultures. Great writers and poets, such as Abraham ibn
Ezra and Judah Halevi, both of whom wrote in Hebrew, lived in both. For a long
transitional period, from 1150 to around 1300, the Jewish culture of al-Andalus
and the emerging Sephardic culture of Christian Spain overlapped as the recurrence of certain literary figures in Scheindlin's and Benjamin Gampel's chapters
demonstrate. But Sephardic culture, as it developed in Christian Spain, which is
Gampel's subject, eventually developed its own singular characteristics.

Gampel takes as his starting point the great watershed in Spanish Jewish history, 1391, when major riots broke out against the Jews and when many converted, either by force or willingly, to Christianity. He asks which elements in
their culture made Jews receptive to Christianity and, conversely, which elements held them to Judaism. Because many of those who converted continued
to follow some Jewish practices, Spain became the cauldron that molded new
forms of Jewish identity. The either/or of medieval identity was shattered in
Spain: the categories of "Christian" and "Jew" were no longer monolithic, and it
was now possible, as it had been in the first centuries of the Common Era, to be

at once a Christian and a Jew. The doctrine of "purity of the blood" (*limpieza de sangre*) that, as of the mid-fifteenth century, Spanish Christians used to distinguish "Old" from "New" Christians, added a racial element to identity that had not existed before. By injecting a racial definition to what had previously been a purely religious identity, "purity of the blood" contributed to the possibility of a hybrid identity in which a converted Jew might not count as a full Christian.

After the expulsions from Spain in 1492 and Portugal in 1497, these Sephardic Jews scattered to safe havens in Italy and the Ottoman Empire (Turkey, the Balkans, North Africa, and Palestine; these latter communities will receive their proper treatment in Volume III). They also established important colonies in Western Europe, particularly in Amsterdam, which, in turn, sent offshoots to the New World. It is this subject that Yosef Kaplan takes up, tracing the contours of a culture that replanted its Sephardic roots in new soil. These Sephardic Jews felt themselves doubly in exile: from the Land of Israel, as tradition taught, but also from the Iberian Peninsula, a homeland that came to define their identity for centuries after the expulsion. Because many of the Jews of the Western Sephardic Diaspora—or their ancestors—had passed through Christianity before returning to Judaism, some, like the philosopher Baruch Spinoza, tended toward heterodoxy, whereas others, such as the Amsterdam Jewish communal leaders, went to the opposite extreme of rigid orthodoxy. This was perhaps the first Jewish community to be acutely aware of itself as "on view" to the outside world, a self-consciousness that foreshadowed the Jewish experience in modernity.

With the expulsion from Spain, Sephardic and Ashkenazic Jews came into direct contact—and often conflict—with each other. At times, the Sephardim even embraced the Spanish Christian doctrine of "purity of the blood" to distinguish themselves from other Jews, thus injecting a racial division in Jewish identity between Jews. For this reason, in communities like Amsterdam, marriage between Sephardim and Ashkenazim was strongly discouraged.

In Italy, the mix of Jewish "ethnicities" was particularly complicated. After the fifteenth century, it was home not only to Sephardic and Ashkenazic Jews but also to the Italianis, the Jews whose Italian ancestry went back to antiquity. By tracing the fortunes of three Italian Jewish families from each of these groups, Elliott Horowitz shows that it is a misnomer to speak of Italian Jewry in the singular and that the Italian Jewish Renaissance was a complex cultural affair, experienced differently by different groups.

Italy is often considered exceptional because the Jews ostensibly shared much more in the majority culture than they did elsewhere. Whatever truth there may be to this claim—and Horowitz's chapter both supports and complicates it—acculturation was by no means the case only for the Italian Jews. The Polish Jews of the late Middle Ages were a seeming counter-example. It is usually assumed that this community, which enjoyed rather considerable privileges at the height of the Polish Commonwealth, nevertheless felt itself quite alienated from Polish culture. Linguistically, for example, the Jews never developed a "Judeo-Polish" but instead added occasional Slavic words to the Judeo-German they brought with them from the West. Yet, despite examples such as Yiddish for the relative isolation and cultural "purity" of the Polish Jews, Moshe Rosman argues that Jews and Poles in the early modern period shared much more of a common culture, especially on the popular and material levels, than either side was probably willing to admit.

The geographical reach of this volume suggests how dispersed the Jews were by the end of the Middle Ages. If the period opened with the center of demographic gravity in the Mediterranean, by its close in the eighteenth century, the center had shifted north and east—away from Spain to Poland and the Ottoman Empire, with smaller outposts in Germany, France, the Netherlands, England, and the New World. This vast Diaspora was, as we have seen, characterized by enormous diversity and even fragmentation. But in order to leave the picture more balanced, we must also take note of its centripetal forces. Even before the invention of printing, the Jewish intellectual elite—primarily rabbis—developed an astonishing international network, laid in part, no doubt, along Jewish trade routes. Although the scholastic traditions of Rashi and the Tosafists in France and Germany differed significantly from those of Maimonides and other Sephardic authorities, they knew of each other's work to an extraordinary extent, much like the international community of medieval Christian scholastics. Given the differences in local culture and custom, it is still remarkable how unified the Jewish world was in terms of its legal practices, testimony not only to the power of the classical texts but also to the authorities who were its custodians. With the exception of the Karaites and the Ethiopian Jews (whose origins remain contested), Jews from Yemen to Poland, from Iraq to France, all followed basically the same halakhah. Moreover, the elite shared a culture of textual study. The study hall was its "playing fields of Eton," the site where the common culture was disseminated to a new generation of scholars for all of whom, Ashkenazim and Sephardim alike, the study of classical texts—Talmud and commentaries—was the highest social value.

With printing, the ability of the rabbinical elite to communicate, influence, and debate with each other grew exponentially, as did their capacity to circulate their interpretations among wider circles of students. Printing also allowed for the popularization of rabbinic literature in the form of works intended for both women and men who could read in their vernaculars (Yiddish, Ladino, and

Judeo-Arabic) much better, if at all, than in rabbinic Hebrew. The culture of the Talmud became increasingly the culture of the folk. But the movement of texts and beliefs was not only from the "top" down. As Shalom Sabar shows in his chapter on childbirth rituals in traditional Jewish folklore, Jews throughout the world shared not only a common legal tradition but also common magical and other folkloric practices. These traditions circulated in books, like the magical text *Sefer Raziel,* and in the mysterious oral channels by which folklore is transmitted by and between cultures. The Jewish Middle Ages, if we are prepared to adopt that term, was thus a period of both unity and diversity on all levels of culture, a peculiar dialectic that would only be shattered by the modern world.

A letter in Arabic by Isaac Ibn Ezra, from the Cairo genizah. The letter is written in Hebrew characters except for its last line, but the cursive Hebrew script is so similar to Arabic writing that the two are almost indistinguishable. (Freer Gallery of Art, Smithsonian Institution, Washington, D.C.; Gift of Charles Lang Freer, F1908.44.21a.)

MERCHANTS AND INTELLECTUALS, RABBIS AND POETS:

Judeo-Arabic Culture in the Golden Age of Islam

RAYMOND P. SCHEINDLIN

Judah al-Ḥarizi—poet, storyteller, and wit—writing early in the thirteenth century somewhere in the Arabic-speaking Middle East, relates the following anecdote:

> Yesterday I spent the day with some friends. We saw a crowd gathered at the city gate and were told by a bystander that they had gathered to watch an astrologer tell fortunes. We pushed through the crowd and found at the center a garrulous old man taking astronomical measurements with an astrolabe and offering his services, advertising himself in elaborate and eloquent speeches. People were coming forward one by one to consult him about their troubles in their work and their private lives, and to learn their own fortunes and those of their children. Each received his answer and paid the astrologer's fee.
>
> I suggested to my friends that we test his powers by agreeing on a question among ourselves: When will the Jews be redeemed from their exile, and when will the Jewish kingdom be restored? When our turn came, we offered him a good fee if he could tell both the question and the answer. The astrologer performed certain rites with sand and lifted his astrolabe. He seemed ready to reply, but instead of launching into his customary eloquence, he sank into a profound and ominous silence. At last, he turned a furious face on us and exclaimed: "I swear by the Creator of the radiant light, the sun and the moon, and every constellation that rises and sets, that you are neither Muslims nor Christians, but members of a despised and lowly people! Could you be Jews?" "Rightly spoken," we replied. He launched into a harangue accusing us of asking about the end of time and history, of wishing for the downfall of the Islamic kingdom, and of rebelling against the state.
>
> The crowd became so enraged that they would have stoned us to death, but someone persuaded them to take us to a judge. The qāḍī was a sensible man

who saw that we weren't revolutionaries but just young people out on the town enjoying ourselves. He kept us in prison overnight until the crowd dispersed, and in the morning sent us on our way. A narrow escape, thank God![1]

This story may serve as an emblem of the style and tone of Jewish life in the Islamic world during the age of Islamic ascendancy. At the beginning of the story, the Jewish boys mix with the crowd in the street. They are unrecognizable as Jews by their speech, bearing, or clothing; they wear no special hat or badge. Even the astrologer, who is supposed to have knowledge of hidden things, says, "Could you be Jews?" indicating that he is not sure. The boys are conscious of being different from the crowd, but the difference they are conscious of is not primarily that they are Jews so much as the social difference. Within the crowd, assembled adventitiously and united only in its fascination with the astrologer, the youths are a preexisting, closed circle of friends. The people in the crowd believe in the astrologer unquestioningly and come forward with serious questions about their lives, but the youths are skeptical intellectuals whose impulse is to test him. Their skepticism has nothing to do with their being Jewish, for belief in astrology crossed religious lines in this period; their test is aimed not at astrology itself but at the astrologer's skill. At the story's beginning, it is not their religion that distinguishes the jaunty youths from the crowd but their class.

The youths openly mark themselves as a group apart from the crowd by going in together on a question. They never actually enunciate the question, for their purpose is to make it as hard as possible for the astrologer to succeed and, if possible, to discredit him. It is only logical that the astrologer should have to guess the question as well as the answer, for if the question were simply "When will Israel be redeemed?" there would be no way to verify the answer; thus, the astrologer has to verify his skill by guessing the question that has been agreed upon. We may assume that the showdown nature of the question would heighten the crowd's attention and would therefore have the effect of isolating the group of youths even more.

The astrologer's speech falls into two parts: the first climaxes with his guess that the youths are Jews; the second is the denunciation. The transition between the two speeches is rich in implications about both parties. The boys' callowness is displayed in their blunt reply (contrasting, as it does, with the astrologer's eloquence): "Rightly spoken!" They acknowledge that they are Jews with no shyness or hesitation, having no inkling of the trouble into which this admission is about to bring them. Are they too surprised by the astrologer's question to lie, or too simple? Whatever the reason, it never occurs to the boys to take advantage of the astrologer's uncertainty, so natural does it seem to them to acknowledge being Jewish.

The moment the astrologer expresses his doubt, he abandons his professional pretension to knowledge of mysteries and is transformed into an ordinary person. And with the vanishing of this illusion, the fun also vanishes, both for the youths in the story and for us readers. Our astrologer may or may not be a con artist at the beginning of the story—the conventions of the genre to which the story belongs would have the medieval reader assume that he is a charlatan—but, at the end, we see him as a Muslim who has been shaken by the Jewish youths' question (no matter how he divines it). It is a fervent believer who, in his second speech, pours his pious rage (in eloquent Hebrew) on the finally frightened boys. The question of the astrologer's sincerity as a fortune teller vanishes into insignificance in comparison with his sincerity as a Muslim. His encounter with the latent messianic hopes of the Jewish youths takes him out of his role as astrologer and turns him into a religious preacher who uses his eloquence to forge the crowd into a group unified in faith and loyalty to their own kind. In the course of this transformation, he ceases to stand above and apart from the crowd—in accordance with the normal role of the protagonist in the genre to which the story belongs—but merges with the crowd and vanishes from the narrative.

The story's depiction of the Jewish characters as externally indistinguishable from the Muslim masses, circulating confidently among them without being aware of any need for caution, corresponds with the reality of Jewish life in the Muslim world for most of the period of this chapter, at least during the era of Islamic supremacy, from the seventh to the thirteenth centuries. The Jews were similar to Muslims in most aspects of style, interests, ideas, and taste, and their leaders were affected by the same intellectual trends in theology, philosophy, and literature; furthermore, Jews of all classes benefited from the prosperity of the Islamic world.

Yet the Jews of Islam were conscious of being members of a group with a different history and a different destiny from those of society at large, as reflected in the question that came most naturally to the minds of the boys: the fate of the Jewish people. Although they moved about comfortably and confidently in their Muslim environment, they were conscious of being in an unsettled state. And, although their people's exile had lasted more than a thousand years, they were still awaiting the Redemption. It turns out that the Jews were not as safe as they thought, for that sustaining hope for redemption was understood by the Muslim majority as implicitly subversive of both the political status quo and the supremacy of Islam. Yet the danger came more from the popular piety of the masses than from the authorities; the official institutions of the state, as represented by the qāḍī in our story, actually protected the Jews. The qāḍī applies classic Islamic law to the boys' case in denying the crowd the right to harm them. In fact, he is generous. Islam extended to the Jews and Christians within its territories protection in the practice of their religion, in exchange for payment of a specific tax and for maintaining a low profile. By raising the question of the messianic redemption, the boys actually come close to breaking this last understanding; they come close enough to the line to enrage the astrologer and the crowd, but since they do not actually cross it (by, for example, openly blaspheming Islam or its prophet), they do not forfeit their protected status (*dhimma*).

The story is typical of the Jewish experience, even its social perspective, for it is written from the point of view of the wealthy, educated elite of the Jewish community. This is typical of the literary sources of the age, which are rich in their testimony of this class's thoughts, beliefs, and imaginations, but whose testimony about the Jewish masses is meager. At the same time, our story affords an exceptionally vivid picture of street life, for literary sources ordinarily tell us little about everyday reality. (As we shall see, we have other sources for such information.)

Finally, our story illustrates the extent to which literary fashions linked Jewish and Islamic culture. Al-Ḥarizi did not aim to provide readers of a later age with a picture of Jewish life in the streets of Islamic cities; he wrote literature of entertainment, and he related this story as a *maqāma*, a kind of story invented by Arabic writers in the tenth century that was widely imitated by Hebrew writers beginning in the twelfth. Not only is al-Ḥarizi's maqāma of the astrologer a perfect example of the Arabic genre in Hebrew, but its line of action and its central motif—a group of well-to-do young men who are out for fun, who in the process cross the boundary of religious propriety, and who thereby nearly come to grief at the hands of a mob—have a close parallel in an Arabic maqāma whose protagonists are all Muslims.[2]

HISTORY

The Jews of Islam may have been highly acculturated to the manners and values of the Islamic world, but they were not an eccentric or marginal community; they were actually in the mainstream of Jewish history. When, in the seventh and eighth centuries, Arab conquerors seized control of the Persian Empire and the Asian and North African territories of the Byzantine Empire and conquered the rest of North Africa and the Iberian Peninsula, they acquired sovereignty over a significant part of the civilized world. Most of the territories conquered at that time—Spain and Sicily were the main losses—have remained Islamic to this very day. Although in modern times the Islamic world has lost to Europe its earlier advantage in economic, technological, and scientific development, in much of the period from the eighth to the seventeenth centuries it was dominant in all these spheres. Indeed, from the seventh through the thirteenth centuries, Islamdom was the center of the Western world and Europe the periphery; correspondingly, the Jews of the Muslim world were the world's leaders in wealth, culture, and intellectual achievement. They were also the bulk—generally estimated as 90 percent—of the world's Jews.

The Jews did not blunder into the Muslim world as immigrants or exiles. They were part of the population of Western Asia, North Africa, and Iberia, now called al-Andalus, where medieval Arabo-Islamic culture developed as an amalgamation of Arabic language, Islamic religion, and local culture. Jews were an intrinsic part of this culture. They resembled their neighbors in their names, dress, and language as well as in most other features of their culture, except, of course, in their religion, their sense of their own distinctness, their view of history, and the institutional affiliations that flowed from these differences.

In view of the above, the Jewish culture depicted in this chapter will be referred to as Judeo-Arabic culture. Although this term is often used to refer to Jewish writing in the Arabic language, it is useful far beyond the domain of language, for the Arabic character of the Jewish culture we are describing is evident not only in the Jews' use of the Arabic language but also in every aspect of their culture during the heyday of premodern Islam—even in their practice of religion and in the ways in which they used Hebrew. Thus, we shall use "Judeo-Arabic" to refer to the culture, and the ordinary language of Judeo-Arabic Jews we shall simply call "Arabic."

To understand the Jews of the Muslim world during the age of Islamic preeminence, the ordinary modern reader is obliged to reorient himself away from Europe and toward the Mediterranean. There he will find a Jewish community quite different from that of either the modern Middle East or medieval Europe: a community that was on the whole prosperous, little subject to persecution, economically well integrated with the environment, and self-confident to the point of being able to adjust to both the external and the internal features of its environment without fear of acculturation. In addition, this community was so productive in its intellectual and literary activities that some of its products have become permanent treasures of the Jewish tradition, and many of them still have the power to fascinate and inspire us with their craft and beauty.

The Islamic conquests created two new conditions that would enable the Jews to flourish and to create the most successful Jewish Diaspora community of premodern times. First, it united them, for the first time since the expansion of the Diaspora in Hellenistic times, hundreds of years before, into one political, economic, and cultural system, a single Islamic empire stretching from the Indus

River in the east to the Atlantic Ocean in the west, including Iberia. Second, it brought relief from persecution, harassment, and humiliation to those Jews who had been living under harsh Christian regimes, especially in Palestine, Egypt, and Spain.

The Arabs did not embark on their conquests with the intention of converting the world to Islam. On the whole, people converted because conditions under Islamic rule were favorable to Muslims; likewise, they adopted Arabic simply because it was the language of government and public life. Implacably hostile to paganism, Islam respected both Christianity and Judaism for possessing a divinely revealed book, and it viewed them as its sisters in monotheism. Therefore, the Muslims permitted Jews and Christians to retain their ancestral religions, provided they adhered to certain conditions.

The Jews and Christians were regarded as *dhimmīs*—protected subjects—and their status was defined by a set of rules known as the Pact of Umar. Dhimmīs were guaranteed their lives and property and were tolerated in the practice of their religion in exchange for payment of special taxes and on condition that they behaved in a manner appropriate to a subject population. They were not to build new churches or synagogues or repair old ones, hold public religious processions, or proselytize. They were not permitted to strike a Muslim, carry arms, or ride horses, and they had to wear distinguishing clothing. In time, other restrictions were added: for example, they were forbidden to build their homes taller than Muslim homes, adopt Arabic names, study the Koran, or sell fermented beverages, and they were excluded from government service.

Putting up with such degrading restrictions—and having to pay for the privilege—was humiliating and burdensome for Christians and Zoroastrians who had formerly lived under their own regimes. For them the Pact of Umar was an incentive to convert to Islam. But for the Jews who had lived under Christendom, the Pact of Umar actually brought relief, because it guaranteed them the protection of the law. Although Muhammad had denounced the Jews in his later career and had persecuted them in Medina, Islam had not, like Christianity, come into being in direct competition with Judaism and had little historical reason for animus against it. Thus, the discriminatory regulations of the Pact of Umar were often disregarded in the first centuries of Islam, or only loosely applied. In general, whenever Islam was in a state of strength, as it was until the tenth century and as it would again be in the Ottoman Empire in the fifteenth and sixteenth centuries, Jews living within its territories would be able to live with dignity, interacting easily with Muslims. Despite the discriminatory regulations, Jews built impressive homes, adopted Arabic names, and studied the Koran, and many Christians owned inns where they sold fermented beverages (often even to Muslims). Nobody minded the rule requiring distinguishing clothing, because that had been customary anyway, and it was hardly enforced in the early centuries.

Another reason the rule of Islam fell lightly on the Jews was that, unlike their situation under Christian rule, they were not the only group subject to discriminatory regulations and certainly not the largest of those groups. That distinction fell to the Christians, whose religious status under Islam was rather more problematic than that of the Jews. Although the Koran put Christians and Jews into the same category of "people of the book,"[3] the doctrine of the Trinity made the Christian religion theologically suspect to the rigorously monotheistic Muslims, and the prominence of crucifixes and icons in Christian worship made its adherents appear to Muslims, who excluded all images in worship, as idolaters. The Jews, a far smaller group, as strictly monotheistic and nearly as averse to images as the Muslims themselves, attracted far less attention and suspicion during this period. Finally, unlike the Christians, the Jews did not have a political identity, for their statehood had long since lapsed. However, facing the Muslim world across the Mediterranean (and adjacent to it in parts of western Asia) was the Byzantine Empire, a Christian theocracy constantly at war with Islamdom. Christian dhimmīs were naturally suspected of being in league with the enemy, or at least of wishing the enemy well. For all these reasons, the lot of Christians was less favorable at first than that of the Jews.

Islam forged a vast, powerful, and prosperous empire, unified by language and religion, much of it on territories formerly belonging to the Roman and Byzantine Empires, in addition to the territories of the Persian Empire and much more. With great scale came great wealth and great culture, as the skills and scholarship of the conquered peoples were incorporated into a new international culture. Thus, Europe's Dark Age corresponds to the Golden Age of Islam. Most of the world's Jews were inhabitants of the Islamic empire and beneficiaries of its success.

But Jews and Christians were not citizens of the Islamic state; as dhimmīs, they owed their loyalty to their own communities, which, upon paying their taxes, were left to govern themselves, as they had under Persian rule. The caliph or the local ruler would recognize as the link between himself and the minority community a Jewish or Christian dignitary who could be held responsible for community affairs; this leader would, in turn, appoint local authorities to manage the affairs of the individual communities. The communal organizations were responsible for raising the money to pay each community's taxes and for its internal management. Jews and Christians had their own court system for the regulation of family law, inheritance, and commercial transactions, though criminal law was generally the preserve of the state. (For the Jews, this meant that talmudic law was in active service for the regulation of the community's affairs.) The communities were also responsible for such social services as education, the care of the poor, widows, orphans, and foreigners, and the ransoming of captives. They also had to maintain religious institutions and oversee questions of doctrine and religious practice.

In Abbasid Iraq, where the Christian community was headed by its catholicos, the Jews were led by the exilarch (*rosh gola* in Hebrew; Arabized as *ra's al-jalūt*), whose appointment had to be confirmed by the caliph. Theoretically he controlled not just the Iraqi community but all Jewish communities under the caliph's sway, which officially embraced most of the Islamic world during the eighth to the tenth centuries. He was, to some extent, treated like royalty. We are told that whenever the exilarch visited the caliph's court, a herald ran before him in the streets crying, in Arabic, "Make way for our master, the son of David!" (for the exilarchs claimed descent from Jehoiachin, king of Judah). But with the fragmentation of the Abbasid empire, the sphere of the exilarch's actual control was progressively reduced, and his authority was recognized in other Islamic territories only as a formality.

The most powerful ecumenical institutions of the Judeo-Islamic world were the *yeshivot*, or academies, two in Iraq and one in Palestine. These academies were schools for the training of rabbis to serve as community administrators, judges, and religious authorities; they also served as high courts to which difficult cases could be directed or to which a dissatisfied litigant could bring an appeal. At first, the yeshivot of Iraq controlled the former Persian territories to the east, and the yeshivah of Palestine controlled the former Byzantine territories to the west; however, the sway of the Iraqi institutions expanded westward at the expense of those of Palestine. The authority of the yeshivot was not merely legal but also administrative, because the yeshivot appointed the heads of the local communities that they controlled, often at great distances. These local heads were generally members (*ḥaver*) of the academy, which sometimes bestowed upon them the Hebrew title *nagid*. They were also sometimes given the Arabic title *ra's al-yahūd* (chief of the Jews) by the Islamic authorities.

The heads of the academies came to be considered the chief expositors and highest authorities of Jewish law, in both its religious and its civil aspects. They bore the title *gaon* (plural, *geonim*); the term derives from a Hebrew word meaning "pride" and is an abbreviated form of the flowery title "Head of the Academy of the Pride of Jacob." From all over the Islamic world, local rabbis would direct difficult cases to the geonim for adjudication, cases that might involve questions of communal organization, business, inheritance, and divorce (then, as today, often more a matter of the division of property than a purely religious one). The answers to such questions are called *responsa* (the Jewish equivalent to the Islamic *fatwā*). The queries were accompanied by donations, which provided much of the upkeep of the academies. In the course of the Islamic age, individual communities (such as Kairouan and Lucena) established their own academies, which competed for funds with the ancient institutions of Iraq and Palestine and contributed to their decline.

The main subject taught in the academies of Iraq was religious law. The chief textbook was, quite naturally, the Babylonian Talmud, the great compilation of the religious tradition that had been made by the predecessors of the geonim, the heads of the academies of Sura and Pumbeditha during the Sassanid period. The authority of the geonim of Iraq, enforced by that of the Abbasid caliphate and the general decline of the Palestinian academy in the course of our period, lent the Babylonian Talmud primacy over the Palestinian Talmud; this explains why the former has become the basis of Jewish law and religious practice worldwide and remains so for Orthodox Jewry to this day. Likewise, the prayer books compiled by the geonim became the standard for Jews worldwide, so that the old Palestinian liturgy has now completely fallen out of use. The geonim put a permanent stamp on many aspects of Jewish religious life, and thus it is only appropriate that the seventh to the eleventh centuries are known to Jewish history as the gaonic period.

The preeminence of the geonim of Iraq was not uncontested; the academies in Palestine occasionally tried to reassert their ancient primacy. But these institutions, though they championed traditions that were at variance with those of the academies of Iraq, functioned within the same religious system, and shared the same doctrines and conception of Judaism and Jewish law. Palestinian and Iraqi authorities recognized each other's religious legitimacy, as did the adherents of the four chief schools of Islamic law. By contrast, resistance to gaonic authority gave rise to a religious schism within Judaism in the form of the Karaite sect, which denied the legitimacy of the entire rabbinic system and became a counterforce to rabbinic Judaism throughout the age of Islamic ascendancy.

This movement, which seems to have crystallized in the ninth century, traced its origins to the decades just after the establishment of the Abbasid empire, when a member of the exilarchic family, Anan ben David, declared the traditions of rabbinic Judaism and rabbinic authority itself to be a fraudulent distortion of the principles of the Jewish religion; in their place, he attempted to reinstate the Bible as the sole religious authority. (The name "Karaite" is derived from the Hebrew word for the Bible, *miqra*). Later, Karaite leaders attributed to him the principle that each individual was free to interpret Scripture independently, limited only by the accumulated traditions of the Karaite community itself. This approach was appealing to distant Jewish communities, like those of Persia and Azerbaijan, which were not firmly under the sway of gaonic authority, but its very nature led to fragmentation. Anan's successors, such as Benjamin al-Nahawendi in the ninth century and Daniel al-Qumisi (who brought the movement to Palestine) in the tenth, modified his doctrine somewhat, developing their own tradition of biblical interpretation and making their own compilations of ritual traditions and legal codes, mostly in Arabic.

The Karaites' devotion to biblical studies made them pioneers in the study of Hebrew grammar and the manuscript traditions of the Bible as well as energetic authors of commentaries on the Bible. It was in the tenth century that the Hebrew text of the Bible was authoritatively fixed, if not by Karaites then at least as a result of the impetus lent to this kind of work by their influence.

Karaism did not rebel against rabbinic Judaism in order to relax the complexity and rigidity of rabbinic law; it was from the beginning a rather conservative, rigid, and even ascetic variety of Judaism. Nevertheless, it attracted followers, many of them well-to-do, in all the territories ruled by Islam, and it became so widespread that it was recognized as an alternate variety of Judaism, so that talmudically oriented Jews acquired the distinguishing title "Rabbanite." Although the two groups considered each other heretical, their adherents intermarried in this period. But because Rabbanites were generally recognized by Islamic governments as the authoritative voice for Jewry as a whole, given the antiquity and prestige of such institutions as the exilarchate and the academies, they were eventually able to suppress the Karaites (without, however, completely eliminating them). The movement declined in the Muslim East in the twelfth century but remained active in Egypt until modern times. It flared only briefly in Islamic Spain. It had an important community in Palestine and Byzantium, concentrated around Constantinople; from there it spread, in the seventeenth and eighteenth centuries, to the Crimea and Lithuania, where it existed until modern times. A small Karaite community still exists in Israel.

One of the most energetic and influential of the geonim was Saadiah ben Joseph (882–942), gaon of Sura. Saadiah left behind a large corpus of writings, and his life and career are far better known to us than any of his predecessors in the gaonate. As the greatest champion of the gaonate, he decisively crushed the ambitions of the Palestinians to regain their authority over Jewish religious life and polemicized relentlessly against the Karaites in their bid to undermine rabbinic authority. In the intellectual sphere, he was a pivotal figure whose oeuvre represents a nearly complete reorganization of Jewish scholarship along the lines of Arabic and Islamic scholarship. I will refer to him often in the ensuing discussion.

After Saadiah, the Jewish community of Iraq gradually declined in importance relative to other Diaspora communities as the Islamic empire broke up
into regional powers and as Iraq lost its dominant position within the Islamic
world. The geonim of the tenth century sent appeals to other Diaspora communities for contributions that would enable them to maintain their institutions,
but the last gaon to enjoy international authority was Hai of Pumbedita (Hai
ben Sherira), who died in 1038. The most important of the other communities
were those of al-Andalus (Islamic Iberia), Northwest Africa, and Egypt. As each
of these regions asserted its independence from the Abbasid empire, its Jewish
communities became centers of rabbinic and Judeo-Arabic culture. A particularly brilliant culture developed in al-Andalus beginning with the reign of
'Abd al-Raḥmān III (912–61), whose capital in Córdoba became a magnificent
metropolis and, for a time, ranked among the great cities of the Islamic world.
Here emerged a class of Jewish courtiers and other public figures (such as Ḥasdai ibn Shaprut and Samuel the Nagid) who sponsored Jewish culture and were
instrumental in the literary developments that will be addressed later in this
chapter.

The Jewish community of al-Andalus came to an abrupt end when, beginning
in 1146, an extremist Muslim sect, the Almohads, arrived from Morocco and
gradually took control of Islamic Spain, outlawing both Judaism and Christianity in its territories. The resultant flight of Jewish intellectuals carried Judeo-
Arabic culture to Christian Spain (which was now expanding southward and
would, by the mid-thirteenth century, occupy virtually the entire peninsula) and
to Provence. Others, like the Cordoban judge Maimon, fled to other parts of the
Islamic world; Maimon went to Morocco and eventually reached Egypt, where
his son, Moses Maimonides (1138–1204), made a distinguished career and established a line of communal authorities that lasted until the fourteenth century.

The Palestinian Jewish community remained relatively unimportant during
the period covered in this chapter. It had its own rabbinical academy, at first in
Tiberias, later in Ramle, that tried to contend for authority with those of Iraq.
Early in the ninth century, the head of this academy had attempted to restore
the patriarchal prerogative of establishing the calendar for Diaspora Jewry, but
this attempt had been quashed by Saadiah. Palestine and its Jews came under
Egyptian rule during the first part of the Fatimid period, until the establishment
of the Crusader kingdom in 1099, and again after Palestine was reconquered
from the Crusaders in 1187.

The Crusades had little immediate impact on the Jews of the Middle East, but
they did have a long-term impact on the Islamic world in that they marked the
beginning of a process of deterioration that would eventually have a deleterious
effect on the status of the Jews. The rapid conquest of Persia and Byzantium in

the seventh century, the tremendous extent and wealth of the Islamic territories, their great cities with their countless mosques and schools, the fame of their scholars, and the brilliance of their intellectual production—all these successes had lent the world of Islam the confidence to tolerate its subject peoples and to leave its dhimmīs to lead their lives in peace. Although the empire had begun to fragment politically as early as the ninth century, the independent and quasi-independent states that emerged remained powerful and confident. But, in the eleventh century, Islamic power began to fray. Sicily was conquered by the Normans even before the Crusades began in 1091. The invasion of the Crusaders in the East coincided with the progressive loss of al-Andalus to Christian conquerors in the West (the process lasted, for all practical purposes, from 1085 to 1248). And the Crusades opened the way for such Italian city-states as Venice, Pisa, and Genoa to take control of trade in the eastern Mediterranean. By the end of the thirteenth century, the Muslims had been driven out of Europe, the coast of North Africa was under constant attack by Europeans, and the Mongols had embarked on their long march across Asia. In 1258, Baghdad fell to the Mongols, putting an end to the caliphate and to any remaining pretensions of an Islamic empire. The balance of power and wealth was shifting in favor of Christian Europe.

Islam reacted partly by turning against its non-Muslim subjects, Christians and Jews alike. The discriminatory rules of the Pact of Umar, generally neglected in the past, were now enforced with rigor. Jews and Christians had to wear distinguishing clothing; they were prohibited from riding even on donkeys within cities; churches and synagogues were vandalized; and Jewish physicians lost the right to treat Muslim patients. Jews and Christians found themselves ever more harassed, humiliated, and subjected to the contempt and violence of the mob. With the progressive decline of the Islamic world's economic power in the fourteenth and fifteenth centuries, the conditions of the dhimmīs deteriorated to the point that many of them simply converted to Islam. The results of these pressures may be gauged by the fact that, by 1481, Alexandria, once one of the most important centers of Jewish life in the world, was left with only 60 Jewish families.

In Iraq, the Mongol conquest of Baghdad brought about a brief amelioration in the condition of the dhimmīs. But after the conversion of the Mongol rulers to Islam, an atmosphere of intolerance and economic stagnation prevailed such that the literary and intellectual productivity characteristic of the heyday of Islam could not be sustained. In Mameluk Egypt (1250–1517), regulations for distinguishing Jews and Christians from Muslims and excluding them from public life were constantly renewed and ingeniously expanded, and a climate of hostility toward "infidels" existed that would have been inconceivable in the days of Islamic expansion.

But the deterioration in Jewish life was not so marked in northwest Africa. The communities of what are now Tunisia and Algeria were stable, and they were even invigorated by an influx of people when Jews began fleeing there from nearby Christian Spain in 1391. Among the refugees were a number of scholars and rabbis, who revived the region's intellectual life. In Morocco, the Merinid dynasty (1286–1465) was more tolerant of dhimmīs than were its Muslim subjects, and it even had Jewish courtiers. But, around 1438, a special walled quarter, called the *mellah,* was set aside for the Jews of Fez to protect them from the popular riots that had already caused considerable unrest. This pattern repeated itself throughout Morocco, with the result that the Jews were progressively segregated from the population at large, and what began as a protective measure ended as a kind of isolation. Nor were the mellahs always effective protection. In 1465, when a Jew was appointed vizier, a wave of massacres occurred throughout the kingdom, a perfect case study in the disparity between the attitudes of the regime and those of the populace toward the Jews.

The second half of the fifteenth century completed the process of change in the Middle East and in Jewish history that had begun with the Crusades. A new power now appeared in the region, sweeping away the decadent old regimes and replacing them with a vigorous Islamic state. This new power was the Ottoman Turks, the last and most important of the series of invaders from central Asia. After progressing through Asia Minor, the Ottomans took Constantinople, the prize that Islam had coveted since the seventh century, in 1453. They went on to take Palestine and Egypt in 1517 and subsequently to seize Iraq and much of the North African coast. By this time, the Jews had been expelled from Spain and most of Western Europe, and their formerly important community in Persia had been reduced to marginality by the advent of the brutally intolerant Shiite Safavid dynasty. But the rise of the Ottomans would provide the opportunity for a new flowering of Jews in the once-again ascendant world of Islam.

The Jews whose story has just been sketched are better known to us than any other premodern Jewish community, thanks to a vast cache of manuscripts found in the *genizah.* This was a room in the Ben Ezra synagogue in old Cairo (still standing, and much visited by tourists) in which manuscripts and manuscript fragments had been allowed to accumulate since the Middle Ages. Among these writings were literary works as well as documents of everyday life—personal and business letters, commercial contracts, bills of sale and lading, marriage contracts, writing exercises, book lists, inventories, and amulets. Thanks to them, it is possible to view daily life in the Judeo-Arabic Mediterranean world, especially from the tenth to the thirteenth centuries, with a degree of detail that is not available even in Islamic sources. The genizah materials provide access to the lives of ordinary people who were not scholars accustomed to expressing themselves in literary works.

The genizah documents confirm that the Jews of the Islamic world became continually more urbanized and were drawn from agriculture toward commerce, in accordance with the empire-wide trend favoring urban life and trade. By the end of the eighth century, it was far more common for Jews in the Muslim world to be town-dwelling craftsmen or businessmen than for them to be farmers, though many townspeople owned farmland. The documents delineate five different social classes among the Jews: peasants; the mass of urban craftsmen and laborers; master artisans; businessmen and professionals; and an upper class consisting of high government officials and agents, doctors, chief judges, and leading businessmen, who might double as community leaders. Jews were found in practically every walk of life from vizier down to blacksmith and tailor, but social trends favored independence and entrepreneurship; in general, it was considered degrading to be merely an employee. Although it was not easy to improve one's social level, upward mobility due to industry and luck was far more common in the medieval Judeo-Arabic world than in feudal Europe.

The unification of the Mediterranean and the Red seas into a single political, cultural, and linguistic sphere facilitated international trade. As individual Jews accumulated wealth, some of them—Maimonides' brother David is a famous example—became active in trade between the Mediterranean and India (where a Jewish community first comes into view near Cochin around the year 1000). The most important industries in the Judeo-Arabic economy were the manufacture of sugar, paper, ceramics, and, especially, textiles. Jews were also prominently involved in the manufacture of glass and metal, especially as silversmiths.

Thanks to the genizah, even the lives of women, nearly invisible in the high literature of the age, can be seen with considerable clarity. Women were widely engaged in remunerative labor, and in many cases they were able to keep the profits for themselves. Textile work—embroidery, spinning, weaving, and dyeing silk—was their main field, but they were also active as doctors (not as formally trained doctors but as practitioners of folk medicine, midwives, and depilators), astrologers, fortune-tellers, brokers engaged in the sale of the products of other women's work, and dressers of brides for weddings and corpses for funerals.

It is satisfying to reflect that, just as the lives and mental habits of this Jewry followed the characteristic patterns of the Arabic-speaking Muslim world, so too was the most generous resource available to us for understanding the community an artifact of Arabo-Islamic practice. Muslims are as sensitive as Jews to the potential holiness of any written text, and the practice of storing unwanted writings in a place of worship rather than discarding them is one that is shared by Judaism and Islam. Thus, the genizah, to which we are so indebted for our knowledge of the Judeo-Arabic world, is itself a perfect representative of that world.

LANGUAGE

The Islamic conquest of the seventh and eighth centuries carried the Arabic language, along with the Islamic religion, to all the territories that it reached. Most of the conquered peoples adopted Islam, as discussed above, and most of them, from Iraq westward to the Atlantic, eventually adopted Arabic as their spoken language (or as one of their spoken languages) and, to a great degree, as their written language too. Although the Jews could not share in Islam without losing their identity as Jews, they could and did share in the common language, using Arabic both for scholarly production and for everyday communication with Muslims and with one another.

By the end of the thirteenth century, Hebrew had replaced Arabic as the normal language of scholarly writing. But this shift did not occur until most of the enduring books of the age had been written in Arabic, especially those destined to become the key texts of systematic Jewish religious thought, such as Saadiah's theological treatise *The Book of Beliefs and Opinions,* Baḥya ibn Paquda's *Guide to the Commandments of the Hearts,* Maimonides' *Guide of the Perplexed,* and Judah Halevi's *Kuzari.* Even the books written in Hebrew—such as Maimonides' *Mishneh Torah* and Abraham ibn Ezra's commentary to the Bible—have a distinctively Arabic flavor. Likewise, the myriad documents and scraps of documents preserved in the genizah are mostly written in Arabic.

How far the language penetrated the inner life of the Jewish community may be judged by the fact that Arabic words were sometimes even used to describe religious ideas and institutions. Thus, when Jews wrote in Arabic, they ordinarily referred to God as "Allah" (always spelled in full) and to the pulpit as *minbar* (later distorted to *almemar* in Sephardic usage). They often referred to the leader of prayers as *imām,* to the Torah as *qur'ān* (though the Hebrew word *Torah* exists in classical Arabic in the form *taura*), to rabbinic traditions as *hadīth,* and to halakhic practice as *sunna.* (However, the corresponding Hebrew terms were also widely used in Judeo-Arabic.) Some Arabic expressions common in Islamic religious parlance entered Hebrew as calques from Arabic and today are not only completely accepted as part of the Jewish heritage but are even used as labels of Jewish authenticity. For example, the practice of following God's name with the Hebrew eulogy *yitbarakh* (may He be blessed) reflects the Arabic *tabāraka,* and the eulogy *alav hashalom* (peace upon him) after the name of a dead person reflects the Arabic *alayhi al-salām.* Most Arabic-speaking Jews (especially women) were ordinarily called by Arabic names, though many had Hebrew names as well.

For Jews, as for many of the conquered peoples, Arabic was not the only language in use; their religion was based on ancient texts written in Hebrew and Aramaic, and some knowledge of these texts was essential to the correct fulfillment of everyday religious duties. Hebrew was learned as part of the process of learning the Bible and other religious works; it was in constant use for the recitation of prescribed daily prayers and for writing liturgical poetry, but otherwise it was not actively employed. Aramaic, the normal spoken language in Iraq and Palestine before the Islamic conquests, declined gradually as a spoken language but continued in use as a written language in connection with talmudic scholarship.

At the beginning of the Islamic period, the Jews of the Middle East and North Africa generally functioned in two languages: a vernacular (Aramaic in Iraq and Palestine, Aramaic and Greek in Egypt, Berber and Latin in northwest Africa, Latin in Iberia), which was used for ordinary conversation, and Hebrew, which was learned as the language of prayers and the classic religious texts but was actively used for little other than the composition of liturgical poetry.

As the Islamic conquests took root and unified the entire region linguistically, Arabic gradually replaced the local languages as the vernacular (except in Iran, where the Jews, together with the rest of the population, continued to speak Persian and do so even today, and Kurdistan, where Aramaic held out in small pockets). Because the two Talmuds, written in Aramaic, were now canonical texts, some knowledge of Aramaic was required of scholars. Accordingly, talmudic scholars in Iraq continued for several centuries to compose their legal writings in Aramaic or in a mixture of Aramaic and Hebrew, so that for a time and in some circles, three languages were in active use.

Saadiah was the first rabbinic leader to make Arabic his main language for scholarly writing, and thus he may be considered the founder of Judeo-Arabic literature. Thanks partly to his influence, and partly to natural development, Arabic took over many of the functions of Aramaic as the language of scholarship, and, as one vernacular replaced another, the original state of diglossia was restored. Arabic now served both as the vernacular and as the language of most scholarly writing and of ordinary correspondence; Hebrew continued to be studied as the language of the Bible and other classical religious texts, especially the liturgy, and was actively employed for the writing of liturgical poetry, the few midrashim that were composed during the gaonic period, and other ceremonial purposes. As the Jews came under the spell of Arabic literature, they adopted some new literary genres from Arabic, using Arabic for some and Hebrew for others, as we shall see.

The balance of Hebrew and Arabic began to shift in the western part of the realm in the twelfth century, as Arabic-speaking Jews began to come into more regular contact with Jews of Christian Europe and as Iberia came increasingly under Christian domination. The first important and truly influential works of Jewish scholarship written in Hebrew by an Arabic-speaking Jew were the commentaries on the Bible by Abraham ibn Ezra (the commentaries were written between 1140 and 1164), who wrote not for his fellow Judeo-Arabic Jews but for the Jews of Latin Europe. This period saw the emergence of a veritable industry of translation of important Jewish writings from Arabic into Hebrew as the communities of Christian Spain, Provence, and Italy woke to the higher culture of the Judeo-Arabic world. Hebrew, heavily influenced by Arabic, now became more prominent as a language of original scholarly writing. By the mid-thirteenth century, Hebrew was the exclusive language of writing by Jews in Spain, which was then being absorbed culturally into Europe and was rapidly losing its Middle Eastern complexion. But in the Islamic East, including Egypt, Arabic remained the dominant language of Jewish scholarly writing until the sixteenth century. And the East remained literarily productive; its products (such as the voluminous writings of Abraham Maimuni) never became part of the general Jewish literary heritage because they were not translated into Hebrew and therefore were not available to the Jews of Christian territories whose communities would in modern times replace those of Islam as the setters of cultural standards.

The outstanding exception to the continued dominance of Arabic in the scholarly writings of the East is Maimonides' code of Jewish law, the *Mishneh Torah,* completed in 1180. This magisterial work is the most important piece of Jewish scholarship written in Hebrew and emanating from the Arabic-speaking sphere during the seventh to the sixteenth centuries. Maimonides may have chosen Hebrew simply to make his book accessible to the Jews of Provence, who at that time were already showing an interest in Judeo-Arabic scholarship and were commissioning translations of Judeo-Arabic works. But other considerations, which will be taken up in the next section below, may also have contributed to this daring decision.

The Arabic spoken by the Jews did not differ markedly from that spoken by Muslims in this period, except insofar as it included terms specific to Jewish religious and legal practice; even these terms were sometimes replaced by words borrowed from Islamic ritual terminology, as we have seen. In most of the period, the spoken Arabic of Muslims and Jews alike already diverged considerably from the classical Arabic used in literary texts. For the purposes of writing, the Jews used several different registers of Arabic. Personal letters between individuals with minimal pretensions to learning might be written in a style approximating the vernacular as it was actually spoken. Most letters and scholarly books, like the great Judeo-Arabic classics mentioned above, were written in Middle Arabic. This register is closer to classical Arabic than the vernacular but includes some vernacular features and abounds in the kind of grammatical lapses that arise when writers try to use a register higher than the one to which they are accustomed. Rare was the Jewish writer who attempted to use true literary Arabic, the register of greatest prestige in the Islamic world, but Jewish writers did sometimes begin books with invocations of God and benedictory formulas couched in rhyming clauses in classical Arabic in the manner of professional Muslim scholars, reverting to the more comfortable Middle Arabic only after the elegant preamble.

One peculiarity of Jewish writing in Arabic is that the Jews normally used Hebrew characters rather than the Arabic script. It is this peculiarity, supported by the tendency of Jewish writers to employ a certain amount of Hebrew vocabulary in their writing, that has caused the Arabic of the Jews to be referred to as Judeo-Arabic. But Judeo-Arabic for much of our period was not, from a purely linguistic point of view, truly a separate language, because no intrinsic difference exists between a language as represented by one alphabet and the same language as represented by another. The Jews were not the only minority community to use non-Arabic script for the majority language: Syriac Christians wrote Arabic in Syriac script,[4] and, after the Christian reconquest of Iberia, crypto-Muslims (Moriscos) remaining in Christian territory often wrote Spanish in Arabic script. The reason for the Jews' use of Hebrew script was probably that it came to them most naturally. Elementary education at the time was nearly always identical with religious education; as the first thing a Jewish child went to school to learn was the prayers and the Torah, Jewish children learned the Hebrew alphabet before they learned the Arabic alphabet. Because Hebrew and Arabic are closely related languages and very similar in their phonetic structures, Hebrew script was well suited to representing Arabic sounds. Thus, when Jews wanted to communicate in writing with other Jews, they wrote in their native language—Arabic—using their native script—Hebrew. Given the large degree of autonomy of the Jewish community and the fact that Jews, like other minority groups, tended to live in their own quarters and to deal primarily with members of their own group, most of their writing took this form. Jews who mixed regularly with Muslims or who wrote for the consumption of Muslims (as did Maimonides in his medical treatises) used the Arabic alphabet, and Jews who had positions at court presumably wrote classical Arabic for official communications, as is reported in the case of Samuel the Nagid.

A curious exception to the Jews' preference for Hebrew script is a group of Bible manuscripts of Karaite origin in which the Hebrew text is written in Arabic characters. No convincing explanation has yet been given for this phenomenon. It has been proposed that Karaites, or at least some of them, represented the wealthiest and best-educated classes of Jewry; being more exposed to Arabic culture, they became more accustomed to the Arabic script than to the Hebrew one.[5] The matter is still contested.

We do not know to what extent the masses of Jews were familiar with Hebrew. Some knowledge of the language was nearly universal for men and was not rare among women, because most people must have known at least the daily prayers. But Hebrew was actively used only by the learned, which ordinarily meant members of the elite classes, and it was not ordinarily used for oral communication except by travelers who sometimes used it outside of Arabic-speaking territory. Thus, most of the letters and documents preserved in the genizah are written in Arabic, though they often begin and end with biblical quotations and formulas of greeting and praise to the recipient couched in sometimes elaborate Hebrew.

Both the attitude toward Hebrew and the role of the language expanded in the course of the seventh to sixteenth centuries. It may seem paradoxical, but just as Saadiah was establishing Arabic as the language of rabbinic writing, he was also propounding a new and exalted view of the Hebrew language. From his time, and beginning with his work, a shift can be discerned not merely in Jewish writers' use of Hebrew, but in their attitude toward it.

Before the early tenth century, there is no evidence that the Jews gave any particular thought to the nature of Hebrew, beyond entertaining the general idea that it was the "holy tongue." By the ninth century, specialists known as the *masoretes* (it is disputed whether they were Rabbanite or Karaite) were already engaged in fixing the text, pronunciation, and cantillation of the Hebrew Bible, providing each word of their meticulously edited manuscripts with symbols indicating its precise pronunciation and rhythmic character in relation to the verse. These studies showed signs of blossoming into the full-scale study of Hebrew grammar. But, beginning with Saadiah, Jewish scholars started to explore Hebrew grammar and lexicography in a systematic way. Saadiah himself composed several books on language. In the introduction to his Hebrew dictionary, *Sefer ha-Egron,* he provides a tendentious sketch of the history of Hebrew and explains the importance of the study of language in terms that would reappear again and again in the works of later writers, both Rabbanite and Karaite:

> This is the book of the *Compilation* [*Egron*] *of the Holy Tongue.* . . . From the time God created man on the face of the earth and bestowed part of His wisdom upon him, the world had but one language . . . until the days of . . . Peleg ben Ever. Then the world was divided up. . . . Languages were distributed in accordance with the number of nations, and the Holy Tongue remained only in the mouths of the descendants of Ever. . . . In the hundred and first year after the destruction of Jerusalem, we began to abandon the Holy Tongue and to speak in the languages of the foreign nations of the land. Three years before the Greek king reigned,[6] in the time of Nehemiah the satrap and his men, he [Nehemiah] saw that we were speaking Ashdodian. He became angry and rebuked the people and quarreled with them.
>
> Then we were exiled after him. In all the cities of the world and the islands of the sea, there was no nation into which our scattered ones did not come; we raised our children in their midst, and they learned their language. Their barbarous languages covered over the loveliness of our own, which was not right. Those in the East spoke Greek and Persian, those in Egypt spoke Coptic, and the people of Kenaz and Spain also spoke foreign languages, as did those who lived in Christian lands, each in accordance with his own nation. . . . Our heart and the living spirit within us are in pain over this, for the Holy speech is absent from our mouths, and the vision of all our prophecies and the speeches of His mouth are like sealed books to us, for our language has become barbarous in the lands of our captivity. It is right for us and all the people of God to study it [i.e., Hebrew], to contemplate it, and to examine it closely, we and our children, even our wives and slaves; it must never depart from our mouths, for [without it] we cannot understand God's Torah. . . .
>
> It came to pass that, in the fourteenth and two hundredth and thousandth year from the sealing of prophecy [i.e., 902 C.E.], the Compiler composed this book to bring wisdom to all the people of God, to all who know the law. He wrote it for those who write . . . and so that the [ordinary] people of God will speak in it [Hebrew] when they go out and when they come in and in whatever they do, in their bedchambers and with their infants. Their hearts must never depart from the intellect, for through it they may know the Torah of God. Thus may God fulfill the word He spoke through Isaiah His servant, "that my words may never depart from Jacob and his seed forever."[7]

Written at the very beginning of the tenth century, before Saadiah even held public office, these words pronounce a visionary program for the revival of the study of Hebrew, even contemplating its restoration as a spoken language. Taken together with Saadiah's many other writings on language and statements by contemporary writers that emphasize the importance of writing Hebrew correctly and beautifully,[8] they amount to a manifesto demanding a new status for Hebrew in the Jewish community. Previous writers had demanded that Jews master Scripture or that they master rabbinic lore, studies that by their very nature would demand some knowledge of the language, but no one before Saadiah had ever made an issue of the study of the language itself, demanding that, for the sake of the Torah, Jews master Hebrew, study its grammar, and even learn to speak in it. No one before him had attempted to explain the status of the Hebrew language in terms of world history.

Saadiah's focus on language was a response to the status of Arabic in the Islamic world, and his writing reflects attitudes that originated in the world of Arabic scholarship. For the Islamic learned classes, the study of language was considered the cornerstone of all scholarship; great emphasis was placed on mastery of classical Arabic, and elaborate rules were propounded for writing it with elegance. This attitude is summed up in the doctrine that Muslim scholars called 'arabiyya, the principle that classical Arabic (i.e., the language of the Koran and of pre-Islamic poetry) is the most perfect of languages and the model for all writing of importance and prestige. The principle of 'arabiyya made a clear distinction between the classical Arabic used for formal purposes and the ordinary Arabic used for normal, informational, written communication (Middle Arabic). In its purest form, classical Arabic was a kind of ceremonial language, the language of poetry, of book introductions, of elegant prose epistles, and of courtly writing; it was used more to impress with a display of linguistic virtuosity than to convey concrete information or to imitate the world of reality outside language itself.

Such thoughts about language were new to the Jews, but they absorbed them and applied them to Hebrew. For Saadiah, the Hebrew of the Bible occupied a position analogous to that of classical Arabic for Arab scholars; for him, the early liturgical poets such as Yannai and Kallir (sixth and early seventh centuries, respectively), with their difficult, even contrived language—far better suited to representing religious and midrashic themes known to the listener in advance than to representing external reality—occupied a position analogous to that of the pre-Islamic poets for Arabic scholars. Accordingly, he tried to encourage Jewish scholars to write Hebrew liturgical poetry in a similar hermetic style, and he himself composed much poetry.

The concept of 'arabiyya, as Hebraized by Saadiah and his contemporaries, gave rise to a division of functions: Hebrew was used for ceremonial communication, where style was most important, and Arabic was used for the ordinary communications in which conveying concrete information was paramount. This division is neatly exemplified by the two introductions to the *Egron*. The Hebrew introduction to the first edition, quoted above, with its ceremonious, quasi-biblical style (Saadiah went so far in imitating biblical style as to provide the text with vowel and trope markings), contrasts strongly with the matter-of-fact Arabic introduction to the second edition, composed 20 years later, in which Saadiah explains his reasons for writing a new version in Arabic. Similarly, he wrote the original version of his *Open Book,* the account of his conflict with the exilarch, in Hebrew. Saadiah later wrote an Arabic version of this work, partly because his Hebrew style had proven too difficult for many readers, and partly because he concluded that Hebrew was not an adequate vehicle for conveying the details of the conflict with sufficient accuracy. In the following centuries, a minor genre arose consisting of *megillot* (scrolls). These were official chronicles composed in Hebrew to commemorate important public events; examples are the *Scroll of Samuel the Third,* the *Scroll of Zuta,* and the *Scroll of Abiathar.*[9]

This distribution of functions—Hebrew as the ceremonial language and Arabic as the language for communication of specific information—is exemplified by letters of condolence or congratulations, which often begin with flowery preambles in Hebrew and then deliver the substance of the message in Arabic, and by collections of Hebrew poetry, in which the poem is in Hebrew but the copyist's introduction explaining the circumstances under which the poem was written is in Arabic.

With this division of functions between Middle Arabic and biblical Hebrew firmly entrenched in Saadiah's circle and reinforced by the Hebraized concept of *'arabiyya,* the stage was set for the introduction of Arabic literary genres into Jewish scholarship and of secular poetry, a literary type adopted from Arabic, into Hebrew.[10]

SCHOLARSHIP

The adoption of Arabic signaled not merely the replacement of one language with another but a reorientation in the intellectual life of Jews in the Arabo-Islamic cultural sphere. Although this shift did not occur simultaneously with the change of languages, the adoption of Arabic made it possible, and perhaps even inevitable.

Once the language of a marginal tribal people, Arabic had become the language of a great and cosmopolitan culture. Muslim scholars absorbed aspects of the literary and intellectual traditions of the ancient civilizations with which they came into contact—India, Persia, Greece—and blended them with the literary traditions native to the Arabian peninsula. Syriac monks had continued studying Greek philosophical works, including works of the church fathers who pioneered the harmonization of Greek philosophy with the Bible. The arrival of Islam spurred debate between Christians and Muslims on the relative philosophical correctness of the two religions and drew Muslims into the attempt to reconcile the koranic revelation with philosophical principles. Intellectual activity was pursued by two different (but often overlapping) classes of Muslims: scholars of the religious tradition, including specialists in the Koran, Ḥadith, and the practice and theory of Islamic law; and members of the court and administrative bureaucracy, composed to a great extent of intellectuals, literati, and poets. Sometimes they were supported in their intellectual activity, especially medical and astronomical study, by the rulers. The great cities of Islam, especially Baghdad, attracted not only poets and scholars pursuing diverse special interests but also a great variety of people representing different religious and ethnic groups, and this encouraged the development of a cosmopolitan intellectual life sometimes referred to as Arabic humanism.[11]

In this atmosphere, members of groups often hostile to one another—Muslims of various sects, Christians, Zoroastrians, Jews, and freethinkers—shared a common heritage of philosophy and science gained from the study of Greek writings in Arabic translation, permitting them to work together and even to discuss their differences of outlook and religion with reasonable toleration. The circles of Abbasid court functionaries included men of culture and refinement who would sometimes meet to discuss religious subjects. Numerous reports describe salons in which Jews, Christians, Zoroastrians, and skeptics debated religion on an equal footing with Muslims; to facilitate debate between adherents of different religious and philosophical systems, such circles adopted the ground rule that no scripture could be adduced in support of a position but only the rules of logic, which were held in common by all. We also have reports of a circle of thinkers who, in the tenth century, composed a kind of encyclopedia, called the *Epistles of the Sincere Brethren*. Although the members of the circle seem to have embraced a form of Ismailism (a branch of Shiism that, in this period, was characterized by relatively tolerant attitudes toward different systems of thought), they cultivated the study of Aristotelian logic and delved into all kinds of scientific and philosophical texts of Greek origin, using translations into Arabic. The Epistles came to be widely disseminated in the Arabic-speaking world, and quotations from them are found in many works of Jewish scholarship after the time of Saadiah; a taste of the cosmopolitan and rationalist atmosphere of the world they represent may be found in a Jewish literary work, *The*

Proverbs of Saʿīd ben Babshād, apparently written in the second half of the tenth century.[12]

Islamic religious life in the Abbasid period was a hotbed of theological debate, with teachers of Islamic law and koranic interpretation attempting to harmonize the contradictions on doctrinal points within the Koran and to codify their system of belief through discussion and debate (known as *Kalām,* which came to be the ordinary term for Islamic theology). Among those who participated in such discussions, a school called the Muʿtazila emerged; its adherents stressed God's unity and justice, leading to exhaustive discussion, on the one hand, of how to understand the Koran's ascription of numerous attributes to a strictly unitary God, and, on the other, of how the principle of free will (the necessary concomitant to God's absolute justice) could be harmonized with the koranic belief in God, who, in His omnipotence, controls all destinies.

Muʿtazilite theology was for a time the official religion of the Abbasid state; later, it was declared heretical. Religion and politics were intertwined; there were times when state policy favored the rationalist, cosmopolitan trends, and other times when it dictated strict orthodoxy of opinion, because the Arabic humanists did not succeed consistently in shaping public policy. Shifts of doctrine could turn into life-and-death issues when inquisitions were established for the detection and punishment of heresy.

Thoroughly versed in Arabic language and literature, and well informed about contemporary intellectual trends, Saadiah was engaged in the problems raised by this kind of intellectual inquiry. We do not know whether he participated in interconfessional salons such as those described above, but he must have received an education in his native Egypt that embraced, besides rabbinic culture, the kinds of studies cultivated by the advanced thinkers of his time. He is thus the first rabbinic figure known to us who was fully educated in both systems.

Saadiah's primacy as the founder of Judeo-Arabic literature was not merely a matter of his choice of language. In a literary career that seems consciously designed to reorganize Jewish intellectual life along the lines of Arabic and Islamic scholarship, his use of the Arabic language appears as only one element in the comprehensive program. Saadiah, the first of the geonim born outside Iraq, was the one who broke the mold of rabbinic writing in the gaonic period. This had consisted mostly of legal responsa and codes organized either haphazardly or in accordance with the order of the Bible or the Talmud, and never reflected a clear authorial hand. Saadiah replaced the making of such compilations with a new literary form: the book. Given that Muhammad had already called the Jews (and Christians) "people of the book," it may sound paradoxical, but it is not too fantastic to claim that Saadiah was the first rabbi to write a book in the modern sense of the word.

Saadiah's works contrasted with the writings of the earlier geonim in that he wrote crafted and closed treatises, conceived and organized not merely by the concatenation of traditions but according to coherent principles. These principles are often stated explicitly in an introduction; this was also an innovation, since no Jewish book written before Saadiah even has an introduction in this sense. The introduction explains the structure of the book and lays out the relationship between the various topics that it treats. Saadiah's books also bear titles that identify their exact contents, another innovation and one in harmony with the principle of coherence.

Finally, Saadiah was the first Jewish author since antiquity to identify himself in his books and to speak directly to the reader instead of merely compiling sources and earlier authorities. We have gotten a taste of this style in the passage quoted above from the *Egron,* in which Saadiah set forth his purpose and even announced the date of his writing the book. Although in the *Egron,* an early work, he spoke of himself in the third person, in later works, like the *Book of Beliefs and Opinions,* he would boldly use the first person. In the *Open Book,* his polemic against the exilarch David ben Zakkai, he would speak even more personally about the events and purposes that led to his writing; he would also make explicit his view of his own role in Jewish life, a view already implicit in the passage from the *Egron* quoted above. As the first Jewish leader to write in Arabic (the *Egron* and the *Open Book* were written in Hebrew and rewritten in Arabic, but most of his other books were written in Arabic from the start), his audience's native language, Saadiah granted himself more exact expression and thus made himself far more intelligible to his readership than was possible in Hebrew or Aramaic. In all these innovations, he was inspired and guided by the example of Muslim writers, who were also writing books according to models not native to the Arabic traditions but inherited from Greek and Syriac writing of late antiquity. Thus, paradoxically, the "people of the book" learned to write books from the very culture that bestowed the name upon them.

Saadiah did not confine himself to religious law; he also wrote on current affairs and on intellectual subjects that had not even been in the curriculum of the academies. By the end of his career, the nature of mainstream Jewish intellectual life had changed significantly and, for the Jews of Judeo-Arabic culture, permanently. A measure of his influence and importance is that he is the first and almost the only one of the geonim who emerges from his own writings and those of others both as a distinct personality and as a human being whose biography can be written.[13] If the same can be done for later Jewish writers of the Arabic-speaking sphere, such as Samuel the Nagid or Maimonides, this is at least partly because Saadiah set the literary precedent of establishing an authorial voice in his writing. But no one else in the gaonic world or, during the period covered by this chapter, outside the Arabic-speaking sphere even attempted to write in the manner of Saadiah.

Saadiah's main philosophical work, *The Book of Beliefs and Opinions,* exemplifies several of his innovations. He was not the first Jew to write on theology, nor was he was the first Jewish philosopher—his immediate predecessors known to us were his contemporaries Isaac Israeli (ca. 855–ca. 955) and the (possibly Karaite) scholar David ibn Marwan al-Muqammis (820–90)—but Saadiah was the first important rabbi to attempt systematically to harmonize Judaism with the dominant intellectual trends of his age. His true predecessor in this endeavor was Philo of Alexandria, who, in the first century, had tried to rethink the Jewish tradition in light of Hellenistic philosophy. Like Philo (who wrote in Greek), Saadiah wrote in the language of his environment; unlike Philo, Saadiah lived long after rabbinic Judaism had become the mainstream form of Judaism and, unlike Israeli and al-Muqammis, was himself one of rabbinic Judaism's great spokesmen. Partly because of his authority and partly because of the cultural climate of the age, his work was widely influential and put a decisive stamp on Jewish communities throughout the Islamic world and beyond it.

The theological treatises of al-Muqammis and Saadiah fit the intellectual atmosphere of the Abbasid age quite well. As might be expected, the themes, organization, and technical vocabulary of their treatises are completely at home in the world of Islamic theology. Saadiah's work reflects extensive knowledge of earlier systems of thought, both from within Islam and from the heritage of antiquity as transmitted by Arabic books. As an extended treatment of the two main themes of Mu'tazilite thought—God's unity and God's justice—it established the problematics and vocabulary of Kalām as the foundation of medieval Jewish philosophy, to be expanded, critiqued, and denounced but never totally abandoned. The concerns and vocabulary of Mu'tazilite thought can be traced in the works of the later geonim, especially in the theological treatises of Samuel ben Hofni (d. 1013), and even in the responsa of the rather conservative Hai ben Sherira (d. 1038), as well as in the works of later philosophers.[14]

Theology became a normal pursuit of Jewish intellectuals in the Islamic world; it came to be seen by many not merely as an adornment of religious life but as an essential part of faith. Baḥya ibn Paquda in al-Andalus (in the second half of the eleventh century) would insist that there can be no sincerity in religious behavior that is not grounded in a theologically correct understanding of religious doctrine. This view itself reflects the rationalism that the Jews acquired by contact with Greek thought as mediated by Arabic and the inclination of philosophically trained religious thinkers to understand specific rituals and doctrines as part of a coherent system resting on or generated by first principles. Baḥya's treatise on the inner life of religion takes as its first principle a brief survey of theology grounded in Kalām. But Baḥya goes on to explain that even a knowledge of doctrine is not enough to guarantee the fulfillment of the inner religious duties. The next condition is to be able to contemplate systematically the ways in which God is revealed in the details of creation. Only by understanding the workings of nature, of animal life, and of the body and soul of man can one come to truly experience gratitude and duty to God. Therefore, a scientific knowledge of the universe is a first step in cultivating the religious life.

Few voices of medieval Jewish thought were as articulate as Baḥya on this subject, but many Judeo-Arabic rabbis of his time would have agreed with his assumption that philosophy is an intrinsic component of religion. This approach was even more elitist than the traditional rabbinic position; from this point of view, the religious virtuoso is not merely one who has mastered rabbinic law and observes it punctiliously, but one who has also mastered the Greco-Arabic philosophical tradition and practices philosophical study and speculation. It also posits a very cosmopolitan ideal, a kind of Judaism that is at least theoretically linked at its philosophical foundations with the other religions and with pure rationalism. A measure of this cosmopolitanism is the fact that much of Baḥya's chapter on the subject is actually lifted verbatim from an Arabic treatise that is now known to have been written by a Christian theologian in the eighth century, a passage that would also be quoted by the renowned Islamic religious reformer al-Ghazzāli (d. 1111). The motion of this passage between Christian, Islamic, and Jewish religious writings is striking testimony to the commonality of intellectual life in certain circles within the Arab-Islamic world.[15]

Besides Muʿtazilism, Jewish thought in the Judeo-Arabic world was formed by the two dominant trends of Greco-Arabic philosophy: Neoplatonism and Aristotelianism. Neoplatonism explains the origin of the universe as a process of emanation—a hierarchical series of spheres of being, leading from an ineffable and unqualified first principle (the One) down to the material world. This "descent" is associated with increasing determination, multiplicity, and imperfection. At the lowest rank of this scale of being is matter, the principle of evil; yet as a reflection of the intelligible world, matter also possesses goodness and beauty, by contemplation of which the human soul can ascend to the spiritual world. The human soul, being spiritual and self-subsistent, is independent of the body; having descended from the supernal world, it can revert to its source by means of ethical and intellectual purification. Thus, release from the fetters of the body in ecstasy or in death is equivalent to salvation. Neoplatonism is thus a religious as well as a philosophical system.[16]

Jewish Aristotelianism differs from earlier types of medieval Jewish philosophy, including Neoplatonism, in its heightened awareness of the boundaries of faith and reason. Jewish Kalām and Neoplatonism used a variety of rational arguments to establish the truth of revelation, without seeing, on the whole, any sharp boundaries between philosophy and religion. By contrast, Jewish Aristotelians held that philosophic speculations must proceed without any regard to theological doctrines. They recognized as valid only demonstrative arguments— that is, those based on the standards for such arguments laid down by Aristotle— and subjected earlier philosophical schools to rigorous critique based on this principle. They held that only after the content of faith and reason had been delineated independently could one ask how the two realms are related. According to the view represented by Maimonides, the teachings of religion and philosophy could be harmonized only in part. According to another view, faith and reason cannot be reconciled.

A central and most crucial issue in Jewish Aristotelianism was the question of creation. Aristotle held that the world is eternal; Maimonides maintained the theory of temporal creation and rejected the emanationist theory. But more radical Jewish Aristotelians veered toward the doctrine of eternal creation. Another important concern of Aristotelians was the complex of questions surrounding divine providence, God's knowledge, and man's free will. A third topic of discussion among these thinkers was the immortality of the soul, given the different views on the nature of the soul attributed to Aristotle.[17]

Jewish Neoplatonism and Aristotelianism cannot be neatly untangled from each other, because the medieval Arabic philosophical works studied by Jews were often composite works that either attempted to harmonize the two schools or failed to notice the potential conflicts between them. But, on the whole, it is safe to say that Neoplatonism predominated until the mid-twelfth century, when, following a shift in philosophical trends among Muslims, Aristotelianism became dominant. The premier representative of the Neoplatonic trend was Solomon ibn Gabirol (1021/22–1058), who wrote his major philosophical work, *The Source of Life,* in Arabic. This work was apparently not designed specifically for a Jewish audience but for the interconfessional class of intellectuals described above, because it contains no reference to any specific Jewish doctrine, attitude, or religious text. The premier representative of the Aristotelian trend is Maimonides, especially in his philosophical work *The Guide of the Perplexed* (written in Egypt and completed in 1190) but in his other writings as well.

The pursuit of philosophy was not confined to metaphysical speculation and the harmonizing of religious tradition with philosophical principles. It also embraced what we would call scientific studies, such as mathematics, astronomy, astrology, physics, and, above all, medicine. Here again, Maimonides is the most famous case. In addition to his rabbinic duties (he wrote hundreds of responsa and may have served as head of the Jews for the Fatimid rulers of Egypt and Palestine), he was the official physician of al-Fāḍil, one of the viziers of Saladin's court. In that capacity, he wrote medical treatises in Arabic (using the Arabic script, as he was writing for non-Jews); early in his career, he had also written a treatise on logic.

Typical of Judeo-Arabic intellectual life was a profound and widespread engagement in the study of the Hebrew language. We have already noted the beginnings of the study of Hebrew in the work of the masoretes. Saadiah must have become acquainted with this study during his stay in Tiberias around 900, but he must have also been familiar with the Arabic manner of studying grammar and lexicography in the course of receiving his own Arabic education, because, while still a young man, he composed the first known dictionary of Hebrew. It is arranged not in alphabetical order of the initial letters of the words, like our dictionaries, but, in accordance with the general practice of Arabic lexicographers, in the order of the final syllables, as an aid to poets in finding rhymes. He also composed a Hebrew grammar. Both Rabbanites and Karaites continued this pursuit; the fact that three languages—Arabic, Hebrew, and Aramaic—were in regular use among Jews enabled Judah ibn Quraysh in North Africa to call attention to the family relationship between them; this recognition led to a great linguistic breakthrough, the observation by Judah ben David Ḥayyuj (ca. 945–ca. 1000) that in Hebrew, as in Arabic, most words are built on a root of three letters. Ḥayyuj's disciple, Jonah ibn Janaḥ (first half of the eleventh century), worked out the implications of the triliteral theory for the paradigms of irregular verbs and nouns, in small treatises and in his masterpiece, a grammar of the Hebrew language. He also composed a dictionary of Hebrew, based on the understanding, which had been growing on Jewish scholars in the preceding century, that these Hebrew roots are similar in meaning to Arabic roots consisting of similar consonants. The subject was religiously controversial—conservative scholars such as Menaḥem ben Saruq (mid-tenth century) rejected the notion that the vocabulary of the Holy Scriptures could be understood by reference to Arabic cognates—but the similarity of Hebrew vocabulary to that of Arabic was too obvious to be overlooked by people who moved so comfortably between the two languages and traditions.

Just as important as the fact that Jews after Saadiah immersed themselves in the same kinds of studies as did Muslims and wrote books on these subjects—philosophy, theology, science, and grammar—was that they read their "modern" learning back into the sources, especially the Bible and liturgy. This process took place on various levels of consciousness: Jewish writers sometimes simply took for granted that the assumptions of the ancient authors were the same as their own, whereas others made a conscious effort to harmonize the ancient source with what they recognized as the rational truth.

This tendency to integrate traditional texts with modern thought is particularly evident in the way in which Jewish intellectuals studied the Bible, another area in which Saadiah was the great innovator. In the schools of the earlier geonim, the Bible had not even been part of the curriculum. Although it was theoretically regarded as the foundation of all of Jewish life, from a curricular point of view the Bible was considered merely elementary knowledge; the earlier geonim rarely bother to explain a passage in the Bible, except in the context of a talmudic discussion, and no one before Saadiah even seems to have thought of writing a commentary on it. Saadiah translated the Bible into Arabic. Most other medieval translators of the Bible produced clumsy word-by-word renditions in their attempts to do justice to the principle that every particle of the sacred text is fraught with religious meaning, but Saadiah did not attempt to reproduce in detail the linguistic peculiarities of the text. He translated it into clear, idiomatic Arabic on the rationalist assumption that the ideas, not the exact words, are what most needed to be conveyed. His translation became so popular that no one attempted to replace it. It is still part of the basic religious education of traditional Yemenite Jews.

Furthermore, Saadiah pioneered a new genre that was destined to become one of the main spheres of Jewish literary activity: the Bible commentary. His commentary is voluminous, because in it he deals with a great variety of subjects that had never been attached to the Bible before. Given his interest in language, he deals with grammar and vocabulary, often explaining the reasoning behind his own translation. But he also deals in detail with theology, geography, dream interpretation, and other subjects, and he draws on a wide range of Greco-Arabic learning to solve problems in the biblical text and to fill in for the readers the information that the elliptical biblical text took for granted or left unexplained. Sometimes, readers get the impression that the information is not strictly needed to explain the text but is thrown in simply for their edification, a practice that recalls the manner of Arabic *adab* works, rambling collections of information loosely grouped around a particular theme or group of themes, and it especially recalls the encyclopedic-type commentary, such as Tabarī's commentary on the Koran.

Saadiah's biblical commentaries and the intellectual assumptions they embodied put the Bible onto the agenda of Jewish scholars in a way that it had never been before. Just as the Jews had revised their attitude toward Hebrew in the wake of their encounter with 'arabiyya, so they reorganized their scholarly hierarchy around their own foundational religious text. This process did not, for the Rabbanites, mean turning their backs on the rabbinic tradition, because by then this was not only considered sacred but was also seen as the foundation of their social organization. Yet the polemic with Karaism may also have contributed to upgrading the position of biblical studies, for it may have been precisely to combat the Karaite appropriation of the Bible that Saadiah focused on it.

Some post-Saadiah Jewish writers followed his example of writing lengthy, miscellaneous commentaries on the Bible, whereas others confined their commentaries mostly to grammatical and lexical matters. Abraham ibn Ezra, one of the last of the great Bible commentators from the Islamic world and, as mentioned above, the first Arabic-speaking Jewish scholar to write Bible commentaries in Hebrew, criticized his predecessors for their penchant for digression; he promised, in his introduction, to confine his comments to the minimal necessary philological information. But, as a true son of the Judeo-Arabic world, even he could not resist writing lengthy excurses on theology, philosophy, science, and liturgical practice. David Kimḥi (ca. 1160–1235), like Abraham ibn Ezra an heir to the Judeo-Arabic tradition who wrote in Hebrew for non-Arabic-speaking Jews (his father had fled Islamic al-Andalus for Provence), confined himself more to matters of language. To Jews of Judeo-Arabic culture, the midrashic approach to the interpretation of Scripture, as represented by their Ashkenazic contemporary Rashi (1040–1105) in France, seemed hopelessly naive, both linguistically and theologically.

In the critical sphere of religious law, the cultural components are even more complex. As in so many other areas, Saadiah was an innovator, composing for the first time monographs on specific topics of rabbinic law, such as inheritance, bailment, and testimony. Like his theological treatise, his halakhic treatises are written in Arabic and, in the manner of Arabic treatises, begin with introductions that spell out the purpose and organization of the material, which is based on a rational, hierarchical principle rather than following the order of the talmudic or gaonic sources or a mere mnemonic principle. Some of the later geonim—such as Samuel ben Hofni and Hai ben Sherira—adopted this model.

But the new types of halakhic writing did not replace the older ways, and gaonic types—responsa collections, compilatory works, unofficial notes—continued to be composed in Aramaic and Hebrew-Aramaic side by side with the new monographs. Later Arabic-speaking scholars such as Nissim ibn Shahīn of Kairouan (ca. 990–1062) continued the gaonic practice of compiling unofficial collections of rulings and commentaries in all three languages; even Samuel the Nagid, though in most respects the very model of the Arabized Jew, used traditional forms and the Aramaic language in his talmudic treatises.

Thus, one of the monuments of halakhic writing of the Judeo-Arabic age, though post-Saadiahnic, is in traditional form. This is the code of Isaac Alfasi (1013–1103), known simply as "The Laws of R. Isaac of Fez." This work is essentially an abridgment of the Babylonian Talmud, made by deleting the Talmud's nonlegal matter and the argumentation supporting nonauthoritative opinions. The work was certainly designed to serve as a code—that is, as a compendium of correct rabbinic practice, with the supporting argumentation. In form, it follows the gaonic practice of simply reusing ancient materials rather than reconceptualizing them in Saadiah's manner. Yet even this work might be said to reflect a practice of Arabic scholarship in that the method of codification is abridgment of a classic text, resulting in what was known in Arabic as a *mukhtaṣar,* or epitome.

Although Alfasi's purpose in making his epitome of the Talmud was probably not to short-circuit the process of reasoning essential to talmudic studies (a practice explicitly objected to in gaonic writings), his act of abridgment did fit very naturally into the academic pattern favored by intellectuals of the more cosmopolitan type in the Judeo-Arabic world, who, unlike the Jewish scholars of the Rhineland, preferred not to devote their lives to talmudic dialectic. They considered a knowledge of talmudic law to be an essential part of higher education but not the main subject for any but future judges and rabbis. Believing science and philosophy to be the pinnacle of intellectual endeavor, they thought it sufficient to master the law as actually practiced, primarily by memorizing the basic texts. Alfasi's abridgment of the Talmud suited this agenda quite well.

By contrast, Maimonides' *Mishneh Torah* embodied a complete upheaval in the history of rabbinic writing. It is interesting to reflect on the place of this work in the literary patterns of medieval rabbinic writing and of Judeo-Arabic intellectual life.[18] Completed in 1180, the *Mishneh Torah* was a project of unprecedented ambition, an attempt to start the history of rabbinic law all over again with a new canonical work. After decades of writing nearly exclusively in Arabic, and turning his back on the practice of rabbinic writers of the preceding nine hundred years, Maimonides wrote his code in Hebrew. Possibly his choice of language was dictated by his growing awareness of the Jewish readership outside the Islamic sphere, given the intensification of intellectual activity among the Jews of Provence in the decades following the immigration from al-

Andalus in the 1140s.[19] But it is also likely that his use of Hebrew was a conscious strategy designed to support the work's bid for canonical authority. We have seen that Jewish writers tended to use Arabic for communicating information and Hebrew for ceremonial writing. By writing in the ceremonial language, Maimonides attached to his code, uniquely among medieval Jewish legal texts, some of the sacred aura of the Bible, the Mishnah, and the liturgy. Specifically, his choice of the rabbinic register of Hebrew would have placed his work soundly in the tradition of the Mishnah, the ancient work that was regarded as the fountainhead of the entire rabbinic enterprise.

Maimonides also mimicked the Mishnah's organization into six orders, each composed of a number of tractates on specific topics, by dividing his work into fourteen large sections, subdivided into treatises on individual topics. But whereas the tractates of the Mishnah plunge into a topic in apparently arbitrary places, organize the material according to mnemotechnical as much as rational principles, and digress extensively into topics not indicated by the title of the tractate, in Maimonides' code the treatises are strictly organized according to rational principles, starting with definitions and first principles and sometimes even a thumbnail sketch of the history of the legal issues involved; they then proceed in the manner of a monograph. The resulting code is a systematic compendium of religious law that lays claim, by virtue of language, form, and, above all, comprehensiveness, to replace and update the Mishnah, nearly a millennium old by the time Maimonides wrote.

Maimonides went further than Alfasi in streamlining the talmudic tradition, by eliminating all the reasoning that underlay the opinions stated in the code and simply enunciating the law, ruling by ruling. To anyone trained in the traditions of rabbinic lore, this is the book's most immediately striking feature, and it is the one that was seized upon by his first critics. Maimonides' intention must have been to make a clean sweep of the tradition and to start it off new. He says in the introduction, "A person who first reads the Torah and then this compilation will know from it the whole of the Oral Law without having occasion to consult any other book between them." For the past eight hundred years, rabbinic scholars have been engaged in undoing Maimonides' intention by laboring to uncover his sources and to explain the basis for his formulations, as is attested by the commentaries that surround and sometimes seem nearly to devour his text in the standard printed editions. With all his reverence for the system of religious law, Maimonides seems bent on freeing the scholar's mind for even higher studies. Only scholars in training to do the practical work of magistrates need to engage in the dialectic underlying the law.

What those higher studies are is indicated by another innovation in the structure of the *Mishneh Torah*. We have already seen repeatedly that one of the innovations of Judeo-Arabic scholarly writing, beginning with Saadiah, was the organization of treatises according to a rational and hierarchic structure. This innovation reached its most consistent fulfillment in the *Mishneh Torah*, the first legal code in the history of Jewish religious writing to begin by enunciating its philosophical principles and to enshrine those principles as part of the legal system. It begins with ringing words: "The foundation of foundations and the pillar of all wisdom is to know that . . . ," announcing itself as embodying the foundational principles of the entire system of religious law and plunging into a summary of philosophical principles on the nature of God, metaphysics, and cosmology. Thus, Maimonides raised the hierarchical principle to a higher level than had ever been done before in Jewish legal writing. The principle that philosophy is a religious duty, as expressed by Baḥya, whose work deals only with the inner life, Maimonides turned into a challenge to the entire world of Jewish scholarship in the sphere of its greatest expertise, the sphere of religious law. The implication is that the mere observance of religious law is slavish adherence to tradition; the real goal is observance of religious law as a step in the process of the perfection of the mind.

To what extent did the heady and sophisticated intellectual life described here affect the lives of ordinary people? Probably very little. The vast majority seem to have had an elementary education designed primarily to prepare them to participate in religious services. For this purpose, they learned to read Hebrew and memorized the prayers and much of the Bible in both Hebrew and Aramaic translation. Elementary education often included Arabic as well, with the emphasis on reading the formal script rather than writing; it seems to have been common that even successful craftsmen and merchants with a good knowledge of Hebrew and Arabic were not able to read the cursive script used in correspondence. Only children destined for the professions—future government officials, physicians, religious scholars, and merchants—were trained to be fluent writers. Arithmetic was also widely taught to children.

Since women did not participate actively in the synagogue service, they were not ordinarily given even this minimal elementary education. Yet the daughters of learned men sometimes received a relatively advanced education. The genizah preserves records of girls attending school and having private tutors to teach them embroidery and the prayers, as well as records of women who were professional scribes and Bible teachers. We even know of one who taught Talmud: the daughter of Samuel ben Ali, gaon of the academy of Baghdad in the twelfth century.[20]

VARIETIES OF RELIGIOUS EXPERIENCE

Many features of religious life in the Judeo-Arabic world recall the manners and customs of the Muslim world in which it was embedded, particularly reverence for and pilgrimage to sacred shrines. In the late Middle Ages, the cult of saints became a mass phenomenon among both Muslims and Jews. In northern Palestine, the tombs of certain famous rabbis of antiquity attracted many pilgrims. In Egypt, where holy shrines were not attributed to saints, certain ancient synagogues were the objects of pilgrimage, and some came to be associated with biblical characters. The most important pilgrim shrine of this type was that of Dammuh. This outlying district of Cairo, a vestige of the city that had existed long before the Muslim conquest, was the site of two annual pilgrimages, one around the spring festival of Shavuot, commemorating the giving of the Torah, and another on 7 Adar, the traditional date of the death of Moses. This latter pilgrimage may have been influenced by the Muslim festivals celebrating the birth and death of Muhammad, which grew in popularity during the thirteenth century.[21] These pilgrimages, to which Jews sometimes invited Muslim friends and which sometimes were even attended by apostates, always threatened to deteriorate into mere pleasure outings. Special regulations had to be issued to put a stop to merrymaking, marionette shows, beer drinking, the presence of unaccompanied women and boys, the playing of chess and instrumental music, and dancing.

In Iraq, two tombs that were objects not merely of local but of international pilgrimage were the ones ascribed to the prophet Ezekiel and Ezra the Scribe. The *Taḥkemoni* by al-Ḥarizi, whose picture of Middle Eastern street life opened this chapter, includes a breathless description of the miraculous properties of Ezra's tomb, put in the mouth of a narrator who purports to have come from Spain. He implies that the tomb was discovered by a Muslim and that it was the object of pilgrimage by Muslims as well as by Jews. In the same rationalist spirit displayed by the youths in the story of the astrologer, al-Ḥarizi's narrator admits to having been skeptical about the miracles attributed to the shrine but then describes how he came to be convinced of their veracity. Al-Ḥarizi follows up the description of his narrator's visit to the tomb of Ezra with a poem in honor of the tomb of Ezekiel.[22]

Arabic culture influenced the practice and theory of religion on a more sophisticated level as well. The Arabization of intellectual life brought about shifts in religious practice and ritual that were evident in the rising prominence of poetry, philosophy (especially in the form of Neoplatonism), and pietism (especially in the form of Sufism). As in so many other areas, the turning point was Saadiah, especially in his contribution to liturgy. The shift from the traditional gaonic style of liturgy to that of the Judeo-Arabic world can be very clearly observed by comparing two of the earliest Jewish prayer books in existence: that of Amram ben Sheshna Gaon, written around 875, and that of Saadiah, written early in the tenth century.[23] A detailed comparison is, unfortunately, not possible, because Amram's prayer book was so frequently and thoroughly revised in the Middle Ages that its original form can no longer be recovered. From what we can tell, it was a compilation of the prose prayers in the order of their recitation, accompanied by halakhic discussions in Aramaic concerning the manner of their recitation, a manner of composition that accords well with the form of pre-Saadiahnic gaonic writing generally. Saadiah, however, and in accordance with his own style as described above, wrote the explanatory matter in the book in Arabic and began his prayer book with an introduction, in this case explaining the nature of prayer and the reasons for the book's composition. He presents the prayers themselves not in the normal order of their recitation but by categories, attempting to superimpose a hierarchical order on material that, unlike the laws of, say, inheritance or bailment, does not naturally lend itself to such means of presentation, and thereby rendering the book difficult to use for actual worship. He also included a large selection of liturgical poetry, some of it his own. In all these respects, Saadiah's prayer book makes the impression of being a "modern" book, as opposed to Amram's more traditional work.

The two prayer books have in common, however, a single goal, one that is consonant with the general tendency of the geonim: to codify and unify Jewish religious practice worldwide. As we have seen, it was through the influence of the geonim that the Palestinian Talmud was relegated to the sidelines of Jewish religious literature and the Babylonian Talmud became both the universally authoritative guide to Jewish life and the chief object of religious study. Similarly, the geonim succeeded in imposing the Babylonian liturgical traditions on most of the Jewish world and suppressing the quite different ones of the Palestinian community. (These are known today mostly thanks to their survival in one synagogue in medieval Fustat, whose prayer texts ended up in the Cairo genizah.) This unifying tendency among the geonim was probably what led some of them to attempt to suppress or restrict the recitation of liturgical poetry as part of public worship.[24]

The synagogue service of Palestine in the period immediately preceding the Islamic conquests was dominated by liturgical poetry (known as *piyyut*). The practice of renewing the synagogue service by constantly rewriting it in poetic form probably began in Byzantine Palestine, though its origins cannot be dated, and it continued to be actively pursued on a large scale well into the twelfth century (with some liturgical poetry still being composed until modern times). Piyyut from pre-Islamic times survives in great quantities, much of it anonymous. It belongs to the same cultural and religious matrix as the Talmud and the midrashim and has points of contact with the midrash as to both its themes and its literary techniques. It would therefore be logical to treat it together with the Talmud and midrash as a third literary product of rabbinic Judaism of the Byzantine age. Yet, for reasons having more to do with the history of scholarship than with the subject itself, it is customary to treat the Talmud and midrash as the end point of Jewish antiquity and the piyyut as belonging to the Jewish Middle Ages.

The earliest poet known to us by name was Yose ben Yose; his dates are unknown, but he must have been preceded by a long tradition of poetic activity. Two later poets, Yannai and Eleazar Kallir, are said to have been master and disciple, and Kallir is thought to have been active no later than the beginning of the seventh century, before the Muslim conquests. Other poets are known to have been active in the same period. Yannai and Kallir are generally thought of as representing the classical period of Byzantine Hebrew piyyut, with Yose ben Yose, together with many anonymous authors, as their forerunner.

The emergence of piyyut is closely connected with the early development of the liturgy. Worshipers probably had the freedom to improvise the text of the prayers so long as they adhered to rabbinic rules regulating the forms and the sequence of themes. Certain formulas came to be adopted that satisfied these requirements, and the formulas emerged as the fixed liturgy that would eventually be canonized by the geonim. But, given the earlier freedom, many different textual realizations of the rules governing prayer existed, and some of these were in verse form. The earliest liturgical poetry is therefore not considered a supplement to the liturgy, or even a replacement for it, but rather a principle of variety within the liturgy's fixed framework, varying as it did from community to community and within each community, from week to week.[25]

The gaonic drive toward unification of religious practice in general and of the liturgy in particular led to attempts to suppress this centrifugal element. Some of the geonim tried to brand it as an unauthorized addition to the texts supposedly sanctioned by the Talmud. Others attempted to undercut it by inventing a historical explanation for its origins, according to which liturgical poetry had been introduced as a subterfuge to permit the public teaching of rabbinic traditions at a time when such instruction had been prohibited in the Byzantine Empire by Justinian; by reformulating the sermon as a prayer, the rabbis of Byzantine Palestine managed to go on teaching in spite of the prohibition. The opponents of piyyut argued that, since the prohibition no longer applied in Palestine and never applied in Iraq, it was time to drop the liturgical poetry. (This polemical reconstruction of the history of liturgical poetry has, unfortunately, been naively adopted in popular histories of Jewish liturgy.)[26]

Despite their success in imposing a canonical liturgy, the geonim failed to banish poetry from the synagogue. For one thing, gaonic opinion was not uniformly opposed to piyyut. Furthermore, many communities had cycles of liturgical poems so well established that they would not give them up, and in other communities the desire for liturgical variation remained strong enough that they refused to give up the practice of commissioning new poetry. The compromise eventually reached, which is still the practice in those traditional communities where liturgical poetry has survived, is to recite the canonical service in accordance with the gaonic regulations but also to insert the liturgical poetry in suitable places—not always the ones for which the poems were originally designed. In this way, the prayer ritual came to be seen as consisting of two elements: a fixed, statutory text mostly in prose and fairly uniform throughout the Jewish world; and a body of poetry regarded theoretically as optional, varying from community to community, and controlled by halakhic safeguards. Poetry remained a major feature of the liturgy throughout the Arabic-speaking world, and it retained much of its freedom and variety well past the point of the gaonic canonization of the liturgy, so that, in some communities, new piyyutim were constantly being written while, in others, old, familiar ones continued to be recited. But the process of canonization turned the piyyut from itself constituting the liturgical service into an optional supplement to the now-standardized prose text. Gradually, the different communities adopted particular sets of poems, and these in turn became fixed, as had the prose prayers before them, so that by the end of the period we find such local rites as those of San'a, Tripoli, Tlemcen, and Aleppo. Even after this process was completed, some genres of liturgical poetry retained their freedom.

The popularity and prestige of liturgical poetry throughout the Jewish world are widely attested by the fact that it continued to be composed throughout the Middle Ages and that many important rabbis tried their hands at it. Its popularity is also attested by descriptions of Jewish liturgy by medieval observers. Of those, one of the most memorable is a satire by al-Ḥarizi of an ignorant cantor and his ignorant congregation. After reporting numerous amusing mistakes in Hebrew pronunciation perpetrated by the cantor, al-Ḥarizi mocks him for reciting such lengthy piyyutim that the congregants gradually lose interest and leave the synagogue before the statutory prayer called the *Shema*. Afterward, his narrator remonstrates with a member of the congregation, who insists—absurdly, from the point of view of religious law—that the piyyut is the essential part of the service and the statutory prayers optional. The implication is that the congregation attended the synagogue more for the sake of the poetry than for the canonical prayers. Al-Ḥarizi's satire presupposes that this preference was widespread, a conclusion confirmed by the memoirs of Samuel al-Maghribi, a twelfth-century apostate in Iraq whose father had been a well-known poet and cantor in Morocco. His description of the synagogue service implies that it was the singing of the piyyutim, rather than their texts, that aroused the enthusiasm of ordinary congregants. Yet al-Ḥarizi's satire makes clear that, for all the enthusiasm of the congregants for piyyut, the cantors often had little understanding of its contents.[27]

Although the Hebrew poets of early gaonic Iraq continued to experiment with the forms of liturgical poetry, they did not innovate much with regard to its functions, its language, or its contents, vis-à-vis the earlier poets of Byzantine Palestine. The types of liturgical poetry cultivated in gaonic Iraq were carried on and further developed by the poets of al-Andalus, who, however, created completely new forms as well, as I will show below. Some poets of al-Andalus, such as Joseph ibn Avitur (d. after 1012), rejected the new developments; Ibn Avitur eventually left al-Andalus and settled in Iraq, where he was doubtless culturally more at home. But even the poets who were most creative in the new modes of liturgical poetry soon to be described, such as Ibn Gabirol, continued to write in forms dictated by the Eastern traditions, with slight modifications.

Saadiah made the writing of poetry in Hebrew an important part of his linguistic agenda. He wrote many piyyutim, often in an extremely difficult style of his own devising. He seems to have done so as an outgrowth of the view that Hebrew liturgical poetry was the part of the Jewish literary heritage that corresponded to classical Arabic poetry within the Arabo-Islamic tradition. By composing liturgical poetry of this very learned kind, he may have been trying to establish Hebrew language and literature within the Jewish community as a cultural force of corresponding weight and prestige. He is the first of the geonim known to have written such poetry, which would put him at odds with the general gaonic attitude; but in liturgical practice, he may have come around to the more conservative view, to judge from the restricted role that poetry plays in his own prayer book.[28]

I have already described the interconfessional nature of philosophical discourse in certain circles of thinkers in the Islamic world, and we have seen that, from the tenth century onward, the minds of Jewish intellectuals were formed not only by the Bible and the Talmud but also by Arabic humanism and philosophy. Their serious thoughts were of the nature of man and the human mind, of the nature of the universe and God, and of the relationship between God and the individual soul. Such thinkers pursued philosophy not merely out of the need to defend Jewish doctrine against competing ideas and religions but also because they saw it as a means of attaining a true account of God, man, and the world. For all the loyalty to the community that such Jewish thinkers displayed in their personal lives, they were also conscious of belonging to the whole race of creatures endowed with reason—humankind—and, within that race, to the class devoted to the fullest cultivation of this endowment, the philosophers.

Such universalism found characteristic expression in a poetic meditation by Ibn Gabirol:

> *Thou art God:*
> *Every creature is Thy servant and devotee.*
> *Thy glory never can diminished be*
> *Because to others some men bend their knee,*
> *For none intends but to come near to Thee.*[29]

This statement represents a radical shift away from the religious exclusivity evinced by both Jews and Muslims when speaking in their more traditional modes. Although such thinkers regarded reason as at least equal, if not superior, to Scripture as a source of truth, they did not reject the basic principles of religion. Following the Neoplatonic tradition, they understood the universe as deriving from a transcendent principle that might be called "The One" or "The Fountain of Life"; though the world we inhabit is removed by many degrees from this source of light and truth in which it originated, we humans, as rational beings, are linked to that divine source by the light of reason that has its temporary seat in our souls and that yearns to return to the source. This view was not merely a theoretical principle; it was a religious conviction that led to new emphasis in the interpretation and practice of Judaism.

Traditional rabbinic thought was based on an essentially anthropomorphic conception of God. Although God was understood to be an invisible, omnipotent, omniscient king and lawgiver, the implications of these qualities had not been thought through to consistency, so that the corporeal descriptions of God in the Bible and rabbinic tradition were, in practice, taken literally. The duty of man was understood to be obedience to God's commands as embodied in a system of positive and negative laws originating in the Bible and elaborated by the rabbinic tradition. The faithful could look forward to eventual material reward for obedience and to punishment for disobedience. Such thinking did not end in the Judeo-Arabic world, but alongside it there arose another, more spiritual, view. Intense preoccupation with logic and philosophical debate led advanced medieval Jewish and Muslim thinkers to refine the concept of God's uniqueness and oneness to the point that nothing positive could be said of Him at all except that He exists. The task of man also changed; in accordance with the prevailing Neoplatonic doctrine, the task was now understood to be the purification of his rational soul through a life of ethical probity, moderate asceticism, and philosophical speculation. This would enable the essentially divine part of him to reascend the ladder of emanation by which it reached its prison in the human body and be reunited with the source. Souls that achieved such union would gain eternal ecstatic bliss, whereas souls that fell short of the goal would be condemned to suffer separation from it.

Thus, Neoplatonism was not merely a system of thought but a spiritualizing program. It was largely foreign to traditional rabbinic Judaism, since the latter was concerned, above all, with maintaining communal institutions and with defining ritual practices, dealt with the inner life only as an afterthought, and never attempted to establish a consistent theological system. The Neoplatonic type of spirituality, which survived even after Aristotelianism replaced Neoplatonism as the dominant philosophical system, compelled cosmopolitan Jews (like Muslims of similar intellectual cast) to engage in a new exegesis of religious traditions to bring the two systems into harmony. This could be done by interpreting the laws and practices of Judaism as a divinely revealed prescription for achieving the Neoplatonic goal of purification of the soul, and by understanding the Torah as an allegory of metaphysical truths.

One of the greatest beneficiaries of the Neoplatonic reevaluation of tradition was the liturgy. Beginning in the eleventh century, religious thinkers such as Ibn Gabirol revolutionized the tradition of piyyut by composing a new kind of poetry that, in effect, provided parts of the standard liturgy with a running poetic commentary. Thus, he was able to shift the meaning of the ancient liturgy into directions indicated by the intellectual preoccupations of the age. These poems provided the opportunity to direct the worshipers' attention to the new themes and the new intentions discovered in or attached to the ancient prayer text. The new poems were sharply distinguished in form and diction from the standard varieties of liturgical poetry, in that they were often composed in accordance with verse patterns adopted from Arabic and in a Hebrew close to that of the Bible, rather than in the distinctive register of Hebrew associated with liturgical poetry. In addition, the new poetry was designed for parts of the service that had never before attracted poetic embellishment. The poets sought a new context because their philosophical interests, especially their concern with the fate of the individual soul, led them to explore the borderline between public liturgy and private meditation. The new genre was called *reshut;* these poems usually allude in their last line to one of the three prayers to which they were to be prefaced. Reshuyot may be short (three to six lines), in quantitative meter, and of intimate tone, or they may be strophic, like the one translated below. They typically deal with the nature and meaning of prayer, with the poet addressing God or his own soul in wonder at the marvelous nature of the two and at the very idea of prayer as a link between them. In this genre, the poets brought together poetic values from Arabic poetry with religious ideas from both the Jewish tradition and the Neoplatonic tradition to create the first Hebrew meditative verse.[30]

The poem translated below is a strophic reshut by Joseph ibn Zaddik (d. 1149) that was designed to introduce the standard prayer of the preparatory liturgy called *Nishmat* (The Soul). The prayer's name derives from its opening, "The soul of every living thing will bless Your name." This sentence enunciates the traditional theme that all creatures praise God as their creator and sustainer and as manager of the universe, but it was particularly congenial to medieval thinkers because of its universality. Furthermore, the opening sentence provided an opportunity to reflect on the meaning of prayer itself, and the opening word was a hook on which to attach meditations on the soul, one of the main objects of their philosophical attention. In this poem, as in many reshuyot, the soul is spoken of as a beloved girl. It is named in the last word of the poem, linking the poem to the prayer.

> *Lovely is the charming girl hidden from every eye.*
> *Consider, men of wisdom, her "where," her "how," her "why."*
>
> *When matter and form were joined, she descended to dwell in clay,*
> *was hidden there against her will, imprisoned in walls of flesh;*
> *enslaved, but by no man's hand; sold, but not for coin,*
> *to till the body's earth, to make man splendid and dread,*
> *as he deserves, to distinguish him from the beasts on account of his mind.*
>
> *O God, how great is Your mystery, great and hard to grasp!*
> *The mightiest of Your creations is man!—Gold joined to stone—*
> *the highest of Your works—like corn mixed with straw.*
> *Your mighty hand it was that connected my body and soul,*
> *fixed the shape of my body, forming it out of clay.*
>
> *This precious girl sought release from her toil,*
> *a day of rest, when her labors would lightly lie.*

For her matter is eternal, she does not perish at death.
She existed already of old, before the body was,
and she is rewarded or punished according to her deeds.

O God, Your word is manna; to praise You, Lord, is sweet;
Your mighty works give a hint of the greatness and might that are Yours.
Take pity on Your folk, joined here in Your house of prayer!
The souls of the world's throngs incline toward You like slaves.
They cry with a voice unceasing: "Praise Him who created every soul!"[31]

The last stanza refers to the specific congregation and the liturgical occasion at which the poem was to be recited, but the first three stanzas are, in effect, a restatement of the Neoplatonic myth of the soul of man as being in captivity in this world and yearning continually for redemption. Here, the assumption of the essential similarity of the soul and God give rise to a new idea of the praise of God; it is essentially the soul's celebration of her own origins and the expression of her yearning to return, a spontaneous impulse that is shared by all the creatures in which she resides. This is the point of the last two lines: the soul's yearning is connected to the words of praise in a sweeping statement that embraces all humanity.

One of the most spectacular rethinkings of the liturgy is embodied in Ibn Gabirol's masterpiece, "The Kingly Crown," a lengthy prose poem constituting a meditation on the confession of sins for the Day of Atonement. This confession, which is recited repeatedly in the synagogue service and is couched in the plural (e.g., "We have sinned"), is part of the public liturgy. But the new emphasis on the soul led naturally to a new inwardness in liturgical poetry, in accordance with which Ibn Gabirol reworded the confession in the singular. He also provided it with a theological-cosmological setting, occupying about two-thirds of the composition, which, for our purposes, is the most important part of the poem. He surveys a number of philosophical themes: the nature of God, the physical properties of the cosmos, and the place of the soul in this complex system. After listing the attributes of the divinity, Ibn Gabirol describes how God's wisdom emanates the cosmos and permeates it all the way down to the four elements. He then describes how the cosmos is built up in concentric spheres in accordance with Ptolemaic cosmology, moving upward from the four elements to the empyrean, the home of the soul in its pure state and the goal to which it yearns to return from its corporeal prison. The purpose of all this scientific information is to ground the confession in a true consciousness of what is at stake, philosophically speaking, in the dialectic of sin and confession; it is nothing less than the fate of the soul. Is the soul to be ruined or purified? Is it to achieve eternal bliss through union with the World Soul? Or is it to be condemned to remain eternally in a corporeal prison? Only at the point in his cosmology when he has clarified philosophically the soul's need for purification does Ibn Gabirol introduce the confession itself, elaborating on it in his own distinctive way.

We should not forget that Neoplatonism was not merely a philosophical system but also entailed an ideal of spiritual fulfillment in the form of ecstasy or illumination achieved by means of intense and prolonged intellectual speculation. In many of his autobiographical poems, Ibn Gabirol asserts that he has devoted his life to achieving his goal; he complains bitterly of the difficulty in obtaining it, swears to pursue it whatever the cost, and expresses gratitude for the glimpses of it that have been vouchsafed to him:

> *Whenever I have hopes, my friends, and look*
> *for moonlight, darkness ruins it,*
> *as if the clouds, for very jealousy*
> *insist on keeping it away from me.*
> *But I look out when it reveals its face,*
> *Rejoicing like a slave whose master shows him grace.*[32]

For all his rationalism, Maimonides, too, hints in the introduction to his *Guide of the Perplexed* that such illumination is the ultimate goal and that it is the equivalent of prophecy.[33] Except for what can be inferred from Ibn Gabirol and other Hebrew poets, we do not have any testimonials to this kind of thinking from Judeo-Arabic writers; given the prevalence of Neoplatonic thinking among them, however, it is reasonable to assume that there were others who subscribed to this essentially religious attitude.

Another manifestation of the increased interest in the spiritual aspects of religion characteristic of the age was the attempt by Baḥya ibn Paquda to reform rabbinic Judaism through a program derived from a combination of Neoplatonism and Islamic pietism. His book, *The Book of the Commandments of the Hearts*,[34] written in Arabic around 1080, quotes extensively from earlier works in Arabic by Muslims (and, in one case, by a Christian) in its attempt to cure his contemporaries of what he saw as their smug conformity to the outward requirements of religious law combined with their unthinking pursuit of material pleasures and ambitions. Baḥya takes aim at two targets in his society: the specialists in religious law, whom he characterizes as concerned mostly with technicalities and casuistry; and the aristocracy, whom he characterizes as concerned mainly with worldly things, despite their adherence to the minimal requirements of law and tradition. Baḥya sought to replace all this with a more inward piety.

In the process, Baḥya introduced into Judaism an entirely new religious vocabulary that had its origins in Islam. The very title of his book, with its implied distinction between the external and the internal life of religion, derives from a Sufi source,[35] and the use of the word "commandments" in the title must have been an intentional challenge to the traditional rabbinic conception of religion. Likewise, several of Baḥya's chapter titles, designating ten basic principles of the religious life, also derive from Islamic pietistic works; thanks to the popularity of Baḥya's *Commandments,* terms such as "trust," "abstention," and, especially, "the soul's reckoning" are now so deeply woven into the fabric of Jewish religious vocabulary that they seem to be native to the Jewish tradition, especially in their Hebrew equivalents *bitaḥon, perishut,* and *ḥeshbon hanefesh.*

Although Baḥya's *Commandments* has deep roots in Sufism, it is not simply a Sufi treatise in Jewish guise. Baḥya's Jewish roots are reflected partly in his technique of attaching biblical and rabbinic prooftexts to every idea raised in the book, which lends authority to his ideas and answers any possible objection that his program is foreign to the Jewish tradition. The Jewish nature of the book is also evident, perhaps paradoxically, in his insistence that his program of piety is based on the rational foundation of theology, because Sufi pietism expressly rejected reason as a source of knowledge and sought authority exclusively in the Koran—the sayings and actions of the prophet, his companions, and the saints of the Sufi tradition—and, of course, in individual experience.[36]

Baḥya begins where Saadiah leaves off, making a knowledge of theology the first step along the religious way. From a rational grasp of the concepts of God's existence and unity, the seeker is required to contemplate the wonders of God's activities in the universe and in the soul of man (that is, the scientific and philosophical program of medieval intellectuals in general). Building on this foundation, the seeker approaches the true service of God through trust, sincerity, humility, repentance, the soul's reckoning, and abstention, so that he reaches the goal of religion, which is love of God. But this love of God falls short of the kind of ecstatic union of full-blown Sufism, and it does not seem that the intermediate states are necessarily a progression of mystical states; for Baḥya, they are simply qualities that one must cultivate in order to reach the goal. Nor does Baḥya commend antisocial, antinomian, or extreme behavior of any kind. Thus, from a Sufi point of view, Baḥya's program is rather middle-of-the-road; its theological underpinnings and constant citing of rabbinic sources show that he is consciously working within the framework of rabbinic Judaism as practiced by the Jewish intellectual class.

The insistence on the inward aspect of religion that is expressed polemically in Bahya's *Commandments* finds lyrical expression in the synagogue poetry of the age. Isaac ibn Mar Saul (active at the end of the tenth century to the early eleventh century) composed a penitential poem, "O God, Do Not Judge Me According to My Sins," that was imitated by many medieval poets (including Judah Halevi) and is still found in the prayer books of traditional Jews of many communities. Though intended for the liturgy, it is very personal in tone, like the reshuyot described above, with the speaker addressing God directly, as if in private conversation. The poem uses Arabic-style rhyme and meter. Although there is precedent for the theme in older synagogue poetry, Ibn Mar Saul's poem is closer in spirit to similar poems written in Arabic by Muslims. It also makes use of terminology derived from Islamic pietistic writing. The same is true of many of the poems composed for the synagogue service in which the precentor addresses the congregation, berating them for their sins and admonishing them to repent; such poems are related to the Islamic tradition of preaching poetry known as *zuhd*.[37]

Whereas Bahya's program and some of the liturgical poetry attest to a tendency for the sensibilities of Islamic piety to slip into the Jewish inner life, evidence of the impact of Islamic piety may be observed in the outward forms of Jewish ritual as well. Thus, in the *Mishneh Torah*, Maimonides, to the lasting bewilderment of readers, students, and commentators, stipulated that a Jew must wash hands and feet before the morning prayer. The washing of the hands in preparation for prayer rested on good talmudic authority, but the additional requirement of washing the feet is not known from ancient sources and is attested only in Jewish communities in the lands of Islam: Palestine, Iraq, North Africa, Egypt, Aden, and Yemen. There is no question that this custom entered Judaism in imitation of the practice of Muslims, whom the Jews could observe daily engaging in extensive ritual ablutions before prayer. As a Jewish poet of Turkey, writing around 1600, said, "Let not the Muslims be holier than you! For they wash their hands and feet and heads with water every morning, afternoon, evening, and night, even when the skies bring down snow and cold." Abraham Maimuni (1186–1237), Maimonides' son and successor as the religious leader of the Jewish community of Cairo, and one of the most prominent Rabbanite authorities of the age, informs us that there were Jews in his time who followed the complete Muslim practice of ritual ablutions, including washing the arms, ears, head, and nostrils.[38] Indeed, Maimonides held the aesthetics of the mosque up as a model and a reproach to the Jews of his own time, much as leaders of the Reform movement in nineteenth-century Germany would reproach their own flock with the decorum of the Protestant Church: "In Muslim lands, where people [i.e., Muslims] are scrupulous about not interrupting, spitting, or speaking during prayer services ... [Jews] speak, interrupt, and spit during the precentor's repetition of the *Amida,* because of which, we have a bad reputation among the Gentiles."[39]

The Karaites had already introduced a number of practices that are more associated with the mosque than with rabbinic prayer, such as kneeling and prostration, sitting on the ankles, lifting the eyes, and spreading the open palms toward heaven. Many of these customs were adopted by Maimuni in his massive religious work, *The Complete Guide for the Servants of God.* Had Maimuni's recommendations been fully carried out, the morning prayer service would have included no fewer than 40 prostrations. He also ordained that, when the congregation rises to recite those prayers that must be said in a standing position, they are to stand in straight rows, a clear imitation of the discipline of the mosque so admired by his father.

Yet the influence of Islam on Maimuni went far beyond these ritual details. His magnum opus was designed to spur a complete renewal of Jewish thought and practice in the spirit of Sufism; it is the most extreme example of the influence of Islamic piety and pietism on the leadership of the Jewish community. Throughout his work, Maimuni acknowledges quite openly his admiration of the practices of the Sufis.

Maimuni's innovations in the sphere of prayer were thus not simply in imitation of the decorum and aesthetics of Islamic ritual, as his father's regulations had been. Rather, Maimuni attempted to turn prayer into an occasion for religious ecstasy. That is why he laid such stress on the posture and gestures of Islamic prayer, which were understood to induce an emotional state of extreme humility and submission; he even recommended that the worshiper aim to induce weeping while at prayer. Anticipating objections on the grounds that his measures were innovations in religious practice and openly imitative of Islamic ways, he asserted that these practices actually originated in the Bible but had been forgotten because of the tribulations of Israel's history and now had to be relearned from non-Jews (an argument that was used to justify many innovations in the Middle Ages, including the writing of poetry and the study of philosophy). Their adoption, therefore, did not fall under the prohibition of imitating the practices of other religions. Despite this defense, his political opponents petitioned the sultan, calling attention to the changes he introduced in the synagogue service, in order to discredit him. The Islamic authorities could be counted on to oppose any measure within the minority communities that might alter the status quo, even if these changes reflected admiration for Islamic practices.

In addition to his public role, Maimuni was the central figure of a circle of Jewish pietists who were inspired by the religious virtuosity of the Sufis; he seems to have intended to establish a Jewish mystical brotherhood similar to those of the Sufis.[40] Since his innovations encountered strong objections, he was unable to impose them on the community at large; nevertheless, he apparently held private worship services for members of his circle. A number of his descendants and successors carried on this family tradition, combining Judaism with a Sufi religious sensibility; even the last member of the Maimonidean dynasty, David ben Joshua Maimuni (1355–1415), wrote a tract in the Sufi spirit. From Egypt and Syria in the fourteenth to sixteenth centuries have come records of Jews joining Sufi brotherhoods, sometimes abandoning Judaism altogether; this same David Maimuni received a petition from a woman requesting that he take steps to restore her husband, who had become infatuated with life in such a brotherhood.[41]

Karaite religiosity differed somewhat from that of the Rabbanites. The Karaites created a completely new prayer ritual consisting entirely of recitations from Scripture and resembling the rituals of the mosque in emphasizing gesture and posture, including prostration. Despite their rejection of the rabbinic tradition and insistence on returning to the religion of the Bible through individual interpretation of Scripture, they did develop a more or less uniform system of ritual law, parallel to that of the Rabbanites but considerably more rigid. Particularly demanding were the rules governing the Sabbath, when the Karaites were prohibited from having light in the house, heating, warm food (the Rabbanites permitted food kept warm from before the Sabbath), or engaging in sexual intercourse. Their understanding of the prohibition of fire on the Sabbath precluded them from even entering a Rabbanite synagogue illuminated by lamps or from lighting Sabbath lamps, one of the most cherished domestic rituals of the Rabbanites.

This austerity may not have been merely the outcome of a peculiar style of exegesis but an expression of an inherently ascetic element in Karaism that can be observed more clearly in its early stages. In the tenth century, Karaites are said to have held vigils in Jerusalem to atone for Israel's sins and bring about the redemption from exile; a tenth-century Karaite author describes pious communities whose members had abandoned their native lands and hometowns and left their families in order to live in seclusion in the mountains.[42] These people wore sackcloth, abstained from meat and wine, and met in assemblies to offer continuous prayers of supplication. This behavior resembles that of Christian hermits, who had long had communities in the mountains of Judaea, as well as that of Muslim pietists. Altogether, the Land of Israel seems to have played a larger role in the religious imagination of the Karaites than in that of the Rabbanites, since the former continued to maintain Jerusalem as a center of religious learning even in the late eleventh century, when conditions in Palestine became so unstable that the Rabbanite academy fled to the greater security of Tyre.[43]

HEBREW POETRY AND BELLES LETTRES

In this world of extraordinary cultural productivity, one of the most striking developments was the discovery of a new set of functions for poetry, resulting in the creation of a whole new literary field, that of nonliturgical poetry.[44] The initiative for this development came primarily from al-Andalus, which remained the most important creative center for Hebrew literature in the Judeo-Arabic age. But the new kinds of poetry were not confined to al-Andalus; the fashion spread quickly to all the lands where Arabic was spoken, and later it would spread to the Christian world as well.

The emergence of the new poetry among the Jews, like the emergence of theology, is part of the story of the Arabization of Jewish culture. The spread of Islam disseminated Arabic poetry along with the language and lent it enormous prestige. This poetry, as it developed in the Abbasid empire, swept away most local literary traditions, just as Arabic had swept away the local languages. Two of the conquered populations—the Persians and the Jews—retained and continued to be creative in their traditional literary languages, but they added to their native repertoires new techniques, themes, and attitudes adopted from Arabic, revolutionizing their own traditions and creating important new hybrid literatures.

In the Arabic-speaking world, poetry played an important role in public life as a vehicle for publicity and propaganda written by professional poets, and it was also a means of entertainment for cultivated amateurs. In the Jewish world, poetry had traditionally been limited to the synagogue; presumably, if Jews had a taste for nonliturgical poetry, they indulged it in their vernaculars, but all records of such activity have been lost. In this, as in so many other areas, the first signs of change occurred in the circle of Saadiah.

In this one sphere, Saadiah was not himself the groundbreaker, but his career and the careers of some of his Iraqi contemporaries show a number of the tendencies that would soon result in innovation. Saadiah wrote some of his Hebrew polemical works in verse, partly in response to heretical writings that were themselves written in verse. Likewise, Karaite opponents responded to Saadiah in verse. The adoption of verse as the medium for these writings probably reflects the Arabic practice of using poetry for writing of a public nature. That members of the Jewish elite were fully aware of this emerges from an anecdote about a Jew who attempted to influence a caliphal appointment by hiring a professional Arabic poet to compose and recite panegyric odes, and by the existence of a fragment of a Hebrew panegyric poem by an older contemporary of Saadiah.[45] Although Saadiah himself did not devise the technical means that permitted Hebrew writers to imitate the rhythms of Arabic poetry, it is perhaps not surprising that the poet who did so began his career as a disciple of Saadiah and received his approval for the invention.

The breakthrough occurred in al-Andalus, which was declared an independent caliphate in 928—in the lifetime of Saadiah—and briefly became a powerful political and economic force. It was also a magnet for scholars and poets, and a cultural center admired throughout the Islamic world. The flourishing of al-Andalus sparked its Jewish community, formerly culturally inert, into life, and its members produced a distinctive and brilliant culture that would last about two hundred years.[46] This period is often referred to as the Golden Age of Hebrew literature. It was the product of the Judeo-Arabic culture I have been describing, with its easy acceptance of the cultural norms of the Arabo-Islamic society, and the culmination of the Arabizing trends set in motion by Saadiah.

The new poetry arose in the circle of Jewish writers around the courtier Ḥasdai ibn Shaprut. As the chief dignitary of the Jewish community of al-Andalus, Ḥasdai adopted the Arabic practice of using poetry and formal, rhetorical prose as the main vehicles of official communication. Like an Arab dignitary, he employed professional writers for this purpose. Since he also seems to have adopted Arabic fashions of entertainment, his Hebrew poets were soon writing about the topics associated with the life of pleasure that were fashionable in Arabic: love, wine drinking, friendship, and the sorrow that these pleasures are so transitory.

If the impulse to write nonliturgical poetry came from Arabic culture, we may well wonder why the members of the Andalusian Jewish elite chose to write their poetry in Hebrew rather than in Arabic. Several reasons have been proposed. It has been argued, for example, that few Jews had sufficiently mastered the classical Arabic literary traditions to be able to write poetry in accordance with the high standards of that tradition. Although this premise is true, the conclusion is not necessarily so, because Jews could have mastered the tradition if it had been important enough to them, or they could have settled for writing in a less classical register of the language, as they did when writing prose.

A more plausible explanation might be that, in the atmosphere fostered by the idea of ʿarabiyya, the religio-cultural doctrine of the perfection of the Arabic language and its classical literary tradition, the Jews had little interest in contributing to the prestige of Arabic by using it in their poetry; they may have chosen Hebrew simply to show that they could reach a similar level of elegance in their own classical language. Thus, the Jews seem to have adopted the essentially competitive idea of the perfection of their own language from the Arabs, and they chose to write poetry in Hebrew as a kind of answer to the Arabic claim.

Finally, it may be that the preference for Hebrew as the language of poetry simply continued the traditional model, according to which the spoken language was used for writing that was intended to convey specific information, but Hebrew was used for communication of a ceremonial, official nature, or writing in which the manner of expression was as important as, or even more important than, the matter being conveyed. In other words, Arabic was the natural language for conveying information, but Hebrew was the natural language of what we would call literature. In adopting the concept of literature from Arabic high culture, the Jews naturally used the language of their own high culture, making use of whatever Arabic techniques and literary devices they could adapt to it.[47]

The work of Ḥasdai's poets marks the beginning of the Golden Age. These poets addressed poetry to him, dedicated books to him, and produced poetry for his use as the chief spokesman for Andalusian Jewry. A twelfth-century Hispano-Jewish writer expressed awareness of the importance of that moment in the history of Hebrew literature by writing, "In the days of Ḥasdai the Chief, they began to chirp, and in the days of Samuel the Nagid, they lifted their voices in song."[48] The achievement of Andalusian Jewry from the tenth to the twelfth centuries was unsurpassed until our own time, when a new Hebrew literature written by the first native speakers of the language since biblical times has finally outshone the Golden Age.

Menaḥem ben Saruq must have served Ḥasdai as a kind of secretary, because he composed the letter that Ḥasdai sent via Jewish merchant-travelers to the king of the Khazars in an attempt to make contact with that community. The letter is written in simple, dignified Hebrew, modeled on the Hebrew of the Bible. It begins with a panegyric poem, secular in the sense that it was written for a nonliturgical purpose; it praises the human being in elaborate—perhaps to us, extravagant—language, in the style of Arabic panegyrics (*madīḥ*) of the time, and uses the typically Arabic technique of monorhyme.[49] Except for the absence of a consistent meter, it closely resembles Arabic political poetry, and, in writing it, Menaḥem was playing the role of a Muslim court secretary within the Jewish community. Thus, despite Menaḥem's conservatism as a lexicographer, this poem may be regarded as the first manifestation of the new Hebrew poetry in Spain.

Menaḥem did not begin his career as a Hebrew poet under Ḥasdai; he had also served Ḥasdai's father, though we do not know what the father's position was. Menaḥem wrote formal mourning poems on the death of Ḥasdai's parents; such poems (*marāthī*) are also part of the Arabic literary tradition. Finally, when, as often happened to courtiers, Menaḥem fell out of favor with Ḥasdai and was treated brutally, he wrote a formal epistle to complain of how he had been abused and to demand justice; it is a long work of sustained power and dignity in nearly perfect biblical Hebrew. Written at the very beginning of the Golden Age, Menaḥem's poems and epistle show great refinement and literary mastery.

Ḥasdai's other protégé was Dunash ben Labrat, who was an author of religious poems, a few of which are still in liturgical use today. Dunash had been a student of Saadiah's in Iraq, where he had devised the technique for imitating in Hebrew the one feature of Arabic poetry that Menaḥem had failed to imitate: quantitative metrics. The system of writing poetry in a metrical pattern based on the alternation of long and short vowels, as in Latin and Greek, was standard in Arabic but had seemed impossible to duplicate in Hebrew.[50] Dunash's innovation aroused a violent debate; he was attacked by Menaḥem's disciples because of the grammatical distortions that his system inevitably caused when it was applied to Hebrew. But these attacks did not prevent the new system from becoming popular immediately. From the time of Dunash on, most secular Hebrew poetry—and some liturgical poetry, as well—written in al-Andalus and in the communities it influenced is in Arabic quantitative metrics.

To judge from the Hebrew poetry, the adoption of literary models from Arabic was only one part of a larger pattern of acculturation; the Jewish grandees of Muslim Spain adopted the manners and social patterns of the Muslim upper classes in many other ways. The poetry depicts a Jewish world that resembles the Muslim one in every respect but religion: a world of luxury, fine manners, and sophisticated entertainment involving music, dance, wine drinking, and flirtation—though to what extent the picture extrapolated from the poetry reflects real life is hard to determine. One of Dunash's poems is about a drinking party given by Ḥasdai; the poet describes enthusiastically the varied sensual pleasures offered by the banquet, and he balances against these worldly delights the more sober reflection that such pleasures are inappropriate for a people undergoing punishment by God in exile:

There came a voice: "Awake!
Drink wine at morning's break.
'Mid rose and camphor make
A feast of all your hours.

'Mid pomegranate trees
And low anemones,
Where vines extend their leaves
And the palm tree skyward towers.

Where lilting singers hum
To the throbbing of the drum,
Where gentle viols thrum
To the plash of fountains' showers.

On every lofty tree
The fruit hangs gracefully,
And all the birds in glee
Sing among the bowers.

The cooing of the dove
Sounds like a song of love.
Her mate calls from above—
Those trilling, fluting fowls.

We'll drink on garden beds
With roses round our heads.
To banish woes and dreads
We'll frolic and carouse.

Dainty food we'll eat.
We'll drink our liquor neat,
Like giants at their meat,
With appetite aroused.

When morning's first rays shine
I'll slaughter of the kine
Some fatlings; we shall dine
On rams and calves and cows.

Scented with rich perfumes,
Amid thick incense plumes,
Let us await our dooms,
Spending in joy our hours."

I chided him, "Be still!
How can you drink your fill
When lost is Zion hill
To the uncircumcised.

You've spoken like a fool!
Sloth you've made your rule.
In God's last judgment you'll
For folly be chastised.

The Torah, God's delight
Is little in your sight,
While wrecked is Zion's height,
By foxes vandalized.

How can we be carefree
Or raise our cups in glee,
When by all men are we
Rejected and despised?"[51]

To readers accustomed to thinking of premodern Judaism mainly as a religion, a Hebrew literature so grounded in values outside that sphere must appear as a bit of a puzzle. But the problem is a modern one artificially superimposed on medieval reality. The Jewish community was, for most purposes and under certain controls, autonomous and self-governing. No matter how freely its members mixed with Muslims—and some must have mixed quite freely, to judge from the cases of Ḥasdai ibn Shaprut and Samuel the Nagid—they spent their lives mostly among themselves. Their Jewish world was a nearly complete one that dealt with life in all its facets, providing them not only with their educational and religious institutions but also with their social services, system of justice, family, friendship, business connections, and means of amusement. They could be as Arabized as they wished without compromising their Jewish identity because that identity was grounded in their corporate status. Under such conditions, and given the attractiveness of Arabo-Islamic culture, it is no wonder that they reached so far outside the sphere of religion in their lives and writing when the cultural climate was conducive to doing so.

The most extreme example of this ability of the Golden Age poets to inhabit two conflicting cultural spheres simultaneously is that of homoerotic love poetry. Medieval and modern readers alike have been offended by poems, like the one quoted a few pages below, in which a male lover addresses a male beloved in erotic terms. Very conservative scholars have even denied that these poems are homoerotic at all, insisting that the masculine language describing the male beloved actually refers to a woman, but the explanations they offer for this strange procedure are not convincing.

In order to understand this phenomenon, it is necessary to reflect that much of the poetry of the Golden Age, even the works of poets known to have been pious and God-fearing, embodies a hedonistic value-system that is at odds with traditional Judaism. Like their Muslim counterparts, these Jewish poets celebrated the life of pleasure precisely because it is in conflict with official religion. When they celebrated homoerotic love, that was hardly worse than when Muslims celebrated wine-drinking, for both practices are absolutely forbidden in their respective religions. Furthermore, from the point of view of Jewish religious decorum, it hardly matters whether love poetry is homo- or heteroerotic: although Jewish law prohibits homosexuality more strictly than it does heterosexual misbehavior, there is no kind of licentiousness that is licit, as Maimonides pointed out in his denunciation of love poetry in general.

Does the existence of homoerotic poetry prove that homosexual behavior was in vogue among the poets and their audiences? There is no concrete evidence in this period for such behavior except the poetry itself, and the stylized kind of poetry produced in this period is a notoriously unreliable source of documentation for historical and social facts. However, we do, when it suits us, accept Hebrew poetry as having documentary value, and if we accept it as evidence that Jews held wine-drinking parties, then what logic permits us to reject its evidence of the practice of homosexuality? Finally, even if the poets did not actually practice homosexuality, the incontrovertible fact that they fantasized about it is a sufficiently blatant break with tradition.

Hebrew homoerotic love poetry is, at the very least, evidence that Jewish poets learned from Arabic poets the pleasures of transgressive poetry. Of all the cultural institutions that the Jews adopted from Arabic culture—language, philosophy, social habits, and communal organization—the most decisive was the Muslim habit of living in allegiance to two complementary principles, the one finding its natural expression in poetry and the other in scriptural exegesis and related genres. The Jewish aristocracy adapted to Judaism the double life lived by sophisticated Muslims, with its contradictions, ambivalences, and occasional pangs of conscience. Some features of the new lifestyle were not compatible with the Jewish religious tradition, being contrary to the spirit, if not always to the letter, of religious law, but neither were they fully in accord with the religious law and spirit of the larger society. The institution that, for Muslims, most clearly

embodied the worldly aspect of their culture was the wine party and its associated entertainments, and it is in the poetry of the wine party that Jews also
show us now and again a glimpse of their own troubled consciences, as we have
just seen.[52]

Thus, the poetry of the Golden Age embraces many genres adopted from Arabic literature. Among these are short poems on themes of pleasure: for example,
wine poems that describe wine and the pleasures of drinking with friends; love
poems that describe beautiful women or beautiful boys, often expressing the
poet's frustration at their coquetry and refusal to be drawn into a love relationship; and poems that lament the brevity of such a delightful life. There are also
short poems of worldly and religious wisdom.

Several genres of longer poems exist as well. Many of these are in the *qaṣīda*-
form characteristic of Arabic poetry of all periods: long odes, opening with a
general theme, often love or the description of nature, and concluding with the
specific purpose for which the poem was written. The two parts are linked by a
transition; part of the poet's skill consists in making this transition a convincing
one. Qaṣīdas are formal poems, often having a public function. Typical themes
are the praise of a patron or friend, praise of a person who has died (in which
case the qaṣīda serves as a formal eulogy of the kind that Menaḥem must have
composed for Ḥasdai's parents), and complaint or reproach. All the poetry is
dominated by conventions borrowed from Arabic. The same features of the
wine, the girls, the gardens, the patron, or the friend are described again and
again, and the same imagery is used and reused in comparisons. The situation of
lovers is always the same. Yet poets exercised great ingenuity in exploiting the
conventions to design lovely artifacts. Furthermore, the fact that they were heirs
to a stylized tradition did not prevent them from striking out on their own; each
of the great poets found ways to exploit the rigid conventions of Arabic poetry
in order to make a personal statement. As a result, they have left us not only a
mass of finely crafted conventional poetry but also a set of precious individual-
ized documents of human imagination and aspiration.

Besides composing poems in classical Arabic verse patterns, the Hebrew poets
used a newer Arabic verse pattern that was invented in al-Andalus. This new
form is thought to have originated in popular song. It differs from the classical
Arabic poem in being sung rather than recited and strophic rather than mono-
rhymed. It also has the peculiarity of ending with a couplet in vernacular Arabic
or Romance; this couplet is called the *kharja* (exit line), and the poem as a whole
is called a *muwashshaḥ* (sash poem). Hebrew muwashshaḥs, like their Arabic
models, originally dealt with the light themes of love, gardens, and wine drinking, but they soon came to deal with most of the themes of secular poetry:
friendship, panegyric, and even religious themes. The muwashshaḥ form was

adopted by liturgical poets as well, without, of course, the colloquial kharja. Here is a secular muwashshaḥ by Moses ibn Ezra (who will be discussed further below); in the original poem, the final couplet is in Arabic:

These rivers reveal for the world to see
The secret love concealed in me.

You who blame me, Ah! Be still.
My love's a stag who's learned to kill.
Arrogant, with stubborn will.
Passion has disheartened me—
Cruel of him to part from me.

A fawn is he with slender thighs.
The sun goes dark when it sees him rise.
Darts are flying from his eyes.
Stole my sleep away from me.
Altogether wasted me.

Never will I forget the night
We lay together in delight
Upon my bed till morning light.
All night he made love to me,
At his mouth he suckled me.

Charming even in deceit;
The fruit of his mouth is candy sweet.
Played me false, that little cheat!
Deceived me, then made fun of me;
I did him no wrong, but he wronged me.

One day when my eyes were filled to the brim
There came to me this little hymn,
So I sang my doleful song to him:
"How dear that boy is to me!
Maybe he'll come back to me."[53]

The kharja is a literary artifact of great interest because it is a link between the three cultural communities of al-Andalus. In composing a muwashshaḥ, the poet—whether a Muslim writing in Arabic or a Jew writing in Hebrew—would ordinarily start by selecting a couplet from an existing song, either in colloquial Arabic or in Romance, using it as the prosodic pattern for the poem as a whole. In the last stanza, the poet would devise a miniature scene with the quotation as a climax. For example, he might describe a girl complaining to her mother about a lover and ending her complaint by quoting the song, so that the vernacular quotation appears in the mouth of a fictional speaker. The little dramatic scene and the shift of language made for a snappy conclusion. Several poets might write muwashshaḥs based on the same kharja, either by coincidence or intentionally, for the sake of competition, so that we find families of muwashshaḥs linked by kharja, all descending from the same popular song. Sometimes the family will include a liturgical muwashshaḥ, which, though lacking the kharja, demonstrates its relationship to the group by the common rhyme and metrical scheme.[54]

The existence of a genre of Arabic and Hebrew poetry based on Romance popular songs is evidence of the fluidity of literary materials between the three literary cultures of the medieval Iberian Peninsula and even overflowing it; for the strophic patterns of the muwashshaḥs also resemble patterns used by the troubadours, and, despite the differences of language and culture, there is considerable overlapping of themes between Arabic and Provençal love poetry. The Hebrew muwashshaḥ is part of the common literary culture of southwestern Europe and thus shares in the movement that gave rise, toward the end of the eleventh century, to the vernacular European love lyric.[55]

Besides imitating Arabic prosody, genres, and themes, the Hebrew poets made extensive use of another set of techniques adopted from Arabic: rhetorical devices and figures of speech. Although present to some extent in all poetry, these had come into vogue in Arabic in the ninth century, and the Arabic poets of al-Andalus who were the immediate models of the Hebrew poets made heavy use of them. Arabic and Hebrew poetry of the age makes extensive use of simile, metaphor, antithesis, parallelism, puns, and wordplay of all kinds. Some poets prided themselves on the density of the rhetorical structures that they were able to devise, though simplicity also was much appreciated.

This sketch of the genres, themes, and techniques of the Golden Age Hebrew poetry of al-Andalus suffices to demonstrate its similarity to Arabic poetry. The Jewish character of the poetry is partly to be found in the fact that it was written in Hebrew. In addition, the choice of Hebrew contributed an element that is central to the poetry of the Jews but hardly has a parallel in Arabic poetry: the constant presence of the Bible. Since the Bible was the basis of Jewish education and was especially prominent in Judeo-Arabic culture, Hebrew poets could count on their readers' ability to recognize any allusion to it. They developed the artful use of biblical quotations as part of their craft, often creating interesting effects by distorting the meaning, expecting their learned audience to respond to the constant manipulation of the quotations. This device was common in Hebrew liturgical poetry before the Jews came into contact with Arabic literature, but the Golden Age poets developed it into one of the mainstays of their art. Arabic poets used quotations from and allusions to sacred writings and classical literature, but there was no single ancient text that underlay their poetry in quite the same way as the Bible underlay Hebrew poetry.

Another Jewish aspect is the values celebrated in panegyric poetry. While these often overlap with values celebrated in Arabic poetry, such as generosity and wisdom, the poems often stress qualities less common in Arabic, such as piety and scholarship, and avoid some that are standard in Arabic, such as military prowess. One reason for this difference is that Hebrew poets were not ordinarily writing in praise of rulers; in fact, most were not even writing to patrons. Some Hebrew poets were paid writers of panegyric, but most such poetry was exchanged among friends who were on the same social level, members of, or aspirants to, the same social class.

The poetry of the Golden Age stands out in the history of premodern Hebrew literature as providing a vehicle of self-expression. Notwithstanding the stylization that marks the poets' choice of language, imagery, and theme, a number of strong individuals were able to exploit it as a means of making distinctive statements of their own visions of their lives, careers, and religious ideas. Several of these poets deserve to be mentioned here as examples.

The first truly great Golden Age poet and the paradigmatic figure of the age was Samuel the Nagid. Besides being vizier in the court of the Kingdom of Granada, Samuel was a scholar who was learned and productive both in the rabbinic tradition and in the new literary fields; he is also said to have composed poetry in Arabic, but none has come down to us. His Hebrew poetry has survived in three substantial collections, one of which contains his long poems recounting the battles he attended in some official capacity and speaking of his personal ambitions, his doubts about the propriety of his public role, his hopes for his son Jehoseph, and his anxiety about old age and death. These poems were probably written with an eye to enhancing his own position vis-à-vis the Jewish community of Granada; they thus serve the same function as panegyrics, but they are written by the subject himself. Arabic poetry knows a genre in which the poet describes his own prowess, and some of the Nagid's boasting tone derives from this type of poem. But he stays close to the Jewish tradition by constant reference to biblical models for his own career, such as the courtier Mordekhai and, especially, King David. He seems to base his claim for religious legitimacy on the parallel between his own career and that of David, who was also a statesman, a warrior, and a poet (for, according to tradition, King David is the author of the Psalms). This typology is probably what suggested to Samuel the idea of calling his collection "The Little Book of Psalms." In one of the greatest of his battle poems, the miracle at the Red Sea provides the typology:

> The day was a day of dust cloud and darkness;
> the sun was black as my heart;
> the clamor of the troops was thunder, like the sea
> and its waves when its rages in a storm. . . .
> Horses were running back and forth
> like serpents darting in and out of their holes.
> The flung spears, as they flew
> were lightning, filling the air with blaze.
> The arrows were like drops of rain,
> the backs of men were sieves,
> the bows were twisting in their hands like snakes,
> and every snake was spitting out a bee.
> The swords above the heads of men were torches,
> but when they fell, they put out someone's light. . . .
> And I—what could I do? No place to flee,
> no one to trust . . . so I poured prayers
> to God . . . who turns the arrows shot
> in battle back upon the foe.
> And as I prayed like one in labor
> bearing her first child
> God heard my prayer.
> He blew on them as once He blew
> on Pharaoh's troops, swept them away;
> they perished in His storm,
> and God made manifest His might.[56]

Ibn Gabirol, a younger contemporary of Samuel, was the first of the great Golden Age poets who was prolific in both secular and liturgical poetry. Some of his secular poetry is addressed to patrons; in his youth, he was apparently supported by a Jewish courtier in Saragossa named Yekutiel ibn Ḥassan. Ibn Gabirol dedicated panegyrics to him and, upon his death, a massive lament as well as a four-line epigram that will keep Yekutiel's name alive so long as Hebrew is still known:

Behold the sun at evening, red
as if she wore vermilion robes.
She slips the wraps from north and south,
covers in purple the western side.
The earth—she leaves it bare and cold
to huddle in shadows through the night.
At once the sky is dark; you'd think
sackcloth it wore for Yekutiel.[57]

He wrote panegyrics to Samuel the Nagid, as well. But Ibn Gabirol also wrote an impressive quantity of personal poetry, in which he presents a complex image of himself: as sickly, orphaned, lonely, and destitute; as a philosopher so obsessed with death and with his philosophical speculations that he neglects worldly concerns, caring nothing for the false honors that this world can bestow; and as a bitter failure who sees that his philosophical attainments have not gained him recognition from his fellow men, and who expresses determination to force the world to grant him fame and glory.

If all I wanted were some little thing,
you wouldn't see me working night and day.
How do you expect me to be happy, to have pleasure,
be content with waiting?—Waiting's a dragged-out thing!
Look how philosophy has eaten up my flesh,
while other people waste their flesh on love! . . .
I struggle on; I wouldn't quit
for all the honors of a Solomon.
I strip off this world's cloak, while Wisdom
wraps herself in robes of light
and gowns of royal blue.
She spurns me, as if she'd given up
on my attaining honors, and having given up,
opened gates of misery for me,
behind me shut the gates of joy. . . .
Tell my detractors
(and let them hold their tongues in front of me)
that I have heard the voice of On,
who plotted to seize Moses' power,
and if the world does not make me its chief,
she does not know who her lover is.

If she would take the measure of my spirit,
you'd see her on her face before my feet! . . .
I sometimes think God put a thing into my mouth—
a jewel when He put it there,
but once in place, it turned into a coal,
or maybe something like a song, which, sung,
reeks with a mix of fragrance and decay.[58]

Moses ibn Ezra (ca. 1055–ca. 1135) held public office in Granada, where he spent the first part of his life; later, for reasons not well understood, he was compelled to wander in the Christian territories in the north of Spain. Much of his secular poetry consists of poems on the life of pleasure and poems of praise to friends, and his muwashshaḥs contain particularly audacious recommendations of the life of pleasure. In his youth, he composed a book of poetic epigrams on such topics as gardens, love, wine drinking, asceticism, and friendship; the little poems all share the device of having homonyms for their rhyme words. Given the fascination of both Arabic and Arabizing Hebrew poets with rhetorical devices, this book was greatly appreciated and was imitated by later poets. Yet Moses ibn Ezra wrote a great deal of religious poetry as well, especially *selihot*, which are as sober and as somber as is customary for the genre. In his secular poetry, he follows the models of formal Arabic courtly poetry even more exactly than do the other Golden Age poets; he is the only one among them, for example, to make use of the desert-encampment theme in the opening part of his qaṣīdas. He put this theme to good use in his exile years, when he wrote many long poems of personal complaint. In these odes, he bewails his isolation in a land of lesser cultural sophistication and describes his longing for the material pleasures of Andalusian courtier life and the sophisticated audience for his poetry that that world afforded:

The abodes of lovers remain desolate,
and their palaces have become like deserts.
They had been designated feeding grounds for girl-fawns,
and had been called a tramping ground for young bucks,
but today, leopards crouch in them
and in them, lion-cubs roar;
in gardens where once the cranes and swallows nested,
hawks and vultures have gathered to mourn.
I wander along walls that lean over,
I go about the torn-down hedges;
I gently yearn for their soil,

I try to revive the stones from their heap,
I pour the tears of my eyes as streams
that no mariner could traverse with his fleet.
I speak to them, but no one hears or answers.
Only the jackal howls laments.[59]

Moses ibn Ezra also wrote several prose works in Arabic, including *The Book of Discussion and Debate,* a treatise on Hebrew poetry, which is one of our main sources of information about the literary theory common to the poets of the age. Another Arabic treatise, *The Book of the Garden: On Figurative and Metaphorical Language,* is a study of figurative language in the Bible and in Hebrew poetry.

Judah Halevi (ca. 1075–1141) was the most prolific of the Golden Age poets. His secular poetry, including the usual light verse on the pleasures of life and qaṣīdas to friends and associates, reflects the witty, outgoing, sensuous personality of a man who took much pleasure in social life. His religious poetry is dominated by an attitude of pious awe and tranquillity, a willingness to let God take over all initiative. But the most distinctive feature of his work is the series of poems connected with his decision, made late in life, to abandon Spain, go on pilgrimage to Palestine, and spend his last years there. This was a shocking, even irrational-seeming plan, for it meant abandoning his family and a comfortable life (Halevi was a physician and a businessman) for a dangerous journey and an old age of hardship in a war zone (this being the period just prior to the Second Crusade) with only a small and poor Jewish community.

In several long poems, Halevi lays out his reasoning and his view of his religious mission, giving the impression that he felt the need to justify his behavior to others and to himself. He also composed several fine poems celebrating Jerusalem and the Holy Land and mourning their desolation (one of these poems, "Zion, Will You Not Greet Your Captives?" not only became part of the liturgy for the Ninth of Av but also inspired many imitations). Finally, he wrote a series of poems describing the ocean voyage itself. Some of these poems may have been products of pure imagination, written in advance of the journey, but others were probably written during his stay in Alexandria during the winter of 1140–41, when he had already experienced the sea, or even on the deck of the ship itself. Not belonging to any existing genre, these poems are a major achievement of individual expression in an age in which most poetic form was dictated by convention:

So pressed by lust for the living God,
to greet the seat of my people's kings,

I never stopped to kiss my wife,
my children, friends, or kin.

I never weep for the orchard I planted,
the garden I watered, my plants that bloomed;
I never think of Azarel and Judah,
my two precious flowers, the best of my blossoms,
or Isaac, the boy whom I counted a son
(he thrived in my sun, my moon made him flourish).

I'll soon be forgetting the house where I worshiped,
where sacred books were once my refreshment;
the pleasure of sabbaths, the splendor of festivals,
Passover's dignity, all are forgotten.
I now turn my dignities over to others;
let idols enjoy the praises once mine!

For chambers, I now have the shade of scrub bushes,
and thickets of thorns for palace gates.
My taste for the finest in perfumes and incense
is satisfied now with the fragrance of brambles.

I am finished, now and forever, with creeping
on palm and face in the presence of men.
I am making my way through the heart of the sea
to the place where God's own feet find rest,
where I can pour out my soul and my sorrow.

His holy mountain will then be my doorsill,
my gate will be facing the gates of heaven.
I will strew the Jordan with my saffron,
put out my shoots on the stream of Shiloah.

What should I fear? God is with me,
His love is the angel that carries my weapons.
As long as I live, I will sing His praise—
till the end of all time, till the end of my days.[60]

Halevi was closely associated with a younger contemporary, Abraham ibn Ezra (ca. 1089–1164), who was also a prolific poet. Abraham ibn Ezra's secular poetry includes some clever epigrams describing his impoverished condition and some good muwashshahs, but it is as a religious poet that he was strongest and most prolific, and it was as the author of commentaries on the Bible that he would achieve lasting fame as a Jewish writer, for he was the first Judeo-Arabic scholar to write Bible commentaries in Hebrew.

With Judah Halevi and Abraham ibn Ezra, the Golden Age proper comes to an end. The Almohad persecution cut Andalusian Jewish culture off at the root. The Jews of Iberia would retain their link with Arabic for at least another century, but signs of change were evident almost as soon as the new Hebrew literature emerged in the triumphant Christian kingdoms. One such sign was the abrupt cessation of Judeo-Arabic literature in Spain. From the mid-twelfth century on, Hebrew predominated as the language of Jewish prose writing in Spain and soon became the sole written language for internal purposes. From this time comes a wave of translations of Judeo-Arabic works into Hebrew for the use of Jews in Christian Europe, as well as for Spanish Jews who were no longer familiar with Arabic. This trend is distinct from the stream of translations of philosophical and scientific works intended for the use of Christians.

But Judeo-Arabic culture did not vanish abruptly. Although the new Jewish communities were technically no longer part of the Islamic world, they were able to carry on Judeo-Arabic culture because the new Christian kingdoms continued to be dependent on their Arabic scholarship and because Iberian Jews maintained their links with the Arabic-speaking world. After a silence of about 50 years, a new generation of Hebrew writers arose in Castile and Catalonia toward the end of the twelfth century. Although the work of these writers is innovative vis-à-vis the Golden Age traditions, they continued to be strongly influenced by Arabic.

Interestingly, just as al-Andalus was becoming Hispanicized, a new genre of Hebrew writing appeared that was derived from Arabic. This was the *maqāma*, a narrative in rhymed prose studded with short poems. In the Arabic maqāma, the narratives follow a fairly regular pattern and are mostly designed to provide an opportunity for an elaborate display of rhetoric. The Hebrew maqāmas, while retaining a strong rhetorical element, tend to have more elaborate narratives.

The great variety of narrative types suggests the growing independence of Hebrew writers from Arabic models as the Arabic culture of al-Andalus gave way to the Romance culture of Spain. With the important exception of Judah al-Ḥarizi (discussed below), we may say that, in form, the Hebrew narrative prose of the period seems to look back to the symbiosis with the Arabic-speaking world, but, in theme, it looks forward to a potential new symbiosis with the belles lettres of Christendom. Certainly, such a shift seemed possible at the end of the twelfth century.

The internal shift from Arabic to Hebrew reflected a significant change in the linguistic situation of the Jews. Throughout the Arabic-speaking world, the daily language of the Jews was merely a variation of the language that also served as the medium of high culture. Vernacular Arabic was not the same as learned Arabic, but knowing the vernacular gave access to the language of philosophical and scientific writings and provided a solid foundation for learning the language of high literature; moving from one register of the language to the other was no more difficult for Arabic-speaking Jews than for their Muslim neighbors. The situation was completely different in Christian Europe, where the Latin vernaculars had diverged so radically from Latin that even knowing a Romance language did not provide access to higher literature. Furthermore, the Islamic world boasted a class of scholars who were not clergy, so that there was much a non-Muslim could study without coming into contact too intimately with religious scholarship. In medieval Christendom, scholarship was almost exclusively the domain of the clergy, so that it was much more difficult for a Jew to become learned in Christian high culture, even if he did manage to learn Latin. With the spread of Christianity throughout the Iberian Peninsula, the linguistic—and therefore the cultural—situation of Iberian Jewry became more like that of the Jews of the rest of Europe. But this process was gradual and did not affect everyone equally. Even as late as the fifteenth century, we still encounter individual Jews in Castile who are learned in Arabic.

Castilian Jewry thus retained its ties to Arabic language and culture longer. Toledo had been a major center of Arabic civilization prior to its conquest by Alfonso VI in 1085, and Arabic continued to be spoken there long after it was forgotten in Aragon. Jews in Castile continued to bear Arabic traditions. Under Alfonso X El Sabio (r. 1252–84), Jews became prominent in the field of translation, because the king encouraged the development of the Castilian language, and under his patronage many works were translated into the vernacular. This project, undertaken for the benefit of non-Jewish scholars, involved mainly scientific works, but Alfonso also sponsored the translation of Jewish and Islamic religious writings for use by the Church. Arabized Hebrew literature continued to flourish, as well. Todros ben Judah Abulafia, a Jewish man of letters who was close to several of Alfonso's court Jews, left a huge body of poetry, including some Hebrew verses addressed to the king that were supposedly engraved on a goblet that Todros presented to Alfonso:

> *Truth beheld revenge on falsehood*
> *when Alfonso was crowned our king.*
> *To wait on you I come; a cup*

engraved with Hebrew verse I bring.
For thus the Lord bade: "Every pilgrim
must bear Me an offering."[61]

Todros's Hebrew poetry is mostly in forms derived from Arabic, but he experimented with verse forms derived from Romance, as in his Hebrew canzone, which is also dedicated to Alfonso. It is a sign of the times that the introduction to his collected poems (which he himself compiled) and the headings to the poems describing the circumstances of their composition are in Hebrew rather than in Arabic. Particularly interesting is his love poetry, which includes, alongside salacious verse, poems that bespeak a more spiritual idea of the nature of love. In a radical break with the traditions of the Golden Age, he even has Love itself speak:

I am Love; as long as I live I will rule all creatures.
My camp and dwelling place is in the hearts and minds of men.
The souls of the great-hearted are my friends,
the souls of villains are my enemies.
Kings may vie with kings in war,
but all submit to me![62]

The main influence of the Hebrew poetry of al-Andalus, however, was in the Arabic-speaking world. Although few poets of stature arose outside of Iberia, Andalusian poetry, especially liturgical poetry, was admired and imitated everywhere. As early as the end of the tenth century, the poems begin appearing in the East. A line of verse by Samuel the Nagid was being analyzed for grammatical correctness in Egypt by the mid-eleventh century. Private letters preserved in the geniza often include poems, some of them badly written, proving that the prestige of poetry reached below the elite class. When Halevi arrived in Egypt, he found admirers who appreciated his poetry and put it into circulation. Isaac, the son of Abraham ibn Ezra, who accompanied Halevi to the East, found a patron for his poems in Syria.

Maimonides arrived in Egypt a generation after Halevi and spent the rest of his life there; though he always thought of himself as an Andalusian, he was untypical for an Andalusian Jewish scholar in not making the writing of poetry one of his chief activities. Egypt did not produce any major poets until the thirteenth century, when Joseph ben Tanḥum Yerushalmi and Moses Darʿi, the latter a Karaite, were active. Iraq also produced few important poets except for Eleazar ben Jacob (1195–1250), but al-Ḥarizi, who relocated from al-Andalus to Iraq, mentions the names of numerous poets whom he met there; he himself managed to find patrons in Iraq and Syria for his maqāmas.

Having begun this chapter with a selection from al-Ḥarizi's maqāmas, I shall conclude it with another. He deserves to frame this chapter, because of his unremitting loyalty to Arabic and Judeo-Arabic culture in an era when historical forces were beginning to erode it; he was the most important Hebrew writer of thirteenth-century Spain who was untouched by new Romance influences. Active as a translator, he rendered many Arabic works into Hebrew, including the maqāmas of al-Harīrī—a notoriously difficult masterpiece of Arabic rhymed prose—and Maimonides' *Guide of the Perplexed.* Al-Ḥarizi followed this achievement by composing his own collection of Hebrew maqāmas, the *Taḥkemoni.* In this work, he reverted to the narrative type of the pure Arabic maqāma, rejecting the new types of narrative and the new values cultivated by the writers of early Christian Spain:

The narrator relates that, when he was a young man, he was driven by restlessness to travel from place to place. One day he found himself in a town in Iraq, where he was invited to an entertainment at the home of a wealthy man, where tables were overflowing with food and drink. Among the crowd was an old man who looked like a vagabond and who gobbled up everything he could reach. He was so crude in those refined surroundings that people began to talk about having him expelled. The man noticed the displeasure of the others, but continued to feed himself. Meanwhile, the guests fell into conversation, and, true to the manners of the age, their conversation turned to poetry. They debated who were the greatest Hebrew poets of the past, while the vagabond continued eating. Yet while he ate, he listened to the conversation with a contemptuous look on his face.

When he had emptied the plates, he asked the narrator what was the subject of the conversation. Upon being told that the topic was the ranking of the great Hebrew poets of al-Andalus, the vagabond fell silent for a moment and then launched into an elaborate speech in which he blamed the company for hating him and despising his gluttony. He said that if it were not for his manners, he would leave the party and abandon the others to their ignorance, but he would forgive them and leave their punishment to God. The company were astonished at this unexpected flow of words and at their eloquence, coming from a man without manners, and they waited eagerly for his speech, which began as follows:

"Men of wisdom, listen to me and open your mouths to the rain of my intellect. I will release every sealed mystery and open whatever is hidden from you. The poets you have named and whose essence you have been trying to uncover—I was once called to do battle with them, and I have arrived here from the very battlefield; my heart is the scroll of their thoughts, and I am the record book of their poems. Pay attention, listen to me; then your spirits will come to life!"

The old man delivered an elaborate lecture on the great poets of the Golden Age, beginning with Menaḥem and Dunash and ending with Judah Halevi, whom he praised as the greatest of all. The company listened in silent astonishment and admiration at his command of the subject and the flow of his words. But the old man had not forgotten the insult. The minute he finished his speech, he vanished from the room, leaving the company to lament their failure to recognize such a master. At the last moment, the narrator recognized him as his old friend, but never even had a chance to speak to him.[63]

Notice how similar in structure this story is to the one with which the chapter opened. The narrator happens upon a stranger who dazzles a company with his verbal skills. A question is posed. Following a silence, a flood of words demonstrates the superior powers of the stranger, who unexpectedly masters the crowd with his eloquence. Here, however, the theme is completely different.

The stranger has magical eloquence and superior knowledge of the history of Hebrew poetry because he is part of that history; he is the last surviving representative of the Golden Age, surrounded by the next generation, who appear to him as philistines. No matter that he is merely a decadent vestige of the glorious age of letters; he demands deference, despite his bad manners, because of where he has been and whom he has known. He is the last one who knew the great men of old, surrounded by members of a generation that may admire but cannot fully grasp their greatness.

Even if we do not judge the Hebrew writing of the twelfth and thirteenth centuries to be inferior to that of the Golden Age—though few readers have considered the writing of the periods to be of equal quality—the differences between the literary mentalities of the two periods, as outlined in the earlier part of this section, are sufficiently interesting. The Hebrew writers of the age showed the mark of the changed cultural circumstances—all but al-Ḥarizi, who, in a world in which romance literature and a new allied Hebrew literature were beginning to take shape, clung to the Arabic models and refused to take the new paths indicated by the models of romance.

The voice of the old man in our story is immediately recognizable as that of al-Ḥarizi himself. Too proud to lament the passing of the Judeo-Arabic age, he sneers at the new generation, asserts his own superiority as a degenerate vestige of that age, and vanishes into the night. Al-Ḥarizi had left Spain and traveled, via Provence, to Syria and Iraq. There he wrote maqāmas (both in Hebrew and in Arabic) and Hebrew poetry in praise of local patrons. He also wrote poetry in classical Arabic for Muslim patrons, who rewarded him appropriately. He may have been a child of al-Andalus, but his heart clearly remained in the Judeo-Arabic East.

NOTES

1. Judah al-Harizi, *Taḥkemoni* (Tel Aviv, 1952), 213–17; the English translation is in *The Taḥkemoni of Judah al-Ḥarizi*, trans. V. E. Reichert, vol. 2 (Jerusalem, 1973), 96–102.

2. The analysis is based on R. P. Scheindlin, "Al-Ḥarizi's Astrologer: A Document of Jewish-Islamic Relations," *Studies in Muslim–Jewish Relations* 1 (1993), 165–75. See also R. Brann, "Power in the Portrayal: Representations of Muslims and Jews in Judah al-Ḥarizi's *Taḥkemoni*," *Princeton Papers in Near Eastern Studies* 1 (1992), 1–22.

3. When Muhammad called Jews and Christians "people of the book" (Koran 2:105 is the first of numerous occurrences of the phrase in the Islamic scriptures), he was referring to their having a sacred scripture as the foundation of their religious systems.

4. S. D. Goitein, *A Mediterranean Society: The Jewish Communities of the Arab World as Portrayed in the Documents of the Cairo Genizah*, 6 vols. (Berkeley, Calif., 1967–93), 1: 15.

5. Salo W. Baron, *A Social and Religious History of the Jews*, 2d ed. (New York, 1952–83), 5: 257. Cited by Joshua Blau, *The Emergence and Linguistic Background of Judeo-Arabic* (Oxford, 1965), 43.

6. By "king," Saadiah means Alexander the Great. His chronology reflects the rabbinic tradition that erroneously accorded only 34 years to the period from the rebuilding of the Temple in 516 B.C.E. to the Macedonian conquest of Palestine in 332 B.C.E.

7. Saadiah ben Joseph, *Sefer ha-Egron*, ed. Neḥemya Allony (Jerusalem, 1969), 156–60. The concluding passage is not an exact quotation from the Bible but a paraphrase of Isaiah 59:21 (my translation). Saadiah apparently interprets "words" in the quotation as meaning "the Hebrew language."

8. Rina Drory, *Reshit ha-Maga'im shel ha-Sifrut ha-Yehudit 'im ha-Sifrut ha-'Aravit ba-Me'a ha-'Asirit* (Tel Aviv, 1988), 48–51.

9. See also the chronicles collected and studied in Zvi Malachi, *Sugyot ba-Sifrut ha-'Ivrit shel Yemei ha-Benayim* (Tel Aviv, 1971), 7–97.

10. The above discussion of the languages of the Jews is based on the following studies: Blau, *Emergence and Linguistic Background*; Drory, *Reshit ha-maga'im*; Goitein, *A Mediterranean Society* 1: 9–16; and David Wasserstein, "The Language Situation in al-Andalus," in A. Jones and R. Hitchcock, eds., *Studies on the Muwashshah and the Kharja* (Oxford, 1991).

11. On Arabic humanism, see Joel Kraemer, *Humanism in the Renaissance of Islam* (Leiden, 1992), esp. chap. 2.

12. Ezra Fleischer, *Mishle sa'id ben babshad* (Jerusalem, 1990).

13. Abraham S. Halkin, "Saadiah (Ben Joseph) Gaon," in *Encyclopaedia Judaica*, vol. 14, cols. 543–47; Henry Malter, *Saadiah Gaon: His Life and Works* (Philadelphia, 1921).

14. Colette Sirat, *A History of Jewish Philosophy in the Middle Ages* (Cambridge, Engl., 1985).

15. George Vajda, *La théologie ascétique de Bahya ibn Paquda* (Paris, 1947). The quotation from the Christian-Arabic text is identified in Amos Goldreich, "Possible Arabic Sources for Distinguishing Between 'Hovot ha-Evarim' and 'Hovot ha-Levavot' " (Hebrew), *Teuda* 6 (1987–88).

16. Paraphrased from J. Kraemer, "Neoplatonism," in *Encyclopaedia Judaica*, vol. 12, col. 958.

17. Paraphrased from Alexander Altmann, "Aristotle," in *Encyclopaedia Judaica*, vol. 3, cols. 446–48.

18. For an authoritative study of the *Mishneh Torah*, see Isadore Twersky, *Introduction to the Code of Maimonides (Mishneh Torah)* (New Haven, Conn., 1980).

19. Twersky, *Introduction*, 333–36.

20. Goitein, *A Mediterranean Society*, 2: 171–90.

21. Ibid., 5: 18–25.

22. Al-Harizi, *Tahkemoni*, 287–94.

23. Amram ben Sheshna Gaon, *Seder Rav 'Amram Ga'on* (Jerusalem, 1971); Saadiah ben Joseph, *Sidur Rav Sa'adia Gaon* (Jerusalem, 1963).

24. In recent scholarship, the attitude of the geonim toward liturgical poetry is seen as being more varied than in older literature; see Ruth Langer, *To Worship God Properly: Tensions Between Liturgical Custom and Halakhah in Judaism* (Cincinnati, 1998), 110–82, and Robert Brody, *The Geonim of Babylonia and the Shaping of Medieval Jewish Culture* (New Haven, Conn., 1998), 121.

25. This standard reconstruction of the history of liturgy has been contested in a series of articles by Ezra Fleischer. For complete bibliography and discussion, see Ruth Langer, "Revisiting Early Rabbinic Liturgy: The Recent Contributions of Ezra Fleischer," *Prooftexts*, 19 (1999), 179–94.

26. On the work of geonim in standardizing the liturgy, see L. A. Hoffman, *The Canonization of the Liturgy* (Notre Dame, Ind., 1979).

27. Al-Harizi, *Tahkemoni*, 223–30; Samau'āl al-Maghribī, *Ifhām al-Yahūd*, ed. Moshe Perlmann (New York, 1964), 57.

28. Yosef Tobi, "Yahaso shel Rav Sa'adia Ga'on Lapiyut," in S. Elizur et al., eds. *Keneset Ezra* (Jerusalem, 1994–95), 325–50.

29. *Keter Malkhut*, section 8, in Hayim Schirmann, *Ha-Shira ha-'Ivrit bi-Sfarad uv-Provans*, vol. 1 (Jerusalem, 1960), 261–262. The translation is my own; for a translation of the entire poem, see D. R. Slavitt, *A Crown for the King* (New York, 1998). For other sources, see R. P. Scheindlin, *The Gazelle: Medieval Hebrew Poems on God, Israel, and the Soul* (Philadelphia, 1991), 142–43.

30. The reshut is the subject of the second part of my book *The Gazelle,* which contains translations of 15 reshuyot with commentary.

31. Yonah David, *Shirei Yosef ibn Ṣadiq* (New York, 1982), 55–56.

32. Schirmann, *Ha-Shira ha-ʿIvrit,* 1: 186–87 (my translation).

33. Moses Maimonides, *The Guide of the Perplexed,* vol. 1 (Chicago, 1963), 7.

34. Translated by Menaḥem Mansoor as *The Book of Direction to the Duties of the Heart* (London, 1973). The usual rendering of the phrase in the title "the Duties of the Heart" derives not from the Arabic original but from the Hebrew translation by Judah ibn Tibbon (ca. 1120–ca. 1190), which tones down the rather provocative Arabic title. The Arabic word translated by Ibn Tibbon into Hebrew by the word *ḥovot* (duties) would be more accurately rendered by *mitzvot* (commandments).

35. See Goldreich, "Possible Arabic Sources."

36. Ignaz Goldziher, *Introduction to Islamic Theology and Law,* trans. Andras and Ruth Hamori (Princeton, N.J., 1981), 150–56.

37. R. P. Scheindlin, "Ibn Gabirol's Religious Poetry and Sufi Poetry," *Sefarad* 54 (1994): 109–42, and Scheindlin, "Old Age in Hebrew and Arabic Zuhd Poetry" (Madrid, in press).

38. Naftali Wieder, *Hashpaʿot Islamiyot ʿal ha-Pulḥan ha-Yehudi* (Oxford, 1946–47), 10–20.

39. Rabbi David ibn Abi Zimra (1479–1573) citing an opinion of Maimonides, as quoted by Wieder, *Hashpaʿot Islamiyot,* 28. No fewer than four extant responsa of Maimonides also deal with this matter.

40. Goitein, *A Mediterranean Society,* 5: 476.

41. Ibid., 2: 253; the story is told in full, with relevant documents, in ibid., 5: 470–74.

42. Ibid., 5: 361.

43. Ibid., 5: 358–72.

44. It is important to limit as much as possible the use of the word "secular" to describe nonliturgical poetry, because this word has caused no end of confusion in the literature on the subject. Much of the nonliturgical poetry is indeed worldly in its themes and attitudes, and it often treats religious themes lightly or irreverently. But in its serious modes, it is not systematically irreligious, freethinking, or anticlerical; indeed, it is often the vehicle for the exploration of serious religious problems.

45. See Nathan the Babylonian's report in Adolf Neubauer, *Mediaeval Jewish Chronicles and Chronological Notes,* vol. 2 (Oxford, 1895), 79, and Nisi Nahrawani in H. Schirmann, *Shirim hadashim min ha-geniza* (Jerusalem, 1965), 25.

46. I prefer to refer to this community as "the Jews of al-Andalus" rather than as "the Sephardim." Although medieval Jews used Sepharad as the term for the Iberian Peninsula, the modern word "Sephardim" usually refers to the diaspora created by the expulsion from Spain in 1492 and its immediate ancestors, the Jews of Christian Spain. Applying it to the Judeo-Arabic Jews of al-Andalus might create a wrong impression about the nature of the latter's culture.

47. Drory, *Reshit ha-maga'im*, 51–53.

48. Abraham ibn Daud in Gerson D. Cohen, ed., *A Critical Edition with a Translation and Notes of the Book of Tradition (Sefer ha-qabbalah) by Abraham ibn Daud* (Philadelphia, 1967), 102.

49. Monorhyme is one among many rhyming patterns of piyyut, but it is the exclusive rhyming pattern and one of the hallmarks of formal Arabic verse.

50. Benjamin Hrushovski, "Prosody, Hebrew," in *Encyclopaedia Judaica*, vol. 13, cols. 1195–1240.

51. Translation from R. P. Scheindlin, *Wine, Women, and Death: Medieval Hebrew Poems on the Good Life* (Philadelphia, 1986), 41; see also the discussion on 43–45.

52. Scheindlin, *Wine, Women, and Death*, 30. The theme of ambivalence toward Arabo-Islamic culture is adumbrated in my article "Rabbi Moshe ibn Ezra on the Legitimacy of Poetry," *Medievalia et Humanistica* n.s. 7 (1976): 101–15, and explored in full in Ross Brann, *The Compunctious Poet: Cultural Ambiguity and Hebrew Poetry in Muslim Spain* (Baltimore, Md., 1991).

53. Scheindlin, *Wine, Women, and Death*, 103; see also the discussion on 104–5.

54. The liturgical poem by Joseph ibn Zaddik quoted earlier in this chapter is in muwashshaḥ form.

55. The extremely complex matter of the relationship between Arabic and Romance strophic poetry is controversial, and it must be admitted that some specialists would take strong issue with this exposition. The strongest case for the interpretation presented here is made by María Rosa Menocal, *The Arabic Role in Medieval Literary History* (Philadelphia, 1987); see also Tova Rosen, "The Muwashshaḥ," in María R. Menocal, Raymond P. Scheindlin, and Michael Sells, eds., *The Literature of Al-Andalus* (Cambridge, Engl., 2000), 165–89.

56. "God of Might," in Schirmann, *Ha-Shira ha-Ivrit*, 1: 86–92 (my translation); see my fuller version in Olivia R. Constable, *Medieval Iberia: Readings from Christian, Muslim, and Jewish Sources* (Philadelphia, 1997), 84–90. A good selection of poems by Samuel the Nagid is available in Peter Cole, *Selected Poems of Shmuel HaNagid* (Princeton, N.J., 1996), and in Hillel Halkin, *Grand Things to Write a Poem On* (Jerusalem, 2000).

57. Scheindlin, *Wine, Women, and Death*, 152–53.

58. Schirmann, *Ha-Shira ha-Ivrit*, 1: 187–88 (my translation). For the rebellious character On, see Num. 16:1ff.

59. Moses ibn Ezra, *Dīwān*, vol. 1, ed. H. Brody (Berlin, 1938), 109–11; my translation is in S. Sperl and C. Shackle, *Qasida Poetry in Islamic Asia and Africa*, vol. 1 (Leiden, 1996), 125.

60. Schirmann, *Ha-Shira ha-Ivrit*, 1: 501–2 (my translation).

61. Schirmann, *Ha-Shira ha-Ivrit*, 2: 441–42; my translation is in "Hebrew Poetry in Medieval Iberia," in V. Mann, T. Glick, and J. Dodds, eds., *Convivencia: Jews, Muslims, and Christians in Medieval Spain* (New York, 1992), 39–59.

62. Schirmann, *Ha-Shira ha-Ivrit*, 2: 426; my translation in "Hebrew Poetry," 56.

63. Al-Ḥarizi, *Taḥkemoni*, 38–48; English translation in Reichert, *Taḥkemoni of Judah al-Ḥarizi*, 1: 69–82.

SELECTED BIBLIOGRAPHY

Brann, Ross. *The Compunctious Poet: Cultural Ambiguity and Hebrew Poetry in Muslim Spain.* Baltimore, Md., 1991.

Brody, Robert. *The Geonim of Babylonia and the Shaping of Medieval Jewish Culture.* New Haven, Conn., 1998.

Carmi, T. *The Penguin Book of Hebrew Verse.* New York, 1981.

Cohen, Gerson D. *A Critical Edition with a Translation and Notes of the Book of Tradition (Sefer ha-qabbalah) by Abraham ibn Daud.* Philadelphia, 1967.

Cohen, Mark. *Under Crescent and Cross: The Jews in the Middle Ages.* Princeton, N.J., 1994.

Cole, Peter. *Selected Poems of Shmuel HaNagid.* Princeton, N.J., 1996.

Frank, Daniel, and Oliver Leaman. *History of Jewish Philosophy.* London, 1996.

Goitein, Shelomo D. *Letters of Medieval Jewish Traders.* Princeton, N.J., 1973.

———. *A Mediterranean Society: The Jewish Communities of the Arab World as Portrayed in the Documents of the Cairo Genizah,* 6 vols. Berkeley, Calif., 1967–93.

Lewy, Hans, Alexander Altmann, and Isaak Heinemann. *Three Jewish Philosophers.* New York, 1969.

Menocal, María R., Raymond P. Scheindlin, and Michael Sells, eds. *The Literature of Al-Andalus.* Cambridge, Engl., 2000.

Pagis, Dan. *Hebrew Poetry of the Middle Ages and the Renaissance.* Berkeley, Calif., 1991.

Scheindlin, Raymond P. *The Gazelle: Medieval Hebrew Poems on God, Israel, and the Soul.* Philadelphia, 1991.

———. *Wine, Women and Death: Medieval Hebrew Poems on the Good Life.* Philadelphia, 1986.

Sirat, Colette. *A History of Jewish Philosophy in the Middle Ages.* Cambridge, Engl.; Paris, 1985.

Twersky, Isadore. *Introduction to the Code of Maimonides (Mishne Torah).* New Haven, Conn., 1980.

———. *A Maimonides Reader.* New York, 1972.

Weinberger, Leon J. *Twilight of a Golden Age: Selected Poems of Abraham ibn Ezra.* Tuscaloosa, Ala., 1997.

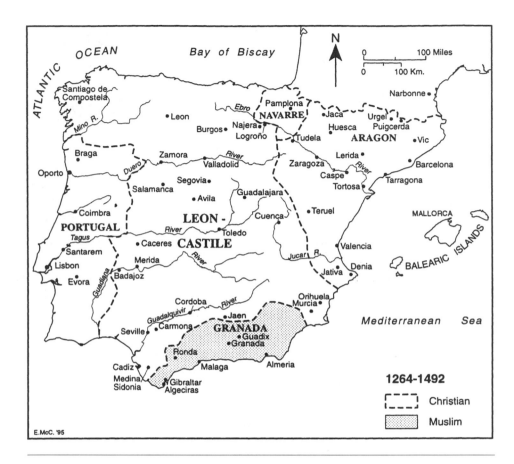

Map of the Iberian Peninsula, 1264–1492.
(From *Medieval Iberia: Readings from Christian, Muslim, and Jewish Sources*,
Olivia Remie Constable, ed., p. 238. Copyright © 1997 University of Pennsylvania Press.
Reprinted by permission.)

A LETTER TO
A WAYWARD TEACHER

The Transformations of
Sephardic Culture in Christian Iberia

BENJAMIN R. GAMPEL

In 1391 in Andalusia and other regions of Castile, and later on within the Crown of Aragon in Valencia, Aragon, and Catalonia, riots broke out against many of the Jewish communities. Jews were killed, their institutions were destroyed, and many Jews were forced to convert to Christianity. When the riots subsided, peninsular Jews and Christians became aware as well of the voluntary conversion to Christianity by many Castilian and Aragonese Jews. One of those converts was Solomon ha-Levi, who had served as rabbi in Burgos and now assumed the name Pablo de Santa María. Joshua ha-Lorki, a young man from the Aragonese town of Alcañiz, wrote an open letter to his former teacher, attempting to discern why ha-Levi, a scholar and leader of the Jewish community, had abandoned his faith for Christianity.[1] Joshua opened his missive as follows:

> After you received an epiphany so wondrous that the ears of all who heard of your discovery tingled with dread, my mind was restless and my heart neither slumbered nor slept. How could I bear to observe who led you to this experience and what motivated you to alter the order of Creation and to rage against us. I reflected to myself that your experience can only be understood within the following analytical categories.

Determined to explore the reasons for ha-Levi's conversion, ha-Lorki proposed four possible motivations. Contemporary chroniclers of Sephardic culture who also wish to analyze why Jews of ha-Levi's generation decided "to alter the order of Creation" would do well to follow ha-Lorki's lead. But the letter can also help us to trace the contours of Sephardic civilization under Christian rule from its very beginnings, when Iberian Jews transformed the culture that they had inherited from their predecessors in Muslim al-Andalus. And, coming at the turning point of 1391, ha-Lorki's letter points ahead to the next century, which ended in the great wave of expulsions from Castile, Aragon, Portugal, and Navarre.

By puzzling over the roots of the behavior of Castilian and Aragonese Jews at this critical juncture, some writers have inadvertently suggested that the history of these Jews under Christian rule led inexorably toward the mass conversion of the late fourteenth century.[2] Indeed, emphasis on the conversions and later expulsions can prevent us from fully appreciating the contours of their lives under peninsular Christianity. Nevertheless, I propose not to avoid concentrating on the events of 1391 but purposefully to use that year as a vantage point from which to look forward to the denouement of the Iberian Jewish communities and backward at the growth of these communities within the medieval Christian kingdoms. It would be willful pretension to imagine that we can reflect upon Sephardic Jewry in Christian Iberia and not let the knowledge of what transpired in the late fourteenth and fifteenth centuries impinge upon our consciousness and influence our reading and interpretation of their culture. So long as we remember that conversion was not their fate from their early years under Christianity or even in the months immediately prior to 1391, probing the response of the Jews in that fateful year affords an effective and convenient means to survey the rich texture of their culture.

The Jews of Iberia first confronted the Christian faith and its adherents when some of the inhabitants of the Roman Empire became Christianized in late antiquity. When the Christian Visigoths who had conquered the Roman provinces of Iberia were themselves defeated by the Muslims in 711, most Jews remained within the broad expanses of the peninsula that fell under Islamic control. Few if any joined the defeated Christians who retreated to the fastnesses of the mountain chains to the north. During the eleventh century, when the Christians began to make significant inroads against Muslim hegemony, an increasing number of Jews came to live in regions dominated by the new rulers. By the middle of the thirteenth century, when the Christians could boast of almost complete military success, the overwhelming majority of Iberian Jews lived within the kingdoms of Castile, Aragon, Portugal, and Navarre.

During the heyday of the *reconquista*—as the victors christened their military triumphs—peninsular Jews identified themselves as Sephardim after the verse in the biblical book of Obadiah that spoke of "the exiles of Jerusalem who are in Sepharad."[3] Already in the tenth century, under Islamic sovereignty, Iberian Jews had viewed themselves as "exiles of Jerusalem"—that is, as the nobility of the

Jewish people who, when their ancient kingdom had been destroyed, left their capital city and created a new homeland in the far western corner of the Mediterranean. These Sephardim, now living in a territory that was the south-westernmost appendage of Christian European civilization, not only drew upon the culture they had created under Islamic rule but were also receptive to both Jewish and Christian ideas arriving from the north. As a result, a new Sephardic civilization emerged on peninsular soil and was expressed in works of mysticism and pietism, in commentaries on the Talmud and the Bible, in polemics against Christianity, in poetry, and in philosophical reflections.

HEDONISTIC TEMPTATIONS

Ha-Lorki began his four-pronged investigation with the following suggestion:

> Perhaps your appetitive soul longed to climb the rungs of wealth and honor which everyone desires and to satisfy the craving soul with all manner of food and to gaze at the resplendent beauty of the countenance of gentile women.

Ha-Lorki challenged ha-Levi, asking whether his decision to convert had been motivated by materialistic or opportunistic considerations. If he imagined that the answer would be affirmative, he would have had no reason to probe further. But for students of Sephardic culture, this is an argument that cannot easily be dismissed. Were Sephardic Jews so content with the material success they had enjoyed during the years of Christian rule that their fear of losing this comfortable existence, to the exclusion of all other considerations, led them to the baptismal font? Simply put, did they convert to enjoy the good life?

To answer this question, we first need to see if opportunistic considerations were an integral aspect of Sephardic culture from its early days within the emerging Christian kingdoms. Although the Jews living in the areas of Christian control during the early years of the reconquista did enjoy a measure of material well-being, they wondered whether the civilization they had fashioned in Muslim-dominated al-Andalus could thrive in the Christian-dominated areas of the peninsula. They had lived under the protection of the Umayyad caliphs, and their symbiotic relationship with Islam had allowed for the efflorescence of a brilliant Andalusian Jewish culture starting in the tenth century. But the situation in the Muslim south had changed. Almoravids, Berber tribes from North Africa who had been invited by local Muslims to help combat the growing Christian strength on the peninsula at the end of the eleventh century, displayed

much harsher attitudes toward the *dhimmī* population (the protected minorities, mainly Jews and Christians) than those of their Umayyad predecessors, who were devoted to building a multiethnic and multireligious society.
With the assumption of power by Almoravids, some Jews, under pressure by the
new government, converted to Islam. Caught between resurgent Christian kingdoms to the north and the increasingly hostile Muslims in the south, Sephardic
Jews struggled to develop a new cultural synthesis. The lives of a few Jewish
intellectuals—two of whom were introduced in the previous chapter—will shed
light on this larger struggle.

One of the avatars of the Muslim-Jewish symbiosis, whose writings incorporated sophisticated notions about the educational curriculum essential for
the development of a well-rounded Sephardic intellectual, was Moses ibn Ezra.
Born into an aristocratic family in the mid-eleventh century, Ibn Ezra enjoyed
a first-rate Andalusi Jewish education. After the entry of Almoravids into his
hometown of Granada (a major locus of Sephardic culture in the Muslim
south), he left the city and, like many other Jews at that time, wandered about
the peninsula and sojourned in lands controlled by the Christians. His poetry,
written while he lived in Christian Iberia, was filled with longing for Granada
and for his beloved Andalusi Jewish culture. He likened his existence in the
Christian north to living among the tongue-tied, surrounded by those who did
not share or even appreciate the cultural values that were the inheritance of the
wealthy Jewish intellectuals under peninsular Islam.[4]

Judah Halevi, one of the most well known of medieval Jewish poets, was a
protégé of Ibn Ezra, and, though born in the north in Muslim Tudela around
1075, studied in the important southern centers of Jewish learning. He too left
Granada, probably in 1090, and traveled. But, unlike Ibn Ezra, Halevi took great
advantage of the emerging Christian states to the north and worked for them as a
diplomat and courtier. He was socially and intellectually flexible enough to realize the potential for the survival of Sephardic culture under Christian political
domination. Yet, in his middle age, he traveled south to the homeland of Sephardic culture and set sail for Alexandria on his way to fulfill a personal religious
pilgrimage to the Land of Israel. Halevi's decision was not a rejection of the potential of an economically successful and politically secure Jewish life in the
Christian north; instead, it was a reflection of a more far-reaching negation of the
symbiosis with Islamic culture that had been the hallmark of Sephardic Judaism.[5]

This was decidedly not the perspective of Abraham ibn Daud. Born in the
early twelfth century in Córdoba (where Andalusian Jewish culture had first
emerged), he settled in the city of Toledo, which was the royal city of the ancient
Visigoths and was also regarded as the capital of the rapidly expanding kingdom

of Castile. Unlike Judah Halevi, Ibn Daud expressed himself in the idiom of Sephardic culture and defended its intellectual orientation, arguing for the continued primacy of its religious values within the Jewish world. He maintained that Jews could thrive in the new atmosphere, contending that their political status was secure under the protective eye of God and his agents, the Christian political leaders. What further comforted Ibn Daud was that the representatives of the Jewish community, the courtier class, were now safely ensconced in the corridors of power under Christendom just as they had been well established in the Islamic south.[6]

Like Ibn Daud, most Iberian Jews made their way north even as Christian domination of the peninsula extended southward. Indeed, by the mid-thirteenth century, the Crowns of Portugal, Castile, Navarre, and Aragon controlled most of the peninsula, and the Muslims had been restricted to their capital city of Granada and the surrounding area. For many Jews, the move to the north was the choice of the good life. While Maimon the judge was preparing to abandon Muslim Córdoba and travel across the Straits of Gibraltar to Morocco with his family and his soon-to-be-famous young son Moses, wealth and honor were the lot of the growing Jewish courtier class in the new Christian kingdoms. And what grand opportunities were available. Jews had become a prized commodity, needed by the Christian monarchs to help them stabilize and populate the newly conquered cities and to provide a ready-made merchant and artisan class within a mainly agricultural society. The Jews, trained in financial administration under Islam, were able to offer these very skills. At the beginning of the reign of Alfonso X the Learned of Castile, Jewish courtiers rose to important positions within the royal government. Moreover, during the thirteenth century in the Crown of Aragon—which grew to include the kingdoms of Aragon, Catalonia, and Valencia as well as parts of southern France and the Italian littoral—Jews occupied significant positions within the royal treasury and the chancellery. They were well respected in the diplomatic arena because of their ability to communicate, both orally and in writing, with the Muslims in Arabic.[7]

Indeed, one of the striking aspects of Sephardic civilization in the Christian period is the degree to which Jews continued to be positively disposed toward Islamic culture. Social and economic relations existed between Jews and Muslims in Christian Iberia, and Arabic food, songs, and decorative designs were part of Jewish households.[8] Our own correspondent Joshua ha-Lorki wrote fluently in Arabic. Even as late as 1482, Jews served as Arabic interpreters to Ferdinand and Isabella upon the fall of Málaga to the Christian forces.

Jews played a crucial role in the court life of the two large Christian kingdoms and were integral to the formation of culture in these emerging societies. Their presence both within the court and on the land was an essential part of the character of these kingdoms, and their lives at times reflected the local mores. Over a century later, in asking the erstwhile Solomon whether his life was governed by hedonistic principles, ha-Lorki first singled out wealth and honor, the commodities enjoyed by many courtiers in Christian territory.

There were built-in stresses in the relationship between the courtier class and other Sephardic Jews, most evident in the dealings that the royal advisers had with leaders of the Jewish community. These tensions, already observable in al-Andalus, can be documented in Christian Iberia up through the last decade of the fifteenth century. From the days of the centralizing Umayyad caliph Abd al-Raḥmān III (early tenth century), who encouraged individuals of all ethnic and religious backgrounds to participate in the creation and functioning of the Andalusian state, the highest-ranking Jew within the administration became the de facto head of the Jewish community and its representative at court. It was the courtier's accomplishments—social, intellectual, diplomatic—that had recommended him to the ruler, attributes that allowed him to rise within the administration. It was not necessarily his attachment to the Jewish community or his adherence to forms of rabbinic Judaism that had brought this individual into the highest councils of state. The Jews and their own chosen leaders had no choice but to rely upon "their man" at court. Although they were relieved to have a Jew at court attending to their concerns, his public lifestyle, which may have been at odds with the behavioral norms prescribed by communal leaders, underscored their worries about how sensitive this individual would be to them, their priorities, and their agenda. And though the courtier was honored by his position, he was loath to be subject not only to the religious principles of the Jewish community but especially to its financial burdens. The courtier often used his status in governmental circles to avoid such responsibilities, even while he was seen as protector of the rights of those communities themselves.[9]

The tensions that prevailed between the leaders of local Jewish communities (not to mention the moralists and rabbinic spokesmen) and the courtier class (usually allied with royal or seigneurial authorities) often erupted into outright hostility. In the writings of the pietist and preacher Jonah Gerondi (d. 1263) and his kinsman the great talmudist, kabbalist, and biblical exegete Moses ben Naḥman of Gerona (known as Naḥmanides, d. 1270), unconcealed anger is expressed at those aristocrats who did not follow the dictates of Jewish law and were overbearing in their use of power. Driven by their ideals and linked with a growing merchant class, influential individuals such as Naḥmanides and Gerondi hoped to engineer a revolt among Barcelonan Jewry in the 1230s, disrupting the rule of courtiers whose authority had been inherited from earlier times.[10]

The ark wall of the synagogue in
Córdoba, Spain, 1314–15.
(Photo: Nicholas Sapieha; courtesy
The Jewish Museum, New York)

A page from the "Sarajevo" Haggadah, a
fourteenth-century Sephardic manuscript,
which is in the National Museum of
Sarajevo in Sarajevo, Bosnia-Herzegovina

It would, however, be misleading to suggest that only the Jewish "aristocracy" benefited from the economic opportunities that developed in the wake of the Christian victories in the thirteenth century. Indeed, the posture of the Jews in the communities of the peninsula reflected the stance of their Christian (and Muslim) neighbors in a number of important respects. In the few items of material culture that have survived from the Sephardic Middle Ages—in the architecture of the synagogues and in the style of rare ceramic objects—the integration of the Jews into Iberian society seems complete, even as these ritual items and spaces reflect Jewish cultural concerns. For example, the Jewish illuminator of a Passover haggadah in fourteenth-century Catalonia included illustrations of noble coats of arms and the armorial bearings of the Crown of Aragon in his depiction of a fortress that dominates an early and significant page of this work. The meaning of the term *convivencia*—the living together of the three faith communities on the Iberian Peninsula—is precisely that the Jews were engaged daily with Christians and Muslims of many different classes and understandably shared some of their values.[11]

There were at least two voices that spoke to medieval Sephardic Jews in their daily lives. One voice warned its listeners about the damage to their Jewish principles if they followed the norms of their non-Jewish neighbors, even as the other voice counseled them—if they needed such advice—that it would be advantageous, if not easier, to comport themselves according to the values of their environment. As early as the tenth century, the poet Dunash ibn Labrat had written of the tension that resulted from the conflict between a life extolling the senses and celebrating the pleasures of the material world and a life following the laws of Judaism, whose sources, both geographical and cultural, lay far from the soil of al-Andalus.[12]

Whether rabbis or laymen, all Sephardic Jews lived within the confines of an elaborate communal system. True, the courtiers, and the wealthy class generally, sought to avoid its rules and its financial demands. But the Jewish community was the organ that controlled behavior and provided services for its members, and it was the channel through which the Jews as a group related to all levels of Christian government—royal, noble, ecclesiastical, and municipal. Communal organization existed in almost all locales of Jewish population; it was known in Hebrew as the *kahal* and in the various Iberian vernaculars as the *aljama, alhama,* or *call.* The court of Jewish law was the central institution within these communities and was empowered to adjudicate most disputes among its members.

Their involvement in the daily lives of their non-Jewish neighbors, however, required a balance between fealty to the community and the demands and benefits of Christian Iberian society. As was true for the communities in Ashkenaz and elsewhere in Christendom, many Sephardim turned to the Christian judicial system if they felt that their case would be heard either more favorably or in a more timely fashion. Any Jew with sufficient economic resources could attend to the royal, municipal, or noble courts for satisfaction of his claims. The rabbis fulminated against the usurpation by the Christian courts of the place of Jewish law within the kahal but realized that they could not prevent any Jew from attending to civil legal needs elsewhere.

The Jewish community distinguished between what it maintained was its authority in ritual and family law and what it conceded fell within the purview of the Christian society—such as the enforcement of law and order and the protection of the financial prerogatives of the various governmental bodies. Although Christian society did not necessarily need the Jews to support its jurisdictional claims, Sephardic Jews applied the talmudic dictum "the law of the kingdom is law" to acknowledge to their own community their willingness to follow the requirements of the Christian legal system. The Jews always tempered their demands for greater legal autonomy by critically appraising the extent of their power and influence among the Christians.[13]

Although clearly identified as members of their own community in Christian Iberia, Sephardim worked both within and without the Jewish legal system. These relatively fluid relations with the surrounding society were also reflected in their sexual activities. Indeed, the sexual proclivities of the Jewish courtier do appear to mirror those of others who inhabited the court. To gaze into the countenance of gentile women, in ha-Lorki's felicitous phrase, was a part of the lives of some of those who pursued wealth and honor, at the very least in the fantasies of some observers.

When Moses of Coucy visited the peninsula from France in 1236, he denounced the sexual practices of the Sephardic Jews as akin to idol worship: "You have thus learned that he who has sexual intercourse with a gentile woman is considered as if he were married to idolatry."[14] Moses later imagined his influence to be equivalent to that of the biblical Ezra, boasting that, in the wake of his sermons, his Sephardic listeners had sent away their foreign wives.[15]

Foreigners were not the only ones dismayed by the sexual mores of Sephardic Jews. The native, albeit Ashkenaz-influenced, Jonah Gerondi was much upset with the practice, left over from Islamic times, of taking concubines—usually Muslim women—without regard for religious niceties or legalities. Naḥmanides, though in many ways a devotee of similar moral strictures, recognized the halakhic permissibility of concubinage and argued that such a practice was a preferred way for a Jewish man to satisfy his sexual needs. Menaḥem ben Zerah, whose family left royal France for the peninsula with the expulsion of 1306, acknowledged the extent of concubinage in his newly adopted culture. Agreeing with Naḥmanides, he suggested in *Tzeidah la-Derekh,* his vade mecum for courtiers, that singling out one woman as a concubine was less objectionable than sexually indiscriminate behavior.[16] In 1281, the Jewish community of Toledo issued a *ḥerem* (ban) that attempted to control sexual promiscuity and especially frowned upon the possession of non-Jewish concubines, but there is little evidence that such limitations enjoyed any success.

Another, more fundamental distinction between Sephardic and Ashkenazic attitudes concerning relations between the sexes can be observed in their stances toward polygamy. The Jews of northern Europe followed their Christian neighbors in not taking a second wife. Yet this practice of monogamy, which was established within the Jewish community allegedly as the result of a ban on polygamy by the early Ashkenazic scholar Gershom of Mainz, was not accepted by Jews within Iberian lands. Having been fashioned in Islamic al-Andalus, Sephardic culture had little difficulty tolerating the taking of more than one wife. The Crown of Aragon, however, maintained stricter laws against polygamy than rulers elsewhere on the peninsula, and those who wished to acquire a second wife had to appeal to the royal authorities for dispensation, as did Ḥasdai Crescas at the end of the fourteenth century.[17]

Still, the writings of the courtier poets and communal preachers within Sepharad itself suggest a real tension between sexual license and restraint. When the thirteenth-century poet Todros ben Judah ha-Levi Abulafia described the lives of the Jewish courtiers, he wrote openly of their amorous activities. Todros, whose poetry exhibits a measure of realism about sexual life as well as a degree of lustfulness not even found in the love poetry of al-Andalus, was consciously aware of his irreverent stance toward traditional values. But when the preacher Todros ben Joseph ha-Levi Abulafia, the poet's namesake, denounced immoral behavior, even Todros ben Judah agreed and composed confessional poetry lamenting the lifestyle and values of his social class.[18]

There is much evidence that Todros's poems reflect actual sexual behavior and were not simply contemporary literary conventions. Nevertheless, we remain in the dark about what this evidence tells us about the lives of Jewish women in Christian Iberian lands. The tradition of misogynist literature prevalent in al-Andalus during the Muslim period also found expression among the Jewish writers in the Christian kingdoms and testifies to the manipulation of these standard literary forms in a new environment. The existence of such a genre tells us that Jewish literary culture allowed for such negative views of women, but it teaches us little about actual relations between men and women.[19]

When ha-Lorki suggested that perhaps Solomon ha-Levi yearned to have sexual relations with non-Jewish women, he was alluding to an attraction that was already acknowledged in the culture. But it was not only Eros in human relations that preoccupied Jews of Sepharad. By the time ha-Lorki wrote his letter to ha-Levi, Iberian Jewish culture had been developing a mystical doctrine of divine love for nearly two centuries. Rather than gaze at "the resplendent beauty of the countenance of gentile women," the kabbalists (as the disciples of this movement that emerged in southern France and Spain in the early thirteenth century came to be known) desired to "behold the beauty of the Lord" (Psalms 27:4) in the form of the feminine aspect of the Deity, the *shekhinah.*

These mystics believed that the human body and its sexual functions could serve as metaphors regarding relationships within the divine realm and that sexual acts were capable of augmenting God's holiness. One early-fourteenth-century Sephardic kabbalist expressed a positive disposition to the sexual act and was excited by the implications of preferred sexual behavior for harmony in the divine realms. The author of this influential "Holy Letter" attempted to regulate many aspects of intercourse between husband and wife as well as to guide the intention of the participants so that their sexual congress would truly be "for the sake of heaven." The greatest work of Sephardic Kabbalah in the Middle

Ages, the *Zohar* (The Book of Splendor), also devoted much effort to the exploration of the sexual relationships between the masculine and feminine aspects of the Deity. According to the *Zohar,* after the soul dies, it frequents the shekhinah, which the text refers to as a "chamber of love." But the *Zohar's* compiler and author, Moses de Leon, was nevertheless ambivalent about the pleasure to be derived from the act itself. Like other Jewish writers of his time, he fulminated against sex with non-Jewish women and was much perturbed by the keeping of Muslim concubines by Jews.[20]

No, ha-Lorki told his mentor, you did not seek to bask in the countenance of alien women; rather, you were careful to observe all the commandments. But gazing into the countenance of the shekhinah did have a profound impact not only on the reasoning offered for a variety of halakhic practices but also, over time, on the nature of the observance of some Jewish laws and rituals. Many observations and discussions of Jewish law—some of Sephardic provenance and others from outside the peninsula—were current in Iberia during the thirteenth century and can be found in the *Zohar*. Although The Book of Splendor was fundamentally a work of mystical thought, it was soon reckoned with by those who saw themselves as expositors of Jewish law.[21]

Even though Sephardic rabbinic culture fostered creativity in a wide variety of disciplines, ranging from biblical and talmudic exegesis to poetry, philosophy, and Kabbalah, halakhic (legal) preoccupations were central. Ha-Lorki, dismissing the possibility that his teacher was seduced by either wealth or women, notes ha-Levi's passion for the law:

> You were always shoring up breaches in the faith, being punctilious with the commandments and their performance, never doubting any of its principles, or being lax in any of its particulars or preventative restrictions as is appropriate behavior for anyone who takes religion seriously.

Rabbinic learning in Sepharad—both in its Andalusi and northern Christian manifestations—was the patrimony of an elite upper stratum within Jewish society, and Solomon ha-Levi was a member of this caste. He shared the assumptions of that culture by demonstrating his concern with the details of Jewish law. Ha-Levi's faithfulness regarding the performance of these obligations proved to his correspondent that the erstwhile Solomon had been sincerely attached to Jewish tradition and to the Jewish community. Moreover, for ha-Lorki, ha-Levi's devotion to the law stood as a refutation of other writers' denunciations of the lax behavior of the courtier class. Here, at least, was one Jewish leader who remained punctilious in his observance.

Moralists had been concerned for many years about the attachment of

A page from *Tur Orah Hayyim* by Jacob ben Asher.
(Library of the Jewish Theological Seminary of America,
New York; Mayer Sulzberger Collection. Photo: Suzanne Kaufman)

Iberian Jews to the *mitzvot* (commandments). When Moses of Coucy, who denounced the lax sexual morality of the Sephardic Jews, arrived on the peninsula in 1236, he also spoke of the neglect of the daily donning of phylacteries and of the placement of *mezuzot* on doorposts (as he had in other locales in Northern Europe). His denunciations, as well as the fulminations of an Iberian-born yet north-European-educated and -influenced moralist like Gerondi, are ample testimony to the halakhic and pietistic ideas that blew in from Ashkenazic lands, but they reveal little of the actual behavioral patterns of Iberian Jews. Although we may never know about their daily religious lives with any certainty, there are some indications that, for those not in the rabbinic elite, the law was also of central importance: the *Sefer ha-Ḥinukh,* an attempt to tease out the 613 principal commandments from the Pentateuch, probably written by a Catalonian scholar in the latter part of the thirteenth century, was wildly popular in Sepharad.[22]

Interest in halakhic matters resulted in a prodigious literary output that was already visible from the early days of the transition of Sephardic culture from its southern Andalus ambience to the Christian north. The main focus of Talmud study in al-Andalus, as for other Jewish communities living within the orbit of Islam, was the extraction of the practical halakhic relevance from those rabbinic writings. After an understandable lull, as Andalusi Jewry gradually made its way to Christian-dominated lands within the peninsula, there was a remarkable outpouring of Sephardic legal writings and talmudic commentaries from the end of the twelfth through the end of the fourteenth centuries. Within the Sephardic communities, a rabbinically learned Jew, *talmid ḥakham,* was a halakhic decisor. Law was central to Sephardic culture, even if those who administered the local Jewish courts were not as well versed in the correct interpretations of the legal materials as the leading rabbinic authorities on the peninsula would have liked.[23]

Over the course of the thirteenth century, there was an observable shift in the study of Talmud, from a stress on practical halakhah to an emphasis on exegesis itself. This process was precisely the reverse of what occurred in the Ashkenazic Jewish communities to the north, where the energy that had long been devoted to talmudic commentary was now directed to practical legal matters. The mutual influence of Ashkenaz and Sepharad is instructive; these two civilizations were not isolated from each other. Not only did Moses of Coucy arrive in Sepharad endowed with his Ashkenazic ideology, but Jonah Gerondi also transmitted the theology of the medieval Ashkenazic pietists to his native Iberia. The Sephardic culture that emerged and developed in the thirteenth century was no less influenced by the creativity of the Jewish communities to the north than it was by the civilization of al-Andalus.

In the early years of the fourteenth century, Asher ben Yeḥiel left war-torn Ashkenaz, where he was a student of the towering halakhic authority Meir of Rothenburg and where he had himself assumed a respected position after his teacher's death. He traveled through southern France in 1303 and arrived the following year in Barcelona, where he spent some days with the great Catalonian talmudist, Solomon ibn Adret. The latter provided him with a personal letter of reference, and in 1305 Rabbi Asher arrived in Toledo, Castile, where he was able to secure an important position.

Asher's rabbinate was distinguished by his loyalty to the teachings of his Ashkenazic teachers and to their communal traditions. But his position within the Sephardic communities influenced his halakhic thinking, even as his legal decisions affected Iberian Jews in their daily lives. Asher found himself reluctantly agreeing to the Sephardic practice of sentencing to death those who, according to the leaders of the Jewish community, had jeopardized the security of the Jewish population. Despite halakhah, he even urged disfigurement as punishment for a widow suspected of having been impregnated by her Muslim lover. He hoped that this decision would help restore the political and religious boundaries that were threatened by the woman's social and sexual behavior. More profoundly for the history of halakhah, Asher—according to Sephardic practice—began to collect and file his legal decisions. This systematization of law reflected developments in contemporary Spanish culture, for it was in the Castilian royal court of Alfonso X that the compilation of legal tradition and practice entitled Las Siete Partidas was composed.[24] Asher's *responsa* were edited by his son Jacob, who had lived in Sepharad for a couple of decades and had preceded his father to Toledo. Jacob's edition of his father's decisions formed the basis for his own *Tur Shulḥan Arukh*, a milestone in the codification of Jewish jurisprudence.[25]

The presence of Ashkenazic ideas in Sepharad was not always as obvious as in the immigration of Asher. The pietistic philosophy of Ḥasidei Ashkenaz had a profound impact on the moralistic tracts written by Sephardic Jews, just as Ashkenazic modes of Talmud commentaries developed by the Tosafistic school revolutionized the methodology of talmudic exegesis practiced by Sephardic scholars. Indeed, the greatest refinement of this dialectical style and its most coherent literary expression can be found in the talmudic commentaries of the Sephardic scholars Naḥmanides and Ibn Adret.

After raising sheer opportunism as a motivation for ha-Levi's conversion, ha-Lorki discounted this possibility as a serious factor and recalled an encounter with ha-Levi at the wedding of a friend:

And ever since the time that I was eagerly drinking your waters when you made your servant one of those who ate at your table, I knew of your comings and goings and I saw in you the intensity of desire, for speculative discourse and for essential truths, and you held back from the pursuit of great deeds and wondrous things. Indeed let me remind your honor about the time I went there to the wedding of your friend Don Meir Benveniste, when you began to occupy yourself with matters of state and you had acquired for yourself a chariot, horses, and runners to do your bidding, you stated privately to me: "I regret that I have subjected myself to the rule of these seeming successes, for they are vanity and works of delusion. They produce nothing but sorrow of heart. If only I could have back as my own that garret where my tent was pitched in those early years and where I spent day and night in diligent study." This was the gist of what you said—rightly—and such expressions were frequently heard from you.

Many Iberian Jews did indeed enjoy the good life, and the courtiers among them probably delighted in these pleasures more than most. But for ha-Lorki such satisfactions did not necessarily lead to legal laxity. Although he seems a bit naive in believing the professions of ha-Levi that he would have forfeited all his worldly success for the garret room where he had spent his youthful days reflecting on religious issues of great moment, ha-Lorki did not view the courtier lifestyle enjoyed by ha-Levi as essentially antagonistic to a life of restraint that entailed the scrupulous observance of the minutiae of halakhah.

PHILOSOPHICAL SEDUCTIONS

Philosophy and Kabbalah, like their literary precursors within the Jewish tradition such as aggadah, served to provide both the motivation and the spiritual underpinning for the practical life that the dictates of rabbinic Judaism ordained. Indeed, the public dissemination of kabbalistic ideas may well have been a response to the rationalists' claim that it was philosophical ideas that contained the secrets of the Torah. But for ha-Lorki as for many others during the Middle Ages, philosophy was seen as an unreliable ally in the goal of persuading the Jews to follow the halakhah and to be loyal to rabbinic Judaism. Ha-Lorki conjectured:

> Or perhaps you were seduced by philosophical inquiry to overturn the bowl and to consider the underpinnings of all faiths to be vanity and works of delusion and so you turned to a religion more conducive to bodily calm and to peace of mind and not accompanied by terrors and fear and dread.

It was not that philosophy led the Jews directly to the baptismal font. Far from making such an assertion, ha-Lorki wondered whether such inquiry weakened the Jews' attachment to the principles of Judaism as well as to those of all other (monotheistic) faiths and lured the Jews to pursue a life more attuned to bodily and spiritual comfort.

Whether philosophical investigation was the acme of the educated Jews' curriculum or at best an uneasy if not treacherous bedfellow in the rabbis' attempt to enforce normative behavior was the subject of intense discussion and even conflict from the very beginning of Sephardic culture. When the Christians were achieving notable success in their military campaigns against the Muslim *taifa* (small states controlled by "party-kings") in the late eleventh century, Moses ibn Ezra feared that the fructifying cultural and social symbiosis enjoyed by the Jews and Muslims in al-Andalus could not easily be transferred to the north. It was the pursuit of philosophical truths that was considered the most praiseworthy intellectual activity in this culture. Indeed, possession of the specialized knowledge born of such inquiry indicated more than anything else that its bearer was a cultured gentleman.

But Ibn Ezra's protégé Judah Halevi asserted that, though philosophy may have at times provided the Jews with a defense of their faith, especially in their encounter with the dominant Islamic culture, it also weakened the attachment to truths that were only in the possession of Judaism. In Halevi's view, echoed over two centuries later by ha-Lorki, such study bred the conviction that the pillars of any inherited faith were not as important as rigorous philosophical inquiry. For Halevi, religions were dissimilar not only in their possession of the truth but also in the ability of their adherents to perceive it. Not all lands were equally conducive to its pursuit, nor were all languages equal to the task of explication. The irony of it all was that Halevi composed his seemingly anti-philosophical treatise, the *Kuzari,* in Arabic, the language of philosophical inquiry for the Andalusi intellectual. Indeed, this work, which was born in a culture known for having raised the systematic study of philosophy to its most exalted form, marked but a new speculative trend.[26]

Philosophical skepticism, according to Halevi, was as threatening to the well-being of the Jewish people as was the belief of many that they could find a comfortable home in *galut,* in any Jewish community outside the Land of Israel. Jewish high society came under Halevi's censure because he believed that the members of this elite, in their attempt to enjoy the benefits of their Andalusi life, were not concerned with particular religious observances, even as they celebrated philosophy. In this sense, the attractions of philosophy, which ha-Lorki suggested as the second possible motivation for the conversion of Solomon ha-Levi, were only an extension of his first argument from hedonism.

With the shift of the Jewish community to the Christian lands, philosophy could no longer be described simply as the most important discipline of Jewish learning. Rather, the conflict over the rightful place of philosophy within the curriculum assumed a central role in the definition of Jewish culture. Abraham ibn Daud, schooled in Andalusian Jewish culture (as was Judah Halevi), hoped that this culture could survive intact its translation to the north. Contrary to Halevi, Ibn Daud maintained that Sephardic culture was still in its prime. Toledo could become the new Córdoba, and philosophical speculation might

still remain a bulwark for the observance of Judaic precepts. Ibn Daud's philosophical magnum opus, *Exalted Faith*, was the first serious attempt to synthesize
Judaism with a mix of Neoplatonism and Aristotelianism (only to be eclipsed by
a far more celebrated work, *Guide of the Perplexed*, by the Córdoba-born Moses
Maimonides, written sometime between 1185 and 1190). *Exalted Faith* was not
only a brave work methodologically but also a triumphant proclamation that
the philosophical curriculum embraced by the Jews of al-Andalus was now
thriving on the Christian side of the divided peninsula.

But Ibn Daud only represented one trend in the intellectual world of the
Sephardim. As Sephardic culture migrated north, it underwent significant
changes, not the least of which was increasing resistance to philosophy, a trend
that found expression in emerging opposition to Maimonides' attempt to wed
Aristotle to Judaism. Judah Halevi was not the only one to reject philosophy as a
threat to traditional religious and social values. Writing from Toledo in the early
years of the thirteenth century, Meir ha-Levi Abulafia perceived Maimonides'
spiritual interpretation of resurrection, in its reflection of a rigid dualism between body and soul and in its tendency to value natural causation over divine
intervention and omnipotence, as a break with some of the fundamental principles of Judaism.[27] The quarrel that ensued over Abulafia's critique was a preview
of the dispute that erupted among Jewish intellectuals in Sepharad, Provence,
and Ashkenaz in the 1230s. Underscoring the change in Sephardic Judaism and
its values, the "Maimonidean controversy" indicated that Sephardic Jewry was
now linked with European Jewish civilization. Writings born of the Muslim-
Jewish symbiosis and the resultant philosophical tradition were destined to be
unsettling to those operating with other cultural assumptions. Some Provençal
scholars feared that, because *Guide of the Perplexed* and the philosophical prole-
gomena to Maimonides' halakhic work, *Mishneh Torah*, attempted to offer a rational basis for all the commandments, commitment to those very precepts
would be undermined. They sent a Sephard intellectual, Jonah Gerondi, who
had studied with the Tosafists of northern France and was then sojourning in
Provence, to elicit support within Sepharad for their anti-Maimonidean campaign. Those in Provence who were offended by this initiative placed these anti-
Maimunists themselves under a ban.[28] The controversy raged on, spreading
north to Ashkenaz as well as to the Iberian Peninsula.

Anti-philosophical positions had been articulated in Sephardic culture under Islam, but the positive valence of philosophical studies was never seriously
questioned. When the Provençal pro-Maimunists chose David Kimḥi to rally
approval among the Iberian Jewish communities for a ban against the anti-
Maimunists, he achieved mixed success in Barcelona but, strikingly, encoun-

tered a deadlocked community in Toledo. Naḥmanides attempted to broker a peace accord by explaining the pro-Maimonidean position to the northern French scholars and attempting to persuade the Sephardic rationalists not to react immediately and enter the fray against the Provençal anti-Maimunists. Abulafia, who earlier had been marginalized by many of the rationalists during the controversy over resurrection, wrote to Naḥmanides about the ultimate futility of his (Abulafia's) own efforts. The debate, however, was abruptly curtailed. Pro-Maimunists asserted that the anti-Maimunists had involved the Dominicans and the newly founded papal Inquisition in Montpellier in this conflict over heresy within the Jewish community. Although there is no independent confirmation of this allegation, the controversy did come to a halt without any attempt to arrive at a reasonable solution.[29]

The Maimonidean controversy signaled both the demise of the Jewish-Andalusian civilization born within the orbit of Islam and the emergence of a new Sephardic culture. Not that the opponents to rationalism in Sepharad were of one mind with either their allies in Provence or the Tosafists, their supporters in northern France. Andalusi traditions did live on in their writings. Unlike their Tosafist brethren, these Sephardim asserted the permissibility of philosophical study and approved of the rationalist ideas in Maimonides' *Sefer ha-Madda* even as they were uncomfortable with some of the implications of the *Guide of the Perplexed*. They merely wished to counter the radical excesses of the rationalist position. Naḥmanides, for instance, presented a modified antirationalist position, suggesting that philosophy only be studied by an elite group of students. He often utilized Maimonides' historical explanations in his own biblical commentary and was sympathetic to Maimonides' critique of rabbinic literature when the ideas of the rabbis ran contrary to reason. Yet when Naḥmanides was confronted with Maimonides' philosophical naturalism, or when Maimonidean comments did not square with kabbalistic interpretations, his criticism was aroused. A well-grounded philosopher simply did not indulge in idle speculation when the Torah, a revelatory source of empirical data, provided clear instruction. Nevertheless, for Naḥmanides, philosophy remained a useful method of clarification.[30] With a similar nuanced sensibility, Naḥmanides, who was one of the early kabbalists, hinted at mystical secrets in his commentary on the Torah even while he opposed the spread of such ideas beyond a small circle of initiates. And, in his talmudic and halakhic works, he was open to the influence of the Tosafists, even though his interpretations were often based on older Sephardic traditions. In all these fields—philosophy, Kabbalah, and talmudic study— Naḥmanides represented the new cultural idiom.

Although the public debate over the role of philosophy within European

Judaism came to an abrupt end in 1233, the issue of whether allegorical interpretations of the Bible led to a disdain for the halakhically observant life remained on the agenda of Jewish intellectuals. Less than a century later, the controversy over rationalism broke out again in Provence, where southern and northern traditions collided and where fear of extreme rationalism troubled a small minority. After much correspondence from anxious and insistent Provençal writers, Solomon ibn Adret, one of Naḥmanides' students and a prodigious halakhist, talmudic commentator, and sometimes kabbalist, declared that one had to be 25 years old before being allowed to study philosophical texts written by non-Jews. Exposing underage students to philosophy, Ibn Adret argued, was akin to feeding hard foods to children incapable of digesting them. Still, this ruling, which was proclaimed in Barcelona following Ibn Adret's suggestion, did not significantly alter the study of philosophy in the Sephardic world.[31]

For many Sephardic thinkers writing in the wake of the conflicts over philosophical study, a moderate position on all these matters seemed in order. Ibn Adret had been troubled only by those extreme rationalists who appeared to view the Bible and its commandments as allegorical teachings. He understood that philosophy was a helpful device to understand Holy Writ so long as basic traditional beliefs were not contradicted. Reason of course had to be subservient to revelation, philosophical reflection to prophecy. In Ibn Adret's commentaries on various aggadot of the Talmud, philosophical ideas were presented, some accepted and others rejected; kabbalistic interpretations, on the other hand, were consciously submerged. This intellectual stance did not represent a new departure; Ibn Adret was, after all, a student of the subtle Naḥmanides.[32] Yet, for Naḥmanides, Ibn Adret, and their later disciples, the lines between philosophy, Kabbalah, and halakhah were not as clearly drawn as they may seem today: each of these disciplines could shed light on the others.

A circle of individuals surrounding Ibn Adret reflected their master's basic approach to the study of Judaism. Following Ibn Adret, who was the most prolific halakhic decisor of the later Middle Ages, they highly valued the study of halakhah and viewed the legal enterprise as central to the curriculum of learned Jews. They were also enamored of Kabbalah and devoted much energy to studying Naḥmanides' occasionally esoteric Commentary on the Torah. Yom Tov ben Avraham al-Isbili, a great halakhist and first-rate talmudic commentator and the most prominent student of Ibn Adret, wrote an analysis of Naḥmanides' commentary entitled *Sefer ha-Zikkaron*. In it, though al-Isbili defended Maimonides against the overt criticisms of Naḥmanides, he repeatedly endorsed the latter's kabbalistically informed conclusions as fundamentally sound.

The students of Ibn Adret also blurred the disciplinary lines between halakhah, philosophy, and Kabbalah. This group did not oppose the study of philosophy. Rational explanations for the mitzvot were welcome in these disciples' popular-legal compilations just as they had been earlier for the author of the *Sefer ha-Ḥinukh.* Open philosophical reflections and judicious hints at kabbalistic truths pepper their writings. There is no sense among these writers that these two approaches to understanding the commandments were fundamentally incompatible. Still, though ideas of philosophical provenance were to be found among this circle, its members resisted the approach of the radical philosophers—those who seemed to suggest that the study of philosophy was theoretically more important to the adept than the observance of Jewish law. Such radicalism continued to encounter fierce opposition among this generation of writers, as it had for their teachers.[33]

The experience of Asher ben Yeḥiel reflects this unresolved tension within Sephardic culture. During his stay in Montpellier in transit to Sepharad, Asher wrote a letter of support for the antiphilosophical party. In Barcelona, where he encountered Sephardic Jews and their culture directly, he argued for a compromise approach. Still, in early 1306, he threw his support behind the ban that was encouraged by Ibn Adret. Although Asher was appointed to a rabbinical post in Toledo, Israel ben Yosef ha-Yisre'eli, the secretary of the kahal and one of his opponents in a communal dispute, argued that a man who did not read Arabic, and was therefore incapable of reading earlier communal statutes, was insufficiently prepared to be a community leader. His legal decisions, according to ha-Yisre'eli, were not binding: the knowledge of the historical culture of the ruling elite, of which philosophical awareness was an essential ingredient, was a necessary credential for a communal judge.[34]

Philosophy therefore remained part of Sephardic culture. But in contemplating whether the corrosive effects of philosophy prompted Solomon ha-Levi's conversion, ha-Lorki dismissed the idea even more quickly than he discarded the argument from hedonism:

> Also of philosophical knowledge, you ate the essence and cast aside the shells.
> And so the first two causes have been dispensed with.

When the rabbis of the Talmud had speculated how the esteemed Rabbi Meir could have associated with the acknowledged heretic Elisha ben Avuyah, one offered the opinion that Meir "found a pomegranate. He ate of its fruit and cast aside its shell." For ha-Lorki, the dangers that philosophy presented were real but manageable. As anyone who pondered the "order of creation" knew, the tree of knowledge of philosophy bore fruit that was both available and tempting. If the serpent was to be believed, it could transform one into a divine being, knowing good and evil. This was not an intellectual opportunity to be forfeited.[35]

THE ENDLESSNESS OF EXILE

Mainstream Sephardic intellectuals viewed halakhah as central to Jewish life and the disciplines of philosophy and Kabbalah as important handmaidens in the study of the Torah. For ha-Lorki, any of the theoretical underpinnings of the observant Jewish life, whether philosophy or Kabbalah, did not necessarily lead to conversion. As a result, he turned his attention elsewhere in contemplating what may have spirited Solomon ha-Levi to the baptismal font:

> Or when you observed the destruction of our homeland and the many troubles that have recently befallen us, consuming us and scattering us—and that God has almost hidden his countenance from us and made us as food to the birds of the heaven and the wild beasts of the earth, it occurred to you that "the name of Israel will be remembered no more."

Did ha-Lorki imagine that ha-Levi's decision was grounded in recent events within Iberia? Or did he think that lengthy reflection on the course of Jewish history had led ha-Levi to conclude that God's presence no longer resided with his chosen people and that they were consequently doomed to disappear?

Despite all the glorious successes of which the Sephardim could rightfully be proud, the saga of Iberian Jewry also contained an important chapter in the history of Jewish suffering. We need not go back to the riots against the Jews of Minorca in the fifth century or to the more widespread and relentless persecution of Jews that marked the last century of Visigothic reign over their southern European lands. When the Jews of medieval Christian Iberia began to emerge in their own right as a significant community, it was as much a result of the invasion of the peninsula by Almoravids and Almohads and their mistreatment of the Jews as it was the economic lure of the invigorated kingdoms of Portugal, Castile, Aragon, and Navarre.

Although Ibn Daud had celebrated the conquest of Toledo by Alfonso VI in 1085, and though thirteenth-century Jews maintained positive relations with the royal court under the militarily successful Fernando III and his son, Alfonso X, Jewish life in Castile was not simply one of unalloyed security. Jews did reach great heights of power and influence at the court of Alfonso X; still, he was unsure of their loyalty. After his hopes of ascending the throne of the Holy Roman Empire were dashed, and after he faced rebellion by both his son and the nobility, the king possibly imagined that the Jewish courtiers were siding with the rebels. He imprisoned all the Jewish tax-farmers in 1279 and hanged one of them, Don Çag de la Maleha. In Toledo—the city of the king—Jews were detained within their synagogues on a Sabbath in January 1281 and large sums of money, twice their annual tribute, were demanded of them.[36] Toledo was where Ibn Daud had reported with great pride that infirm Jews had been brought inside its walls because of the high esteem in which Judah ha-Nasi ibn Ezra was held by Alfonso VI.

So how secure did the Jews feel? Living under the rival monotheisms of Christianity and Islam, they had long realized that both harbored unflattering views of them and their religion. If they did not adopt the faith of the rulers and of the majority population, Jews were, at best, second-class citizens. So when Alfonso X composed poems and compiled an anthology of verse entitled *Cantigas de Santa María* that featured many anti-Jewish stereotypes, the Jews well may have understood that he was not expressing any particular animus toward them. He was simply repeating attitudes prevalent in medieval Christian Europe about the Jews and their behavior.[37]

Aragonese Jews held significant posts at the court of Jaume I the Conqueror in the fields of administration, diplomacy, colonization, and finance, and yet they too found their situation somewhat insecure. In 1283 Pere II, Jaume's son and successor, dismissed the Jews from royal service. Although they continued unofficially to work at the court and at positions that had been declared off-limits, they were surely stunned by the reversal in their fortunes. Additionally, the Jews suffered from other economic disabilities. Subject to accusations of usury, they could not set the rates of interest they wished to charge. Furthermore, the king declared moratoria on the loans that they had tendered, and taxes became increasingly onerous. As the crucial role that the Jews had played in the conquests diminished, they were eliminated from significant sectors of the economy, such as the burgeoning maritime trade. Although their connection to the monarch remained intact despite repeated attacks, the growing competition and animosity from other groups within the kingdoms—whether from the growing bourgeois class or from segments within the church—reminded the Jews that their success was not admired or approved of by all.[38]

The Jews were the objects of royal economic aggrandizement in all the Christian Iberian kingdoms, but they generally viewed themselves as economic free agents, capable of influencing governmental decisions. They did not expect to have unimpeded success in their interventions, but they were relatively confident of access to the monarch. One of the professions through which they were able to flex this influence, albeit irregularly, was that of medicine. In al-Andalus the Jewish courtiers, aside from those possessing skills as financial administrators and diplomats, were often physicians whose entrée to the ruler was perhaps more informal than that of other royal advisers. This intimacy was greatly prized by the Jews; the physician garnered much prestige among his peers and in turn was the recipient of attempts to influence him. He was often resented by others, Jews and Christians alike. The Church at Rome manipulated traditional suspicions, declaring that Jewish physicians should not be employed by rulers, even though the popes themselves frequently turned to Jewish doctors.[39]

The success of the Jews extended beyond Castile and Aragon to the kingdom of Portugal. Blessed with long-reigning monarchs of the same dynasty until the penultimate decade of the fourteenth century, Jews played an important role within the economy of Portugal and could boast of their share of courtiers and advisers to the king. In 1373, after King Fernando intervened in the war that the other peninsular kingdoms were waging against Enrique II of Castile and his French allies, Portugal was invaded by the Castilians, and the kingdom's stability was challenged. With the death of Fernando in October 1383, revolts swept the countryside, and pressure was applied by the cities to oust the Jews from some of their more prestigious posts at the royal court. This unrest, which included an assault on the main Jewish quarter in Lisbon, was soon overshadowed by another Castilian invasion, which was finally repulsed by the Portuguese at Aljubarrota. Jews continued at their old posts under the new monarch, João, despite his promises and that of his regent mother to the contrary. Security may have been the condition of Portuguese Jews, but anti-Jewish tension constantly lurked beneath the surface.[40]

Toward the end of the fourteenth century, Navarrese Jews began to enjoy relative prosperity. They had endured the excesses of the Shepherds' Crusade, which had also harmed Aragonese Jews; scores of Jews in Estella and the surrounding area had been massacred in 1328 with the eclipse of the Capetian dynasty; and, like the Portuguese, they suffered from the Castilian civil war. A powerful centralizing monarch, Carlos III, came to the Navarrese throne in 1387. He inaugurated what was arguably one of the most tranquil periods in the history of the small Pyrenean kingdom.[41]

During the fourteenth century, the Jews of Castile were able to maintain the status that they had enjoyed a hundred years earlier, probably because a Christian middle class had not emerged within the kingdom as it had in the Crown of Aragon. Indeed, in the mid-fourteenth century under Pedro I, Samuel ha-Levi Abulafia was appointed treasurer of Castile, a sure sign that the influence of prominent Jews had not waned within royal circles. The architecturally fine synagogue that Abulafia had built in Toledo was perhaps a further indication of

the physical security that some Jews felt within the kingdom. Although the synagogue may only have been intended for the use of his family and its entourage, it
seemed to reflect the famed convivencia of the three faith-cultures in Castilian
society. It was constructed in the *mudejar* style, and in all likelihood the plaster
work and decoration were executed by Muslims. The synagogue was dedicated
in honor of the monarch, Abulafia's employer, and the lavish encomia bestowed
upon Pedro could probably be interpreted not only in light of his role as Abulafia's patron but also in his capacity as defender of Jewish rights and security.

It is hard to know how these signs of well-being were understood by Castilian
Jewry. After all, when Jews emerged from the synagogue of Samuel Abulafia or
from their other houses of worship in Toledo and gazed skyward, they could not
fail to miss the large cathedral towering over them from the highest point within
the city. Their minority status was made clear to them with just one glance. Yet
from all indications they had every reason to trust Pedro's devotion to their concerns and had no compelling reason to doubt their security. Even when Abulafia
and his retinue fell out of favor with the king, other Jews soon occupied themselves with the diplomatic and financial tasks that Abulafia had performed.

Following the policy of his father and predecessor, Alfonso XI, Pedro relied
upon the Jews and kept the nobility distant. But this course of action did not secure his hold on the Castilian throne. He had to contend with a rebellion that,
after initial setbacks, he was able to quash. He then embarked upon a war with
the Crown of Aragon that he appeared to be winning until France, allied with
the Castilian nobility led by his half-brother Enrique, came to Aragon's aid and
ultimately emerged victorious. The climax of the Castilian civil war came when
Enrique murdered Pedro at Montiel in March 1369 and founded the Trasta-
maran dynasty.

Enrique was able to gather support among the nobility, city-dwellers, and
others within the kingdom through his use of blatantly anti-Jewish messages.
He continually called for the dismissal of Pedro's Jewish advisers and forced Jewish communities to support his side during the civil war; the Jews of Burgos
were threatened twice during his campaign. Upon Enrique's ascension to the
throne, he immediately declared a moratorium on the repayment of Jewish
debts. Surprisingly, though, Jews were again appointed at court to fill some of
the same roles as they had played under Pedro. While it was clear that the Jews
were essential to the sure functioning of the kingdom, the hatred for them could
not be dismissed.[42]

In Aragon, latent anti-Jewish attitudes were also revealed in a violent manner
during the outbreak of the plague in 1348. Not only did Jews die in the same proportions as the rest of the Aragonese population, but they were also killed dur-

ing popular upheavals in the wake of this terrible scourge. The Jewish cemetery at Lleida, for example, could not contain the bodies of all those who had died of the epidemic, and local Jews appealed to King Pere III for an additional plot of land.[43]

Was ha-Lorki correct, then, that the tale of endless suffering which seemed to be the fate of the Jews had persuaded ha-Levi that his former coreligionists could never be assured of God's protection? In considering this possible motivation for ha-Levi's conversion, ha-Lorki addressed the specific question of whether the decline of Sephardic Jewry should cause Jews to wonder about their ultimate survival as a people:

> And I cannot argue that the third reason, that is the destruction of the people, may have deluded you, because I am confident that you are not ignorant of the fact that is well-known amongst us from the travelogues of those who have journeyed the length and breadth of the world, or from the letters of Maimonides of blessed memory, or from the accounts of merchants who voyage across the seas—that at present most of our people are to be found in the lands of Babylonia and Yemen, where the exiles of Jerusalem settled at first, besides the exiles of Samaria who today are as numerous as the sands on the seashore and who dwell in the lands of Persia and Media. Some of these exiles live under the domination of a king who is called the Sultan of Babylonia and of the Ishmaelites, some in districts where the yoke of no other people is upon them, such as those who live on the border of the lands of the Cushites which is called al-Habash adjacent to the Edomite prince called Prester John, who have a treaty with him that is renewed annually. And that is an irrefutable fact.
>
> And furthermore all the Jews who dwell in Christian lands are only descended from those who returned to Jerusalem [under Ezra and Neḥemiah] who without doubt were not of the leaders of the Exile but rather of the humblest people. As the rabbis have said about them, "Ezra did not ascend from Babylonia to Israel until he left Babylonian Jewry like pure sifted flour."
>
> Following this assumption, even if it were God's decree to destroy and exterminate all the Jews who live within Christendom, the people would remain alive and intact, so this should not lead to a weakening of faith.

Even if all the Jews in Sepharad and the rest of Christendom were destined for extinction, ha-Lorki argued, the faith of the observant Jew should remain unaffected. This is a far cry from what Ibn Daud, living in Christian Toledo, wrote about his community and its future in the twelfth century. For Ibn Daud, the Sephardic Jews were not only the nobility of the Jewish people but also the ones amongst whom the eschatological drama would first unfold. Whereas Ibn Daud employed the biblical phrase "exiles of Jerusalem that are in Sepharad" to refer to his peninsular coreligionists, ha-Lorki employed a talmudic citation in the name of Rabbi Eliezer to indicate that the Jews of Sepharad, like all Jewry living in Christian lands, were a genealogically mixed group whom Ezra the Scribe had taken against their will to Judaea. Indeed, for ha-Lorki, it was Babylonian Jewry purged of these impure individuals that remained the refined essence of the Jewish people. Unlike Ibn Daud, Judah Halevi had no such exalted notion of his native Andalusi community. The purifying essence of the Jewish people was the Land of Israel where Ezra had taken the Babylonian exiles. There was no place, east or west, where Jews could find rest; only their homeland afforded spiritual security. But ha-Lorki parted company with Halevi on the Land of Israel: the Jews' ancestral home could not provide the answer for Solomon ha-Levi's theological crisis.

Sephardic Jewry was not insulated from world Jewry, either in reality or in their imagination. Ha-Lorki assumed that the literate population in Iberia would be aware of Diaspora communities from the letters of Maimonides and from merchants' reports and travelers' accounts. For example, in the late twelfth century Benjamin ben Jonah, for reasons that are not immediately apparent, famously departed from his hometown of Tudela on a trip that took him through the Mediterranean world, the Middle East, and the Near East.[44] From the beginnings of Sephardic Jewry, peninsular Jews were conscious of their place within the Diaspora. Whereas the Jews of al-Andalus were part of the Islamic world and their community maintained links to the centers of Jewish life in Qayrawan, Baghdad, or the Land of Israel, the Jews in the Christian kingdoms mainly turned their gaze northward to the other Jewish communities of Western Europe.

The connections between the peninsula and the Jews of Ashkenaz and Provence, as we have seen, were many. The talmudic glosses of Rashi and the Tosafist school, less so their halakhic rulings, were influential in the writings of Naḥmanides and Ibn Adret. Naḥmanides and Gerondi were also much impressed with the penitential and mystical ideas of Ḥasidei Ashkenaz, the German pietists. With the arrival of Asher ben Yeḥiel and his family, Ashkenazic halakhic decisions made a significant foray into the thickets of Sephardic legal literature. And in the debates over the valence of philosophical studies, the ideas of these centers flowed, albeit polemically, between these areas of Jewish life. Sephardic Jews exported not only philosophical ideas but also grammatical monographs, legal decisions, and codes of Jewish law. Despite the obvious differences in the elite written culture of these Jewish communities, they did not develop in isolation from each other.

The role in this process of the flow of Jews across political borders cannot be underestimated. As noted, Iberian merchants traveled abroad and brought back tales of foreign communities. The persecutions and especially the expulsion of the communities of Western Europe also caused many individuals from different Jewish cultures to seek refuge on the peninsula. Of particular import was the banishment of Jews from France in 1306. The Jews of *reconquista* Iberia came to constitute a West European culture.[45]

Sephardic Jews devised neat categories for the various diasporas, referring to the Jews settled in Christian-dominated countries as living under Edom (the biblical name for Esau, Jacob's brother, and a symbol, for the rabbis, of the Roman Empire and therefore of its heirs, the Christians). Those under Islam dwelt within the domain of Ishmael (biblical half-brother of Isaac). Christian lands provided a haven for the Jews when the intolerant Berber tribes overran al-Andalus, but even during this period some Jews, including Maimonides and Moses ibn Ezra, viewed north European civilization as irremediably backward. In the late thirteenth century, with most of Sephardic Jewry living comfortably within the Christian states of the peninsula, Baḥya ben Asher, a kabbalist and biblical exegete living in Saragossa, transformed the old rabbinic saying "Better under a gentile than [an] Ishmael[ite]" into "Better under Edom than under Ishmael." Christendom, at least in its Iberian format, was recognized as far more hospitable to Jews and Judaism than Islamic civilization.[46]

Ha-Lorki's fears for the future of the Jewish people were not allayed by his knowledge of European communities but rather by his awareness of Eastern Jews. Some Sephardim had fled Iberia for Muslim territories in the wake of the riots of 1391. But when ha-Lorki turned his gaze eastward, he saw not only these Jews, whether in the Land of Israel or in Babylonia and Yemen, but also the "irrefutable fact" of the Jews who lived a politically independent existence in the far-off land of the Cushites, linked by treaty with an Edomite prince by the name of Prester John. Edom was still seen as an ally in the land of al-Habash.

The fantasy of a Jewish community free of the overlordship of non-Jews was rife both within and outside of the peninsula. In ninth-century al-Andalus, people had been taken with Eldad ha-Dani, who had presented himself as having come a great distance with news of Jews—indeed, the ten lost tribes of the Bible, who were living in a place far removed from the Islamic world and were alleged to be militarily powerful and politically dominant. In the century following Eldad's appearance, Ḥasdai ibn Shaprut, diplomat at the court of Abd al-Raḥmān III in al-Andalus, sent a letter to the Jewish king of the Khazars eagerly seeking information about his people and asking as well about the whereabouts of the "ten lost tribes" and the far-away lands they inhabited.

The notion of a Christian prince living in distant lands was similarly prevalent within European Christendom. In the second half of the twelfth century, this prince, also called Prester John, ruled the ten lost tribes and was readying himself to avenge the enemies of the Cross. By the early fourteenth century, his abode was located in the land of the Cushites in Ethiopia (al-Ḥabash).[47] The Jewish version of the story had a particular polemical valence vis-à-vis Christianity. For Jews living under the rival monotheistic civilizations of Christianity and Islam, and especially for those dwelling under Christendom, the reality of their political subservience to others was a constant challenge to their faith. If indeed God was on the Jews' side, the argument went, why were they not favored with a politically independent state? The Bible shared by Jews and Christians had declared that the "scepter will not depart from Judah." The Jews would only maintain political sovereignty, according to Christian exegetes, "until Shiloh comes"—that is, until Jesus the Messiah would arrive. For the Christians, the subjection of the Jews was clear proof of the advent of their Messiah. Even the proud Jews of Sepharad, who reveled in their power (and Ibn Shaprut was a wonderful embodiment of such sentiments), were painfully aware that they were politically dependent. Stories of Jewish kings, such as those who ruled the Khazars, or, more fantastically, of places where the ten lost tribes not only dwelt but wielded military power and levied taxes—the clearest sign of authority for medieval Jews—circulated among the Sephardim. These tales afforded an important psychological boost and helped stock the polemical arsenal against the Christians and Muslims. For Judah Halevi, the legend that the king of the Khazars had embraced Judaism was the point of departure for the *Kuzari*, his classic defense of his faith (which ha-Levi himself described as "the despised religion") against the rival claims of Islam and Christianity. Along with his mystical attachment to the Land of Israel, he was able to imagine another land where, in ha-Lorki's words, "the yoke of no other people is upon [the Jews]."

The state of affairs described by ha-Lorki—that "many troubles have . . . come but recently, that have consumed us and scattered us"—indicated, according to Christian theology, "that God had . . . given us as food to the birds of the heaven and the wild beasts of the earth." The Christians concluded and never ceased to remind the Jews that "God has hidden [and not "almost has hidden" as ha-Lorki was piously obliged to write] his countenance" from the Jews, indeed that God had rejected the Jewish people, and that the name of Israel would be remembered no more. Earlier in the fourteenth century, the physician Abner of Burgos, born a Jew and later a convert to Christianity, wrote that when he had beheld the oppressed Jews, burdened by taxation and generally afflicted, he had been pained by Christians asking his people why it seemed that God was not watching over them.

The third motivation that ha-Lorki offered for Solomon ha-Levi's conversion reflected the Christian argument that God had deliberately rejected the Jews—Israel in the flesh—as punishment for their rejection of Jesus and had therefore chosen another people—*verus* Israel, those who confessed Christ. Ha-Lorki confidently asserted in response that the "exiles of Samaria"—the ten tribes of the northern biblical kingdom of Israel—were "as numerous as the sands on the seashore and dwelled in the biblical lands of Persia and Media." In medieval Jewish thought, ruminations about the whereabouts of the ten lost tribes were always connected with the coming of the Messiah. The discovery of these ten lost tribes would be a sure sign that the messianic advent was near. No, ha-Lorki appeared to be saying to ha-Levi, not only were the Jews flourishing in many countries, but the advent of the Jewish Messiah was also imminent. Admittedly, this was a far cry from Ibn Daud's contention that the messianic drama would begin with the redemption of Sephardic Jewry. Ha-Lorki expected both the site of flourishing Jewish communities as well as the provenance of the Messiah himself to be far away from this western corner of the Mediterranean.

THE SPECTER OF CHRISTIANITY

Or perhaps there were revealed to you the secrets of prophecy and the basic principles of faith and their proofs, such as were not revealed to the pillars of the world amongst our people during all the days of our long Exile, and you concluded that our forefathers had inherited falsehood because of their limited understanding of the Torah and of prophecy and therefore you chose what you chose because it is true and certain.

The specter of Christianity had loomed over ha-Lorki's discussion of whether the Jews would continue to survive as a people, and now it explicitly became the fourth way to justify ha-Levi's decision to alter the order of creation. Ha-Lorki's formulation of this possibility was cloaked simultaneously in cynicism and yearning. The notion that the erstwhile rabbi from Burgos had been the recipient of a revelatory experience was unsettling to ha-Lorki and consequently had to be held up to ridicule. He had only to go back a few years in time to when Abner of Burgos (ha-Levi's hometown) was also beset by doubts. In a dream, Abner claimed to have beheld an individual who rebuked him for sleeping and who explained that the Jews were mired in the galut because of their inability to recognize the ultimate truth. After first ignoring the evident import of his dream, Abner continued to reflect on the meaning of the Torah and its prophecies until visited yet again by this Christ-like figure, who this time induced him to embrace Christianity.

Abner's contemporaries wondered about his decision to convert and questioned his motivation. Abner had read widely in philosophy and mysticism. In the final analysis, despair over the suffering of the Jews and the failure of their messianic prophecies were the decisive factors in bringing him to the Cross.[48] For those faithful to Judaism, the most chilling idea to contemplate was that their forefathers, the pillars of the world, had inherited falsehood. The Christians who sought to convert the Jews had been arguing for years that the Jews did not truly understand the meaning of the Torah and the prophecies. As ha-Lorki concluded, "you chose what you chose because it is true and certain."

This was not an indirect argument. Ha-Lorki had dismissed the idea that ha-Levi's conversion derived from hedonistic motives or from a relativist position regarding religious truth that had resulted in turn from devotion to philosophy. Rather, he proposed that ha-Levi had decided that the Christians were right and the Jews were wrong:

> Therefore only the last reason remains for me to consider and that involves the study and weighing of opinions regarding religions and prophecies, especially since I know that you are acquainted with the rarest of the books of the Christians—and their interpretations and their principles—since you are proficient in their language, books of which no contemporary scholar is familiar. In addition, about two months ago, the text of the letter which you sent to Yosef Orabuena in Navarre came into my possession via Saragossa; in it I saw that you believe of the man who came during the last years of the Second Temple that he is the Messiah for whom our people have waited from then until now, and that all the prophecies which speak of the Messiah and the redemption fully conform with his particulars; that is to say with his birth, his death, and his resurrection.

Competitive tension with the two monotheistic religions under which the Jews lived during the Middle Ages was one of the central features of their lives. In Iberia, where the three religions cohabited, these tensions assumed more complex and variegated forms. When Judah Halevi, who lived in both Muslim and Christian states, wrote the *Kuzari,* his first few pages were openly devoted to the truth-claims of Christianity and Islam. Not surprisingly, he found the arguments for their religious beliefs to be wanting.

Even during the heyday of Jewish life in Christian Iberia in the thirteenth century, the Jews faced and responded not only to the literary accounts of this conflict but to personal and state-sanctioned challenges to their faith as well. A concerted movement by Christians to missionize among the Jews had found its most significant early expression in France in the 1230s. Fueled by the zeal of Jewish converts who set out to vindicate themselves among their former coreligionists, a new methodology was developed and implemented in the attempt to actualize the age-old dream of the conversion of the Jews. In this view, rabbinic literature, which formerly had been seen as lacking any religious value because Christ had already come, was now perceived as the main obstacle to the Jews' recognition of the truth of the Christian message. Possessed of this understanding, the Talmud was put on trial in Paris on a variety of charges, including blasphemies against God and the Holy Family, abuse of Christianity, and the promotion of absurd ideas. The Talmud was found guilty, and as a result many copies of this text were burned in the streets of the city.

Just as Jewish learning crossed the Pyrenees and altered the texture of Sephardic Judaism, so Christian ideas about conversion traversed political boundaries and dramatically affected Jewish-Christian relations. Even in thirteenth-century Aragon, where Jaume I employed Jews at the highest levels of government, the king compelled Jews (and Muslims) in 1242 to attend conversionary sermons, and new ideas were promoted about how best to convince the Jews of the truth of Christianity. Turning the Parisian stratagem on its head, friars of the newly founded Mendicant orders argued that a thorough study of rabbinic literature would yield important proofs of the truth-claims of Christianity. This audacious new approach, first pioneered in Provence, emerged on the peninsula in 1263.[49]

Nahmanides, whose intellectual brilliance was acknowledged by both his Christian and his Jewish contemporaries, was called upon by the king to debate these new ideas with the Dominican friar Pablo Cristiani (Pau Christià), formerly Saul, a Jew from Montpellier. They had already confronted each other in Girona, Nahmanides' hometown. But in the royal palace of Barcelona, with noble, ecclesiastical, and municipal worthies as well as King Jaume himself in attendance, the setting was far more dramatic. After the opening session on Friday, July 20, 1263, three additional meetings were held, and the disputation was concluded the following Friday. In the immediate aftermath of the debate, Cristiani and the king, joined by other Christian dignitaries, visited a Barcelonan synagogue on the Sabbath and preached there to those assembled. Nahmanides briefly responded to their comments. The encounter in the synagogue indicated that this disputation was part of a larger effort to bring the gospel to the Jews of Aragon.

Two years later, Nahmanides wrote an account of his debate with Cristiani. Aside from wishing to promote his perspective on the proceedings and to stem

Detail of a page from *Cantigas de Alfonso X,*
showing a disputation between a Catholic
prelate and a group of Jews wearing distinctive
pointed hats. (Library of the Monastery of
El Escorial, Madrid. Photo: Institut Amatller
d'Art Hispànic, Barcelona)

any criticism of what might have been perceived as an inadequate performance, Naḥmanides may have also intended his report as a handbook for Jews in their future encounters, public and private, with Christian neighbors and missionaries. In the wake of the publication of his account, the Dominicans charged that Naḥmanides had defamed the Christian faith. This accusation may have forced him to leave Sepharad for the Land of Israel.[50]

There were other public disputations between Jews and Christians. The merchants and travelers of the Mediterranean world served as the channel through which the Christian-Jewish debate was brought to the island of Majorca in 1286. There was a debate in Avila, Castile, in the 1370s, and another in 1375 in Pamplona in Navarre. There is much evidence of private debates as well. In these encounters, the climate of ill-will was far more muted than in the public confrontations, and the prevailing atmosphere of greater tolerance allowed for more open and less scripted interchanges between the protagonists.

Some of the Jewish accounts of actual disputations are found in much larger polemical works whose authors only used the debates as a point of departure for their anti-Christian arguments. Moses ha-Kohen of Tordesillas wrote an expanded record of a disputation in which he had argued with two converts to Christianity in the cathedral of Avila, after these proselytes had delivered conversionary sermons to their former coreligionists. The Jewish community had encouraged ha-Kohen to write an account of the event in commemoration of what had transpired and as a guide and sourcebook to assist them in future disputations. The debates occurred in 1373 or 1374; ha-Kohen first penned his account in 1375 and added to it in 1379, including a refutation of the interpretations of biblical and talmudic passages that the converts had used as proofs for the truth of Christianity. Ha-Kohen's expanded work also served to combat the arguments found in *Pugio Fidei,* the massive compilation of Raimundus Martini written in the previous century and directed against Jews and Muslims, and the more recent writings of Abner of Burgos and his disciples. Indeed, one of Abner's students threatened ha-Kohen with another public debate unless he responded to a list of accusations that the man had leveled against a number of objectionable talmudic passages. This individual argued menacingly that, since these paragraphs reflected anti-Christian hostility, it did not behoove Christians to tolerate Jews in their society, even as this same writer had brought other talmudic citations as support for Christian truth-claims.

What distinguished the work of ha-Kohen from efforts by other Jewish apologists was the tone he adopted toward his interlocutors and toward the sacred texts he attempted to defend. Jewish biblical exegetes in the Middle Ages had always been concerned with the conflicting claims of Christianity, and Jewish commentators on the talmudic aggadot were conscious of the uses to which the Christians put these rabbinic texts. From Naḥmanides' report on the Barcelona disputation to the aggadic commentaries written by Ibn Adret (who may have debated some of these issues with Martini himself), such an awareness is clearly in evidence. Admittedly, it was difficult for Jewish writers to argue that some talmudic passages needed to be reinterpreted or that the ideas they contained were not central to rabbinic theology. But the confident assertiveness noticeable in the behavior and writings of the earlier Sephardic defenders of the faith was not in evidence in the work of ha-Kohen. Toward the end of the fourteenth century, this apologetic genre of Jewish literature had become even more defensive, exhibiting a deeper fear of the Christians and a concomitantly greater desire to please the host society that had been calling into question the modicum of tolerance shown to the Jews.[51]

The polemical literature reflected the concerns of all Jews living in the Iberian Christian kingdoms. The debate with Christianity writ large was in some ways a constant of daily life and not only a concern of the Jewish intellectual elite. In these wars of attrition, the identity of the Messiah appeared at the vanguard of both the Christian and the Jewish initiatives. If the Messiah had already arrived in the person of Jesus, as the Christians had argued at Barcelona in 1263, then the laws and ceremonies of the Jews had ceased to possess any theological meaning, and the entire order of creation for medieval Jews had come to an end. If there is much writing about the Messiah among Sephardic Jews, it is mainly because the notion of the Redeemer was essential to justify their continued existence as a separate community living under the aegis of Christianity.

The hopelessness engendered among the Jews because of the endlessness of the exile and the frightening conclusion that God might no longer be a watchful presence on their behalf, expressed so clearly by ha-Lorki in the third possibility for ha-Levi's conversion, was directly connected with his astonishment that his mentor believed that the man who had come toward the end of the Second Temple period was "the Messiah for whom our people have awaited from then until now." Naḥmanides had taken such concerns as his point of departure in his essay *Sefer ha-Geulah*. As the Bible was often the site where rival interpretations about the Messiah warred with each other, the exegesis of scriptural passages formed the centerpiece of his arguments. Naḥmanides argued against the Christian position that the messianic promises had already been fulfilled. Even the intensification of aspects of the messianic idea within Jewish mystical writings of the thirteenth century can be understood against the background of the Christian attempt to convert the Jews. When moderate rationalists in the fourteenth century viewed some of the messianic core beliefs as metaphors for the stages in the intellectual development of man, it might have reflected their desire to move away from the actual messianic debate with Christians that had proved such a problematic issue for the Jewish community.[52]

Ha-Lorki recalled that ha-Levi was fluent in "their" language, a reference not to the Iberian vernaculars in which Jews had been conversant since the thirteenth century but, rather, to Latin. In al-Andalus the Jews had not only spoken Arabic but were well versed in the Koran and in the literature of the Muslim intellectuals. Indeed, Jews composed works in Arabic ranging from philosophical treatises to verse. Hebrew was still employed for a variety of genres in al-Andalus, but it was not the exclusive language of Jewish creativity, as it was in Ashkenaz and in Christian Iberia as well. In the large-scale translation projects sponsored by Alfonso X in thirteenth-century Toledo, Jews aided in translating works from Arabic into Latin and then into the Iberian vernacular. Arabic, or more correctly Judeo-Arabic, was still current among Sephardic Jews even in the fourteenth century. Jews did not have the same relationship with Latin as they had with Arabic, probably because Latin was predominantly a sacred language but Arabic functioned both as a literary medium and as a spoken tongue. The symbiosis that developed between the Hebrew and Arabic languages among the Jews never emerged between Hebrew and Latin. Nevertheless, there were individuals, a subset of the intellectual class such as astronomers, physicians, and philosophers, who did read Latin works. Ha-Lorki may therefore have been exaggerating when he wrote to ha-Levi that "you are aware of the ideas—and their interpretations . . . which are . . . in the books of the Christians . . . , ideas of which no contemporary scholar is cognizant." Nissim Gerondi, who lived in the mid-fourteenth century, was aware of the current philosophical literature available in Latin, and we know that ha-Kohen knew Latin and read the New Testament and later Christian writings.[53]

Ha-Lorki inserted the particulars of Jesus' life into his monologue with the erstwhile Solomon ha-Levi by introducing Yosef Orabuena of Navarre, to whom ha-Levi as Paulus de Sancta Maria (Pablo de Santa María) had written a letter about the Messiah. Orabuena was the physician of Carlos III of Navarre, and he also served as tutor to members of the royal family, an efficient tax collector, and the chief rabbi of Navarrese Jewry. As a prototypical Sephardic courtier, he was expected to be involved in the cultural conversations of the time. The letter he received from ha-Levi was copied and distributed to all who were engaged in the debate over whether the prophecies of the Bible had been fulfilled in Jesus. Ha-Levi, like Abner of Burgos before him, continued to write to Jews even after his conversion. Although written by someone who was now a Christian, and therefore formally as a piece of Christian-Jewish polemic, ha-Levi's letter to Orabuena also seemed to be part of an internal Jewish debate.[54]

While ha-Lorki may have designed his letter as a private missive, it was also intended for a public audience intrigued by ha-Levi's conversion and his possible motivations. Ha-Lorki's letter therefore needs to be seen as yet another volley in the long polemical match between European Jews and Christians. Still, the personal element for ha-Lorki is abundantly clear in his closing remarks. After offering ha-Levi four options for explaining his behavior and analyzing all of them, ha-Lorki concluded:

> If only I were as in earlier times, I would fly away and find rest in the shadow of your halls and you would teach me and tell me that which was revealed to you about these matters, one by one. Perhaps you would quiet the throbbing of my heart and you would remove the surging doubts that are my constant companions. And God knows that from the moment, close to four months ago, when the changes that transformed you were announced and came to our attention, I have thought to confront you face to face so that my ears may hear directly from your mouth the reasoning and opinions that moved you to cross the boundaries set by the ancestors, your fathers and your fathers' fathers, the holy and distinguished ones among our people. I [would have done so] except for the fact that the attempt to travel there would lead to harm, about which it is not appropriate to put in writing. A word to the wise should suffice.

Ha-Lorki stands here in all of his many contradictory reactions to his teacher's conversion. He simultaneously yearned for the erstwhile ha-Levi yet battled against his truths, was cynical about ha-Levi's possible revelatory experiences yet could imagine the tenderness he would feel should they meet again. The religious devastation caused by ha-Levi's change of faith reminded ha-Lorki of the physical destruction his people had just endured. Ha-Levi had dared to cross the boundaries of faith set by their ancestors; the borders of the Christian Iberian kingdoms were more easily traversed by rioters and by polemicists. Ha-Lorki's cryptic remark about the dangers inherent in traveling to ha-Levi is not easy to interpret. Ha-Levi lived in Castile, ha-Lorki in Aragon, and their mutual correspondent Orabuena resided in Navarre. Was the danger physical or theological? And from whom in his imagined audience was he protecting himself with his remark that a hint sufficed for the wise?

Ultimately, ha-Lorki wished his audience to understand that all his speculation regarding the motivation for ha-Levi's conversion had served simply as an introduction to yet another confident polemic against a challenging Christian adversary. After explaining to ha-Levi that a face-to-face interview was not in the offing, he wrote with the demanding mien of a prosecuting attorney yet softened by a touch of subservience. "And therefore I saw fit to write your honor an outline of those doubts. My teacher and master, I am in need of instruction. After appropriately begging your pardon, I will set out my case before you; I will put questions and you shall respond to me." What followed at great length were a variety of challenges to many aspects of Christian theology, including arguments that Jesus could not have been the Messiah. No innovative ideas were introduced in these paragraphs; their content was similar to other Sephardic polemics against Christianity fashioned over the previous 150 years.

Only after the completion of this extensive polemic did ha-Lorki return to his biblically and rabbinically laden personal remarks. He wrote that Christian theological claims had been intruding on his thoughts since his teacher's conversion and that neither Christian nor Jewish scholars had been helpful in silencing the tremors of his heart about whether individuals were obligated to seek the true religion.[55] But since ha-Levi has mastered "the Scripture of both Torahs more than any of the learned men of our time," ha-Lorki wrote hopefully, "I knew that you would quench my thirst and therefore to you I lifted my eyes." Ha-Lorki concluded his letter:

And since Time has decreed to settle me in the remote regions of this land and there my dwelling is established, inaccessible to travelers, I cannot write when the spirit moves me. Therefore, my lord, I beseech your eminence to answer me at length on all the particulars of this letter. Also if perchance your refined intellect has recently composed a new treatise on these matters, please send it to me by letter courier. "May the Lord open up for you his bountiful store," the treasure-house of intellect and wisdom, so that you may gaze upon the beauty of true things and that you may behold the path in which precious illumination lies. As someone who is wholeheartedly with you, whose soul lies down in fear and rises in horror, and who is bound to you with cords of love, I will not abandon your service even to swallow my spittle.

Infatuated with and struggling against the former ha-Levi, ha-Lorki was nevertheless lured and repelled by Christianity. He wrote to ha-Levi without a trace of self-consciousness about "our people" and "our Torah" even as he described him as learned in "the Scripture of both Torahs," referring to the Old and New Testament (and not to the rabbinic notion of a Written and Oral Law). The details of the polemical arguments that ha-Lorki amassed and with which he interrogated the erstwhile ha-Levi may have eluded most Sephardic Jews, and Iberian Christians for that matter. But the realization available to all living on the peninsula was that the truth of Christianity was predicated on the falsehood of Judaism, on God having chosen a new Israel, and on the erstwhile chosen people being bereft of divine protection. That was a conclusion the Jewish community in the wake of 1391 surely found profoundly unsettling. Sephardic culture had been created within the boundaries of Christian society and shaped by the daily competitive struggles between the peninsular monotheisms. The devastation wrought by the attacks had left the Jews reeling both physically and religiously.[56]

In a brief response,[57] ha-Levi chose only to address the question of whether those who were raised within false religious systems such as Judaism and Islam were obligated to search for the true faith. Unsurprisingly, ha-Levi answered this query in the affirmative and then concluded his missive in a manner that would leave no doubt—either to ha-Lorki or to anyone else—about his stance on the relative truth-claims of Judaism and Christianity:

> Do not scrutinize the words, only the ideas, for, in truth, I have actually turned away from the Hebrew language and I am too occupied with my studies to find the time to produce something properly edited. From your brother the Israelite, once a Levite, who, owing to the disqualification of the first is seeking another Levitical role—and dearer is the latter than the former—to serve in the name of his God, his righteous Messiah, to be sanctified with the holiness of Aaron. Formerly in Israel when he did not know god, Solomon of the House of Levi, and now since his eyes have beheld God, he is called Paulo de Burgos.

Ha-Levi probably imagined that this response would settle any and all speculation about his motivation to convert. He claimed that it was only after having renounced his former Levitical priesthood that he was sufficiently unencumbered to actually behold the God of Israel, as did Moses, Aaron, and their elite entourage at Mount Sinai.[58] So it was not lust or radical philosophical speculation that drew him to sanctify himself with this new priesthood but rather his reflections on matters of faith that led him to believe in the truth of Christianity and enabled him to gaze upon the Divine. Such an assured response must have struck terror in the hearts of its recipients. The Jewish community was unraveling as a result of the physical destruction and religious coercion of 1391, and this display of faith, exhibited by a former rabbi, surely did little to shore up its crumbling identity.

The confidence that peninsular Jews may have possessed in the continuity of Sepharad must have been further shaken by the observation that the kingdoms of Castile and Aragon were incapable of protecting their Jews or of restoring their communities. In the Crown of Aragon, many Jewish communities simply disappeared as their numbers drastically declined through emigration and conversion. Many Castilian Jews abandoned the large urban centers where they had established their important communities and moved to the smaller towns and villages of the kingdom. The Jews of Portugal and Navarre, on the other hand, living in kingdoms possessed of strong centralizing monarchs during the last decade of the fourteenth century, were able to emerge from this catastrophe relatively unscathed. Indeed the Portuguese João I, and probably Carlos III of Navarre as well, permitted Jews fleeing Castile to cross their borders, and the Portuguese king even permitted those who had converted in Castile to return to Judaism within his lands.[59] Even though, as we shall see, the Jews who remained on the peninsula reestablished many elements of their earlier culture, the wave of mass conversions created unsettling new social and religious dynamics.

FROM 1391 TO 1498

Some two decades after ha-Levi had left ha-Lorki reeling from his decision to abandon the Jewish faith and adopt Christianity, ha-Lorki himself took the waters of baptism along with a new name, Gerónimo de Santa Fé (Hieronymus de Sancta Fide). In 1412, he had encountered Vicente Ferrer, a fiery preacher who spoke of the end of days and described in hair-raising detail the glories of the Last Judgment, and who had been sent by the Avignon pope Benedict XIII on a mission to convert mankind prior to the arrival of the Antichrist. On his tour of Aragon, Ferrer found ha-Lorki in his hometown, Alcañiz. For almost 20 years, since he had written his open letter, ha-Lorki had been thinking deeply about why Sephardic Jews had converted to Christianity. Now, he too zealously embraced the Christian faith and, like ha-Levi and Abner of Burgos, sought to demonstrate its truth to his former coreligionists. So it was not opportunism and it was not philosophy that led ha-Lorki to the baptismal font. Instead, he had acquired a profound sense, from a theological understanding of Jewish history both past and present, that God had indeed forsaken the Jewish people and had chosen a new Israel. It was his realization as well that all the biblical prophecies about the messianic future were indeed bound up with the person of Jesus. To this end, ha-Lorki compiled midrashim that relied heavily on Martini's *Pugio Fidei* and were designed to prove to the Jews that the Christian prophecies regarding the Messiah were true.[60]

Armed with these newly acquired beliefs, ha-Lorki sought to stage a public disputation in Alcañiz. But the debate, which was first seen as a modest affair, became projected as a major confrontation between representatives of the Jewish communities of Aragon and the Christians led by ha-Lorki. The pope himself addressed letters to each of the Jewish communities toward the end of 1412, asking them to send their most learned scholars to the papal court at Tortosa to participate in this debate. For the Aragonese Jews, who had not yet recovered from the riots of 1391 and the ensuing wave of conversions (whether by force or choice), the timing could not have been worse. They were well aware that the disputation was being staged in order to encourage even more of their people to convert. And what an extravaganza it was. When the Jews arrived at the papal court on February 7, 1413, for the formal opening of the debate, they found 70 seats in the large courtyard occupied by cardinals, bishops, and archbishops, all turned out in their finest vestments. The audience, which numbered almost a thousand people, included distinguished members of the papal court and of the local nobility and municipality. Jewish intellectual and political leaders from the entire kingdom of Aragon were also in attendance.

The methodology employed by the Christian as well as the Jewish disputants had not changed much since 1263, when Pablo Cristiani had confronted Naḥmanides. Unlike the debate at Barcelona, however, this dispute dragged on for months. The disputation appeared to have ended with ha-Lorki's final address on April 19, but the debate over the Talmud resumed in June 1414 in the village of San Mateo, midway between Tortosa and the pope's fortress in Peñiscola, and it only reached a conclusion on November 10, 1414, nearly two years after it began.

The Tortosa disputation was a sign that the intense polemics characterizing Jewish-Christian relations before 1391 were to continue, but now against the backdrop of the violence and mass conversions of that fateful year. As we have seen, these formal disputations were part of a larger conversation between Jews and those who had abandoned Judaism for Christianity. Although the events of 1391 had eroded the Jewish communities, this conversation continued to flow between those who remained Jews and their former coreligionists. The exchange of letters between ha-Lorki and ha-Levi was not an isolated occurrence. Isaac bar Sheshet Perfet, one of the leading halakhists among Sephardic Jews and a rabbi in Valencia, was blackmailed into converting to Christianity during the riots. Some of Valencia's Christians had hoped that other Jews would follow him. After more than a year had passed, Perfet fled the peninsula and resumed his professional calling, serving as a rabbi to communities in North Africa. There he was asked to determine the legal status of Jews who had converted and had lived their lives, privately and publicly, as Christians before fleeing the peninsula. At first, Perfet displayed great sensitivity to the psychological, familial, and financial dynamics that would cause a Jew to convert and live as a Christian on the peninsula rather than emigrate immediately. Eventually, though, he argued that even those who were forcibly baptized could not be assumed to be loyal to the Jewish people or to Judaism unless they behaved in ways consistent with halakhah.[61]

On the peninsula, the conversations continued. Ḥasdai Crescas, Saragossan rabbi and royal adviser, worked with the Aragonese king and queen to rebuild the communities of their realm. Crescas was an innovative philosopher who attempted to diminish the role of Aristotelian thought in Jewish philosophical reflections. He sought to substitute his own work on philosophy and halakhah, *Or Adonai,* in place of the *Mishneh Torah* of Maimonides, that essential building block of Sephardic culture. As Crescas assembled his magnum opus, he willingly confronted the population of those newly converted. By arguing that the title of heretic could not be applied to one who was a forced worshiper of idols, he gave encouragement to those who had converted under duress and did not wish to be read out of the Jewish community. Crescas stressed as well that the sincere impulse to behave according to Jewish principles was at times even more meritorious than to adhere to the positive and negative commandments themselves.[62]

The fight for the souls of Jews, those who remained in the faith and those who had converted, prompted Crescas to write a polemical pamphlet entitled "A Refutation of Christian Principles." In this complexly argued work, written in an Iberian vernacular and focused on Christian theological principles such as the Trinity, the Virgin Birth, Transubstantiation, and, of course, the Messiah, Crescas broadened his reading audience to include those Jews who were philosophically sophisticated yet not fluent in Hebrew. Ha-Levi made it known that he wished to debate Crescas; these two intellectuals were at the center of the battle over the souls of the Jews.[63]

The debate was also joined by thinkers whose religious identity was not immediately apparent. Isaac ben Moses ha-Levi, also known as Profiat Duran or Efodi, the Hebrew acronym of his name, furnishes us with an intriguing example of this phenomenon. Duran was born in the mid-fourteenth century, probably in Perpignan, in the northern reaches of Catalonia. He made his way to the major intellectual centers in pursuit of the study of sciences and languages and found a home personally and intellectually with Crescas in Saragossa. During 1391 or in its immediate aftermath, he converted to Christianity; whether he was forced or chose to do so voluntarily is not clear. He lived in Perpignan until 1393, and probably for over a decade more, as the Christian Honoratus de Bonafide. He was a man of considerable wealth, thanks especially to his money-lending activities. He may have at times left the kingdom, especially for southern France, as did other erstwhile Jews of Perpignan, but he returned to his native Catalonia and lived as a Christian.

About four years after his conversion, Duran wrote a letter in Hebrew entitled "Do Not Be Like Your Fathers," which announced that his intellectual and emotional ties remained both with Judaism and the Jewish people. Joseph ibn Shem Tov, who translated Crescas's "Refutation of Christian Dogma" into Hebrew in the mid-fifteenth century, explained how the letter came to be written. According to Ibn Shem Tov, Duran and his friend Bonet ben Goron, both of whom had converted to Christianity, decided to travel to the Land of Israel and to resume their Jewish identity. While Bonet was preparing to set sail and Duran had already left, Bonet encountered the erstwhile Solomon ha-Levi in Avignon, who persuaded him of the truth of Christianity. Having decided not to meet up with his friend, Bonet wrote a letter to Duran, outlining his new theological stance, to which "Do Not Be Like Your Fathers" was a rejoinder.

Whatever the truth of this story, some of its details do find an echo in the letter itself. The presence and influence of ha-Levi is referred to explicitly. Ha-Levi's decision to convert clearly loomed large for the entire coterie of Jewish intellectuals of that generation. Bonet's original conversion to Christianity was understood; his sincere belief in Christian dogma, though, clearly rankled Duran. Filled with anger at his friend's betrayal, and surely aware of the delicacy needed in writing an open letter attacking his friend's newly appreciated religious faith, Duran resorted to a missive infused with biting sarcasm.

Duran wrote that his own faith had not wavered since his conversion and that his friend's current rejection of his theological and actual Jewish ancestors was a rejection of the Jewish people and of Judaism. Duran's own discomfort with his conversion is apparent in a letter he wrote about the same time to his friend En Yosef Avram in Girona upon the death of his father, the poet Abraham ben Isaac ha-Levi. According to Duran, God knew what was in the hearts of those who had been forcibly converted and did not eliminate them from the category of "the seed of Abraham." Conversion could only be justified, according to Duran, if, as a nominal Christian, Bonet would strive to "give praise and thanks to Him."

Duran was not content to leave these personal and theological issues alone. At the suggestion and encouragement of Crescas, with whom he apparently kept in contact during these years, Duran wrote a profound anti-Christian polemic entitled *Kelimat ha-Goyim* (Shame of the Gentiles) in which he attempted to show the correctness of Judaism. Dedicated to Crescas, whose presence as the "glory of the rabbis" he constantly evoked, Duran hoped that this penetrating essay on Christianity, based on a learned familiarity with the New Testament and the writings of the significant Christian authorities of the Middle Ages, would be of use. His audience consisted of those who were contemplating conversion to Christianity as well as those who were reexamining their outward Christianity and wondering if they should commit themselves intellectually as well as practically to their new faith-community. That certain individuals—some of them as distinguished as Duran himself—continued to embrace both identities in different arenas of their lives was puzzling to many of their contemporaries, but it was a dramatic demonstration of a key aspect of a new Iberian culture that emerged after 1391.[64]

Although the conditions would admittedly never be the same for the peninsular Jews after the events of 1391–1416, did the deaths and the conversions of those years spell inevitable doom for their culture? Would it be fair to describe the fifteenth century simply as a period of uninterrupted decline for them? Or did the hallmarks of Sephardic civilization as highlighted by ha-Lorki in 1391 remain prominent features of the Iberian landscape, despite the large-scale abandonment of Judaism during those years?

Despite the trauma of 1391–1416, there was still wealth and honor to be attained by Jews in the various kingdoms. The rapidly expanding opportunities of these societies in the immediate aftermath of the thirteenth-century conquests may have been perceived by both Jews and Christians as ancient history, but the good life could still be enjoyed by fifteenth-century Sephardim. The anti-Jewish legislation of the first two decades was rescinded as the Jews legally regained the status that was theirs prior to the riots. Some communities that had dissolved under the pressure of events were able to reconstitute themselves by mid-century. Their economic activities, though mainly local in scope, were diverse.[65] The courtier class continued to mix with Christians and Muslims as part and extension of its official duties—activities that may have guaranteed their community's security in the minds of many Jews—and in fact Jews of all classes interacted with their social and economic counterparts from the other faiths. Despite the riots and the conversions, or possibly because of them, Iberian society and its norms, including its class prejudices, were a constant in the daily lives of the Sephardim. A particular familiarity with Iberian culture is reflected during these years. When Isaac Caro wrote his Hebrew commentary on the Bible, he utilized words in the vernacular and geographical features of the peninsula to help his readers understand his interpretation of the texts. Caro's references to military matters and the fine points of swordsmanship reflected the interests of a politically savvy inhabitant of the peninsula during the 1470s and eighties, when the Christian reconquista geared up for its final successful forays against Muslim Granada.[66]

Remarkable connections can be observed between Sephardim and Christians after 1391, even on matters central to the Jewish-Christian debate. The master of the Order of Calatrava commissioned Moshe Arragel of Guadalajara to translate the Hebrew Bible into the vernacular and to pen a commentary to accompany the volume. Initially hesitant to accept the commission, Arragel finally agreed and worked on the project from 1422 to 1433. In his commentary, he not only cited a wide array of Jewish authors but included the exegesis of Christian scholars as well. The tone of his work was generally impartial, and at times he even appeared to support the Christian interpretation of specific passages. The Bible was published with illustrations executed by Christians because Arragel refused to be involved in this aspect of the project. The volume reflected the two religious traditions whose exegesis was cited in the commentary. Although the illustrators depicted Arragel in an honored fashion, they dressed him in identifiably Jewish costume with the distinguishing mark that had been ordained two centuries earlier by the Fourth Lateran Council.[67]

Jews were familiar with the vernacular Romance languages that were used in each of the Christian kingdoms; indeed, they used these languages in their daily lives. Songs, liturgical texts, proverbs, and other compositions reflecting Christian models were written in Romance languages and at times were even appropriated wholesale from Christian culture. Vernacular literature in Castilian and Catalan had thrived during the late fourteenth and fifteenth centuries, and the Jews' interest in creating in these languages mirrored the current style in Iberian society. Hebrew, which had been developed in Sepharad following Arabic models, remained stuck in its classicist mode and in its learned traditions, and, with a few exceptions, it was not able to adapt itself to the new modes of poetry being pioneered on the peninsula.[68]

Although battered by Christianity during the period 1391–1416, late-medieval Sephardic Jewry was intimately involved with Iberian society and its written and oral culture. But was this immersion pursued at the expense of an interest in the older forms of Jewish learning? Did the persecutions and conversions result in a decline in the traditional subjects of Jewish study? Sephardic Jewish culture in the fifteenth century did not deteriorate as much as it exhibited a change in its emphases. Although the older forms of Talmud commentary—such as the distinguished *novellae* (brief episodic commentaries) of Naḥmanides and Ibn Adret—were no longer being systematically pursued, there was no decline in talmudic exegesis. Drawing on philosophical discourse and especially ideas about logic, Isaac ben Jacob Campanton, who founded a yeshivah in Zamora, Castile, promoted an innovative methodology with which to study the Talmud. Assuming that the talmudic text was written with great care and precision, Campanton argued that its words needed to be carefully examined in order to elicit the range of meanings embedded within a particular passage. Campanton read the exegesis of medieval commentators by associating their comments with the options available within the text itself. Although little information is available on Campanton's life, we do know that he, along with Ibn Shem Tov, the son of Abraham Benveniste (a communal reformer), and two wealthy Jews, were involved as a group in assessing the taxes of the Castilian Jewish communities. One can easily argue that the presence of such individuals in powerful positions within the communities indicate that the older Sephardic style of leadership still prevailed. For this group, philosophy was not only (to paraphrase ha-Lorki) a fruit whose essence should be eaten while its shell is cast aside; speculative reasoning could also serve as the source to discover the truth about the Talmud, the foundational document of rabbinic Judaism.[69]

In the wake of 1391, there were those who argued that excessive devotion to the study of Talmud to the detriment of other traditional subjects was one of the reasons that many Jews deserted the faith. Duran maintained that the educational curriculum of Sephardic Jewry had to be reformed. Greater emphasis had to be given to the study of the Bible and to the mastery of the Hebrew language—subjects, he suggested, that would make the Jews more steadfast in their faith. Writing in 1403, Duran censured the talmudists themselves, not only because they refused to study other subjects, including the Bible, but also because they possessed overweening pride and felt that "all should stand up before them." The Aragonese philosopher Abraham Bibago also vehemently decried those talmudists who, while steeped in rabbinic knowledge, did not possess sophisticated ideas about their faith.[70]

Biblical study was not neglected; it remained central to the profile of the Jewish intellectual. Exegesis was alive and well in the moderate philosophical commentaries of the Aragonese Isaac Arama, in the kabbalistically tinged writings of Abraham Saba, who wrote in Portugal after his departure from Castile in 1492, and in the works of Saba's contemporary, the Lisbon rabbi Joseph Ḥayyun. The most distinguished exemplar of fifteenth-century commentators was the prolific Isaac Abravanel, who composed commentaries on almost all of the biblical books. Abravanel's writings reflect the beginnings of a profound shift away from medieval modes of thinking. This turn was not surprising for a man who was born in a Portugal influenced by humanist ideals and who moved in the last decades of the fifteenth century to Castile, where Renaissance modes of thought had permeated court culture. His exegesis indicated a sophisticated grasp of geography and a chronological awareness that supported a profound distinction between past and present. Abravanel subjected the Bible to the same stylistic questions he would have posed to any other literary text. He wondered in a letter to Ḥayyun (who may have been a teacher of his) whether the book of Deuteronomy had been written by God or by Moses. Although he wrestled with the authorship and the dating of biblical books as well as of rabbinic sources, Abravanel never undermined the idea of the Torah of Moses in his own commentaries.[71]

Many new educational institutions were founded over the course of the fifteenth century on the northern half of the peninsula (reflecting the demographic shift), where a burgeoning cadre of students was enrolled. These were yeshivot that emphasized the study of the Talmud and of the halakhah, as was the tradition among Sephardic yeshivot in previous centuries. Yet other subjects such as Kabbalah were also included in the curriculum, and some students may have been encouraged to pursue their mystical studies in greater depth. Campanton's academy in Zamora may have been one of these institutions. Philosophical topics were often explored in institutions separate from the talmudic academies. Students would leave their regular studies and travel to these schools to pursue the disciplines of physics and metaphysics.[72] Yeshivot served as copying centers for manuscripts that, presumably, were studied in their institutions. Although manuscripts were also produced elsewhere on the peninsula, the printed Hebrew book made its appearance in towns that may have also hosted these educational institutions. A variety of repositories existed for these books and manuscripts, such as private libraries owned by Jews and Christian converts and those managed by social institutions such as confraternities.[73]

The study of philosophy and Kabbalah was cultivated in the fifteenth century, though their precise place within the curriculum of Sephardic Jews is not clear. These disciplines offered important prisms through which to view the foundation works of rabbinic culture and to look at the greater world. Toward the end of the century, there were thinkers who combined both of these fields of study into a unified perspective on Judaism and the Jewish people, even though some kabbalists demonized philosophy as the root of all evil.[74] The study of philosophy had taken a new turn with the writings of Crescas and his attack on Maimonides. Although many philosophers defended Maimonides and his ideas about free will and determinism, they followed Crescas by retreating from Maimonides' contention that the ultimate end of human life was the perfection of the intellect. Crescas's disciples argued in opposition that what led to the immortality of the soul was fealty to the word of God as expressed in the Torah and to the performance of the commandments. The works of Maimonides, as in previous years, remained the focal point around which the arguments about the appropriate place of philosophy within the Sephardic curriculum continued to swirl. The physician Abraham Shalom, writing in Catalonia in the mid-fifteenth century, agreed with the Maimonidean position on the creation of the world and defended the role of philosophy (that is, Aristotle's writings) within Judaism. But Shalom departed from Maimonides by asserting that it was knowledge of halakhah and not metaphysics that was necessary for the perfection of human beings. By arguing that the Law was an expression of Divine Love, he was espousing a Jewish particularism in the fashion of ha-Levi, Naḥmanides, and Crescas. Further, by asserting the importance of Divine Law, he was supporting those who had refused to convert to Christianity and had been willing to suffer because of that conviction.[75]

The beginning of the fifteenth century proved to be a time of renewed interest in kabbalistic ideas after mystical creativity had suffered a decline during the fourteenth century. This attention was expressed in the study of works such as the *Zohar*. As a result of the fascination it held for its readers, this book earned a quasi-canonical status. So great was the focus on the written word as opposed to oral transmission that Shem Tov ibn Shem Tov bemoaned the fact that he could find no one to teach him Kabbalah. The philosopher Joseph Albo also decried this reliance on the texts. But the goal of this student of Crescas (Albo was also one of the chief disputants at Tortosa) was to limit those mystical ideas that could serve as a springboard for further philosophical speculation to those that were received as oral communications from a master. Kabbalah was achieving status as authoritative rabbinic interpretation even for those who were not kabbalists by training. We have already observed how mysticism was accorded an important place in the curriculum in the philosophically oriented school of talmudic studies founded by Campanton.

Some of the kabbalists' specific attitudes, such as Shem Tov ibn Shem Tov's scathing critique of the philosophical enterprise, grew out of internal intellectual developments, but the general interest in Kabbalah may well have been a reaction to the theological quandaries posed by the events of 1391. The author of the mystical *Pokeaḥ Ivrim*, living near Burgos in 1439, boasted not only of the superiority of the study of the Kabbalah (philosophy was deemed inferior, not dangerous) but also of the greatness of Castilian Jewry, who had endured the disasters of the turn of the century. This author viewed the survivors who remained within the Jewish faith as "sanctifiers of the name," possessing the same spiritual stature as that generation of Israelites who had received the revelation at Sinai.[76]

The options for an imaginative mystic, in the absence of reliable oral transmissions and in the face of the seemingly sterile world of speculative exegesis, were severely limited. In response to this predicament, a small and highly idiosyncratic group of mystical writers emerged toward the end of the century whose teachings were grounded in part on revelatory experiences that had been stimulated by acts of magic. These authors, fierce antirationalists all, blamed the ills of Jewish society on the study of philosophy. During the last few decades of Iberian Jewish life, however, some kabbalists eschewed this radical path and were well integrated into the intellectual mainstream. Among them were Abraham Saba, the great exegete who was exiled to Portugal from northwest Castile in 1492, and those who studied in Campanton's yeshivah in Zamora, also in northwest Castile. Indeed, at the end of the century there were also those who combined both philosophical and mystical reflections in establishing their worldview. Isaac Arama and Joel ibn Shua'ib utilized philosophy and Kabbalah in their exegetical works in such a fashion that it is not easy to disentangle these intellectual strands within their writings.[77]

After the destruction and the conversions of the late fourteenth and early fifteenth centuries, some Jews reevaluated their cherished notion that their people fared better in Christian lands than in Islamic countries. A Saragossan Jew wrote a letter of introduction for a friend who had decided to emigrate to the Land of Israel from Tudela, Navarre—which had barely been affected by the events of 1391–1416. He let loose a string of invective against the accursed soil of Sepharad, and he praised the Land of Israel as a land of bounty. Sephardic Jews did emigrate to the Land of Israel as part of a general migration in the Mediterranean world. There was a small but consistent stream of emigrants after 1391, but it was only after 1453, in the wake of the Turkish conquest of Constantinople and amid speculation about the reorganization of the political and religious world order, that the ancient homeland became a magnet for a larger number of emigrants. Yet even as some counseled their friends to leave the paradise of Sepharad for the humiliation and poverty of the Jewish communities of the Islamic Diaspora, it remained axiomatic for these Sephardim that there was less hatred toward the Jews in Christian lands than there was under the Muslims.[78]

As Sephardic ideas and people began to spread to the eastern Mediterranean and even to central Europe, the Iberian Sephardim paid close attention to events taking place outside the peninsula. Their continued interest during the fifteenth century in the mythical figure of Prester John and his exploits not only reflected a broadening of geographical horizons, which was symptomatic of Renaissance culture, but also indicated the desire of Jews to imagine that their redemption was in the offing. Ḥasdai Crescas demonstrated curiosity in stories regarding the whereabouts and adventures of Prester John, and Isaac Abravanel was devoted to news about the ten lost tribes and their settlement in far-away lands.[79]

As before 1391, speculations about distant Jewish communities served as a psychological buffer against the arguments of the rival faith. Issues of Jewish sovereignty and the location of the ten lost tribes were intimately connected to Jewish expectations about the coming of their Messiah and to their assertion that God had not forgotten his chosen people. Crescas may have been supportive of a messianic pretender in the 1390s. According to our correspondent ha-Lorki, speaking as Gerónimo de Santa Fé during the proceedings at Tortosa, Crescas had "preached in the synagogue" about reports of a Messiah born in the northern Castilian village of Cisneros. Nevertheless, there is scarcely any indication that Sephardic Jews participated in a messianic movement. Indeed, Crescas maintained that belief in the Messiah was not a dogma within Judaism, and his student Joseph Albo argued, contra Maimonides, that one who denied the Messiah was a sinner but not an infidel. Still, ruminations about the Messiah and recommendations about the activities Jews might perform to hasten his coming were crucial in maintaining the equilibrium of the community within an ever more confident Christian society.[80]

Preoccupation with Christian truth-claims shadowed and informed Jewish life in Christian Iberia, and understandably cast an even more intense pall during the fifteenth century. A half-century after Crescas composed his vernacular *Refutation of Christian Principles*, Joseph ibn Shem Tov, a Castilian courtier who was engaged in polemical activities with Christian scholars, translated it into Hebrew, presumably to serve as a sourcebook for Jewish specialists. Ibn Shem Tov understood that the Jewish-Christian debate was not confined to strictly polemical treatises but informed philosophical and exegetical works as well. The arguments ha-Lorki made while a Jew to the erstwhile Solomon ha-Levi were still being combated over 40 years later in the latter's magisterial biblical commentary, *Scrutinium Scripturarum*.[81]

Toward the end of the fifteenth century, the virulence of Jewish literary attacks against Christianity intensified. A noted kabbalist, Abraham ben Eliezer ha-Levi, asserted the demonic nature of the Christian faith. The author of an anonymous contemporaneous work, the *Book of the Answering Angel*, which claimed to be a product of divine revelation, derided Christian theology and expressed deep and unmitigated hostility to the person of Jesus. Yet this same writer adapted Christian ideas about the birth and nature of the Messiah in his own description of the redeemer. He foretold that at the end of days the power of Christianity would be destroyed, but Christianity would prove to be an ally of Judaism at the time of the redemption. The juxtaposition of this author's hatred of the historical expression of Christianity with his attraction to its theology strikingly underscored the complex and paradoxical attitude of Sephardic Jews to Christian society at the end of the fifteenth century.[82]

This convoluted attitude was even more emblematic of those who had converted to Christianity during the last decade of the fourteenth century and the first two decades of the fifteenth. Whether willingly or forcibly converted, these individuals had formed, unawares, another religious grouping within the Christian Iberian kingdoms: the *conversos.* The variegated religious behavior of these converts and the response of Jews and Christians to their activities profoundly affected the fortunes of Sephardic Jewry and proved to be crucial factors in the development of Spanish and Portuguese civilization.

As the fifteenth century continued to unfold, some of the conversos had become socially and religiously integrated into the older Christian community, while others had remained as faithful as they could to the Judaism they had willingly or forcibly abandoned. Given the failure of the host Christian society to assimilate them and the prohibition in canon law against their return to Judaism, the vast majority of conversos led a double religious existence distinguished by practices characteristic of both Judaism and Christianity. When riots broke out against the "New Christians" (a designation that reflected their incomplete acceptance within Christian society) in southern Castile in the 1460s and 1470s, Iberian Christian society recognized that the conversos presented not only a religious problem but a social one as well. In response to this challenge, some Christian writers argued for educational initiatives to assist the conversos in their Christianization. Others asserted that, as judaizers, these New Christians were heretics deserving of the death penalty. Ferdinand and Isabella charted a position between the two views by founding a papal Inquisition under Crown control to investigate the behavior of converts in Castile and Aragon.[83]

Some Jews (on and off the peninsula) viewed their converted brethren as members of their own community, deserving both friendship and religious encouragement. Others viewed the apostates with little sympathy and asserted that the conversos' daily behavior undermined their status as members of the Jewish people. These Jews criticized the converts for their unwillingness to observe the laws of Judaism in private and for their reluctance to embrace a public as well as private Jewish existence by emigrating from the peninsula. Although social and religious ties between Jews and conversos were maintained in the immediate aftermath of the conversions, changing occupational and residential patterns of the New Christians and the ever-widening gaps between the religious expressions of these two groups over the course of the fifteenth century loosened and frayed those earlier bonds.[84]

After a few years of operation, the tribunals of both the Castilian and the Aragonese Inquisitions concluded that a majority of the conversos were following Jewish practices and posed a religious threat to the "old Christians" as well as to their own souls. In the late 1480s, senior inquisitorial officials began to promote a solution to this seemingly intractable problem. By preventing Jews from associating with conversos, they suggested, the Jews would not be able to influence their former coreligionists to practice Jewish rituals. Free of this negative influence, the conversos would be free to turn to the Christian faith with great sincerity and devotion.

Gradually, the idea of a kingdom-wide expulsion of the Jews gained support within government circles as the most effective means of resolving the social and religious difficulties raised by the converso population. The Jews were completely surprised by this development. After all, their position within Iberian Christian society had been relatively stable ever since the 1420s. In addition, the king and queen had displayed a conservative stance in domestic affairs, a posture that had reassured the Jews that their political status would not be altered. To be sure, Ferdinand and Isabella had separated Jews from New Christians in a number of towns and cities within Castile and Aragon and had even expelled the Jews from Andalusia in order to prevent their religious contamination of the conversos. But the monarchy had, for the most part, continued to support the rights and privileges of the Jewish community.[85]

On March 31, 1492, only a few weeks after Ferdinand and Isabella had brought the centuries-old reconquista to a successful conclusion, they signed the edict banishing the Jews from their realm. The Jews had until the last day of July 1492 to leave Castile and Aragon or to convert to Christianity and remain within their homes. Many Jews chose to convert, but others decided to cross the borders into Portugal and Navarre or to reestablish their lives outside of the peninsula.[86] As the fifteenth century drew to a close, however, the two kingdoms that had provided refuge for the exiled Jews followed the example of Castile and Aragon. At the end of 1496, King Manoel decreed the expulsion of the Jews from Portugal. Because of the absence of a substantial converso population that could have filled some of the economic roles left vacant by the departing Jews, the expulsion evolved into a forced conversion of all of Portuguese Jewry. At the end of 1497 or the beginning of 1498, King Juhan and Queen Catalina of Navarre decided to expel their Jews to prevent the invasion of their kingdom by powerful neighbors to the south. Unable to leave the country without traveling through off-limits territory, almost all the Navarrese Jews converted.[87]

And so the saga of Iberian Jewry came to a close. Sephardic Jews would continue to build their communities and to fashion their traditions, albeit no longer within the geographical boundaries where their culture was born and where they had cultivated their unique identity. Exiles took with them not only their well-developed Sephardic culture but also their personal perspectives on the past and the future. The Portuguese-born Abravanel, who served at the court of Ferdinand and Isabella, remained convinced that peace and prosperity had been the lot of Sephardic Jews even on the eve of the expulsion. But others, such as Abraham ben Eliezer ha-Levi and his brother-in-law, the chronicler Abraham Zacuto (who was imprisoned in Portugal upon refusing to convert in 1497), held a much darker view of the last two decades of peninsular Jewish life. Similarly, though some exiled Sephardim recalled their Iberian past and its cultural accomplishments with great pride, others remained dejected and pessimistic and did not find in their history anything that might augur well for the successful regeneration of their community.[88]

The fear that God had turned His countenance away from His people haunted the exiles as it had ha-Lorki. For some of the refugees, the messianic exegesis of biblical texts and of rabbinic commentaries allowed for a defense against despair and encouraged the suppression of the frightful conclusion that Christianity might indeed have triumphed. Living on the Italian peninsula in the wake of the expulsion, Abravanel composed three treatises devoted to the rehabilitation of the messianic prophecies of Judaism. In "Salvations of His Annointed," his exploration of rabbinic reflections on the messianic advent, Abravanel expressed nothing but contempt for ha-Lorki, "the chief of all heretics, may his name and memory be blotted out."[89]

Let Abravanel, the great exemplar of the Sephardic courtier tradition, have the final word. He may have summarized the conflicted perspectives of the exiles when they looked back at the glories of Sephardic Jewry and their ignominious exile. He asserted, in his commentary on Jeremiah 2:24, that the last day Jews were permitted to reside in Castile and Aragon was the ninth of Av, the day on which they commemorated the destruction of the First and Second Temples in Jerusalem. With this calendrical sleight of hand, he taught us much about Sephardic Jews and their culture. Abravanel surely knew that July 31, the last official day of Jewish presence in Castile and Aragon, was the seventh of Av. (The actual ninth of Av, two days later, was a day that, for many of the exiles or even those remaining on the peninsula, was decidedly horrific.) But by identifying the ninth of Av as the date of expulsion, Abravanel gave voice to the Sephardic perception that the downfall of the community—"the exiles of Jerusalem who are in Sepharad"—was to be equated with the great national tragedies that the Jewish people had suffered. Even as he viewed the trauma that befell his people, he was also suggesting a parallel between the grand accomplishments of Sephardic Jewry and the glories of the distant past.

NOTES

1. The translation here—and throughout this chapter—is mine. For the Hebrew text and a German translation, see L. Landau, *Das Apologetische Schreiben des Josua Lorki* (Antwerpen, 1906). See also the University of California dissertation by Judith Gale Krieger, *Pablo de Santa María: His Epoch, Life and Hebrew and Spanish Literary Production* (1988), in which the Hebrew text is accompanied by an English translation on pp. 262–309, and Michael Glatzer, "Between Joshua Halorki and Shelomo Halevi—Towards an Examination of the Causes of Conversion Among Jews in Spain in the Fourteenth Century," *Pe'amim* 54 (1993): 103–16.

2. See, for example, Yitzhak Baer, *A History of the Jews in Christian Spain*, 2 vols. (Philadelphia, 1966), 2: 95–169 and *passim*.

3. Samuel Krauss, "The Names Ashkenaz and Sepharad" (Hebrew), *Tarbiz* 3 (1931–32): 431, 435.

4. Raymond P. Scheindlin, "Rabbi Moses ibn Ezra on the Legitimacy of Poetry," *Medievalia et Humanistica*, n.s. 7 (1976): 101–15.

5. Two recent articles of note on Judah Halevi, whose life has attracted much scholarly attention, are Yosef Yahalom, "The Leningrad Treasures and the Study of the Poetry and Life of Yehuda Halevi" (Hebrew), *Pe'amim* 46–47 (1991): 55–74, and Ezra Fleischer, " 'The Essence of Our Land and Its Meaning'—Toward a Portrait of Judah Halevi on the Basis of Geniza Documents" (Hebrew), *Pe'amim* 68 (1996): 4–15.

6. The classic work on Abraham ibn Daud is Gerson D. Cohen, ed., *Sefer ha-Qabbalah (The Book of Tradition) by Abraham ibn Daud* (Philadelphia, 1967).

7. See, for example, José S. Gil, *La escuela de traductores de Toledo y los colaboradores judíos* (Toledo, 1985); Robert I. Burns, ed., *The Worlds of Alfonso the Learned and James the Conqueror* (Princeton, N.J., 1985); and, on courtiers in Aragon, the work of David Romano, especially his *Judíos al servicio de Pedro el Grande de Aragón* (Barcelona, 1983).

8. Eleazar Gutwirth, "Hispano-Jewish Attitudes Toward the Moors in the Fifteenth Century," *Sefarad* 49 (1989): 237–62.

9. Eliyahu Ashtor, *The Jews of Moslem Spain*, 3 vols. (Philadelphia, 1973–84), and Yom Tov Assis, *The Golden Age of Aragonese Jewry* (London, 1997), 13–18 and *passim*.

10. For a re-creation of these events, see Bernard Septimus, "Piety and Power in Thirteenth-Century Catalonia," in Isadore Twersky, ed., *Medieval Jewish History* (Cambridge, Mass., and London, 1979), 197–230.

11. On the physical remains of the Sephardic communities on the Iberian Peninsula, see José Luis Lacave, "Material Remains," in Haim Beinart, ed., *The Sephardi Legacy*, vol. 1 (Jerusalem, 1992), 452–73. For an introduction to a facsimile edition of the fourteenth-

century haggadah, see Cecil Roth, *The Sarajevo Haggadah* (Beograd, Yugoslavia, 1975), 7–45, esp. 15, 21–22, and the illuminated pages.

12. Ross Brann, *The Compunctious Poet: Cultural Ambiguity and Hebrew Poetry in Muslim Spain* (Baltimore, Md., 1991).

13. On the relationship of the Jewish community and governmental authorities during the Middle Ages, see Shmuel Shilo, *Dina de'Malkhuta Dina* (Jerusalem, 1974). On the judicial system of the Jews in medieval Iberia, see, generally, Abraham Neuman, *The Jews in Spain*, vol. 1 (Philadelphia, 1942), 112–46. On the situation in the Crown of Aragon, see Assis, *Golden Age*, 145–63, and especially his "The Jews of Spain in Gentile Courts (XIIIth–XIVth Centuries)" (Hebrew), in Menahem Ben-Sasson et al., eds., *Culture and Society in Medieval Jewish History* (Jerusalem, 1989), 399–430.

14. Moses of Coucy, *Sefer Mitzvot ha-Gadol*, Prohibition 112, no. 3. On the sexual mores of the Spanish Jews, see Yom Tov Assis, "Sexual Behaviour in Mediaeval Hispano-Jewish Society," in Ada Rapoport-Albert and Steven J. Zipperstein, eds., *Jewish History: Essays in Honour of Chimen Abramsky* (London, 1988), 25–59.

15. See Assis, "Sexual Behaviour," 37.

16. Reference to the herem of 1281 is in *Zikhron Yehudah* (Berlin, 1846), no. 91, fol. 45b. See Mordechai A. Friedman, "Menahem ben Aaron Ibn Zemah's Anti-Polygyny Torah Commentary from the Geniza," in Marc Z. Brettler and Michael A. Fishbane eds., *Minhah le-Nahum* (Sheffield, Engl., 1993), 103–16.

17. Assis, *Golden Age*, 299–307.

18. Brann, *Compunctious Poet*, 143–57.

19. Talya Fishman, "A Medieval Parody of Misogyny: Judah ibn Shabbetai's 'Minhat Yehudah sone hanashim,' " *Prooftexts* 8 (1988): 89–111. See also Assis, "Sexual Behaviour," 28. The beginnings of a discussion of medieval Sephardic women, relying on scattered data, can be found in Renée Levine Melammed, "Sephardi Women in the Medieval and Early Modern Periods," in Judith R. Baskin, ed., *Jewish Women in Historical Perspective*, 2d ed. (Detroit, 1999), 128–49.

20. Monford Harris, "Marriage as Metaphysics: A Study of the *Iggereth Hakodesh*," *Hebrew Union College Annual* 33 (1962): 197–220. See also Isaiah Tishby, *The Wisdom of the Zohar*, vol. 3 (New York, 1989), 1371, and David Biale, *Eros and the Jews* (New York, 1992), 101–20.

21. Jacob Katz, "Halakhic Statements in the Zohar" (Hebrew), *Tarbiz* 50 (1980–81): 405–22, reprinted in his *Halakhah and Kabbalah* (Jerusalem, 1984), 34–51. See also Israel Ta-Shma, *Ha-Nigle She-Banistar* (Tel Aviv, 1995), and the review by Yehuda Liebes in *Tarbiz* 64 (1995): 581–605.

22. See Israel Ta-Shma, "The Author of Sefer 'Ha-Hinnukh' " (Hebrew), *Kiryat Sefer* 55 (1980): 787–90.

23. Abraham Grossman, "Legislation and Responsa Literature" and "Relations Between Spanish and Ashkenazi Jewry in the Middle Ages," in Beinart, ed., *Sephardi Legacy*, 1: 188–239.

24. A mixed attitude toward the Jews prevailed in Las Siete Partidas. Alfonso devoted an entire section to the Jews and, in so doing, acknowledged their important presence within his kingdom. Although his rules understandably reflected classical Christian theological attitudes toward the Jews and the influence of the newly resurgent Roman legal system, Alfonso also expressed particular views about this minority. For while the code gave voice to the blood libel that had appeared in mid-twelfth-century England for the first time, Alfonso did not claim that such crimes had ever occurred and further asserted that only he and his royal judiciary would sit in judgment on these matters. And while he ordered the Jews to wear a distinguishing mark on their clothing so that they could be identified, in accordance with the proceedings of the Fourth Lateran Council in 1215, he also explained, contrary to traditional Christian teachings, that the reason no one could deface a synagogue was that the name of God was praised therein. See Dwayne E. Carpenter, *Alfonso X and the Jews: An Edition of and Commentary on Siete Partidas* (Berkeley, Calif., 1986), 7, chap. 24 "De los judíos."

25. The convenient Hebrew translation of Alfred Freimann's German articles on Rabbi Asher and his family is *The ROSh, Rabbenu Asher ben R. Yehiel and His Descendants* (Jerusalem, 1986). See also Israel Ta-Shma, "Rabbenu Asher and his Son R. Ya'akov Ba'al ha-Turim—Between Ashkenaz and Sepharad" (Hebrew), *Pe'amim* 46–47 (1991): 75–91, where on p. 88 he discusses the relationship between Las Siete Partidas and Tur.

26. Cohen, *Sefer Ha-Qabbalah*, 295–300. See also Jan D. Katzew, "Moses ibn Ezra and Judah Halevi: Their Philosophies in Response to Exile," *Hebrew Union College Annual* 55 (1984): 179–95.

27. Bernard Septimus, *Hispano-Jewish Culture in Transition* (Cambridge, Mass., 1982), 39–60.

28. Daniel Jeremy Silver, *Maimonidean Criticism and the Maimonidean Controversy, 1180–1240* (Leiden, 1965).

29. Septimus, "Piety and Power."

30. See the articles by Bernard Septimus, Moses Idel, and David Berger in Isadore Twersky, ed., *Rabbi Moses Naḥmanides (RaMBaN): Explorations in His Religious and Literary Virtuosity* (Cambridge, Mass., 1983).

31. A convenient summary is David Berger, "Judaism and General Culture in Medieval and Early Modern Times," in Jacob J. Schacter, ed., *Judaism's Encounter with Other Cultures* (Northvale, N.J., 1997), 100–108.

32. See the unpublished master's thesis of David Horwitz, "The Role of Philosophy and Kabbalah in the Works of Rashba" (Yeshiva University, 1986).

33. Dov Schwartz has written voluminously on these issues. See, especially, his "Theology and Learning in Medieval Jewish Philosophy: A Chapter in Maimonidean Influence" (Hebrew), *Da'at* 37 (1996): 153–79, and "A Study of the Philosophical Variety in Spain and Provence Before the Expulsion" (Hebrew), *Pe'amim* 49 (1991): 5–23.

34. Israel Ta-Shma, "Philosophical Considerations for Halakhic Decision-Making in

Spain" (Hebrew), *Sefunot*, n.s. 3, no. 18 (1985): 99–110, and reprinted in his *Ritual, Custom and Reality in Franco-Germany, 1000–1350* (Jerusalem, 1996), 79–93.

35. See Schwartz, "Theology and Learning" and "A Study of the Philosophical Variety." See also Warren Harvey, *Hasdai Crescas' Critique of the Theory of Acquired Intellect* (Ph.D. diss., Columbia University, 1973), 2: 86–89 and *passim*.

36. Norman Roth, "Two Jewish Courtiers of Alfonso X Called Zag (Isaac)," *Sefarad* 43 (1983): 75–85.

37. Dwayne E. Carpenter, "The Portrayal of the Jew in Alfonso the Learned's *Cantigas de Santa María*," in Bernard Dov Cooperman, ed., *In Iberia and Beyond: Hispanic Jews Between Cultures* (Newark, Del., 1998), 15–42.

38. Assis, *Golden Age*.

39. See Joseph Shatzmiller, *Jews, Medicine and Medieval Society* (Berkeley, Calif., 1994), and Yom Tov Assis, "Jewish Physicians and Medicine in Medieval Spain," in Samuel S. Kottek and Luís García-Ballester, eds., *Medicine and Medical Ethics in Medieval and Early Modern Spain* (Jerusalem, 1996), 33–49.

40. Maria José Pimenta Ferro, *Os judeus em Portugal no século xiv* (Lisbon, 1979).

41. Beatrice Leroy, *The Jews of Navarre in the Late Middle Ages* (Jerusalem, 1985).

42. Julio Valdeón Baruque, *Los judíos de Castilla y la revolución Trastámara* (Valladolid, 1968).

43. See the perceptive remarks of David Nirenberg, *Communities of Violence* (Princeton, N.J., 1996), esp. 231–45.

44. See Marcus Nathan Adler, *The Itinerary of Benjamin of Tudela* (London, 1907).

45. See, generally, Grossman, "Relations Between Spanish and Ashkenazi Jewry."

46. Bernard Septimus, "Hispano-Jewish Views of Christendom and Islam," in Cooperman, ed., *In Iberia and Beyond*, esp. 43–48.

47. Abraham Gross, "The Expulsion and the Search for the Ten Tribes," *Judaism* 41 (1992): 130–47.

48. Baer, *History of the Jews in Christian Spain*, 1: 327–31.

49. Robert Chazan, *Daggers of Faith: Thirteenth-Century Christian Missionizing and Jewish Response* (Berkeley, Calif., 1989).

50. Robert Chazan, *Barcelona and Beyond: The Disputation of 1263 and Its Aftermath* (Berkeley, Calif., 1992).

51. See, generally, Hanne Trautner-Kromann, *Shield and Sword* (Tübingen, 1993), and Jeremy Cohen, "Towards a Functional Classification of Jewish Anti-Christian Polemic in the High Middle Ages," in Bernard Lewis and Friedrich Niewöhner, eds., *Religionsgespräche im Mittelalter* (Wiesbaden, 1992), 93–114. Ora Limor has written on the disputation in Mallorca in 1286; see her "Missionary Merchants: Three Medieval Anti-Jewish Works from Genoa," *Journal of Medieval History* 17 (1991): 35–51. On Ibn Adret's involvement in the Christian-Jewish debate, see Jeremy Cohen, "The Christian Adversary of Solomon ibn Adret," *Jewish Quarterly Review* 71 (1980–81): 48–55. David Berger, "Christians, Gentiles and

the Talmud: A Fourteenth-Century Jewish Response to the Attack on Rabbinic Judaism," in Lewis and Niewöhner, eds., *Religionsgespräche im Mittelalter*, 115–30, analyzes the work of ha-Kohen.

52. Dov Schwartz, "The Neutralization of the Messianic Idea in Medieval Jewish Rationalism" (Hebrew), *Hebrew Union College Annual* 64 (1993): 37–58 in the Hebrew numbered pagination.

53. Yom Tov Assis, "The Judeo-Arabic Tradition in Christian Spain," in Daniel Frank, ed., *The Jews of Medieval Islam: Community, Society, and Identity* (Leiden, 1995), 111–24, and E. Gutwirth, "Actitudes judías hacia los cristianos en la España del siglo xv: Ideario de los traductores del latín," *Actas del II Congreso Internacional. Encuentro de las tres culturas* (Toledo, Spain, 1985), 189–96. On Nissim Gerondi, see Warren Zev Harvey, "Nissim of Gerona and William of Ockham on Prime Matter," *Jewish History* 6 (1992): 87–98; on ha-Kohen, see Trautner-Kromann, *Shield and Sword*, 148.

54. Beatrice Leroy, "Le Grand Rabbin de Navarre Josef Orabuena," in Carlos Barros, ed., *Xudeus e 'conversos' na historia* (Santiago de Compostela, 1994), 153–67.

55. On ha-Lorki's view, see Colette Sirat, *A History of Jewish Philosophy in the Middle Ages* (Cambridge, Engl., 1985), 348–50.

56. See Nirenberg, *Communities of Violence*, esp. 200–230, on Holy Week violence. His ruminations about the riots of 1391 are in ibid., 248–49.

57. Ha-Levi's letter to ha-Lorki can be found in Landau, *Das Apologetische Schreiben*, 19–21. The Hebrew text, accompanied by an English translation, is in Krieger, *Pablo de Santa María*, 311–17.

58. See the writings of the second-century bishop Melito of Sardis, as reported in Jeremy Cohen, *Living Letters of the Law* (Berkeley, Calif., 1999), 10–11.

59. See Elias Lipiner, *Two Portuguese Exiles in Castile: Dom David Negro; Dom Isaac Abravanel* (Jerusalem, 1997), 20, and, generally, Pimenta Ferro, *Os judeus em Portugal*. For Navarre, see Beatrice Leroy, "From 1390 to 1460, King Charles III of Navarre, Protector of Foreign Jews in his Kingdom" (French), *Sefarad* 52 (1992): 463–71.

60. Moisés Orfali, "Jerónimo de Santa Fé and the Christian Polemic against the Talmud" (Spanish), *Annuario di Studi Ebraici* 10 (1980–84): 157–78.

61. Jaume Riera i Sans, "On the Fate of R. Isaac Bar Sheshet (RIBaSh) During the Persecutions of 1391" (Hebrew), *Sefunot*, n.s. 2, no. 17 (1983): 11–20. The most recent discussion of Perfet's attitudes toward the Iberian conversos is in Norman Roth's argumentative *Conversos, Inquisition and the Expulsion* (Madison, Wisc., 1995), 35–38.

62. See Natan Ophir, "A New Reading of R. Ḥasdai Crescas' *Or ha-Shem*: The Conversos' Perspective" (Hebrew), *Proceedings of the Eleventh World Congress of Jewish Studies*, vol. 3/2 (Jerusalem, 1994), 41–47.

63. Daniel J. Lasker, *The Refutation of the Christian Principles by Ḥasdai Crescas* (Albany, N.Y., 1992).

64. Frank Talmage, "The Polemical Writings of Profiat Duran," *Immanuel* 13 (1981): 69–95.

65. For Aragon, see the many articles by Miguel Angel Motis Dolader, among them "The Disappearance of the Jewish Community of Daroca in the Beginning of the 15th Century," *Proceedings of the Tenth World Congress of Jewish Studies,* vol. 2/2 (Jerusalem, 1990), 143–50. See also Mark D. Meyerson, "The Economic Life of the Jews of Murviedro in the Fifteenth Century," in Cooperman, ed., *In Iberia and Beyond,* 67–95.

66. Eleazar Gutwirth, "Contempt for the Lower Orders in 15th-Century Hispano Jewish Thought," *Miscelánea de estudios árabes y hebraicos* 30 (1981): 83–93, and Gutwirth, "Isaac Caro in His Time," ibid. 40 (1991): 119–30.

67. Jocelyn N. Hillgarth, *The Spanish Kingdoms,* vol. 2 (Oxford, 1978), 159–60.

68. See Eleazar Gutwirth, "Towards Expulsion: 1391–1492," in Elie Kedourie, ed., *Spain and the Jews* (London, 1992), esp. 58, and Raymond P. Scheindlin, "Secular Hebrew Poetry in Fifteenth-Century Spain," in Benjamin R. Gampel, ed., *Crisis and Creativity in the Sephardic World* (New York, 1997), 31–37.

69. Daniel Boyarin, *Sephardi Speculation: A Study in Methods of Talmudic Interpretation* (Jerusalem, 1989).

70. Eleazar Gutwirth, "Conversions to Christianity Amongst Fifteenth-Century Spanish Jews: An Alternative Explanation," in *Shlomo Simonsohn Jubilee Volume* (Tel Aviv, 1993), 103–21.

71. Abraham Gross, *Iberian Jewry from Twilight to Dawn: The World of Rabbi Abraham Saba* (Leiden, 1995), and his *Rabbi Joseph ben Abraham Hayyun* (Ramat Gan, 1993). See also Eric Lawee, "On the Threshhold of the Renaissance: New Methods and Sensibilities in the Biblical Commentaries of Isaac Abarbanel," *Viator* 26 (1995): 283–319, and his "The Ways of Midrash in the Biblical Commentaries of Isaac Abarbanel," *HUCA* 67 (1996): 107–42.

72. Joseph R. Hacker, "On the Intellectual Character and Self-Perception of Spanish Jewry in the Late Fifteenth Century" (Hebrew), *Sefunot,* n.s. 2, no. 17 (1983): 21–95, and Abraham Gross, "A Sketch of the History of Yeshivot in Castile in the Fifteenth Century" (Hebrew), *Pe'amim* 31 (1987): 3–21.

73. Michael Riegler, "Were the Yeshivot in Spain Centers for the Copying of Books?," *Sefarad* 57 (1997): 373–98, and Menahem Schmelzer, "Hebrew Manuscripts and Printed Books Among the Sephardim Before and After the Expulsion," in Gampel, ed., *Crisis and Creativity,* 257–66. On libraries, see Eleazar Gutwirth and Miguel Angel Motis Dolader, "Twenty-six Jewish Libraries from Fifteenth-Century Spain," *The Library,* Sixth Series 18 (1996): 27–53, and Jocelyn N. Hillgarth, "Majorcan Jews and Conversos as Owners and Artisans of Books," in Aharon Mirsky et al., eds., *Exile and Diaspora: Studies in the History of the Jewish People Presented to Professor Ḥaim Beinart* (Madrid, 1991), 125–30.

74. Shaul Regev, "About the Problem of the Study of Philosophy in Fifteenth-Century Thought; R. Joseph ibn Shem Tov and R. Abraham Bibago" (Hebrew), *Da'at* 16 (1986): 57–85.

75. Hava Tirosh-Rothschild, "Political Philosophy in the Thought of Abraham Shalom" (Hebrew), *Jerusalem Studies in Jewish Thought* 9 (1990): 409–40. See also Eric Lawee, "The

Path to Felicity: Teachings and Tensions in *'Even Shetiyyah* of Abraham ben Yehudah, Disciple of Ḥasdai Crescas," *Mediaeval Studies* 59 (1997): 183–223.

76. Schwartz, "A Study of the Philosophical Variety in Spain and Provence," and Boaz Huss, "On the Status of Kabbala in Spain After the Persecutions of 1391" (Hebrew), *Pe'amim* 56 (1993): 20–32.

77. Moshe Idel, "Inquiries in the Doctrine of *Sefer ha-Meshiv*" (Hebrew), *Sefunot*, n.s. 2, no. 17 (1983): 185–266, and Abraham Gross, "Satan and Christianity: The Demonization of Christianity in the Writings of Abraham Saba," *Zion* 58 (1993): 91–105. See also Isaiah Tishby, *Messianism in the Time of the Expulsion from Spain and Portugal* (Jerusalem, 1985).

78. Haim Beinart, "A 15th-Century Hebrew Formulary from Spain" (Hebrew), *Sefunot* 5 (1961): 116–17; Joseph R. Hacker, "Links Between Spanish Jewry and Palestine, 1391–1492," in Richard I. Cohen, ed., *Vision and Conflict in the Holy Land* (Jerusalem, 1985), 111–39; and Septimus, "Hispano-Jewish Views of Christendom and Islam," 48–50.

79. Gross, "The Expulsion and the Search for the Ten Tribes."

80. Warren Zev Harvey, "The Messianism of Rabbi Ḥasdai Crescas" (unpublished paper delivered at Yeshiva University conference, "Creativity in a Community in Decline," 1992), and Eric Lawee, " 'Israel Has No Messiah' in Late Medieval Spain," *The Journal of Jewish Thought and Philosophy* 5 (1996): 245–79.

81. Lasker, *Refutation of the Christian Principles*, and Glatzer, "Between Joshua Halorki and Shelomo Halevi."

82. Moshe Idel, "The Attitude to Christianity in the *Sefer ha-Meshiv*," *Immanuel* 12 (1981): 77–95.

83. Haim Beinart, "The Converso Problem in 15th-Century Spain," in R. D. Barnett, ed., *The Sephardi Heritage* (London, 1971), 425–56.

84. The literature on this subject is abundant and frequently contentious. The following are but a sampling: Haim Beinart, *Conversos on Trial* (Jerusalem, 1981); Benzion Netanyahu, *The Origins of the Inquisition* (New York, 1995); Roth, *Conversos, Inquisition and the Expulsion;* David M. Gitlitz, *Secrecy and Deceit: The Religion of the Crypto-Jews* (Philadelphia, 1996); and Renée Levine Melammed, *Heretics or Daughters of Israel?* (New York, 1999). The remarks of Hillgarth, *Spanish Kingdoms,* 2: 410–83, on the religion of the conversos and generally on late-fifteenth-century Iberian Jewry are persuasive.

85. Maurice Kriegel, "The Making of a Decree: The Expulsion of the Jews of Spain in 1492" (French), *Revue historique* 260 (1978): 49–90.

86. Haim Beinart, *The Expulsion of the Jews from Spain* (Hebrew) (Jerusalem, 1994); Miguel Angel Motis Dolader, *La expulsión de los judíos del reino de Aragón,* 2 vols. (Saragossa, 1990); Benjamin R. Gampel, *The Last Jews on Iberian Soil: Navarrese Jewry 1479–1498* (Berkeley and Los Angeles, 1989), 89–119; and Pimenta Ferro Tavares, *Os judeus em Portugal no século xv,* vol. 1 (Lisbon, 1982 and 1984), 252–57.

87. Maria José Pimenta Ferro Tavares, "Expulsion or Integration? The Portuguese Jewish Problem," in Gampel, ed., *Crisis and Creativity,* 95–103, and Benjamin R. Gampel, "Ferdi-

nand and Isabella and the Decline of Portuguese and Navarrese Jewries," in Yom Tov Assis and Yosef Kaplan, eds., *Jews and Conversos at the Time of the Expulsion* (Jerusalem, 1999), 65–92.

88. Haim Hillel Ben-Sasson, "The Generation of the Spanish Exiles Considers Its Fate," *Binah* 1 (1989): 83–98, and Joseph R. Hacker, "Pride and Depression—Polarity of the Spiritual and Social Experience of the Iberian Exiles in the Ottoman Empire" (Hebrew) in Menahem Ben-Sasson et al., eds., *Culture and Society in Medieval Jewry*, 541–86.

89. Benzion Netanyahu, *Abravanel* (Philadelphia, 1968), 195–257.

SELECTED BIBLIOGRAPHY

Ashtor, Eliyahu. *The Jews of Moslem Spain*, 3 vols. Philadelphia, 1973, 1979, and 1984.

Assis, Yom Tov. *The Golden Age of Aragonese Jewry*. London, 1997.

———.*Jewish Economy in the Medieval Crown of Aragon*. Leiden, 1997.

Baer, Yitzhak. *A History of the Jews in Christian Spain*, 2 vols. Philadelphia, 1961 and 1966; available in paperback with an introduction by Benjamin R. Gampel, Philadelphia, 1992.

Beinart, Haim, ed. *The Sephardi Legacy*, 2 vols. Jerusalem, 1992.

Gampel, Benjamin R. *The Last Jews on Iberian Soil*. Berkeley and Los Angeles, 1989.

———, ed. *Crisis and Creativity in the Sephardic World*. New York, 1997.

Hillgarth, Jocelyn N. *The Spanish Kingdoms*, 2 vols. Oxford, 1976 and 1978.

Kedourie, Elie, ed. *Spain and the Jews*. London and New York, 1992.

Leroy, Beatrice. *The Jews of Navarre*. Jerusalem, 1985.

Mann, Vivian B., et al., eds. *Convivencia. Jews, Muslims, and Christians in Medieval Spain*. New York, 1992.

Motis Dolader, Miguel Angel. *La expulsión de los judíos del reino de Aragón*, 2 vols. Saragossa, 1990.

Neuman, Abraham A. *The Jews of Spain*, 2 vols. Philadelphia, 1942.

Pimenta Ferro Tavares, Maria José. *Os judeus em Portugal no século xiv*. Lisbon, 1979.

———, *Os judeus em Portugal no século xv*, 2 vols. Lisbon 1982 and 1984.

Singerman, Robert. *The Jews in Spain and Portugal: A Bibliography*. New York, 1979.

———. *Spanish and Portuguese Jewry: A Classified Bibliography*. Westport, Conn., 1993.

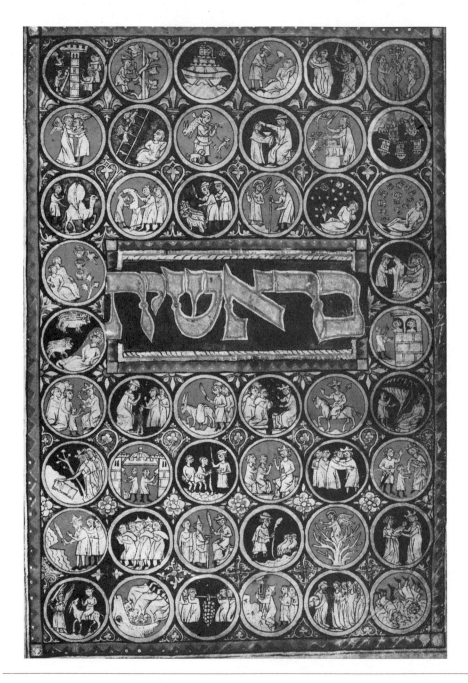

"Bere'shit" page from the *Schocken Bible*. Southern Germany, c. 1300.
Vellum, produced in the workshop of the scribe Ḥayyim. (Private collection)

THREE

A JEWISH-CHRISTIAN SYMBIOSIS:

The Culture of Early Ashkenaz

IVAN G. MARCUS

*When people look around for a place to reside, they should take stock of
the residents of that town—how chaste are the Christians there?
Know that if Jews live in that town, their children and grandchildren
will also behave just as the Christians do. For in every town,
at least in most parts, Jews act just like Christians.*
—Sefer Ḥasidim[1]

The Jews of early Christian Europe did not live in ghettos but mixed socially with their more numerous Christian neighbors. Even though the most learned advocated that Jews resist the lures of the majority culture, the very process of cultural resistance involved the appropriation and adaptation of Christian symbols as a means of building up Jewish solidarity. By parodying or taking over Christian images for their own purposes, Jews created a strong self-image as a Christ-like community, made up of "holy families" of married Jewish mothers, fathers, and their children, ready to suffer and even die as witnesses to the truth of Judaism in a Christian society. Living or dying in the German Empire, northern France, and England, the Jews of "Ashkenaz" (as they came to call themselves) fashioned tiny self-governing local communities and developed and transmitted to later generations the ideals and customs that shaped the Jewish culture in western and, eventually, eastern Europe until the Nazis destroyed it there a thousand years later. Even today, Ashkenaz is the root culture of a vast number of Jews around the world, from the United States to Israel.

The name Ashkenaz is mentioned in Genesis 10:3 and 1 Chronicles 1:6 as the land of a descendant of Noah's son Japheth. It also appears in Jeremiah 51:27 as an Asian kingdom, possibly in Anatolia or in the Caucasus, between the Black and the Caspian Seas. Although Jews in the early Middle Ages appropriately referred to German lands as "rinus" (the Rhineland) and "lotir" (the land of Lotharingia/Lorraine), the name Ashkenaz inexplicably emerged sometime in the twelfth century and eventually displaced the earlier ones.[2] In the course of time, it came to include not only western German settlements but also the Jews of northern France and England, to the west, and those of central and eastern Europe as well. How this occurred is still not understood.[3]

Can we make sense of how Jews actually lived among Christians in those centuries that historians call the European Middle Ages? To be sure, the Middle Ages have generally had bad press since the fifteenth century, when printing was invented. We dismiss them as a time of prejudice, violence, and intolerance, and we take for granted that Jews in the Middle Ages were worse off than most, huddled together in squalid ghettos, deprived of rights, constantly persecuted.

But this is misleading. Built on the legacies of the ancient world, much of Western civilization as we know it was refashioned or even created in the Middle Ages. For Christians, Muslims, and Jews, it was a time of great creativity, which had a lasting influence. In Europe, parliamentary representative government was invented and nurtured; the towns in which most Europeans live today were founded and expanded; magnificent Gothic cathedrals were built; universities, too, were begun in medieval Paris, Oxford, and Cambridge; stories about King Arthur's court expressed a new conception of romantic love that only modern feminism has challenged and that Hollywood, mass culture, and romance novels insist is still very real.

Although many writers have emphasized the violence and insecurity that beset the Jews of Ashkenaz, Jews would not have survived there, let alone created what they left us, had that been the main story. Christian persecution was usually the exception rather than the rule, and it characterized some times, not others. The norm may be described as different patterns of social mixing between Jews and Christians: social-economic (trade, medicine, moneylending) and social-religious (conversion, sexual liaisons, arguments over religion), among others.

Jews in medieval Europe confronted Christians there in two senses. On the one hand, hostile conflicts sometimes pitted members of one community against the other. This is what we usually think Jewish life was like in this period. On the other hand, members of each culture lived literally face to face with members of the other on a daily basis. This is the part of the story that is often unappreciated.

In fact, the two aspects of Jewish-Christian confrontation were closely related. One of the primary underlying and persistent reasons that the power elites of both cultures tried to separate Jews and Christians from time to time was the reality of their everyday social mixing. Jews lived closely and at times intimately with members of the Christian majority, so much so that Christian leaders thought Jews were dangerously influencing the faithful, and rabbis thought the same was true of Christian influence. Jews and Christians usually needed each other and were so attracted to one another that they persisted in interacting closely despite all but the most drastic measures designed to halt that social reality.

This social interdependence does not mean that Jews and Christians as a rule liked or even respected one another. Far from it. Though sometimes attracted to the point of fascination with what they saw, each looked down on members of the other culture as a matter of principle. Much of Jewish culture was even involved with countering Christian images and claims by using or subverting those symbols into anti-Christian arguments and values. For its part, the culture of the Christian majority did not simply dismiss the presence of the Jews, who constituted only a tiny minority of the population. Instead, Christians constantly seemed to focus on the Jews, either to win them over or to restrain them so that they would not influence or harm the much larger and more powerful majority.

Despite the social closeness members of the two cultures enjoyed, historians of medieval Europe have focused on the story of the Christian majority. Historians of the Jews, in contrast, usually pay attention to Christian authorities and their laws or to officials or mobs only when they are hostile and aggressive agents of "a persecuting society."[4]

Why has this been so? In the wake of the first horrific anti-Jewish riots in Europe at the beginning of the First Crusade, in the spring of 1096, liturgical texts did record the Jews who died then as witnesses or martyrs for their religion in central Europe. Traditional Jews recite these texts to this day. As a result of the ideology of remembrance and martyrdom that synagogue poets created in the early twelfth century, Jews in Ashkenaz remembered only those times when they were persecuted and forgot others when they were not. Modern historians proceeded to construct their accounts based on those preserved records and have forgotten that they were not the norm. Influenced by their own contemporary agendas as well, they lost track of the fact that they were relying on how medieval survivors wanted their own past to be remembered as part of a strategy to build group solidarity. That ideology of persecution does not express the past itself in all of its complexity.

To the cliché of constant persecution, add that of demographic segregation, which has also helped shape the dominant view that the Jews of medieval Europe were culturally isolated and backward. Because it is usually taken for granted that north European Jews were chronic victims who lived in isolation from Christian townsmen and women, it is also assumed that they did not share a common social and cultural setting, permeated with Christian symbols. They were parochial, confined to their Jewish parish within a hostile Christian environment. How could Jews have been actively engaged in any significant cultural exchange with those who supposedly hated and constantly persecuted them? Moreover, it is argued, since the rabbis did not read Latin, the language of the learned enemy elite, how could they have learned anything from Christian books? Besides, why would they have wanted to? Shifting ground, apologists for Jewish learned culture contrast urban rabbis with illiterate Christian peasants. Thus, the picture of culturally and socially isolated, beleaguered medieval Ashkenaz emerges.

As we re-examine the complex historical culture of Ashkenaz and test the view just outlined against the evidence, as well as common sense, we will see that the assumptions of the widely accepted view are not believable. Nor are they accurate. Although there were significant persecutions of Jews in north medieval Europe, especially from the fourteenth century on (which was a time of widespread general violence in the region), this experience was not unique to north European Jewry. There had been major outbreaks in the ancient world, as well as in Muslim Spain, where Jews were massacred by the thousands in 1066 and 1146, and in Christian Spain in the catastrophic riots of 1391. But in those ancient and medieval cases, not to speak of modern Jewish history, Jews were not persecuted most of the time. Had that been the case, Jewish survival would indeed have been a miracle. Precisely because persecutions were irregular occurrences, we must look at each incident as a special situation requiring contextual analysis, and we must not assume, with the ideology of martyrdom in Ashkenaz, that it was typical.[5]

THE EMERGENCE OF ASHKENAZ

Although Jews had moved in and out of the western provinces of the Roman Empire and would later remember a story that Charlemagne (d. 814) founded the Jewish community of Mainz, long-lasting communal settlements began not in Carolingian times but only in the mid- to late tenth century. There are no signs of continuity from late Roman northern settlements such as Cologne, where Jews lived in the fourth century. As international merchants, Jews followed the trade routes north from Byzantine or Muslim Italy across the Alps into the Rhineland or migrated from the Mediterranean coast of southern France up the Rhone Valley into the northern county of Champagne and, in some cases, continued farther east into the Rhineland. There, members of former Italian Jewish families quickly married Jews who had come to Germany from France. In the newly melded society, Jews brought with them ancient Palestinian and Babylonian lore, law, and especially customary patterns of local Jewish living (*minhagim*). Ordinary parents and learned individuals alike recommended following not only ancient sacred books but also what came to be called "the custom of our ancestors" (*minhag avoteinu*), which both groups regarded as sacred, no different from ancient texts.[6]

Between 950 and 1100, Jews lived in all the politically and economically important towns in the German Empire. First in Mainz (around 950), located where the great north-south medieval superhighway of the Rhine River meets up with the east-west water route of the Main. Soon also in Magdeburg, Merseburg, Prague, and Regensburg, in the east; Bamberg on the Main River; Cologne, Worms, and Speyer, on the Rhine farther west; and Trier, on the Moselle. Although the Jewish settlements in the east reflect the early beginnings of the empire in the tenth century, Jewish demography increased in the west, along the Rhine. This pattern reflects the shift in German politics from the era of the Saxon emperor Otto the Great based in the tenth century in the northeast, to the eleventh- and twelfth-century centers of power of the Salian and Staufen houses farther west.[7]

In contrast to Germany, where settlement was disrupted in late antiquity, Jews in France left traces in inscriptions from the fifth century on. They had a synagogue already by the sixth century in Paris and Orléans. In the south, Jews settled early in Narbonne, Agde, Avignon, and Arles, among other locations. As the feudal barons grew in power after the collapse of the Carolingian Empire in the ninth century, Jewish communities began to grow in places like Le Mans, near the County of Champagne, and in that county's capital towns of Troyes and Provins. Much of rabbinic intellectual achievement took place during the twelfth century in the small towns of Champagne—Ramerupt, Vitry, Dampierre, as well as in the larger Troyes—and then shifted to Paris, where Jews settled at the center of political and ecclesiastical protective power, on the Ile de la Cité, near Notre Dame, and a bit later along the narrow streets of the Left Bank close by, such as today's Rue de la Harpe. Although Jewish merchants had moved in and out of Roman Britain, Jews settled in England only after the Norman conquest in 1066, and they remained closely linked to the Norman and Angevin rulers, for better or worse, and spoke French for generations.

In the early Middle Ages, Christian monarchs promoted the economic vitality of their domains by inviting Jewish and other merchants into the new towns that were developing. Later on, Christian monarchs would be responsible for expelling entire Jewish communities, as in England, France, and Spain. Between royal invitation and expulsion, Jews lived for the most part on intimate social terms with their Christian neighbors, often in small towns.

The earliest royal policy toward the Jews in northern Europe dates from Charlemagne and especially from his son, Louis the Pious (r. 814–40). He issued three private charters (*privilegia*) to individual Jewish merchants around 825. These texts indicate that Jews were among the international traders doing business in the Carolingian empire and were granted protection of their lives, exemption from tolls, guarantees of religious practice, and communal autonomy, including the right to use their own rabbinical courts to settle internal disputes. Subsequent rulers of the German empire also pursued this Carolingian policy toward Jewish merchants, and it encouraged the Jewish immigration that became a factor in the demographic and urban expansion of early medieval Europe.

Of special significance was the Kalonymus family from Lucca, Italy. As their Greek name implies, they originally hailed from southern, Greek-speaking Byzantine Italy (Magna Graecia), and ultimately from Roman Palestine. Another branch was the Abun family, descended from a Rabbi Abun from Le Mans in northern France. Other families also came from France, perhaps Metz, and together they became the nuclei of the Mainz Jewish elite, the first important settlement that recorded its new beginnings.

At first, local family customs, not authoritative shared ancient religious texts, played an important role in practicing Judaism. True, some northern French rabbinic pioneers would later travel to far-off centers in Palestine or Babylonia, and even maintain contacts with the Jewish political and religious authorities in those lands or with Muslim Spain. But the geographical distance of Ashkenaz from other centers often gave the leaders of the Mainz community considerable room to improvise and experiment with new patterns of autonomous local governance.[8]

From the beginning, communal leadership assumed two overlapping but distinct forms. On the one hand, legal decisions were rendered by religious judges or rabbis, unpaid scholars who acquired expertise in custom and the written traditions of Jewish law, especially the Talmud. On the other hand, communal control over public affairs devolved upon the "elders," whose authority derived from their age, wealth, family lineage, perhaps government favor, and other personal qualities, and in some cases also from their Torah learning. The elders maintained public order, collected taxes for the Christian authorities and for the support of Jewish social services, and were the liaison between the community and the Christian central and local rulers. In the period of first settlement, rabbis were merchants like most of the rest of the male Jewish community, and they were among the elders who decided public policy.

As part of a general demographic and urban expansion in eleventh- and twelfth-century Christian Europe, the first tiny Jewish communities grew in size and became more complex. Communal roles got more differentiated and specialized. Eventually—exactly when is a matter of interpretation and even of definition—a paid rabbinate developed, perhaps in embryo as early as the thirteenth century, certainly by the fifteenth.[9]

The location of the early north European communities on a Jewish frontier prompted religious leaders and elders alike to be innovative. We see this in the legal decisions of Rabbenu Gershom ben Judah (d. 1028), the first major rabbinic figure in Mainz. Gershom functioned as an appeals judge on matters of Jewish law, and his legal opinions (*t'shuvot* or *responsa*) rarely mentioned the decisions and precedents of the Babylonian *geonim*, the contemporary legal masters who resided in southern Mesopotamia from the seventh century on. Rather, he answered questions by interpreting and directly applying talmudic, earlier mishnaic, or even biblical passages, thereby imitating, rather than following, the geonim.[10]

We also find signs of improvisation in the actions of the early communal board (*kahal*) and communal leaders (*parnasim*) contemporary with Gershom. They undertook to maintain law and order, supervise the weights and measures in the market, and provide for the indigent. As the Jewish population grew, members of the founding families tried to limit immigration. As early as the tenth century, local communal boards placed bans on new settlement (*herem ha-yishuv*) to prevent excessive economic competition.

By the middle of the eleventh century, questions about the limits of local autonomy between towns arose in newer areas of settlement, like the County of Champagne. Rabbi Judah ha-Kohen, Gershom's successor in Mainz, replied to a question that the elders of Troyes (Champagne) sent him. The case involved the community's decision to impose a six-month boycott on hiring a particular Christian maid who had been abusive to the Jewish plaintiff. In the areas of general public welfare and security, he ruled, each local community was completely autonomous. But if one Jewish community violated religious law, another community or outside religious authority could hold it accountable and impose sanctions, such as excommunication of its guilty members. Moreover, individual Jews in one community did not have the right to claim immunity from decisions reached by the elders there, even if those elders constituted a numerical minority of voting members.

Another sign of new communal development occurred in 1084, when some Mainz Jews fled the fire that broke out in the Jewish quarter there, and Ruediger, bishop of Speyer, issued them a formal charter of privileges in his town. It was the first community charter granted to a Jewish community in Christian Europe, though in principle it was no different from the charters of protection (*tu-itio*) Louis the Pious had issued to individual Jewish merchants over 250 years earlier. The Speyer charter extended to its new community guarantees of life, religious protection, self-government, and exemption from tolls. Just before the bishop died, he arranged for three Jewish communal leaders from Speyer to seek the confirmation of his episcopal charter from his temporal superior, the German emperor, Henry IV, who granted it in 1090. The Carolingian policy of royal and imperial protection of Jewish local self-rule, first developed in the German towns, became the model for Jewish communities in the regions of royal France, England, Christian Spain, and Central Europe down to early modern times.

Occasionally, support broke down. It happened twice in the eleventh century. Both times it was triggered by rumors that Jews were guilty when Muslims took over Christian holy sites in Jerusalem. The first occurred sometime between 1007 and 1012, and it included the temporary expulsion of the Jews from Mainz and the conversion of Gershom's son.[11]

The second instance is better documented in Hebrew and Latin sources; it involves the anti-Jewish riots that broke out in the Rhineland and elsewhere in central Europe in the spring prior to the departure in August 1096 of the main armies that launched the First Crusade. Again, Jews were drawn into what was essentially a far-off Christian-Muslim conflict. While the German Jews' main protector, Henry IV, was in Italy, thereby creating a power vacuum in the empire, murderous Crusader knights and rabble triggered a remarkably agitated response in some Jews who ritually killed their own families and themselves to avoid being forced to convert to Christianity. Jewish men and women are described as using a special slaughtering knife and reciting a blessing before doing the act, as though they were latter-day priests in the ancient Temple in Jerusalem, where only priestly males ritually slaughtered animals. This innovation shocked Christians and some other Jews, when they heard about it, but it remained a sacred option for Jews to martyr themselves when threatened with the horrors of forced baptism well into the seventeenth century.[12]

The deaths or martyrological behavior of perhaps as many as a thousand German Jews in 1096 had been anticipated on a smaller scale in Italy and in northern France in 1007.[13] Like those earlier events, the violent episodes of 1096 were local and regional, limited to central Europe, and did not spread to most of France, where the call to a Crusade had taken place, or to Italy, northern Spain, or England—all Christian lands, too. In addition to being limited in geographical scope, the violent events of 1096 did not unleash an ongoing "age of Crusades" characterized by anti-Jewish persecution throughout Christian Europe. The number of Jews who were killed 50 years later in Germany in 1146, in the wake of the call to a second Crusade, did not compare in scope or significance to 1096, nor did the violence that occurred another 40 years later, at the time of the third Crusade in the late 1180s.

In England, anti-Jewish accusations did not necessarily trigger violence. For example, in 1150 a second-rank cleric named Thomas of Monmouth, who wanted to create a local Christian martyr cult, accused the Jews of Norwich of having killed a Christian boy after ritually violating his body in a mock crucifixion during Easter week of 1144, as a re-enactment of the Passion. Indeed it was Thomas who invented the "ritual murder accusation," but no violence took place on this occasion; nor did it when the canard resurfaced in Gloucester in 1168 or in Bury St. Edmunds in 1181. Consequently, we need to distinguish anti-Jewish accusations or libels from outbreaks of anti-Jewish violence and not assume they are necessarily linked events.

The riots that did do serious damage to English Jewry—never counting more than 5,000 persons at any time—occurred in the context of a political transition, during the coronation festivities of Richard II in London. Subsequent to the king's departure for the continent in December 1189—creating another power vacuum, reminiscent of 1096 in Germany—riots erupted in Norfolk, Norwich, and Lincoln, only some of which caused fatalities. By March 1190, however, a major episode occurred in York, a center of Jewish moneylending that included some immigrants from the Rhineland. Some Jews seeking security in the tower of York committed suicide, as had German Jews in 1096. Altogether, we know of a handful of murderous incidents that took place during the 200 or so years that Jews lived in medieval England (ca. 1066–1290).

In France, from Jewish settlement in the early Middle Ages to the major expulsion of 1306, a minor outbreak may have occurred in 1096 in Rouen, in the County of Normandy, but only a few significant violent episodes are known up to the expulsion of 1306. Violence did occur in Blois in 1171, after a Jew there was accused of killing a Christian, even though no body was produced and no one there at the time claimed that the alleged killing had been a ritualized re-enactment of the death of Jesus. This resembles an incident that occurred in Würzburg, Germany, in 1147, when Jews were accused of killing a Christian and some Jews were killed.[14] Strictly speaking, these were accusations of murder, not of ritual murder.[15]

At first, then, violence tended to accompany only accusations that Jews had killed a Christian. The newly invented allegation of ritual murder did not precipitate violence when it first appeared in the twelfth century. But in 1235, in Fulda, Germany, violence did follow the first blood libel, the new accusation that Jews not only killed Christians but also ritually ingested Christian blood, at first, for medicinal purposes. Later this accusation would be elaborated that Jews used Christian blood to produce Passover matzah. This canard is an inversion and projection of the newly strengthened rite of the Eucharist.[16]

Other minor riots occurred in France in the royal town of Brie in 1192 (fewer than 100 killed) and in Brittany, Anjou, and Poitou in 1236. When a ritual murder accusation took place in Valréas in 1247, in the atmosphere of Louis IX's Crusade preparations, Jews were burned in public, and again in royal Troyes, in 1288. These and a few other incidents were horrendous but not everyday events. They were exceptional, which is one reason Jews or Christians or both chose to remember them.

Jewish moneylending at immoderate interest, or usury, became a major factor in the impoverishment of the Jewish communities in England and France in the thirteenth century. Although papal policy condoned Jewish lending at moderate rates of interest, canon lawyers and theologians opposed it absolutely, and in the late thirteenth century the English and French kings implemented policies based on the stricter interpretation.[17] In reality, this policy to eliminate Jewish moneylending met with limited success, because credit was always needed at all levels of society, especially consumer credit, which Jews provided. The measures taken against usury were usually economically and politically motivated, but other factors were involved, such as asserting royal prestige or Christian piety, and each case must be treated individually.

In royal France, Jewish moneylending with interest was made illegal in 1230 but persisted anyway. To support his Crusade, Louis IX (r. 1226–70) confiscated Jewish loans, as provided by the Council of Lyon (1245), expelled only Jewish usurers from France in 1248–49, and confiscated their property. In England, Edward I (r. 1272–1307) issued his Statute on the Jews (1275), which outlawed Jewish lending completely but was so ineffective that he finally yielded to pressure from the English knights and expelled the two or three thousand Jews from his kingdom in 1290 as a quid pro quo for a huge grant from his knights. His queen took over the loans and effectively collected them for herself.[18]

Philip IV the Fair (r. 1285–1314) expelled perhaps as many as a hundred thousand Jews from royal France in 1306—a number probably not much different from those expelled from Spain in 1492—mainly for religious reasons. Most of the French Jews never returned, even when they were permitted to do so temporarily in 1315. A subsequent expulsion (1322), the readmission of a small group of Jews (1359), and a final expulsion (1394) involved relatively insignificant numbers compared to 1306, which marked the effective end of northern French Jewry. Moreover, unlike the Jews of Spain in 1492, the Jews of royal France did not maintain a broad collective identity as Tzarfatim (Jews from France, based on Obadiah v. 20) but blended into the Jewish communities in parts of Aragon or the German Empire. The fact that some individual authors would add to their name "ha-tzarfati" is not the same as the persistence of French Jewish communities in exile. It is not clear why they did not retain their own collective cultural identity, as the Jews of Germany and Spain did.

As the Jewish communities were eliminated by royal edict in England and France, organized Jewish life in the north shifted increasingly eastward to the politically fragmented German Empire, the central and east European territories of Bohemia, Moravia, Hungary, Poland, and Lithuania. The thirteenth and early fourteenth centuries were a time of nearly continuous demographic expansion in Europe, and the Jewish communities in central and eastern Europe were augmented by natural increase and new immigration from the west. By the turn of the fourteenth century, most of the European Jewish population outside of the Iberian Peninsula lived in parts of Italy, the German Empire, and farther east. The late thirteenth through mid-fourteenth centuries were a time of growing social unrest among the lower classes in Europe prior to and accompanying the great famine of 1315 and the Black Death toward mid-century.

Contrary to the impression created by the martyrological ideology of 1096, the major demographic turning point for north European Jewry was not that year but the 50-year period of violence that stretched from the Rintfleisch massacres in 1298 to the devastation of the Black Death of 1348–50. The latter was a general trauma that reduced the population of many areas of Christian and Jewish Europe by as much as half.

In France, the protagonists of the Shepherds' Crusade of 1320, and in Spain, the Lepers Plot of 1321, did not set out to attack only Jews, but the rioters killed many. The peasants' revolt in England in 1381, a social upheaval against royal officials and ecclesiastical authorities, offers an instructive comparative context. It broke out as part of the climate of lower-class protest movements, ultimately futile, and had nothing to do with anti-Jewish animus, because the Jews had already been expelled in 1290. But it shows that complex factors were also at work in those riots when Jews were involved. The social and religious-ethnic motivations of the riots in Iberia in 1391 have been debated as well.[19]

It was in the German Empire that a series of violent episodes broke out that made a major dent in the Jewish population of many towns and areas. First came the Rintfleisch massacres in 1298, then the Armleder riots in 1322, and finally the anti-Jewish massacres that accompanied the panic that broke out in Germany as word of the plague approached. It is often thought that the main Christian explanation for the plague was that the Jews had poisoned the wells, but, in fact, Christians actually offered many other causes.

Ecclesiastical leaders attributed the death wrought by the plague to the sinfulness of Christian society. More scientific and medical persons referred to the air as a conduit of the plague, without knowing about microbes as the mechanism of contagion. Others blamed it on the stars. There were abundant explanations without mentioning the Jews. Nevertheless, unable to explain a catastrophe of the magnitude of the plague, some Christians blamed the Jews for poisoning the wells and rivers in parts of Europe even before the plague arrived. This explanation before the fact created a panic or fear that may be compared to the early modern witch craze against women, to aspects of the anti-communist hysteria of the 1950s, or to anti-gay panic that accompanied the early days of the AIDS epidemic in the 1980s.[20]

The result of this panic was a truly devastating toll in human life above and beyond the Jewish deaths brought about by the plague itself when it finally arrived and, with it, the elimination of several communities in the empire.[21] No other event would compare to it until 1391, when (as Benjamin Gampel recounts in his chapter) riots broke out from Seville to Barcelona and several Jewish communities, including the latter, were permanently destroyed by conversion, emigration, or death.

As a gradual demographic and economic recovery slowly began, Jews were readmitted for specified periods into towns of early settlement, like Speyer, and into newer Jewish communities in Austria and Bohemia. The decline of imperial protection of the Jews is reflected in the growing influence of the Christian burghers, who reserved the right to expel "their" Jews at will. The elimination of effective royal authority added to the communities' increased political vulnerability in the later Middle Ages in the West. The simultaneous weakening of the papacy from the time of Boniface VIII (d. 1303) also meant the removal of a formerly reliable and constant source of protection.

Despite weakened central controls, the very proliferation of independent principalities and cities in the German Empire constituted a safety valve for the Jews there. Whenever residents of one particular community were expelled, they could find refuge in another until the earlier edict was rescinded. As economic instability reduced the demand for Jewish moneylending in the towns, some Jews began to settle in villages and on rural estates. Gradually, they entered new occupations as agricultural merchants and middlemen. The decline in economic opportunities in the empire also led many Jews to join the eastward emigration of German Christian burghers attracted to Poland and Lithuania, still another frontier. They brought the vernacular of Middle High German with them, and this language would become the basis of Yiddish in Eastern Europe.

INWARD ACCULTURATION

Despite occasional eruptions of violence, it is remarkable that during almost 350 years of Jewish life in Ashkenaz, roughly from 950 to 1300, Jews and Christians increasingly lived together in small towns, fully aware of one another and the ways they behaved. Although we do not yet know enough about many aspects of everyday life there, much of the evidence suggests just how familiar the Jews were with their Christian environment and how they tried to resist the pressures of the majority culture. They did so by what I call "inward acculturation." That is, Jews who did not convert or flirt with converting retained a strong collective Jewish identity and sometimes expressed it by internalizing or transforming various genres, motifs, terms, institutions, or rituals of Christian culture in a polemical, parodic, or neutralized manner. They did so even when signs of ambivalence and doubt surfaced.[22]

A fundamental paradox lies at the heart of the culture of Ashkenaz. Most of the time, everyday closeness had the effect of confirming Jewish cultural and religious superiority. Even when Jews appropriated Christian religious symbols and rites, they often transformed them into rituals of self-confidence that also expressed contempt for their neighbors. Based on the conviction that Judaism is truly the will of God and that the Jews are God's elect, the Jews of Ashkenaz had a strong, positive religious self-image and an attitude of contempt for Christianity, which they thought was false. This posture was a direct response to the prevailing Christian culture's parallel stance that it and it alone embodied the truth of God's will and that Jews without Christ were a rejected people practicing an obsolete religion. Given that the learned and faithful of each culture, to varying degrees, imposed a hierarchical or graded view of itself in relation to the other, confrontation was inevitable.

However, in tension with the hierarchical and exclusivist view of Jew and Christian toward one another, another stance coexisted in each and could be dominant in individual cases. Members of each culture were sometimes attracted to the other one, despite the official party lines and repeated efforts of the elites to remind the faithful to keep the members of the other culture "in their place"—meaning, in relative dependence to themselves. Jews were sometimes attracted to Christianity, even enough to convert, and some Christians converted to Judaism, even though it was a capital offense. From its earliest days in Palestine, Christian groups had an ambivalent attitude toward the mother religion from which they eventually broke away. Some insisted on visiting synagogues as well as going to church, celebrated the Jewish Sabbath as well as the

Christian Lord's Day, and even partook in the Passover as well as in the Easter sacrifice, all to the chagrin of church leaders whose preaching fell on deaf ears.[23]

The social setting for Jewish-Christian confrontation was widespread daily interaction. Accompanying this backdrop were the salient features of Ashkenaz, especially the strong solidarity-building ideology of holiness that generated a readiness to die for Judaism out of the belief that God loves the Jews despite appearances; a feisty willingness to resist triumphalist Christian pressure by turning Christian cultural images into counter-polemical actions, views, rites, commentaries, and debates taking for granted that Judaism is true and Christianity is no better than ancient idolatry; and a positive attitude toward Jewish women, expressed in law and collective memory. In addition, the Jews of Ashkenaz were never under the governance of any central or even regional Jewish authorities but instead fended for themselves in local communities.

Consider an early example of Jewish-Christian economic and social mixing in the town of Mainz. In the late tenth and early eleventh centuries, the Jewish community there probably numbered in the hundreds of families, perhaps a thousand individuals by the time of the death of Gershom ben Judah in 1028. The Jewish quarter of the city has not survived, but we know that it was near the cathedral and market in a central part of the old town, not too far from the Rhine. Mainz was the first of the towns on the river to boast of a Jewish cultural elite, well ahead of the growing towns of Worms and Speyer, farther to the south, that developed signs of tiny Jewish communities in the mid- and late eleventh century, respectively.

Many of the Jews who arrived in Mainz from northern Italy or northern France were merchants engaged in trade with Christian clients. An institution emerged that allowed one Jew to establish an exclusive business relationship with a particular Christian client. He might be the head of a monastery or a secular priest, or a layperson. This trade monopoly was known as a "maarufia," a term probably imported from Arabic-speaking North Africa that meant "familiar client."[24] It was widespread in the Rhineland, and community boards adopted measures to protect it.

Much of our first-hand knowledge of Jewish merchants in early Europe are based on the rabbinic responsa and decisions attributed to Gershom, who was the most learned rabbinic Jew of northern Europe in his day. His responsa reflect close business dealings between Jews and Christians at different levels of society. For example, a Jew lends money against the collateral of ecclesiastical vestments used in Christian worship;[25] a Jewish winemaker hires a Christian employee to handle barrels of wine;[26] a Christian woman asks a Jew about to travel abroad to buy her expensive clothes and gives the Jew the money, but asks for collateral while he is away;[27] a Jew mortgages his vineyard to a Christian and agrees to pay him a fixed amount of wine each year.[28]

CRISIS AND ASHKENAZIC SELF-FASHIONING AS RESISTING MARTYRS

The relatively close ties that Jewish merchants had with Christian clients and neighbors were rudely shattered toward the end of the eleventh century. On November 27, 1095, at a church council held in Clermont, Pope Urban II called upon the knights of France to embark on an unprecedented armed pilgrimage to Jerusalem to liberate the Christian holy places in that city from the polluting presence of the infidel Seljuk Turks and to assist their Christian brothers who were living in the eastern Christian lands. The Seljuks had recently converted to Islam and were zealously prohibiting Christian pilgrims from the west from visiting the holy places in Jerusalem.

Before well-organized armies of knights left for the east in the late summer of 1096, other knights and mobs marched from France and areas of Germany into the Rhineland. In the late spring and early summer, they attacked the growing Jewish communities living in Speyer, Worms, and Mainz, Trier on the Moselle River, the villages on the lower Rhine to which the Jews of Cologne had fled, and Regensburg on the Danube. With the exception of the Jews of Speyer, most of whom were saved, and those of Regensburg, farther southeast, in Bavaria, who were forced into the Danube and baptized en masse, most Jews either died or temporarily converted. The attackers killed some, and others engaged in acts of ritual killing of other Jews and committed suicide rather than be forcibly converted to Christianity.[29]

The riots and acts of martyrdom and conversion are known to us from short passages in Latin chronicles of the Crusaders' trek to Jerusalem and from three types of Hebrew sources: liturgical poems, memorial lists of martyrs, and unusually detailed narratives or chronicles. Together, the Hebrew texts created a liturgically structured, lasting collective memory of the very character of the culture of Ashkenaz. For this reason we need to dwell on their significance.

The oldest genre is the liturgical poetry (*piyyutim*) written in the form of dirges (*kinot*). Perhaps as many as 25 such laments were composed in the early twelfth century about the 1096 martyrs. Some have remained in the German and Polish/Lithuanian liturgies for the Ninth of Av, the fast day that marks the destruction of both ancient Temples in Jerusalem, now linked to Germany in 1096 as well.[30]

Although most of these new poems refer to Jewish suffering in general, a few mention the names of Mainz, Worms, and Speyer and the dates of the Christian attacks. This detail serves to assimilate the destruction and martyrdom of those places with ancient Jerusalem, a two-way process that also made Mainz into a latter-day Jerusalem in Europe. This linkage serves as well to identify the Crusaders with ancient Roman soldiers, both understood in Jewish memory as descendants of Esau, the boorish and violent elder brother of Jacob (Israel). Over time, the collective memory of the three Rhineland communities came to form the central consciousness of martyrological heroism for the entire culture of Ashkenaz.

The liturgical poems were crucial in achieving this collective group consciousness, which persisted in special ways among the Jews of Frankfurt am Main, for example, into the twentieth century. One of the poems written about 1096 entered the Sabbath liturgy. Called "Merciful Father" (*Av ha-Raḥamim*), it is still recited on most Sabbaths in the Polish/Lithuanian rite, but in the synagogues of Germany it was said only twice a year: on the Sabbath prior to Tisha Be-Av and on the Sabbath before Shavuot, when the Jews of Mainz were attacked in 1096. It reads in part:

> *May the Father of mercies, Who dwells on high, in His mighty compassion,*
> *   Remember those loving, upright, and blameless ones,*
> *The holy congregations, who laid down their lives for the sanctification of the*
> *   divine Name,*
> *Who were lovely and pleasant in their lives, and in their death were not divided;*
> *Swifter than eagles, stronger than lions to do the will of their Master and the*
> *   desire of their Rock.*
> *May our God remember them for good with the other righteous of the world,*
> *And render retribution for the blood of his servants, which has been shed.*[31]

Lists of memorialized martyrs, too, were recited annually. The names were not combined into a long list but were arranged according to the communities to which the martyrs belonged and the dates of the attacks in which they died. This arrangement of the names by community reflected and reinforced local consciousness in Ashkenaz.[32]

The custom of reciting annually the lists of the local righteous dead—and, later on, the anniversary of one's parents' deaths—is mainly derived from the Christian monastic practice of compiling and reading necrologies, lists of the dead arranged by date of death. The Jewish books of martyrs came to be called *Memorbücher*, after the Christian record books known as the *Libri memorialis*. They reflect the Jews' close awareness of their Christian neighbors' rites, which they turned into an implicit cultural polemic. Reading out the memorial lists on the anniversaries of the martyrs' deaths was a way of affirming the truth of Judaism and denying any Christian claims to truth.

The mourner's recitation of a version of the ancient *kaddish* prayer, originally a declaration of God's sanctity recited after studying Torah, came into prominence in Ashkenaz after 1096 as well. After the massive trauma of the Black Death riots and expulsions in central Europe (1348–50), Ashkenazic Jews not descended from the martyr communities of 1096 began to remember annually the deaths of their own parents and refer to that time of year as the *yahrtzeit*. They also expanded the liturgical remembrance of departed parents from the traditional once a year, on the Day of Atonement, to four, adding Sukkot, Passover, and Shavuot as times when one read the memorial prayers that begin with the word *yizkor* (may He remember).[33]

Thus, out of the liturgical remembrance of the local martyrs in the Rhineland, the culture of Ashkenaz developed a nearly universal cult in memory of the dead. It has lasted to the present and was even accepted to some extent by Iberian Jews who never experienced the violence of 1096. Complementing these rites, Ashkenazic Jews created a cult of the dead. It involved the practice of visiting cemeteries to pray to the dead to assist the living and seek to ameliorate the dead's suffering with prayer. In thirteenth-century Germany, *Sefer Ḥasidim* (The Book of the Pietists), attributed to Rabbi Judah ben Samuel the Pietist (d. 1217), justifies these visits "because the dead derive benefit when their loved ones visit their graves and pray on behalf of their souls, improving their lot in the next world. And also, when they are asked, they pray on behalf of the living."[34]

The localism of Ashkenaz is also seen in the third type of Hebrew source: three Hebrew narratives about 1096 that have survived. Of the three, two were written anonymously, almost as a collective record of local events. The longest of them is misleadingly attributed to an otherwise unknown Solomon ben Samson because his name appears in the middle of the text, where it is attached to a particular local event. The long anonymous narrative is composed of many small units arranged according to the communities that were attacked, including not only Speyer, Worms, and Mainz but also others, such as Cologne, Trier, and Regensburg. This pattern of communal organization is consistent with the way the memorial lists are organized. The shorter anonymous text breaks off in the middle and only contains reports about Speyer, Worms, and Mainz, which are at the center of all three texts.[35]

The one narrative that probably can be attributed to a known author of considerable stature is unique in other ways as well. It contains piyyutim and short narrative introductions for each of the four Rhineland communities of Speyer,

Worms, Mainz, and Cologne. In the liturgical poems about each community, the author has included his name in the form of an acrostic. The first letters of each line spell out his name, Rabbi Eliezer ben Nathan, the most important Jewish legal scholar of early twelfth-century Mainz. It was copied many times and preserved the memory of 1096 along with the piyyutim.[36]

There is a clear bias in these texts in favor of detailing, quantifying, and praising the behavior of the martyrs, who are viewed as ancient Temple priests who behaved better than Abraham at the near sacrifice of Isaac (described in Genesis 22, the *Akedah,* or Binding of Isaac). It seems at first that the Jewish martyrs alone are counted up in the Hebrew chronicles because, to the narrators, they alone matter.[37] But the long anonymous account in particular goes out of its way to praise the forced converts, even though the martyrs, not the converts, stand at the center of the narrative: "It is now fitting to recount the praises of those who were forcibly converted. . . . He who speaks evil of them, it is as though he spoke thus of the Divine Countenance."[38]

The emphasis on the martyrs' acts and the praise of the forced converts are mutually reinforcing if we assume that the authors and much of the audience for these texts were those who were themselves either temporary converts or their relatives living in the Rhineland in the early twelfth century, when the narratives and poems were written. The point of the chronicles is to enumerate the martyrs' acts of religious loyalty and saintliness, to invoke their meritorious behavior as a reservoir of vicarious atonement for those who survived, and to pray for the speedy punishment of the perpetrators. As the long anonymous narrative says, "May the blood of His devoted ones stand us in good stead and be an atonement for us and for our posterity after us, and our children's children eternally, like the Akedah of our Father Isaac when our Father Abraham bound him upon the altar."[39] And Eliezer ben Nathan's dirge for the community of Cologne cries out, "May their death be a source of forgiveness and pardon for us."[40]

Moreover, the texts explicitly tell us that many of the testimonies came from former converts: "Thus have attested those few survivors who were forcibly converted."[41] Although the narrators pray for God to avenge the dead, they do not claim that the acts of the martyrs were motivated to trigger the messianic era when that revenge would take place. The narrators stress personal reward in the hereafter for the Jewish martyrs, just as Pope Urban II had to his Christian audience at Clermont. Divine revenge on the perpetrators is left in God's hands, though the hope is expressed that it will come soon.[42]

We have no way of knowing if each episode is exactly true. Although the ideology of martyrdom colors the selection and reworking of the editors' sources, it is still clear that some Jews ritually killed their families and themselves. This act is portrayed in several accounts. In one, a Samuel the elder asks Menaḥem the sexton to take a sword:

"Slaughter me with this very sword that I used to slaughter my son Yeḥiel. I have thoroughly inspected it, and it possesses no defect that would disqualify the ritual slaughter." So Menaḥem took the sword in his hand, inspected it carefully, and slaughtered Samuel the elder as he had slaughtered Samuel the bridegroom. Menaḥem pronounced the benediction of ritual slaughter, and Samuel answered, "Amen."[43]

Albert of Aix is one of the few Latin narrators to mention the riots at all, and he explicitly tells us that Jews killed each other, even though his understanding of the motive differs from that of the Jewish writers and he did not pick up all of the nuances of the ritualization of the act:

The Jews, seeing that their Christian enemies were attacking them and their children, and that they were sparing no age, likewise fell upon one another, brothers, children, wives, and sisters, and thus they perished at each other's hands. Horrible to say, mothers cut the throats of nursing children with knives and stabbed others, preferring them to perish thus by their own hands rather than to be killed by the weapons of the uncircumcised.[44]

Because of the heavy hand the editors imposed on the events of 1096, we learn more about the writers' cultural self-perception than about the details in the events themselves.[45] It was this perspective that created the image and self-image for centuries to come of the culture of Ashkenaz as centered on martyrs and saints. The Jews who fashioned this ideal were aware of the larger culture in which they lived, drew their inspiration from familiar Christian symbols and rhetoric, and proceeded to argue with and resist those Christian ideals by internalizing, subverting, or transforming them.

One example of this awareness is the way Crusader and martyr alike claimed that their unprecedented behavior accorded with the will of God. The spirit of both participates in the same moment of hysterical religious enthusiasm: both justify their extreme behavior as flowing from a spontaneous ability to decipher God's will independent of ordinary institutional channels. The zealous knights and mobs that sought to avenge the death of Christ by killing his "enemies" did so despite explicit prohibitions in secular and ecclesiastical law and tradition about killing Jews. Although Pope Urban II had promised remission of punishment to Crusaders who killed the enemy Turks, one of the Hebrew chronicles offers a revealing distortion of this promise and has Urban saying, "whosoever kills a Jew will receive pardon for all his sins."[46] This anti-Jewish version suggests the kind of rumors that circulated in an atmosphere of heightened Christian zeal.

The reconstructions of the pope's speech and the Hebrew narratives give the will of God a special role that may explain the spontaneous and potentially unrestrained behavior exhibited by both Crusaders and martyrs. Although the speech itself has not been preserved, accounts of it convey something of the passion of Urban II's remarks as well as his surprise at the reception his call evoked, as the crowd signaled its agreement by shouting, as though with one voice, "Deus vult! Deus vult!" (God wills it, God wills it).[47]

Although Urban never specifically mentioned the Jews in his speech, it was not a big leap for some knights, let alone the rabble, to work themselves up against the enemy "in our very midst," as a Jewish chronicler described the Crusaders' thoughts.[48] The enemy within merged with the one in the East, and, in a frenzy of religious enthusiasm, knights set out on a vendetta to avenge the crucified Christ.[49] What is especially significant for our understanding of the culture of Ashkenaz during the First Crusade riots in Germany is that the writers of the Hebrew narratives were aware of the spontaneous and unprecedented character of Christian behavior toward the Jews of the Rhineland.

The Jews who were about to be attacked internalized this fervor, especially the knights' conviction that one might intuit the will of God. The Hebrew narrators' rationale for the acts of sacrificial martyrdom refers to this intuitive knowledge. The narrator of the longer anonymous text first details the political bribery and the other prudent measures the Jews took for self-protection. But, at a certain point, it becomes clear that they must die. How do they know? According to the narrators, "when the people of the Sacred Covenant saw that the Heavenly decree had been issued and that the enemy had defeated them . . . they wept for themselves and for their lives and proclaimed the justness of the Heavenly judgment."[50] Or, in Eliezer ben Nathan's version, "all wholeheartedly accepting the judgment of Heaven upon themselves."[51] The short anonymous narrative, about the attack on Worms, says: "They saw that the decree had been issued in Heaven and that there was no escape and no recourse."[52]

How did the Jews of the Rhineland know that God wanted them to stop resisting by political or military means? Why did they suddenly revert instead to behavior that acted out ancient literary models of ritualized homicide and suicide in the face of idolatrous coercion, like the martyrs of Masada, whose deeds they knew from *Sefer Yosipon*, a Hebrew paraphrase of Josephus?[53] They seem to have intuited the will of God no less than had the knights who decided on their own that the pope's call to arms against the Turks was also an exhortation to kill the Jews. The events of 1096 suggest a mentality shared by all the participants.[54]

In addition to this shared assumption that the will of God can be fathomed directly, the Latin and Hebrew sources are strikingly similar in the way they make use of the rhetoric of insult.[55] The Jewish narrators use metaphors of pollution about Christians similar to the pope's description of the Muslim Turks, each contrasting the impure enemy—a source of sexual pollution and sacrilege—to his own group, the locus of purity, holiness, and goodness.

Here is Robert of Rheims's version of Urban's accusations against the Turks in far-off Palestine:

> [A] foreign race, a race absolutely alien to God . . . has invaded the land of those [Byzantine] Christians. . . . These men have destroyed the altars polluted by their foul practices. They have circumcised the Christians, either spreading the blood from the circumcisions on the altars or pouring it into the baptismal fonts. . . . What shall I say of the appalling violation of women . . . ? On whom, therefore, does the task lie of avenging this?[56]

The horror aroused in ecclesiastical writers by visions of sexual pollution and un-Christian rituals such as circumcision indicates how Christian cultural boundaries can be erected by positing an enemy that behaves in an un-Christian way. The Hebrew chroniclers use the same rhetoric, applying imagery of pollution to the Christians, even in speeches purporting to be the thoughts of the Crusaders themselves! Here is a version of a speech attributed by the author of the longer anonymous Hebrew narrative to the Crusader knights' motives:

> Now it came to pass that, as they passed through the towns where Jews dwelled, they said to one another: "Look now, we are going a long way to seek out the profane shrine [Church of the Holy Sepulchre] and to avenge ourselves on the Ishmaelites [Muslim Turks], when here, in our very midst, are the Jews—they whose forefathers murdered and crucified him for no reason. Let us first avenge ourselves on them and exterminate them from among the nations so that the name of Israel will no longer be remembered, or let them adopt our faith and acknowledge the offspring of menstrual impurity."[57]

The Jewish narrator has the Crusaders, as it were, refer to the Church of the Holy Sepulchre, their goal, as "the profane shrine," the holiest of places in Christian imagination. Even more striking, he portrays them speaking of Jesus and Mary as "offspring of menstrual impurity."

In 1096, Mary is repeatedly described not only in the language of immorality, just as she had been in isolated passages in the Talmud and midrash, but also as menstrually impure (*niddah*). The language of anti-Christian rhetoric even appears in Jewish business documents and was a common way Jews referred to Christian sancta. Sometime in the Middle Ages, these and other motifs were combined into a vituperative counter-Gospel or Gospel parody in the various Aramaic and Hebrew texts known collectively as the *Life of Jesus* (*Toledot Yeshu*).[58]

In the later Life of Jesus narratives, one Miriam (Mary) is betrothed to a very pious man but is seduced, while menstrually impure, by a robber named Joseph. Thus the Christian Mother of God becomes the quintessentially impure Jewish woman, and herself a source of impurity. Jesus is described in relation to her as the bastard son of an adulteress, and a ritually unclean one at that.[59]

Implied by this strategy is a contrasting claim about Jewish women: the Holy Family of the Church is polluted and immoral; the Jewish family is the true holy family. Far from revealing a distance between Jews and their Christian environment, this language shows how closely they were aware of Christian symbols, so aware that they were able to turn Christian images upside down and claim for their own women a higher religious standing than the Virgin Mary.

The strategy of praising the holy Jewish family emphasizes an innovative and central role for Jewish women as activist martyrs. Although the Jews who tried to avoid being polluted by the Christians by being forcibly converted or killed compare themselves to ancient male Temple priests, some of whom killed each other and themselves, a number of the active martyrs in 1096 were women. Albert of Aix could not get over the fact that Jewish mothers killed their own children. This motif appears in several episodes, none perhaps more poignant than the story of a Mistress Rachel who is described in the two anonymous accounts as participating in the killing of her four children. The names of this mother and her four children also appear in the Mainz memorial list.[60]

Other women are given especially prominent mention, such as at Speyer, the first community to be attacked, according to all three narratives: "a distinguished pious woman there . . . was the first among all the communities of those who were slaughtered."[61] Whereas Temple priests in ancient Jerusalem were not only men but also members of the priestly caste, the martyrs of 1096 are both men and women, young and old: the narratives repeatedly stress the diverse ages of those who died.

In part, the broad social spectrum of the martyrs is meant to convey the ruthlessness of the killers, who spared no one. But the social inclusiveness of the chroniclers, especially their emphasis throughout on the active role of women, is yet another way of contrasting the Jewish family to the obscenely impure Christian Holy Family based on sin and lust, which we may compare to the very kind of sexual impurity Pope Urban II decried in the Turks.[62]

A sign of the polemical character of the way women are presented in the m tyrologies is the fact that, despite the prominence of Jewish women who are portrayed engaging in ritual slaughter of their children as though they were Temple priests, none of the narratives mentions Christians raping Jewish women or girls. A possible hint in that direction is in the account of the long anonymous text about Trier, where Crusaders attempt to lure a Jewish woman but are foiled by her suicide.[63] One piyyut about 1096 has been mistranslated as referring to Crusaders raping Jewish women, but the phrase probably means "they compelled my pious ones to be baptized" (*tzenuai anasu*), not "they raped my modest women."[64]

In contrast, the reports of Urban's speech repeat lurid details of gruesome acts of sexual violence perpetrated on Christian women as well as men in the East. Says the account of Robert of Rheims: "What shall I say of the appalling violation of women . . . ?" Is it possible that Christian mobs were only interested in converting or killing, maiming, or torturing the Jews, but none succeeded in sexually abusing them? Instead, the Jewish narrators go out of their way to refer to their women as being beautiful, wholesome, chaste, and pure.

The motif of the beautiful "Jewess" is well known in Christian writings and has a long history, including such modern figures as Rebecca in Sir Walter Scott's *Ivanhoe*. Several of the moralistic stories, or *exempla,* of the Cistercian monk Caesarius of Heisterbach, writing around 1220 in the Rhineland, describe sexual encounters between clerics and "beautiful" Jewish maidens. The theme occurs also in medieval Spanish literature, where it is an important Christian representation of Jewish women. In the 1096 accounts, we have yet another example of a polemical use of this motif, internalized from Christian writings and turned against Christian images of Mary.[65]

Contrasting images of Jewish family purity and Christian pollution are strongly expressed in polemical juxtapositions. For example, in the long anonymous account:

The women girded their loins with strength and slew their own sons and daughters, and then themselves. . . . The young maidens, the brides, and the bridegrooms looked out through the windows and cried out in a great voice, "Look and behold, O Lord, what we are doing to sanctify Thy Great Name, in order not to exchange You for a crucified scion who was despised, abominated, and held in contempt in his own generation, a bastard son conceived by a menstruating and wanton mother."

Shortly afterward, the negative Christian image precedes the positive Jewish one:

> Refusing to gainsay their faith and replace the fear of our King with an abomi-
> nable stock, bastard son of a menstruating and wanton mother, they extended
> their necks for slaughter and offered up their pure souls to their Father in
> Heaven. The saintly and pious women acted in a similar manner, extending
> their necks . . . and each man likewise to his son and brother, brother to sister,
> mother to son and daughter, neighbor to neighbor and friend, bridegroom to
> bride, fiancé to his betrothed.[66]

It is likely that both the later version of the Life of Jesus narratives and the Hebrew narratives of 1096 were fashioned in the early twelfth century, just as the
stories about Mary were being collected and disseminated to elevate her to the
highest level of sanctity.[67] The Jewish rhetoric of resistance reflects this trend by
inverting it. The juxtaposition of an impure Mary and the pure Jewish women
also suggests why there is no mention of rape in any of the narratives of 1096. If
human nature did not radically change that year, we may well assume that Jewish women were sexually abused, but the Jewish narrators apparently ignored
any sources containing that information.

The Jewish chroniclers thus turned the female martyrs into married Madon-
nas, for, though virginity was a Jewish as well as a Christian value, Jews considered marriage and motherhood an even higher state. For a mother to kill her
children embodied a level of holiness that could never be attained by Mary. Such
acts of familial piety trumped any Christian claim that God sacrificed His only
begotten son, a view Jews rejected as blasphemous.[68]

LIVING AND REMEMBERED
JEWISH WOMEN IN ASHKENAZ

Although the image of Jewish women as paragons of purity and family life in
the 1096 narratives is stylized and polemical, occasionally the condition of real
women surfaces. The social place of women in Ashkenaz was a prominent feature of the responsa of Gershom ben Judah. His influential ordinances prohibiting polygyny and requiring a Jewish wife's consent to be divorced have
lasted for a millennium in Ashkenaz, and they were accepted in Sephardic lands
as well.

When Jewish merchants traveled to Muslim Spain or North Africa, or farther
to the East, and were away for years at a time, their wives and children were left
in Germany with only the wife's parents to offer support. It sometimes hap-

pened that a man would marry a second time in some distant land and start a second family.

From biblical times, there had been no prohibition for a Jewish man to take more than one wife. It was relatively rare, even in the Bible, though there are signs that rabbis in the Talmud took more than one wife. For example, the Babylonian sages Rav and Rav Naḥman: "When Rav went to Darshis, he used to say, 'Who will be my wife for a day?' And when Rav Naḥman came to Shekunziv, he would say, 'Who will be my wife for a day,' " that is, while they were staying over in that town.[69]

Real polygynous marriages existed among the Jews who lived in Muslim lands, where men were permitted to take up to four wives, if they could afford it. We get a sense of the seriousness of this situation from a set of communal decisions or ordinances (*takanot*) promulgated in mid-twelfth-century France. They were issued to protect Jewish women whose husbands traveled abroad to earn a livelihood, as they were likely to do especially if the marriage went sour. We can assume that the practice also existed in the early eleventh century, when Gershom issued his ordinance against polygyny, and that the norm of monogamy in Christian Europe influenced him to change the talmudic norm:

> We have decreed . . . that no [Jewish man] shall be permitted to leave his wife for more than eighteen months without permission of the Court of the nearest city, unless he receive the consent of his wife in the presence of proper witnesses; we have permitted the absence of eighteen months only to such as leave out of necessity to earn and provided the husband is at peace with his wife. . . . When the husband returns from his journey he must remain at home for no less than six months before undertaking a second journey; but in no case may he forsake his wife as the result of a quarrel or with bitter feelings, but only with the consent of the Court in the manner described. Each man must send his wife the means for her livelihood every six months. He must make payment through the Court for whatever debts were contracted in his absence in order to maintain his family and give his children their education in accordance with the law of the Talmud [Ketubbot 50a]; one who is able to do so must before leaving on a journey give his wife sufficient means for the support of the family.[70]

At first, Gershom issued the ordinance with the concurrence of the other rabbis of Mainz just for that community in order to protect a de facto abandoned wife whose merchant husband was living abroad for years at a time. The text that has survived refers indirectly to the ordinance and deals with the ways it may be suspended:

The ban [ḥerem] of [someone who violates] the ordinance of the communities established by R[abbenu] Gershom, Light of the Exile, against marrying two wives may not be suspended except by one hundred men. These men shall not agree to suspend the ban unless a cogent reason is given for the request and unless the payment of the marriage contract [*ketubbah*] is assured either by cash or other guarantee.[71]

Although this ruling was originally binding only in Mainz, where it was promulgated, by the middle of the twelfth century it was widely accepted in northern France, in England, and throughout the German Empire. Even in the eleventh century, none of the many references to family life in responsa, liturgical poems, historical narratives, and lists of martyrs from 1096 mentions a man with more than one wife. Jews from France and Germany who moved to Muslim lands or even to Christian Spain, which had a Muslim minority population, might ignore the ban there, but, in Ashkenaz, men maintained monogamous households. Gershom's enormous prestige created a social change that became a universal feature of north European Jewish family life.

Another ruling, also reliably attributed to Gershom, was that a Jewish woman could no longer be divorced without her consent, a practice permitted by talmudic law. Based on Deuteronomy 24:1 and 24:3, the Jewish law of divorce requires a husband who wants to divorce his wife to initiate the action and assigns a passive role to his wife. Gershom introduced the revolutionary idea that a wife must agree to her husband's initiative: "Here are the excommunication bans of our ancestors from Rabbenu Gershom Light of the Exile, may he rest in peace. . . . One may not give a bill of divorce [*get*] to his wife against her will."[72]

This decision, too, began in Mainz and first applied to the three Rhineland communities of Mainz, Worms, and Speyer. Eventually, it became a region-wide requirement for all north European Jewish communities and was widely accepted there along with the ban on polygynous marriages.

The second ordinance plugged a loophole in the ban on polygyny. Without this, if a Jewish merchant's first wife discovered he had started a second family, he could avoid being shunned by the community simply by sending her a writ of divorce; with it, he could not send it without her consent. This added force to the original ban, since a merchant who was found out now risked excommunication, and it made a Jewish woman more secure in her marriage, since it could not be dissolved against her will. It would also inhibit wealthy husbands who did not mind paying her the ketubbah settlement that a divorce usually required.

Complementing Gershom's innovative rulings is a rare portrait of one of the few well-educated Jewish women of the times. Often as not, these women were members of rabbinical families. For example, there is a tradition that the great Bible and Talmud commentator Rashi of Troyes (1040–1105), who had no sons, taught at least one of his daughters Torah, and two of them married distinguished rabbinic scholars.[73] Although there is a traveler's report that the daughter of the twelfth-century Baghdad rabbi Samuel ben Ali taught his daughter, who was "expert in Scripture and Talmud" and gave "instruction in Scripture to young men through a window,"[74] she too may have benefited from not having male siblings and is one of two rare cases from the medieval Muslim world. The other is a short but elegant Hebrew poem possibly written by the wife of the tenth-century Andalusian Jewish court poet Dunash ibn Labrat (see Raymond Scheindlin's chapter).[75] Otherwise, one looks in vain, for example, for any reference to the learning of the wife of Maimonides (d. 1204) or the wife of Rabbi Judah Halevi (d. 1141).

In Germany, such a woman was Mistress Dulcea, the wife of Rabbi Eleazar ben Judah of Worms (d. ca. 1230). Eleazar writes that, as he was studying at his table, on November 15, 1196 (22 Kislev 4957),[76] men marked (with crosses?) came into his house and attacked his family, killing his wife and two daughters (ages thirteen and six) and wounding his son and him. Their deaths moved husband and father to write three elegies. The one to his wife is modeled on Proverbs 31, the "Woman of Valor." Despite the stylization of the language and its heavy dependence on the biblical text, Eleazar manages to give us something of his wife's character and her role as the mainstay of the household in Worms.[77]

In part, he stresses the special economic role his wife and daughters played in supporting the family. But he also indicates how his wife, in particular, supported the students who boarded in their house. In effect, a Jewish woman becomes a partner in running a school, the abbess of a Jewish monastery. Rabbi Eleazar teaches, and Mistress Dulcea provides food and material support. She teaches women and is learned herself in liturgy and many aspects of the Jewish laws involved in the sewing together of ritual objects and customs associated with marriage and death.

This is how Eleazar begins:

Who can find a woman of valor [Proverbs 31:10a] like my pietist wife, Mistress Dulcea?
A woman of valor, her husband's crown, a daughter of aristocrats,
A God-fearing woman [30b], renowned for her good deeds;
Her husband trusts her implicitly [11a], she fed and clothed him in dignity
So he could sit among the elders of the land, and provide Torah study and good deeds [see v. 23].

The scholar credits his free time to study the Torah to his wife's labors,[78] which is why she can be considered a pietist (*ḥasidah*). This is a rare example of a woman being included among the pietists of Ashkenaz (Ḥasidei Ashkenaz), a group of religious virtuosos (discussed later in this chapter). Even allowing for hyperbole and a stylized allegiance to the rhetoric of the biblical text, much of her sacrifice and learning comes through in Eleazar's glosses:

> *She always treats him well* [12a] throughout their life together;
> Her labor provides him with books, her very name means "pleasant";
> *She looked for white wool* [13a] with which to make ritual fringes [*tzitzit*],
>   she spun *with enthusiasm* [13b];
> *She foresees* [16a] how to do [many] commandments, all who see her
>   praise her.

The female occupations par excellence were spinning and weaving; hence, the notion of a woman as the "distaff side." Here this commonplace is exemplified by Dulcea's manufacturing of religious items such as the ritual fringes of the prayer shawl usually worn by men. The issue of whether a woman is permitted to make fringes comes up in a rabbinic question addressed to Rabbi Meir ben Barukh of Rothenburg in the late thirteenth century. Clearly Eleazar permitted it, and it must have been a common practice, even if some people objected or were unclear about its religious justification.[79]

Eleazar conducted a boarding school for his students, who were of various ages and some of whom came to study with him from far away. Meir ben Barukh did the same thing in the late thirteenth century, though no such arrangement is known, for example, about Isaac Alfasi or Maimonides, in Muslim Spain or Egypt. In Ashkenaz, rabbinic wives had to feed their own families and also take care of the students' needs. The theme of economic productivity by making religious objects related to spinning and sewing, and Dulcea's support of the household including the boarders, are major leitmotifs in this elegy. Moreover, she was not producing these objects only for her local community. Although Jewish women (especially widows) engaged in business dealings in Muslim as well as Christian Europe, it was unusual for them to produce liturgical objects as a commercial venture:

> *She is like the merchant ships* [14a]: she feeds her husband [so he can] study
>   Torah;
> Daughters saw her [see 29a] and declared her happy, *her wares were so
>   fine* [18a];
> *She gives food to her household* [15a] and bread to the [school]boys [15a end];

See how *her hands held the distaff* [19a] to spin cords for [binding] books;
Zealous in everything [she did], she spun [cords] for [sewing] tefillin and
    megillot, gut for [stitching together] Torah scrolls;
Quick as a deer she cooks for the young men and attends to the students'
    needs;
She girded her loins with strength [17a], and sewed some forty Torah scrolls;
She prepared the feast, set the table for all the Fellows;
She adorned brides *in good taste* [18a] and brought them in honor [to the
    wedding];
"Pleasant" would bathe the dead, sew their shrouds;
Her hands [19a] sewed the students' clothes and torn books;
See how she distributes [the fruits of] her labor among Torah scholars;
She extends a hand to the poor [20a],
Feeding her boys, daughters, and husband;
She freely did the will of her Creator, day and night;
Her lamp will not go out in the night [18b]—she makes wicks
For the synagogue and schools, and she says Psalms.

The author now shifts his attention to his late wife's learning and synagogue
piety. It is difficult to know how extraordinary Dulcea of Worms was in this regard. Most likely she was like other daughters and wives of learned Jews, a distinct minority of men or women. Occasionally we get hints of how irregularly
even men, let alone women, attended synagogue. The long anonymous Hebrew
First Crusade chronicle says about Abraham, son of Yom Tov, of Trier: "He was a
faithful man, righteous, upright, and beloved of God. It was his custom to attend
the synagogue both in the morning and in the evening."[80] This comment is
highly suggestive and makes Eleazar's praise of his wife all the more remarkable.
Consider now Dulcea:

She sings hymns and prayers, she recites petitions;
Daily [she says] confession, [*nishmat kol ḥai*] "the breath of every living
    being" and [*ve-kol ma'aminim*] "all who believe";[81]
She says [*pittum ha-ketoret*] "the compound forming the incense"[82] and the
    ten commandments;
In all the towns she taught women [so that they can] chant songs;
She knows the order of the morning and evening prayers,
And she attends synagogue morning and evening;
She stands throughout Yom Kippur, sings and prepared the candles
    [beforehand];[83]
She honors the Sabbaths and Holidays as well as Torah scholars;

She openeth her mouth with wisdom [26a] and she knows what is forbidden,
   what permitted.

Dulcea's attendance at the synagogue, not required of women, seems unusual,
since she had two young daughters and a son.

Apart from her synagogue piety and learning, a woman needs to know the
laws that affect her life as a female. These Dulcea knew, her husband notes, including the laws of kashrut for the kitchen, the rules about menstrual impurity
that affected conjugal relations, and the Sabbath regulations for lighting lamps
or preparing the dough offering (*ḥallah*) beforehand, among others. Thus Dulcea had learned what the author of *Sefer Ḥasidim* said a Jewish girl should be
taught. For, as he observed pragmatically, "If she will not know the Sabbath laws,
how can she observe them?" One might add, How will her family as well?[84]

   On the Sabbath she sits and listens to her husband's sermon;
   More modest than everyone she is wise and faithful—[one is] fortunate [to be
      in] her company;
   When [doing] all the commandments she is zealous, selfless, gracious;
   She bought milk for the students, and hired [them] tutors from her earnings;
   Known and wise, she serves her Creator joyfully;
   She ran to visit the sick, to fulfill her Creator's commandments;
   And she feeds her boys, urges them to study, and serves the Name, may He be
      blessed, out of [proper] fear;
   She is happy to do her husband's will, she never angered him;
   "Pleasant" are her deeds; may the Hidden Rock remember her;
   May her soul be adorned, bound in the bond of light of the [eternally] living;
   Give her of the fruit of her hands [31a] in Paradise.

Despite the high style of this elegy, much of Dulcea's everyday activities comes
through: making wicks for synagogue lamps, sewing shrouds, supplying milk for
the boarders. Above and beyond all the facts about her learning, piety, and productivity, something genuinely moving about a husband's love for his wife is expressed in this elegy. So far as we know, Eleazar did not marry again.

JEWISH CULTURAL ASSERTIVENESS AS
CHRISTIAN BLASPHEMY

Eleazar's portrait of his wife's virtues is an open celebration of Jewish motherhood, and it echoes the polemical juxtaposition in the 1096 narratives between

the sanctity of Jewish family roles and the impurity and immorality of the Christian Holy Family. The range of Jewish polemic was not limited to insulting the Christian claims about Jesus and Mary in Hebrew narratives, and it is not clear how familiar Christians were with these kinds of Hebrew writings. There was always the possibility that a Jew who converted would reveal them and endanger the Jewish community.

That it was dangerous for a Jew to speak openly about such matters in the presence of Christians can be learned from the early-twelfth-century abbot Guibert of Nogent, from northern France. In his collection of stories about his life, he describes an eccentric nobleman, Jean, the Count of Soissons: "He practiced the perfidy of the Jews and heretics to such an extent that he said blasphemous things about the Saviour, which through fear of the faithful the Jews did not dare to do. . . . Although he supported the Jews, the Jews considered him insane, since he approved of their religion in word, and publicly practiced ours."[85]

Guibert thinks Jews would not dare to blaspheme aloud as the Count of Soissons did. As this case indicates, some Christians moved between the communities and could pass along incriminating information about Jewish blasphemy to the Christian authorities. Occasionally a marginal Jewish figure appeared who played the role of semi-Jew and semi-Christian. Thus, from thirteenth-century Germany, Rabbi Meir of Rothenburg refers to "those despicable creatures who wander from town to town and alternately appear as Jews or as fanatical Christians," who "call themselves Jews in order that people should give them food, and that they should have a chance to steal and to indulge their base appetites."[86] Whether nominally a Jew or a Christian, such figures could endanger the Jewish community by passing along how Jews actually talked about Jesus and Mary.

Jews blasphemed Christian sancta by their actions as well as by their words. One of the accusations Christians made against Jews in medieval Ashkenaz was that they insulted images of the Holy Family by connecting them to a latrine. A passage in the Talmud already makes a special association between Jesus and excrement: "Onkelos son of Lolonikos, the son of Titus's sister, raised Jesus[87] from the dead by magic and asked [him]: . . . What is your punishment? They replied, With boiling excrement, since a Master said, Whoever mocks the words of the Sages is punished with boiling in hot excrement."[88] This rhetoric continued in Eliezer ben Nathan's 1096 account, where he says about the martyrs of Worms, "in the end they regarded the object of the enemy's veneration as no more than slime and dung."[89]

This motif led to elaborations in behavior as well as rhetoric associating Jesus with bodily elimination in various forms, a point not lost on medieval Christian authorities and writers. The claim that Jews blaspheme by foul deeds is made by Rigord, the ecclesiastical court biographer of King Philip Augustus of France. Among the reasons for the king's brief expulsion of the Jews in 1182 from his growing domains, Rigord mentions the following:

> At that time, the Jews were afraid that their houses might be ransacked by royal officials. It happened that a certain Jew, who at the time was staying in Paris, held certain ecclesiastical objects as pledges. He had a gold cross marked with gems, a book of the Gospels decorated with gold and precious stones in an extraordinary manner, silver cups, and other vessels. He placed them all in a sack and vilely threw it into the deep pit where he used to relieve himself (for shame!).
>
> A short time afterward, Christians discovered the objects in that very place—God having shown the way. The objects were all returned to their own church with great joy and honor, and a fifth of the debt having been paid to the lord king of all that was owed.[90]

Another gesture connecting the body of Christ with latrines is found in a letter that Pope Innocent III wrote in 1205 to the archbishop of Sens and the bishop of Paris, asking them "to restrain the excesses of the Jews." In detailing what he had in mind, he wrote that he had heard that the Jews,

> whom the kindness of princes has admitted into their territories, have become so insolent that they hurl unbridled insults at the Christian Faith, insults which it is an abomination not only to utter but even to keep in mind. Thus, whenever it happens that on the day of the Lord's Resurrection [Easter] the Christian women who are nurses for the children of Jews, take in the body and blood of Jesus Christ, the Jews make these women pour their milk into the latrine for three days before they again give suck to the children.

The pope continues without further elaboration, "they perform other detestable and unheard of things against the Catholic faith."[91] By this gesture, Jews were placing Jesus himself into a latrine, since Jews seemed to think that the milk contained the digested body and blood of Christ. Christian illuminated manuscripts portrayed Jews placing images of the Virgin and Child into latrines or show a chamber pot with pseudo-Hebrew lettering on it, as in the Isenheim altarpiece, a Christian association of Jewish culture with bodily elimination.[92]

The linkage in Jewish writing between Jesus and Mary and latrines or other scatological imagery is well grounded in an expressed disgust at the thought that God could enter a human body. The language of latrines is associated in some Jewish polemics against the Incarnation, by claiming that the Christian worship of Jesus is much worse than the Israelites' worshiping the Golden Calf—because Christians "err in saying that something holy entered into a woman in that stinking place—for there is nothing in the world as disgusting as a woman's stomach, which is full of feces and urine, which emits discharge and menstrual blood and serves as the receptacle for man's semen."[93] The attributed latrine gesture mocks the Incarnation, the Virgin Birth, and insults the body of Christ by linking Jesus and his mother with human physicality in its most obnoxious form.

Although Christian sources claim that Jews insulted Christian images by linking them to latrines or feces, the Jewish texts about 1096 do not portray Christians placing Jewish symbols into latrines or defiling Jewish bodies or synagogues with feces or urine, and it is likely they did not do so. The typical act that the Jewish writers describe both in 1096 and in the 1147 narrative of Rabbi Ephraim of Bonn is of Christians attacking Jews with knives or swords, and occasionally

A Jew desecrating a picture of the Virgin and Child is punished by a Christian,
who then prays to the image as it miraculously produces holy oil.
French, fourteenth century. (Bibliothèque Royale, Brussels; Ms. 9229-2930, folio 34v)

dragging them through the muddy streets. The Jews also portray Christians tearing apart Torah scrolls or stomping on them in the dirt. The victims' naked bodies are compared to the Torah scrolls, sacred objects also made of skin; like the scrolls, which the perpetrators undress (unwrap) before tearing, they strip the Jews naked and trample both underfoot.[94]

Why latrine blasphemy for Jews but attacks on people and Torah scrolls for Christians? Each culture chooses a specific kind of target that reflects an awareness of the sancta in the other culture that must be destroyed or degraded in a uniquely polemical way. A basic difference in attitudes toward the body is reflected in the 1096 Hebrew texts and the Christian ones about Jewish latrine blasphemy. Jews equate Jesus and Mary with bodily elimination, a parody of the Christian claim that its sancta, though human, are really spiritual. Some Christian thinkers even tried to remove any association of bodily elimination of ingested sacred symbols. A thirteenth-century preacher rejected the idea that the eucharistic wafer could be physically digested and eliminated and wrote that the host became "not bodily food but food of the soul; not of the flesh but of the heart."[95] By the late Middle Ages, Christians were associating Jews, women, and other marginal groups with feces and latrines.[96]

Compare this view with that of Judah Hasid, who objected to the local custom of feeding small children honey cakes on which biblical verses were written because "it is not proper to excrete (biblical verses)," which is related to the ancient rabbinic claim that the biblical manna, heavenly food God provided the wandering Israelites in the desert, was not excreted after being eaten.[97] The contrast between the medieval positions is instructive: the Jewish author does not doubt the physical process, though the rabbinic tradition about manna does. The Christian view spiritualizes the eaten host by denying that it is subject to physiological processes.

Did any of acts of latrine blasphemy in fact occur? It is important to be cautious when weighing any charge of blasphemy leveled against Jews in medieval Europe and look to the evidence. Each type of accusation must be assessed separately. In addition to the ritual murder accusation and the blood libel mentioned earlier came the charge in Paris in 1290 that Jews attack and otherwise desecrate the consecrated host, which embodies for the faithful the body of Christ. Each of these accusations is a different version of a claim that Jews reenact the archetypal sin, which Christian writers persisted in reconfiguring from the Gospel accounts of the Passion—that Jews are killers of "the Body of Christ." That could be understood as Christ then, or as a Christian or as Christ in the host now.[98]

Although there are no Jewish discussions of whether Jews should kill Christians, or ritually ingest their blood in their services, or desecrate the host, Jews do discuss carrying out acts of latrine blasphemy, and it is possible that some Jews did this, in addition to hurling written Hebrew attacks on Christian sancta when they thought it was safe to do so. In a polemical tract written by the northern French rabbinic figure Joseph Official in the thirteenth century, the author offers a parable to justify this behavior. Jews in parts of Ashkenaz were discussing and debating this at the time:

Once my lord and father, Rabbi Nathan, may he rest in Paradise, was riding alongside the Count of Sens. The count got off his horse opposite a bush in order to urinate. My lord and father saw this, and he got off his horse opposite an abomination [a cross] and urinated on it.

The count saw this and objected. He said to him, It is not proper to do that, to make the cross smell bad. My father replied, On the contrary, *"It was a foolish thing for you to do"* [Genesis 31:28]. You urinated on a bush, on which the Holy One, blessed be He, radiated His presence in order to bring salvation [that is, at the burning bush, Exodus 3:1–3]. But this [cross], on which you [Christians] say that [the god] you fear was defeated, stank, and rotted, it is right that you should expose yourself and pee all over it![99]

The idea of insulting Christianity by eliminating on its symbol is discussed but rejected in another Jewish source that is nearly contemporary with Official. *Sefer Ḥasidim* is a collection of exempla and comments exhorting Jews to follow the author's intuitive understanding of the hidden will of God. It laid out for the people of Ashkenaz ancient ascetic and exclusivist norms of behavior of Jew toward Jew and Jew toward Christian, and it had a great influence on the conduct of Jews in Germany and later in Eastern Europe. The fact that *Sefer Ḥasidim* recommends that Jews not insult Christian icons by eliminating on them indicates that the issue was a live one and that Jews were debating it:

A [Jew] wanted to eliminate [on or near a Christian image]. His companion said to him, They might kill you [if you do it there]. He said, It is for the sanctification of the Name [of God]! The other one replied, You will have no reward but only sin if you jeopardize your life. Moreover, don't endanger your children and the other [Jewish] residents of the town. That which is written, *I should be sanctified in the midst of the children of Israel* [Leviticus 22:32] refers to when gentiles are oppressing one [by threatening], If he doesn't do such and such they will kill him. It is also written, *It is for Your sake that we are killed all day long* [Psalms 44:23]. But if one causes himself to be killed, about him it is

written, *But for your own life-blood I will require a reckoning* [Genesis 9:5], and
it is [also] written, *Preserve well your life* [Deuteronomy 4:9].[100]

Because Jesus and Mary were viewed by Jews as no better than feces and urine
anyway, the polar opposite of Jewish sancta, it was considered appropriate to put
their images into latrines or to eliminate on their images. The only inhibiting
factor in any of this seems to have been the fear of reprisals, not any sense that it
was the wrong thing to do. In this regard, it may just be a matter of degree as to
how many times Christians accused Jews of these acts and the times Jews actually managed to say or do them. It is reasonable to guess that some Jews did it
some of the time and thought it was the right thing to so. As the argument in
Sefer Ḥasidim indicates, some Jews thought that desecrating Christian images
was an act of sanctification of God's Name, a form of self-affirmation of cultural
truth and purity.

In addition, there is evidence that Jews acted out anti-Christian rites on
Purim, when they symbolically equated Haman in the Book of Esther with
Jesus. From the fifth century, Jews were accused of hanging Haman as Jesus on
wooden crosses, and we have records about such behavior from medieval Europe as well.[101] Purim, which takes place during the Hebrew month of Adar,
when Jews are urged to rejoice, often coincided with the Christian Lent, a time of
mourning and sobriety. The climax of Adar is Purim, when Jews are enjoined to
become drunk and carnivalesque. In defiance of Christian sobriety, the Jews
celebrated their own Mardi Gras during Lent as Purim and even borrowed the
Christian custom of wearing elaborate costumes, first in late medieval Germany
and then in Italy and elsewhere.[102]

The Crusaders of 1096 had innovated by attacking not only Muslims but also
Jews as enemies of Christ; then, in the later Middle Ages, it was not a big leap for
Christians to mix together what Jews in fact did with what the Christians fantasized about them. This fantasy, this "invented Jew," had a most pernicious effect
on Jewish life in Europe even into the twentieth century.

THE SUBCULTURE OF ASHKENAZIC PIETISTS
AND THEIR CHRISTIAN NEIGHBORS

The passage in *Sefer Ḥasidim* advising Jews not to insult Christian images is but
one of several that deal with the interaction of pietist Jews with Christians. Descendants of the Kalonymos family of Lucca and southern Italy, one of the first
families to migrate to Germany, the Ḥasidei Ashkenaz were rabbinic scholars
who claimed to have received ancient Palestinian and Babylonian secret tradi-

tions about God, the universe, the Hebrew Bible, and the liturgy, all of which could be harmonized by properly interpreting the numerical values of Hebrew words and phrases. They produced thousands of pages of esoteric writings, most of which have yet to be published, and a smaller collection of moralistic tales, exegetical and homiletical commentary that advocated a perfect life, beyond the demands of Jewish law, for the select few who joined their community in the Rhineland towns of Speyer and Worms and in Regensburg, to the southeast.[103]

Their most important anthology, *Sefer Ḥasidim,* is composed of some 14 topically arranged books that together express the worldview of an ascetic, hierarchically self-confident subculture of supercilious Jews who consider themselves holier than other Jews and head and shoulders above Christians. They have been compared, without exaggeration, to contemporary Ultra-Orthodox (*ḥaredi*) Jews. These unusual sources also suggest the close social relations between Jews and Christians in Ashkenaz; in their insistence that pietists avoid Christian influences, the authors reveal just how intimately familiar they were with their surroundings. In their hierarchical vision, the pietists were to shun Christians and also other Jews, but only if the pietists were in a position of relative weakness or vulnerability. If they were in a position of dominance, they could and should try to influence other Jews and even Christians.[104]

According to *Sefer Ḥasidim,* a Jew should think of being a pietist as analogous to the way Christian knights go into battle to win fame and glory:

> Pay attention to how some people risk their very lives for the sake of personal honor. For example, knights go into the thick of battle and even sacrifice themselves to enhance their reputations and to avoid being humiliated. . . . How much the more should [a pietist] be resourceful for the sake of his Creator's honor.[105]

The author compares a knight's willingness to sacrifice his life in battle not to a Jew's readiness to die as a martyr, as in 1096, but merely to his willingness to be a pietist—that is, to control his desires and passions. If he does this, he surely will earn so great a reward that the knight's efforts will pale in significance. The ideal act of combat is not resistance to anti-Jewish violence; it is the inner struggle of the pietist's will.

Elsewhere, the author explicitly tells us that one can be a pietist only when the period is not one of violence:

> Think about the following. If it were a time of persecution [which it is not], you would [undergo] suffering or death for the Holy One, blessed be He.

[Thus the verse] *maidens* [*alamot*] *have loved you* [Song of Songs 1:3] is interpreted as though it said, "To the death [*al mavet*], they have loved you." If they
wanted to kill you or torture you, so that death would be preferable, you would
endure the worst. You certainly should follow [acts of pietism], which are not
as onerous [a demand] and which only involves resisting the passions that
tempt you [to disobey God's will].[106]

Thus the pietist world is presented as one of relatively peaceful coexistence
between Jews and Christians. The late twelfth and early thirteenth centuries
were not like 1096, let alone 1298–1350 or the fifteenth century. And precisely because of the close social interaction during this period, Jews were just as concerned about resisting Christian culture as the Christians were worried that Jews
would influence them. As with Ashkenaz in general, the pietists were concerned
about affirming their Jewish cultural identity by denigrating Christianity.[107]

Far from being isolated in a ghetto, the Ḥasidei Ashkenaz, like other Jews,
lived side by side with Christians, so much so that Judah the Pietist reminds his
readers that the Jews' morality in any given place is no different from that of
their Christian neighbors.[108] He tries repeatedly to elevate his pietists and remove them from temptations. For example, Jews were aware of the vernacular
literature known as "romances," adventure tales about heroic knights and beautiful ladies in distress, such as the stories of King Arthur and other story cycles
that were popular in northern France and Germany. The pietists were tempted
to read them, but Judah warns his readers that they should not even cover a holy
Jewish book with parchment that has such tales written on it, employing the
French word "romances" spelled out in Hebrew letters.[109] Opposition to stories
written in the vernacular was also expressed by Judah's contemporary, Rabbi
Judah ben Isaac, known as Sir Leon, of Paris (1166–1224).[110] Obviously there were
Jews who enjoyed reading them as much as Christians did.

Judah Hasid's concern for the welfare of Jewish women is reflected in one of
the many exempla that are found throughout *Sefer Ḥasidim*. He advises those
who travel to disguise themselves as nuns or as Christian women for their own
protection, not from anti-Jewish persecution but from a random sexual attack
on the road:

A [Jewish] woman who travels abroad and hears that Christians might violently harm her, fearing that someone might rape her, may disguise herself as a
nun so that they will think she is a nun and will not rape her. If she heard that
lawless Jews might harm her she also may wear a Christian woman's clothes,
say that she is a Christian woman, and [tell them] that [if they harm her] she

will scream and turn them over [to the Christian authorities]. She may even scream before [they actually attack her] to get Christians to come to her aid, even if they kill the lawless Jewish men.[111]

The assumptions behind this prescription for "cross-dressing" illuminate many aspects of intergroup relations. One is Judah's view that Christian men would not rape nuns. Another is that "lawless" Jewish men might attack a Jewish woman but would hesitate if they thought she was a Christian. The author further believes that a woman may scream and turn over such Jews to the Christian authorities even if it results in their death.

In another story, a Jewish woman's son is ill, and a Christian woman brings her a stone that is supposed to have healing powers derived from the Church of the Holy Sepulchre, where Jesus was buried. The mother rejects the remedy because of its source, but the story indicates that Jewish and Christian women were in social contact. The story ends: "The Jewish woman said, Since she said it is from Jesus [the word is censored in the printed edition of Sefer Ḥasidim], I do not want my son to drink over the stone. She did not want any medication to be performed with the stone. This is [the meaning of] *with all your soul* [Deuteronomy 6:5], *to love the Lord your God* [19:9]."[112]

The author interprets a verse that often was used to justify acts of martyrdom— "with all your soul," meaning to love God even in situations when you have to give up your soul, that is, your life—as referring to everyday contact with Christian holy places, which he regards as dangerously contaminating.

At times, the author suggests that a Jewish doctor should not cure a Christian when the cure will result in the patient's worship of Christianity, which the writer views as idolatry—for a Jew is not allowed to aid and abet anyone in false worship. A Jew goes to a Jewish doctor to get a remedy for a hoarse throat and a cough. When he arrives,

> a monk was sitting there and he understood the vernacular, the same language that the Jew was speaking. The Jewish sage said to the doctor in Hebrew, Do not tell me the remedy until the monk leaves. After the monk had left, the sage said, If the monk asks you the remedy, do not tell it to him because he will prepare it for the monks who shout in their house of foolishness [insulting for: pray in church]. The monk did ask the Jew what [the doctor] had told him, but he did not want to disclose it to him.[113]

Apart from everyday contact between Christians going to Jewish doctors and the tactic of a Jew reverting to Hebrew in order not to be understood by a Christian, this exemplum also prescribes the ideal hierarchy of Jews in Ashkenaz in relation to Christians. Not all contact is to be avoided, but only that in which a Jew is subordinate to a Christian. If a Jew is the doctor and the monk is dependent on him, there is no prohibition of contact. The same applies when Jews lend money to Christians. Again, the Christian is dependent on the Jew. Hierarchical thinking also lies behind ecclesiastics who protest when Jewish moneylenders take church objects as pawns. From their point of view, such practices violates proper hierarchy by placing Jews over Christian sacred vessels.[114]

In these interactions, the Jews gained firsthand knowledge of Christian behavior, religious images, and beliefs. Jews and Christians talked to each other frequently, not only about business but also about their religious beliefs. In the exempla of Caesarius of Heisterbach, a Cistercian monk who was a contemporary of Judah the Pietist, the tale is told of a cleric who was in the habit of "going to the house of a Jew to argue with him about the Christian faith. [The Jew's] daughter, then a little girl, would often listen very eagerly to the discussion, and would weigh as well as her intelligence allowed both the arguments of the Jew her father and those of his clerical opponent; and so, little by little, she became by the providence of God, imbued with the Christian faith."[115]

An encounter between unequals was dangerous for the weaker party, and *Sefer Ḥasidim* tries to limit such encounters:

> Suppose a monk or a priest or a learned and erudite [Jewish] sectarian or a Jew learned in Talmud who is not a pietist and busily chases after his own reputation approaches a pietist who is not as learned; or a learned person encounters a witch to debate Torah. If he debates them, they might persuade him to follow them. About such a situation it is written, *Answer not a fool according to his folly, lest you also be like him* [Proverbs 26:4]. . . . Even if you are more learned than he, do not permit a less learned person to listen to your debates because that person might be persuaded [by your opponent], since he does not understand [which position is] the true one. . . . But if you are so learned that you are confident that you will win the argument . . . [then apply the verse] *Answer a fool according to his folly, lest he be wise in his own eyes* [Proverbs 26:5].[116]

Sefer Ḥasidim assumes that daily contact took place between Jews and Christians even in churches: "A Christian who is walking in a house of abomination [a church] said to a Jew, 'Exchange this garment for me.' [Because it will be used] in an idolatrous sacrifice [the Mass], the Jew should not give it to the Christian."[117] The only issue at stake is if the Jew will sell the Christian liturgically related objects, a prohibition often violated, not if they will meet in a church.

We also see that some Jews tried to avoid entering churches and that one who did so could earn disapproval, but the discussion itself reinforces the impression that it was a frequent occurrence. "A Jew went into a courtyard of [a place of] idolatry [a church]. When he left, he heard an oracular voice that said, '*Me you have cast behind your back*' [1 Kings 14:9], and he fasted regularly for the rest of his life."[118] Or again, "A Jewish man once went into a house of idolatry and was sorry [about it]. He asked an Elder to tell him what [penance] to do. He told him that he should fast every year on that same day, and he did so."[119]

A clever Christian might even take advantage of this well-known taboo, as when "a monk owed a Jew money, and the monk knew that [the Jew] would not follow him into an abomination. When the Jew came to collect his debt, the monk went into the house of abomination, but the Jew did not want to follow him."[120] Clearly, then, though some Jews did go into churches, others did not. The extensive preoccupation in the sources with this question reflects the porous social boundaries between the two cultures.

To discourage Jews from doing business with clerics in their religious institutions, the author of *Sefer Ḥasidim* warns,

> Most Jews who do business with clerics do not become wealthy their whole lives, because their wealth will not last. [This is] because [the Jews] are supplying [the clerics] with the [liturgical] necessities for idolatry [which Jews may not do]. Such a person also transgresses [the verse], *Do not bring an abomination into your house* [Deuteronomy 7:26]. That is why in the end they will lose that which they earned from the clerics.[121]

Jews sold to Christians the very objects that the medieval Talmud scholars said they must not sell. In his comments to the first part of Talmud Tractate Avodah Zarah (Foreign Worship), Rabbenu Jacob ben Meir, also later known as Rabbenu Tam (d. 1171), ruled that the Mishnah seems to prohibit all business dealings with "idolators" and hence with contemporary Christians on the three days prior to their festivals, but actually it only prohibits the selling of articles needed for religious services, such as the Mass.[122] Yet Jews evidently insisted on engaging even in this very limited area of commerce, because it is a prominent subject of discussion in *Sefer Ḥasidim* as well as in ecclesiastical legislation. Consider the following: "It once happened that a [Jewish] man used to sell to priests all the [liturgical] necessities for a house of foolishness [church]. When he died, it happened to be the day Christians marched [outside] with all of their images [All Saints Day], and the uncircumcised brought [them] near his [funeral] bier. [The Jews] said, He has been paid back in kind!"[123] It does not matter that this is merely an exemplum and not a factual report of a "real event." The point of the story is that this kind of behavior was known and opposed by both Jewish and church officials, apparently without much success by either.

Jews sometimes came into possession of Christian liturgical objects that were forfeited for nonpayment of debts. Although the Jew was in control, *Sefer Ḥasidim* sometimes decries this practice, such as when the object is a book, going so far as to urge that a pietist burn a forfeited Christian book he inherited or otherwise acquired,[124] despite the loss resulting from the destruction of a valuable handmade object.

Behind this recommendation is the assumption that Christian images have negative potency and can contaminate Jewish worship or activities that are dedicated to God, and thus they should be isolated (if not destroyed). For example, "If a Jewish man is in the synagogue and sees a house of idolatry [a church—i.e., through a window], he should cover the window with something so that he can no longer see [the church]."[125] Consider the association evoked in a related teaching by the same author: "When a man sits down to write or think about Torah in front of a window, he should not look out at pigs or feces."[126] Or: "People asked why a Jewish man did not go out to greet the king. He replied, They are bringing their image there and also incense of idolatry [which is] an abomination. That is why I won't go there."[127]

Avoidance of Christian contamination can take other forms as well, such as not sharing the same flowing water, which is required for Jewish ritual bathing. To share it would be a desecration of God's Name:

> In a certain town there was not a lot of [flowing] water, for [ritual] bathing. There was much vacant land around, and some Jews wanted to live on it. The sage said to them, "Since there is no other water except that in which they test thieves [by ordeal], when monks pronounce over it the names of their idolatry, [Jewish] women must not bathe in it [to purify themselves ritually after they menstruate]. And [it is not proper] even to cleanse knives and metal or glass utensils in the same water. For one must not say a blessing where they mentioned the name of idolatry."[128]

A RITUAL OF CHILDHOOD

The idea of protecting a purified Jewish person from outside contamination by covering him or her up is an early medieval Palestinian custom that was associated with Jewish women who bathed in the ritual bath and risked being contaminated when returning home.[129] A similar motif is found in medieval

Ashkenaz in connection with the initiation ceremony when a Jewish boy is first introduced to his Hebrew letters.

This ceremony, like many other liturgical practices in medieval Ashkenaz, point to the central place of custom (*minhag*) in the culture of Ashkenaz. Often they are referred to as ancestral (*minhag avoteinu*), without any reference to a written source. As mentioned earlier, the early Jews of Italy, Germany, and northern France followed a form of Judaism that consisted of practices passed down from parents to children and was less dependent on the written words and teachings of contemporary rabbis. Even when the rabbinical leadership became concerned over discrepancies between the Talmud and how Jews were actually living, especially in their commercial dealings with Christians, most went out of their way to square the sacred text with behavior that the rabbis held to be equally holy.

The initiation ceremony is a case in point. Although the texts that describe it refer to it as an ancestral custom, it is attested for the first time in twelfth-century Germany and France. It builds on elements found in talmudic mnemonics and early medieval traditions of magical study. Jews in Ashkenaz took these elements and their awareness of the Christian images and rituals around them and fashioned a ritual as a polemical denial of the efficacy of Christian liturgical rites. The rite affirms the central importance of the study of Torah, expressed through food symbols and their associations with the Torah, God's word.

A boy of three, four, or five is taken from his house to the synagogue or to the teacher's house on the first day of Shavuot (Pentecost). He is wrapped in a cloak or a prayer shawl (*talit*) when he is carried through the street, so that he does not see and is not seen by "a gentile [= Christian] or a dog"; another version has, "a dog, pig, ass, or gentile [= Christian]."[130] Again, we see the idea of contamination by sight and the contrast of opposing cultural values.

The ceremony of the boy's initiation reflects other aspects of Jewish-Christian acculturation as well. In the illumination that has been preserved of this ceremony, the teacher sitting on a chair resembles a type of Madonna on the Throne of Wisdom. The teacher of Torah is the Jewish polemical replacement for Mary; the boy becomes a Jewish Jesus figure embodying Torah wisdom, which he symbolically ingests in the form of special foods.

In addition, in the panel that portrays an adult bringing the child to the teacher, the boy caresses the cheek of his father or the learned Jew who carries him. This image is an internalization and transformation of the *madonna amabilis,* or lovable Madonna. It conveys a strong affective family bond between the boy and his father or guardian before he is transferred to the keeping of the teacher and the rigors of disciplined study and memorization. As in the case of

Initiation into Torah of a Jewish schoolboy. Center: the father or elder brings the child
to the teacher; Left: the boy sits on the teacher's lap in imagery based on the Child Jesus
sitting on the Madonna's lap; Right: the teacher takes the boy to the river, which is
compared to the everflowing waters of Torah. The children hold round honey cakes
and eggs, which are eaten in the ceremony. Leipzig Mahzor. (Universitätsbibliothek,
Leipzig; Hebrew Ms. Vollers 1102, vol. 1, f. 131r. Photo: Suzanne Kaufman)

family imagery in the 1096 narratives, here too a Christian symbol of celibate
sanctity is transformed into a Jewish family relationship.

To make the first day of school a pleasant one, the child is fed eggs and cakes
baked with honey on which verses of Scripture are written, thus enacting the
prophet's vision when he eats God's scroll and says, *"I ate it, and it tasted as sweet
as honey to me"* (Ezekiel 3:3). The idea of eating God's words in the form of sweet
cakes, which are also compared to sweet manna, is a Jewish transformation
of the central liturgical mystery of the church, the Eucharist. The Gospel of
John (1:1) equates Jesus with the "Word," but the Jewish ceremony proclaims that
the Torah is the word of God and symbolically creates an equivalent to the central ritual of the Mass.

Did Jews know about the eucharistic sacrifice and its requirements? Of course
they did. We have seen that they sold Christians everything they required to
enact it.[131] We also have an interesting complaint by Rigord, court biographer of
King Philip Augustus, about Jewish behavior that he regards as blasphemous
mocking of the Eucharist. It overlaps at least in part with elements of the children's initiation ceremony:

Certain ecclesiastical vessels consecrated to God—the chalices and crosses of
gold and silver bearing the image of our Lord Jesus Christ crucified—had been
pledged to the Jews by way of security when the need of the churches was
pressing. These they used so vilely, in their impiety and scorn of the Christian

religion, that from the cups in which the body and blood of our Lord Jesus Christ was consecrated they gave their children cakes soaked in wine.[132]

Although the Jewish initiation ceremony does not make use of wine, Rigord's report from the same time and place makes it plausible to interpret the cakes as part of a mock Eucharist. Of related interest are references in early-fourteenth-century Ashkenazic Hebrew manuscripts to a Jewish magical ceremony designed to enhance one's memory, one of the purposes mentioned for the cake ceremony. Here, adults eat small honey cakes inscribed with the Hebrew alphabet and some of the same verses used in the children's ceremony. But, because the ceremony is to be performed on the eve of a festival, the celebrant is also to drink a cup of wine over which special formulas are to be recited.[133] Wine and honey cakes are thus used together, as in the Eucharist.

There is enough overlap among the various references to cake and wine ceremonies to suggest that the boy's initiation ceremony, Rigord's accusation, and the magical memory rite share a vocabulary that makes use of the symbols of the Christian Mass. Those elements are directed toward Jewish purposes, and some of the time they also serve as a mock Eucharist in a polemical confrontation with Christian sancta. Once again, we see how closely linked the two cultures were in these times of relative peace. And yet, the Jews of Ashkenaz were also actively resisting Christian culture even when it was not persecuting them.

ASHKENAZIC RABBIS AS TRUE CHRIST FIGURES

Even in peaceful times there were pressures on Jews to convert, and we catch glimpses of their awareness of this pressure and even of the attractiveness of Christianity in narratives that reveal the permeable membrane between the two cultures in the twelfth and thirteenth centuries.

The first is the story of Jacob ben Meir, the most important French talmudist of the twelfth century. It appears in *Sefer Zekhirah* (Book of Remembrance) by Rabbi Ephraim of Bonn, a relative of Eliezer ben Nathan, the author of one of the 1096 narratives. The episode, placed within the context of events surrounding the call for a Second Crusade in 1146, depicts a Crusader attack on "our rabbi Jacob." From the highly allusive overtones of the narrative, this story illustrates how a Jewish author imagined a Jew as a Christ figure and Crusaders as New Testament Jews who nearly kill their intended victim. Significantly, this same Jacob was later called "Rabbenu Tam." In Genesis 25:27, the adjective *"tam"* is attached to the patriarch Jacob. There it means "simple" or "plain," but it can also mean "the innocent one," as in Job 1:1 (*ish tam*), a description of someone who is innocent but suffers a divinely arranged trial.

Of all the prominent scholars named Jacob in Jewish tradition, why should only Rabbenu Jacob ben Meir get this nickname? Why was he not called "RYbaM," an acronym for Rabbenu Ya'aqov ben Meir, for example? Perhaps an awareness of his story, imagined or actual, lies behind the tagging of this towering rabbinic and communal figure as "the innocent one." Although we do not know if the episode occurred as described, the memory of this story was preserved in several manuscripts.[134]

> On the second festival day of Shavuot, French Crusaders gathered at Ramerupt and came to the house of Rabbenu Jacob, may he live, and took all that was in his house. They ripped up a Torah scroll before his face and took him out to a field. There they argued with him about his religion and started to assault him viciously. They inflicted five wounds on his head, saying: You are the leader of the Jews. So we shall take vengeance upon you for the crucified one and wound you the way you inflicted the five wounds on our god.[135]

By presenting the attack on Jacob as an act of revenge for the crucifixion of Jesus, the narrator equates what the Christians are inflicting on Jacob with what they accuse the Jews of having done to Jesus. This conforms to the kind of religious vendetta the narrators of the 1096 chronicles attributed to the earlier Crusaders who, they claimed, were killing Jews to avenge the killing of Christ. The association in the story of Jacob with Jesus is reinforced when the Christians refer to the rabbi as "the leader of the Jews," an echo of Jesus' mock title, King of the Jews. Within the Jewish narrative, Jacob alternates between being the leader of northern French Jewry and a substitute Christ figure.

There is something ironic about attacking the great student of the Talmud and his Torah scroll, as though Judaism were only a biblical religion. With few exceptions, that was the Christian perception of Judaism until the thirteenth century. In medieval Christian illuminations, a Jew debating a Christian holds a scroll, representing the Old Testament, whereas the Christian holds a book, the embodiment of Christian truth.[136] That Jewish writers understood the Christian perspective comes across in the narratives about 1096 and the attack on Jacob. There is no sign that the Christians realized who Jacob was, because they had not yet discovered the central importance of talmudic studies in northern Europe. They viewed him simply as the leader of the Jews, a communal rather than a special intellectual or religious role.

The story also indicates that the Christians wanted to argue with Jacob and hoped to convert him. This idea is a prominent one in Jewish-Christian relations throughout the ages. According to Ephraim, Christians thought even Jewish leaders were ambivalent about their faith and were vulnerable to persuasion. Although the idea of Jacob converting may seem preposterous, members of rabbinic families, such as Gershom ben Judah's son, in early-eleventh-century Germany, as well as some rabbis in late-medieval Spain, did convert. So, the idea itself was never outlandish to Christians.

One sign of the ambivalence that some Jews may have felt toward remaining Jewish or being tempted to cross over is reflected in a narrative about Rabbi Amnon of Mainz that was also preserved by Ephraim. Unlike the story of Jacob, it features not a real historical leader but a completely imaginary one.[137] The narrator refers to Amnon, as he did to Jacob, as "the leading Jew of his time." He describes the repeated efforts by a local bishop to convert him, a motif we saw in the encounter between the Crusaders and Jacob. Finally, exhausted by the process, Amnon lets down his guard for an instant and tells the bishop, "Give me three days and I will let you know." German imperial charters permitted Jews to have three days to decide if they did in fact wish to convert even after saying they did.[138]

Amnon immediately realizes that his hesitation implies doubt, and that he has signaled a possible triumph for the Christian leader. For even appearing to have had a moment's doubt and having allowed the Christian community to think his conversion might follow, Amnon becomes a martyr. Although he offers to have his sinning tongue pulled out, the bishop disagrees. The tongue spoke well, by indicating a possible interest in conversion. It was his body that sinned by not coming to the church when he said he would.

Amnon is dismembered, and when Rosh Hashanah arrives he is brought into the synagogue and supposedly composes the piyyut known as "U-Netaneh Tokef," which is recited just before the Sanctification Prayer, or *Kedusha*. The narrative also plays with the rabbinic term for martyrdom, *Kiddush ha-Shem*, the sanctification of God's Name.

The story ends with a clear reference to the Gospel accounts of Jesus' appearance before his disciples three days after his death and his instructions to them to teach his word. Now the three days of hesitation at the beginning of Amnon's story are transformed into three days of ultimate triumph; Amnon appears to a leader of the Mainz community three days after his death and tells him to disseminate the prayer that he has composed. Christianity itself has been bested: another Jewish Christ figure has suffered for the truth, which will be perpetuated after his death.[139]

We see here how Jewish writers represent Christians (Jacob's story) or Jews (Amnon's) as imagining that an important Jew might be attracted to Christianity. By wrestling with this perception, the authors of the narrative transform overt Christian symbols into anti-Christian polemic. Once again, this rhetorical palette reveals the degree to which Jewish writers were aware of Christian images and used them in order to bolster morale in the face of an aggressive culture. Violence was not the only means by which Christians tried to pressure Jews toward the baptismal font, and Jews raided the Christian rhetorical arsenal in self-defense.

VISUAL POLEMICAL CONFRONTATIONS

A good example of Christian visual assaults on Jews is the personification of Jews and Christians in the form of two women known as *Synagoga* and *Ecclesia*, the Synagogue and the Church. In antiquity, Roman coins portrayed Israel as a stooped woman with the caption *Judaea Capta* ("Judah Defeated") after the Romans destroyed the Temple in 70 C.E., but the personification of Jews and Christians as two women began in the Middle Ages in Europe. The figure of Synagoga draws on biblical motifs of defeat including a broken staff, being blind and with fallen crown (Lamentations 5:16–17 and Jeremiah 48:16). Ecclesia wears her crown, is not blind, and her staff is intact, embodying Christian power and rule. The contrasting pair appear everywhere for Jews and Christians to see them: in stained-glass windows or sculpted upon or inside Christian buildings or in illuminations and bas reliefs that Jews saw when they came into possession of Christian books or vessels as pledges for loans.

Jews resisted this image in various ways. One visual polemic of Synagoga's claims against Ecclesia is found in a Hebrew manuscript illumination that seems to depict the protagonists of the Song of Songs as an allegory: Israel is the female figure, God the male. The Hamburg Maḥzor contains a single illumination, and it accompanies a piyyut based on a verse from the Song of Songs and written for the Sabbath preceding Passover. A man wearing a pointed Jewish hat faces a woman wearing both a crown and a blindfold. (See page 496.)

The image is incongruent. It seems to portray the two lovers in the Song of Songs as a Jewish man and woman, but it is not clear why she wears a crown topped by cross-like figures as well as a blindfold. As in many cases of Jewish inward acculturation, an earlier model in the Talmud refers to wreaths or crowns worn by Jewish brides. But there is no continuous history of this custom, and the illustrations appear for the first time when Mary is becoming increasingly important in Christian piety.

This motif is a polemical adaptation of the Christian coronation of Mary, sometimes portrayed as the Bride of Christ. The depiction of a crowned Jewish bride is the Hamburg Maḥzor's challenge to the idea of Mary as the Virgin, simi-

Christian representation of (a) victorious Christianity (*Ecclesia*, left) and
(b) defeated Judaism (*Synagoga*, right) on the west façade of Notre-Dame de Paris.
(Courtesy Ivan G. Marcus)

lar in purpose to the 1096 narratives' images of Jewish women. The image of a
crowned Jewish bride also is a riposte to the Synagoga depiction of the crownless
Jew. Despite the political reality that Jews have little collective power, the crowning of a bride serves to place cultural power in the institution of marriage and
procreation.[140]

But what of the Synagoga-like blindfold right under the crown? This seems to
combine the crown of Ecclesia with the blindfold of Synagoga. Which is it?

In light of all that we have seen thus far about the Jews' keen awareness of
Christian images and even texts, it is highly unlikely that they were unaware of
the meanings of a crowned bride who is also depicted as a Synagoga figure. It is
in fact very rare for medieval Ashkenazic Jews to think of themselves as anything
other than superior to Christians. Given their proclivity to transform Christian
symbols into anti-Christian polemics and pro-Jewish ideas, it would be surprising if that is not happening here as well. If we look at the text that the illumination accompanies, we will understand what is at stake.

The poem is a reworking of a verse in Song of Songs 4:8 that was traditionally understood to mean, *From Lebanon come with me; From Lebanon my bride, with me! Look down [tashuri] from Amana's peak, from the peak of Senir and Hermon.* The poet changes the order of the biblical words and compares the Jews to God's beloved and crowned one. Rashi of Troyes understood the verse to refer allegorically to the romance between God and Israel: "From the time you left here until when you return here, I am with you through all your comings and goings." And, specifically on the word "tashuri," Rashi says: "When I gather together your scattered ones, you will *see* and *understand* the reward of your work from the earliest trust you put in me, when you followed Me in the desert" (see Jeremiah 2:2). The central image in both the verse and the accompanying piyyut is sight.

The Jewish image proclaims that, although the Christian world may think the Jews are blind to what Christians claim to be the truth, it is the Jews who see and understand God. The blindfold is there ironically as a way to represent the Jews from a Christian perspective, which the artist judges to be false. Jews are the true crowned bride who is God's beloved, and Jewish women are the wives of real, mortal husbands with whom they form Jewish family units. The crown does not belong on the head of the imitation bride, Mary, the false Christian celibate female ideal.

Like the Jewish comparisons to Christ in Jacob's stigmata or Amnon's rising from the dead to communicate with his disciples in Mainz, the image of the crowned, blindfolded bride is another internalization of Christian symbols turned against Christianity and subverted into a pro-Jewish message of triumph. A further sign of ironic symbolism is the depiction of the male groom figure, an allegorical representation of God, wearing the Jewish man's pointed hat. Both the hat and the blindfold are ironic indicators that Jews triumph over Christians despite appearances.

This very dichotomy between appearance and reality is itself a Christian worldview of flesh and spirit that the Jewish writers, artists, and patrons have turned against Christian truth claims. God really is with us, not with them, despite appearances. In the Hamburg Maḥzor image, what seems to be blind really sees God. The blindfold on the Synagoga-bride is only appearance. This is the burden of the entire commentary of Rashi on the Song of Songs.[141] It is not only that God, the male figure, is in love with Israel, the female, but Rashi also reads the songs as an unchanging historical allegory of the constant relationship between God and Israel. It begins with the revelation of the Torah at Mount Sinai, often portrayed as a marriage between God and the Jewish people; it continues through the periods of exile, when it seems as though God has rejected Israel; and it will conclude with the arrival of the true Messiah.

Jewish portrayal of a seemingly blind *Synagoga* as the truly triumphant, crowned, Jewish bride of God, depicted as a medieval Jewish man. Hamburg Mahzor. (Staats- und Universitätsbibliothek, Hamburg; Hebrew Ms. Levy 37, folio 169v)

Like the victorious, crowned Synagoga, Rashi's comments are reactions to an aggressively persistent, Christian culture that Jews understand and are determined to resist. A polemical thrust is found in much of Rashi's biblical commentaries as well as in those of other northern French Bible exegetes who are denying Christian interpretations of Hebrew scriptures.[142]

A related but different matter is why Jews sometimes produced or commissioned manuscripts illuminated with unattractive beaked faces. This peculiarity of several Hebrew manuscripts from Germany has led scholars to speculate about the second commandment's restrictions on the portrayal of human faces and about the pietists' alleged opposition to representational art. But, in fact, there is no blanket opposition in Jewish tradition to representational art, only to certain ways of depicting the deity, and the pietists had specific problems in mind when they commented on the subject.[143]

The second commandment does not explain why medieval German Jews permitted unflattering images to appear in their manuscripts. The presence of such images raises the issue of how Jews imagined themselves aesthetically compared to the Christians whom they saw all around them. The familiar contrast between a negative surface appearance and a deeper unseen truth is indicated in related comments that appear in thirteenth-century Hebrew polemical texts from France and Germany. The latter, *Sefer Nitzaḥon Yashan* (The Old Polemical Handbook), says:

> The heretics ask: Why are most gentiles fair-skinned and handsome while most Jews are dark and ugly? Answer them that this is similar to a fruit; when it begins to grow it is white but when it ripens it becomes black, as is the case with sloes and plums. On the other hand, any fruit which is red at the beginning becomes lighter as it ripens, as is the case with apples and apricots. This, then, is testimony that Jews are pure of menstrual blood so that there is no initial redness. Gentiles, however, are not careful about menstruant women and have sexual relations during menstruation; thus, there is redness at the outset, and so the fruit that comes out, i.e., the children, are light. One can respond further by noting that gentiles are incontinent and have sexual relations during the day, at a time when they see the faces on attractive pictures; therefore, they give birth to children who look like those pictures, as it is written, *And the sheep conceived when they came to drink before the rods* (Genesis 30:38–39).[144]

The author of this passage takes for granted the Christian accusation that Jews are ugly, Christians fair and beautiful.[145] But he also believes that appearances are deceiving. Although some Jews in Ashkenaz may have thought of themselves as physically unattractive compared to Christians, they had no doubt that they and they alone knew the truth. Christians stereotyped Jews as both ugly and false when they depicted them with beaked noses, for example, in graffiti or in illuminations. Rather than assume that Jews were unaware of these negative images, we have reason to think that they reinterpreted them as unattractive but misleading appearances to be distinguished from a higher, invisible truth.

CONCLUSION

This chapter has not been about the culture of some of the learned Jews of Ashkenaz, fascinating as that story is, but about all of the Jews there viewed collectively as a religious culture. Composed of rich and poor, men, women, and children, the small Jewish communities in Ashkenaz were closely involved with ordinary Christians as well as with ecclesiastic and temporal leaders. Above all, it was this daily interaction between Jews and Christians that helped to shape each religious culture.

When the Jewish authors of the early-twelfth-century Rhineland towns of Mainz, Worms, and Speyer constructed a martyr profile of what being a Jew in Ashkenaz meant, they ignored the peaceful social realities of everyday life. And yet, the liturgical and narrative texts that they wrote about 1096 shaped the self-image of Ashkenazic Jews as being ready to die as a witness to the one God. This ideology of martyrdom was a very powerful source of communal sustenance, helping Jews live as Jews while actively resisting the blandishments of the Christian society around them. But because Ashkenazic martyrdom is an ideology, it is not an adequate description of the complex and dynamic exchanges that took place between members of two strong cultures.

Jews as well as Christians could go on the offensive, even if only in words and occasional gestures of contempt. Jews also actively challenged members of the other culture to define themselves, so much so that an anonymous twelfth-century writer rebuked his fellow Christians in northern France: "We write, therefore, not to extol our [faith] but rather so that we give the Jews no cause to jeer at our ignorance. They frequently confront us and like Goliath they say: *Give me a man, that we may fight together*" (1 Samuel 17:10).[146] Jewish Goliaths? Were not the Jews little Davids resisting the might of Christian Goliaths all around them? In truth, they were both.

NOTES

1. *Sefer Ḥasidim,* ed. Jehudah Wistinetzky (1892; 2d ed. with Hebrew introduction by Jacob Freimann, Frankfurt am Main, 1924), par. 1301; hereafter cited as *SH,* followed by the paragraph number. For the facsimile edition, see Ivan G. Marcus, ed., *Sefer Ḥasidim: Ketav yad parma H 3280* (Jerusalem, 1985), 239. Unless otherwise noted, translations from *Sefer Ḥasidim* are mine.

2. References to Ashkenaz as Germany in the widely used commentaries of Rashi of

Troyes (1040–1105) may have contributed to its acceptance. See Rashi on Deut. 3:9, on B. Ḥulin 93a, and on B. Bava Mezia 73b, among others.

3. Samuel Krauss, "The Names Ashkenaz and Sefarad" (Hebrew), *Tarbiz* 3 (1932): 423–35.

4. R. I. Moore, *The Formation of a Persecuting Society: Power and Deviance in Western Europe, 950–1250* (Oxford, 1987).

5. David Nirenberg, *Communities of Violence: Persecution of Minorities in the Middle Ages* (Princeton, N.J., 1996). Daniel Lord Smail, "Hatred as a Social Institution in Late-Medieval Society," *Speculum* 76 (2001): 118–20.

6. Basic studies on the history and culture of Ashkenaz include Moritz Güdemann, *Geschichte des Erziehungswesens und der Cultur der abendländischen Juden*, 3 vols. (1880–88; rpt. Amsterdam, 1966); Bernhard Blumenkranz, *Juifs et chrétiens dans le monde occidentale, 430–1096* (Paris, 1960); Cecil Roth, ed., *The Dark Ages: Jews in Christian Europe, 711–1096* (New Brunswick, N.J., 1966); Kenneth R. Stow, *Alienated Minority: The Jews of Medieval Latin Europe* (Cambridge, Mass., 1992); Mark R. Cohen, *Under Crescent and Cross: The Jews in the Middle Ages* (Princeton, N.J., 1994); Avraham Grossman, *Ḥakhmei Ashkenaz ha-Rishonim* (Jerusalem, 1981); Avraham Grossman, *Ḥakhmei Zarfat ha-Rishonim* (Jerusalem, 1995); Israel Ta-Shema, *Minhag Ashkenaz ha-Qadmon* (Jerusalem, 1994); Michael Toch, *Die Juden im mittelalterlichen Reich* (Munich, 1998); Ephraim Kanarfogel, *"Peering Through the Lattices": Mystical, Magical, and Pietistic Dimensions in the Tosafist Period* (Detroit, 2000).

7. See Michael Toch, "The Formation of a Diaspora: The Settlement of Jews in the Medieval German *Reich*," *Aschkenas: Zeitschrift für Geschichte und Kultur der Juden* 7 (1997): 57, 71–72.

8. See Avraham Grossman, "The Ties of the Jews of Ashkenaz to the Land of Israel," in Richard I. Cohen, ed., *Vision and Conflict in the Holy Land* (New York, 1985), 78–101.

9. On the emergence of the paid rabbinate in Ashkenaz, see Simon Schwarzfuchs, *Etudes sur l'origine et le développement du rabbinat au moyen âge* (Paris, 1957), 17–38, and Israel Yuval, *Ḥakhamim be-doram* (Jerusalem, 1989), 11–15. Compare the evidence from southern France and the Crown of Aragon from the early fourteenth century in Joseph Shatzmiller, "Rabbi Isaac Ha-Cohen of Manosque and His Son Rabbi Peretz: The Rabbinate and Its Professionalization in the Fourteenth Century," in Ada Rapoport-Albert and Steven J. Zipperstein eds., *Jewish History: Essays in Honour of Chimen Abramsky* (London, 1988), 61–83.

10. See Robert Brody, *The Geonim of Babylonia and the Shaping of Medieval Jewish Culture* (New Haven, Conn., 1998).

11. See Robert Chazan, "1007–1012: Initial Crisis for Northern-European Jewry," *Proceedings of the American Academy for Jewish Research* 38–39 (1970–71): 101–18; Kenneth Stow, *The '1007 Anonymous' and Papal Sovereignty: Jewish Perceptions of the Papacy and Papal Policy in the High Middle Ages*, Hebrew Union College Annual Supplements, 4 (Cincinnati, 1984); Richard Landes, "The Massacres of 1010: On the Origins of Popular Anti-Jewish Violence in Western Europe," in Jeremy Cohen, ed., *From Witness to Witchcraft: Jews and Judaism in Medieval Christian Thought* (Wiesbaden, 1996), 79–112.

12. On the blessing, see Haim Hillel Ben-Sasson, *Perakim be-Toledot ha-Yehudim bimei ha-Beinayim* (Tel Aviv, 1958), 179, and Shraga Avramson, "The Text of the Blessing on Martyrdom" (Hebrew), *Torah she-be-'Al Peh* 14 (1972): 156–64. For the seventeenth-century legacy of 1096, see Yehezkiel (Edward) Fram, "Between 1096 and 1648/49: A Re-examination" (Hebrew), *Zion* 61 (1996): 159–82, which is a revision of Yaakov (Jacob) Katz, "Bein Tatnu le-Tah-Tat," in Shmuel Ettinger et al., eds., *Sefer Yovel le-Yitzhaq Baer* (Jerusalem, 1961), 318–37.

13. See Ivan G. Marcus, "Hierarchies, Religious Boundaries and Jewish Spirituality in Medieval Germany," *Jewish History* 1, no. 2 (Fall 1986): 24, n. 27, and Avraham Grossman, "The Cultural and Social Background of Jewish Martyrdom in Germany in 1096," in Alfred Haverkamp, ed., *Juden und Christen zur Zeit der Kreuzzüge* (Sigmaringen, 1999), 74, n. 3.

14. See the Latin description in Annales Herbipolenses, Monumenta Germaniae Historica, Scriptores 16:3–4, ed. Georg Pertz (Hanover, 1859), translated in Robert Chazan, *Medieval Stereotypes and Modern Antisemitism* (Berkeley, Calif., 1997), 61–62.

15. The Hebrew accounts do not refer to an accusation of a "ritual murder" at Blois, nor is the time of year stipulated as being around Easter or Passover, as in other accusations. It was Robert of Torigny who wrote in his Latin chronicle that Blois was a ritual murder like Norwich and Gloucester, in England, and Pontoise, in France, and that it took place around Easter. See William C. Jordan, *The French Monarchy and the Jews: From Philip Augustus to the Last Capetians* (Philadelphia, 1989), 18, and Robert Stacey, "From Ritual Crucifixion to Host Desecration: Jews and the Body of Christ," *Jewish History* 12, no. 1 (Spring 1998): 23. For translations of prose Hebrew sources about Blois, see Robert Chazan, ed., *Church, State, and Jew in the Middle Ages* (New York, 1980), 114, 296, 300–304; for the Latin account, see *Chronique de Robert de Torigni* (Rouen, 1873), 2: 27. On the incident, see Robert Chazan, "The Blois Incident of 1171: A Study in Intercommunal Organization," *Proceedings of the American Academy for Jewish Research* 36 (1968): 13–31.

16. R. Po-chia Hsia, *The Myth of Ritual Murder: Jews and Magic in Reformation Germany* (New Haven, Conn., 1988), and Miri Rubin, *Gentile Tales: The Narrative Assault on Late Medieval Jews* (New Haven, Conn., 1999).

17. Kenneth R. Stow, "Papal and Royal Attitudes Toward Jewish Lending in the Thirteenth Century," *Association for Jewish Studies Review* 6 (1981): 161–84.

18. Robert Stacey, "Parliamentary Negotiation and the Expulsion of the Jews from England," in *Thirteenth Century England*, vol. 6 (Woodbridge, 1997), 77–101.

19. Nirenberg, *Communities of Violence*, chaps. 3 and 4, and Philippe Wolfe, "The 1391 Pogrom in Spain: Social Crisis or Not?" *Past and Present* 50 (1971): 4–18.

20. František Graus, *Pest-Geissler-Judenmorde: Das 14. Jahrhundert als Krisenzeit* (Göttingen, 1987), and the sources in Rosemary Horrox, ed., *The Black Death* (Manchester, 1994), 95–226.

21. See the graph of anti-Jewish violence in the German Empire that spikes during the Black Death by several hundred percent over anything before or after between 1090 and 1529, in Toch, *Juden im mittelalterlichen Reich*, 57.

22. See Ivan G. Marcus, *Rituals of Childhood: Jewish Acculturation in Medieval Europe*

(New Haven, Conn., 1996), chap. 1. On doubt in medieval Ashkenaz, see Ivan G. Marcus, "A Pious Community and Doubt: Jewish Martyrdom Among Northern European Jewry and the Story of Rabbi Amnon of Mainz," in Zvia Ginor, ed., *Mikra le 'Avraham* (New York, in press); Jeremy Cohen, "Between Martyrdom and Apostasy: Doubt and Self-Definition in Twelfth-Century Ashkenaz," *The Journal of Medieval and Early Modern Studies* 29, no. 3 (Fall 1999): 431–71.

23. For a good example of the attraction of Judaism for gentile Christians in the late fourth century, see Wayne A. Meeks and Robert L. Wilken, eds. and trans., *Jews and Christians in Antioch in the First Four Centuries of the Common Era* (Missoula, 1978), 83–127.

24. *Teshuvot Rabbenu Gershom Meor ha-Golah,* ed. Shlomo Eidelberg (New York, 1955), esp. no. 68, p. 159, and no. 70, p. 162, and elsewhere.

25. Ibid., no. 21, p. 75.

26. Ibid., no. 23, p. 79; translated in Irving Agus, *Urban Civilization in Pre-Crusade Europe,* 2 vols. (Leiden, 1968), 750–52.

27. Eidelberg, *Teshuvot,* no. 24, p. 81.

28. Ibid., nos. 27 and 28, pp. 89–91.

29. Yom Tov Assis, Michael Toch, Jeremy Cohen, Ora Limor, and Aaron Kedar, eds., *Yehudim Mul ha-Zelav: Gezeirot Tatnu ba-Historiah u-va-Historiografiah* (Jerusalem, 2000).

30. See *Seder ha-Kinot le-Tishah be-Av,* ed. Daniel Goldschmidt (Jerusalem, 1972), nos. 23, 26, 30, and 34; for English translations, see *The Authorised Kinot for the Ninth of Av,* trans. and ed. Abraham Rosenfeld (New York, 1979), 127–28, 132–34, 139–42, and 148–49.

31. The translation is based on Joseph H. Hertz, *The Authorised Daily Prayerbook* (New York, 1955), 510–15. For the German custom of reciting it only twice a year, see *Seder Avodat Yisrael,* ed. Seligmann Baer (Rödelheim, 1868), 233.

32. Siegmund Salfeld, ed. *Das Martyrologium des Nürnberger Memorbüches* (Berlin, 1898), 5–12 (Hebrew) and 101–19 (German).

33. See Ismar Elbogen, *Jewish Liturgy: A Comprehensive History,* trans. Raymond P. Scheindlin (Philadelphia, 1993), 82 (mourner's kaddish and yahrtzeit) and 163 (yizkor).

34. *SH* 1537, translated in Elliott Horowitz, "Speaking to the Dead: Cemetery Prayer in Medieval and Early Modern Jewry," *The Journal of Jewish Thought and Philosophy* 8 (1999): 310.

35. The three Hebrew narratives were published together for the first time by A[dolph] Neubauer and M[oritz] Stern, eds., *Hebräische Berichte über die Judenverfolgungen während der Kreuzzüge,* with a German translation by Seligmann Baer (1892; rpt. Hildesheim, 1997 hereafter, NS). The edition has some deficiencies but is more careful than A. M. Habermann, *Sefer Gezeirot Ashkenaz ve-Zarfat* (1945; rpt. Jerusalem, 1971; hereafter, H). A new edition is being prepared for the Monumenta Germaniae Historica by Eva Haverkamp. English translations of the three texts are in Shlomo Eidelberg, *The Jews and the Crusaders* (1977; rpt. Hoboken, N.J., 1996; hereafter, E), and the two anonymous texts are in Robert Chazan, *European Jewry and the First Crusade* (Berkeley, Calif., 1987; hereafter, C).

36. This account, like the two anonymous ones, contains material not found in either of the others and has parallels that contain significant variations (see, for example, n. 43 below). This fact means that each was edited independently based on different oral informants and from short written accounts that are no longer preserved, as proposed in 1892 by Harry Bresslau in his introduction to Neubauer and Stern, *Hebräische Berichte*, xiii–xxix. For other views that do not fully account for the evidence, see Anna Sapir Abulafia, "The Interrelationship Between the Hebrew Chronicles of the First Crusade," *Journal of Semitic Studies* 27 (1982): 221–39; Chazan, *European Jewry*, 43; and Robert Chazan, *God, Humanity and History: The Hebrew First Crusade Narratives* (Berkeley, Calif., 2000), 101–2. Each anonymous account survives in a single manuscript; Eliezer ben Nathan's narrative is found in at least nine, probably because of his fame and the piyyutim it contains. See Abraham David, "Zikhronot ve-hearot al gezeirot tatnu—bi-defus u-ve-khitvei yad ivriyim," in Yom Tov Assis et al., *Yehudim Mul ha-zelav*, 194–46. Manuscript Breslau no. 189 is no longer missing. It is now in the Beinecke Rare Book Library, Yale University, New Haven, Conn.

37. The numbers are not reliable. Of those who died in Mainz, the Latin chronicler Albert of Aix records 700 deaths (Edward Peters, ed., *The First Crusade: The Chronicle of Fulcher of Chartres and Other Source Materials*, 2d ed. [Philadelphia, 1998], 110); the longer anonymous Hebrew text has 1,100 deaths (NS 8, H 32, E 33, C 256); and Rabbi Eliezer b. Nathan lists 1,300 deaths (NS 39, H 75, E 83). But when we add up the names of the martyrs mentioned in the more reliable memorial lists, we get just over a thousand Jewish martyrs for all of the Rhineland communities, not for any one of them. This number assumes that most plural forms for unnamed "children" usually mean two or three, because when a family had four or more children that is noted. On the small nuclear family size in Ashkenaz, see Kenneth R. Stow, "The Jewish Family in the Rhineland in the High Middle Ages: Forms and Function," *American Historical Review* 92, no. 5 (Dec. 1987): 1085–1110, esp. 1088.

38. NS 29, H 57, E 68, C 294. Translations here and below are from Eidelberg's edition of the three texts.

39. NS 17, H 43, E 49, C 273.

40. NS 45, H 81, E 92.

41. NS 17, H 43, E 49, C 273, and see NS 22, H 49, E 57, C 282.

42. I agree with Robert Chazan, *Medieval Stereotypes*, 75–77, that there is no evidence in these sources to support Israel Yuval's claim that an activist messianic motivation was behind the actions of martyrs or the authors of the chronicles. Nor is there textual support for Yuval's speculation that Christian awareness in the early twelfth century of Jewish ritual homicides in 1096 prompted some to invent the libel that Jews went about ritually killing Christian children. In fact, Willis Johnson correctly points out that the inventor of the ritual murder accusation, the monk Thomas of Monmouth, explicitly says that Jews ritually kill Christian boys, but that neither Jews nor Christians would do such a thing to their own children. See Israel Yuval, "Vengeance and Damnation, Blood and Defamation: From Jewish Martyrdom to Blood Libel Accusations" (Hebrew), *Zion* 58, no. 1 (1993): 33–90;

Yuval, 'Shenei Goyim Be-Vitnekh': Yehudim ve-Nozrim—Dimuyim Hadadiyim (Tel Aviv, 2000); Yuval, "Christliche Symbolik und jüdische Martyrologie zur Zeit der Kreuzzüge," in A. Haverkamp, ed., *Juden und Christen*, 87–106; and Willis Johnson, "Before the Blood Libel: Jews in Christian Exegesis After the Massacres of 1096" (Master of Philosophy diss., Cambridge University, Aug. 1994), 60–61. The text is in Augustus Jessopp and Montague Rhodes James, eds., *The Life and Miracles of St. William of Norwich by Thomas of Monmouth* (Cambridge, Engl., 1896), 24–25. On Thomas, see Gavin Langmuir, "Thomas of Monmouth: Detector of Ritual Murder," in his *Toward a Definition of Antisemitism* (1984; rpt. Berkeley, Calif., 1990), 209–36. For Christian influence on the personal afterlife of the martyrs, see Shmuel Shepkaru, "From After Death to Afterlife: Martyrdom and Its Recompense," *Association for Jewish Studies Review* 24, no. 1 (1999): 1–44, esp. 37–41.

43. NS 19, H 45–46, E 52, C 277 (long anonymous text), and compare the parallel, without the ritual details, in NS 42, H 77, E 87 (Eliezer b. Nathan). This is one of many examples of details that are in the Eliezer account that are not found in parallels in the long anonymous text, an indication that the former cannot simply be derived from the latter. For other examples of ritual slaughter, see NS 9, H 34, E 36, C 259; NS 41, H 77, E 86; and NS 50, H96, E 103–4, C 230.

44. Peters, ed., *The First Crusade*, 110. See also the Gesta Treverorum, Monumenta Germaniae Historica, Scriptores 8, ed. Georg Pertz (Hanover, 1848), 190–91 and Gross, "Al maasei kiddush ha-shem," in Assis, et al., eds., *Yehudim Mul ha-Tzlav*, 176.

45. On the accuracy of the details in these texts, see Ivan G. Marcus, "From Politics to Martyrdom: Shifting Paradigms in the Hebrew Narratives of the 1096 Crusade Riots," *Prooftexts* 2, no. 1 (Jan. 1982). The texts' literary character means that they can be viewed as "fictions," *not* in the sense of complete inventions but rather as shaped narratives. On this meaning of the word "fiction," see Natalie Zemon Davis, *Fiction in the Archives* (Stanford, Calif., 1987), 3, and Ivan G. Marcus, "The Representation of Reality in the Narratives of 1096," *Jewish History* 13, no. 1 (Fall 1999): 37–48. Robert Chazan expresses a similar point of view in his *Medieval Stereotypes*, 138–39. An important study that confirms the historical background of some of the everyday details in the Trier episode, though not necessarily the details of the acts of martyrdom, is Eva Haverkamp, " 'Persecutio' und 'Gezerah' in Trier während des Ersten Kreuzzüges," in A. Haverkamp, ed., *Juden und Christen*, 35–71.

46. NS 48, H 94, E 100, C 226.

47. See Ivan G. Marcus, "Mi-'deus vult' ve-ad 'retzon ha-borei': idiologiyot datiyot kitzoniyot u-metziut historit bi-shenat tatnu ve-etzel hasidei ashkenaz," in Yom Tov Assis et al., eds., *Yehudim Mul ha-Zelav*, 92–100.

48. NS 1, H 24, E 22, C 244.

49. That knights as well as mobs were involved and that the former thought of the attack on Jews as a vendetta for the death of Jesus, see Jonathan Riley-Smith, *The First Crusade and the Idea of Crusading* (Philadelphia, 1986), 48–57.

50. NS 6, H 31, E 31, C 253.

51. NS 38, H 74, E 81.

52. NS 48, H 95, E 101, C 228.

53. On this tradition, see Grossman, "Cultural and Social Background of Jewish Martyrdom," 73–86, esp. 81–83.

54. See Robert Chazan, "The Early Development of Hasidut Ashkenaz," *Jewish Quarterly Review* 75, no. 3 (Jan. 1985): 199–211, and his *European Jewry,* esp. 80–81.

55. See Anna Sapir Abulafia, "Invectives Against Christianity in the Hebrew Chronicles of the First Crusade," in Peter W. Edbury, ed., *Crusade and Settlement* (Cardiff, 1985), 66–72.

56. Louise Riley-Smith and Jonathan Riley-Smith, eds., *The Crusades: Idea and Reality, 1095–1274* (London, 1981), 43.

57. NS 1, H 24, E 22, C 243–44. Eidelberg, following Habermann, has "promiscuity" (*zimah*), but the manuscript, former London Rabbinical Court ms. 28 f. 151a, reads "niddah." Neubauer and Stern unnecessarily amend the text to *niddah;* that is the actual reading.

58. Jordan, *French Monarchy,* 16; Siegfried Stein, "The Development of the Jewish Law on Interest from the Biblical Period to the Expulsion of the Jews from England," *Historia Judaica* 17, no. 1 (Apr. 1955): 39; and B. Avodah Zarah 46a. For Toledot Yeshu as a counter-history, see Amos Funkenstein, "History, Counterhistory, and Narrative," in his *Perceptions of Jewish History* (Berkeley, Calif., 1993), 39–40; David Biale, "Counter-History and Jewish Polemics against Christianity: The *Sefer Toldot Yeshu* and the *Sefer Zerubavel,*" *Jewish Social Studies,* n.s. 6 (1999): 130–45. According to Yaakov Deutsch, the earliest Jewish association of the epithet "bastard" (*mamzer*) with "son of the menstruant" (*ben ha-niddah*) is found in a post-talmudic text. See Michael Higger, ed., *Masekhet Kallah* (New York, 1970), 146–48. Although Jesus is not mentioned there by name, the reference seems likely to allude to him.

59. See Samuel Krauss, *Das Leben Jesu nach jüdischen Quellen* (1902; rpt. Hildesheim, 1977); William Horbury, *A Critical Examination of the Toledot Jeshu* (Doctor of Philosophy diss., Cambridge, Engl., 1970); "The Life of Jesus," translated by Bernard S. Bachrach in his *Jews in Barbarian Europe* (Lawrence, Kans., 1977), 98–102; "The Acts of Jesus," translated by Herbert W. Basser, in Barry Walfish, ed., *The Frank Talmage Memorial Volume,* vol. 1 (Haifa, 1993), 273–82. The earliest text of the Life of Jesus narratives does not have the impure Mary imagery, and it may be contemporary with the Hebrew 1096 narratives themselves as Jewish polemical responses to the growing influence of the cult of Mary in medieval Christendom. See Yaakov Deutsch, "Evidence About an Early Version of 'Toledot Yeshu'" (Hebrew), *Tarbiz* 69, no. 2 (2000): 177–97, where the Hebrew text is presented and analyzed.

60. NS 9–10, H 34, E 35–36, C 258–59; NS 54–55, H 101–2, E 111–12, C 238–39; and Salfeld, ed., *Das Martyrologium,* 12 (Hebrew) and 117 (German). In the long anonymous account, Rachel's husband Judah seems to appear, but this is a misunderstanding on the part of that editor, who constructed his version of this episode from the source found now in the shorter anonymous and from a piyyut that mentions a generic Jew called Judah. See Marcus, "Representation of Reality," pp. 37–48. See Abraham Gross, "Al maasei kiddush ha-shem

be-magenza bi-shenat tatnu: piyyutim u-kheronikot," in Yom Tov Assis et al., *Yehudim Mul ha-Zelav*, 187–91.

61. NS 2, H 25, E 22, C 244. See Marcus, "From Politics to Martyrdom," 45.

62. This polarity is developed for the first time in an undergraduate seminar paper written by K. Connor Martin, "Virtuous Women: Virgins and Wives in the Hebrew Chronicles of the First Crusade and Christian Hagiography," Yale University, Dec. 1998; see also Shoshanna Gershenzon and Jane Litman, "The Bloody 'Hands of the Compassionate Women': Portrayals of Heroic Women in the Hebrew Crusade Chronicles," in Menachem Mor, ed., *Crisis and Reaction: The Hero in Jewish History* (Omaha, Neb., 1995), 73–91, esp. 84.

63. See NS 28, H 56, E 66, C 292–93. Martin, "Virtuous Women," discusses this episode as well.

64. "Evel aOrer" (I raise lamentation) by Menahem ben Makhir in Rosenfeld, ed., *Authorised Kinot*, 148.

65. Compare the use of this motif in Christian writings about Jews, such as Edna Aisenberg, "La jud'a muy fermosa: The Jewess as Sex Object in Medieval Spanish Literature and Lore," *La Crónica* 12 (Spring 1984): 187–94. On Caesarius, see Ivan G. Marcus, "Jews and Christians Imagining the Other in Medieval Europe," *Prooftexts* 15 (1995): 209–26. See also Shlomo Noble, "The Jewish Woman in Medieval Martyrology," in Charles Berlin, ed., *Studies in Jewish Bibliography, History, and Literature in Honor of I. Edward Kiev* (New York, 1971), 347–55, and Alfred Haverkamp, "Baptised Jews in German Lands during the Twelfth Century," in Michael Signer and John Van Engen, eds., *Jews and Christians in Twelfth-Century Europe* (Notre Dame, Ind., 2001), 269–73, esp. 270.

66. NS 7, H 31–32, E 32, C 255. See also NS 9, H 33, E 35, C 258; in Eliezer ben Natan, NS 38, H 73, E 81; and in the short anonymous, NS 54, H 101, E 110, C 237–38.

67. See R. W. Southern, "The English Origins of the 'Miracles of the Virgin,' " *Medieval and Renaissance Studies* 4 (1958): 176–216.

68. On this motif in Judaism and Christianity, see Jon D. Levenson, *The Death and Resurrection of the Beloved Son* (New Haven, Conn., 1993), and Shalom Spiegel, *The Last Trial*, trans. Judah Goldin (Philadelphia, 1963).

69. B. Yoma 18b and the parallel in B. Yevamot 37b.

70. Louis Finkelstein, ed., *Jewish Self-Government in the Middle Ages* (1924; rpt. New York, 1964), 168–70.

71. Finkelstein, ed., *Jewish Self-Government*, 142–43; R. Meir ben Barukh of Rothenburg, *Sh'eilot u-Teshuvot* (ed. Prague), ed. Moshe Aryeh Bloch (Budapest, 1895; rpt. Tel Aviv, 1968), 159c.

72. Finkelstein, ed., *Jewish Self-Government*, 205–6. See also R. Meir ben Barukh of Rothenburg, *Sh'eilot u-Teshuvot*, ed. Prague, 159d; Avraham Grossman, "The Historical Background to the Ordinances on Family Affairs Attributed to Rabbenu Gershom Me'or ha-Golah ('The Light of the Exile')," in Rapoport-Albert and Zipperstein, eds., *Jewish History*, 15.

73. *Sefer Shibbolei ha-Leqet,* part 2, in Oxford, Bodleian Library, Hebrew Ms., Michael 535 (Neubauer Catalogue no. 657), f. 57, cited in Güdemann, *Geschichte,* 1: 232.

74. See the itinerary (*sibbuv*) of R. Petahia of Regensburg, in *Jewish Travellers: A Treasury of Travelogues from 9 Centuries,* 2d ed., ed. Elkan Nathan Adler (New York, 1966), 71.

75. See Shirley Kaufman, Galit Hasan-Rokem, and Tamar S. Hess, eds. and trans., *The Defiant Muse: Hebrew Feminist Poems from Antiquity to the Present* (New York, 1999), 62–63. For the possibility that she did not write it, see Ezra Fleisher, "On Dunash ibn Labrat, His Wife and His Son: New Light on the Beginnings of the Hebrew-Spanish School" (Hebrew), *Mehqerei Yerushalayim be-Sifrut Ivrit* 5 (1984): 189–202. My thanks to Joel Kraemer for the reference.

76. See Eduard Mahler, *Handbuch der jüdischen Chronologie* (Leipzig, 1916), 564.

77. The text is printed in Habermann, *Sefer Gezeirot,* 165–166, based on Oxford, Bodleian Library, Hebrew Ms., Michael 448 (Neubauer Catalogue no. 2215), f. 30r, but one must consult the better manuscript, also at the Bodleian, Opp. 757 (Neubauer Catalogue no. 2289), f. 292v, which is the basis of the translation that follows. It is also found in a third Oxford Hebrew Ms., Opp. 712 (Neubauer Catalogue no. 2240), f. 25r. For an annotated version of this translation, see Ivan G. Marcus, "Mothers, Martyrs, and Moneymakers: Some Jewish Women in Medieval Europe," *Conservative Judaism* 38, no. 3 (Spring 1986): 34–45. For a translation of Eleazar's prose introduction and the laments for Dulcea and their two daughters, see Judith Baskin, "Dulce of Worms: The Lives and Deaths of an Exemplary Jewish Woman and Her Daughters," in Lawrence Fine, ed., *Judaism in Practice: From the Middle Ages Through the Early Modern Period* (Princeton, N.J., 2001), 429–37.

78. Eleazar says in his prose introduction, though not in the poem, that Dulcea also supported the family "from other people's money" (*mi-kesef aheirim*), apparently a reference to her activity as a moneylender. See Habermann, *Sefer Gezeirot,* 164, and Baskin, "Dulce of Worms." Possibly she was among those Jewish women who made small consumer loans to Christian women. See *SH* 465 and 1265 and William C. Jordan, "Jews on Top: Women and the Availability of Consumption Loans in Northern France in the Mid-Thirteenth Century," *Journal of Jewish Studies* 29 (1978): 39–56.

79. Meir ben Barukh of Rothenburg, *Teshuvot Pesaqim u-Minhagim,* 3 vols., ed. Yitzhaq Zeev Kahanah (Jerusalem, 1957–63), 1: 49.

80. See NS 27, H 55, E 65. I follow Eidelberg's translation here. Compare C 291.

81. The former, now recited only on Sabbath mornings, was recited daily in medieval Ashkenaz by German pietists. The latter was and is still recited only on Rosh Hashanah and Yom Kippur. For references to these and other prayers mentioned here, see Marcus, "Mothers, Martyrs, and Moneymakers."

82. B. Keritot 6a, recited at the end of the Sabbath Musaf service.

83. On the possibility that this refers to a special kind of ritual involving making wicks and candles for the atonement of family members, see Chava Weissler, *Voices of the Matriarchs: Listening to the Prayers of Early Modern Jewish Women* (Boston, 1998), 134–35, and, for

the texts, see Chava Weissler, "Measuring Graves and Laying Wicks," in Fine, ed., *Judaism in Practice.*

84. *SH* 835.

85. The Memoirs of Guibert de Nogent 3:16 in John F. Benton, *Self and Society in Medieval France* (Toronto, 1984), 210.

86. Mordecai ben Hillel, *Sefer ha-Mordecai* to B. Ketubbot par. 306, translated in Irving Agus, *Rabbi Meir of Rothenburg* (1947; rpt. [2 vols. in 1] New York, 1970), 290–91. On such vagrants, see Edward Fram, "Perception and Reception of Repentant Apostates in Medieval Ashkenaz and Premodern Poland," *Association for Jewish Studies Review* 21, no. 2 (1996): 299–339, esp. 313–15 and notes there.

87. This is the reading in the uncensored Munich Ms. of the Babylonian Talmud at B. Gittin 57a, and see Ch. Merchavia, *Ha-Talmud bi-Rei ha-Nazrut* (Jerusalem, 1970), 276. The older, censored editions read "the sinner" (*ha-poshea*), and the modern Vilna edition reads "the sinners" (*ha-poshim*). See R. Travers Herford, *Christianity in Talmud and Midrash* (1903; rpt. New York, 1975), 67, 404.

88. This passage was included in an anthology of talmudic quotations prepared by Nicholas Donin, a convert to Christianity, for Pope Gregory IX, who appended it to a letter he sent to the Bishop of Paris and others in June 1239 concerning the books of the Jews, especially the Talmud. The heading of this passage says: "That the same Jesus was punished in Hell in burning excrement because he mocked the words of the sages." See Merchavia, *Ha-Talmud*, 276, quoting Paris, Bibliothèque Nationale, Latin Ms. 16558.

89. NS 38, H 73, E 81. Compare 2 Kings 10:27, where the pagan Temple of Baal is turned into a latrine.

90. *Oeuvres de Rigord et de Guillaume le Breton,* ed. H. François Delaborde (Paris, 1882), Bk. 1, sect. 14: 27 (my translation). For additional examples, see Alfred Thomas, "Alien Bodies: Exclusion, Obscenity and Social Control in *The Ointment Seller,*" in Jan M. Ziolkowski, ed., *Obscenity: Social Control and Artistic Creation in the European Middle Ages* (Leiden, 1998), 214–307. In addition, see Denis Meehan, ed., Adamnan's *De locis sanctis* (Dublin, 1948), 118–19; Henry Richardus Luard, ed., *Matthaeus Parisiensis, Chronica Maiora* (London, 1880), 114–15; Alfonso X, el Sabio, *Cantigas de Santa Maria:* Cantigas 1 a 100, ed., Walter Mettmann (Madrid, 1986), 143–44, noted in and discussed by Peter Schäfer, *Mirror of His Beauty: Feminine Images of God from the Bible to the Early Kabbalah* (Princeton, N.J., 2002), chap. 9.

91. Solomon Grayzel, *The Church and the Jews in the XIIIth Century* (1938; rpt. New York, 1966), 115.

92. For a discussion of the figure on p. 479, see Eric M. Zafron, "An Alleged Case of Image Desecration by the Jews and Its Representation in Art: The Virgin of Cambron," *Journal of Jewish Art* 2 (1975): 63, fig. 1, and see "the miraculous recovery of an *ymagete de Nostre Dame* put down a latrine by a Jew," Paris, Bibliothèque Nationale, Ms. français 22928 (Gautier de Coincy's *Miracles de Nostre Dame*), fol. 76r, reproduced in Michael Camile, *The Gothic Idol*

(Cambridge, Engl., 1989), 186, fig. 103. For the chamber pot, see Ruth Mellinkoff, *The Devil at Isenheim* (Berkeley, Calif., 1988), 64. The motif of the Jew-Pig, including the image of a Jew licking a sow's anus, is discussed in detail in Isaiah Shachar, *The Judensau: A Medieval Anti-Jewish Motif and Its History* (London, 1974), and see Claudine Fabre-Vassas, *The Singular Beast: Jews, Christians, and the Pig,* trans. Carol Volk (New York, 1997).

93. *The Jewish-Christian Debate in the High Middle Ages,* ed. and trans. David Berger (Philadelphia, 1979), 68, par. 39. Compare B. Shabbat 152a about women in general.

94. Compare Aztec rites of flaying enemies and ceremonially wearing their skins, as interpreted in David Carrasco, *City of Sacrifice: The Aztec Empire and the Role of Violence in Civilization* (Boston, 1999).

95. James de Vitry, "De sacramentis," 214, quoted in Miri Rubin, *Corpus Christi: The Eucharist in Late Medieval Culture* (Cambridge, Engl., 1991), 38.

96. See Thomas, "Alien Bodies," and Shachar, *Judensau.*

97. For Judah's statement, see *Sefer ha-Asufot,* London, Jews College, Hebrew Ms. 134 (Montefiore 115), f. 67b; for the rabbinic sources, see *Sifrei be-Midbar,* Baha'alotekha, sec. 88, ed. H. S. Horowitz (1917; rpt. New York, 1947), 87; B. Yoma 75b.

98. See Stacey, "From Ritual Crucifixion to Host Desecration," 11–28; Rubin, *Gentile Tales;* and Jeremy Cohen, "The Jews as the Killers of Christ in the Latin Tradition, from Augustine to the Friars," *Traditio* 39 (1983): 1–27.

99. R. Yosef b. Natan Official, *Sefer Yosef ha-Mekaneh,* ed. Judah Rosenthal (Jerusalem, 1970), 14 (my translation). See Elliott Horowitz, " 'Ha-zelav ha-doker' vihudei eiropah bemai ha-beinayim," in Assis et al., eds. *Yehudim Mul ha-Tzlav,* 118–40.

100. *SH* 1365.

101. See Theodosian Codex 16.8.18 (May 29, 408) in Amnon Linder, ed., *The Jews in Roman Imperial Legislation* (Detroit, 1987), 236–38; Brie/Bray in Chazan, ed., *Church, State, and Jew,* 305–6; and Elliott Horowitz, "The Rite to Be Reckless: On the Perpetration and Interpretation of Purim Violence," *Poetics Today* 15, no. 1 (Spring 1994): 9–54.

102. See Elimelekh (Elliott) Horowitz, " 'The Opposite Happened': Jews Against Their Enemies in Purim Celebrations" (Hebrew), *Zion* 59 (1994): 155 and the sources mentioned there.

103. Joseph Dan, *Torat ha-Sod Shel Ḥasidut Ashkenaz* (Jerusalem, 1968); Elliot Wolfson, "Demut Yaakov Ḥakukah be-Kisei ha-Kavod: Iyyun Nosaf be-Torat ha-Sod Shel Ḥasidut Âshkenaz," in Michal Oron and Amos Goldreich, eds., *Massu'ot: Mehqarim be-Sifrut ha-Kabbalah u-ve-Mahshevet Yisrael Muqdashim le-Zikhro shel Prof. Ephraim Gottlieb* (Jerusalem, 1994), 131–85.

104. Jacob Katz, *Exclusiveness and Tolerance: Jewish-Gentile Relations in Medieval and Modern Times* (New York, 1961), 93–105, argues that the pietists were always supposed to avoid contact with Christians but everyday life made it impossible. The ideal, however, was to avoid contact whenever a pietist was not in a position of relative advantage and influence. See Marcus, "Hierarchies, Religious Boundaries."

105. *SH* 985.

106. *SH* 2, pp. 4 (bottom) and 5 (top). Elliott R. Wolfson, "Martyrdom, Eroticism, and Asceticism in Twelfth-Century Ashkenazi Piety," in Assis et al., eds., *Yehudim Mul ha-Tzlav,* 171–220, compares 1096 and pietism, but his emphasis on eros in both is not in the sources.

107. See Ivan G. Marcus, "The Dynamics of Jewish Renaissance and Renewal in the Twelfth Century," in Michael Signer and John van Engen, eds., *Jews and Christians in Twelfth-Century Europe* (Notre Dame, 2001).

108. *SH* 1301, quoted in the epigraph at the beginning of the chapter. On Christian influence on the pietists, see Talya Fishman, "The Penitential System of Hasidei Ashkenaz and the Problem of Cultural Boundaries," *The Journal of Jewish Thought and Philosophy* 8 (1999): 210–29.

109. *Sefer ḥasidim* (Bologna, 1538), 142.

110. See Tosafot to B. Shabbat 116b, s.v. *ve-khol she-ken.* My thanks to Susan Einbinder for the reference.

111. *SH* 261.

112. *SH* 1352; compare Tosefta Ḥulin 2:22–23; Jerusalem Talmud Shabbat 14:4, 14d; B. Avodah Zarah 27b, and see Joseph Shatzmiller, "Doctors and Medical Practice in Germany Around the Year 1200: The Evidence of 'Sefer hasidim,' " *Journal of Jewish Studies* 33 (1982): 593.

113. *SH* 1368.

114. For papal disapproval, see Solomon Grayzel, *The Church and the Jews in the Thirteenth Century* (1933; rev. ed., New York, 1966), 34–35.

115. Caesarius of Heisterbach, *The Dialogue on Miracles,* Bk. 2, chap. 25, trans. H. von E. Scott and C. C. Swinton Bland (London, 1929), 1: 107.

116. *SH* 811.

117. *SH* 1363.

118. *SH* 1357.

119. *SH* 1358.

120. *SH* 1362.

121. *SH* 1349.

122. Tosafot to B. Avodah Zarah 2a, "asur."

123. *SH* 1359.

124. *SH* 1351.

125. *SH* 1364.

126. *SH* 799 (end).

127. *SH* 1361.

128. *SH* 1369.

129. See Shaye J. D. Cohen, "Menstruants and the Sacred in Judaism and Christianity," in Sarah B. Pomeroy, ed., *Women's History and Ancient History* (Chapel Hill, N.C., 1991), 273–98 and the references there.

130. See Marcus, *Rituals of Childhood,* 28, 31.

131. For other examples of Jewish awareness of the Eucharist, see ibid., 155, n. 89.

132. *Oeuvres de Rigord,* 1:13, p. 25; translated in James Harvey Robinson, ed., *Readings in European History* (Boston, 1904), 1: 427, cited in Joseph Shatzmiller, "Mi-Gilluyehah Shel ha-Antisheimiut bi-Ymei ha-Beinaim: Haashamat Yehudim be-Ḥillul ha-Tzlav," in B. Oded, ed., *Mehkarim be-Toledot Am Yisrael ve-Eretz Yisrael,* vol. 5 (Haifa, 1980), 160 n. 3, and Christoph Cluse, "Stories of Breaking and Taking the Cross: A Possible Context for the Oxford Incident of 1268," *Revue d'histoire ecclesiastique* 90, nos. 3–4 (1995): 396–441.

133. See Parma, Biblioteca Palatina, Hebrew Ms., De Rossi no. 1033, fol. 25 col. 2, which Elisheva Baumgarten pointed out to me.

134. According to Jacob's nephew, Rabbi Isaac of Dampierre, his uncle moved from Ramerupt to Troyes. See R. Isaac ben Moses of Vienna, *Sefer Or Zarua,* 2 parts (Zhitomir, 1882), part 1, par. 442, f. 63d. Scholars have assumed that he moved because of the attack, but there is no independent confirmation of Ephraim's story of the attack, and Jacob could have moved for any number of reasons. The fact that his nephew was still living in Ramerupt suggests that a threat of violence was not the reason. For the proposed causal link, see E. E. Urbach, *Baalei ha-Tosafot,* 4th ed. (Jerusalem, 1980), 66.

135. NS 64, H 121, E 130. On Jewish awareness of the stigmata, see Berger, ed., *Jewish-Christian Debate,* 78, par. 54.

136. See Bernhard Blumenkranz, *Le juif médiéval au miroir de l'art chrétien* (Paris, 1966), p. 51, fig. 52, and p. 61, fig. 65.

137. The text is in Isaac ben Moses, *Sefer Or Zarua,* part 2, par. 276, f. 63b. See Marcus, "A Pious Community and Doubt."

138. See the charter issued by Emperor Frederick Barbarossa (1157) to the Jews of Worms, Monumenta Germaniae Historica, Legum Sectio IV (9 vols. in 12; Hanover, 1893–1976), 1: 227–29, no. 163, translated in Chazan, *Church, State, and Jew,* 64. See also Marcus, "Jews and Christians Imagining the Other," 215.

139. See, for example, Matt. 27:11, 29, 37, 42.

140. Naomi Feuchtwanger, "The Coronation of the Virgin and of the Bride," *Jewish Art* 12–13 (1986–87): 213–24, esp. Fig. 1, from the Leipzig Mahzur, fol. 64v.

141. See Ivan G. Marcus, "The Song of Songs in German Hasidism and the School of Rashi: A Preliminary Comparison," in Walfish, ed., *Frank Talmage Memorial Volume,* 1: 181–89.

142. Grossman, *Ḥakhmei Tzarfat,* chaps. 4 and 5; Ivan G. Marcus, "Rashi's Historiosophy in the Introductions to his Bible Commentaries," *Revue des études juives* 157 (janvier–juin 1998): 47–55.

143. Kalman Bland, *The Artless Jew: Medieval and Modern Affirmations and Denials of the Visual* (Princeton, N.J., 2000); Vivian Mann, ed., *Jewish Texts on the Visual Arts* (Cambridge, Engl., 2000).

144. Berger, *Jewish-Christian Debate,* par. 238, pp. 159 (Hebrew) and 224 (English) and

the notes on p. 340. This passage is indebted to Official, *Sefer Yosef ha-Mekaneh,* par. 104, p. 95, from thirteenth-century France. Rosenthal (Official, *Yosef ha-Mekaneh,* p. 95, n. 1) notes yet another parallel from Oxford, Bodleian Library, Hebrew Ms., Opp. 757 (Neubauer Catalogue no. 2289), pp. 50–51. See David Berger, "Al tadmitam ve-goralam shel hagoyim be-sifrut ha-pulmus ha-ashkenazit," in Assis, et al., eds., *Yehudim Mul ha-Tzlav,* esp. 75–79.

145. Haim Hillel Ben-Sasson, ed., *A History of the Jewish People* (Cambridge, Mass., 1976), 557. A hint of this view is also found in the early-fifteenth-century polemical handbook by Rabbi Yom Tov Lipmann Mühlhausen, *Sefer ha-Nitzaḥon,* par. 239 (1644; rpt. New York, 1979), 134, called to my attention by Yisrael Yuval and Ora Limor. This comment, like the parallel passages, accepts the Christian claim that Jews during the Exile are less attractive than Christians, but they do not concede that Christians also have the truth. They maintain that Jews have the truth and will also regain their beauty in messianic times. On physical ugliness as a sign of religious truth or falsehood, see Haverkamp, "Baptised Jews in German Lands," 270, and compare Giuseppe Mazzotta, *Dante's Vision and the Circle of Knowledge* (Princeton, N.J., 1993), 140 and 237, on the "aesthetics of ugliness," an important theme in Jewish and Christian representations of the Other.

146. J. P. Migne, ed., *Patrologiae cursus completus,* Series Latina, 221 vols. (Paris, 1844–64), vol. 213: 749.

SELECTED BIBLIOGRAPHY

Baumgarten, Elisheva. *Mothers and Children: The Medieval Jewish Experience.* Princeton, N.J., forthcoming.

Bonfil, Robert. "Aliens Within: The Jews and Antijudaism." In Thomas A. Brady, Jr., Heiko Oberman, and James D. Tracy, eds., *Handbook of European History 1400–1600.* Leiden, 1994.

———. "Cultural and Religious Traditions in Ninth-Century French Jewry." In Joseph Dan, ed., *Binah,* vol. 3: Jewish Intellectual History in the Middle Ages. Westport, Conn., 1994.

Chazan, Robert. *European Jewry and the First Crusade.* Berkeley, Calif., 1987.

———. *God, Humanity, and History: The Hebrew First Crusade Narratives.* Berkeley, Calif., 2000.

———. *In the Year 1096 . . . The First Crusade and the Jews.* Philadelphia, 1996.

———. *Medieval Jewry in Northern France: A Political and Social History.* Baltimore, Md., 1973.

———. *Medieval Stereotypes and Modern Antisemitism.* Berkeley, Calif., 1997.

———, ed. *Church, State, and Jew in the Middle Ages.* New York, 1980.

Cohen, Jeremy. *The Friars and the Jews.* Ithaca, N.Y., 1982.

———. "The Jews as the Killers of Christ in the Latin Tradition, from Augustine to the Friars." *Traditio* 39 (1983): 1–27.

———. *Living Letters of the Law: Jews and Judaism in Medieval Christianity.* Berkeley, Calif., 1999.

Cohen, Mark R. *Under Crescent and Cross: The Jews in the Middle Ages.* Princeton, N.J., 1994.

Einbinder, Susan. *Beautiful Death: Jewish Poetry and Martyrdom in Medieval France.* Princeton, N.J., 2002.

Finkelstein, Louis, ed. *Jewish Self-Government in the Middle Ages.* 1924. Reprint, New York, 1964.

Hirschler, Gertrude, ed. *Ashkenaz: The German Jewish Heritage.* New York, 1988.

Horowitz, Elliott. "The Rite to Be Reckless: On the Perpetration and Interpretation of Purim Violence." *Poetics Today* 15, no. 1 (Spring 1994): 9–54.

Hsia, R. Po-chia, and Hartmut Lehmann, eds. *In and Out of the Ghetto: Jewish-Gentile Relations in Late Medieval and Early Modern Germany.* Cambridge, Engl., 1995.

Jordan, William Chester. *The French Monarchy and the Jews: From Philip Augustus to the Last Capetians.* Philadelphia, 1989.

Kanarfogel, Ephraim. *"Peering Through the Lattices": Mystical, Magical, and Pietistic Dimensions in the Tosafist Period.* Detroit, 2000.

Katz, Jacob. *Exclusiveness and Tolerance: Jewish-Gentile Relations in Medieval and Modern Times.* New York, 1961.

Langmuir, Gavin. *Toward a Definition of Antisemitism.* Berkeley, Calif., 1990.

Lipton, Sara. *Images of Intolerance: The Representation of Jews and Judaism in the Bible moralisée.* Berkeley, Calif., 1999.

Marcus, Ivan G. *Piety and Society: The Jewish Pietists of Medieval Germany.* Leiden, 1981.

———. *Rituals of Childhood: Jewish Acculturation in Medieval Europe.* New Haven, Conn., 1996.

Marcus, Jacob R., ed. *The Jew in the Medieval World.* 1938. Reprint, Cincinnati, 1999.

Metzger, Thérèse, and Mendel Metzger. *Jewish Life in the Middle Ages.* New York, 1982.

Mundill, Robin R. *England's Jewish Solution: Experiment and Expulsion, 1262–1290.* Cambridge, Engl., 1998.

Nirenberg, David. *Communities of Violence: Persecution of Minorities in the Middle Ages.* Princeton, N.J., 1996.

Rubin, Miri. *Gentile Tales: The Narrative Assault on Late Medieval Jews.* New Haven, Conn., 1999.

Schäfer, Peter. *Mirror of His Beauty: Feminine Images of God from the Bible to the Early Kabbalah.* Princeton, N.J., 2002.

Schreckenberg, Heinz. *The Jews in Christian Art.* New York, 1996.

Shatzmiller, Joseph. *Shylock Reconsidered: Jews, Moneylending, and Medieval Society.* Berkeley, Calif., 1990.

Signer, Michael, and John Van Engen, eds. *Jews and Christians in Twelfth-Century Europe.* Notre Dame, Ind., 2001.

Soloveitchik, Haym. "Three Themes in the *Sefer Hasidim.*" *Association for Jewish Studies Review* 1 (1976): 311–57.

Stow, Kenneth R. *Alienated Minority: The Jews of Medieval Latin Europe.* Cambridge, Mass., 1992.

Wolfson, Elliot R. "The Mystical Significance of Torah Study in German Pietism." *Jewish Quarterly Review* 84, no. 1 (July 1993): 43–78.

Hanukkah lamp, Poland, eighteenth century. Bronze, cast and engraved.
The eagle at the top symbolizes Polish sovereignty.
(The Israel Museum, Jerusalem; Stieglitz Collection of Judaica 118/868)

FOUR

INNOVATIVE TRADITION:

Jewish Culture in the

Polish-Lithuanian Commonwealth

MOSHE ROSMAN

In 1655, as part of his attempt to convince Oliver Cromwell and the political and economic leadership of Revolutionary England to readmit the Jews, who had been expelled in 1290, the Dutch Sephardic rabbi Menasseh ben Israel published a small book called *The Humble Addresses*. In it he surveyed the state of Jewish communities in various parts of the world. In describing the Jews of the Polish-Lithuanian Commonwealth, he observed:

> [T]hey have the jurisdiction to judge amongst themselves all causes, both criminal and civil; and also great and famous academies of their own. . . . [T]here is a Iew, called Isaac Iecells, who built a synagogue, which stood him in one hundred thousand francs, and is worth many tons of gold. . . . There is in this place such infinite number of Iews; that although the Cosaques in the late warres have killed them above one hundred and fourscore thousand; yet it is sustained that they are yet at this day as innumerable as those were that came out of Egypt. In that Kingdome the whole Negotiation is in the hand of the Iews, the rest of the Christians are either all Noble-men, or Rustiques and kept as slaves.[1]

Menasseh emphasized four distinguishing features of Polish Jewry of his time: its ramified legal autonomy; outstanding institutions of Torah learning; commercial importance and consequent economic strength; and its large numbers. During the "classical" period of Jewish history in Poland (from around 1500 until the late eighteenth century partitions of Poland by its neighbors Russia, Prussia, and Austria), the Commonwealth was home to what became the largest Jewish settlement in the world, dominating Jewish culture of the period and serving as a linchpin in the European Jewish economy. Essential factors in the attainment of this status were the relative freedom granted the Jews in

Poland to practice their religion and the opportunity given them to engage in most occupations. This freedom and opportunity, greater than anywhere else in Europe, was one facet of the unique character of early modern Poland.

At its peak in 1634, the Polish-Lithuanian Commonwealth, as it was known after 1569, stretched from the Oder River in the west to some 100 miles beyond the Dnieper River in the east, and from the Baltic Sea in the north to the Dniester River in the south. This was the largest geopolitical entity in Europe. Permanent Jewish settlement took root in the twelfth century and, as the Commonwealth developed, Jews flocked there in large numbers over the centuries: more than 250,000 by 1648 and approximately 750,000 by 1764, the largest Jewish community in the world and half of the Commonwealth's urban population.

Poland-Lithuania was superficially similar to the countries to the west whence the Jews had been expelled or, beginning in the sixteenth century, restricted to ghettos. A king, who was in constant negotiation with the nobility, headed the political system. The Catholic Church was the established religion, and its institutions played an official role in politics and a central role in the economy. That economy was based on feudally organized agriculture, with land ownership concentrated in the hands of the king, the Church, and the nobles. Serfs, bonded to the landowners, still carried out the work through the period under consideration here. Cities and towns were chartered by their royal, ecclesiastical, or noble owners and governed by a tripartite municipal council elected and run by taxpaying male residents. The Jews were a separate estate whose rights and obligations derived legally from charters granted them over the centuries by the kings and nobles.

Upon closer inspection, however, early modern Poland appears different from contemporary European nations, particularly with regard to its cultural foundations. The nobility in countries like England and France constituted 1 or 2 percent of the population and were coextensive with the upper class. Polish nobles constituted some 10 percent of the populace and might be rich or poor, great landowners, middling landlords, or landless. Regardless of economic standing, each nobleman enjoyed various privileges and the right to participate in the political process by electing representatives to the local councils, or dietines (*sejmiki*), which in turn chose delegates to the national diet (Sejm). The nobles also had the right to participate in the election of the king upon the demise of the reigning monarch. Thus, 10 percent of the Polish male population was enfranchised, which was unique in Europe.

This enfranchisement was but one expression of a general antiauthoritarian political ethos. The ideal of equality, at least among the nobility, though far from realization, was a standard political and social slogan. Polish noblemen of all classes were passionately devoted to defending their "Golden Freedom" from any absolutist pretensions that the king might entertain. The king could not make appointments, raise an army for war, or levy new taxes without the approval of the Sejm. Moreover, on his or her own feudal estate, each noble landlord was a virtual king, unanswerable to any higher authority.

Although Catholic bishops had a defined political role to play as senators in the Sejm and the Polish primate served as Interrex when royal elections were pending, the Polish Church had less effective power than many of its sister national churches to the west. Poland was a multiethnic, multireligious country where only some 40 percent of the population was ethnic Polish. The Lithuanians, Belarusans, Ukrainians (Ruthenians), Latvians, Germans, Armenians, Italians, Scots, Turks, and Jews with their Calvinism, Arianism, Lutheranism, Eastern Orthodoxy, Uniate Greek Catholicism, Islam, Armenian Catholicism, and Judaism all enjoyed official sanction to practice their respective religions, more or less freely, most of the time. Even among the ethnic Poles were Protestants and a sprinkling of Orthodox. In this situation, religious toleration was the theoretical norm. As expressed in the declaration of the 1573 Confederation of Warsaw: "We who differ in matters of religion will keep the peace among ourselves, and neither shed blood on account of differences in faith or kinds of church, nor punish one another by confiscation of goods, deprivation of honor, imprisonment or exile." Poland has been described as "a state without stakes" and was never riven by a civil war based on religious differences.[2]

The Church's discriminatory requirements frequently had to bend before the necessity of toleration. Indeed, the economic interests of Church institutions often dictated tolerance on their part. For example, the fact that Jews were forbidden to occupy positions of authority over Christians did not prevent some Church institutions from leasing their holdings to Jews, who in their administrative capacity would of necessity be superior to serfs and other Christians.[3]

To be sure, Polish religious tolerance, rooted more in utility than in a systematic, philosophically sophisticated, noble-minded ideology, was ambivalent. It was an imperfect, sloppy toleration, with many examples of backsliding into discrimination and persecution. Orthodox, Protestants, and even the small Muslim population were variably subject to such actions as administrative limitations on office-holding and other privileges, forced participation in Catholic worship services, violence, and conversionary pressures. In 1667 the Arians were expelled from the country, and in the eighteenth century mob actions against Protestants became fairly common.

Nowhere is the ambivalence of Polish policy toward a minority group—its religion and culture—more evident than in relation to the Jews. Their relatively felicitous status in Poland was not achieved without resistance. Churchmen were officially committed to the traditional policy of maintaining the Jews in an inferior position. A host of Church-inspired restrictions mandated a large measure of physical segregation and limited commerce and daily intercourse with them. Townspeople were opposed to a more benign policy primarily because of the commercial competition Jews posed to Christian businesses. As the Jarosław burghers put it in 1571:

> We have come to the opinion that a large number of Jews living in a city never bodes well for Christian people. On the contrary, it causes them much damage and loss. Their plots bring catastrophe to Christians and encourage people to abandon dignified work. As a result many have reached their last piece of bread.[4]

Polish ambivalence toward the Jews was given a concrete form that could be altered through negotiations and payments. This codification took the shape of two classes of documents: privileges and pacts. Privileges were granted to Jewish communities by kings and nobles. These charters, usually formulated in consultation with Jews, assumed that they were a vulnerable minority group, requiring defense from various hostile forces in society. Their physical security, religious freedom, and potential livelihoods needed to be safeguarded; their culture required a supportive infrastructure. The assumption was that if Jewish life were allowed to flourish, the royal or seignorial interests would be served.[5]

The counterpoint to privilege was the pact. Pacts were agreements negotiated between the Jewish communities and the Christian municipalities when the aim of the city fathers was opposite to that of the privilege-givers. They were intended to serve as a tool of containment, both geographic and economic. One of the earliest was the 1485 agreement that the Jews of Cracow would refrain from any commercial activity except the sale of forfeit pawns and the products of poor Jewish women who made hats and collars. Another example is the 1645 agreement in Przemyśl that the Jewish community would pay an annual fee in exchange for limited commercial privileges: Jews would be allowed to sell most types of textiles wholesale, but not retail; Jewish barbers, tailors, and bakers could service Jewish customers only. Frequently, pacts set quotas on the number of Jews who could settle in a town. In some cases, Christian townspeople were not satisfied with a pact and pressed the king to grant their town a "privilegium de non tolerandis Iudaeis" (privilege not to tolerate Jews in their midst).[6]

Pacts and privileges delimited the parameters of a process of negotiation that

hinged upon a complex calculus of economic considerations, cultural and sociological factors, political maneuvering, and personal relationships. Consequently, Poland was a place where, as Rabbi David ben Samuel Halevi, known
as the Taz, averred, "most of the time the gentiles do no harm; on the contrary
they do right by Israel." However, some of the time, it was a place where Jews
were disproportionately victims of crime and casual violence, where blood and
desecration-of-the-Host libels occurred with some frequency, and where there
were anti-Jewish mob attacks.[7]

Privileges promised Jews the right to live by their traditions and protection
from hostile treatment. Pacts demonstrated that the gentile population wanted
the Jews in its midst to impinge on their lives as little as possible. Ironically, these
two apparently contradictory tendencies converged, creating a space where all
agreed that the Jews should continue to articulate the medieval institutions of an
autonomous Jewish community. Jewish circumstances in Poland might be characterized, then, as a consequence of the permutations of various tendencies in
Polish culture. To what extent did Polish Jews share this culture?

JEWS AND POLISH CULTURE

Traditionally, a dichotomy has been drawn between "authentic" Jewish culture
that grew out of the Jewish past and alien "influences" from Polish culture that
might divert or blur the authentic vector. Both Polish and Jewish scholars, until
very recently, have emphasized how little Polish culture influenced Jewish society. For Poles this was a sign of the Jews' alienation from Polish society—and by
implication a partial explanation for whatever bad treatment they suffered. For
Jews, cultural isolation was an indicator of the genuineness of Jewish culture in
Poland and an excuse for some scholars to downplay the importance of the Polish context. Certainly, in discourse about Jewish assimilation, Polish Jewry in all
ages is usually held up as one of the most "Jewish" of Jewries, only minimally affected by its surroundings.

The view that Jews were alienated from Poland culturally certainly has evidence to marshal in its support. Economic behavior is a good example. The
main criticism of Jews by townspeople was that they did not honor the conventions of commerce. At a time in Europe when competition was a dirty word and
merchants were expected to respect each other's divinely apportioned market
share, Jews engaged in competitive, capitalistic commercial tactics. Jewish merchants traveled to distant suppliers at source, rather than purchase from middlemen. Jews organized syndicates to buy in volume and sometimes even cornered
the market on certain commodities. They exploited Jewish solidarity to gain

commercial credit, avoided and evaded paying staple duties that towns had the right to impose on all doing business within their confines, lowered profit margins, and advertised and promoted their products.

Endorsing these capitalist practices in commerce conducted with non-Jews, Jewish communal authorities sought—even if they were usually unsuccessful—to circumscribe their application within the community. There staple rights were to apply; local merchants were to be preferred to outside Jews; established retailers were to be protected from incursions by upstarts. Dealings within the Jewish zone were supposed to follow accepted European norms of limited competition; only business with gentiles was open to competitive methods. This double standard might well indicate that the Jews' mentality was one of alienation. It might also imply that they felt themselves *in* their towns but not *of* them.

Another illustration is language. The vernacular of Polish Jewry was Yiddish, a language that had grown out of Middle High German and accompanied the Jews to Poland when they came to settle. No Judeo-Polish language developed (though Yiddish in Poland did come to incorporate many Polish and other Slavic terms). As a rule, Jewish knowledge and use of Polish was not a standard cultural accoutrement but a function of one's contacts with non-Jews. Merchants could speak it with some fluency, whereas rabbis could not express themselves adequately. There were some Jews who could read Polish for commercial purposes and even some who could sign their names on legal documents in Latin letters, but full literacy in Polish was rare. Even fewer non-Jewish Poles knew any Yiddish. With no real common language, it would seem that Jews and Christians were operating in separate cultural universes.

Both in fact and in consciousness, the Polish Jews were Jews in a Christian land. They often did feel alienation and even fear. Privileges and judicial records provide ample proof that such feelings were not mere paranoia. There is little question that Jewish culture in Poland was leavened by an underlying perception of insecurity and powerlessness. Gentiles in general were viewed as potential persecutors, and salutary Jewish circumstances were regarded as fragile and contingent. This perception prompted Jews to adopt a political strategy of accommodation to the primary loci of power in the country: the king and the high nobility.[8] It also led to Jewish culture encoding a stance of *kabdehu ve-ḥashdehu* ("respect, but suspect") with regard to their Christian neighbors. This attitude was expressed by rabbinic laws and communal ordinances restricting contact with non-Jews and by Jewish folklore that often assigned a demonic role to its gentile characters.

To say that Jews in Poland felt and acted alienated to a significant degree is not, however, the same as saying that they did not share in Polish culture. Despite cultural distancing, there is reason to consider them as part of the Commonwealth in the cultural sense. From medieval times, Jews defined their circumstances in Poland as qualitatively different from the rest of Ashkenaz— that realm of Jewish culture, marked by Yiddish speech, stretching from the Loire to the Dnieper. One of the earliest sources for Jewish history in Poland is a letter (ca. 1200) from Rabbi Eliezer of Prague to Rabbi Judah Hasid in Regensburg in the Rhineland. Eliezer urged the German rabbi to understand that the frontier conditions of eastern Europe called for a para-rabbinic religious leadership that would not be paid a regular salary by the Jewish community as Judah mandated for religious functionaries in the west.[9] In the rough state of the new communities of the east, providers of religious services had to subsist on contributions. This was but an early stage in the development of Polish variants of standard Ashkenazic institutions and customs relating to liturgy, ritual, education, and communal organization. While still recognizable as Ashkenazic, the Polish versions were sufficiently differentiated from the originals that in Jewish legal and exegetical discourse it became necessary to change the accepted term "Ashkenaz" to the formulaic expression "Ashkenaz and Polin," in which Ashkenaz denoted the Ashkenazic Jewish communities west of Poland. Rabbinic literature contains a number of observations on the differences between Jewish life in Poland and in Ashkenaz, particularly with regard to the more hospitable legal and social environment in the former.[10]

For Jews, Poland was different, and some of them demonstrated a rather sophisticated knowledge of the realities that made Poland what it was. For example, Rabbi Eliezer Ashkenazi, writing in Gniezno in 1580, chose to interpret the story of the Tower of Babel not as a challenge to divine power to which God responded by dividing the human race linguistically, but as an attempt to establish a universal religious regime which God "was obliged to separate . . . since the proliferation of doctrines aids and stimulates the investigator to attain the desired truths." That is, unanimity in religion is undesirable because religious pluralism, as the Italian-born Eliezer witnessed in Poland, is conducive to the exploration of truth.[11] It does not seem coincidental that it was in religiously pluralistic Poland that this well-traveled rabbi gave expression to such sentiments.

Seventy years later, Nathan Hannover, analyzing the background to the Chmielnicki Uprising, understood that the Jews of Ukraine, in principle a disdained minority, had gained power over the Ruthenian serfs as a result of the pro–Roman Catholic discriminatory policies of Zygmunt III and his appreciation for the Jews' administrative capabilities:

The King . . . loved justice and loved Israel. In his days the religion of the Pope gained strength in the Kingdom of Poland. . . . King Zygmunt raised the status of the Catholic dukes and princes above those of the Greek Orthodox so that most of the latter abandoned their faith and embraced Catholicism. The masses that followed the Greek Orthodox Church became gradually impoverished. They were looked upon as lowly and inferior beings and became the serfs of the Polish people and the Jews . . . [and thus] the lowliest among the nations became their overlords.[12]

Note that, to Hannover, "loving justice" was equally compatible with loving Israel and with enserfing Ruthenian peasants. This strong identification with the ruler was shared by many Jews.

The eighteenth-century Jewish wine merchant Ber of Bolechów wrote a memoir in which various Polish political and economic developments figure prominently. Observe Ber's admiration for the Commonwealth's High Tribunal at Lublin:

This Tribunal was the supreme court over all the courts which existed in each *starostwo* [an administrative unit]. Each province and district used to elect a number of wealthy noblemen, learned in the law, who assembled at Warsaw . . . and there the Diet chose from among them men known for their high character, fear of God, love of truth and incorruptibility.[13]

In outward behavior, Jews were differentiated from Christian inhabitants of the Commonwealth. Religious rituals, especially food restrictions, were vivid boundary markers that had the potential for limiting social contacts. The Jewish calendar guaranteed different evaluations of time, dates, and seasons as well as a contrasting rhythm to life. Based on their respective theologies, Jews and Christians shared an assessment of the Jews' fundamental Otherness within the dominant society. Yet, an expression of Polish values such as Eliezer Ashkenazi's, the identification with the rulers implied by Hannover, and the respect for Polish institutions expressed by Ber, all bespeak a profound Jewish engagement with Polish cultural categories. There was a Polish-Jewish mentality that drew upon the Polish experience.

Both Poles and Jews recorded legends of a woman named Esterka who was the queen (in the Jewish version) or the mistress (in the Polish version) of King Casimir the Great (fourteenth century). Notably, the two traditions were independent of each other. Even on a topic of such obvious popular and mutual interest, Poles and Jews referred to disparate sources of knowledge and seemed unaware of one another's ideas on the subject. This is another example implying that Jewish and Polish cultural creativity had different sources of inspiration and parallel lines of development.

Nevertheless, what is striking is the trend within Polish-Jewish tradition that the Esterka legend represents. This is but one of the stories in which Jews—who could not be official participants in Polish political institutions and could not put up a candidate for king—exert a decisive influence on the kingship. There was the tale of Abraham Prochownik, who in the days of Poland inchoate was offered the crown by the bickering lords of Great Poland, but he refused it, engineering instead the choice of the founder of the Polish state, Piast. Or the story of Saul Wahl, who, upon the death of Stefan Batory in 1586 and subsequent deadlock in the succession process, was chosen regent; serving for one day only, he instituted legislation favorable to the Jews, ruled justly over the Poles, and finished that super day by effecting the election of Zygmunt III Wasa as king of the Commonwealth. And then there was the Hasidic leader Dov Ber of Mezhirech; in 1764 it was he, in consultation with another rabbi, who decided that Stanisław August Poniatowski should be king. Approved by God, his choice was ratified, unwittingly, by the noble Polish electorate.[14]

These fantasies are typical of subordinate minorities. A form of what sociologists call "expressive hostility," they express a frustration with powerlessness and a hunger for empowerment. They say, in effect: our weakness is only apparent; we exercise a fateful influence on the key institutions of the country. All appearances to the contrary notwithstanding, we count! (Ironically, antisemites said the same thing about Jews, based on different fantasies and for different purposes.)

Jews *wanted* to count in Poland. They conceived of meaningful power and the trappings that accompanied it in exquisitely Polish terms. These people were not dreaming about the army of the ten lost tribes south of the Sahara about to organize and sweep through Europe, carrying them off to the Land of Israel. They did not prepare for the messianic Shabbtai Zevi to return after his conversion to Islam and show the Polish monarch what a king with true divine rights could do.

They also did not look to some alternative or competing non-Jewish political-cultural system as a source of comfort. There was no praise or longing for the Ottoman Empire, which had taken in so many Iberian Jewish exiles and allowed some of them to attain riches and prominence. There were no invidious comparisons made between Poland, on the one hand, and Muscovy or countries to the west, on the other—except to praise Poland. For a Polish Jew to feel empowered, empowerment had to be legitimated and recognized in a specifically Polish context.

Although incidents of forced baptism did occur, the Poles had no systematic program of Jewish polonization analogous to their attempts with other minority ethnic and religious groups. Yet, despite their lack of assimilation to Polish culture, Jews saw themselves functioning as part of the system. They were concerned about demonstrating the depth of their roots in Polish soil and the legitimacy of their rights, without trying to escape their Jewishness. Given the range of responses to domination available to subordinated minority groups, they chose accommodation, eschewing the extremes of revolt and assimilation.

But Polish and Jewish culture had more in common than collective identification of the dominated people with the dominators. Both cultures—and the cultures of most of the other minority groups in the Commonwealth—were part of a larger European heritage, and thus many of the unexamined axioms that shaped daily life were common property. This was not a question of "influence," for Jews did not divide their culture into "native" and "borrowed" categories; to the bearers of this culture all of it was authentic. The inherent authority of both the rabbi, whose status evolved from talmudic precedents, and the *parnasim* (communal elders), who closely resembled the medieval German *burgomeister* and Polish *burmiśtrzowie*, were taken for granted, endowed with religious significance, and regarded as "Jewish."

Jews and Christians agreed on such fundamental political concepts as the function of local political leadership: not to represent the people, but to serve as guardians or conservators whose job it was to determine the public interest and then act upon it without explicit consideration of the popular will. With regard to economic life, both Jews and Christians believed in the regnant notion of a regulated market within stable conditions and restricted competition, and they applied it, as noted above, within their communities. For Christians, one way to restrict competition was to reduce the number of competitors, and a convenient way to do this was to exclude or impede Jews. For Jews, who could not block Christian competition by law, the combative tactic of choice was, as we have seen, aggressive commercial practices.

Another example of shared cultural axioms is the sphere of what is usually called popular religion. We might define this, in the present context, as popular understanding of causation. For all peoples of the Commonwealth, the world was a dangerous place. Life was fragile, threatened at every turn by human violence and natural calamities. Such disasters when experienced on the public level—floods, famine, fires—were usually attributed directly to God as divine punishment for sin. On the personal level, however, intermediate agents—demons—were often blamed for bringing on disease, infertility, stillbirth, injury, and other misfortunes. Frequently, the response to trouble was mystical magic. As the Polish-Jewish expatriate physician Tobias Kohn wrote about Poland in 1707:

"Even if demons had never been created, they would have had to be created for the people of this country; for there is no land where they are more occupied with demons, amulets, oath formulas, mystical names, and dreams."[15]

These tools of theurgy had to be wielded by experts, shamans who specialized in supernatural defense. Christians had their exorcising priests and other mystical experts; Jews had *ba'alei shem* (masters of the divine name). Significantly, in some contexts each group believed the holy men of the other to possess genuine theurgic power. Poles and others, for example, addressed the most famous Jewish ba'al shem, Israel ben Eliezer (ca. 1700–1760), as "Doktor," and in some Ukrainian folktales Christians consult Jewish wonder workers. Conversely, Jewish stories about Israel ben Eliezer, who was known as the Ba'al Shem Tov, assert that he credited the powers of certain Christian holy men. In one tale, concerning a particular priest, the Ba'al Shem Tov declares: "I do not want to provoke him because he is a great sorcerer; he will sense it the moment that I begin to deal with him."[16] These crossover beliefs, encompassing the vicissitudes of life and the magic that could deal with them effectively, created a shared band of discourse among all the Commonwealth's groups. People understood reality in a common way and showed a grudging respect for the magical rituals of others.

Concrete material evidence exists for a core shared culture among majority

Masonry Izaaka Synagogue built in 1644 in Cracow. The photograph was taken in 1936. (Photo: Archiwum Panstwowe w Rzeszow; courtesy United States Holocaust Memorial Museum Photo Archives, Washington, D.C.)

Wooden synagogue built in the mid-eighteenth century in Glebokie (today in Belarus).
The photograph was taken in 1924. (Photo: Jack Kagan; courtesy United States Holocaust
Memorial Museum Photo Archives, Washington, D.C.)

and minority groups. The northern Renaissance and Baroque style of urban
masonry synagogues built in the fifteenth through eighteenth centuries fit well
into the architectural fabric of Polish cities. Wooden synagogues, in vogue in
smaller cities and towns in the seventeenth and eighteenth centuries, were distinctive buildings yet obviously shared the architectural and artistic vocabulary
of local wooden churches, manor houses, and other structures. Jewish clothing,
ritual and household objects, food, and music were typically variations on conventional Polish styles.[17] For Polish Jews, the aesthetic standard was Polish.

PRINTING AND THE EVOLUTION OF
POLISH-JEWISH CULTURE

Like Europeans in general, Jews were profoundly affected by the spread of
printing. During the sixteenth and seventeenth centuries, the technology came
into its own, and it had a democratizing effect. With books so much cheaper
than they had been in the days of manuscript, many more sectors of society, in
addition to the professionally learned and the wealthy, could find their way to
knowledge. Groups formerly unassociated with book culture, such as artisans,
merchants, women, and children, constituted new audiences. Rather than acquire only such knowledge as the clergy or the teachers decided to impart, they
could now study on their own and believed that they had the right to do so.

Detail of the ceiling of the synagogue in Chodorow, near Lvov, Poland. The synagogue was built in 1652; the ceiling was painted by Israel Ben Mordekhai Lisnicki, of Jaryczow, in 1714. Some of the twelve signs of the zodiac can be seen in this detail. (Photo [b/w print of color original] © Beth Hatefutsoth Photo Archive, Tel Aviv; no. 228, Permanent Exhibition)

This new state of affairs altered the relationship between knowledge and authority. Formerly, the transmitter of knowledge had nearly complete control over it. Only he had the book; he conveyed its contents by way of an oral interpretation that was automatically authoritative to his listeners. He even decided which knowledge was appropriate to transmit and which was to remain esoteric. Yet once people could read the books for themselves, they could listen to interpretation critically. The authority of the teacher was no longer guaranteed. In fact, the necessity for a teacher was reduced. A person's encounter with the wisdom of the past could be direct, without an intermediary. Knowledge could not be reserved by an elite for itself. People could choose whether to learn, what they wanted to learn, and how they wanted to learn it.[18]

They also had the potential for comparing different views and traditions. There was a new cross-fertilization of knowledge across geography and between fields. French, German, and Italian interpretations of the Bible, for example, could all be read by the same person. The implications of new theology and language studies for the understanding of the Bible became apparent much more quickly and to a wider audience. Printing also led to the dissemination of many more types of knowledge. It was no longer only the most weighty of classical tomes and learned dissertations that were published, but now also less serious and less lasting works such as abridgments, story collections, chapbooks, practical guides, even humorous tracts.

In addition to creating new audiences for new kinds of knowledge, printing opened the field to new authors. With a broad-based commercial market for books, people who were not part of the learned elite could be convinced that what they had to say might attract a paying audience and financially justify the expense of publication. Members of the secondary intelligentsia—popular preachers, ba'alei shem, and scribes, for example—now tried their hand at writing and publishing for profit.

All of these changes affected Polish Jews as much and—because of the relatively higher rates of literacy among Jews than among Christians—probably even more than they did the population in general. The presence of these changes in Jewish culture is epitomized by the figure of David ben Menashe Darshan.

David was born in Cracow circa 1527. He studied for a time at one of the premier yeshivot of his era, that of the Rabbi Moses Isserles in his native city. But, as he noted bitterly, for reasons he could not explicate, David could not complete the course of study:

The light of my intellect was progressively dimmed, for I was barred, against my will, from the academies of Torah. In several provinces, those great in

learning and in wealth turned against me, and prevented me from studying
Torah in the proper time, because I was considered a pariah among them . . .
"and David's place was empty" [1 Samuel 20:25] in the academy.[19]

David was an outsider to the world of the Torah elite. Though apparently ordained a rabbi, he never served in any formal rabbinic capacity or as a teacher in
a yeshivah. He earned his meager living as an itinerant popular preacher, yearning for a permanent position and a decent livelihood. There were doubtless
many semi-intellectual figures like him throughout the ages whose failure to
excel meant that their voices were never heard. Thanks to printing, David's fate
was different.

Unable to become a complete scholar within the elitist institutions, David
pursued a novel path to advanced Jewish education that would have been impossible before the advent of print. He collected 400 books and built a personal
library. If he could not sit at the feet of his generation's leading scholars, he
would still be able to learn from the greatest scholars of all the ages by studying their books. The knowledge denied him by institutions he would acquire
through self-study. Moreover, his library would serve as the basis not only of his
personal knowledge but also of his status in the community and his work. David
proposed establishing a new type of bet midrash (study academy), with his
library as its foundation.

To appreciate his proposal and its ramifications, it is first necessary to understand the institutional structure of Jewish education in Ashkenazic communities, including Poland, in this period. Following the traditional model, Jewish
education was organized on three levels. The first was elementary, where boys
from the age of three or four were educated in a series of schools (hadarim; sing.
heder), moving from learning to read and write, through Bible and basic commentaries, to Talmud and halakhah. A heder could be either public, sponsored
by the community, or private, financed by the parents of the boys. As a rule, in
the public heder the classes were large and the quality of instruction inferior. In
a private heder, the wealthier the parents, the more they could afford to pay the
teacher (melamed), the better trained he would be, and the smaller the class
would be. The class was heterogeneous in terms of the students' ages and ability,
and the teacher spent most of the eight-to-ten-hour day moving from small
group to small group, instructing each according to its level. Often he had an assistant (behelfer) who tended to the physical needs of the younger children and
dealt with disciplinary and other problems.

At around the age of puberty, most boys completed their education and entered the world of work, mainly as assistants in their parents' businesses or
trades, but also as workers for others and apprentices. Some, however, continued

on to the next level of education, the yeshivah. A yeshivah could also be either public, supported by a local Jewish community, or private, sponsored by a wealthy family, usually the parents or parents-in-law of the *rosh yeshivah* (head of the yeshivah). Two prominent rabbis of the seventeenth century described the circumstances leading to the establishment of the yeshivot they headed, one public, the other private. David ben Samuel Halevi (the Taz) described his institution in Ostróg:

> Three years ago the holy community council of the holy community of Ostróg engaged me to teach Torah among them. They established a great bet midrash for me, a place of meeting for the gathering of scholars. All good and favor to said council, who pour money from their pocket to give me enough to support myself and my large and important yeshivah.[20]

Yehoshua Falk recalled how his dream of heading a large yeshivah was fulfilled:

> And [God] placed in the heart of my father-in-law, the noble and generous head and leader of the community of Lvov and its vicinity, the famous Rabbi Yisrael bar Yosef, of blessed memory, [who] spoke with me heart to heart and said: "I have the opportunity of performing a *mitzvah,* hold on to it and I will stand at your side. I will supply you with worthy students as you desire." He decided, declared, and did it. He was my guide, giving me his stone house, beautifully built with three floors and attics, so that flocks [of students] could gather there and on it would be "hung the shields of the heroes" [Song of Songs 4:4].[21]

The curriculum of the yeshivah consisted primarily of two subjects: Talmud and its associated classical commentaries, Rashi and the Tosafists; and halakhah as explicated in several canonical works, most notably the *Arba'ah Turim,* the *Mordekhai,* the *Sha'arei Dura,* the *Sefer Mitzvot Gadol,* and the *Sefer Mitzvot Katan.* The main objective of yeshivah learning was to train a rabbi who could determine what the law should be in any given circumstances. To do this he had to be versed in the Talmud, the relevant canonical halakhic texts, and the branch of Ashkenazic custom represented by his own community. The measure of a scholar was his ability to make a halakhic ruling that took all of these sources of authority into account.

There were teachers (*alufei ha-yeshivah*) who taught Talmud and halakhah to formal classes in the yeshivah, but most of the time was devoted to tutorial-style study, with advanced students coaching those who had not reached their own level. The rosh yeshivah, in addition to teaching text to a regular class, offered a daily lesson for all students and teachers in the yeshivah. Here he engaged all present in a dialectical analysis of the section of the Talmud they had learned, challenging their understanding of the text and trying to get them to see its multiplicity of levels.

Support for a yeshivah meant providing a space, paying its head and other teachers, providing stipends for advanced students, and making provision for feeding and housing the single students, who usually numbered in the dozens and mostly came from out of town. Their accommodations were modest, typically consisting of meals taken with a local family and sleeping in that family's or another's home or in the study hall.

The single students were divided into two groups: beginners (*na'arim*) and advanced (*baḥurim*), with the latter serving as tutors to the former. At any point during their years in the yeshivah, students might leave it and enter the market and workplace. At around the age of 18, a baḥur would likely marry and receive the title *ḥaver*. This signified that he was no longer a student, learning the techniques and basic texts of Torah, but an independent scholar who could study on his own and even teach others.

Most ḥaverim left the yeshivah when they married, utilizing the dowries their brides brought to set up households and invest in commerce or income-producing concession leases, such as on inns, mills, or tax collection, which could provide a livelihood. Some went to work as religious functionaries (*kelei kodesh*): preachers, teachers, scribes, rabbis' assistants, or even rabbis in small, outlying communities. Constituting a secondary intelligentsia in Jewish society, they did not write the learned books nor teach the future leaders. They were, however, a group that could read the books and serve as a constituency for ideas set forth by the intellectual leadership. They could also popularize ideas through their contacts with the public. David Darshan was a typical member of this class.

Ḥaverim who remained in the yeshivah, supported usually by their (wives') families, belonged to the group called *lomdim* or *ḥakhamim* and represented the third level of traditional Jewish education. They did not require instruction but studied for the most part independently, though they would normally attend the rosh yeshivah's general lesson. After several years spent perfecting their skills and knowledge, the rosh yeshivah would grant them the title *moreinu*, which signified advanced rabbinic ordination. This qualified them to be communal rabbis, halakhic judges, and even yeshivah headmasters (*rashei yeshivah*) themselves.

From the seventeenth century in Poland, it became common to separate the married lomdim, institutionally, from the single students. Lomdim who continued their studies past marriage and the acquisition of the title of ḥaver attended

post-graduate institutions that were also divided into public and private. Those
under the aegis of the community were called bet midrash, whereas those supported by a wealthy patron were called kloyz. The bet midrash was open to all
lomdim, whereas the kloyz, being private, was selective. For several years a student would have to support himself, usually with funds provided by his wife's
family. After gaining the title moreinu, he was considered a permanent member
of the bet midrash or kloyz and was granted a stipend by either the bet midrash's
sponsoring community or the wealthy kloyz founder. Young lomdim fresh out
of a yeshivah would typically try to be accepted into a kloyz where there was a
prominent scholar so as to be able to learn from him.[22]

The yeshivah, bet midrash, and kloyz were elitist institutions. As students
progressed from ḥeder through yeshivah to bet midrash and kloyz, their number
was constantly being reduced. Those who managed to stay the course were progressively mastering a body of knowledge that was universally respected but unfamiliar to most people. The great authority and honor accorded this knowledge
lent its masters high social status. Attendance at institutions of advanced Jewish
learning was one sign of a person's membership in the elite.

David's proposed bet midrash was not aimed at such people. His institution of
learning was to be completely different from the traditional schools. Rather than
attract the highly educated few, it was to be open to all. As David described it:

Blessed be the Lord of the universe, Who has motivated me to establish a place
of study in honor of the God of Israel in whatever place God will prepare for
me. I shall bring into it, for the honor, glory and splendor of the God of heaven
and earth, more than four hundred choice books. . . . And these books will be
ready and available for all who desire knowledge and understanding of God
from them. God willing that among them there will be found some new kinds
of books that have been hidden away for some years. And though modest my
worth, I will not leave the place except on Sabbath eves to prepare for the Sabbath, always being on hand for anyone seeking to know or to delve into God's
Torah, to the best of the ability of my modest intelligence and limited understanding. This is why Divine Providence saw fit to enable me to come by these
books, and established me in this study, despite my lowly status, in order that
attachment to God might be strengthened and the life-line not ruptured completely, heaven forbid, by the excessive weight of the anxieties of subsistence
and taxes and imposts, and the troubles and the uprooting and the hardships
that we endure in our exile because of our many sins.

And there is no time [for a person] to be engaged in the study of Torah, in
order to know the commandments thoroughly. On some occasions he has the

time but no book; on others he has the book, but no understanding. Thus, when he enters the bet midrash his deficiency, whatever it may be, will be supplied. And if he understands better than I do, I shall not be ashamed to learn from him. And if there be something too difficult both for the one who asks and for me, I shall take the trouble to consult the great scholars.

. . . And I also undertake to be prepared every day, regularly, for at least an hour, to instruct the simple folk about some commentator or some decisor or about the Bible, in accordance with their desires and at such time as they choose, which will be of great benefit to the children of the indigent. In addition I shall outline the fine points of a book for the teachers of children, and this will be of tremendous benefit for schoolchildren who learn from them.

In general, I shall not be too lazy to undertake whatever my appointed duty may be. And from this will flow many advantages for the educated and uneducated alike. The advantages to the totally uneducated have already been made clear; as to the advantages for those who have a little learning, when they come home tired and worn out from their effort to make a living, each one can take a book home with him and read it, and if he is baffled by the meaning of some text, or by some difficult word, he can jot it down on paper, even in [Yiddish], and he may send it to the bet midrash, and the messenger need not reveal the name of the person involved. And I shall explain it if I know it, and if I don't I shall make inquiry about it. . . . And sometimes even a sharp-witted and expert scholar who needs to find a saying or law or a verse, or needs to look up something in the books of wisdom or Kabbalah or the like, and he does not happen to be in possession of these books, may write it on paper, send it to the bet midrash and I shall take the trouble to look for it and find it.[23]

The study material was David's 400 books, which went far beyond the standard yeshivah curriculum of Talmud, classic commentaries, and halakhic codes. The students were not to attend classes or study in groups in the bet midrash full-time, but rather study at their leisure, on their own, from books of their choosing from the library's collection, either learning at the bet midrash or at home. If they had questions, David was to be available to answer them, and anything he could not answer he offered to forward to the local rosh yeshivah. Those with the least education, who might not feel comfortable confronting the content of the books on their own, could benefit from popular lessons that David would offer on their level. Overworked and undereducated teachers could obtain summaries of books they felt they should know about without having to read them themselves. Accomplished scholars could use the new bet midrash as a reference library, looking up verses, laws, and citations.

What David wanted to establish was a popular learning resource center, similar in concept to a modern community public library, where the printed book, rather than the teacher, was at the heart of the educational process. In principle, the student was independent of a teacher, learning by himself from books. The teacher was to enter the educational process only when the student decided to call for him in response to some difficulty. In this bet midrash, the relationship between the student and the book was to replace, to a large extent, the relationship between the student and the teacher. The role envisioned for the teacher was supplementary. There was no need for an erudite master teacher; a middling scholar like David was sufficient as tutor and manager of studies. Since the books, not the teacher, were the arbiters of knowledge, David did not need to establish his intellectual authority and was perfectly willing to entertain the possibility that the users of the books would have something to teach him. In this way, those, like him, who were low in the scholarly hierarchy could find an intellectual and educational role in a community that promised them a permanent position and a livelihood. The proposed bet midrash offered knowledge to all comers, not just to those who had advanced through the hierarchy of institutions and proven themselves worthy members of the learned elite—though these latter, too, could find the library useful. The curriculum was to include a much broader selection of texts than those routinely studied in established institutions.

David's bet midrash was evidently never established, but his proposal demonstrates new trends in learning that printing and the general accessibility of new knowledge facilitated in all sectors of education: the growing importance of books; new contexts of learning outside of children's schools and elitist institutions; new types of people seeking instruction, not just the young and the elite; the increasing popularity of independent study without benefit of a teacher; the enlarging of the canon of books to be studied and the curriculum based on it and the need for even members of the learned elite to be aware of new genres and knowledge outside of their own particular stream of tradition; and the activities of new disseminators of knowledge who required neither the credentials nor the institutions of the elite.

David also explored the new possibilities offered by print in his book, *Shir ha-Ma'alot le-David* (Cracow, 1571). This book was unique in the history of Jewish literature up to that time. It was essentially a prospectus, presenting samples of scholarly, religious, and social services that David was prepared to offer in his quest to secure a reliable livelihood. In it he gave examples of sermons, answers to legal questions (*responsa*), magical amulet inscriptions, form letters, and poems that he could write to help people get through their lives. His objective was to showcase his talents with the hope that some influential readers would invite him to take up residence in their community, where he could offer the services demonstrated in the prospectus, for suitable remuneration.

Shir ha-Ma'alot le-David offers a glimpse into the areas of Jewish religion and learning, other than halakhah, that interested Polish Jews of the early modern period. David's writing, unsophisticated and aimed at a poorly educated audience, paralleled emphases in the intellectual activity of his elitist peers. With both types of writers adopting similar modes, we can be reasonably certain of the cultural trends they were attempting to address. For example, David's featuring his sermonic skills suggests the importance of oral sermons, homiletic books, and commentaries on nonhalakhic works during this period. Rabbis who were David's contemporaries showed intensive interest in Bible exegesis, producing a large number of supercommentaries on the classic medieval commentary of Rashi. By expatiating on the well-known explanations of the great medieval authority, they advanced their own interpretation of the biblical text. There was also direct exegesis of the Bible; best known is the homiletic commentary of Shlomo Ephraim Lunshitz, *Keli Yakar* (Lublin, 1602), even today one of the standard biblical commentaries printed in many Hebrew editions of the Bible. Interestingly, virtually all of these commentaries focused on the Pentateuch or the popular narrative books (*megillot*) of Ruth and Esther, implying thereby that both writers and readers were not concerned with Bible study per se but with rendering meaningful those parts of the Bible that were most closely connected to regular Jewish ritual life. By explaining the weekly Torah portion from the Pentateuch and the stories that were closely associated with the important festivals of Shavuot and Purim, the writers afforded their audiences fresh interpretations that could heighten the interest and significance of what was routine.

Another way of relating the Torah to life was through sermons. A class of religious functionary, the preacher (*darshan*), was not usually a full-fledged rabbi with the moreinu title but had a fixed role in the Polish communities. A sermon was not normally part of the worship service proper but an appendix at the end of the service or an event in its own right on a Friday evening, a Saturday afternoon, or a special occasion during the week. Listening to sermons was a way to pass the day without being drawn to sinful pursuits or slothful waste of time. In some communities (*kehillot*; sing. *kehilla*), there was a permanent preacher on the communal payroll whose job it was to give weekly sermons loosely connected to the themes of the weekly Torah portion as well as discourses on public occasions (such as weddings, funerals, and communal meetings) as required. It was to such a position that David aspired. While waiting for fortune to smile upon him, however, he worked as an itinerant preacher. Perusal of their budgets reveals that many *kehalim* (sing. *kahal*, governing councils of the kehillot) hired such men to spend a Sabbath or even several in their communities. Town rabbis—whose main duties were to serve as judge (the standard formal designation of a community rabbi was *av bet din*, or chairman of the court), halakhic decisor, and teacher—were not primarily responsible for giving sermons. Therefore, when the rabbi did speak in public, his appearance was a sign of the importance of the occasion. Customarily, he would give a sermon on the Sabbath before Yom Kippur (Shabbat Shuvah) and the one before Passover (Shabbat ha-Gadol) in order to introduce these upcoming holy days with their special halakhic requirements (particularly fasting on Yom Kippur and refraining from leaven on Passover) and profound religious messages in as serious and thoroughgoing a manner as possible. In addition, if the community was faced with some catastrophe or success, it was typically the rabbi who marked the event. Although the oral, Yiddish, topical, and occasional natures of the genre were obstacles to transferring sermons to print, there were famous preachers and some important collections or adaptations, most notably, the books of Rabbi Lunshitz mentioned above.

Sermons usually involved moral exhortation. This was a main motif in Jewish literature of the age in both Hebrew and Yiddish. (Many of the books were printed in dual-language editions.) Whether in the form of ethical wills, text interpretations, monographs (or their abridgments) on the moral life, codes of ethical behavior, or manuals of ritual behavior, moral and conduct literature flourished in Poland. Examples are *Yesh Nohalin* (Prague, 1615), Avraham Horowitz's famous ethical will distilling the wisdom of his life experience for his descendants; Isaac ben Elyakum's *Lev Tov* (Prague, 1620), detailing the proper attitudes and behavior that a person should display in family and social life; and *Kav ha-Yashar* (Frankfurt am Main, 1705) by Tzvi Hirsh Kaidanover, a passionate exhortation to live a life full of the fear of God.

A NEW CANON

Shir ha-Ma'alot le-David is a significant cultural document, however, not only for what it presents but also for what it represents. A book such as this would be inconceivable in manuscript form. It has no content in the sense of a thesis to be explicated or a classic text to be elucidated. It was not written with the intention that its wisdom would take on permanent form and be available to future generations. This is a book providing information about erudition, not erudition itself, and presumes that there is an audience seeking such information. *Shir ha-*

Ma'alot le-David could only be justified economically because printing made publication relatively inexpensive and because the outlay that was required was an investment for David, akin to advertising or to sending a portfolio to a range of prospective employers. The book's contents would not enshrine David in the annals of scholarship but would attract attention to his talents and, he hoped, secure him a lucrative position in a community.

David's activities show that, in Poland by the sixteenth century, both the form and the function of the traditional Ashkenazic canonical texts had changed. In the late medieval period, such texts were utilized as the basis for the lessons of the teachers in the yeshivah. Each teaching scholar transmitted the text to his students along with his own interpretations, explanations, and excursuses. It was this teaching that was the real text. This explication, called *hagahot* (glosses), was recorded by disciples in the margins of the manuscript page. When the text was later re-copied, these comments were often incorporated into the main body of the text.[24] The individualization of canonical texts by those who taught them explains why the manuscript era produced multiple recensions of the same work, such as the Mordekhai of Rabbi Samuel, the Mordekhai of Rabbi Samson, the Rhenish Mordekhai, and the Austrian Mordekhai.

With the advent of print, the text as written by the author, or edited by the editor, was set permanently. The distinction between text and commentary could not be blurred. Once printed, the book stood on its own, detached from the rosh yeshivah. He was no longer the single authoritative agent of transmission nor, in effect, an editor or secondary author of the work. As David's proposal illustrates, the book was no longer a repository of tradition for the learned; it was now available to anyone to study and teach it. The very suggestion of the new, popular bet midrash with no bona fide scholar to act as central authority shows how printed books had the potential to threaten the authority of inherited traditions, established institutions, and vested leaders.

In addition to broadening the audience for learning and enabling students to become independent of teachers, printed books also introduced new subjects and new information to all, both the learned and the half-learned. In Jewish terms this meant that, thanks to the intensive activity of the printing houses of Italy, the yeshivot of Ashkenaz and Poland of the sixteenth and seventeenth centuries became awash in books by medieval Sephardic scholars who had previously been only names or occasional citations. Maimonides, Naḥmanides, Saadiah Gaon, Don Isaac Abravanel, Rabbi Isaac Arama, Rabbi Abraham ibn Ezra, Rabbi David Kimḥi, Rabbi Solomon ibn Adret, Rabbi Baḥya ibn Paquda, and many others could now be studied directly and in depth. Ashkenazic readers now had access to books of philosophy, biblical and midrashic interpretation, medieval science, Kabbalah, homiletics and morality, Hebrew grammar, Talmud study, and halakhah that broadened the range of subjects and introduced new approaches to studying them. Some of these books emphasized rationalism; others promoted mysticism.[25]

Moreover, scholars would now have to consider many more authorities of the past when producing new knowledge. In effect, a new library of canonical texts was created, much larger in scope and variegated in terms of the traditions it drew upon than the medieval Ashkenazic works that had served as the basis of the traditional Ashkenazic intellectual endeavor. This new canon had far-reaching ramifications for Polish-Jewish culture. It had the potential to alter the study curriculum, the methods of study, the process by which Jewish law was determined, and the practice of Judaism itself.

Sometime in the third quarter of the sixteenth century, Rabbi Solomon Luria (ca. 1510–1573), who was known as the Maharshal and who served as rabbi in several important Polish-Lithuanian communities, wrote a letter to Rabbi Moses Isserles in response to his mention in passing of an Aristotelian concept. What Luria wrote may strike the outsider as an overreaction:

> I received your message. . . . I saw in it piercing words and I felt as if a razor were in my flesh, for I was surrounded by clusters of wisdoms, most of them foreign in strange vessels, while the native wisdoms are deserted. . . . I said, "Woe is me, that my eyes have seen in addition to what my ears have heard, that the main delight and fragrance are the words of the unclean one, and it has become like a perfume to the holy Torah in the mouths of the sages of Israel, may Heaven save us from this great sin." . . . And now I have seen written in the prayers and prayerbooks of the students the prayer of Aristotle and this is the fault of the leader like you who encourages them since you mix Aristotle with the words of the living God.[26]

The intensity of this outburst is probably due to its being part of a major controversy that originated in the sixteenth-century yeshivot of Poland and Ashkenaz but soon went public. It is usually referred to as the polemic over "philosophy." However, another vehement expression of this argument makes it clear that the dispute was not over the question of the legitimacy of philosophic study but over the legitimacy of the newly developing canon.

In April 1559, the rabbi of Poznan, Aaron Land, in a sermon delivered on Shabbat ha-Gadol, launched an attack on this new canon. The original sermon has not survived, but it was paraphrased by Abraham Horowitz in his bitter diatribe against Land and his like-minded son-in-law, Joseph Ashkenazi:

And not as was preached by the great ass, the father-in-law of the said fool, on the Shabbat ha-Gadol of the year [1559], who said in his impudence that no Jew should study anything but the Talmud alone, and that all other books are books of Homer. Why he even said that no Jew should study the Twenty-four [books of the Bible] frequently or closely.[27]

Land was proposing a departure from the accepted new trend of broadening the legitimate Jewish canon with books on new subjects. Branding anything nontalmudic as "Homer" or "philosophy"—and hence illegitimate—he advocated that Polish Jews narrow their field of study to the Talmud only. He even sought to deflate the newfound interest in Bible study. As often happens, his conservative response to the perceived danger of a new intellectual trend was no less radical than the innovation; even non-Talmud books that were traditionally studied in the yeshivot, such as Maimonides' *Guide of the Perplexed,* were to be jettisoned.

Notably, for cultural conservatives like Land and Luria, the books that represented the greatest threat to the traditional cultural constellation were not "philosophical" at all, but halakhic—namely, the new halakhic codes of the Sephardic Rabbi Joseph Karo. The problem with these books was not the introduction of alien ideas but something more ominous: a fundamental change in the way halakhah was decided and in how the practice based on those decisions would look.

The basic book of Jewish law, the Talmud, is a dense text that is not organized according to a strictly logical order but consists of complicated discussions between authorities attempting to determine what the law in any given situation should be. It includes arguments, logical exercises, anecdotes, legal and historical precedents, legends, exegesis, and homiletics. It is often difficult to follow the discussions, and the final determination of the law is not readily apparent. It is understandable, then, that throughout the Middle Ages there had been attempts to codify Jewish law in part or in whole. Typically, an author would organize the laws by topic in logical categories, summarize the laws in each category, and present them in straightforward form with little or no discussion. However, since manuscript books were intended as instructional tools for the yeshivah teachers and their students, and as research aids for rabbis deciding legal questions, they were not really the "final" version of the texts. The text was what was *taught* and not what was originally *written.* With regard to determining contemporary halakhah, these books were part of an array of resources, including individual decisions by noted authorities in responsum form, in manuscript, that rabbis used to resolve legal problems on an ad hoc basis. The leading early-sixteenth-century Polish rabbis, Jacob Polak and Shalom Shakhna, consciously refrained from writing general halakhic summaries so as not to displace the medieval works and short-circuit the traditional decision-making process. They believed that rabbis should continue to consult the Talmud and all subsequent sources regarded as canonical in the Ashkenazic tradition.

With the popularization of print in the sixteenth century, new attempts were made to codify all of halakhah. The most successful were those of Karo, who as a child was one of the Jews expelled from Spain and Portugal. He lived in various places in the Ottoman Empire and by 1538 was in Safed. In 1555, Karo published the *Bet Yosef.* Ostensibly a gloss on the canonical *Arba'a Turim* code, this was really an attempt to trace the origin of each rule, present alternative opinions, and decide what the final law should be. Ten years later, Karo produced his most influential work, the *Shulḥan Arukh* (lit., prepared table). Much briefer than the *Bet Yosef,* presenting the bare law without sources and without alternative opinions, Karo insisted that this book was to serve as a practical guide to proper religious behavior for untutored students and a convenient review tool for the learned. Its outstanding feature was that it presented "the fixed, final law, without speech and without words."[28]

To those who objected to the new canon that printing was helping to impose, Karo's books were anathema. They were not, in fact, mere study or legal aids intended to serve a supplementary role in helping teachers and legal authorities perform their duties. They set the text, admitting of no modification through oral transmission, and emphasized Sephardic legal traditions. Moreover, they put the law into the hands of all comers. Anyone who could read might think that he knew what the law should be. This implied the possibility of a "cookbook" approach to deciding halakhah; look up the law by topic in the code and then apply it by deduction to the situation at hand.

To this Luria protested:

> From the days of Ravina and Rav Ashi [the editors of the Talmud] there is no tradition to decide according to one of the geonim or later sages; rather according to he whose words prove to be clearly based on the Talmud.[29]

In other words, there can be no one rabbi and no one code that should be regarded as *a priori* authoritative in every situation. An authority must be judged on his fidelity to the original talmudic sources and the cogency of his reasoning. Sometimes it is one sage who succeeds in arriving at the best result and sometimes another. The law cannot be determined by facile deductions and analogies made on the basis of putatively archetypal rules. Every situation must be carefully weighed on its own merits in the light of talmudic law and its authoritative interpretation throughout the ages.

Therefore, rather than summarize or codify the laws, Luria composed his *Yam shel Shlomo*, going through the Talmud section by section (he did not complete the entire work) and adducing what every canonical authority had to say about each section. In this way he hoped to refocus attention on the Talmud, reinforce loyalty to the Ashkenazic halakhic tradition, and assert the principle that halakhah should be decided by a process of painstaking erudition with the Talmud always at its foundation.

Luria's approach countered the new code by rejecting it and the methodological assumptions that underlay it. Other Polish rabbis also thought Karo's work problematic but considered codification in the age of print unavoidable and even desirable. Isserles objected to Karo's privileging of Sephardic halakhic tradition, realizing that, because of the nature of print, inexperienced students would read the *Shulḥan Arukh* on their own and assume that its rulings were normative "without controversy."[30] However, Isserles did agree that a new code was necessary. He had already made his view clear in a previous book, *Torat ha-Ḥatat,* an attempt to synthesize ritual law that was to replace the medieval *Sha'arei Dura:*

> One says this and another says that . . . one prohibits and one permits . . . whoever has not the palate to taste their sweet but largely obscure words cannot reach conclusions from these numerous glosses [on *Sha'arei Dura*]. . . . Time comes to an end, but their words are endless, for they have composed for that book commentaries and appendices and many students have jumped up and attributed nonsensical things to it.[31]

The problem with *Sha'arei Dura,* and with the entire medieval Ashkenazic halakhic corpus, was centuries of accumulated confusing glosses and commentaries. From this jumble it was next to impossible to learn the law in a systematic manner. Isserles' solution was to coopt the *Shulḥan Arukh.* He wrote a companion work, called the *Mappa* (lit., tablecloth), which introduced Ashkenazic traditions and took into account customary practice. He did not publish this as a separate book. Instead, he created a post-printing version of a traditional medieval annotated manuscript. Beginning with the Cracow edition of the *Shulḥan Arukh* that appeared in the 1570s, Isserles' glosses were printed as a natural continuation of Karo's text, paragraph by paragraph. Isserles took advantage of the *Shulḥan Arukh* to create a new Ashkenazic law book that would replace the confusion of medieval codes and commentaries, presenting "the proper order of all the laws . . . in a manner easily comprehensible to every man be he small or great."[32] This new canon would not be merely a manual to guide everyday practice, as Karo had proposed, but would serve as the textbook of halakhah in the yeshivot. The success of the *Shulḥan Arukh* cum *Mappa* (i.e., set table plus tablecloth) in becoming the standard source for Jewish law in Ashkenaz and Poland is evident in the appearance over the next two centuries of new editions of the *Shulḥan Arukh–Mappa* that included the glosses of various rabbis adjacent to the main text.

With this new compendium of halakhic sources available for study, the nature of Talmud study in the yeshivah now changed. Traditionally, the lesson was directed toward deriving the law. With the *Shulḥan Arukh–Mappa* and attendant commentaries now the main source for determining practical law, this function became secondary. Those who needed to know the law so as to be able to serve as communal rabbis concentrated on the new code with its accumulating glosses.

Talmud study in the yeshivah was now directed at explicating the text from every conceivable angle. The objective was no longer to understand how the text formed the foundation for a particular area of halakhah; instead, it was to uncover the subtleties of the text itself: its logic, its internal consistency, the relationship between various passages even if they were ostensibly unconnected, and the contradictions entailed by competing interpretations of the text. This analysis was accomplished by means of *pilpul* (casuistry). Although it had always been a component of the yeshivah curriculum, used to sharpen students' thinking skills, pilpul now became the central mode of study and the focus of bitter dispute.

Earlier I mentioned that the rosh yeshivah customarily gave a daily lesson in which he probed and challenged students' understanding of the text and tried to get them to think about it more profoundly. By the mid-seventeenth century, this central lesson consisted of a lecture by the rosh yeshivah during which, in the manner of pilpul, he posed numerous difficulties inherent in the passage under study and then proposed an interpretation that would resolve the logical, textual, and interpretive problems. Often such resolution entailed far-fetched assumptions and hairsplitting reasoning; it did not necessarily bear a connection to the practical legal implications of the passage. With pilpul at its core, the main track of yeshivah study—Talmud—became a quintessentially intellectual endeavor, study for study's sake. Study for the practical purpose of knowing or deciding the halakhah, based on the code literature, was secondary.

This innovation met with opposition. As the chronicler David Gans of Prague noted, this style of pilpul study "was not acceptable to all the scholars and men of integrity. Many of the heads of the exile, the great men of the world, the elders and paragons of our generations do not agree with it." The two most prominent opponents were Luria in Poland and Rabbi Judah Loew (the Maharal) in Prague. In their institutions they retained both the traditional medieval halakhic canon and the nexus between Talmud study and determination of the halakhah. For them, pilpul continued to be an ancillary tool, and the objective of learning the Talmud text was to derive the law.[33]

The tremendous energy expended in the Polish institutions of learning of the sixteenth and seventeenth centuries on controversies over the canon of study, the proper means for learning the law, and the objective of yeshivah study be-speaks the central place of rabbinic texts in Polish-Jewish society. The denizens of the yeshivot were an elite, relatively small in number, but the primary cultural message to all Jews was that obedience to God's commands was the central task of life, in theory at least, for everyone. The general consensus was that the sacred texts constituted the articulation of God's commands and that the accepted method of studying these texts was the way to comprehend their import. Even those who did not study were convinced that "the tiny letters" (referring to the print of the holy books) were the map to the path of righteousness and holiness. Not all of the holy books were, however, part and parcel of the normal yeshivah curriculum.

JEWISH MYSTICISM IN POLAND

In 1598 in Cracow a boy named Abraham Rapoport (destined to become one of the leading rabbinic lights of seventeenth-century Polish Jewry) delivered his bar mitzvah homily (*derasha*). At the climax of the sermon, when he sought to drive home the point that a person is obligated to struggle with his evil inclina-tion and purify his soul, this thirteen-year-old quoted a prooftext from the *Zohar,* the chief text of Jewish mysticism—Kabbalah.[34]

Kabbalah (lit., reception) was traditionally the most elitist area of Jewish study. Hoary teachers who had received the mystical tradition from their own mentors would carefully select from among the most advanced students those who were to be instructed out of manuscripts that had been copied by trusted initiates. Mystical adepts who were both ascetic and punctilious in their ritual observance were viewed as the spiritual avant-garde of the Jewish community. By the late seventeenth and eighteenth centuries, conventicles of such ascetic, mystical pietists were to be found in many larger communities. Supported by the official kehillot, these small groups of men bore an aura of holiness and engaged in Kabbalah-inspired study and ritual practice that was believed to redound to the credit of all of the Jews of their locale. They were the spiritual elite of their communities; even rabbis sought their insights. How, then, did a bar mitzvah boy gain casual familiarity with the *Zohar*?

Rapoport's bar mitzvah speech is a minor expression of an important cultural phenomenon in Jewish communities of the sixteenth and seventeenth centuries: the popularization of mysticism.[35] We can recall that David Darshan, a good indicator of nonelite interests, had singled out Kabbalah both as a discipline for which his library could serve as a resource and as an area in which he had expertise. For the Jewish elite, the fact that members of the secondary intelligentsia like David could claim familiarity with Kabbalah was an issue equal in rank to the dispute over "philosophy." It became a perennial topic of debate for Ashkenazic Jewry as a whole. In the mid-seventeenth century, the official preacher of the Cracow Jewish community, Berekhia Berakh, in his book *Zera Berakh* deplored

> ... the scandal of Kabbalah study ... for thus it was called "Kabbalah," its name shows its nature, that it was transmitted from person to person going back to Moses who received it from Sinai and there is no warrant to reveal it except to "one in a city and two from a family" [Jeremiah 3:14] and no one may innovate in Kabbalah on his own but rather must hint at [new ideas] by way of allusion from scripture or rabbinic sayings. But now a few people who are famous in their own eyes use the crown of Torah as a tool to earn a living and compose books about Kabbalah and they get permission to print these books and go around the towns distributing them ... and they reveal the hidden and the mysterious before the great and the small. Moreover they mix their own words that they invent from their heart with the words of the Kabbalah to the point where one cannot tell which are the words of the true sages and which the words that were added.[36]

Berekhia was bemoaning a phenomenon that had begun in 1558, when the *Zohar* first began to roll off the press in Mantua. This "hidden midrash" was the fundamental text of Kabbalah; its appearance in print removed it from the sphere of the elite initiates and threw it into the public domain. In addition, the recrudescence of mystical activity, centering on the figures of Rabbi Moses Cordovero and Rabbi Isaac Luria in the sixteenth century in Palestine, radiated to Europe in the seventeenth and eighteenth centuries. There had always been a tacit assumption that Kabbalah was the key to the divine secrets. Now anyone could achieve esoteric access; especially since, as Berekhia complained, a whole secondary literature—in print—developed. Study aids in the form of lexicons, introductions, summaries, and indexes lowered the threshold of preparation needed to embark upon the study of Kabbalah. Works of interpretation, explanation, commentary, and even Yiddish paraphrase of the *Zohar* and other works put the kabbalistic message in more comprehensible form. In addition, manu-scripts were both widely copied and printed. All of this literary activity testifies to widespread and intense demand for Kabbalah knowledge. As Mordekhai Yaffe, rabbi of Poznan, explained in defending his decision to write a commentary on the works of the fourteenth-century Italian kabbalist Menahem Recanati:

> What can I do in the face of the insistence of wise and understanding ones, who say to me every day "Why do you hide them [kabbalistic teachings] like pearls? Is not the entire people supreme holy beings, perfect in faith, and God, the master of masters, resides among them? Bring out [the teachings] to us that we may know those revelations."[37]

A plethora of specifically kabbalistic books was published; moreover, kab-balistic doctrines, terms, references, and interpretations began appearing in conventional homiletic and halakhic rabbinic works. By the early seventeenth century, Rabbi Joel Sirkes could assert that the Kabbalah was "the source of all the Torah and its essence." Rabbi Sheftel Horowitz, in his ethical will to his chil-dren, declared, "I order you to learn the wisdom of Kabbalah because a man who does not learn this wisdom is not God-fearing. . . . *Sefer ha-Pardes* should be for you like the *Shulhan Arukh*."[38]

The popularization of Kabbalah reached its peak in the second half of the sev-enteenth century, in the wake of the Sabbatian messianic episode—which, notwithstanding its failure, did much to spread Lurianic kabbalistic doctrines—with the publication of religious manuals prescribing both ethical and ritual be-havior based to a large extent on kabbalistic lore. The flourishing of this conduct literature in both Hebrew and Yiddish is proof that not only scholars and semi-scholars like David Darshan but also the rank-and-file members of the commu-nity wanted a share in the Kabbalah. These people were not about to study Kabbalah, but they did believe in its importance and its authority and therefore wanted their ritual practice to reflect its doctrine. It is the adoption of Kabbalah-based practices that is the true measure of the integration of kabbalistic modes into the culture of Polish Jewry.[39]

The desire of most people to behave in accordance with requirements set forth in kabbalistic books explains the great popularity of abridgments of Kabbalah-inspired works. For example, the *Shenei Luhot ha-Berit* (popularly known by the Hebrew acronym *SheLaH*), written by Isaiah Horowitz and first printed in Amsterdam in 1649, is a collection of moral instructions, homilies, interpretations, theology, and customs based on kabbalistic sources that was widely studied in Poland and elsewhere in Ashkenaz until the modern period. It-self a popular reworking of kabbalistic ideas, the *SheLaH* was later made even more accessible to the poorly educated by means of several abridgments pub-lished in both Hebrew and Yiddish. The most popular Yiddish one was reprinted more than 40 times. Abridgments left out the theory and kept in the practice. Common people did not need to understand the philosophy of the doctrine; they trusted the rabbis and intellectuals to do that. They needed to know the ramifications of the theory for everyday life: what prayer to say for a sick person, how to guarantee a safe birth, what mourning ritual to observe, how to arrange one's estate prior to death, what the proper meditation was to intone before per-forming a particular mitzvah—in short, what the Kabbalah had to add to every halakhic category that appears in the *Shulḥan Arukh*.[40] People wanted to feel that they were doing the right thing in accordance with the most authoritative (i.e., kabbalistic) approach to Judaism.

They also believed that, as the key to divine secrets, Kabbalah could be applied in a practical manner to solve life's problems. It was the demand for so-called practical Kabbalah that underlay the seventeenth- and eighteenth-century pro-liferation of ba'alei shem. These Jewish shamans used practical Kabbalah to es-tablish contact with the divine spheres and affect the course of life here on earth. Ba'alei shem were specialists in magical defense, knowing how to wield kabbalis-tic knowledge and rituals to protect people from the machinations of the demons who lurked everywhere. Whether it was healing disease, exorcising dyb-buks, inducing fertility, guaranteeing material success, or preventing stillbirth, ba'alei shem offered men and women a means for dealing with the exigencies of life.

For example, Hillel Ba'al Shem, who traveled around communities in Volhy-nia and Poland in the 1730s and 1740s, detailed the various names of God (and even illustrations of supernatural beings) that must be written into different types of amulets in order to gain protection in dangerous situations, such as sickness, birth, or travel. In a different vein, Hillel offered the following means of dealing with epilepsy: the person with the problem should take a mixture of cer-tain herbs "and smoke it all together until the smoke goes into his mouth and nose and into his entire body. In this way we weaken the alien powers and all the demons; and the magical spells and evil spirits and the forces of defilement are made to flee and driven away from a person's body." With regard to love, his ad-vice to a woman seeking to gain a certain man's affections was: "If you wash your breasts in wine and give it to him to drink, he will love you with a great love." To a man: "If you smear your genitals with goose or wolf bile mixed with oil and have relations with the woman, she will love you."[41] The Ba'al Shem Tov (Israel ben Eliezer), the putative founder of Hasidism, went beyond helping individuals, employing his connections with the divine to try to avert or attenuate plagues and persecutions facing the Jewish community as a whole. This was apparently one of the features of his activity that singled him out as a ba'al shem par excellence.[42]

Ba'alei shem were either itinerants like Hillel or they settled in one town, as the Ba'al Shem Tov did in Międzybóż in Podolia, and people spent a considerable amount of time consulting them and following their instructions in an attempt to keep life on an even keel. In *Shir ha-Ma'alot le-David*, David Darshan, ostensibly a preacher, gave sample amulet inscriptions (*kameot*) that he had written as a further qualification for being granted a position in a community. His easy mixing of homiletics and magic and his presumption that expertise in practical Kabbalah was a recommendation for public employment are indications of how much a part of normal life Kabbalah and the magical theurgy it entailed had become. In the yeshivot, the rabbis were integrating kabbalistic considerations into their textual interpretations. In synagogues, marketplaces, and homes, ordinary people were integrating Kabbalah not only into their prayers and ceremonial observances but also into their dealings with other people and with the forces of nature and the Divine. Life was lived in a kabbalistic idiom.

GENDER DISTINCTIONS

In consonance with traditional Jewish culture, gender distinctions were omnipresent in the culture of the Polish Jews. Each sex had a sphere in which it was dominant: men were in charge of the public arena, both the synagogue and the communal institutions, and women managed the home and family life. Both appeared in the marketplace but, taking the family as the typical economic unit, usually the husband was the senior partner and the wife the junior one. For example, if the family leased a tavern, the woman would be primarily responsible for preparing the food and sleeping quarters and serving the customers, while her husband would handle the supplies and finances. Perhaps they would supplement their income with side occupations such as petty moneylending, typically a woman's responsibility, and some kind of mercantile activity, usually conducted by a man. If the couple were storekeepers, it was common for the wife to manage the store in the marketplace while the husband secured credit and went on buying trips. If he were a tradesman, a baker or a tailor, for example, his wife was often his chief assistant without benefit of title.

The overall cultural goal was for people of both sexes to subscribe to the same beliefs and values, to understand and practice the basic halakhic obligations incumbent on all Jews, and to perpetuate these in the family setting. One of the consequences of the spread of printing was the creation of new tools to enable both men and women to arrive at this goal, albeit via different paths. For women, especially, the religious library, largely produced in Poland and fully available there, signified a new sense among communal leaders of the importance of cultivating female participation in religious life, and it signified their concerted effort to do so.

Different tools for religious expression were placed at the disposal of men and women, respectively. A boy went to a ḥeder, where the curriculum prepared him to participate in the public religious life of the community. Literacy in Hebrew enabled him to take an active part in worship services, follow the Torah reading, understand learned discourse, and perhaps belong to a study group. If he continued on to yeshivah study, he might gain the facility for independent study of rabbinic texts. His basic religious books were the *Siddur* (prayer book), *Ḥumash* (Pentateuch) with Rashi's commentary, Mishnah, Talmud, and, from the late sixteenth century on, the various Kabbalah-based manuals of devotional practices, alluded to in the previous section of this chapter.[43]

For a girl, the basic religious vehicle was Yiddish. She learned to read through informal instruction by a family member, the efforts of a private tutor, or, on occasion, short-term enrollment in a ḥeder—just long enough for her to master phonetic Hebrew reading that she could apply to the already familiar Yiddish language, written in Hebrew characters. Women (and uneducated men) could concentrate on the message of the Bible thanks to the Bible-inspired printed Yiddish books that began to appear in the sixteenth century.

The very first of these, *Mirkeves ha-Mishne* (Cracow, 1534), was a dictionary and concordance of the Bible. There were also translations and epic poems, like the *Melokhim Bukh* (Augsburg, 1543) and *Shmuel Bukh* (Augsburg, 1544), that retold biblical stories in a contemporary language and style. Other books purported to be translations but were actually reworkings of the biblical text with midrashic interpretations, legends, and explanations woven into the narrative. The most famous of these, *Tzeno u-Reno* (Lublin, before 1622), was specifically aimed at women. It is one of the Jewish bestsellers of all time, having gone through more than 200 editions from its initial publication, around the turn of the seventeenth century, through the twentieth.[44]

In addition, books like *Azhoras Noshim* (Cracow, 1535), *Seder Noshim* (Cracow, 1541), and *Seder Mitzvos Noshim* (Cracow, 1577) were devoted to analysis and explication of commandments (*mitzvot*) especially incumbent upon women. Morality anthologies and manuals, such as the *Brantspiegel* (Cracow, 1596) and

Menekes Rivka (Prague, 1609), contained moral admonitions, instructions for daily conduct, and illustrative didactic anecdotes. The collections of prayers called *tehines* contained occasional prayers to be said at times of religious significance. Pious story anthologies like the *Mayseh Bukh* (Basel, 1602) provided entertainment with a message.[45]

These two corpora, the Hebrew one written exclusively by men and the Yiddish one primarily by them, were calculated to convey to those who studied them fundamentally similar religious knowledge and values. A male who learned Ḥumash with Rashi and a female who read the *Tzeno u-Reno* would both be familiar with the rabbinic interpretation of Scripture that formed the foundation of the Jewish religion. The famous dicta of *Pirkei Avot,* learned by males directly from the text, were translated and transmitted to females in the Yiddish books. The *Mayseh Bukh* included many of the famous rabbinic tales. The *Brantspiegel,* an encyclopedic handbook aimed to guide Jewish women's thought and action in daily life and through the seasons of the year, presented much halakhically derived material. Some tehines contained passages, based on the *Zohar* and other classic kabbalistic works, that were adapted from the Yiddish paraphrases of kabbalistic sources.[46]

The texts aimed at women, and popular among them, display a virtually complete internalization of the fundamentals of religious faith and categories, including those that are male-oriented. Women's prayers display a highly developed concept of a personal, immanent God who is accessible and merciful. Judging from women's liturgy and religious literature, they were familiar with biblical cosmogony and cosmology. Women understood the Jewish system of divine reward and punishment and the connection between proper ritual observance and Redemption. Morality books addressed to women urged them to find vicarious fulfillment by supporting the religious activities of their husbands and sons.

If, to the conceptual knowledge that could be gained from books, we add the practical knowledge of ritual observance—such as *kashrut,* the Sabbath, and holidays—that was learned mostly by example or through oral instruction, we can assert that Polish-Jewish women and men in the sixteenth through eighteenth centuries started off with a common body of knowledge, commitments, and practices. They were members of the same religion, willing to accept the same basic obligations and believing in the same theology.

However, as they acquired their religious edification differently, they also expressed their religious commitment differently. Take prayer. Men prayed mainly in public as part of a thrice-daily quorum in the synagogue, according to a fixed liturgy, composed by anonymous ancient authors, with variety in the service governed by a predetermined ritual calendar. The whole point was to pray as one's fathers had, to perpetuate the liturgical tradition. Changing the formula of the prayers would disqualify them, and even the introduction of cantorial melodies that necessitated the repetition of certain words could be an issue of controversy.

Women, however, typically attended the synagogue only on the Sabbath and holidays. Mostly they prayed individually at home, in the ritual bath (*mikveh*), or at the cemetery. Even when they did come to the synagogue, women did not usually join in the Hebrew liturgy with the men. They responded aloud to prayers led by a female leader (*zogerke*) or recited newly composed, individual prayers in Yiddish, the teḥines. Originally popular in western Ashkenaz and later also published in Poland, collections of teḥines began appearing in the late sixteenth century. Teḥines of Polish origin, some of them written by women, date from the eighteenth century. These tend to concentrate on women's ritual obligations and customs (the three female mitzvot: *ḥallah,* separating a portion of baking dough; *hadlakah,* Sabbath and festival candle-lighting; and *niddah,* ritual purification after menstruation), on such female customs as *kneytlakh legn* (measuring graves with candlewick), and on events in the synagogue and the liturgical calendar. Central to Polish teḥines were the themes of penitence and redemption, especially in connection with the penitential season preceding the High Holy Days in the autumn.[47]

Teḥines offered women a means of religious expression that paralleled men's but was much more directly reflective of eighteenth-century beliefs and women's particular consciousness and concerns than were the texts of the classical prayers said primarily by men. Although they contain no overt feminist protest against the male monopoly of the prestigious roles in Judaism (priest, prophet, sage), teḥines do at times imagine women in more powerful and honored roles than was their experience in real life. Thus, while retaining the custom of supplicating God in the name of the patriarchs Abraham, Isaac, and Jacob, the teḥines often add the matriarchs Sarah, Rebekah, Rachel, and Leah and beseech them to play an active role in turning God's favorable attention to the supplicant. Some teḥines make comparisons between the woman engaged in the feminine religious activities of ḥallah and hadlakah and the high priest offering sacrifices or lighting the Temple menorah.[48] For example, the very popular cycle of prayers called *Teḥine Shloyshe She'orim* contains passages like the following:

[From teḥine to be said when lighting Sabbath candles:]
Master of the Universe, may the mitzvah of my lighting candles be accepted as equivalent to the mitzvah of the High Priest when he lit the candles in the pre-

cious Temple. As his observance was accepted so may mine be accepted. "Your words are a candle at my feet and a light for my path" means that Your words are a candle at my feet so that all my children may walk in God's path, and may the mitzvah of my candlelighting be accepted so that my children's eyes may be illumined by the precious holy Torah.

May the merit of the beloved Sabbath lights protect me, just as the beloved Sabbath protected Adam and kept him from premature death. So may we merit, by lighting the candles, to protect our children, that they may be enlightened by the study of Torah, and may their planets shine in the heavens so that they may be able to earn a decent living for their wives and children.

[From teḥine to be said when preparing candles for Yom Kippur:]
Through the merit of preparing a wick for the sake of our mother Rachel, and because of her merit, may You fulfill the verse "And the children will return to their borders," which means, through the merit of Rachel, God—praised be He—will return us to our land. Amen.

[From teḥine for the monthly new moon:]
Upon me, so-and-so, rests the responsibility to praise Your Holy Name with fear and awe, so that I may benefit from Your mercy. I am filled with sins, with our many sins, and You are called the Lord of Mercy and You teach us the way of penitence, for You are compassionate and You have taught us the way of repentance. So I, so-and-so, come before Your venerable Name to pray for myself and my husband and children. . . . May this be a favorable time before the throne of Your glory for You to forgive our sins as You promised Moses our Teacher at that holy moment: "I have forgiven as you requested." Forgive our sins as we confess them and receive our prayers as You received the prayer of Hannah when she said: "I am a woman bitter of soul. A woman of bitter spirit am I." . . .

May God grant that in our days and in the days of our children, we may live to see the Temple built and the High Priest perform the service there.

May I, so-and-so, and all the righteous women live to pray there through the merit of our matriarchs Sarah, Rebekah, Rachel, and Leah.[49]

The difference between the male and female religious spheres is also expressed in the key domain of study, a primary activity. Men usually studied in a public bet midrash in the company of peers. Their Hebrew or Aramaic study texts, many composed centuries earlier, required a hefty investment of time and effort just to be read with comprehension. The women's Yiddish texts posed no such linguistic problem; women could study them on their own and often read them aloud to their children on Saturday afternoons. These texts provided a good foundation for the knowledge and practice of Judaism, but women's study, which consisted only of Yiddish reading, was not considered to be study at all; it was an act of piety, akin to prayer. In the social configuration of the time, men studied, women prayed. This, reciprocally, both expressed and perpetuated men's greater social prestige.

A further expression of the difference between male and female religious life is the ideal image of the sexes proffered by prescriptive texts and eulogies. A man was supposed to be a tireless scholar, or at least an honest—and successful—businessman, and, in either case, a rigorous performer of the commandments. A woman was expected to live up to the 20 or so ideal characteristics sketched out in chapter 31 of the Book of Proverbs, known by its opening words, *Eishet Ḥayil* (A Woman of Valor). In the period under discussion, however, several of these traits were typically emphasized. The ideal woman was to be clever, wise, energetic, of good family pedigree (meaning she was related to scholars), beautiful, modest, pious, and charitable. The last attribute probably reflected the charity customs of the time, which consisted primarily of providing meals for poor people who were sent to one's home by communal officials.

A sense of the differences in religious life for men and women can be gleaned from some autobiographical writings dating from the late eighteenth century. The Polish-Jewish wine merchant Ber of Bolechów (1723–1805) described his religious behavior when he was in his early twenties thus: "[I] conducted myself as a God-fearing man, attending every morning and evening the service of the synagogue and praying with great devotion. I was deeply engaged in studying the Bible, the Mishnah, the *Gemara,* and the laws of the *Shulḥan Arukh,* besides other, ethical works."[50]

Compare this brief profile, with its emphasis on public ritual and the study of canonical texts, to what another eighteenth-century figure, Elijah ben Solomon Zalman, the Gaon of Vilna, mandated for his daughters in a letter to his wife. From his words, it is clear that the ideal female would concentrate on her character and morals, with a minimum concern for the classic study texts, and would prefer private rather than public ritual behavior. He wrote:

> I also make an especial and emphatic request that you train your daughters to the avoidance of objurgations, oaths, lies, or contention. Let their whole conversation be conducted in peace, love, affability, and gentleness. I possess many moral books with Yiddish [translations]; let them read these regularly; above all on the Sabbath—the holy of holies—they should occupy themselves with

these ethical books exclusively. For a curse, an oath, or a lie, strike them; show no softness in the matter. . . . [U]se your utmost rigor in their moral training, and may Heaven help you to success! So with other matters as the avoidance of slander and gossip; the regular recital of grace before and after meals, the reading of the Shema, all with true devotion. The fundamental rule, however, is that they not gad about in the streets, but incline their ear to your words and honor you and my mother and all their elders. Urge them to obey all that is written in the moral books. . . .

It is also better for your daughter not to go to synagogue for there she would see garments of embroidery and similar finery. She would grow envious and speak of it at home, and out of this would come scandal and other ills. Let her seek her glory in her home, cleaving ever to discipline, and showing no jealousy for worldly gauds, vain and delusive as they are.[51]

While the Vilna Gaon's instructions to his wife project a clear ideal image of women's proper religious tasks, there was a gap between this and what actual, normatively religious women practiced and believed. For example, though the Gaon railed against the potentially negative effects of synagogue attendance, it is obvious that women did go to the synagogue. Few shared his jaundiced view, though others did point out the possible pitfalls. Similarly, the Gaon's horror at the prospect of his daughters strolling in the street could not be a guide for the many women who spent their days pursuing their family's livelihood in the marketplace.

Beyond the sphere of ritual behavior, a woman was expected to fulfill a religious role analogous to her social function and reflecting her status in society— that is, woman as religious facilitator. As succinctly put by Isserles, the sixteenth-century Polish halakhic authority, "a woman is not obligated to teach her son Torah, but in any case if she helps her son or her husband study Torah she gets part of their reward."[52] This ideal was put into practice by women like Miriam Ashkenazi, daughter of the famous Ḥakham Tzvi Ashkenazi, sister to Rabbi Jacob Emden, and wife of Rabbi Aryeh Leib ben Shaul. Emden, writing in the mid-eighteenth century, noted that his brother-in-law could concentrate on his studies because "he had a wife [Miriam] who was very good in the precious attributes of love, morality, fear of heaven, and modesty. She was a great, pious person with strong love for her husband, with submission and modesty; in addition to her beauty and great pleasantness and cleverness in woman's work, in managing the household in cleanliness."[53] Women were expected quietly to create the atmosphere that would enable their menfolk to reach the religious summit.

In the early modern period, however, men realized that women ought not to be relegated to a facilitating role and taken for granted. There was at least tacit recognition that, in cultural terms, women needed to be actively nurtured and reinforced. The Yiddish religious literary genres mentioned earlier that were aimed, in the words of the *Brantspiegel,* at "women, and men who are like women"—that is, the unlearned nonelites—all flourished beginning in the sixteenth century. The production of this literature was an admission by the scholarly class (still the dominant, though no longer exclusive, authors) that, religiously speaking, women and other nonelites should not be dismissed lightly. Their spiritual concerns and religious life were significant and it was important that they be informed; otherwise there was a risk that they would be led astray by new, radical ideas and social movements that arose among Jews as well as Christians (for example, Sabbatianism and Frankism) in Reformation and post-Reformation Europe. The gap between the educated elite and the common people must not grow too big.

The profound shift in attitudes implied by the appearance of Yiddish religious literature was captured by the printer of the Yiddish translation and midrashic paraphrase of the Book of Esther, *Di Lange Megilla* (Cracow, 1589). This man, Isaac ben Aaron of Prostitz, noted that "the way of the world is that women especially are considered nothing at all and regarded as good for nothing. Whether they are young or old they are done much injustice and violence. This is contrary to God's will that one should mock and play with his creation." Thus, in contrast to the conventional approach, Isaac declared that "Women are also obligated to learn. This includes the Pentateuch and the 24 [books of the Bible], and all of the laws of ritual purity and what is prohibited and what is permitted—just like the men."[54] It is no accident, then, that most of these books in Yiddish were addressed to women, either exclusively or in tandem with nonlearned men. They represented a new consciousness of the cultural status of women. Women's particular mitzvot were newly codified, analyzed, and explicated.

Conversely, in the early modern period it seems that stereotypes of women's sins developed as well. As the teḥine author Sarah bas Tovim put it: "I, the woman Sore [= Sarah], beseech the young women not to converse in the beloved holy shul, for it is a great sin."[55] As we have seen, the Gaon of Vilna also took a dim view of purported female talking and ostentatious sartorial display in the synagogue. So did the eighteenth-century teḥine author Leah Horowitz, who observed that "women are talkative, gabbing in the synagogue on the Sabbath . . . and talk in the synagogue makes women jealous of each other. . . . When she comes home she argues with her husband about finery, for she says, 'In the synagogue I should be like the woman dressed in attractive clothes.'"[56]

As we have seen, teḥines (some of which may originally have been part of an oral tradition) were also codified and routinized beginning in the late sixteenth century. The advent of teḥine books marks the institutionalization of women's prayer. Even the editing and publication of the didactic story collections indicated a new awareness of women's cultural importance. The stories they read should be "religiously correct" and dovetail with the messages preached by the elite texts and their propagators. Overall, the appearance of new Yiddish religious genres in the early modern period meant that the role of women was a prominent item on the Jewish cultural agenda. They had to be properly prepared to take their place in that culture.

This new emphasis on the potential contribution of women apparently also had a practical effect. There is at least a hint that the male stereotype of women as religious ignoramuses began to change as the opportunities grew for women to acquire knowledge. In the mid-sixteenth century, Isserles could note that women who eat with men must listen in to the ritual introduction to the grace after meals "even though they don't understand"; but about a century later, Rabbi Abraham Gombiner, citing an earlier source, insisted that "most women understand a little."[57] Moreover, there are some signs that women were beginning to enter the public religious field. Isserles, for example, pointed out that a series of medieval restrictions on menstruating women, excluding them from the synagogue and public worship, were not in accord with the letter of the halakhah. He also legitimized at least partial circumvention of these restrictions, thus making it easier for women to attend synagogue regularly—a practice that was apparently gaining popularity.[58]

Physically, beginning in the late sixteenth century in Ashkenaz and spreading to Poland, synagogues began to be remodeled and new ones constructed with women's sections (*ezrat nashim*) that were an integral part of the building. Thus, the women were brought into the synagogue rather than being excluded or relegated to adjacent annexes, cellars, or temporary designated areas.[59] This gave them a place, albeit a secondary one, within the synagogue itself and made their attendance there normative. It was an important early milestone in a subsequent four-centuries-long trend for women to become more and more part of synagogue and public ritual life. The emphasis of some eighteenth-century Polish teḥines on aspects of the synagogue service and the liturgical calendar reflects more female prayer in the synagogue setting and is another sign of women's— very gradual—integration into the public domain.

The idea that women should be included in the main arena of Jewish religious life reached a new level in mid-eighteenth-century Poland when Leah Horowitz wrote the Hebrew introduction to her prayer compilation, *Teḥine Imohos*. She believed that the well-known rabbinic maxim—that the crown of the priesthood belonged to Aaron and the crown of kingship belonged to David but the crown of Torah was obtainable by anyone—applied to women as well as men. Her own Talmud study and participation in halakhic dialectic was, in her opinion, a means of "bringing merit to the many." Moreover, all women had the power to offer redemptive prayer, but to do so they must attend the synagogue for the three daily services. Leah offered a twist on the conventional notion that a woman's relationship to Torah study should be as facilitator. The essence of a woman's duty in this regard was not passive support but, she held, was actively to prevent her husband and sons from neglecting their obligations.[60] Although Leah's was a lone and lonely voice, it was a harbinger of developments in the religious life of Jewish women over the next two centuries.

A NEW TRADITION

By the eighteenth century, Polish-Jewish culture had undergone a significant transformation from the medieval Ashkenazic culture in which it originated. The canon of sacred books to be studied had been expanded. There were new genres and levels of books and a corresponding variety in the types of people who studied or read them. In particular, new provisions were made for including women in the circle of the religiously informed and involved. The emphasis of the yeshivah curriculum had shifted from determining the law to analyzing the text. There were now new tools for deciding halakhah, and life was suffused with the beliefs and practices of Kabbalah.

The popularity of Kabbalah partly explains the development of a new type of Hasidism by the late eighteenth century. As mentioned above, many seventeenth- and eighteenth-century communities hosted conventicles of ascetic, mystical pietists. The members of these elitist groups were called Hasidim (lit.: beloved [of God]), denoting their special relationship with things holy and spiritual. In the course of the eighteenth century, some of the leaders of these groups made significant changes in their beliefs, practices, and organization. A new type of Hasidism arose that eventually developed into a mass religious and social movement that caught the imagination and commanded the loyalty of a large proportion of Polish Jewry.

The man usually considered to be the founder of the new Hasidism, the Ba'al Shem Tov, lived in the town of Międzybóż, where he headed a small group of mystical virtuosos. He was a charismatic figure whose attraction and authority derived from his confident and intelligent personality, success at healing, and expertise in mystical communication with the Divine—not from prodigious talmudic erudition. He innovated by insisting that communion with God (de-

vekut) could be achieved without asceticism and without mastery of the content of dense Talmud texts. The path to devekut, according to him, included the spiritualizing of Torah study through mystical contemplation of the letters of the texts, and the achieving of ecstasy in prayer. In contrast to the rabbis and mystics of his day, he provided an example of religious leadership that was not only aloft in the world of the spirit but also down-to-earth, involved in mundane problems. He took responsibility for both the physical and the spiritual needs of the members of his extended family and household, including grandchildren, stepson, in-laws, and some nonrelatives: the mystics in his intimate group as well as disciples who lived elsewhere and with whom he had only sporadic contact. Beyond his duty to them, the Ba'al Shem Tov felt responsible for the fate of all the Jewish people, and much of his communication with the Divine was aimed at averting collective disasters such as persecution and plague. Although he did not establish any new institutions, his ideas and behavior set precedents that his disciples and others developed into the new Hasidic movement after his death.[61]

The early stages in the crystallization of this movement are typified by the activities of one of the Ba'al Shem Tov's associates, Rabbi Dov Ber, the maggid of Mezhirech (d. 1772). Unlike the Ba'al Shem Tov, Dov Ber was an accomplished talmudist, but he was also a maggid, a popular preacher, involved with the life of the community. Dov Ber settled in the Volynian town of Mezhirech in the 1760s and established a group of new-style Hasidim. He made a concerted effort to attract followers to his court, where he preached the new doctrines and used his virtuosity in Torah to address people's spiritual needs. The philosopher and memoirist Salomon Maimon—who arrived in Mezhirech in the late 1760s, intrigued by emissaries whom Dov Ber had sent out to spread the word of his new approach—described how the latter connected with potential Hasidim:

[O]n Sabbath I went to th[e] solemn meal, and there found a large number of respectable men who had gathered together from various quarters. At length the great man appeared, his awe-inspiring figure clothed in white satin. Even his shoes and snuff-box were white, this being among the kabbalists the color of grace. He greeted each newcomer with "Shalom." We sat down to table and during the meal a solemn silence reigned. After the meal was over, the superior struck up a solemn inspiring melody, held his hand for some time upon his brow, and then began to call out, "Z. of H., M. of R., S.M. of N." and so on. Each newcomer was thus called by his own name and the name of his residence, which excited no little astonishment. Each as he was called recited some verse of the Holy Scriptures. Thereupon the superior began to deliver a sermon for which the verses recited served as a text, so that although they were

disconnected verses taken from different parts of Scripture they were combined with as much skill as if they had formed a single whole. What was still
more extraordinary, every one of the newcomers believed that he discovered in
that part of the sermon which was founded on his verse something that had
special reference to the facts of his own spiritual life. At this we were of course
greatly astonished.[62]

As this passage demonstrates, Dov Ber's leadership was not limited to one geographic area. Attracting people—particularly Talmud students and established
householders—from far and wide, he evinced a deep concern for the identity
and needs of the individual. Torah, Kabbalah, and visual and aural devices (impressive appearance, silence, and music) were all utilized to pierce the veil of
worldliness and bring the Hasidim close to God. Dov Ber's followers were distinguished by their obedience and devotion to him and by their joyous singing and
dancing. Intensive Talmud study was neglected in favor of Kabbalah and ecstatic
prayer. They adopted kabbalistic customs such as the donning of white on the
Sabbath, the use of so-called polished knives to slaughter animals for consumption, and worship according to the Lurianic order of prayer, rather than the traditional Ashkenazic one.

In the 1770s and 1780s, similar Hasidic courts developed around leaders like
Aaron of Karlin, Elimelekh of Lyzhansk, Levi-Yitzḥak of Berdichev, Menaḥem
Mendel of Vitebsk, Abraham of Kalisk, Shneur Zalman of Ladi, Naḥum of Cher-
nobyl, and Zusya of Annapol. Each developed a regional following and a particular style of leading and teaching his disciples. All, however, propagated the
basic doctrines of Hasidism.[63]

The primary means of doing this was oral teaching; orality, rather than textu-
ality, was a hallmark of Hasidism. However, certain Hasidic texts circulated in
manuscript and in published form in the last two decades of the eighteenth century. Jacob Joseph of Polonne, a disciple of the Ba'al Shem Tov, published three
books of biblical homiletics: *Toldot Ya'akov Yosef* (Koretz, 1780), *Ben Porat Yosef*
(Koretz, 1781), and *Tzofnat Pa'ane'ah* (Koretz, 1782). A fourth book by him, *Ke-
tonet Passim*, was not published until 1866. Other important publications included *Noam Elimelekh* (Lvov, 1787) by Elimelekh of Lyzhansk; *Maggid Devarav
le-Ya'akov* (Koretz, 1781) and *Zava'at ha-Rivash* (Ostrog, 1793), based on the
teachings of Dov Ber; and *Keter Shem Tov* (n.p., 1794–95), a digest of the Ba'al
Shem Tov's teachings as found in the books of Jacob Joseph and elsewhere. From
books such as these, it is possible to understand the essence of early Hasidism.

The early Hasidic teachers emphasized two main doctrines. The first is encapsulated in the oft-repeated slogan that combines the biblical verse "The
whole earth is full of His glory" (Isaiah 6:3) and a saying of the *Zohar:* "There is

no place empty of Him" ("*Melo kol ha'aretz kevodo ve-let atar panui minei*"). God is immanent in everything in creation. Everything reflects the divine and expresses the divine. Everything can serve as a path to devekut. There is nothing profane; all is holy. The fact that many things appear divorced from holiness is only apparent. The task of the Hasid is to discover the divine root of every object and every act and thereby turn them into vehicles of communion. This can be accomplished through "nullification of the existent" (*bitul ha-yesh*) or "stripping away materiality" (*hafshatat ha-gashmiyut*)—viewing and understanding everything from the perspective of its connection to God, rather than from its physical appearance. Thus, not only study and prayer are religious acts but also commerce, artisanship, eating, and sex; all human behavior has the potential to reveal God to His people, and each person can aspire to that revelation.[64]

Crossing the divide between the corporeal and the spiritual is not easy; for many it is virtually impossible. This is where the second basic doctrine is crucial: the teaching of the *tzadik*. The tzadik was the leader of each Hasidic group. Also referred to as "Rebbe" or "Admor" (an acronym for the Hebrew phrase "Our master, teacher, and rabbi"), his role was to bring the individual Hasid to devekut. If the Hasid could not so easily cleave to God, he could cleave to his tzadik. By obeying him in all things, thirstily imbibing his teachings, concretizing his relationship to the tzadik by supporting him materially, and adopting his mode of dress and other customs, the Hasid expected to be carried along when the tzadik made contact with God. Since the holy must be discovered in all aspects of life, the tzadik must be involved in every facet of the life of his people. He must take responsibility for them both on earth and in heaven and ensure that each and every one will achieve his spiritual potential.[65]

The emergence of these Hasidic institutions and doctrines and the increasing loyalty of a significant number of people to various tzadikim elicited opposition to the new movement. The Vilna Gaon, Elijah ben Solomon Zalman, is famous as one of the greatest rabbinic scholars in history. He was also an old-style, mystical-ascetic Hasid. He lived in an ivory tower of Talmud study, with no defined duties, supported by a stipend from the Vilna community. He was largely uninvolved with the rank-and-file members of the community, teaching only an elite circle of advanced scholars. His leadership was exerted through his overpowering mastery of all of rabbinic literature, as expressed through his teaching and writings, and his towering example of total devotion to learning and strict observance of the law. The only way to come closer to him was to become more like him. His style of communion with God was necessarily limited to the few who could devote themselves, mind and heart, to full-time, sophisticated study of the Torah.[66]

Early in 1772, the Gaon became aware of the teachings and practices of the new Hasidism. He considered its appeal to the uninitiated as a vulgar perversion of the true mystical-ascetic Hasidism. He and others who agreed with him attempted to suppress the new movement with bans against its practices and persecution of its leaders. Eventually these opponents, the Mitnagdim, developed new institutions and doctrines of their own that competed with those of Hasidism. The conflict between Hasidism and Mitnagdism emerging in the late eighteenth century was a harbinger of the dislocations that were to wrack Polish-Jewish culture from the end of the eighteenth century until the Shoah.[67]

Traditional Jewish culture operated on the foundation of a God-oriented universe in which all of a person's deeds were done "for the sake of Heaven." In Poland-Lithuania in the early modern period, the means for individuals to prepare themselves to live in this spirit were greatly enhanced. This multicultural country offered the Jews sufficient toleration and freedom to allow for the emergence of new cultural ideas and forms directed toward the fulfillment of their divinely mandated obligations. With a new (and newly accessible) library, more people in Jewish society could feel closer to God and be confident that, personally, they had an intelligent grasp of what God demanded of them. With the popularized tools of Kabbalah, more people had the means to religiously calibrate their every action. Armed with their culture, Jews could be confident that life had divine meaning; they could face its different aspects—whether mundane, tragic, or triumphant—secure in the belief that they had the power to discern God's purpose. Ironically, however, where developments in the early modern period had fostered the rooting and spread of traditional culture throughout Jewish society, the ethos of modernity that was to explode over East European Jewry in the nineteenth century shook this self-confident culture, threatening it with obsolescence.

NOTES

1. L. Wolf, ed., *Menasseh ben Israel's Mission to Oliver Cromwell* (n.p., 1901), 87. This characterization is not accurate in all details: Jewish courts did not have official jurisdiction in criminal matters, though sometimes they did deal with criminal cases; and the number of Jewish victims of the Chmielnicki Uprising in 1648–49 ("the Cosaques in the late warres") was probably less than a quarter of what Menasseh posited.

2. The quote appears in *Volumina Legum* (St. Petersburg-Cracow-Peznari, 1859–1952), II:124; on the Polish-Lithuanian Commonwealth and its institutions, see J. Tazbir, *A State Without Stakes* (Warsaw, 1973), and J. K. Federowicz, *A Republic of Nobles* (Cambridge, Engl., 1982).

3. On the Polish Church and the Jews, see J. Goldberg, "Poles and Jews in the 17th and 18th Centuries: Acceptance or Rejection," *Jahrbücher für Geschichte Osteuropas* 22 (1974): 252–57; J. Kalik, "The Catholic Church and the Jews in the Polish-Lithuanian Commonwealth in the 17–18th Centuries" (Hebrew), (Ph.D. diss., Hebrew University, Jerusalem, 1998).

4. M. Steinberg, *Żydzi w Jarosławiu* (Jarosław, 1933), 6–7, translated into Hebrew in S. A. Cygielman, *Yehudei Polin Ve-Lita Ad Shenat Tah (1648)* (Jerusalem, 1991), 216–17.

5. J. Goldberg, "The Privileges Granted to Jewish Communities of the Polish Commonwealth as a Stabilizing Factor in Jewish Support," in C. Abramsky et al., eds., *The Jews in Poland* (Oxford, 1986), 31–54.

6. Cygielman, *Yehudei Polin,* 193–223; J. Goldberg, "*De non tolerandis Iudaeis:* On the Introduction of Anti-Jewish Laws in Polish Towns and the Struggles Against Them," in S. Yeivin, ed., *Studies in Jewish History: Presented to Professor Raphael Mahler on His Seventy-fifth Birthday* (Merhavia, 1974), 39–52.

7. The quote is from *Divrei David* (1689; rpt. Jerusalem, 1978), on Deuteronomy 7:22, p. 525 (my translation). On the persecution of Jews in Poland, see B. D. Weinryb, *The Jews of Poland* (Philadelphia, 1972), 152–53; H. Węgrzynek, "*Czarna legenda Żydów*": *Procesy o rzekome mordy rytualne w dawnej Polsce* (Warsaw, 1995); and Z. Guldon and J. Wijacka, "The Accusation of Ritual Murder in Poland, 1500–1800," *Polin* 10 (1997): 99–140.

8. G. D. Hundert, *The Jews in a Polish Private Town: The Case of Opatów in the Eighteenth Century* (Baltimore, Md., 1992), 39; M. J. Rosman, "Jewish Perceptions of Insecurity and Powerlessness in 16th–18th Century Poland," *Polin* 1 (1986): 19–27; Rosman, "A Minority Views the Majority: Jewish Attitudes Towards the Polish-Lithuanian Commonwealth and Interaction with Poles," *Polin* 4 (1989): 31–41 (reprinted in A. Polonsky, ed., *From Shtetl to Socialism: Studies from Polin* [London, 1993], 39–49).

9. Yitzhak ben Moshe of Vienna, *Sefer Or Zaru'a,* part 1 (Zhitomir, 1862), 113; Weinryb, *The Jews of Poland,* 24.

10. M. Rosman, "The Image of Poland as a Center of Torah Learning After the 1648 Persecutions" (Hebrew), *Zion* 51 (1986): 439–47; M. Rosman, *Polin: Perakim be-Toledot Yehudei Mizrah Eiropah ve-Tarbutum,* vols. 1–2 (Tel Aviv, 1991), 72.

11. Eliezer Ashkenazi, *Ma'ase Hashem,* (Venice, 1583), fol. 56v, quoted in H. H. Ben-Sasson, "The Reformation in Contemporary Jewish Eyes," *Proceedings of the Israel Academy of Sciences and Humanities* 4 (1969–70): 258–59.

12. N. Hannover, *Abyss of Despair,* trans. and ed. A. Mesch (1950; rpt. New Brunswick, N.J., 1983), 27 (translation slightly modified). The book was originally published in Hebrew as *Yeven Metzulah* (Venice, 1653).

13. B. Birkenthal, *The Memoirs of Ber of Bolechow,* trans. and ed. M. Vishnitzer (1922; rpt. New York, 1973), 124; see Exodus 18:21.

14. C. Shmeruk, *The Esterke Story in Yiddish and Polish Literature* (Jerusalem, 1985); B. D. Weinryb, *The Beginnings of East European Jewry in Legend and Historiography* (Leiden,

1962), 1–11; G. Karpeles, "A Jewish King in Poland," in his *Jewish Literature and Other Essays* (Philadelphia, 1895), 272–92; A. J. Heschel, *The Circle of the Baal Shem Tov*, trans. and ed. S. Dresner (Chicago, 1985), 22.

15. T. Kohn, *Ma'ase Tuvia* (Venice, 1707), 110d (my translation).

16. The quote is from D. Ben-Amos and J. Mintz, trans. and eds., *Shivhei ha-Besht: In Praise of the Ba'al Shem Tov* (Bloomington, Ind., 1970), 149. See also M. Rosman, *Founder of Hasidism* (Berkeley, Calif., 1996), 17–26, 56–62, and O. Pritsak, "Ukraine as the Setting for the Emergence of Hasidism," in S. Almog et al., eds., *Israel and the Nations: Essays Presented in Honor of Shmuel Ettinger* (Jerusalem, 1987), lxxxi–lxxxii.

17. M. i K. Piechotkowie, *Bramy Nieba: Bóżnice drewniane* (Warsaw, 1996); T. Hubka, "Jewish Art and Architecture in the East European Context: The Gwoździec-Chodorów Group of Wooden Synagogues," *Polin* 10 (1997): 141–82.

18. E. L. Eisenstein, *The Printing Press as an Agent of Change* (Cambridge, Engl., 1980), and E. L. Eisenstein, *The Printing Revolution in Early Modern Europe* (Cambridge, Engl., 1983).

19. David Darshan, *"Shir ha-Ma'alot le-David" (Song of the Steps)* and *"Ktav Hitnazzelut l'Darshanim" (In Defense of Preachers)*, translation (with modifications) and annotation by Hayim Goren Perelmuter (Cincinnati, 1984), 138. See also E. Reiner, "Itinerant Ashkenazic Preachers in the Early Modern Period" (Hebrew), unpublished paper. I wish to offer my gratitude to Elḥanan Reiner for sharing his research and insights with me. As will be obvious to the reader, I am heavily indebted to his work, together with that of Jacob Elbaum and Zev Gries, in my discussion of rabbinic culture.

20. *Turei Zahav* (Lublin, 1646), intro., on *Shulḥan arukh* (my translation).

21. *Sefer Me'irat Einaim* (Prague, 1614), intro., on *Shulḥan arukh* (my translation).

22. For descriptions of the higher institutions of Jewish learning, see D. Assaf, *Olam ha-Torah be-Polin* (vols. 5–6 of *Polin* [Tel Aviv, 1990]); M. Breuer, "The rise of Pilpul and Hillukim in Ashkenazic Yeshivot" (Hebrew), in *Sefer zikaron le-Rabbi Ya'akov Yehiel Weinberg* (Jerusalem, 1970), 241–55; E. Reiner, "Wealth, Social Position and the Study of Torah: The Status of the Kloiz in Eastern European Jewish Society in the Early Modern Period" (Hebrew), *Zion* 58 (1993): 287–328; E. Reiner, "Changes in the Yeshivot of Poland and Ashkenaz in the 16th–17th Centuries and the Controversy over Pilpul" (Hebrew), in I. Bartal et al., eds., *Ke-Minhag Ashkenaz u-Polin: Sefer Yovel le-Chone Shmeruk* (Jerusalem, 1993), 9–80; E. Reiner, "The Ashkenazi Elite at the Beginning of the Modern Era: Manuscript Versus the Printed Book," *Polin* 10 (1997): 85–98; and E. Reiner, "The Attitude of Ashkenazi Society to the New Science in the Sixteenth Century," *Science in Context* 10 (1997): 589–603. For a summary of the important personalities, issues, and achievements of rabbinic culture in early modern Poland, see M. Shulvass, *Jewish Culture in Eastern Europe: The Classical Period* (New York, 1975).

23. D. Darshan, *Shir ha Ma'alot le David* (Cracow, 1571), intro., translation (with modifications) from the Perelmuter edition (see n. 19 above), 39–41.

24. Reiner, "The Ashkenazi Elite," 91.

25. J. Elbaum, *Petiḥut ve-Histagrut* (Jerusalem, 1990); Reiner, "The Attitude of Ashkenazi Society," esp. 600–601.

26. Rama (Moses Isserles), *Responsa* no. 6 (my translation). For all of the texts reflecting this dispute between the two rabbis, see A. Siev, *Shut ha-Rama* (Jerusalem, 1971), pp. 18–38, nos. 5–7.

27. Horowitz's polemic was published by P. Bloch, "The Controversy Over Maimonides' *Guide* in the Poznań Community in the Mid-16th Century" (German), *Monatsschrift für Geschichte und Wissenschaft des Judentums* 47 (1903): 153–69, 263–79, 346–56. The selection translated here is from Reiner, "The Attitude of Ashkenazi Society," 590 n. 7; in that work, Reiner was the first to recognize that what was in dispute was the content of the canon of study and not the subject of philosophy.

28. On the content and significance of the *Shulḥan Arukh,* see I. Twersky, "The *Shulḥan Áruk:* Enduring Code of Jewish Law," in J. Goldin, ed., *The Jewish Expression* (New York, 1970), 323–43 (originally appeared in *Judaism* 16 [1967]; the translated quote appears on p. 332).

29. Solomon Luria, *Yam Shel Shlomo,* vol. on *Ḥullin,* (Cracow, [1533–35]) second intro. (my translation).

30. Moses Isserles, *Mappa,* intro. in *Shulḥan Arukh,* (Cracow, 1579; rpt. Jerusalem, 1974).

31. Moses Isserles, *Torat ha-Hatat* (Cracow, 1569), intro.; this passage is translated in Reiner, "The Ashkenazi Elite," 94.

32. Ibid.

33. Reiner, "The Changes"; the quote from Gans appears on p. 48 (my translation).

34. Neki Kapaim, cited in Elbaum, *Petihut,* 151–52 and according to the index.

35. See, for example, F. A. Yates, *Giordano Bruno and the Hermetic Tradition* (Chicago, 1971); R. J. W. Evans, *Rudolf II and His World: A Study in Intellectual History, 1576–1612* (Oxford, 1973); and B. P. Copenhaver, *Symphorien Champier and the Reception of the Occultist Tradition in Renaissance France* (The Hague, 1978).

36. Berekhia Berakh, *Zera Berakh* (Cracow, 1662), part 2, intro.; quoted in Elbaum, *Petihut,* 217 (my translation).

37. Mordecai Yaffe, *Levushim* (Venice, 1620), intro.; quoted in Elbaum, *Petihut,* 215 (my translation).

38. Both quoted in Elbaum, *Petihut,* 218–19 (my translation); the *Sefer ha-Pardes* referred to is Moses Cordovero's *Pardes Rimmonim.*

39. Z. Gries, *Sifrut ha-Hanhagot* (Jerusalem, 1989), intro., chap. 2.

40. For discussion of the *Shelah,* see I. Zinberg, *A History of Jewish Literature* (Cincinnati, 1975), 6: 115–20; Gries, *Sifrut,* chap. 2.

41. Hillel Ba'al Shem detailed his remedies, incantations, inscriptions, exorcism, advice, criticism, and medicaments in his 300-page manuscript called *Sefer ha-Ḥeshek,* now in the Vernadsky Library, Kiev, Jewish Division, Or 178, and discovered there by Yohanan Petrovsky. The quotes are my translations from pp. 27a, 146a.

42. For a summary of the Ba'al Shem Tov's activities, see M. Rosman, *Founder of*

Hasidism (Berkeley, Calif., 1996), 173–86, and I. Etkes, *Ba'al Hashem* (Jerusalem, 2000), 266–74.

43. S. Stampfer, "Gender Differentiation and the Education of the Jewish Woman in Nineteenth-Century Eastern Europe," in Polonsky, ed., *From Shtetl to Socialism,* 187–211.

44. On early Yiddish Literature, see Zinberg, *A History of Jewish Literature,* vol. 7; C. Shmeruk, *Sifrut Yiddish: Perakim le-Toledoteha* (Tel Aviv, 1978), 9–71; and C. Shmeruk, *Sifrut Yiddish be-Polin* (Jerusalem, 1981), 11–116.

45. D. Roskies, "Yiddish Popular Literature and the Female Reader," *Journal of Popular Culture* 13 (1979): 852–58; A. Segal, "Yiddish Works on Women's Commandments in the Six- teenth Century," in *Studies in Yiddish Literature and Folklore* (Jerusalem, 1986), 37–59; Shmeruk, *Polin,* 11–74, 147–64; C. Turniansky, "On Old Yiddish Biblical Epics," *International Folklore Review* 8 (1991): 26–33; Zinberg, *A History of Jewish Literature,* vol. 7. On women's prayers, see C. Weissler, *Voices of the Matriarchs* (Boston, 1998).

46. Stampfer, "Gender Differentiation," 194–95; Weissler, *Voices,* 36–44, 89–103.

47. Weissler, *Voices,* 23–28.

48. Ibid., 89–103.

49. Translations taken, with modification, from T. G. Klirs et al., trans. and eds., *The Merit of Our Mothers* (Cincinnati, 1992), 12–42.

50. Birkenthal, *Memoirs of Ber of Bolechow,* 79.

51. This letter was translated and published by I. Abrahams, *Hebrew Ethical Wills* (Phila- delphia, 1976), 316–17, 321 (here slightly modified). In order to avoid the sin of slander, the Gaon also urged his sons to stay at home as much as possible and "even in synagogue make but a very short stay and depart. It is better to pray at home, for in synagogue it is impossi- ble to escape envy and the hearing of idle talk" (321).

52. *Mappa* on *Shulḥan Arukh* Yoreh Dei'ah 246:6. For precedents to this position, see J. R. Baskin, "Some Parallels in the Education of Medieval Jewish and Christian Women," *Jewish History* 5 (1991): 43.

53. Y. Emden, *Megillat Sefer,* ed. Y. Bick (Jerusalem, 1979), 93.

54. The quotes are translated in Zinberg, *A History of Jewish Literature,* 7: 126; see also Shmeruk, *Polin,* 89.

55. Klirs et al., trans. and eds., *The Merit of Our Mothers,* 28 (see also 12); Weissler, *Voices,* 126–46.

56. Quoted from the rarely printed Hebrew introduction to her Aramaic-Yiddish *Tehine Imohos.* See Jewish National and University Library R8° 41A460 *Tehines,* vol. 6, no. 2. See also Weissler, *Voices,* 104–25. For more on Leah Horowitz, see H. Liberman, *Ohel Rahel* (Brooklyn, 1980), 432–34, 437.

57. *Mappa* and *Magen Avraham* on *Shulḥan Arukh* Oraḥ Ḥaim 199.7.

58. Mappa on *Shulḥan Arukh* Oraḥ Ḥaim 88:1. On the history, development, and ha- lakhic status of these restrictions, see A. Grossman, *Ḥasidot u-Mordot: Nashim Yehudiyot be-Eiropah bi-Ymei ha-Beinayim* (Jerusalem, 2001), 47–51, 318–19, and esp. the literature

cited p. 48 n. 106; see also J. R. Woolf, "Medieval Models of Purity and Sanctity: Ashkenazic Women in the Synagogue," in M. J. H. M. Poorthuis and J. Schwartz, eds., *Purity and Holiness: The Heritage of Leviticus* (Leiden, 2000), 263–80.

59. C. H. Krinsky, *Synagogues of Europe* (Mineola, 1985), 28–31; R. Krautheimer, *Mittelalteriche Synagogen* (Hebrew edition: *Batei Kenesset bi-Ymei ha-Beinaim,* trans. A. Goren [Jerusalem, 1994], 84–93). For further studies of women and the synagogue, see S. Grossman and R. Haut, eds., *Daughters of the King: Women and the Synagogue* (Philadelphia, 1992).

60. L. Horowitz, *Tehine Imohos,* intro.; see also Weissler, *Voices,* 110–16.

61. See note 42 above and I. Etkes, *Tenu'at ha-Ḥassidut be-Reishitah* (Tel Aviv, 1998), chaps. 2–5.

62. *Solomon Maimon: An Autobiography* (New York, 1967; based on translation by J. Clark Murray [London, 1888]), 54. For more on Dov Ber, see R. Schatz-Uffenheimer, *Hasidism as Mysticism* (Princeton, N.J., 1993).

63. See A. Rapoport-Albert, "Hasidism After 1772: Structural Continuity and Change," in A. Rapoport-Albert, ed., *Hasidism Reappraised* (London, 1996), 76–140, and Etkes, *Tenu'at ha-Ḥassidut,* chaps. 6–8.

64. R. Elior, *Ḥeirut al ha-Luḥot* (Tel Aviv, 1999), chaps. 6, 8, 9.

65. *Noam Elimelekh,* ed. G. Nigal (Jerusalem, 1978); Elior, *Ḥeirut,* chaps. 10, 11; Etkes, *Tenu'at ha-Ḥassidut,* chap. 7.

66. H. H. Ben-Sasson, "The Personality of the Vilna Gaon and His Historical Influence" (Hebrew), *Zion* 31 (1966): 39–86, 197–216.

67. Elior, *Ḥeirut,* chap. 7; Etkes, *Tenu'at ha-Ḥassidut,* chap. 10; A. Nadler, *The Faith of the Mithnagdim* (Baltimore, Md., 1997).

SELECTED BIBLIOGRAPHY

Baron, Salo W. *A Social and Religious History of the Jews,* vol. 16, Poland–Lithuania, 1500–1650. Philadelphia, 1976.

Birkenthal, Ber. *The Memoirs of Ber of Bolechow.* Trans. and ed. M. Vishnitzer. New York, 1973.

Davies, Norman. *God's Playground: A History of Poland,* 2 vols. New York, 1982.

Fram, Edward. *Ideals Face Reality: Jewish Law and Life in Poland, 1550–1655.* Cincinnati, 1997.

Goldberg, Jacob. *Jewish Privileges in the Polish Commonwealth.* Jerusalem, 1985.

Hundert, Gershon David. *The Jews in a Polish Private Town: The Case of Opatów in the Eighteenth Century.* Baltimore, Md., 1992.

———, ed. *Jews in Early Modern Poland.* London, 1997 [= *Polin,* vol. 10].

Polonsky, Antony; Jakub Basista; and Andrzej Link-Lenczowski, eds. *The Jews in Old Poland, 1000–1795.* London, 1993.

Rosman, M. J. *The Lords' Jews: Magnate-Jewish Relations in the Polish-Lithuanian Commonwealth.* Cambridge, Mass., 1990.

Rosman, Moshe. *Founder of Hasidism: A Quest for the Historical Ba'al Shem Tov.* Berkeley, Calif., 1996.

Shulvass, Moses. *Jewish Culture in Eastern Europe: The Classical Period.* New York, 1975.

Teller, Adam, ed. *Studies in the History of the Jews in Old Poland in Honor of Jacob Goldberg.* Jerusalem, 1998 [=*Scripta Hierosolymitana,* vol. 38].

Weinryb, Bernard Dov. *The Jews of Poland: A Social and Economic History of the Jewish Community in Poland, 1100–1800.* Philadelphia, 1972.

———. *Texts and Studies in the Communal History of Polish Jewry.* New York, 1950 [=*Proceedings of the American Academy for Jewish Research,* vol. 19].

Zamoyski, Adam. *The Polish Way: A Thousand-Year History of the Poles and Their Culture.* London, 1987.

Ketubbah, Lugo, Italy, 1746 (dated 15 Adar II 5546).
Gouache, metallic paint, graphite on vellum.
(In the permanent collection of The Magnes Museum, Berkeley; 67.1.6.3.
Photo: Ben Ailes)

FIVE

FAMILIES AND THEIR FORTUNES:

The Jews of Early Modern Italy

ELLIOTT HOROWITZ

In 1509 Elijah Capsali of Crete, which had been under Venetian rule for over three centuries, journeyed to Padua in the hope of studying at the renowned yeshivah of Rabbi Judah Minz. Barely a week after his arrival, however, the great rabbi, who had been the undisputed spiritual leader of Ashkenazic Jewry in northern Italy, fell ill and died. Capsali was able to be present at Minz's deathbed and to participate in his unusually (and controversially) elaborate funeral, concerning which he later composed a detailed account, possibly the first such account in Jewish literature.[1] His decision to include a detailed description of these events in the history of the Venetian republic he composed, in Hebrew, after his return to Crete, suggests that while witnessing Minz's death and burial Capsali felt himself, perhaps for the first time, to be experiencing history.

As Minz lay dying, we are told, he summoned the rabbis of Padua to his bedside in order to deliver before them a final exhortation. Afterward, he conferred special ordination upon one of them and blessed some of the others present, including Capsali himself. At that point Rabbi Abraham, Minz's son and presumed successor, approached, together with two of his own sons. Minz placed his hand upon their heads, kissed them, and then embraced them. He began to bless them as well, but suddenly drew his feet up onto the bed and expired. This, we are told, all occurred on a Friday evening.

On the following day, the leaders of Padua's Jewish community met in the synagogue in order to deliberate "what should be done for the man whom the King wishes to honor" (Esther 6:6). It was decided that the entire community, young and old, should observe a fast on the next day, the day of the burial, and that all stores and businesses should be closed then as well. It was further agreed that the wooden furnishings of the yeshivah would be broken and a coffin fashioned out of them; also that torches would be kindled and held aloft around the deceased while he was being eulogized, though not (by implication) in the procession itself.

On the following Sunday morning, the entire community gathered in the courtyard outside Minz's home. The coffin containing his body was placed in a raised position, upon which were placed his books as well as a Torah scroll. Shortly afterward, wrote Capsali,

> Forty enormous torches of white wax, each costing . . . nine *marcelli,* were brought out and distributed to all the rabbis and notables, and to the distinguished students of the yeshivah. Each stood with his partner, the eldest in accordance with his age and the youngest in accordance with his youth [Genesis 43:33]. And I, the humble, was also among those holding torches . . . and we positioned ourselves around the coffin and then lit them.[2]

The "enormous torches of white wax" referred to by Capsali were apparently *doppieri*—torches formed of several wax candles fastened together. In 1494 the pilgrim priest Pietro Casola, passing through Venice on his way to Jerusalem, described the impressive procession on the festival of Corpus Christi from the church of St. Mark into and around the adjoining Piazza San Marco, focusing on the role therein of the city's famed confraternities, or *scuole*. Third among these on that occasion was the Scuola di San Marco. "Before their cross," wrote Casola, "walked at least thirty-six brethren with their candlesticks." Each was of gilded wood and contained a doppiero of white wax weighing at least two pounds.[3] Capsali himself, in his later "Chronicle of Venice," described the experience of watching the 120 senators emerge late one night from a meeting in the Ducal Palace:

> And then I saw the glory of the Venetian state, for each of the *pregadi* had his slaves and servants waiting for him below in the courtyard of the [ducal] palace, each with enormous torches of white wax, and when it came time for the *pregadi* to descend, a bell would ring . . . and they would immediately light the torches they were holding, and the courtyard would be flooded with light. Then I saw the grandeur and glory of Venice.[4]

Combining Capsali's observations with those of Casola, we can see how "the enormous torches of white wax" held aloft during the eulogies for Minz could be perceived by those present as symbols of grandeur, but also as icons of an alien religion. Upon the conclusion of the eulogies, Capsali reported, the torches were extinguished and Minz's coffin was carried alternately by students and scholars of the yeshivah and distinguished members of the community to Padua's Jewish cemetery, where "we rekindled the torches, and there he was eulogized further." After Minz was buried together with a Torah scroll, to the accompaniment of much weeping, the torches were again extinguished and the mourners were accompanied home.

Capsali's account reveals a powerful sense of ambivalence on the part of Paduan Jewry with regard to the ritual use of torches. On the one hand, they were deliberately chosen for use in the ceremony as a means of conveying the extraordinary degree of respect felt for the deceased rabbi. On the other, great pains were clearly taken to avoid actually carrying the large white torches in procession. Despite these efforts, voices of criticism were heard in the community upon the conclusion of the seven days of mourning. After Abraham was chosen by the community council (following an extremely close vote) to succeed his father, his first action upon being installed in office was to deliver an address in Padua's synagogue:

> To stifle the voices of those who criticized the custom he had instituted of having the torches lit, objecting that . . . this was the custom of the gentiles. He justified his action on the basis of talmudic sources, demonstrating that this was how scholars were honored in ancient times. Thereafter, the hostility toward him subsided somewhat.[5]

Although Abraham cited talmudic evidence (evidently Avodah Zarah 11a) in order to silence his critics, he evidently shared their feeling that funerary torches were not quite "Jewish"—otherwise he would have done his great father the greater honor of having the torches accompany his coffin to burial. Capsali's account, with its detailed description of the successive kindling and extinguishing of the torches, provides a poignant illustration of the mixture of attraction and repulsion felt by the Jews of northern Italy in the early sixteenth century toward the impressive public processions of their Catholic environment. In the pages that follow, I shall examine the complex and often dialectical relationship between the cultural world of Italian Jewry and that of the surrounding environment, steeped in varying doses of Mediterranean Christianity and Renaissance Humanism.

It is important to stress, however, that during the early modern period there was no single monolithic Italian Jewish culture but, rather, three varieties thereof, corresponding to the three distinct "ethnic" groups among which the Jews of Italy were divided. The *Italiani* Jews of local origin, who traced their ancestry (not always persuasively) to the Roman Empire, were known in Hebrew as *lo'azim* (vernacularists) because they alone, at least until the seventeenth century, spoke Italian (or rather, Judeo-Italian) between themselves. The Ashkenazim, who hailed from north of the Alps, were concentrated, as one might

expect, in northern Italy, especially in the towns of the Veneto. During the fifteenth and sixteenth centuries they still tended to speak Yiddish between themselves and to use the language for literary purposes. Between 1545 and 1609, no
fewer than 35 Yiddish books were printed in Italy.[6]

Third were the Sephardic Jews of Iberian origin, who were often former *conversos*, or descendants thereof. Their piquant presence was first felt during the
sixteenth century, after the spate of expulsions from Spain, Sicily, Portugal,
and the Kingdom of Naples (1492–1541), especially in such communities as
Rome, Ancona, and Ferrara.[7] By the beginning of the seventeenth century the
Sephardim had come, at least economically, to dominate the Jewish community
of Venice, where they were divided into two subcommunities, the "Levantines"
and the "Ponentines." The former had come to Italy by way of Turkey, or other
parts of the Ottoman Empire, whereas the latter, whose Iberian roots were more
pronounced, arrived from elsewhere on the continent.[8] One way of recapturing
these three cultures, to which we shall return shortly, is by tracing the fortunes of
four families: The "Italiani" Finzis, the "Ashkenazi" Carmis, and, among the
Sephardim, the aristocratic Abravanels in the sixteenth century and the rabbinical Aboabs in the seventeenth.

WIGS, WATER, AND WINE

The delicate balance between embrace and rejection reflected in the funeral rites
of Minz is evident also in the striking set of decrees that, with the support of his
rabbinic colleagues, he issued shortly before his death. These decrees were intended to rectify what were perceived to be widespread religious failings among
the predominantly Ashkenazic Jews of the Veneto. Of the decrees relating to female modesty, one stipulated that married women must wear traditionally
opaque head-coverings rather than resorting to wigs or diaphanous silk veils (a
Bolognese specialty),[9] both of which had become fashionable in the fifteenth
century. Casola, when passing through Venice in 1494, was convinced that the
elaborate coiffures of its women were composed largely of false hair, since he
had seen "quantities of it on poles, sold by peasants in the Piazza San Marco.[10]
Minz's decree, despite his great authority, was evidently not very effective, as
may be seen from a sermon preached several decades later by his own great-
grandson, Rabbi Samuel Judah Katzenellenbogen. The latter castigated the
Jewish women of Venice for their laxity, contrary to Ashkenazic tradition, in resorting to flimsy head-coverings or wigs; he compared them unfavorably with
Catholic nuns who, he claimed, were considerably stricter in such matters.[11]

Another of the issues raised by Minz and his colleagues was the immodest conduct of Jewish women in the public bathhouses: "No woman shall permit herself to be washed by a non-Jewish man in a bathhouse," they declared (recognizing that Jewish men were not likely to be employed in such establishments), "and no [Jewish] man shall be permitted to enter a place where women bathe in the nude."[12] The latter part of the decree sought to keep Jewish men out of the sorts of bathing establishments, then quite common in parts of Europe, that did not practice strict separation of the sexes. This arrangement had made possible such works of art as Albrecht Dürer's 1496 drawing "Bathing Women," executed just after his first stay in Venice. Earlier in the fifteenth century, the Catalan traveler Pero Tafur was struck by the mixed (nude) bathing he encountered in such cities as Basel and Bruges, reporting with unconcealed amazement that "the bathing of men and women together they take to be as honest as church-going with us."[13] The decree issued by Minz and his colleagues was intended to prevent Jewish men from frequenting such establishments, but it remained significantly silent about their use of female bath attendants, a practice that medieval Ashkenazic halakhists had curiously condoned.[14] (The frequent exposure to female nudity [or semi-nudity] in these circumstances undoubtedly contributed to the relaxed attitude among northern Italian Jews toward the generous representation of female flesh in such ritual objects as Esther scrolls or Hanukkah lamps,[15] clearly intended for family use.)

Just as Tafur gave trenchant expression to his sense of having entered a different culture when he crossed the Pyrenees, so too did Rabbi Obadiah of Bertinoro express, in his 1488 letter from Jerusalem to his father (who had remained in Città di Castello), the profound sense of having entered a different Jewish world when he arrived, in one of the earlier legs of his pilgrimage from central Italy, on the island of Sicily. Particularly striking was his account of Jewish life in Palermo. After describing the various occupations of the Palermitan Jews and their impressive synagogue, he commented on the rampant problem of informers, and then added laconically: "In the matter of menstrual purity they are also very lax, and most brides enter the marriage canopy already pregnant. They are extremely zealous and meticulous, however, in observing the prohibition regarding wine of the gentiles."[16]

These two sentences, which seem at first glance to be at variance with each other, actually form a coherent whole. More than seeking to praise Palermitan Jews for their stringency in one area or find fault with their laxity in another, Obadiah sought to highlight the sharp differences between two Jewish religious cultures, each of which was characterized by different kinds of "normal exceptions"—a term coined by the Italian historian Eduardo Grendi.[17] In central and northern Italy, the rabbinic prohibition regarding "wine of the gentiles"

Megillat Esther (Purim scroll), Italy, ca. 1675. (Library of the Jewish Theological
Seminary of America, New York. Photo: Suzanne Kaufman)

Hanukkah lamp, Italy, sixteenth century. Bronze, cast.
(The Israel Museum, Jerusalem; Stieglitz Collection of Judaica 118/852)

(*setam yenam*) was treated with considerable laxity, whereas monthly immersion was practiced by Jewish women with persevering regularity, even when this entailed, especially in smaller communities, compromising their modesty. Early in the seventeenth century, when a bitterly contested struggle developed among the Italian rabbis concerning the ritual bath in Rovigo, Rabbi Abtalion of Consiglio, one of those who deemed it ritually unacceptable, was accused by an opponent of being "stringent in water and lenient in wine."[18] Despite the tone of sarcasm in this accusation, it did reflect, if somewhat obliquely, the dominant religious tendency throughout the early modern period among the Jews of northern Italy. Several decades earlier, when asked about the permissibility of eating ricotta cheese, Rabbi Moses Provenzale of Mantua (d. 1576) replied diplomatically that there was, to his knowledge, one variety in the production of which (wine) vinegar was used, and this variety of the cheese was "prohibited to the strictly observant." By this he meant the minority of north Italian Jews, mostly of the rabbinical class, who abstained from *setam yenam*.[19]

In Sicily, however, the religious mores of the Jews, in both wine consumption and other matters, were far closer to those of the eastern Mediterranean than to those of their coreligionists in central and northern Italy. Indeed, in his letter from Jerusalem, Obadiah observed that "in all the communities" that he had visited on his way to Jerusalem "except for Italy, Jews are extremely careful to abstain from wine of the gentiles."[20] Yet in the Jewish communities of the eastern Mediterranean it had been widely customary, since the Middle Ages, for women to forgo ritual immersion in the halakhically prescribed manner (indoors in a *mikveh*, or outdoors in a river or the sea) in favor of the local bathhouse.[21]

The greater stringency with which married Jewish women in central and northern Italy performed their monthly immersions seems to have been related to their more casual approach to matters of modesty, reflected in Minz's aforementioned decree regarding mixed bathing. Similarly, in one of his responsa, Minz attempted to convince the Jews of Treviso, whose wives had been practicing outdoor immersion, of the need to construct a proper ritual bath in a discreet location so that the women could purify themselves monthly "with proper care and without fear of harassment" from either Jews or gentiles. He was not the only Italian rabbi of his time who feared that women performing their monthly ablutions outdoors, albeit in the dark, might fail, after undressing, to inspect their bodies with the requisite care.[22] But what is striking is that no one in northern Italy complained that women in small towns, where many Jewish loan-bankers and their families dwelt, were abstaining from monthly immersion under such challenging circumstances—as was evidently the case in Sicily at the time of Obadiah's visit. One historian, in describing the Tuscan ladies of the early Renaissance, has written that they "did not worry . . . about the neighbors who watched through windows kept wide open."[23] These aristocratic women evidently had more in common with their Jewish countrywomen than they may have realized.

STRANGE BEDFELLOWS

The prevalence of bridal pregnancy that Obadiah encountered in Palermo did not necessarily mean that young Jewish men in Sicily were having more premarital sex than their young coreligionists to the north—but only, perhaps, that they were having it with their future wives. When the representatives of the leading Italian communities had met in Forli, in May 1418, to review a set of sweeping proposals put forward in Bologna some two years earlier, considerable alarm was expressed concerning carnal relations between Jewish men and Christian women, which were described as having become widely accepted.[24] Although the individual communities were encouraged to identify and punish such perpetrators, sexual relations across religious lines, a problem during the fifteenth century also north of the Alps,[25] continued to plague many Italian Jewish communities.

The ubiquity of such relations is also evident through the efforts of civil authorities to control them. In July 1424, the Republic of Venice issued a formal decree prohibiting cohabitation between Jewish men and Christian women, under penalty of fine and imprisonment, the length of which depended on the woman's status. "If she were a prostitute on the Rialto," Benjamin Ravid has noted, "then the Jew was to pay a fine of 500 *lire* and spend six months in jail," whereas for relations with "non-professional" Christian women the fine was the same but the jail sentence was doubled.[26] In Florence, nearly half of the criminal offenses for which Jews were prosecuted during the fifteenth century seem to have been related to sexual relations with Christians.[27] This may not, as noted above, have diverged significantly from the situation north of the Alps, where in a relatively small community such as Nuremberg seven Jews were fined in a single year (1430) for having sexual relations with Christian women.[28]

Nonetheless, there are indications that in Italy such behavior, if not condoned, was nonetheless realistically anticipated as a fact of life. Thus, in 1491 Jewish bankers in Mantua arranged, as part of their *condotta* (charter) with the local authorities, that if they were caught cohabiting with Christian women they would not be held in prison for more than five days.[29] Both sides seem to have recognized that such incidents were not likely to be rare. Less than a century later, the 25-year charter extended by Duke Emmanuel Filibert of Savoy in 1572 to Jews and other merchants stipulated that Jews convicted of sexual relations with a Christian woman would pay 50 scudi for the first offense and 100 for the second—which seems to have been anticipated as confidently as the first.[30]

In March 1580, just around the time of Carnival, the Jewish community council of Padua (whose Jews had not yet been ghettoized) issued two directives, one unanimously and one nearly so, attempting to prevent intimate contact between Jews and Christians. The first, noting that the local bishop had been complaining, apparently not without justification, about rampant sexual relations between Jewish men and Christian women in the city, imposed a ban of *herem* (temporary excommunication) upon any transgressor. The second directive prohibited both Jewish men and women from dancing with Christians of the opposite sex, whether in their own homes or in those of Christians. A fine of two (gold) scudi was imposed, half of which would go to the informer. The decision of the council some 15 years later to permit only married men to hold positions of communal authority may well have been rooted in the suspicion that those who were not married would be more susceptible to such temptations.[31]

The earliest knowledge we have, for example, of Salomone, son of the legendary Venetian banker Asher Meshullam (Anselmo del Banco), who was considered to be the wealthiest Jew in early-sixteenth-century Italy, is that in 1515 he was condemned in his absence to a heavy fine for having sex with a Christian prostitute in the home of a Jewish procuress. Several decades later, a Venetian Jew named Daniele was reported to have slept regularly with a Christian prostitute, known as "la Rossa," in the ghetto home of his fellow Modenese, Giovanni.[32] Such habits could begin early. Isaac Modena, through his second marriage the future father of the Venetian rabbi Leone Modena, settled accounts with the papal chamber in 1539 for having fornicated with a Christian woman in Bologna when he was eighteen—shortly after (as we know from his son's celebrated autobiography) having given up his religious studies to begin a career in loan banking and commerce. Three years earlier, a certain Salvatus Montelupone of Civitnova Marche, a small town south of Ancona on the Adriatic coast, was fined a single ducat (being understandably unable to pay more) for having fornicated with a married Christian woman when he was fourteen.[33]

One prominent historian of Italian Jewry has recently issued a rather scathing and wholesale critique of "current historiography" for allegedly presenting "the evidence of sexual relations between Jews and Christians as proof of social integration encouraged by the general climate of permissiveness that is supposed to be typical of Renaissance Italy." Yet it is worth noting that as early as 1926 another historian, Cecil Roth, pointed to "that sexual looseness which was always one of the cankers of Italian Jewry."[34] The historiographical question turns not on the extent of sexual intimacy between Jews and non-Jews in Italy but, rather, on the causes and consequences thereof. Did such relations stem simply from occasional weakness of the flesh, or were they, like the frequently lascivious liaisons between Jewish masters and maidservants of their own faith (a subject to which we shall return), part of a network of "normal exceptions"? I would argue for the latter position.

AMULETS AND ASTROLOGY

A related realm of less than reputable activity whose role in the culture of Italian Jewry has been debated by scholars is that of magic. In 1930 Roth, himself then barely 30 years old, took particular delight in describing the lifestyle and career of Leone Modena (1571–1648), whom he felt "more than any other person . . . represents his age to the modern mind." He listed, for example, all 26 professions that Modena, by his own admission, practiced at one point or another, including the writing of flowery letters, laudatory poems, rhymed epitaphs, legal deeds, comedies, and amulets—in which, Roth added dryly, "he can hardly have believed."[35]

Roth may have been alluding to the critique of amulets, rooted in the rationalistic teachings of Maimonides, which Modena had included in his anti-kabbalistic *Ari Nohem*. That polemical work, however, which Modena had not dared to publish in his lifetime (it was first printed in 1840), was written when he was nearly 70 years old and did not necessarily reflect the author's attitudes during his younger years.[36] When Roth himself returned, some three decades later, to the subject of superstition, his approach was considerably more nuanced. "One of the paradoxes of intellectual life in this period," he wrote in *The Jews in the Renaissance* (1959), "was the manner in which skepticism and even rationalism of a kind were combined, sometimes in the same person, with the grossest superstition." Even the most erudite and ostensibly levelheaded scholars, Roth noted, "sometimes showed the utmost credulity and harbored the greatest superstitions, much as was the case with some of the leaders of Italian intellectual life at this time." Not surprisingly, he now described Modena himself as "an individual who was intensely superstitious, paid preposterous respect to omens . . . and displayed unswerving optimism in his belief in alchemy."[37]

By the late 1950s, the traditional image of Renaissance rationalism, which had been first problematized by the pioneering studies of Aby Warburg and Fritz Saxl, was further undermined by their disciples D. P. Walker and Frances Yates.[38] In a pathbreaking monograph published just one year before Roth's *Jews in the Renaissance,* Walker quoted a striking passage from Marsilio Ficino's influential

1489 medical treatise *Libri de Vita*. The passage from Ficino, who was both a priest and a physician, also sheds considerable light on how and why even "enlightened" Renaissance rabbis might have been involved in the preparation and/or prescription of magical talismans:

> If you do not approve of talismans, which were however invented to benefit men's health, but which I myself do not so much approve of as merely describe, then dismiss them with my permission. . . . But at all events, unless you disregard life itself, do not disregard medicines strengthened by some celestial support. For I have long since discovered by frequent experiment that there is as much difference between medicines of this kind and those made without astrological selection as between wine and water.[39]

Ficino was used in the early sixteenth century by his countryman Pietro Pomponazzi as an authority in defending talismans against the criticisms of Thomas Aquinas. In the following century, Modena's controversial contemporary Tomaso Campanella followed Ficino in paradoxically using Aquinas as an authority in support of those magical practices (such as the use of talismans) that St. Thomas himself had condemned.[40] It is not surprising, therefore, that learned Italian Jews of the sixteenth and seventeenth centuries, including physicians, continued to prescribe and produce both amulets and talismans, for which there was considerable popular demand.

Many Italian Jews were in the habit of wearing small decorative cases of silver and/or gold, sometimes carrying inscriptions or even encrusted with gemstones, within which a parchment with a protective text would be inserted—a custom common also among Italian Christians. In fact, from a late-seventeenth-century exchange between two Italian rabbis regarding the permissibility of selling used amulets to Christian silversmiths, it is clear that many, if not most, of these amulets were then being produced by Christian craftsmen, who often did the external Hebrew inscriptions as well.[41] Although some of these amulets were to be worn (either by adults or by children) as pendants, the larger ones were intended for hanging on a baby's crib, one of the childbirth rituals discussed by Shalom Sabar in his chapter.[42]

Leone Modena's older contemporary, the physician and kabbalist Abraham Yagel, wrote in 1579 that "one should not be surprised if well-known men possess wonderful amulets . . . to cure sick patients and to perform wonders in the heaven and on earth." Early in the seventeenth century, he carried on a correspondence with the banker Daniel Modena (no relation) concerning the treatment of the latter's son, whom Yagel diagnosed as suffering from a form of

Amulets, Italy, seventeenth–nineteenth centuries.
(The Jewish Museum, New York; catalog nos. 186, 223–227.
Photo copyright © The Jewish Museum of New York / Art Resource, New York)

melancholia. Although he felt the chances of effecting a cure were slim, he prescribed a regimen of purgatives and bloodletting, sending on also a chart with
the relevant astrological data. In addition, the young patient was ordered by
Yagel to hold in his hand a specially crafted copper amulet immediately after
performing the purgation.[43] Around the same time, Leone Modena's student
Joseph Hamiz was criticized (possibly by Modena himself) for abetting fornica-
tion by providing non-Jews with amulets to be encased in copper so that "they
might have their way with harlots."[44]

Yagel's combined use of astrology and an amulet for healing a fellow Jew is
hardly surprising in light of his own comments in *Gai Ḥizayon,* an account (recently published in English translation) of a heavenly journey taken allegedly by
his soul. There Yagel had no less an authority than Job declare, in contradistinction to the view of the talmudic sage Rabbi Yohanan: "Know well that Israel has a
constellation [*mazal*]." In fact, it even had two constellations, Capricorn and
Aquarius, both of which were related, as "Job" knew from two medieval Hebrew
astrological works, to the planet Saturn, widely associated with the Jews.[45] The
role of amulets in Renaissance astral magic has been lucidly explained by Eugenio Garin: "The celestial powers . . . come to be caught . . . or used by imprison-

ing them in fictitious material representations, talismans and amulets, capable of absorbing and concentrating astral forces."[46]

The use of magical amulets extended, it should be noted, also to Ashkenazic circles in Italy. The Yiddish work composed for women, *Mitzvot ha-Nashim,* first published in Venice in 1552 and republished in 1588, informed its readers that amulets need not be removed when performing ritual immersion. Similarly, Rabbi Meir Katzenellenbogen of Venice (d. 1565), who was probably the most respected Ashkenazic rabbi of his generation in Italy, composed a work of practical Kabbalah that included many medical remedies, and he was even recognized in his later years as a *ba'al shem* (master of the name).[47] Early in the 1570s, Moses Carmi of Cremona, son of the wealthy Ashkenazic banker Saul Raphael Carmi (to whom we shall return) and son-in-law of the Italiani banker and rabbi (a common combination) Isaac Foa of Reggio, wrote to one of the latter's sons expressing concern over his health, as well as that of two of his siblings. Moses mentioned that his father had sought from a "friend" an amulet that would cure the particular fever from which the Foas were suffering, but he took the precaution of having it "tested" before sending it on to Reggio, so as not to expose his relatives to the potentially pernicious effects of holy names that would not heal. The senior Carmi's "friend" may have been the anonymous Jewish astrologer who, according to the report of an apostolic visit to Cremona in 1575, continued to predict the future and to practice palmistry though he knew these were forbidden.[48]

Similarly, in the spring of 1580 Stella Diana Levi (née Norzi), who had been married to the Ferrarese banker Samuel Levi for nearly a decade, sent a moving letter in highly learned Hebrew and Aramaic to Rabbi Abraham of Sant' Angelo, her former tutor, who had left Ferrara for Asti some eight years earlier. In her letter, which was composed for her "professionally," Stella Diana requested that Abraham send her an amulet, which he himself had prepared and tested, in order to safeguard the health of her infant son. The latter had been given the name Isaac Jedidiah at birth but his name had been changed to Ishmael during his first illness, and he was again facing grave danger.[49]

In 1583 we find young Ishmael among the three children who were listed as members of Ferrara's Hevrat Gemilut Ḥasadim ("the society for deeds of loving-kindness"), the oldest known Jewish confraternity in Italy, which was concerned primarily with caring for the sick and burying the dead. We do not know if Abraham had dispatched the amulet or, if so, whether it had proved effective, but it is quite striking that after attempting to improve the infant's delicate health through such methods as changing his name and hanging an amulet around his neck, his parents eventually took the step of enrolling him in a pious confraternity. Since it is unlikely that they were interested in having Ishmael pay nocturnal visits to the sick or construct coffins for the dead, it would appear that the Levis were drawn to Gemilut Ḥasadim—and motivated, moreover, to pay its monthly dues—by the belief that confraternal membership itself possessed potentially redeeming sacral significance.

PIETY AND IMPROPRIETY

The confraternity in which the Levis enrolled their son was apparently the earliest such Jewish institution to emerge in Italy, having been founded shortly before Rosh Hashanah in 1515 by 57 men and 14 women in the synagogue of Ferrara. The synagogue had been established in the 1480s in a building that had been given to the community by Ser Samuel Melli of Rome, who had purchased it from a member of the Norzi family, into which the future Stella Diana Levi would be born. The conversion of the building into Ferrara's first permanent place of Jewish worship had been authorized by Duke Ercole I of the House of Este. In 1473, Ercole had extended his protection to resident Ferrarese Jews, in opposition to papal demands, and two decades later he allowed 21 families of Spanish exiles to settle in the city under rather favorable conditions. By the early sixteenth century, Ferrara was a modest-sized though fairly heterogeneous Jewish community, which, despite periodic tensions with the local Christian populace, had benefited from unusually good relations with the ruling dynasty.[50]

In its inaugural statutes of 1515, Gemilut Ḥasadim gave a concise and concrete description of the confraternity's major aims:

> to care for the infirm poor when necessary, and to attend them day and night, nursing them, for the glory of God, until they regain their health. Also to attend the dying . . . and, after their deaths, to prepare a coffin . . . to wash their bodies, to carry them to the cemetery, to bury them, and, afterwards, to accompany the mourners home.[51]

Its primary orientation, then, was toward acts of benevolent piety connected with sickness and especially death. These concerns, common among contemporary Catholic confraternities in Italy, had also been dominant among the only Jewish pious (as opposed to mutual aid) associations known with certainty to have existed in late medieval times, those of Spain and southern France. Gemilut Ḥasadim, founded not long after the expulsions of the Jews from Spain in 1492 and from Provence in 1500–1501, and including among its ranks no small number of refugees from both, would seem to have drawn upon these traditions of confraternal benevolence. The Jews arriving from some of these areas, moreover, had witnessed a proliferation of Christian confraternities in their midst. Abraham Farissol, the first scribe of Gemilut Ḥasadim, had come to Italy from Avignon, where 64 Christian confraternities had emerged during the fifteenth century alone. In Rome two confraternities for Torah study were organized among the local Spanish exiles before 1540, one associated with the Aragonese community and the other with that of the Castilian Jews. Jews coming from these areas to Ferrara in the late fifteenth or early sixteenth century seem to have brought with them certain Mediterranean habits of sociability that had been translated, in their former communities, into forms of confraternal piety. Their own inclinations in this direction could only have been fortified by the Italian environment, where during the sixteenth century there was a marked proliferation of confraternities serving a variety of social and religious aims.

Whereas its Jewish predecessors in Spain and southern France devoted themselves to the care of the sick *or* the dead, the Ferrarese confraternity chose to widen its focus so as to provide both kinds of charity to the wider community, providing burial in all instances and sick-care in cases of financial need. Yet, not all of the services provided by Gemilut Ḥasadim were directed toward the larger community—some, as was also the case in many Italian Catholic confraternities, were reserved for its members alone. This symbolically important distinction had also been part of the late-medieval traditions of confraternal piety among Spanish and southern French Jewry. Thus, the inaugural statutes of Gemilut Ḥasadim stipulated that upon a member's death the confraternity would care for and comfort the mourners, but no such provision was included in the services it offered to the general Jewish community.

The 1515 document stipulated no criteria for admission, other than willingness to abide by the confraternity's statutes including payment of monthly dues, nor was a selection process for new members mentioned. By 1552, however, the confraternity's egalitarian character diminished considerably, and the distinction between the services offered to members and those offered to the general community widened further. Initially there had been no such thing as nonpaying members, and consequently no set of activities reserved for a confraternal underclass. According to the revised statutes of 1552, those who did not pay monthly dues were expected to perform a wider range of activities than those who did. Some of those activities, such as burial, were quite demanding.

Moreover, whereas funeral attendance was originally seen as part of the confraternity's general service to the community, by 1552 attendance was required only at the funeral of a fellow member or one of his/her relatives. Another exclusive service offered then to members was that confraternal officials were required, when visiting a member who had been ill with fever for three days, "to encourage him to confess his sins before God and to deliver his final testament before his family." In the latter case, the confraternity saw itself as standing somewhere between God and the family, dutifully reminding the moribund member to fulfill his responsibilities toward both. And in involving itself in a member's deathbed confession, as in fasting for his recovery, the confraternity used ritual as a means of both reflecting and intensifying the fraternal bonds between its members. The concern with confession went beyond the functional level, however, because the Jews of Italy were much concerned with this aspect of the deathbed rite, mirroring a basic shift with regard to this "sacrament" that had occurred in Catholicism after the Council of Trent.[52]

The confraternity's increasing concern with the soul and its salvation came at the cost of decreasing concern with the body and its interment. Whereas the inaugural statutes had seen burial as a core, and perhaps the most central, activity of the confraternity, those of 1552 no longer regarded it as a task in which all members need, at some time or another, take part. It was assigned rather to "a Jew from among the nonpaying members," who would perform the burial free of charge. Gemilut Ḥasadim was thus becoming a confraternity in which membership, while it had its rewards for all, meant different things to different people.

Much can also be learned about changes in the Ferrarese confraternity's social character by comparing its 1552 list of members with that of 1515. Whereas none of the 57 men listed as charter members bore honorifics before their names, three of 36 were so honored in 1552, as were two of the eight women who were there listed. Although this does not necessarily mean that none of the original members were deserving of such honor, it does indicate that no point was then seen in officially distinguishing between one member and another, just as no distinction was yet made in 1515 between paying and nonpaying members.

Gracing the top of the right-hand column of the 1552 list appear the names "Don Jacob" and "Don Judah" Abravanel, each with the princely epithet *ha-Sar* preceding their Iberian-style honorific. These two brothers, scions of "what was perhaps the outstanding [Jewish] family in all Europe in that age," were grandsons of the exegete, philosopher, and statesman Don Isaac Abravanel.[53] Their parents, the illustrious couple Samuel and Benvenida Abravanel, had moved north upon the expulsion of the Jews from the kingdom of Naples in 1541, settling in Ferrara, where Samuel died some five years after their arrival. His three sons—Isaac, Jacob, and Judah—represented, more than any of their contemporaries, the transplantation of Iberian Jewish aristocracy to Italian soil.

Of these the latter two were, as sons of Benvenida, treated more favorably in his will than Isaac, who had been born to a woman (quite possibly a Jewish maidservant) to whom Samuel was not married.[54] After his father's death, Jacob, the elder of the two, took control (together with his mother) of the family's lucrative loan-banking business, which extended as far as Tuscany, where they maintained no less than five banks. Both mother and son were on especially close terms with the ducal family, Jacob with Cosimo de Medici and Benvenida with his wife Leonora, whose tutor she is reported to have been during her family's sojourn in Naples. Jacob, who seems to have inherited not only his father's money but also his libido, had also been on rather close terms with a number of Christian women, with whom he was accused of having had frequent carnal relations—acts for which he managed to gain absolution in Rome in October 1547.[55]

Whether on account of his venerable background, or because such peccadilloes were relatively common among the scions of Italian Jewish banking families, Jacob's venereous affairs prevented him neither from gaining admission to Ferrara's Gemilut Ḥasadim nor from being listed, together with his brother Judah, in a place of honor among its members in 1552. Conspicuous, however, for their continued absence in 1552 were the leading members of the Norzi clan, the first family of Ferrara's Jewish community. Isaac Norzi, described by a contemporary as "a powerful figure in his town, deferred to on account of his wealth and fortune, and feared by all," never joined Gemilut Ḥasadim, nor had his father before him, the legendary and equally feared Immanuel.[56] True to family tradition, Isaac's sons (the eldest of whom, Abraham Immanuel, had been ennobled by Duke Ercole II in 1543) also remained outside the ranks of the confraternity, as did their brother-in-law, Joshua Modena. The latter's father, Eliezer, was one of the most respected members of the community, having distinguished himself through both learning and philanthropy, yet he too seems to have kept his distance from Ferrara's only Jewish confraternity.[57]

Ferrara was not the only sixteenth-century community in which the local Jewish elite distanced themselves from efforts to establish a pious confraternity—an institution that could potentially serve as a competing source of power. In Recanati, south of Ancona, a group of Jews managed, in 1545, to gain permission from papal authorities to establish a confraternity very much like Gemilut Ḥasadim despite the opposition of the local Jewish communal leadership.[58] In Bologna, however, where by the middle of the sixteenth century approximately 20 percent of Catholic adults were members of pious confraternities, there were by 1546 two Jewish confraternities, Raḥamim and Nizharim. The former, whose name corresponded closely with the Italian *misericordia* (mercy), seems, like the unnamed confraternity in Recanati, to have followed the benevolent orientation of Gemilut Ḥasadim. The latter, however, was considerably more eclectic in orientation, concerning itself also with avoiding (at least among its members) such transgressions as blasphemy, late arrival for morning prayers, and idle chatter in the synagogue. Nizharim ("the scrupulous") allowed both women and children into its ranks and included in its statutes a special appendix for its female members. Children were to pay the same entry fee as adults (half a scudo) but were unable to vote and exempt from all confraternal obligations until reaching the age of thirteen.[59]

Why their parents might choose to enroll them as children, despite the considerable expense, can perhaps be explained by looking at the names of the boys who were listed, for the first time, among the members of Ferrara's Gemilut Ḥasadim in 1552. One of the two was "the blessed child 'Oh that *Ishmael* might live' (Genesis 17:18) b. Azariah Finzi, may God protect him." Ishmael's father, who was not a member of the confraternity himself, evidently enrolled his young son in the hope that the spiritual benefit conferred by membership would improve his chances of survival. Ishmael did indeed survive, long enough, at least, to still be listed among the members of the Gemilut Ḥasadim in 1583. He proved, in fact, in line with the prophecy for his biblical namesake, to be something of a "wild man" (see Genesis 16:12), being provoked in 1577, after no less than 15 years' membership in a pious confraternity, to slay his sister on account of her alleged sexual misconduct. Just as Jacob Abravanel's sexual escapades did not prevent him from being listed, in a place of honor, among the members of Gemilut Ḥasadim in 1552, so too (following the double standard) did Ishmael Finzi's execution of his sister not jeopardize his standing in the same confraternity some three decades later.

Azariah (Bonaiuto) Finzi, the bereaved father of both the slayer and his victim, saw fit, as we learn from his friend Abraham Yagel, to defend Ishmael's deed, asserting that it was "inappropriate for one calling himself a Jew, especially a member of one of the most prestigious families [*la-meyuḥasin she-bahem*], to suffer a veil of shame upon his face, being mocked by all who see him for the blemish attached to his family's reputation."[60] The Finzis, both Azariah's immediate family and the members of his extended clan (which constituted several branches), did, in fact, enjoy considerable repute, having distinguished themselves as loan-bankers throughout northern Italy since the late fourteenth century and having contributed significantly to the rich intellectual life of its Jewish communities. The family's fortunes between the fourteenth and seventeenth centuries (to which the following pages will be devoted) reflect, sometimes directly and sometimes obliquely, many of the most significant trends that shaped the lives of early modern Italian Jews.

THE FINZIS: BANKING AND BOOKS

The earliest Finzi known to us is Gaio (Isaac), a native of Rome who had emigrated north to Bologna, where he was selling used clothing in 1353. By 1368 two of his grandsons, Musettino and Gugliemo, were partners in a local loan bank, and the family's ascent from rags to riches had begun. Musettino Finzi's three sons, Manuele, Salomone, and Gaio, later entered their father's banking partnership and by 1390 had extended its loan activities to Mantua. Salomone Finzi, who was also a physician, served as one of Bologna's representatives to the synod of 1416, which took place in Bologna, and that of 1419, which took place in Forli. At these synods, matters of mutual concern to Italy's Jewish communities (such as excessive spending on luxuries and dangerous liaisons with Christian women) were discussed, and sumptuary laws were enacted. These limited, for example, the amount of jewelry that could be worn by men or women in public, and the number of guests other than close relatives one could invite to a wedding or circumcision feast. Another representative at the two synods was Isaac ben Moses Finzi of Padua, where members of the family who had arrived there from Ancona had been active in loan banking since 1369.[61]

From the early fifteenth century, members of the Finzi family played an important role in the lives of the Jews of Mantua and the surrounding region. The brothers Mordekhai/Angelo and Isaac, grandsons of Salomone Finzi, opened a lending bank in Mantua sometime before 1434 and lived together in the city's Cammello district, but within several years they dissolved their business partnership, holding in common only portions of a household in Bologna. Mordekhai/Angelo moved his family, his bank, and his extensive library to a separate home in Mantua's Orso district, where he remained for about a dozen years, before moving to nearby Viadana. There, in addition to continuing his loan banking, he found time for such activities as copying a Hebrew translation of an Arabic philosophical work by the Aristotelian Ibn Tufayl, with a fourteenth-century commentary by Moses Narboni, which Finzi completed in late January 1460. Among earlier works he had copied were two treatises of Averroes' *Middle Commentary* on Aristotle, translated from Arabic into Hebrew by Narboni's older contemporary, Kalonymos ben Kalonymos of Arles.[62]

Mordekhai/Angelo was much more than a mere copyist and may, in fact, be considered the leading scientific savant of fifteenth-century Italian Jewry. Shortly before Rosh Hashanah of 1441, he had completed in Mantua, "with the help of a non-Jew," a Hebrew translation from Latin of an important medieval astronomical work—John Batecombe's planetary tables, drawn up for the city of

Oxford in 1348. Other astronomical works by Mordekhai/Angelo include an extended commentary on the Alfonsine tables as well as treatises on the Jewish calendar and on the diameters of the sun and the moon. In the field of mathematics he translated two works by Abu Kamil, his "Book of Rare Things in the Art of Calculation" and his "On the Pentagon and the Decagon" (both of which were probably consulted in a Latin or Romance translation), and composed his own Hebrew commentary on an important algebraic work by the same Arab author. Mordekhai/Angelo also produced a number of original mathematical treatises, one of which dealt with nonintersecting lines. Moreover, he dabbled in less scientifically rigorous subjects, such as Hebrew alphanumerics and numerology, a treatise concerning which he completed during the intermediate days of Passover in 1447.[63]

Like his distinguished contemporaries among Italy's Christian humanists, Mordekhai/Angelo combined a deep commitment to science with an abiding interest in disciplines that have since come to be considered "magical." Thus his oeuvre includes a Hebrew treatise of 14 chapters on the arcane subject of geomancy—a method of divination in which "by marking down a number of points at random and then connecting or canceling them by lines, a number or figure is obtained which is used as a key to sets of tables or to astrological constellations." Mordekhai/Angelo was aware that these forms of divination were often disparaged, but he adopted a position that may be described as sympathetically agnostic: "We shall refrain from elaborating on the verification of these arts, which would be out of place here," he wrote in his introduction, "since their verification is a loftier art than this."[64]

Mordekhai/Angelo was not the only member of his family who was drawn to both scientific and esoteric knowledge. As a consequence of a complex 1454 lawsuit in which Mordekhai/Angelo, his son Salomone, and his daughter-in-law Brunetta (daughter of Daniel Finzi) were named as defendants, a list of 226 Hebrew manuscripts that were part of a Bolognese property they owned jointly has survived. The list includes 18 prayer books, 21 philosophical works, and 31 medical treatises. Yet 35 works, the largest number, were described as kabbalistic in character.[65] Other Finzis of the fifteenth century also shared these wide interests. Abraham ben Yoav Finzi, of the Recanati branch of the family, had a copy of David Messer Leon's introductory Hebrew textbook on logic, *Mikhlal Yofi*, copied for him in Ancona very shortly after the work itself was composed, in early 1455.[66]

The marriage of Salomone and Brunetta (who shared a great-grandfather) was characteristic of the endogamous trends among the Finzis—and among other Jewish banking families in northern Italy. In 1474, David ben Manuele

Finzi, a member of the family's Padua branch, who maintained a loan bank in San Giovanni in Persico, a town on the outskirts of Bologna, betrothed his son Bonauito (Azariah) to Devota, the granddaughter (through her mother, Poma) of Benjamin Finzi, also of the family's Padua branch, who had been a banker in Vicenza. Both bride and groom were, like Salomone and Brunetta, descendants of Musettino Finzi of Bologna. Devota's aunt Rosa (née Finzi), who had twice been widowed (both her husbands had been named Musetto) was a formidable matron who managed her own loan bank, evidently the only such concession in Bologna to be granted to a woman.[67] Although Rosa was considered by Jewish law to be a *katlanit* (killer widow), and thus technically barred from remarriage, her financial attractiveness probably helped overcome such considerations. As Ariel Toaff has noted, among the Jews of nearby Umbria, "second and even third marriages of widowers and above all widows . . . were widespread." Particularly striking is the case of Brunetta da Sarnano of Perugia, whose considerable dowry (which she collected from the heirs of her first two husbands after their deaths) allowed her to marry three times between 1547 and 1554.[68]

Although marriages between relatives had their merits, they did not necessarily mean lower dowries. David Finzi received 220 ducats from Poma when his son was betrothed to her daughter Devota in November 1474, but a month earlier he managed to betroth his own daughter, Presiata, to Solomon ben Moses of Urbino (scion of a well-known Mantuan banking family) while promising a dowry of only 180 ducats.[69] Nor did endogamous marriages assure monogamous fidelity. One year earlier, in 1473, Salomone Finzi of Mantua, who had been married to his cousin Brunetta for some two decades, was imprisoned for three weeks, together with a Jewish servant who resided in his home, on the charge of cohabiting with a Christian woman. The two were freed only after Salomone's elderly father Mordekhai/Angelo, who had at first denied the charge in a letter to the Marquis of Mantua, paid an enormous fine of 2,000 ducats on their behalf. In 1508, Salomone's nephew Joshua (Salvatore) Finzi was among the five Mantuan Jews granted "absolution" by the authorities for such behavior.[70]

In 1507, Isaac Norzi, a son of the "overbearing" Ferrarese banker Immanuel (as aptly described by Cecil Roth), confessed to having carnally known a Christian woman, evidently a prostitute, in Bologna while operating under disguise— either by having removed his Jewish badge or by wearing masquerade during Carnival (a common strategy for illicit liaisons).[71] Isaac was married, perhaps not very happily, to Consiglia, a daughter of the noted Bolognese banker Abraham Raphael ben Jacob Finzi, whose partnership with Isaac's formidable father, which had begun in 1494, had recently been rather unpleasantly terminated—a matter that might have affected relations between Isaac and his wife. Nonethe-

less, in the spring of 1520 Isaac presented her with an elaborately illustrated Hebrew codex of the (Italiani) prayer ritual and the Passover haggadah. Curiously,
however, the scribe's testimony in the colophon that he had copied it for Isaac
Norzi, to be used by him and his sons, is contradicted by Consiglia's statement,
apparently in her own hand, that it was she who commissioned the manuscript
"to bring me joy when I come to bow before the Lord, [both] on holidays and
on all days of the year."[72] This was probably not the only disagreement between
husband and wife. Nonetheless, from their marriage (one of two between offspring of the two bankers—Isaac's sister Diamante was married to Abraham's
son Isaac) emerged four sons. The eldest of these, Abraham Immanuel Norzi
(named after his two living grandfathers), would eventually be ennobled by
Duke Ercole II of Ferrara.[73]

Isaac's mildly embarrassing escapade in his father-in-law's native Bologna
took place shortly after the latter had formally, though secretly, declared before
witnesses, on February 28, 1507, that he had been coerced by Immanuel Norzi to
sell, for an artificially low price, his share of the Ferrarese bank they had previously held in common.[74] When, some 12 years later, Abraham Finzi's declaration
was submitted to a rabbinical court and made public, a major controversy ensued, which turned largely on the question as to whether the case could be
impartially tried in Ferrara, over whose rabbis, it was widely (and plausibly)
claimed, Norzi wielded considerable influence.[75]

Ten days before Abraham made his secret declaration in Bologna, he had pru-
dently requested permission to establish a synagogue in Sermide, southeast of
Mantua, to which he apparently planned to relocate. Jewish loan bankers had
been active in Sermide since 1414, and during the late fifteenth century it had
boasted such prominent figures as Samuel da Pola, for whom Abraham Farissol
(who lived in the banker's home and probably also served as tutor to his children) copied several Hebrew manuscripts during the early 1480s, and whose
bank Abraham Finzi eventually purchased. Prior to the latter's arrival, however,
organized Jewish life in the town seems to have been rather weak. Within several
months after arriving in Sermide, Farissol copied the three manuscripts most
necessary for maintaining a minimal Jewish existence: a codex comprising the
Torah, five *Megillot,* Psalms, Proverbs, Job, and the *Haftarot;* Rashi's commentary on the Torah; and a prayer book of the Italiani rite. Abraham Finzi may not
even have found a *minyan* of 10 men to pray with him in his synagogue. After
just over four years, in August 1511, he sold his bank and home in Sermide to Angelo (Mordekhai) da Colonia.[76]

It is against this peregrinatory background that we can perhaps best understand why the inscription on the Torah binder (*mappa*) that Abraham Finzi's

wife made (but did not quite complete) in his honor (currently in New York's Jewish Museum) explicitly stipulated that "wherever it may be, may it be our right to take it out without restraint."[77] She probably began work on the binder just before their departure to or from Sermide, and in the haste of moving never managed to complete it. The couple eventually returned to Bologna, where Abraham's charter to lend money was renewed in 1522 and again in 1530. By 1538 he was evidently no longer among the living, for a five-year extension was then granted to his heirs. One of them, Vitale (Ḥayyim), decided to return to Sermide, where in 1540 he was chartered to operate a loan bank—apparently the one his father had sold to Angelo da Colonia nearly three decades earlier. In October 1541, around the time of the High Holy Days, Vitale was also granted permission to make changes in the synagogue and to conduct services there as in the past.[78]

Synagogues in private homes, especially in those of wealthy bankers, were quite common in Italy's smaller communities. In the fifteenth century, Rabbi Joseph Colon ruled that the members of a small community (apparently in the Piedmont) that barely managed to gather a minyan during the High Holy Days could not transfer their synagogue from one person's home to another's without the consent of the former. Even in Padua there was a lavish private synagogue that the wealthy banker Herz Wertheim had constructed in his home sometime around 1500. According to Elijah Capsali, the costly curtain (*parokhet*) of the synagogue's Torah ark was embroidered with pearls and even its walls were originally gilded—until some of Wertheim's coreligionists informed the local authorities of his egregious ostentation.[79] In Spoleto, where Jews had resided since the late fourteenth century, the synagogue was still situated, early in the sixteenth century, in the centrally located home of the venerable de Pomis family, whose members had included many prominent bankers and physicians. It was there that, in 1508, a young mother named Eva was killed by her husband Servadio (Ovadia), who claimed that she had been beating him continually. He was fined 300 florins by the governor of Spoleto, a considerable sum (and more than most local Jewish husbands received as dowries), and banished from the town for a year. Upon Servadio's return, in the winter of 1510, he managed to marry again. His was hardly the only act of violence, or even murder, perpetrated in an Italian synagogue.[80]

Such brazen acts of violence, whether carried out in the synagogue or in other public places, often need to be seen as part of ongoing feuds or disagreements, frequently involving issues of honor, rather than as isolated or random incidents. Thus in Spoleto, in April 1480, the banker Moses di Ventura was attacked one morning with kicks and punches by two other Jews, Musetto and his son

Isaiah, as he was crossing the town's main square. Witnesses reported that Musetto accused the banker of having earlier caused the death of two of his children by plague when he provoked the family's expulsion from Recanati. Seven years later, in 1487, Angelo (Mordekhai) di Gugliemo, one of the wealthiest Jews in Perugia, was killed in the local synagogue by a coreligionist named Deodato, who had earned his living as a dancing master. The murderer, who later returned to ask forgiveness of his victim's daughter, had probably been her teacher, and may have been brazen enough, despite his lowly status, to ask her prosperous father for her hand in marriage.[81]

SERVANTS, SONS-IN-LAW, SODOMY, AND SLAUGHTER

Not all members of the Finzi family had been affluent loan-bankers. In 1494, Benvenuta, daughter of Gugliemo Finzi of Bologna, was working as a maid-servant in the home of Ventura di Abramo, the leading Jewish banker in Perugia.[82] Her annual wage was only four ducats, but it is likely that her wealthy employer was also committed, at least implicitly, to marrying her off and providing her with a dowry. During the sixteenth century, cases appear in the responsa of Italian Jews who married off their "concubines" to others, and it is quite clear that these young women had officially entered their homes as servants.[83]

In 1575, Rabbi Moses Provenzale of Mantua was consulted by a Roman colleague about the case of a childless *kohen* (a man of priestly descent) who had been married 10 years and who, rather than divorce his barren wife and take another, as Jewish law would have preferred, decided to impregnate (with his wife's knowledge) a young Jewish woman who worked (and lived) in their home. When his "natural son" came of age, the kohen was eager for the young man to be called first to the Torah and to participate in the "priestly blessing," as befitted his paternal lineage, but there were those who felt that the boy's priestly standing had been marred by his illicit birth. The Roman rabbi, who was a kohen himself, ruled unequivocally that the young man's priestly credentials allowed him even to serve in the Holy Temple of Jerusalem, and Provenzale heartily agreed.[84] Some four years earlier, Provenzale had been asked a related question of some delicacy by his former student (and uncle of the sororicide Ishmael), Rabbi Ḥananiah Finzi, then residing in Ferrara. A married woman, who had borne her husband both sons and daughters, had an extended affair with her Jewish manservant. Her husband, who had repeatedly exhorted her to desist, eventually divorced her—after she acknowledged the sexual character of her relationship. The wayward woman was now determined to accept her young lover's offer of marriage, threatening that, if the local rabbis denied them permission to wed, as mandated by traditional Jewish law, then they would apostasize and marry in a Christian ceremony. Provenzale acknowledged that the lovers should optimally be harshly punished, so as to deter others from following their lead, but advised his former student, whose own niece would soon sin in a similar manner, to treat the errant couple gently for fear of driving them from adultery into apostasy.[85]

Although sexual affairs with Jewish maidservants were considerably more common among Italian Jewry than with manservants, the case described by Hananiah was not quite unique. Some three decades earlier, during the early 1540s, a young man serving as a banking apprentice and living in his employer's home seduced one of the latter's engaged daughters and, after she became pregnant, fled to Rome. There he was hired by another Jewish banker, again as a live-in apprentice. Not surprisingly, he continued his sexual adventures, this time with the married daughter-in-law of his employer. Her preoccupied husband, however, was quite slow in recognizing that the two had been conducting an affair, even when his mother reported finding them in bed together in their home one night. Only after repeated reports from several sources who had seen the couple together (especially during the evening prayers, when the male members of the household were in the synagogue), and after his wife gave birth to a second child (of uncertain paternity), did the cuckolded husband turn for advice to Rabbi Isaac de Lattes.[86]

Lattes, who had recently emigrated to Rome from his native Provence, may have been a bit surprised by certain aspects of Jewish marriage Italian-style, but after a quarter-century he certainly learned, in at least one aspect, to do as the Romans did. Late in the 1560s, after having successfully married off two of his daughters,[87] Lattes betrothed a third, Simḥa (Allegra), to the young scholar Rabbi Mordekhai da Foligno but found himself unable to deliver the entire sum of the promised dowry by the day of the wedding—a frequent cause of protracted engagements among Italian Jewry.[88] The groom nonetheless proceeded with the ceremony (which was not always the case), but his short-lived relationship with his father-in-law, who died a year later, proved to be a rather stormy one. Replying to a letter of Mordekhai's penned shortly after the wedding, Lattes called attention to the fact that he had refrained from addressing him as "father-in-law" and had failed also to sign off as "your son-in-law." To the former's obvious reluctance to acknowledge the familial bond between them, Lattes responded sharply: "Are you from an elevated family and is mine inferior to yours, or are you wiser than I am, or have you perhaps found me guilty of immoral conduct, or is your wife refusing to sleep with you?" If the last remark clearly aimed below the belt, the letter's conclusion did so even more blatantly:

"Here, take my daughter like a piece of meat," wrote Lattes, alluding to a well-known talmudic phrase (Nedarim 20b), "eat her roasted if you like, or eat her cooked; to me she is a stranger."[89]

Earlier in the sixteenth century Rabbi Joseph Arli, who preceded Lattes as tutor in the household of the formidable Sienese banker Ishmael da Rieti, wrote to his future son-in-law asking him to accept a dowry of only 150 scudi rather than the 250 he had initially promised, citing the need to educate his son in addition to marrying off his daughter. In the early seventeenth century, Leone Modena of Venice pledged a dowry of no less than thrice his annual salary upon the engagement of his first daughter, Diana, at the age of thirteen—relying, as he later wrote in his autobiography, "on heaven's mercy." The engagement, as was then common, lasted more than two years, primarily in order to allow time to raise the promised funds—something Modena managed only by the skin of his teeth. Nonetheless, he soon promised an even higher sum for the dowry of his second daughter, Esther, whose wedding date was, not surprisingly, twice postponed on account of her father's failure to raise the necessary funds.[90]

The problems presented by the need to amass a considerable dowry for daughters (if not quite as considerable as the sum that was promised) frequently found expression already at their birth. Like the Jews of the medieval Mediterranean before them, and like their Christian neighbors, Italian Jews of the Renaissance strongly preferred male offspring to female,[91] a preference that could be expressed in a wide variety of ways. A half-serious yet highly literary letter of consolation attributed to Ishmael da Rieti sought to comfort a friend to whom a daughter had just been born.[92] In 1556, Lattes appended to the (limited) license he granted a young Mantuan woman to perform ritual slaughter the invocation that, in return for performing the commandment, she be blessed with "male children who will teach Torah and faithfully observe God's commandments."[93]

Early in the sixteenth century, the founders of Ferrara's aforementioned Gemilut Ḥasadim society had required that members make a contribution upon the marriage of *either* a son or a daughter, but upon the birth *only* of a son.[94] Similarly, in 1576 the newly established dotal society in the ghetto of Venice, Ḥevrat Hasi Betulot (the first of its kind among Italian Jewry) required its members to contribute 50 percent more upon the birth of a son than upon the obviously less auspicious birth of a daughter.[95] As its members were especially well aware, daughters eventually had to be amply dowered.

But as its later scribe (and beneficiary) Leone Modena also learned, sons could present particular problems of their own. His eldest, Mordekhai, who died young and never married, seems to have been involved in a number of homosexual affairs, one of them with the banker Raphael Spira, in whose home he was employed from the age of 18 as tutor and banking assistant. Leone's guilt about the relationship, expressed in his autobiography, may well have derived from the fact that he himself had been the unsuspecting intermediary between the two. In that same work, Leone reported having exiled his son Isaac to Morea for "behaving improperly" as a 17-year-old, and he acknowledged also that the murder of his youngest son, Zebulon, by fellow Jews in the Venetian ghetto had been motivated by jealousy over the favors of a Jewish prostitute—Simḥa (Allegra), daughter of Nissim Shoshan. Unlike his grandfather Isaac, who had been fined for patronizing a Christian prostitute in Bologna during his youth, Zebulon Modena had fallen for a fallen woman of his faith, and he paid for it even more dearly.[96]

Simḥa/Allegra was neither the only Jewish woman in Venice nor the first of her faith in Italy to practice the world's oldest profession. According to the 1526–27 census of the city of Rome, which had an abnormally high male-to-female population ratio, about 30 of the city's prostitutes (who then numbered somewhere between 750 and 1,500) were Jewish.[97] In 1575, the organist of the Cathedral at Cremona was denounced for having "made love" with a Jewish woman known as "la Zenoeza," which would appear to have been her professional name. Late in the sixteenth century, three Jewish prostitutes (including the mother-daughter team Nahla and Gila) were operating in Mantua, where, according to the 1598 ban issued jointly by the rabbis and the council of the Jewish community, "many [Jews] had been confounded by them." Some five years later efforts were made, with the encouragement of the duke, to collect a dowry for Gila so that she could marry.[98] In 1620, there were also at least three Jewish prostitutes in Venice, which, like Rome, was internationally famous for its courtesans. Later in the seventeenth century, each of the two Frances brothers, Jacob and Immanuel, composed a Hebrew poem about a Jewish prostitute.[99]

No contemporary poems were written about Jewish slaughteresses, but they have attracted the attention of modern historians, some of whom saw them as reflecting the prominent position of women in Italian-Jewish society. Yet, as Robert Bonfil has shown, authorizing women to slaughter (which was technically permitted by the leading medieval halakhists but frowned upon in practice) simply reflected the realities of Jewish life in northern Italy, where communities were often small and men were often away on banking business. The latest license known to us was issued to Isota, daughter of Elḥanan Yael Fano and niece of the kabbalist Rabbi Menaḥem Azariah da Fano, shortly after her marriage in 1623. Nearly a decade earlier she had been issued a limited license permitting her to slaughter fowl, but not sheep or cattle. After her marriage to a member of the celebrated Foa family, she was authorized to perform the porging (*nikur*—removal of prohibited fat) of those animals but not the more strenuous act of slaughter. The latter license, which was issued by the official porger (*menaker*) of the Mantuan community, was countersigned by two of its rabbis, Baruch Gallico and Ḥananiah Finzi.[100]

Although both rabbis appended the epithet "the youthful" before their names, in the case of Finzi this was clearly a gesture of modesty, for he had been serving in the rabbinate for over half a century. In 1570, for example, he had consulted his former teacher, Moses Provenzale, concerning a woman who, prior to her marriage, shaved her head and had a wig made out of her own hair. Might

Ritual slaughter (porging) license granted to Isota, daughter of Elḥanan Fano, by Eliah ben Joseph of Forli. Mantua, 25 Kislev, 5375 (November 27, 1614). (Library of the Jewish Theological Seminary of America, New York. Photo: Suzanne Kaufman)

such a wig, he asked, serve as an acceptable head covering in place of the custom-ary veil or shawl? Provenzale admitted that he was unhappy with the use of wigs as a form of head covering for married women, but he acknowledged that "it was difficult to alter accepted practice."[101] Finzi was clearly able, on the basis of his teacher's responsum, to give the brave young woman, who had already shaved her head, permission to wear her own hair in a fashionable wig. It is not unlikely that he also permitted his wife to adorn her own head with false hair in accor-dance with "accepted practice."

ḤANANIAH FINZI AND HIS GENERATION

Ḥananiah Finzi belonged to that class of Italian rabbis who not only were born into banking families but were also themselves active loan bankers. He main-tained a partnership in the Mantuan region with his brothers Azariah/Bonaiuto (father of Ishmael) and Mordekhai/Angelo. Their father Salomone and grand-father Samson had operated a bank in the same region as well. As was common in such families, their sister, Simḥa/Allegra, also married a loan banker.[102] Ḥana-niah, despite serving in the rabbinate, was clearly affluent enough in 1581 to have a Torah scroll written for him by the noted Mantuan scribe Rabbi Meir Padua.[103]

Within six years, Ḥananiah had extended his economic activities to the sphere of Hebrew printing. In 1587, he was instrumental in the publication of five sepa-rate liturgical works in Venice. Of these, the edition of *Ma'amadot* was probably the least profitable, for eight years later no fewer than 1,268 copies were still in his possession. Ḥananiah's decision to print so many copies was the typically rash move of an over-enthusiastic novice. As Paul Grendler has observed, in late-sixteenth-century Venice "the normal press run of a title of ordinary or modest sales potential was about 1,000 copies; a major publisher with a title of assured high demand ordered press runs of 2,000 or 3,000 copies." In 1559, for example, the famed Aldine press published a number of learned titles for the Accademia Venetiana in print runs mostly ranging from 825 to 1,125 copies, but in 1572 it printed "six press runs of 3,300 copies, each in various formats, of a liturgi-cal work, the Little Office of Our Lady."[104] Ḥananiah seems to have believed that a liturgical work such as *Ma'amadot* would have a similar appeal among his coreligionists.

We know of the number of volumes in his possession because in 1595 the bishop of Mantua, acting on instructions from Rome, ordered the libraries of local Jews to be searched for books containing anti-Christian material, which re-sulted in the preparation of 430 detailed inventories. Consequently, we know considerably more about the libraries of Mantuan Jews, both male and female, than we do about those of any other early modern community.[105] Although Hananiah's list of some 2,500 tomes reflected only the "remainders" of his Venetian publishing venture, others, including those of his Finzi kinsmen (and kinswomen), reflect broader cultural interests. For example, 18 copies of Petrarch's sonnets and 31 copies of Ariosto's *Orlando Furioso* (of which the young Leone Modena had produced a partial Hebrew translation) were found in the homes of Mantuan Jews in 1595.[106] Petrarch's work appeared in the libraries of three members of the Finzi family: Judah ben Uziel, Raphael, and Yekutiel. Whereas Yekutiel Finzi possessed the largest of these libraries, comprising 225 printed Hebrew books and 15 Hebrew manuscripts, he owned only one other Italian book—a translation of Aristotle's *Ethics*.[107]

Raphael Finzi, who owned 22 Hebrew books and 6 in Italian, also included in his collection works by Ariosto and Tasso. One wonders whether he might have been the same Raphael Finzi who, nearly 30 years earlier, on the eve of Shavuot (May 13) 1567, had completed copying a kabbalistic commentary on the prayers by his father, Jacob Israel Finzi da Recanati—a controversial figure to whom we shall return. This would reflect an interesting—and, for the late sixteenth century, characteristic—symbiosis between Kabbalah and Renaissance culture.[108]

Judah Finzi's library reflected the impact of the Renaissance to an even greater degree. He owned only 17 Hebrew books and one manuscript, but 10 volumes in Italian. In addition to Petrarch's sonnets, his library included such popular works as Ovid's *Metamorphoses,* a basic source concerning classical mythology, and Baldesar Castiglione's *Book of the Courtier.* The former was quoted by such sixteenth-century Jewish savants as Azariah de Rossi, Judah Moscato, and Abraham Yagel, and it was also to be found in the Mantuan library of Graziosa Finzi. The latter, which has been justly described as "one of the best known and best-loved texts in the Renaissance," had been composed (in Italian) late in the first decade of the sixteenth century, and by century's end it had appeared in more than 100 editions (including translations into Spanish, French, Latin, German, and English).[109] A similar work in Judah Finzi's library, also owned by three other Mantuan Jews, was Antonio de Guevara's popular *Vita di Marco Aurelio,* a fictionalized and very rhetorical biography of the Roman emperor that had been written in Spanish during the second decade of the sixteenth century, when Guevara was in the service of Emperor Charles V. Twenty-one editions appeared in Italian translation alone between 1544 and the end of the sixteenth century, and the *Vita,* which the polymath Mantuan native de Rossi cited in his *Meor Enayim,* was also a popular item in the vernacular curriculum of Italian schools. Among the practical teachings the author, a former Franciscan, sought to inculcate, was that the attractions of the flesh have their season in life but should be subordinated to reason when youth has passed—advice useful to both Christians and Jews in Renaissance Italy.[110]

De Rossi may well have followed a lifestyle consonant with Guevara's advice, for when he was examined, in his mid-thirties, by the Marrano physician Amatus Lusitanus, the latter found him to be "slender and emaciated" (with his face the color of a lemon) and suffering from "melancholic sleeplessness." The latter symptom was seen by the physician to have resulted largely from de Rossi's habit of "study at night, which is harmful and contrary to nature." After following for four months the rigorous course of treatment prescribed by Lusitanus, however, "his strength increased to that of a boxer." Some two decades later, in the wake of an earthquake that shook Ferrara, where de Rossi was then living, in late 1571, he was able to produce (within just 18 months) his three-part *Meor Enayim,* which has justifiably been described as "the most remarkable Jewish work of the Renaissance period." It was less a book than a loose collection of essays, most of which dealt, in rather pioneering fashion, with aspects of Jewish antiquity considered in the light of Greek and Latin literature. De Rossi, who was the first Jewish writer to cite his ancient coreligionist Philo of Alexandria, was also familiar with such medieval Christian authors as Isidore of Seville, Thomas Aquinas, and Dante.[111]

Like other antiquarian scholars of his generation, he also consulted ancient coins, one of which came from the collection of a prominent Mantuan Jew, David ben Raphael Jacob Finzi da Fontanella. The collecting of ancient coins and medals had become enormously popular in Italy during the second half of the sixteenth century with the publication of such influential works as Enea Vico's *Discorsi sopra le medaglie de gli antichi* (1555) and Sebastiano Erizo's *Discorso sopra le medaglie,* which first appeared in 1559. David Finzi, to whose name the Mantuan scribe Meir ben Ephraim appended the honorific "the magnificent" (*ha-mefoar*) in his list of customers, also found other outlets for his wealth, ordering a particularly large and undoubtedly expensive Torah scroll in May 1566, just before the holiday of *Shavuot.*[112]

From another member of the Finzi family, however, emerged one of de Rossi's sharpest rabbinical critics—Rabbi Isaac ben Raphael Finzi of Pesaro, a former resident of Mantua. Like his former townsmen Moses Provenzale and Judah Moscato, Isaac was particularly upset about the section of *Meor Enayim* dealing with chronology, concerning which he sent de Rossi a detailed 13-point critique prior to the book's publication. The latter responded in an appendix he called *Ma'amar Tzedek 'Olamim.*[113] Nonetheless, on the eve of Passover in 1574, Isaac joined four other rabbis of Pesaro in signing the proposed ban on de Rossi's work that had been forwarded from Venice.[114]

KABBALISTS AND CONVERTS; FATHERS AND SONS

Rabbi Jacob Israel ben Raphael Finzi (of the family's Recanati branch), who is sometimes confused with the above-mentioned Isaac (who may have been his brother),[115] was a key figure in an earlier book-related controversy in Italy. This was the fierce debate that took place during the late 1550s over the publication of the *Zohar*—which, despite his own kabbalistic leanings, Jacob Israel vigorously opposed. Pesaro, the community in which he resided, was at the center of the controversy because its leadership was sharply divided over the issue. The physician Rabbi Judah (Laudadio) de Blanis, one of Pesaro's two community leaders (*parnasim*), supported the exoteric tendency characteristic of the Kabbalah's more philosophically inclined adherents, and he advocated publishing the *Zohar*, as did Isaac de Lattes, who then served as head of the local yeshivah—and whose responsum supporting publication was to appear in the book's first edition. However, Rabbi Menaḥem da Foligno, the community's other leader, opposed publication of the *Zohar*, and it was he who encouraged Jacob Israel, a respected kabbalist who often fused halakhah and Kabbalah in his responsa, to take a public position on the matter.[116]

In May 1558, shortly after the publication of the *Tikkunei ha-Zohar* and the *Ma'arekhet ha-Elohut*, but just before the *Zohar* itself appeared, Jacob Israel penned a vigorous responsum condemning the publication and dissemination of any kabbalistic works. Its opening lines, which convey a deep sense of isolation and sorrow, drew upon both the words of the prophet Elijah (I Kings 19:10, 14) and the liturgy for the Ninth of Av:

> I have been very jealous for the Lord and his holy Torah—the teachings [*Torah*] of the Kabbalah, trodden underfoot by the impudent and devoured by legions, published in the streets and marketplaces [and placed] before worthless persons . . . while she dons sackcloth and brings her grievance before her Creator.[117]

Jacob Israel was worried about kabbalistic material coming into the hands not only of uneducated Jews but also of Hebraically learned Christians who might "do with it what they wish," an allusion to the Christian Kabbalism that had been thriving in Italy for nearly a century. He may have been particularly concerned about the possibility that Christians would utilize the Kabbalah for missionary purposes.[118]

Later in the sixteenth century, the former Isaac Pugliese of Venice, who became Marcantonio degli Eletti ("of the elect") upon his conversion to Catholicism, mentioned that one of the books urged upon him during his deliberations was *De arcanis catholicae veritatis,* by the Italian Franciscan Pietro Galatinus. This work, which marshaled a variety of Hebrew sources (including kabbalistic ones) in support of Christianity, was first published, somewhat paradoxically, by the pioneer Jewish printer Gershom Soncino in 1518. It was republished in 1550 and proved quite popular for over a century. It was while chatting in a bookstore about *De arcanis* that the physician Amatus Lusitanus first met Azariah de Rossi, who was familiar with the Latin work. And Leone Modena's anti-Christian treatise *Magen va-Ḥerev,* composed during the 1640s (but not published until the twentieth century), was largely a response to the work of Galatinus, whose enormous influence he ruefully acknowledged.[119]

Unlike *De arcanis,* of which no copy was to be found among the 430 libraries of Mantuan Jews in 1595, the *Zohar* itself, first published in Mantua (1558–60) and then in Cremona (1559–60), could be found in more than 10 percent of their libraries—51 copies in all.[120] Whether or not its publication had any actual effect on conversionary efforts is not clear. True, Moses Provenzale of Mantua had advised caution when asked by Ḥananiah Finzi, in 1571, about an adulterous couple who threatened to apostasize if action were taken against them. It is also true that two years later he received a curious inquiry (from Siena) as to whether a clause might be introduced into the wedding ceremony canceling the marriage in the event of the groom's conversion to Christianity.[121] These, however, were not particularly new problems, and even members of the Finzi family had fallen victim to the various temptations of conversion. In 1454, for example, an Isaac Finzi, who resided in the Piedmont, decided to convert to Christianity. To this end the Duke of Savoy granted a letter of safe-conduct to a former Jew, Ludovico of Chambéry, whose task it was to escort Isaac to several prayer shrines on his way to the king of France, in whose presence he was to be christened.[122]

A responsum penned in 1470 by Rabbi Joseph Colon, who himself had been born in Chambéry, reflects the relative fluidity between Jewish and Christian worlds that characterized urban life in Italy before the era of the ghetto, and that facilitated religious conversion—in either direction. Falcone, an Ashkenazi Jew residing in Pavia who served as innkeeper of the hostel maintained (with difficulty) by the local Jewish community, wrote to Colon asking whether he, as a kohen, was permitted to resume relations with his errant wife. After six months or so of steady complaining about her husband's occupation (with good reason, he candidly acknowledged), she had finally walked out one afternoon, on the New Moon of Adar, while Falcone was studying with one of their daughters. One suspects, in fact, that their having been "blessed" with daughters who needed one day to be dowered contributed in no small measure to her dissatisfaction with her husband's job.

Taking with her some of her best clothes and some of the family silver, she ran, reported Falcone, with their four-year-old daughter in tow, into the home of a Christian neighbor whom she knew well, as she had sewn clothes for members of the family and had also taken in their laundry. Falcone noted in his letter to Colon that, since he had been deeply immersed in study with his older daughter, half an hour passed before he noticed his wife's absence. After checking the homes of some Jewish neighbors, he finally knocked on the door of the Christian woman. When her husband saw him at the door he attempted to shut it, but Falcone managed to force himself inside, where he came face to face with the assistant bishop, who welcomed him and told him not to worry, as well as four other local Christians—two men and two women.

The assistant bishop explained politely to Falcone that his wife had been imbued with a "different spirit" and that she was considering conversion to Christianity, to which end they were seeking to persuade her. He added, however, that if she chose not to convert "we shall advise her to return to her people and her God." Falcone asked for permission to speak with her in Yiddish and asked her why she would not come home, to which she replied unequivocally that she was no longer willing to be an innkeeper's wife. When Falcone assured her that she would have her wish, she replied tartly, "Do not mock me, for you have already lied to me ten times, and I no longer trust you." She did, however, agree to let him take their small daughter home. As Falcone was leaving, the clergyman assured him that his wife would not be coerced into hasty conversion, but that she would be sent to live among young nuns in a secluded convent for a trial period of 40 days, during which time she would make her final decision.

As Falcone reported to Colon, she did in fact enter the convent, to which she was escorted by seven women and two men, but after spending a day and a night there "her spirit was agitated" (Genesis 41:8). She sent word to the bishop expressing her wish to leave and explaining, moreover, that she was the wife of a kohen, "and if I remain for another day or two, I shall no longer be able to seek refuge beneath his wings, for he will banish me from his home."

Colon, in a decision seconded by two other rabbis (Judah Minz and Jacob of Mestre), ruled that Falcone could indeed accept his wife back into his home and bed, since there was no reason to suspect that she had been sexually violated while she flirted briefly, in mostly celibate surroundings, with the possibility of conversion. Even more striking than the sympathetic understanding shown by the three rabbis for the predicament of the priestly innkeeper and his wavering wife is that which had been shown by the local bishop when Zalman, a member of Pavia's Jewish community, approached him on the morning after Falcone's wife had entered the convent, hoping to recover whatever property she had taken with her. When the bishop informed him that she had already expressed her desire to leave, Zalman, thinking that it was a ruse, asked that she be given three, or perhaps even ten days, in order to make her mind up fully. To this the bishop is reported to have replied indignantly: "How can your mouth and heart allow you to utter such a thing? She has made it clear that if she remains another night her husband, who is a kohen, will never be able to take her back." The bishop also asked Falcone, when he came to fetch his wife from the convent, not to punish her or even reprimand her for what she had done.[123]

This fifteenth-century non-conversion story, which seems to cry out for conversion into a screenplay, even has an amusing aftermath. Some nine years later Falcone, as his wife (who, ironically, seems to have been named Gentile) had predicted, was still running Pavia's Jewish inn, but he had finally found a way of supplementing his income. In August 1479 the duke of Milan acceded to his request to allow Jews to gamble at the inn. It was stipulated, however, that if a Christian were to be found gambling there, Falcone himself would be fined the hefty sum of 50 ducats.[124]

Shortly before Falcone's wife left him and found temporary refuge in the home of a Christian neighbor, another female conversion saga, which ended rather differently, had begun elsewhere in the duchy of Milan. Sometime late in the 1460s, Caracosa, a daughter of the banker David of Castelnuovo, was baptized in Cremona by a layman using ordinary well water. Nonetheless the town's bishop gave his blessing to the act and proclaimed her a Christian, bestowing upon her the name of Archangela. On Good Friday and Easter Saturday of 1469, several Jews—despite being confined, in theory, to their quarters on those solemn days—demonstrated noisily in front of the bishop's palace and outside the convent in which Caracosa had been held. They had apparently been heartened by the duke's decision to send her to Milan so that the archbishop could ascertain whether she sincerely desired to convert. Some of the Jews were subsequently arrested. Despite their optimism, the archbishop decided, in fact, that Caracosa/Archangela had become a Christian and would remain one. After she announced her plans to marry a servant of the duke of Milan, the duke issued an order to have her father provide her with a dowry of 250 ducats—the same sum he had allocated for his other daughters. Adding insult to injury, the unfortunate father was eventually charged another 40 ducats for her wedding expenses.[125]

Around the same time, a Sicilian-born Jew, who was later to achieve fame as a Christian kabbalist under the name Flavius Mithridates, converted to Christianity through the sponsorship of Gugliemo Raimondo Moncada, count of

Aderno, and took the latter's name. By 1477 or thereabouts, after teaching Arabic and Hebrew in Palermo, he moved to Rome, where he became a protégé of Bishop Giovanni Battista Cibò, the future Pope Innocent VIII. On Good Friday in 1481, Gugliemo of Sicily, as he was then known, preached the "Sermon of the Passion" in the presence of Pope Sixtus IV and the College of Cardinals in the Vatican. The sermon was based chiefly, as Chaim Wirszubski has shown, "on Christological interpretations of Jewish or ostensibly Jewish texts" and sought to demonstrate that "what happened to Jesus had been foretold or foreshadowed by the Prophets and the Rabbis." Although Gugliemo/Flavius soon became familiar enough with the pope to dine regularly at his table, he eventually fell out of favor and was forced to flee north of the Alps, where he taught Hebrew and Kabbalah in Louvain, Cologne, Tübingen, and Basle. Upon returning to Italy he became, in 1486, the teacher of the celebrated and controversial humanist Pico della Mirandola and, consequently, as Wirszubski has stressed, "the first known translator of Kabbalah on a large scale." His Latin translations for Pico alone amounted to some 40 books of varying size "written by different authors, belonging to different periods, and representing different types of Kabbalah."[126]

During the sixteenth century, converts from Judaism continued to play an important and often dominant role in the various worlds of Christian Hebraism in Italy, which extended from the teaching of Hebrew and Aramaic to the censorship and burning of Hebrew books. In his *Emek ha-Bakha,* the first version of which was completed in 1558, Joseph ha-Kohen named three former coreligionists who had been, in his opinion, most responsible for instigating Pope Julius III against the Talmud and causing many copies to be confiscated and burnt throughout Italy. These were Ḥananel da Foligno, Joseph Moro, and Solomon Romano.

The biography of the first is particularly interesting. Before his conversion, he was a moneylender and businessman in the Umbrian towns of Foligno and Spoleto. A condotta between the residents of the former and the brothers Ḥananel/Graziadio and Gamliel/Camillo was approved by the papal chamberlain (on orders from Clement VII) in June 1530. Some eight years later, the chamberlain approved a similar condotta between Ḥananel/Graziadio, his wife Giusta, and the commune of Spoleto. After the decline of his business fortunes during the early 1540s, he went to Rome, where he was baptized by none other than Ignatius Loyola, founder of the Jesuit order, in the church of Santa Maria della Strada, taking the name Alessandro Franceschi. By 1548 he was serving as Hebrew scribe of the Vatican library, and within a few years he also became lecturer of Hebrew at the University of Rome. At the time of his conversion, Ḥananel/Graziadio/Alessandro's wife, who refused to become a Christian, was pregnant with their first child. Although she fled from the Papal States in order to avoid having the unborn child raised as a Christian (as Church policy required), Giusta was eventually tracked down—as a consequence of her husband's appeal to Pope Paul III. Her son, who was given the name Ottavio, was brought up by the Jesuits of Rome and eventually joined the Dominican order, but he also acquired enough of his ancestral language to succeed his father as Hebrew scribe of the Vatican library. Later in life he was bishop of Forli.[127]

Another noted father and son "team" of converts in sixteenth-century Rome were Elia Corcos, who had been one of the leaders of the local community, and his son Moses, both of whom took the surname Ghislerio after being baptized personally by Pope Pius V (r. 1566–72). Moses also took on his sponsor's chosen papal name and was henceforth known as Pio Ghislerio. It was under that name that he served as the pope's agent for the distribution of dowries to female converts.[128]

Farther to the north, in the duchy of Milan, a no less interesting conversion saga may be found among the Ottolenghi, an Ashkenazic banking family in Lodi. Abraham Ottolenghi was 14 when his father, Yeḥiel/Michele, died at the age of 50 in 1567, leaving all his ample assets to his eight children, most of whom were still minors, as well as to the one being carried by his pregnant wife. By the time Abraham came of age, some four years later, to draw his share of the inheritance, he had converted to Christianity and changed his name to Vespasiano de Canibus. By 1598, however, Abraham/Vespasiano had apparently returned to the faith of his father(s), for in that year he married a Jewish widow from Lodi, where he had continued to reside after his conversion.[129]

Abraham was not the first Jewish convert in Italy to take the flamboyant name of Vespasiano. Earlier in the sixteenth century, Jacob Meshullam, a son of the legendary banker Anselmo del Banco, became the Cavalier Marco Paradiso upon converting to Christianity in 1533, having received from the Venetian doge Andrea Griti the coveted status of Cavalier di San Marco as part of the package. As early as 1531, Pope Clement VII had authorized Jacob, who had been one of the most prominent members of the Paduan Jewish community (having participated, as Capsali noted, in the 1509 election of Abraham Minz as head of the local yeshivah), to retain his property after being baptized, but he seems to have intentionally waited until after his father's death before leaving his ancestral faith. This was not true of Jacob's own sons, two of whom preceded him to the baptismal font. A third joined Jacob when he himself converted to Christianity on July 15, 1533. Unlike the Cavalier Marco Paradiso, at least one former Jew named Jacob was content to change his name merely to Giacomo. Many converts chose, like Gugliemo Raimondo Moncada (a.k.a. Flavius Mithridates) and

Pio Ghislerio, to take the names of their Christian sponsors, but there were sometimes other onomastic considerations. A Venetian Jew who entered the local Casa dei Catecumeni on St. Bartholomew's Day (August 24), 1595, became Bartolomeo after his baptism.[130]

THE CARMIS OF CREMONA

In the will in which Yeḥiel/Michele Ottolenghi provided for the future Vespasiano de Canibus, he had also stipulated that his daughter Marta would receive the handsome sum of 2,000 gold scudi upon her marriage to Yekutiel/ Consiglio, the eldest son of the distinguished banker Saul Raphael Carmi. The Carmis of Cremona, a wealthy Ashkenazic banking family whose fortunes will occupy much of our attention in the coming pages, tended to intermarry during the sixteenth century with two other banking families—first with their fellow Lombardians (and fellow Ashkenazim) the Ottolenghi, and then with members of the Italiani Foa family of Reggio Emilia. Saul Raphael's father, Menaḥem Carmi, had arrived in Cremona from Venice during the early 1540s and appears in archival documents as the banker Emanuele Carmine (or Carmini), son of the late Moise of Casalmaggiore. His big business breakthrough had come in 1542, when he managed to become sole inheritor of his late father's loan bank— a matter considerably facilitated by the fact that his only surviving brother had been insane for 14 years. Four years later, he was among the eight Cremonese Jews who were responsible for deciding the share each of their coreligionists would pay of the tax annually levied by the local commune upon the Jewish community. Menaḥem/Emanuele's growing status as a banker in Cremona is clearly reflected in the fact that, in 1557, he contributed a full 20 percent of the 3,000 scudi mandatory loan levied by the commune upon the Jews—the largest single contribution by any member of the community.[131]

Menaḥem/Emanuele Carmi had married the sister of Joseph Ottolenghi, a prominent rabbi active in both loan banking and Hebrew printing whose family had evidently originally hailed from Ettlingen in Germany, though it is possible that their name, like that of the Carmis, was derived from an Italian town.[132] In April 1559, when the Inquisition confiscated many cases of Talmud tomes from the Jews of Cremona, the bulk were taken from these two Ashkenazic brothers-in-law.[133] Marital ties between their two families continued for at least two more generations: Menaḥem/Emanuele Carmi's younger son Yeḥiel/Michele married his cousin, a daughter of Joseph Ottolenghi. His grandson Yekutiel/Consiglio, the eldest son of his own elder son Saul Raphael, later married Marta, the orphaned daughter of Yeḥiel/Michele Ottolenghi, as noted above. In October 1580 another of Saul Raphael's sons, Abraham, married his cousin Kilah Carmi, who was a granddaughter of both Menahem Carmi and Joseph Ottolenghi. The family diary Abraham began to keep after that event, together with the letters he and his brothers (under the guidance of their tutors) had earlier begun to exchange in Hebrew, provide an unusually intimate glimpse of the worlds, both male and female, of late-sixteenth-century north Italian Jewry.

Early in the 1570s, Yekutiel/Consiglio, by then already married to Marta, penned a letter to one of her brothers who was then studying in Vercelli with the Carmi family's former in-house tutor, Rabbi Zanvil (David Samuel/Simone) Pescarol, alongside his own younger brother Abraham. "I believe," he wrote, "that the path you have chosen—to embrace the foreign [= Italian] tongue without forsaking the German [= Yiddish] tongue—is a good one, for both are useful in study." Yekutiel/Consiglio predicted that his brother-in-law would therefore fare better linguistically than he had, who remained, he claimed, inadequate in both spoken languages. He expressed surprise, however, that his young correspondent had arranged with Pescarol to pursue their biblical studies in Yiddish and their talmudic studies in Italian: "For, in my modest opinion, the opposite would seem more appropriate, since the Ashkenazim exceed the Italian Jews in incisive and elaborate talmudic argumentation [*ha-pilpul veha-harifut*], while the Italians are vastly superior in grammatical analysis and precise interpretation."[134]

This cultural distinction between the two ethnic groups was widely noted. Earlier in the sixteenth century, Rabbi Israel of Perugia, an Ashkenazi Jew who had emigrated with his sons to Jerusalem, wrote back proudly to his Umbrian benefactor that his Hebrew speech and writing were of sufficient merit that he was thought by the local Jews to be an Italiani rather than an Ashkenazi. The dichotomy noted by Yekutiel/Consiglio between the intellectual skills of Ashkenazic and Italiani Jews would be echoed, from a different perspective, in the seventeenth century by Judah Asael del Bene in his *Kissot le-Veit David* (1648). Del Bene was a proud representative of the Italiani cultural tradition, and he was highly critical of those Ashkenazic Jews in Central Europe who found much time for rabbinic literature but hardly any for biblical and grammatical studies.[135]

The choice of Pescarol as young Abraham Carmi's mentor was hardly an arbitrary one, for he had earlier served as in-house tutor to Abraham's older brothers Yekutiel/Consiglio and Moses.[136] Both brothers, when writing to Abraham in Vercelli, closed by asking him to "kiss the hands" of their former teacher. And Pescarol, in a letter sent during the mid-1570s to the joint household of Saul Raphael and Yekutiel/Consiglio Carmi in Cremona, congratulating them on the

birth of a baby girl, inserted the words "I kiss your hands" before signing off as
their "loyal servant."[137]

Although Pesacrol, like the youths he taught, came from an Ashkenazic banking family based in Lombardy, his had recently fallen on hard times. His father,
Kalynomos (Clemente) ben Moses, had been a loan banker in Cremona since
the 1530s, and in 1546 had served alongside Menaḥem/Emanuele Carmi as one of
the eight bankers responsible for deciding how much each of the local Jews
would pay in taxes. Less than a decade later, however, Pescarol was imprisoned
on account of his numerous unpaid debts to coreligionists in a number of Italian communities, and in October 1556 the bank belonging to him and his two
sons was sold to cover those debts.[138] This forced sale seems, therefore, to have
indirectly launched Pescarol's career as a teacher to the Carmi boys and other
young members of their class—and his.

Such a position, though technically that of a glorified servant,[139] would have
provided a learned young man of straitened circumstances with free room and
board, a respectable address, and some spending money. In 1571, the newly married but impecunious Mordekhai da Foligno, who had recently quarreled with
his noted father-in-law Isaac de Lattes after having been shortchanged on his
dowry, joined (without his wife) the joint household of the brothers Saul
Raphael and Yeḥiel/Michele Carmi. Mordekhai, who unlike his predecessor
Pescarol was not of Ashkenazi background, may also have intentionally sought
by entering such a household to rankle his father-in-law, whose sharp criticisms of Italy's Ashkenazic rabbis (for allegedly favoring their fellow Ashkenazim) had been openly expressed in responsa written only a few years earlier.[140]
Mordekhai's prime responsibility (or, rather, challenge) was to tutor Saul Raphael's son Abraham, then a few months short of his bar mitzvah, in both religious and secular subjects. Writing to Abraham some years later, Mordekhai
reminded him of his profound ignorance at the time, noting also that many had
sought to dissuade him from taking on the bratty young aristocrat as a student,
since previous masters had been unable to tame him, finding that "even if beaten
with a rod he budges not from mischief."[141]

Yet within a decade, by October 1580, Abraham Carmi had become a reasonably learned and quite respectable young man, marrying his Cremonese cousin
Kilah, who was also a granddaughter of his own godfather (*sandak*), Joseph Ottolenghi. When joyfully recording their marriage in the Hebrew family diary he
then began to keep, Abraham was able, with apparently little effort, to quote
Psalms 68:7 ("God restores the lonely to their homes . . .") in an allusion to a talmudic passage (Sanhedrin 22a) referring to God's matchmaking virtuosity. And
when recording the death in early 1582 of his uncle and father-in-law Gideon

Yeḥiel/Michele Carmi (who had acquired an additional name, as was customary, during a previous illness—and rabbinic ordination, as was less customary, after his death), Abraham was able to cite the talmudic teaching (Shabbat 153a) that the manner in which a person was eulogized reflected the manner in which he would be received into the next world. One suspects that the posthumous ordination that Abraham's late uncle received on the day of his funeral had been awarded by the rabbi and banker Isaac Foa of Reggio, in whose home the deceased had been nursed during a previous illness—and to whose daughter Eugenia his son (Abraham's cousin) Menaḥem had become engaged by Purim of 1581.[142]

Marital relations between the Carmi and the Foa families had begun during the early 1570s, when Saul Raphael's second son Moses married Isaac Foa's daughter, Esther/Stellina. When Saul Raphael died in Reggio late in the summer of 1591, he too had acquired an additional name, Israel, and he too was honored upon his death with rabbinic ordination; in his case, however, the supreme title of gaon was bestowed upon him, in recognition of his decades of service to the Jews of Cremona and the duchy of Milan.[143] Since Isaac Foa was then no longer living, it would seem likely that his distinguished son-in-law, the great kabbalist Menahem Azariah da Fano (who would later be named executor of Saul Raphael's will), had bestowed the honor.[144]

By the time of Saul Raphael's death, his family, including his son Abraham and daughter-in-law Kilah, had been living in the small town of Brescello, north of Reggio, for several years. Shortly before their departure from Cremona, Abraham had an Ashkenazic *mahzor* for the High Holy Days copied for him, apparently expecting such items to be harder to come by in Brescello. It was in that prayer book, completed shortly before Rosh Hashanah in 1585, that Abraham eventually entered the information that constituted his family diary. And it was in Brescello, during the 1580s, that Abraham and Kilah's first child was born while Abraham was in Venice on business. Sadly, the child died after only eight days and never received a name. When recording his daughter's birth and death, Abraham consoled himself with the hope, alluding to yet another talmudic teaching (Baba Kama 141a), that her arrival would augur the future birth of sons.[145]

Yet, when after 14 years of marriage, in October 1594, Abraham Carmi, his pregnant wife Kilah, and their nearly three-year-old daughter Simḥa/Allegra moved into their own home, a step he took only after his father's death, the prayers he expressed in the family diary did not include the hope that he would be blessed with male children. His wife's chronic obstetric difficulties and the fact that their only son (named after Abraham's late uncle and father-in-law,

Circumcision bowl, Italy, seventeenth century. Silver, gilded, with inscription from Joshua 5:3. (In the permanent collection of The Magnes Museum, Berkeley; 2000.7.1. Photo: Ben Ailes)

Yeḥiel/Michele) had survived only 16 months, clearly contributed to his readiness to regard even the birth of a daughter as an unmitigated blessing. When this short-lived son was born in early 1589, Saul Raphael Carmi had performed the circumcision, just as he had performed Abraham's over three decades previously.[146] Rather than asking one of his brothers or another male relative to serve as sandak, however, Abraham (rather unusually) kept the "honor" for himself—perhaps in order to keep a close eye on his aged father's hand.

There was, of course, no godmother—a role by then long obsolete in Ashkenazic circumcision ceremonies,[147] but still quite common among the local Italiani. Recording his impressions of Rome in 1581, the vast majority of whose Jews were Italiani,[148] Michel de Montaigne described in great detail a circumcision ceremony, which he witnessed "very attentively and with great profit." Montaigne reported that the Jews "give the boys a godfather and godmother, as we do. . . . The godfather sits down on a table and puts a pillow on his lap; the godmother brings him the infant there and then goes away."[149] Perhaps the best source we have for the custom of double godparenthood among the Italiani, however, is the celebrated autobiography of Leone Modena, to which we have already turned repeatedly.

Modena mentioned both his godparents among the major participants in his own circumcision ceremony, which took place in 1571. On that occasion the "noted kabbalist Rabbi Menaḥem Azariah Fano" had performed the procedure, while Leone's own father Isaac and a female relative from his father's side, "Sarah, the daughter of my uncle Shemaiah," served as his godparents. When Leone's wife Rachel (née Simḥa) gave birth to their first son, Mordekhai, in 1591, both paternal grandparents served as the child's godparents—reflecting, perhaps, the apparently Europe-wide convention of grandparents having a special claim to the godparenthood of firstborn children. At the circumcision of their next son, Isaac, two years later, it was the turn of the two maternal grandparents to serve as godparents. When in March 1595 a third son, Abraham (who died soon of smallpox), was born to Leone and Rachel, her uncle and aunt were the godparents. And upon the birth of Zebulon, in May 1601, the two godparents were Rachel's brother Moses Simḥa and his wife. In all four instances, it should

be noted, both godparents were from the same side of the family, contrary to
what John Bossy has called the "obligatorily bilateral" system common throughout Western Christendom, whereby a godparent on one side of the family "must
be balanced" by a godparent of the opposite sex on the other.[150]

The custom of double godparenthood among Jews seems, at least in the early
modern period, to have been uniquely Italian. In their respective accounts of circumcisions performed in late-sixteenth-century Prague and Avignon, neither
Fynes Moryson nor Felix Platter (in contrast to Montaigne in Rome) mentioned
the existence of a godmother.[151] Similarly, when Abraham Carmi was away in
Vercelli during the early 1570s, his older brother Yekutiel/Consiglio wrote from
Cremona informing him that he would soon be going to nearby Lodi in order to
serve as sandak for his brother-in-law's newborn son. Although this was an event
in his wife's family (the Ottolenghi), no mention was made of her joining him to
serve as godmother. And when one of Abraham's younger brothers was born,
apparently in 1575, the child's father (Saul Raphael), who was away on business,
instructed his brother (and partner) Yehiel/Michele to "kiss the hands" of their
distinguished relative by marriage, Isaac Foa of Reggio, and invite him to Cremona, "to hold the child on his knees when he was brought into the covenant."[152]
Although Foa was invited to bring his wife along, she was clearly not invited to
serve alongside him as godmother. The Carmi would gladly intermarry with
such prominent Italiani families as the Foa, just as they would with their other
kinsmen the Ottolenghi, but like the latter they adhered steadfastly to their
Ashkenazic traditions.

Nonetheless, some non-Ashkenazic traditions crept into Carmi family practice. The brothers Yekutiel, Moses, and Abraham were all in the habit, as we have
seen, of concluding their letters with references to ritualized hand-kissing of a
deferential nature, which in the early seventeenth century was still seen as foreign to Ashkenazic practice.[153] And when Abraham and Kilah's only child to survive infancy was born, in early 1592, she was named Simha/Allegra after his
mother, who was, clearly, still alive. Nearly six years later, in late December 1597,
Abraham recorded another birth—a son named Raphael, after his formidable
father Saul Raphael. Abraham's eldest brother Yekutiel/Consiglio, who had some
years earlier acquired the additional Hebrew name of Benjamin (probably during a serious illness),[154] served as his nephew's circumcisor, and one of the child's
maternal uncles, Vardimas Samson Foa,[155] held him on his knees. With a younger
circumcisor this time, Abraham did not insist on doing the honor himself. Like
many previous circumcisions in the Carmi family, however, a prominent Italiani
relative was selected as godfather but was not "teamed" with a godmother. Sadly,
six weeks later the infant Raphael was dead.[156]

THE END OF AN ERA

The infant's death came in the midst of other difficulties, both for the Carmis and more generally for the Jews of the duchy of Milan. In December 1596, Yekutiel/Consiglio Carmi had been one of the two recipients of a letter from the governor of Milan informing them, in the name of the Spanish Crown, that the Jews of the duchy had two months in which to leave. Several months later Yekutiel/Consiglio, following in the footsteps of his father, was named one of the four representatives of the duchy's Jews who were given permission to remain behind in order to collect debts and liquidate businesses. The three rabbis who were given responsibility, in 1600, for settling these accounts of Jewish former residents of the duchy of Milan were Menḥem Azariah da Fano (a Carmi relative by marriage), Vitale Meli, and Ḥananiah Finzi of Mantua. Yekutiel/Consiglio and his family had a number of opportunities for relocating, but it was ultimately to Brescello, under the rule of the Este, where his late father Saul Raphael had moved during the 1580s, that he decided to take his family, joining his brothers Abraham, Menaḥem/Emanuele, and Yom Tov/Bondieo by the beginning of 1601. The brothers seem to have diversified their economic pursuits while residing in Brescello and to have consulted Menaḥem Azariah about the ritual permissibility of profiting from the rental of land upon which pigs were being raised.[157]

The turn of the seventeenth century was also difficult for the Jewish community of Ferrara, where during the early 1590s Menaḥem Azariah, who resided with his father-in-law in Reggio, had sent two of his young sons to be educated and even enrolled them in the local Gemilut Ḥasadim. From a peak of approximately 2,000 in 1590, the Jewish population of Ferrara fell to 1,530 in 1601. The community's decline was precipitated by the death of Duke Alphonso II in 1597, after which time Ferrara was lost to the Este dynasty and incorporated into the Papal States. As a result of the stricter measures imposed upon the community by the new authorities, which included a drastic reduction in the number of synagogues, Jews began to leave Ferrara in considerable numbers. One institution that benefited, paradoxically, from this instability was the venerable Gemilut Ḥasadim confraternity. Between 1598 and 1601, four new members joined its ranks, all of them children—three of whom were entered by their anxious parents on the very day they were circumcised. All in all, the confraternity grew from 44 members in 1583 to 64 two decades later, an increase of 45 percent. This, however, reflected the concomitant decline of the community's other institutions. Although the Jews of Ferrara were not forced into a ghetto until 1626, from the early seventeenth century the city ceased, as Cecil Roth noted, "to be a great center of Jewish life."[158]

Nor was this an easy time for the Jews of Mantua. In 1595, as noted above, the bishop of Mantua, acting on instructions from Rome, had ordered more than 400 libraries of local Jews, including four belonging to members of the Finzi family, to be searched for books containing anti-Christian material. In August of that same year, Jewish attendance at compulsory Christian sermons,[159] which in the past had never been strictly enforced in Mantua, came under the exacting, and painfully ironic, enforcement of the Jewish community. Anyone unable to attend would not be permitted to send a replacement but would be required to go on another occasion. Furthermore, anyone refusing to attend the missionary sermons would have his name proclaimed in the community's synagogues and would not be allowed "to join a minyan of worshipers, nor be called to the Torah as long as he persists in his refusal."

On a Saturday morning in April 1600, a 77-year-old Jewish woman was burned at the stake in Mantua's cathedral square, in the presence of more than 10,000 people (including Duke Vincenzo and his wife, Lady Eleanora), for having engaged in witchcraft. Among the alleged targets of her sorcerous spells was a local nun who had been born Jewish. In August 1602, seven Mantuan Jews, all male, were hung by their feet in the same cathedral square, before an even larger crowd, after having allegedly staged in their synagogue a mock sermon by a visiting fiery Franciscan monk. Later that month the duke, who had ordered the execution of the men and the banishment from Mantua of their widows and children, began negotiations with the Jewish community concerning the establishment of a ghetto, which was completed within a decade.[160]

Shortly before its completion, Menaḥem Azariah da Fano, who was then in his sixties, moved from Reggio to Mantua, where his younger brother Elḥanan Yael was a leading member of the community. Elḥanan Yael had previously resided in Ferrara, where his elder brother had circumcised three of his sons between 1590 and 1596. Their sister Isotta, whose date and place of birth are not known, did not, of course, have the distinction of being circumcised by a great kabbalist, but she did eventually receive, as noted above, formal permission first to slaughter fowl and then, after her marriage in 1623, to perform the ritual porging of sheep and cattle. Isaac Berechia da Fano, the eldest of her brothers, elected (perhaps with some pressure from his father) to have two of his own sons circumcised by his renowned, but aging, uncle. The younger of the two was born in Mantua in February 1619 and was the last child to be circumcised by Menaḥem Azariah—whose *pinkas mohel* (circumcisor's register) has fortunately survived. Within 18 months the great kabbalist was dead.[161]

According to the dirge composed after his death by the young Modenese kabbalist Rabbi Joseph Jedidiah Carmi, Menaḥem Azariah died at the age of 72, in
Ab (August) 1620. Later that summer, Joseph Jedidiah, who might have wished
to receive his *moreinu* (advanced rabbinic ordination) title from the foremost
Italian kabbalist of his time, received it instead from the controversial Venetian
rabbi Leone Modena, whose anti-kabbalism was later to be expressed in his *Ari
Nohem* (The Roaring Lion). Modena, however, had at least been one of Menaḥem Azariah's 169 circumcisees over more than half a century, a fact that he
proudly noted in his autobiography. In granting Joseph Jedidiah's ordination,
Modena cited not only his learning but also the "eminent family" from which he
came.[162] By this the Venetian rabbi seems to have alluded less to Joseph Jedidiah's
father (Benjamin Yekutiel Carmi) than to his two grandfathers, both eminent
bankers, who had been among the leading figures of late-sixteenth-century Italian Jewry and who had arranged a number of marriages between their offspring.
Saul Raphael Carmi of Cremona and later Brescello, Joseph Jedidiah's paternal
grandfather, had, as noted above, been awarded the title of gaon after his death
in 1591. Isaac Foa of Reggio, his maternal grandfather, had been learned enough
to be a gaon in his lifetime, and he perhaps best exemplified the Italian model of
the banker-rabbi.

Joseph Jedidiah, who was also a silversmith, achieved no small measure of
renown through his controversial collection of Cordoverian kabbalistic liturgy,
Kenaf Renanim. Completed in 1625 and published in Venice two years later, his
work sparked a bitter conflict, even before its publication, between its author
and his Modenese neighbor, the influential kabbalist Rabbi Aaron Berechia,
who had recently published a similar work, *Ashmoret ha-Boker* (1624), which
reflected the emergent Lurianic orientation.[163] As in many Italian-Jewish controversies, there were financial disagreements in the background as well as a network of family connections, which complicated matters even further. One of the
letters of approbation that appeared in *Kenaf Renanim* had been written by the
kabbalist Rabbi Moses Foa, a great-uncle of the author, who was the younger
brother of his maternal grandfather, Isaac Foa of Reggio.[164] Another was contributed by Ḥananiah Finzi of Mantua, who had recently approved the authorization of his townswoman Isotta Foa as a ritual porger. Yet Isotta's husband
Matzliaḥ Menaḥem had generously supported the publication, in Mantua, of
Berechia's *Ma'avar Yabok* (1626), a kabbalistically tinged handbook of death-
related rituals and liturgy that was to become the standard guide of Jewish
thanatological practice for centuries.

When Judah Minz died in Padua during the first decade of the sixteenth century, Elijah Capsali felt the need to transcribe the precise manner in which the

great rabbi departed the world, and the members of Minz's yeshivah, together with leaders of the community, devoted much deliberation to the details of the funeral. After 1626, however, such deliberations became increasingly obsolete, because the *Ma'avar Yabok*—which reflected popular practice as much as it shaped it, and which appeared in numerous popular abridgments—gradually became the guide both for those preparing to cross the narrow river from life into death and for those who were seeing them off on their final journey.

This was only one of the respects in which the seventeenth century witnessed a narrowing of options, cultural as well as religious, for the Jews of northern Italy. Within the increasingly ubiquitous ghettos, distinguished families continued to marry according to predictable patterns, and fortunes continued to be made and unmade according to the unpredictable vicissitudes of vicars and dukes. In the evenings, learned scholars would still take out their weighty tomes, frustrated husbands would flirt hopefully with their maidservants, and promenading young men would continue to cast amorous glances at coquettish courtesans. But there was a recurrent sameness to these well-rehearsed steps in the dance of life—and death.

When Mordekhai Bassani, the chief rabbi of Verona who had served the community in various capacities since 1660, died there in 1703, the communal scribe made a point of noting, while describing the rabbi's funeral, that "he had been purified according to the order prescribed in *Ma'avar Yabok*." He also noted, for the record, that the rabbi's soul "had expired with [the word] *eḥad* [one]," the ringing last word of the opening verse of the *Shema*.[165] Both statements were essentially a form of scribal shorthand for saying that Bassani had departed the world in the (by then) officially prescribed manner.

The literary motif of uttering the *Shema* with one's dying breath is, of course, an ancient one, going back to talmudic times, but it was not always standard practice. Capsali, for example, made no mention of Judah Minz uttering the *Shema* in his detailed description of the great Paduan rabbi's death in 1509. However, Leone Modena, in one of the two accounts he wrote of his son Mordekhai's premature death in 1617 (as a result of alchemical experimentation), reported that "psalms and confessions did not leave his lips until his soul departed with *eḥad*."[166] One senses that, even if these words were not literally true, they were, by Modena's time, what must be said about someone who had died well. By the same token, in 1703, when Bassani died in Verona, it was appropriate to report that his funeral rites had followed the order prescribed in Berechia of Modena's by-then-classic *Ma'avar Yabok*. And when another rabbi of Verona, Nathan Pincherle, died there precisely half a century later, his contemporary biographer reported that he was surrounded at the moment of death by more than a dozen members of the community, who were "reciting Psalms, as well as verses contained in *Ma'avar Yabok*."[167]

In fact, even a century later, Anna Morisi, the servant of the Mortara family in Bologna whose alleged baptism of young Edgardo in 1852 led to the international incident known as "the Mortara affair," testified that she became aware of the severity of the infant's illness when she saw members of the family, "sitting, sad and crying, at a little table next to Edgardo's crib, reading from a book in Hebrew that the Jews read when one of them is about to die." There is little doubt that the Hebrew book was *Ma'avar Yabok,* or one of its abridgments. Anna knew how to interpret this somber scene since she had learned from her sister Monica, who worked for the Mortaras for four years before her, "that when a Jew was about to die, they stood over him and read a book in Hebrew."[168]

A FINAL FUNERAL

In contrast to the Veronese rabbis Bassani and Pincherle, however, when Rabbi Samuel Aboab, the great Venetian rabbi of converso descent, died in 1694, neither the rituals of dying nor the funeral arrangements, as later described by Samuel's son and successor Jacob, adhered closely to the dictates of Berechia's work. In fact, no mention at all was made of *Ma'avar Yabok* in Jacob's account of his father's very ritualized and very public death. Samuel Aboab, "the story of whose life," as Cecil Roth remarked, "was in itself a romance," was born in Hamburg, where his father and other members of the family traded under the name Faleiro. In 1623, at the age of 13, Samuel was sent to Venice to study with Rabbi David Franco, who soon died and "whose portionless daughter Mazzaltob," noted Roth, Aboab "gallantly married."[169] In 1637 he moved, together with his wife, father, and brothers, to Verona as part of the first contingent of Sephardic Jews to enjoy some measure of autonomy in that traditionally Ashkenazic enclave—at the expense, however, of participation in the affairs of the community at large. By 1650 Samuel was back in the city of the lagoons as rabbi of its Ponentine community.[170]

Even before his departure for Venice, Aboab's considerable standing as a halakhist led other Italian rabbis, Sephardic as well as Italiani, to turn to him for advice. His Venetian colleague Rabbi Azariah Figo, for example, consulted him on subjects ranging from the permissibility of wearing decorative spurs on the Sabbath (concerning which both took a lenient position) to the thorny case of a kohen who was living with a divorcée (and former prostitute) as his concubine. Although the latter relationship was multiply problematic in ritual terms, it did have the salutary effect of keeping the woman off the streets of the ghetto. Another delicate question that came to Aboab from Venice was sent by his future colleague Rabbi Moses Zacuto, who asked in 1646 whether a rabbinic scholar who abstained from setam yenam at home, but not when traveling, might be deemed trustworthy concerning the provenance of a cask of wine in his own possession. Zacuto himself had been of two minds on this question and had composed two conflicting responsa, but Aboab, who clearly felt a need to make a statement condemning the rampant permissiveness, ruled against the itinerant imbiber's reliability.[171] Two decades later, during the manic messianic fervor that affected most Italian communities, he shrewdly charted a cautious course of prudence with regard to the Sabbatian movement, a course that bolstered his position of leadership, within the ghetto of Venice and beyond it, during the post-Sabbatian era.[172]

One senses that, for the heavily Sephardic community of Venice, the death of Aboab in 1694 was no less momentous an occasion than was the demise of Judah Minz for the Ashkenazim of early-sixteenth-century Padua. In both instances, protocol seems to have required, paradoxically, that a new protocol be invented. Whereas in Capsali's account of Minz's funeral it is the latter's yeshivah that dominates throughout the entire ceremony, at the rites surrounding Aboab's death in Venice a wider variety of participants were involved. His sons, together with the city's leading rabbis, prepared the body for burial. The late rabbi's students were then the first to carry his coffin from his yeshivah through the streets of the ghetto, all of whose shops were closed. Waiting to accept the coffin from them were the seven members of the community's "small council," who carried it to the entrance of the Ponentine synagogue, where Aboab had customarily prayed. There the coffin was placed on the shoulders of the Ponentine *ma'amad*, or council, whose members carried it to the synagogue's courtyard, where he was eulogized for the first time. After much weeping, the members of the Levantine ma'amad carried Aboab's body to their house of study to be eulogized again. From there he was taken by the leaders of the Scuola Tedesca (Ashkenazic synagogue), where the third eulogy took place. Representatives of the entire Venetian community, clothed in black and carrying burning torches, then escorted the deceased rabbi by boat from the ghetto to the Jewish cemetery on the Lido, where he was eulogized for the fourth time.[173]

Minz's funeral had moved, as Capsali noted, between two sites at which torches were kindled—the courtyard outside his home and yeshivah, and the cemetery. In Padua's homogeneously Ashkenazic community, there were no other sites with which ritual contact had to be made. Aboab's procession, by contrast, stopped three times along the way—at the synagogues of each of Venice's three communities, whose members and leaders were thus able to give ritual expression to their link with the deceased. His four sons found a different way of giving ritual expression to their more intimate and yet more deferential relationship to the deceased—kissing his feet.

From their reading of the *Zohar* and related works, Aboab's sons could have been inspired to kiss the hands of their dead father, just as Rabbi Eleazar had kissed the hands of Rabbi Simeon bar Yoḥai. And, indeed, parting with such a kiss from one's close relatives, shortly before or after their death, was common enough in Italy for Leone Modena to have mentioned in passing that he managed to kiss the hands of his grandfather Solomon "in Ferrara, in the month he died."[174] But kissing their feet was quite another matter. Had Jacob Aboab and his brothers developed a taste for Renaissance art, however, they might have known of the kissing of the foot depicted by such Quattrocento artists as Gentile da Fabriano or Domenico Veneziano in their versions of the *Adoration of the Magi*, or, more appositely, of Fra Angelico's famous *Deposition from the Cross*, in which the feet of the dead Jesus are being kissed.[175] Even if they did not develop such a taste, which is most probably the case, they lived in a world in which such extravagant gestures of deferential respect (enacted, for example upon the inauguration of a new pope) were very much in evidence.[176] Like the processional torches described by Capsali in the early sixteenth century, they could inspire both attraction and repulsion. But when the greatest rabbi of your generation, who happened also to be your father, was leaving the world, the greatest possible sign of respect had to be shown, even at the risk of appearing a bit "too goyish."

NOTES

1. On Capsali's account of Minz's funeral, see M. A. Shulvass, *Between the Rhine and the Bosporus* (Chicago, 1964), 180; Robert Bonfil, *Jewish Life in Renaissance Italy*, trans. Anthony Oldcorn (Berkeley, Calif., 1994), 268–75; and A. Toaff, *Love, Work, and Death: Jewish Life in Medieval Umbria*, trans. Judith Landry (London, 1996), 55 n. 65.

2. Eliyahu Capsali, *Seder Eliyahu Zuta*, 3 vols., ed. Aryeh Shmuelevitz et al. (Tel Aviv, 1976–83), 2: 254–55 (my translation). For a somewhat different translation of the passage, see Bonfil, *Jewish Life*, 269.

3. The other confraternities, Casola noted, carried doppieri of different colored wax. See M. M. Newett, ed. and trans., *Canon Pietro Casola's Pilgrimage to Jerusalem in the Year 1494* (Manchester, 1907), 149–50.

4. Capsali, *Seder Eliyahu Zuta*, 2: 271 (my translation); see also p. 307 on Capsali having witnessed more than 1,500 tonsured priests carrying torches of white wax at the funeral of Iacomo Michiel

5. *Ibid.*, 2: 255 (my translation). Further on processions in Venice and the Veneto, see

E. Horowitz, "Processions, Piety, and Jewish Confraternities," in R. C. Davis and B. Ravid, eds., *The Jews of Early Modern Venice* (Baltimore, Md., 2001), 231–47.

6. See M. A. Shulvass, "Ashkenazic Jewry in Italy," *YIVO Annual of Jewish Social Science* 7 (1952): 110–31 (reprinted in Shulvass, *Between the Rhine and the Bosporus,* 158–83), and E. Horowitz, "I Carmi di Cremona: Una famiglia di banchieri ashkenaziti nella prima Eta moderna," *Zakhor* 3 (1999): 155–70, and the sources cited there. On Yiddish literature in Italy, see Shulvass, *The Jews in the World of the Renaissance,* trans. E. I Kose (Leiden, 1973), 222–27, and Chone Shmeruk, "Yiddish Printing in Italy" (Hebrew), *Italia* 3 (1982): 112–75.

7. See Renata Segre, "Sephardic Settlements in Sixteenth-Century Italy," *Mediterranean Historical Review* 6 (1991): 112–37 (reprinted in A. Meyuhas Ginio, ed., *Jews, Christians, and Muslims in the Mediterranean World After 1492* [London, 1992]), and R. Bonfil, "Ha-Yehudim ha-Sefardim veha-Portugalim be-Italya," in H. Beinart, ed., *Moreshet Sepharad* (Jerusalem, 1992), 543–59.

8. See Cecil Roth, *Venice* (Philadelphia, 1930), 63–71 (reprinted in 1975 as *History of the Jews in Venice*); Y. H. Yerushalmi, *From Spanish Court to Italian Ghetto* (New York, 1971), 194–206; B. Pullan, *The Jews of Europe and the Ghetto of Venice, 1550–1670* (Oxford, 1983), chaps. 10–13; Benjamin Ravid, "The Establishment of the Ghetto Nuovissimo of Venice," in H. Beinart, ed., *Jews in Italy: Studies Dedicated to the Memory of U. Cassuto* (Jerusalem, 1988), 35–54; and Benjamin Ravid, "Les séfarades à Venise," in Henry Méchoulan, ed., *Les Juifs d'espagne: Histoire d'une diaspora* (Paris, 1992), 283–94.

9. See J. Herald, *Renaissance Dress in Italy, 1400–1500* (London, 1981), 87, 195, and J. Backhouse, *The Illuminated Page* (London, 1997), 224–25 (no. 200).

10. Newett, trans., *Canon Pietro Casola's Pilgrimage,* 144; P. Molmenti, *Venice: Its Individual Growth . . . to the Fall of the Republic,* trans. H. F. Brown (Chicago, 1907), 2: 2, 92.

11. L. M. Epstein, *Sex Laws and Customs in Judaism* (New York, 1948), 52–54; R. Bonfil, "Aspects of the Social and Spiritual Life of the Jews in the Venetian Territories at the Beginning of the Sixteenth Century" (Hebrew), *Zion* 41 (1976): 86–90.

12. Bonfil, "Aspects of the Social and Spiritual Life," 71.

13. *Pero Tafur: Travels and Adventures, 1435–1439,* ed. and trans. M. Letts (London, 1926), 184–5, 200. See also Philip Braunstein, "Toward Intimacy: The Fourteenth and Fifteenth Centuries," in G. Duby, ed., *A History of Private Life: Revelations of the Medieval World,* trans. A. Goldhammer (Cambridge, Mass., 1988), 600–610, and, for some other remarkable illustrations, R. van Marle, *Iconographie de l'Art Profane au Moyen-Age et à la Renaissance* (n.p., 1931; reprt, New York, 1971), 1: 497–515. Dürer's drawing is reproduced in J. R. Hale, ed., *Renaissance Venice* (London, 1973), plate 15.

14. See Epstein, *Sex Laws,* 30, and the sources cited there.

15. See, for example, the sixteenth-century Italian bronze lamps in Jerusalem's Israel Museum reproduced in Chaya Benjamin, ed., *The Stieglitz Collection: Masterpieces of Jewish Art* (Jerusalem, 1987), nos. 120, 125. This phenomenon was especially common in Italian illustrated ketubbot, though generally of a later period. See, for example, ibid., no. 216, and

Shalom Sabar, *Ketubbah: Jewish Marriage Contracts of the Hebrew Union College Skirball Museum and Klau Library* (Philadelphia, 1990), no. 66, both from the eighteenth century.

16. For the latest edition of the letter, see M. A. Artom and A. David, "R. Obadia Jare of Bertinoro and His Letters from the Land of Israel," in Beinart, ed., *Jews in Italy*, 55. See also E. Horowitz, "Toward a Social History of Jewish Popular Religion: Obadiah of Bertinoro on the Jews of Palermo," *Journal of Religious History* 17 (1992): 140.

17. Grendi has argued that some kinds of transgressive acts may be seen as exceptions "to the norms defined by political or ecclesiastical authorities" and yet, at the same time, "perfectly representative of their own social milieu." See Edward Muir, "Introduction: Observing Trifles," in E. Muir and G. Ruggiero, eds., *Microhistory and the Lost Peoples of Europe* (Baltimore, Md., 1991), xiv.

18. Horowitz, "Toward a Social History," 143.

19. A. Y. Yani and A. Yosef, eds., *Responsa of Moses Provenzale*, vol. 2 (Jerusalem, 1998), no. 136.

20. Ibid., no. 142; Artom and David, "R. Obadia Jare of Bertinoro and His Letters," 72.

21. In the thirteenth century, Rabbi Isaiah of Trani observed with unconcealed vexation that "all the Romaniote communities [of the eastern Mediterranean] have become accustomed to laxity with regard to the immersion of a menstruant, and there is not to be found in all of Romaniote Jewry a single community where the women immerse themselves other than in the stench of the [public baths]; and most [men] therefore, cohabit with menstruants." See Steven Bowman, *The Jews of Byzantium: 1204–1453* (University, Ala., 1985), 213–14; Horowitz, "Toward a Social History," 144.

22. Yani and Yosef, eds., *Responsa of Moses Provenzale*, 2: no. 146.

23. See Charles de La Roncière, "Tuscan Notables on the Eve of the Renaissance," in Duby, ed., *A History of Private Life*, 195.

24. See Louis Finkelstein, *Jewish Self-Government in the Middle Ages* (New York, 1924), chap. 10, and Bonfil, *Jewish Life*, 111–13.

25. See, for example, S. W. Baron, "The Jewish Factor in Medieval Civilization," in L. A. Feldman, ed., *Ancient and Medieval Jewish History* (New Brunswick, N.J., 1972), 246; Y. Y. Yuval, *Ḥakhamim be-Doram* (Jerusalem, 1988), 329–30.

26. Benjamin Ravid, "The Legal Status of the Jews in Venice to 1509," *Proceedings of the American Academy for Jewish Research* 54 (1987): 185–86; Riccardo Calimani, *The Ghetto of Venice: A History*, trans K. S. Wolfthal (New York, 1987), 10. For a similar decree enacted some 15 years later, see Shlomo Simonsohn, ed., *The Jews in the Duchy of Milan*, 4 vols. (Jerusalem, 1982–86), 19, 21.

27. See Baron, "The Jewish Factor," 245–46; and Cecil Roth, *The Jews in the Renaissance* (Philadelphia, 1959), 44, both based on the data of M. Ciardini, *I banchieri cbrei in Firenze nel secolo XV* (Borgo San Lorenzo, 1907).

28. Yuval, *Ḥakhamim*, 330 n. 15.

29. S. Simonsohn, *History of the Jews in the Duchy of Mantua* (Jerusalem, 1977), 208, 212.

30. If unable to pay, the Jew would receive two lashes publicly for the first offense and four for the second. See R. Segre, ed., *The Jews in Piedmont*, 3 vols. (Jerusalem, 1986–90), 483. The charter was originally published by M. Lattes, "Documents et notices sur l'histoire politique et littéraire des juifs en Italie," *Revue des Etudes juives* [hereafter *REJ*] 5 (1882): 223–37.

31. Daniel Carpi, ed., *Minutes Book of the Council . . . of Padua*, 2 vols. (Jerusalem, 1973–79), 1: 117 (nos. 60–61), 334–35 (no. 572). On dancing with Christian women during Carnival, see Simonsohn, ed., *Milan*, 1615, doc. 3663 (1575). On the status conferred by marriage, see E. Horowitz, "The Worlds of Jewish Youth in Europe, 1300–1800," in G. Levi and J.-C. Schmitt, eds., *A History of Young People*, vol. 1 (Cambridge, Mass., 1997), 95–96.

32. Roth, *History of the Jews in Italy* (Philadelphia, 1946), 176; David Jacoby, "New Evidence on Jewish Bankers in Venice and the Venetian Terraferma (c. 1450–1550)," in A. Toaff and S. Schwarzfuchs, eds., *The Mediterranean and the Jews: Banking, Finance, and International Trade* (Ramat-Gan, 1989), 163–65; Nicholas Davidson, "The Inquisition and the Italian Jews," in Stephen Haliczer, ed., *Inquisition and Society in Early Modern Europe* (London, 1987), 23.

33. *The Autobiography of a Seventeenth-Century Venetian Rabbi*, ed. and trans. M. R. Cohen (Princeton, N.J., 1988), 80; Shlomo Simonsohn, ed., *The Apostolic See and the Jews*, 8 vols. (Toronto, 1988–91), 2046 (doc. 1806), 2124–25 (doc. 1921).

34. Bonfil, *Jewish Life*, 111; Cecil Roth, "Venice and Her Last Persecution of the Jews," *REJ* 82 (1926): 416. On the contrast between the historiographical stances of Roth and Bonfil, see David Ruderman, "Cecil Roth, Historian of Italian Jewry: A Reassessment," in David Ruderman and David Myers, eds., *The Jewish Past Revisited: Reflections on Modern Jewish Historians* (New Haven, Conn., 1998), 128–42.

35. Roth, *Venice*, 212, 218–19. For the actual list, including a facsimile in Modena's hand, see Cohen, ed., *Autobiography of a . . . Rabbi*, 160–62.

36. Cohen, ed., *Autobiography of a . . . Rabbi*, 153, 261. For the relevant passage in *Ari nohem*, see P. Naveh, ed., *Yehudah Aryeh Modena: Leket Ketavim* (Jerusalem, 1968), 231.

37. Roth, *Jews in the Renaissance*, 59–60.

38. Saxl, Walker, and Yates had all worked at the Warburg Library, which became the Warburg Institute upon its removal from Hamburg to London. On the "Warburg" approach to Renaissance culture, see, among others, Carlo Ginzburg, "From Aby Warburg to E. H. Gombrich: A Problem of Method," in Ginzburg, *Clues, Myths, and Historical Method*, trans. John and A. C. Tedeschi (Baltimore, Md., 1989), 17–59; E. H. Gombrich, *Aby Warburg: An Intellectual Biography* (London, 1970); and Felix Gilbert, "From Art History to the History of Civilization: Aby Warburg," in Gilbert, *History: Choice and Commitment* (Cambridge, Mass., 1977), 423–39.

39. D. P. Walker, *Spiritual and Demonic Magic from Ficino to Campanella* (London, 1958), 168. On Ficino's magic, see also F. A. Yates, *Giordano Bruno and the Hermetic Tradition* (London, 1964), chap. 4, and Wayne Shumaker, *The Occult Sciences in the Renaissance* (Berkeley,

Calif., 1972), 120–33. Historians of magic have generally distinguished between amulets and talismans, with the latter term often being reserved for objects that have written words or letters inscribed on them. See R. Kieckhefer, *Magic in the Middle Ages* (Cambridge, Engl., 1989), 77.

40. Walker, *Spiritual and Demonic Magic,* 107, 214.

41. Roth, *Jews in the Renaissance,* 63. On the Christian practice of amulets for young children, see Christiane Klapisch-Zuber, *Women, Family, and Ritual in Renaissance Italy,* trans. L. G. Cochrane (Chicago, 1985), 149–50. On Christians producing amulets for Jews, see the exchange between Rabbi Yohanan Ghiron of Florence and Samuel Aboab in the latter's *Responsa Devar Shmuel* (Venice, 1702), no. 332, excerpted also in *Mekorot le-toldot ha-hinnukh be-yisrael,* ed. Simha Assaf, 4 vols. (Tel Aviv, 1925–42), 3: 141. Aboab mentioned having heard that only in Mantua were there some Jews who insisted on having the "holy names" inscribed by a fellow coreligionist.

42. For some of the surviving Jewish amulets, see R. D. Barnett, *Catalogue of . . . the Jewish Museum, London* (London, 1974), nos. 593–95, 603–5; Benjamin, *The Stieglitz Collection,* nos. 264–66; and V. B. Mann, ed., *Gardens and Ghettos* (Berkeley, Calif., 1989), nos. 186, 223–229.

43. David Ruderman, *Kabbalah, Magic and Science: The Cultural Universe of a Sixteenth-Century Jewish Physician* (Cambridge, Mass., 1988), 29, 37.

44. Roth, *Jews in the Renaissance,* 61; Shulvass, *Jews in the World of the Renaissance,* 153 n. 4; Gershom Scholem, *Sabbatai Sevi: The Mystical Messiah,* trans. R.J.Z. Werblowsky (Princeton, N.J., 1973), 744–45 n. 154.

45. David Ruderman, ed. and trans., *A Valley of Vision: The Heavenly Journey of Abraham ben Hananiah Yagel* (Philadelphia, 1990), 170–71. For contrasting views among other Jewish thinkers, see David Ruderman, *The World of a Renaissance Jew: The Life and Thought of Abraham ben Mordecai Farissol* (Cincinnati, 1981), 126–27.

46. Eugenio Garin, *Astrology in the Renaissance: The Zodiac of Life* (London, 1983), 46.

47. Joshua Trachtenberg, *Jewish Magic and Superstition* (New York, 1939), 295 n. 1; E. Horowitz, "Speaking of the Dead: The Emergence of the Eulogy Among Italian Jewry of the Sixteenth Century," in David Ruderman, ed., *Preachers of the Italian Ghetto* (Berkeley, Calif., 1992), 138–39.

48. Yacov Boksenboim, ed., *Igrot Beit Carmi: 1570–1577* (Tel Aviv, 1983), 287–88; Simonsohn, ed., *Milan,* 1617; Cohen, *Autobiography of a . . . Rabbi,* 111. On Jewish palmistry (=chiromancy), see Gershom Scholem's useful entry "Chiromancy," in *Encyclopedia Judaica,* vol. 5, cols. 477–79 (reprinted in Scholem, *Kabbalah* [New York, 1974], 317–19).

49. Yacov Boksenboim, ed., *Igrot Melamdim (1555–1591)* (Tel Aviv, 1985), 310–11, 388.

50. On Ferrarese Jewry during this period, see Ruderman, *The World of a Renaissance Jew,* 21–26; and Segre, "Sephardic Settlements," 122–26.

51. David Ruderman, "The Founding of a Gemilut Hasadim Society in Ferrara in 1515," *Association of Jewish Studies Review* 1 (1976): 233–68, esp. 259. The next several paragraphs draw heavily on this work by Ruderman and on E. Horowitz, "Jewish Confraternal Piety in

Sixteenth-Century Ferrara: Continuity and Change," in Nicholas Terpstra, ed., *The Politics of Ritual Kinship: Confraternities and Social Order in Early Modern Italy* (Cambridge, Engl., 2000), 150–71.

52. See also E. Horowitz, "The Jews of Europe and the Moment of Death in Medieval and Modern Times," *Judaism* 44 (1995): 271 and the sources cited there.

53. For this characterization of the family, see Roth, *Jews in the Renaissance*, 54. On the Abravanel family in Italy, see also, more recently, A. di Leone Leoni, "New Information on the Abravanel" (Italian), *Zakhor* 1 (1997): 153–206, and R. Segre, "Sephardic Refugees in Ferrara: Two Notable Families," in B. R. Gampel, ed., *Crisis and Creativity in the Sephardic World* (New York, 1997), 164–85.

54. Roth, *Jews in the Renaissance*, 45; E. Horowitz, "Bein adonim le-meshartot ba-hevra ha-yehudit ha-Eiropit bein yemei he-beinayim le-reshit ha-eit ha-hadasha," in Y. Bartal and I. Gafni, eds., *Eros, Erusin, ve-Issurim* (Jerusalem, 1998), 198–99. Segre, "Sephardic Refugees in Ferrara," 172, oddly refers to Benvenida as Samuel's "second wife."

55. Simonsohn, *The Apostolic See,* 2604–5 (doc. 2716).

56. On Immanuel and Isaac, see P. Norsa, *Una famiglia di banchieri: I Norsa,* 2 vols. (Naples, 1951–59), chaps. 1–2. On the fear of Immanuel, see Azriel Diena, *Responsa*, ed. Yacov Boksenboim, 2 vols. (Tel Aviv, 1977–79), 2: 27, and on the fear of Isaac, see E. Kupfer, "R. Abraham b. Menahem Rovigo and His Removal from the Rabbinate" (Hebrew), *Sinai* 61 (1967): 151–55.

57. On Isaac Norzi's sons, see Norsa, *Una famiglia,* 2: chap. 3. On Abraham Immanuel's ennoblement, which applied also to his heirs, see Simonsohn, *Mantua,* 32 n. 115. On Joshua Modena, see Boksenboim, ed., *Igrot Melamdin,* 22 and the sources cited there. On Eliezer Modena, see Diena, *Responsa,* 1: 279ff and 2: 172.

58. Simonsohn, *The Apostolic See,* 2503 (doc. 2563).

59. B. Rivlin, "The 1547 [sic] Statutes of Hevrat Nizharim in Bologna" (Hebrew), *Asufot* 3 (1989): 357–96; M. Perani, "Poiché da Bologna uscirà la Torah e la Parola del Signore dalla Hevrat Nizharim: Una confraternità religiosa nella Bologna ebraica del cinquecento," in M. G. Muzzarelli, ed., *Verso l'epilogo di una convivenzia: Gli ebrei a Bologna nel XVI secolo* (Florence, 1996), 129–53.

60. Abraham Yagel, *Bat Rabim* Ms., Moscow-Guenzberg 129, no. 67 (Institute of Microfilmed Hebrew Manuscripts, JNUL, no. 6809), 57a–b. The incident has been mentioned by David Ruderman (*Kabbalah, Magic and Science,* 21), who graciously made the manuscript available to me, but my reading of the text (and hence translation) differs somewhat from his. On parental desire for the "execution" of an adulterous daughter, compare, for the medieval Ashkenazic world, I. A. Agus, *Rabbi Meir of Rothenberg* (New York, 1947), 283–85 (no. 246). For a case in fifteenth-century Sicily of a (Catholic) father who cut his adulterous daughter's throat—and subsequently received a royal pardon—see Allan Ryder, "Crime in Sicily," in Trevor Dean and K. J. P. Lowe, eds., *Crime, Society, and the Law in Renaissance Italy* (Cambridge, Engl., 1994), 68.

61. See V. Colorni, "Genealogia della famiglia Finzi: Le primi generazioni," in V. Colorni, *Judaica Minora: Nuove ricerche* (Milan, 1991), 330–36 (for the Hebrew version, see Beinart, ed., *Jews in Italy,* 219–25), and Antonella Campanini, "A Jewish Family in Bologna between Medieval and Modern Times: The Finzi" (Italian), *Zakhor* 3 (1999): 79–93. On the synods of Bologna and Forli, see Finkelstein, *Jewish Self-Government,* 281–95.

62. Simonsohn, *Mantua,* index s.v. "Finzi, Angelo"; Malachi Beit-Arié, "Mordecai Finzi's Copy of a Work by Averroes," in A. K. Offenberg et al., eds., *Bibliotheca Rosenthaliana: Treasures of Jewish Booklore,* 2d ed. (Amsterdam, 1996), 36.

63. See Roth, *Jews in the Renaissance,* 20, 231–32, 236; M. Levey, ed., *The Algebra of Abu Kamil . . . in a Commentary by Mordecai Finzi* (Madison, Wisc., 1966), 8–9; and, especially, Y. T. Langermann, "The Scientific Writings of Mordekhai Finzi," *Italia* 7 (1988): 7–44.

64. Trachtenberg, *Jewish Magic,* 217–19; Langermann, "Scientific Writings," 42–44. On medieval and early modern geomancy, see also Keith Thomas, *Religion and the Decline of Magic* (New York, 1971), index s.v. "geomancy."

65. Carlo Bernheimer, "A Private Collection of 200 Hebrew Manuscripts in the 15th Century" (Italian), *La Bibliofilia* 26 (1925): 300–325; Simonsohn, *Mantua,* 677–78; Colorni, "Genealogia," 224–25; M. Perani, "Spigolature sul patrimonio librario degli ebrei a Bologna tra medioeveo e rinascimento," in M. G. Muzzarelli, ed., *Banchi ebraici a Bologna* (Bologna, 1994), 261–63. The 1454 list was misleadingly described as an inventory of Salomone Finzi's library by Roth, *Jews in the Renaissance,* 327, and (probably as a consequence) by Shifra Baruchson, *Sefarim ve-Korim: Tarbut ha-Keriah shel Yehudei Italia be-Shilhei ha-Renaissance.* (Ramat Gan, 1993), 85.

66. See Judah Messer Leon, *The Book of the Honeycomb's Flow,* ed. and trans. Isaac Rabinowitz (Ithaca, N.Y., 1983), xx n. 17. In 1595 there were four manuscript copies of this (unpublished) work in Mantuan Jewish libraries. See Baruchson, *Sefarim ve-Korim,* 234.

67. Campanini, "A Jewish Family in Bologna" (Italian), 85–89.

68. Toaff, *Love, Work, and Death,* 30–31. On the negative attitude toward remarriage of widows in both Jewish and Christian tradition, see E. Cohen and E. Horowitz, "In Search of the Sacred: Jews, Christians, and Rituals of Marriage in the Later Middle Ages," *Journal of Medieval and Renaissance Studies* 20 (1990): 243–48.

69. P. Cremonini, "Presenza ebraica a San Giovanni in Persiceto tra XIV e XV secolo," in Muzzarelli, ed., *Banchi ebraici a Bologna,* 212–14. Benjamin, one of the two sons of the banker Manuele Finzi (great-grandfather of David), had moved his own loan bank from Padua to Vicenza early in the fifteenth century; see Simonsohn, *Mantua,* 199–200. On the bankers of the Urbino family, see Simonsohn, *Mantua,* 203–4, 211.

70. Simonsohn, *Mantua,* 647 n. 216.

71. Roth, *Italy,* 176; Norsa, *Una famiglia,* 14–15. For another sixteenth-century instance of a Christian prostitute claiming that she thought her Jewish client was a Christian, see Simonsohn, *Milan,* 1390 (doc. 3188).

72. For the 1520 manuscript, now in Paris (Bibliothèque Nationale), see M. Beit-Arié and

C. Sirat, *Manuscrits médiévaux en caractères hébraiques,* vol. 3 (Paris, 1986), no. 69; M. Garel, *D'une main forte: Manuscrits hebreux des collections françaises* (Paris, 1991), no. 143.

73. Norsa, *Una famiglia,* 21; Simonsohn, *Mantua,* 32 n.115.

74. The document is reproduced in Yacov Boksenboim, ed., *Parashiot* (Tel Aviv, 1986), 83–85 (and see also 4–29).

75. See A. Marx, "A Jewish Cause Célèbre in Sixteenth-Century Italy," in *Abhandlungen zur Errinerung an Hirsch Perez Chajes* (Vienna, 1933), 149–93 (reprinted in A. Marx, *Studies in Jewish History and Booklore* [New York, 1944], 107–54); and Norsa, *Una famiglia,* 7–21.

76. V. Colorni, "Gli ebrei a Sermide," in *Scritti in memoria di Sally Mayer* (Jerusalem, 1956), 35–38; Simonsohn, *Mantua,* 16–17, 570; Ruderman, *The World of a Renaissance Jew,* 23, 158.

77. Cissy Grossman, "Womanly Arts: A Study of Italian Torah Binders in the New York Jewish Museum Collection," *Journal of Jewish Art* 7 (1980): 40–41; C. Grossman and B. Kirshenblatt-Gimblett, eds., *Fabric of Jewish Life: Textiles from the Jewish Museum Collection* (New York, 1977), no. 17.

78. Simonsohn, *Mantua,* 223; Simonsohn, *The Apostolic See,* 1493–94 (doc. 1191), 1627 (doc. 1297), 1783 (doc. 1462), 2104 (doc. 1882), 2236 (doc. 2051).

79. Joseph Colon, *Responsa* (Jerusalem, 1988), no. 113; Capsali, *Seder Eliyahu Zuta,* 2: 257–58.

80. Toaff, *Love, Work, and Death,* 24, 31–32, 91, 95–97; A. Toaff, *The Jews in Umbria,* 3 vols. (Leiden, 1993–94), 3: doc. 2204.

81. Toaff, *Love, Work, and Death,* 96, 108, 111; Toaff, *The Jews in Umbria,* 2: 939 (doc. 1779).

82. Toaff, *Love, Work, and Death,* 250–51.

83. Horowitz, "Bein Adonim le-Meshartot," 200–201. On the relatively low penalties in Italy for sexual relations with servants, see Nicholas Davidson, "Theology, Nature, and the Law: Sexual Sin and Sexual Crime in Italy from the Fourteenth to the Seventeenth Century," in Dean and Lowe, eds., *Crime, Society, and the Law in Renaissance Italy,* 94.

84. Yani and Yosef, eds., *Responsa of Moses Provenzale,* 2, no. 111.

85. Ibid., no. 114. On another case of a woman marrying her former servant, see Yacov Boksenboim, ed., *Igrot Rabbi Yehudah Aryeh mi-Modena* (Tel Aviv, 1984), 197.

86. M. Z. Friedlander, ed., *Responsa of Isaac de Lattes* (Vienna, 1860), 53–56; Horowitz, "The Worlds of Jewish Youth," 112.

87. One was married to Rabbi Abraham d'Angelo, and another to Salomone Corcos of Rome. See Boksenboim, ed., *Igrot Melamdim,* 21.

88. See E. Horowitz, "The Dowering of Brides in the Ghetto of Venice: Between Tradition and Change, Ideals and Reality" (Hebrew), *Tarbiz* 56 (1987); 347–71. For some additional instances of engagements lasting as long as eight years, see Kenneth Stow, "Marriages Are Made in Heaven: Marriage and the Individual in the Roman Jewish Ghetto," *Renaissance Quarterly* 48 (1995): 467, 478, 484.

89. See Boksenboim, ed., *Igrot Melamdim,* 278–79, and E. Horowitz, "*Yeshiva* and *Hevra:*

Educational Control and Confraternal Organization in Sixteenth-Century Italy," in Daniel Carpi et al., eds., *Shlomo Simonsohn Jubilee Volume* (Tel Aviv, 1993), 130–31. For another case, during the same decade, of a father who never managed to pay the dowry he had promised, see Stow, "Marriages Are Made in Heaven," 475.

90. Horowitz, "The Dowering of Brides," 360–65; Horowitz, "The Worlds of Jewish Youth in Europe," 101–3.

91. See, for example, S. D. Goitein, *A Mediterranean Society,* 5 vols. (Berkeley, Calif., 1967), 3: 227–28; and Shulamith Shahar, *Childhood in the Middle Ages,* trans. Chaya Galai (London, 1990), 43–44.

92. Yacov Boksenboim, ed., *Igrot Beit Rieti* (Tel Aviv, 1987), 309–10. On Ishmael Rieti, see Horowitz, "*Yeshiva* and *Hevra,*" 126–29 and the sources cited there.

93. Friedlander, ed., *Responsa of . . . Lattes,* 139–40. Compare Bernardino of Siena, as cited by Shahar, *Childhood,* 43–44.

94. See Ruderman, "The Founding," 261. This was still the case in the confraternity's statutes of 1552 and 1583.

95. ASV, Fondo Scuole Piccole 733 [Central Archives for the History of the Jewish People, HM 5948d], 7a (May, 2, 1576). On the confraternity, see Horowitz, "The Dowering of Brides," 347–71.

96. N. Z. Davis, "Fame and Secrecy: Leon Modena's Life as an Early Modern Autobiography," in Cohen, ed., *Autobiography of a . . . Rabbi,* 63–64; E. Horowitz, review of Cohen, ed., *Autobiography, Jewish Quarterly Review* [hereafter: *JQR*], n.s. 81 (1991): 456–57. On Jewish homosexuality in sixteenth-century Italy, see also Roth, *Renaissance,* 45, and Simonsohn, *Mantua,* 544 n. 114.

97. Toaff, *Love, Work, and Death,* 13; Peter Partner, *Renaissance Rome: 1500–1559* (Berkeley, Calif., 1976), 98–99. On prostitution in Rome, see also E. S. Cohen, "Seen and Known: Prostitutes in the Cityscape of Late-Sixteenth-Century Rome," *Renaissance Studies* 12 (1998): 392–409.

98. Simonsohn, *Milan,* 1613; Simonsohn, *Mantua,* 543–44.

99. Pullan, *The Jews of Europe,* 162, 277; Horowitz, "The Dowering of Brides," 355–56.

100. C. Dushinsky, "May a Woman Be a Shohetet," in B. Schindler, ed., *Occident and Orient: [Moses] Gaster Anniversary Volume* (London, 1936), 96–106; Robert Bonfil, "The Historian's Perception of the Jews in the Italian Renaissance: Towards a Reappraisal," *REJ* 143 (1984): 71–75.

101. Yani and Yosef, eds., *Responsa of Moses Provenzale,* 1: no. 90.

102. Simonsohn, *Mantua,* 226–28, 236; R. Segre, *Gli ebrei lombardi nell'età spagnola* (Turin, 1973), 125.

103. D. Kaufmann, "Meir b. Ephraim of Padua, Scrollwriter and Printer in Mantua," *JQR* n.s. 11 (1899): 282, 290. On Meir of Padua, see also Simonsohn, *Mantua,* 725–26.

104. P. F. Grendler, *The Roman Inquisition and the Venetian Press, 1540–1605* (Princeton, N.J., 1977), 9–11.

105. Simonsohn, "Books and Libraries of Mantuan Jews, 1595" (Hebrew), *Kiryat Sefer* 37 (1962): 103–22, esp. 114.

106. Baruchson, *Sefarim ve-Korim*, 180; Cohen, ed., *Autobiography of a . . . Rabbi*, 20.

107. Simonsohn, "Books and Libraries," 114–15; Yekutiel's Italian copy of *Ethics* was not the only one then owned by a Mantuan Jew. See Baruchson, *Sefarim ve-Korim*, 188.

108. Ms. Cambridge Add. 512. See S. C. Reif, *Hebrew Manuscripts at Cambridge University Library: A Description and Introduction* (Cambridge, Engl., 1997), 268–69. On the combination of Kabbalah and Renaissance culture, see Moshe Idel, "The Magical and Neoplatonic Interpretations of the Kabbalah in the Renaissance," in B. D. Cooperman, ed., *Jewish Thought in the Sixteenth Century* (Cambridge, Mass., 1983), 186–242, and Moshe Idel, "Major Currents in Italian Kabbalah between 1560–1660," *Italia Judaica* 2 (1986): 243–62 (both reprinted in D. B. Ruderman, ed., *Essential Papers on Jewish Culture in Renaissance and Baroque Italy* [New York, 1992]. See also Ruderman, *Kabbalah, Magic, and Science*, esp. chap. 9.

109. H. G. Koenigsberger, G. L. Mosse, and G. Q. Bowler, *Europe in the Sixteenth Century* (rev. ed. London, 1989), 418; Peter Burke, *The Fortunes of the Courtier: The European Reception of Castiglione's Cortegiano* (Oxford, 1995); Simonsohn, "Books and Libraries," 114; Azariah de Rossi, *Meor Enayim*, ed. David Cassel (Vilna, 1866), 160, 379; Shulvass, *Jews in the World of the Renaissance*, 294; Ruderman, *Valley of Vision*, index.

110. See Simonsohn, "Books and Libraries," 114; Baruchson, *Sefarim ve-Korim*, 185–86; P. F. Grendler, *Schooling in Renaissance Italy* (Baltimore, Md., 1989), 300–305, 422–24; and de Rossi, *Meor Enayim*, ed. David Cassel, 260.

111. Harry Friedenwald, "Two Jewish Physicians of the Sixteenth Century," in Harry Friedenwald, *The Jews and Medicine: Essays,* 2 vols. (Baltimore, Md., 1944), 2: 391–403; L. A. Segal, *Historical Consciousness and Religious Tradition in Azariah de'Rossi's Meor Einayim* (Philadelphia, 1989), 14; Roth, *Jews in the Renaissance,* 318–27. For a well-annotated selection of passages from the *Meor Enayim,* see R. Bonfil, ed., *Kitve Azariah min ha-Adumim* (Jerusalem, 1991), 334. An annotated English translation of the entire work has been published by Joanna Weinberg, *The Light of The Eyes* (New Haven, 2000).

112. Kaufmann, "Meir b. Ephraim," 277, 287; Roth, *Jews in the Renaissance,* 329; Simonsohn, *Mantua,* 264, 348, 637. On numismatics in sixteenth-century Italy, see F. Haskell, *History and Its Images: Art and the Interpretation of the Past* (rev. ed. New Haven, Conn., 1995), chaps. 1–2.

113. Roth, *Jews in the Renaissance,* 209, Simonsohn, *Mantua,* 636; *Mazref la-Kesef,* ed. David Cassel (Vilna, 1864), 123–39. On the criticisms of Provenzale and Moscato, see R. Bonfil, "Some Reflections on the Place of Azariah de Rossi's *Meor Enayim* in the Cultural Milieu of Italian Renaissance Jewry," in Cooperman, ed., *Jewish Thought in the Sixteenth Century,* 26–29; and Bonfil, ed., *Azariah de Rossi: Selected Chapters,* 101–17.

114. Just over a month later, the ban was signed by six Ferrarese rabbis; among them the brothers Moses and Aaron, sons of Israel Finzi—of the family's Reggio branch. See Bonfil, ed., *Kitve Azariah,* 134–36.

115. For the confusion between the two, see, for example, I. Elbogen's entry "Finzi" in the *Jewish Encyclopaedia;* and Robert Bonfil, *Rabbis and Jewish Communities in Renaissance Italy,* trans. J. Chipman (Oxford, 1990), 79. Note also Bonfil, "The Place of de Rossi's *Meor Enayim,*" 46 n. 34, where he strangely refers to Isaac Finzi as a "rather famous" kabbalist.

116. On the situation in Pesaro, see Horowitz, "Speaking of the Dead," 142–43. On Jacob Israel Finzi's studies with the Spanish exile Rabbi Eliezer ibn Zur and on his use of kabbalistic teachings in his responsa, see M. Benayahu, "Kabbalah and Halakha—A Confrontation" (Hebrew), *Da'at* 5 (1980): 93–95. On other aspects of his (still largely unpublished) writings, see Bonfil, *Rabbis and Jewish Communties,* 53–54, 61, 78–79.

117. S. Assaf, "La-pulmus al hadpasat sifrei Kabbalah," in S. Assaf, *Mekorot u-Meḥkarim be-Toledot Yisrael* (Jerusalem, 1946), 241 (originally published in *Sinai* 5 [1939–40]).

118. Ibid., 245–46. On the scholarly debate concerning Jewish reactions to Christian Kabbalah, see Ruderman, *The World of a Renaissance Jew,* 51–56.

119. Pullan, *The Jews of Europe,* 248–50; Friedenwald, *The Jews and Medicine,* 2: 392–93; David Amram, *The Makers of Hebrew Books in Italy* (1904; rpt. London, 1963), 122–24; F. Secret, *Les Kabbalistes chrétiens de la Renaissance* (Paris, 1964), 102–6; Leone Modena, *Magen va-herev,* ed. Shlomo Simonsohn (Jerusalem, 1960), esp. 50–54.

120. Baruchson, *Sefarim ve-Korim,* 160–63.

121. For the latter case, see Yani and Yosef, eds., *Responsa of Moses Provenzale,* 1: nos. 82–83.

122. Segre, *The Jews in Piedmont,* 267 (doc. 581). It is quite possible that this Isaac was a nephew of the aforementioned loan banker, Abraham Finzi. For other Finzi converts in later centuries, see, for example, Simonsohn, *Mantua,* 71, 156.

123. Colon, *Responsa,* no. 160; H. H. Ben-Sasson, ed., *A History of the Jewish People* (Cambridge, Mass., 1976), 567; Simonsohn, *Milan,* 506–7. On the problems involved in a kohen's wife resuming sexual relations with him after having (even possibly) been violated, see Maimonides, *Mishneh Torah: Issurei Biah,* chap. 18.

124. Simonsohn, *Milan,* 798–99, 890.

125. Ibid., 448, 468–70, 473–77, 480, 482, 484, 489, 491, 493, 486.

126. Chaim Wirszubski, ed., *Flavius Mithridates: Sermo de Passione Domini* (Jerusalem, 1963); Chaim Wirszubski, *Pico della Mirandola's Encounter with Jewish Mysticism* (Jerusalem, 1989); Shlomo Simonsohn, "Some Well-Known Jewish Converts During the Renaissance," *REJ* 148 (1989): 20–26.

127. Simonsohn, "Some Well-Known Jewish Converts," 31–38.

128. Piet van Boxel, "Dowry and the Conversion of the Jews in Sixteenth-Century Rome: Competition Between the Church and the Jewish Community," in Trevor Dean and K. J. P. Lowe, eds., *Marriage in Italy, 1300–1650* (Cambridge, Engl., 1998), 125.

129. Segre, *Gli ebrei,* 23, 53; Roksenboim, ed., *Carmi Family,* 33–38, 316–17; Simonsohn, *Milan,* 1474–75, 1537–38, 2021; Horowitz, "I Carmi di Cremona," 160.

130. Simonsohn, *The Apostolic See,* 1707 (doc. 1357); Pullan, *The Jews of Europe,* 265–66;

Jacoby, "New Evidence," 168–69, 176–77. For other instances in the sixteenth century of sons delaying apostasy until after their father's death, see Hava Frankel-Goldschmidt, "Mumarim yehudim be-Germania be-Tekufat ha-Reformazia," in M. Ben-Sasson, R. Bonfil, and J. R. Hacker, eds., *Tarbut ve-Hevra be-Toledot Yisrael bi-Mei Ha-Beinayim* (Jerusalem, 1989), 629.

131. Simonsohn, *Milan*, 1090, 1100, 1087–88, 1100, 1216, 1275, 1288, 1299, 1322–23; Horowitz, "I Carmi di Cremona," 158–59.

132. For the traditional claim that the Ottolenghi originally came from Ettlingen, see Roth, *Italy*, 360; Shulvass, *Between the Rhine*, 174. For the more recent claim that their name derived from the town of Odalengo in the Piedmont, see Colorni, *Judaica Minora*, 72. On the derivation of the name Carmi from the town of Crema in Lombardy, see Horowitz, "I Carmi di Cremona," 156.

133. On the Carmi-Ottolenghi marriage and the confiscation of books, see Segre, *Gli ebrei*, 18–19, 35, and Boksenboim, ed., *Carmi Family*, 32 n. 62. On Joseph Ottolenghi's role in Hebrew publishing, see Isaiah Sonne, "The Expurgation of Hebrew Books—The Work of Jewish Scholars: A Contribution to the History of Censorship of Hebrew Books in Italy in the Sixteenth Century," *Bulletin of the New York Public Library* 46 (1942): 993–99, and Meir Benayahu, *Ha-Defus ha-ivri be-Cremona* (Jerusalem, 1971).

134. Boksenboim, ed., *Carmi Family*, 142. Part of this letter was first published by B. Chapira, "Les manuscrits de la bibliothèque de l'Alliance israélite," *REJ* 105 (1939–40): 56, and cited by Shulvass, *Between the Rhine*, 172.

135. Abraham Ya'ari, *Igrot Eretz Yisrael* (Ramat Gan, 1971), 173; Assaf, ed., *Mekorot le-Toledot ha-Hinnukh be-Yisrael*, 2: 138.

136. Boksenboim, ed., *Carmi Family*, 38–39. On Zanvil as a name for Samuel among Ashkenazic Jews, see Colorni, *Judaica Minora*, 784.

137. Boksenboim, ed., *Carmi Family*, 134, 140–41, 196. On Pescarol's relationship with the Carmi family, see also Horowitz, "*Yeshiva* and *Hevra*," 123–47, upon which some of the following paragraphs draw as well.

138. Simonsohn, *Milan*, 1064, 1100, 1280–81, 1307, 2362.

139. On the close link between the status of household tutor (*melamed*) and that of the banking apprentice (*manhig*) in sixteenth-century Italy, see Diena, *Responsa*, 1: 245; Boksenboim, ed., *Carmi Family*, 39; Segre, *Piedmont*, docs. 1052, 1058 (1572), 475, 478.

140. At around the same time (and in connection with the same controversial case), Rabbi Abraham Rovigo of Ferrara went so far as to accuse Ashkenazic rabbis of "deeming the blood of an Ashkenazi redder than that of an Italiani." See Shulvass, *Between the Rhine*, 168; Bonfil, *Rabbis and Jewish Communities*, 108 n. 29; and Boksenboim, ed., *Parashiot*, 424.

141. Boksenboim, ed., *Carmi Family*, 313–14.

142. Ibid., 286–87, 317–18, 329–30. On Foa, see Abraham Ya'ari, *Mehkerei sefer* (Jerusalem, 1958), 334–35.

143. Boksenboim, ed., *Carmi Family*, 34, 322–23. On the title of gaon, and on awarding

rabbinical titles on special occasions, see Bonfil, *Rabbis and Jewish Communities*, index s.v. "titles."

144. On Menaḥem Azariah's residence in Reggio from ca. 1580, see R. Bonfil, "Yediot haddashot le-toledot hayyav shel R. Menaḥem Azarya mi-Fano u-tekufato," in Etkes and Salmon, eds., *Perakim be-Toledot ha-Hevra ha-Yehudit . . . Mukdashim le-Professor Ya'akov Katz* (Jerusalem, 1980), 112f. On his role as executor of Saul Raphael's will, see Boksenboim, ed., *Carmi Family*, appen. IV.

145. Boksenboim, ed., *Carmi Family*, 319–20, 341–42; Aldo Luzzatto, ed., *Hebraica Ambrosiana* (Milan, 1972), no. 16.

146. Boksenboim, ed., *Carmi Family*, 319, 324.

147. See Daniel Sperber, *Minhagei Yisrael* 1 (Jerusalem, 1989), 65–66.

148. Toaff, *Ghetto Roma ba-Meah ha-16* (Ramat Gan, 1984), 36–37. Toaff estimates that in 1571 approximately 70 percent of the community was of Italiani origin.

149. D. M. Frame, trans., *The Complete Works of Montaigne* (Stanford, Calif., 1967), 944–45.

150. Cohen, ed., *Autobiography of a . . . Rabbi*, 82, 93, 96–97, 100–101; John Bossy, "God-parenthood: The Fortunes of a Social Institution in Early Modern Christianity," in K. von Greyerz, ed., *Religion and Society in Early Modern Europe* (London, 1984), 198.

151. For Moryson, see the excerpt in A. Cohen, ed., *An Anglo-Jewish Scrapbook, 1600–1840* (rpt. Westmead, 1969), 290–91. For Platter, see Salomon Kahn, "Thomas Platter et les juifs d'Avignon," *REJ* 25 (1892): 84–86.

152. Boksenboim, ed., *Carmi Family*, 38, 138, 285.

153. See Joseph Hahn Nordlingen, *Sefer Yosef Ometz* (Frankfurt, 1928), 281.

154. Boksenboim, ed., *Carmi Family*, 324, 338–39.

155. On Vardimas Samson, see Ya'ari, *Mehkerei sefer*, 330.

156. Boksenboim, ed., *Carmi Family*, 316, 319, 327.

157. See Horowitz, "I Carmi di Cremona," 168–69 and the sources cited there.

158. Roth, *Italy*, 320–21; S. W. Baron, *A Social and Religious History of the Jews*, 18 vols. (New York, 1952–83), 14: 89–90; Bonfil, *Rabbis and Jewish Communities*, 318–20; Horowitz, "Jewish Confraternal Piety in Sixteenth-Century Ferrara," 170–71.

159. On these sermons, see, for example, Roth, *Italy*, 138, 315–16, and Davidson, "The Inquisition," 25–26.

160. Simonsohn, *Mantua*, 32–43.

161. Bonfil, "Yediot Hadashot," 98–135. The extensive family tree composed by Bonfil (ibid., 134) omits Elhanan Yael's daughter Isotta.

162. Leone Modena, *Responsa Ziknei Yehuda*, ed. S. Simonsohn (Jerusalem, 1956), 61, 184 (second pagination); Cohen, ed., *Autobiography of a . . . Rabbi*, 82, 153; Horowitz, "I Carmi di Cremona," 169.

163. On the controversy, see Isaiah Tishby, "The Confrontation Between Lurianic and Cordoverian Kabbalah in the Writings and Life of R. Aaron Berechia of Modena" (Hebrew),

Zion 39 (1974): 25–81 (reprinted in Isaiah Tishby, *Hikrei Kabbalah u-Sheluhoteha,* vol. 1 [Jerusalem, 1982], 194–250). For selections from *Kenaf Renanim,* see J. Schirmann, ed., *Anthologie der Hebräischen Dichtung* (Berlin, 1934), 265–66.

164. See Tishby, "The Confrontation," 26–34, 49–52, and Horowitz, "I Carmi di Cremona," 167–68.

165. *Minute-book of the Verona Community,* ms. Jerusalem 4° 553.

166. Horowitz, "The Jews of Europe and the Moment of Death," 275–78.

167. Menahem Navara, *Yemei Temimim* (Venice, 1753), 12a–b.

168. D. I. Kertzer, *The Kidnapping of Edgardo Mortara* (New York, 1997), 206, 217.

169. Roth, *Venice,* 231–32. Roth erroneously wrote that Aboab had studied with Franco in Verona.

170. Yerushalmi, *From Spanish Court,* 198–208.

171. Moses Zacuto, *Responsa* (Venice, 1761), nos. 50–51; Aboab, *Responsa Devar Shmuel,* nos. 7, 48, 55. On the problem of setam yenam, see also ibid., nos. 49, 69, 175, and the comments in *Sefer ha-Zikhronot* (1650) attributed to Aboab, 26b–35b.

172. Scholem, *Sabbatai Sevi,* 497–99.

173. See Jacob Aboab's introduction to his father's posthumously published *Responsa Devar Shmuel,* quoted (without attribution) in M. S. Ghirondi and H. Neppi, *Toledot Gedolei Yisrael . . .* (Trieste, 1853), 366–70, and paraphrased by Roth, *Venice,* 235–36.

174. Cohen, ed., *Autobiography of a . . . Rabbi,* 78; E. Horowitz, "On Kissing the Dead in the Mediterranean World" (Hebrew), *Tarbiz* 67 (1997); 131–34.

175. See John Hale, *The Civilization of Europe in the Renaissance* (New York, 1994), 223–25, and, for additional references, Horowitz, "On Kissing the Dead," 132.

176. Peter Burke, *The Historical Anthropology of Early Modern Italy* (Cambridge, Engl., 1987), 172–73; Peter Burke, "The Language of Gesture in Early Modern Italy," in Jan Bremmer and Herman Roodenburg, eds., *A Cultural History of Gesture* (Oxford, 1991), 71–83. On kissing the foot of the pope, see also Lucien Wolf, *Jews in the Canary Islands* (London, 1926), 227 (1678).

SELECTED BIBLIOGRAPHY

Bonfil, Robert. *Rabbis and Jewish Communities in Renaissance Italy.* Trans. J. Chipman. Oxford, 1990.

———. *Jewish Life in Renaissance Italy.* Trans. Anthony Oldcorn. Berkeley, Calif., 1994.

Cohen, Mark, ed. *The Autobiography of a Seventeenth-Century Venetian Rabbi.* Princeton, N.J. 1988.

Davis, Robert, and Ravid, Benjamin, eds., *The Jews of Early Modern Venice.* Baltimore, 2001.

Mann, V. B., ed. *Gardens and Ghettos: The Art of Jewish Life in Italy.* Berkeley, Calif., 1989.

Roth, Cecil. *The History of the Jews in Italy.* Philadelphia, 1946.

———. *The Jews in the Renaissance.* Philadelphia, 1959.

Ruderman, David. *Kabbalah, Magic and Science: The Cultural Universe of a Sixteenth-Century Jewish Physician.* Cambridge, Mass., 1988.

———, ed. *Preachers of the Italian Ghetto.* Berkeley, Calif., 1992.

———, ed. *Essential Papers on Jewish Culture in Renaissance and Baroque Italy.* New York, 1992.

Shulvass, Moses. *The Jews in the World of the Renaissance.* Trans. E. I. Kose. Leiden, 1973.

Simonsohn, Shlomo. *History of the Jews in the Duchy of Mantua.* Jerusalem, 1977.

Toaff, Ariel. *Love, Work, and Death: Jewish Life in Medieval Umbria.* Trans. Judith Landry. London, 1996.

Emanuel de Witte, *Interior of the Portuguese Synagogue of Amsterdam*, 1680. Oil on canvas. (Rijksmuseum, Amsterdam)

BOM JUDESMO:

The Western Sephardic Diaspora

YOSEF KAPLAN

"The men are most of them of a tawny complection with black hair; some have clearer skins, and are scarce discernable from the Dutch, etc. They carry much perfume about them."[1] With these words Philip Skippon, an English traveler who visited the Dutch Republic, described the Sephardic Jews of Amsterdam, whom he encountered during the week he spent there in June 1663. Although he emphasized that it was difficult to distinguish between them and the Dutch, he was quite aware of their special presence, both in the Exchange building, where he noted that "Men of several nations resort hither, but the most frequent strangers are the Jews, who fill one walk [of it],"[2] and in the streets of the city where their lives were centered. Their presence in Amsterdam so impressed him that he estimated their number at 20,000, nearly ten times the actual size of the community.

Skippon was one of many travelers who reached Amsterdam during the seventeenth century and whose curiosity drew them to the residential quarters of the Portuguese Jews and led them to visit their houses of worship. Even before the great Sephardic synagogue was dedicated in 1675 and became a major attraction chosen by many travelers as their first stop in Amsterdam, Christian tourists from Holland and elsewhere visited the first Jewish houses of worship in the city. Amsterdam had then become a thriving metropolis and the center of the Sephardic Diaspora in western Europe and the New World, a window through which Europeans, including travelers and exiles from many other countries gathered in the Dutch Republic, could observe the "New Jews." These former New Christians, the descendants of Jews who had been baptized as Roman Catholics, some by force and some willingly, during the last century of Jewish presence in the Iberian kingdoms, had openly returned to Judaism after generations of isolation. For a significant number of visitors, this was their first exposure to living Jews, and certainly to a wealthy and flourishing Jewry, whose social elite was entirely immersed in European cultural activity, whose members spoke many languages, and who had direct acquaintance with the Christian religion and theology.

The ancestors of the Sephardic Jews of the west had abandoned the Jewish world during the fifteenth century, especially at the time of the decree of 1497 requiring the mass conversion of the Jews of Portugal, including the exiles from Spain who had fled there in 1492. Their separation from that world attenuated, sometimes even emptied, the Jewish heritage of the *converso* community. The great majority of them assimilated into Iberian society, though even the committed assimilationists among them were forced to cope with rejection and opposition that their presence aroused within the Christian establishment, and their particularity marked their intellectual, theological, and literary work in Spanish and Portuguese, which often expresses a subversive attitude toward dominant values in Iberian society such as honor and pure Christian lineage.

The yearning of many conversos for a spiritual and antiritualistic Christianity attracted them to Erasmian humanism. Prominent among those with such leanings were the Augustinian monk and poet Luis de León and the most important humanist thinker in sixteenth-century Spain, Juan Luis Vives. Almost all of the Hebraists at the Universities of Salamanca and Alcalá de Henares during the sixteenth-century were of converso origin, as were several prominent members of the Jesuit Order such as Diego Laínez and Juan de Polanco.

However, even conversos who retained a bond of some sort with the Jewish religion, those crypto-Judaizers who sought to observe certain customs in secret, had only pale and faint knowledge of Jewish sources. Although geographic separation was not sufficient to sever all the latent ties that connected them with the Jewish world, the vigilant surveillance of the Inquisition greatly limited their ability to develop true Jewish life, even clandestinely. They did not possess Jewish literature, and what they learned and internalized regarding Judaism was mainly taken from hostile Christian sources, which they interpreted with a subversive reading. Their problematic social reality created a vacuum in their Judaism, which was sometimes filled by popular beliefs in which Christian and Jewish concepts and symbols were intermingled. The conviction that *faith* in the Law of Moses grants salvation, indicating their skepticism regarding the redemptive power of the Christian church, became a guiding principle in their religious life. Yet, among the educated class, this vacuum was often filled with questions and doubts, which sometimes broke through the barriers of established religion and led them to adopt a critical attitude toward all religious particularism, including Judaism, and even toward religious faith as such. The files of the Iberian Inquisition show that people with Averroistic or nihilistic tendencies were always present among the *judaizantes*, denying belief in the immortality of the soul and divine providence. Some people with proto-Deist tendencies were apparently to be found among them as well, claiming that salvation could be attained by different religions.

One such person was Juan de Prado, who returned to Judaism in 1654 and was excommunicated in 1658 for his heterodox views by the Sephardic community of Amsterdam a couple of years after the excommunication of his younger companion Baruch Spinoza. At the University of Alcalá de Henares, while still a Christian, Prado was active among a group of converso students who observed certain Jewish commandments. Together with some of them he believed that Jews, Muslims, and Christians could all attain salvation, because all three religions had the same goal: to bring the believer to awareness of God. The conversos who left Spain and Portugal and wished to rehabilitate themselves within Judaism took with them these intellectual differences and contradictions. Hence, some of the ideological ferment that affected the communities of Sephardic Jews in the west reflected ideological tensions that already existed beforehand among the Iberian conversos.

Not all the New Christians who left Spain and Portugal wished to return to Judaism. There was no lack of emigrants whose departure afforded them an opportunity to free themselves completely from the restrictions entailed by their Jewish origins. Quite a few New Christian families managed to flee from the dread of the Inquisition and the social discrimination imposed upon them by the Statutes of Purity of Blood adopted in many Iberian institutions. They migrated to Italy, France, the southern Netherlands, England, and the Americas, and within a relatively short time shed all signs of their origins and ancestry and integrated within the host culture. Only an experienced historian can sometimes succeed in locating a few of them, on the basis of certain identifying marks (such as engagement in professions such as medicine and in financial activities such as international commerce, expressions of religious nonconformism, and the like), though these can often be deceptive. However, for those conversos who emigrated and chose to return openly to Judaism, the threatening presence of others who sought to efface their own affiliation with Judaism could not be ignored; rather, it was an ideological challenge with which they were forced to cope. For the entire converso Diaspora, the assimilationists symbolized the possibility of escaping Jewish fate, and they attracted others to follow in their footsteps. Moreover, those who left Iberia, including refugees from the Inquisition who escaped from its talons by the skin of their teeth, continued to foster ties with their homeland, which some of them viewed as a "lost paradise." The poet Daniel Levi (Miguel) de Barrios, a converso who returned to Judaism in the early 1660s and was active in Amsterdam until the early eighteenth century, wrote in one of his later works: "All of Spain is not called Celtiberia on account of the Celts and the

Iberians, as many say, but rather the name is taken from the Hebrew word for ribs (*tzela'ot*) in the second chapter of Genesis: 'and the Lord caused a sleep to fall upon Adam, and he slept, and He took one of his *tzela'ot*,' for the Garden of Eden was located in Spain."[3]

Even stronger was the tie to Portugal, which recovered its independence in 1640, firing the imagination of many in the Sephardic Diaspora who yearned to return to their beloved country. Significantly, after the establishment by former conversos of the Sephardic community in London in the early days of the Restoration (1660), a minority of the Portuguese Catholics of Jewish origin who had found their way to London chose to live on the margins of the new community without converting to Judaism. Despite their strong ethnic and cultural ties with the Portuguese Jews, they remained Catholic. Some of them had escaped from the Portuguese Inquisition, and others had arrived in London with the retinue of Catherine of Braganza to assist in her marriage to Charles II (r. 1660–85). One of the latter, Fernando Mendes da Costa, wrote from London in 1663 to his brother Jorge in Rome, asking him to assist Manoel de Melo, who had just then left London for Rome to negotiate with the pope regarding the recognition of Portugal. The last paragraph of Fernando's letter is extremely revealing: "We have told him [de Melo] that when the business is concluded, 8 or 9 hundred people now in Castile and France will go to that kingdom [Portugal], and many from the North here."[4] Fernando, dwelling within the safe confines of London, was toying with the idea that many New Christians from Portugal would return to their homeland if it were to change its policy toward them—that is, if it ended social discrimination and persecution by the Inquisition. Among those who might emigrate to Portugal, Fernando also included many people from "the North here" (that is, England) who, in his opinion, would be prepared to return to their place of origin, with all that this implied, including reversion to the Catholic religion.

It is well known that, during the first generations after the expulsion, a stream of conversos from Spain, and even more so from Portugal, headed for the Sephardic Jewish centers that had been established in Islamic lands—in North Africa and especially in the Ottoman Levant. Emigration continued throughout the sixteenth century and did not cease during the seventeenth, though it decreased to some degree. Absorbed by the Sephardic communities, the Iberian exiles created an organizational and educational infrastructure for the restoration of *ba'alei teshuva* (penitents) to the bosom of Judaism. Their presence was quite notable in Izmir during the entire seventeenth century, and they occupied a prominent place among the enthusiastic followers of Shabbtai Zevi. Groups of former conversos arose in Safed and Jerusalem as well, seeking ways to "atone

for their sins" as Christians. Similarly, in Italy during the sixteenth century, especially in Ferrara, and for a short time also in Ancona in the Papal States, more
than a few conversos returned to Judaism. For reasons of economic profit, the
Christian authorities, including the popes, related to them as Jews in every respect, ignoring their Catholic past and the fact that they had received the sacrament of baptism.

In contrast to them, however, conversos who returned to Judaism in western
Europe during the seventeenth century and founded communities there had to
create their own organizational infrastructure. Thus, toward the end of the sixteenth century a community of Sephardic *ponentini*, or former New Christians,
was established in Venice, and similar communities were established in Pisa and
in Leghorn. The Italian communities of former conversos were very concerned
with maintaining their independence and particularity, and they kept aloof
from the other Jewish communities on Italian soil. However, they were not acting in a vacuum and could not avoid being influenced by the Jewish life around
them. The situation was quite different in northwest Europe. Since there was no
Jewish life in that region before the arrival of the conversos, generally the first
Jewish community they encountered was the one they established themselves, in
their own figure and image. Such was the situation in Amsterdam, Hamburg,
and London as well as in southwest France, where there were centers of *nou-
veaux chrétiens portugais* at least from the time of the *lettres patentes* that the
kings of France began to grant them in the mid-sixteenth century. However,
these individuals did not begin to express their Judaism outwardly until the
1660s, and they were not recognized officially as Jews until the early eighteenth
century.

Even when the Sephardic communities began to be consolidated in western
Europe with official recognition by the authorities, not all the conversos who arrived there immediately returned to Judaism. Some preferred to retain their
Christian identity, living as Catholics or even as Protestants. Moreover, not all
those who officially returned to Judaism did so from clear religious motivation.
Along with those motivated by ideological conviction, there were others for
whom a return to Judaism was an effective means of retaining family and ethnic
ties within the Sephardic Diaspora. Certainly, financial interests were involved in
their decision. The Jewish religion provided a common denominator, uniting
families dispersed in many countries and helping to keep the family capital intact. Furthermore, poor opportunists found a form of security in the Sephardic charity organizations, which granted them rather generous support and a
chance to improve their conditions of life.

THE JEWISH PROFILE OF FORMER CONVERSOS

On their own initiative, the "New Jews"—who had never previously tasted Jewish life as it was lived in a traditional society—established new frameworks to supply basic socialization for themselves and for those who would arrive in their wake. Of course they were assisted by veteran Jewish communities from other countries that were willing to extend a helping hand, and they even managed to gain significant support throughout the Sephardic Diaspora in the Ottoman Empire and Italy. They were strongly influenced by the Sephardic community in Venice, because until the 1630s Venice was the capital of the western Sephardic world, serving as a bridge between the European Jews and their brethren in the Levant.

Not only were most of the members of the western Sephardic Diaspora new to Judaism, but their special character as former conversos or the descendants of former conversos was also notable for generations in the Jewish profile of their communities. They were the first Jews in the early modern period who were forced to redefine their Jewish identity and mark its boundaries, and they could only do so with the intellectual tools they had acquired in their Christian socialization. Indeed, quite a few of them had received an excellent education in the best Iberian universities—Alcalá de Henares, Salamanca, Valladolid, and Coimbra—and in Jesuit seminaries and monastery schools. The proportion of physicians among them was relatively high, and their theological and philosophical background was quite extensive. Paradoxically, these former conversos drew definitions of their Jewish identity and justification for acceptance of the yoke of Jewish law from Iberian neo-scholasticism, Jesuit pedagogy, and fideistic philosophy. Some of them advanced claims similar to those of the Catholic fideists, who sought to justify the unchallenged supremacy of the pope and the church tradition against the attacks of Protestants and early modern skeptics. In their own arguments against neo-Sadducees and neo-Karaites, who were gaining a following among the intellectual class of former conversos, these thinkers maintained that acceptance of the authority of the talmudic and rabbinic tradition was necessary to avoid plunging into the abyss of religious uncertainty. One such thinker was Isaac Orobio de Castro, a physician and philosopher who returned to Judaism in Amsterdam in 1662 and argued with Spinoza and with Juan de Prado after they were excommunicated by his community. Orobio de Castro regarded the Oral Law as the factor that could guide the Jewish believer, given the existence of uncertainty, because, he said, the human intellect is limited by its very nature and unable to gain unequivocal knowledge.

The new communities of the "Spanish and Portuguese Jewish Nation" did not ostensibly deviate from the framework established by halakhic Judaism over the generations; they explicitly declared their loyalty to the "faith of the Sages." The syndics who led them claimed "supreme authority over all" (*superioridade sobre tudo*), but they consistently accepted the professional authority of the rabbis in halakhic matters. Yet, during the seventeenth century, fissures appeared in the traditional framework that the "New Jews" sought to define. Although officially they were committed to applying the principles of the halakhah in all matters, in the face of reality this application became quite partial and problematic. Their connection with halakhic norms became weak in various areas of life, notably, first of all, in their extensive economic activities. An indication of this tendency is the almost complete lack of regulations on economic matters among the ordinances instituted by these communities during the seventeenth and eighteenth

B. Picart, *The Circumcision Ceremony of the Portuguese Jews*, 1722. Engraving.
The legend indicates (A) the father, (B) the mother and godmother in another room
at upper right, (C) the godfather, holding the infant, (D) an empty seat for Elijah,
(E) the mohel, and (F) a rabbi, relative, or friend holding the cup.
(Jewish Historical Museum, Amsterdam; JHM 03966)

Romain de Hooghe, *Burial of a Sephardi Jew* in the Portuguese-Jewish
Cemetery of Ouderkerk, near Amsterdam, c. 1680. Etching.
(Jewish Historical Museum, Amsterdam; JHM 01104)

centuries. Moreover, questions on economic matters are hardly to be found in
the responsa of their rabbis, which are not particularly impressive in any event.
Among these Jews, religion was increasingly limited to ritual matters, Sabbath
and holidays, and the synagogue. Secular activity expanded into the space left
vacant after the scope of Jewish law was narrowed. However, since this impressive process took place unintentionally, without any public challenge, and in
places where the rabbinical establishment was rather weak and subject to the
domination of the Mahamad (the executive committee of syndics of the community), it failed to arouse stiff ideological resistance.

  To a degree, the Sephardic Jews of western Europe can be seen as harbingers
of the individualism that emerged in modern Jewish life. Since their Judaism
was not self-evident, they had to fill it with new content and to determine its
boundaries. Various alternatives were available to them in defining their Jewish
identity. Many of them clung to the halakhic tradition with devotion and some-

times even with the fanaticism typical of penitents (in common speech those who were scrupulous in observing the commandments were known derisively as *mitzvoteros*), whereas others held critical, subversive, and antinomian views, thoroughly rejecting talmudic Judaism. Uriel da Costa, a converso from Porto who returned to Judaism in Hamburg around 1616, and who confronted the local Sephardic communities there and in Amsterdam, after rejecting the Oral Law and rabbinical authority, wrote an autobiographical work shortly before taking his own life in 1640. There he states:

> I observed, that the customs and ordinances of the modern Jews were very different from those commanded by Moses. Now if the Law was to be strictly observed, according to the letter, as it expressly declares, it must be very unjustifiable in the Jewish doctors to add to it inventions of a quite contrary nature. This provoked me to oppose them openly, nay, I looked upon it as doing God service to defend the law with freedom against such innovations.[5]

Quite a few conversos who returned to Judaism regarded it as a religion rather than an all-embracing way of life. Since they were used to experiencing their Judaism in secret, they became accustomed to distinguishing between inner, intimate religious reality and the outer way of life they had led in Spain and Portugal according to the values prevalent in the Iberian Christian world. When they returned to Judaism, some of them came to the conclusion, as it were, that spiritual identification with the tradition was more important than the punctilious observance of the Torah and the commandments—a version of the Iberian converso principle that faith in the law (and not necessarily its observance) promises life in the world to come. This view challenged rabbinical Judaism and opened the way for all kinds of individualistic interpretations of the Jewish tradition. Other former conversos were more radical and joined circles of atheists and libertines or of Christians who denied the confessional character of Christianity. The political and social atmosphere of the Dutch Republic created fertile ground for this trend: in the conditions of relative tolerance that prevailed there, the Jewish community lost part of its authority as a corporation, and its coercive power was blunted.

Spinoza, the son of conversos who returned to Judaism in Amsterdam, was excommunicated by the community there in 1656. Later to become one of the most influential philosophers in modern times, Spinoza not only opposed rabbinical authority and the idea that the Jews are the Chosen People but he also laid the foundations of biblical criticism. The ideas he expressed at the time of his excommunication were later developed in his *Tractatus Theologico-Politicus*

(first published anonymously in 1670). Until his death in 1677, he remained outside of Judaism without converting to Christianity. Like quite a few *chrétiens
sans Eglise* in the Dutch Republic, he was unattached to any church or religious
denomination, though he was very close to circles of collegiants, nonconformist
Christians of a rationalistic bent, with whom he found much in common.

A fair number of Jews removed themselves from the community without
any struggle or opposition—and many of them did so without converting. In
London this tendency was even more pronounced, because from the start the
communal organization of the Sephardic Jews was not a corporation. The community was powerless to deal with Iberian conversos who retained their social
connections with it but refused to be circumcised, so that their "Judaism" was, in
their view, a matter of identity of interests with the ethnic group and nothing
more. Wishing to imitate the lifestyle of the English gentry, some of the wealthiest among them moved to rural estates, far from the supervision of the community in London, and their attachment to Judaism weakened.

However, along with individualism, another phenomenon—that of ethnic
awareness—is manifest in the western Sephardic Diaspora. The Sephardim
did not refrain from offering financial and even political assistance to other
groups of Jews in central and eastern Europe; nevertheless, their religious identity could not give full expression to their social identity. They regarded themselves as part of the *Nación* (Nation), a vague concept that they used to signify
the entire Iberian Jewish community, including the various groups of conversos
and New Christians who remained in Spain and Portugal and their colonies.
The Nación, though it did not express nationalism as it developed later in Europe, was based on components of identity such as ethnicity, culture, language,
and common fate, making it a precursor of a new development that became increasingly problematic in the modern period.

Despite the criticism in principle voiced by the Sephardic leaders against remaining in the "lands of idolatry" (the term they used for Spain, Portugal, their
colonies, and, in general, Catholic countries where Jews were forbidden to live),
these Jews continued to view the people of Jewish descent who remained there as
an integral part of their ethnic group. Connections of family and business, history, and common cultural affinities strengthened the ties among the various
parts of this Diaspora and sometimes even masked the differences and religious
and ideological conflicts among them. Although the religious leadership never
granted ideological legitimacy to members of the Nación who remained, willingly or under duress, outside of Judaism, the Sephardic Jews of western Europe
did accord them social legitimacy by maintaining connections with them in
various areas and on different levels.

Thus a unique Diaspora emerged, whose past and Jewish origins were a common denominator, though not all its members were of the same faith and not all of them had a real connection with Judaism. In the historical context of early modern Europe, the ideological struggles among the various segments of this Diaspora and the connections and solidarity that existed within it were two sides of the same coin.

THE ECONOMIC ELITE AND ITS CULTURAL IDEALS

"Some of them are rich, but most are very poor."[6] Thus Skippon summed up his impression of the social composition of the Sephardic community in Amsterdam. Indeed, in the entire western Sephardic Diaspora, the presence of the poor was constant and oppressive. The communities invested considerable effort in reducing poverty and concealing its manifestations from outside eyes. The Sephardic charity funds offered large sums of money to prevent the poor members of the community from emerging in the city streets and damaging their decorous collective image. These considerations led them to the conclusion that it was preferable to keep away poor people with no profession, and this gave rise to the phenomenon of the *despachados,* poor Jews who were sent to distant countries, first eastward to the Levant and Palestine, later to the New World. The concentration of despachados in the Jewish communities of the Caribbean colonies, such as in Curaçao, Surinam, Jamaica, and Barbados, had a deep influence on the social composition of the Sephardic population in those colonies and on their Jewish culture, emphasizing their marginality in relation to European Jewish centers.

The mass emigration to western Europe of refugees from Germany and Poland-Lithuania following the Thirty Years' War and the wars in eastern Europe between 1648 and 1660 augmented the tendency among the Sephardic Jews to keep apart from the Ashkenazim, and they employed various strategies of segregation to remain separate and rid themselves of the humiliating presence of the *tudescos* and *polacos.* Toward the end of the seventeenth century, this separatism reached a peak when regulations were passed in the Sephardic communities forbidding interethnic marriage. The Jewish economist and philosopher Isaac de Pinto summed up this attitude very well in a letter to Voltaire in 1762, in response to the latter's harsh words on the Jews in his *Dictionnaire philosophique:*

The distance between them and their brethren is so great that if a Portuguese Jew dwelling in Holland or England were to marry an Ashkenazic Jewish woman, he would immediately lose all his special privileges: he would no longer be considered as a member of their synagogue . . . and he would be completely removed from the Nation.[7]

In general it may be said that the image projected by the Portuguese Jews was determined by the huge effect made by the wealthiest of them. The western Sephardim corroborated a well-known sociological rule, which maintains that groups of high status are assessed according to their elites, in contrast to groups of low social status, which are judged according to their lowest strata. A Frenchman named Maximillian Misson, who visited Amsterdam in the 1680s, wrote that "the Portuguese Jews here are extraordinary Rich," but what impressed him more than anything was the fact that "notwithstanding the Inquisition against the Jews in Spain and Portugal, a Portuguese Jew (Don Jerome Nunez de Costa) was Agent of Portugal, at Amsterdam. And another (Don Emanuel de Belmont) Resident of Spain. This last received the title of Count from the Emperor."[8]

However, these two were not isolated cases. In Hamburg, Amsterdam, the Hague, and London, and later also in Bordeaux, a number of Sephardic magnates were active, the descendants of conversos who claimed venerable aristocratic origins and whose return to Judaism added great economic power to the communities of the Nación. These wealthy merchants established an extensive network of economic connections between northwestern Europe, Iberia, and the colonies in the Caribbean. Those of vast wealth sought to translate their economic power into values of social status, including imitation of the external manners and way of life of the French aristocracy. The fabulous wealth and financial experience of the most prestigious families, who stood at the peak of the Jewish social pyramid, brought them to the royal courts of Europe. Their emotional and cultural ties with the Iberian world were not obscured even after they left the peninsula, and their economic connections with Spain and Portugal led the most prominent members of this elite to serve the interests of those countries. By virtue of this activity, some of them received diplomatic appointments and even titles of nobility.

The Portuguese Crown, after it was liberated from the Spanish yoke in 1640, honored several members of the prominent Curiel family with the exalted title of *"cavaleiro fidalgo da casa real."* The first of these was Jacob Curiel of Hamburg, who worked in the service of the Conde Duque de Olivares in establishing the Spanish military fleet for the war against the Dutch and later became a supplier of munitions to the Portuguese and a dynamic agent in their secret diplomatic service. His son Moses, also known as Geronimo Nunes da Costa, received a similar title in Amsterdam, as did David, Jacob's brother. The latter, also known as Lopo Ramírez, changed sides in 1645 and passed into the service of the Spanish. Similarly, the magnate Manuel de Belmonte served as diplomatic representative of the Spanish monarchy in Amsterdam, and, to avoid embarrassing the Spanish diplomats, who were accustomed to visiting him, he chose as his private dwelling a splendid mansion outside the quarter where most of the Jews of the city lived. Abraham (Diego) Teixeira entertained Queen Christina of Sweden in his house in Hamburg for 15 days after her abdication. In gratitude for financial services, Antonio Lopes Suasso, who was raised in a New Christian family in Bordeaux and then changed his name to Isaac Israel Suasso when he returned to Judaism in the 1650s, received from King Carlos II of Spain (r. 1665–1700) the barony of Avernas-le-Gras in the southern Netherlands. His son Francisco, who became Abraham Israel Suasso, inherited the title from his father. Just as the father had increased his property by marrying a daughter of the wealthy Pinto family, so, too, the son doubled his possessions and expanded his business by marrying a daughter of the Teixeiras of Hamburg.

Romain de Hooghe, *House of Baron Belmonte*, 1700–1705. Etching.
(Jewish Historical Museum, Amsterdam; JHM 07051. Collection J. v. Velzen)

In this manner, by weaving marriage connections, the financial aristocracy of the Sephardic Diaspora reinforced its position and heightened the aura of prestige that surrounded it. Individuals from the Pinto, Pereira, and Cortisos families in Amsterdam, the Lima and Seneor families in Hamburg, and the Mendes da Costa, d'Aguilar, and Pereira-Lopes families in London gained honors and marks of distinction from kings and princes. Sir Solomon de Medina was the first Jew in England to receive an English knighthood, and King William III (r. 1688–1702) paid him the honor of visiting him at his home. Some members of the aforementioned families became court Jews in every respect and maintained sumptuous lifestyles, as befit their status. Their splendid homes were well-known meeting places for high society, where the local elite circles and representatives of the European aristocracy visited them.

These court Jews sought to embellish their position by offering what they viewed as a dignified presentation of the riches of the Jewish heritage. They purchased old books and manuscripts, commissioned manuscript copies of works by contemporary authors who enhanced the heritage, and collected rare and valuable ritual objects. They displayed these treasures before their non-Jewish visitors to impress them with the virtues of Jewish culture and to demonstrate that it was not alien to the European heritage but, rather, fit into it well. A considerable number became patrons of Jewish authors and poets and supported the publication of books—mainly in Spanish—that were meant not only for the readership of the Nación but also for the educated Hispanic community at large. Thus, they aspired to a status as patrons of culture equal to that of anyone in the Iberian world. Some of the works they sponsored, including those of Daniel Levi de Barrios, Joseph Penso de la Vega, Manuel de Leão, and Joseph Henriques Almeida, were devoid of signs of Judaism, and their content also does not reveal the authors' religious affiliation.

THE "BOM JUDESMO" OF THE "GENTE POLÍTICA"

This economic elite played a considerable, sometimes even decisive role in erecting splendid and impressive houses of worship in the centers of the Sephardic Diaspora in Amsterdam, the Hague, and London. Aware of the curiosity that Jewish synagogues aroused among Christian travelers, some of whom had never witnessed Jewish religious services, they sought to present Jewish worship in its full glory and give it traits similar to the dignified atmosphere that prevailed in Christian churches, especially those of the Protestants. Indeed, the French diplomat Charles Ogier, who visited two of the Sephardic synagogues in Amsterdam in 1636, was surprised to discover a great similarity between them and the Calvinist churches of the city.

The splendor that characterized the members of the Portuguese Jewish economic elite, and their outward grandeur, was very evident to visitors to their synagogues, especially their magnificent new sanctuary, the Esnoga in Amsterdam, which was dedicated in 1675. William Mountague, who saw it in the late seventeenth century, wrote that it was "the largest [synagogue] in Europe (if not in the World) being much superior to those we our selves saw in many other Parts, where the Jews are most numerous."[9] According to another famous visitor, Gregorio Letti, "The synagogue of the Portuguese seems to be a seat of noblemen, a well-made people, almost all civil, well dressed, rich, and who make a fine impression."[10]

This synagogue was indeed the most impressive—both in size and in magnificence—in all of western Europe, and nowhere else did a Jewish house of worship occupy such a prominent place in the urban landscape. The Dutch architect Elias Bouman, who designed the building, appears to have been influenced to some degree by the model of King Solomon's Temple that was built by Rabbi Jacob Juda León Templo and that became an attraction for travelers who visited the small museum Templo established in his home. The interior of the Esnoga was reminiscent of Calvinist churches in Holland, and everyone who entered it was drawn to the beauty of the Holy Ark (*Heikhal*) which was constructed of jacaranda wood from Brazil, a gift from the magnate Moses Curiel. The interiors of the synagogues that were erected afterward in London (Bevis Marks, 1701), in the Hague (on the initiative of Abraham Israel Suasso, 1726), and on the island of Curaçao (1732) were smaller-scale replicas of the Esnoga, expressing the wish to imitate the dignified impression it aroused.

The Sephardim of western Europe realized that they were exposed to observation by a large and distinguished European community. In general, the members of the Nación showed great openness toward Christian visitors. In the congregation of Amsterdam, the worshipers sitting behind the reader's platform (*tebah*) functioned as ushers when necessary, to permit non-Jews to sit in the synagogue, on condition that this was arranged in an orderly manner, such as in a theater. Indeed, to some degree those Jews felt that the synagogue service was similar to theater, and they, the actors, were supposed to arouse a feeling of earnestness in the visitors. Their leadership viewed the gentiles as a group whose values, culture, manners, and aesthetic taste had to be taken into consideration, so that the spectacle performed before them would please them.

Various community regulations in Amsterdam, Hamburg, and London emphasized the need to display good manners and restraint in the synagogue, condemning what "appears to be behavior more appropriate to barbarians than to people of good breeding [*gente política*]."[11] Indeed, they wished to be seen as gente política: well-bred, courteous people, whose behavior bespoke cultivation and good taste. At times the worshipers were asked to behave in a manner that would not arouse distaste or ridicule among the gentile visitors, "who whisper about these things and others which constitute a desecration of [the name of] heaven."[12]

Just as the collections of Judaica that were maintained with such care by the Sephardic court Jews in the salons of their splendid houses were meant to present Jewish culture as equal in value to that of the Christian elite, so, too, the severity regarding the behavior required in the synagogue and public places where the Jews were exposed to the attention of non-Jews was intended to present Judaism as civilized and cultured, with features befitting the patterns of behavior that had crystallized within European courtly society and been transferred to the bourgeoisie. Since the play had to follow the rules of the theater, the first principle to be observed was the prevention of anything that might disturb the audience's concentration and enjoyment. Therefore, a regulation adopted by the Sephardic community of Amsterdam at the end of the seventeenth century aimed to prevent the disorder caused by "certain people [who] are accustomed to stand while the entire holy congregation is sitting, which arouses great reproach among the strangers."[13] A similar regulation, instituted in London, condemned this conduct because of "the scandal that this raises among those who come from outside."[14]

In London, however, unlike Amsterdam, the Sephardic Jews were reluctant to invite gentiles to the synagogue, and as early as 1664 they stated explicitly:

> [T]o avoid the scandal and hindrance that it caused . . . when English ladies came to see the ceremonies of our religion, it is forbidden, and ordained that from this day henceforth no *Yahid* of this *Kahal Kados* may bring them to it, nor rise, nor move from his place to receive them, nor [persons] of any other nation that may be, in order to accompany them, or give them place; and the same applies to the gentlemen who may come to this Synagogue, reserving to the members of the *Mahamad* the power to act as they ought according as may seem good to them.[15]

Thus only the Mahamad had the prerogative of inviting strangers to the synagogue. Nevertheless, other regulations show that outsiders did visit the London synagogue frequently, and there was great sensitivity toward their presence and caution to maintain dignified conduct during prayers so as not to give them grounds "to be able to blame." In 1711 this sensitivity even led to the cancellation of the ceremony of dancing with Torah scrolls on Simḥat Torah, because this causes "more of a scandal than any benefit."[16] This strange decision appears to be a late reaction to Samuel Pepys's remarks following his visit to the first synagogue of London in Creechurch Lane, on the evening of Simḥat Torah in 1663. In his diary, which had meanwhile received considerable publicity, Pepys wrote that he was horrified by what seemed like a barbaric ceremony to him. One gets the impression that he thought dancing with the Torah scrolls was the ordinary manner in which the Jews worshiped their God.

In similar spirit, ordinances were passed in all of these communities against pounding with hammers on Purim, which was viewed as "barbaric behavior" (in Amsterdam) and as "an indecent custom" (in London), or because of "the damage that was liable to arise from this commotion" (in Hamburg).

However, the cultural pretensions of the social elite were not restricted to the desire to present the congregation's religious services in a grand and dignified fashion before strangers. Let us not forget that, from the moment Judaism ceased to serve as a comprehensive way of life and became restricted increasingly to the religious sphere, the synagogue service gained central significance in the lives of the Portuguese Jews. Hence, many regulations concerning this subject were instituted in all the congregations of the Nación. For example, 40 percent of the regulations of the Sephardic congregation of Surinam, which were reconfirmed in 1754, deal with synagogue matters. Similarly, it must not be forgotten that one of the main ambitions of the elite was to educate the Sephardic community (and in some way also to have a similar influence on the Ashkenazim) in what they called *bom judesmo,* or "worthy Judaism." In this context, the proper presentation of synagogue services was meant to reflect the internalization of the values of bom judesmo in their own view and that of their surroundings.

In a certain sense it may be said that, in the western Sephardic Diaspora, an extremely heavy yoke was borne, the demands of which were in some respects more severe than those of Jewish law. That yoke, in the image of the culture that the social elite wished to inculcate, required obedience and restraint, the control of instincts, and maximal consideration for the taste and inclinations of the surrounding society. This "civilizing process" imposed severe discipline on the members of the western Sephardic communities and demanded constant and rigid control from the leadership. The high rates of excommunication and other public punishment during the early modern period, especially in Amsterdam and Hamburg, show that this process did not go forward smoothly and that the norms of the gente política and their ideals of bom judesmo were not easily internalized.

RELIGIOUS AND SECULAR EDUCATION

The kabbalist Shabbetai Sheftel Horowitz, an Ashkenazic Jew from Prague, visited Amsterdam during the seventeenth century and publicly expressed enthusiasm for the educational system run by the community of former conversos. Other visitors from central and eastern Europe, who came from the most important centers of Jewish learning of that time and were rather critical of the scholastic and elitist systems of study practiced therein, were not sparing in praise of what appeared to be an excellent method, one that took the pupil's abilities into account and presented the subjects systematically, according to a rational pedagogical plan. The well-known bibliophile Shabbetai Bass, who came to Amsterdam in 1675, expressed his amazement at what he saw in the school of the Sephardic Jews: division into six classes, each in a separate classroom. In the first classroom,

small boys study until they can read the prayers; and then they are sent to the second classroom, where they study Torah with singing the cantillation until they are familiar with the five books of the Torah . . . and then they enter the third classroom, where they study Torah until they are expert in commenting on it in the vernacular, and every week they learn Rashi's commentary well, with the entire portion. Then they come to the fourth classroom, and there they study prophets and the writings in order, with singing the cantillation, and one boy reads the verse in the Holy Tongue and then explains it in the vernacular, and all the boys listen to him, and then he explains the next one, too, and so do they all. Then they go to the fifth classroom and they accustom the boys to read Jewish law by themselves . . . and there they speak no language other than the Holy Tongue, but they interpret the halakhah in the vernacular. And they learn the science of grammar well, and also every day they also study a different halakhah from the *Gemara*. And when they come to a holiday or festival all the students study the *Shulḥan Arukh* concerning it: the halakhot of Pesaḥ on Pesaḥ, and every holiday in turn, so that all of the boys are knowledgeable about the laws. And then they go to the sixth classroom of the yeshivah, the House of Study of the rabbi, the head of the religious court, may God preserve him, and there they sit in a classroom and learn one halakhah every day with grammar, Rashi, and *Tosafot*, and they also debate the fine points of every matter of the law in Maimonides and the *Tur* and *Bet Yosef* and the other halakhic authorities. . . . And the time of study is the same for all of the rabbis and teachers, and in the morning when the clock strikes eight all the teachers and students come to their classrooms, and they study for three hours until eleven comes, and then they all leave at once. And when the clock strikes two in the afternoon they all also come as before and study until it strikes five, and during the winter until they gather in the synagogue. And in those hours when the boys are not in school every householder has a man who teaches the boy to write in the vernacular and in the Holy Tongue, and to review the studies in his home, and to make poems and witticisms and to act in the right way, and to teach each one what he wishes.[17]

Although the roots of some of the points emphasized in the program of study are to be found in the medieval Spanish tradition, which emphasized the importance of studying correct Hebrew, grammar, and the Bible, the pedagogical views of these educators certainly derived from the humanistic principles that were gaining a foothold in European society. They might even have been familiar with the *Didactica Magna* of Comenius. It cannot be doubted that the organization of the Amsterdam school was quite similar to that of the Jesuit schools in Iberia at the time, because several of the men who laid down the guidelines for the Sephardic community in Amsterdam had been educated in Jesuit institutions. This is notable, among other things, in placing the pupils in six classes, the division of the school day into morning and afternoon sessions (among the Jesuits, the morning session was two and a half hours, the afternoon session three and a half hours), and in the great value attributed to repetition, to reading with cantillation, and to recreational activity.

Yet this method was incapable of producing halakhic authorities who could compete with the products of the great Sephardic centers of learning in the Levant, and therefore during the seventeenth and part of the eighteenth centuries Amsterdam had to hire Sephardic rabbis from the Ottoman Empire, North Africa, and Italy. (Rabbi Saul Levi Mortera, the Italian Ashkenazic rabbi who was active in the Sephardic community of Amsterdam for more than 40 years and played a central role in forming the religious life of the community until his death in 1660, was in this respect an exception that proved the rule.) As early as the 1630s, however, local figures who had been educated in Amsterdam began to gain prominence, including Rabbi Menasseh ben Israel, Rabbi Isaac Aboab da Fonseca, and Rabbi Moses Raphael d'Aguilar, all of whom had arrived with their parents from Portugal as children. The varied works of these three rabbis testify to the breadth of the schooling offered by the Sephardim to the most gifted of their young men. In addition to ordinary studies in the Talmud Torah and at the Etz Haim Yeshivah, they studied Latin with private teachers, both Jewish and non-Jewish, and expanded their abilities in the areas of theology, philosophy, and rhetoric. A thin stream of young men from the Portuguese community even undertook university studies in Holland, in Franeker and Hardewijk, but mainly in Leiden, where about a dozen of them received degrees in medicine during the seventeenth century. The open system at that university, which did not require membership in any college or prolonged residence, permitted them to prepare for examinations with the physicians of the Jewish community of Amsterdam, who also guided them in writing their dissertations. Thus the students only had to be present at the university for short periods.

Although it did not stress talmudic erudition, the Etz Haim Yeshivah became a central source providing rabbis for other Sephardic communities in western Europe and the colonies in the Americas. It must be emphasized that the function of the rabbis in the communities of the Nación was mainly professional and advisory, because in the Amsterdam community, like those of the western Sephardic Diaspora in general, judicial power lay in the hands of the *parnasim* (the syndics of the community, members of the Mahamad). However, in order for the parnasim to judge "according to the law and close to the law," they had to consult rabbinical authorities. Over time it became customary for the parnasim in these communities to bring all of the questions and claims addressed to them before the rabbinical court (*Ḥakhamim*). But of all the communities of the Nación, only in Amsterdam did a rabbinical court manage to consolidate a degree of power. In the first half of the eighteenth century it even grew stronger, though then, too, it remained subordinate to the Mahamad of the community. Resort to the rabbinical court brought with it the development of a responsa literature. Beginning in 1728, after Rabbi David Israel Athias and Rabbi Isaac Ḥaim Abendana de Britto were appointed as rabbis of the community, the Etz Ḥaim Yeshivah began more or less regularly to publish responsa written by its senior students and by those whom it had ordained as rabbis, in a series called *Pri Etz Ḥaim.*

However, the increased strength of the community rabbinate is liable to create an illusion. One cannot conclude from the fact that the influence of the rabbinical court increased in Amsterdam during the eighteenth century that the community had become more disciplined with respect to Jewish law. On the contrary: because a significant part of the community had parted from it, and because the tie between part of the economic elite and the institutions of the community had become weaker, the presence of the pious segment loyal to Jewish law was more strongly felt. The control of the rabbis did increase, but now this control affected a diminished community, a large proportion of whose members had become marginal. These tendencies were even stronger in other Sephardic communities. There, too, educational systems were established with pedagogical underpinnings that were similar to those of the Talmud Torah in Amsterdam, but neither in Hamburg nor in London, nor of course in Bayonne, Bordeaux, or the Caribbean communities, was it possible even to approach the level of the institution in Amsterdam.

Emigration from Iberia and the transition from Christianity to Judaism decreased the education of women to some degree. In Spain and Portugal a considerable proportion of the *conversas* had learned to read and write, and sometimes far more than that, but in the communities of the Nación, where no formal education was available to them during the seventeenth century, many were illiterate. And later, in contrast to the broad education of boys, such schooling as girls did receive was very limited. Only the daughters of wealthy families were given private tutoring, including the study of languages. Just a few women reached the level of independent creativity, and their presence is barely felt.

In England, the Talmud Torah for boys, Sha'arei Tikva, had functioned since 1664, in a form quite similar to that of the Talmud Torah in Amsterdam, though on a modest scale. A special school for girls, Villa Real, was established there in 1730, named for the philanthropist who endowed it. At that very time English and arithmetic were first introduced into the curriculum of Sha'arei Tikva. In Amsterdam, boys from affluent families received instruction from private tutors in languages, including Latin and Dutch, as well as the elements of arithmetic and basic principles of commerce and accounting.

LANGUAGES, LITERATURES, AND LIBRARIES

Portuguese was generally the lingua franca of the Nación. Since most seventeenth-century conversos were more or less of Portuguese origin, and even those who emigrated to Spain after 1580 continued to use Portuguese in communications within the family and their ethnic group, it became the private idiom of the various branches of the Nación, both among Jews and among conversos. However, Spanish was occasionally predominant in certain centers of this Diaspora during the seventeenth century. Thus, though the community regulations in Amsterdam and Hamburg were written in Portuguese, the language used in daily conversation among the Sephardim in those cities, the first community statutes in London were written in Spanish (though later they were written in Portuguese), because Spanish was the language of some of the first prominent conversos in England, who came from decidedly Spanish-speaking areas, especially the Canary Islands. In the French communities that were not established until the early eighteenth century, the main spoken language was French; since the mid-sixteenth century the New Christian communities in

France had undergone a pronounced process of local acculturation. Nevertheless, Spanish was used to a significant extent in some of their written regulations, in religious services, and in their contacts with the Sephardic world. Perhaps in this case proximity to the Spanish border had a significant influence on the predominance of Spanish over Portuguese.

In general it may be said that these two Iberian languages constantly encountered one another in the discourse of the Nación. The suffocation of both languages (to use the term developed by the Dutch linguist B. N. Teensma, who studied the phenomenon in Amsterdam) is sometimes in evidence in their idiom. Many Spanish words and syntactic forms penetrated the Portuguese of the Jews of Amsterdam as a result of their intensive and daily contact with Spanish speakers, and especially because of the influence of the Ferrara Bible translation, prayers, and Jewish catechisms that were written in Spanish. Thus, for example, the Portuguese word *judeu* (Jew), which is *judío* in Spanish, often appears in documents as *judeo;* the Portuguese word *quantidade* (quantity), which is *cantidad* in Spanish, appears there as *cantidade;* or the Portuguese word *dezembro* (December), which is *diciembre* in Spanish, sometimes appears as *deziembre.*

In time, Dutch words and expressions also penetrated the language of the Amsterdam Jews, and some French influence is felt as well, because that was the language they mostly used in communication with local scholars, at least at first. From the beginning of the eighteenth century a gradual decline in knowledge of Iberian languages naturally took place, both because the stream of conversos from Spain and Portugal dwindled and because of a marked acculturation process within Dutch society. In 1730, Daniel de la Penha wrote in Amsterdam: "Nevertheless one finds that with the passage of time there are many among us who experience difficulty in understanding this [Portuguese] very well and proportionate to their having been born in this country, they have mastered the Netherlandish tongue as if it is their own mother tongue."[18] Similar processes, sometimes even more rapid, took place in the other centers of this Diaspora. In England, for example, English became the main language of the community, though the regulations and ordinances were still written in Portuguese. Knowledge of Spanish possibly remained stronger, because it continued to be used as the internal language of culture and literature, and contact with it was fostered by means of the method used to teach the Bible, which included reading the Spanish translation.

Although relatively few of the works by Jews of the western Sephardic Diaspora were written in Hebrew, such as their relatively modest halakhic literature and some theological works, a number of the men trained in the educational institutions of the community proved their ability as rhymesters in Hebrew, using it when called upon for occasional writings. A few of them attained more significant achievements, such as Isaac Aboab da Fonseca, who translated the philosophical-kabbalistic works of Abraham Cohen Herrera from Spanish to Hebrew. Although he often distorted the philosophical character of the original to no small degree, the translation does demonstrate his excellent command of the Hebrew language. Joseph Penso de la Vega wrote an allegorical drama in Hebrew, when he was seventeen years old (*Asirei Hatikva*, printed in Amsterdam in 1673). Outdoing them all was Rabbi Moses Zacuto, whose command of biblical Hebrew was outstanding. Nevertheless, it is doubtful whether Hebrew penetrated the consciousness of these Jews in significant fashion, and more than anything one gains the impression that it served as a central tool for halakhic inquiry only for a limited group of rabbinical scholars and students, though for them as well it was not a spoken language. Public sermons in the synagogues were given in Spanish or Portuguese, depending on the personal background of the rabbi or preacher who gave them. Although more than 400 Hebrew sermons by Rabbi Saul Levi Mortera are extant in manuscript, and the printed collection of his sermons (*Giv'at Shaul*, Amsterdam, 1645) is also in Hebrew, it appears that in the synagogue he was forced to preach in Portuguese, a language he managed to learn very well during the more than 40 years that he served as a rabbi in Amsterdam. Nevertheless, one notes traces of Italian in his major work, which he wrote in Portuguese, *The Eternity of the Law of Moses* (the original manuscript of 1659–60: *Tratado da verdade da lei de Moisés*).

A relatively high number of lexicographical treatises and grammar books were written about the Hebrew language by members of the Sephardic communities, and Hebrew flourished in the many printing houses of Amsterdam that were owned by Sephardim. In the seventeenth century, Amsterdam replaced Venice as not only the capital city of Jewish literature in Spanish and Portuguese but also the most important center of Hebrew printing. However, most of these books were intended for export, including the famous editions of the Talmud printed by Immanuel Benveniste and the vocalized Mishnah printed by Menasseh ben Israel. And many of the proofreaders employed by the printers came from outside the Diaspora of former conversos, including German and Polish Jews.

In the area of cultural creativity, it is difficult to point to a Jewish society in the early modern period whose production was so wide-ranging and varied as that of the Sephardic Jews in the west, especially in the Dutch metropolis. The need to define their new identity gave rise to extensive literary activity that set itself the goal of translating the doctrines of Judaism and the elements of rabbinic law into Spanish and Portuguese and into the philosophical and theological terms with which these Jews were familiar. Thus they translated and printed daily and holiday prayer books, ritual study texts, books of regulations and customs, and classical works by Judah Halevi, Solomon ibn Gabirol, Maimonides, Jonah Gerondi, and others.

Sephardic intellectuals, former conversos who, as Catholics, had acquired their education in Iberian and French universities, aroused great interest among theologians, Hebraists, and various other types of Christian scholars. Their excellent command of Latin (and sometimes French as well) permitted them to hold a lively and animated dialogue with the representatives of the *République des Lettres.* Many Protestant theologians sought to renew the Jewish-Christian argument in western Europe by means of the Sephardim. Despite the Mahamad's opposition to theological disputes, for fear of arousing anger among orthodox Protestant circles, conversations and arguments did take place between Jewish scholars and spokesmen for the different Christian denominations.

Only a few of these disputations have been published. Official censorship in the host countries and the internal censorship imposed by the Sephardic communities themselves prevented them from being printed. However, many polemical works by Eliahu Montalto, Saul Levi Mortera, Moses Raphael d'Aguilar, Isaac Orobio de Castro, and others were circulated around the western Sephardic Diaspora in dozens of manuscript copies, serving not only as a defense against the anti-Jewish arguments advanced by Christian spokesmen but also as a primary means to strengthen the self-definition and identity of the conversos who returned to Judaism.

Indeed, the encounter between Sephardic and Christian intellectuals in Amsterdam was not limited to theological discussion. On various levels, Jews and Christians cooperated against the "common enemies" who threatened the religious stability of both camps: Deists, skeptics, libertines, and Spinozists. Not only were some of the philosophical and theological works written by Sephardim intended for both Jewish and Christian readers, but they were also sometimes written explicitly for a non-Jewish audience, which the authors viewed as their principal audience on certain topics. The physician Isaac Cardoso, who returned to Judaism in Venice in the mid-seventeenth century, wrote a voluminous scientific and philosophical encyclopedia in Latin, *Philosophia Libera* (Venice, 1673), which was dedicated to the Senate of the Venetian Republic and mainly intended for a Christian public. Menasseh ben Israel wrote a few treatises in Latin on theological questions, which were primarily intended for Calvinist scholars. A few of his books appeared simultaneously in Latin and Spanish for gentile and Jewish audiences, respectively. In similar spirit, Isaac

Orobio de Castro joined a circle of philosophers who set out to combat the philosophy of Spinoza, composing a Latin work, *Certamen Philosophicum,* that was widely circulated among Dutch philosophers.

The intellectual cooperation between Sephardic Jews and their Christian hosts in western Europe was expressed in various cultural fields. Menasseh ben Israel did not hesitate to cooperate with the Millenarians, and some of his works promoting the return of the Jews to England were written on their initiative and with their assistance. Adam Boreel, an indefatigable Hebraist, not only dwelt for seven years in Middelburg with the Sephardic rabbi Jacob Juda León Templo, laboring with him to publish a Latin and Spanish translation of the Mishnah, but he also financed the vocalized Hebrew edition of the Mishnah, edited by Menasseh ben Israel and published in Amsterdam in 1646. Boreel also paid for the model of King Solomon's Temple built by Templo in Amsterdam. Visitors flocked to see it, and Templo's books on the Tabernacle and Solomon's Temple were translated into many European languages and reached a huge audience.

Although most of the literary works written and printed in Amsterdam and the other Sephardic communities can be classified as religious, with didactic and ethical or else polemical and apologetic purposes, an impressive variety of secular works were also produced, especially in Spanish and Portuguese. Iberian literature continued to be the model: even those writers who were born as Jews in the new Sephardic communities can be categorized mainly as imitators of *culteranismo* and *conceptismo,* which were predominant in Spain. This remained the case at least until the beginning of the eighteenth century, when French literature began increasingly to influence their taste. Some of the works written by poets and authors such as Manuel de Pina, Daniel Levi de Barrios, and Abraham Gómez Silveyra were intended not only for a Jewish audience but also for a larger, Christian Hispanic readership in the southern Netherlands and even in Spain itself. Some of these works were printed in Brussels in order to circumvent community censorship and to obscure the Jewish identity of the authors from Christian readers.

Some of the authors of the western Sephardic Diaspora were multilingual: they wrote in Hebrew for Jewish rabbinic scholars and for a Jewish audience beyond the borders of the Nación, and they used Portuguese for works addressed to their own communities. Spanish was used similarly, though works in that language sometimes appealed to the whole Sephardic audience and also to Christian Hispanic readers in the Spanish territories. For example, Joseph Penso de la Vega wrote his *Confusión de Confusiones* (Amsterdam, 1688) in Spanish because it was intended as a critique of the behavior of members of his community in stock trading, though in the book they are alluded to only indirectly. The Spanish newspaper that was printed in the Jewish printing house of Castro Tartas, *Gazeta de Amsterdam,* beginning in 1675, was intended to provide Sephardic merchants with economic and political information, though nothing Jewish was mentioned in its pages. Finally, western Sephardic Jews also wrote in Latin, the language of discourse among the learned in Europe. Menasseh ben Israel wrote in all four of these languages, and he even published a book in English, which was apparently translated for him. In any event, he claimed to have mastered nine languages.

Baron Manuel de Belmonte was one of the principal patrons of Daniel Levi de Barrios, and he also sponsored two literary academies established by intellectuals and poets of the Sephardic community in Amsterdam: *Temor Divino* in 1676 and *Los Floridos* in 1685. These flourished in the style of the academies in Spain and Portugal, with a certain Italian flavor. The participants belonged to the economic and cultural elite of the community, and in their discussions they emphasized rhetoric rather than the ideas conveyed. Because of their decidedly secular character, these academies were distinct from the various religious study groups, which were sometimes also founded on the initiative of the community magnates. These were called *jesibot,* and they were essentially charity confraternities that also held regular sessions to study Torah and rabbinical literature.

We have indications of organized theatrical activity within the Sephardic community of Amsterdam dating from at least the end of the seventeenth century, when a warehouse was rented for the production of plays in Spanish. The theater, which received enormous impetus in the Hispanic society of the Golden Age, could not be absent among the western Sephardim, who were so deeply immersed in Iberian culture. In this field, too, members of the social elite played a dominant role. It was their custom to have theatrical troupes and opera singers hold performances in their homes and to invite a large audience from the community.

Some of the leading Sephardic authors of this period, most prominently Daniel Levi de Barrios, wrote plays in Spanish. However, we have no proof that they were ever staged. In this area, as well, it is notable that the vast majority of the original plays do not deal with Jewish subjects at all and were not specifically intended for a Jewish audience.

In 1708, a group of devotees of Spanish comedy asked permission from the Amsterdam municipality to present plays in Spanish in Schouwburg, the city theater, on Wednesdays, when the theater was dark. Their request was rejected for the interesting reason that Jewish spectators would stop attending the theater on other days.

The Sephardic Jews also met the local residents at places of less elevated entertainment, including coffeehouses, taverns, gaming houses (*casas de juego*), and even brothels. However, even in these popular areas, separate entertainment centers were also established to supply the social needs of the members of the Nación on their own. Here, too, strict class distinctions were maintained.

More impressive even than the variety and multilingual character of the works of the intellectuals was the rich culture of reading among them. For example, their philosophical and theological writings show impressive mastery of Christian theology, neo-scholastic philosophy, classical literature, medicine, geography, contemporary Iberian literature, and political thought. Isaac Aboab da Fonseca left behind an impressive library with 373 Hebrew books and another 179 books in other languages, including Latin and Greek. These included works in philology, classical literature, history, and Christian theology. Even more impressive was the library of Rabbi David Nunes Torres, who was the rabbi of the Sephardic congregation of the Hague at the beginning of the eighteenth century and whose library included 1,500 non-Hebrew books. Among these volumes was the banned work of Uriel da Costa, *Exame das Tradiçoes Phariseas,* published in Amsterdam in 1624, denying belief in the immortality of the soul. This book found safe refuge, hidden from the severe eye of the Mahamad on the Sephardic rabbi's bookshelves. However, no less impressive was the library of Rabbi Samuel Abbas, a native of Hamburg, who died in Amsterdam in 1693. It included nearly 1,100 books, of which 236 were Hebrew works and the rest were divided as follows: 421 in Latin, 168 in Spanish and Portuguese, 248 in French, and 113 in Italian. A look at this Sephardic rabbi's library brings out the diversity of his intellectual world. In addition to Jewish law and rabbinic literature, he was interested in Kabbalah and philosophy, biblical exegesis, Jewish chronology and historiography, Hebrew grammar, and ethical literature. The vernacular books touch upon almost every area of science and knowledge of the age: from the writings of Aristotle to those of Calvin and the works of Hippocrates, Avicenna, and Fernelius; lexicons and dictionaries in many languages; Boccaccio's *Decameron* in French translation and the works of Petrarch in Spanish translation; the writings of Hebraists such as Buxtorf and of anti-Jewish polemicists such as Hoornbeek; works of the classical and modern historians; an extremely rich selection of Iberian literature of the Renaissance and Baroque periods; and, of course, many contemporary Sephardic Jewish works.

It is interesting that this library, like those of Aboab da Fonseca and Nunes Torres, was sold at public auction after its owner's death. It appears that no one in the Sephardic communities followed in the footsteps of these cultivated rabbis, multilingual scholars who were not reluctant to take up "gentile wisdom" and to bring "the beauties of Japhet into the tents of Shem." Over time this synthesis fell apart, and the rabbinical culture of the western Sephardic Diaspora detached itself from European culture. The Jewish education of those among the elite who remained involved in community life and did not assimilate into the majority society became pale and superficial—as is demonstrated, for example, by the library of David Nassy of Surinam in the late eighteenth century. Between this library and that of Samuel Abbas extends not only an ocean but also a hundred years of rapid acculturation. Conversely, among the rabbinical establishment and those associated with it, a process of self-segregation and isolation behind the walls of orthodoxy took place. Whereas the library of Abbas contained 236 Hebrew volumes, somewhat more than 20 percent of its contents, and most of these were rabbinical works, it would be hard to find any Hebrew books among the 433 volumes in Nassy's library, except for a few Bibles and prayer books. Nassy did remain loyal to the variety, the eclecticism, the multilingualism, and the wide-ranging intellectual curiosity that is reflected in the libraries of the Sephardic rabbis and Jewish scholars of the seventeenth century. However, with regard to books of Jewish content, he was forced to make do with philosophical and ethical works that had been translated into Iberian languages and with apologetic treatises in Spanish and Portuguese that had been written during the prior century in the centers of the Nación in western Europe. His distance from rabbinical culture denied him any access to the sources of Hebrew religious literature. Moreover, the writings of Sephardic rabbis in the second half of the eighteenth century show an astonishing diminution of intellectual breadth.

The heyday of the Sephardic Diaspora had passed both in international trade and in the creation of original culture. The economic stagnation that prevailed among the Sephardic international traders during the eighteenth century very much detracted from the importance of the western Sephardic Diaspora. Colonial trade in general and the Sephardic mastery of the trade routes between the Caribbean and northwestern Europe lost the importance they had previously enjoyed in the European economy. Similarly, just as the processes of modernization were seen early in that Jewry, so, too, did pronounced tendencies toward assimilation develop among them. The relatively comfortable conditions that prevailed in several of the countries where they were active and their integration into the surrounding society ultimately impelled many of them to leave the framework of Judaism. The sharp decline in the number of conversos who left Iberia after the 1730s also dealt a significant blow to the demographic development of the communities of the Nación. Of the splendor that had characterized its great centers, only the myth remained, and bom judesmo became a faint memory. Although it was still capable of arousing the sympathy and enthusiasm of the Jewish Enlightenment movement in central Europe, it waned in the Sephardic Diaspora itself.

NOTES

1. Ph. Skippon, "An Account of a Journey Made Thro' Part of the Low Countries, Germany, Italy, and France (1663)," in *A Collection of Voyages and Travels,* vol. 6 (London, 1732), 406.

2. Ibid., 405.

3. Daniel Levi de Barrios, *Imperio de Dios, en la Harmonia del Mundo* (Amsterdam, n.d.), 40.

4. Published by L. Wolf, "The Jewry of the Restoration 1660–1664," *Transactions of the Jewish Historical Society of England* 5 (1902–5); 30–31.

5. *Uriel da Costa's Own Account of His Life (Exemplar humanae vitae),* trans. John Whiston (London, 1740). See also Uriel Acosta, *A Specimen of Human Life* (New York, 1967), 12–14.

6. Skippon, "An Account of a Journey," 406.

7. [I. de Pinto], *Apologie pour la nation juive ou Réflexions critiques sur le premier chapitre du VII Tome des Oeuvres de Monsieur de Voltaire au sujet des Juifs* (Amsterdam, 1762), 16.

8. M. Misson, *A New Voyage to Italy, with Curious Observations on Several Other Countries, as, Germany, Switzerland, Savoy, Geneva, Flanders and Holland . . . Done out of French.* 2d ed., vol. 1 (London, 1699), 25.

9. W. Mountague, *The Delights of Holland, or a Three Months Travel About That and the Other Provinces with Observations and Reflections on their Trade, Wealth, Strength, Beauty, Policy, etc.* (London, 1696), 146.

10. G. Letti, *Il ceremoniale historico e politico, opera utilissima a tutti gli Ambasciatori, e Ministri publici,* vol. 5 (Amsterdam, 1685), 728 (my translation).

11. *Livro de Ascamot* A (Book of Ordinances and Statutes) of the Talmud Torah community of Amsterdam, in the Municipal Archives of Amsterdam, PA 334, No. 19, fol. 143 (my translation, here and for all archival works below).

12. Ibid., fol. 391.

13. *Livro de Ascamot* B, ibid., No. 20, fol. 248.

14. *Libro do Mahamad* of the Sephardic Community of London, in the Community Archives, No. 103, Vol. I, fol. 34r.

15. *El Libro de los Acuerdos, Being the Records and Accounts of the Spanish and Portuguese Synagogue of London, from 1663 to 1681,* trans. L. D. Barnett (Oxford, 1931), 15.

16. *Libro de Acuerdos,* in the Community Archive of London, Ms. No. 129, Vol. II, fol. 36.

17. Shabbetai Bass, *Siftei Yeshenim* (Amsterdam, 5440 [1680]), fol. 8v.-r.

18. Quoted by B. N. Teensma, "The Suffocation of Spanish and Portuguese Among Sephardi Jews," *Dutch Jewish History,* vol. 3 (Jerusalem and Assen-Maastricht, 1993), 138–39.

SELECTED BIBLIOGRAPHY

Berger, Shlomo. *Classical Oratory and the Sephardim of Amsterdam: Rabbi Aguilar's 'Tratado de la Retórica.'* Hilversum, 1996.

Bodian, Miriam. *Hebrews of the Portuguese Nation: Conversos and Community in Early Modern Amsterdam.* Bloomington, 1997.

Boer, Harm den. *La literatura sefardí de Amsterdam.* Alcalá de Henares, 1996.

Cohen, Robert. *Jews in Another Environment: Surinam in the Second Half of the Eighteenth Century.* Leiden, 1991.

Hyamson, Albert M. *The Sephardim of England: A History of the Spanish and Portuguese Jewish Community, 1492-1951.* London, 1951; repr., 1991.

Israel, Jonathan I. "An Amsterdam Jewish Merchant of the Golden Age: Jeronimo Nunes da Costa (1620–1697), Agent of Portugal in the Dutch Republic," *Studia Rosenthaliana* 18: 1 (1984): 21–40.

———. *European Jewry in the Age of Mercantilism, 1550-1750.* Oxford, 1985.

———. "Gregorio Leti (1631–1701) and the Dutch Sephardi Elite at the Close of the Seventeenth Century." In A. Rapoport-Albert and S. J. Zipperstein, eds., *Jewish History: Essays in Honour of Chimen Abramsky.* London, 1988.

Kaplan, Yosef. *From Christianity to Judaism. The Story of Isaac Orobio de Castro.* Translated from the Hebrew by Raphael Loewe. Oxford, 1989.

———. *An Alternative Path to Modernity: The Sephardi Diaspora in Western Europe.* Leiden, 2000.

———, Henry Méchoulan, and Richard H. Popkin, eds. *Menasseh ben Israel and His World.* Leiden, 1989.

Nahon, Gerard. *Métropoles et périphéries sefarades.* Paris, 1993.

Popkin, Richard H. "Some Aspects of Jewish-Christian Theological Interchanges in Holland and England, 1640–1700." In J. van den Berg and E. G. E. van der Wall, eds., *Jewish-Christian Relations in the Seventeenth Century: Studies and Documents.* Leiden, 1988.

Révah, Israel S. "Les Marranes." *Revue des études juives* 118 (1959): 29–77.

Salomon, Herman P. "The 'De Pinto Manuscript': A 17th Century Marrano Family History." *Studia Rosenthaliana.* 9:1 (1975): 1–62.

———. *Portrait of a New Christian: Fernão Alvares Melo (1569–1632).* Paris, 1982.

Studemund-Halevy, Michael, ed. *Die Sefarden in Hamburg. Zur Geschichte einer Minderheit.* 2 vols. Hamburg, 1994–97.

Swetchinski, Daniel M. "The Portuguese Jews of Seventeenth-Century Amsterdam: Cultural Continuity and Adaptation." In F. Malino and Ph. Cohen Albert, eds., *Essays in Modern Jewish History: A Tribute to Ben Halpern.* New York, 1982.

בֶּ צִימֵה לֵיהֶם פְּ קַר קוֹדְ וְהוֹב פִּ ילֵס לֶהָיֹב

———. *Reluctant Cosmopolitans: The Portuguese Jews of Seventeenth-Century Amsterdam*. London-Portland, 2000.

Swetchinski, Daniel M., and L. Schönduve. *The Family Lopes Suasso, Bankers to William III*. Zwolle, 1988.

Teensma, Benjamin N. "The Suffocation of Spanish and Portuguese among Sephardi Jews." In J. Michman, ed., *Dutch-Jewish History*, vol. 3. Jerusalem, 1993.

Yerushalmi, Yosef H. *From Spanish Court to Italian Ghetto. Isaac Cardoso: A Study in Seventeenth-Century Marranism and Jewish Apologetics*. New York and London, 1971.

ספר רזיאל

ברוק ומנוסה לשמירה ליולדה ולולדה מן הכישוף ומן עין הרע ובשעת הלידה שלא ישלוט בה ובולדה שום
שד ומזע רע · שיר המעלו' וכו' · שמות היוצאי' מש'יר המעלה המה אשא עיני אל ר'ת ע'ב זהו
שם הוי'ה כמלוי יורן וכן ס'ת עני אל ההרים מאין ק'ל זהו ה' רוכב על ע'ב ק'ל וגם ס'ח ההרי' מאין יבא אדנ'י הוי'ה
משולבות עזרי עזרי מעם ה' עושה ה'ת אד'ני שמים וארץ ס'אקנ'ל דתה לא'ינם ר'ת הוי'ה כמלוי אדם עליון
יד ימינך יומם ג'יורין משם של ע'ב שהוא כלה רחמי' לעורר רחמי'אדם עליון הוי'ה במלוי אלפין וחתו השם' לא יכבה
ר'ת הוי'ה כמלוי אלפין ונם כל אות אחר חשם הוי'ח נוטריקון עשצי'ו · זה השם מוב מאוד לשמירה גם בכל ליל'ה
קודם שינה צריך לומר כל אדם והישר המעלות ולכוון זה השם · ואח'כ ויעבר את מעבר יב'ק · ויעבר ע'ב ר'י'ו זהו
ע'ב שמות שהם רי'ו אותיות יב'ק אדנ'י הוי'ה אחיה משולכות · ואח'כ שם של ע'ב כאשר תמצא ברף כ'ד עמוד ב'
ואח'כ פסוק יברכך וגו' עם השמות כאשר תמצא ברף מ'ב עמוד ב' · ואח'כ עמור העיגול זה ציורו ביסין העיגול שמע
משולב עם ויהי נועם ברף הנ'ל והצד השני יענך ה' ביום צרה וגו' · ויוצא מזה המזמור ד' פעמי'יב'ק כי עזרה ישגבך
קרשו בגבורות ישע ונפלו ואנחנו קמנו יענגו ביום קראינו וב'ק הוא'ו ג' שמות ארני הוי'ה אה'יה משולבות וד' כתות
לשמרה שלא יזיק שום כשוף הנה צרה ח'נה ח' רוכב · והשמו' היוצאים מזה הפסוק מוב מאוד
ע'י כלי ע'ב שם של ע'ב הוא משובר כל הקליפות כירוע וא'כ לישועתך כל ג' אותיות הוא שם בפני עצמו וברף שם כבוד
וגו' א'כב ג' אותיות שם בפני עצמו ואח'כ כן פרת יוסף בן פרת עלי עין בנות צעדה עלי שור בשם יל'ר ר'ה ס'ן
וש'ר נ'ח עש'ל נמ'ם רה'ע אלו שמות טוב מאד לעין הרע ויוצאן מן הפסוק ב? פרת וראי'ה לרבר עש'ל בנים עין רע
וגם נמ'ם רה'ע בני'מטרי עין הרע' · ואח'כ שבעים שמות מלאכים המה מוב מאור לכל השמירות כירוע ואחר כן אלו
השמות וציוריהם כאשר ראה וחקק אדם הראשון את צורוהן ומוב מאוד לשמירת היולדת עם הולד :

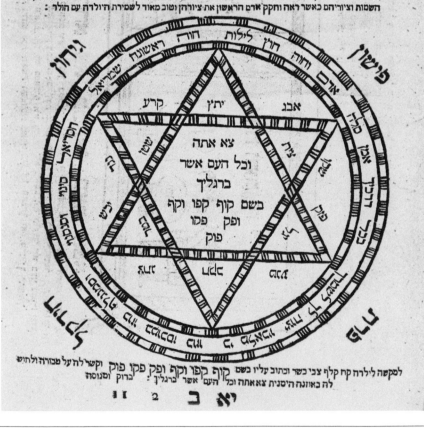

למקשה לילדה קח קלף צבי כשר וכתוב עליו בשם קוף קפו וקף ופק פקן פוק וקשר לה על טבורה ולחוש
לה באוזנה היסנית צא אתה וכל העם' אשר ברגלין · ברוק ומנוסה :

יא ב 2

SEVEN

CHILDBIRTH AND MAGIC:

Jewish Folklore and Material Culture

SHALOM SABAR

Let us imagine the birth of a Jewish baby in a remote shtetl in Poland or Russia before the onslaught of modernity: a woman is in labor in her bedroom, surrounded by a midwife and a few other women. No man is allowed in the room, not even the husband or a doctor. Fearful of the grave dangers of childbirth, shared by all people in the pre-modern world, the room is provided with protective amulets and other magical objects. The midwife or perhaps a member of the family slips a mysterious book under the pillow of the woman in labor. This book contains magical formulas against the murderous spirits and evil demons, such as Lilith, who threaten the newborn and his mother.

Let us now shift our gaze to a similarly traditional Jewish household in an Islamic town—be it Teheran, Baghdad, or Zakho in Iraqi Kurdistan. The scene is the night before circumcision—believed to be the most dangerous night for the newborn and his mother, because this is the last opportunity for the demons to attack the male child before the protective ceremony of circumcision would take place. As a measure of protection, the chair of Elijah—a chair with magical functions among the Jews of Islam—stands in the center of the room. The chair is ornamented with Torah finials, ḥamsas, healing plants, and holy books—including at times the book of magic formulas. Inscribed metal and paper amulets in the room are based on the formulas in this book, *Sefer Raziel ha-Mal'akh* (Book of Raziel the Angel).

It is thus clear that, side by side with the normative and written system of the halakhah, Judaism developed what we may call "folk religion." Although comprehensive codes such as Joseph Karo's *Shulḥan Arukh* (The Prepared Table; Venice, 1565) set out to cover every aspect of the life of the Jew, there was sufficient room for unofficial, often unwritten, beliefs and practices. The reality of daily life, the deep religious beliefs of the common people, and close contacts with the host societies and their varied cultures gave rise to popular beliefs, patterns of behavior, customs and practices, and the production of religious artifacts that could not be always accounted for in the "official" halakhic sources.

The popular beliefs and practices were not limited to a particular Jewish community or section thereof. In fact, they played a major role in the life of Jewish communities under Christianity in Europe and under Islam in Arab lands and the Ottoman Empire. Life as a religious minority in these countries shaped, to a large degree, the two main components of the Jewish folk tradition: the cultural and spiritual heritage of the Jewish people, and the influence of the host culture. In contrast to the national heritage of other people, we may thus trace similar Jewish traditions in Germany and Yemen, but they often bear variations reflecting the local culture.

In the following pages, I will discuss this phenomenon in the context of an important event in the life cycle—childbirth. This crucial period of transition was accompanied, like other rites of passage in human life, with sociopsychological fears and anxieties. These gave rise to the creation and adaptation of numerous customs and practices, the purpose of which were primarily to fight the evil and hostile forces believed to cause the "crises." Every possible method, expressed in different media, was used for this purpose. In so doing, the Jews were no different from other traditional societies. Of special interest, however, is the usage and transformation of traditional Jewish origins that concern such practices and objects. The Jewish elements demonstrate that, though the rabbinical authorities did not always sanctify this folk culture, it did rely heavily on accepted, normative Jewish sources, such as the Bible and the Talmud. It is this mixture of "high" and folk cultures, enhanced by the trends and practices of the surrounding society, that is reflected in the traditions and objects examined in this chapter. The culture they represent proves that, in many cases, the folkloristic beliefs were more universal and stronger than the practices of the "official" religion—creating fascinating bonds across wide geographical distances.

THE WITCH WHO STRANGLES CHILDREN

Prior to the major changes in medicine and hygiene in nineteenth-century Europe, the danger of childbirth was great. The possibility that either the mother or her newborn would not survive the traumatic event was a fact of daily life. Moreover, even the period following the delivery was considered critical, both for the mother, who was still very weak, and for the infant. Statistics from eighteenth-century France show that about 250 babies out of 1,000 did not survive their first year, and only about 575 out of 1,000 reached the age of five; the numbers of deaths was even larger among the lower classes, who were generally not included in these records. In the Middle East, where modern medicine arrived late, this situation continued to dominate until recent times. An average family, especially a poor one, could expect that as many as half of its children would not survive their early years.[1]

Trying to fight these phenomena, folk beliefs and traditions gave rise to many customs and practices, amulets and talismans, incantations and conjurations—all of which aimed to protect the mother, and even more so the baby. Such protective measures are universally known from every traditional society, and the monotheistic religions are not exceptional. Jews in Christian Europe and the Islamic East were likewise involved to various degrees with such practices.[2] While relying heavily on the accepted practices among the host society, the Jewish methods of protection, such as the use of amulets, were often deeply rooted in tradition. It is within this realm that the folk religion of the Jews developed and played a major role in the daily life of the people.

A case in point is the early medieval anthology of Hebrew legends known as the *Alfa Beta of Ben Sira,* which was apparently composed in Babylonia in the late ninth to early tenth centuries.[3] One of the legends presents as the main enemy of babies Adam's first wife, Lilith, whose jealousy of Eve drives her to kill the newborn and endanger its mother.[4] Although Lilith is mentioned in the Bible only once, in another context (Isaiah 34:14), Jewish legendary sources connect this demonic figure—who is known as Lilitu in ancient Babylonian demonology—with the creation stories in Genesis.[5] As Bible and folklore scholars have noted, the first and second chapters of Genesis present two different, even contradictory, accounts of the creation of the world. The first one (Genesis 1 and 2:1–3) is a rather harmonious picture: God creates the world in seven days according to a well-thought-out plan, in which man and woman are the summit of the process—having been created after the plants and trees, birds and animals. In the second version (Genesis 2:4–22), the order of Creation markedly changes: man is created before the trees and animals, and the first woman, Eve, is created last, after Adam could not find a suitable mate. Folklorists have also pointed out that, whereas the Creator in the first story is rather remote and abstract, in the second story He is more active and "tangible"—walking in the Garden, talking, and consulting with the angels.[6]

The rabbis of old did, in fact, notice the differences between the two stories. In attempting to solve the problem of the simultaneous creation of man and woman in the first version ("male and female He created them"—Genesis 1:27), they brought up the legend of "First Eve," who parted from Adam—explaining that it is she who is created with Adam in the first chapter of Genesis, whereas Eve is created in the second. According to later midrashic sources, "First Eve" is identified as the ancient demon Lilith, and since she was created as equal to

Adam, she required equal rights, including, for example, to be positioned over him during intercourse.[7]

The author of the *Alfa Beta of Ben Sira* used some of the old midrashic sources to amplify the story and add to it the magic-amuletic elements. According to these accounts, Adam could not accept the demands of Lilith, and so she pronounced the Ineffable name and left him. Realizing he cannot live without a woman, Adam asks God to bring Lilith back. Three mysterious angels, Sanoi (or Sanvai), Sansanoi (or Sansanvai), and Semangalof, are sent to fetch her. They find her near the Red Sea, but Lilith does not agree to their plea. She tells them she is not coming back; the sole purpose of her creation is to harm newborn babies—males until the eighth day after birth, and females until the twelfth day. When their attempts to threaten Lilith fail, the angels succeed in convincing her that, wherever she sees their image illustrated or their names written on an amulet, she and the other demons who accompany her will not enter a house to harm a baby or its mother.

This legend was apparently created to justify the use of amulets,[8] but it also contributed to the dissemination of the story of Lilith and the need for such amulets. An important tool in this process was yet another book, *Sefer Raziel ha-Mal'akh*, which contains, inter alia, explanations on how to prepare amulets, including one for childbirth. *Sefer Raziel* contains portions of several Hebrew works dealing with various aspects of magic, cosmology, and mystics.[9] According to the introduction, the angel Raziel revealed the secrets contained in the book to Adam to assist him in his despair following the expulsion from paradise. The name of the angel is derived from the Hebrew words *RAZ* and *EL*, literally meaning "secret" and "God," respectively—because Raziel is the angel connected with the secrets and mysteries of God. As he sits behind the divine curtain, Raziel also hears everything that happens in this world.

The material collected in *Sefer Raziel* was written over a long period, with some sections dating back to talmudic times. However, because of its special nature, the book was not printed until 1701 (in Amsterdam), and, even then, the publisher did not intend the book to be read by everyone. Rather, simply possessing it would protect the owner and his home from misfortunes and dangers (such as fire and robbery). It would drive away evil spirits and even work as a charm to raise "wise and intelligent sons." Polish and Russian Jews put the book under the pillow of a woman in childbed, and in Baghdad, as noted above, it was placed on the chair of Elijah. Although *Sefer Raziel* is not unique in these aspects and messages, it gained unusual popularity, and since its first appearance it was issued in numerous editions, both in Ashkenazic and Sephardic communities. In fact, the book continues to be popular to this day in Israel, and in recent years it has been published many times, mostly in miniature format (or on microfiche the size of a credit card) to be kept in one's pocket or car as a means of personal protection.[10]

Sefer Raziel provides formulas for amulets both for a woman who has a difficult delivery and for the newborn. The amulet in Figure 1 (p. 670), according to the text, should be prepared from the skin of a deer, upon which are inscribed incantations and diagrams.[11] The inscriptions on this amulet are, as on many others, composed of kabbalistic formulas, *shemoth* (or "names" of God), as well as biblical verses that were considered appropriate at the time, though their original meaning has been altered. Here the verse is from the story of Moses and Pharaoh in Egypt: "Get thee out [of Egypt], and all the people that follow thee" (Exodus 11:8). In the original Hebrew, the last section of the verse literally reads "and the people at your feet," which is understood as an incantation for safe delivery (i.e., get out from between the woman's legs). These sympathetic words should be whispered in the woman's right ear while the amulet is placed on her navel.

Reciting these words with no reference to God is considered useless. Two kabbalistic names of God are inscribed on this amulet. The first is "In the name of *Kuph*," which is written in six anagrammatic forms. This strange name is derived from a peculiar method of giving Hebrew letters "abbreviated" numerical value, which add up to 15—the equivalent of the powerful contracted name of God, YAH. The second "name" is much more common in Jewish magic: it is the 42-letter name, beginning with *ABAG YATATZ*, which is derived from the abbreviations of the prayer hymn *Anna be-Kho'ah*. This name has supposedly been known since Mishnaic times, and the prayer *Anna be-Kho'ah* is attributed to the first-century *tanna* (sage of mishnaic times), Rabbi Neḥunyah ben ha-Kana.[12] The name is considered especially powerful in the context of childbirth because it contains the abbreviated expression *kera Satan* (lit. "rend Satan"), which is understood as a call to God to protect the baby or his mother from the evil powers and demons seeking to harm them.

The second childbirth amulet in *Sefer Raziel* is specifically aimed against Lilith and thus gained more widespread popularity (Figure 2).[13] This amulet is clearly derived from the legend in *Alfa Beta of Ben Sira,* which is actually narrated in the text below the illustration. The legend calls for a visual and/or written depiction of the names of Sanoi, Sansanoi and Semangalof, so two alternative forms are provided in the pair of rectangles that are joined together. The appearance of the angels is indeed bizarre: in the right rectangle they are made of geometric forms, whereas at left they are more reminiscent of birds, however strange. As an extra measure, an abbreviated formula of the protective Priestly Benediction (Numbers 6:24–25), which invokes God to bless and guard His followers, is written next to the angels at right.[14]

Fig. 2. Amulet for childbirth; *Sefer Raziel ha-mal'akh*, Amsterdam, 1701.
(Library of the Jewish Theological Seminary of America, New York)

DURING DELIVERY IN EIGHTEENTH-CENTURY GERMANY

A rare glimpse of childbirth practices in eighteenth-century Germany appears in an etching included in the book *Jüdisches Ceremoniel* (first illustrated edition: Nuremberg, 1724) by the convert Paul Christian Kirchner, who led people to believe he was a rabbi before he was baptized (Figure 3).[15] The detail at upper right shows a common practice at the time: childbirth took place at home, in the presence of women only. (Hospital childbirth with male doctors in attendance did not become customary until much later.)[16] The woman in labor is shown seated next to her bed on a special chair used for this purpose, as four midwives surround her.

Although the procedure of childbirth in Kirchner's book is not different from contemporary non-Jewish ceremonies, the etching includes two significant details. On the walls are written (apparently with charcoal), in Hebrew letters, *"Adam Ḥava. Ḥutz Lilit. Senoi Sansenoi Sanmangelof [sic]"*[17] (Adam, Eve, Out Lilith / Sanoi Sansanoi Semangalof)—the same words as those seen in Figure 2 in the *Sefer Raziel* amulet. The meaning is clear: the three angels are invoked to protect the woman against Lilith, who should not come into the room, whereas

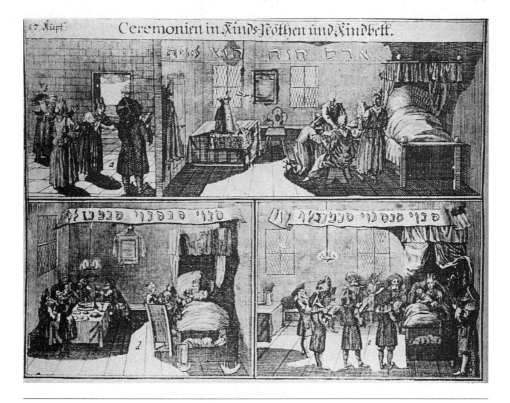

Fig. 3. "Ceremonies for women in labor and confinement" by P. C. Kirchner, *Jüdisches Ceremoniel*, Nuremberg, 1724. (Library of the Jewish Theological Seminary of America, New York)

Adam and Eve, the alternative couple, whose seed continued the human race, are "invited" to enter.

The other interesting element is the object standing on a cloth-covered table (Figure 4). Marked with the letter C, this object is, according to Kirchner, a Torah scroll brought from the synagogue.[18] Indeed, an eighteenth-century German Torah scroll was customarily "dressed" with just such a wide piece of textile, called a *me'il* ("mantle"), which covered the parchment scroll from top to bottom, and the round object placed at top is obviously a typical Ashkenazic Torah crown. But why was a Torah scroll brought from its natural environment, the Holy Ark in the synagogue, to this room? Like the inscriptions on the wall, it is there to protect the occupants. Because this is the holiest object in the Jewish space, it was believed that its sanctity would exert sympathetic powers, ease the delivery, and shield the mother and child.[19]

The presence of a Torah scroll in the delivery room should not be considered lightly. Despite its supposed sympathetic influence, the rabbinical authorities

Fig. 4. Detail of Fig. 3 showing the delivery at home.
(Library of the Jewish Theological Seminary of America, New York)

could not ignore the fact that the Holy Book was placed in the vicinity of blood and other body fluids involved in childbirth. Moreover, though according to halakhah "the words of the Torah are not susceptible to ritual uncleanness [*tuma'h*]" (BT, Berakhot 22a),[20]—or, in another translation, "the words of the Torah do not contract uncleanness" (or "contamination")—the rabbis feared that the Torah would itself be defiled in the delivery room. After all, in the eyes of the biblical lawgiver, a mother is unclean and ritually impure for certain periods, depending on whether the newborn is male or female (see Leviticus 12). Judaism shares this concept with some other traditional societies, such as those in Sri Lanka or Sierra Leone, where childbirth takes place in an isolated booth.[21] Accordingly, it is not surprising that the placing of a Torah scroll in the delivery room caused problems related to "proper usage," if not official law, for both the Ashkenazic and Sephardic authorities whose communities followed this custom.[22]

Although it was impossible to do away with this extremely popular practice, alternatives were offered in several places. For example, when a woman of the Alexandrian community of Egypt had a difficult labor, the men went to the synagogue, recited Psalms in front of the opened Ark, and blew the Shofar. In Pinsk (in Russia), a long string was tied to the doors of the Ark and rolled down through the streets of the shtetl to the house where a woman was in labor. The string's other end was put in her hand to pull, in the belief that this would ease the birth. The same custom was followed by the Sephardim in Safed—with the significant difference that at the crucial moment of birth, the string was cut, "because she is impure and is forbidden to be tied to the Torah scroll."[23]

Similar practices at the time of delivery, with curious variations, were also known among the Jews of Islamic lands. The Torah case was used to ease a woman's labor pains, as were other ceremonial objects related to the holy scroll. Obvious examples are the Torah finials (*rimmonim*). A typical Kurdish rimmon is composed of two hinged, hemispheric silver parts that can be opened in the center. During a difficult labor, the husband would go to the *ḥakham* (the name used for a rabbi in Islamic lands; plur. *ḥakhamim*), who filled the rimmon with flowing water while reciting Psalms. The husband then hurried home and, without saying a word, gave the rimmon to his wife so she could drink the blessed water.[24]

EUROPEAN CHILDBIRTH AMULETS

Despite widely held beliefs to the contrary, European Ashkenazic Jews used amulets for various occasions, almost like their brethren in Islamic lands. Here, again, German or Polish Jews were no different from the local Christian population, except that their amulets had a Jewish context and Hebrew writing. It should be noted, however, that the presence of Hebrew writing does not by itself necessarily indicate that an amulet is Jewish. Many Christian amulets were also written in Hebrew letters, occasionally even using standard kabbalistic formulas, which were considered magical and protective. Thus, the Jewish context of a Hebrew amulet always has to be examined carefully.

European Jewish amulets were generally written or printed on one side of a single piece of paper. Naturally, the handwritten paper amulets represent a more personal, even unique, object, whereas the printed examples appeared in many copies and were used in many homes. In both types, the text is often accompanied by a popular illustration, appropriate for the context. Much can be learned from these accompanying images about the views and ideology of a particular community. This is especially important in view of the fact that standard formulas of the text were widely used in many countries.

SEVENTEENTH-CENTURY HOLLAND

Figure 5 comes from early-eighteenth-century Holland.[25] The standard Hebrew text here seems secondary to the many images that surround it. Moreover, the connection of these images to the function and usage of the amulet is not always

Fig. 5. Childbirth amulet made by Abraham bar Jacob, Amsterdam.
Copper engraving printed on paper. (Library of the Jewish Theological
Seminary of America, New York)

clear (e.g., the top left scene depicts Isaac blessing Jacob). A partial explanation
for this somewhat peculiar phenomenon is found in the identity of the folk
artist who produced it and, unusually enough, inscribed his name at bottom
center. This is Abraham bar Jacob, who was, as implied by his name, a proselyte
who was attracted to the cultural and fairly well-to-do Jewish community
of late-seventeenth-century Amsterdam. However, his Christian background is
reflected in the works he produced for the local community (such as his well-
known haggadah of 1695—the first illustrated edition with copper engravings).[26]
Here, the central image shows Adam, Eve, and the serpent in Paradise, surrounded by animals. The episode is reminiscent of typical Christian depictions
of the "Original Sin"—which has no such meaning in Judaism. Indeed, Abraham copied this scene from a Protestant Bible illustrated by the Swiss artist
Matthaeus Merian (1593–1650).[27] In Merian's Bible, the scene is attached to the
appropriate text in Genesis, and Abraham bar Jacob, who was apparently
brought up on this edition, used it to illustrate Adam and Eve, though their
names appear in the Jewish amulet in a totally different context.

Fig. 6. Childbirth amulet for a boy, Germany, eighteenth century.
Printed on paper. (Library of the Jewish Theological
Seminary of America, New York)

EIGHTEENTH-CENTURY GERMAN AMULETS

Printed amulets from eighteenth-century Germany were generally produced by
Jewish printers. Separate pages were prepared for male and female children—
each accompanied by appropriate images.[28] The small woodcuts show what is
expected of the child when he or she grows up. Thus, the amulet for a boy depicts a small male figure dressed in the typical costume of an urban German Jew
of the time, holding an open book (Figure 6).[29] This is most likely a prayer book
or a talmudic text. Men in contemporary German-Jewish art are customarily
shown holding a liturgical book; in fact, they are ordinarily depicted participating in a religious ceremony or performing the commandments.[30]

Fig. 7. Childbirth amulet for a girl, Germany, eighteenth century. Printed on paper.
(Library of the Jewish Theological Seminary of America, New York)

And what is expected of baby girls? The childbirth amulet for a female leaves no doubt (Figure 7). At bottom center appears a cartouche inscribed with the Hebrew words *niddah, ḥallah, hadlakah*. These terms refer to the three commandments incumbent on the Jewish woman: ritual immersion, setting aside a portion of the dough, and kindling the Sabbath lights. In the context of childbirth, these commandments are of special importance, for it is written in the Mishnah, "On account of three transgressions women die in childbirth: because they are not observant of [the laws of] Niddah, Ḥallah, and the kindling of the [Sabbath] lights" (BT, Shabbat 31b). Of the three, the amulet in Figure 7 shows in the upper central cartouche the lighting of Sabbath candles. We see a room in which a typically garbed woman is lighting the special Sabbath lamp of German Jews. This is a hanging metal lamp, consisting of a central shaft and a star-shaped oil container, which gave it the name *Judenstern* ("Jews' star").[31] Undoubtedly this scene was selected for representation because, in the folklore of German Jews, it was believed that the lights expel demons that may destroy the pleasure of Friday night. In addition, the time of kindling was considered a most opportune moment for a woman's supplications (*tkhines*).[32] It is thus clear that, despite the folk nature and simple production of these paper amulets, much thought was invested to make them meaningful for those who used them.

EASTERN EUROPE

Unlike the Jews of Germany, those of Poland generally avoided figurative representation. Obviously, they interpreted more severely the Second Commandment's prohibition of the making of "graven images." Instead of human figures, their visual arts are filled with such Jewish symbols as the seven-branched menorah and the Tablets of the Law, intricate geometric and floral decorations, and a wide selection of animals, which—under the influence of locally popular non-Jewish images—included mythical creatures such as the unicorn. However, even in this last category, animals that have symbolic meaning in Jewish tradition are more prominent. For example, the leopard (tiger), eagle, deer, and lion, which appear more frequently than other animals, stand for their "qualities" as explained in the Mishnah: "Judah, the son of Tema, said 'Be bold as the leopard, light as the vulture [eagle], fleet as the deer, and strong as the lion, to do the will of Your Father in heaven' " (Pirkei Avot, 5, 23).

The selection of pictorial motifs for Polish childbirth amulets clearly fits the general style and iconography of local Jewish art. They were customarily made by yeshivah boys in the technique of papercuts, which was extremely popular among both the Jews and their neighbors.[33] The charming and colorful childbirth papercuts were called in Yiddish *Kimpetbrivl* (lit.: "letter for the childbed") or *shir hama'losl* (as the main text on them is Psalm 121, which begins with the Hebrew words *shir ha-ma'alot* ["A song of ascents"]. The text of this Psalm, which is also written on childbirth amulets from other countries (see, for example, the Dutch amulet of Abraham bar Jacob mentioned above), is considered magical and protective because it contains such verses as "The Lord is your guardian, the Lord is your protection at your right hand.... The Lord will guard you from all harm.... The Lord will guard your going out and coming in now and forever."[34]

Other typical formulas include mentioning the name of biblical couples, chiefly the patriarchs and matriarchs, which serve as models for fertility and bringing up "good children." The "presence" of these couples in the room is considered to have a good influence on the laboring woman, and it is for this reason that Rachel is rarely mentioned (since she died giving birth to Benjamin). This is in contrast to Lilith and her retinue, who is also referred to, according to popular belief, by the biblical verse "You shall not live a *witch*" (Exodus 22:17), which may also be translated as "You shall not allow a witch to live." To make the spell work, this verse is written four or even six times, each time with the three words that make up this verse in Hebrew (*mekhashefa lo te'haye*) arranged in a different order. It is this combination of the incantations and the pictorial

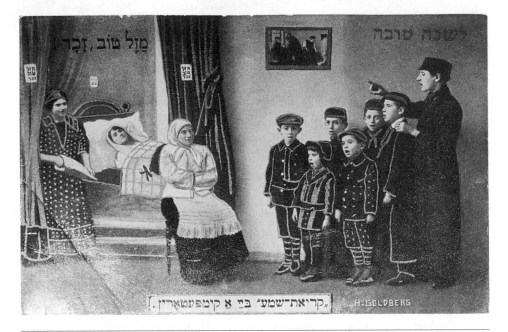

Fig. 8. "Reciting the Shema near a woman in childbirth" (after she delivered the baby);
New Year postcard designed by H. Goldberg, Warsaw, 1910s. (Collection Shalom Sabar)

and cutout symbols that gave the page its supposed effectiveness. The attractive
pages were hung over the mother's bed or the child's crib, or next to the doorway
of the room (as can be seen in a New Year's postcard from Warsaw, 1910s—
Figure 8).

Other Jewish circles in eastern Europe, which were even less lenient in their
approach to figurative representation, did not avoid the use of paper amulets.
However, the amulets were unadorned, with the text as the central and only
component of the small page. Yet among other Hasidic circles, the portrait of a
noted rabbinical authority or even a local venerated rabbi may appear prominently on an amulet. In Figure 9, such a portrait was not drawn with lines and
colors; instead, the maker used a sacred Hebrew text, whose miniature letters
were shaped into designs in a technique called "micrography." It is by virtue of
the portrayed rabbi that the mother and her baby are protected.

The explanation for this phenomenon is simple: the rabbi or tzadik (righteous sage) was given a special status and at times venerated as a miracle worker.
Large tablets with portraits of holy rabbis were produced as colorful litho-
graphic prints (and in other techniques) in many copies and hung in the houses
of their followers. These were often the only human representation permitted in
the house. Some prints show just one or two tzadikim, whereas others depict a

"group portrait" of selected figures from different places and times. The justification is found in a biblical verse often quoted on these tablets: "And your eyes shall see your teachers" (Isaiah 30:20).[35] It should be noted, finally, that this phenomenon is today even more widespread among the ultra-Orthodox in Israel.

BETWEEN EAST AND WEST: JERUSALEM OF THE LATE OTTOMAN PERIOD

During the nineteenth and early twentieth centuries, Jerusalem was a small town on the edge of the dying Ottoman Empire. At the beginning of the nineteenth century, the entire population of Jerusalem numbered no more than 9,000, of which about 2,500 were Jews. Their number increased steadily, and by 1900 there were some 35,000 Jews in a total population of about 50,000. The Jewish community was composed of two major groups: Sephardim, who arrived early on from other parts of the empire, and Ashkenazim, who came mainly from eastern Europe. In the second half of the century, Jewish immigrants from Islamic lands—chiefly Persia, Bukhara, Morocco, and Yemen—joined the Sephardim.[36]

Each of these groups, and later also the Jews from Islamic lands, brought with it particular customs, rituals, culture, and art. Yet a new folk and visual culture was also created of the mixture of the communities and their contacts with the local population and the land. This new culture is reflected in the numerous objects and souvenirs created locally. Only a small portion of these objects was produced for local consumption; most were either sold to tourists or sent to Diaspora Jews. They served as reminders of the poor Jews of Jerusalem, who required financial and other support. Using a few typical visual symbols, these souvenirs and ritual objects were instantly identified with Jerusalem and the Holy Land.[37]

Fig. 9. Childhood amulet with micrography; image of R. Akiva Eger of Posen by Zvi ben Jacob, Budapest, late nineteenth century. Printed on paper. (Library of the Jewish Theological Seminary of America, New York)

Fig. 10. Childbirth amulet with the Temple Mount, Jerusalem, late nineteenth century. Printed on paper. (Library of the Jewish Theological Seminary of America, New York)

Childbirth amulets clearly reflected this local tradition. Thus, while the text was basically the same as that used in the other countries, the images produced a new concept as to how mother and child may be protected—by depicting the holy sites of the Land of Israel, in particular of Jerusalem. The images of the primary pilgrimage sites evoked pious feelings and the belief that their sanctity would protect those who beheld them. The same sites, it should be noted, appeared on the souvenir objects, where they served as a reminder of the poor who lived near them and helped future pilgrims plan their itineraries in the Holy Land.

The most popular site on the Jerusalem amulets was the Temple Mount. A small black and white picture at bottom center of Figure 10 depicts a conventional image of the Mount, showing a brick wall that represents the Wailing Wall. The cypress trees above the Wall are symbolic of the "cedars of Lebanon" from which Solomon's Temple was built (see 1 Kings 5:20ff). The trees are flanked by two monuments, usually identified as "School of Solomon" (right) and "The Temple" (left). A close examination of these structures reveals that they are, surprisingly enough, modeled on the early Muslim structures that stand on the Temple Mount: al-Aqsa mosque and the Dome of the Rock, respectively. This anachronistic identification is rooted in European art of centuries earlier. The Crusaders were the first to misidentify the Muslim structures they found on the Temple Mount with the biblical monuments. The visual stereotypes they created infiltrated European art and, in the course of time, were adopted chiefly by Italian and Sephardic Jews who "imported" them back to the Holy Land.[38]

Another curious paper amulet of Jerusalem points at a mixture of totally different artistic traditions. This colorful page was created during the first decade of the twentieth century by Moshe Shah Mizrachi, a native of Teheran who came to Jerusalem around 1890. Mizrachi opened a shop for frames and mirrors in the spice market of the Old City, and he also produced votive tablets, amulets, and naive biblical scenes.[39] His amulet (Figure 11), based on formulas from *Sefer Raziel* (as also declared in the arch at top), features a combination of motifs. In the large oval at center is the Dome of the Rock, captioned with the words of Jeremiah (17:12), "High from the beginning, Your place of our sanctuary." This image is surrounded by 12 tombs of holy men buried around Jerusalem, Tiberias, and Shechem. In the four corners of the amulet are the four animals of *Pirkei Avot*. Their depiction, totally foreign to Jews of Islam, clearly indicates east European influence on Mizrachi, whereas the holy sites reflect the local tradition. Mizrachi's Persian background is especially evident in the color scheme of the page and the ornamental elements. This mixture of traditions was possible at the time only in the Land of Israel, in Jerusalem in particular.

Fig. 11. Moshe Shah Mizrachi, Home amulet based on *Sefer Raziel*, Jerusalem,
early twentieth century. Colored lithograph. (Gross Family Collection, Tel Aviv)

ISLAMIC LANDS DURING RECENT CENTURIES

Whereas the Ashkenazim in Europe mainly used paper amulets to protect the
newborn, in the lands of Islam the Jews preferred objects made of metal, especially gold and silver. The use of paper and parchment amulets was widespread as
well, but the metal ones were more highly regarded and sought after in both Is-

lamic and Jewish communities. Beyond their prophylactic function, the costly metal amulets served an additional, no less important, purpose: as jewelry.[40] Whether she was Muslim or Jewish, urban or rural, rich or poor, a Middle Eastern woman considered jewelry to be an essential component of her daily appearance. Skilled craftsmen invested great effort in the creation of attractive and intricate pendants, necklaces, bracelets, and rings, which both beautified her and protected her from the evil eye and other dangers (Figure 12). Naturally, however, not all the jewelry used in a given time, place, and society was the same, and the selection of pieces, their richness, quan-

Fig. 12. Amulet necklace, North Africa or Persia, nineteenth century. Silver. (In the permanent collection of The Magnes Museum, Berkeley; 69.3. Photo: Ben Ailes)

tity, and quality, served to indicate the status of the owner. Moreover, wearing inscribed amuletic jewelry prominently engraved in distinctive square Hebrew letters gave the bearer not only protection but also a sign of identification.

Amuletic jewelry was not worn only by women. From the moment a baby was born, he or she was adorned with protective metal amulets (Figure 13). As we can see in photographs of children taken prior to the 1940s, both boys and girls continued to wear them till the age of five or six (Figure 14).[41] The dangers awaiting the newborn did not end with the circumcision ceremony, as was believed among some Ashkenazic communities; the difficult reality of life dictated that such amulets would be used in later years as well. Amulets were attached to the child's clothing, used as pendants and anklets, or even attached to the hair above the forehead with wax.[42] The double function of these objects can be demonstrated, for example, by ankle rings, which usually had suspended drop-shaped bells whose sound helped a mother to keep track of her child.

Handwritten parchment childbirth amulets, and in recent times printed paper ones, were also used by the Jews of Islamic lands. The more traditional parchment examples were individually inscribed on long, narrow "scrolls," which were usually rolled up and inserted into cylindrical metal cases. Such amulet cases, common also among the Muslims, have survived from many Jewish communities in these regions.[43] Printed amulets became common especially in North Africa (Morocco, Tunisia, and Algeria) in the 1920s and 1930s and were in popular demand there until the immigration of these communities to Israel.

And what about the texts inscribed on the amulets in these countries?

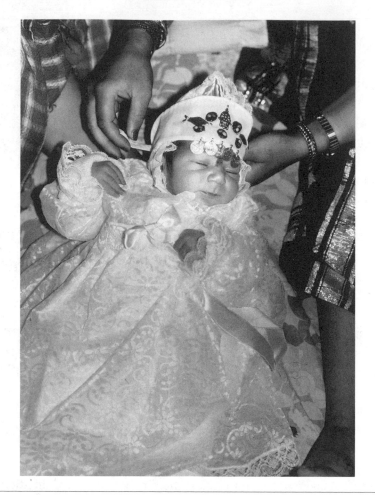

Fig. 13. Eight-day-old boy on the morning of his *brit milah* (circumcision).
Symbols to ward off the evil eye are sewn to his special headband.
(Photo: Keren Tzionah Friedman. © 1987)

Perhaps the most distinct feature of the inscriptions, which sets the amulets of the Jews of Islamic lands apart from their European counterparts, is the way they were personalized. Thus, unlike the simple paper amulets of Europe, the metal and elongated parchment amulets in Islamic lands were in many cases—if not most—prepared for a specific person and specific occasion. Along with the familiar formulas, we thus find the name of the person for whom the amulet was made. In the metal examples from Kurdistan and Iran, for example, the name is often inscribed on the back, while the front bears the significant Hebrew abbreviation *lenokaz*—standing for *le-noseh kameah zo* ("To the bearer of this amulet").[44] This inscription means that the protection is provided only for the baby or woman who wears it. The purpose for which the amulet was manufactured is at times mentioned as well. Apparently for lack of space, the jewelry/metal amulets are usually brief in this respect and many do not mention anything (though the selected formulas are commonly indicative of the specific protection needed). The elongated parchment scrolls, however, contain long and detailed inscriptions that list the "remedies" required and thus open a window to the personal desires, beliefs, and needs of the Jews in these regions. An important point in this context is that, once the child grew up or the person specified in the text had been cured, a metal amulet would often be discarded (usually melted down for the silver), and a parchment amulet would be put in a *genizah* (storage facility).

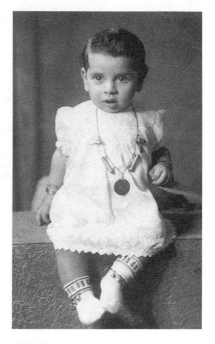

Fig. 14. Jewish girl with amulets, Baghdad, 1940s. (Photo courtesy Folklore Research Center Archives, The Hebrew University of Jerusalem)

Notwithstanding the differences between east and west in materials, shape, and usage of the amulets, the basic textual formulas inscribed on them, especially on the printed childbirth amulets, are practically identical. Let us look, for example, at a paper amulet from Casablanca of the late 1930s or early 1940s (Figure 15).[45] It was printed by Joseph Lugasy, who continued to print such materials in Jerusalem after his family immigrated to Israel. Like the Polish Kimpetbrivl (see Figure 8), the amulet contains Psalm 121 followed by *"Shaddai kera' Satan"* and the names of the three angels who dealt with Lilith. Also like the Polish example (and some found elsewhere) are the names of the "good biblical couples" and the verse "You shall not allow a witch to live," written again in its six possible forms. Even more curious is the subtitle of this amulet, announcing it is using a formula sanctioned by the renowned Hasidic Rabbi Israel ben Eliezer (the Ba'al Shem Tov).

In addition to familiar formulas, the aforementioned kabbalistic shemoth were ubiquitous in Islamic lands, where they were considered most appropriate. In Kurdistan, for example, silver amulets were often topped by a large inscription, *be-shem Shaddai* ("In the Name of the Almighty"), and the amulet itself was simply referred to as *Shaddai*. Another common one is the so-called "Eight-letter Name," *YAHDWNHI*. This powerful name is composed of the four letters

Fig. 15. Joseph Lugasy, childbirth amulet, Casablanca, Morocco,
late 1930s–early 1940s. Printed on paper. (Shalom Sabar Collection)

of the Ineffable Name or *Shem ha-Meforash* (i.e., the Tetragrammaton *YHWH*),
alternating with the other common name of God: *Adonai*.[46] The combined holy
name is commonly written as a superscription in hollow letters, several times
larger than the rest of the lengthy text. It is found in the same form, though
much larger, at the top of the decorative menorah tablets that were hung on the
walls of Kurdish, Iraqi, Afghani, and other synagogues—thus they brought the
sanctity of the holy space into one's personal realm.[47] God's names were also hid-

den in secretive kabbalistic formulas, known only to the initiated, as well as in magic numerical squares, which have been popular on Arabic amulets (for example, in Morocco).

Another important category concerns angelology. Invoking sympathetic powers—in particular angels, who are believed to possess healing and protective energies—is common on the eastern amulets. The names of these angels are commonly copied from kabbalistic works, in particular *Sefer Raziel*. Names of angels are either fully spelled out or alluded to in one form or another. Childbirth amulets (though other types as well) would naturally be inscribed with the names of Sanoi, Sansanoi, and Semangalof. In some lands (e.g., Yemen, Iran, Iraq), these angels are illustrated in the same form as in *Sefer Raziel* (see Figure 2). Kurdish and Persian amulets often feature the mnemonic name *Argaman,* standing for the five important angels: Uriel, Raphael, Gabriel, Michael, and Nuriel. Each one of these popular angels has a different function related to his name. Thus, for example, Raphael is the healing angel, as his name means literally "God is healing," whereas Michael is considered the greatest guardian archangel, for his name translates "Who is like God?"[48]

It should be noted, finally, that though the text on an amulet was given such importance, it apparently was not and could not be deciphered by most of those who used these objects. They were not supposed to read the inscriptions, or to understand their hidden meaning. In this respect the Jews of Islamic lands were not different from their brethren in Europe. On the title page of *Sefer Raziel,* it is clearly stated that the book itself serves as protection against every possible mischief. The understanding of the text contained in it and its proper employment was preserved for those few learned kabbalists or the ḥakhamim.

THE "JUDAIZATION" OF THE *KHAMSA*

Notwithstanding the astonishing similarity in the texts inscribed on Hebrew amulets from Europe and the Middle East, the pictorial designs on the latter are of an entirely different character. In the Middle East, as in Europe, the local culture played a decisive role. The borrowed designs were given a new meaning fitting Jewish ideals and their immediate function.

The best example to illustrate this process is the typical Muslim *khamsa* plaque, also known in Arabic as "the hand of Fatima."[49] This object became an extremely popular type of amulet among several Jewish communities under Islam—in particular, in Morocco, Tunisia, Persia, Kurdistan, and Iraq. The khamsa thus shows how an element universally identified as representing the deep religious ideas of one culture can be adapted by another and used as its

Fig. 16. Home amulet, Jerusalem, early twentieth century. Painted on glass, possibly by Moshe Shah Mizrachi. (Einhorn Collection, Tel Aviv)

Fig. 17. Islamic home amulet, Morocco, twentieth century. (Shalom Sabar Collection)

inherent symbol, even in the sacred space of the synagogue, without any hesitation.

The "Judaization" of the khamsa was actually very simple and direct. Judaism offers sufficient associative resources to make this process almost obvious, as we can see by comparing a Jewish tablet made to protect a house in early-twentieth-century Jerusalem with a Muslim one with the same purpose (Figures 16 and 17). The two objects share a similar composition: a large hand in the center, flanked by two circles above. Most likely the Jewish tablet is based on the extremely popular Islamic type. However, the Jewish example is imbued with concepts and ideas that derive from traditional Jewish sources.

For example, the five fingers of the hand are separated in the traditional form of the blessing

Fig. 18. "Heh" amulet, Gibraltar, late nineteenth century. Cast and engraved silver. (Gross Family Collection, Tel Aviv)

hand of the priest (*kohen*) in the synagogue. This gesture is known to any traditional Jew, and thus looking at the hand illustrated in this way makes a totally different impression than the Muslim one. In fact, there are many ceremonial objects for the synagogue from Islamic lands that prominently feature a hand in this priestly position (for example, a Torah Ark curtain from Istanbul, a pointer to read the Torah [*Yad*] from Iran, and rimmonim from Azerbaijan).[50]

Another important point concerns the Hebrew letter "Heh," which is emphatically written as a large capital at the center of the hand in the tablet. "Heh" is the fifth letter in the Hebrew alphabet, and accordingly its numerical value is five. Simultaneously, it signifies the amuletic number five (*khamsa* in Arabic) and is a single-letter name of God ("monogrammaton"). As such, "Heh" has a particularly holy status to this day. Many metal Jewish amulets made for various purposes are frequently inscribed predominantly or solely with this letter (Figure 18).[51] Another feature of the "Judaized" khamsa in the context of "Heh" is its association with the figure of Joseph, as we shall see below.

THE SWORD AMULET AND THE NIGHT BEFORE CIRCUMCISION

The high mortality rate of babies in Islamic lands kept the fears and beliefs in the demonic powers of Lilith alive until modern times. The specter of a woman who strangles babies is, in fact, immanent in Islamic society at large, and the Muslims

Fig. 19. Amulet for mother and newborn child (with Lilith "bound in chains"), possibly Persia, nineteenth century. Engraved silver. (In the permanent collection of The Magnes Museum, Berkeley; 67.1.1.3. Photo: Ben Ailes)

usually call her Karina (lit. in Arabic, "escort").[52] Every possible method of magic was employed to fight Karina and Lilith.[53] The Jewish practices were not limited to inscribing the names of the three angels or the popular formula *Ḥutz Lilit* ("Lilith get out!"). Although the Ashkenazic childbirth amulets of Europe often mention her name with all its known variations, among the Jews of Islamic lands this was not always deemed sufficient. One curious image, common in particular on Persian amulets, whether made as paper (or parchment) scrolls or silver plaques, is that of Lilith "bound in chains" (Figure 19). The crudely drawn figure is shown with her mouth wide open, revealing large teeth. On the belly of this frightening image appear the words "*Shemira* [a protection] to the child that is born, so that no harm would ever afflict him. Amen. [In the name of] Sanoi, Sansanoi, and Semangalof." Additional protection is provided by inscribing around the figure an imaginary fence, which is formed by the protective 22 letters of the Priestly Benediction (Numbers 6:24–25). The importance of such an amulet and many others like it is further heightened in view of the fact that figurative imagery was not common among the Jews of Islamic lands.

Precautions against Lilith and the evil eye were augmented on the eve of circumcision. It has traditionally been believed that, on this night, Lilith and her retinue would do anything possible to harm the child. In nearly every Jewish community, people stayed awake to "guard" the baby and its mother. Early illustrations and descriptions of the customs associated with this vigil appear in the books of Kirchner and another eighteenth-century German Hebraist, Johann Christoph Bodenschatz (see Figure 3, bottom right panel).[54] In Germany, where the night was known as *Wachnacht* ("watch night"), the men would light candles, recite prayers, and read Psalms; in Islamic lands, they more commonly read the *Zohar*.[55] In many communities, east and west, children and women participated in these activities, as can be seen in the aforementioned postcard from

Poland (see Figure 8), where children are gathered outside the mother's room, reciting the Shema—which was believed to provide protection for the newborn through the sacred prayer itself and the participation of strong, healthy boys in the ceremony.[56]

Many other customs associated with the eve of circumcision have been instituted in the course of time (for some additional practices, see the subsection on Elijah, below). Here, I will briefly examine a curious object that unites the folk beliefs of the Jews under Islam with those of the European Ashkenazim. This object is a sword used to "fight" the evil spirits, in particular Lilith. This custom is in fact common in many other societies, where swords, knives, scissors, and even needles, fishhooks, and other sharp metal objects are believed to aid in this purpose. The preferred metal in most cases is iron (though other substances have been used as well), because iron is commonly believed to be the best charm against the forces of evil.[57]

The strong belief in the power of the sword in the context of childbirth is best demonstrated by a popular custom of the Iraqi Kurdish Jews, who used a miniature symbolic sword for an extended period in

Fig. 20. Seipa (sword) amulet, Iraqi Kurdistan, early twentieth century. Engraved silver. (Gross Family Collection, Tel Aviv)

the life of the child. This object is known in the special neo-Aramaic dialect of Kurdish Jews as a *seipa* (cf. the Hebrew term *sa'yif*, "sword") (Figure 20).[58] In order to fight the evil eye in every way possible, the material for the seipa was customarily acquired from three silversmiths: a Jew, a Muslim, and a Christian. The silver obtained from these sources was then melted down and reworked by a Jewish silversmith who prepared a small sword with one, two, or three holes at the ends. The ḥakham would inscribe on it the protective formulas, such as Psalm 121, shemoth, protective angels with meaningful names (e.g., Azriel, Shamriel), and the three angels who combat Lilith. The crowded and lengthy inscription significantly ends with the words: "a barrier and fence to the bearer of this amulet." The sword was sewn to the cap of the child, who wore it everywhere for several years. In some cases the lad would wear the cap with the seipa until he started to don tefillin (perhaps as a sort of replacement for the protection provided by the sword).

In Kurdistan the symbolic and psychological function of the sword dominated, but the battle waged against Lilith in other communities was more fierce.

In Morocco and Ashkenaz, for example, a much larger sword was used, preferably one that had shed blood—as if an actual fight were under way. Known as *sif* ("sword") *d'tahdid,* the Moroccan sword was thought to be the best weapon against the enemies of the newborn. The *tahdid* is a ceremony conducted every evening between childbirth and circumcision. Before the ceremony begins, a large, real, iron sword, preferably one that has "proved itself" in the past, is placed under the pillow of the woman in childbed.[59] A celebration is then held at home, with relatives and other guests present. The festive meal is accompanied by the reading of selections from various sources, with special emphasis on the *Zohar,* which is to Moroccan Jews an extremely sacred and protective text.[60] At midnight the windows and doors are closed and the sword is removed from under the pillow. The master of the house brandishes the weapon in all directions, as if he is dispelling Lilith and the other demons, while he and all others loudly recite protective verses.[61]

The Moroccan tahdid ceremony is strikingly similar to the German Wachnacht. A close examination of the lower right scene in the engraving in Kirchner's book (see Figure 3) clearly shows a small sword hanging behind the woman who reclines in the bed, holding an infant. This type of sword, called a *Kreismesser,* was used among German Jews for 30 days following the birth.[62] Every night during this period the mother would stand in the center of her room holding the sword and thrust it in the four directions, to dispel Lilith. Although the description and illustration in the Kirchner book may seem quite fantastic to the modern spectator, such Ashkenazic swords did survive. A late-eighteenth-century example from Alsace (where it was called *Krasmesser*) is preserved in the Collection Société d'Histoire des Israélites d'Alsace et de Lorraine in Strasbourg.[63] Just like the Moroccan and German swords, the Alsatian one is made of iron. Significantly, it is engraved with the same unequivocal verse: "You shall not allow a witch to live." As in Morocco, a sword that had already proved itself was preferred. Thus, according to one source, in the nineteenth century the Jewish community of Hessen-Kassel used for this ceremony swords that had belonged to Napoleon's artillerymen.[64]

BIBLICAL FIGURES AND CHILDBIRTH

Heroes from the remote and mythical past constitute a major source for the creative folklore of many peoples. In Judaism, this place of honor is preserved primarily for biblical figures, but this is not to belittle the role of post-biblical figures. In the realm of magic, for example, such sources as the Talmud and midrashic literature are replete with wondrous tales and legends about the supernatural powers of rabbis who could perform miracles, cure incurable diseases, and even reverse the laws of nature. (For example, Ḥoni *ha-Me'aggel* ["the circle drawer"], who lived in the first century B.C.E., was able to make the rain come down.) This tradition continued to flourish in later periods with figures such as Maimonides or Rabbi Judah Loew ben Bezalel of Prague, to whom legend attributes the creation of the Golem (a mythical human figure created artificially by using holy names in a magical way). Even today, miraculous stories are told about recently deceased personages like the Ḥabad (Lubavitcher) Rebbe or the Moroccan saint Baba Sali.[65]

Most post-medieval Jewish folk heroes arose in local communities, and the folk culture created around them was not always known in other lands. But the biblical heroes were obviously widely known, and even people who could not read the Scriptures were closely familiar with their stories. True, the extra-biblical stories told about them were not the same everywhere; each community emphasized the points that were important locally and reflected its own attitude, aspirations, and beliefs. Yet some basic characteristics of the biblical hero, which shaped its image for generations to come, have been shared by many communities.

In this process, the talmudic and midrashic literature played a decisive role as well. The rabbis of old set the general outlines along which a given biblical figure developed later on. A typical example of this process is King David. The story of the second king of Israel as it appears in the books of Samuel and Kings presents a controversial figure with extreme strengths and weaknesses: a great commander and superb ruler of the nation, who also shows great religious zeal, but also a man who cannot manage his own family and who commits adultery. This problematic picture changes in the midrashic literature, where the king is idealized. He is presented as a pious and most righteous man, praised for his devotion, poetry, and zeal, and exonerated from all blame (in his relationship with Bathsheba).[66] To this day the image of David, from whose seed the Messiah will come, is central in Jewish folklore, and the talmudic dictum "David King of Israel is alive and existing" is recited with great zeal. The six-pointed star called the "Shield of David" has been central in practical Kabbalah (the use of kabbalistic symbols for magical purposes) since the early Middle Ages, and in the past hundred years has been identified as the primary visual symbol of Judaism.[67]

"BEN PORAT YOSEPH": JOSEPH AND CHILDBIRTH

Joseph was an especially popular figure in the folklore of the Jews in Islamic lands, where he acquired the image of protector of children and fertility. In order to understand how Joseph was "selected" for this curious role, the background of this phenomenon must be briefly described. Joseph was unusually popular among the Muslims, being the only biblical personage whose life story gets a full *sura* (section or chapter) in the Koran. The *Surat Yusuf* begins with the statement, "We shall tell you the most beautiful story." The Koranic account, which draws on extra-biblical legends and other sources (including Jewish ones), is replete with many details of the numerous miracles wrought by Joseph and praise of his unusual character. We should also note that popular Islamic literary accounts of his life, such as the famous epic *Yusuf and Zulaykha* composed in 1483 by Abd al-Rahman Jami of Heart, draw on many rabbinical sources.[68]

Of course, Joseph also held a place of honor among the Jews of Islamic lands. In fact, even in medieval Spain his story has a highly unusual visibility in Jewish folklore and art. For example, two important Sephardic haggadah manuscripts, the *Sarajevo* and *Golden Haggadot*—both produced in the fourteenth century—contain many miniatures dedicated to Joseph, despite the fact that he is not an essential part of the Exodus story.[69] Joseph is also prominently featured in the manuscript art of the Jews in Iran. Under the influence of Persian miniature painting, the local Jews allowed themselves to use figurative representations. Here, indeed, the story of Joseph appears in a manner closely resembling Muslim book decoration. Several Jewish illuminated manuscripts with Jami's *Yusuf and Zulaykha* transliterated into Judeo-Persian (the dialect of Persian Jews written in Hebrew letters) are known (Figure 21).[70] Clearly, in these miniatures Joseph emerges as Jacob's most beloved, appreciated, and successful son. Paraphrases of Jami's work were written by Iranian Jews and, like Esther plays in Europe, were performed in the Jewish neighborhoods.[71]

The profound admiration of Islamic Jews for Joseph and his exemplary character is reflected best, however, in the realm of childbirth and magic. The selection of this one among the 12 sons of Jacob to be the protector of children and fertility seems most appropriate—because Joseph's mother had a difficult time giving birth to him; he suffered as a child; and his brothers even attempted to kill him. But despite all these misfortunes, Joseph grew up to be beautiful and successful—every mother's dream.

The ḥakhamim, however, inquired deeply into the sources to justify this image. Evidence for Joseph as protector of fertility was found in talmudic sources, which were mixed with popular beliefs and symbols of the time and place. Thus, practitioners of Kabbalah in the lands of Islam indicated that the evidence for the power of the *ḥamsa* as a charm (*segulah*) for barren women, or those who had difficulties during childbirth, comes directly from the story of Joseph in Egypt. The somewhat intricate explanation is based on lending a new

Fig. 21. "Zulaykha's Dream of Joseph," Persia, 1853. Miniature in Judeo-Persian manuscript of Jami's *Yusef and Zulaykha.* (Library of the Jewish Theological Seminary of America, New York)

meaning to the familiar story, and to a wordplay in the original Hebrew version. The story goes that, following the cycle of famine years and drought, Joseph was able to provide bread (i.e., food) to the Egyptian people as a result of his agrarian policies (Genesis 47). In our context, the drought is taken to mean barrenness, and providing the seed for the bread is obviously understood as fertility (in

Hebrew the word for "seed" is the same as for "semen"). Moreover, the symbolic meaning of Joseph's words to the Egyptians, "Here is seed for you to sow the land" (Genesis 47:23), becomes especially significant because the word for "here" in Hebrew is "heh."[72]

Many objects of Judaica—votive tablets dedicated to the synagogue, for example, or amulets for the home and the person—that were produced in the lands of Islam strongly emphasize the connection of Joseph to fertility and the protection of children, and they were believed to bring good luck to people who beheld or used them. For example, the fingers of the hand in Figure 18 are inscribed with the blessing of Jacob to his beloved son Joseph: *ben porat Yoseph ben porat alei ayyin banot tza'ada*. In standard English translation this verse appears as "Joseph is a fruitful bough, even a fruitful bough by a fountain" (Genesis 49:22). These words were given deep figurative meaning in the context of magic and fertility. In tractate Berakhot of the Babylonian Talmud (page 20a), it is said of Rabbi Johanan, who was famous for his exceptional beauty, that he was accustomed to go and sit at the gates of a bathing place.

> He said: When the daughters of Israel come up from bathing they look at me and they would have children as handsome as I am. Said the rabbis to him: Is not the Master afraid of the evil eye? He replied: *I come from the seed of Joseph, over whom the evil eye has no power.* For it is written "Joseph is a fruitful vine . . ." Rabbi Abbahu said with regard to this, do not read *alei ayyin* ("by a fountain") but *olei ayyin* (i.e., "rising above the [power of the evil] eye").

This talmudic reference to the ability of Joseph to "rise above the evil eye" has been extremely instrumental in shaping his image as protector of children. Thus, on some old metal amulets for children, the only text is the blessing of Jacob to Joseph (Figure 22), and on others it appears in the vicinity of other familiar formulas or in an abbreviated form.[73] To this day, the most common blessing of a Sephardic ḥakham to a child is "Ben Porat Yoseph" (said while the rabbi puts his hand on the head of the child). Similarly, the words of Johanan ("I come from the seed of Joseph . . .") are fully quoted in the two circles of the home amulet, and many other examples exist (for instance, an Italian-Sephardic tablet that hung in a room where a circumcision was to take place.

The image of Joseph as a supreme protector is enhanced by yet another important motif: the fish. In the home amulet in Figure 16, for example, a pair of fish flank the ḥamsa with Jacob's blessing. The fish is a symbol of fertility in several cultures. In Jewish sources, this is clearly based on Jacob's blessing to Joseph's sons, Ephraim and Manasseh: "The angel who has redeemed me from

all harm, bless the lads . . . and may they be teeming multitudes upon the earth" (Genesis 48:16).
In Hebrew, "be fruitful and multiply" is *ve-
yidggu la-rov*, which literally means "[multiply]
like fish." Moreover, in the Talmud, it is said:
"Just as the fishes in the sea are covered with
water and the evil eye has no power on them, so
the evil eye has no power over the seed of
Joseph" (BT, Berakhot, 20a).[74]

The fish as a metaphor for fertility is, in fact,
further elaborated in classical Jewish sources.
The Talmud discusses, for example, what the
Israelites in the desert meant when they complained to Moses, "We remember the fish [*daga*]
that we used to eat free in Egypt" (Numbers
11:5). According to the authority Rav, *daga* is indeed simply "real fish"; however, Rav's rival,
Samuel, says: "*daga* means 'illicit intercourse' "
(BT, Yoma 75a). The great medieval commentator Rashi explains the words of Samuel, "*daga*
is the name for sexual intercourse." Obviously
these commentators refer to an extremely popular midrash concerning the incredible fertility of

Fig. 22. *Ben Porat Yosef*
amulet, Morocco or Palestine,
c. twentieth century.
Engraved silver. (Photo courtesy
Folklore Research Center
Archives, The Hebrew University
of Jerusalem)

the Hebrews in Egypt. According to this legend, despite the hardship of bondage
and despite Pharaoh's decree to cast all the male infants into the river, the Israelites continued to multiply, and every woman bore six children in every pregnancy. This idea surfaces also in Jewish legends concerning messianic times, in
which fertility would have no limits. Accordingly, the name given to the Messiah
in one of these legends is *Nun*—meaning, in Hebrew, "fish."[75]

This tradition continued in the Islamic lands among both the Jews and the
Muslims. The Jews in Morocco, for example, used to throw a live fish at the feet
of the bridal couple during their wedding, as a symbol and a wish for their fertility. Moreover, among North African Jews, Tunisians in particular, names of
various fishes were given to boys in order to protect them. It is not surprising,
therefore, to find in Hebrew amulets the image of the fish illustrated in the
vicinity of Jacob's blessing to Joseph. Separate fish amulets were common as
well, whether illustrated or three-dimensional. In the island of Djerba, blue
fishes are painted on the facade of the whitewashed walls of Jewish houses (Figure 23). Also, life-size, stuffed textile fishes with gilt decorations are extremely

Fig. 23. Paintings on a wall in Djerba herald the celebration of a Jewish wedding with symbols that are amulets to safeguard the home, bring good luck, and ensure fertility. (Photo: Keren Tzionah Friedman. © 1980)

common among both Jews and Muslims in Tunisia, where they are hung as protective amulets at the entrance of the house.[76]

Finally, the association of Joseph with protection continues to this day in Israel, especially among families who emigrated from Islamic lands. Contemporary amulets "for guarding against the evil eye, and for success in livelihood and [good] health" are emphatically inscribed with the verse concerning Joseph ("Ben Porat Yoseph . . .") in large capitals atop the letter "Heh" and the open hand at center (Figure 24). Sometimes a fish is included as well. It is noteworthy that portraits of kabbalists and modern saints from Morocco (e.g., the Baba Sali) or Iraq (e.g., Rabbi Joseph Ḥayyim of Baghdad) are frequently included in these amulets. Thanks to Joseph and his powers, symbolized by the fish and ḥamsa, and to these holy figures, one can still get the traditional protection from the evil eye.

"ELIYAHU ZAKHUR LA-TOV": ELIJAH AND CHILDBIRTH

Another important figure who has been "enlisted" to protect the infant against demons and evildoers is Elijah. Unlike the case of Joseph, belief in the powers of Elijah is common to Jewish communities everywhere. In fact, a survey of the items assembled in the Archives of the Jewish Folktale in Haifa reveals that there are more stories concerning Elijah than any other hero of the Jewish people. His biblical status as a miracle worker and as a person who did not physically die undoubtedly contributed to his popularity. In the folktales, however, he does not appear in his biblical role as a zealous prophet and religious leader but rather as a heavenly messenger who remedies social injustices. Accordingly, he is the one who benefits the pious poor, impoverishes the wicked rich, punishes the

Fig. 24. Political amulet of the Shas party with portraits of Rabbis Yitzhak Kadoorie (*left*), Simon Bar Kokhbar (*center*), and Ovadiah Yosef (*right*). Israel, 1990s. Printed on cardboard. (Shalom Sabar Collection)

unjust, cures the sick, provides the needed food on Friday (for the Sabbath) or the eve of a holiday (Passover in particular), and he may even appear miraculously as the tenth person needed for a *minyan* (Jewish liturgical quorum).[77]

Aside from these social roles of Elijah, a number of customs related to him emerged in the course of time. For example, although he is not connected directly to the Passover night, he is prominently represented in it. Thus, a relatively late custom is to place on the Seder table a wine cup for Elijah, in addition to the four cups that are drunk by every participant.[78] This custom may reflect the rabbinical controversy over whether one should drink four or five cups of wine at the Seder, but the association of the fifth cup with Elijah is most probably due to the popular Jewish belief that "when Elijah comes" all disputes and doubts will be resolved. The "visit" of Elijah at every Seder thus became a standard feature of the night celebrating past deliverance—fitting well the traditional expectation that the prophet is the one who will bring the message of final redemption at the end of days (based on Malachi 3:23). This messianic hope is also expressed in the beloved hymn chanted fervently in many Jewish communities on the conclusion of the Sabbath: "Elijah the prophet, Elijah the Tishbite, may he soon come to us with the Messiah, Son of David."

In medieval and early printed haggadot, especially from Germany and Italy,

Fig. 25. Wall decoration for circumcision room, with Elijah ascending to heaven (*top*),
the binding of Isaac (*center*), and Elijah heralding the arrival of the Messiah (*bottom*);
Italy, c. 1800. Parchment, printed and inscribed. (Library of the Jewish
Theological Seminary of America, New York)

Elijah is frequently illustrated as a hero of the Passover story. Depicted as an old
man blowing the Shofar, he usually appears on the page beginning with the Hebrew word *shefokh* ("Pour out Your fury upon the nations that do not know
You" [Psalms 79:6]), which is recited while the door is opened for him. Despite
the biblical origin of the verse, Jews who read it in these haggadot understood it
to be a call for God to redeem them and take revenge on the contemporary nations who persecuted them. Elijah's social role here is to comfort his suffering
people and lead them to the heavenly Jerusalem of the end of days (Figure 25).
Accordingly, in one Italian manuscript haggadah of the fifteenth century, a
bearded young man holding a cup of wine is shown opening the door for Elijah-
Messiah combined in one person, while the head of the household and all the
other family members, including the servant, are riding behind him on the
white (actually gray) ass.[79]

ELIJAH IN THE CIRCUMCISION ROOM

The immortal wanderer visits Jewish homes and brings with him good messages not only on the Seder night but also during the circumcision ceremony. The association of Elijah with the newborn begins, however, even earlier. The prophet is considered in Jewish sources to be the guardian of children from the moment they come into this world, and throughout the early "critical" period of their lives. This curious role of Elijah is in fact derived from a biblical source. In Malachi 3:1 he is called *Mal'akh ha-Berit*—namely, "The Angel [or messenger] of the Covenant," which in rabbinic sources is interpreted as "circumcision" (because in Hebrew *Berit* means both "covenant" and "circumcision").[80] This quality, combined with his supernatural powers and miracle working, in particular the resurrection of the widow's child (1 Kings 17:17–24), made Elijah the ideal "guardian angel" of children in Jewish folklore.[81]

He appears, to begin with, in some versions of the Lilith legend, which are reminiscent of the story of Lilith and the three angels. In these versions, Lilith and her retinue are on their way to the house of a woman in childbirth when they encounter Elijah. Upon learning that she intends to kill the woman and "drink the blood" of her baby, Elijah paralyzes Lilith on the spot and forces her to take an oath not to harm any mother or child wherever she sees or hears her own 13 names. Subsequently, Lilith gives the prophet a complete list of her bizarre names, the meaning and origin of which is not entirely clear.[82]

The Lilith-Elijah story is inscribed in its entirety on many paper amulets, both from Christian Europe and the Islamic East.[83] Eighteenth-century German ones, for example, contain the story, plus the 13 names printed in large capitals (see Figures 6 and 7). Moreover, each name is provided with full vocalization marks—as if to assure the user that he or she will make the correct identification of Lilith when and if she turns up. The story similarly appears on Jerusalem paper amulets, and popular specimens from Morocco (see Figure 16), Tunisia, and Algeria.

Elijah is also connected with an object used by some Sephardic and other Jewish communities in Islamic lands: a large metal tray with many candles and protective plants (Figure 26), which is brought in festive parade to the room of a woman on the night before her son's circumcision (see the section on the sword amulet, above). In the Sephardic and the Islamic communities, Elijah has a prominent protective role on this night. In fact, among the Jews of Morocco and the Mountain Jews ("Tats") of East Caucasus (Dagestan and neighboring areas), the eve of circumcision is explicitly called "The Night of Elijah the Prophet."[84]

Fig. 26. *Siny'yat Eliyahu Nabi* with candles; made in Jerusalem, 1934, and used by a local Kurdish community to this day. (Courtesy of Gallit-Siman Tov)

The ornamental tray is known as *Siny'yat Eliyahu Nabi* (Elijah's tray) or *Kandilat Eliyahu Nabi* (Elijah's candelabrum). "Magical" plants, in particular ruta (in Arabic, *roda*), are put in a dish or glass of water in the middle of the tray, surrounded by as many candles as possible, each one lit by a guest. Light is believed to have sympathetic power in the context of childbirth, for fire is considered in Judaism a sacred symbol of fertility and life (see the biblical aphorism "The spirit of man is the light of God" [Proverbs 20:27]). In talmudic times, the lighting of candles was considered such an important protective measure during delivery that rabbis allowed women to do it even on the Sabbath (BT, Shabbat, 128b). For the same reason, one was not allowed to extinguish the fire in a room in which there was a newborn, or remove anything that was burning. This belief also persisted in Ashkenaz, and among Polish Jews in modern times it was even considered bad luck if a person smoking a cigarette left the confinement room.[85]

A lively description of the customs connected with Elijah's tray is found in the work of Abraham Moses Luncz (1854–1918), who immigrated to the Holy Land from Kovno and described the "bizarre" customs of "our Sephardic brethren in the land of the Orient":

> On the night before circumcision, the relatives and acquaintances of the family, and others that are honored in this mitzvah, bring an olive-oil lamp, which will be lighted throughout the night. And the custom among our Sephardic brethren is that members of the household of the *sandak* ["godfather," or the man who traditionally holds the child on his knees during the circumcision ceremony] carry such an oil lamp with many spouts, decorated with kinds of aromatic plants, and parade with it in the streets of the town, led by the loud noise of a drum, while they sing cheerful songs, until they reach the house where the circumcision will take place.[86]

Finally, events in the life of the prophet are frequently depicted on circumcision implements and Hebrew illustrated manuscripts associated with childbirth and circumcision. These scenes do not necessarily refer to childbirth but show the prophet in his finest hours. Figure 25 (p. 706) is a good example: a large parchment panel from Italy (ca. 1800) that was apparently used as a wall decoration for the circumcision room and is calligraphically inscribed with a liturgical hymn for the occasion.[87] Elijah is shown at top being carried off to heaven in his fiery chariot, and below we see him blowing the Shofar, heralding the arrival of the Messiah. In the center appears the *Akedah* (the Binding of Isaac). Although this scene is seemingly unrelated to circumcision, it should be noted that actually Isaac is the model for all Jewish boys—being the first Jewish baby to be circumcised, when he was eight days old. However, it is not this event that appears on circumcision objects and manuscripts but rather the Akedah—which, like the episodes selected for Elijah, is the most exemplary moment of Isaac's life in Jewish tradition.[88]

ELIJAH AND HIS CHAIR

The "participation" of the biblical prophet in the first days of life culminates at the circumcision ceremony. He has been directly associated with this rite since the early gaonic period. Thus, according to the eighth-century midrashic work *Pirke de-Rabbi Eliezer* (chapter 29), when Elijah complained to God that "the Israelites have forsaken Your covenant" (1 Kings 19:14), he was "ordered" by God to be present in every circumcision ceremony (here, again, *Berit,* "covenant," is understood as "circumcision"). Thus, a special chair called *kisei Eliyahu* (chair of Elijah) is prepared for the symbolic presence of "The Angel of the Covenant" at the ceremony.[89]

Over time, distinctive local traditions developed regarding the chair of Elijah—its form, size, and ornamentation. In some communities it is difficult to distinguish between this chair and that upon which the sandak sits. In most places, however, the elaborate seat of Elijah remains unoccupied and is centrally positioned in the circumcision room. The *mohel* (circumciser) usually lays the child on the symbolic chair and subsequently hands him to the sandak. Among Ashkenazic Jews, it became common to join the two seats together into a bench divided in the center: on one side (usually the left) sits the sandak, while the other remains empty for Elijah. The Sephardim in Europe, in contrast, generally used two chairs placed next to each other. Noteworthy for their attractive designs are the Italian Elijah chairs, which are enhanced with gilt decorations and carved with elaborate motifs, including three-dimensional lions. A rather small, almost toy-like chair of Elijah was the norm in some communities—chiefly in Islamic lands (Yemen, Kurdistan, Libya)—but it is also known from Europe (small chairs are preserved in the old synagogues of Carpentras and Cavaillon in Provence).[90]

The chair of Elijah represents his symbolic presence in the circumcision cere-monies of all Jewish communities, but it is especially among the Jews of Islamic lands that the virtues of the mystical prophet imbued his chair with magic and miraculous healing and protective powers. Moreover, Elijah's presence was nearly tangible in the ceremony and beyond. Thus, in a number of communities, songs welcoming his arrival into the circumcision room were, significantly, sung in the vernacular by both women and men.[91] Many folk stories "testify" to the miracles performed by Elijah during his visits. Belief in his actual presence may also be indicated by a special ornamental staff prepared by the Jews of Afghanistan and Bukhara for the elderly prophet, who runs from one house to another and obviously needs to rest.[92]

In Islamic lands, the chair of Elijah was festively decorated for the circumci-sion ceremony, entirely changing its otherwise plain appearance (Figure 27). When not in use, the chair was customarily preserved "naked" (without any or-naments or decorations) in the synagogue—inside the Ark of the Torah. Unlike the Ark in most European synagogues, in these regions it was not a piece of fur-

Fig. 27. Dressed Elijah chair; made in Baghdad, 1940s, and in use in an Iraqi synagogue in Ramat Gan, Israel. (© Society for Jewish Art, Hebrew University of Jerusalem; Sc_15, no. 23)

niture but several large niches or an actual room at the end of the synagogue's wall closest to Jerusalem. Within such a niche or room, the Elijah chair (often several of them) was, significantly, placed next to the Torah cases (*tikim*),[93] and this proximity provided the chair with both spiritual sanctity and physical ornaments. Thus, for example, the rimmonim would be taken from the tikim and placed on four nails or posts in the corners of the chair. Similarly, costly silk scarves, which were loosely draped on many tikim, would be removed and put on the chair. These scarves were donations of pious women, who wished in this way to form an indirect contact with the holiest object in the synagogue, commonly handled only by men. The placing of the scarves on the holy chair was another important mediator, now connecting the mother, her offspring, and the Torah. To these scarves and other tex-tiles and cushions that covered the chair, women in some communities added various protective amulets and talismans, such as silver ḥamsas, wolf's-tooth amulets (common in Iraq and Kurdistan), healing plants, and other kinds of magic objects.

Once the chair was fully "dressed," it was ready to fulfill its role. In order to utilize fully the miraculous, protective "presence" of Elijah, the use of the chair was not limited to the time of the circumcision proper. Among the Jews of Iraqi Kurdistan, for example, the chair of Elijah would be brought to the room of the mother shortly after she gave birth, or at the latest the night before the circumcision.[94] As discussed above, that night, which in Kurdistan was known as *lelshashe,* was considered the most dangerous for both child and mother.[95] The presence of the miraculous chair in the room during the eight days before circumcision, and especially on the sleepless lel-shashe, was thought to provide maximum protection.

The chair attracted everyone's attention. In Kurdistan, a visitor would first approach the holy object and kiss it. In Morocco, a cup of water was put under the chair and then given to barren women or sick people. In Tunisia, a barren woman would sit under the chair (especially during the circumcision), in the belief that the prophet would give her a child. In Libya, a cup filled with oil was placed on the chair and later used as ointment for various diseases. Elsewhere in Libya, two plates were put on the chair—one containing clean sand, the other, two eggs. Following the circumcision, the sand plate was used in the burial of the foreskin; the eggs were given to barren women who drank their contents raw.

To return to the Kurdish custom: on the morning of the circumcision day, the highly ornamented chair would be paraded back to the synagogue, where the ceremony was commonly held. Carrying the chair was considered a big merit, and the mitzvah was actually publicly auctioned. During the parade, the men and boys danced and sang around the chair. Once inside the synagogue, the chair was given an honored place on the bimah (known among Jews of Islamic lands as the *teivah*),[96] the platform in the synagogue from which the Torah is read. The congregation then waited for another festive parade to arrive, that of the women bringing the infant to be circumcised. It was believed that Elijah accompanied this group, and, when they entered the synagogue, everybody rose in honor of the prophet. In other communities, for example in Morocco, while the mohel was doing his work, women would seize the opportunity to supplicate the prophet, who was believed to be present in the room, with many requests for good health, livelihood, and male children. A typical supplication, which was originally recited in the Moroccan-Arabic dialect of the local Jews, reads in translation as follows:

O dear Elijah, as you came to visit this house, may you come and visit the houses of all the miserable women. And may you visit the home of my daughter [full name], so that I may be privileged to see her embracing a male child. And please make me fortunate, O Merciful One, to see the circumcision day of this child.[97]

CONCLUSION

In this chapter, we have seen how the grave problems and risks of childbirth in the pre-modern world led to the creation of a system of Jewish folk beliefs and traditions. This system is deeply rooted in Jewish sources, though it is also nourished by local customs and the practices of the surrounding society. Biblical verses, talmudic passages, and other "official" texts were always readily quoted on amulets.

The system of folk beliefs crossed chronological and geographical borders. In fact, in many cases it was stronger than the accepted "high" culture of Jewish law. The fear of Lilith and the use of the protective angels to fight her began many centuries ago and continue almost uninterruptedly to this day. The curious formulas found on amulets, though never officially sanctioned, were practically the same from Germany and Poland to Morocco and Tunisia, and from Holland and Italy to Palestine, Iran, Kurdistan, and Yemen.

In this process, rabbis or ḥakhamim, especially those versed in the secrets of practical Kabbalah, played an important role as mediators between the normative and folk cultures. They were considered to have access to the holy and secretive texts, which were commonly not read or understood by the men, women, and children for whom such amulets were prepared. Although some authorities, most notably Maimonides, fiercely spoke against such customs, the "official" representatives of Jewish law, by and large, collaborated with the needs of their communities. In Islamic lands, for example, the writings on the silver amulets were carried out by the ḥakhamim, who would wash themselves in preparation and observe the same laws of purity required for writing a Torah scroll or other sacred texts. The psychological needs behind the practice of giving amulets were apparently understood as well. This point is nicely illustrated in the following folk story, which emanates from the Kurdish community of Zakho (Iraq), one of the major centers for the creation of amulets before the mass immigration to Israel:

This is a story about a woman from Zakho whose son had a sudden attack of weeping. He could not stop weeping all day and all night, and nothing could calm him down. The woman was at a loss and finally went to consult the sage Shabbethai 'Alwan, of blessed memory. The sage entered his room and after a few minutes came out and gave the worried mother an amulet, saying "Hang this around your son's neck, and he will calm down."

The mother did as he said, and after several hours the child calmed down and fell asleep. When the child grew up and no longer needed the amulet, the mother, out of sheer curiosity, opened it and found a blank piece of paper with nothing written on it. She thought that perhaps the holy letters had flown away or were written in invisible ink. So she went to the sage Shabbethai and asked him about the mystery. He replied, "Is it important to you whether the paper in the amulet is written on or not? It is sufficient that your son's illness disappeared, and thank God for that."[98]

NOTES

1. See F. Lebrun, *La vie conjugale sous l'Ancien Régime* (Paris, 1975), 139ff. Similar figures also appear in the case of 12 parishes in eighteenth-century England; see E. A. Wrigley and R. S. Scofield, *The Population History of England: 1541-1871. A Reconstruction* (Cambridge, Mass., 1981), 249. Regarding the world of Islam, elderly Jewish women from these lands who were interviewed in Jerusalem confirmed this unfortunate situation. An example is this writer's mother, of Zakho in Kurdish Iraq. Prior to the immigration of the family to Israel in 1951, she gave birth to ten children, of whom only four survived.

2. See R. Patai, *On Jewish Folklore* (Detroit, 1983), 337–443 (the chapter "Jewish Birth Customs").

3. For a study of this work, see E. Yassif, *Sippure Ben Sira bi-Ymei ha-Beinayim* (Jerusalem, 1984).

4. For two versions of the legend, see Yassif, *Sippure Ben Sira*, 230–34.

5. See L. Ginzberg, *The Legends of the Jews*, 7 vols. (1st ed., 1909–38; Philadelphia, 1968), 1: 65–66, and G. Scholem, "Lilith," in *Encyclopaedia Judaica*, 16 vols. (Jerusalem, 1972), vol. 11, cols. 245–49 (and see there for the earlier literature).

6. See, e.g., J. G. Frazer, *Folk-Lore in the Old Testament: Studies in Comparative Religion, Legend and Law* (New York, 1923), 1ff.

7. The appellation "First Eve" is found in the Midrash Genesis Rabbah 22:7 (for an English translation, see *Midrash Rabbah—Genesis*, vol. 1, trans. H. Freedman [London, 1983], 187). For the development of the legend in Jewish sources, see Yassif, *Sippure Ben Sira*, 64–67, and Ginzberg, *The Legends of the Jews*, 5: 87–88.

8. See G. Scholem's review of the book by H. A. Winkler, *Salomo und die Karina* (Stuttgart, 1931), in *Kirjath Sepher* 10 (1933–34): 69. See also Yassif, *Sippure Ben Sira*, 67,

and J. Trachtenberg, *Jewish Magic and Superstition: A Study in Folk Religion* (New York, 1939), 101.

9. On *Sefer Raziel,* see Trachtenberg, "Raziel, Sefer," in *Jewish Magic,* s.v. index; T. Schrire, *Hebrew Amulets: Their Decipherment and Interpretation* (London, 1966), 3, 61–63, 110 (some of the information there, however, should be modified); and the entries on the angel and the book by Scholem and J. Dan in *Encyclopaedia Judaica,* vol. 13, cols. 1591–93.

10. On folk medicine in contemporary Jewish society, especially in Israel, see H. Matras, "Jewish Folk Medicine in the 19th and 20th Centuries," in N. Berger, ed., *Jews and Medicine: Religion, Culture, Science* (Tel Aviv, 1995), esp. 123ff, and H. Matras, "Contemporary Amulets for Mother and Child" (Hebrew), *Rimonim* 5 (1997), 15–27. See also M. Reines-Josephy, "The Use of Amulets in Contemporary American Jewish Society," *Proceedings of the Ninth World Congress of Jewish Studies,* Division D, vol. 2 (Jerusalem, 1986), 175–80.

11. *Sefer Raziel ha-Mal'akh* (Amsterdam, 1701), 43a.

12. Cf. Schrire, *Hebrew Amulets,* 97–98. *Anna be-kho'aḥ,* however, was apparently created in Medieval Spain. See *Encyclopaedia Judaica,* vol. 3, cols. 25–26.

13. *Sefer Raziel,* 43b. Cf. Trachtenberg, *Jewish Magic,* facing title page and 139, and Schrire, *Hebrew Amulets,* 118.

14. Schrire, *Hebrew Amulets,* 97. It should be noted that the Priestly Benediction appears on Hebrew amulets regardless of their design and material. It is also common on Ashkenazic paper amulets. See, e.g., a childbirth amulet from Germany in 1834, preserved at the Israel Museum (no. 103/400) and reproduced and described in I. Shachar, *Jewish Tradition in Art: The Feuchtwanger Collection of Judaica,* trans. R. Grafman (Jerusalem, 1981), no. 5: 22–23.

15. P. C. Kirchner, *Jüdisches Ceremoniel, oder Beschreibung derjenigen Gebräuche, welche die Juden . . . in Acht zu nehmen pflegen . . .* (Nuremberg, 1724), plate facing p. 148 (the childbirth ceremonies are discussed on 149–54).

16. See E. Shorter, *A History of Women's Bodies* (Harmondsworth, Engl. 1982), 35ff.

17. Note that the transliteration of the names of the three angels is the one used by Kirchner, *Jüdisches Ceremoniel,* 155.

18. Ibid., 149.

19. On the folk customs that relate magical powers to the Torah scroll in Jewish tradition, see S. Sabar, "Torah and Magic: The Torah Scroll and Its Accessories as Magical Objects in Jewish Culture in Europe and in Muslim Countries" (Hebrew), *Pe'amim: Studies in Oriental Jewry* 85 (2000): 149–79 (on the Torah in childbirth ceremonies, see 153–58).

20. See, e.g., the statement of Maimonides: "All who are ritually unclean, *even women in their menstruating period,* and even a non-Israelite, may hold a scroll of the law and read in it, for the words of the Torah do not contract uncleanliness, provided that the holder's hands are not soiled." See *Mishneh Torah,* "Book of Adoration" 10:8 (ed. and trans. M. Hyamson [Jerusalem, 1965], 139b).

21. See, e.g., D. B. McGilvray, "Sexual Power and Fertility in Sri Lanka," and C. P. MacCor-

mack, "Health, Fertility and Birth in Moyamba District, Sierra Leone," both in C. P. Mac-Cormack, ed., *Ethnography of Fertility and Birth* (London, 1982), 58 and 121, respectively. See also R. I. Coughlin, "Pregnancy and Birth in Vietnam," in D. V. Hart et al., eds., *Southeast Asian Birth Customs* (New Haven, Conn., 1965), 238.

22. For example, the renowned rabbi of Ferrara, Isaac Lampronti (1679–1756), wrote in his talmudic encyclopedia *Paḥad Yitzḥak:* "It is forbidden to bring the Torah scroll *near* a woman who has difficulty in labor—but only to the entrance of her house; perhaps the merit of the Torah will protect her, and not because it is a charm" (vol. 3, pt. 4 [Venice, 1798], 11a; my translation). Similar opinions were expressed by Ashkenazic rabbis, such as the German rabbi Judah Leib ben Enoch Zundel (1645–1705) in his responsa book *Ḥinnukh Beit Yehudah* (Frankfurt am Main, 1708), responsum 71. See also Patai, "Jewish Birth Customs," 379–80, and Sabar, "Torah and Magic," 156–57.

23. For these incidents, see Patai, "Jewish Birth Customs," 380.

24. See E. Brauer, *The Jews of Kurdistan* (Detroit, 1993), 155 (translated from the original Hebrew edition [Jerusalem, 1947]).

25. See Shachar, *Jewish Tradition in Art*, no. 1: 20–21.

26. See Y. H. Yerushalmi, *Haggadah and History* (Philadelphia, 1976), 43–46 and plates 59–62, 66–69.

27. On the artist and his Bible, see the facsimile edition (based on a hand-colored German edition of 1630): *The Bible in Word and Art* (New York, 1988).

28. See Shachar, *Jewish Tradition in Art*, nos. 2–3: 20–21.

29. For the costume of eighteenth-century German Jews, see A. Rubens, *A History of Jewish Costume* (London, 1973), 124–25.

30. See U. Schubert, *Jüdische Buchkunst*, vol. 2 (Graz, 1992), 83ff.

31. See I. Shachar, *The Jewish Year* (Leiden, 1975), 3–4 and plate I.

32. See C. Weissler, *Voices of the Matriarchs: Listening to the Prayers of Early Jewish Women* (Boston, 1998), s.v. index *"Hadlakat Haner"*).

33. On this craft and for a large selection of Jewish papercuts from eastern Europe, see G. Frankel, *The Art of the Jewish Paper-cut* (Tel Aviv, 1996), and J. Shadur and Y. Shadur, *Jewish Papercuts: History and Guide* (Berkeley, Calif., 1994).

34. The Book of Psalms has generally been used in Jewish magic for such purposes. An early work that lists the potential "uses" of various sections of the Psalms is the kabbalastic work *Shimmush Tehillim* (The [Magical] Use of Psalms), which was first printed in Sabbioneta, Italy, in 1552. See Trachtenberg, *Jewish Magic*, 109.

35. For an analysis of this phenomenon and its historical development, see R. I. Cohen, "The Rabbi as Icon," in *Jewish Icons: Art and Society in Modern Europe* (Berkeley, Calif., 1998), 114–53.

36. For the sociocultural and urban background of the old city of Jerusalem in this formative period, see Y. Ben-Arieh, *Jerusalem in the 19th Century: The Old City* (Jerusalem and New York, 1984).

37. See *Omanut ve-U'manut be-Eretz Yisrael ba-Me'ah ha-19,* exhibition catalog, The Israel Museum (Jerusalem, 1979); S. Sabar, "On the Difference in Attitudes Toward Visual Arts between Sephardim and Ashkenazim in Eretz Israel in the Late Ottoman Period" (Hebrew), *Pe'amim* 56 (1993): 75–105.

38. For the image of the Dome of the Rock in European art, see, e.g., C. H. Krinsky, "Representations of the Temple of Jerusalem before 1500," *Journal of the Warburg and Courtauld Institutes* 33 (1970): 1–19. For this representation in Jewish art, see S. Sabar, *Mazal Tov: Illuminated Jewish Marriage Contracts from the Israel Museum* (Jerusalem, 1993), 43ff, and S. Sabar, "Messianic Aspirations and Renaissance Urban Ideals: The Image of Jerusalem in the Venice Haggadah, 1609," *Jewish Art* 23/24 (1998): 294–312.

39. On Mizrachi and his artistic career, see S. Sabar, "The Binding of Isaac in the Work of Moshe Shah Mizrachi: A Jewish Folk Artist from Persia in Early 20th Century Jerusalem," in Amnon Netzer, ed., *Pādyāvand* ("Judeo-Iranian and Jewish Studies Series") (Costa Mesa, Calif., in press).

40. See Y. K. Stillman, "The Middle Eastern Amulet as Folk Art," in I. Ben-Ami and J. Dan, eds., *Studies in Aggadah and Jewish Folklore* (Jerusalem, 1983), 95–101.

41. For these and other images of Jewish children and women wearing amulets, see O. Shwartz-Be'eri, ed., *The Jews of Kurdistan: Daily Life, Customs, Arts and Crafts,* exhibition catalog, The Israel Museum (Jerusalem, 2000), 179–81.

42. A wide selection of such amuletic jewelry is described and reproduced in Shachar, *Jewish Tradition in Art,* nos. 804–1092, pp. 252–317; and C. Benjamin, *The Stieglitz Collection: Masterpieces of Jewish Art* (Jerusalem, 1987), nos. 258, 267–69, 275–78, pp. 388ff. The examples reproduced in Schrire, *Hebrew Amulets,* are also mostly from the lands of Islam.

43. The length of some of these scrolls can be over a meter. For examples, see Shachar, *Jewish Tradition in Art,* nos. 776–79: 241–45 (silver cases are reproduced on pp. 253, 255, 257). For parallel Islamic examples, see R. Hasson, *Early Islamic Jewellery* (Jerusalem, 1987), 40–42, and R. Hasson, *Later Islamic Jewellery* (Jerusalem, 1987), 90–91.

44. See Schrire, *Hebrew Amulets,* 122.

45. See A. Müller-Lancet, ed., *La vie Juive au Maroc,* exhibition catalog, the Israel Museum (trans. from the 1973 Hebrew edition; Jerusalem, 1986), fig. 160, p. 97.

46. See Schrire, *Hebrew Amulets,* 96, and plates 1–4, 8. Additional examples are reproduced in Shwartz-Be'eri, *Jews of Kurdistan,* 170ff.

47. On these tablets, see E. Juhasz, "The Amuletic Menorah: The Menorah and Psalm 67," in Y. Israeli, ed., *In the Light of the Menorah: Story of a Symbol* (Hebrew original, 1998; English edition, Jerusalem, 1999), 147–51.

48. For the names of the angels found on the amulets and their function, see Schrire, *Hebrew Amulets,* 104–11.

49. See J. Herber, "The hand of Fatima" (French), *Hespéris* 7 (1927): 209–19; E. A. Westermarck, *Pagan Survivals in Mohammedan Civilisation,* 2d ed. (Amsterdam, 1973), chap. 2 (esp. 27–28); and the entries *"Ayn"* and *"Khamsa"* in *The Encyclopaedia of Islam,* new ed., 10 vols. (Leiden, 1960–2000), 1: 786, 4: 1009.

50. Some examples can be found in E. Juhasz, ed., *Sephardi Jews in the Ottoman Empire*, exhibition catalog, The Israel Museum (Jerusalem, 1990), 88, 89, 99, 107, and col. pl. 17 (Torah Ark curtains); B. Yaniv, "The Mystery of the Flat Torah Finials from East Persia," *Pādyāvand* 1 (1966): 70–71 and figs. 21–22; Sabar, "Torah and Magic," 171–72 and figs. 12–13 (*rimmonim* and a Torah pointer).

51. See, e.g., Shachar, *Jewish Tradition in Art*, nos. 934, 935, 959–62, 965–66.

52. Evidently the figure of Karina in Arabic demonology is closely related to Lilith. See Winkler, *Salomo und die Karina* (and see Scholem's review of the book in *Kirjath Sepher* 10 (1933–34): 68–73).

53. For parallel figurative influences in the realm of magic, see R. Shani, "A Judeo-Persian Talismanic Textile," in S. Shaked and A. Netzer, eds., *Irano-Judaica: Studies Relating to Jewish Contacts with Persian Culture Throughout the Ages*, vol. 4 (Jerusalem, 1999), 251–73.

54. Kirchner, *Jüdisches Ceremoniel*; J. C. Bodenschatz, *Kirchliche Verfassung der heutingen Juden, sonderlich derer in Deutschland* (Erlang, 1748–49), pt. IV, fig. 5.

55. For the Ashkenazic *Wachnacht*, see, e.g., Trachtenberg, *Jewish Magic*, 170–71, and H. Pollack, *Jewish Folkways in Germanic Lands (1648-1806)* (Cambridge, Mass., 1971), 19-22. In other communities the night was given various names. For example, in Italy it was called *veglia;* for the ceremonies of the Italian Jews, see E. Horowitz, "The Eve of the Circumcision: A Chapter in the History of Jewish Nightlife," *Journal of Social History* 23 (1989): 45–69. For some customs in Islamic lands on this night, see the subsection on Elijah later in this chapter.

56. For this custom, see Y. D. Weisberg, *Otzar ha-Berit: Dinei u-Minhagei Millah*, 2 vols. (Jerusalem, 1991), 2: 211–12.

57. See J. G. Frazer, "Taboo and the Perils of the Soul," in *The Golden Bough: A Study in Magic and Religion* (New York, 1951), 232–36, and T. H. Gaster, *The Holy and the Profane: Evolution of Jewish Folkways*, 2d ed. (New York, 1980), 10–11.

58. For a description of this custom, see Brauer, *Jews of Kurdistan*, 173–74 (the Hebrew inscription on the *seipa* on p. 174 is copied with mistakes), and fig. facing p. 203. Additional examples are reproduced in Shwartz-Be'eri, *Jews of Kurdistan*, 173.

59. For an example from Marrakech (95 cm. long), see the sword reproduced in Müller-Lancet, *La vie Juive au Maroc*, 97.

60. See H. Goldberg, "The Zohar in Southern Morocco: A Study in the Ethnography of Texts," *History of Religions* 29 (1989–1990): 233–58.

61. Note that the ceremony is conducted with some variations in the different towns in Morocco. See R. J. Bensimon, *Yahadut Maroko: Havai u-Masoret be-Maḥzor ha-Ḥayyim* (Lod, 1994), 55–58.

62. See Kirchner, *Jüdisches Ceremoniel*, 154, and Bodenschatz, *Kirchliche Verfassung*, pt. IV, p. 57.

63. Reproduced in E. Muchawsky-Schnapper, *Les Juifs d'Alsace: Village, Tradition, Emancipation*, exhibition catalog (bilingual), The Israel Museum (Jerusalem, 1991), no. 59.

64. Reported by J. Dahlberg, "Volkskunde der Hessen-Kasseler Juden," in R. Hallo et al.,

eds., *Geschichte der jüdischen Gemeinde Kassel* (Kassel, 1931), 1: 157 (quoted by Patai, "Jewish Birth Customs," 412).

65. See E. Yassif, *The Hebrew Folktale: History, Genre, Meaning* (trans. of the Hebrew edition of Jerusalem, 1994; Bloomington, Ind., 1999), 106ff, 321ff, 406–7; on Israeli legends of saints, see ibid., 407–29.

66. See A. Shinan, "Al demuto shel David ha-melekh be-sifrut Ḥazal," in Y. Zakovitch, ed., *David me-ro'eh le-mashiah* (Jerusalem, 1995), 181–99.

67. For these designs, see Schrire, *Hebrew Amulets,* 59–68. It should be emphasized that the usage of the Magen David in Hebrew amulets has no relation to national or Zionist sentiments and is based on old magic-astrological signs. See G. Scholem, "Magen David," *Encyclopaedia Judaica,* vol. 11, cols. 687–97, and G. S. Oegema, *The History of the Shield of David: The Birth of a Symbol* (Frankfurt am Main, 1996), esp. 51–64.

68. See B. Heller, "Yusuf b. Ya'kub," *The Encyclopaedia of Islam* (Leyden, 1934), 4: 1178–79. For the various episodes of the story as they appear in Islamic miniature painting, see R. Milstein et al., *Stories of the Prophets: Illustrated Manuscripts of Qiṣaṣ al-Anbiyā'* (Costa Mesa, Calif., 1999), 124–30.

69. In the *Sarajevo Haggadah,* the Joseph miniatures occupy folios 11v to 20r—a total of 19 miniatures; for their reproductions and brief descriptions, see the facsimile edition: *The Sarajevo Haggadah,* intro. E. Werber (Belgrade, 1985), 28–30. In the *Golden Haggadah,* the Joseph story is on folios 5r to 8v (13 miniatures with 18 scenes); see B. Narkiss, *The Golden Haggadah* (London, 1997), 28–35.

70. For descriptions of three Judeo-Persian *Yusuf and Zulaykha* manuscripts (preserved at the Jewish National and University Library, Jerusalem, and the Library of the Jewish Theological Seminary, New York), see V. Basch Moreen, *Miniature Paintings in Judaeo-Persian Manuscripts* (Cincinnati, 1985), 21–29, and A. Taylor, *Book Arts of Isfahan* (Malibu, Calif., 1995), 34, 36–37.

71. See A. Netzer, "The History of the Forced Converts of Mashed According to Ya'akov Daylamgan" (Hebrew), *Pe'amim* 42 (1990): 151.

72. Some printed sources of Sephardic rabbis and ḥakhamim of Islamic countries who quote this and other curious traditions connecting Joseph with the magical number five include Rabbi Ḥayyim Joseph David Azulai, *Petaḥ einayim* (Jerusalem, 1959 [first ed.: Livorno, 1790]), 18b, and Rabbi Abraham Khalfon, *Ḥayyei Avraham: Sefer ha-Te'amim ve-ha-Minhagim lefi Minhagei ha-Sefaradim u-Vnei Edot ha-Mizraḥ* (Jerusalem, 1965 [first ed.: Livorno, 1826]), 198–99. A contemporary example is Rabbi Isaac Peḥa, *Sefer Olei Ayyin* (Jerusalem, 1990), 206–10.

73. See, e.g., Schrire, *Hebrew Amulets,* plates 2, 5, 12, 14, 16.

74. See Patai, "Jewish Birth Customs," 348–49.

75. Ibid., 348.

76. For these practices, see Bensimon, *Yahadut Maroko,* 451, and C. Z. Hirschberg, "The Fish in the Mosaic of the Synagogue at Naro and in the Jewish Folklore of Modern Tunisia

and Tripolitania" (Hebrew) *Eretz Israel* 8 (Jerusalem, 1967): 305–11 and plates 43–44 (English summary on pp. 78*–79*).

77. See, e.g., the selection of articles in *Yeda-ʿAm (Journal of the Israel Folklore Society)* 7, no. 25 (1961), which was dedicated to "Elijah the Prophet in Folklore, Traditions and Folk-Life" (Hebrew).

78. For the history and development of this custom, see Y. Avida, *Koso Shel Eliyahu ha-Navi: Naftulei Minhag be-Hitrakmuto* (Jerusalem, 1958).

79. This haggadah is preserved at the Library of Congress, Washington, D.C. ("The Washington Haggadah"); see B. Narkiss, *Hebrew Illuminated Manuscripts* (Jerusalem, 1974), plate 50. See also J. Gutmann, "The Messiah at the Seder: A 15th-century Motif in Jewish Art," in S. Yeivin, ed., *Studies in Jewish History Presented to Raphael Mahler* (Tel Aviv, 1974), 29–38. The image of Elijah heralding the Messiah in the circumcision tablet (see Figure 26) is derived from the printed Venice Haggadah of 1609; see S. Sabar, "Messianic Aspirations and Renaissance Urban Ideals: The Image of Jerusalem in the Venice Haggadah, 1609," *Jewish Art* 23/24 (1998): 294–312.

80. See N. Rubin, *Reshit ha-Ḥayyim: Tiksei Leida, Millah u-Fidyon ha-Ben bi-Mekorot Ḥazal* (Tel Aviv, 1995), 95–96.

81. See A. Wiener, *The Prophet Elijah in the Development of Judaism* (London, 1978), 58–59 (and 136–40 on "Elijah in Jewish Folklore").

82. Yassif, *Sippure Ben Sira*, 68. See also Scholem, "Lilith," in *Encyclopaedia Judaica*, vol. 11, col. 248.

83. For some Ashkenazic examples, see Shachar, *Jewish Tradition in Art*, no. 3: 21, and Matras, "Jewish Folk Medicine," 121. Printed amulets with the Elijah-Lilith legend from Islamic lands are especially known from North Africa (Morocco and Tunisia). For published examples, see ibid., 130 (from Djerba); and Müller-Lancet, ed., *La vie Juive au Maroc*, 97, no. 160 (from Casablanca).

84. Known as *Lilt Eliyahu Nabi* in the Moroccan-Arabic dialect of the Jews. See Bensimon, *Yahadut Maroko*, 81ff.

85. See Patai, "Jewish Birth Customs," 400–402, and Gaster, *The Holy and the Profane*, 11–12.

86. Abraham Moses Luncz, "The Religious and Folk Customs of Our Brethren in the Holy Land," in Lunez, ed., *Yerushalayim (Jerusalem: Yearbook for the Diffusion of an Accurate Knowledge of Ancient and Modern Palestine)*, vol. 1 (Vienna, 1882), 3 (my translation); reprinted in *Yeda-ʿAm* 13, nos. 33–34 (1968); 4 (English summary, p. I).

87. See *Kehillat ha-Kodesh: Creating the Sacred Community*, exhibition catalog, The Library of the Jewish Theological Seminary of America (New York, 1997), no. 33, p. 43.

88. For example, the Akedah is depicted in the carved wooden handle of a circumcision knife from eighteenth-century Italy, preserved at the Israel Museum; see Benjamin, *The Stieglitz Collection*, no. 206, pp. 310–11. Note that the combination of the *Akedah* with the Ascension of Elijah appear on other objects related to the circumcision ceremony. An exam-

ple is the title page of a circumcision book from Vienna, 1728, preserved at the Jewish Museum, Prague; see D. Altshuler, ed., *The Precious Legacy: Judaic Treasures from the Czechoslovak State Collections* (New York, 1983), fig. 193, p. 197.

89. See R. Jacoby, "The Small Elijah Chair," *Jewish Art* 18 (1992): 70–77, and R. Jacoby, "The Relation Between Elijah's Chair and the Sandak's (Godfather) Chair" (Hebrew), *Rimonim* 5 (1997): 43–53.

90. See Jacoby, "The Small Elijah Chair" and "Elijah's Chair and the Sandak's." The small Elijah chair apparently reflects the old Land of Israel tradition.

91. Some songs in honor of Elijah that have been published are from Morocco and Libya. For Morocco, see Bensimon, *Yahadut Maroko,* 85; for Libya, see F. Sou'aretz, "*Yeled youlad lanu,*" in F. Sou'aretz et al., eds., *Yahadut Luv* (Tel Aviv, 1960), 388 (reprinted [Hebrew] in *Yeda-'Am* 7, no. 25 [1961]: 62–63). A few exemplary lines from the Libyan song (my translation) are: "Here comes to us Elijah the Prophet! / Here comes to us the splendor and the circumcision / Cheer up for Elijah . . . Let us sing / And raise our voice / In honor of Elijah / Who sits here on the chair." And, from the Moroccan: "Who is the one who enters through the doorway of our house? / If I am not mistaken, it is our Master Elijah who comes to us / How happy I am Oh mother!"

92. Most of the Elijah staffs that survived are from the Jewish community of Herat in Afghanistan. See Z. Hanegbi and B. Yaniv, *Afghanistan: The Synagogue and the Jewish Home* (Jerusalem, 1991), 34–35, and items 57–59, 156–58. The Afghani staff has healing powers as well; see Z. Kurt, "The Staff of Elijah the Prophet" (Hebrew), *Yeda-'Am* 7, no. 25 (1961): 64 (English summary, p. v). On a recent visit to the Jewish communities in Bukhara, I saw a few staffs of the same nature, used at the circumcision ceremony. However, after many years of Soviet rule, the Bukharan Jews I met did not know about the association of the staff with Elijah.

93. See Shwartz-Be'eri, ed., *Jews of Kurdistan,* 239, and Jacoby, "The Small Elijah Chair," 76, fig. 8.

94. Brauer, *Jews of Kurdistan,* 164, and M. Yona, *Ha-Ovedim be-Eretz Ashur: Yehudei Kurdistan ve-Zakha* (Jerusalem, 1989), 64, report that the chair was brought on the night before circumcision. However, in interviews with mothers from Zakho, they told me they vividly remember the chair being brought to their room several hours after the baby was born (and thus the chair served to protect the baby throughout the seven days before circumcision).

95. For the ceremonies connected with the Kurdish *lel-shashe,* see Brauer, *Jews of Kurdistan,* 163–66 (the transliteration of the name in the book should be corrected). The etymology of the name is not clear, and the hypothesis that it is derived from the number six (*shesh*) is uncertain. Thus, though the Kurdish Jews of Sena (Iran) did indeed typically celebrate this ceremony on the sixth night, it is more plausible to associate it with the Kurdish spirit *sheshe,* "a female demon . . . who lays traps for the children" (Brauer, *Jews of Kurdistan,* 163, and see A. J. Maclean, *A Dictionary of the Dialects of Vernacular Syrian* [Oxford, 1901], 313: "*Shasha*—a jinn or malignant sprite, said to haunt mothers and infants"). Note that the

lel-shashe, ceremonies are also known from the Muslim Kurds and Iraqi (Baghdadi) Jews in both Iraq and India.

96. See Brauer, *Jews of Kurdistan,* 164–66; Yona, *Ha-Ovedim be-Eretz Ashur,* 64.

97. See Bensimon, *Yahadut Maroko,* 98 (my translation).

98. Translated by Yona Sabar and quoted in his book *The Folk Literature of the Kurdistani Jews: An Anthology* (New Haven, Conn., 1982), 189–90.

SELECTED BIBLIOGRAPHY

Bialer, Yehuda L., and Estelle Fink. *Jewish Life in Art and Tradition,* 2d ed. Jerusalem, 1980.

Brauer, Erich. *The Jews of Kurdistan.* Comp. and ed. R. Patai. Detroit, 1993.

Budge, E. A. Wallis. *Amulets and Superstitions.* London, 1930; New York, 1978.

Dundes, Alan. *Interpreting Folklore.* Bloomington, Ind., 1980.

Gaster, Theodor Herzl. *The Holy and the Profane: Evolution of Jewish Folkways,* 2d ed. New York, 1980.

Gennep, Arnold van. *The Rites of Passage.* Paris, 1909; Chicago, 1960.

Gutmann, Joseph. *The Jewish Life Cycle.* Leiden, 1984.

Horowitz, Elliott. "The Eve of the Circumcision: A Chapter in the History of Jewish Nightlife." *Journal of Social History* 23 (1989): 45–69.

Jacoby, Ruth. "The Small Elijah Chair." *Jewish Art* 18 (1992): 70–77.

Matras, Hagit. "Jewish Folk Medicine in the 19th and 20th Centuries." In N. Berger, ed., *Jews and Medicine: Religion, Culture, Science.* Tel Aviv, 1995.

Patai, Raphael. "Jewish Birth Customs." In *On Jewish Folklore.* Detroit, 1983.

Pollack, Herman. *Jewish Folkways in Germanic Lands (1648-1806). Studies in Aspects of Daily Life.* Cambridge, Mass., 1971.

Sabar, Shalom. "The Judaization of the Khamsa." In N. Behrouzi, ed. *The Hand of Fortune: Khamsas from the Gross Family Collection and the Eretz Israel Museum Collection.* Tel Aviv, 2002 (in Hebrew and English).

Scholem, Gershom. "Lilith." In *Encyclopaedia Judaica,* vol. 11. Jerusalem, 1972.

Schrire, T[heodore]. *Hebrew Amulets: Their Decipherment and Interpretation.* London, 1966.

Shachar, Isaiah. *Jewish Tradition in Art. The Feuchtwanger Collection of Judaica.* Trans. R. Grafman. Jerusalem, 1981.

Shorter, Edward. *A History of Women's Bodies.* Harmondsworth, Engl., 1982.

Stillman, Yedida K. "The Middle Eastern Amulet as Folk Art." In I. Ben-Ami and J. Dan, eds., *Studies in Aggadah and Jewish Folklore.* Jerusalem, 1983.

Trachtenberg, Joshua. *Jewish Magic and Superstition: A Study in Folk Religion.* New York, 1939.

Turner, Victor W. *The Ritual Process: Structure and Anti-Structure.* Chicago, 1969.

Ungerleider-Mayerson, Joy. *Jewish Folk Art from Biblical Days to Modern Times*. New York, 1986.

Yassif, Eli. *The Hebrew Folktale: History, Genre, Meaning*. Trans. J. S. Teitelbaum. Bloomington, Ind., 1999.

Yoder, Don. "Folk Medicine." In R. M. Dorson, ed., *Folklore and Folklife*. Chicago, 1972.

Part Three

MODERN

ENCOUNTERS

INTRODUCTION TO PART THREE:
MODERN ENCOUNTERS

DAVID BIALE

"The Jews should be denied everything as a nation, but granted everything as individuals. They must be citizens." So declared Count Stanislas of Clermont-Tonnerre in 1789 as the French National Assembly debated the emancipation of the Jews. It was this clarion call that set the political stage on which modern Jewish cultures acted out their many roles. Jewish identity from antiquity through the Middle Ages was quintessentially collective: to be a Jew meant to belong to the community (*ethnos* in Greek, *corporatio* in medieval Latin) called Jewish, a community regarded as "foreign" both religiously and ethnically. In the Greco-Roman world, a Jew might adopt Hellenistic culture, but he or she could never shake off Jewish ethnic identity. In the Middle Ages, the only escape lay in conversion—joining, that is, another religious community. Only modernity promised the possibility of an individual identity within a state of equal citizens.

But this was a promise not always kept. The historian Jacob Katz at one time argued that modernity can be defined as the emergence of a "neutral" society, a public sphere in which one's religious or ethnic identity might be left at the door. But Katz himself came to recognize that, even after the separation of church and state in the French Revolution, religion continued to play a central role in the lives of modern nations. Even if many Jews, for perhaps the first time in their history, shed religion in favor of a purely secular identity, the societies in which they lived often did not do so at the same rapid pace: Christianity and Islam continued to be dominant forces in the way modern nations treated their Jewish minorities. And, even more ominously, modern nationalism often fostered ethnic exclusivism in which those of foreign origin could not gain membership in the *Volk*. Radical nationalism secularized religious hostility to Jews, transforming it alchemically into the new racial antisemitism. Jewish culture in the modern period had to meet these two challenges: the promise of individual assimilation, on the one hand, and the threat of the new antisemitism, on the other.

What, we may ask, is modern about modern Jewish culture? Is it secularism? Perhaps so, but then surely the "secular" Hebrew poetry of medieval Spain would have to be defined as modern. Or is it, rather, the embrace by Jews of non-

Jewish cultures as their primary sources of identity? Again, this is surely the case, but our earlier forays into biblical, Hellenistic, and medieval Jewish cultures suggest that Jews in earlier times frequently immersed themselves in cultures not their own. Is it, finally, that Jews felt a new sense of belonging to the countries in which they lived? Once again, this is undoubtedly true, whether in Weimar Germany, republican France, postwar America, or Israel, but wasn't it also the case for the Jews of Babylonia and Spain?

What may be the most defining characteristic of modern Jewish culture is precisely the question of *how* to define it. During all periods and in all places before the modern, Jewish culture was, almost by definition, the culture produced by the Jews. Not so in modernity. Just because many Jews participated in creating modern physics does not make that science "Jewish." And, just because a disproportionately high number of Jews work in Hollywood does not make all movies part of Jewish culture. It is only in the modern period that this very question arises, because only in modernity has it been possible for Jews to contribute to the majority cultures in which they live without their Jewish identities playing an explicit role in doing so. To be sure, there may well be something in modern Jewish culture that has produced so many Jewish physicists or filmmakers, but the sum total of their work does not necessarily belong to the culture that produced them. So, such an expansive definition of modern Jewish culture seems too broad, but, at the very least, such a definition—even if we reject it—is only possible in the modern period.

Let us try, instead, a much more limited definition: Jewish culture on all levels—literary, religious, and popular—is culture grounded in Jewish sources. But this definition begs the question of what a Jewish source really is. Surely, a religious definition of Jewish sources would be far too limiting, because it is one of the premises of this history that Jewish culture is broader than just religion. If this were true for periods before modernity, how much more so for an age when religion is only one force competing among many. Indeed, one part of a definition of modern Jewish culture is that it has unmoored itself from the canonical texts of the Bible, Talmud, and medieval legal, philosophical, and mystical traditions. Yet this "unmooring" or, in some cases, forcible divorce from the canonical tradition was often accomplished in full consciousness of that tradition. Richard I. Cohen, for instance, shows how, in Western and Central Europe, the different translations and editions of the Bible played central roles in defining modern Jewish identities. At times, these editions reflected radically modern sensibilities, quite alien to premodern mentalities, but they used the traditional text as their vehicle. At other times, modern Jewish identities required the inversion of the tradition, turning heretics into heroes. In my chapter on East European Jewish culture, I show how some East European writers and artists turned to the figure of Jesus as a symbol for expressing the modern Jewish experience. But those in Eastern Europe—and elsewhere—who came to be called "orthodox" often unwittingly defended tradition against such heresies by using very modern arguments and methods. Finally, in describing how Jews created a new national, Zionist culture in the Land of Israel, Ariel Hirschfeld charts a two-fold movement: the return to the geographic place of the Bible in order to create a new nation often involved the conscious rejection of traditional Jewish texts, but the simultaneous revival of the Hebrew language as a secular language required drawing from those religious sources themselves.

Perhaps, then, these three examples bring us closer to a usable definition: Jewish culture in the modern age is that which expresses the modern Jewish experience, frequently drawing the raw materials for such expressions from the historical tradition, either directly or by inversion. These expressions were born of confrontations with the new world in which Jews found themselves. Thus, Stephen J. Whitfield describes how American Jewish culture involved repeated translations of the Yiddish culture that Jews brought with them from Eastern Europe into an American idiom. Yet the American case suggests that the world in which Jews found themselves was also a world they made: Jews shaped American culture in the twentieth century as much as it shaped them. Similarly, in Europe, both Western and Eastern, the migration of Jews to the cities transformed both the Jews and their urban cultures.

There is, however, another side to modern Jewish cultures that is often ignored when we view the subject primarily through the lens of Western and Central Europe or North America. The process of emancipation and modernization was extraordinarily uneven throughout the Jewish world. If the French and American revolutions conferred equal citizenship on their Jews, the same was not the case elsewhere. The Jews of Germany, Austria-Hungary, and Italy had to wait until the second half of the nineteenth century when emancipation came as the belated fruit of national unification. For the Jews of Eastern Europe, it required a cauldron of war and revolution, which led to the overthrow of the Russian czar and the creation of the new state of Poland, to bring equal citizenship. And, in the Muslim world, the Jews remained second-class citizens: the Ottoman *millet* system persisted, except where European imperialism or the fall of the Ottoman Empire brought it to an end. For each of these communities, the differing pace of political emancipation was reflected in different patterns of cultural change. Thus, we can begin to speak of national Jewish cultures in a more precise sense than in the Middle Ages: where once, for example, Ashkenazic culture spanned political borders, now it devolved into the different cultures of the

German Jews, Polish Jews, Hungarian Jews, and so forth. The broad chapter on Western and Central Europe by Cohen, and on Eastern Europe by me, are each filled with cultural varieties corresponding to the new, modern nation-states.

No picture of modern Jewish culture can be complete without examining those communities, once the majority of the world Jewish population but now a much reduced minority, who lived in the Ottoman Empire, North Africa, Yemen, Iraq, and Iran. Many of the Jews of the Ottoman Empire were Sephardic speakers of Ladino, and Aron Rodrigue devotes his chapter to an investigation of the rise and fall of Ladino culture as these Jews confronted modernity, especially as it was imported from France. Lucette Valensi examines Jewish cultures in North Africa, focusing especially on Tunisia and Morocco, where the communities consisted of Jews from Sephardic, Italian, and Berber backgrounds and where modern ideas brought in primarily by the French confronted traditional Jewish cultures that shared much with their Muslim neighbors. Yosef Tobi ranges widely—from Yemen to Iraq, Iran, Afghanistan, and Central Asia—over Middle Eastern Jewish cultures, most of which, though not of Sephardic origin, adopted Sephardic liturgy and rituals from the mystical community of Safed. Thus, the descendants of the Babylonian Jewish community, whose Talmud and liturgy had shaped so much of the Jewish world to the West, now became, in a sense, "Sephardic." Although these Jewish communities of the Middle East remained largely traditional well into the twentieth century, they were not immune from modern influences, especially in urban settings such as Baghdad, or in Soviet Bukhara.

The twentieth century witnessed the disappearance of most of these North African Middle Eastern communities, partly as a result of the rise of Zionism and the violent Arab reaction against it. Although substantial numbers of these Jews, especially those from North Africa, emigrated to France and elsewhere, the largest concentration came to the new State of Israel, where, until the recent immigration of Russian Jews, they and their descendants formed over half of the population. "Mainstream" Zionist culture, as Hirschfeld describes it, was largely an Ashkenazic creation, but the new state was much more culturally diverse than its founders were willing to admit, and the confrontation with this unexpected reality became a major challenge to the very concept of a monolithic mainstream. The folk culture of Israel, the subject of Eli Yassif's chapter, reflects the influence of these North African and Middle Eastern Jews as well as other, more recent immigrants. Yet it would be a mistake to divide the culture of Israel between the "high" or "elite" culture of Ashkenazim and the "popular" or "folk" culture of the Mizraḥim and Sephardim. As Yassif shows, all of Israeli culture exhibits elements of the folkloric.

The State of Israel has absorbed a number of Jewish communities that have long been considered among the most exotic, such as those of India and Ethiopia. Hagar Salamon takes up the culture of the latter, a group whose origins are shrouded in mystery and whose very identity challenges the definition of who is a Jew. In Ethiopia, the way these Jews understood themselves was bound up in their dense cultural interactions with their Christian neighbors, a pattern that can be found as well in better-known Jewish cultures throughout the ages. When they came as immigrants to Israel, the Ethiopian Jews continued to challenge traditional Jewish identities, adding yet more complexity to the culture of modern Israel.

The rise of a truly indigenous popular Israeli culture, partly fashioned by Zionist myths but partly fashioned against them, represents an entirely new stage in the history of Jewish culture. Israeli Jews have perhaps more "agency" in fashioning their culture, in all its registers, than in any other place in the modern world. But no culture in a global world can be entirely insulated. Moreover, despite the hostility between Israel and its Arab neighbors, Middle Eastern Arab culture has left its mark on Israeli Hebrew, cuisine, and other, less tangible realms of its culture. In perhaps the most perplexing challenge, what does it mean for an Israeli Jewish culture that a Palestinian writer like Anton Shamas writes in the "Jewish" language of Hebrew? By becoming the culture of the majority, Israel faces the reversal of the Diaspora Jewish dilemma: where does the identity of the majority culture end and that of the minority begin?

In Israel, the modern and traditional mix and interact in surprising ways. Israel is at once a modern culture and the heir of the traditional cultures of Eastern Europe, North Africa, and the Middle East. The example of Israel demonstrates in a vivid way that Jewish culture can never break entirely free from its historical moorings, just as the representatives of "tradition" are often, themselves, scarcely immune from the modern. And, far from solving the problems of Jewish identity and "belonging," the State of Israel, like its contemporary Diaspora counterparts—and, most especially, its counterpart in North America—has given them a multiplicity of new expressions.

Interior of the synagogue in Oranienburgstrasse, Berlin, 1866.
(Photo: Leo Baeck Institute, New York)

ONE

URBAN VISIBILITY AND BIBLICAL VISIONS:

Jewish Culture in Western and Central Europe in the Modern Age

RICHARD I. COHEN

Could Moses Mendelssohn (1729–86), the Enlightenment Jewish philosopher and originator of the *Bi'ur* (a translation of the Bible into German in Hebrew characters), have seen what a Galician-born Jewish artist used for the frontispiece of an illustrated Bible at the beginning of the twentieth century, he would certainly have been shocked and uncomfortable. But whether Ephraim Moses Lilien (1874–1925) was out to stun his audience or was just deeply engrossed in the *art nouveau* style is at present of little significance. However, by placing the renowned thinker alongside the less-known, erstwhile Zionist artist, we get a fuller view of the cultural transformation of West and Central European Jewry during a century and a half. Jewish sensibilities and concerns were radically transposed as the engagement with a panoply of cultural orientations superseded earlier pinnacles of Jewish integration, such as Muslim Spain. Even the Bible, the Old Testament, the touchstone of Judaism, would be refracted and refashioned in a multitude of expressions, showing the shifting boundaries of Jewish life and the Jews' profound acceptance of the surrounding environment. The tightrope Mendelssohn walked between traditional Judaism and European culture was long forgotten or discarded when Lilien brazenly incorporated into the frontispiece of his Bible (1908,[1] 1923) two androgynous figures holding an extended Torah scroll that covers their genitalia. In Lilien's day, the tightrope stretched between European culture and a Jewish nationalist agenda.

Juxtaposing these texts highlights other contrasts in the modern Jewish experience in Western and Central Europe. Whereas Mendelssohn continued an internal tradition of commentary and exegesis in written form, Lilien offered a visual interpretation, much less common or conscious of tradition. The former claimed the original text through intricate discourse, the latter playfully experimented with it. The written text was directed to Jews, to widen their horizons and concerns; the visual one was an ecumenical effort (which originated among German Lutherans), to engage both non-Jews and Jews. Whereas Mendelssohn's Bible demanded distinctness, Lilien's celebrated the nonsectarian, but constantly alluded to the exclusive. Combined, the texts merge rationalism, visibility, universalism, uniqueness, traditional scholarship, and modern skepticism, as well as encounters with the "other," contemporaneously and historically. They are contrasting expressions of the ways Jews have tried in the modern period to integrate their culture into a larger category of civilization, but both reveal inner tensions within those paths. By studying the issues emanating from the oeuvres of Mendelssohn and Lilien, we will chart some of the roads that led from one to the other. Although today neither Mendelssohn nor Lilien are cited as the pioneers of new horizons, of modernism, in the way Marx, Freud, or Kafka are perceived, they and their works frame the confrontation with modernity that Jews of different religious, cultural, and social backgrounds faced.

Mendelssohn's age saw the political and social barriers between Jews and non-Jews challenged by voices within European society and governments, though not overcome. Joseph II (r. 1780–90), the Habsburg emperor, was the first to make a serious change in the political status of European Jews. He promulgated a series of Toleration Acts that promised to integrate the Jews into the general

Title pages of the Bible illustrated by Ephraim Moses Lilien, 1908.
(Courtesy Richard I. Cohen)

polity, and in the case of the recently occupied province of Galicia (1789) came close to extending equal rights to its more than 200,000 Jews. Joseph's actions generated a warm-hearted response from some Enlightenment Jews (*maskilim*), who viewed them as an opportunity to encourage an intensification of secular education and openness to different occupations. More traditionally minded Jews demurred, fearing the consequences of increased proximity to Christian society and culture. But it was the French Revolution (1789) that raised the ante of change, emancipating the Jews as full citizens of France (1790, 1791) and in other regions conquered by the revolutionary forces and ideology. Offered equality of opportunity and faced with nascent nationalist spirit and a strong centralistic orientation, Jews in France rapidly began to refashion themselves, experiencing both dramatic demographic change and social mobility.

Within a generation, from place to language, from traditions to style, from occupations to status, Jews moved from a more exclusive world to one permeated with a French disposition. Once begun, the political emancipation of the Jews continued unabated for several decades throughout Western and Central Europe, leaving in its wake (or at times even anticipating) similar internal changes in France. Fashioning a German, Italian, English, Dutch, or Austrian/Hungarian identity was an integral part of the modern Jewish experience, the contours of which were different from country to country, affected by the unique process of emancipation in each and by each particular system of government and concept of citizenship. Yet there were similarities in the ways that Jews juggled conflicting loyalties and feelings of belonging. Nationalism in its variegated forms engrossed them and shaped their allegiances but also challenged and provoked the sense of their own nationhood. By the time Lilien appeared on the scene, the political and cultural situation was a far cry from the days of Mendelssohn. Emancipation had been secured; Jews were intensely engaged in their surroundings and diversified in their interests and networks of associations. They had become involved, and disproportionately represented, in pursuits that were rarely considered their traditional domain—music, art, theater—and individual Jews figured prominently, or as leaders, in new areas of science, culture, and intellectual interests. Their economic pursuits made Jews forces to contend with in diverse spheres.

Mendelssohn's friendship with the German playwright Gottfried Ephraim Lessing, mythologized in the nineteenth century as a symbol of German-Jewish symbiosis, did not find its sequel in that century. In the social sphere, the relationship between Jews and non-Jews remained remote. Jews were still excluded from various societies and associations, though some individuals had broken these barriers in almost every country. The animosity that left its imprint on Mendelssohn and several of his seminal texts became more caustic and organized from the 1870s on, jeopardizing the success of emancipation and jolting many Jews out of their sense of accommodation in their native countries. More or less intense expressions of antisemitism flourished in the last quarter of the century throughout Western and Central Europe. Although he was reared in emancipated Galicia, Lilien, like most Central European Jews, endorsed modernity but was not oblivious to these troubling developments. At times he lashed out at them in his illustrations.

Notwithstanding the shadows on the horizon, most Jews in these parts of Europe continued their quest for full integration. They spoke a European language, grew distant from the traditions of their parents and grandparents, and quite remarkably acculturated to the surrounding society. In multinational countries, such as in the Austro-Hungarian Empire, Jews swung between adopting the German language and showing allegiance to the rising currents of Czech and Hungarian nationalism by learning Czech or Magyar. In this period of some 150 years, the boundaries of Jewish belonging were seriously redefined and remapped. Individually and collectively, the Jews embarked on many new projects that often placed them in conflict with their traditional past, though elements of that past were forever gnawing at the core of these new forms of understanding and consciousness.[2] Myriad different attachments—religious, social, cultural, and philanthropic—anchored them to their ancestral moorings (which only vaguely resembled traditional Judaism), while, politically, the nascent Jewish nationalist movements (including Zionism) that challenged the commitment to acculturation engaged only a smattering of adherents. Thus, if an urban Jew in Western or Central Europe were to purchase a Bible at the beginning of the twentieth century, chances are that neither Mendelssohn's German-language *Bi'ur* nor Lilien's Bible with its Zionist flavor would be the most likely choice. Probably a translation in a European language, with or without the Hebrew original, would be preferred, because both Mendelssohn's and Lilien's efforts hardly reflected the mainstream of Jewish life at the time. Contemporary Jewish reality and culture were being refashioned in the European languages, accentuated by a growing commitment to the country of residence and buttressed by a distancing from the ways of the past and a frenetic movement to the urban hub. Nonetheless, a resilient Jewish voice could be detected in many areas and countries.[3]

CONSTRUCTING PUBLIC AND PRIVATE SPACE

The increasing openness of the modern age offered a new temptation for Jews: to be at the center of the cultural, economic, and social arena, where politics were played out and where one enjoyed freedom of movement and association. Major European cities in the late-eighteenth and nineteenth centuries underwent dramatic economic, demographic, structural, and cultural changes. Physical and economic expansion encouraged an influx of new elements—merchants, intelligentsia, petty traders, public officials, and others. This mobility weakened the stratified or quasi-feudal structures as agrarian society waned. The populations of Paris, Budapest, Vienna, and Berlin multiplied many times. National groups—Slovaks, Romanians, Germans, French, Serbs, Italians, Armenians, and Greeks—were on the move, and Jews joined this migratory movement with eager anticipation. They sought with equal passion the haven of cities that were predominantly Protestant or Catholic, surpassing the attraction to these cities of other ethnic or national minorities. A city such as Prague or Amsterdam that had previously had a major Jewish community became even more attractive; those at the periphery of Jewish activity because of legislation (such as Vienna and Pest) or small Jewish populations (such as Paris) turned into magnets, drawing Jews throughout the nineteenth century in increasing numbers. The statistics of Jewish urbanization in this period are staggering, and the process became especially pronounced after 1850. For example, the Jews in Paris and Vienna numbered between 900 and 1,000 in the latter part of the eighteenth century, but by 1870 these populations had grown to 30,000 and 40,000, respectively. In a new milieu with untold possibilities and attractions, a clear departure from more restricted and confined living spaces, Jews were confronted very clearly with options for constructing their individual and collective space, a clear hallmark of their growing freedom.[4]

The cities to which Jews gravitated gradually ended residential segregation. Toleration became the rule of thumb (though privileged elements in society continued to prevent Jews from living in particular neighborhoods). The freedom to live where they wished required the Jews to make decisions of wide cultural and social implications concerning where they would reside, with whom, and how they would create their public and private spaces and system of values. Should Jews mask their identity, for fear of being seen as clannish, or should they accept their new freedom and congregate openly with both Jews and non-Jews? How would they use the freedom to build their public and private space? What would happen to the former center of Jewish life—the synagogue—when previous restrictions on its construction were almost completely removed?

We ourselves may also ask some questions: What meanings can we attach to the interest at the end of the nineteenth century in creating an arena for Jewish art—within the synagogue or within a separate institution, a museum? What transpired in the private sphere, in the home? How did gender figure into the

roles men and women assumed in these different situations? How did the home
now function as a transmitter of values and as the mediator between acculturation and preservation of a Jewish cultural identity, and who assumed the responsibility for this? Did the home create or break down barriers between Jews
and non-Jews? Put differently, was the oft-quoted remark by the Russian-Jewish
maskil Judah Leib Gordon that one should be "a person outside of the home and
a Jew in one's home" a viable way of life for Jews in Western and Central Europe?
And how were Jews able to preserve their traditional form of life in this new
context?

Upon their return to England in the seventeenth century, the Jews encountered a society that by and large enabled them to integrate and acculturate fully
into its fabric. The memories of the medieval past and the expulsion of 1290
faded into oblivion. Although London was home to only a small number of Jews
prior to 1700, its Jewish community grew significantly in the eighteenth century.
The mere 750 Jews at the beginning of the century grew through waves of immigration to more than 15,000 (of a population of some 800,000) at its end.[5] Jews
gravitated to London from Germany, Holland, and Poland and brought with
them diverse living patterns, levels of religious behavior, economic status, and a
predisposition to acculturation with the surrounding society. Because neither
legal restrictions nor Jewish communal organizations existed at this time, London offered the immigrants the remarkable freedom to live where they pleased.
The city's "complex and largely unregulated patterns of urban life allowed persons with ambition and drive much room for manoeuvre."[6] London was not
Berlin, where even Mendelssohn lived under a special dispensation.

The newcomers seized the opportunities offered by the "unregulated patterns
of urban life." Both the poor and the wealthy lived initially in the eastern end of
the city. But class and money quickly became a factor: the elegant living quarters
of the West End enticed Sephardim and Ashkenazim of means, whereas the
more traditionally minded and lower-class Jews remained in the City. Moving to
the West End carried with it a clear demarcation from association with Jewish
organizational life and synagogue attendance. Moreover, it is remarkable that
Jews of wealth were already in the 1720s, in their emulation of English gentry
style, purchasing lavish country homes and estates, at times with sprawling acres
of land. As Todd Endelman has shown, living like "a country gentleman . . .
meant a physical separation from the mass of the Jewish community."[7]

Samson Gideon, who was born in London in 1699, is an example of this cut of
Anglo-Jewish society. The son of Rehuel Gideon Abudiente, of Marrano stock, a
trader in Barbados who was the first Jew to become a freeman in London, Samson inherited a sizable sum on his father's death. Brought up traditionally, he

used this legacy to purchase (in the 1720s) a home in a fashionable area, where people of the noble and gentry classes lived. Following his marriage to a non-Jewish woman in the 1740s, he acquired several country estates. Although he maintained a minimal connection with the Bevis Marks synagogue, he did everything possible to attain the status of an English aristocrat and shunned any connection with the efforts in 1753 to improve the political status of the Jews by an act of naturalization.[8] Indeed, for the wealthy—as the case of Gideon shows—physical distance could contribute in time to almost total estrangement, including conversion, from Jewish life. The choice of where to build one's home was at times a determining factor in the maintenance of connection with Jewish mores, but at times it also stemmed from a predisposed attitude toward those mores—alternatives that did not exist for the lower middle class.

By the mid-nineteenth century, some 13,000 of England's 35,000 Jews lived in London. A sizable number of them (approximately 5,000) had moved to the western part of the city, and later to the north, taking the same path as the wealthier Christians. In 1842 a group of elite families, both Sephardim and Ashkenazim, who actively supported political emancipation established the West London Synagogue of British Jews. In response to external criticism and internal motivations, they introduced many aspects of the radical reform that were common in Germany and cited these changes, as well as the "advancement of British Jews" in different areas, when they lobbied for emancipation before Prime Minister Robert Peel in 1845. Believing in political reform and asserting their sense of belonging to English society, they did not forgo their expectations from the system, nor did they deny their affiliation with some form of Jewish nationhood.[9] Thus a move to a better neighborhood did not always result in total disengagement from Jewish concerns or in abandonment of Jewish identity. Yet, when large waves of Russian and Romanian immigrants began stampeding into London in 1881, they presented a direct contrast to the form of acculturation that the English Jews had sought.

The East End, though not a clearly defined geographic area, had remained throughout the century the home of the Jewish poor and lower middle class: the peddlers, old-clothes dealers, itinerant traders, and petty traders. It now turned into the hub of London Jewry. From 1881 to 1914, the city received more than 60 percent of the Jewish immigrants to Britain, and by the turn of the century some 120,000 of the 144,000 Jews in London lived in the East End. In the public mind, justifiably so, Anglo-Jewry became synonymous with the occupations of the East European Jews: the garment trade, leather work, and furniture making. This development turned the tables on the goals of the "elite"—now a minuscule minority in a sea of non-Anglicized Jews. This concentration of occupation and neighborhood raised the public visibility of the Jews beyond what the establishment deemed judicious for acculturation. In what became a common reprimand on the part of established Jews to newcomers in the face of mass migration in the twentieth century in different countries, the leading Anglo-Jewish newspaper, the *Jewish Chronicle,* editorialized in 1888:

> If poor Jews will persist in appropriating whole streets to themselves in the same district, if they will conscientiously persevere in the seemingly harmless practice of congregating in a body at prominent points in a great public thoroughfare like Whitechapel or Commercial Road, drawing to their peculiarities of dress, of language, of manner, the attention which they might otherwise escape, can there be any wonder that the vulgar prejudices of which they are the objects should be kept alive and strengthened?[10]

The division between the haves and have-nots was so pronounced that the haves felt threatened by a visual reminder of an "obsolete" way of life, exacerbated by its mass and concentration.

Established Jews perceived their economic success, organizational clout, involvement in English society, and lavishness and monumentalism in the synagogue space as evidence of their acculturation; they did not see themselves as flaunting a Jewish presence in England. They would have preferred the East European Jews to have been dispersed more widely throughout the British Isles. On encountering these newcomers in London, en masse, in one area, their misgivings rose to the surface. There can be no better indication of this fear of being misrepresented by the immigrants, or of being identified with them, than the fact that Jewish agencies sent more than 24,000 Jews back to Eastern Europe during the period 1881–1906. Yet, as the historian David Feldman has cogently argued, not only Jewish interests were involved in such an act but also the assumptions of the "propertied classes concerning the provision of poor relief, the organisation of charity and the consequences of unlimited immigration."[11] These considerations of visibility and representation were foreign to the immigrant Jews, both non-urban and urban in origin. Their notions of private and public space had been shaped by a context in which the concentration of Jews and notions of visibility were internally framed and understood. They migrated intentionally to the East End, where they found a large Jewish population of similar background, traditions, and services, close to the docks, where they could obtain employment in the occupations they knew.

London provides an example of the ways in which the migration of East European Jews to major cities in Western countries in the nineteenth and twentieth centuries (France, the United States, and Germany to a lesser extent) clashed with the native Jews' sense of public/private space and overturned the process of acculturation. In each country the political context and nature of the state's orientation fueled the particular sensitivity of the native Jews to "eastern visibility." The natives desired the immigrants to speak the local tongue, dress accordingly, act patriotically, minimize their organizational efforts, and avoid overzealous behavior in the areas of politics and religion. But the immigrants did not accept the patronage of the elite Jews in London, just as they would not accept it a generation later in Paris. This unique situation, the "unregulated patterns of urban life" that had enabled the Anglo-Jewish elite to emulate the aristocracy and be molded by Georgian and Victorian society, was rudely challenged. London was now in a different phase of development, and its immigrant population was to open up new avenues of identity and visibility born of the interplay between the liberal concept of a nation and the immigrants' rearing in Eastern Europe. Urbanization did not spell the doom of Jewish presence in cities like London, which were energized by mass immigration.

Whereas London was by and large an open city from the days of resettlement, Vienna in the Habsburg Empire was almost hermetically closed to Jews after their expulsion from the city in 1670. Under the strong centralist Catholic rulers, the number of Jews remained very small for more than 150 years. Those allowed to reside there came from the successful class of Court Jews, who served the court in one form or another. The Habsburg attitude toward Vienna was clear: as the capital of a Catholic empire, and under the influence of feudal magnates, it must be protected from Jews and unbelievers. Only when a bourgeoisie emerged in the mid-eighteenth century did this notion begin to change, challenged by those who saw in a Jewish presence an economic and cultural blessing. But the real breakthrough came after the Revolution of 1848, when new legislation ended Jewish residential restrictions.

Over the next 50 years, Vienna witnessed a tremendous growth of its Jewish population. Coming from all areas of the empire, Jews—rich and poor, traditional and acculturated—turned to Vienna in increasing numbers. The capital attracted them for many reasons: cultural, economic, political, and even psychological. Some were fleeing poverty and rising nationalism, others were looking for economic and cultural opportunities and for freedom. Emperor Franz Joseph, the mythic father figure who hovered over this period, loomed in the minds of many as a protector. All told, the number of Jews rose to as much as 10 percent of the entire population in 1880, and by World War I to almost 200,000 (about 8.5 percent of the population), nearly 28 times the 1860 population.

Marsha Rozenblit has shown that, notwithstanding upward mobility and distancing from the traditional way of life, immigrants in the second half of the nineteenth century preferred the areas of the city where other Jews lived, and thus they mingled in a social context almost entirely with other Jews. This division was widened during the modernization and economic expansion that Vienna experienced during this period. Leopoldstadt, where the ghetto stood in the seventeenth century, was again the center of Jewish life in the nineteenth, at times housing over half of the Jewish population of Vienna. Within this quarter, divisions clearly existed between the wealthier and the poorer areas, but by and large the Jews did not prefer to live in sections that were marked by a particular social class. The fact that many of them changed their occupations during this period affected only slightly their choice of neighborhood. "Jewishness," Rozenblit argues, was then the "primary criterion in neighborhood selection," and individuals were little concerned where the other Jews came from—Hungary, Bohemia, Galicia, etc.—so long as they were Jews.[12] Or, as Robert Wistrich put it, "there were no rigidly definable 'uptown' and 'downtown' Jews in Vienna," and notwithstanding the anti-Jewish animus of the late nineteenth century, the city "continued to attract Jews, to provide fertile ground for their talents and for their hope of successful integration as respected and cultured members of society."[13]

Living in such proximity, Jews from different countries tended to remain associated with others of similar class and orientation. Acculturation in Vienna was unlike that experienced by the elite Jews of eighteenth-century London; it transpired among Jews going in similar professional directions. Sigmund Freud's revealing correspondence with his colleague Karl Abraham in 1908 resonated with a sense of this shared existence/fate, as opposed to their relationship with the Swiss analyst Carl Jung. As Freud wrote to Abraham in one letter: "You are closer to my intellectual constitution because of racial kinship"; then, in another, "May I say that it is consanguineous Jewish traits that attract me to you? We understand each other."[14] Indeed, Freud was deeply concerned with the issue of "visibility," fearing that psychoanalysis would be perceived as "a Jewish national affair."[15] But "visibility" notwithstanding, this pattern of acculturation and relationships most certainly prevailed among other, far less integrated Jews than someone like Freud.

The Jews were indeed a significant presence in Vienna; their physical concentration was mirrored by occupational groupings in the areas of the free professions, the liberal press, commerce, banking, and industrial capitalism. Acculturation was rampant and the conversion rate higher than in all of Europe at the turn of the twentieth century, though pockets of traditional Judaism maintained themselves and a certain assertion of identification with the Jewish people continued even among the more deeply acculturated. Once again Freud provides a penetrating observation on this continuing link. In his fascinating introduction to the Hebrew translation of *Totem and Taboo,* written in Vienna in 1930, Freud states:

> No reader of [the Hebrew version of] this book will find it easy to put himself in the emotional position of an author who is ignorant of the language of holy writ, who is completely estranged from the religion of his fathers—as well as from every other religion—and who cannot take a share in nationalist ideals, but who has yet never repudiated his people, who feels that he is in his essential nature a Jew and who has no desire to alter that nature. If the question were put to him: Since you have abandoned all these characteristics of your countrymen, what is there left to you that is Jewish? He would reply: "A very great deal, and probably its very essence." He could not now express that essence clearly in words; but someday, no doubt, it will become accessible to the scientific mind.[16]

Yet the city often contributed strongly to the obliteration of the traditions immigrating Jews brought with them, though not enough either for the political antisemitism that flourished from the 1870s on or for the persistent religious antisemitism of Catholic Vienna. Within the culture of this pulsating and dynamic city, the Jews' dwindling connection to tradition, and the assertive antisemitism they faced, individuals like Franz Werfel, Otto Weininger, Freud, and Gustav Mahler were energized to seek new forms of expression in which the element of Jewishness was moot. But even they, who were far removed from the community, its affairs, and its ideologies, could not, it seems, avoid the imputations of their Jewishness.

Urban life certainly ate away at Jewish religious life. Franz Kafka, who wrote in early-twentieth-century Prague, placed the onus for this development on the move from the villages to the city. In a penetrating letter to his father, Kafka described the difference between the latter's Judaism and his own:

> You had really brought some traces of Judaism with you from that ghetto-like little village community; it was not much and it dwindled a little more in town and while you were doing your military service, but still, the impressions and memories of your youth did just about suffice to make some sort of Jewish life, especially since you did not, after all, need much of that kind of help.... [I]t all dribbled away while you were passing it on. In part it was youthful memories of your own, of a kind that could not be conveyed to others.... It was also im-

possible to make a child . . . understand that the few flimsy gestures you performed in the name of Judaism, and with an indifference in keeping with their
flimsiness, could have any higher meaning. . . . It was much the same with a
large section of this transitional generation of Jews, which had migrated from
the still comparatively devout countryside to the towns.[17]

Indeed, Jewish Prague of the nineteenth and twentieth centuries had only
memories and physical remnants, in its historic cemetery, of the luminaries
of rabbinic scholarship that it once had harbored. In the seventeenth and eighteenth centuries, Prague hosted the largest single Jewish population in the world:
between 10,000 and 11,000 souls, whose rabbis and scholars were recognized
near and far. By Kafka's day, the Jews of Prague had embraced modernization
and German culture and had totally distanced themselves from traditional Jewish life. Prague had also lost its crown as the largest Jewish community in the
world. Habsburg legislation and an ignominious expulsion in 1745 had ended
the Prague community's central role, which it never recovered. It was only in the
last quarter of the nineteenth century, when demographic changes in Bohemia
led to a large migration of Czechs to Prague, that Jews—conversant in Czech
and rural in origin—again flocked to the city, their number rising to 27,000 by
1900 and constituting 7.9 percent of the city's population. Prague asserted itself
further in the next decades as the center of Bohemian/Czech Jewry; according to
the 1921 census, almost half of all Bohemian Jews were residents of the city. Although traditional life was minimal, most of the Jews preferred to live in apartment buildings that were extensively inhabited by other Jews. In a highly volatile
nationalist atmosphere, the clustering of a particular ethnic group in one neighborhood was uncommon, but Gary Cohen has shown that Jews maintained a
high degree of association with other Jews, preserving a shared value system and
common habits.[18]

Prague thus offers another variety of Jewish accommodation in an urban setting, though it was much smaller than either London or Vienna, numbering less
than 700,000 people in 1921. From the middle of the nineteenth century, Prague
was the epicenter of the rising Czech nationalist spirit, which was driven by a desire to assert the Czech language and culture and limit German domination of
culture, politics, and education. The nationalist movement's goal of sovereignty
stood at odds with the German orientation of the Habsburgs, with which the
Jews had strongly aligned themselves from the time of Joseph II—and especially
in Prague, where they gained a modern education, adopted the German language, cultivated a bourgeois existence, and were at peace with Habsburg rule.
They had become an integral element of civic bodies—such as the casinos—that

celebrated a German synthesis. But as the clash between the Germans and the Czechs surged forward in Bohemian life, and as rural Jews attached to Czech traditions and the nationalist movement migrated to Prague, the Jewish population became embroiled in a serious struggle over its affiliation similar to that which permeated the rest of the populace. Several vocal societies and associations emerged in this period, asserting a Czech-Jewish political and cultural alliance. The growing identification with Czech culture and language resulted in a significant decline in German-Jewish schools.

The relative ease with which Jews had found a home in Prague and integrated comfortably into German culture, leaving much of their Judaism behind, was an experience of the past. They now entered a more complex situation, a struggle between strong, competing ethnic and national identities. They were necessarily pulled into these controversies and found themselves criticized and attacked by both German and Czech nationalists. Antisemitic outbursts—though rarely in a violent form—in the 1890s strained the nature of their integration into the urban setting. Within this nationalist tug-of-war and economic antisemitism, Jewish nationalism found a niche as intellectuals and shopkeepers, small merchants and university students turned to Zionism. Figures securely adapted to Prague and Bohemian life and culture were at the center of this realignment, evidence of the fascinating cultural and political evolutions in the urban crucible of the nineteenth and twentieth centuries. Still others tried to create bridges between the Czech and German worlds by becoming significant cultural conduits of the literature written in one or the other language. As mediators, struggling to preserve a common voice for the society, Jews insisted "that the tone of the national debate be modulated, that broad areas of understanding and mutual cooperation be established, and that the ethnic, religious, and linguistic diversity of the state be preserved."[19] Moreover, from the position of this "in-betweenness" emerged Kafka, whose writings are often seen as the epitome of the modern experience and at times the quintessential expression of the modern Jewish predicament. His writings have become synonymous with Prague as Freud's were with Vienna.

Jews moved to the amorphous cities with great expectations for a more neutral polity and wider cultural and economic horizons. Often they remained in close proximity to other Jews, either through the choice of neighborhood or through the particular buildings in which they lived, as the historian Steven Lowenstein observed of German Jews, who "demonstrated a noticeable tendency to congregate in certain sections of the municipality."[20] This enabled them to preserve elements of their communal life and organization, and it served as a comfortable cushion for those who had moved from a small city, town, or more rural area where their predominant contact had been with other Jews. It did not necessarily impede the process of acculturation to the surrounding society. The work space was often separated from the residential zone, and upward mobility encouraged at least a modicum of interaction with non-Jews, though more for the men than the women. Migrations, modernization, national and ethnic feuds, and new gender roles fueled the interrelations between Jews and others and among the Jews themselves and created patterns of identity and belonging that transformed the city into a formative framework of Jewish life in the modern period. Indeed, in some countries the less turbulent character of rural society did not guarantee the preservation of Jewish tradition and identity; sometimes it even threatened that identity more than urban life did. Yet, when we view the changes in city life in the nineteenth and twentieth centuries, it is difficult to ignore the marked presence of the Jews. Their physical concentration in particular areas was mirrored by clear characteristics of their cultural dilemmas and patterns of behavior.

These vignettes of urban acculturation reveal that Jews in emancipated Europe were generally not encumbered by a negative stereotype of clannishness. Although they were aware of their visibility, sensed their "otherness," and were conscious of discrimination, they managed to forge new forms of Jewishness. Preoccupied by their sense of belonging (what Kafka called the Jew's tightrope) and yet desiring to live with their own kind, feeling a "racial kinship" (as Freud put it), they placed their trust in the openness of the city and its promise for the future. Residence within the urban space was characterized by hope and energy. Nowhere could this be appreciated better than in the ways in which some Jews affirmed the public space in constructing imposing houses of worship.

AFFIRMATION OF THE PUBLIC SPACE

Jews built synagogues even before the destruction of the Temple in the first century C.E., but following that event the synagogue became the very center of Jewish religious life and ceremony. Throughout their history, Jews have created institutions in a wide variety of architectural styles, often with striking similarity to Christian or Muslim holy places. However, nothing surpassed the transformation that took place in this cultural domain from the days of Moses Mendelssohn.

Germany is a case in point. Lowenstein has refined our thinking on the impact of urbanization on Jewish life. Although it was the dominant mode throughout the nineteenth century, the urbanization process was much more gradual than generally regarded. Lowenstein's work has also overturned the received truth that urbanization was the cause of the dramatic changes in German-Jewish lifestyle (a truism applicable for other European countries as well), from religion to economics. He argues that the move to the cities took place more often than not only *after* a distinct move away from traditional religious practice, occupation, and cultural interests. Yet that development was incremental, and the major move from the rural to the urban setting took place only as of the second half of the nineteenth century. Once that process took over, it was remarkably consistent. Seven cities (Leipzig, Hamburg, Munich, Berlin, Frankfurt, Breslau, and Cologne) were, by 1925, the home of more than half of German Jewry—a development not paralleled among Christian Germans, who remained about half as urbanized as the Jews. Berlin was the premier choice. Already in the eighteenth century it had become a Mecca for Jews seeking economic advancement and, through the presence of Mendelssohn, a home of the Jewish Enlightenment; it was also the center of much religious turbulence and conversion.

Berlin's growth in the nineteenth century as the center of Prussian society intensified. It gradually emerged from the heavy economic burden of the Napoleonic wars and was soon to become the cultural and architectural center of Germany. The inspiration came from the renowned architect Karl Friedrich Schinkel (1781–1841), who in the 1820s designed the building that would house the masterpieces belonging to Prussia. Opened in 1830, the museum (now called the Altes Museum) was built in the square that already included the royal palace, the Zeughaus, and the cathedral, according art a space commensurate with the monarchy, the army, and the church. This monumental structure helped Berlin to rival Vienna, Dresden, and Kassel in cultural importance. Together with its political and economic vitality and a rather liberal civic society, such cultural growth enhanced Berlin's growing attraction to Jews. The city became a hub of Jewish life.[21] According to Bruno Blau (1881–1954),[22] Berlin's Jewish population multiplied sixfold between 1840 and 1871, rising to 36,000, and became 4 percent of the city's population. By 1925 it had risen to 172,000. German Jews gravitated to the north central part of the city and figured there prominently. In the developing city, Jewish neighborhoods were distinct, with myriad institutions and synagogues. Because the Jews had no communal monuments of their own and were not represented in German public monuments—even the proposal to incorporate the figure of Mendelssohn into a joint public monument in Berlin had been rejected[23]—it would seem that their synagogues served that function.

The Oranienburgstrasse synagogue, a creation of the mid-nineteenth century, was the largest in the world at that time (see p. 730). Designed by Schinkel's student Eduard Knoblauch (1801–65), it was built in the Moorish style that had captured the imagination of German Jews. In close proximity to the museum quarter, the synagogue granted Berlin Jewry a resounding sense of presence in the city. There was room for 1,400 men and for 800 women, who were to sit in an open gallery. The choir loft would accommodate 60 people. Built with the most modern technology—iron construction and gas lighting—the sanctuary soared 23 meters high and measured some 57 meters in length and 40 in width. It took 10 years to complete the building, as costs soared ever higher. Not wedged into a narrow space, the synagogue with its two matching cupolas and large dome was clearly visible, accentuating the sense of economic and civic accomplishment of the congregants. Contemporaries often compared the synagogue to the Alhambra in Granada, noting its overall appearance, the nave where the *aron kodesh* was ensconced and overshadowed, the lush gold ornamentation, and the myriad shapes and designs on the walls and ceiling.[24] Others compared the synagogue— some positively, some negatively—to the Temple of Solomon, intimating that this was, symbolically, the new temple in a new Fatherland.

An elaborate inauguration ceremony was attended by many public figures, including Count Bismarck. The Jews came dressed in formal attire to hear a program of music, speeches, and expressions of goodwill by local officials. Precisely planned, the ceremony emphasized the participation of non-Jews and the decorum and breaking of boundaries between the public and the Jewish space. Young and old congregants proceeded to the synagogue, holding Torah scrolls and accompanied by local and national dignitaries. Onlookers, both non-Jews and Jews, lined the streets to watch. The inauguration with all its pomp was truly a communal rite designed to gain for the Jews the respect and confidence of Berlin society.[25] To mark the importance of this event, reproductions of Emile de Cauwer's painting of the synagogue's façade (1865) were widely sold.[26] As for other distinguished nineteenth-century edifices, secular and ecclesiastical, a medal was struck to commemorate the inauguration, soon followed by other memorabilia to safeguard the memory and showcase the success. Reports on the ceremony appeared in Jewish newspapers in Europe and America, and the sense of a breakthrough in the grand production was duly noted.

The establishment of the Oranienburgstrasse synagogue had an impact on other synagogues in other countries. Its cultural message was one that bourgeois Jews in many cities wanted to convey: optimism, belief in the process of integration and emancipation, and above all a sense of belonging. Its Moorish style emphasized the congregants' relationship to another country, another period, but, as the historian Ismar Schorsch has astutely observed, the Spanish influence "dovetailed so completely with the overriding Spanish bias of German Jewry."[27] It took on a kind of sacred style.[28] Oranienburgstrasse was a total reversal of the diasporic mentality often imputed to the Jews of Central and Western Europe. There was no masking here of identification, of success, of allegiance (now even an outright connection to a Spanish past). These Berlin Jews were forthrightly affirming that, like their brethren elsewhere in the Reich, they were willing to be seen and had the wherewithal to establish a presence in their city.[29] A contemporary Jewish commentator took note of the implications of such a building. "The Jews," he wrote, "can show what power they possess."[30] Let us remind ourselves before looking at another vignette that this was 1866, even before the growth of Berlin's Jewish population.

Like Berlin, Paris ("the capital of the nineteenth century," in Walter Benjamin's phrase) had also witnessed from the beginning of the century a growing Jewish population. Jews numbered a mere 1,000 at the time of the Revolution, but, by 1861, 25,000 (26.3 percent) of the Jews in France lived in Paris, showing a proportionately higher growth rate than the non-Jews of the city. Jewish migration to Paris had been spearheaded by the members of the economic and professional elite, who sought to rise in a variety of occupations, including public office—the most notable being Adolphe Crémieux (1796–1880), who twice served as minister of justice in French governments.[31] In 1859, when the Oranienburgstrasse synagogue was being built in Berlin, the official leadership of French Jewry, the Central Consistory established during the Napoleonic period (1808), negotiated with the minister of the interior the construction of two new synagogues in Paris, which was then in the midst of its tremendous redevelopment under the famed prefect and architect Georges-Eugène Haussmann. A dispute quickly arose over the space that would be allotted. The Consistory, often seen as the driving force behind "assimilation" tendencies and by then under a leadership more lay than rabbinical, wished to have a synagogue located on an attractive street, rue Ollivier, with great visibility, but the prefect dismissed their request. The Consistory rejected his alternative suggestions. Having successfully raised money from a significant number of Parisian Jews, the leadership of the community and its upper echelon were united in their demand for a space they felt appropriate for such an undertaking. Haussmann, who retired in 1870, remained as adamant in his opposition as Empress Eugénie, who objected to a synagogue exit on the same street as the church of Notre-Dame-de-Lorette. The community was left with no choice but to build on Rue Victoire, a narrow and far less impressive street than the Rue Ollivier.[32] But what they could not achieve in their location they tried to make up in the construction of the interior.

The Jewish architect, Alfred Aldrophe (1834–95), used a Romanesque style for the internal space, more in the tradition of French architecture than the Moorish style prevalent in many other contemporary synagogues. In order to accommodate the growing population and seat a very large audience—as many as 5,000 people—the dimensions of the sanctuary exceeded those of most Parisian churches and public edifices. Forty-four meters long and 17 meters wide, it soared over 28 meters high, culminating in a barrel-vaulted ceiling. The central focus was on the ark and *bimah,* a setting that shows the influence of the Reform temples of early-nineteenth-century Germany, in which the orderly service was handled by professionals. To accentuate the importance of the ark area, the entrance to it was made from marble columns, and synagogue and Consistory officials were given designated seats nearby. Behind the ark were twelve windows upon which the tribes of Israel were inscribed, and above them were five windows with the Star of David in the center and the names of the books of the Pentateuch. Following the decision of a rabbinical council in 1856 to allow organs in consistorial synagogues, one was built with the hope of enticing larger participation in the services. Notwithstanding these changes, Hebrew remained the language of prayer.[33]

The main area of the synagogue was defined by a combination of expansive arches and two levels of supports. Women were seated in aisle galleries not covered by grids. All in all, the synagogue created an uncommon setting for those Jews who had moved to Paris from Alsace-Lorraine and were accustomed to smaller structures and less rigid arrangements. The new space carried a specific meaning: to become acculturated to the urban center, one should feel at home in a house of worship that placed the rabbi far from his congregants, required orderly, formal appearance and presentation, and offered a certain aesthetic appreciation.[34] Likened to a cathedral without its gloomy interior,[35] the synagogue opened in 1875, five years after the French were defeated by Prussia. The political context encouraged the Grand Rabbi of France, Zadoc Kahn, to proclaim that the dedication of the synagogue was "proof that France . . . has the right to take off its mourning clothes and celebrate anew the feasts of the spirit, of art, and of religion."[36] Such a public space enabled French Jews to feel that they had a center. Indeed, the Victoire, the congregation of the Grand Rabbi, was a most representative location. It offered a place for aristocratic Jews to hold weddings,[37] a site where the community might commemorate special events (such as memorial services for French Jews killed in battle), and one in which the model of integration and collective identity—*patrie et religion* (country and religion)—could be seen and emulated. Ushers in the synagogues wore hats with a tricolor badge, the emblem of the Revolution, whereas the rabbis were garbed in dress very similar to that of French Catholic priests (clerical robes, long white bands from the neck down, and three-cornered hats).

Yet cultural values were far from the only ones involved in creating such a

Interior of the synagogue in Rue Victoire, Paris, 1861–74.
(Photo: © Roger-Viollet Agence Photographique, Paris)

public space: throughout the nineteenth century, the Consistory had waged a battle against private *minyanim* (quorums of 10 men for service). Although the attempt to curtail these services was presented to the French authorities as an issue of "the dignity of religion and the security of the state,"[38] economics and authority were an intrinsic part of the campaign. The Consistory understood its mandate to be to regulate private services and guarantee its own financial status through payment for seats in synagogues and functions performed by its accredited functionaries. The struggle against private services was unrelenting, and the Consistory often sought the intervention of the French authorities to support its demands, but its efforts were not crowned with great success.[39] The building of the Victoire could thus be seen as an outgrowth of the Consistorial drive to regulate and shape Jewish religious life, but, on no less a scale, the creation of the synagogue—and others with similar directives—helped promote the image of French Jewry to Parisians and to Parisian Jews.

The Victoire highlights the ways in which many internal tendencies within a community came into play in constructing a public space, and how that space helped fashion those who interacted with it. Indeed, two generations later, in 1913, Russian-born Jews supported the erection of a synagogue in *art nouveau* style in the Marais district—which was inhabited by a growing number of East European Jews—apparently to sidestep the consistorial-Romanesque style and to express their independence of the established leadership.[40] But the interplay of architecture, communal and political identity, and economics can also be seen in a city that was beginning to undergo both a major demographic change and the emergence of a new religious orientation. Pest, in nineteenth-century Hungary, provides this illuminating mixture.

Following the law of 1840 that enabled Jews to settle throughout the country and buy urban real estate, the move to towns and privileged urban residences took off. Pest was at the center of this demographic change. Jews had settled there from the 1780s but now found it an especially welcome place for commerce and industry, where they could fill a function that was inappropriate for the strong aristocratic nobility and the weak, dispossessed masses. Whereas in the 1830s some 6,000 Jews lived in the city, by 1857 the number had risen to 14,000, and the Jews figured prominently in the commercial realm in what was still a preindustrial, backward economy.[41] Pest was also open to new cultural and religious currents. It hosted a "rabbinic Haskalah" (Orthodox rabbis who were interested in secular learning and yeshivah education) as well as a reform movement that opened a school in 1814 and a reform service (*chorschule*) in 1827.[42] With the coming to Pest in 1836 of the Moravian-born Löw Schwab (1794–1857), a scion of distinguished yeshivot, to serve as chief rabbi, a new phase in the city's religious history began. Schwab gradually pushed forward a platform that regarded Reform's rejection of basic halakhic issues (such as circumcision and conversion of the Jewish Sabbath to Sunday) as untenable, while upholding its attempts to aestheticize Judaism by changing the place of the bimah and introducing a choir and modern methods of preaching. This middle-road position, which Schwab developed in close collaboration with his son-in-law, the scholar

Leopold Löw, became known in Hungary as the Neolog orientation. On the basis of this innovative approach, Schwab was instrumental in bringing the Orthodox and Neologs in Pest to accept a plan to build a joint synagogue that incorporated a traditional Hebrew service, a male choir, an organ, and vernacular sermons. Having paved the way for this agreement and having developed a certain following, lay and rabbinic, Schwab could count on the rising Jewish financial interests in Pest to bring to fruition his goal of a combined space.

Ludwig von Förster (1797–1863), a distinguished Viennese architect known for his work on other synagogues, was chosen in 1853 to design the building. Once again a Moorish style was proposed. The architect evoked certain associations with the Alhambra, in its decorations, composition, and form, but also incorporated Turkish influences, as he had done in other buildings in other contexts. The Förster creation was not typically "Moorish." Though influenced by recent excavations in historic Mesopotamia, Förster did not allow this style to dominate but rather integrated it into other classic ones—namely, the Greco-Roman and the medieval Romanesque and Gothic. Granted an attractive but somewhat unwieldy space, the initiators and Förster undertook an ambitious synagogue. Its two impressive towers (over 41 meters high) resonated for some with Boaz and Jachin, the biblical pillars, reflecting Förster's desire to re-create the Temple of Solomon. The architect also introduced the use of colored brick on building façades in Budapest. Although a lack of funds prevented the completion of Förster's original plan, the outcome was remarkable in many of its details—the size of the sanctuary (55×26×26 meters), the elaborate area of the ark (designed by Frigyes Feszl [1821–84], a Hungarian architect), the double gallery, and the large round windows. Appropriately for Schwab's compromise plan, the organ was installed behind the ark, though its large pipes could be seen on either side of the cupola that surmounted the ark.

The Dohány synagogue, which was completed in 1859, seated 3,000 people (more than 20 percent of the Jewish population of Budapest at the time). Schwab was no longer alive, but the site was commensurate with his goal—the creation of a more liberal service that attended to the aesthetic and social demands of a growing bourgeoisie. On the inauguration day, September 6, 1859, Jewish businesses were closed and a very large gathering came to a punctiliously prepared ceremony. The consecration was extensively reported by the Hungarian newspapers and inspired several visual mementos (engravings and lithographs), but, most important, the synagogue itself attracted many sightseers who were awed by its appearance. Over the years, the edifice fulfilled Schwab's hope that it would be at the vanguard of Hungarian Jewish life.

The Dohány inspired the creation of other "Moorish" synagogues in Budapest, and its style and ornamentation were often emulated outside of Hungary. In its own day it was considered one of the most impressive buildings in Hungary; it figured prominently in an 1873 guidebook to Budapest, the year the towns of Buda, Pest, and Obuda (ancient Buda) joined to become one municipality.[43] Well situated in the heart of the city, the Dohány, which was built prior to the tremendous surge forward in the city's public construction, emphasized the preeminent role that the Jewish middle class was already playing in the urbanization process. Situating themselves so centrally and visibly in the public sphere in the 1850s, a mere decade after the liberalizing laws, Pest's Jews showed their burgeoning identification with the city and its future. Not deterred from embarking on such a monumental project even though they still lacked equal rights and were far from the level of influence they would eventually attain in Budapest's economy, the supporters of Dohány paved the way for a commanding Jewish presence in the public sphere. Indeed, the synagogue was the site of many central communal gatherings and "symbolized the endeavor of the majority of Pest Jews to become part of the Hungarian nation."[44]

The three synagogues highlighted here (Oranienburgstrasse, Victoire, and Dohány), among many dozens in cities across Central and Western Europe, were built while Jewish migration to the urban centers was in motion but far from the level it reached during the last quarter of the century. This chronology underscores the dramatic change already taking place in the self-consciousness of Jews in the region—their unmistakable and uncompromising demand to be visible. The contrast to the pre-Emancipation period is illuminating. Prior to 1789, legislation in various countries often confined Jewish services to the home or placed severe restrictions on the dimensions of the synagogue. In building monumental edifices in the nineteenth and twentieth centuries, Jews collectively affirmed their presence in the public space. What stands out in these structures is the preoccupation with a dignified and impressive undertaking. Certainly the men behind these endeavors were successful in their financial pursuits, craved involvement in the societies they inhabited, were aware of lingering forms of rejection and antisemitism, and were growing more distant from Jewish ceremonial observance. The buildings carried meanings for them. These individuals wanted to refute notions of the "artless Jew," to assure the larger society that the Jewish bourgeoisie was loyal to principles of religion and civility, and to establish a public space that could enhance their own stature in the eyes of their fellow citizens. Worship was secondary. Thus, studying the way public space was chosen or negotiated for these and many other synagogues, and the discussions that ensued over the style of the sanctuary, enables us to see how religion, politics, economics, and cultural identification were intertwined in such processes.[45]

The sense that the public space was a venue in which Jews could give free rein to their economic strength and aspirations would grow as the movement from rural to urban settings intensified. But public space was not limited to the synagogue. In the last quarter of the nineteenth century, Jews in several countries began to use the public space to conserve artifacts of Jewish visual culture. This began moderately, with the exhibition of the Strauss collection of Judaica at the Universal Exhibition in Paris in 1878, where some 82 objects of ceremonial art were placed on display amid countless artifacts from different cultures. The immediate response was slight, confined to a few articles by writers interested in Jewish visual culture—most prominently, Vladimir Stasov, the Russian art critic, and David Kaufmann, the distinguished Hungarian-Jewish scholar. Exhibiting these heirlooms of Jewish ritual art—to be seen by all—in a clearly defined non-Jewish space was a statement on the part of Isaac Strauss (1806–88), a composer of popular music for Napoleon III's court balls at Vichy, that they had a legitimate place among other works of art.[46] Showing art implied that one had culture and civilization. Strauss was one of a small number of Jews in Western and Central Europe who were then collecting Jewish objects of art; his collection would later be shown in the 1887 Anglo-Jewish Historical Exhibition in London and then purchased by and stored in the Cluny Museum of Paris, where it was seldom seen until after World War II.

Nowhere else were the issues of visibility and public celebration of things Jewish so well emphasized as in the discussions that preceded the 1887 exhibition in London's Royal Albert Hall. The organizers hoped that such a large undertaking would in some way legitimize the Jewish community in the eyes of English society and temper antisemitic views, but some individuals voiced their concern at such a public manifestation of Judaism. In a sense, the modern predicament of Jewish integration into European society was being played out on the stage of this exhibition. Was Judaism a private affair—meant only for the home and synagogue? Was "Jewish art" sufficiently attractive and engaging? Clearly, for the supporters of the exhibition, visibility implied acceptance and recognition, or, as England's chief rabbi Hermann Adler put it, the exhibition "would remove something of the mysteriousness which, in the mind of the outer world, seems to encompass everything related to our observances."[47] What those who objected to the visibility inherent in the exhibition were possibly enunciating was a sense that such "performative" Judaism went beyond the strict context of religion. But it was precisely this nexus that such distinguished scholars as Heinrich Graetz and Joseph Jacobs found so attractive in the undertaking: in Graetz's words: "You wished to display the inner connection of your past and your present. You wished to show that while you, as English patriots, are attached to this happy isle with every beat of your hearts, you wished to preserve your connection and continuity with the long series of generations of Israel."[48] Although Graetz minimized the art itself and compared it unfavorably with that of European cultures, he placed much value in the enterprise itself, which was greater than the sum of its parts.

In 1907 the sculptor Alfred Nossig (1864–1943), who had been born in Lemberg, coordinated an extensive exhibition of works by artists of Jewish origin from Europe and Palestine, together with a large number of Jewish ceremonial objects, in a public gallery in Berlin. A smaller exhibition had been mounted at the Whitechapel Free Art Gallery in East London in 1906, but the Berlin show was unprecedented for the continent. Indeed, this was the first time that European Jewish artists were presented in a non-Jewish venue, which enabled Nossig to assert, in the accompanying catalogue, the idea that these disparate artists shared a common spirit, a view that smacked of Jewish nationalism. The ambitious show included the works of some 60 artists, including Camille Pissarro (France), Jozef Israëls (Holland), Isidor Kaufmann (Austria), Maurycy Gottlieb (Galicia), and Samuel Hirszenberg (Poland). The implication was that, in unison, they evoked a Jewish concern with the plight of their people—consciously and subconsciously. Of the leading artists of Jewish origin of the day, only Max Liebermann refused to have his work shown in this context, though two decades later he would head a committee for the creation of a Jewish museum in Berlin. His absence did not detract from public interest in the exhibition, which would certainly have given Graetz satisfaction.

These breakthroughs in exposing Judaism publicly through art were unlike the constant stream of self-congratulatory comments by Jewish newspapers in the nineteenth century on the participation of individual artists of Jewish origin in salons, exhibitions, and fairs. The joint exhibitions were attempts to present a collective identity and announced a new category of Jewish culture and creativity. But none of their efforts led to the institutionalization of art in the form of a permanent collection—a museum. It was not until 1997 that Paris, which hosted the Strauss collection in 1878, opened a Musée d'art et d'histoire du Judaïsme, made possible by a significant gift from the city of Paris. Notwithstanding the support that the Anglo-Jewish Historical Exhibition received and the subsequent creation of a Jewish Historical Society in London in 1893, a permanent institution of Jewish art lagged far behind. That was established only in 1932, and then within the context of a new community center. As for Berlin, 10 years after the Nossig exhibition the Jewish community dedicated two rooms in its building on Oranienburgstrasse, next to the synagogue, to the Judaica collection bequeathed to it by Albert Wolf. Efforts to turn this collection into a "museum" were stymied until one was ultimately opened on January 24, 1933—a week before Adolf Hitler rose to power—in a building that had been donated to the community and was adjacent to the communal center.

These situations tell us much about the different Jewish communities. To create an art museum in a public space required both a determined constituency totally dedicated to this endeavor and a great sense of comfort about showcasing Judaism outside the realm of religion. Apparently, what was regarded as a legitimate and valuable use of public space—a fashionable and impressive synagogue—was less valued and more troublesome in regard to an institution that went beyond the purview of religion proper. The bourgeois values to which these Jews aspired when they mounted temporary exhibitions fit well with an emerging museum culture but conflicted with their concerns about integration within the body politic. Moreover, even in those cities where a Jewish museum had been established in earlier years—such as Vienna, Danzig, Frankfurt, and Prague—there were no buildings specifically dedicated to the enterprise; they were all housed in communal institutions or in private homes. The efforts of collectors such as Salli Kirschstein (1869–1935) in Berlin and Lesser Gieldzinski (1830–1910) in Danzig to engage the community in the creation of a museum of Jewish art encountered opposition and indifference.

The contrast between the visibility of the synagogue and that of the museum is striking. Museums, though ever more important to nineteenth-century European cities, had not yet won the popularity they assumed after World War II, nor were there any that specialized in particular themes and areas of art and ethnic categories. The Jews would have certainly been cautious to create such an institution prior to others in the society. Reluctant to regard this area of culture as central to Jewish life, and concerned about the controversial ethnic implications of a "Jewish museum," they relegated their art to private and communal spaces, where it would not counteract the process of acculturation. Nevertheless, the existence of such collections was in itself an impressive indicator that Jews had begun to think of these objects as having wider cultural and social meanings.

MAKING A PRIVATE SPACE IN THE CITY

Trieste, an Italian city in the Habsburg Empire that harbored no more than 1,000 Jews at the end of the eighteenth century, tore down its ghetto in 1785 and was exceptionally receptive to its Jewish community. Trieste was the home of Rachel (Luzzatto) Morpurgo (1790–1871), a descendant of a distinguished line of Italian Jews that included the venerable scholar Samuel David Luzzatto (with whom she studied) and Rabbi Moses Ḥayyim Luzzatto, an eighteenth-century poet and mystic who died long before Rachel was born. She received an unsystematic Jewish education that included some biblical and talmudic studies, and she developed an interest in Kabbalah. She showed herself to be a determined woman who rejected her parents' attempt to choose her husband and, at age 29, married the man she desired. Between pursuing her occupation as a seamstress and raising four children, she occasionally wrote and published Hebrew poetry that attracted interest and encouragement. Her poetry was concerned with her spiritual search while it evoked the struggle between a life devoted to verse and one tied to the obligations of family and gender. In one particularly poignant poem, written in 1847, she sounded frustrated and resigned to the life of anonymity as well as to the fate of women and their context:

> *I've looked to the north, south, east, and west:*
> *a woman's word in each is lighter than dust.*
> *Years hence, will anyone really remember*
>
> *her name, in city or province, any more*
> *than a dead dog. Ask: the people are sure:*
> *a woman's wisdom is only in spinning wool.*
>
> *Wife of Jacob Morpurgo, stillborn.*[49]

Rachel Morpurgo understood that the accepted pattern for women was domestic: support of one's spouse and rearing of one's children. She did not write an ode to motherhood—it was the struggle between the worlds that she recorded ("I took stock and hid my book, / my pen and said: go away"). Her Hebrew was fine enough that she preferred it to Italian, opting like her distinguished cousin Samuel to rekindle expressions and associations with traditional literature. By using Hebrew, she was also asserting that she belonged to a private realm. She was not trying to make her mark in an acculturated world but was staying within the traditional boundaries. In this sense she continued an Italian-Jewish tradition of profound connection to the Hebrew language and literature that persisted through the nineteenth century and prevailed against reform attempts to replace Hebrew with Italian for prayer. Clearly, Trieste held in its midst a comfortable mix of enlightened and traditional Jewry that fit neatly with Morpurgo's duality. Considered the "first modern woman poet" to write in Hebrew, she remained peripheral to the development of Hebrew letters, but her poetry goes far in evoking the predicament of a woman struggling with her spiritual inclinations and attempting to find her place within a male-dominated society.

Morpurgo did not come from ordinary stock, and she received unusual support for her uncommon undertaking, but even she had more stops than starts in her literary career. Domestic life was the overriding female preoccupation among both traditional and acculturated women, and anything that would compromise the centrality of the family was frowned upon. Urbanization did not create this situation, but it somewhat changed its contours. The blessing for women composed by Rabbi Arnaud Aron, the grand rabbi of Strasbourg, in his very popular *Prières d'un coeur israélite* (The Prayers of an Israelite Heart, 1848), at about the same time Morpurgo was writing her poetry, consecrated the domestic as the ultimate experience: "May I never forget that man's labors overload his soul with cares and pains, and that the duty of a woman, her most sacred mission, is to restore calm and serenity in the heart of her spouse through her obligingness, her submission, her indulgent character."[50] The essence of Aron's blessing was no different from what all of enlightened and bourgeois society in Western and Central Europe cherished, what has come to be known as the "cult of womanhood." Yet several Jewish women tried to break out of the pattern, and some have left us a wider variety of texts in European languages than Morpurgo did in Hebrew. Many of them dealt with the struggles expressed in her verse, especially the conflicting situations between expectations of the home and one's inner desires. Others, such as Rahel Varnhagen (1771–1833) and Fanny Lewald (1811–89) in Germany and Grace Aguilar (1816–47) in England, went beyond these themes and were more troubled with the boundaries of belonging than with other concerns. Although they wrote in German and English, indicating their greater acculturation and their adoption of the values of middle-class life, they were not free of Morpurgo's inhibitions.

Almost universally restricted to the home, Jewish women generally lacked the opportunity men had for acculturation and access to non-Jewish society. Higher education, independent professions, and economic pursuits were denied them until the beginning of the twentieth century; they were not very different in this regard from non-Jewish women. As the pillars of the home, women were expected to inculcate in their children the values of bourgeois society, culture, and religion; teach them manners, taste, and language; and introduce them to classical and contemporary literature and music.

Music was encouraged in Jewish homes in the eighteenth century, but it became even more important in the nineteenth; according to Ezra Mendelsohn, it became a central integrating element for European Jews.[51] Piano and violin lessons became *de rigueur* in German-Jewish homes, and in other countries the involvement of Jews in one form or another of music was deeply encouraged and realized. Whether or not there were seven pianos in the childhood home of the

Viennese philosopher Ludwig Wittgenstein (1889–1951) is of little concern, but that legend shows how families of different levels of integration were determined to make music part of the education of both boys and girls. In acculturating to bourgeois standards, Jewish middle-class women took up the piano as part of their effort to create pleasant social and familial events. The German-Jewish artist Moritz Oppenheim (1800–1882) captured this ambience in a painting (1879) showing his grandson taking a cello lesson in a well-established home while one of the lad's sisters accompanies him on the piano.[52] Although there were women who became accomplished pianists, this activity was first and foremost a way of supplying entertainment for the family, much as it was for the non-Jewish bourgeoisie. It also served as a bridge to the public sphere, leading Jewish women to become actively involved in patronizing the arts. This phenomenon was not limited to Germany. Vignettes describing Jewish girls playing the piano, "learning scales and Strauss waltzes," commonly appear in memoirs of life in Hungary.[53] There, at the turn of the twentieth century, the Jewish bourgeoisie was deeply entrenched in the music world at all levels and was central to its musical culture, especially in Budapest. This deeply troubled Béla Bartók, the leading Hungarian composer of the day, who responded with outright anti-semitism to the fact that his audience and supporters were overwhelmingly Jewish. Indeed, as Judit Frigyesi has argued: "What is important . . . is not simply that Jews were actively involved in Hungarian art music but the fact that they were largely responsible for the creation of the musical environment in which the new Hungarian musical culture emerged."[54] Certainly, the preponderance of Jews within that setting emerged from Jewish women's encouragement of music as a cultural value; thus, they helped grant Jewish society a role in defining the urban space.

Their influence, however, was felt not just in the realm of culture. The Jewish identity of the children was seen to be dependent on the rearing they received from their mothers, who were apparently more prone to keep alive aspects of traditional observance than were their husbands, in the home and in the synagogue. As Paula Hyman has argued, "Religion fell naturally within women's domain, for it drew upon emotion to disseminate morality and fortify social order."[55] As "the guardian angel" or as "priestess of the home," the Jewish woman contributed significantly, some argue indispensably, to the preservation of specific Jewish values. In attempting to alleviate acculturation, she served as a vital mediator between the process of integration and the preservation of aspects of Jewish tradition. Oppenheim, whose famous representations of the traditional family were highly popular in the late nineteenth and early twentieth centuries among German Jewry, immortalized this ideal woman. Her centrality to the home looms large in his paintings.[56] According to Schorsch, "Oppenheim projected her as a commanding presence, a person of stature, wisdom, warmth, and piety. The nobility and harmony which marked the homes he painted were her accomplishment. From the very outset in his *Return of the Volunteer* Oppenheim assigned the mother pride of place by locating her at the very heart of the scene."[57] Yet we must add that, when the artist painted a mother and her children at a gallery of antique art (1865), he refrained from hinting at her ethnic or religious origin.[58] That mother was widening the horizons of her children, in the true bourgeois spirit of the "educating mother," an act that the Jewish mother is never seen performing in his oeuvre. Oppenheim confines her to the private space, unlike the non-Jewish women who are seen in other contexts and cultural settings. His glorification of the domestic Jewish mother was pursued but somewhat transformed by Alphonse Lévy (1840–1918), who liked to represent her as a heavyset woman in rural Alsace. His figure is dominated by her domestic cares (in particular those of the kitchen, which Morpurgo needed to leave to write "Again I'll try / to offer song, / I've left the kitchen / behind in anger"), but she is full of warmth and simplicity and is concerned with religious principles. She teaches her son or grandson his daily prayers, but she too remains within the familial context.

The urban Jewish woman did not remain confined to the home in the period of Emancipation. She was active in social institutions, tackling issues of poverty, education, professional training, philanthropy, and spiritual leadership. The new roles of women in society became much more diverse in the second half of the twentieth century, generating new alignments, concerns, and directions. But what may have been the most significant development in this period is that men relinquished more and more "Jewish areas" to women, who became more than ever "responsible for maintaining the integrity of the Jewish family as the locus of the formation of Jewish identity."[59]

Yet the home was far from a monolithic entity, and women were not responsible for all aspects of the private sphere. Depending upon country, class, religious orientation, gender relationships, and cultural influences, the home took on various forms and styles, and based on these divisions its character and appurtenances were distinctly disparate. In the seventeenth century, several generations before the rise of an elite class of Jews in Germany, one encountered remarkable financial discrepancies among the Jews in various cities, but a characteristic many shared was their attitude toward art. Contrary to accepted notions, Jews did not shy away from visual portrayals and showed little reluctance to hanging works of art in their homes.

The Jews of Amsterdam wanted to have their synagogues painted by leading artists, and they cherished portraits of their rabbis, which they hung in their synagogue offices.[60] Paintings and portraits also hung in their homes. They had their own portraits painted (one of the earliest is of Simcha Vaz of the esteemed Belmonte family, painted by her son), and some of them were avid collectors of art both Jewish and non-Jewish. In their patrician homes in the northeastern part of the city, several of which captured the attention of contemporary artists, they housed fine works of art that attracted much interest. The German author Johannes J. Schudt, whose noted work *Jüdische Merckwürdigkeiten* (1714–18) offers much insight into Jewish life at the beginning of the eighteenth century, wrote of Moses de Pinto: "In the Amsterdam home of the rich Portuguese, Moses de Pinto, are found precious paintings to the total value of one ton of gold."[61] In a will dated 1687, David de Abraham Cardozo bequeathed to another Dutch Jew a painting of the Portuguese synagogue by the well-known artist Emanuel de Witte. Although we have little information as to whether Jews purchased sculpture at this time in Amsterdam, the first existent statue of a Jew is of Don Antonio Lopez Suasso (1614–85), one of the most successful merchants in the Hague in this period. Born and baptized a Roman Catholic, Suasso converted to Judaism in 1654. He was granted the title of baron and an estate in Brabant and probably had the bust commissioned for his home in the way in which later Suassos commissioned family paintings for their residences.[62] The presence of such art and elegance in these homes does not seem to have aroused any objections from the rabbinate or the Mahamad, the governing board of Amsterdam's Portuguese Jews. "Subversive" ideas and habits that were the source of excommunication and other punishments did not apparently include behavior related to ostentatious possessions and the act of viewing.[63]

This was not always the case. Azriel Shochat has collected a considerable amount of eighteenth-century moralistic and halakhic literature in which German Jews are castigated for their pretentious way of life, excessive consumption, and reckless pursuit of *objets d'art*. The distinguished rabbis Jacob Emden and Jonathan Eybeschutz, who were locked in controversy for decades, were at least in agreement about one thing: Jewish homes were full of relief sculptures, paintings with immodest figures, and scenes of emotional expression. Moses Mendelssohn seems to have shared the rabbis' distaste, yet even he possessed paintings and cherished a bust of his dear friend Lessing.[64] Mendelssohn's relationship to it offers an insight into the changing attitude toward objects in the Jewish home. He kept the piece in his drawing room, where he received friends and guests. When he became mortally ill, he asked to have the sculpture moved to a new position so that he could constantly see it. And Mendelssohn, as we recall, was an observant Jew who knew the meaning of the phrase "know before whom thou stand." He wanted to have Lessing close to him, to remind him of their friend-ship; he wanted to have the physical proximity of his deceased friend during his own last days. Mendelssohn's students felt that way about him; it is not inciden-tal that they had a bust of the philosopher made a year before he died. Subse-quently they made copies of it for their private space. Rabbinic injunctions against sculpture would continue to carry weight in Jewish society but only with certain traditional elements, as more and more people desired, like Mendelssohn and his students, to have tangible and visual mementos of their loved ones.

Moralistic and halakhic literature rebuked both observant and less observant Jews, who from the beginning of the modern period were attracted to the deco-rative and fine arts. Glikl bas Leyb (better known as Glückel of Hameln), a per-spicacious and observant widow who left behind an engaging portrayal of German Jews at the beginning of the eighteenth century, described with relish, homes that were "decorated like those of a minister." Such comments were in-dicative of an acceptance of fine possessions and had a basis in the social frame-work of Jewish life. Indeed, the Court Jews and their large entourages had a penchant for elegant objects, of Jewish and non-Jewish provenance, and spent large sums to acquire them. The ambience of the courts attracted them in many ways, not the least of which was the way they embellished their private space, their homes. Samson Wertheimer (1658–1724), a distinguished Court Jew under several Habsburg rulers, was granted at the outset of his service to Leopold I (1640–1705) the ruler's portrait, an imperial chain of grace, and a thousand ducats to acquire "silver or golden dishes." Wertheimer, who traveled in a great chariot to his various residences, was not alone in his worldliness nor in his ex-tensive possessions. Indeed, in some of the grander homes of this era, one might see paintings by Rubens, Caravaggio, Poussin, and Watteau. Isaac Daniel Itzig was so enamored of his palatial space that he had it depicted on a saucer accom-panying a cup which bore his portrait, showing him clean-shaven and fully acculturated to Prussian society in his stylish wig, jabot, and frock coat. Few im-ages offer such a precise perspective on how the sense of excess and luxury was being internalized by this group, and this well before they had received a sem-blance of equality. Nothing of their success was hidden; their trust in the au-thorities was considerable. The palaces of the Fliess, Ephraim, and Itzig families were considered some of the finest of the period, their gardens as magnificent as those of the Berlin aristocracy; yet, unlike Samson Gideon, they were not neces-sarily distanced from their adherence to Jewish tradition by their extravagant lifestyle. Itzig had a synagogue in his home, as did other Court Jews of great wealth (such as Samson Wertheimer, Alexander David in Braunschweig, and Es-ther Liebmann in Berlin). This duality—wealth and tradition—failed miserably in the next generation. Tradition invariably lost out. Yet contradictions were common, as in the case of Fliess, who possessed a wine cellar with nonkosher wines that, in a most modern touch, he willed not be sold to Jews.[65]

Such exceptional private spaces and patterns of behavior indicate that traditional norms were beginning to lose their universal acceptance. The values, manners, dress, and style of the milieu in which Jews lived found their way into their homes, and halakhic and moralistic literature was left behind. But these striking examples of the way eighteenth-century Jews appreciated the worlds of art, music, and possessions enable us to further comprehend the desire of nineteenth-century Jews to build a certain kind of synagogue. The new lifestyle paid greater attention to and expended larger resources on cultural attributes outside the specific Jewish realm, in the public space as in the home. Handling all these innovations while preserving aspects of Jewish tradition presented a profound challenge; in meeting it, men and women assumed different roles. Whereas women, as we have seen, were the "priestesses of the home," men were the guardians of possessions and texts.

The choice of books that were read and could be found in Jewish homes definitely widened during this period. Hebrew and Yiddish increasingly lost their hold on nontraditional Jews; subjects in the humanities and natural sciences replaced the sacred texts, while newspapers and literature—classic and popular—found avid readers and writers. Attendance at public schools grew extensively and fueled a vast crisis for traditional learning and interests. With this transition of loyalties, concerns, and pursuits, the place and meaning of the Bible in the home and the public sphere were also reassessed and totally revamped. An inquiry into the way the holy text was treated in this new context serves as a bridge between the private and public sphere, for indeed it was a book that touched at the root of Jewish self-consciousness, individually and collectively.

REPOSSESSING THE BIBLE

In reinterpreting, retranslating, and reconfiguring the Bible—the Old Testament, for our purposes—Jews across Central and Western Europe were engaged in a process of repossession. Clearly, their experiences differed from country to country, but some common patterns emerged. Having acculturated to one degree or another, be they Orthodox Jews in Germany offering a German translation and commentary or English Jews rejecting the revelation at Mount Sinai, Jews saw in the Bible the foundation of their modern existence, their source of belonging to the larger society. Their concern with biblical figures, Moses above all, expressed their need to identify with a tradition and present to others a link to their past glories, still relevant to that society. Some energetically argued that only Jews could be authentic interpreters of the Bible, because they possessed the most intimate connection with Hebrew. Praising Hebrew as the mother of all languages, dramatizing the role of Moses as the supreme spokesman of a just and equitable society, and reaffirming the Jewish distinctness of the sacred text, Jews across countries and ideologies asserted a cultural identification with that text, not necessarily commensurate with religion or tradition. In doing so they also countered and engaged with Christian interpretations of the Bible and constructions of history that fossilized Judaism with the coming of Jesus. Herein lay the nexus of the acculturation process and the Jews' preoccupation with the Bible: to forget their original source and place in the world was tantamount to abandoning themselves completely to the majority. Thus, as the Talmud and traditional life lost ground, Jews turned of necessity to the Bible, where they met head-on the Christian evaluations of their "portable Fatherland" (Heinrich Heine's felicitous formulation). They found these interpretations wanting and untenable. The Bible, so it appears, could not be a simple bridge between Judaism and Christianity.

In fact, controversy about the Bible, a struggle over authority and interpretation, raged from the eighteenth through the early twentieth centuries in Western and Central Europe. The arguments had been churned many times previously, but the debate took on new and vital contours in the modern period. As the Jews began to stake their claim to citizenship while diluting their religious identification to a nonpolitical ethnicity—such as "German Citizens of the Mosaic Faith"—and integrating into all walks of society, they left behind large elements of their traditional education. The Bible, or its cultural, social, and even political meaning, loomed larger in their attempt to distinguish themselves from their cultural setting. Thinkers, writers, and artists from almost every cultural or religious strand in modern Jewish life tried to stamp the Bible with their own, special imprimatur. Moreover, as part of the European canon, the Bible was not the domain of Jews alone; its interpretation was part and parcel of the public consciousness. A significant challenge to the position of the Jews came not only from the cultural and political forces that opposed their integration and emancipation but also from scrutiny of the Talmud and the Bible. These books were reassessed by Christian scholars of Judaism in the sixteenth century (the phenomenon known as Christian Hebraism) and continued to undergo an intensive reevaluation in the eighteenth century.[66] Furthermore, prominent European philosophers—Thomas Hobbes, Benedict Spinoza, and John Locke, to name but a few—challenged, each in his own way, basic beliefs about the Bible and its authorship, lending strength to the assault on the Masoretic text. Although influential thinkers still celebrated the biblical teachings, others challenged the very legitimacy of the book upon which Judaism had built its basic premise and created its link to the past.

Often it is claimed that the bitter tone of the Jewish confrontation with Christianity subsided in the Napoleonic period. Jewish leaders in the Assembly of Notables, when questioned by Napoleon in 1807 about their community's level of commitment to the French state and people, responded, with a degree of circuitous rhetoric, that they no longer harbored classical conceptions of Christians as idolators and saw them as "brothers."[67] In a similar vein, it has been argued that the "turn" to the Bible on the part of the maskilim was a means of finding a common source with their Christian counterparts. Notwithstanding these accepted truths, the question remains whether in their "use" of the Bible Jews were indeed building a bridge to the Christians. Moreover, as the vernacular was adopted by European Jews and their ability to read the Bible in the original language dwindled, their unique position as "the People of the Book" was challenged. Others could equally claim this title, as the German Protestants did. For generations they had used Luther's translation, and they clearly regarded the Bible as theirs. How then could German Jews, whose language was now German, sense a unique attachment to the Bible? Furthermore, Moses, the Jews' lawgiver and leader, was being seriously minimized by biblical commentators in Germany and England. His historicity was challenged by many scholars (Spinoza was an important exception) and his contribution to monotheism questioned. Such arguments demanded a concerted response by Jewish thinkers and educators, who were taxed and concerned. In this sense, Freud's *Moses and Monotheism,* published in 1939, can be seen as a continuation of the individual and collective discourse that engaged Jewish writers of earlier decades. The challenges to their people's origins opened up a whole series of issues. The discussions often took place in the vernacular and reverberated throughout the modern period; they all underscore the fact that the integration of Jews into European society also necessitated their cultural adaptation, and, for many, this included charting a position toward the Jewish past.

Scholars and other commentators have pointed out that the study of history, which had been strikingly underplayed in Jewish learning, became an essential element in the self-conscious nature of modern Jewish society.[68] It appears, however, that the "turn" to the Bible ought to be seen not only as an extension of the awakening interest in history but as an independent phenomenon with remarkable offshoots. As the roots of Jewish identification were being attacked from within and without, and as Jewish cohesiveness was weakened by integration, negotiation with the biblical text helped Jews enunciate another form of belonging and erect new boundaries with their cultural habitat.

Why the Bible, and what did it offer these people? If we examine some known texts, and others less canonical, within the sociocultural and political context of the modern period, the nature of their engagement with the Bible appears less monolithic. Key figures of the Jewish Enlightenment aimed to strengthen the Bible's place in the home and within the educational system, in contrast to the traditional hierarchy that emphasized first and foremost the study of the Talmud. But saying that is not enough. The nature of the Bible was what was at stake. Naphtali Herz Wessely (1725–1805), a Hamburg-born Jew who was educated in Copenhagen and then lived in Amsterdam before moving to Berlin, focused intensively on the Bible. In later years, writing to the Jews of Trieste, he recalled that when he was nine years old and a student in a *bet midrash,* the five books of Moses were considered taboo, and he had not studied them. Under the influence of his teacher Rabbi Shlomo Zalman Hanau, Wessely developed a love of grammar and the Hebrew language, and gradually, writing in Hebrew, he sought a literal explanation of the Bible and tried to offer rational, linguistic commentary on various sections. He composed *Shirei Tiferet* (Songs of Glory, 1789–1802), a five-volume epic on Moses, responding also to Johann Gottfried Herder's call for some poetic treatment of Moses. Wessely's engagement with secular education and cultural evolution pushed him to treat the Bible in ways that asserted its pride of place in the development of culture. From his first work, *Gan Na'ul* (The Locked Garden, 1765–66), Wessely was concerned with distinguishing between synonyms in order to show the genius of the Hebrew language, and inter alia to reveal the brilliance of rabbinical exegesis. In a textual and linguistic commentary that tacitly upheld that exegesis, he responded to currents in European thought and to the contemporaneous rationalistic and Enlightenment criticisms of the rabbinic interpretation of Scripture. His ability to mask the inner dialogue was remarkable. Those readers not versed in the contemporary debate could have remained oblivious to its intended direction.

Wessely was an important social and cultural innovator. His famous Hebrew tract *Words on Peace and Truth* (1782), written in response to Joseph II's first Edicts of Toleration (1781–82), was a significant breakthrough in the prevailing attitude toward the course of Jewish education and the study of the Bible, in particular. Although he dramatically prioritized *Torat Adam* (the law of man) and secular studies over religious teachings and study, what he called *Torat Elohim* (the law of God), Wessely upheld the centrality of revelation of the Torah to Moses—the kernel of *Torat Elohim*—and the necessity of learning Hebrew in order to study the Bible. Failure to know the language, he warned his fellow Jews, leads to a state of depravity. Wessely's agenda, exegetical and social, was clearly designed to bring Jews into the orbit of the European Enlightenment with the Bible serving as the basis of study and moral direction. But he also had a political goal. Such a step would further legitimate their right to an improved political status and maybe even to equality with the Christian majority.[69]

Wessely affirmed the textual authenticity of the Hebrew Bible, the authority of revelation to Moses, and his greatness as a leader, and he defended Judaism from critiques of these positions. He envisaged the future education of Jewish boys and girls as different from his—the Bible would be at the center, and study of the Talmud would be relegated to a select few. The *Bi'ur*, the translation of the Bible into German written in Hebrew characters in which he himself was engaged, would be their primer. Published from 1783 over a period of several years, the *Bi'ur* became a basic text for the Jüdische Freischule, the first maskilic school in Berlin, established in 1778. Wessely also intended the *Bi'ur* to counter the rising tide of German and English biblical criticism, which questioned the authority of the Masoretic text and the nature of rabbinic exegesis.

Mendelssohn, the architect and guiding force behind the project, turned to this translation in the last decade of his life. Mendelssohn's controversies with various Christian figures, starting with his public confrontation with the Swiss theologian (and leading theorist of physiognomy) Johann Caspar Lavater in 1769, encouraged him to assert himself in the Jewish terrain. Fearing that Prussian society might envelop Jewish tradition altogether, he embarked on this scheme, wanting to leave behind a Bible translation that relied on traditional Jewish interpretations rather than on Protestant scholarship. He opposed the Christians' disregard for the Masoretic text, even if at times he showed a close affinity with its critics. Caught in the crossfire between Protestant biblical scholarship and traditional Jewish exegesis, Mendelssohn hoped that his translation would enable German Jews "to understand sayings of wisdom [and they] may go and seek the word of the Lord without [relying on] the translations of Christian scholars." He minced no words about the challenge to the Masoretic text, remarking in his introduction:

> Our rabbis have prepared for us a Masora and created a fence for law and justice so that we will not flounder like blind people in the darkness. And from now on we have no right to move from their ways and to reorient a way of life. One does not go according to this or that interpretation but only after the Masora.[70]

Thus Mendelssohn anticipated what many Jews would do in different countries throughout the nineteenth century: offer a new vernacular translation that would preserve in some form a Jewish outlook on the text, repossessing it for Jews and reclaiming it for Judaism.

Mendelssohn went even further than one would have expected. He elegantly wove into his translation many commentaries from medieval writers—from Rashi to Maimonides—to highlight their sophisticated reading of the text and to celebrate the harmonization of rabbinical interpretations with "the literal text." Moreover, he revealed little inclination to waver in his belief in the authenticity and oneness of the Bible, intimating the position to which he would later subscribe in his important philosophic work *Jerusalem* (1783). Clearly preferring a Jewish "presentation" of the Bible, Mendelssohn added the *tikkunei soferim* (corrections of the copyists) that accompanied all traditional editions. Consciously, and maybe ideologically, he was thinking of a traditional audience while addressing a much broader one. But had he stopped here, the *Bi'ur* would have failed in its other purposes. Certainly Mendelssohn wanted to facilitate language study and improve comprehension by translating the Bible into "the German customary at this time among our nation" while lavishing praise on the literary beauty of the Hebrew text. This integrated approach upheld, almost completely, notions of revelation and halakhic Judaism even as Mendelssohn and his colleagues worked to produce an elegant translation with annotations both literary and grammatical.[71]

The success of the Mendelssohn translation had wide-reaching implications. Initially opposed by rabbinical figures outside of Berlin, the *Bi'ur* gradually penetrated many different communities and levels of Jewish society. Even Rabbi Jacob Mecklenburg (1785–1865), a leader of German Orthodoxy and the chief rabbi of Königsberg, showed deep respect for Mendelssohn's translation and methodology. In his own commentary on the Bible, Mecklenburg upheld Mendelssohn's notion that midrashic and talmudic passages offer clear and exact exegesis of the biblical text. Although the *Bi'ur* was by no means universally accepted by Orthodox and ultra-Orthodox circles, noted rabbis such as Akiva Eger of Posen either endorsed or subscribed to later editions. Mendelssohn's Bible eventually assumed a distinguished place in the homes of German Jews as a holy text to be studied.

The battle over the Bible was intense. By the middle of the nineteenth century, six other German versions were on the market, three in Hebrew script and three in German script. Moreover, a host of commentaries and other translations (both of individual books and of the Pentateuch) vied for the authoritative position on the text, all of them seeking to engage German Jews with the Bible. The *Bi'ur* easily won out over most of these translations, going through more than 20 editions by the middle of the nineteenth century. A measure of competition was offered by the indefatigable labors of the Reform rabbi and editor of the *Allgemeine Zeitung des Judentums,* Ludwig Philippson (1811–89). Interestingly

enough, though coming from a much less traditional position than Mendelssohn, Philippson showed great respect for the *Bi'ur,* even as he presented a more
popular edition of the entire Old Testament to the acculturating Jewish community. Like the Orthodox Mecklenburg, Philippson shied away from confronting
the aggressive biblical criticism that severely minimized the role of Moses and
challenged the authenticity of the Masoretic text. In fact, Philippson adhered to
a fully traditional viewpoint when it came to the thorny issues of creation, authorship of the text, and the Egyptian period.

In three editions (1854, 1859, and 1878), one of which was heavily illustrated
with English engravings (1859, published in Leipzig), and in a later edition
(1875) with engravings by the French artist Gustave Doré, Philippson tried to
bring the biblical period to life by including images and commentaries that anchored the text in Egyptian lore and romantic visions. His exegesis focused on
linguistic issues and ethical concerns but was designed for a Jewish readership
that would take pride in the glory of the text. (Freud's father apparently used the
illustrated version of 1859 to educate young Sigmund, an indication of the penetration of Philippson's work even into traditional homes.) Philippson incorporated Doré's work because it abounded in dramatic realism and offered the
reader gripping and true-to-life depictions of biblical figures and stories, unencumbered by complex symbolism.

Other Bibles with particular agendas continued to be published, but both the
Mendelssohn and the Philippson projects certainly enabled German-speaking
Jews to receive a rather traditional Jewish approach to the Bible for a good part
of the nineteenth century. Neither, of course, could satisfy the likes of Samson
Raphael Hirsch (1808–88), a militant Orthodox leader, as being sufficiently God-
fearing. In the 1860s he produced his own Pentateuch translation and commentary, free of any scientific orientation and addressed to his followers. And it goes
without saying that in none of these versions was there any attempt to use the
Bible as a bridge to Christian understanding and fellowship.[72]

The drive to safeguard a specifically Jewish approach to and interpretation of
the Bible was not limited to Germany. What happened there was not a catalyst
but indicates a type of strategy that developed as the battle over interpretation
intensified. It was in England that a major challenge to the Old Testament
emerged, first and foremost (but not exclusively) among the eighteenth-century
Deists. Though Deists like Thomas Chubb and Thomas Morgan were at odds on
many issues, they agreed that the Old Testament had no validity for Christianity
and the New Testament. Their arguments were supplemented by the research of
Benjamin Kennicott and others who tried to establish a new text of the Old Testament that would supplant the Masora. These devastating criticisms, which

spread through English society, questioned the veracity of Jewish roots. It is thus
not incidental—as the late Anglo-Jewish scholar David Daiches noted in 1942—
that just around the time that Mendelssohn perceived the necessity of doing battle in Germany over the Bible and began to publish the *Bi'ur* (in 1783), there
appeared in England the first Hebrew-English Bible (1785) to be produced under
the auspices of a Jew, Alexander Alexander. Using the authorized King James
Version (1611), Alexander did not stray greatly from an English-Hebrew Bible
that had been published 11 years earlier, but he included *haftarot* (portions from
the Prophets read in synagogue following the reading of the Torah on Sabbaths
and other designated days), as an aid to the synagogue-goer. Even more important, during this period several thinkers emerged in England who sensed the
need to "repossess" the Bible for Judaism by disclaiming and refuting the tendencies of the Deists, Kennicott, and other writers on the Old Testament.[73]

David Levi, Abraham Tang, Raphael Baruh, Solomon Bennett, and Isaac Del-
gado all attempted to withstand the tidal wave of Christian criticism of the Old
Testament and assumptions about the nature of the Jewish prophecy and Moses.
Levi and Tang rejected Kennicott's challenge to the Masoretic version, pointed
out the ways in which English biblical criticism was deeply wanting, and denied
the aspersion that the Jews had allowed many mistakes to penetrate their Bible.
(Interestingly, this issue had already surfaced in the Mendelssohn-Lavater controversy of 1769–70.) Levi, in his three-volume *Dissertation on the Prophecies*
(1793–1800), vigorously upheld Moses' authority as a prophet—rejecting the notion popularized in the radical deistic text *The Three Imposters: Moses, Jesus, Mohammed.* Writing in English, Levi condemned those who thought that they
could translate the Bible without first acquiring the intimate knowledge of Hebrew that Jews possessed from birth. Here was another polemical argument that
Jews in the modern period were to employ to discredit non-Jewish research or
study of the Bible and to claim the sacred text for themselves: only Jews could
deal seriously with the Bible because only they possessed the necessary linguistic
skills. Both Levi and Tang further argued that the Torah would never require
anyone to believe in fantasies unsubstantiated by reason and that it would never
contradict reasonable moral instincts. (Incidentally, this too was an issue at
the heart of Mendelssohn's response to Lavater.) Although they did not, like
Mendelssohn, produce a translation of their own, Levi and Tang constantly
commented on the Bible and corrected the prevailing versions, showing how
much meaning their engagement with this text contributed to their self-identity.[74]

In this heated dialogue, Levi was pushed to establish what one may almost call
a dogmatic attitude toward Judaism. Not only did he declare that one who does
not accept Moses' authorship of the Bible ceases to be regarded as a Jewish be-

liever, but he also urged other Jews to enter the fray and contest the Christian attempt to usurp their rightful ownership of the text. His "articles of faith" show the Enlightenment tradition in full force, supplemented by a traditionalist attitude toward the Bible. For Levi, it was a rational book, God-given and Moses-authored, and the Hebrew prophets (unlike Jesus) were prophets of truth. Moreover, the persistence of Jewish survival is evidence of providential history. For Levi and this circle, it was almost as if the Bible had become, to re-turn to Heine, a "written Fatherland." Claiming its Jewish roots had become a way to create a sense of belonging, presaging what the Galician-Jewish sculptor Alfred Nossig would later depict in his Moses-like description of the *Wandering Jew* (1901).[75] There, the eternal wanderer holds a *Sefer Torah*—the Pentateuch— intimating that what enabled Jews to endure over time and place was their sa-cred book. The key, then, to their survival was their internal, spiritual source, not the external pressure or situation, as the myth of the Wandering Jew—con-demned to walk the earth eternally for refusing assistance to Christ on his way to Calvary—commonly maintained.[76]

In the nineteenth century, several English Jews, faced with attacks on the Old Testament and negative assessments of its contribution to society, felt the need to offer a defense.[77] Even Claude Montefiore (1858–1938), who stood at the center of ecumenical discussions and was a proponent of an open attitude toward the New Testament and Christian teachings, remained adamant in claiming the Old Testament for Judaism. Montefiore, who was a founder of the Liberal Jewish movement along with the magistrate and social worker Lily Montagu, was a strong advocate for attaching oneself to a nonrabbinic form of Judaism while remaining identified with the community. His book *Bible for Home Reading* (1896) offers a unique glimpse of the way a highly acculturated Jew attempted to combine modern biblical criticism and research, appreciation and regard for Christian moral and religious teachings, and a "Jewish perspective." Wholly un-orthodox in his approach to the presentation of the text—for example, not be-ginning with the Creation story, which was "too full of grave moral and religious difficulties to form a suitable beginning" and was not "the best and noblest chapters"—Montefiore made it clear from the outset that the Old Testament was not a uniquely "universal" book but one that "was written by Jews, about Jews, and for Jews." Comparing the Jews' attachment to the Bible to the English sentiment for Shakespeare, he emphasized time and again that, though Moses was not the sole author of the Bible, and though it is permeated with historical inaccuracies and replete with unoriginal and untenable tales and varying de-grees of ethical and religious teachings, it is the Jews who have been the great world-teachers about goodness and God. And . . . most of what men believe about God, and a very great deal of the very best of what they know and believe about goodness, was written by Jews and is found in the Bible. It is the Bible, and through the Bible it is the Jews, who have taught men not only to love God and to love goodness, but to see that the love of goodness is part and parcel of the love of God.[78]

In this Bible, which stresses moral teachings above all, Montefiore allowed himself homiletic devices that assumed significant moral lessons: for example, the fact that Moses, the founder of Judaism, had no grave is understood as an indirect protest against that stage in history when idolatry reigned and the spirits were worshiped. Montefiore took it for granted that the Jewish religion had evolved over time and that modern rabbis could contribute to further growth. Like the leaders of Reform Judaism in Germany, and in common with Simon Dubnow's theory of national autonomism in Russia, Montefiore claimed that Judaism became much purer and freer when it was separated from the national soil. Rather than decay with the fall of Jerusalem, Judaism rose and developed through its exile in Babylon. The Bible thus became its source of strength, emerging once again as a "written Fatherland"—replacing the national-political-geographic connection.[79]

Montefiore, in his classical Reform exegesis, had little empathy for books in the Bible that failed to meet his moral standard: the Book of Esther was unrepresentative of Jewish tradition and could easily be removed from the canon. Yet with great inner satisfaction he guided the reader carefully through the Psalms "as we breathe a purer air," leaving behind national limitations. But in the three-way struggle between universalism, scientific criticism, and a "Jewish perspective," even Montefiore's *Bible for Home Reading* fails to eliminate completely the tone of Jewish superiority: for example, "Many races have contributed, each in its own degree, to the total store. The Jewish race has made, as we believe, the largest and most fruitful contributions."[80]

In his attempt to reread the Bible rationally, expunging all the fantasies that Levi and Tang had also rejected, Montefiore espoused the notion that all men are God's creatures. God cares for all without distinction of race or creed and allows for religious and spiritual development outside the Hebrew Scriptures. But Montefiore stopped there. He concluded his second volume with a lukewarm approach to the New Testament, claiming that its best sections can be found in their pristine form in the Old Testament. Eventually he chose not to include the New Testament in his Bible "for home reading," because when all was said and done, he was convinced that it is in the Hebrew Scripture that "we can still gather those essential doctrines by which the purest faith in the Divine can be quickened and sustained, and by which the noblest life among and for our fellow-men can be lived in the realized presence of God."[81]

Montefiore's engagement with the Bible illuminates a phenomenon common among Jews whose sense of belonging was very much challenged by their growing attachment to the majority culture. This was especially pronounced among German Jews, who from Mendelssohn onward grappled with the implications of acculturation for their identity. No one more than Heinrich Heine (1797–1856) epitomized this dilemma. Allusions have already been made to Heine's "written/portable Fatherland," a notion that seems to convey the ambivalence sensed by Jews who detached themselves from traditional Judaism but remained in some manner associated to their Jewish roots. Regardless of the changes in Heine's feelings about the Bible and its personages over the decades of his tumultuous life, he consistently evoked its images and ideals, personalities and mysteries. Like Germans in general, he was deeply engaged with the Lutheran translation and praised the Protestant Reformation for making the Bible more accessible to the public.[82] Indeed, Heine understood the Bible to be a carrier of cultural and moral traditions, and, as Protestantism, it allowed people to reconnect through the Bible with the morality of ancient Judaism. Scots and Americans, Danes and Northern Germans imbibed this tradition. The Protestants succeeded where the Jews trailed far behind, because the Jews were constrained by their isolation in society. Nonetheless, and especially after his conversion to Lutheranism in 1825, he saw the Bible as an integral part of Jewish civilization. The ancient Hebrews, unlike the Jews of the Ghetto, were proud and noble individuals, and the Bible was a foundation text of civilizations, which survived the encounter between historic rationalism and theology. In one of Heine's unique constructions:

> What a book it is! As great and wide as the whole world rooted deep in the abysses of creation and reaching far upward into the blue mysteries of heaven. . . . The Jews can take comfort—they lost Jerusalem, it is true, and the Temple, and the Ark of the Covenant, and the golden vessels and trinkets of Solomon, but all that is of little weight when compared with the Bible, the indestructible treasure which they saved.[83]

Then, after mentioning that it was Muhammad who designated the Jews the "people of the book," Heine offered a view of the Bible that granted the text a metahistorical meaning, central to the repossession of the Bible in modern times: "A book is their fatherland, their property, their ruler, their good and evil fortune. Within the boundaries of this book they live: here they can exercise an inalienable right of citizenship, here they cannot be expelled or despised, here they are strong and admirable."[84] In a sense Heine thus countered his own aversion to one aspect of modern Jewish behavior—crass commercialism—with praise of the Jews who at the time of the destruction of the Temple left all the gold and silver behind, saving only the Bible, which they bestowed on humanity as a gift:

> As they spread the Bible throughout the whole world, and deliver it, as it were, into the hands of all mankind, by means of mercantile stratagems, smuggling and barter, and leave it for its exegesis to the understanding of the individual, they are founding the great commonwealth of the spirit, the commonwealth of religious feeling, of neighborly love, of purity and true morality. These cannot be taught by dogmatic perception patterns, but by image and example such as are contained in the lofty and holy Book of instruction for little and big children—the Bible.[85]

The Bible granted the Jews inner freedom, even if they were later to be subjugated, and a sense of value, even while they were being devalued. It was this perspective that brought German Jews to use the Bible extensively for educational purposes in the nineteenth century. Scores of books based on the Bible were published for children and young men, and toward the end of the century compilations of stories about women in the Bible were published for the edification of young women.

Heine returned at several points in his life to the figure of Moses and his contribution to the world. In his youth, when he was enthralled by the Greeks and their aesthetic sense, Heine showed no sympathy for Moses' character and his "hostility to art," but in later years his position changed dramatically.[86] Moses loomed in his mind as the great artist who created the people of Israel, the "human pyramids," both "colossal and indestructible." This glowing change of heart, in clear opposition to German thinkers and biblical scholars of his day, resonated among Jews in other countries, where the role of Moses as lawgiver and creator of a moral system was significantly emphasized. Thus, the "portable Fatherland" had become for Heine a form of belonging, one that never overtook his sense of being a German or a European but clearly played a role in shaping his persona and the minds of others who read him diligently for generations.[87]

Heine's notion, though significant for many in the throes of developing their German-Jewish consciousness, was challenged by a leftist-Jewish thinker, Moses Hess (1812–75). Hess was disturbed by the thrust of rationalism that pervaded many German-Jewish attempts to interpret the Bible. In his drive to rekindle the spirit of patriotism imbued in the ancient lawgivers, Hess tried to reinstate the connection between the Bible and the Land of Israel, just as the Christians had. The effort of the maskilim to replace the national ethos with humanistic ideals ran roughshod over ideas essential to the biblical story. For Hess, the historic right of the Jewish people to the Land of Israel emerged from the story of Abraham, and without this pivotal connection, and until such time as Jews returned to their land and settled there, all acts of reform should be postponed. Hess was one of the first acculturated Jews in nineteenth-century Western and Central Europe to make this political connection, rejecting the thrust of much biblical interpretation that sought to repossess the Bible without political or national overtones. Moreover, Hess had profound respect for Moses' leadership and his role in engineering the evolution of the people, and he completely opposed a Judaism based on the Bible alone, without the Talmud, the Oral Law. He claimed that Moses and the Oral Law were on the same level and that Diaspora Jewry survived through this connection.

Notwithstanding his strong advocacy of the interrelationship between the Bible and the Land of Israel, Hess continued to see the Bible as the source of monotheism and humanism. He believed deeply in its moral, social, and universal-historical value. He also saw the Bible as the root of Jewish genius and the Jewish contribution to civilization. In his post-1850 writings, the sense of Jewish superiority rings clear, and the attuning of Judaism to the majority culture and religion is rejected.

Hess's concern with the nature of the Jewish contribution to society continued to feature prominently in the writings of German Jews during the Second Reich (1870–1914). Jewish apologists, historians, theologians, and thinkers were concerned by the debates over the nature of Christian teachings: could Jesus be seen as superseding the Mosaic tradition? Even before the heated controversy (ca. 1900) over Adolf von Harnack's disassociation of Liberal Protestantism from the Old Testament—positing Jesus as the authentic continuation of biblical Judaism—Jews quoted the French scholar Ernest Renan's opinion that Christianity was deeply dependent on Judaism as its original source. Similarly, they described Jesus' message as no more than a continuation of Mosaic law. The ideas of Matthew and Luke on prayer were also considered mere derivations from biblical Judaism. The fact that such a wide variety of Jewish thinkers (Leo Baeck, Heinrich Graetz, Leo Eshelbacher, Martin Schreiner, Ludwig Geiger, and Martin Buber, to name but a few) hotly upheld the primacy of the Jewish Bible—minimizing the originality and independence of Christian thinking—gives us an indication of how central this was to their sense of Jewish uniqueness, "the history of Jewish consciousness" and superiority.[88]

While men like Montefiore, Baeck, and Geiger were increasingly defining themselves as Citizens of the Mosaic Faith, creating a clear delineation between their loyalty to their countries and their allegiance to Judaism—depoliticizing their religious attachment—the Bible became a source of moral edification. It would appear, however, that within this new dichotomy the universalist message of the Bible—the bridge between Jews and non-Jews—was not simply achieved; it had its own deficiencies and limitations.

As acculturation progressed and Jews moved firmly into the orbit of the German language and culture, another major Bible project emerged. It was spearheaded by the philosopher Martin Buber (1878–1965), who sensed the growing distance of his fellow German Jews from the original Hebrew text and was cognizant of the continuing criticism of Protestant thinkers on the value and virtue of the Old Testament. Buber's interest in this project began prior to World War I, but it was only after the war and at the initiation of a Christian publisher, Lambert Schneider, that he undertook the translation with the distinguished, but then paralyzed, Jewish philosopher Franz Rosenzweig. Before the latter's death in 1929, the two men translated 10 books of the Bible, innovatively asserting the distinct nature of the biblical text while granting priority to its "oral" quality. Underlying these objectives were their contentions that the Bible was originally spoken and that it constituted a single unified text. Though fully aware of Christian and Jewish exegesis, the translators were less concerned with producing a philologically correct version or one with a literary voice than in rendering it true to its Hebrew cadence and to what Buber called "the natural laws of human breath and human speech." The ultimate purpose was to guide the German-Jewish reader back to the original language and to engage that reader in an intimate, spiritual dialogue with the speaker of the text. In Gershom Scholem's words, the translation "found a creative compromise between the traditional Jewish awe that forbids the pronouncing of the name of God and the obligation to make the biblical word readable, i.e. audible."[89] Indeed, Rosenzweig used the term *verdeutschen* to refer to the translation into German, rather than the more common *ubersetzen,* implying their desire to turn the German into a Jewish language by capturing the oral layer of the Hebrew in their translation.

In creating this Hebraized German text, Buber and Rosenzweig recognized the boldness of their endeavor. The first books of their Bible were welcomed by many German Jews, particularly the youth of various ideological leanings. Recalling the impact of this translation, a leader of the student movement commented: "There was hardly a meeting, a seminar, a conference, or a camp of Jewish youth organizations where Bible study was not part of it."[90] Yet the translation was far from being universally accepted, given the ideological differences that continued to mark German Jewry in the waning years of the Weimar Republic. Alas, the project was not finished for decades. On its completion in Israel in 1961, Scholem wondered for whom it remained relevant because Buber continued with the translation even after his intended readers were no longer among the living. It would appear that, for Buber, the original philosophic and spiritual design had not lost its purpose. Through the "first genuine encounter of the Jewish-Hebrew Bible and the spirit of the German language," he rejected attempts to devalue the Old Testament and the God of Creation. He still hoped to lay the groundwork for what he called a "shared primal truth" between Judaism and Christianity.[91] Neither the Holocaust nor the creation of the State of Israel nullified these spiritual goals.

We have seen how some Jews in Protestant England and Germany contended for the sovereignty of the Bible. Could Jews in a Catholic country with a strong centralist orientation—France, for example, where religion and *patrie* were incorporated in the spirit of the state—feel the same freedom to engage openly in a debate over the nature of the Bible and its relation to Jewish continuity? What role could the Bible play in Jewish self-definition in the presence of a formidable Catholic establishment?

Unlike in England and Germany, in France significant currents of thought had very positive ideas about Moses and the pattern of rule of the ancient Hebrews. Jean Bodin, the distinguished political philosopher of the late sixteenth century, wrote glowingly of the State of the Hebrews and saw it as one to be emulated. Bodin was soon followed by others who drew parallels between natural law and the law of Moses. Abbé Claude Fleury, a popular seventeenth-century writer and Louis XV's confessor, was especially laudatory of the Hebrews so long as they followed Moses' law and institutions. In an extensive tract on the customs of the Israelites, republished in dozens of editions, he wrote:

> The people God chose to conserve the true religion until the preaching of the Gospel are an excellent model for a human life most in conformity with nature. We see in their mores the most reasonable ways to survive, to occupy oneself, and to live in society: we can learn not only morality, but also economics and politics from them.[92]

Other Catholics, such as Abbé Guénée and the dedicated supporter of Jewish emancipation Abbé Grégoire, drew parallels between the Mosaic system and republican ideals, and praised their attitudes toward slavery, women, and the unfortunate. These opinions did not run counter to their Catholic belief that, with the coming of Jesus, the torch was passed to the "true Jews." Moreover, they coincided with ideas voiced by leading Enlightenment thinkers such as Jean-Jacques

Rousseau, who forcefully presented Moses as a great leader and lawmaker who showed the highest respect for his constituents. For Rousseau, Moses was a fore-runner of the republican order. Similar views redolent of the pre-revolutionary period appeared during the Restoration (1815–48), though often couched in a conservative attack on revolutionary ideals. In upholding the political tradition of the Hebrews, these diverse voices encouraged Jews in France, in a period marked by rapid acculturation to French society, to embark on their negotiation with the Bible.

The individual who most energetically presented an unabashed defense of the Mosaic law and the pristine nature of the Bible was the French-Jewish writer Alexandre Weill (1811–99). The publication in the early 1890s of his *Five Books of Moses* (*Les cinq livres [mosaïstes] de Moïse*) was possible, he claimed, only in the liberal Third Republic, created in the 1870s. A man whose life spanned much of the nineteenth century and who flirted with various ideologies and professions, Weill had been a staunch believer in the revolutionary vision. Almost reiterating the Deist platform, he envisaged in 1847 a revolution bringing an end to all par-ticular religions and eventually creating one people, "only brothers and disciples of Jesus." However, when the Revolution of 1848 failed to realize the utopian dream, Weill became engaged in mysticism and raged against anti-Jewish ex-pressions, past and contemporary. But his "turn" to the Bible, often overlooked, is revealing, because he revisited some themes from his earlier writings, though now in much less refined and at times extremely caustic language directed at both Christians and Jews, contemporary and historic.[93]

Weill presented his five-volume work as the product of 60 years of involve-ment with the Bible. His autobiographical comments, interspersed throughout, add a certain prophetic tone. He wanted the reader to recognize the significance of his reencounter with the original text, after he had been preoccupied for years with other issues: he had come face to face with the Bible's absolute universal truth and had recognized that Hebrew was the "mother of all languages, ancient and modern." Echoing the writings of other French authors, he designated Moses "the single and unprecedented legislator of all times and periods," who admitted no royalty, no tyranny other than the law of God. Weill spoke admir-ingly of Moses' attitude toward women and toward the notion of divorce, com-paring it most favorably to that found in the texts of other religions, especially the Hindu Mahabharata. He praised the liberal nature of the Jewish religion, and opposed it to idolatrous religions, including Christianity(!), which are unable to come to terms with the glaring fact that all things good, such as liberty and progress, extend from Moses and the Jews. The overriding superiority of the Mosaic law, reiterated time and again by Weill, makes the other religions view

Judaism with discomfort and feel strangled by it. Weill left no issue untouched. He denied the place of the supernatural in Jewish religion and life, which is based on natural law and rooted in historic certitude and experiment. It is therefore no wonder that the philosophic-religious position of Moses appeared to him to be not only "the absolute truth about God and man" but also the solution to all the problems of the nations.

Weill was at least aware that, in both his paean to Moses and his vitriolic denunciations of those who wrote critically of Moses and the Bible, from Voltaire to Ernest Renan (whom he portrayed as the most ignorant writer of the nineteenth century), he was unusually bold. In time, he assumed, his ideas would be vindicated, even as he admitted that anyone who would have dared previously to speak as he did would have been burnt at the stake. His ability to express such uncommon views stemmed from the "absolute freedom of religion of the Third Republic and in the French language." Here, then, is the epitome of Jewish self-confidence. On the eve of the Dreyfus Affair, as antisemitism surfaced once again in France, a Jewish writer boldly affirmed his right to extol the Mosaic law as the progenitor of 1789—of liberty, equality, fraternity—of the American Revolution, and of Cromwell's teachings. In his desire to return to the pristine Mosaic tradition for the welfare of French society, Weill railed against the prophet Ezra's damnable influence ("the vulgar Pharisees") on rabbinic Judaism in contaminating the Mosaic text, and against the Christians' misunderstanding of Judaism and their false beliefs. One wonders whether the anticlerical mood of the Third Republic further fueled Weill's militancy and led him to believe that the demise of Christianity was imminent. Interestingly, he added a Hebrew postscript to the fifth volume in which his vigorous position had no filters or boundaries. A characteristic quotation from this harangue brings some of the flavor and intent of his conclusion:

> I sing to God song and thanks for having bestowed on me strength and power to raise Moses from the grave of the trinity in which Ezra and the first Sanhedrin, followed by the Pharisees and after them the disciples of Jesus, buried him: I said I will smite them, I will remove their memory from mankind. I broke the yoke of the Ezraites, nullified Christian strength. I opened to the nation the chimneys of truth in the Pentateuch, and their gates will never close again![94]

Yet Weill hoped that "the day will come when there will be no more preachers, and as Moses said, where the people will be the teacher, religion and the truth will be born from the ashes and from the filth." Moreover, in returning the Bible to its true safekeeper—the pure Mosaic tradition—and reinstating Moses as the sole prophet and Messiah, Weill also hailed the tradition of 1789, the true reincarnation of the Mosaic law, now being reestablished in the Third Republic. Filled with outrage against attempts to tamper with the noblest of virtues and political systems, Weill remained a devout adherent to French Jewry's dyarchy of Religion and Fatherland.

Was Weill inordinately out of line, dramatically off base? Even before the Revolution of 1789, Beer Isaac Berr (1724–1828), a fellow traveler of the Jewish Enlightenment and the translator of Wessely's *Words on Peace and Truth* into French, had called for improvement in the teaching and studying of the Bible. Responding in his 1791 pamphlet *Lettre d'un citoyen* (Letter of a Citizen) to the revolutionary emancipation decrees, Berr spoke of the Bible as the bridge between citizenship and Judaism, asserting the Jews' ability to integrate into society. He hoped to see a French translation in the spirit of the *Bi'ur*—engagement with the original text, accompanied by French commentary. But during the Restoration, amid the very articulate Saint-Simonian circle, emerged Joseph Salvador (1796–1873). Born in Montpellier to a mixed marriage and highly acculturated parents, Salvador stepped into the fray with several works on the nature of the Mosaic law and its institutions that directly challenged Christian claims on the nature of the state and the role of Judaism in the progression of mankind. His work was to leave a deep imprint on other Jewish writers (such as Gustave d'Eichtal, Léopold Dukes, and Adolphe Franck) and to arouse the ire of prominent French writers, most notably Renan.[95]

Salvador went much further than his predecessors. Returning to the Bible and to Moses in the 1820s, he showed unstinting belief in the centrality of Mosaic teaching and the Mosaic system. Not only was the decalogue the foremost contribution to mankind but it also lay at the foundation of the Revolution's triad of equality, fraternity, and liberty. The Hebrew Republic was the most advanced system of public order, the wisest and simplest, and none had superseded it. But Salvador proceeded another step forward. While taking the Roman Church to task for appropriating the mission of the Bible, he envisioned a time when its rule would be overturned. To the claim that the Bible and Judaism had been inherited by Christianity, Salvador responded:

> Your argument is erroneous. You have power on your side for the present, but we have time. Your world is ephemeral, you are not the last stage of salvation. The day will come when nations will rise up and reject the yoke of the Roman Church, will lay claim to a new world of justice, or, in the words of the Bible, a new Jerusalem.[96]

Salvador thus upheld Judaism's mission to the world by positioning the Bible in its Jewish framework. Other Jewish Saint-Simonians adopted this radical view, which granted Judaism's political origins a new significance for the evolution of society. During the Restoration, rabbis and scholars echoed these themes, often exalting Mosaic law in Bodinian fashion as the model of a democratic society. To these deeply acculturated figures, Judaism was "the mother of religions," Moses was the great figure who conceptualized a God of reason and universality, and the prophets strove to spiritualize the Bible's concepts and vision. As Hippolyte Rodrigue wrote in his *Les trois filles de la Bible* (The Three Daughters of the Bible, 1856), "The religion of Israel . . . which is monotheistic in its essence, rationalist in its existence, absolutely represents the two victorious principles, the foundations of the current philosophical movement." Rodrigue and other French Jews who were reevaluating their sense of belonging, thanks to their unique political situation, used the Bible to enunciate universalist beliefs and republican values and break the vise in which Christian writers had gripped their religion and their sacred text.

At this time, Samuel Cahen's multivolume Bible translation, initiated in 1829, during the period of the Restoration, when Jewish academics were still shunned and biblical criticism was dominated by Christian scholars and theologians, was gradually drawing to completion. Cahen (1796–1862), like Mendelssohn and Levi before him, felt the need to reassert the Jewish hold on the Bible. His version immediately drew criticism from the *Archives de Christianisme*, the journal of Christian Bible scholars, which attacked his rationalist method and rejection of Christian interpretations. Cahen's approach was indeed rationalist. The translator's deliberations were diligently documented, and he sneered at Jewish customs occasioned by what he regarded as misunderstandings and/or superstitions. And, certainly, Cahen sifted through many translations of the text, including those of Christian writers; yet his preference clearly lay with Jewish commentators, medieval as well as modern.[97] Cahen's efforts do not seem to have had much impact on his coreligionists, but they further indicate that there was a concerted attempt in this period to reinvigorate Judaism by offering a modern biblical text that took its inspiration from internal Jewish sources.

In the same spirit, the Alliance Israélite Universelle, established in Paris in 1860, energetically waged a campaign to "regenerate" the Jews of North Africa, Turkey, and the Middle East. Striving to modernize these populations by changing their educational systems, the Alliance followed the maskilic approach and moved biblical education to the center of attention, reducing talmudic studies to a bare minimum. The leaders of the Alliance were inspired by the ideas of Salvador and Weill: they saw the Bible as a source of societal transformation. The

Bible was not just a list of commandments interpreted by the Mishnah, the Talmud, and the rabbis but a rudimentary text upon which the foundations of the modern order could be established. Alliance leaders gave the Bible, which encapsulated their notions of an ideal society, a preeminent place in the education of Jews under Islam.[98]

The triumphalism that prevails in much of the Jewish biblical exegesis that we have examined was present even in the first Bible fully illustrated by a Jewish artist in the modern period. Ephraim Moses Lilien was born in 1874 in Drohobycz, a thriving city in eastern Galicia that produced two other notable Jewish artists, Maurycy Gottlieb and Bruno Schulz. Lilien is well known for his work in connection with the early Zionist Congresses and for his depictions of Theodor Herzl. Less is known of his ambitious plan to illustrate both the Old and the New Testaments.[99] Eventually only three of a projected seven volumes were published, covering mostly the Old Testament. Two identical editions of the work were published in 1908–12 and 1923 and were accompanied by a translation by the Protestant biblical scholar Eduard Reuss (1804–91). The abbreviated translation was based on Reuss' extensive translation, previously published in both French and German, which though conservative in tone clearly rejected the single-authorship hypothesis.

Lilien undertook this project in Berlin in 1907, after returning from his first visit to Palestine deeply enraptured by the holy places he had seen and by the diversity he observed in the Jewish and Arab populations. He had been part of the tremendous development in graphics in Berlin at the turn of the century and was influenced by Jugendstil and Aubrey Beardsley. Lilien's Bible is filled with daring allusions and dramatically original interpretations capped by a celebration of masculinity and strength, eroticism and nudity. This was not a Bible to be brought to synagogue! It was intended for an audience that appreciated art and would not be aghast when it encountered Lilien's ploys and designs. On the opening page (see p. 30), the Creation of the World shows God seated, attended by two nude male angels whose wings cover His face, in accord with the Jewish tradition that God's face should not be seen. A halo behind His covered head is partially visible. God's lower body can be seen, though it is covered in a full robe, and His fingers are spread in the gesture of the Priestly Blessing—a way for Lilien to include himself in the image, because he traced his lineage to the priestly class. Before proceeding too far into his Bible, we are presented with another leap of Lilien's homoerotic and secular imagination when he presents an angel as Herzl, or Herzl as an angel. The angel/Herzl—homoerotic, powerful, masculine—banishes Adam and Eve from Paradise. (Lilien could have very easily based this image on a painting by the Munich artist Franz von Stuck

[1863–1928], completed in 1897 and published in *Ost und West* in 1905, in which a forceful, naked figure with a halo holds a large stick in a similar position to Herzl's sword as he gazes directly at Adam and Eve, seen only from the back.) Clearly feeling that he had the artistic license to mold the Bible within his own ideological framework, Lilien also merged the figures of Moses and Herzl, two visionaries who changed the course of history. He depicts Herzl as Moses when he is about to destroy the tablets—unconventional tablets of law, possibly in pseudo-cuneiform style, which Lilien used to assimilate the classical tradition with the visionary future.[100] He also merged the figure of Herzl with the angel who was destined "with a drawn sword" to stop Balaam from cursing Israel. His strong body contrasts sharply with the figure of Balaam, depicted as an aging Arab on a donkey: the past cannot curse or contend with the virile future. In these and other images of Herzl, Lilien cast the recently deceased leader of the Zionist movement as the savior and guardian of Israel's future.

Lilien also offered a rare visual interpretation of the hanging of Haman, one of two images he used to illustrate the Book of Esther. Rather than simply hang Haman on a tree, the artist felt no compunction about hanging him on a cross, as Mordecai, looking old and sated, gazes away. Haman's head is covered by a large cloth, but his brawny body is naked except for a loincloth, as Jesus was often depicted. Haman's legs are tied to the stake. This was not the first time Lilien associated Christ and the fate of Jews. His painting *Dedicated to the Mar-*

The expulsion of Adam and Eve from the Garden of Eden,
in the Bible illustrated by Ephraim Moses Lilien, 1908. (Courtesy Richard I. Cohen)

tyrs of Kishinev (1903) showed an aged Jew, draped in a *talit* and bound to a stake, embraced and kissed by an angel holding a *sefer torah*. The angel's wings and the Jew's body form a cross.[101]

In hanging Haman on the cross, Lilien invoked an association between him and Jesus, a provocative element in his interfaith Bible project. Whether Lilien was aware of a practice among some Jews to burn on Purim an effigy of Haman that resembled the crucified Christ, in a form of "ritual reversal," is unclear, but the similarity between the images is haunting.[102] Lilien stands at the polar opposite to Montefiore's strong reservations about the Book of Esther. Montefiore viewed it as a purely national book with little to no moral or religious value. Had he his choice he would clearly have opted for eliminating the book from the Bible and expunging the holiday from the Jewish calendar.[103] Yet neither the German nor the Jewish reception of Lilien's Bible made any reference to his provocative image of Haman, nor to those that incorporated the likeness of Herzl.[104]

Lilien's Bible, like the others represented here, was part of the dramatic outpouring of cultural creativity by urban Jews in Central and Western Europe. The political, social, and religious currents that transformed Jewish life during this period are inextricably interwoven in these texts, illuminating the challenges Jews encountered as they sought integration, straddling different worlds and accepting a certain form of identification with Judaism that had all the appurtenances of a "modern" construction. Our focus on the Bible, while overlooking wholly rejectionist or radical assimilationist ideologies and silent attempts by individuals to completely hide their identity—not insignificant in this period—enables us to witness the struggle of Jews to reinterpret their sense of belonging and to reassess the meaning of their cultural heritage for themselves and society. Inevitably this led them to consider the import of Judaism as opposed to Christianity, an encounter that often yielded more conflicting assessments than mediating ones. The Bible thus offered Jews a way to break with their traditional past and forge a new vision of the future within the European urban setting.

The crucified Haman, in the Bible illustrated by Ephraim Moses Lilien, 1908. (Courtesy Richard I. Cohen)

REJECTING THE CITY JEW

At home in the city, privately and publicly, Jews concentrated in the thriving capitals of Central and Western Europe and in areas where other Jews lived. They made dramatic advances in the economic, cultural, and political arenas of their respective countries and played a significant role in defining the modern metropolis. The success of Jewish elites in the various capitals did not go unnoticed. As the process of emancipation continued throughout the nineteenth century and covered all of Western and Central Europe, it gradually encountered voices of opposition among a wide range of individuals and political parties. These focused on characteristics of behavior and physiognomy, often racially interpreted; the concentration of Jews in certain professions; images of power and intent; and national or cultural allegiances. The urban setting—especially in the nineteenth and twentieth centuries—was seen by non-Jews as the anvil upon which the Jews constructed their identity and webs of power.

In eighteenth-century London, the Ashkenazic immigrants were depicted as sellers of old clothes, peddlers, and petty tradesmen, shabbily dressed and disheveled, conversing in a foreign tongue. They were clearly viewed as "others," alien to English life. Yet they were not impugned with the derogatory epithets of the nineteenth century. As Jews achieved impressive economic success and Jewish migration to the cities mushroomed, the tone changed. "The Jews are the rulers of the age," went one adage; "the Jews are our misfortune," went another. Baron Rothschild was called "king of the Jews." The new visibility of the Jews and their bold entrepreneurial manner underlay an imaginative trope that merged timeworn images of them to fit their evolving situation. From the middle of the nineteenth century, the concentration of resources in the hands of Jews was increasingly regarded as inimical to the welfare of society. The imagining of Jewish power went far beyond the fact of it. In France, this trope was directed at the banking families that were involved in the extension of the railroad system: Foulds, Rothschilds, Cohens. Socialists and antisocialists joined in this perception of the Jews. The sense of being dominated by the Jews grew in the second half of the century. Several writers expressed the fear of national defeat at the hands of the Jews (enunciated in such titles as *La France Juive* and *Der Sieg das Judentum*),[105] whereas others subscribed to a more encompassing fear of Jewish world domination (epitomized by *The Protocols of the Elders of Zion*). The implication was that, through their international connections, Jews could control the economic, political, and cultural scene.

But domination was not the only motif. Another that was more subtle but highly charged was the claim that Jews were rootless, belonged nowhere, and were driven by their insatiable restlessness to disrupt the basic social order. Jews came to the city because they had no roots in the soil of the land. No one depicted this idea better than the talented graphic artist Adolphe Willette (1857–1926). In 1893 he portrayed a stereotypical Jewish capitalist—corpulent, hook-nosed, a cigar in one hand and an umbrella in the other—donning a crown (a symbol of rule and wealth). He stands next to sacks of money and an emaciated peasant. The terrain is arid; the caption below leaves nothing to the imagination: "It's drying up, this old land of France. He [the Jew] thirsts again for blood and tears. It will be necessary to irrigate it incessantly."[106]

Whereas Willette caricatured the effect of Jewish urbanism and capitalism on the land, the arch-nationalist Maurice Barrès zeroed in on the interrelationship of rootlessness and politics. In 1902 he wrote in his *Scènes et doctrines du nationalisme:*

> The Jews do not have a country in the sense that we understand it. For us, the fatherland is our soil and our ancestors, the land of our dead. For them, it is the place where their self-interest is best pursued. Their intellectuals thus arrive at their famous definition: the fatherland it is an idea! But which idea? That which is most useful for them—for example, the idea that all men are brothers, that nationality is a prejudice to be destroyed.[107]

Barrès made the significant connection between the rootlessness of the Jew and the way in which it serves his political and economic aspirations and ideological predilections. According to Barrès, the Jews became believers in a republican ideal and patriotic causes without actually knowing the true meaning of a Fatherland. Similar arguments would later be directed at Jewish artists of the Paris School—such as Amedeo Modigliani, Marc Chagall, Moïse Kisling, Jacques Lipschitz, and Chaim Soutine—whose work was criticized in the interwar period for lacking a sense of the French terrain and for promoting degeneracy and corruption.[108] In some ways this attack echoed turn-of-the-century Germany, when the Secessionist movement and one of its leading representatives, Max Liebermann, were vilified viciously. Cosmopolitan modernism—that is, the Secessionist movement—was seen as the antithesis to German patriotic art and culture, and Liebermann as a man lacking "any specifically German character" who could be living anywhere.[109] Moreover, the charge of rootlessness was at the heart of the antisemitic attacks on Léon Blum, France's first prime minister of Jewish origin, when he came to power in 1936. Said Xavier Vallat, a leading antisemite though not a racist: "To govern this peasant nation that

France is, it would be better to have someone whose origins, however modest, are deep in our soil, than a subtle Talmudist."[110] Indeed, Blum, who never failed to acknowledge his dual consciousness—as a Frenchman and as a Jew—would become the subject of a remarkable gallery of caricatures that depicted him as a "Wandering Jewess," a prostitute, a dandy, a bohemian, and an inciter of lascivious behavior. These images were part and parcel of Blum's otherness.

Another element that became associated with Jewish character in the nineteenth century was probably best enunciated by the great German composer Richard Wagner in his 1850 critique, *Judaism in Music*. His wrath was focused on the writers Heinrich Heine and Ludwig Börne and the composer Felix Mendelssohn-Bartholdy. Lacking inner peace, they could not achieve true creative originality and were forced to engage in a form of parasitical art that did not emerge from the depths of the German spirit. Lacking cultural authenticity, they necessarily had to live off the work and creativity of others. In the same way, Jewish entrepreneurs and capitalists, journalists, and owners of newspapers would be maligned for profiting from the suffering of others. These accusations touched upon the nature of the Jews' activity in the urban setting, be it their engagement in banking and the stock market, their penetration of the liberal professions, or their involvement in art dealing and collecting. These fields were viewed by the antisemites as inherently parasitic and dominated by a Jewish network. Similarly, parliamentary and republican ideals were regarded as synonymous with Jewish principles and motivations.

Antisemitism took many routes, of course, some less extreme and violent than others. But when one ponders the connection between the venom Hitler unleashed in *Mein Kampf* after he saw traditionally dressed Jews walking in the streets of Vienna, and the book-burnings in 1933, the boycotts of Jewish department stores, and the burnt synagogues on Kristallnacht (November 9, 1938), Jewish visibility in the city looms large. The urban setting had enabled Jews to flourish in areas that were closed to previous generations and to promote areas of creativity with which they were not historically associated. In the interwar years, forces of nationalism and fascism threatened to push Jews back into the ghetto. The space they had relied on and trusted became an ominous portent of future disaster.

CONCLUSION

In *The Interpretation of Dreams,* Freud recalled walking with his father when he was "ten or twelve years old." This was in 1866 or 1868, in Vienna, to which the family had moved in 1860. His father spoke to him, on this occasion, of the improved conditions for Austrian Jews and related this bit of personal history: "When I was a young fellow, one Saturday I went for a walk in the streets of your birthplace, beautifully decked out, with a new fur cap on my head. Along comes a Christian, knocks off my cap into the muck with one blow, and shouts, 'Jew, off the sidewalk!' " Freud asked how he had responded, and his father replied: "I stepped into the road and picked up my cap." Commenting on this, Freud remarks that this "did not seem heroic to me."[111] This story exemplifies the predicament Jews encountered in the modern period, one to which they often reacted by accepting their inferior condition and avoiding confrontation. Other scenarios in a host of different contexts could be brought to reinforce this narrative, and still many others would emphasize patterns of dealing with one's inferior situation—radical assimilation, self-denial or self-deprecation, rejection, or exit. The story stands in sharp contradiction to the spirit of this chapter, in which these tropes or strategies have not been accorded a central voice.

The voices heard and the images seen in this chapter did not function in isolation. Building a synagogue was a public act that necessitated negotiations with the civic authorities about style, size, location, and visibility. When directed to prefer one style over another, to remove an architectural element, or to restrict themselves to one area, the Jews did not simply yield. They claimed the public space as their own, asserting their right to act in the open. Negotiations led to compromises on both sides, not to unilateral decisions.

The Bible translations of this period were another way that Jews in Western and Central Europe asserted their historic lineage and unique role in Western civilization. The translators drew from many sources, classical and contemporary, non-Jewish and Jewish, to protect Jewish memory from becoming wholly integrated in the European culture.

In the growing metropolises of Europe, the Jews tended to congregate in certain neighborhoods. As they moved quickly up the economic ladder (Freud's family itself being an example of this), their homes became a setting wherein bourgeois cultural values were absorbed and enunciated. Adopting the vernacular, they ceased using Hebrew and Yiddish; secular music, art, theater, and literature replaced Jewish song and devotion. They developed a sense of belonging to their native countries, which fit neatly with the growing nationalist spirit of the times. Women, still functioning mainly in the home, created a bridge between the worlds and strove to preserve some form of Jewish identification.

At the same time, the Jews were becoming more visible in the realms of politics, economics, and culture, and their visibility was becoming of less concern to the acculturated Jew. Though perturbed by the cold winds of antisemitism, they trusted the city's openness to ideas, to potential, to the future. Many behaved like

Freud's father, accepting the lot dealt them, but many others were like Freud himself, exploring new frontiers, wary of over-visibility but rarely acting to avoid it. In the 1930s, Léon Blum was advised to relinquish his candidacy for prime minister of France lest there be troublesome repercussions for French Jewry, but Blum hardly gave it a thought. He believed in the Revolutionary vision that had laid the groundwork for acculturation, and he believed that one could be "happy as God in France." He was not alone. Until the Nazis came to power, Jews across Western and Central Europe could apply that phrase to their own countries and feel that they were an integral part of the society in which they lived.

NOTES

1. Ferdinand Rahlwes, ed., *Die Bücher der Bibel,* vol. 1 (Braunschweig, 1908). The other volumes were published between 1908 and 1912. No changes were made between the first edition and the 1923 edition published in Berlin and Vienna.

2. Jonathan Frankel, "Assimilation and the Jews in Nineteenth-Century Europe: Towards a New Historiography?" in Jonathan Frankel and Steven J. Zipperstein, eds., *Assimilation and Community: The Jews in Nineteenth-Century Europe* (Cambridge, Engl., 1992), 1–37.

3. Pierre Birnbaum and Ira Katznelson, eds., *Paths of Emancipation: Jews, States, and Citizenship* (Princeton, 1995), 3–36.

4. Ezra Mendelsohn, ed., *People of the City: Jews and the Urban Challenge. Studies in Contemporary Jewry,* vol. 15 (New York, 1999).

5. Todd M. Endelman, *The Jews of Georgian England, 1714–1830: Tradition and Change in a Liberal Society* (Philadelphia, 1979).

6. Todd M. Endelman, "The Chequered Career of 'Jew' King: A Study in Anglo-Jewish Social History," in Frances Malino and David Sorkin, eds., *From East and West: Jews in a Changing Europe, 1750–1870* (Oxford, 1990), 151.

7. Endelman, *Jews of Georgian England,* 127.

8. Barbara C. Gilbert, "Anglo-Jewish Art Collectors of the Victorian Period: Patterns in Collecting" (Ph.D. diss., University of Southern California, 1986), 32–39; James Picciotto, *Sketches of Anglo-Jewish History,* ed. Israel Finestein (London, 1956), 55–59.

9. David Feldman, *Englishmen and Jews: Social Relations and Political Culture, 1840–1914* (New Haven, Conn., 1994), 48–71.

10. *Jewish Chronicle,* Sept. 28, 1888, p. 9; quoted in Geoffrey Alderman, "English Jews or Jews of the English Persuasion? Reflections on the Emancipation of Anglo-Jewry," in Birnbaum and Katznelson, eds., *Paths of Emancipation,* 145. See also Vicki Caron, *Uneasy Asylum: France and the Jewish Refugee Crisis, 1933–1942* (Stanford, 1999).

11. Feldman, *Englishmen and Jews,* 306.

12. Marsha L. Rozenblit, *The Jews of Vienna, 1867–1914: Assimilation and Identity* (Albany, N.Y., 1983), 94–98. The above paragraph is based on her statistical analysis of the changing nature of the Viennese Jewish population.

13. Robert S. Wistrich, *The Jews of Vienna in the Age of Franz Joseph* (Oxford, 1989), 58, 61.

14. Freud to Abraham, May 3 and July 23, 1908; both are in *A Psycho-Analytic Dialogue: The Letters of Sigmund Freud and Karl Abraham, 1907–1926*, ed. Hilda C. Abraham and Ernst L. Freud, trans. Bernard Marsh and Hilda C. Abraham (London, 1965), 34, 45. For this notion of acculturation, I am indebted to Marsha Rozenblit's work; see also her essay "Jewish Assimilation in Habsburg Vienna," in Frankel and Zipperstein, eds., *Assimilation and Community*, 237.

15. Yosef Hayim Yerushalmi, *Freud's Moses: Judaism Terminable and Interminable* (New Haven, Conn., 1991).

16. Sigmund Freud, *Totem and Taboo* (London, 1950), xi.

17. Franz Kafka, *Dearest Father: Stories and Other Writings*, trans. Ernest Kaiser and Eithne Wilkins (New York, 1954), 173–74; see also Ezra Mendelsohn, *The Jews of East Central Europe Between the World Wars* (Bloomington, Ind., 1987), 135.

18. Gary B. Cohen, "Jews in German Society: Prague, 1860–1914," *Central European History* 10 (1977): 28–54.

19. Hillel J. Kieval, "Autonomy and Independence: The Historical Legacy of Czech Jewry," in David Altshuler, ed., *The Precious Legacy: Judaic Treasures from the Czechoslovak State Collections* (New York, 1983), 104; Kieval, *The Making of Czech Jewry: National Conflict and Jewish Society in Bohemia, 1870–1914* (New York, 1988); and Kieval, *Languages of Community: The Jewish Experience in the Czech Lands* (Berkeley, 2000). See also Mendelsohn, *The Jews of East Central Europe*, 132–46.

20. Steven M. Lowenstein, "Was Urbanization Harmful to Jewish Tradition and Identity in Germany?" in Mendelsohn, ed., *People of the City*, 80–106.

21. Steven M. Lowenstein, *The Mechanics of Change: Essays in the Social History of German Jewry* (Atlanta, 1992); Lowenstein, *The Berlin Jewish Community: Enlightenment, Family, and Crisis, 1770–1830* (New York, 1994); Emily D. Bilski, ed., *Berlin Metropolis Jews and the New Culture, 1890–1918* (Berkeley, 1999).

22. Bruno Blau, *Die Entwicklung der jüdischen Bevölkerung in Deutschland, 1800–1945*, 2 vols., unpublished manuscript.

23. Alexander Altmann, *Moses Mendelssohn: A Biographical Study* (Philadelphia, 1973), 754–55.

24. Harold Hammer-Schenk, *Synagogen in Deutschland: Geschichte einer Baugattung im 19. und 20. Jahrhundert (1780–1933)* (Hamburg, 1981), 1: 290.

25. See Michael A. Meyer, " 'How Awesome Is This Place!': The Reconceptualisation of the Synagogue in Nineteenth-Century Germany," *Leo Baeck Institute Year Book* 41 (1996): 51–63.

26. Andreas Nachama and Gereon Sievernich, *Jüdische Lebenswelten Katalog*, vol. 1

(Berlin, 1991), 194 (no. 9/66); for an example of such a procession that took place in Prague at the turn of the twentieth century, see Altshuler, ed., *The Precious Legacy*, 105.

27. Ismar Schorsch, *From Text to Context: The Turn to History in Modern Judaism* (Hanover, N.H., 1994), 81.

28. Hammer-Schenk, *Synagogen in Deutschland*, 1: 293.

29. See Shulamit S. Magnus, *Jewish Emancipation in a German City: Cologne, 1798–1871* (Stanford, 1997), 216–17 and illustrations following p. 190, which show the sense of excitement involved in building the Glockergasse synagogue, where "no expense was spared."

30. Quoted in Carol H. Krinsky, *Synagogues of Europe: Architecture, History, Meaning* (New York and Cambridge, Mass., 1985), 268.

31. Michael Graetz, *The Jews in Nineteenth-Century France: From the French Revolution to the Alliance Israélite Universelle*, trans. Jane Marie Todd (Stanford, 1996), 41–78.

32. David Cohen, *La promotion des juifs en France à l'époque du Second Empire (1852–1870)* (Aix-en-Provence, 1980), 2: 783–95; Dominique Jarrassé, *Une histoire des synagogues françaises: Entre Occident et Orient* (Arles, 1997), 218–25; Krinsky, *Synagogues of Europe*, 247–50; Simon Schwarzfuchs, *Du juif à l'israélite: Histoire d'un mutation, 1770–1870* (Paris, 1989), 301. On Haussmann's influence on nineteenth-century Paris, see Vanessa R. Schwartz, *Spectacular Realities: Early Mass Culture in Fin-de-Siècle Paris* (Berkeley, 1998), 16–26.

33. Schwarzfuchs, *Du juif à l'israélite*, 297–301.

34. Phyllis Cohen Albert, *The Modernization of French Jewry: Consistory and Community in the Nineteenth Century* (Hanover, N.H., 1977), 192. Albert points out that, as of 1840, the Central Consistory became stricter in imposing order in the synagogue during services and, following 1870, instituted a uniform prayer for the French government.

35. Israel Cohen, *Travels in Jewry* (New York, 1953), 309.

36. Quoted in Krinsky, *Synagogues of Europe*, 249.

37. Michael R. Marrus, *The Politics of Assimilation: A Study of the French Jewish Community at the Time of the Dreyfus Affair* (Oxford, 1971), plate 1, shows an image of a Rothschild wedding held in the Victoire in 1876.

38. Cohen Albert, *Modernization of French Jewry*, 212.

39. Ibid., 196–221.

40. Carol Herselle Krinsky, "Hector Guimard's *Art Nouveau* Synagogue in Rue Pavée, Paris," *Journal of Jewish Art* 6 (1979): 105–11.

41. Peter I. Hidas, "Hidden Urbanization: The Birth of the Bourgeoisie in Mid-Nineteenth-Century Hungary," in Michael K. Silber, ed., *Jews in the Hungarian Economy, 1760–1945: Studies Dedicated to Moshe Carmilly-Weinberger on His Eightieth Birthday* (Jerusalem, 1992), 135–57; see also Silber's introduction, 3–22.

42. Michael Silber, "The Historical Experience of German Jewry and Its Impact on the Haskalah and Reform in Hungary," in Jacob Katz, ed., *Toward Modernity: The European Jewish Model* (New Brunswick, N.J., 1987), 107–57.

43. Géza Komoróczy, ed., *Jewish Budapest: Monuments, Rites, History* (Budapest, 1999),

108; John Lukacs, *Budapest 1900: A Historical Portrait of a City and Its Culture* (New York, 1988).

44. Komoróczy, *Jewish Budapest*, 111.

45. This was true not only for Western and Central Europe. See, e.g., the discussion over the St. Petersburg synagogue in late-nineteenth-century Russia in Benjamin Nathans, "Conflict, Community, and the Jews of Late-Nineteenth-Century St. Petersburg," *Jahrbücher für Geschichte Osteuropas* 44 (1996): 208–14; an expanded version can be found in Mendelsohn, ed., *People of the City*, 104–48.

46. Richard I. Cohen, *Jewish Icons: Art and Society in Modern Europe* (Berkeley, 1998), 155, 187; Barbara Kirshenblatt-Gimblett, *Destination Culture: Tourism, Museums, and Heritage* (Berkeley, 1998), 81–85. Strauss was the great-grandfather of the distinguished anthropologist Claude Lévi-Strauss.

47. R. Cohen, *Jewish Icons*, 196.

48. Heinrich Graetz, "Historical Parallels in Jewish History," trans. Joseph Jacobs, in Ismar Schorsch, ed., *Heinrich Graetz: The Structure of Jewish History and Other Essays* (New York, 1975), 264.

49. Rachel Morpurgo, "On Hearing She Had Been Praised in the Journals," trans. Peter Cole, in Shirley Kaufman, Galit Hasan-Rokem, and Tamar S. Hess, eds., *The Defiant Muse: Hebrew Feminist Poems from Antiquity to the Present* (New York, 1999), 79. Morpurgo's poetry was collected and published in 1890 in Kraków with several letters and was reprinted in Tel Aviv in 1953.

50. Quoted in Paula E. Hyman, *The Emancipation of the Jews of Alsace: Acculturation and Tradition in the Nineteenth Century* (New Haven, Conn., 1991), 62.

51. Ezra Mendelsohn, "On the Jewish Presence in Nineteenth-Century European Musical Life," in E. Mendelsohn, ed., *Modern Jews and Their Musical Agendas: Studies in Contemporary Jewry*, vol. 9 (New York, 1993), 3–16.

52. The painting is reproduced in Georg Heuberger and Anton Merk, eds., *Moritz Daniel Oppenheim: Jewish Identity in 19th Century Art* (Frankfurt, 1999), 230.

53. Susan Rubin Suleiman, *Budapest Diary: In Search of the Motherbook* (Lincoln, Neb., 1993), 49.

54. Judit Frigyesi, "Jews and Hungarians in Modern Hungarian Musical Culture," in Mendelsohn, ed., *Modern Jews and Their Musical Agendas*, 47.

55. Paula E. Hyman, *Gender and Assimilation in Modern Jewish History: The Roles and Representation of Women* (Seattle, 1995), 25.

56. Heuberger and Merk, eds., *Moritz Daniel Oppenheim, passim.*

57. Schorsch, *From Text to Context*, 102.

58. Heuberger and Merk, eds., *Moritz Daniel Oppenheim*, 229.

59. Hyman, *Gender and Assimilation*, 154.

60. Yosef Kaplan, "For Whom Did Emanuel de Witte Paint His Three Portraits of the Sephardic Synagogue in Amsterdam?" *Studia Rosenthaliana* 32 (1998): 133–54.

61. Quoted in Mozes H. Gans, *Memorbook* (Baarn, 1977), 64. It appears that this was the

same Pinto of whom Joseph Shaw remarked that the home was "pav'd with duccatoons or crownpieces and these enlayed edgewise" (quoted in Kaplan, "For Whom Did Emanuel de Witte Paint," 141 n. 32).

62. See the Suasso catalogue for his sculpture and the various paintings. Two of the paintings are also in Alfred Rubens, *A History of Jewish Costume* (London, 1973), 143, 147.

63. Yosef Kaplan, "The Social Functions of the Herem in the Portuguese Jewish Community of Amsterdam in the Seventeenth Century," *Dutch Jewish History* 1 (1984): 111–55.

64. Mendelssohn seems to have frowned on the behavior of the wealthy. See Steven M. Lowenstein, "Jewish Upper Crust and Berlin Jewish Enlightenment: The Family of Daniel Itzig," in Malino and Sorkin, eds., *From East and West*, 188–89.

65. Ibid., *passim*. See also Vivian B. Mann and Richard I. Cohen, eds., *From Court Jews to the Rothschilds: Art, Patronage, and Power, 1600–1800* (Munich, 1996), 101, 201.

66. Frank Manuel, *The Broken Staff: Judaism Through Christian Eyes* (Cambridge, Mass., 1992).

67. Jacob Katz, *Exclusiveness and Tolerance: Studies in Jewish-Gentile Relations in Medieval and Modern Times* (New York, 1962), chap. xv. Both the Assembly of Notables and the Sanhedrin were Napoleon's initiative.

68. Yosef Hayim Yerushalmi, *Zakhor: Jewish History and Jewish Memory* (Seattle, 1982); Schorsch, *From Text to Context*.

69. I refrain from claiming that Wessely expected the change in Jewish life to contribute to the emancipation of the Jews as this political concept developed in a later period. See Edward Breuer, "Naphtali Herz Wessely and the Cultural Dislocations of an Eighteenth-Century Maskil," in Shmuel Feiner and David Sorkin, eds., *New Perspectives on the* Haskalah (London, 2001), 27–47.

70. Moses Mendelssohn, "Introduction," *Netivot Hashalom* (Berlin, 1784).

71. Eddy Breuer, *The Limits of Enlightenment: Jews, Germans, and the Eighteenth-Century Study of Scripture* (Cambridge, Mass., 1996). For a brief discussion of the Buber-Rosenzweig translation, see the text below.

72. Lowenstein, *The Mechanics of Change*, 29–64; Steven M. Lowenstein, "The Social Dynamics of Jewish Responses to Moses Mendelssohn (with Special Emphasis on the Mendelssohn Bible Translation and on the Berlin Jewish Community)," in Michael Albrecht, Eva J. Engel, and Norbert Hinske, eds., *Moses Mendelssohn und die Kreise seiner Wirksamkeit* (Tübingen, 1994), 333–48; Edward Breuer, "Between Haskalah and Orthodoxy: The Writings of R. Jacob Zvi Mecklenburg," *HUCA* 66 (1995): 259–87; Yerushalmi, *Freud's Moses*, 64; Mordechai Breuer, *Modernity Within Tradition: The Social History of Orthodox Jewry in Imperial Germany*, trans. Elizabeth Petuchowski (New York, 1992), 184–91.

73. Henning Graf Reventlow, *The Authority of the Bible and the Rise of the Modern World* (Philadelphia, 1985); David Daiches, "The Beginnings of Anglo-Jewish Biblical Exegesis and Bible Translation," *Miscellanies of the Jewish Historical Society of England* 4 (1942): 20–24.

74. David B. Ruderman, *Jewish Enlightenment in an English Key: Anglo-Jewry's Construc-*

tion of Modern Jewish Thought (Princeton, 2000); Richard Popkin, "David Levi, Anglo-Jewish Theologian," *Jewish Quarterly Review* 87 (1996): 79–101.

75. See Richard I. Cohen, "Exhibiting Nineteenth-Century Artists of Jewish Origin in the Twentieth Century: Identity, Politics, and Culture," in Susan T. Goodman, ed., *The Emergence of Jewish Artists in Nineteenth-Century Europe* (New York, 2001), 154.

76. For these images, see R. Cohen, *Jewish Icons*, 227–28.

77. Feldman, *Englishmen and Jews*, 62–65, 82–89, 121–27. Feldman claims that the turn to the Bible among certain elements of English Jewry in the mid-nineteenth century was to counter the charges of Judaism's "rabbinism."

78. Claude Montefiore, ed., *The Bible for Home Reading* (London, 1896), 5.

79. Montefiore's work (ibid.) was published in two volumes in London and New York, 1896 and 1899. Various editions of it were published during the pre–World War I years.

80. Ibid., 776.

81. Ibid., 781.

82. See Heine's comment in his 1827 edition of the Luther translation, in Joseph A. Kruse and Michaël Werner, *Heine à Paris, 1831–1856* (Paris, 1981), 166.

83. Heinrich Heine as quoted in Prawer, *Heine's Jewish Comedy*, 348.

84. Ibid., 348.

85. As quoted in Tabak, *Heine and His Heritage*, 86.

86. Kalman P. Bland, *The Artless Jew: Medieval and Modern Affirmations and Denials of the Visual* (Princeton, 2000), 16–19, 23–27.

87. Heinrich Heine, *Über die Bibel* (Munich, 1912); S. S. Prawer, *Heine's Jewish Comedy: A Study of His Portraits of Jews and Judaism* (Oxford, 1983); Israel Tabak, *Heine and His Heritage: A Study of Judaic Lore in His Work* (New York, 1956). For a list of books on biblical personalities designed for educational purposes, see Gabriele von Glasenapp and Michael Nagel, *Das jüdische Jugendblich: Von der Aufklärung bis zum dritten Reich* (Stuttgart, 1996). See also Jacques Ehrenfreund, *Mémoire juive et nationalité allemande: Les juifs berlinois à la Belle Époque* (Paris, 2000), 92–95.

88. Schorsch, *From Text to Context*, 318; Uriel Tal, *Christians and Jews in Germany: Religion, Politics, and Ideology in the Second Reich, 1870–1914*, trans. Noel Jonathan Jacobs (Ithaca, N.Y., 1975); Paul Mendes-Flohr, "Martin Buber and the Metaphysicians of Contempt," in Jehuda Reinharz, ed., *Living with Antisemitism: Modern Jewish Responses* (Hanover, N.H., 1987), 133–64; Michael A. Meyer, "Judaism and Christianity," in Michael A. Meyer, ed., *German-Jewish History in Modern Times*, vol. 2 (*Emancipation and Acculturation, 1780–1871*) (New York, 1997), 184–90.

89. Gershom Scholem, "At the Completion of Buber's Translation of the Bible," in his *The Messianic Idea in Judaism and other Essays on Jewish Spirituality* (New York, 1971), 317. See also Mendes-Flohr, "Buber and the Metaphysicians," 151–57.

90. Ernest M. Wolf, "Martin Buber and German Jewry," *Judaism* 1 (1952): 350. Quoted in Michael Brenner, *The Renaissance of Jewish Culture in Weimar Germany* (New Haven,

Conn., 1996), 107. See also Maren Ruth Niehoff, "The Buber-Rosenzweig Translation of the Bible Within German-Jewish Tradition," *Journal of Jewish Studies* 44 (1993): 258–79.

91. The first quotation is from Buber's devoted student Ernst Simon, as cited in Brenner, *The Renaissance*, 108; for Buber's remark, see Mendes-Flohr, "Buber and the Metaphysicians," 155.

92. Claude Fleury, *Les moeurs des israélites où l'on voit le modèle d'une politique simple et sincère pour le gouvernement des Etats et la réformation des moeurs* (Bruxelles, 1769); over a hundred editions were published during the following century. Quoted in Graetz, *The Jews in Nineteenth-Century France*, 183. See also S. Ettinger, "The Beginnings of the Change in the Attitude of European Society Towards the Jews," *Scripta Hierosolymitana* 7 (1961): 196–218.

93. The title of his work is revealing in its own right. Each title page had a different declaration on the uniqueness of the Bible and its language. Here I have added Weill's comments on the title page of volume five. Alexandre Weill, *Les cinq livres (mosaïstes) de Moïse. Traduit textuellement sur l'hébreu avec commentaires et Étymologies avec Élimination des falsifications qu'Esra et la Grande Synagogue ont frauduleusement mises dans la bouche de Moïse. . . . Nul, à moins de lire cette traduction textuelle et rationelle . . . ne comprendre le génie incommensurable et incomparable de Moïse, à la fois humain et divin, Un et Unique, d'où sont sorties la Réforme, la Révolution de Quatre-vingt-neuf et dont l'idéal social n'a jamais été atteint* (Paris, 1890–91). The last sentence with the reference to 1789 appeared only in the fifth volume.

94. Ibid., vol. 5 (1891), 317.

95. For a detailed discussion of Salvador's ideas and the French response, see Michael Graetz, *The Jews in Nineteenth-Century France, passim,* and Paula E. Hyman, "Joseph Salvador: Proto-Zionist or Apologist for Assimilation," *Jewish Social Studies* 34 (1972): 1–22.

96. Quoted in Graetz, *The Jews in Nineteenth-Century France*, 228–29.

97. Based on random observations of his 18-volume Bible. S. Cahen, *La Bible, traduction nouvelle, avec l'hébreu en regard . . .* (Paris, 1829–58).

98. Aron Rodrigue, *French Jews, Turkish Jews: The Alliance Israélite Universelle and the Politics of Jewish Schooling in Turkey, 1860–1925* (Bloomington, Ind., 1990).

99. Milly Heyd, "Lilien: Between Herzl and Ahasver," in Gideon Shimoni and Robert S. Wistrich, eds., *Theodor Herzl: Visionary of the Jewish State* (Jerusalem, 1999), 265–94; Michael Stanislawski, *Zionism and the Fin de Siècle: Cosmopolitanism and Nationalism from Nordau to Jabotinsky* (Berkeley, 2001), 98–115.

100. Milly Heyd, "Lilien and Beardsley: 'To the pure all things are pure,' " *Journal of Jewish Art* 7 (1982): 58–69; M. S. Levussove, *The New Art of an Ancient People: The Work of Ephraim Mose Lilien* (New York, 1906).

101. Ziva Amishai-Maisels, "The Jewish Jesus," *Journal of Jewish Art* 9 (1982): 91. The association of Haman and Christ has a rich Jewish lineage to it in midrashim and poetry from the pre-Byzantine and Byzantine period. We have no idea if these were known to Lilien.

102. Elliott Horowitz, "On the Rite to Be Reckless: On the Perpetration and Interpretation of Purim Violence," *Poetics Today* 15 (1994): 9–54.

103. Claude Montefiore, ed., *The Bible for Home Reading,* vol. 2 (London, 1914), 406–408. Previous editions were published in 1899, 1900, and 1907.

104. Heyd, "Lilien: Between Herzl and Ahasver," 284–89.

105. These are the names of two seminal works in late-nineteenth-century antisemitism. The former, *France Judaized* by Edouard Drumont, was first published in 1886 and went through more than 200 editions; the latter, by Wilhelm Marr, *The Victory of Judaism over Germanism,* was published in 1878 and became a significant antisemitic text in Imperial Germany.

106. *La Libre Parole,* 17 July 1893; published in Norman L. Kleeblatt, ed., *The Dreyfus Affair: Art, Truth, and Justice* (Berkeley, 1987), 77.

107. Paula E. Hyman, *The Jews of France* (Berkeley, 1999), 107.

108. Romy Golan, *Modernity and Nostalgia: Art and Politics in France Between the Wars* (New Haven, Conn., 1995).

109. Peter Paret, *The Berlin Secession* (Cambridge, Mass., 1980), 178–79; Bilski, *Berlin Metropolis Jews.*

110. Quoted in Hyman, *The Jews of France,* 148.

111. Peter Gay, *Freud: A Life for Our Time* (New York, 1988), 11–12.

SELECTED BIBLIOGRAPHY

Birnbaum, Pierre. *Jewish Destinies: Citizenship, State, and Community in Modern France.* New York, 2000.

Birnbaum, Pierre, and Ira Katznelson, eds. *Paths of Emancipation: Jews, States, and Citizenship.* Princeton, 1995.

Cohen, Richard I. *Jewish Icons: Art and Society in Modern Europe.* Berkeley, 1998.

Endelman, Todd M. *The Jews of Georgian England, 1714–1830: Tradition and Change in a Liberal Society.* Philadelphia, 1979.

Frankel, Jonathan, and Steven J. Zipperstein, eds. *Assimilation and Community: The Jews in Nineteenth-Century Europe.* Cambridge, Engl., 1992.

Gans, Mozes H. *Memorbook: Pictorial History of Dutch Jewry from the Renaissance to 1940.* Baarn, 1977.

Graetz, Michael. *The Jews in Nineteenth-Century France: From the French Revolution to the Alliance Israélite Universelle.* Trans. Jane Marie Todd. Stanford, 1996.

Hyman, Paula. *The Jews of Modern France.* Berkeley, 1998.

Katz, Jacob. *Out of the Ghetto: The Social Background of Jewish Emancipation, 1770–1870.* Cambridge, Mass., 1973.

———, ed. *Toward Modernity: The European Jewish Model.* New Brunswick, N.J., 1987.

Kieval, Hillel J. *The Making of Czech Jewry: National Conflict and Jewish Society in Bohemia, 1870–1914.* New York, 1988.

Lowenstein, Steven M. *The Mechanics of Change: Essays in the Social History of German Jewry.* Atlanta, 1992.

Marrus, Michael R. *The Politics of Assimilation: A Study of the French Jewish Community at the Time of the Dreyfus Affair.* Oxford, 1971.

McCagg, William O., Jr. *A History of Habsburg Jews, 1670–1918.* Bloomington, Ind., 1989.

Mendelsohn, Ezra. *The Jews of East Central Europe Between the World Wars.* Bloomington, Ind., 1987.

Meyer, Michael A., ed. *German-Jewish History in Modern Times.* 4 vols. New York, 1997.

Roth, Cecil. *A History of the Jews in England.* Philadelphia, 1979.

Rozenblit, Marsha L. *The Jews of Vienna, 1867–1914: Assimilation and Identity.* Albany, N.Y., 1983.

Ruderman, David B. *Jewish Enlightenment in an English Key: Anglo-Jewry's Construction of Modern Jewish Thought.* Princeton, 2000.

Salberstein, Michael C. N. *The Emancipation of the Jews in Britain.* London, 1982.

Schorsch, Ismar. *From Text to Context: The Turn to History in Modern Judaism.* Hanover, N.H., 1994.

Wistrich, Robert S. *The Jews of Vienna in the Age of Franz Joseph.* Oxford, 1989.

Yerushalmi, Yosef Hayim. *Zakhor: Jewish History and Jewish Memory.* Seattle, 1982.

The writer, activist, and ethnographer S. Ansky (Solomon Rapoport) in 1888, at age twenty-five. (YIVO Institute for Jewish Research, Photo Archives, New York; YIVO RG 121)

A JOURNEY BETWEEN WORLDS:

East European Jewish Culture from the Partitions

of Poland to the Holocaust

DAVID BIALE

In an undated autobiographical fragment composed early in the twentieth century, the Russian Jewish folklorist, writer, and social revolutionary S. Ansky (Solomon Rappoport) wrote of his circuitous path away from and back to Jewish life:

> A young man, born and raised in the thick of Jewish life, underwent a very paradoxical evolution; works in the Hebrew language forcefully and violently tore me away from ancient Judaism and its traditions and awakened within me a hatred and contempt for its traditions, thrusting me [instead] toward Russian letters, so that later, in the Russian language, I would discern the splendor of the poetry that lies buried in the old historical foundations and traditions [of Jewish culture].[1]

This compact statement, written, significantly, in Russian, might be multiplied many times for several generations of East European Jews. Here Ansky traced the contours of Jewish culture in Eastern Europe after 1800, encompassing the traditional Jewish world and the many forms of rebellion against it. Born in 1863 in the White Russian town of Vitebsk, which boasted both an outstanding Lithuanian-style yeshivah and a strong community of Ḥabad (Lubavitch) Hasidim, Ansky was steeped in both of the branches of nineteenth-century East European Jewish Orthodoxy. Like many of his generation, he abandoned talmudic study for Haskalah (the movement of Jewish Enlightenment) but soon passed further on the road to acculturation by embracing social revolution. While agitating among Russian miners, he adopted a Russian-sounding name (but one that also drew from the Yiddish custom of forming last names from the first name of one's mother) and soon began writing solely in Russian. After a period of exile in Paris, he came back to Russia in the wake of the 1905

Revolution. By the end of the Paris period, Ansky had begun the return to his people, and he returned as well to writing in Yiddish, the language in which he had started writing some 20 years earlier. Once back in Russia, he threw himself into the Jewish national revival that was in full swing in response to the wave of pogroms accompanying the Revolution. In 1912, Ansky organized and led the first expedition of the Jewish Ethnographic Society, which collected a vast array of stories, folk beliefs, songs, manuscripts, photographs, and ritual objects. In the years before his death in 1920, he wrote the work for which he is most famous, *The Dybbuk,* a play that, as we shall see, combined many of the themes of his life's journey. In the pages that follow, I will use the stages of Ansky's life—Orthodoxy, Haskalah, Russian acculturation, and return to the folk—as markers of the various cultural paths that the Jews pursued in their confrontations with the peculiar forms modernity took in Eastern Europe.

Although Ashkenazic Jewish culture goes back at least a thousand years to the Jews of the Rhineland, the culture produced by the nineteenth-century East European Jews is frequently seen by many today, through a kind of optical illusion, to be equivalent to a timeless Ashkenazic culture. The Jews who are our subject here inherited much from their Central and East European ancestors—their language, religious customs, popular practices, and forms of communal organization—but on this foundation they created something new, which became, by the twentieth century, *the* culture of Ashkenaz.

As Ansky's journey suggests, the nineteenth century for East European Jews was an age of border crossings between competing identities. This was a period of enormous internal divisions: between Hasidism and the Lithuanian yeshivah culture, between *maskilim* (disciples of Enlightenment) and Orthodox authorities; between those who wanted to develop Jewish culture in Hebrew or Yiddish and those who found their cultural homes in one of the non-Jewish languages of Eastern Europe; and, finally, between "assimilationist" revolutionaries who sought Jewish salvation in a Russian or Polish revolution and "nationalists" who wanted to preserve Jewish identity and find a Jewish solution to the "Jewish Question," either in Palestine or in Europe. All sides of these disputes contributed toward the formation of a unique culture, one that encompassed competing and contradictory voices. Despite their differences, however, these voices also shared certain surprising affinities. All of them, even the most ostensibly conservative or "Orthodox," were responses to the peculiar conditions of Jewish life in Eastern Europe, and particularly in the Russian Empire, in the period between the partitions of Poland in the late eighteenth century and the Holocaust. All of them contributed toward the formation of new Jewish identities—identities that still echo and even persist today.

In 1772, Russia annexed the White Russian provinces of Polotsk and Mogilev from the tottering Polish-Lithuanian Commonwealth. Among the towns in Polotsk that now fell under Russian rule was Vitebsk, which was to be Ansky's birthplace nearly a century later. Although Vitebsk was the home of probably no more than a few thousand Jews, the total population of Jews that the Russian state inherited was about 45,000. At the same time, Poland's other powerful neighbors, Austria and Prussia, swallowed up other districts of the Polish Commonwealth. Thus began a process that, by 1795, was to dismember the medieval Polish state and transfer the Jewish population to new political rulers. By the end of the partition process, at least 800,000 Jews would come under Russian rule, some 260,000 would fall under Austria, and an additional 160,000 under Prussia.[2]

The cultural implications of these dramatic political developments were not immediately apparent but would become increasingly so in the course of the nineteenth century. For the Jews in the vast and variegated region of what has been called "East Central Europe"—the Austrian Habsburg Empire and eastern Prussia—a window was open toward the West and, with political emancipation in the last third of the nineteenth century, increasing numbers were to abandon Jewish tradition and adopt modern forms of life. In Czernowitz, the capital of Bukovina, on the eastern border of the Habsburg Empire, for example, many Jews enthusiastically embraced the German language and German culture, as they did in Bohemia and Moravia, the Czech lands in the empire. In the Hungarian part of what would become (after 1867) the Dual Monarchy of Austria-Hungary, a process of "Magyarization" took place throughout the nineteenth century, particularly in the cities, in which Jews embraced the Hungarian language and culture.

In Russia, which took control of the largest number of Jews, the process of acculturation was more delayed, circuitous, and complicated. The Pale of Settlement, created by the Russian state in several steps after the partitions of Poland, prevented most Jews from living in the main Russian cities, thus precluding the kind of rapid acculturation that occurred farther to the West when Jews moved in the first half of the nineteenth century to Berlin, Vienna, Prague, and Budapest. Only very few were able to enter the wealthy merchant guilds and escape the Pale. Needless to say, they could not join the aristocracy, which, at least in the cities, was often the Westernized element in Russian society, nor could they identify with the peasants. Russian society lacked a strong, emerging middle class, so the Jews did not find a social base for assimilation as they did in Germany, Austria, Hungary, France, Italy, and England. The Russian state failed to emancipate the Jews, as had the nations of Western and Central Europe in the course of the nineteenth century; the Jews of the Russian Empire remained subjects, but not full citizens, until the 1917 Revolution. In this respect, the status of the Jews scarcely differed from that of other peoples in the empire: all were subjects, since the modern category of citizen was not allowed to cross the borders of the czarist state.

In Poland, which was a semiautonomous kingdom under the czar and in which Jews were subject to fewer disabilities than in Russia proper, a process of Polonization occurred earlier in the century as a new Jewish middle class adopted Polish language and culture. Joining with their Polish neighbors in the insurrections against Russia of 1831 and 1863, some Polish Jews, particularly in the cities, were able to turn this political alliance into an avenue for acculturation. But here, too, Polonization was limited to the larger cities; the vast majority of Jews, scattered in smaller villages and towns in the countryside, would remain far less affected by Polish culture.

Whereas in Western and Central Europe it became increasingly possible for Jews to identify themselves as, for example, "Germans of the Mosaic faith," such a purely religious identity was all but impossible for the Russian Jews: they were seen by others, and largely viewed themselves, as a distinct and separate national group within a multinational empire. Blocked from assimilating directly into non-Jewish society, many young Jews chose instead to align themselves with the groups seeking to overthrow the old order. Revolutionary politics became its own form of assimilation and acculturation. To take the case of Ansky: as a result of reading the literature of Russian populism, he discovered new ways of defining Jewish culture. But the "Russian" culture that he, like many young Jews, absorbed was that of resistance and revolution, itself—like Marxism—at least partly imported from the West.

For all of these reasons, what appears to us in perhaps distorted hindsight as the "inexorable" waves of modernization that were sweeping up Jews in Western and Central Europe produced very different, even contrary, results in Russia. In fact, we should probably avoid using the term "modernization" altogether for Imperial Russia because it raises more questions than it answers. Although the Russian state, starting with Peter the Great in the first half of the eighteenth century, began to take steps to Westernize, the nineteenth century witnessed significant moves to resist the European Enlightenment and the doctrines of political liberalism that it preached. Under Nicholas I (r. 1825–55), the slogan of "autocracy, orthodoxy, and nationalism" captured the desire of the regime to insulate itself from the winds of modernity behind a high wall of "Slavic" identity. Nicholas's regime adopted far-reaching policies to try to "Russify" the Jews, but these often coercive measures were quite different from the forces of assimilation in the West.[3]

Lengthy conscription (25–30 years) into the Russian army, the attempted dissolution of Jewish communal self-government in 1844, and government regulation of Jewish educational and rabbinical institutions all created enormous hostility to the Russian state among most Jews. The czarist government set up two official rabbinical seminaries and a system of official rabbis (*ha-rabanut me-ta'am*) with authority over matters like divorce. Poorly trained, these rabbis received little popular legitimacy, and they contributed to the undermining of communal authority. Because the authorities were forced to deliver up conscripts—many of them kidnapped children—to the army in order to fulfill draft quotas, popular hostility was further directed against them and especially against those thought to be "informers" to the government. The policies of Nicholas thus shattered the cohesiveness and solidarity of the Jewish community, leaving an increasing leadership vacuum with profound implications for Jewish culture. Some have even argued that the tendency of Russian Jews to embrace revolutionary causes later in the century was at least partly a result of the abiding hatred of the state engendered under Nicholas. Yet, despite these harsh measures, Russification of the Jews remained limited to very small groups; Russification failed but it paradoxically may have planted the seeds of revolution.

The regime of Alexander II (r. 1855–81) abolished many of the policies of Nicholas I, and it was during Alexander's reign that Jewish acculturation in Russia began in earnest.[4] Starting in the 1860s, his government promulgated a series of liberal reforms that allowed many more Jews to migrate to urban centers such as St. Petersburg and Moscow: from a mere 11,980 in 1858, the numbers in the main Russian cities rose to 59,779 in 1880 and 128,343 in 1897.[5] Young Jewish students, both male and female, who were allowed to attend the gymnasia and universities were exposed for the first time to Russian culture and politics. Russian became the native tongue for increasing numbers of Jews, rising, in St. Petersburg, from 2 percent in 1869 to 37 percent by 1900. Yet the government, even in its most liberal days, scarcely contemplated the full emancipation of the Jews, and most Jews remained trapped in the Pale of Settlement, still speaking Yiddish as their mother tongue.

It was under these conditions in the Pale that East European Jewish culture developed its peculiar and particular forms. Despite increasing adoption of Russian or Polish culture as the nineteenth century wore on, the vast majority of Jews who did not migrate to the big cities cultivated an indigenously Jewish culture in which the primary languages were Hebrew and Yiddish. In Ansky's Vitebsk, for instance, Yiddish was still known—and probably spoken as their main language—by 99.2 percent of the Jews as late as 1897.[6] With Western influences seeping through the borders of the empire, some Jews began to rethink their traditional culture, but because few joined Russian society fully, the new "modern" or "secular" movements tended to develop their own singular forms in which the "Jewish" elements predominated over the "non-Jewish." For this reason, terms like "modern" or "secular" may be misleading. Even though Jews elsewhere in the modern world also developed their own subcultures, in Eastern Europe this subculture was insulated enough from the surrounding cultures as to feel often more like a separate culture. As we shall see, even the strand of this culture that we call "Orthodoxy" or "ultra-Orthodoxy" today was not equivalent to pre-modern or traditional Jewish culture in Eastern Europe because, like its various critics, it was born from the encounter with the singular conditions of the nineteenth century.

Prior to the Polish partitions, the Jews regarded themselves and were regarded by others as a separate and distinct group, but, as Moshe Rosman has shown in his chapter on the pre-modern Polish Jews, the walls segregating the Jews from non-Jewish society did not preclude cultural interchange. In the nineteenth century, various internal and external forces demanded that the Jews change their traditional culture and adopt that of the non-Jewish society, but this challenge often resulted paradoxically in new forms of distinctive self-identification and new feelings of difference among both the traditionalists and their opponents.

The deepening sense of a separate Jewish culture was due, in part, to the demographic preponderance of Jews in the Pale. Reversing an eighteenth-century trend to spread out into the countryside, Jews in the nineteenth century concentrated more and more in small cities and towns; by the end of the century, as we have seen, they were moving into the larger cities as well. Throughout Europe, a population explosion was under way, but the Jews of Eastern Europe increased, for reasons still debated by demographers, at a greater rate than their non-Jewish neighbors. The countryside may have been Ukrainian, Belorussian, or Polish, but the urban settlements were Jewish: in many of the *shtetlach* and cities of the Pale (with exceptions in Ukraine), the Jews often constituted the majority of the population. To take Vitebsk, again, as our example, in the middle of the nineteenth century there were only 9,417 Jews in the town. In the period of Ansky's boyhood, from his birth in 1863 to his departure from the town in 1881, the population jumped from about 14,000 to approximately 24,000. By 1897, when the most authoritative Russian census was taken, the Jews of Vitebsk constituted 34,420 out of a total population of 65,719. So, the second half of the nineteenth century witnessed a nearly fourfold increase, reflecting both the enormous natural growth of the population and the movement of Jews—like Ansky's father—from the surrounding countryside into urban centers.[7] It was perhaps partly as a result of this feeling of living in a preponderantly Jewish world that the modern movements of Jewish nationalism arose at the end of the nineteenth century in Russia. If Zionism, to take the most prominent of these movements, wished to create a Jewish nation, then it did so because such a nation was already coming into being demographically and culturally in Eastern Europe.

THE INVENTION OF EAST EUROPEAN
JEWISH ORTHODOXY

A young man, born and raised in the thick of Jewish life . . .
ancient Judaism and its traditions.

Vitebsk lay on the border between the provinces of Mogilev and Polotsk—the first, at the beginning of the nineteenth century, a stronghold of the Lithuanian yeshivah culture, and the second a center of Hasidism, the eighteenth-century pietistic movement. In Vitebsk itself, both of these competing movements found representation. Already in the eighteenth century, an important early Hasidic teacher, Menaḥem Mendel of Vitebsk, gathered followers in the town (he eventually led a group of Hasidim to emigrate to Palestine), and, later, the Lubavitch or Ḥabad sect of Hasidism made Vitebsk one of its centers. But the town also boasted a flourishing yeshivah in the Lithuanian style, headed by a number of learned rabbis who were the authors of widely distributed rabbinic commentaries. For a Jewish boy, to grow up in Vitebsk in the last third of the nineteenth century entailed exposure to both of these religious movements that had dominated Eastern Europe for nearly a century.

Any account of the culture of nineteenth-century Ashkenaz must start with these manifestations of Orthodoxy. We must, however, distinguish between tradition—Ansky's so-called "thick of Jewish life"—and Orthodoxy. Many Jews, probably the overwhelming majority, continued to live traditional lives throughout the nineteenth century in terms of their daily practices, values, and aspirations. But the articulation of that tradition changed dramatically as its defenders confronted the challenges of the age. The result of this confrontation was the "invention" of Orthodoxy, which was a culture every bit as "modern"—in the sense of "new"—as that of the modernizers. And rather than only opposing the modernizing movements, Orthodoxy often interacted with them in complicated and entangled ways.

The creation of this new Orthodox culture had its roots in the second half of the eighteenth century with the rise of Hasidism and its opponents. Yet neither Hasidism nor Mitnagdism (from *mitnaged* or "opponent") was a fully coherent movement at this time, and it is only from the vantage point of their later development that we imagine them so in their early years. In the nineteenth century, disciples of these two movements shaped the images of their founders—Elijah ben Solomon, the Gaon of Vilna (1720–97), and Israel Ba'al Shem Tov, or "the Besht" (ca. 1700–60)—as exemplifying the values of the movements. These images were based, to some degree, on historical truth, but they also embodied the primary cultural values that the early-nineteenth-century leaders tried to instill in their followers.

The Lithuanian Yeshivot   Let us begin with the Gaon of Vilna and see how his biography played itself out in the culture of the Lithuanian yeshivah movement, the institutional setting for the Mitnagdim.[8] The Gaon was the greatest talmudic scholar of the eighteenth century but held no rabbinical office. He headed neither a communal rabbinic court nor a yeshivah. Instead, he cultivated a reclusive lifestyle for which he developed a kind of theological justification. Although he did play a significant role in the polemics against Hasidism, primarily by instigating one of the first bans against the movement, he was only a public figure in a limited sense. It was, rather, his sons and students who turned him into the titular leader of the anti-Hasidic forces and the founder of the Lithuanian yeshivah system. Indeed, as the nineteenth century wore on, the Gaon increasingly became something like a Hasidic *rebbe* (or *anti-rebbe*) for the Lithuanian opponents of Hasidism. He was seen as the mirror image of the Besht, a founder of a movement who, like the Hasidic leader, could perform magical acts of intercession for his disciples.

After the Gaon's death in 1797, two of his sons, Abraham and Judah, published his commentary on the *Shulḥan Arukh* (Joseph's Karo sixteenth-century legal code that had become the standard for Jewish law) with an introduction that contains a fascinating biographical sketch of their father. Among its many interesting features is the way this biography creates a kind of individual personality, an exemplary one, to be sure, but still a personality with a sense of individual subjectivity that we usually identify with the Enlightenment. Indeed, the emergence both in the yeshivah world and in Hasidism of biographies—often accompanied by portraits—of great rabbinic figures was a new phenomenon, though it also drew from the medieval tradition of hagiography.

The Gaon is portrayed as a cloistered and ascetic scholar, perhaps more so than any spiritual figure from the Middle Ages. But he is also said to have developed a new ethos. Rather than cultivating "fear of God" as a primary value, he elevated the study of Torah to a position of absolute importance. The virtues of study had been, of course, central to rabbinic Judaism since late antiquity, and, indeed, the Mishnah proclaimed that "the study of Torah is equal to all [the commandments]." But the Gaon and his disciples raised such statements to a new theoretical level, even above the commandments: "The Torah is like bread, upon which man's heart feeds . . . and it is needed constantly, like bread. . . . But the mitzvot [commandments] are like a confection, which is good periodically and in the proper time, like a confection which one eats from time to time."[9]

If the commandments are understood as reflecting also a person's social involvement, the Gaon here resolutely proclaims the superiority of solitary study. Never before had pure study been valued more highly than prayer or the performance of commandments. Yet it must be emphasized that study for the Gaon meant not only talmudic study but also kabbalistic. The Gaon was no less a mystic than were the leaders of Hasidism. He saw no contradiction between the rational argumentation of the Talmud and the esoteric speculations of the Kabbalah.

This fierce ideology of intellectual immersion plays a central role in the biographical sketch written by the Gaon's sons. Referring directly to both Hasidism and the Haskalah, they wrote that, through his single-minded devotion to study, he was able to "always worship God through joy [the Hasidic ideal] . . . [and] every day true Enlightenment [*haskalah amitit*] was strengthened through his hands." By coopting the values of these two competing movements, the Gaon's sons reinforced the centrality of traditional study. They recount with awe that their father never slept for more than two hours in any twenty-four-hour period and never for more than half an hour at a time. During these brief naps, his lips continued to whisper words of "law and legend" (*halakhot ve-aggadot*). To illustrate that study even crowded out familial affection, they tell a story of how the Gaon's favorite son, Solomon Zalman, was taken ill at the age of five or six. The Gaon nevertheless followed his customary practice of traveling some distance from Vilna in order to seclude himself in study:

> There [in this secluded study spot] the springs of nature were dammed up to the point that he forgot his house and his children for more than a month. Once, he went to the bath house and, since, as is known, it is forbidden to meditate on the Torah there, he began to think about personal matters and in this way he remembered that he had been away from home for more than a month. And he also remembered his beloved son who was lying on his sick bed. [At once] his compassion was aroused and he ordered his carriage prepared to take him home so that he could seek after his son's welfare.[10]

Since talmudic times, elite Jewish culture had exhibited persistent tensions between domesticity and study: both were given high value, but the lure of intellectual study frequently won out over family. So it was also with the Gaon, but here his ability to literally erase any thought of his family—and even of his beloved son who was ill—while he was studying is held up as a kind of heroic ideal. And this is not the only story in this text or in others about the Gaon's extraordinary ability to do so. We cannot, of course, determine whether such stories are true or are hyperbolic inventions. But even if they are fictions, it is remarkable that it is the Gaon's own sons who relate this account in celebratory tones, even when the story involves their father's neglect of themselves. Their paradoxical intention was clearly to turn the Gaon—who, as the text makes clear, was an intensely private man—into a public icon of scholarship. In so doing, they created a radical distinction between the realm of domesticity and the realm of Torah study, one that had its roots in earlier Jewish tradition but was also similar in function to the distinction emerging in European culture between the "private" and the "public." Even though the Gaon's sons were unlikely to have been responding to these new ideas, their account fits well into a larger cultural trend.

If the Gaon himself considered study a private affair, his preeminent student, Ḥayyim of Volozhin, was to translate his ideas into a public institution, the yeshivah of Volozhin, founded in 1803. It does not appear that the Gaon instructed Rabbi Ḥayyim to create this school. But Volozhin became the setting for a new type of educational institution that would, in turn, reshape the culture of the traditional Jewish world of the Russian Empire. Generations of the brightest young Jewish men passed through its doors as well as the doors of other yeshivot inspired by its example, such as Telz, Mir, and Slobodka. The poet of the nationalist revival, Ḥayyim Naḥman Bialik (1873–1934), celebrated Volozhin as the "school where the soul of the nation was formed," by which he meant the institution that trained not only rabbinical authorities but also those who later became maskilim or, like Bialik himself, Zionists, as well as poets, mystics, philosophers, novelists, and folklorists. Although earlier rabbinical academies in Eastern Europe sometimes attracted students from a distance, none ever achieved the prominence of the great Lithuanian yeshivot, which drew them from a wide geographical range and, like nineteenth-century European universities, contributed to the creation of a national elite not tied to a specific locale.

The curriculum of the yeshivot also resembled the classical, humanistic training of the German or English university systems, albeit in a Jewish idiom. For the most part, the goal of talmudic study was not primarily to train rabbis or to investigate legal questions for their practical significance. The *rosh yeshivah* (yeshivah head) was neither a legal authority nor a communal rabbi; this new institutional figure resembles in Orthodox Jewish terms something like a university academic, an "ivory tower" scholar. In the second half of the nineteenth century, this tendency reached new heights of abstraction in the so-called "analytic" school of Ḥayyim Soloveitchik of Brisk and others, which focused on the logical ramifications and linguistic formulations of talmudic arguments rather than either textual erudition or legal applications.[11] Some have compared this method to the school of analysis developed by English philosophers at Oxford and Cambridge in the twentieth century in which the linguistic meaning of propositions became the core of philosophical investigation. Although the yeshivah method itself grew at first out of an internal development in the history of the halakhah starting in the eighteenth century, by the second half of the nineteenth century it became an intellectual alternative to the historical approach to Jewish texts championed by the Haskalah.

Far from a mere continuation of traditional methods of study, the Lithuanian yeshivot represented a powerful, theoretical response on similar intellectual grounds to modern skepticism and rationalism. Indeed, some of the opponents of the analytical method from within the Lithuanian yeshivah world were disturbed by its very innovative and, one might even say, "modern" character. The sheer intellectual attraction of this method found perhaps its most eloquent expression in the essay *Halakhic Man*, written by Ḥayyim of Brisk's grandson, Joseph B. Soloveitchik, considered by many the most brilliant exponent of the Lithuanian yeshivah system in the twentieth century. Soloveitchik, himself trained in Western philosophy as well as rabbinics, argued that the analytic school's method of study was similar to modern science, even though its terms of reference were quite different.[12]

This doctrine of absolute intellectualism owed its origins to the Gaon, who, as we have seen, argued that love of God is best expressed by engaging in the rational exercise of talmudic discourse. Because of this emphasis on critical inquiry, the Lithuanian system encouraged constant questioning of all dogmatic answers. Ḥayyim of Volozhin taught that "a disciple is forbidden to accept the statements of his teacher when he questions them, and sometimes the truth is on the side of the disciple, just as a small tree ignites a large one. . . ."[13]

Although rabbinic discourse since the Talmud encouraged questioning and disagreement, Ḥayyim raised such freedom to a new level. This faction of the new Jewish Orthodoxy encouraged the very opposite of conservative "traditionalism" even as it defended the superiority of traditional learning. The very value of free inquiry, which was to inform the Jewish Enlightenment, can be found in the schools of its opponents. However, this free inquiry was itself limited by the abstract, theoretical questions that were central to the Lithuanian yeshivah culture: since such questions generally had no practical application, they provided a safe outlet for the intellectual curiosity that might otherwise turn toward heretical modernity.

The Lithuanian yeshivah movement made another major contribution toward the later rise of secular Jewish culture in its promotion of book publishing. One

impetus behind the establishment of the Volozhin yeshivah was a sense among
the Lithuanian scholars that knowledge of Torah in Eastern Europe had diminished and that part of the problem was the lack of books. Few of the yeshivot
of the day possessed full copies of the Talmud, and the libraries of most rabbis
were probably even more meager. With the regeneration of talmudic study in
Volozhin came a dramatic increase in the publishing of rabbinic texts. Eager for
business, publishers sought out new markets of readers, to whom we will return,
from Hasidim in search of tales of rebbes, to maskilim interested in translations
of European literature and science, to female consumers of romantic chapbooks
and religious manuals. Perhaps the most famous of these publishers was Romm
of Vilna, established at the end of the eighteenth century. During the reign of
Nicholas I, Romm was one of only two Jewish publishers officially allowed to
operate, and it gained a virtual corner on the market, publishing the famous
Vilna Talmud in thousands of copies as well as works of Hebrew and Yiddish literature. During its most active period, Romm was directed by a woman, the
widow of the original proprietor, with her brothers; the firm became known as
"the press of the widow and the brothers Romm."

In the late eighteenth and early nineteenth centuries, there was, then, a certain
overlap between the Lithuanian scholarly tradition and the beginnings of the
East European Jewish Enlightenment. An example of this overlap is Joshua
Zeitlin (1742–1821), a wealthy merchant from Shklov who supported both the
work of proto-maskilim like Barukh Schick (1744–1808) and traditional rabbinic
scholarship, including the establishment of the Volozhin yeshivah. Schick, a disciple of the Gaon who spent time in Moses Mendelssohn's circle in Berlin and
tried to promote scientific knowledge among East European Jews, claimed that
the Gaon himself favored learning science: "I heard from his holy tongue that for
every deficiency of knowledge a man has in the sciences, he will have ten deficiencies of knowledge in the science of the Torah; for Torah and science are
closely related."[14] According to some of his disciples, the Gaon was knowledgeable in mathematics and music, because he believed these disciplines necessary
for solving problems in the Torah. Statements of this kind by the Gaon—
whether real or fictive—were seized upon by those of his disciples inclined
toward Haskalah to prove the importance of studying modern science, a preoccupation of the Haskalah throughout the nineteenth century. There was a strong
sense among these proponents of the Enlightenment that lack of scientific knowledge made the Jews look like fools in the eyes of the world. As one member of the
early Haskalah circle in Shklov, Judah Leb Margoliot (1747–1811), wrote:

For it does not befit the honor of the Lord's religion and congregation for us to
be fools in the eyes of the Gentiles and to be considered like wild beasts. Does

the Lord wish for [the sciences] to be honored in the hearts of our enemies and for us to be considered fools and idiots?[15]

From the vantage point of the early twenty-first century, it seems incredible that the Jews, so preeminent in the sciences today, considered themselves only 200 years ago utterly ignorant of scientific knowledge, something that could not be said of Italian, Spanish, or Middle Eastern Jews in earlier periods, or even of sixteenth-century Prague Jews like Judah Loew (the Maharal) and David Gans.

It would, however, be a mistake to argue that the Gaon and his tradition were primarily responsible for the rise of the Jewish Enlightenment in Eastern Europe. Schick's statement about the Gaon's interest in science became a bone of contention between maskilim and traditionalists through the nineteenth century. As time went on, the Gaon's spiritual heirs tried to restrict the meaning of such putative positions and, like other Orthodox authorities, to forbid the study of any non-Jewish books. Similarly, in the face of Haskalah demands to leaven the study of Talmud with study of the Bible and Hebrew grammar, they suppressed the Gaon's own advocacy of such a broadened curriculum. Increasingly threatened by modernity, they seized upon the Gaon's insistence on the exclusive value of Torah study to label all foreign sciences *bitul torah* (annihilation of Torah). In fact, the Volozhin yeshivah was closed down in 1892 because it refused to bow to the Russian authorities' demand to limit the number of hours of Torah study and increase the hours spent on secular subjects in its curriculum. (It was reopened three years later, but on a much reduced scale.)

The Gaon's legacy was therefore double-edged: the Lithuanian yeshivot cultivated an intellectualism that resembled the Haskalah, but the single-minded focus on Torah study led to a total ban on any other type of learning, a position that was not so much traditionalist (since Jewish intellectuals in previous times had often learned sciences) as it was an innovation. In this rejection of "worldly sciences," all of the branches of East European Jewish Orthodoxy in the nineteenth century—from the Lithuanian yeshivot to Hasidism and Hungarian Orthodoxy—were in general agreement (although some of the leaders of these movements were not entirely ignorant of intellectual developments outside their world, and one exceptional yeshivah, at Lida, was founded by Isaac Jacob Reines in 1907 to include secular subjects). If the nineteenth century began with some cautious openness to "foreign books," by the end of it, to be an Orthodox Jew in Eastern Europe meant overwhelmingly to be opposed to any secular study outside of Jewish texts.

The intellectualism of the Lithuanian yeshivot was not the only development within the traditional world of the nineteenth century; despite its self-image as the monolithic defender of tradition, the new Orthodoxy took many forms.

Within the Lithuanian world itself, a reaction took place in the form of the *musar* (ethical) movement of Israel Salanter (1810–83).[16] Salanter, who was a product of the yeshivah culture, developed a doctrine of personal introspection and ethical self-restraint that built on medieval ethical literature and the teachings of the Gaon but addressed nineteenth-century issues in an acute way. Although he did not explicitly deny the centrality of Torah study, he placed alongside it—and perhaps even above it—the importance of *yir'ah* (fear of God). In a way that seems remarkably modern, he shifted the struggle against the Evil Impulse (*yetzer ha-ra*) from the theological to the psychological realm. Here was a doctrine that added to rational talmudic discourse a preoccupation with the self and its emotional states. Salanter also broke with the prevailing elitism of the Lithuanian yeshivot and addressed his teachings to a wider audience, taking into account the material sufferings of the Russian Jews. In this respect, as well as in offering a spiritual ethos beyond textual study, Salanter's doctrine resembled Hasidism, though his was a movement within the yeshivah world. Another resemblance to early Hasidism was the way his followers, usually adolescents studying in yeshivot, formed radical fellowships.

Salanter's main source for this new psychology was a work called *Ḥesbon ha-Nefesh* (An Accounting of the Soul) by Mendel Lefin (1741–1819), one of the first East European maskilim, again pointing to an overlap between "traditional" and "modern" Jewish cultures. Although Salanter's *musar* movement did not arise primarily as a reaction against the Haskalah, it undoubtedly functioned, like Lithuanian intellectualism, as a traditionalist alternative to modern cultivations of the self. Its solutions may have been different, but it was addressing the same new consciousness of individualism.

It was Salanter's seemingly "modern" emphasis on the self and the doctrine of introspection that excited the opposition of the leaders of the Lithuanian yeshivot. One of the preeminent rabbinic authorities of Eastern Europe in the early twentieth century was Abraham Karelitz of Kossov (1878–1953), known better, after one of his works, as the *Ḥazon Ish* (The Vision of a Man). Like the Gaon of Vilna, the Ḥazon Ish never held any institutional position, but, due to his charisma, he is widely considered to be one of the founders of the Ḥaredi, or ultra-Orthodox, community in Israel (he arrived in Palestine in 1933). The Ḥazon Ish rejected musar's focus on the self and argued instead that the best way of conquering the Evil Impulse was by super-punctilious observance of Jewish law. For this reason, he insisted on the most stringent interpretations of the law so as to make observance as difficult as possible. Absolute submission—and not personal autonomy—was the goal (although such submission was characteristic of certain tendencies in musar as well). Yet this extremism was itself not so much traditional as new, a product of the peculiar dynamics within the Lithuanian yeshivah world in the face of new challenges.

A similar ultra-Orthodox culture of extreme rigidity developed in Hungary. Perhaps in no other country of Eastern Europe was the process of modernization from the mid-nineteenth century on as dynamic as in Hungary. In the 1850s and 1860s, the introduction of compulsory secular education and "Magyarization" (linguistic nationalism) transformed Jewish culture there to a degree unheard of elsewhere in Eastern Europe. Even among Jews who retained a traditional way of life, Hungarian or German sometimes replaced Yiddish as the primary language, a development uncommon elsewhere. At a time when the majority of Jews in the Russian Empire continued to be traditional in their way of life, the Orthodox in Hungary, like their counterparts in Germany, were threatened with becoming a minority within the Jewish community. Against the religious innovations of the Reformers and modern Hungarian culture, Jewish traditionalists, especially in the eastern regions of Hungary, developed an ultra-Orthodox response. Indeed, it was precisely because of the immediate threat of modernity that such an extreme reaction developed much more in Hungary than in Russia, where, as we have seen, the challenge of modernity was significantly more distorted and delayed.

The titular founder of Hungarian ultra-Orthodoxy, Moses Sofer (1763–1839), also known as "the Ḥatam Sofer"), who was the chief rabbi in Pressburg (Bratislava), where he founded a large and enormously influential yeshivah, declared in his ethical will:

> Do not touch the books of Rabbi Moses [Mendelssohn] of Dessau and your foot will never slip. . . . The daughters may read German books, but only those which have been written in our own way. . . . Be warned not to change your Jewish names, speech, and clothing—God forbid. . . . Never say "Times have changed." We have an old Father, praised be His name, who has never changed and never will change.[17]

Sofer opposed the reading of any foreign books by men, and even women—who were typically allowed greater latitude in their reading—were only to be permitted German (by which he probably meant Yiddish) books if they were written in the traditional manner. Adapting several rabbinic midrashim which claimed that the biblical Israelites survived exile in Egypt because they did not change their names, speech, or clothing,[18] he stipulated that the same standard should apply in the nineteenth century. Although throughout the centuries Jews had in fact adopted non-Jewish names, languages, and costume, the nineteenth-century Hungarian ultra-Orthodox, in contrast to the Orthodox in Germany, took the midrash literally and as a commandment. Questions of language and dress would become critical markers of identity in the wars between different groups of Orthodox and modernizers in Eastern Europe.

Like the Ḥazon Ish in the twentieth century, Sofer opposed any liberal innovation in the law. He argued that God "granted authority to the sages in each generation to establish customs in Israel, and once they are spread, it is forbidden to uproot them,"[19] a position that seems on the face of it self-contradictory but was intended to reconcile the legislative freedom of the rabbis of each generation with unwavering conservatism. Akiva Joseph Schlesinger (1837–1922), the leader of Hungarian ultra-Orthodoxy in the latter part of the nineteenth century, went even further. He elevated the *Shulḥan Arukh* into a canonical text in which "every rule . . . is equal to the Ten Commandments; and every Jewish custom is equal to the Ten Commandments."[20] By giving such authority to this body of law, Schlesinger cast implicit aspersions on the traditional talmudic culture—as well as the Lithuanian yeshivah culture—valuing disagreement and debate. These tendencies to equate law with custom and to favor rigid codes over talmudic discourse were to become characteristics of East European ultra-Orthodoxy and its twentieth-century heirs. Yet, as with the Ḥazon Ish, these ostensibly "traditional" positions were themselves radical innovations.

The culture of the yeshivot was predominantly elitist. Not only did they explicitly appeal to the most talented boys of the Jewish world, but they did so based on an elitist ideology. According to the theology promulgated by the disciples of the Gaon, the spiritual capabilities of most men (about women there was hardly any question!) were limited, and only the select few might attain true learning. Kabbalistic teachings were certainly part of legitimate wisdom (like the Gaon, Ḥayyim of Volozhin and other Lithuanian authorities were themselves Kabbalists), but the Kabbalah was to be transmitted as an esoteric doctrine because only the few could understand it. As opposed to the Hasidic teaching of divine immanence, which might make God accessible to all Jews, the Mitnagdim typically taught that God was transcendent and unknowable. Only the Torah provided access to divine wisdom, but full understanding of the Torah was only possible for a small religious elite—a classically medieval position. In this regard, Mitnagdism positioned itself both against the Haskalah, with its Enlightenment zeal for universal education, and against Hasidism, the movement of popular piety that became, in the early nineteenth century, a mass movement.

Hasidism   Let us turn now to Hasidism, the other major component in the emerging Orthodox culture of Eastern Europe.[21] Hasidism, as Moshe Rosman shows in volume II of this series, dates back to the middle of the eighteenth century, but because many of the sources from that period are either apologetic or polemical, it is hard to estimate just how widespread it was in its first half-century. It is likely that the Hasidic communities were no more than scattered, small worship circles organized around charismatic leaders. Although these *tzadikim* may have attracted followers from distant places, the sects had not yet acquired the wide geographic scope and broad popular allegiance that would be the case in the nineteenth century. In part, this was due to the power still wielded by their opponents, who typically controlled the local communal institutions (the *kahal*). The initial spread of Hasidism may have profited from the Polish government's abolition of the Council of the Four Lands in 1764, which prevented traditional communal authorities from enforcing a nationwide ban on the sect. But with the partition of Poland, the governments of Austria and Russia, which had inherited the areas where Hasidism flourished, sought to weaken local communal power as well. The growing strength of Hasidic groups in the early nineteenth century may have had something to do with this new political atmosphere. Indeed, the bans against Hasidism promulgated in the last quarter of the eighteenth century by the Vilna Gaon and his allies had no counterparts in the nineteenth century. The weakening of the kahal and its formal abolition (it continued to function unofficially, however) by the government of Nicholas I in 1844 created a leadership vacuum that not only Hasidism but also the Haskalah and later movements tried to fill.

Like the Mitnagdic use of the Gaon, the nineteenth-century Hasidim also shaped the image of their founder, the Besht, as a way of advancing the identity of the movement. The collection of stories entitled *Shivḥei ha-Besht* (In Praise of the Ba'al Shem Tov), published in 1815, is less a historical source for the life of the Besht than it is a mirror of how early-nineteenth-century Hasidism wished to portray its founder and itself. Let us consider one story from this hagiography that concerns turning the teachings of Hasidism into written texts, perhaps an echo of the struggle against the textual culture of the Mitnagdim:

> There was a man who wrote down the teaching of the Besht that he heard from him. Once the Besht saw a demon walking and holding a book in his hand. He said to him: "What is the book that you hold in your hand?" He answered him: "This is the book that you have written." The Besht then understood that there was a person who was writing down his teaching. He gathered all his followers and asked them: "Who among you is writing down my teaching?" The man admitted it and he brought the manuscript to the Besht. The Besht examined it and said: "There is not even a single word here that is mine."[22]

As in many of these stories, the Besht is clairvoyant, in this case because he can see demons. Those who write down the Besht's teachings are like demons, and what they write bears no relationship to the actual teaching. Like many popular movements and like early rabbinic Judaism itself, Hasidism began with oral doctrines. The Besht himself never actually wrote anything systematic, beyond a few letters. By the time *Shivhei ha-Besht* was composed, many oral teachings attributed to him had appeared in written form. In the case of the Besht and other Hasidic masters, whose primary form of communication was oral, the written versions were all translations from the Yiddish, in which they were told, into Hebrew. Even if these teachings were authentic—and this story questions their authenticity—the very act of translation would naturally change their meaning. The story thus appears to take issue with the emergence of a literary Hasidic culture in Hebrew in favor of a more popular oral culture, which would have been primarily in Yiddish, a tension between an "elite" and a "popular" language that would be replicated by the Haskalah writers later in the century. This criticism is particularly ironic, because Hasidism itself played a major role in the increase in printing of Jewish books that took place in the nineteenth century and that contributed to a veritable revolution in reading among East European Jews.

In fact, one of the books most often published in both Hebrew and Yiddish editions was *Shivhei ha-Besht.* So, an additional irony is that this story is a written version of a teaching of the Besht, even though it teaches us not to write down his teachings! *Shivhei ha-Besht* therefore has a peculiar status as a work of folklore that tries to preserve the oral character of its sources. It is well known that Hasidism raised storytelling to a spiritual art, as, indeed, one tale in *Shivhei ha-Besht* makes explicit:

> When there was a circumcision ceremony in the house of the head of the court of the holy community of Horodnya, I heard from the rabbi of the holy community of Polonnoye and then from the rabbi of our community that the Besht said: "When one tells stories in praise of the *tzaddik,* it is as though he were engaged in *ma'ase merkavah* [mystical speculation on the nature of God]."[23]

Here is a story that legitimizes the telling of stories about the tzadik as equivalent to kabbalistic speculation about God and thus turns the tzaddik into something close to God. It is as though the author of *Shivhei ha-Besht* is quoting the Besht himself as the warrant for his own creation. In the last third of the nineteenth century, there would be a veritable explosion of this kind of literature of the "deeds of the tzaddikim" (*ma'asei tzaddikim*). Like the *Shivḥei ha-Besht*, these were tales collected long after their subjects had lived by Hasidim motivated by an impulse similar to that of secular folklorists. In fact, it was in this same period, as we shall see later, that secular writers were also to "rediscover" Hasidic tales and undertake their own collections of folklore. Hasidim, secularists, and even Mitnagdim were all engaged, for different but interrelated reasons, in a culture of remembrance.

Many Hasidic storytellers borrowed from older Jewish folktales, but they used traditional motifs to express the particular struggles and anxieties of their age. Traditional stories about children taken captive by non-Jews might give voice to the need to fight against the allure of a non-Jewish world now beginning to tempt Jewish children. Another threat was the Jewish Enlightenment and other manifestations of modern culture. One story, published in 1866, tells how Satan ensnares a young man and promises to let him return home only if he agrees to read one page of a certain book every day. The young man takes an oath to do so, but after he reads one page, he loses all desire to study. With each succeeding day, he reads another page and gradually gives up obeying one commandment after another.[24] The tale clearly deals with the dangers of reading a work of Haskalah, but the maskil who tries to corrupt the youth is transmuted into a traditional demon. Interestingly, the youth's slide into heresy comes from that most traditional activity, study, but here studying a heretical book causes him first to lose all desire to study, including, presumably, even to study the heretical book! In this way, the story implicitly recognizes the overlap between traditional and modern Jewish cultures: both are based on books, but books of radically different meaning. And, finally, the story also resonates against the tale from *Shivḥei ha-Besht* in which a demon reads a book ostensibly written by the Ba'al Shem Tov but really written by a demon. Taken together, these tales suggest a culture quite anxious about books and their potentially dangerous consequences. Hasidism undertook an uneasy and tense mediation between books, which represented the intellectual elite, and oral tales, which represented the *vox populi*.

Tales like these were one of the ways in which Hasidism developed its own particular brand of popular culture. The growth of Hasidism as a truly popular movement took place in the first half of the nineteenth century in far-flung corners of Eastern Europe: White Russia, Ukraine, Poland, Galicia, and Hungary. The courts of the tzaddikim became sites of pilgrimage from miles around and transformed the very character of the towns in which they were located. For example, when the small town of Gora Kalwaria in Poland became the seat of the rebbe of Ger (the Yiddish name for the town), the town's population exploded.[25] Like the Lithuanian yeshivot, the courts of the tzaddikim became supra-local institutions that filled the vacuum left by the disbanded Council of the Four Lands by creating links between communities and by contributing to the emergence of a new form of Jewish national identity in Eastern Europe.

Perhaps the most successful of the early-nineteenth-century Hasidic leaders was Israel of Ruzhin (1796–1850), the great-grandson of one of the Besht's primary disciples, Dov Ber, the Great Maggid of Mezeritch. Starting in 1813, Israel built an extraordinary Hasidic empire, first in Ukraine and then, as of 1841, in Sadagora, in the Galician province of the Austro-Hungarian empire, to which he escaped after having been accused of involvement in the murders of two Jewish "informers." Though cut off from the majority of the Ruzhin Ḥassidim in Russia, Israel and his dynastic successors built an opulent palace in Sadagora where they received visitors from far and wide, including maskilim and curious non-Jews. Unlike other Hasidim, the Ruzhin rebbes dressed in semimodern garb and imitated the lifestyle of the Galician nobility. Alluding to the messianic tradition, Israel styled himself as a kind of Jewish king, which undoubtedly increased his appeal to Jews living under the absolutist monarchs of Russia and Austria.

Israel's success as a leader owed little to either his learning or spiritual gifts, which by all accounts were quite minimal, but rather to a kind of charisma as well as great organizational ability. His charisma was pastoral rather than mystical, and his Hasidim regarded him primarily as a devoted father to his vast flock. Israel himself made no secret of his lack of learning and, in fact, created a theory to legitimize his style of leadership:

> When the early *tzaddikim* had to improve the lot of their followers [*le-hativ la-olam*], they did so by teachings and prayer, because at that time the world was in a loftier state [*beḥinat gadlut*]. But now that the world is in a state of decline [*beḥinat katnut*], when the tzaddik has to improve the lot of his community, he can only do so by means of stories of the deeds [of the earlier tzaddikim] and other simple devices.[26]

With the age of Hasidic greatness over, the tzaddik can only use the stories from that past rather than original doctrines, a development that already begins, as we have seen, with the *Shivḥei ha-Besht*. In another place, Israel speaks of himself in Yiddish as a "coarse Jew" (*grobiyon*) and explains that this is because his work involves dealing with material matters in order to raise them up to their source.[27] The doctrine of the "raising of sparks" from the material world was central to eighteenth-century Hasidism, but Israel of Ruzhin clearly intended to justify both his materialistic lifestyle and his often crude and provocative behavior. Beyond the idiosyncrasies of the Ruzhin dynasty, however, teachings like these capture the transformation of Hasidism from small pietistic sects to a mass movement concerned less with esoteric spirituality than with the material and pastoral needs of its followers. As traditional or premodern community institutions declined, Hasidism in the nineteenth century filled an increasingly felt vacuum.

The various types of East European Jewish Orthodoxy that developed in the nineteenth century—the Lithuanian yeshivah movement, Hungarian ultra-Orthodoxy, musar, and Hasidism—all should be considered self-conscious articulations of traditional ways of life in the face of a changing world. Yet, as much as this new Orthodoxy was a "conservative" or "reactionary" response to modernity, the development of this response often involved the use of very modern techniques and tools. Examples can be found in a wide variety of spheres. The Orthodox came to understand the importance of political organization and, in 1912, formed the Agudat Yisrael party, which became a particularly vigorous force in electoral politics in interwar Poland. The Orthodox also adopted the Haskalah's means of dissemination of ideas through newspapers and journals such as *Ha-Levanon* and *Ha-Tevunah*.

Yet another "modern" or new phenomenon in the Orthodox world were portraits of rabbis, which became popular throughout Eastern Europe in the nineteenth century, as they had in the previous century in Germany.[28] As both Hasidism and the yeshivah world came to venerate their charismatic leaders through virtual "cults of personality," the visual images of these rabbis assumed ritual importance, something almost unknown in the Jewish Middle Ages. Because the followers were spread over great distances, those who could not be immediately in the presence of the rabbi often found that a portrait on the wall served as a handy substitute. These portraits might take the form of lithographs or even, in one unusual case, an image made of micrography (miniaturized writing that formed the lines of the picture and thus combined the visual with the textual). A scandal broke out in Hungary in 1866 when the venerated Rabbi Yehuda Aszod died; his followers, intent on preserving some memento, propped him up on a chair with a book and took his photograph, which was reproduced and then widely circulated. In these surprising ways, visual culture found a place in the Orthodox world of Eastern Europe—and, as we shall see, in the secular.

Even synagogue architecture reflected the influence of contemporary trends.[29] In the seventeenth and eighteenth centuries, Jewish communities in Eastern Europe adapted the architecture of the traditional wooden churches to create a distinctive type of wooden synagogue; these structures, which had their own singularly Jewish features, represent the interplay between Jewish and Christian culture in pre-modern Poland (see Moshe Rosman's chapter on this period). But in the nineteenth century, with the growth in the Jewish population throughout Eastern Europe and particularly in the cities, the traditional synagogues were often inadequate for their congregations. The communities where Hasidic courts were located also needed large buildings to accommodate the many worshipers on important holidays, as well as to lodge the households of rebbes like those of the Ruzhin dynasty. In early-nineteenth-century Poland, the civil authorities enforced a classical style on large buildings. Many of the synagogues built from then through the 1920s boasted Doric or Tuscan pilasters. In the larger towns and cities, the Jews considered it appropriate to follow the architectural canons of their surroundings, and thus many of the synagogues of the time bore striking resemblances to neighboring churches. Later on, as urbanization accelerated and communities became more prosperous, synagogues increasingly became vehicles for Jewish self-expression. Some styles, like the classical, neo-Gothic, neo-Renaissance, and neo-Romanesque, suggested the connections between Jewish and historical European culture. Others, pioneered in 1854 by the synagogue in Wloclawek, in western Poland, demonstrated the Jews' "Oriental" identity by adopting motifs from Islamic architecture, a trend these Polish Jews borrowed from their German cousins during this period. And these developments were not limited to Poland. In Russia proper, similar architectural styles might be found, as we can observe from a picture of the great synagogue of Vitebsk with its columns, arches, and towers.

In this way, the Orthodox Jews of Eastern Europe, who may have insisted on their isolation from the contagion of modernity and the non-Jewish world, demonstrated in their buildings, as in many other features of this new traditionalism, that the walls against the outside world were often quite permeable. The very invention of Orthodoxy—the resolute denial of change in Jewish tradition—was itself the innovative product of a creative interaction with the surrounding world. When Ansky spoke about "the thick of Jewish life" in which he grew up, he scarcely imagined how different this culture already was from "ancient Judaism and its traditions."

THE CULTURE OF ENLIGHTENMENT

[W]orks in the Hebrew language forcefully and violently tore me away
from ancient Judaism and its traditions and awakened within me a
hatred and contempt for its traditions.

In an autobiographical fragment from 1910, Ansky remembered that, when he left Vitebsk in 1881, he took with him a bundle of Haskalah works that he had read during the previous year: Moses Leib Lilienblum's *Sins of Youth,* Isaac Ber Levinsohn's *Zerubavel,* Abraham Mapu's *The Love of Zion,* and Peretz Smolen-

The Izhorier synagogue of Vitebsk, which was the "Grand Synagogue" of the *mitnagdim* (opponents of Hasidism), photographed in 1910. It became a meeting place for Zionists and was the site for a memorial for Theodor Herzl after his death in 1905. Typical of nineteenth-century Eastern European synagogue architecture, it combined an eclectic array of styles to convey a sense of churchlike grandeur. (YIVO Institute for Jewish Research, Photo Archives, New York; YIVO R 1 Vitebsk 46)

The Hasidic Ziretsheir synagogue in Vitebsk, constructed in a grand manner like that of its *mitnagdic* competitor. As opposed to the usual image of Hasidism, the synagogue was known for its cantor and large choir. It stood directly opposite the family home of the socialist writer Chaim Zhitlovsky. (YIVO Institute for Jewish Research, Photo Archives, New York; YIVO R 1 Vitebsk 45)

skin's *A Donkey's Burial.* It was these "works in the Hebrew language" that had such a violent effect on the young Ansky, as they did on so many other Jewish youths of the nineteenth century, creating not simply a disillusionment with "ancient Judaism and its traditions"—or, better, the new world of nineteenth-century Orthodoxy—but "hatred and contempt."

By the time of Ansky's youth, the Haskalah had become a relatively well-established literary movement, which produced significant numbers of novels, poems, memoirs, newspapers, journals, and translations of European literature and science—all in the peculiar, cumbersome Hebrew style that the maskilim developed. The Haskalah did not start with the intention of overthrowing the Jewish religion, but, as the nineteenth century wore on, it became increasingly radical and secular. This secular "moment" in Jewish history was the product of the singular constellation of political, economic, and social barriers that largely prevented the kind of bourgeois assimilation that Italian, German, Austrian, and French Jews experienced in the course of the nineteenth century. With these avenues blocked, the Jews developed their own intense, internal culture that sought a variety of solutions to the dilemmas posed by Eastern Europe. This secular culture ultimately found expression not only in Hebrew but in Yiddish and East European languages as well.

Although the Haskalah in Germany quickly became the credo of the growing middle class, the political and social stagnation under which the East European Jews suffered left the maskilim of the East an embattled minority for most of the nineteenth century; in fact, the challenge they posed led to a virtual "cease-fire" between Hasidim and Mitnagdim. Out of their struggle for survival against censorship of their books and communal persecution, the maskilim became intent on redistributing power within Jewish society. They advocated a new kind of community in which power would be shared between an enlightened state and enlightened, acculturated intellectuals like themselves, a common move among subject intellectuals in colonial societies. Following this approach, some of the early maskilim even sought an alliance with the repressive regime of Nicholas I. The reordering of power they envisioned went hand in hand with a new form of knowledge: secular learning would take the place of rabbinic learning, just as modern leaders would take the place of rabbis.

Much of Haskalah literature was oppositional in character, permeated with a hatred of traditional Jewish life that, given its authors' own origins in that world, suggested self-loathing. Beginning with satirical anti-Hasidic literature early in the century, such as Joseph Perl's *Revealer of Secrets,* the fiction and journalistic writings of the modernizers typically featured harsh criticisms of traditional Jewish communal and religious life, reminiscent of the French Enlightenment's vituperative anticlericalism. Some of these works, like Smolenskin's *A Donkey's Burial,* thematized the struggle between maskilim and their benighted opponents against the backdrop of the shtetl. The only relief from the dreary portraits of traditional Jewish life came from escapist romances set in biblical times, like the first Hebrew novel, Mapu's *Love of Zion.* Because most of the writers who attacked shtetl culture were by then writing in cities like Odessa or Vilna, this literature also expressed urban contempt for rural culture.[30] For a boy in a town like Vitebsk (itself more urbanized and sophisticated than a backwater shtetl), such "works in the Hebrew language" constituted a revolutionary manifesto against tradition indeed.

The maskilim were interested in the integration of the Jews into Russia, even though the Hebraists among them envisioned a Jewish subculture in Hebrew; their position might be considered "proto-nationalist." After the pogroms of 1881–82, many became disillusioned with this vision and turned toward other forms of national regeneration. But the maskilic culture of self-criticism infected the revolutionary political movements of the end of the century, from Zionism to Bundism: for these political ideologies, the common Jews of the vast reaches of the Pale were a pitiable and contemptible lot who had to be radically transformed, transported away, or a combination of both.[31] Perhaps never have movements of national regeneration held such disparaging views of their subjects: uncompromising criticism of tradition itself became a tradition. The Orthodox themselves contributed to the culture of criticism and schism, labeling the maskilim heretics by applying to them the names of historical "deviants" like "Karaites" and "Sadducees." As the traditional authorities lost their power to ban the maskilim and their books, they became no less embattled than their opponents. In the modern State of Israel, where the heirs of these parties still struggle for cultural and political hegemony, this extraordinarily contentious culture struck new roots in ancient soil.

The East European Haskalah had started as a moderate enough movement within Jewish learned culture, spreading eastward from Germany as the nineteenth century progressed. This process was partly the result of the way Poland was partitioned. The area of Galicia, which was taken over by Austria, began to absorb Western influences before the areas annexed by Russia. Although, as we have seen, there were a few aspiring maskilim who traveled from the Russian Empire (particularly from Shklov, in Volhynia) to Mendelssohn's Berlin, the first real East European Haskalah developed in mercantile towns like Brody around such figures as Joseph Perl, Solomon Judah Rapoport, and Nahman Krochmal. The "Russian Mendelssohn," Isaac Ber Levinsohn (1788–1860), whose apologetic work against Christian missionizing, *Zerubavel,* found a place in Ansky's suitcase, spent a number of years in these circles in the early nineteenth century before returning to Russia and publishing his Haskalah manifesto, *Te'udah be-Yisrael*, in 1828.

Although these early maskilim absorbed Western Enlightenment ideas, their writings were often cast in rabbinic forms of argument. *Te'udah be-Yisrael* begins with the approbation (*haskamah*) of an important Vilna rabbinical authority in the manner of traditional books.[32] Yet Levinsohn dedicated the work to Czar Nicholas I, received a 1,000-ruble prize, and thus ensured its publication; the dedication and the book's publication history point to the attempt by the Russian Haskalah to serve as a bridge between the Jews and the state. Echoing arguments from earlier maskilim, Levinsohn argues for the study of foreign languages and sciences, but his arguments are couched in traditional style, using proof texts from rabbinical sources. Like Moses Maimonides, the great medieval hero of the Haskalah who had tried to reconcile the Bible with Greek science, Levinsohn sought to show that the tradition itself is on the side of Haskalah. In its defense of studying foreign sciences, *Te'udah be-Yisrael* spoke the language of at least some of the disciples of the Gaon of Vilna and, perhaps, the Gaon himself. Here we can observe the proximity between the learned culture of the Lithuanian yeshivah movement and the early Haskalah. It was not uncommon for full-fledged disciples of the Haskalah later in the century to speak of their own fathers as "maskilim," which probably meant that the fathers were steeped in the traditional intellectual values shared by the Haskalah and Mitnagdism. The similarities between the two groups, at least initially, shows not so much that the Haskalah "grew out of" the yeshivot as that they were virtually simultaneous developments of nineteenth-century Jewish culture.

Yet maskilim and Lithuanian scholars quickly parted company as the yeshivot became increasingly hostile to foreign books. Levinsohn's manifesto already departs radically from the culture of the Mitnagdim, even though he uses traditional proof texts. He opens with a panegyric to Pallas Athene, hardly a theme one might expect in a rabbinic text. In a barely concealed attack on the exclusive study of Talmud in the yeshivot, Levinsohn argues—as had the earlier German Haskalah—for systematic training in Hebrew grammar and the Bible, two disciplines that had disappeared from the educational curriculum in Eastern Europe but had been part of Spanish Jewish culture in the Middle Ages. And, in his argument for studying foreign sciences, he liberally laces his text and footnotes with words in Latin characters, thus pointing the way to a new synthesis between Jewish and non-Jewish cultures.

As we have seen, the Orthodox frequently defended their tradition by adopting literally the midrash that the Jews had been preserved in exile by not changing their "names, language, and clothing." These were three of the features of Jewish culture that were particularly under attack during the nineteenth century. Absolutist regimes, in an effort to extend bureaucratic control over the Jews, required them to take on proper last names, as opposed to the traditional first name and patronymic. They also attempted to impose the use of European languages and dress. These were measures favored by the maskilim as well. Levinsohn was the first in Eastern Europe to argue for learning foreign languages, although he, like most maskilim, also favored the revival of Hebrew as the national Jewish language.

In choosing either Hebrew or a European language, the maskilim were almost deliberately constructing an elite culture, because the vernacular of the vast majority of Jews was Yiddish and few could read Russian or German or the flowery, artificial Hebrew of the Haskalah. It was only later in the century that a secular literary culture was to emerge in Yiddish. Levinsohn set the tone that was to prevail among the intelligentsia toward the language of the "folk" when he wrote in *Te'udah be-Yisrael* that Yiddish could not be the language of Enlightenment because it was not pure: "This language which we speak in this land, which we borrowed from the Germans, is called 'Jewish German' [*yehudit ashkenazit*], and it is thoroughly corrupt since it is intermixed with words taken from Hebrew, Russian, French, Polish, and the like as well as from German and even the German words are mispronounced and slurred."[33] This characterization of Yiddish, epitomized later as a "jargon," was more ideological than linguistic since all languages are to some extent "intermixed." Ironically, maskilim like Levinsohn rejected the "fusion" character of Yiddish while demanding that modern Jewish culture become a hybrid between Jewish and European traditions: language must be pure, but culture needed to be mixed.

In fact, depending on the region, by the second half of the nineteenth century many Jews had become increasingly familiar with multiple Jewish and non-Jewish languages, a sign of the growing hybridity of their culture. In the larger cities and towns especially, they read Hebrew and spoke and read Yiddish and the local language (Polish, Russian, Hungarian) and, not infrequently, some German as well. The memoirs of one Polish Jew about his father, born in 1882, relates:

> Father, who went only to *ḥeder* . . . knew five languages: Hebrew, Yiddish, German, Polish and Ukrainian, although he apparently could not write Ukrainian. No one thought of this as anything extraordinary. . . . "True" foreign languages were French and English. If you asked my father before World War I, he would certainly have answered that he knew no foreign language.[34]

Whether he actually "knew" all of these "non-foreign" languages, he at least had some familiarity with them. Although Jews in many places throughout the ages were "multilingual" in this sense, the century or so before the Holocaust in Eastern Europe may have been one of the most multilingual periods in all of Jewish history.

The question of clothing was also a critical marker that divided maskilim from the Orthodox and especially from the Hasidim. The Hasidim in particular regarded adoption of modern dress as a sign of apostasy, and they elevated "traditional" garb (itself borrowed from eighteenth-century Polish fashion) to virtually the status of law. This acute sensitivity to clothing and appearance as signs of identity stemmed from the attempts of governments and maskilim alike to modernize the Jews by changing how they looked. Israel Aksenfeld (1787–1866), who wrote the first Yiddish novel in the 1840s, *Dos Shterntikhl* (The Headband), satirized traditional Jewish life by making the central symbol of his book one of the characteristic pieces of Jewish dress, the jewel-encrusted headband that wealthy married women wore. In Aksenfeld's novel, women represent traditional culture and the maskilic hero, Mikhl, symbolically defeats this bankrupt world by marrying the heroine but presenting her with a shterntikhl made of false pearls.[35]

Samuel Joseph Fuenn (1818–90), the maskil who edited the important Hebrew journal *Ha-Karmel*, gave a historical explanation for Jewish dress:

[T]he foremost cause of the distance and enmity between the children of Israel and the Christians in our state is the difference of dress. . . . The division and difference in dress derive not from reasons of religion, but rather from a corrupted source, the hatred of the nations during the Middle Ages toward Israel. Wanting not to mingle with the children of Israel they placed a seal on the brow of the Jew which established his religion. . . . In the course of time this became a distinguishing mark among the children of Israel, setting them off from their oppressors. From this isolation they took comfort. . . . In the course of time, when the original reason had been forgotten, they claimed it was for their benefit and was freely chosen.[36]

Against the Orthodox claim that Jewish dress was a traditional, indeed commanded, marker of identity, Fuenn argued that it is a relic of medieval hatred of the Jews. It was the Christian oppressors, not the Jews, who wanted such an external sign of difference. In a time theoretically free of such medieval prejudice, neither Christians nor Jews ought to need such signs.

Fuenn's argument suggests that, in the public culture the maskilim tried to create, the Jews would not be immediately identifiable by appearance. In the words of the Hebrew poet Judah Leib Gordon (1831–92), the goal of the Haskalah was to be a man on the street and a Jew at home.[37] This ideology was entirely unrealistic in Eastern Europe, where such a "street" (or "neutral society") devoid of ethnic, class, and religious differences did not exist for Russians or Poles any more than it did for Jews; there was no single "Russian" or "Polish" form of dress since different social castes—aristocrats, peasants, and merchants—all dressed differently. But if the maskilim could not make the Jews look like Russians or Poles, homogeneous categories that were still imaginary, the debate over dress did create visible signs of party affiliation *within* Jewish culture: a maskil was distinguishable from a yeshivah student who was in turn distinguishable from a Hasid. Russia's inability to fulfill Gordon's slogan created a paradoxical effect: a Jewish public culture of remarkable vitality, but one whose vitality might be measured by the fierce battles between its many factions.

Memoirs and the Cultivation of Modern Jewish Identities   Among the library of Haskalah books that Ansky mentions taking with him from Vitebsk, he cites one in particular as having a disproportionate influence on him and his comrades: Moses Leib Lilienblum's (1843–1910) *Sins of Youth*, first published in 1876. Lilienblum's autobiography, written when he was less than 30 years old, was a wholesale attack on traditional Jewish life as exemplified by what he portrayed as the tragedy of his own life: the personal as political. Regarding himself as already an "old man," Lilienblum blamed the traditional family life of the East European Jews—especially childhood and early marriage—for eradicating his ability to fulfill himself in the modern world. This indictment—so far from contemporary sentimental portraits of the family as the foundation of a healthy Jewish life—was a key plank in the Haskalah's platform: only by transforming the family might it be possible to begin transforming the Jews as a people.[38]

By paying new attention to the domestic sphere, the maskilim developed an entirely new concept of individual Jewish identity. This new "self," based on Enlightenment ideas of individuality, also required a thoroughgoing assault on traditional definitions of the self. The maskilim undertook both of these tasks most frequently by writing autobiographies, a genre itself based on the modern idea of the individual, which they adopted with the greatest enthusiasm.[39] The idea that an individual might have a unique history had no real precedent in earlier Ashkenazic Jewish culture, and neither biography nor autobiography had played important roles. (Two exceptions in the eighteenth century can be found in Germany: the autobiography of the Rabbi Jacob Emden, and that of the wealthy merchant woman, Glückel of Hameln.) The first Haskalah autobiography, which was to become a model for most nineteenth-century East European writers of the genre, was Salomon Maimon's *Lebensgeschichte,* written and published in German in 1792. Following Jean-Jacques Rousseau's *Confessions,* Maimon (ca. 1753–1800) eschewed traditional formulas and set out to tell what he advertised as the unvarnished truth about his life. The result is a kind of mélange of the picaresque and the *Bildungsroman,* as he describes his adventures escaping the world of Lithuanian talmudism and becoming a child of the Berlin Enlightenment. The outrageous character of many of the episodes in the book suggests that Maimon was less intent on telling his life history as it actually happened than in constructing a literary persona shaped by Enlightenment ideology.[40]

This was also to be the case for Maimon's successors in Eastern Europe, such as Mordecai Aaron Guenzburg, Abraham Ber Gottlober, Ephraim Deinard, Yehzkel Kotek, and Lilienblum himself. These authors used the stories of their lives as portraits of traditional Ashkenazic culture and as arguments for why and how it should be overturned. They claimed that talmudic study and early, arranged marriage impoverished and stifled the individual's self-expression. As with Maimon's autobiography, their works need to be seen as ideological statements, based, to be sure, on their own lived experiences and not as accurate generalizations about how all other Jews of their world in fact experienced their lives. But for aspiring rebels like Ansky, these memoirs provided a narrative into which they could insert their own lives, a model for how they came to understand themselves and the world they rejected.

The memoirs focus typically on two major traumas: the *ḥeder* (or primary school) and marriage. In line with their argument for new types of schools and their cooperation with the czarist regime's attempt to impose such schools on the Jews, the maskilim typically portray the ḥeder in the most horrific terms, with the *melamed* (teacher) a barely educated brute who physically abused his pupils. Going to the ḥeder was an experience of being wrenched out of the security of the family and thrown into the callous arms of one of the traditional community's stock institutions. This was a boy's first encounter with the unremittingly hostile Jewish public world.[41]

The next such encounter was marriage, an institution no less publicly sanctioned and controlled than education. For centuries, it had been the ideal custom among Ashkenazic Jews to marry off their children at the beginning of adolescence (13 for boys and 12 for girls), though probably only the wealthy could afford to do so consistently. Because most of the future maskilim came from relatively well-off families, their engagements, arranged by the traditional *shadkhan* (marriage broker), were typically made at age 11 or 12 and their mar-

A. Trankowsky, *The Jewish Wedding,* late nineteenth century. Oil on canvas. (In the permanent collection of The Magnes Museum, Berkeley; 75.19. Photo: Ben Ailes) Note the combination of traditional clothing (the father of the bride) and modern "bourgeois" clothing (the man wearing a top hat). The traditional Eastern European "klezmer" musicians are portrayed on the left.

riages took place a year or two later. They were then packed off to the houses of their in-laws, where they lived with their young wives for several years (determined by the dowry), during which time they were expected to study.

The memoirs devote considerable attention to the conflicts with in-laws, for it was frequently during this period that the young men began to discover the writings of the Haskalah. The first to do so was Maimon himself, who describes in his characteristically caricatured and comic manner the beatings he suffered at the hand of his mother-in-law and the tricks with which he amply repaid her. Lilienblum attributes the very writing of *Sins of Youth* to his conflict with his mother-in-law: "It was my mother-in-law who in a real sense was the creator of this autobiography, that is, of the tragic part of it."[42] The struggle against the traditional world therefore took the form of an intergenerational battle, not between "fathers and sons" (the title of the Turgenev novel that resonated with many Jewish intellectuals) but between parents-in-law and sons-in-law.

Little wonder that, when the maskilim later came to write their memoirs and ideological tracts, the institution of early marriage should figure so prominently as something that needed radical change. According to their ideals for an enlightened Jewish society, marriage would follow European ideas of free choice and romantic love. Young boys would learn productive professions and only marry when they could support their families. Their wives would no longer go out to the marketplace while the men studied but would find their true roles within the home in the image of European bourgeois domesticity. By revolutionizing marriage and the family, the maskilim hoped to create a new private sphere that, in their view, was utterly absent in traditional Jewish culture. The Haskalah also pioneered a critique of the traditional role of women as the breadwinners in their families and as captives of the patriarchal system of law, an ironic proto-feminism since it was an attack on a system in which women had considerable economic power. Judah Leib Gordon's famous poem "On the Point of a Yod" attacked the way the law discriminated against women abandoned by their husbands without a *get* (writ of divorce), which left them destitute and unable to divorce or remarry. These proto-feminist arguments reflect the influence of nascent Russian feminism as the maskilim came into greater contact with Russian intellectual currents in the more liberal reign of Alexander II. Yet this primarily male movement was equally ambivalent about the independent, modern woman. A number of maskilim expressed hostility toward women writing in Hebrew, an unusual phenomenon represented by figures like Yente Kalman-Wohlerner (1810–91) and Miriam Markel Mosesohn (1841–1920).[43]

Although it was not until the twentieth century that women began to contribute in large numbers toward the secular Jewish culture of Eastern Europe, the nineteenth century witnessed a revolution in their education.[44] In traditional society, girls were typically taught to read prayers and moralistic literature like the midrashic *Tsene u-Rene* primarily in Yiddish. They were usually taught at home, but, if they did attend a ḥeder, it was for fewer years than the boys. It was not uncommon by the mid-nineteenth century for families with bourgeois aspirations to hire tutors to teach their daughters Russian. As the maskilim and the Russian government established "modern" schools, more girls were given formal education and, by the 1897 Russian census, nearly a third of Jewish females aged 10–29 could read some Russian, as against almost half of males. The Orthodox world itself came to recognize the importance of female education in the early twentieth century with the establishment of the network of Beis Yaakov schools for girls. From the 1860s, small numbers of women began to make their way to universities. Here is a description of student life at the University of Kiev in the 1870s:

The [student nihilists] favored complete equality of rights for women, and they decided that men had no right to rule over them.... The male and female students would gather together and read forbidden books.... Here the question of women was easily solved, like all other social questions: there is no God, no law or etiquette, there is no rich or poor, no race or nationality, no difference in status or gender. Young men and women from our people went almost crazy from the complete freedom that they encountered here ... and gradually all restraints were cast off. The laws of modesty and etiquette were violated.... The Jewish girls would sleep in student apartments of the members of the new party [that is, the revolutionaries], not distinguishing between Jews and Christians.[45]

Although the maskilim believed that their proposals for change fell on deaf ears in the traditional world, major changes such as these were, in fact, under way in Jewish culture in the second half of the nineteenth century. The age of marriage rose among all Jews, including the Orthodox, so that the early marriages denounced by the maskilim became increasingly rare. The values of romantic love and free choice in marriage not only captured the imagination of secular university students but infiltrated popular culture as well. Yiddish chapbooks sold by itinerant booksellers became the source for "modern" ideas, often wedding traditional practices with romance. For example, a girl and a boy might fall in love, only to discover at the end of the story that they were destined for each other by the traditional vow (*tekias kaf*) sworn between their respective parents at birth.

One remarkable anonymous tale tells of the daughter of a rabbi from Constantinople who is engaged to a rabbi's son from Brisk, a geographical improbability that is typical of this kind of literature.[46] She is the best student in her father's yeshivah in Constantinople, also an improbable detail because, of course, women were not allowed to study in yeshivot. The engagement with the boy in Brisk takes place when she is 12, and she and he exchange the traditional formulaic letters. But curiosity gets the better of her and, disguised as a boy, she travels to Brisk, where she enrolls in her fiancé's yeshivah. This story was to be repeated by later authors, among them, most famously, Isaac Bashevis Singer in his "Yentl the Yeshivah Boy." What is fascinating here is the way this nineteenth-century popular fiction collapses the traditional gender separation of family life and yeshivah: instead of waiting for her betrothed, the girl conceals herself as a boy and enters his world. It was perhaps through such literature that popular culture might register covert protest against the rigid values of elite Lithuanian scholarship.

Jewish folklore and folksongs from the nineteenth century attest to the attenuation of traditional values on the popular level. One folksong relates how a girl who falls in love with a boy commits suicide as a result of opposition from her parents. In another song, which may have been based on an actual incident in Moldavia in the early 1870s, a boy, enraged at the opposition of his girlfriend's parents, kills her and then attempts, unsuccessfully, to kill himself. The parents regret their opposition and warn other parents not to interfere in their children's romantic affairs.[47] That this kind of romantic literature and folksong, mixing traditional and modern elements, began to affect the way people lived can be seen in the following rabbinic court case from 1879:

> The boy Chaim said that for a long time, perhaps four or five years, the soul of the virgin [Neḥama] had adhered to him in love . . . and, once, the two of them found themselves by chance together . . . and they talked together day and night. She said to him that it seemed to her that their love was eternal. During this whole time, she wrote him many letters containing statements of love and affection.[48]

Clandestine love was, of course, nothing new (the girl here was already engaged to someone else) and romantic love was certainly not absent from traditional Jewish life.[49] But this case does contain some modern elements. Engaged couples were encouraged to use form letters (*egronim*) to communicate; the maskilim themselves wrote such letters to try to infiltrate modern values into traditional culture. Here, the girl uses one of these Haskalah formularies or even writes in her own voice.

In addition, traditional society would have tried (not always successfully) to prevent any meeting between young men and women. By the second half of the nineteenth century, young Jews developed new spaces in nature for escaping traditional strictures. As the Hebrew writer M. J. Berdichevsky (1865–1921) wrote in a short story at the end of the century: "A generation went and a generation came and a new generation rose in Israel, a generation that began to walk on the Sabbaths at the borders of the city."[50] Traditional Jewish culture was contained within the boundaries of towns, and the vast regions separating the towns were the realm of the peasants; now, Jews ventured forth into nature, symbolically crossing over into the non-Jewish world, a world where the Sabbath laws were no longer observed and all manner of transgression of boundaries suddenly became possible.

For the maskilim themselves, the new Jewish identities and family values they preached often seemed out of reach. The marriages of these ideologues rarely went well, and a high percentage of them either divorced their wives voluntarily or were forced to do so when their in-laws discovered their heretical leanings. Some never succeeded in achieving a happy domestic life. And, despite their advocacy of equality for women, many, like Lilienblum, who conducted an ultimately fruitless epistolary affair with a young female disciple of Haskalah, never fully realized their ideology in their own lives.

In fact, the experience of these young maskilim reflected the implosion of Russian Jewish family life in general.[51] Even in the first half of the nineteenth century, the divorce rate among Russian Jews was surprisingly high, probably reflecting increasing economic deprivation. Toward the end of the century, it dropped, but not because family life became more stable: desertion became more common as husbands, partly by emigrating to America and other destinations, separated from their wives without formal writs of divorce. Although before the partitions of Poland the Jewish communities had usually been able to control marriage and divorce through the powers granted to them by the Polish government, this form of stability collapsed in the nineteenth century. The Russian government increasingly intervened in Jewish family law, either through making its own court system available to Jews disgruntled with rabbinic courts or through the state rabbis, whose authority paralleled that of traditional rabbis. The result of this confusion of authority created a social and cultural vacuum in which individuals might pursue their own desires. The scenes of free love such as we saw at the University of Kiev were but one example of this breakdown of traditional authority.

In the wake of this breakdown, the cultural self-perception of many young Jews was often more gloomy than liberated. In the literature produced by the heirs of Haskalah, the writers of the national renaissance of the turn of the century, the protagonists were typically incapable of fulfilling their romantic longings: the failure of Eros became a metaphor for a growing culture of pessimism and despair. The stock-in-trade of this literature was the figure of the *talush*— meaning "uprooted"—typically a young maskil, alienated from both his people and the non-Jewish culture he wished to enter, his intellectual and cultural impotence symbolized by sexual impotence. The talush was a passive and masochistic figure, tormented by erotic longings but unable to fulfill them. It was the talush who, more than any heroic figure, was the most representative of the literature of national renaissance, a symbol of the presumed national impotence of the Jewish people.

Consider the unnamed protagonist of Joseph Hayyim Brenner's (1881–1921) Hebrew novella, *In Winter* (*Ba-Ḥoref*), published in 1904: he is no longer a part of traditional Jewish society, but neither can he find solace in the Haskalah or in any political movement, remaining a wanderer between two worlds, unable to put down roots. At the end of the story, he finds himself penniless and without a ticket on a train. After being discovered by the conductor, he is roughly thrown off with a hail of antisemitic curses. A village lies some three miles away, but he is told that there are no Jews there. The novella ends with the protagonist lying on the ground as rain beats down and snow envelops him. If, as we shall presently see, the train represents the modern world in which the Jewish intellectuals sought to integrate, then the implication of Brenner's story is that they will not stay on for long. Once on the train, they will travel too far from the traditional Jewish world ever to return to it, and, thrown off by the antisemites, they will perish on cold and alien ground. In Brenner's dark tale, the Haskalah's attempt to create a new Jewish self seems doomed: his talush, anonymous and incapable of coherent action, has lost both his creative individuality and his tie to a community. Such was the culture of despair that paradoxically accompanied the political movements of Jewish national awakening.

SHEM AND JAPHET ON THE TRAIN

. . . thrusting me toward Russian letters. . . .

In 1912, Ansky wrote a short story in Yiddish under the title "A Goyisher Kop" (Gentile Mentality) that, like Brenner's, takes place on a train.[52] The story involves a meeting in a railway car between the first-person narrator and an old revolutionary acquaintance who had previously taken a Christian name and tried to pass as a Russian; now he was dressed in the European style but had reverted back to his Jewish name, Moses Silberzweig. A discussion about conversion ensues between the two, with an elderly Jew in the compartment joining in. The travelers recount several tales of conversion, the purpose of which seems to be to demonstrate the absurdities of identity in the Russian context. The first story concerns the mass expulsions from Moscow in 1891–92, when many Jews tried to escape the edict by converting to Russian Orthodoxy. One clever fellow, having mastered the catechism, became a "professional" convert: for a hefty fee, he would appear with someone else's identity papers and go through the conversion for him. In this way, he went through 55 conversions and earned hundreds of rubles—without actually converting himself! The second story deals with a non-Jewish girl working for the revolution who infiltrates into St. Petersburg with a phony Jewish passport. When the police challenge her residency papers and repeatedly demand that she pay them bribes, Silberzweig (the narrator of this story) attempts to persuade her to convert to Christianity, which would obviate the need for papers. But the irreligious girl refuses to convert, even though she was always a Christian! The narrator of the frame story concludes: "For the first time in my life I felt that it wouldn't be such a bad idea to talk to a goy."

Both of these stories within the story suggest the sometimes bizarre and fuzzy borders between Jewish and non-Jewish identity in late-nineteenth- and early-twentieth-century Russia. For those, like Ansky himself, who had undergone the process of acculturation—had turned to "Russian letters"—a certain fluidity of identity became possible: one could slip out of one's Jewish clothing and into Russian, perhaps later changing back. For the vast majority of Russian Jews, still mired in the largely Yiddish-speaking Pale of Settlement, such fluidity was, of course, not possible. But in the revolutionary movements, as in the second story, as well as in the description of student life in Kiev, Jews and non-Jews might mix promiscuously even to the point of adopting one another's identity. Yet Ansky's story also reinforces the boundaries between Jew and gentile: in all three cases (Silberzweig himself, the expulsions from Moscow, and the revolutionary girl), conversion does not work as it is meant to. The convert reverts to his previous identity, or he does not really convert, or she cannot convert because she really had a different identity to begin with. No matter how much a Jew might adopt Russian culture, Ansky seems to suggest, he or she could never really become Russian.

Written after he had already made his journey back to the Yiddish language and Jewish life, Ansky's criticism of the possibility of changing identities in the Russian context reflected his own partisan point of view. But by the early twentieth century, there were those who had made the journey without turning back. The young Vladimir Jabotinsky (1881–1940), who would later become the leader of the Revisionist Zionists, was born into a Russified Jewish family in Odessa, ignorant of all Jewish languages and determined, until he saw the Zionist light, to make his career in Russian letters. He was not alone. As the statistics from the beginning of this chapter show, the opening up of the Russian universities and major cities under Alexander II produced an ever-increasing Jewish population educated in Russian culture, a process that took place in the other national cultures of Eastern Europe as well. Many young people, like Ansky, found inspiration in the new traditions of Russian revolutionary populism and devoured such writers as Pisarev, Chernyshevsky, and Lavrov (Ansky was Lavrov's personal secretary in Paris). But not all became revolutionaries: Jabotinsky is an example of a young Jewish intellectual less moved by Russian politics than by Russian literary aesthetics.

Conversion symbolizes the ultimate assimilation into another culture, and, though far less common among Russian Jews than among their contemporaries in Germany or France, it did take place and it is evidence for more widespread Russification than is frequently assumed. In the first decade of the twentieth century, Pauline Wengeroff (1833–1916), the wife of a wealthy Lithuanian merchant, wrote her autobiography, a rare occurrence for a woman, and published it in Berlin in German under the title *Memoirs of a Grandmother: Pictures Out of the Cultural History of the Jews of Russia in the Nineteenth Century*. Wengeroff's husband had abandoned much of Jewish religious practice, and her children had all converted to Russian Orthodoxy. Her memoir is at once an exercise in nostalgia and an amateur ethnography of Russian Jewish life during the transition from tradition to modernity. Quoting her own mother in a kind of Yiddishized German, she writes:

"I [that is, Wengeroff's mother] and my generation will certainly live and die as Jews; our grandchildren will certainly not live and die as Jews. But what our children will be I cannot foresee." The first two parts of this prophecy came true. The third is now coming true, for our generation is some kind of mongrel (*Zwitterding*). . . . [The Jews] could not acquire the new, the alien, without renouncing the old, what was most unique and holy to them. How chaotically these modern ideas swirl about in the minds of Russian Jewish men! . . . The old family values disappeared without anything new taking their place. For most Jewish women of that time, religion and tradition suffused their inner essence . . . and for that reason, a difficult struggle took place in their most intimate family circle.[53]

Wengeroff describes this destruction of the old world as a consequence of the great liberalization of the 1860s and 1870s, although her own husband, who is clearly the model of the confused Jewish man, had renounced tradition even earlier, apparently out of disillusionment with Hasidism. Largely ignoring the rising feminism of Jewish women, she sees them as the guardians of tradition and men as its destroyers. But she herself came into her marriage already literate in Russian and German and was actually responsible for teaching her husband German. Wengeroff's exaggerated portrait of a generation of Jews rushing headlong into assimilation and apostasy was based on her own experience as a woman in the wealthy merchant class, but she nevertheless gives us insight into an aspect of East European Jewish culture that, in the shadow of pogroms and persecution, has too often been played down.

Ansky's story of the misadventures of identity takes place significantly on a train, a metaphor for many Jewish writers (like Brenner) for the modern sites, such as cities, where Jews might encounter non-Jewish culture under new circumstances, sometimes positive and sometimes negative.[54] For the nineteenth century, the train represented modernity in several ways. The railway altered conceptions of time; journeys that, from time immemorial, had taken days could now be compressed into hours. Of equal importance was the new space created by the railway carriage, a territory that was at once private and public. Perfect strangers found themselves thrown together for long periods. Although the first-, second-, and third-class divisions of trains reproduced the class divisions of society, the railway car could still serve as a kind of social leveler and as the territory, at once intimate and anonymous, for a new kind of social discourse between strangers. As Tolstoy reflected in his famous story "The Kreutzer Sonata," the train setting allowed passengers to tell their private stories in a public space.

For Jews, too, the train represented a new social space in which some of the intimacy of the shtetl might be reproduced but not necessarily with familiar faces. Although East European Jews were accustomed to an active public sphere in the synagogues, study halls, and marketplaces of their communities, this public domain remained a localized one. As the isolation of communities was overcome, the train contributed greatly toward the new sense of the Jews as an interconnected nation within the Russian Pale. This development registered not only on modernizing Jews but on the traditionalists as well, as railway lines served to bring farflung Hasidim in closer proximity to the courts of their rebbes. For example, the small town of Gora Kalwaria, which, as we have already seen, housed the court of the rebbe of Ger, became much more accessible to the sect's disciples when a special rail line was built to connect it with the main railway system.

But the train also served as the vehicle for destruction of the old world of the shtetl, providing, as it did, the means for escape to the big cities and the foundation for a new market economy that would destroy the shtetl's main function. Both for Jews in their everyday experiences and for writers of fiction, the train mirrored the urbanization of their life: in the cities of Eastern Europe, as in the trains, an anonymous existence became possible, though not always one in which a person might hide his identity as a Jew. The railroad car came to symbolize the creation of what was called in Yiddish the *yidishe gas* (Jewish street), a new public place where secular politics and culture could strike roots and flourish, yet dramatically opposed to the old "Jewish street" of the shtetl.

The railroad also created a new territory for encounters between Jews and non-Jews. Here, the complex traditional relations between Jewish merchants and innkeepers, Ukrainian peasants, Polish noblemen, and Russian petty officials (all of whom were stock figures in Jewish literature of the nineteenth century) might be reproduced but also transformed, not necessarily in a better way. A classic exposition of this issue is Mendele Mokher Sforim's "Shem and Japhet on the Train," written in 1890, just a year after Tolstoy's train story. Mendele was the pseudonym as well as the fictitious narrator (Mendele the Bookseller) of the great Hebrew and Yiddish writer Sh. Y. Abramowitsch (ca. 1836–1917).[55] Mendele distinguishes between the Jews of the third-class compartment and the gentiles who ride in second and first class, and in so doing he weaves together the question of Jewish-gentile relations and the train as a new form of transportation symbolizing modernity. He contrasts the train with the wagon on which he used to tour the countryside selling pious books to the common Jews. Here he engages in a striking linguistic inversion. Many of Abramowitsch's stories start with Mendele the Bookseller traveling on his wagon, the term for which, in both Hebrew and Yiddish, is *agalah* or *agoleh*. Indeed, the most prevalent form of transportation in the East European countryside was the wagon, and the *ba'al agoleh* (wagon driver) was a stock figure in life as in literature. But in the present story, Abramowitsch uses this word to signify the railway carriage; conversely, when he refers to a horse-drawn wagon, he uses the word *karon*, which most Hebrew writers employed to signify a railway car. By using a term with primitive and homey associations to refer to the technological marvel of the railway, Abramowitsch mocks the ostensible power of modern inventions to change the Jews' fate: no matter what vehicle may convey them, Jews will always remain Jews.

Mendele, the narrator, makes the train a symbol for all the evils of modern urban life—alienation from nature and class conflict:

> [T]he railway train . . . is like a whole city in motion with its tumult, its populations split into classes and sects, who carry with them their hatred and envy, their bickerings and rivalries and petty deals. Such passengers may traverse the whole world without regard to the grandeur of nature, the beauty of the mountains and plains and all the handiwork of God.[56]

The horse-drawn coach, like the shtetl it stands for, represents by contrast a kind of freedom, even if the passengers are "jammed together like herrings in a barrel." As insecure as the shtetl may have been, it was being replaced by an even more uncertain and unfamiliar reality.

Like the shift from shtetl to city, the story within the story deals with the new encounter between Jews and gentiles. Reb Moses and his family are riding on the train, having been expelled from Bismarck's Prussia. Moses explains that they are victims of the new racial antisemitism—hence the ironic reference to the biblical Shem and Japhet, the sons of Noah who were construed as the eponymous ancestors of the Semites and Aryans. They are traveling with a Polish Christian, who was also expelled from Germany. This Pole was an old acquaintance of the Jew but had become an antisemite himself, a commentary on the vicissitudes of historical relations between Jews and Poles. Now united in the train of exile, the two become friends again, and Moses proposes to teach the Pole the lessons the Jews have learned over the centuries in order to survive. These lessons involve begging and deference to all authority. Mendele is so struck by the solidarity between the Jew and the Pole (perhaps an allusion to the Jewish participation in the Polish revolts against Russian rule in 1831 and 1863) that he ends his story with a prayer: "Lord of the Universe! Grant us a few more such disciples—and Shem and Japhet will be brothers—and peace will come to Israel!"

As is often the case in these Mendele stories, Abramowitsch stands at an ironic distance from his pseudonymous narrator. Mendele's logic is terribly askew, for even if modernity subjects other peoples to the terrible sufferings and exiles experienced by the Jews, it is highly unlikely that Japhet will come, in the biblical phrase, to "dwell in the tents of Shem." Abramowitsch ridicules the hoary tactics of begging and licking the boots of the authorities. Indeed, Abramowitsch is no more sympathetic to Mendele's nostalgia for his coach and shtetl than he is sanguine about the ostensible alliance of Jew and goy on the train. True Jewish survival can only come by changing this approach to the world—getting off the train, as it were, and starting afresh. Or, perhaps, it requires getting on a different sort of train that would take the Jews out of Europe and to a life in Palestine (as the nascent Zionist movement advocated) or to America (as many Russian Jews were already voting for with their feet).

The onset of modernity in Eastern Europe had indeed changed relations between Jews and non-Jews but often in directions that scarcely seemed better. Violent attacks on Jews were nothing new in the late nineteenth century, but the pogroms (the word itself became current at this time) of 1881, 1903, and 1905–6, as well as the revival of the medieval ritual murder accusation, seemed to signify at once an unexpected return to the Middle Ages and something different: not only riots that got out of hand and that the authorities could not control but possibly the products of a new antisemitic ideology and governmental collusion. Although Western and Central Europe witnessed attacks on Jewish emancipation in the forms of the Dreyfus Affair and the rise of antisemitic political movements, only in Russia did antisemitism take on the flavor of mass violence. Thus, Jewish/non-Jewish relations in Eastern Europe were caught in a vise between growing acculturation and political identification with the state, on the one hand, and new forms of violence, prejudice, and segregation, on the other. It was precisely this tension that Abramowitsch captured in his train story.

Another sign of the ambivalent relationship with Russian culture was the recurring fantasy in literature of erotic relations between Jews and Christians. Bialik, the poet laureate of the national renaissance, devoted a disturbing story to the subject. "Behind the Fence" tells of the love between a Christian girl, Marinka, and a Jewish boy, Noah; their love stands in opposition to the brutality and xenophobia of his parents and of her witch-like stepmother. At the end of the story, he is forced to marry a Jewish girl, having left Marinka pregnant. On one level, the story is an indictment of traditional Jewish society and of the "fence" between Jews and gentiles—a rather shocking position, no doubt, for readers of the Hebrew national poet! On another level, however, the figure of Marinka's stepmother hints at the demonic potentialities of the gentile world, a theme with strong echoes in popular folk culture.

Indeed, fascination with the erotic attraction of the non-Jew was often bound up in literature with a fear of the demonic Other. Devorah Baron (1888–1956), one of the early female writers of Hebrew and Yiddish fiction, explored this theme in a bizarre fable about a female "Jewish" dog. Dogs have negative associations in Ashkenazic folklore and are generally associated with the gentile world. Baron's dog is a symbol for the vexed relations between Jews and gentiles in Eastern Europe. She bears puppies sired by a dog belonging to a local nobleman, but her offspring are stolen from her. She is kidnapped by gentiles and gang-raped by their dogs. Finally, she falls in love with a "gentile" dog, becomes as vicious as the gentiles, and betrays the Jews to whom she had once belonged. The story ends with the Jews strangling her: such is the violence, the story suggests, that attends on those who would cross the borders between Jews and their neighbors.

The ambivalent relationship to Russian culture found expression not only in literature but also in visual art, in which Jews in Eastern Europe began to engage by the last part of the nineteenth century. Here, we may return to Vitebsk, whose academy of art (a very unusual institution in a town of the Pale and a sign that Vitebsk was already modernizing), established by the painter Yehuda (Yuri) Pen, turned many young Jews into artists, the most celebrated of whom was Marc Chagall (1887–1985). In his autobiography, Chagall recounts his escape from academic failures at the Russian gymnasium to Pen's School of Painting, which in turn prompted him to go in 1907 to St. Petersburg to pursue a career as a painter. For Chagall and others, art became a vehicle for mediating between Jewish and European culture.

Perhaps nothing in the work of Chagall and other Jewish artists (such as Maurycy Gottlieb, Mark Antokolsky, and Samuel Hirszenberg) captured the relationship to the attractions of "Japhet" more than the figure of Jesus, to which they returned again and again in their art. Just as historians and writers like Joseph Klausner, Lamed Shapiro, Uri Zvi Greenberg, and Sholem Asch, in very different ways, tried to reappropriate Jesus for the Jews, so the visual artists sought to wrench him out of Christianity and make him over into a Jewish symbol.[57] These works were equally subversive toward traditional Jewish belief, for which Jesus was a black magician. (East European Jews would traditionally play cards or dice on Christmas eve and refrain from studying Torah in the belief that the demonic spirit of Jesus was abroad and could only be countered by sacrilegious activities.) For these modernist writers and artists, Jesus as Jew became a palimpsest for a new Jewish identity, at once universal and particular.

Three brief examples will suffice. In 1873, Mark Antokolsky sculpted his *Ecce Homo,* which represents Jesus with East European Jewish features, side curls, and a skullcap. Anticipating criticism by both Christians and Jews for appropriating a Christian theme, Antokolsky wrote that he identified with Jesus as a revolutionary—a model, he implied, for rebellion against both the Russian and Jewish establishments. Here was Jesus not so much as a figure of reconciliation between Jews and Christians but as a prophet of transformation of both worlds. In the wake of the pogroms, other artists applied Christian symbols to Jewish suffering. Samuel Hirszenberg's (1865–1908) *The Wandering Jew,* painted in 1899, depicts a bearded figure, clad only in a loincloth, who runs with a terrified expression over heaps of sprawled corpses scattered in a forest of crosses.[58] He is the only survivor, it would seem, of the pogroms/crucifixions that had destroyed and mutilated his brethren: the Jews are the suffering Christs tortured by the Christian world. Finally, Chagall's own preoccupation with Jesus, from his *Golgotha* in 1912 to his *White Crucifixion* in 1938 and other Christological paintings from the World War II period, completes the appropriation of Jesus as the symbol of Jewish suffering. It is possible that Chagall's first depiction of Jesus in *Golgotha* (originally named *Dedicated to Christ*) was intended as a reference to Mendel Beilis, the Russian Jew who had been accused of ritual murder.[59] In *White Crucifixion,* a Christ clad in a prayer shawl for a loincloth hangs on a cross in the middle of the painting; surrounding him are scenes of Jews fleeing burning towns. The destruction of Jewish life in Europe thus found its ultimate, ironic expression in the primordial symbol of Christianity, a symbol also of that acculturation which many Jews so fervently sought.

If the train of Ansky's story "A Goyisher Kop" had originally symbolized the ambiguous promise of modernity and cultural integration, within a few years of Chagall's *White Crucifixion* painting it would become the predominant symbol of the deportation and murder of so many East European Jews. There was, of

Marc Chagall, *White Crucifixion*, 1938. Oil on canvas.
(The Art Institute of Chicago, Gift of Alfred S. Alschuler, 1946.925. All rights reserved.)
Chagall's painting reflects the artist's use of the Jewish Jesus to represent the destruction of
Eastern European Jewish life through pogroms and flight, even before the Holocaust.

course, no inevitable trajectory from acculturation to the Holocaust, nor should
one be implied. On the contrary, the tensions and struggles over the attempts to
adopt non-Jewish cultures in Eastern Europe, and the incomplete and frustrated
nature of those struggles, were to produce Jewish cultures of remarkable vitality
in the decades before the Great Destruction.

TO THE FOLK!

*I would discern the splendor of the poetry that lies buried in the old
historical foundations and traditions.*

For those, like Ansky, who imbibed the Russian populist traditions of "going to
the people," a return to the Jewish folk (if it did take place) was frequently based
on images of the folk refracted through "Russian letters." The folk whom these
intellectuals discovered, often as a response to the pogroms and persecutions of
the latter part of the nineteenth century, was a folk they, in a sense, created. As we
have already observed, most of the intellectuals of the Haskalah had fled the
shtetl for the cities—Odessa, Vilna, Warsaw—and their critical and satirical portraits of Jewish village life were written at a distance, both geographical and
mental. Now, the return to the people involved going back to the countryside,
as Ansky and his collaborators did in the ethnographic expeditions that he
launched in 1912. In a programmatic essay written in 1914, Ansky described Jewish folklore as an "oral tradition": "like the Bible [it is] the product of the Jewish
spirit; it reflects the same beauty and purity of the Jewish social, the same modesty and nobility of the Jewish heart, the same loftiness and depth of Jewish
thought."[60] Ansky clearly intended his characterization of Jewish folklore as an
"oral tradition" to usurp the rabbinic idea that the Talmud was the oral law; for
an intellectual alienated from the world of talmudic scholarship, rabbinic culture had become a fossilized "written" tradition. The oral tradition of Jewish
folklore, rather than the written traditions of the rabbis, might unite the secular
intellectual with the people, but the ravages of modernity threatened to destroy
this culture at precisely the moment when it was most needed.

By the late nineteenth century, the effects of urbanization, mass emigration,
and impoverishment convinced many that the traditional culture of the folk was
doomed to extinction. Although at this time the majority of Jews, though fewer
than before, still lived in small towns, followed religious tradition, and spoke
Yiddish, some intellectuals became caught up in a culture of nostalgia for the
world of their fathers and mothers.[61] This had its parallels in neo-Romantic, nationalist movements in Russia and elsewhere in Europe to memorialize the life
of the folk before it was irretrievably lost. Writing in the 1880s, Abraham Ber
Gottlober (1810–99), who was one of the founders of the Haskalah in Odessa,
constructed his autobiography in the form of an ethnography of customs that
were rapidly becoming unfamiliar:

Before I relate the history of my life from the time I became a bridegroom, I will place before the eyes of the reader the customs of our people in those days (and, with some small changes, these are still today the customs of many of our people) . . . in order that they should be available in the future for the next generation which will forget the ways and customs of the days that have passed.[62]

The tone of Gottlober's memoir is distinctly different from that of his younger colleague in the Haskalah, Lilienblum, in *Sins of Youth*. Gottlober mixed criticism with sentimentality for a vanishing world, and what is fascinating about his statement is that, like Wengeroff, Gottlober wrote in a period in which, as he himself says, many of the traditional customs persisted; although some practices, like adolescent marriage, had indeed disappeared, the accelerating processes of urbanization, proletarianization, and Russification had still not totally eradicated traditional life. His nostalgia, like that of others in this period, might be called "anticipatory nostalgia," a prophecy of a time when all that would be left would be memories.

The culture of nostalgia spawned historical, literary, and folkloristic enterprises that contributed greatly toward the creation of a popular secular culture. Simon Dubnow (1860–1941), the dean of Russian Jewish history, put out a call for documents and records from small communities throughout the Pale; he enlisted a small army of amateur researchers who sent him a treasure trove of materials that became the first historical archive of East European Jews. In the first decade of twentieth century, a Society of Jewish Folk Music and a Jewish Ethnographic Society were formed to recover and preserve the culture of the folk. Some writers, like Berdichevsky, Y. L. Peretz (1852–1915), and Martin Buber (1878–1965), rebelled against the Haskalah's contempt for Hasidism by collecting and rewriting Hasidic stories, a movement of "neo-Hasidism" that found a romantic echo especially among German Jews in search of authentic Jewish roots.

The culture of nostalgia touched many diverse groups, not all of them secular. Among the Hasidim, as mentioned earlier, a desire arose to collect and publish tales of the tzaddikim.[63] Many of the stories that would be retold by the secular "neo-Hasidic" writers had their origins only slightly earlier in the Hasidic world. The Hasidic collectors were engaged in a kind of folkloristic and historical enterprise of their own that implicitly reflected a surprisingly modern sensibility. And within the world of the Lithuanian yeshivot, biographies of great talmudic scholars became an accepted genre, attesting to a similar kind of historical impulse: Orthodox culture, like its secular opponent, became preoccupied with its own history and with remembering a vanishing past.

The attempt to create a marriage between secular intellectuals and popular culture had its origins in the emergence of modern Yiddish literature in the middle of the nineteenth century. As we have seen, the maskilim regarded Yiddish as a disreputable hybrid language that could not serve as the vehicle for modern Jewish culture. But since Hebrew or Russian were not accessible to most Jews, any author seeking a real audience had no choice but Yiddish. A ready market for literature of all kinds in Yiddish existed throughout the Jewish world of Eastern Europe due to two factors: widespread literacy, especially female literacy; and printing, particularly after Alexander II loosened censorship on Jewish books. Much of Yiddish literature had for centuries been directed primarily toward women or toward uneducated men, but it was limited in variety and scope. By the second half of the nineteenth century, there was a proliferation of such literature. Some of it was devoted to traditional religious themes and to Hasidic tales of the tzaddik, but certain maskilim writing in Yiddish began to appropriate the popular forms of romance and adventure to spread their doctrines to the masses. One example is Azik Meyer Dik (1814–93), who claimed, at one point, that "one hundred thousand copies of my books have already been sold and new orders from the booksellers arrive daily."[64] Dik wrote scores of pulp romances aimed primarily at female readers and often designed to inculcate the new bourgeois values of domesticity. Thus, in his *Words of Righteousness* (1863), Dik states that "if, with God's help, you really obtain a good apartment with all the amenities, which is as difficult to obtain as a good match, then it is incumbent upon the housewife to keep it clean and tidy."[65] He makes this argument sound traditional by scattering a variety of biblical and rabbinic proof texts, a rhetorical style that had trickled down from the yeshivah into popular culture (and that would later be much satirized by Mendele Mokher Sforim and Sholem Aleichem).

The new journals and newspapers published by the maskilim served as important conduits, in addition to books, in bringing popular literature to a wide audience. Although the Hebrew and Russian Jewish publications necessarily had limited scope, their Yiddish supplements had greater circulation. Alexander Zederbaum (1816–93) was one of the great pioneers of both the Hebrew and Yiddish press. His Hebrew newspaper *Ha-Melitz* was the most important organ of the Haskalah, but in 1862 he began to publish a Yiddish weekly, *Kol Mevasser,* first as a supplement to *Ha-Melitz* and later as an independent journal. In 1867, Zederbaum serialized Y. Y. Linetski's satiric Yiddish novel (which appeared as a book two years later), *Dos Poylishe Yingl* (The Polish Boy). Whereas the Hebrew Haskalah had lampooned Hasidism in a parodic style accessible only to a highly educated audience, Linetski's text accomplished the same goal in much more popular fashion. In fact, as evidence that this kind of literature was read not only by a secular audience but also by Hasidim themselves, here is Zederbaum's testimony:

> The story caught the interest of the public to such an extent that people, wait-ing impatiently from week to week for the new installment, would read it im-mediately whenever the most recent issue arrived, even before they read the latest news. . . . More than that: Hasidim, who are enemies of *Kol Mevasser* in general—let alone of the author of this story, whom they would gladly see dead—even they would look every week for the new issue and read *Dos Poylishe Yingl* with pleasure.[66]

This passage suggests that perhaps we would be too hasty to divide this read-ing public into "religious" and "secular." Just as the lines between yeshivah cul-ture and the Haskalah were often fuzzy, so the readership of a spoof on Hasidism might include the Hasidim themselves.

It was on this foundation that the "classicists" of nineteenth-century Yiddish literature—Mendele Mokher Sforim, Sholem Aleichem (Shalom Rabinovitz, 1859–1916), and Peretz—created their great works. All of these authors started out writing in Hebrew or, in the case of Peretz, Polish. The switch to Yiddish was undertaken with a certain ambivalence, captured in part by the assumption of folksy pseudonyms. Mendele, who published his first Yiddish story in 1864, later claimed that he had lowered himself from the lofty heights of Hebrew in order to save the folk from the trashy novels of writers like Dik and the extraordinarily prolific Shomer (N. M. Shaykevitsh, 1846–1905). The ambivalence of writers like Mendele suggests the complex relationship between the intelligentsia and popu-lar culture that informs the history of Yiddish literature in its so-called classi-cal age.

Yiddish culture was, then, not so much the culture of the folk as it was the culture that intellectuals wished to attribute to the folk. As a variety of political movements emerged at the end of the nineteenth century to attempt to find col-lective solutions to the problems of the Russian Jews, culture became a weapon in the battle. In opposing Zionism, which in Eastern Europe championed He-brew culture, Bundists and other so-called "territorialists" (those who advocated the realization of Jewish national rights in Eastern Europe) often embraced Yid-dish. A leader in this effort was Ansky's boyhood friend from Vitebsk, Chaim Zhitlowsky (1865–1943), who, like Ansky, had joined the populist Narodniki in his youth but, following the pogroms of the 1880s, returned to the Jewish folk. He became one of the ideologists of the socialist Bund in 1898 and later joined the more moderate territorialists (he would go on in the United States to adopt and then shed a variety of other ideologies). Zhitlowsky's "Yiddishism" was an attempt to construct a secular culture of the East European Jews as the foundation for Jewish national rights.

The term *yiddishkeit* became a secular substitute for traditional religious culture. It is interesting to note that the term was also taken up by the Orthodox to evoke the world of tradition. Thus, for Akiva Schlesinger, the ideologue of Hungarian ultra-Orthodoxy, beyond the traditional realm of the halakhah lay the category of "Jewishness" (*yahadut*—here the Hebrew equivalent of yiddishkeit), which he contrasted with "gentileness" (*goyut*): these were no longer mere religious categories but instead something like essential national or ethnic characteristics. The traditional notion of *am yisrael* (the people of Israel) now began to take on secular, nationalist associations, once again complicating the conventional dichotomy between the secular and the Orthodox.

The return to the folk was inextricably bound up with identification with Jewish suffering. Here, folk memory might serve the needs of those intellectuals whose attitude toward popular Jewish culture now shifted from satire to sentiment. In 1901, two of the new ethnographers, S. M. Ginzburg and P. S. Marek, published a collection of "Yiddish Folksongs in Russia," some of which purported to go back to the conscription of Jewish children into the army of Nicholas I. We recall that Jewish communal leaders were often complicit with the government in kidnapping poor boys into the Cantonist brigades. Now, the protesting voice of the people found its place in print:

> *Little children are ripped from the ḥeder*
> *And dressed in soldiers' garments.*
> *Our leaders, our rabbis*
> *Help to give them up as soldiers.*[67]

The maskilim of the time of Nicholas had also deflected blame for this terror away from the czarist government and onto the communal authorities. Later in the century, though, in the wake of the pogroms, the conscription came to be seen as an early stage in the unremitting czarist hostility toward the Jews.

Yet the military reforms of Alexander II significantly changed the Jewish military experience. A beautifully illustrated minute book of a Jewish prayer fraternity in the Russian army, composed between 1864 and 1867, suggests that some draftees continued to adhere to their religious traditions.[68] Although anti-Jewish opinion argued that the Jews were draft evaders—and many, no doubt, were—conscription into the Russian army from the 1860s on served as another road to acculturation but not necessarily to complete loss of Jewish identity.

In response to the pogroms of the last decades of the nineteenth century and the first decades of the twentieth, a whole literature of lamentation emerged in Hebrew and Yiddish.[69] At times, lamentation was mixed with protest, as in Bialik's famous poem "The City of Slaughter," which took the Jews of Kishinev to task for not defending themselves against the pogromists (an accusation actually contradicted by some of the evidence; in fact, this was a time when Jews began to organize armed self-defense). During World War I, massive pogroms in Galicia prompted Ansky, who undertook a campaign to aid the victims, to chronicle the devastation. His account became the inspiration for other, similar chronicles of pogroms during the Russian Civil War.

Another cultural response to the perceived passive suffering of the Jews and the need for self-defense was the development of a new literary hero, the *ba'al guf*—meaning "he who has a [strong] body"—who represented the exact opposite of the talush, a Jew with vitality and strength and perhaps even a dose of violence. The figure takes his name from Bialik's 1899 Hebrew short story "Aryeh Ba'al-Guf" and was elaborated by a panoply of Hebrew, Yiddish, and Russian writers, from Sholem Asch to Isaac Babel. In Asch's famous Yiddish story "Kola Street," tough Jews defend their community against the pogromists, but their own violence is partially responsible for the pogrom. Asch glorifies the bloody, anti-intellectual nature of his Jewish gangsters, but there is almost a comic-book quality to their violence that throws some doubt on just how the author understands them.

Berdichevsky developed the ba'al guf figure in his works of fiction; as an ethnographer, he searched for real-life models of the underside of Jewish society: violent butchers and muscular hewers of wood instead of emaciated yeshivah students. Berdichevsky's biography reflects many of the different cultural forces we have been following. Born of a Hasidic family in Ukraine, he studied at the Volozhin yeshivah, a sign that, by the last part of the nineteenth century, the old antagonism between Hasidism and Mitnagdism had waned considerably. At Volozhin, Berdichevsky discovered Haskalah, but he went past it to embrace a radical form of Jewish cultural nationalism. He denounced the "religion of the book" in favor of a "new Hebrew man" who would follow a "religion of the sword." Under the influence of Nietzsche, he turned to the folk as the ostensible representative of a vitalistic culture opposed to the ethical intellectualism and passivity of elite rabbinic culture. Here, then, was an example of an intellectual who, like the Russian Narodniki, sought an alliance with "the people" (or, to be more precise, his *image* of the people) against the official establishment: only the folk, in their elemental vitality, could defend against Jewish suffering and construct a new collectivity based on nationalist virtues.

The return to the folk was therefore never direct and uncomplicated but instead always shaped by the modernist and secular ideologies of the intellectuals. All of these themes now came together in Ansky's last work, *The Dybbuk*, first put on the stage in 1920, after its author's death. *The Dybbuk* wedded folklore with Jewish modernism. Ansky based the play on folktales about dybbuks, the restless spirits of the dead that, in Jewish folklore, might inhabit the bodies of the living, but he wove the traditional tale into a "modern" story of romantic love. *The Dybbuk* takes the typical Haskalah form of a conflict between romantic love and the traditional engagement (*shiddukh*), but Ansky goes a step further by creating an alliance between popular Jewish culture, the culture of the folk, and modern values against a repressive rabbinic establishment. Following a standard theme from popular culture, Chanon, the brilliant young kabbalist, is promised to Leah in an oath sworn by their parents before their birth. But following Chanon's sudden death, Leah's parents betroth her to another boy for purely pragmatic considerations. In revenge, Chanon possesses her in the form of a dybbuk and refuses to let her marry the husband her father has chosen for her. Leah becomes both male and female when the dybbuk enters her, and this gender confusion subverts the marriage. Possession by the dybbuk, with its sexual overtones, symbolizes a kind of erotic revolt against the reactionary establishment of rabbis and parents, but, because of the prior pledge between the parents, it is also a revolt that has divine—or traditional—backing.

A 1921 production of Ansky's *Dybbuk* in Vilna. (YIVO Institute
for Jewish Research, Photo Archives, New York; YIVO RG 119 Vilna Troupe 016)

Chanon is a kabbalist, but his Kabbalah is really a camouflaged form of erotic modernism. He says of himself: "I am one of those who searches for new ways."[70] He propounds a doctrine of the "holiness of sin" and asserts that the greatest sin, lust for a woman, can be purified into the greatest holiness. However, the tragic end of the story, in which Leah, too, dies and is now united with Chanon in the "other world," suggests that romantic love cannot yet find a home in this world. Although tragedy of this sort could be found in the Yiddish romances of the late Middle Ages, Ansky's play is a contemporary commentary on the power of the establishment as against the counter-culture of the folk or the revolutionary doctrines of modernity. The original title of the play, "Between Two Worlds," suggests not only the obvious "world of the living" and "world of the dead" but also the dilemma of Jews caught between the vanishing world of popular culture and the world of modern values still struggling to be born.

A romantic tragedy ending with the death of the "star-crossed" lovers, *The Dybbuk* also reverberates with more ominous overtones. Ansky wrote the play during World War I, which had witnessed some of the worst pogroms against the Jewish communities of Eastern Europe since 1648–49. Although *The Dybbuk* does not allude directly to these events, the deaths of Chanon and Leah are prefigured by the slaughter of a bride and groom in 1648 by Chmelnitski Cossacks as the couple was being led to the wedding canopy. According to the folk custom of the town, at every wedding thereafter the guests danced around the grave of these martyrs and invited them to take part in the festivities. This implicit identification with the martyrs of a past pogrom hints that the untimely end of Chanon and Leah is more than a romantic tragedy: it also points to the pogroms of the era in which *The Dybbuk* was written, the horrors of which would ultimately be overshadowed by the Holocaust.

BETWEEN THE WARS

The Bolshevik Revolution aborted an attempt to premiere *The Dybbuk* in Moscow; although the reasons were not immediately political, Ansky's turn to the magical elements of Jewish folk culture was clearly not in line with a politically correct view of the people's consciousness. Ansky himself fled to Vilna, which was to become part of the newly independent Polish Republic. Between the two world wars, the Russian Revolution and the rise of an independent Poland were the two political events of the greatest importance for East European Jewish culture, which, like a supernova star, burned perhaps most brightly just before it was snuffed out. In both Russia and Poland, but for different reasons, a vibrant Jewish culture flourished for a limited time and all of the rich tensions and conflicts that we have followed in this chapter found their final expressions.

In the new Soviet Union, the policy articulated by the regime shortly after the Revolution called for a culture that was "national in form and socialist in content." The Jewish Sections of the Communist Party (known by the abbreviation Yevsektsia) took on the task of revolutionizing Jewish culture in line with party ideology.[71] The parameters of this new culture were dictated by what the party considered bourgeois versus what it considered progressive. Because Hebrew had become the language of the Zionist movement, which was judged a bourgeois-nationalist deviation, the Bolsheviks rejected it as a legitimate Jewish national language. Schools conducted in Hebrew were shut down, and Hebrew writers banned and harassed. Nevertheless, for nearly a decade after the Revolution, Hebrew culture struggled to survive in the Soviet Union. The Habimah theater was perhaps its greatest vehicle. Its production of *The Dybbuk,* in Bialik's Hebrew translation and heavily influenced by Expressionism, became a sensation, attracting the attention of prominent non-Jews. But despite the support of such luminaries as Konstantin Stanislavsky, the director of the Moscow Art Theater, and the writer Maxim Gorky, Habimah was forced to shut down and its company had to go into exile in 1926.[72] In a sense, the Yevsektsia's war on Hebrew culminated in an extreme way the language wars of the Haskalah period, but now with those favoring Yiddish armed with state power.[73] Indeed, it is ironic that Yiddish should have won the war in light of its original reputation among modernizers as a medieval "jargon." But the fact that a secular Yiddish culture had developed by the turn of the century made it possible to conceive of a Communist war against the shtetl and its religious culture carried on in the primary language of that culture.

Let us return again to Vitebsk to observe briefly how that war was waged. Immediately after the Bolshevik Revolution, Chagall came back to his hometown as the commissar of fine arts and as director of a Free Academy of Art, a successor to Pen's academy where he had gotten his start. From 1918 to 1920, when he went to Moscow to work with the new Yiddish State Theater, Chagall led a populist Jewish cultural renaissance in Vitebsk. But Vitebsk also became an important Yevsektsia center, and it was there that the Jewish Communists published their Yiddish organ *Der Royter Shtern* (The Red Star), the purpose of which was to agitate for Bolshevik policies on the "Jewish street." The Yevsektsia launched attacks against institutions of traditional Jewish life in Vitebsk, confiscating synagogues and banning study houses. In 1921, they staged a public trial of the heder, which, as we have seen, had also been one of the Haskalah's main targets. Throughout the 1920s, this campaign continued; it culminated in 1930 with the closing down of the Lubavitch yeshivah. Here was the realization of the Haskalah's most extreme agenda, but never in the nineteenth century had the maskilim mustered the power to carry out such a far-reaching revolution. Whether the maskilim or their successors would have used such extreme and brutal tactics against their traditional opponents if they had been able to do so is hard to know. But now their critique had been taken over by an ideology even more hostile to the culture of Jewish tradition. Because many of the leading Bolsheviks were themselves assimilated Jews, the new policies reflected the confluence of all of the cultural trends we have followed in this chapter.

The official endorsement of Yiddish as the national language of Jewish culture created a brief but intense renaissance in theater and literature, but now the multilingualism that characterized the nineteenth century came to an end. The Yiddish State Theater, where Chagall designed the sets, performed plays based on the works of Mendele, Peretz, and Sholem Aleichem, but these were staged to emphasize the most anticlerical and proletarian aspects of the writers. Yiddish prose and poetry also flourished. If earlier generations of writers had been influenced by the Russian literary tradition of rural sketches, often based on satirical or neo-Romantic realism, the new generation imbibed European modernism: Introspectivism, Expressionism, and Symbolism. A group that formed in Kiev before World War I that included David Bergelson, Pinchas Kahanovich (Der Nister), David Hofstein, and Peretz Markish continued into the Soviet period. Younger writers, such as Itzik Feffer, composed works of "socialist realism" in Yiddish. By the end of the 1920s, these authors were subjected to increasing political criticism and forced to write in conformity with party dictates. Yet this was clearly a period of extraordinary literary activity. Daily newspapers and journals appeared in Yiddish in many cities, including Kiev, Odessa, and Minsk. In 1928, 238 Yiddish books were published, with a total circulation of 875,000. The 1930s witnessed a significant decline as Stalin consolidated power, but there was again a Yiddish cultural renaissance during World War II and immediately after, as part of the wartime ideology of antifascism. Between 1948 and 1953, however, Jewish culture in the Soviet Union suffered its death blow with the shutting down of Yiddish theaters, newspapers, and publishing houses and with the execution of 24 of the most important Jewish writers on August 12, 1952.[74]

Events in Russia narrowed the Jewish cultural system to Yiddish, but a more multilingual process took place in Poland, where Jewish life flourished perhaps with the greatest intensity in the interwar period.[75] Let us consider one particular community, the city of Wloclawek, which lies some 185 kilometers northwest of Warsaw, along the Vistula River. At the beginning of the twentieth century, it had a Jewish population of 4,000, which rose to some 10,000 by the 1930s (out of a total population of 56,000). At a time when Jewish culture in Vitebsk was undergoing coerced constriction, Wloclawek enjoyed a veritable renaissance.[76] The community was run by a kahal board, chosen in hotly contested elections by all male Jews in the town. A wide range of political parties represented all the cultural options that I have traced here, including the Hasidim of Strykow and the Agudah representing the strictly Orthodox, the religious Zionists (Mizrahi), socialist Zionists (Poale Zion), Revisionist Zionists, and the Bund (non-Zionist socialists). Most of these political parties were associated with a school system: Tarbut and Yavneh (Hebrew), TSYSHO (Central Yiddish School Organization), Horev and Beis Yaakov (Orthodox schools for boys and girls, respectively), as well as Polish public schools. Several gymnasia (including one for girls) were opened at the end of World War I, and many of the young people of the town joined the range of youth movements—Betar, Hashomer ha-Tzair, He-Halutz—paralleling the political parties. A Jewish press, a theater, and sports organizations flourished. Although the foundations for this rich and varied culture were laid before World War I, it was in the two short decades of Polish independence that it achieved its full vitality.

Two contradictory linguistic trends determined the course of Jewish culture. On the one hand, although Yiddish remained the mother tongue of the majority, increasing numbers of Polish Jews received their education in Polish (most of the Jewish schools mentioned above were required to teach some subjects in Polish), and this became their primary language of communication with friends and even parents. This tendency toward Polonization, which existed to some degree before World War I, gained enormous impetus with the emergence of an independent Poland. (The same adoption of the indigenous language can be seen in the new Czechoslovak Republic, where Jews who had previously identified primarily with German now embraced Czech.) On the other hand, increasing Polish nationalism was accompanied by significant new antisemitism that sought to exclude the Jews (who constituted 10 percent of the population) from many corners of Polish life. Faced with mounting barriers, the Jews developed their own complex culture, which took place simultaneously in Hebrew, Yiddish, and Polish.[77] Although the Tarbut network of schools—dedicated to teaching Hebrew—existed throughout Poland, Hebrew culture had perhaps the greatest difficulty. Neither a Hebrew press nor Hebrew theater succeeded in putting down roots, and most Hebrew writers and poets left for Palestine. Hebrew culture in Poland was primarily imported; a significant market existed for Hebrew newspapers and books produced in Palestine as well as Berlin (at least during the 1920s). Yiddish culture had an easier time, with significant literary centers emerging in the interwar period in Warsaw and Vilna. The Yung Vilna

circle of the 1930s made a particular mark with the poetry of Abraham Sutz-
kever, Leyzer Wolf, and Chaim Grade. Yiddish newspapers flourished, reflecting
all of the different political and religious movements; 11 were published in Warsaw alone. The theater staged Yiddish classics plus translations into Yiddish of
great dramas from world literature.

It was the growth of Jewish culture in Polish, however, that signified the singular nature of Jewish Poland between the wars. In Warsaw, Cracow, and Lvov,
daily papers appeared in Polish that were published by Jews and intended for
Jewish audiences.[78] It appears that Jews preferred to get their general news—and
not only news of the Jewish world—from a Jewish source, even if their preferred
language was Polish. Similarly, a Polish Jewish theater emerged in 1925 under the
directorship of Mark Arnshteyn (1879–1943), producing, among other works, a
Polish translation of Ansky's *Dybbuk* steeped more in Polish romanticism than
in Jewish folklore.[79] It was in developments such as these that a Jewish subculture
in Polish took shape in the years before the Holocaust.

The Great Destruction swept away this remarkable culture, just as Stalinism
did in the Soviet Union. To be sure, East European Jewish culture did not end
with its demise in Europe. It had already sent strong offshoots to both North and
South America as well as to what was to become the State of Israel. The flourishing of Yiddish or Hebrew culture in those places continued the legacy of Eastern
Europe in new forms that lie beyond the scope of this chapter. Today, our
memory of that culture is caught between the horror in which it died and nostalgia for a harmonious past that never existed. Immediately after the Holocaust,
Abraham Joshua Heschel, the scion of a great Polish Hasidic dynasty, eulogized
East European Jewish culture in a Yiddish address later translated and published
as "The Earth Is the Lord's." There is much in Heschel's beautiful evocation of
the spiritual grandeur of this culture that still rings true, but, in one sense, he
failed to capture the full measure of the Jews whose cultural variety we have followed here. For, like Ansky's journey "between two worlds," the culture of the
East European Jews was neither static nor seamless. Instead, the secret to its vitality lay precisely in its fissures, conflicts, and struggles in search of new identities in a fragmenting world.

NOTES

1. Quoted in David Roskies, "S. Ansky and the Paradigm of Return," in Jack Wertheimer,
ed., *The Uses of Tradition: Jewish Continuity in the Modern Era* (New York, 1992), 247.
Roskies translates to English from a Yiddish translation of a Russian manuscript from

Ansky's literary remains left in St. Petersburg. The Russian was published in *Evreiskiya Starina* 2 (1924). The Yiddish appeared in Moyshe Shalit, "Maye protim vegen Sh. Anski," *Literarishe Bleter* 340 (1930): 839. I have slightly altered Roskies' English translation based on the Yiddish. For my overall analysis and use of Ansky, I am very much indebted to Roskies, especially his introduction to S. Ansky, *The Dybbuk and Other Writings* (New York, 1992), and his "The Maskil as Folk Hero," *Prooftexts* 10, no. 2 (1990) : 219–35.

2. These figures are anything but exact and are based on unreliable census data, some of which is a projection forward of the 1765 Polish census. See John Klier, *Russia Gathers Her Jews: The Origins of the "Jewish Question" in Russia, 1772–1825* (Dekalb, Ill., 1986), 19.

3. See Michael Stanislawski, *Tsar Nicholas I and the Jews: The Transformation of Jewish Society in Russia, 1825–1855* (Philadelphia, 1983).

4. On this period, see John Klier, *Imperial Russia's Jewish Question, 1855–1881* (New York, 1995).

5. See Benjamin Nathans, *Beyond the Pale: The Jewish Encounter with Late Imperial Russia* (Berkeley, 2002).

6. See Baruch Karu, ed., *Sefer Vitebsk* (Tel Aviv, 1957)—a translation into Hebrew of the article on Vitebsk from the Russian *Jewish Encyclopedia.*

7. See ibid., 4; Jacob Lestchinsky, "Vitebsk and the District in the Nineteenth Century" (Hebrew), 5–21; and Aronson, Gregor, ed., *Vitebsk amol; geshikhte, zikhroynes, hurbn* (New York, 1956).

8. On the Gaon, see Immanuel Etkes, *Yaḥid be-Doro: Ha-Gaon me-Vilna—Demut ve-Dimui* (Jerusalem, 1995). On the culture of the Mitnagdim, see Alan Nadler, *The Faith of the Mitnagdim: Rabbinic Responses to Hasidic Rapture* (Baltimore, Md., 1997). On the Lithuanian yeshivot, see Shaul Stampfer, *Ha-Yeshiva ha-Lita'it be-Hithavutah* (Jerusalem, 1995).

9. *Be'ur ha-GRA le-Mishlei* (Psalms), 4:4, in Immanuel Etkes, *Rabbi Israel Salanter and the Musar Movement,* trans. Jonathan Chipman (Philadelphia, 1993), 24.

10. Introduction to *Bi'ur ha-GRA*, Oraḥ Ḥayyim.

11. See Norman Solomon, *The Analytic Movement: Hayyim Soloveitchik and His Circle* (Atlanta, Ga., 1993).

12. Joseph B. Soloveitchik, *Halakhic Man,* trans. Lawrence Kaplan (Philadelphia, 1983).

13. Hayyim of Volozhin, *Ruaḥ Ḥayyim al Avot,* chap. 1, mishna 4, p. 7. See also H. H. Ben Sasson, "The Personality of Elijah, Gaon of Vilna, and His Historical Influence" (Hebrew), *Zion* 31 (1966) : 199.

14. Barukh Schick, *Uklides* (The Hague, 1780), intro., translated in David E. Fishman, *Russia's First Modern Jews: The Jews of Shklov* (New York, 1995), 22. Fishman's book is the best treatment of the relationships between the Gaon, his disciples, and early Russian Haskalah.

15. Judah Leb Margoliot, *Bet Midot* (Shklov, 1786), 20b; translated in Fishman, *Russia's First Modern Jews,* 115.

16. See Etkes, *Rabbi Israel Salanter.*

17. Translated in Paul Mendes-Flohr and Jehuda Reinharz, *The Jew in the Modern World*, 2d ed. (New York, 1995), 156.

18. *Mekhilta*, ed. H. S. Horowitz (Jerusalem, 1960) 14, Bo, par. 5; *Midrash Rabba Leviticus, Emor* 32:5; *Pesikta de-Rav Kahanah*, ed. Solomon Buber (Lyck, 1868), Vayehi be-shalaḥ 83b and *Pesikta Zutarti* Shmot 6.6 (for not changing clothing), Numbers Rabba 13.19, 20.22, Midrash Rabba on Song of Songs 4.25.

19. Moses Sofer, *Derashot*, ed. Yosef Naftali Stern (Cluj, 1929), 2:243a–b, translated in Jacob Katz, "Towards a Biography of the Hatam Sofer," in Frances Malino and David Sorkin, eds., *From East and West: Jews in a Changing Europe, 1750–1870* (Oxford, 1990), 253.

20. Akiva Joseph Schlesinger, *Lev ha-Ivri*, vol. 2 (Lemberg, 1868), f. 846, n. 23, translated in Michael Silber, "The Emergence of Ultra-Orthodoxy: The Invention of a Tradition," in Wertheimer, ed., *The Uses of Tradition*, 49.

21. For a summary of recent scholarly views of Hasidism, see Ada Rapoport-Albert, ed., *Hasidism Reappraised* (London, 1996).

22. *Shivḥei ha-Besht*, 123; trans. in Dan Ben-Amos and Jerome Mintz, eds. and trans., *In Praise of the Baal Shem Tov* (Bloomington, Ind., 1979), 179.

23. *Shivhei ha-Besht*, 133, trans. in Ben-Amos and Mintz, eds., *In Praise*, 199.

24. *Sefer Sippurei Kedoshim*, ed. G. Nigal (Jerusalem, 1977), 34. See also Elie Yassif, *Sippur ha-Am ha-Ivri* (Jerusalem, 1994), 429–30.

25. See Elonora Bergman, "Gora Kalwaria: The Impact of a Hasidic Cult on the Urban Landscape of a Small Polish Town," *Polin* 5 (1990) : 3–23.

26. Israel of Ruzhin, *Irin Kadishin* (Bnei Brak, 1983), 106. See also David Assaf, *Derekh ha-Malkhut: R. Yisrael me-Ruzhin u-Mekomo be-Toldot ha-Ḥasidut* (Jerusalem, 1997), 146–47.

27. *Keneset Yisrael* (Warsaw, 1906), 8a.

28. See Richard I. Cohen, *Jewish Icons: Art and Society in Modern Europe* (Berkeley, 1998), 114–53.

29. See Maria and Kazimierz Piechotka, "Polish Synagogues in the Nineteenth Century," in Antony Polonsky, ed., *From Shtetl to Socialism: Studies from Polin* (London, 1993), 212–31.

30. On the special character of the new city of Odessa and its role in nineteenth-century Russian Jewish culture, see Steven J. Zipperstein, *The Jews of Odessa: A Cultural History, 1794–1881* (Stanford, 1985).

31. On the culture of Jewish politics in the late nineteenth century, see Jonathan Frankel, *Prophecy and Politics: Socialism, Nationalism, and the Russian Jews, 1862–1917* (Cambridge, Eng., 1981), and Ezra Mendelsohn, *Class Struggle in the Pale: The Formative Years of the Jewish Workers' Movement in Tsarist Russia* (Cambridge, Eng., 1970).

32. Isaac Ber Levinsohn, *Te'udah be-Yisrael* (Vilna, 1828; rpt., Jerusalem, 1977). On Levinsohn and the early Russian Haskalah, see Immanuel Etkes's introduction to the 1977 edition of *Te'udah be-Yisrael*. For the relationship between the early Haskalah and the regime of Nicholas I, see Stanislawski, *Tsar Nicholas I and the Jews*.

33. Levinsohn, *Te'udah*, 34.

34. Roman Ziman, "Gatunek: Podroz," *Kultura* 11 (1983): 24, quoted and translated in Chone Shmeruk, "Hebrew-Yiddish-Polish: A Trilingual Culture," in Yisrael Gutman, Ezra Mendelsohn, Jehuda Reinharz, and Chone Shmeruk, eds., *The Jews of Poland Between Two World Wars* (Hanover, N.H., 1989), 289.

35. See Dan Miron, *Ben Ḥazon le-Emet* (Jerusalem, 1979), 177–216.

36. Letter from Samuel Joseph Fuenn to Bezalel Stern (1840) in *Pardes* (Odessa, 1897), 3: 149–56, trans. in Mendes-Flohr and Reinharz, *The Jew in the Modern World*, 382–83.

37. A paraphrase of the line in Gordon's poem "Awake My People" ("Hakitza ami"), published in 1866. On Gordon, see Michael Stanislawski, *For Whom Do I Toil? Judah Leib Gordon and the Crisis of Russian Jewry* (New York, 1988).

38. See David Biale, *Eros and the Jews* (Berkeley, 1997), chap. 7.

39. On Haskalah autobiographies, see Alan Mintz, *"Banished from Their Father's Table": Loss of Faith and Hebrew Autobiography* (Bloomington, Ind., 1989).

40. My student, Abraham Socher, has completed a doctoral dissertation on Maimon's autobiography and its relationship to his philosophical work (Berkeley, 2001).

41. On the ḥeder and its image, see Steven J. Zipperstein, *Imagining Russian Jewry* (Seattle, 1999), chap. 2.

42. Moses Leib Lilienblum, *Ketavim Autobiografim* (Jerusalem, 1970), 1 : 108.

43. See Shmuel Feiner, "The Modern Jewish Woman: A Test Case of the Relations Between the Haskalah and Modernity" (Hebrew), in Israel Bartal and Isaiah Gafni, eds., *Eros, Erusin ve-Issurim* (Jerusalem, 1998), 253–304.

44. See Shaul Stampfer, "Gender Differentiation and Education of the Jewish Woman in Nineteenth-Century Eastern Europe," in Polonsky, ed., *From Shtetl to Socialism*, 187–211.

45. M. Kamionski, "Jewish Nihilists in the Seventies" (Hebrew), *Ha-Shiloaḥ* 17 (1907): 257–63.

46. Anonymous, *Ayn Sheyne Historye fun aynem Ekhtikn Rovs Tokhter fun Konstantinopl un fun ayn Rov Zayn zun fun Brisk* (n.p., n.d.).

47. See Meir Noy, "The Theme of the Canceled Wedding in Yiddish Folksongs: A Bibliographical Survey" (Hebrew), in Issachar Ben-Ami and Davnoy, eds., *Studies in Marriage Customs* (Jerusalem, 1974), 61–65.

48. Abraham Landau Bornstein, *Avnei Nezer* (Pieterkov, 1916), *Even HaEzer,* pt. 1, no. 119.

49. On this theme, see Biale, *Eros and the Jews,* chap. 3.

50. M. J. Berdichevsky, "In Their Mothers' Womb" (Hebrew), in his *Kitve M. J. Bin-Gorion* (Tel Aviv, 1965), 1: 102. The borders of the city represent the farthest reaches Jewish law allowed one to walk on the Sabbath: these Jews were walking past the very boundaries of the halakhah.

51. See ChaeRan Freeze, *Between Marriage and Divorce: The Transformation of the Jewish Family in Imperial Russia, 1825–1914* (Hanover, N.H., 2001).

52. Translated under the title "Go Talk to a Goy" in S. Ansky, *The Dybbuk and Other Writings,* ed. David Roskies (New York, 1992), 145–50.

53. Pauline Wengeroff, *Memoiren einer Grossmutter,* 2d ed. (Berlin, 1919), 2: 138–39.

54. See the introduction by Ruth Wisse to Sholem Aleichem, *The Best of Sholem Aleichem* (New York, 1979).

55. On Mendele, see Dan Miron, *A Traveler Disguised: A Study in the Rise of Modern Yiddish Fiction in the Nineteenth Century* (New York, 1973).

56. "Shem and Japhet on the Train" (Hebrew), in *Kol Kitve Mendele Mokher Sefarim* (Tel Aviv, 1947), 399. The story is translated in Robert Alter, ed., *Modern Hebrew Literature* (New York, 1975), 15–40.

57. See Zivia Amishai-Maisels, "The Jewish Jesus," *Journal of Jewish Art* 9 (1983): 84–104, and David Roskies, *Against the Apocalypse* (Cambridge, Mass., 1983), 258–312. My student, Matthew Hoffman, has completed a dissertation on this theme: "Reclaiming Jesus and the Construction of Modern Jewish Culture" (Berkeley, 2000).

58. Cohen, *Jewish Icons,* 217, 223–27.

59. Zivia Amishai-Maisels, "Chagall's *Dedicated to Christ:* Sources and Meanings," *Journal of Jewish Art* 21 (1995): 69–94.

60. S. Ansky, *Dos yidishe etnografishe program,* ed. L. I. Shternberg, vol. 1 (Petrograd, 1914), 10, quoted in Roskies' introduction to Ansky, *The Dybbuk and Other Writings,* xxiv.

61. For a discussion of how Russian Jewish intellectuals pioneered the nostalgic image of the shtetl that would later surface in such works as *Life Is With People* and *Fiddler on the Roof,* see Zipperstein, *Imagining Russian Jewry,* chap. 2.

62. Abraham Ber Gottlober, *Zikhronot u-Masa'ot* (Jerusalem, 1976), 85.

63. See Israel Bartal, "True Knowledge and Wisdom: On Orthodox Historiography," in J. Frankel, ed., *Studies in Contemporary Jewry* 10 (1994): 178–92, and Ada Rapoport-Albert, "Hagiography with Footnotes: Edifying Tales and the Writing of History in Hasidism," *History and Theory* 27 (1988) : 119–59.

64. A. M. Dik, introduction to *Maḥaze mul Maḥaze* (Warsaw, 1861).

65. Quoted in Naomi Seidman, *A Marriage Made in Heaven: The Sexual Politics of Hebrew and Yiddish* (Berkeley, 1997), 20.

66. Zederbaum's introduction to the 1869 Odessa edition of *Dos Poylishe Yingl,* quoted in Dan Miron, *A Traveler Disguised: A Study in the Rise of Modern Yiddish Fiction in the Nineteenth Century* (New York, 1973), 5.

67. S. M. Ginzburg and P. S. Marek, eds., *Evreiskie narodniye pesni v Rossii* (St. Petersburg, 1901), no. 50. See the rhymed translation in Roskies, *Against the Apocalypse,* 59.

68. Michael Stanislawski, *Psalms for the Tsar: A Minute-Book of a Psalms-Society in the Russian Army, 1864–1867* (New York, 1988).

69. See Roskies, *Against the Apocalypse,* for a comprehensive and nuanced account of this aspect of the culture.

70. S. Ansky, *Der Dybbuk,* in *Di Yidishe Drame fun 20sten Yorhundert* (New York, 1977), 44.

71. On the Yevsektsia, see Mordechai Altshuler, *Ha-Yevsektsyah bi-Verit-ha-Mo'atzot (1918–1930): Ben Le'umiyut le-Komunizm* (Jerusalem, 1980).

72. On Jewish theater in the Soviet Union, see Mordechai Altshuler, ed., *Ha-Te'atron ha-Yehudi bi-Verit ha-Mo'atzot: Mehkarim, Iyunim, Te'udot* (Jerusalem, 1996).

73. See Jehoshua A. Gilboa, *A Language Silenced: The Suppression of Hebrew Literature and Culture in the Soviet Union* (Rutherford, N.J., 1982).

74. On Jewish culture in the Soviet period, see Zvi Y. Gitelman, *A Century of Ambivalence: The Jews of Russia and the Soviet Union, 1881 to the Present* (New York, 1988); Nora Levin, *The Jews in the Soviet Union Since 1917* (New York, 1988); and David Shneer, "Reinventing *Yiddishkayt:* Yiddish and the Creation of Soviet Jewish Culture, 1917–1930" (Ph.D. diss., University of California, Berkeley, 2001).

75. See Gutman et al., eds., *The Jews of Poland Between Two World Wars;* Antony Polonsky, Ezra Mendelsohn, and Jerzy Tomaszewski, eds., *Jews in Independent Poland, 1918–1939* (London, 1994); and Celia Heller, *On the Edge of Destruction: Jews of Poland Between the Two World Wars* (New York, 1977). More generally, see Ezra Mendelsohn, *The Jews of East Central Europe Between the World Wars* (Bloomington, Ind., 1983).

76. For information on this community, see Katri'el P. Tkorsh and Me'ir Koz'an, eds., *Vlotslavek ve-ha-Sevivah: Sefer Zikaron* (Tel Aviv, 1967).

77. See Chone Shmeruk, "Hebrew-Yiddish-Polish," in Gutman et al., eds., *The Jews of Poland Between Two World Wars,* 285–311.

78. See Michael Steinlauf, "The Polish Jewish Daily Press," in Polonsky, ed., *From Shtetl to Socialism,* 332–58.

79. See Michael Steinlauf, "Mark Arnshteyn and Polish-Jewish Theater," in Gutman et al., eds., *The Jews of Poland Between Two World Wars,* 399–411.

SELECTED BIBLIOGRAPHY

Dawidowicz, Lucy, ed. *The Golden Tradition: Jewish Life and Thought in Eastern Europe.* Northvale, N.J., 1989.

Etkes, Immanuel. *Rabbi Israel Salanter and the Musar Movement,* trans. Jonathan Chipman. Philadelphia, 1993.

Fishman, David E. *Russia's First Modern Jews: The Jews of Shklov.* New York, 1995.

Frankel, Jonathan. *Prophecy and Politics: Socialism, Nationalism, and the Russian Jews, 1862–1917.* Cambridge, Eng., 1981.

Freeze, ChaeRan. *Between Marriage and Divorce: The Transformation of the Jewish Family in Imperial Russia, 1825–1914.* Hanover, N.H., 2001.

Gitelman, Zvi Y. *A Century of Ambivalence: The Jews of Russia and the Soviet Union, 1881 to the Present.* New York, 1988.

Gutman, Yisrael, Ezra Mendelsohn, Jehuda Reinharz, and Chone Shmeruk, eds., *The Jews of Poland Between Two World Wars.* Hanover, N.H., 1989.

Kieval, Hillel J. *Languages of Community: The Jewish Experience in the Czech Lands.* Berkeley, 2000.

Mendelsohn, Ezra. *The Jews of East Central Europe Between the World Wars.* Bloomington, Ind., 1983.

Mintz, Alan. *"Banished from Their Father's Table": Loss of Faith and Hebrew Autobiography.* Bloomington, Ind., 1989.

Miron, Dan. *A Traveler Disguised: A Study in the Rise of Modern Yiddish Fiction in the Nineteenth Century.* New York, 1973.

Nadler, Alan. *The Faith of the Mitnagdim: Rabbinic Responses to Hasidic Rapture.* Baltimore, 1997.

Nathans, Benjamin. *Beyond the Pale: The Jewish Encounter with Late Imperial Russia.* Berkeley, 2002.

Polonsky, Antony, ed. *From Shtetl to Socialism: Studies from Polin.* London, 1993.

Roskies, David. *Against the Apocalypse.* Cambridge, Mass., 1983.

Seidman, Naomi. *A Marriage Made in Heaven: The Sexual Politics of Hebrew and Yiddish.* Berkeley, 1997.

Solomon, Norman. *The Analytic Movement: Hayyim Soloveitchik and His Circle.* Atlanta, Ga., 1993.

Stanislawski, Michael. *For Whom Do I Toil? Judah Leib Gordon and the Crisis of Russian Jewry.* New York, 1988.

———. *Tsar Nicholas I and the Jews: The Transformation of Jewish Society in Russia, 1825–1855.* Philadelphia, 1983.

Wertheimer, Jack, ed. *The Uses of Tradition: Jewish Continuity in the Modern Era.* New York, 1992.

Zipperstein, Steven J. *Imagining Russian Jewry.* Seattle, 1999.

———. *The Jews of Odessa: A Cultural History, 1794–1881.* Stanford, 1985.

ספר
מעם לועז
חלק שלישי ספר ויקרא

Isaac Magriso, Title page of *Sefer Me-am Loez* (Leviticus),
Constantinople, 1753.
Published by Nisim Ashkenazi.

THREE

THE OTTOMAN DIASPORA:

The Rise and Fall of Ladino Literary Culture

ARON RODRIGUE

Judeo-Spanish is the preeminent language of the people, and it will remain so for quite some time whatever we might do. Everyone agrees that we should do away with Judeo-Spanish, that there is no reason to preserve the language of our former persecutors . . . and nevertheless, the lower classes, the bourgeoisie, and even the "aristocracy," as they are called here, everyone still speaks and reads Judeo-Spanish and will continue to do so. In committee meetings where all the members are well educated and everyone knows French, a discussion started in correct, even elegant French will, often in an instant, inexplicably move into Judeo-Spanish jabbering. The most "select," dignified Jewish ladies when paying a call on a friend will be politely chitchatting in French and suddenly break into jargon. Turkish is like a borrowed suit; French is gala dress; Judeo-Spanish is the worn dressing gown in which one is most at ease.[1]

This excerpt, from a report on the Sephardim[2] of Constantinople written in 1908 by Moïse Fresco, the director of one of the Alliance Israélite Universelle schools in the city and himself an Ottoman Jew, highlights some of the major themes of the cultural transformation of Sephardic Jewry in modern times. Written at a decisive moment in the history of these communities, the year of the Young Turk Revolution, it captures the new complexities of their cultural profile after decades of change brought about by growing Western economic and political presence in the Middle East, reforms initiated by Ottoman rulers, and attempts at educational and cultural reform undertaken by French Jewry intent on "civilizing" "Eastern" Jewries. Multilingual, and performing different linguistic strategies in different settings, hesitating between the glittering prizes offered by Paris and loyalties to the local Ottoman rulers, and soon to face new Zionist and new Turkish nationalist demands pulling in yet different directions, the Sephardic world was unprepared for the triumphant nationalisms that would gain the upper hand in the Levant after the fateful events of 1908.

As Fresco's text makes amply clear, Judeo-Spanish, or Ladino, had remained one of the most distinctive features of the Sephardic diaspora in the Levant that had come into being after the expulsions and mass departures of the Jews from the Iberian Peninsula at the end of the fifteenth century. Ladino was to remain the hallmark of this diaspora until its mid-twentieth-century destruction and dissolution. Ladino marked deeply all aspects of the cultural life of Levantine Jewry. Its core culture area was situated in the Balkans and Asia Minor, with small offshoot communities in the Eastern Mediterranean such as those of Egypt, Palestine, and Syria.

The reconstituted Sepharad that spoke Ladino in the Levant was an integral part of the mosaic of religious and ethnic groups that lived under Ottoman rule for centuries, sometimes in harmony, sometimes in conflict, but generally in a coexistence that operated according to parameters which were to obtain until new developments in the nineteenth century. In this respect, Ladino culture is inseparable from the Ottoman context of Levantine Jewish life.

Jews lived as a recognized and officially tolerated group under the classical Ottoman political system. The Islamic tradition of toleration of "the people of the book" underpinned the broad contours of Muslim/non-Muslim relations in the empire, with a quasi-contractual "pact" (*dhimmā*, or *zimmet* in Turkish) that protected non-Muslims in return for their payment of special taxation and acceptance of inferior status. Nevertheless, this Islamic legal regulation was, as in all religious traditions, subject to constant interpretation and was implemented with various degrees of elasticity in different periods and under different rulers. Yet its discursive framework provided a political language and vocabulary to fundamental divides and boundaries in Ottoman society, the most notable of which was the exclusion of non-Muslims from formal political rule, though the rich and influential among them could frequently exercise enormous power informally.

The clear political boundary between Muslim and non-Muslim that could be transcended only by conversion should not obscure the fact that, in many areas of social existence, such boundaries were porous. Through economic and social interaction, especially in the major cities such as Salonica, Constantinople, Izmir, and Adrianople (Edirne), as well as in numerous smaller towns, the Jews came to share much with their neighbors in realms such as dress, food, and music. It is interesting to note that a great part of Sephardic cuisine (adapted to Jewish laws of *kashrut*) is built on the template of Turco-Balkan food culture. Perhaps most strikingly, Sephardic synagogue music is essentially the same as Ottoman high court music, with Sephardic musicians participating in and contributing to the repertoire of high Ottoman classical music. The numerous words of Turkish and Greek origin in Ladino confirm the receptivity of this culture to outside influences.

Nevertheless, the engagement with external cultural modes did not have the same corrosive effect on group identity that was to accompany it in the modern Western or Westernized nation-state with its nation-building policies of cultural homogenization. Like other empires, the pre-modern Ottoman state was singularly uninterested in such a project. Indeed, the reverse was true, with "difference" rather than "sameness" as the normative and even prescriptive configuration of sociopolitical organization. Each major ethnic and religious group was recognized, whether formally or informally, as a distinctive group, with no expectation of the eventual dissolution of its cultural specificity. The acceptance of difference did not entail equality, because the ruler/ruled divide that usually corresponded to the Muslim/non-Muslim divide brought with it hierarchy and power stratification. This acceptance also provided to large areas of social existence a degree of autonomy that is unimaginable in the modern Western polity.[3]

In the Levantine city, where most Sephardic Jews lived, with its multilingual, multiethnic, multireligious social fabric, different groups engaged in a daily give-and-take in the cultural as well as the economic realm. In the city, the Jewish man, like others, was able to communicate in a pastiche of languages such as Turkish, Greek, Armenian, and Bulgarian. The Jewish woman, operating in the sphere of the home, was exposed less to outside influences, which nevertheless did frequently manage to make an incursion. Linguistic hybridity was limited to the market place—the bazaar—and stopped at the gates of the household and of the community. Outside influences did exist, but these were domesticated, coopted, adapted, and naturalized by the different communities, losing any corrosiveness for group identity as a whole. Ethnic boundaries were fluid, and they shifted constantly. Nevertheless, the primacy of group distinctiveness and identity remained. The Levantine Sephardim, using strategies common to Jewish diasporas everywhere, Judaized the influence from the outside. And it was Ladino that operated as a powerful tool for the domestication of the "other." Hence, until the modern period, a distinctive culture, transplanted from medieval Sepharad, but now in full mutation, could evolve and flourish in the mosaic that was the Ottoman Levant.

LADINO

There is no consensus among scholars about the existence of major differences between the language spoken by the Jews in Spain and that of the surrounding population. It would be safe to assume that Jews were conversant with the many regional dialects that proliferated there before Castilian imposed its supremacy in the sixteenth century. There were, nevertheless, some words that were particular to Jews, such as *Dio* for *Dios,* reflecting the concern not to attribute a plural nature to God, and *Alhad* for Sunday, originating from the Arabic instead of the Spanish *Domingo* with its Christian connotations. Hebraic religious vocabulary, of course, left its imprint in those areas of the language that touched upon ritual and learning.

The Jews took Spanish and Portuguese with them as they left the Iberian Peninsula. In Western Europe, communities of Marrano origin kept these languages until well into the eighteenth century, replenishing them with constant contact with the peninsula. Nevertheless, Ladino never existed among these communities, and the Spanish and Portuguese in use in these Western Sephardic centers never evolved into a distinctive Jewish language and was never written with Hebrew script. Proficiency in these languages was eventually to die out except for sporadic usage during religious ritual, to be replaced by the languages spoken by the surrounding populations. In areas such as North Africa, where the arriving Sephardim were not numerically superior to indigenous Jewish communities, Spanish also disappeared. Judeo-Arabic was adopted by the descendants of the Iberian exiles, with the exception of a few small communities in northern Morocco, such as Tangier and Tetuán, where a distinctive form of Judeo-Spanish known as Haketia was to survive until the twentieth century. It was in the Ottoman Levant, most notably in the Balkans and in Asia Minor where the exiles swamped demographically the local Greek-speaking Romaniot Jews, that Spanish embarked upon the path that transformed it into a Jewish language proper, Ladino. As the influx diminished, and as the links between Levantine Jewry and the West grew weaker, this language evolved on its own, maintaining many words that had become archaic in Spain and borrowing extensively from Hebrew and surrounding languages, such as Turkish and Greek. An important contributing factor to the distancing from the Spanish spoken on the Iberian Peninsula was the usage by Eastern Sephardim of the Rashi Hebrew script. The lack of standardization in transliteration accentuated the differences with Iberian Spanish. Nevertheless, in all its essential features, Ladino retained its Hispanic character.

There has been considerable controversy about the designation of this language. The very term "Ladino," though widely accepted, has been contested by some scholars. According to some interpretations, the term should be used exclusively for the highly stylized, fixed *written* language for the literal, word-by-word, one-to-one translations of sacred and liturgical texts from the Hebrew. As is seen in the Istanbul translation of the Pentateuch in 1547, and in the numerous translations of the prayer book and the Passover haggadah, this was a language that reproduced the order of words as in the Hebrew original, and, once having fixed the corresponding word in Spanish, it never changed it down the ages.

Ladino, then, according to this interpretation, is essentially a *calque,* a copying language used only for translations from the Hebrew.[4] In fact, its very name originates from the term *enladinar,* meaning "to render into a Latin tongue." Ladino in this respect is the counterpart in Spanish of other Jewish translating languages, such as Taytsch in Yiddish or Sharh in Judeo-Arabic. To confuse matters even more, in modern times Eastern Sephardim have given many appellations to the language that they spoke, ranging from *Espaniol* (Spanish), *muestro Espaniol* (our Spanish), or, less frequently, *djudezmo.*

The Ladino linguistic situation of these communities corresponded to that of diglossia, where "higher" and "lower" variants of the language coexist. As with many diglossic cultures, for a long time there existed a high-culture, written literary language, initially used by the educated rabbinical elite for translation of the sacred texts. This was Ladino proper, and it was heavily influenced by Hebrew syntax. In time the translations, such as those of the Bible and the Passover haggadah, assumed a sacred quality themselves. The spoken language of quotidian speech was much more fluid and evolved in a dynamic dialectical relationship with the surrounding cultures and with the high-culture language of the sacred translations. Eventually, in the eighteenth and nineteenth centuries, as free translations of rabbinical texts gained currency, many of the translators used the term Ladino on the title pages of books, in spite of the fact that this was no longer the archaic translating medium. The written language and the popular spoken language represented different stages in a wide spectrum. And, of course, Hebrew reigned supreme as the most prestigious mode of rabbinical literary production. Some familiarity with the surrounding languages added to the linguistic repertoire of the Levantine Sephardim, whose polyglot cultural profile was to remain distinctive until modern times.

Ladino, used to denote both translated calque texts and, eventually, free translations from the Hebrew, was the term most commonly employed by Sephardic writers to refer to the language in which they were publishing in the formative period of Sephardic literary creativity. Although Judeo-Spanish is a neologism that gained currency at the end of the nineteenth century as a result of Westernization, Ladino has the benefit of continuing the usage of the Sephardim themselves, and it is the preferred term here.

The confusion in the very name of this language points to the open-ended and fluid nature of its literary development. No academy, no regulating structure, no conference, no state imposed order on the language or standardized its usage. Unlike their Yiddish-speaking counterparts in the north, Ladino-speaking populations lacked the demographic critical mass that might have opened this matter to debate and resolution in the modern period. The variety that has existed in the names of the language bears testimony to the overshadowing of Sephardic culture in the modern period by other Jewish and non-Jewish cultural modes and spheres of influence that have demoted its status until our own day.

HEBREW AND LADINO

Throughout its existence, most writing in Ladino consisted of translations, initially from Hebrew, and in the modern period from European languages. Very few publications existed in Ladino in the first two centuries of the implantation of the Sephardim in the Levant. Rabbinical culture produced works exclusively in Hebrew, even if many Ladino words are to be found in these texts, most notably in the *responsa* literature. Ladino, like Yiddish in the same period, simply lacked the prestige of Hebrew and came lower in the hierarchy of the rabbinical value system. None of the great works of Sephardic creativity in the sixteenth and seventeenth centuries were written in the language. Its usage remained mostly in the oral and commercial spheres.

Indeed, the sixteenth and seventeenth centuries after the expulsion saw an extraordinary output by the rabbinical elite in Hebrew. Sephardim established the first printing press in the Ottoman Empire in Istanbul in 1493. The cities of Istanbul, Salonica, and Edirne emerged as important centers of Hebrew publishing and, together with Safed, rose to become the principal centers of Jewish intellectual life. Important Yeshivot and Talmudei Torah were established in all four. The Talmud Torah of Salonica attracted students from as far away as Poland. Great halakhic sages such as David ibn Yahya, Jacob ben Habib and his son Levi ben Habib, Samuel de Medina, and Joseph Taitazak taught in these institutions and produced numerous works of Jewish religious law. Joseph Karo, educated entirely in the Sephardic culture area of the Ottoman Balkans, moved to Safed after teaching in Istanbul, Edirne, Nikopol, and Salonica, and prepared the celebrated and authoritative *Shulḥan Arukh,* which became the standard accepted code of law for Jewish communities in the empire and in Europe. Biblical exegesis and homiletics, as well as philosophy (mostly in the sixteenth century), remained important areas of creativity for figures such as Joseph Taitazak and Moses Almosnino. Kabbalistic thought, usually part of the repertoire of Hebrew learning among the Sephardim, rose to particular prominence from the mid-sixteenth century onward, most notably in Safed, where Moses Cordovero, Salomon Alkabez, Isaac Luria, and Ḥayyim Vital studied and taught.

In contrast to this intellectual achievement in Hebrew, whatever existed in writing in Ladino came into being because of some perceived utility. For example, the very first work to be published in the language in the Levant was the *Dinim de Shehita y Bedika,* which appeared in Istanbul in 1510, a book on ritual slaughter and inspection of animals, obviously of great use for a migrating population. Reinforcing the religious rectitude of the masses remained of paramount concern. In this vein, works on ethics would emerge as an especially popular genre, the most notable in the sixteenth century being the *Regimiento de la Vida* of Moses Almosnino (Salonica, 1564). (The same author's *Extremas y Grandezas de Constantinopla,* an account of the city of Istanbul, though written in Ladino, appeared only in Spanish in Latin script in Madrid in 1567.) Baḥya ibn Paquda's *Duties of the Heart* was translated from Hebrew into Ladino at the same time by Tzadik ben Joseph Formon under the title *Obligasion de los Korasones.* The Ladino translation of extracts from another important book of great utility, Karo's *Shulḥan Arukh,* was published in Istanbul under the title *Meza de Alma* in 1568.

But the foundational text was the famous translation into Ladino of the Pentateuch in Istanbul in 1547 from the press of Eliezer Gershon Soncino; the same translation appeared in Latin characters in Ferrara in 1553. The latter version was designed for the Western Sephardim, who were used to the Latin script. This was the first major translation of the most fundamental texts of Judaism, following word for word the Hebrew original and setting the modalities of the future translation enterprise. It was followed by translations of the Passover haggadah and of the prayer book, again in calque form. No doubt this translation of the Pentateuch represented the final fruition of Sephardic attempts to translate the sacred texts, the origins of which went back to the Middle Ages in Spain. It was to assume as sacred a quality as the original text, and it remained the most significant work in Ladino for two centuries. During this period it was Hebrew, and literary production in Hebrew, that provided the determining template of Ladino literature.

SABBATIANISM AND ITS CONSEQUENCES

Ladino writing, as a palimpsest of Hebrew texts, was to break free from its calque relationship to Hebrew in the course of the eighteenth century and evolve into a full-fledged literary enterprise. Translation from Hebrew was still an important activity, but new works written directly in Ladino became significant. The precedent-setting work that allowed the flowering of Ladino literary creativity was without any doubt the *Me-am Loez* of Jacob Hulli, which began to be published in 1730. The single most important work in Ladino literature, this vast, multivolume compendium of rabbinical lore (which was to be developed, after the premature death of Hulli in 1732, by a host of other writers during the next century and a half) was organized as a commentary on the books of the Bible, beginning with Exodus. Utilizing all available rabbinical material, halakhic and aggadic sources as well as past commentaries, histories, philosophical writings, and moderate kabbalistic interpretations to explicate the biblical text in the language of the masses as well as impart knowledge about the world and how to live a righteous life, the *Me-am Loez* represented the continuity with the past function of Ladino literature as the medium to moralize and educate the average Sephardic Jew. It established the new genre of rabbinical writing directly in Ladino, giving legitimacy to original creativity in the language.[5]

This seems to have been a direct outgrowth of the Sabbatian crisis that had wreaked havoc in the Jewish world in general and among Sephardic communities in particular in the second half of the seventeenth century. Shabbtai Zevi, born in Izmir, was a native son of the Eastern Mediterranean diaspora, and nowhere was his influence more directly felt than in the Sephardic heartland. New developments in kabbalistic thought and practice among the elite as well as undercurrents of messianism that had been with the Sephardic exiles since the expulsion fused in the person of Zevi to produce a messianic explosion. In 1665 he claimed to be the messiah and announced the beginning of redemption. He attracted a huge following from all sections of the Jewish population inside and outside the Ottoman Empire, being greeted with extraordinary mass enthusiasm wherever he traveled. Many Jews stopped work and sold all their belongings in preparation for the ingathering of the exiles in the Holy Land. Although at first the authorities ignored the movement, its revolutionary implications were brought to their attention by some of its opponents. In 1666 they gave Zevi a choice between conversion to Islam or death; he chose the former. A stunned Jewish world woke up from its dreams, though substantial numbers continued to believe in Zevi and many chose to follow him in his conversion to Islam. These formed the *dönme* (from the Turkish word "to turn") sect that was to survive until the twentieth century in Salonica.[6]

A symptom of intellectual and social crisis and malaise, intimately linked to the socioeconomic dislocations experienced by the Jewish communities of the Eastern Mediterranean, Sabbatianism made the crisis even deeper and cast a pall on Sephardic rabbinical creativity. There seems to be considerable evidence of demoralization and a closing of horizons among the rabbinical elite in the generations that followed the Sabbatian trauma, as well as a decline in religiosity and knowledge among the Jewish masses of the East. As Hulli explained in his introduction to the *Me-am Loez*, it was to remedy this latter condition that he embarked upon his work. Bemoaning the lack of knowledge of Hebrew and of the archaic nature of Ladino texts impenetrable to the masses, Hulli aimed at nothing less than to reacquaint the average Sephardic Jew with the religious tradition and to revive traditional faith and practice. And the medium to do this was to be the everyday language that was easily understood.

Although the rabbinical establishment received Hulli's first volume with suspicion, the book's extraordinary success soon won it support. Hulli died before completing his work on Exodus. His second volume appeared posthumously in 1733, completed by Isaac Magrisso, who then continued to finish Exodus with a final volume in 1746. Magrisso went on to treat Leviticus (Istanbul, 1753) and Numbers (Istanbul, 1764). Isaac Arguete launched upon the explication of Deuteronomy (Istanbul, 1773) but did not live to finish it. These texts constitute the classical *Me-am Loez,* which went through scores of printings in the next century and were widely disseminated in the Levant; even poor households possessed a copy. Indeed, if there were to be one book that a Sephardic family owned, it was likely to be a volume of the *Me-am Loez.* In time, these texts assumed a sacredness of their own, and both men and women learned sections of them by heart.

Other writers, such as Raḥamim Menaḥem Mitrani (Joshua, 1851, 1870), Raphael Hiya Pontremoli (Esther, 1864), Raphael Isaac Meir Benveniste (Ruth, 1882), Isaac Judah Aba (Isaiah, 1892), Nissim Moshe Abud (Ecclesiastes, 1898), and Ḥayyim Isaac Shaki (Song of Songs, 1899), continued the *Me-am Loez* project in the next century. Though of a lesser quality than the first series, these works added to a lively enterprise of religious writing that offers the best insight into the Sephardic tradition. Paraphrasing and commenting, the volumes of the *Me-am Loez* represented in the vernacular the intertextuality of the larger Jewish religious scholarship, and they acted as powerful vectors of transmission down the generations by rendering this tradition comprehensible—and Judeo-Hispanicizing it in the process. Much bigger in scope then the Ashkenazic *Tzena Urena* to which it has been often compared, the *Me-am Loez* appealed to both men and women yet remained prestigious for the rabbinical elite, a status not shared by similar endeavors in Yiddish.

NEW TRANSLATIONS AND ORIGINAL WRITINGS

The emergence of an original Ladino literature was accompanied by the rise of translation that was no longer a calque of the Hebrew. The golden age of classical Ladino, the eighteenth century, was also the one in which arguably the best of the translators, Abraham Asa, produced scores of important works, the most important of which was the new translation of the Bible published between 1739 and 1744. This replaced the old translation of 1547, which had now become too archaic and utilized, like Hulli's work, quotidian Ladino. Following in Hulli's footsteps in rendering the classical Hebrew texts available for the masses, Asa also produced a new translation of sections of the *Shulḥan Arukh* that appeared under the title *Shulḥan ha-Melekh* (Istanbul, 1749). All these, together with the first volumes of the *Me-am Loez,* were supported by subsidies from philanthropists in Istanbul and benefited from the success of the major new printing press in the city, established by Jonah Ashkenazi.

The impetus given to free productivity in Ladino and its legitimization led to the first printing of religious poetry, a genre that had remained oral until now. The most significant works in this domain were the *Coplas de Yosef Ha-Tzadik* of Abraham de Toledo (Istanbul, 1732) and *Los Maasiyot del Sinior de Yaakov Avinu* (Istanbul, 1748). Purim poems, which were part of this progression from oral to published poetry, were printed in collections known as *Coplas de Purim.*

Ethical writing, a genre that had been popular in the past, was also revived in the new medium. Works on how to lead a just existence steeped in religion, mixed with tales of science and sometimes of Kabbalah, emerged as a favorite genre for the rabbinical elite whose books in this domain would be published first in Hebrew and, soon thereafter, in Ladino. Arguably the most important of these was the *Sefer Shevet Musar* of Eliyahu Hakohen of Izmir, which appeared in Hebrew in 1712 (Istanbul) and was translated into Ladino by Asa in 1742 (Istanbul), with numerous reprints in the next century. One should also note, among others, the *Sefer Tikunei ha-Nefesh* of Reuben ben Abraham (Salonica, 1775) and the hugely popular *Pele Yoetz* of Eliezer Papo (Istanbul, 1824; Ladino translation by his son, Vienna, 1870; and Salonica, 1899–1900). Translations of similar works that saw the light of day in the Ashkenazic world were also significant: Zvi Hirsch Kaidanover's *Kav Ha-Yashar* and Pineḥas Elijah Hurwitz's kabbalistic *Sefer ha-Berit* enjoyed great popularity in Ladino.

By the middle of the nineteenth century, the Ladino repertoire included the whole range of rabbinical literature with the exception of halakhah, which remained exclusively in Hebrew. The latter language continued as the central referent. In many ways, until this period Ladino literary creativity can be said to have produced a mimesis of Hebraic literature, a situation symbolic of the unequal relationship between the two. Writing was the domain of the educated class, the rabbinical elite, whose first preference was Hebrew. The shock of the Sabbatian phenomenon led to the first major departure from this norm—the appearance of the *Me-am Loez*—which nonetheless remained firmly in the religious sphere. Although the *Me-am Loez* opened the path to original works produced in Ladino, even these emulated and shadowed Hebrew texts, explicating the tradition in the vernacular spoken and understood by the masses. Hebrew and the rabbinical heritage hence marked deeply all aspects of Ladino writing. The link between the two languages would be weakened and indeed in many cases snapped altogether with the rise of a new value system. Fundamental changes in the Ottoman Empire in the nineteenth century dethroned religion in the Sephardic communities and, with it, the primacy of Hebrew.

NATIONALISM AND FRAGMENTATION

The nineteenth and early twentieth centuries saw major changes in the Ottoman Empire that altered Jewish existence irrevocably. The rise of nationalist movements among the non-Muslim peoples of the Balkans, the overthrow of Ottoman rule with the rise of new nation-states, the irruption of Western power into the area, and new cultural and political orientations all left their mark. The Sephardic community, which had constituted itself as a distinctive culture area under one Ottoman rule, was now fragmented as different states established suzerainty over the various Jewish centers. The Sephardim of Belgrade were now ruled by Serbia, *de facto* independent since 1830 (*de jure* in 1878). Sarajevo fell under Habsburg rule in 1878. The state of Bulgaria came into existence in the same year and encompassed most of the Jewish communities of Northern Thrace and south of the Danube. Greece, independent since 1830, had a relatively small Jewish population until it annexed Salonica during the Balkan Wars of 1912–13. The Macedonian communities of Monastir and Uskup became part of the Serbian state at this time. Of all the Sephardic communities of the Balkans, only Edirne (Adrianople) and a few others in Eastern Thrace remained under Turkish rule on the eve of World War I and would continue to do so with the establishment of the Turkish republic after the war.

Both the institution of reforms by the Ottomans and the creation of new states in areas where their rule was overthrown went in tandem with the massive incursion of Western power into the region. The Ottoman state tried to put its house in order with a series of reforms such as the *Tanzimat* (Reforms) proclamation in 1839, the Reform Decree of 1856, and the constitution of 1876. The latter remained unimplemented under Abdulhamid II but was reinstituted after the Young Turk Revolution of 1908. Centralization and state-building policies were the main impetus behind most of these developments. Nevertheless, largely under Western prodding the Ottoman state improved the civil status of the non-Muslims, eventually granting them equal rights in 1856 (though they were not subject to compulsory conscription until 1909). The reforms, however, also eroded the autonomy of the non-Muslim groups, whose members were now subject to the new Western-inspired secular courts of criminal and commercial law. Still, education and culture remained within the purview of each group; until the Balkan Wars and World War I, the overwhelming majority of non-Muslims still attended their own schools. The Jews were no exception. Although successive governments slowly moved toward the creation of a state-sponsored Ottoman Turkish educational structure, a process that received an increased nationalist impetus after the Young Turk Revolution, the goal was far from being reached at the demise of the empire after World War I. Hence, Turkicization remained rather weak for the Jews.[7]

THE ALLIANCE ISRAÉLITE UNIVERSELLE

It was the educational institutions of the Alliance Israélite Universelle that came to provide the Sephardim with mass European-style schooling after the third quarter of the nineteenth century. The Alliance was founded in 1860 in Paris to fight for Jewish rights throughout the world and to combat anti-Jewish prejudice wherever it made itself manifest. It lobbied actively for Jewish emancipation with the authorities both in Paris and in the countries where the issue emerged. In addition to its political work, the Alliance was a major force in the field of education. Believing deeply in the moral emancipation of the Jews alongside their political emancipation, it cast its attention on the communities around the Mediterranean basin where, in contrast to the Russian Empire, the political situation made action possible. Attempting to improve the lot of Sephardic and Eastern Jews and also to reform, modernize, and Westernize them, the Alliance gradually created a vast school network in this area. At the height of its influence, in 1913, this network had 183 schools with 43,700 students from Morocco to Iran. Dispensing modern French and Jewish instruction, the schools came to replace much of the traditional education among the Jews in these lands and were a potent force in the emergence of a Jewish middle class in the Middle East and North Africa.

As members of the first Jewish community to be formally emancipated, French Jewish intellectuals and eventually much of the French Jewish elite came to perceive themselves as in the vanguard of Jewish modernity. Grafting the universalism of the French revolution onto a secularized version of Jewish messianism, they came to see it as their mission to spread the message of emancipation throughout the world so that all Jews would emerge into the promised new world of modern civilization. This would naturally entail increased openness to the outside world by the Jews and the reforming of Jewish society. Such a perspective was the guiding principle of the work of the Alliance across the Mediterranean basin.

The Alliance exercised a very powerful influence into the second half of the twentieth century among the Sephardic and Eastern Jewish communities. The history of the organization in this context is at the heart of the decisive encounter of East and West that led to the fundamental cultural, social, and economic reorientation of these Jewries. Working separately but sometimes in tandem with French colonialism, the school network of the Alliance was responsible first and foremost for the spread of the French language among the Jews of the Middle East and North Africa by offering them a modern French primary and lower secondary education. But it also laid great emphasis on the teaching of Jewish religious knowledge, biblical and prayer-book Hebrew, and Jewish history. Indeed, the Alliance schools were most certainly not secular institutions but primarily religious ones, with Judaism taught according to the principal tenets of modern Franco-Judaism. Furthermore, the Alliance was deeply concerned with the status of women and attached a great deal of importance to their education. In this it was at its most revolutionary. Its creation of a mass educational system for girls was a first in the history of Sephardic and Eastern Jewries. The education imbibed in these schools offered many new vistas to Jewish women and led to their individual social mobility but also contributed to the transformation of their status.

The Alliance message was received unevenly in communities far removed from the French sociopolitical context that had produced this form of Judaism. Nevertheless, the education imparted in its schools led to a growing awareness among the Sephardim of newer versions of Jewish existence than obtained in Europe and to a reevaluation of their place and belief-system in their own lands. The reorientation of Middle Eastern and North African Jews away from their traditional moorings in their local societies in the direction of the European metropole was a long secular development that accompanied the irruption of the West in the area. The economic interests of the Jews, a classic intermediary group between East and West, lay certainly in the overall Western presence, and increased trade with Europe led to considerable upward social mobility in major Jewish centers such as Salonica, Istanbul, and Izmir. The Alliance's work contributed to this larger process and played an important role in the creation of a Francophone Jewish bourgeoisie in the Levant.[8]

Familiarity with French became a hallmark of Sephardic Levantine culture. Even the surviving traditional schools emulated the programs of the Alliance and introduced French, which came to pervade all aspects of cultural life. Many upper-class families began to abandon Ladino at home, and the language itself underwent a dramatic change, succumbing to the invasion of hundreds of French words. These usually replaced words of Hebrew or Turkish origin, as is amply clear in any Ladino newspaper of the time that began to put the older words in brackets after the newly introduced French ones, eventually dispensing with the older words altogether. By the first decade of the twentieth century, the language was quite different from what it had been a century earlier.

One of the paradoxical results of this engagement with the West in general and with French in particular was the remarkable efflorescence of Ladino literature around the turn of the century. Whereas the number of people proficient in French increased swiftly, the language of the masses, in spite of the inroads made by French at school, remained Ladino. Intellectuals, publicists, and writers all needed to use Ladino in order to reach a sizable audience for their works. French may have altered elements of Ladino but did not replace it. French became an additional language, that of culture, added to the polyglossic repertoire of the Sephardim of the Levant. And it acted as the central conduit for the transmission of new genres of literature that it rendered familiar and that were then incorporated into the Ladino canon.

THE SEPHARDIC HASKALAH AND NEWSPAPER CULTURE

Even before the massive incursion of French, new influences had started to make inroads among Sephardic intellectuals. Italy, on the borders of the Ottoman Empire, had long constituted a major area of contact between the Eastern Sephardim and Europe. Trade relationships remained significant, with movements of Jews in both directions. These links were strengthened even more with the establishment of hundreds of Italian Jewish families in some of the major port cities of the Ottoman Empire in the course of the eighteenth century to develop trade and commerce. These Francos, as they were known, and the trade networks that they created were responsible for some degree of familiarity with Italian among the mercantile elements in Sephardic communities. Francos such as the Camondo, Allatini, and Modiano families were important allies of the reformist projects in centers such as Salonica and Istanbul that were pushed by the Alliance in the second half of the nineteenth century.

It is noteworthy, in this context, that David Moses Attias, a Sarajevo-born author living in Livorno, the port of origination of most of the Franco families, wrote arguably the very first book in Ladino echoing some of the themes of the European Haskalah (Jewish Enlightenment). His *Guerta de Oro* (1778) was essentially a secular treatise on the new spirit that must be introduced among the Sephardim of the East, highlighting the importance of learning secular subjects and of becoming more acquainted with developments in Europe through the learning of European languages. In order to facilitate this task, the book offered an introduction to Italian.

Following Attias, the systematizing of language study as well as elementary education emerged as a major preoccupation of writers in Ladino. Scores of textbooks appeared in the course of the nineteenth century, beginning with the *Otsar ha-Ḥayim* of Yisrael Ḥayim (Vienna, 1823), which introduced readers to elements of German, Ottoman Turkish, Hebrew, mathematics, and geography. Many an author turned his hand to education manuals, such as *Kuntres Darkhei Noam* by Judah Alkalay and *Livriko de Primera Klasa* by Moses David Alkalay. In addition, many books on Hebrew grammar were published in Ladino, the most important of which were Menaḥem Farhi's *Rav Pe'alim* and Isaac Bekhor Yehudah's *Yavi Mi-piryo*.

Until well into the second half of the nineteenth century, Hebrew continued to be a major conduit for the circulation of ideas between the Ashkenazic and Sephardic worlds, but it now became important in the secular as well as the religious domain. Ideas of the Haskalah made their way and influenced leading Sephardic figures such as Judah Nehama and Abraham Danon. European Hebrew newspapers such as *ha-Magid* were read and commented upon regularly, and letters sent by Sephardim and published in their pages attested to an important readership in the East.

Haskalah-oriented agendas combined with curiosity about different Jewish communities and personalities gave rise to Ladino editions of books about famous Jews such as Moses Montefiore, Adolphe Crémieux, and the Rothschilds. Not only were the new Hebrew classics translated but so were the works of Yiddish literature produced by authors such as Y. L. Peretz, Sholem Aleichem, and Sholem Asch.

However, the most important transmitters of information as well as of new genres of literature were the newspapers, in whose columns almost all of the new books in Ladino appeared first in serialized form. Like the Turkish, Greek, Armenian, and other communities, the Jews created a lively Ladino newspaper culture from the middle of the nineteenth century, closely related to the growing importance of news about economic and political developments. The rise of Ladino journalism was broadly contemporaneous with that of the European Jewish press. The first Ladino newspaper, *La Buena Esperansa,* appeared in Izmir in 1842, to be followed by the *Puertas del Oriente* in 1845–46 in the same city, and *La Luz de Israel* in Istanbul in 1853. These had a brief existence but were soon replaced by much longer-lasting publications. One was the *Jurnal Israelit,* which appeared in Istanbul during the entire decade of the 1860s; its editor, Ezekiel Gabay, and his son Isaac Gabay continued the enterprise in the 1870s with *El Nasional* and with *El Telegrafo.* The latter was to last, appearing several times a week, until 1930. Equally long-lived was *El Tiempo,* edited by David Fresko, a redoubtable polemicist and radical Westernizer, from the 1870s until the early

1930s. His counterpart in Izmir was Aaron Ḥazan, who published *La Buena Esperansa* from 1871 to 1922. In Salonica, Saadi Halevi and his son Sam Levy brought out *La Epoka* from 1875 till 1912. Sofia also had a lively Ladino press, *La Voz de Israel* becoming the most significant Jewish newspaper in Bulgaria between 1877 and 1899. All told, 389 Ladino newspapers were founded, most of them between 1880 and 1920.

These newspapers were important not just for the circulation of information. In continuity with the overall framework of moralization of the masses that had been the mission of traditional Ladino writers, the new journalists were deeply engaged with the reform of Sephardic society, attacking "obscurantist" and "superstitious" habits and spreading new ideas about dress, food, and hygiene. Such preoccupations eventually led to overt politicization, and the whole gamut of political stances such as Ottomanism (patriotism for a united, liberal Ottoman polity), local nationalism in the successor states to the empire, Zionism, and socialism were represented in the columns of the press. By World War I, not only was the Sephardic world fully cognizant of the political movements in the wider Jewish and non-Jewish arenas but it was participating in them.

The Ladino newspaper constituted the most fertile form of creativity in the Eastern Sephardic world in the modern period and created a public sphere in Ladino. The transmission of news was only one among its many goals. Equally important was the omnipresent voice of the editor, who would frequently write most of the news columns but also editorialized throughout the paper, giving his own take on events and developments, polemicizing and militating for his agenda, which was usually in the direction of promoting reform. To further this goal, much space was given to acquaint the reader with the latest developments in the fields of science, technology, dress, and food occurring in Europe. Indeed, in many cases supplements devoted to this task emerged as newspapers in their own right, such as *El Instruktor, El Sol,* and *El Amigo de la Famiya,* which were created by David Fresko, the editor of *El Tiempo.* The papers ran advertisements for European products and gave advice on their use.[9]

The attention of the reader was held by serialized translations of popular European novels that would later be published in book form. The newspaper was hence the site of the introduction of entirely new genres in Ladino.

Hundreds of such novels were to appear in the late nineteenth and early twentieth centuries, translations eventually accompanied by some original works by local writers. Nowhere is the Judeo-Hispanicization of outside influences more apparent than in the pages of these translated novels and novellas. The title pages already announced the process with words such as *imitado, adaptado, rezumido* (imitated, adapted, summarized). The translators rarely searched for an exact equivalence with the original; rather, these were the products of acts of rewriting.[10] Plots were adapted, transformed, and frequently given a local hue, usually in far fewer pages than the original. The line between what was recognizable as a translation and an original work of fiction blurred and frequently disappeared in this new literature. The new Ladino work of fiction emerged in the interstices of genres. *Manon Lescaut,* by Abbé Prevost, was reduced to 82 pages; *Paul et Virginie,* by Bernardin de Saint-Pierre, to 23 pages. Alexander Ben Ghiat, Elia Karmona, and Shelomo Israel Sherezli were the most prolific of the translators/authors.

Works of drama also gained in popularity. Many of the plays of Shakespeare and Molière were translated, rewritten, and adapted, again rather freely. Original works, some on biblical but also some on secular themes, also emerged. Zionist societies as well as socialist organizations in Salonica were particularly active in fostering this activity. Many plays were published in the Jewish press, which also developed other genres, such as poetry. The Salonican Jacob Jona became famous throughout the Sephardic world with his satirical poems and songs on the events and personalities of the day; he also collected anecdotes, proverbs, love songs, and short stories.

The converse of this increase of secular writing in Ladino was accompanied by a decline in the number of publications of religious import. Sephardic rabbinical culture, ever more anemic, could not withstand the rising tide of cultural adaptation. By the end of the nineteenth century, new Hebraic and religious Ladino works had shrunk to a handful. Secularization had arrived with a vengeance.

The development of new genres in Ladino illustrates an important point about the dynamics of Westernization in this context. Westernization was not just an act of mimesis, with a triumphant West as the subject and a subservient Sephardic East as the object. Rather, it was a dynamic process with the local frequently coopting and domesticating the new, creating new hybrid genres in many domains of cultural creativity ranging from literature to music. The Sephardim, like many of their non-Jewish counterparts in the region facing the same challenges, "imitated" and "adapted" and transformed the Western, creating a complex bricolage of cultural modes that married "East" and "West."

CHALLENGES TO LADINO

Paradoxically, the burning issue in this period of efflorescence was the question of the status of Ladino and whether it should be abandoned. The language was threatened by the very process of change that had seen its emergence as a secular medium. Accused from all sides of being nothing more than a "corrupt jargon," Ladino steadily lost its legitimacy among Sephardic Jews as a proper language of discourse.

As part of its "civilizing mission," the Alliance was determined to eradicate the usage of Ladino. Like the European reformers for whom Yiddish was an unwholesome relic of the past that must be discarded, the Alliance's Central Committee and the teachers were hostile to all local Jewish languages and dialects. By the early 1880s, some teachers were fining students if they used Ladino in the schools. In 1884, the Central Committee formally banned the language from all its educational establishments. It is doubtful whether this was ever really implemented. Because Hebrew and religious instruction were taught by local rabbis who used Ladino as a teaching medium, its presence in the schools continued. But by frowning upon it and discouraging its usage as much as possible, the schools contributed to its delegitimization in the eyes of the people.

This was aided considerably by the overriding emphasis given to French in the Alliance schools. Apart from the hours devoted to Hebrew, Turkish, and, in some schools, to one other European language, and apart from religious instruction, where Ladino crept in, subjects from natural sciences to geography and arithmetic were taught in French, which the students began to study in the lowest grades.

The next challenge to Ladino came from Turkish. The official view of the Alliance was that a good knowledge of the language of the country was essential if Jews were to deserve emancipation. It was a moral imperative for the Jews of Turkey to learn Turkish. Furthermore, it was indispensable for social advancement, because many careers in the civil service would be accessible to Turkish-speaking Jews. The Alliance had been shocked to see how difficult it had been to find a Jewish leader of any stature who could speak enough Turkish to become a member of the Council of State in 1876, when the abortive first Ottoman constitution was put briefly into effect. For many Alliance teachers, the example of the Armenians who had advanced in the Ottoman administration because of their intimate knowledge of Turkish was one that had to be emulated by the Jews. The Central Committee inquired several times as to how to train Jews to become civil servants, but no adequate means were found. Indeed, though the Alliance paid lip service to the importance of learning the language of the country, in reality it did not make great efforts in this direction. French was the language of civilization, and the Alliance's first priority was civilizing the Jews.

The language issue emerged with acuity as a result both of reform and of the pressure on the state to stem the tide of local nationalisms. Turkicization was adopted as state policy under the Young Turks. But, by the end of the nineteenth century, increasing emphasis was already being put on control of the foreign schools and on the spread of Turkish among the non-Muslims of the empire. In 1894, the state decreed that the teaching of some Turkish in all non-Muslim schools would be compulsory, and it began to send out Turkish teachers paid by the government. However, the decree did not make Turkish the language of instruction. The Jews and the Alliance could not remain insensitive to this development, and the hours devoted to Turkish were increased in many schools. In the meantime, the Chief Rabbinate began to concern itself with this matter. A commission was created to oversee the ways in which Turkish could be introduced into the Talmudei Torah. An old Talmud Torah in Istanbul was transformed into a school where the language of instruction was Turkish.

The Young Turk Revolution of 1908, which abolished the last inequalities between Muslims and non-Muslims and which instituted compulsory military service, increased substantially the demands for more Turkish in the schools. All of the Alliance teachers pointed out the new possibilities now open to the Jews in the civil service. The Alliance was quick to respond and, in a new decree, increased the hours of Turkish studied in each school. There were by now better teachers of Turkish available, and the aim was to direct the best students to pursue the rest of their secondary education in government schools, a route taken by increasing numbers. Nevertheless, no other major changes in the curriculum were undertaken in the Alliance institutions. The primacy given to French subverted all efforts. Ladino lost out from all points of view. No defender of the language emerged in the educational system in which three languages already took precedence: French as the language of civilization; Hebrew as the language of the religion; and Ottoman Turkish as the language of the country.

Sephardic journalists had been engaged with the language problem since the beginning of their enterprise. Raphael Uziel, the publisher of one of the first newspapers in Ladino, *Puertas del Oriente* in 1845–46, commented in its pages on the "mixed" nature of the language, its lack of standardization, and its inferior status. Similar concerns were to be voiced by almost all Sephardic journalists expressing themselves in the Ladino press. Many, such as the editor of Vienna's *El Nasional*, proposed the outright abandonment of Ladino in favor of modern Spanish, whereas others argued for the adoption of the language of the state, abhorring a return to the tongue of the "ancient persecutors" whose distant offspring, Ladino, was itself distasteful because of its Iberian baggage. Fresko, who was closely aligned to the Alliance, was the strongest critic of Ladino, arguing for increased efforts for the learning of Turkish. Fierce polemics broke out in the pages of *El Tiempo* on this subject after the 1880s. The lone defender of Ladino emerged in the person of Sam Levy, the co-editor of Salonica's *La*

Epoka, who argued for the retention of a modernized and standardized form of the language.

Growing familiarity with political movements such as the emergent nationalisms in the Ottoman Empire made the small but highly vocal Sephardic intelligentsia increasingly uncomfortable with the proliferation of languages in the community. From the 1890s onward, the columns of the Judeo-Spanish newspapers such as *El Tiempo, El Telegrafo, El Meseret,* and *La Buena Esperansa* are full of polemics about the language question. Sephardic writers, all of them graduates of the Alliance schools, became deeply concerned about the languages that should be taught in these institutions. Writing in Ladino, the journalists nonetheless agreed that it constituted a corrupt medium, did not suit the requirements of the age, and had to go. Although most remained convinced that a knowledge of French was indispensable for an understanding of "civilization," many agreed that the future lay with Turkish—and that both were indispensable for the modern Ottoman Jew.

In 1900, the Tamim-i Lisan-i Osmani Cemiyeti (Society for the Propagation of the Ottoman Language) was founded by Jews in Istanbul. Similar societies sprang up in the aftermath of the Young Turk Revolution, which was greeted with great enthusiasm by Ottoman Jews. Ladino newspapers, beginning with the *Ceride-i Lisan* of 1891, had begun to publish a few of their pages in Turkish. An increasing number of Jews began to attend Ottoman secondary schools and institutions of higher education, though these were still a minority of Jewish students on the eve of World War I.

The nascent Zionist movement among Sephardic Jews after 1908 propagandized in favor of Hebrew but was not particularly successful. In theory, most Jewish public figures were convinced of the need for Turkish but, in practice, the move toward it remained limited to a relatively small minority of Jewish students. The educational infrastructure created by the Alliance remained in place; French remained popular as the language of civilization par excellence. Although more Jews were now continuing their education after the Alliance schools in Turkish institutions, the majority of the Jewish population remained satisfied with the Alliance. The multiethnic nature of the empire, the existence of many different educational systems associated with the different religious and ethnic minorities, and the relative weakness of the Turkish educational infrastructure were all contributing factors to the relative slowness of Turkicization among the Jews of the Ottoman Empire.

Nevertheless, Ladino continued to be the object of attack and derision among those who earned their livelihood by writing in it daily. It suffered, on the one hand, from the prestige of French and, on the other, from the necessity accorded to Turkish by Ottomanist patriotism. The nation-states that carved up the Ottoman Empire and succeeded it after World War I eroded even further a language whose status had already been weakened considerably. In Serbia, Bosnia, and Bulgaria, and later in Greece and Turkey, the Jewish school systems were eventually nationalized, with the language of the country holding pride of place. In Bulgaria, which had a successful Zionist movement, Hebrew instruction in Jewish schools emerged as a significant alternative. The decline of the traditional educational system and the policies of the Alliance and later modern state schools, all linked in one way or the other to the vagaries of the process of transformation undergone by the Ottoman Levant, converged to sever the chain of transmission of Ladino from generation to generation in a written form and relegated it exclusively to the home. The same process that begat the explosion in Ladino literary activity was also eventually to be responsible for the demise of the language.

By the 1930s, the number of Ladino speakers had begun to diminish. Serbo-Croatian newspapers had already replaced the last Ladino newspaper of Sarajevo, *La Alborada,* in 1901. In Bulgaria, the interwar period saw a precipitous decline in the number of publications in Ladino. In Turkey, the move toward Latin script in the 1920s prompted the Jews to switch to this script in Ladino. This led to cutting off new generations from the centuries-old literature written in Hebrew Rashi script. Creativity and literary activity in the language declined dramatically in Turkey in the twentieth century.

Salonica, the largest Sephardic center, held out the longest. Publishing in Ladino continued in the interwar years. Nevertheless, there too the decline in the number of publications was quite evident. "National" languages were replacing Ladino as the mother tongue of the Sephardim, and the new value system continued to valorize European languages to the detriment of the local "jargon." The latter was also under attack from Hebrew, promoted by significant Zionist movements in Bulgaria and Greece. The last Ladino newspaper in the world printed in traditional Rashi script, *El Mesajero,* was closed down by the occupying German forces in Salonica in 1941.

The Holocaust destroyed Ladino together with the communities that had seen it flourish over the centuries. The Jews of Salonica, with the rest of Greek Jewish communities, were decimated. Most of the Sephardim of Belgrade and Sarajevo perished. Bulgarian Jewry, which survived the war, was deeply traumatized and left en masse for Israel after 1948. Turkish Jewry, which survived intact, had also suffered major trauma during the war years and also migrated in large numbers. By the second half of the twentieth century, only small remnants were to be found in the old heartlands of the Eastern Sephardic diaspora. Most were transplanted to Israel.

Ladino did not survive the transition to Israel, meeting yet another nation-state with demands for an exclusive national language—in this case, Hebrew. Today, there is no serious literary creativity in the language that is spoken and understood mostly by the older Sephardim. Writing in Ladino survives here and there in a few periodicals, and in a page devoted to it in each issue of the Turkish Jewish newspaper *Shalom.* No young Sephardim speak it as their mother tongue. Having lasted for five centuries, the language is for all intents and purposes dead, a casualty of the Holocaust and of the long-term, secular processes of political, social, and cultural change that destroyed the transnational Levant in which it had developed and flourished.

NOTES

1. Archives of the Alliance Israélite Universelle, France XVII.F.28, M. Fresco, Rapport annuel 1907–1908.

2. The term Sephardim is used here to refer to the direct descendants of the Jews of the Iberian Peninsula who retained Judeo-Iberian traditions and languages.

3. For a discussion of these points, see Aron Rodrigue, "Difference and Tolerance in the Ottoman Empire: Interview by Nancy Reynolds," *Stanford Humanities Review* 5 (1995): 81–90. For a general history of the Sephardim, see Esther Benbassa and Aron Rodrigue, *Sephardi Jewry: The Judeo-Spanish Community, 14th–20th Centuries* (Berkeley, 2000).

4. The principal modern proponent of this view is Haim Vidal Sephiha, *Le Ladino: Judéo-espagnol calque* (Paris, 1973).

5. For an overview of the *Me-am Loez,* see Michael Molho, *Le Me-am Loez: Encyclopédie populaire du séphardisme levantin* (Salonica, 1945).

6. The most comprehensive book on this episode is still Gershom Scholem, *Sabbetai Sevi* (Princeton, N.J., 1973).

7. See Aron Rodrigue, "From *Millet* to Minority: Turkish Jewry in the 19th and 20th Centuries," in Pierre Birnbaum and Ira Katznelson, eds., *Paths of Emancipation: Jews Within States and Capitalism* (Princeton, N.J., 1995), 238–61.

8. For the latest overview of the Alliance's activities, see Aron Rodrigue, *Images of Sephardi and Eastern Jewries in Transition, 1860–1939: The Teachers of the Alliance Israélite Universelle* (Seattle, 1993).

9. For this and for a case study of Ladino newspaper culture, see Sarah Abrevaya Stein, "The Creation of Yiddish and Judeo-Spanish Newspaper Cultures in the Russian and Ottoman Empires" (Ph.D. diss., Stanford University, 1999).

10. For a study of this phenomenon, see Olga Borovaia, "Translation and Westernization: *Gulliver's Travels* in Ladino," *Jewish Social Studies* n.s. 7, no. 2 (Winter 2001): 149–68.

SELECTED BIBLIOGRAPHY

Benbassa, Esther, and Aron Rodrigue. *Sephardi Jewry: The Judeo-Spanish Community, 14th–20th Centuries.* Berkeley, 2000.

Borovaia, Olga. "Translation and Westernization: *Gulliver's Travels* in Ladino." *Jewish Social Studies* n.s. 7, no. 2 (Winter 2001): 149–68.

Molho, Michael. *Le Me-am Loez: Encyclopédie populaire du séphardisme levantin.* Salonica, 1945.

Rodrigue, Aron. "Difference and Tolerance in the Ottoman Empire: Interview by Nancy Reynolds." *Stanford Humanities Review* 5 (1995): 81–90.

———. "From *Millet* to Minority: Turkish Jewry in the 19th and 20th Centuries." In Pierre Birnbaum and Ira Katznelson, eds., *Paths of Emancipation: Jews Within States and Capitalism.* Princeton, N.J., 1995.

———. *Images of Sephardi and Eastern Jewries in Transition, 1860–1939: The Teachers of the Alliance Israélite Universelle.* Seattle, 1993.

Romero, Elena. *La Creacíon literaria en lengua sefardí.* Madrid, 1992.

Scholem, Gershom. *Sabbetai Sevi.* Princeton, N.J., 1973.

Sephiha, Haim Vidal. *Le Ladino: Judéo-espagnol calque.* Paris, 1973.

Stein, Sarah Abrevaya. "The Creation of Yiddish and Judeo-Spanish Newspaper Cultures in the Russian and Ottoman Empires." Ph.D. diss., Stanford University, 1999.

Jewish men on the Tunisian island of Djerba discuss business in the village marketplace. Black stripes sewn to traditional Tunisian trousers commemorate the destruction of the Temple in Jerusalem. (Photo: Keren Tzionah Friedman. © 1980)

MULTICULTURAL VISIONS:

The Cultural Tapestry of the Jews of North Africa

LUCETTE VALENSI

In October 1824, the Englishman Joseph Greaves arrived in Tunis, where he planned to stay for a time, and looked for a tutor to teach him Arabic. The man he found was not a Muslim but a native Jew, Mordekhai Naggiar. The two men toured the city together, visiting the slave market, exploring the Jewish and Christian quarters, and exchanging opinions on a variety of subjects. Naggiar had a regular job as a translator with the Tunisian government and enjoyed the friendship of the prime minister. Bitterly evoking the situation of the Jews, he judged their condition to be worse than that of slaves. At the same time, he denounced Judaism as riddled with superstition and accused the rabbis of being tyrannical. He claimed that he was hated by other Jews because of his subversive ideas on the Jewish religion.

Naggiar and Greaves communicated in Italian. In Tunis, this language was in current use and served in exchanges between individuals of all backgrounds. (The Bey Ahmad himself, who would rule the country from 1837 to 1855, had a Sardinian mother and spoke fluent Italian.) Naggiar also spoke French, having lived for several years in Paris, where he had established relations with the greatest Orientalist of the day, Silvestre de Sacy.

Naggiar told his companion that he had completed a work on the Berber language at the behest of an agent of the Dutch consulate in Tunis. He had worked on this project with a Kabyle (a native of a mountainous area of Berber-speaking population east of Algiers), spending several months with him, and had composed a Berber grammar and lexicon on the basis of phrases in Arabic transcribed in Arabic characters. The whole thing had been sent to Amsterdam. Naggiar hoped to extend this work with a study of the Berber of Aurès (in present-day Algeria) and was prepared to do it at his own expense if he did not obtain support from the academy in Amsterdam to which he had applied.

A strange story. It is commonly accepted that indigenous Jews, a majority of the Jewish population of Tunisia, were generally more attached to tradition and less open to the outside world than their Livornese coreligionists, who constituted a minority of some 2,000 individuals in Tunis and played a much more important role in the great Mediterranean trade. Yet Naggiar contradicts this received idea. Far from being immersed in traditional religious culture, he was involved in an intellectual project that signals an entry into secular culture. From a social perspective, he had established contacts with transnational European circles interested in the progress of scientific knowledge. As a translator with the Tunisian government, Naggiar occupied a position that the Jews in North Africa and minorities in the whole of the Muslim Mediterranean have always occupied, that of the *drogman* (intermediary), the mediator between two worlds. In the world of commerce, this was usual. In the world of knowledge, it was less so and has, in this case, a modern inflection.

And what was Greaves doing in Tunisia? He had not come as a merchant or a traveling naturalist, as numerous Europeans had done under the ancien régime, nor as an Orientalist in search of strong emotions and picturesque views, as many did in the nineteenth century. Nor was he one of the various experts and adventurers who, beginning in the nineteenth century, offered their services to the rulers of the region in the name of technical and economic progress. Greaves was a Protestant missionary who set out to convert not only the Greeks and Catholics living on these Muslim shores of the Mediterranean but the Jews and even Muslims as well. He brought with him many Bibles in Arabic and Italian and various pamphlets, which he sold through workers recruited for this purpose. Most important, he engaged in lengthy discussions with those who were willing. In Tunisia, he was a complete failure among the Jews. He soon gave up on learning Arabic, and in January 1825 he packed his bags and returned to Christian lands.

A double failure: the missionary work Greaves—and other such clerics—attempted in Tunisia and Morocco came up against the condemnation of the rabbis and the hostility of ordinary believers. The attraction that Western culture began to exercise in the nineteenth century was increasingly powerful but only in its secular aspects. If Jews distanced themselves from local practice, it was not to adhere to another religion but to modify their relationship with their own tradition. As for Naggiar, he adopted a critical stance with regard to rabbinical tradition, on the one hand, and opened himself to secular intellectual activities, on the other: the study of languages, the composing of dictionaries, the dialogue with European non-Jewish scholars. Was this entirely new? Were these challenges to tradition the constituent elements of modern Jewish culture? We should remember that this kind of intense intellectual exchange had occurred in the Middle Ages, too, when Islamic civilization flourished. For the period under discussion in this chapter, it would be easy to ascribe the first contribution of modernity to the West: to attribute the role of transmitters of innovation to the circles of Jewish traders who maintained close relations with Europe—specifically, to the Livornese Jews in the case of Tunis or Algiers. This would be true in part, but only in part. From Greaves's Tunisian experience, we learn that a native Jew might speak four languages: Arabic, Hebrew, Italian, and French. Though instructed in Jewish tradition, he would be interested in new disciplines independent of that tradition. It will be objected that Naggiar's entry into Western culture took place after the Napoleonic wars, so rather belatedly. This is a hypothesis that will have to be tested by closer examination of the relations that the Jews of the Maghreb maintained with their coreligionists in the rest of the Diaspora.

Naggiar has not left a description of his milieu, unlike other Jews of the Arab world who accompanied European visitors and eventually set down their own vision of their society in writing. But his encounter with Greaves at least allows us to formulate some of the issues that will be discussed in the following pages. The first concerns the particular coloration of North African Judaism. North African Jews, Greaves tells us, wore the same garments, apart from color, as their Muslim neighbors, and they spoke Arabic. He might have made the same observations in Libya, Algeria, and Morocco. But beyond dress and language, what did these Jews and Muslims share? What was specifically North African in the Jews' culture? These questions soon suggest others: What was Jewish about that culture? Embedded in their Muslim environment, what did they share with the rest of the Diaspora beyond common religious references to the basic texts of Jewish tradition? What did they know about the social practices, the dreams, and the expectations of other Jews around the world?

Naggiar and the Jews, like the Muslims, lived through a historical period during which pressure from European countries was increasingly felt in North Africa. Under these conditions, did the history of the Jews encapsulate the more general history, or did the changes that intervened have a different impact on different segments of the society? Because the Jews formed a religious minority, did they work out in different ways the new opportunities that presented themselves or the restrictions they endured?

NORTH AFRICAN JEWS IN
THEIR MUSLIM ENVIRONMENT

Before answering these questions, it is appropriate to set the scene and situate the position of the Jews in the region during the eighteenth to twentieth centuries. Of the four countries of the Maghreb (Libya, Tunisia, Algeria, and Morocco), only the last never came under the sway of the vast Ottoman Empire, which controlled the greater part of the Mediterranean world between the sixteenth and the nineteenth centuries. The Alaouite dynasty, descendants of the Prophet and as such designated as Shorfa, have governed Morocco since the seventeenth century. Although the sultan's religious legitimacy was never challenged, this vast country was geographically and socially fragmented, and various regions or tribes attempted to escape the political and fiscal control of the Sherifian state. Formally part of the Ottoman Empire since the sixteenth century, Libya, Tunisia, and Algeria became practically autonomous, signing treaties with foreign countries and minting their own currencies. From 1711 to 1835, Libya was ruled on the model of the Ottoman state by the Qaramanly dynasty, with the same tension as in Morocco between the central government and a number of fragmented tribal structures that were the basis of social and political life in the countryside. In Tunisia, the Husaynite dynasty, in power since 1705, would rule until the establishment of the republic in 1957. Whereas the Bey surrounded himself with a Turkish political and military elite, he had established and institutionalized a pacific relationship with the local society. In Algeria, however, the Turkish militia that governed in Algiers was never transformed into a stable dynasty or sought real integration into the local society; it maintained the military character of the political regime.

In a primarily rural population—in part village-dwelling, in part tribal and nomadic—the Jews formed the only non-Muslim minority in the Maghreb, and a small minority at that, nowhere reaching 3 percent of the total. They were nonetheless all the more visible for being essentially urban, with the largest communities concentrated in the capital cities and commercial ports. Still, numerous, much smaller Jewish communities were scattered throughout the interior of the Maghreb, even as far south as the Sahara. The population of Algeria at the time of the French conquest (1830) is estimated at three million and that of the Jews there at around 15,000. In Tunisia, out of a population that scarcely exceeded a million in the middle of the nineteenth century, Jews numbered 25,000 to 30,000 individuals, more than half of them in Tunis itself. In Morocco, which was home to the most important Jewish community, the population of the country at the beginning of the twentieth century is estimated at five million and the Jewish population at 100,000. Finally, Libya numbered only around 16,000 Jews in 1916. Everywhere, the Jews were generally artisans and small tradesmen. Nearly everywhere, they lived in separate neighborhoods known as *mellah*s in Morocco and as *hara*s in the rest of the region. And everywhere most of them lived in grim poverty, which remained the case until the virtual end of their presence in North Africa.

In Tunis, the Jewish population—15,000 to 20,000 individuals, out of a total of around 100,000—was divided between an indigenous Arabic-speaking majority and an Italophone minority. The members of the two communities frequented different synagogues, maintained separate cemeteries, managed their resources separately, and defended their identity through strict endogamy. The native Jews, *Twansa* (Tunisians), cultivated local tradition, and their references were mostly Eastern. The others, called Grana in Arabic, Portuguese in Hebrew, and Livornese in the Romance languages, maintained commercial and familial relationships with the Italian port cities, especially Livorno. Speaking and reading Italian, they were more directly exposed to the currents of ideas in Christian Europe and more open to non-Jewish circles. At least this was a general tendency, though the reality was certainly more fluid, as the case of Naggiar demonstrates. As happens everywhere, lines that divide are also shared: social differentiation operates, specific identity is formed, precisely at the points of contact and confrontation between various groups. Lines that divide are also tempting to cross when they establish hierarchy, not only contiguity: if one group is considered superior, members of the inferior group will seek access to it or use it as their model. A rich Tunisian Jew would therefore act like an Italian and marry an Italian Jewish woman if he could. A native Jew who did business in Italy would return Italianized. In the much smaller communities in the interior of the country, the partition was necessarily more porous. In daily life, finally, the Grana had to mix with the natives and tended to share with them practices and beliefs.

This dualism of Jewish society was found again in Tripoli and Algiers. Farther west, the population was divided between *Megorashim* (Jews expelled from the Iberian peninsula) and *Toshabim* (native Jews), but over time the descendants of the first took over the leadership of the large urban communities, set the tone in matters of law, and to some extent Hispanicized the indigenous Jews. Beyond these explicit distinctions (which were sometimes legal, as in the case of the Grana and Twansa in Tunisia starting in the eighteenth century), we find the same kind of differentiation within every Jewish community. Even in remote places such as the Libyan villages studied by the social anthropologist Harvey Goldberg, we find outward-looking "cosmopolitan" elements and inward-looking Jews more strongly attached to localism. There was a kind of division of labor between the two: tension but also complementarity. Besides, such a polarization was far from rigid, because social and geographic mobility allowed people to compete for economic advantage and social prestige.

Social mobility became even stronger with the important changes that intervened in the nineteenth century, both in the system that governed relations between the state and its subjects and in connections between the Maghreb and Europe. The commercial and financial capitals of the world economy at the time were in Europe. The integration of the Maghreb into international trade at the end of the eighteenth century resulted in an intensification of economic relations with the ports of Marseilles, Livorno, London, and Amsterdam and an expanded sphere of action for commercial circles—city-dwellers in the great ports more generally and Jews in particular.

In the political arena, the Ottoman regime regained control of Libya in 1835, and the great reform movement known as the Tanzimat was extended to this country. The imperial decrees of 1839 and 1856, in particular, granted civil equality to non-Muslims and in effect abolished the discriminatory practices of the traditional system. Reforms of the provincial and local administration allowed non-Muslims to take part in the management of public affairs. Inspired in part by the Ottoman example but also ceding to European pressures, Tunisia in turn adopted the Fundamental Pact in 1857 and a constitution in 1861, which improved the legal and economic position of the Jews. Such reforms were not extended to Morocco, where the sultan resisted foreign pressure and refused to follow the Ottoman example.

Soon, however, all the countries of the Maghreb would be subjected to colonial rule: Algeria first, in 1830, although France's conquest of the whole country would take more than 40 years; then Tunisia, which became a protectorate under French tutelage in 1881; followed by Morocco in 1912. The northern part of Morocco came under Spanish control at the same moment, while Libya became an Italian colony. The imposition of colonial rule introduced major changes in the political system and in the position held by every segment of society. Traditional forms of social organization were shattered—and even destroyed, especially in Algeria—and new social forces emerged with the growth and diversification of the urban population. A sizable Christian population coming from every port of Mediterranean Europe superimposed itself on the local population of Muslim and Jews. This colonial society provided new patterns of interaction and ways of living while remaining stubbornly resistant to giving the Muslim population access to equal rights. Culturally, Western models became dominant, and the French language became the symbol of high culture. Such developments must be kept in mind as we try to appreciate the cultural history of one of the segments of this complex society, namely the Jewish one, and as we seek answers to the questions outlined above.

THE POLYGLOSSIA OF NORTH AFRICAN JEWISH CULTURE

Let us broach the first set of questions. To what extent was North African Judaism part of a broader Jewish culture? What means did North African Jews have at their disposal to maintain the Orthodox tradition they shared with the rest of the Diaspora? Did they exchange people and ideas with other centers of Jewish life? Did they receive men, ideas, and products that were bearers of innovation? Internally, what was the position of North African Judaism in the global culture of this region?

In the Maghreb, as in the rest of the Muslim world, Jewish communities were equipped to maintain and transmit the religious scholarly tradition. Muslim authorities allowed them, as People of the Book, to practice their religion, to organize their systems of education and social assistance, to maintain their religious buildings and cemeteries, to distribute their prayer books and ritual objects, and, finally, to dispense justice. As a matter of fact, from Morocco to Libya the intellectual leadership of the rabbis remained remarkably powerful in the larger communities; some of the most famous of them were teachers, judges, and authors and, posthumously (if not during their lifetimes) were considered saints who had also worked miracles for their congregants. Such were Isaac ben Sheshet Barfat (Ribach, 1326–1408) and Simon ben Semah Duran (Rachbatz, 1361–1444) of Algiers, or Itshaq Hai Taieb Lo Met (1743–1837) and Yehoshua Bessis (1773–1860) of Tunis, who became recipients of fervent popular respect and the subjects of numerous legends.

Education remained a private affair, with local synagogues housing teachers and rabbis who offered instruction to youngsters in return for a weekly fee paid by the parents. More affluent families could hire teachers to come and teach in their own homes. Adults could also form groups that came together to study the Talmud and the *Zohar*. Yeshivahs, established by private donors, offered teaching designed for literate professionals, future rabbis, judges, tutors, and various officiants. Exclusively organized for the male population, this system was not equally accessible everywhere: schools and teachers were more available in the larger cities, such as Tunis, Algiers, Constantine, Fez, and Rabat, where Jews who were successful in long-distance trade or in business of any sort could support philanthropic activities. Education was also more advanced in places where a tradition of study had already existed for a long time. In 1773, the rabbi-emissary Azoulay, who spent several months in Tunisia, counted 300 learned rabbis among the Jews of the capital.[1] In the middle of the nineteenth century, the traveler J. J. Benjamin found more than 800 trained talmudists in Tunis alone and a high level of literacy among indigenous Jews.[2] The scholarly scriptural tradition remained solidly intact.

Maghrebi Jewish scholars had constant contacts with their counterparts in Europe and the Holy Land. From the latter they received emissaries who brought them books and introduced the halakhic views and practices of Palestine into North Africa. The travelers also shared what they knew about the Haskalah in Europe. The *Shulḥan Arukh* and the Lurianic tradition remained powerful influences on all of North African Jewry throughout the eighteenth and nineteenth centuries, and the contagion and turmoil of the Sabbatian movement was as strong in Morocco and Tunisia as it was in the Near East. Books printed in Italy and even in Poland also reached North Africa.

In turn, some North African Jews traveled abroad. It was not uncommon for pious individuals to settle in Palestine at the end of their lives. Scholars were familiar with the centers of Jewish intellectual life in Europe, and some went to the New World. As early as 1540, a Tunisian-born Jew, Jacob ben Haim, served as a proofreader at Daniel Bombergo's famous Hebrew press in Venice. Jacob bin Aaron Sasportas, born in Oran in 1610, became a rabbi in Tlemcen, then went to Fez and Safi in Morocco, and eventually to Amsterdam. Summoned back to Morocco by the sultan, he was sent on a diplomatic mission. Later, he was a rabbi in London, Hamburg, and Amsterdam and played an active role in the debate against Shabbtai Zevi, a debate that was the subject of one of his numerous works. Moses ben Isaac Ed-Derʿy, born in Morocco in 1774, concluded an unhappy marriage in London, published several books in Amsterdam between 1807 and 1818, then went to Paris, where, like Naggiar soon after, he met the Orientalist scholar Silvestre de Sacy. From Europe he went to Smyrna, Jaffa, and finally Jerusalem, where he died in poverty in 1841.

The first book in Hebrew published in North America was by a Jew from Algiers, Judah Monis. Having studied in Italy, he immigrated to Boston at the beginning of the eighteenth century, converted to Christianity in 1722, and in 1735 published *A Grammar of the Hebrew Tongue, Being an Essay to Bring the Hebrew Grammar into English*. In a later period, the Tripolitan scholar Mordekhai Hakohen, who never traveled outside his native Libya, published articles between 1904 and 1914 in Jewish journals in London, Warsaw, and Palestine. Spread out over several centuries, these examples of geographic mobility and close contacts with other centers of the Diaspora should challenge the idea, all too often expressed, of the closed nature of the Jewish communities of North Africa between the sixteenth and eighteenth centuries, and of the notion that a watershed appeared with the changes in the nineteenth century. Other indications point in the same direction.

In the Maghreb itself, learned Jews, whether they devoted all their time to study or simultaneously practiced a trade or craft, kept busy writing. In the region of southern Morocco alone, including the Tafilalt, far removed from any great urban center, hundreds of manuscripts were left by local scholars from the seventeenth to the nineteenth centuries. They worked in every genre, from the exegesis of the great traditional texts to collections of poetry and historical chronicles of their community. Until the mid-nineteenth century, however, there were no printing presses in North Africa. At the beginning of the sixteenth century, Jews exiled from Portugal had introduced printing in Fez, but their experiment was short-lived. In Tunis, presses were introduced in 1769, with no greater success. Many works therefore remained in manuscript form, as did those of Muslim scholars, and consequently they enjoyed limited distribution. Certain genres lent themselves to oral transmission, such as the poetic compositions of *piyyutim* and *bakkashot* that were regularly performed in the synagogues. Yet from the beginning of the eighteenth century, Jews from Constantine, Algiers, Tunis, and Morocco sent their manuscripts to Livorno—sometimes to Amsterdam—to have them printed.[3] An early work of Samuel of Avila (born in Meknes, Morocco, ca. 1687) was published in Amsterdam in 1725; another, consisting of the collection *The Ten Commandments,* by a Tunisian scholar, was also published in Amsterdam in 1737 (this book was not in Hebrew but in Tunisian Judeo-Arabic). In Livorno, the *Zerah Emet,* by Messaoud Zerbib, a rabbi from Constantine, was published in 1715, followed in 1748 by the *responsa* of the Algiers rabbi Raphael Yedidiah Seror (1681–1737). The first Tunisian work published in Livorno in 1759 was a talmudic commentary by Samuel Al-Adawi of Tunis. Finally, the first Djerbian author, Isaac Haddad, had his notes on the Talmud published in Livorno in 1761, at the behest of his sons. More than a hundred books by Tunisian authors would be published in the next hundred years, mostly works of biblical and talmudic exegesis, commentaries on earlier treatises, and kabbalistic commentaries on the Bible or other canonical texts. Among them we also find juridical consultations, such as the *Mishkenot ha-Roim* of Ouziel Elhaik, an eighteenth-century Tunisian rabbi and judge whose 1,499 *Shehelot u-Tshuvot* were published in 1869.

It is tempting to see this innovation as the sign of a change in the social foundation of literate culture. In this view, learned men who produced books that conformed to the Orthodox tradition could hope for wider distribution and greater didactic efficacy, thanks to printing. That they had recourse to this technology seems also to suggest that they were seeking to reach (and had at their disposal) a public of men who knew how to read, and that they were therefore responding to an increased demand. This, however, is unclear. The texts were not generally composed with a view to publication but for social, pedagogical, or practical purposes. The point was to demonstrate that every generation made its contribution to the scriptural patrimony and ensured its continuity. Often the texts were published after the death of their author, at the behest of his descendants, who simply put together handwritten notes. It seems that such works had very limited printings, as if their distribution were answering mostly a familial need. Their publication must be seen, then, as an act of filial piety. As the anthropologist Shlomo Deshen, who calls this the "ritualization of literacy," was able to observe among the Jews of North Africa who settled in Israel, publishing was a prophylactic act and the book was a prophylactic object that prolonged the memory of the deceased while securing for his descendants the effect of his posthumous *berakhah,* or blessing.

Such works, which made no claim to renew the scriptural tradition, nonetheless contributed to giving North Africa its specific coloration. In a study of the literary culture of Muslim scholars in the same period, I proposed the notion of cultural diglossia, which meant that local scholars, without ever breaking with the classical culture of Islam, developed a vernacular Islam rooted in their own environment. Just as there is, from the linguistic point of view, a classical Arabic shared by all scholars and literate people, and vernacular languages specific to different regions, so Islam as a religious tradition became differentiated into regional schools, proud of their scholars, of their saintly figures, and of their accomplishments. Such schools produced works that did not mean to innovate or even expand classical knowledge. Their purpose was to transmit the message of universal Islam while rooting it in the local environment. Something similar occurred in Jewish culture with the development of a local written tradition connected to the common high tradition. Trained in the general, classical tradition, North African Jewish scholars developed a specific variety, with its own set of references—other local scholars—and its own particular audience to which they aimed their prescriptions, norms, and commentaries. Convinced of the centrality of their own community, they rarely tried to measure themselves against other centers of the Diaspora. In the process, a kind of introversion of the common culture occurred, together with its embeddedness within local settings. Inscribed in the continuity of Orthodox Judaism and unfailingly referring to it, this vernacular Judaism was the product of a local history and cultural environment.

A similar process was at work in other manifestations of religious life, notably with the local variety of mysticism. The two major figures of Jewish mysticism were Shimon bar Yohai and Meier Ba'al Ha-Nes, second-century Palestinian rabbis who were shared as references by all the communities. But their cult in

North Africa was often associated with a third figure, a local male or female saint. The commemoration of the death of the two rabbis on *Lag ba'Omer* coincided with celebrations around the tomb of the native saint. Here again, religion was expressed with reference to common tradition but in a vernacular form.

This was also true of literary creation. Although the genre of piyyut was common to all of Judaism, its concrete form was local. In Morocco, where this poetic form was highly developed between the seventeenth and twentieth centuries, it alternated between Hebrew and Judeo-Arabic within the same passages. There is even a word, *matruz* (braided), to designate this weaving together of two languages.[4] A piyyut collected and published by Haïm Zafrani shows how the Hebrew and Arabic strophes are enmeshed. The first exalts God's greatness in Hebrew, and the poet deplores the straying of his soul; the second sings of "lost loves and separation from the beloved" in Arabic:

> *May the name of God be exalted in the mouths of all living creatures. [Hebrew]*
> *My heart is gone and I have no one to turn to. [Arabic]*
> *My only one did not find for herself a nest of freedom. [Hebrew]*
> *You came closer my soul, but with no strength to carry the burden. [Arabic]*
> *As soon as my heart was hooked, I felt it. [Arabic]*[5]

Each of these expressions also has a third, non-Jewish dimension borrowed from the Arabic and Muslim traditions, or shared with them. A Hebraizing Jew from another region of the Diaspora might have read the couplets in Hebrew without understanding the oral expression. He would understand their biblical, talmudic, or midrashic references and their ritual connotations. The strophes in Arabic, however, would escape him. An Arabophone Muslim from the same country could hear them but not read them, since they were transcribed in Hebrew. He might even hum them, because they followed the metrical form of the Arabic *qaṣīda* or the prosody of Andalusian musical pieces that were equally familiar to the Jews and Muslims of Morocco. He could grasp the hagiographic contents, because these songs celebrated local saints. What would escape him, however, were the specifically biblical and talmudic references.

The Jews spoke the Arabic of the region where they lived, and it was their normal means of communication, but the Livornese Jews also spoke Italian, and in the towns in northern Morocco there were Spanish-speaking Jews. Besides these languages, they spoke Berber in some regions of Morocco and had recourse to it for the peddling trade. They used Spanish in Morocco, Italian and the lingua franca elsewhere for trade with Europe. As for written language, literate Jews learned Hebrew (and some Aramaic) in the course of their religious studies but not Arabic, the written language of all literate Muslims, whether Berberophone or not. These usages drew dividing lines, indeed lines of reciprocal exclusion, between Jews and Muslims. But they do not tell us about the Jews' intellectual horizon or whether it coincided, even partially, with that of the Muslims. If exchanges between Jews and Muslims were confined primarily to technical and economic matters, did this affect their vision of the world, their system of values, their ways of interpreting experience? Evidently yes, where economic ethics were concerned. But where was the boundary drawn between the economic domain and other activities? If only to exercise their professions, the Jews also needed to respect prevailing codes concerning the division of sexual roles, acceptable behavior according to each person's rank and tradition—in short, a whole set of social rules that assume common notions of categorization and thinking. It would therefore be reductive to limit the zones where the representations of Jews and non-Jews overlapped to the economic sphere, as is often done, because economic practice bears on other areas of social life.

It is generally agreed that a zone of culture common to Jews and Muslims existed that was not directly inspired by religion. Folktales, for example: characteristically, among the earliest experiments in the modern use of printing in Tunisia, a café owner named Hai Sarfati had the idea, sometime around 1860, of making several loose-leaf copies in Judeo-Arabic of tales belonging to the corpus of the *Thousand and One Nights* for his clients to read while consuming their coffee. Thus, some of the best-known stories of the Oriental literary patrimony circulated, in Arabic transcribed into Hebrew characters, in the cafés of Tunis. Similarly, evoking the collections of poetic compositions and Andalusian music, Zafrani observes that "we are witness to the same literary creation, the same text, the same discourse, to which both societies brought minor modifications" in order to make them fully compatible with their own religious tradition.[6]

More broadly, the overlapping between Jewish and Muslim cultures even affected ritual practices: those concerning the meals for religious holidays, in particular, beginning with one of the Sabbath meals, and those concerning the marriage rite. These overlappings also affected religious and intellectual activities involving methods and conditions of teaching or the style and content of scriptural production. Wherever we look, Jewish culture, in its regional diversity, was one of the constituent elements and variants of the larger culture of the Maghreb.

RESTRICTED LITERACY, COMMON MEANINGS, SHARED EXPECTATIONS

I have already discussed who was literate and how they acquired this skill within the traditional system. The result was, as in most societies of the period, a restricted literacy, a minimal and oral education for boys, and nothing for girls. Nonetheless, we must question the usual dichotomies of high culture and low; Orthodoxy and practices considered, depending on the instance, to be heretical, superstitious, or popular and folkloristic; the piety of women and the humble and the religious life of the educated elite. A case in point is the seasonal pilgrimage to the tombs of the saints, a widespread practice among all the Jews of the Maghreb. The most visible public manifestations, on the one hand (meals, drink offerings, dances, and songs), and their equally visible kinship with visits to the *mawsim* of the Muslim saints, on the other, cast a veil of suspicion over the orthodoxy of this practice. Let us look at the Jewish communities of Djerba, which reveled in this ritual with a particular intensity.

First, let us consider the place: a synagogue that, until recently, had been isolated in the countryside, at some distance from the village of Hara Sghira, to which it was attached. Why this unusual location? Because it was here, according to local legend, that Jews from Judaea took refuge after the destruction of the Temple, on this strange island (in Arabic, *ghrība*) where they built a village and a synagogue. The Ghrība, according to another legend, was a mysterious young girl (in Arabic, also *ghrība*) who lived alone some distance from the village. One evening, flames surrounded her hut, and in the morning the young girl was found dead but with her features intact. People understood that they were dealing with a saint and built a synagogue on the place where she had lived. The Ghrība, for the Jews of Djerba as well as for those who come to visit or invoke its blessing from afar, is a holy place. It is also a place of annual pilgrimage, which takes place on Lag ba'Omer, 33 days after Passover, between the fourteenth and the eighteenth day of the month of Iyyar (April–May). These two dates correspond, respectively, to the deaths of Meier Ba'al Ha-Nes and Shimon bar Yohai—omnipresent figures, as already mentioned, in North African Judaism.

The rituals begin on the evening of the fourteenth of Iyyar, when the Jews of Hara Sghira come to the synagogue of the Ghrība to commemorate Meier by lighting candles and reciting prayers. On the following day, pilgrims who have come from elsewhere have their turn in the synagogue; they make donations, light candles, then silently make the wishes they have come to express. Under the ark is a niche hollowed out in the ground that marks the place where the body of the mysterious girl was found. Here women place lit candles and eggs, each egg bearing the name of a girl of marriageable age. In the warmth of the candles, the egg hardens. It is brought to the girl who, after eating it, is supposed to find a husband within the year. The pilgrims, continuing their course, leave the synagogue and recite a prayer in memory of their family dead. This is followed by a distribution of dry fruits and brandy to the rabbis, who chant Bar Yohai's hymn. Thus the visit, the course, the prayers, and the gifts respond to the individual and familial demands of the pilgrims. They allow everyone the discreet expression of desires and expectations. They connect the pilgrims with their descendants (through the marriageable maidens) as well as with their deceased elders. And in all these actions they are counting on the intercession of the Ghrība and of Meier. These actions may not obey the norms of the strictest orthodoxy, but the motivation—continuity between the living and the dead—is in no way transgressive.

The *hillula* of Bar Yohai initiates a broader collective celebration. It begins with a long vigil, during which the men of Hara Sghira read passages from the *Zohar* exalting the life of this teacher of mysticism. The night ends with songs dedicated to him. (Indeed, all the texts of this ritual have been collected in Djerba itself in a work published in 1929.) On the following day, Jews from Djerba and the pilgrims gather to prepare for a procession with a huge candelabrum (menorah) that they dress for the occasion. The candelabrum represents, ranked on its different levels, all the symbols of local Jewish identity: the tablets of the law and the *shaddai,* symbol of almighty God; the names of the two rabbis being honored, great biblical figures, and the most famous Tunisian rabbis; and, finally, the 12 tribes of Israel.

The dressing of the candelabrum is auctioned off publicly, marked by lavish distributions of brandy and accompanied by the music of the local orchestra. After every winning bid, squares of silk and chiffon are attached to the candelabrum, sprayed with perfume, and decorated with flowers and various jewels that finally cover the candelabrum entirely until it resembles a bride ready to be led to her husband's house. And the candelabrum, secured to a cart, is actually borne to the village, preceded by musicians and followed by a large procession of men, women, and children, Djerbians and others, between two lines of onlookers who are present en masse for the whole spectacle. At the village, the procession makes a stop at every holy place. Then the candelabrum is brought to the Ghrība, where, divested of all its finery, it is lit with hundreds of candles. The crowd fills the synagogue, mingling men and women, Jews and Muslims, and residents of the island and visitors who exchange drinks and various fruits until nightfall.

The candelabrum represents, ranked on different levels, all the symbols
of local Jewish identity: the tablets of the law and the *shaddai*,
symbol of Almighty God; the names of the two rabbis being honored,
great biblical figures, and the most famous Tunisian rabbis; and finally the
twelve tribes of Israel. (Photo: Keren Tzionah Friedman. © 1980)

Singing the hymn of Bar Yohai, adorning and parading the candelabrum, participating in the procession, displaying one's joy through dance and music—all
of these actions have a meaning that is not easy to decipher in the heat of the festival, and perhaps they do not have the same meaning for all participants. Speaking only of the residents of Djerba, we must remember that they live normally
under the sign of separation. Even while tacitly knowing and respecting the
practices and beliefs of members of the other religious community, Jews and
Muslims live apart. They cannot, for example, eat in each other's homes, because
the Jews are strict followers of the requirements of *kashrut*. They cannot exchange written messages, because Muslims write in Arabic or French whereas

Jews write in Hebrew or transcribe the Arabic language into Hebrew characters. They cannot take spouses from the other community. Each group follows the rituals of its own calendar and frequents its own resorts, and, even in their professional activities, the men choose trades in fields in which other members of their religious and local community already work. Nor do the two Jewish villages of Djerba (Hara Sghira and Hara Kebira, literally the "small" and the "large" Jewish quarters) form a homogeneous community. On the contrary, they live in a competitive relationship. So long as the size of their population allowed it, they had separate rabbinical courts, independent religious schools, and persons entrusted with ritual slaughter and social assistance. The three and a half miles separating them authorized economic and professional relations between the two communities but also allowed each to keep to itself.

In each of the two villages, finally, the world of women was complementary and in solidarity with that of the men but stood in an asymmetrical relationship in which girls and boys were assigned distinct roles and attributes from early childhood. Whereas the boys always received a religious education, learning Hebrew and participating in rituals celebrated at the synagogue, the girls assumed a Jewish identity by default, without reliance on the knowledge of sacred texts, and were confined to the domestic space. Traditionally, a daughter did not leave her father's house except to be led, with her face entirely covered, to the house of her husband.

When the candelabrum is clothed in silk and adorned with jewels, it resembles, as we have seen, the bride being led to her husband. This is why one calls it the *a'rusa*, the bride. Its march toward the various synagogues of Hara Sghira (all masculine spaces) is similar to the course followed by the bride. Its procession, in which men and women mingle in the presence of Muslims, is similar to the wedding procession. What is being celebrated on Lag ba'Omer, then, is a wedding: the union of the feminine principle and the masculine principle in Hara Sghira; the symbolic union of the two Haras; the meeting of Jews and Muslims; and, finally, the meeting of residents of the island and visitors from elsewhere. All the barriers, carefully built and maintained during the year, fall during the festival.

The social significance of this great spectacle covers yet another meaning, this time a religious one, which leads us back to the figure of Bar Yohai, who supposedly received the revelation of the *Zohar*, The Book of Splendor, the fundamental text of kabbalistic mysticism. In a mystic sense, the death of Bar Yohai is called *hillula*, an Aramaic word that means wedding, because the soul of the rabbi is going to join God. In addition, one of the main themes of mysticism is that of the religious experience as a mystic union with the divinity. Beyond the dogmatic knowledge contained in the Torah, beyond the institutional forms of religion, mysticism seeks a direct relationship between the believer and God, living and hidden. And, in the symbolism of the *Zohar,* the community represents the feminine principle that is united with God, the masculine principle. Leading the candelabrum in its bridal costume is therefore leading the community to the meeting with its divine husband. Some deep, secret messages are being passed on, not through written or even verbal expression but through a powerful performance that excludes no one. Not even the worried rabbis, who, while denouncing what seems to them excessive, put a finger on what lies in the very heart of the ritual.

In emphasizing the similarities in the devotional practices of Jews and Muslims around the tombs of their saints, scholars have generally neglected to observe important differences. The popularity of the cult of saints among the Jews was directly related to the diffusion of kabbalistic mysticism. In addition, this was developed in one center, Safed, and by one major figure, Isaac Luria. It does not seem that the cult of the saints in Islam rested on analogous supports. Conversely, the network of *zawiya*s (shrines) constructed around the tombs of the Muslim saints often provided the framework for Islamic brotherhoods: nothing like this is found among the Jews, who had no brotherhood organization and for whom the local community offered the chief framework of religious life. Similarly, though the zawiyas often became places of study, this was not the case for the tombs of Jewish saints. It is also likely that the expansion of Jewish practices of pilgrimage dates from the nineteenth century, contemporary with the greater safety of the highways and greater ease of communication. The cult of the saints and practice of pilgrimages perhaps achieved their fullest flowering when the Judaism of the Maghreb was about to disappear.

The flourishing of poetry and song in Morocco illustrates another aspect of cultural continuity between the learned and ordinary believers. As such, it cannot be read as simply folkloric: both are inseparable from mysticism. Although knowledge of the fundamental texts of mysticism was confined to restricted circles, kabbalistic activity, in its manifestations and modes of expression, involved a much larger public. In 1712, Moses Aben Sur introduced his poetry anthology, *Tsiltsele Shama',* with an argument for singing about God, justifying song and poetry by their "contribution to the sefirotic world and to the restoration of universal harmony." Another illustration of this continuity between learned culture and popular expression is the hymn of Bar Yohai, one of the best-known pieces of music in the communities of the Maghreb. The version that Zafrani presents, collected in the Atlas Mountains in the 1960s, consists of 36 strophes of four verses (*rub'iyya*), each written in Hebrew characters in the local Arab dialect, directly inspired by the *Zohar* but also by the Talmud and midrash. So the themes of esoteric knowledge, like those of the learned tradition, circulated as much among the literate as among the mass of the faithful, who had no access to scriptural knowledge.

The generally established dichotomy between learned culture and popular culture in practical terms excludes the uneducated elements of the communities from the formation or the transmission of Jewish culture, at least as active elements. According to this view, these elements of society were ruled by the prescriptions of Jewish law, guided by their legitimate leaders—rabbis and scholars—and were the docile (or not-so-docile) executors of norms pronounced by those leaders and of the rituals prescribed by tradition. At best they are said to practice Judaism in a form that is often considered to be corrupted by ignorance and responsible for making religion sink into superstition.

The examples presented above indicate that, through songs and poetry, ordinary believers rephrased the knowledge of the sages in their own way. They did it in a space beyond the synagogue and the study house: in the mixed and public space of festivals and gatherings or the mixed space of the family. Through pilgrimage, procession, and vigil at the tomb of a devout figure, they recast in yet another way the expectations of the literate elite, while sharing them. And they did more: they performed the censored, repressed, unavowed aspects of those expectations. They made visible what the mystic scholars whispered in an esoteric tongue.

In fact, the actions and modes of intervention of these ordinary believers have a broader scope. Let us consider, and swiftly reject, the Sartrean thesis (which Spinoza had formulated differently before him): these agents reproduced Jewish identity because the non-Jewish Other designated them as such; it is the contempt of others that made Jews Jews. The Muslims, who sweepingly stigmatized certain lowly occupations (those of peddler, singer and musician, dancer, tinsmith and blacksmith, pawnbroker) and the individuals who exercised them, ordered Jews to behave like Jews. Thus, one was a Jew by default, ready to escape if historical and political conditions changed. In this view, when the practices of segregation and exclusion disappeared, this identity would also disintegrate: this happened in Europe, and especially in France. Indeed, Jews are no longer peddlers or pawnbrokers. Yet they remain Jews, nonetheless, in their new roles. In what respect?

Those faithful deprived of scriptural knowledge played a more active role than has been recognized. They inculcated norms, values, and practices. Through the vernacular means of gestures and management of the body, they exercised a didactic function in their own way. They also translated religious prescriptions into practices. They performed the time-bound rites of the day, of the week, and materialized the prescriptions relating to ritual purity. This role of executor, which is readily acknowledged by the champions of high culture, might be formulated as a tautology: "practicing Jews practice Judaism." But the uneducated also confirmed the validity of dogma by turning its usage into a living language learned without formal means, like a mother tongue. Without this, religion would become a dead letter. The women of North Africa never had access to written religious knowledge—except for abridgments in Spanish written for the use of women in a few communities of northern Morocco. They never read Leviticus or the Book of Genesis, and at best they might have heard these translated into Arabic in the synagogues. But generation after generation they respected and transmitted the laws of kashrut. Generation after generation they based the organization of family time and all their activities on the distinction between weekdays and days of rest. In this way, women contributed to the construction of Jewish social identity and to the differentiation between Jews and non-Jews. As Joëlle Bahloul showed in a seminal study, the dietary and culinary practices of the Algerian Jews involved not only perpetuating biblical commandments but also elaborating a logic of social and cultural differentiation that guaranteed the specific place held by Jews among the other elements of society.[7] By making a distinction between foods meant for feast days and those for ordinary days, differentiating menus according to moments of the Hebrew calendar and making distinctions in modes of hospitality, it was the world around them that they arranged and, hence, relations between Jews and the surrounding society.

Perhaps they also preserved the most archaic elements in each of the local traditions. This has been observed elsewhere. Sidney Mintz, when he studied the use of sweets, for example, noted that holiday meals are the refuge of lapsed practices: think of the elaborate confection of wedding or birthday cakes, which pick up practices invented in the Middle Ages.[8] In the eastern part of North Africa, two practices were current in all the Jewish communities. The first was the preparation and consumption of a couscous for the Friday night dinner. In other words, the Sabbath was welcomed by this specifically North African dish, common to Jews and Muslims. Their attachment to traditional Judaism, then, was expressed through an attachment to a deeply Maghrebian tradition. The second practice, however—the slow preparation for the Saturday meal of an exclusively Jewish dish, the *tfina*—brought together two series of basic symbols. First, agricultural symbols: different grains and vegetables were combined with meats to form a complete dish, a summation of the earliest domestication of nature, as if the Sabbath meal preserved the archaeological trace of times past. And second, eminently Jewish symbols: the ingredients included not just kosher meat but beef as well, the pinnacle of the hierarchy of licit animals, and especially the foot of the ox, as if the meal must illustrate and concretize the commandments of Leviticus. To distinguish beef and to devalue lamb, when the majority Muslim population preferred the latter, was also to state difference and affirm identity and otherness in terms of taste.

In this game of distinction between self and others, by these practices that constructed difference and maintained identity, ordinary Jews contrived to stamp the culture of their community with its particular style. In the Diaspora, Judaism is diverse. Continuing reference to the same stock of texts, maintenance of rabbinical authority, and respect for the holy history suspended since the destruction of the Temple do not, as we know, preclude the infinitely diverse ways of living a Jewish life. The greater or lesser degree of fervor, the particular form taken by expressions of faith, were not the result of a more or less rigid adherence to orthodoxy but of a relationship of both neighborliness and oppression, cooperation and exclusion, cohabitation and extended competition with the dominant Muslim majority.

Having established continuity and interdependence between elements too readily viewed as opposed and hierarchical, I would like to venture one more observation on the position of Jews in the overall culture of North Africa. The assumption that Jews, wherever they lived, were not only the borrowers of cultural features from the larger society but also participants in the shaping of the more comprehensive regional (or national) culture has become a widely accepted postulate. Yet though it would be easy to see how such an active contribution operates today in some parts of the Diaspora (particularly in the United States), it might be more difficult to grasp how it was possible in the past, in other places. The notion of "cultural symbiosis" has been extensively used to designate elements shared by Jews and Muslims. Expressions of it have been found, as we have seen above, in several aspects of musical or poetic production. We might go one step further in this respect, with a few simple observations. The stigmatization in Muslim society of performing arts such as dancing, singing, and playing musical instruments left these activities to inferior, outsider groups, namely blacks and Jews. We may assume that, because of this division of labor, it was such debased groups that forged, sustained, and renewed the musical tradition. Similarly, certain crafts were specifically, if not exclusively, Jewish, such as jewelry making. Although Jewish jewelers obviously adjusted their products to the resources and tastes of their Muslim patrons, it may be assumed that they had their say technically and aesthetically and that North African jewelry embodied the imagination, desire, and taste of these craftsmen even as they responded to the expectations of their customers. All of this evidence supports the assumption that the Jews made a specific contribution to the culture of their region that was not dictated by their religious membership but by the interstices reserved for them in the larger social fabric.

MODERN MUTATIONS

In the nineteenth century, internal changes in the sociopolitical systems of the Maghreb, like the changes imposed by the West European countries, posed a double challenge for the Jews. First, an intellectual and spiritual challenge. Knowledge and technologies independent of religion were at last within reach. A secular knowledge was offered to the Jews that opened doors and expanded their horizon. As in other regions of the Diaspora, Jews in Muslim countries had maintained the traditional hierarchies, placing religious knowledge above knowledge borrowed from the majority society. In Islamic societies, rabbis, like their Muslim counterparts, the *'ulama*, enjoyed religious, moral, and intellectual authority as teachers, judges, and religious leaders. To a certain extent, rabbis also exercised some form of political authority within the limits of their local community, defining and sanctioning what was licit or illicit, acceptable or not, and in some cases mobilizing their congregation for public action. The hierarchy was reversed, or at least shaken, when the West introduced new areas of knowledge, new technologies, and new values and when eminent members of the Jewish community started to promote secularization of teaching and of economic, intellectual, professional, and other practices. The traditional religious leadership was unable to mount an effective opposition, except in rare cases such as Djerba.

Likewise, this process posed a social challenge. Jews adopted practices that broke barriers and changed the conditions that regulated social relations between them and non-Jews, as well as among themselves (relations between men and women, for example, with women slowly gaining access to instruction and nondomestic space). Similar modifications took place between the learned religious and educated lay people, who were increasingly valued for their secular knowledge. A good Jewish mother, recounts a Tunisian Jew educated between the world wars, already dreamed of her son becoming a doctor rather than a rabbi. In Tunis in the 1930s, three of the four presidents of the Bar were Jews; in the society of medical sciences, eight of the twenty presidents were Jews. They were following a movement begun by the Algerian Jews, and the Jews of Morocco would follow the Tunisians.

At this point we should inquire into the relations between Jewish history and

culture and the other sociopolitical forces at play. Were Jewish history and culture simply a reduced version of those of the majority culture (in our case, Muslim)? Or did they mirror the dominant culture (French, in the colonial context,
for Morocco, Algeria, and Tunisia; Italian for Libya)? We know the end of the
story: only a few thousand Jews remain in Tunisia and Morocco today, and none
in Algeria and Libya. It would be tempting—and it has become a trend in the nationalist narrative of postcolonial North Africa—to see the history of the Jews
in this region as merely a development of colonial history and to see their near-
disappearance as part of the complete eradication of colonial society. Yet such a
view would be largely misleading and requires further debate. One may assume
that the Jewish experience in the age of European empires, though different (and
in many respects diverging) from the experience of the native Muslims, remained quite specific. The differences concern the conditions and nature of the
Jewish experience, the opportunities offered to Jews and the barriers that channeled their course and redirected their choices.

The social conditions of Jews in the pre-modern Middle East and North
Africa have been aptly summarized by Harvey Goldberg:

> The place of the Jews may be seen as a function of a specific religious world
> view, assigning them a position which limited their access to certain roles and
> resources and prescribed public behaviors marking those limitations. At the
> same time, this religious principle was congruent with and reinforced general
> features of traditional societies. Islamic countries, like pre-modern Europe,
> placed groups, defined by some rule-of-birth or other ascriptive principle, into
> slots in the social order and assumed the fixity of social and cultural bounda-
> ries separating the members of those groups.[9]

He adds, "The clear lines separating segments of society were an aspect of
traditionality but, at the same time, allowed elements of 'modernity' to operate,"
insisting then on the role played by Jewish merchants engaged in broad international trade in this opening to modernity. Actually, what made possible the advent of modern ways or principles varied according to place and period. It is
difficult to accept without amendment Norman A. Stillman's assertion:

> Oriental Jewry's confrontation with modernity was a direct result of the im-
> pact of an ascendant Europe upon the economic, political and cultural life of
> the Islamic world from the end of the eighteenth century onward. The increas-
> ing European encroachments upon, and eventual hegemony over, most Mus-
> lim societies were generally welcomed by the native Jewish and Christian

minorities, whereas they were deeply resented and frequently opposed by most of the majority population.[10]

This assertion calls for two major objections—which the author anticipates in the course of his analysis. The first bears on the idea of the direct effect of European pressure. For the impact of Europe to be felt in the cultural and intellectual domain required local mediators and internalization by local agents, and it could not have imposed itself as directly as Stillman asserts. The second objection bears on the dichotomy established between members of the majority and minority populations, the first being uniformly characterized by their hostility to the European presence. If the majority society indeed "resented" and "opposed" the political and economic domination of the European powers, they did so, as early as the beginning of the twentieth century, with the means and in the name of principles borrowed from European political culture. However, they put up no resistance to adopting—when they had the means to do it—the language and cultural forms introduced by the colonial regimes, from the novel to the theater, cabaret songs, and film, to mention only the products of popular culture. Similarly in the domain of education: members of the colonized society did not refuse to attend the secular French school, it was simply not open to them. At the end of the colonial regime in Algeria, most men and women were illiterate. The acculturation of Jews and Muslims was therefore not synchronic and was, for both, highly differentiated.

In Tunisia in the eighteenth and the beginning of the nineteenth centuries, the innovators and mediators were first the Livornese Jews of Tunis, who took part in the great European and Mediterranean trade and were in close contact with the Jewish communities of Livorno and Italy in general. Through them, germs of innovation penetrated and challenged tradition. By the 1770s, we see some of them being won over by freemasonry (and denounced as heretics by their coreligionists). A few years later, sensitive to the political culture of the French Revolution, which made Jews equal citizens along with other members of society, they displayed the tricolor rosette when Livorno, along with all of Tuscany, became part of the Napoleonic empire. Some time later they abandoned their distinctive dress, clothing themselves like Europeans to assert their social status and bourgeois values. Similarly in Morocco, between the first half of the eighteenth century and the end of the nineteenth, Jewish merchants from the port of Essaouira borrowed elements of their material culture from the British, with whom they had active economic relations, though their intellectual culture remained embedded in their tradition.

In the nineteenth century, these mediations were joined by changes introduced in the political system that authorized a redistribution of roles between different religious segments of society and a redefinition of relations between groups. Simultaneously, the local economic and political elite, Jews included, were exposed to European consuls and their circles, as well as to European merchants and businessmen, and were thus introduced to new ways of life—from their furniture and dress to activities like piano playing and opera singing. The French writer Chateaubriand could not help expressing his disappointment when he visited Tunis in 1807: the city looked more like a provincial French town than the Oriental capital he expected to find.

Soon, however, institutional changes that further modified the social and legal position of the Jews were not spontaneously introduced by local rulers but were imposed by foreign powers competing for dominance in each of the regions of the Muslim Mediterranean. It would be wrong, however, to see in these changes merely the expression of a relationship forced by and favorable to the European powers, with local authorities impotently ceding to external injunctions. The local society, or at least important elements of its elite, was profoundly engaged in intense reflection on the necessity and nature of reforms. The Tunisian historian Ben Dhiyaf brings us invaluable testimony on this point. He was one of the redactors of the first Tunisian constitution in 1861. As is well known, the constitution was imposed on the monarchy by the emissaries of France and England. But Ben Dhiyaf fully considered the implications of this institutional change and threw himself body and soul into the enterprise. To an observer astonished at his zeal, he replied that, for him, it was like a new religion.

As noted above, the Fundamental Pact of 1857, then the constitution of 1861, affirmed the judicial equality of all subjects, regardless of religion. These documents therefore put an end to the regime of the *dhimmā,* which, as in all of Islam, imposed discriminatory and humbling measures on the Jews. In the same reform movement, an Upper Council was established, some of whose members were named by the Bey and the rest drawn from among the prominent citizens of the country by the first councillors named. Yet despite the supposed equality of all subjects, no prominent Jew figured in the first council. We do not know if the Jews expressed their disappointment, or if they inspired Ben Dhiyaf to address a written question to the council—of which he was a member:

> We ask the Upper Council why it has not chosen any Jews during the last recruitment of this assembly. Are the Jews not part of this realm? Is there no one among them whose human worth is perfect? Is there no one among them who, from the temporal point of view, occupies a distinguished rank, is there no single one among them who counts among the elite? . . . How shall we not admit

them as servants of a realm to which they belong, participating in its advantages as well as its inconveniences, by the same right as Muslims?[11]

Ben Dhiyaf's request received a negative response. This example illustrates, nonetheless, that progressive changes were produced in the local political culture before the establishment of the colonial regime; the currents of reform were ready to revise the rules governing the rights of minorities and relations between them and the Muslim majority. Acquainted with the attempts at reform introduced at the center of the Ottoman Empire and inspired by it, equally acquainted with the new political thought in Europe (especially in France), the reformists sincerely sought to ameliorate the functioning of their own institutions. The problem of compatibility between modern law and the religious bases of the *sharia* (Islamic law) was inevitable. But a learned man like Ben Dhiyaf confronted it openly, as did the other liberal intellectuals of his day, and far from a religious clinging to the letter of past principles, he was determined to demonstrate that the spirit of these principles was more fully realized in the modern law. Similarly, we should not ignore the attraction, indeed the fascination, that Europe exercised over the elite governing Algeria and Tunisia. From the 1830s onward, the reformist beys of Tunisia were directly inspired by European models to modernize their army and their administration. When Algiers was conquered by France, the Dey found refuge for several years in Livorno before departing for Egypt. And this was true, later on, for the Bey of Constantine. The minister Kheireddine went to Europe to repair a damaged Tunisian career and subsequently returned to Istanbul, where he was once again prime minister. And General Hussein, who had given an unfavorable answer to Ben Dhiyaf's question to the council, spent the last years of his life in Livorno. Jews attracted by the West were not alone, then, in thinking that the Promised Land was now Europe rather than Palestine.

We must place the Jews' eager welcome of all aspects of modernity in this context. Not only was the center of gravity of existence displaced from a religious to a secular framework, but a whole set of distinct yet simultaneous social changes took place, including diversification of activities, greater social and geographical mobility, a renewal and secularization of the educational system, greater participation in social and extra-community life, greater freedom from the traditional constraints of community life, and a voluntary Westernization of social practices. The majority Muslim society would experience these changes in turn, sooner and more pervasively for urban dwellers, more slowly for the rural regions or those far from centers of decision making; sooner for men, with more difficulty for women. The rural exodus, urbanization, the immigration of Algerian workers to France at the time of World War I, and service in the French army accelerated entry into modernity—willing or not—for certain segments of the majority population.

Without reviewing the history of these changes, let us single out those, at least, that affected Jewish culture and specifically the social conditions of its production and transmission, the institutional vectors and agents of change. Each of these vectors had a different social basis. Each appeared at a different date and was of different duration, but they exercised cumulative and, for some Maghrebian Jews, irreversible effects. Beginning in the 1830s, the most effective and powerful agent of acculturation was the school: because of what it taught; because of what it demoted (traditional teaching dispensed in Jewish schools); but also because secular education offered access to new knowledge, to unforeseen professional activities, and to positions favorable to more continuous contact with non-Jews. The intellectual horizon was profoundly modified but so were the values of educated Jews, their expectations, and their conception of relations between men and women, Jews and non-Jews, people and God.

In Algeria, Jewish schools teaching in French were opened in the major towns in 1832. From 1870 onward, Jewish girls and boys were in principle admitted to public education, because they had become French citizens under the Crémieux Decree of that year. The school system underwent major growth starting in 1881, when primary education became obligatory and free.

On a reduced scale, missionary schools opened by groups of Protestants and Catholics were the first agents of acculturation through an apprenticeship in European languages and secular disciplines in the other countries of the Maghreb. Later on, a number of French Jews, having experienced emancipation themselves, became active in extending their model to Jewish communities in the Ottoman Empire and in the Arab world. Assuming that their "Oriental" brethren were living in abject conditions of subjugation and ignorance, they aimed to spread enlightenment and extend "the benefits which had been bestowed upon them just two or three generations earlier."[12] A regeneration of the Jews was at stake, by which Oriental Jews would be technically and intellectually prepared for modern times. Western gods were thus shaping Oriental man in their own image.

Based in Paris, the Alliance Israélite Universelle proposed a modern curriculum in French, following the French model, which was implemented in 1862 in Morocco, 1866 in Libya, and 1878 in Tunisia. The paradox, however, often emphasized by historians of the period, is that the regeneration planned by French Jews did not contribute to a better integration of Oriental Jews into the larger society. Instead, it deepened the divisions and competition between them and their Muslim neighbors.[13] Yet the impact of the Alliance schools should not be overstated. Until World War II, only 15,000 children were educated in Alliance schools in Tunisia and Morocco, a small proportion of the school-age population. In Tunisia, the French public system was more open to the Jews than in Morocco, and it soon offered free education to the children of families who could pay for the minimal equipment required. The Alliance network of schools became the refuge of children from the poorest Arabophone neighborhoods, whereas those who could afford them preferred the French middle schools and high schools as a safer avenue for social mobility, by way of access to further studies and hence to the liberal professions. The French high school also provided a space of meeting and confrontation with non-Jewish students, and it opened the way to participation in public life. Evoking his school days between the world wars, the writer and journalist Jean Daniel writes these lines, which his contemporaries might have endorsed:

> In this little town in French Algeria where I was born, whose average intellectual level was nothing compared to any of the communities of what was then called the metropolis, in this "College colonial de Blida" there were not only one or two or five adolescents but dozens of them who were awakened, and with great ardor, to all forms of cultural curiosity and political struggle.[14]

Another expression of the process of acculturation was the flourishing of Jewish printing activity. The first presses were started in Algeria, first in Algiers (1853) and three years later in Oran. They published works in Hebrew and in Judeo-Arabic. Also worth mentioning is the sustained work of Joseph Ghenassia, of the Constantine community, who published between the 1920s and the 1950s translations into Judeo-Arabic of almost all the religious classics. The readership of his work, however, remained rather limited. Starting at the end of the nineteenth century, the workshops in Algeria also published newspapers and generally ephemeral weeklies in Algiers, as well as in Oran and Constantine. The first of this type was *Adziri: Jurnal bilyahud wa-bilfransis* (The Algerian: Journal in Jewish and French), published by Nessim Benisti. In Tunisia, Hebrew printing developed after the establishment of the protectorate, first in Tunis, then in Djerba, and, to a lesser extent, in Soussa. The first Hebrew printing press in Morocco was set up in 1891 in Tangiers, and Libya had its first press in Tripoli in 1917.

The print shops in Tunis did not attempt to produce scholarly books, which could be procured by other means, but cheap books meant for ordinary members of the congregation. These were prayer books, *haggadot* presenting the translation of the Hebrew text into the Arabic vernacular, and other works required for the principal religious rituals. Loose-leaf, single-page summaries of the calendar of holidays and their accompanying ritual and dietary prescriptions were published for popular consumption, as were prophylactic notices meant to be attached to the door of a birthing room to avert the evil eye from a newborn. Tunisian presses also printed texts that, while meant for an exclusively Jewish public, were not directly religious: newspapers in Judeo-Arabic, to which we shall return below, and secular texts that indicate the emergence of a nonreligious written literature alongside the oral tradition. The very first book produced in Tunis in 1862 was a Judeo-Arabic text of the constitution, the *Qanun al-Dawla al-Tunisiya*, published so that Jews might be better informed of the institutional innovations that granted them new rights. The second work produced in Tunis was a collection of tales in Judeo-Arabic. Informed of what European Jews were publishing, and receiving their books in Hebrew, the Tunisian printers also translated some of these works, at once absorbing and reflecting echoes of the Haskalah and Hasidism. Responding to their initial exposure to Western secular literature, they translated popular novels such as Alexandre Dumas's *The Count of Monte Cristo*, Eugène Sue's *Les Mystères de Paris*, and Daniel Defoe's *Robinson Crusoe*.

The Hebrew presses of Djerba, which started in 1903, were based on another model—less open to secular culture, more anchored in Orthodox and regional tradition. But it is all the more remarkable that this activity arose in a community of modest size (fewer than 5,000 inhabitants at its height, just after World War II) and at such a distance from the great currents of economic and cultural exchange. The Djerba printers published books by Moroccan and Algerian rabbis. They filled orders from southern Tunisian, Libyan, and Algerian communities, with whom relations were close and constant. Altogether, however, this was still only a regional market. It is unlikely that these books reached other parts of the Diaspora, especially as they contained passages in Judeo-Arabic accessible only to Arabophone readers and described specific holiday rituals that were exclusive to the Djerbian communities and their satellites.

Recent research has taken inventory of the abundant production printed in Hebrew and Judeo-Arabic. These works have not yet been evaluated for their literary quality, and, if some have been recently reissued, it is because of their documentary interest. To this day we have not discovered any overlooked masterpiece, and perhaps there is none. But the breadth of this outpouring still deserves special mention and analysis. For Tunisia, there are nearly 1,500 titles in Judeo-Arabic alone, an indication of the effervescent intellectual activity of literate Jews as well as a strong local demand. Above all this number marks a major innovation that is reminiscent of the change of status that the Yiddish language

underwent in Europe around the same period. The publication of books in
Judeo-Arabic bears witness to the promotion of local dialects to the rank of
written language, capable of translating aspects of the liturgy but also adapted to
a fictional literature and the communication of news in the press. This movement, however, had no counterpart in the majority Muslim population, whose
elites, attached to classical Arabic, never resolved to promote the local dialects
into national languages. The literary flowering of Judeo-Arabic lasted a little less
than a century, from 1860 to the mid-twentieth century. The turn of the century
saw its fullest burgeoning. After World War I, only the perseverance of Makhlouf
Nadjar, in Soussa, allowed popular literature in Judeo-Arabic to continue to
meet the demands of Arabophone Jews. French, in fact, became dominant in
oral and especially in written communication, which demoted writings in Arabic. It was in French that young Jews would launch the first information dailies,
in order to address themselves to a public who were the products of French and
secular schools, and it was in French that the first novelists would begin to measure themselves against non-Jewish writers.

Until that point, Jewish writers had used Hebrew, in conformity with tradition. When they wrote in Hebrew, they could in principle share their thoughts
and their knowledge with other Jews of the Diaspora. These literate circles were
no doubt a restricted elite, but they devoted much of their time to study, and
they read works meant to last. Writing in Hebrew meant communicating with a
timeless audience that spread over potentially the whole space of the Diaspora.
It meant initiating a dialogue with writers of the past, whom the author would
never have known except through their works, as well as with present and future
readers equally unknown. Writing in Judeo-Arabic belongs to an entirely different strategy. The educated man was now addressing himself to secular readers,
who perhaps read little and then with difficulty, and who in any case did not devote all their leisure time to reading. Yet these were individuals whom the author
might know and identify. By introducing Judeo-Arabic as a written language,
the educated class enlarged its audience, most of which was Arabophone, and
anchored the local Jewish culture more firmly in its surroundings. Unlike the
learned Italian Jews, who since the Renaissance had written in Italian to address
non-Jews, the Maghrebian authors remained within their own milieu. They cultivated an increasingly local—hence increasingly fragile—form of Jewish culture. In the 1920s, shifting to French, they entered for the first time into an
intellectual space that was shared by other French-speakers, whatever their religious affiliation. For the first time, they addressed readers who were in principle undifferentiated from the religious or ethnic point of view. (Interestingly
enough, during the same period authors from Muslim circles launched them-

selves into literature and theater in both Arabic and French.) Their public was nonetheless ranked in a social and cultural hierarchy: to write in French was to turn one's back on the Arabophone populace and demote indigenous expressions of written culture.

We should not, however, underestimate the importance of low-priced works published in Judeo-Arabic for Jews belonging to circles only weakly influenced by the French or educated in traditional rabbinical schools. From fieldwork conducted in the 1990s by Yosef Tobi among Jews from Tunisia who settled in Israel, it appears that books in Judeo-Arabic were present in many homes, a sign that, when the émigrés gathered the few things they could carry away with them, such books were among their most prized possessions. Tobi was also able to verify that the owners of these books read them often. "These owners," he writes, "were not necessarily highly educated people, one counted among them 'simple folk' as well. I am able to testify to the very wide distribution of this literature and to the refusal of the books' owners to part with them."[15]

Another vehicle for cultural change was the development of newspapers, which corresponded to the tentative opening of a public space. Under the colonial regime, freedom of expression and association were intermittent and political activity closely watched. But this close surveillance could not prevent the proliferation of an increasingly diversified press. The growth of the Jewish press was part of this movement and expresses, as it does for the majority population, a powerful process of acculturation and secularization. In Tunisia, more than 120 newspapers and periodicals were published between 1878 and 1961 in Judeo-Arabic, Hebrew, and French. The Jewish press was at its height between 1880 and World War I. These newspapers were sometimes political and informative, sometimes cultural or humorous, and often short-lived. At least one of them, however, had great staying power and reached a broader audience: the weekly *El Nedjma* (The Star), founded in Soussa in 1920 by Leon Tubiana and Makhlouf Nadjar. This paper was distributed throughout North Africa and continued until 1961.

The titles of these newspapers alone convey the republican and egalitarian political values their founders borrowed from the contemporary French press: *El Huriya* (Liberty), *El Estaoua* (whose subtitle in French was *L'Egalité*), *La Fraternité*, and *L'Aurore*, no doubt inspired by the French daily that had published Zola's famous "*J'accuse*" letter during the Dreyfus Affair. All of these newspapers were published before World War I. But readers had already begun to shift to the French-language newspapers. Their greater staying power testifies to the existence of a stable public and currents of divergent opinion: the traditionalist *L'Egalité* (1911–34) took a stance against *La Justice* (1907–35), in which Mardochée Smadja called for the extension of French jurisdiction to the Tunisian Jews and the suppression of the rabbinical court. There were also Zionist newspapers (such as *Le Reveil juif,* 1924–32, allied with the revisionist movement of Jabotinsky, *La voix des juifs,* and *L'Echo juif*). In a third period, Jews came to own general newspapers addressed to the entire Francophone reading public. These were signs of a more direct entry into the public space shared with non-Jews. The most popular were *Le Petit Matin* and *La Presse.* From the 1920s until 1956, there was a socialist evening paper, *Tunis socialiste,* founded by Dr. Albert Cattan, among whose regular contributors were Dr. Cohen Hadria and Serge Moati. The latter launched Montmartre-style revues and managed a movie house before devoting himself full time to journalism. Of course, Jewish readers did not restrict themselves to the local Jewish press. They passionately followed the newspapers and magazines published in France that expressed the most varied currents of political life, though especially those that espoused secular and antiracist views. The Italian Jews, in turn, were tempted for a time by the fascist-inspired press.

Acculturation and modernization were not restricted to the inspiration of Western models. With the help of radio and records, the musical fashions of the Middle East, especially from Egypt, modified indigenous tastes and practices. Between the wars, Jewish musicians not only played privately (for family and religious celebrations) but also were featured for the first time in public places (theaters and café-concerts) alongside Muslim musicians. The names Saliha and Ali Riahi now appeared on the same bill with the Jewish singer Raoul Journo in Tunisia, and Reinette l'Oranaise appeared with Fadila Dziri in Algeria.

Dependence on the colonial metropolis, however, meant that the cultivated bourgeois of North Africa awaited theater and opera troupes, orchestras, and books primarily from Paris, and they soon expected records and current films as well—especially from America. Jews not only became promoters of these media but also took an active part in the formation of local amateur troupes. Again, these activities promoted encounters with non-Jews. One such cultural society in Tunisia was l'Essor, in which Jews provided the majority of the actors, the audience, and the speakers. Typically, at one of the lecture-debates organized by l'Essor in the 1930s, the militant Zionist Elie Louzoun was followed at the rostrum by a young Tunisian lawyer, Habib Bourguiba, who was already the leader of the chief nationalist party and would become the first president of the Tunisian Republic in 1957.

CHANGES IN THE POLITICAL CULTURE

One of the most decisive changes was access to a new political culture in a context marked, first of all, by the imposition of colonial regimes in the region, then by the emergence of nationalism in each of the countries of the Maghreb and the

Arab world and of Jewish nationalism in the form of Zionism, and finally by the collapse of the colonial systems after World War II.

The political culture of the Jews in the traditional context combined the messianic expectation of a future that promised their liberation with, for the present, an apolitical stance that was assumed as much out of caution as because of their condition as protected subjects of the Muslim sovereigns. Furthermore, tradition had enjoined them since the talmudic period that *dina de-malkhutah dinah* (the law of the kingdom is the law), and therefore they had to respect the law of the state that sheltered them. Involvement in the political sphere was reduced to the minimum, except for the few prominent Jews who took part in financial administration, in Tunisia and Morocco, or those who were coopted for diplomatic missions in Morocco. The Libyan Jewish community under the Turkish regime, which lasted until 1912, was viewed as a single political entity. The community was jointly responsible for the regular payment of taxes, and its leader, the sheikh, for the assessment and collection of these taxes. This sheikh was usually a member of the communal elite appointed by the local governor. He was the representative of the community in external affairs, its main political broker embodying the institutional mechanism that linked it to the wider society and to the central authority. Most noteworthy in this system is that, despite the numerous changes Libya underwent, the status and the role of the sheikh in the small communities remained practically unchanged after the shift from the Ottoman regime to the Italian colonial administration and then to English military rule. Moreover, this description applies equally to the Muslim population, whose sheikhs were chosen among the prominent families (*a'yan*) of each community and served as political brokers between their people and the representative of the central government. This description is also valid for other parts of the Maghreb, where communal affairs were overseen by a council formed by members of the learned and commercial elites, whereas the *nagid* (or *moqaddem,* local Jewish community leaders) provided the link between the community and the local or central authorities.

The elite combined material wealth with an opening onto the world beyond the community, both the Muslim world of the political authorities and the non-Muslim world of international commerce. Within the boundaries of the community, the linkage between this tight circle of the elite and the poorer elements of the Jewish population was accomplished through relations of patronage, through philanthropic support of communal institutions, and through the authority granted the elite by their wealth, by the role they played as mediators in conflicts within the community, and, when possible, by their religious merit and their attachment to local values. As secular leaders, they were nonetheless expected to protect the representatives of religion and to defend their values and teachings. Beyond the communal boundaries, these prominent men formed the main link between the government and the Jewish population. In this framework, ordinary Jews had no political claims. Under normal circumstances, there were no conflicts of interest with the Muslims and the local system. Jews developed only defensive tactics to avoid trouble and reduce the risk of excessive taxation or other arbitrary exactions. Individually, they might engage in a patron-client relationship with a Muslim—if circumstances or their professional activity made it necessary. It was a matter of honor for the patron to protect and defend his client, because Jews could not bear arms, ride horses, or take part in any violent action. The Jewish client was thus, in this respect, in a position similar to that of Muslim women, whose safety and honor were the responsibility of their menfolk.

By the mid-nineteenth century, the reforms introduced by local authorities, without erasing the boundaries that separated Jews and Muslims, at least allowed openings favorable to the Jews. As already mentioned, such reforms provided Jews with new opportunities in Libya and Tunisia and gave them quasi-equal status with Muslims. They could abandon the stigmatizing symbols associated with their status as dhimmī, such as special clothing and headgear. They could acquire real estate. There were Jewish representatives appointed (and salaried) to the new courts. However, not all changes were welcomed by the Jews; for example, they were not eager to accept military conscription in Libya. And not all the changes were welcomed by the Muslim population. Traditionally, Muslims wore red caps, Jews black or dark ones. When the reforms abolished the restrictive regulations in Libya and Tunisia, Jews were prompt to trade their dark caps for red *chechias,* so that they could not be distinguished from Muslims. But Muslims reacted violently in several places in both countries, tearing the head-coverings off the Jews who frequented the markets and displayed themselves publicly in their new garb.

In Morocco, members of the elite facilitated the action of European Jewish organizations, and they were the first to support the institutional reforms introduced under foreign influence. As a matter of fact, support for Western ideas and the exhibition of more material manifestations of foreign culture (clothing, furnishing, culinary habits) became symbols of power for the Jewish elite and strategic tools to enhance their social and political position. By the end of the nineteenth century, it was obviously the colonial regime that put Jews (and Muslims) in direct contact with the principles of republican and democratic culture. Not that this culture was applied in the colonies and protectorates, but it was constantly held up as a horizon to be reached. Moreover, in spite of the close control to which the regime subjected the colonized population, it could not prevent the emergence of a public space, a place where convergent or contradictory aspirations could be expressed, negotiated, and debated. Through the institutional and economic changes it introduced, the colonial regime itself produced a decompartmentalizing of the society and opened places for socializing independent of religious differences, whether these were schools, outdoor cafés, theaters, or athletic clubs. These new spaces, once again, did not erase the old partitions between religious communities, but they opened breaches in the walls. And within each religious community, they permitted a certain freeing of individuals from the constraints of their group and their religion. These changes were produced as the colonial authorities changed the institutional framework of the Jewish communities, weakening the rabbinical leadership by depriving it of some of its features and functions.

As for the Jews, one reason for their adherence to the principles of the political culture of democratic and republican France was their integration into the French political community through citizenship. Actually, bestowal of French nationality or citizenship varied widely from country to country. A policy of complete political assimilation of the Jews was imposed in Algeria with the promulgation in 1870 of the Crémieux Decree, which granted French citizenship to all of them. This policy ultimately resulted in divorcing the aspirations and status of the Jews from those of the Muslims. But the antisemitism of the colonial population, which took particularly virulent forms during the Dreyfus Affair in 1896–98, and the Vichy legislation in the 1940s reminded the Jews of Algeria that they had not become entirely French and subsequently influenced their political positions.

The Jews of Algeria, then, were not able to undergo, with due allowance for time lag, the same process of secularization and integration into French society as did the Jews of France. French society in its colonial manifestation had specific features: "provincial" in its manner, it depended on the home country for intellectual innovation and always took its social and cultural models from Paris. Above all, imbued with a sense of superiority over the colonized population by virtue of their situation and jealously protective of the advantages that this relationship gave them, the French of Algeria were often racists (toward Muslims) and antisemites, which forced the Jews into strategies of defense and withdrawal. Nonetheless, when North African Jews had access to the same modes of social evasion as the Jews of France, like them they adopted the universalist values of the Enlightenment and became those "Republic's madmen" described by Pierre Birnbaum. He observed that, with the separation of church and state, which authorized minority access to the highest ranks of public administration solely on the basis of diplomas and merit, the Jews of France devoted themselves entirely to their duty in the civil service and cultivated a true religion of the homeland. The Jews of Algeria were not admitted into the high ranks of the colonial administration, but their entrance into the polity with the Crémieux Decree and their experience in the army and the state schools made them, too, religious adherents to a similar cult; taking up arms and spilling one's blood became the ultimate proof of one's patriotic attachment to the homeland.

One episode is particularly illuminating in this respect: the reaction of the Algerian Jews to the anti-Jewish policy of the Vichy regime and to the American landings in North Africa during World War II. These years of crisis and action deserve attention, for they crystallize within a relatively short period many elements that characterized the political culture in the colonial situation. As we know, the promulgation of racist laws in the autumn of 1940 by the regime of Marshal Philippe Pétain was not imposed by the occupying Germans. And this was even truer for their extension to North Africa, which was still under the control of France without any interference on the part of the Germans. In Algeria, the promulgation of the statutes of October 1940 came along with the abolition of the Crémieux Decree. From one day to the next, Algerian Jews lost the French citizenship that had automatically been theirs since 1870, and they fell to the rank of French subjects like the rest of the indigenous population. In June 1941, a second statute aggravated the earlier legislation. Jews were dismissed from the civil service (2,169 of the 2,638 civil servants lost their jobs) and from the fields of journalism, radio, theater, and cinema. A *numerus clausus* reduced their presence in the medical profession to 2 percent, and the same applied to lawyers, architects, midwives, and dentists. Similarly, a quota system reduced the number of Jewish students to 14 percent in secondary education, and to 3 percent in higher education. Finally, the Aryanization of businesses threatened to deprive the majority of Jews of their livelihood. This policy as a whole was not simply the result of applying to Algeria measures that had been taken in France. It was a response to the repeated demands of antisemitic elements in the colonial population of European origin, elements that had been organized in the 1930s and found conditions under the Vichy regime favorable to their interests. The colonial administration, on its side, fully adhered to Pétain's program of national revolution, one of whose effects was the creation of a French Legion of combatants and a Service d'ordre legionnaire, the French equivalent of the Nazi S.S. Jews were not only excluded from these groups but became their targets, because the legionnaires regarded it as their task to fight against "democracy, Gaullist dissidents, and against the Jewish scourge."[16]

Not surprisingly, under such dramatic circumstances Jews became the most important component of French resistance in Algeria. When the Allies decided that American forces would land on the Algerian shore, they had to rely on the Jews to prevent armed opposition from the French local authorities. In fact, the only heroic action that took place to support the landing of the American forces on November 8, 1942, was mainly the work of young men who belonged to the elite of Jewish society in Algiers. The main leaders of the resistance were Jewish, as well as most of the 377 conspirators who took an active part in the fall of Algiers by paralyzing French forces loyal to Pétain. They soon fell victim to the ambiguous position of the American government, whose main concern was to use the North African coast as a base to open a second front against the Germans. Robert Murphy, then adviser to General Dwight Eisenhower and in charge of the whole operation, engaged in negotiations with Admiral Jean Darlan and the local representatives of the Vichy government. After Darlan's assassination, many of the Jewish fighters were arrested, imprisoned, or deported to the south of the country.

This episode is rich in lessons about the culture of the Jewish elite, two features of which are particularly salient. First of all, the young men's action was motivated chiefly by the abolition of the Crémieux Decree. They suffered most from having been excluded from the French political community. They aspired primarily to reestablish their citizenship. This question was at the center of the protests they addressed to the Vichy government, as it was in the approaches they made toward the Americans. They obtained satisfaction only in October 1943, nearly a year after the Allied landing, when General Charles de Gaulle finally succeeded in ousting Henri Giraud, whom the Americans supported and who was opposed to the reestablishment of the Crémieux Decree.

Second, their action was characterized by patriotism driven to extremes precisely because it was denied by their Pétainist and antisemitic adversaries. They desired to recover their rights as citizens in order to do their duty as citizens, meaning in this case to fight on the European front against the Axis forces. To give their life for the homeland would demonstrate that they were really French. They displayed no feeling for their European coreligionists, whose fate, it is true, was not yet known in its full horror. After the crisis, Algerian Jews (like those in France) hastened to impute Algeria's antisemitic policy to the Germans, and to the illegitimate Vichy regime, in order to be reconciled with the French community in the broadest sense. They kept intact their faith in a political culture that was republican, secular, and universalist, although it had no application in colonial Algeria. Having directly suffered a racist policy did not make them more sensitive to the analogous suffering of the Muslim population or to the aspirations expressed by the nationalist groups. They showed only a tepid sympathy when the Algerians suffered a merciless repression on the very day when the war ended in Europe on May 8, 1945. Only a few of them, finally shaken by the humiliation they had suffered, would be engaged by the Zionist project. So patriotic faith, the cult of France and the republic, triumphed among the Jews of Algeria over solidarity with the European Jews and over any possible solidarity with the Algerian Muslims.

The policy of Jewish political assimilation was carried out even more reluctantly in Tunisia than it had been in Algeria. It is estimated that only 15 percent of Tunisian Jews acquired French nationality beginning in 1923. But without demanding or obtaining the status of French citizens, Tunisian Jews nonetheless clung to a culture that would free them from the old constraints and equip them for new activities. As in Algeria, the antisemitism of the colonial population and the press that was openly expressed at the end of the 1930s made the Jews the most ardent defenders of universalist values. Adherence to those values was not just a feature of the intelligentsia; its echo could be heard even in modest circles. Nor was it exclusive to the Jews. In the three countries controlled by France, those Muslims who had attended French schools and universities had acquired the same principles. Both groups retained the lessons of their secular schooling, and both shared the ideology of the Enlightenment, of secular and republican values as a model for living together.

But, in the end, their paths diverged, especially those that led to nationalism, with its religious component, whether wanted or not. Nationalism in the Maghreb, as in the rest of the Arab world, naturally included Muslims but in practice almost no Jews. The first delegation to the Tunisian nationalist party congress in Paris, in 1919, did include an Arabic-speaking Jewish lawyer, Elie Zerah, but he could not attract anyone else like him and did not stay in the movement. The Jews judged the Destour movement from the outside, sometimes with suspicion, sometimes with respect. They more easily participated in local sections of the French parties of the left, at first radical or socialist. In Tunisia, during the period of the Popular Front in France, the rise of antisemitism in the late 1930s mobilized an increasing number of young Jews into trade unionism, socialism, and finally communism. These activists were employees, mostly intellectuals and bourgeois, to whom communism promised more universalism than the Enlightenment, a messianic ideology, and perhaps a sense of community and belonging that was a substitute for the Jewish community. In the end, the Jews who rallied around nationalism formed but a tiny minority and had little influence on their peers. Zionism made its appearance as an ideology at the beginning of the century but became a political movement only between the world wars, when the authorities of the protectorate authorized the creation of a Zionist

Federation in 1920. This led to the development of a Zionist press, youth movements, and the teaching of Hebrew, clearing the way for an action that World War II and the events in Palestine would amplify. And it was finally in Tunisia that the Zionist movement became most developed.

French policy toward the Jews was still more reserved in Morocco, where the protectorate meant to leave indigenous institutions intact and tried not to alienate the Muslim population by granting the Jews a distinct status. They simply could not acquire French nationality so long as they remained in Moroccan territory. The colonial regime, moreover, was of shorter duration here, and hence there was less French influence through the schools and other means of acculturation. The fascination with French culture was a powerful force, but for many fewer people. As for an appeal to Jewish nationalism, Zionism could only encounter the hostility of the Muslims. The first Zionist group in Essaouira was founded *even before* the institution of the protectorate, in 1900, in response not to Arab or Moroccan nationalism but to European political Zionism, which seemed compatible with the internal reform that had begun in local Jewish society.

HYPHENATED IDENTITIES

Under precolonial and colonial conditions, the entrance into modernity of each of the countries of the Maghreb was not, finally, synonymous with the entrance of the Jews into global society. This society remained partitioned according to the old cleavages. Hence, despite the Westernization and progressive acculturation of North African Jews, the process of individualization developed only with difficulty. Traditional culture, whether Jewish or Muslim, did not leave much space for individual affirmation. As for the Jews in particular, the name assigned at birth, which ought to constitute the singularity of the individual, in fact inscribed him or her in a community and separated him or her from the surrounding society. It also inscribed the person in a temporal continuity that referred to both the Hebrew patrimony and the family genealogy. A newborn was therefore straightaway someone reborn. Similarly, the inculcation of practices and roles offered the individual the possibility of excelling in conformity with the proposed models, not of distinguishing himself or herself from them. Nonconformity was at once a transgression and an outrage; it meant exposure to hostility if not sanction.

Since the emergence of literary fiction among the Jews of the Maghreb, the genre of autobiographical fiction has flourished, especially since the 1950s. This might have signaled the emergence and affirmation of the "I," access to autonomy by the individual who dares to speak in his or her own name. The truth is that, from the first novels of Albert Memmi (born in Tunisia in 1920) to those of Albert Bensoussan (born in Algeria in 1935) and of Marcel Benabou (born in Morocco in 1939), "I" speaks of "we." The novel of the singular individual is in fact the family and ethnic novel, always a novel of collective identity. It is simultaneously the novel of an always riven identity: Jew *and* Arab, French *and* Maghrebian, secular *and* Jewish, an identity hyphenate, which may be the mark of modernity but is nonetheless fully inscribed in the continuity of Jewish culture in North Africa. Turning this into a joke, *Gagou,* an autobiographical novel by Guy Sitbon, ends with the following dialogue:

Albert Memmi.
(Photo: L. Hoffman.
Reprinted with permission)

"Let's be clear: are you Jewish or Arab?"
"Both."
"Half and half?"
"No, both, fully."
"And when they fight each other, what side are you on?"
"On the wailing side."[17]

CONCLUSION

In David Biale's chapter in the present volume, he reminds us that "several rabbinic midrashim . . . claimed that the biblical Israelites survived exile in Egypt because they did not change their names, speech, or clothing," and because they did not intermarry and did not collaborate with the gentile government. In the twentieth century, North African Jews, including members of the less Westernized strata, changed their names by widely adopting Western first names. Yet in the second, hidden position, they most often maintained a biblical name or local one, or both. Even the Western first names were selected to mark the Jews' distinction from their Christian or French neighbors—hence their predilection, for a time, for Slavic or Germanic names, and later for American names made popular by the movies. The abandonment of recognizably Jewish first names or their relegation to a second position thus attenuated the visibility of the Jews but

did not signal a renunciation of their identity. They also changed languages, losing the use of Hebrew as the language of written expression, losing Arabic as the
language of spoken communication, and preferring French as the vernacular
and the language of high culture in ever greater numbers. And yet, they pronounced French with their own accent, and they subjected it to serious recasting
that made it unrecognizable to non-Jews. Writers such as Roland Bacri from Algeria and Katia Rubenstein from Tunisia tried to immortalize their distinctive
speech in their work, thus fixing the trace of a speech that at once marked a
boundary between themselves and the non-Jews and created the conditions of
an intense and immediate communication between Jews themselves.

Did the Jews of North Africa abandon religious endogamy? In great numbers,
no. But for men who took wives from among the Christians, the patrilineal principle was so strong that it never put in question the Jewish identity of the children born of such "mixed" marriages. Wrote Jean Daniel: "So confident, too
confident perhaps, of his Jewish faith to believe that anything could ever damage
his descendants, my father paid no special attention to my brothers' marriages to
women who were not born into his religion."[18]

Finally, did they involve themselves in politics? Actively, not many did. But as
in other Arab and Muslim countries, the members of religious minorities—
in our case, the Jews—did espouse secular and universalist ideologies more
readily than the Muslim majority. Jews were represented in greater numbers,
proportionally, than Muslims in secular social movements; they were more often
tempted by cultural and political cosmopolitanism than by nationalism.

If we extend the statements of the rabbinic midrashim, we also note that Jews
escaped from the ghettos, wherever they existed and whenever they could, in
order to invest in newly built neighborhoods, encouraging the introduction of
the latest and most fashionable architectural forms. Their impact is still visible
in the urbanism of the great cities like Tunis or Casablanca, where the Jews made
up about a fourth of the population in the interwar period. Social exclusion had
permitted self-segregation and provided Jewish communities with a territorial
base. Having moved out of the ghettos, Jews continued to group together voluntarily in neighborhoods where they formed the majority, in order to stay near
their families, to benefit from the services necessary to fulfill religious obligations, or to conform to colonial conditions that de facto, if not by law, assigned a
specific space to each of the national and religious components of the society.
When it came to an involvement in sports or the formation of theater troupes,
the choice of vacation resorts or cafés, innovation and the adoption of new fashions were done with tacit respect for the old confessional cleavages.

Even in private, domestic space, more protected from outside influences, the modifications introduced were modulated by the inherited practices of religious tradition. Until their departure from the Maghreb, thousands of Jews lived in utter destitution. The memoirs they have published, as well as the medical and sociological investigations conducted at the time, agree on the great material distress of vast segments of the communities, in disadvantaged regions as well as in the big cities.

Albert Memmi recalls that

Our real kingdom, where we lived and died, was the world of tuberculosis, which permanently affected three quarters of the population, of typhoid, which every summer, like some monster out of the Apocalypse, carried off beautiful young people who only the week before had been playing, laughing, and shouting on the beaches . . . of gastroenteritis, of intestinal fevers, which gathered to the divine bosom half the year's nursing infants, scarcely emerged from the maternal womb.[19]

We must not lose sight of these facts, for if Westernization and modernization did indeed take place, they hardly affected the Jewish masses—or the greater part of the Muslim population. But in bourgeois homes, Western fashions and tastes prevailed. By reading fashion magazines, traveling, or observing the practices of the French of North Africa, one learned the aesthetic conventions of one's class and hurried to adopt them. Art nouveau, art deco, and even the audacious furniture of the Bauhaus style successively invaded the apartments of the Jews. The bride's trousseau, the household goods with which the new couple was equipped, were chosen according to the norms of the Western bourgeoisie. But this did not dictate their use. Fine china and linens would still be reserved for the celebration of the Sabbath and religious holidays. The Westernization of daily life in no way implied the attenuation of religious practices: on the contrary, it made them more splendid.

In this general movement, which affected the style of the Jewish table and way of life as well as the uses of time and space, colonial society opened escape hatches in communal and confessional barriers without altogether destroying them. In turn, even as they were living through all these changes, the Jews of North Africa sustained subtle strategies to differentiate themselves from non-Jews, continuing to maintain a distinct identity and reproducing it. They would renew these strategies of reproduction and differentiation once they had immigrated to France, with means adapted to their new condition.

NOTES

1. "Le rabbin Azoulay à Tunis, 1773," in Robert Attal and Claude Sitbon, *Regards sur les Juifs de Tunisie* (Paris, 1979), 31–37.

2. J. J. Benjamin, *Eight Years in Asia and Africa* (Hanover, N.H., 1859).

3. Robert Attal, "Littérature hébraïque tunisienne," in Attal and Sitbon, *Les Juifs de Tunisie*, 197–202.

4. See Joseph Chétrit, "Shlomo Gozlan: Un poète bilingue de Tamgrût dans le Drâa," in Michel Abitbol, ed., *Communautés juives des marges sahariennes du Maghreb* (Jerusalem, 1982), 427–52, and Haïm Zafrani, *Littératures dialectales et populaires juives en Occident musulman* (Paris, 1980).

5. Zafrani, *Littératures dialectales*, 246.

6. Ibid., xviii.

7. Joëlle Bahloul, *Le culte de la Table dressée: traditions de la table juive algérienne* (Paris, 1983).

8. Sidney W. Mintz, *Sweetness and Power: The Place of Sugar in Modern History* (New York, 1985).

9. Harvey E. Goldberg, ed., *Sephardi and Middle East Jewries: History and Culture in the Modern Era* (Bloomington, Ind., 1996), 3.

10. Norman A. Stillman, "Middle Eastern and North African Jewries Confront Modernity: Orientation, Disorientation, Reorientation," in Goldberg, ed., *Sephardi and Middle East Jewries*, 60.

11. L. Bercher, "En marge du Pacte 'fondamental': Un document inédit," *Revue tunisienne* (1939): 67–86.

12. Goldberg, ed., *Sephardi and Middle East Jewries*, 14.

13. Ibid., 15.

14. Jean Daniel, *Le Temps qui reste* (Paris, 1973), 12.

15. Yosef Tobi, "The Flowering of Judeo-Arabic Literature in North Africa, 1850–1950," in Goldberg, ed., *Sephardi and Middle East Jewries*, 213–25.

16. Michel Abitol, *The Jews of North Africa During the Second World War* (Detroit, 1989), 53.

17. Guy Sitbon, *Gagou* (Paris, 1980).

18. Jean Daniel, *Le Refuge et la source* (Paris, 1977).

19. Albert Memmi, *Ce que je crois* and *Le juif et l'autre* (Paris, 1995), 54.

SELECTED BIBLIOGRAPHY

Les Juifs d'Algérie: Images et textes. Paris, 1987.
Les Juifs de Tunisie: Images et textes. Paris, 1989.

Abitbol, Michel. *The Jews of North Africa during the Second World War.* Detroit, 1989.

———. *Le passé d'une discorde: Juifs et Arabes du VIIe siècle à nos jours.* Paris, 1999.

———, ed. *Communautés juives des marges sahariennes du Maghreb.* Jerusalem, 1982.

Allouche-Benayoun, Joëlle, and Doris Bensimon. *Juifs d'Algérie hier et aujourd'hui: Mémoires et identités.* Toulouse, 1989.

Anski, Michel. *Les Juifs d'Algérie du decret Crémieux à la Libération.* Paris, 1950.

Appelfeld, Aharon. *"What Is Jewish in Jewish Literature."* The Max and Irene Levy Memorial Lecture, Harvard University Library, Cambridge, Mass., 1993.

Assaraf, Robert, and Michel Abitbol, eds. *Perception et réalités au Maroc: Relations judéo-musulmanes.* Paris, 1998.

Attal, Robert. "Les missions protestantes anglicanes en Afrique du Nord et leurs publications en judéo-arabe à l'intention des juifs." *Revue des études juives* 132 (Jan.–June 1973): 95–118.

———. *Regards sur les Juifs d'Algérie.* Paris, 1996.

Attal, Robert, and Joseph Avivi. *Registres matrimoniaux de la communauté juive portugaise de Tunisie aux XVIIIe et XIXe siècles.* Jerusalem, 1989.

Attal, Robert, and Claude Sitbon. *Regards sur les Juifs de Tunisie.* Paris, 1979.

Avrahami, Itshaq. *Pinhas ha-Kehilah ha-Yehudit ha-Portugezit be-Tunis (1710–1944).* Lod, 1997.

Ayoun, Richard, and Bernard Cohen. *Les Juifs d'Algérie: Deux mille ans d'histoire.* Paris, 1982.

Bacri, Roland. *Le Beau temps perdu: Bab-el-Oued retrouvé.* Paris, 1978.

Bahloul, Joëlle. *Le culte de la Table dressée: traditions de la table juive algérienne.* Paris, 1983.

Bar-Asher, Shalom. "The Jews of North America and the Land of Israel in the XVIII and XIX Centuries: The Reversal in Attitude Toward *Aliyah*." In Lawrence A. Hoffman, ed., *The Land of Israel: Jewish Perspectives.* South Bend, Ind., 1986.

Benabou, Marcel. *Jacob, Menahem and Mimouni: A Family Epic.* Lincoln, Neb., 1998.

———. *Why I Have Not Written Any of My Books.* Lincoln, Neb., 1996.

Benjamin, J. J. *Eight Years in Asia and Africa.* Hanover, N.H., 1859.

Bercher, L. "En marge du Pacte 'fondamental.' Un document inédit." *Revue tunisienne* (1939): 67–86.

Birnbaum, Pierre. *Les Fous de la République: Histoire politique des Juifs d'Etat de Gambetta à Vichy.* Paris, 1992.

Chatelain, Yves. *La Vie littéraire et intellectuelle en Tunisie de 1900 à 1937.* Paris, 1937.

Chérif, Mohamed-Hédi. "Ben Dhiâf et les Juifs tunisiens." *Confluences Méditerranée,* no. 10 (Spring 1994): 89–96.

Chétrit, Joseph. "National-Hebrew Modernity Against French Modernity: The Hebrew Haskalah in North Africa at the End of the Nineteenth Century" (Hebrew). *Miqqedem Umiyyam* 3 (1990): 11–76.

———. *Piyut ve-Shirah be-Yahadut Maroko.* Tel Aviv, 1992.

———. "Shlomo Gozlan: Un poète bilingue de Tamgrût dans le Drâa." In Abitbol, ed., *Communautés juives*, 427–52.

———. *Ha-Shirah ha-'Arvit-Yehudit Shebi-khetav bi-Tzefon-Afrikah*. Jerusalem, 1994.

Chouraqui, André. *Marche vers l'Occident: Les Juifs d'Afrique du Nord*. Paris, 1952.

Cohen-Hadria, Elie. *Du Protectorat à Indépendence tunisienne: Souvenirs d'un témoin socialiste*.

Daniel, Jean. *Le Refuge et la source*. Paris, 1977.

———. *Le Temps qui reste*. Paris, 1973.

De Felice, Renzo. *Jews in an Arab Land: Libya, 1835–1970*. Austin, Tex., 1985.

Deshen, Shlomo. *The Mellah Society: Jewish Community Life in Sharifian Morocco*. Chicago, 1989.

———. "The Work of Tunisian Scholars in Israel." *American Ethnologist* 2 (1975): 251–59.

Goldberg, Harvey E. *The Book of Mordechai: A Study of the Jews of Libya*. Philadelphia, 1980.

———. *Cave Dwellers and Citrus Growers: A Jewish Community in Libya and Israel*. Cambridge, Engl., 1972.

———. *Jewish Life in Muslim Libya: Rivals and Relatives*. Chicago, 1990.

———. "Ottoman Rule in Tripoli as Viewed by the History of Mordechai Hakohen." In Miége, J. L., ed., *Les relations entre juifs et musulmans en Afrique du Nord, XIXe-XXe siècles, actes du colloque international de l'Institut d'histoire des pays d'Outre-mer*. Paris, 1980.

———. "The Zohar in Southern Morocco: A Study in the Ethnography of Texts." *History of Religions* 29 (1990): 233–58.

———, ed. *Sephardi and Middle East Jewries: History and Culture in the Modern Era*. Bloomington, Ind., 1996.

Hazan, Ephraim. "Rabi Musa Bujnah Paytan of South Libyan Jewry." In Abitbol, ed., *Communautés juives*, 453–68.

Hirschberg, H. Z. *History of the Jews in North Africa*. 2 vols. Leiden, 1974.

Jowett, William. *Christian Researchers in Syria and the Holy Land in 1823 & 1825 . . . , with an Appendix Containing the Journal of Mr Joseph Greaves on a Visit to the Regence of Tunis*. Boston, 1826.

Kenbib, Mohammed. *Juifs et musulmans au Maroc, 1859–1948*. Rabat, 1994.

Laskier, Michael M. *The Alliance Israélite Universelle and the Jewish Communities of Morocco, 1862–1962*. Albany, N.Y., 1983.

———. *North African Jewry in the Twentieth Century: The Jews of Morocco, Tunisia and Algeria*. New York, 1994.

Memmi, Albert. *Ce que je crois*. Paris, 1995.

———. *Le juif et l'autre*. Paris, 1995.

Miège, Jean-Louis, ed. *Les relations entre juifs et musulmans en Afrique du Nord, XIXe–XXe siècles*. Paris, 1980.

Mintz, Sidney W. *Sweetness and Power: The Place of Sugar in Modern History*. New York, 1985.

Romanelli, Samuel. *Travail in an Arab Land*. Trans. and ed. Yedida K. Stillman and Norman A. Stillman. Tuscaloosa, Ala., 1989.

Rubenstein, Katia. *Mémoire illettrée*. Paris, 1979.

Schroeter, Daniel J. *Merchants of Essaouira: Urban Society and Imperialism in Southwestern Morocco, 1844–1886*. Cambridge, Engl., 1988.

Schroeter, Daniel J., and Joseph Chetrit. "The Transformation of the Jewish Community of Essaouira (Mogador) in the Nineteenth and Twentieth Centuries." In Goldberg, ed., *Sephardi and Middle East Jewries*, 99–116.

Schwarzfuchs, Simon. *Les juifs algériens et la France*. Jerusalem, 1981.

Sebag, Paul. *Histoire des Juifs de Tunisie des origines à nos jours*. Paris, 1991.

Simon, Rachel. *Change Within Tradition Among Jewish Women in Libya*. Seattle, 1992.

Sitbon, Gui. *Gagou*. Paris, 1980.

Stillman, Norman A. *The Jews of Arab Lands: A History and Source Book*. Philadelphia, 1979.

———. *The Language and Culture of the Jews of Sefrou, Morocco: An Ethnolinguistic Study*. Manchester, 1988.

———. "Middle Eastern and North African Jewries Confront Modernity: Orientation, Disorientation, Reorientation." In Goldberg, ed., *Sephardi and Middle East Jewries*, 59–72.

Taïeb, Jacques. *Etre juif au Maghreb à la veille de la colonisation*. Paris, 1994.

Tobi, Yosef. "The Flowering of Judeo-Arabic Literature in North Africa, 1850–1950." In Goldberg, ed., *Sephardi and Middle East Jewries*, 213–25.

Tsur, Yaron. "Haskala in a Sectional Colonial Society: Mahdia (Tunisia) 1884." in Goldberg, ed., *Sephardi and Middle East Jewries*, 146–67.

Udovitch, Abraham L., and Lucette Valensi. *The Last Arab Jews: The Communities of Jerba, Tunisia*. Photographs by Jacques Pérez. London, 1984.

Valensi, Lucette. "Espaces publics, espaces communautaires aux XIXe et XXe siècles." *Confluences Méditerranée*, no. 10 (Spring 1994): 97–110.

Valensi, Lucette, and Nathan Wachtel. *Jewish Memories*. Berkeley, 1991.

Zafrani, Haïm. *Ethique et Mystique: Judaïsme en terre d'Islam*. Paris, 1991.

———. *Les Juifs du Maroc: Vie sociale, économique et religieuse. Etude de "Taqqanot" et "Responsa."* Paris, 1972.

———. *Littératures dialectales et populaires juives en Occident musulman*. Paris, 1980.

———. *Pédagogie juive en terre d'Islam: L'enseignement traditionnel de l'hébreu et du judaïsme au Maroc*. Paris, 1969.

———. *Poésie juive en Occident musulman*. Paris, 1977.

Jewish woman from Habban with typical hairdo, makeup, hair net, and jewelry, c. 1950.
(The Israel Museum, Jerusalem)

CHALLENGES TO TRADITION:

Jewish Cultures in Yemen, Iraq, Iran,

Afghanistan, and Bukhara

YOSEF TOBI

In the 1860s, the Alliance Israélite Universelle began its activity among the Jewish communities in the countries of the Middle East (Yemen, Iraq, and Iran) with the establishment of modern schools, thus opening a new cultural era in their history. The endeavor was generally welcomed by the communities themselves, which, since the Middle Ages, had been open to ideas from the "secular" culture of the surrounding Muslim society. But the reaction of religious leaders was more negative, especially when they realized that the purpose of the Alliance did not match the requirements of the accepted Jewish tradition in those communities. Rabbi Joseph Ḥayyim (1834–1909) was the foremost religious leader of Iraqi Jewry in the mid-nineteenth century. His legal *responsas* showed a remarkable readiness for halakhic adaptation to the modernizing innovations of his age.[1] However, he resisted the Alliance schools when he realized that reinforcement of religious life was not their primary concern. When a representative of the Alliance sought authorization to open a technical school for girls, Ḥayyim published a "ban" jointly with all the rabbis of the community forbidding its members to send their children to the Alliance schools. In Persia the rabbis responded similarly, but this occurred only at the end of the century, by which time many children had already been educated at these schools.[2] The ambivalence of the Middle Eastern communities to modernist trends, and in a different context to the new Zionist idea of Theodor Herzl and his followers, with its goal of migration to the Land of Israel, characterizes these communities throughout the modern period. This ambivalence was also apparent later to the State of Israel. The immediate response was positive and, to some degree, even enthusiastic. Disappointment set in, however, after these Jews concluded that modernity

My thanks to Murray Rosovsky at the University of Haifa, who translated this from the Hebrew.—Y.T.

and Zionism were not to be attained in conformity with the Jewish religious tradition. Before engaging in a detailed perusal of the culture of the Middle Eastern Jews in the modern age, let us consider the factors that shaped it prior to its entry into that age.

THE FORMATION OF THE COMMUNAL CENTERS OF MIDDLE EASTERN JEWRY

At the height of the Middle Ages, Jewish culture had two main branches: the Babylonian branch, led by the exilarchs and the *geonim* (heads) of the yeshivot who resided in Baghdad, the capital of the Abbasid caliphate; and the branch led by the heads of the yeshivah in Palestine. These two centers engaged in a fierce struggle, with regard to issues of prayer and law and to the collection of funds for the yeshivot. Signs of this conflict were clearly evident in the communities of Egypt, North Africa, and Yemen, as these were under the common influence of both centers. During the twelfth century, the Babylonian center seemed to gain the upper hand in respect to liturgy and halakhah. Its influence became consolidated not only in the lands of the Middle East but also in Palestine itself, in Egypt, in North Africa, in Spain, and even in the Jewish communities of southern Europe and Germany. But in all these countries, most notably Spain, Italy, and Germany, independent cultural centers arose as the Jews shed their obligations to the Babylonian or the Palestinian centers, and as they submitted to some degree to the influences of the surrounding culture. The direct link to the Jewish culture that had formed in gaonic times was preserved only in the countries of the Middle East.

However, as the institutions of the exilarchate and the *geonim* weakened, the power of the Babylonian center could not be maintained in the Middle Eastern countries. This decline had already begun by the end of the twelfth century, when the Jewish center in Egypt was consolidated under the leadership of Moses Maimonides, who was not an adherent of the geonim of Babylonia. He was succeeded during the thirteenth century by his son, Rabbi Abraham Maimuni, and his grandson, Rabbi David Ha-Nagid. Maimonides' writings, especially his halakhic code *Ha-Yad Ha-Ḥazakah* (or *Mishneh Torah*), whose like no Babylonian *gaon* could match, steadily eliminated the need to consult the works of the geonim. True, Maimonides' teachings were not readily accepted in the communities of the Middle East, as is attested by the polemical exchanges between him and the Jews of Yemen and Babylonia, conducted by the head of the Baghdad yeshivah, Samuel ben Ali. In time Maimonides' teachings overtook those of the geonim, although the latter did not disappear entirely, remaining evident principally in the liturgy.

The Maimonidean legacy itself came under pressure during the sixteenth century, when a great Jewish center arose in Safed after the expulsion of the Jews from Spain in 1492. The Spanish sages were dispersed among the Jewish communities of the Mediterranean basin, especially in North Africa, Egypt, Palestine, and Syria. Wherever they went, these exiles utterly transformed Jewish society, demographically and culturally. Even where they did not settle, their influence was enormous. The center at Safed, though small in population, was, for over a hundred years and especially in the second half of the sixteenth century, the most important spiritual hub of Jewry. After first settling elsewhere, many of the exiled rabbis of Spain, or their sons, eventually arrived in Jerusalem or Safed. In the mighty struggle for leadership that ensued between these two centers, the rabbis of Safed triumphed. It was here, in Palestine, that the deep feeling welled up that the hour of redemption had come, precisely in the aftermath of the great crisis. This was sensed not only by the "visionaries," the kabbalists, but also by the halakhists (legal authorities), whose feet were planted firmly on the ground. Rabbi Jacob Berav, the greatest of the halakhists in the generation following the Spanish exile, sought to reinstitute the rabbinic ordination (*semikha*) that had lapsed in the fifth century as the most significant step toward the realization of the messianic idea. No rabbi had dared to contemplate such an act since the cessation of semikha. Berav's ambition was not realized, but this did nothing to undermine the special status of Safed and its sages in the eyes of the Jewish communities generally, and particularly those that were nearby.

The Safed center embraced a vast number of scholars, who wrought a revolution in almost every domain of Jewish spiritual creation: liturgy, poetry, biblical exegesis, halakhah, and, above all, Kabbalah, from the school of Rabbi Moses Cordovero and Rabbi Isaac Luria (the Ari). The *Shulḥan Arukh* of Rabbi Joseph Karo became the accepted halakhic code of the Jews of the Middle East, the *piyyutim* (liturgical poems) of Rabbi Israel Najjārah spread rapidly among them, and their own writers of piyyutim adopted his literary method. Cordovero's kabbalistic composition *Pardes Rimmonim* (The Pomegranate Orchard) and Luria's Kabbalah, presented through the writings of his colleague and pupil Rabbi Ḥayyim Vital, became an inseparable part of the spiritual tradition of the Middle Eastern Jews. The liturgy, too, which had retained many remnants of the gaonic tradition, especially from the *siddur* (prayer book) of Saadiah Gaon, was likewise entirely altered, as a result of the siddurim produced by Jewish printers in Italy according to the liturgy formulated in Safed following Luria's teaching. The absolute submission of the Middle Eastern communities to the Safed doctrine resulted principally from spiritual weakness and the decline in the numbers of local scholars, especially in the Persian-speaking communities. Safed's influence was further strengthened by the Shaddarut, a fund-raising agency established in Safed in the second half of the sixteenth century for the dispatch of emissaries. These agents traveled annually to the Middle Eastern communities to collect contributions for the support of the center in Safed; in the process they also disseminated the teachings of this center. The influence of Safed was also extended by the invention of printing. The works of Karo and of Najjārah were printed during their lifetimes and distributed in commercial quantities among the Middle Eastern communities, where they replaced the works of the geonim and of Maimonides, which survived only in a limited number of manuscript copies.

The last historical event shared by all the Middle Eastern Jewish communities, one that sent a violent tremor through most of them, was the Sabbatian eruption in the 1660s. The movement led by Shabbtai Zevi, a native of Izmir, was all-embracing, the most powerful messianic movement in Jewish history. In the end, the heights of hope were equaled by the depths of disappointment. The longed-for "messiah" did not accomplish his goal; what is more, he even converted to Islam, to the bewilderment of his followers. This grave spiritual and social crisis plunged the Middle Eastern Jewish communities into a long period of confrontation between the old and the new, or, more accurately, into a process of eventual adaptation to the new.

The most important spiritual center of the Middle Eastern communities before and during the Middle Ages was the one in Baghdad. This center bore the relics of its ancient glory as late as the fourteenth century, as emerges from the comprehensive *dīwān* (collection of poems) of Aharon Ḥakīmān, an important poet whose work constitutes the main, if not the exclusive, source for the Babylonian communities of his day.[3] During the fifteenth century, however, the community almost totally disappeared. Only following the Ottoman conquest in the sixteenth century was there something of a revival, when ties with the Safed spiritual center were developed. Nevertheless, Baghdad only regained cultural importance after 1774, when Rabbi Ṣedaqah Ḥūṣīn was called there from Aleppo by the heads of the community. An outbreak of plague had carried off many of the people, leaving no rabbinical figure, and Ḥūṣīn was asked to resurrect the spiritual life of the community. His arrival in Baghdad was a turning point in the reconstruction of the Baghdad community as a spiritual center for the Iraqi communities and also for those of most of the neighboring countries. Henceforth, Baghdad would enjoy an unbroken chain of outstanding rabbis and Torah scholars, of whom the leading figures were Rabbi ʿAbdallah Somekh (1813–1889) and his pupil Joseph Ḥayyim, to both of whom we shall return later. The arrival of Ḥūṣīn was the catalyst that brought Baghdadi Jewry into line with the modern Spanish tradition as this took shape in Safed in the sixteenth century. This is the only way to understand the seemingly puzzling statement of Somekh about the Jews of Baghdad when he expounded the halakhic obligation to follow the *Shulḥan Arukh:* "It is a certainty that for us, the Sephardim who have acted like our master, of blessed memory, it is forbidden to do anything except as according to our master, of blessed memory."[4] Although the Jews of Iraq are the descendants of the ancient exiles who went there at the end of the biblical period, this spiritual custom defines them as Sephardim (Spanish Jews), obligated to observe the halakhah according to the ruling of Karo and to reject the actions of any who do not do so. Even the linguistic usage of Hebrew known as the Babylonian tradition was not upheld by the Jews of Iraq, and apart from slight remnants such as the *Seder ʿAqedat Yitzhak,* recited on the eve of the second day of the New Year and based on the ancient gaonic legacy, nothing of this tradition exists in modern religious practice in what was once Babylonia.

Here we may note that, during the period of decline of the Baghdad community in the fifteenth century, a separate culture crystallized in northern Iraq, where the Jewish communities spoke neo-Aramaic. It is not precisely clear when the deep rift occurred between the Arabic-speaking communities centered in Baghdad in the south of the country and the neo-Aramaic-speaking communities in the north, with their hub at Mosul.[5] We do have evidence from the seventeenth century of Torah scholars in the neo-Aramaic-speaking communities, the leading ones being members of the renowned Barazāni family. But after the study of Torah was renewed in Baghdad at the time of Ḥūṣīn, the neo-Aramaic-speaking communities were overshadowed by those who spoke Arabic. Still, a unique local culture developed in which neo-Aramaic was both the spoken and the written language, principally for the *sharḥs* (expanded translations) of the Bible, midrashim, and classical liturgical texts. In any event, the Kurdish communities also adapted to the new Spanish tradition, although relics of the Babylonian tradition were preserved in their form of oral Hebrew expression.

The Persian-speaking communities of this period included those of Persia itself (modern Iran), Afghanistan,[6] and Bukhara, in central Asia, where Tajik, a Persian dialect, was spoken.[7] The Persian-speaking communities reached the peak of their cultural and spiritual development in the fourteenth and fifteenth centuries, in the epics of ʿAmrānī and Shāhīn, written in Judeo-Persian. But after the rise to power of the Shīʿite dynasty in 1499, the political status of the Jews deteriorated, and as a consequence so did their social, economic, and cultural condition. This decline reached its nadir under Shah ʿAbbās II (1642–66), who reacted harshly to the way the Jews of Persia embraced the messianic movement of Shabbtai Zevi.[8] Iranian Jewry also suffered sorely from the absence of a spiritual center for the communities dispersed throughout that vast state and from the isolationist policy of the Shīʿite rulers and their enmity with the Ottoman Empire, perceived as heretic because it belonged to the Sunni branch of Islam (the Ḥanafi school). The Jews of Persia, and all the more the Jews of central Asia, were cut off from the great centers of Jewish culture, including Baghdad. Yet precisely for that reason the Persian Jews retained early traditions, such as the prayer book, which until the eighteenth century was based on Saadiah Gaon's siddur. However, when under the Sunni Zand dynasty (1736–94) the country opened up to foreigners, including Jews, the Persian and central Asian Jews very soon cast off the shreds of their ancient traditions. They became entirely subject satellites of the Jerusalem and Baghdad communities. In Persia the old prayer book was replaced by the Spanish siddur. In Bukhara an interesting spiritual struggle ensued in the last decade of the eighteenth century between Zekharya Matzliyaḥ, a Yemenite Jew who advocated the retention of the old prayer book, and Rabbi Joseph Maman, an emissary of the Safed community, who favored the Spanish tradition. Absolute victory went to Maman; moreover, at the request of the Bukhara community, he settled in the city and became its spiritual leader. From that time forward all the rabbis of Bukhara were Maman's pupils and descendants.

The Jewish community of Yemen was unique in the degree to which it preserved its ancient traditions instead of absorbing the new customs from Palestine. But the Safed doctrine nevertheless spread in Yemen, too, thanks to the Yemenite poet and kabbalist Rabbi Zekharya al-Ẓāhirī, who visited Safed in the 1660s, and the printer Rabbi Abraham Ashkenazi of Safed, who visited Yemen to sell his books at around the same time. These two men introduced the Safed teachings to Yemenite Jewry, but the local sages, under the spiritual leadership of the dominant community of Ṣanʿā, did not consequently abandon the legacy of the geonim and Maimonides. The older tradition (the *baladi*) and the new one (the *shāmi*), which derived from the kabbalists and the sages of Safed, dwelt side by side. During the sixteenth and seventeenth centuries, the Safed influence gradually sank in, mainly in the areas of the liturgy and halakhah. Many of the Yemenite rabbis were drawn to Kabbalah, beginning with Isaac Wannah in the seventeenth century. This influence grew steadily greater, squeezing out the old tradition and meeting less and less resistance. There are several reasons for this development. First, many Hebrew books published by Jewish printers in the Ottoman Empire and Italy reached Yemen, which was known as a good market for them. A considerable number of printers and booksellers visited the country regularly from the sixteenth century on, to promote their business.[9] Second, emissaries from Palestine came often and were customarily received with great admiration and respect. To these factors we may add the serious political at-

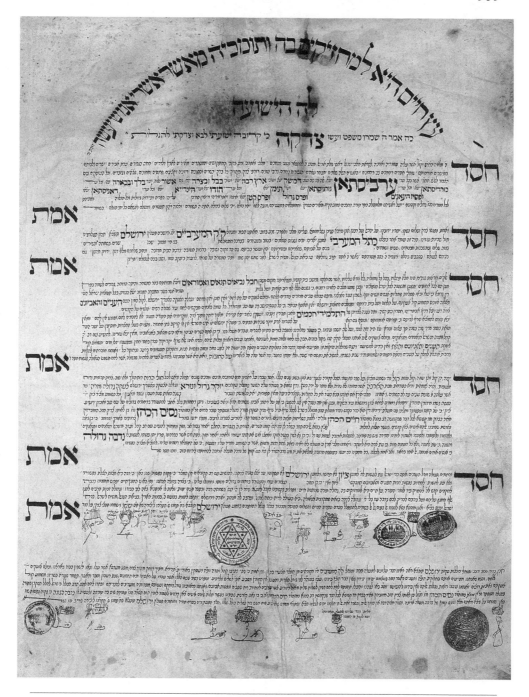

Document of a rabbinical emissary (*shadar*) from Jerusalem, sent to Jewish communities
in the East in 1866. (Einhorn Collection, Tel Aviv. Photo: Ron Erde)

tenuation of the community after the Sabbatian turmoil of 1667–69, which culminated in the sequestering of the Jews in the town of Mawzaʿ on the Red Sea;
the loss of many of their ancient manuscripts; and the undermining of the spiritual ways of life that were based on the ancient heritage. On their return from
exile, the Jews were unable to restore their lives according to that heritage. It was
not until about 1740 that the head of the community, Shalom ʿIrāqi, sought to
enforce the customs of Palestine (shāmi) on Yemenite worship and halakhah
and to displace entirely the old medieval tradition. However, the Ṣanʿā rabbis
rose in opposition and prevented ʿIrāqi from executing his scheme. This struggle
finally ended in a compromise reached at the communal court of Ṣanʿā, which
found literary expression in the essays of Rabbi Yiḥye Ṣāliḥ the greatest of the
Yemenite sages in the second half of the eighteenth century. His writings are
the best reflection of the character of Yemenite Jewry to this day. As we shall
see below, the interaction between these two schools was one of the principal
impulses behind the spiritual creativity of the Jews of Yemen in the twentieth
century.

The compromise between the two schools was accepted primarily in the Ṣanʿā
community and those nearby. But most of the other communities adapted almost completely to the new school; the *Shulḥan Arukh* replaced Maimonides'
Mishneh Torah as the halakhic code binding on the courts, and the imported
printed siddur replaced the original *tiklāl* (the Yemenite prayer book), which
was preserved in manuscript copies. (The printed prayer books were copied out
by hand for the use of the worshipers.) Adaptation to the Spanish school was
most evident in the Aden community. This community differed in its origins
from others in Yemen, but, following the conquest of Aden by the British in 1839,
it grew closer to the outside world, and Jews from other countries joined it. Foreign influences, both British and Indian, grew stronger, so that Aden became the
most Sephardic community in Yemen.

Such were the circumstances of the Jewish communities in the lands of the
Middle East at the advent of modern times. The very small community of Aden
was the first of them to be freed in the year 1839 from the status of protected people (*dhimmī*) under Muslim rule and to be granted equal rights under either European or Ottoman rule;[10] it was the second in all Muslim countries, after
Gibraltar, which was also tiny, to win these advantages before the close of the
eighteenth century.

RABBINIC LITERATURE

In recent centuries, there have been only two important Jewish religious centers,
Baghdad and Ṣanʿā, in all of the Middle Eastern countries. Ṣanʿā reached its peak

at the time of Ṣāliḥ. After his death in 1805, no fresh rabbinic literary creativity arose until the end of the century. The few essays written by his pupils, and their pupils, were purely epigonic, resting on his work in one way or another. His grandson, Rabbi David Ṣāliḥ, wrote notes to his commentary on the siddur (*'Etz Ḥayyim*); Rabbi Jacob Ṣāliḥ and Rabbi Shalom Ḥibshūsh wrote abbreviated versions of his responsa (*Pe'ullat Tzaddiq*); and several other sages wrote short compositions on the halakhic rules of ritual slaughter and forbidden foods, based on the works of Yiḥye Ṣāliḥ. Other rabbis, such as Yeudah Jisvān, Pinḥas Meghori Ha-Cohen, Yiḥye Ha-Cohen, and Ḥayyim Koraḥ, adopted the method of his commentary to the *megillot*. They also wrote commentaries on the Pentateuch and other biblical books (such as *Minḥat Yehudah, Or Torah,* and *Ḥayye Shalom*) by compiling extracts from the books of various sages early and late, chiefly the kabbalists. Yet they were never able to integrate their commentaries into a composition with a direction and an originality of its own. The use of these late summaries of traditional Judaism largely prevented the Yemenite Jews from directly engaging the classic literature such as the Talmud, gaonic literature, the work of Maimonides, and medieval philosophical writings.

By contrast, Baghdad in the nineteenth century, especially in the latter years, was at its zenith in terms of rabbinic literary output because of the wide-ranging activity of the great sage Joseph Ḥayyim. His mastery of Torah and spiritual authority caused his many and varied compositions to tower over anything produced before and to make the creative power of rabbis who came after him seem small. His work included important essays in halakhah, especially his great collection of responsa (*Rav Pe'alim*), his many compositions on Kabbalah (such as *Benayahu*), homilies, poems, *piyyutim,* and much more. Of all his books, the essay *Ben Ish Ḥay* was the most renowned. This work, which is an arrangement of halakhic rules of the *Shulḥan Arukh* according to the weekly Torah portions in two annual cycles, was intended to bring Torah study closer to the wide strata of the people. This was in fact the aim of much of the spiritual writing of Ḥayyim, who never was willing to assume a position of institutional authority over the community. His books of homilies, short essays on halakhic rules on defined subjects, were meant for women as well as for men and were written in the vernacular (*Qānūn al-Nisā'*). He often incorporated tales and fables into his writing for the same purpose, like the sages of earlier generations, who also felt a divide opening between the elite (who possessed some knowledge of Torah) and the common people. For example, as discussed in Aron Rodrigue's chapter, at the end of the eighteenth century, Rabbi Jacob Khulli began a comprehensive work called *Me-'am Loez,* a collection of commentaries in Ladino on the books of the Bible, and in the middle of that century Ṣāliḥ wrote *Sha'are Ṭahrah* primarily for women in the Arabic spoken by the Jews of Yemen.

Earlier and more far-reaching popularization occurred in Persia, Kurdistan, and Bukhara, where there were no important centers of learning. In Persia, a transition to writing in Judeo-Persian had occurred as early as the fourteenth century. From that time on, hardly anything of value was composed in Hebrew, and even Judeo-Persian writings contain only translations and reworking of classical literature, especially in the domains of liturgy and ethics, for the use of the masses, who did not understand Hebrew.[11] Akin to the *tafsīrs* (translations) of the Torah and the Persian epics of Shāhīn and ʿAmrānī of the fourteenth and sixteenth centuries, tafsīrs and epics were written in Kurdistan, to a much more limited extent, in neo-Aramaic, the local spoken language. These usually remained as oral literature, and the members of these communities were educated in this literature of translation.[12] Tafsīrs in Judeo-Arabic were also used by the teachers of young children in Iraq, but they did not constitute canonical literature and were hardly ever committed to writing. For the most part they were only an educational tool and remained in the oral tradition. In any event, in these communities—Persia, Bukhara, and Kurdistan—no rabbinic literature of any standing was created in the nineteenth century or the first half of the twentieth.

It is hard to say that this popularization of doctrine was linked to the political and social changes experienced by the Jewish communities because of the entry of the Western powers and the equalization of civil rights. A likelier conjecture is that this was a late stage in the spiritual decline of these communities, a deep contrast to their splendor in the Middle Ages. The flourishing of later sages in one place or another indeed arrested the deterioration to a greater or lesser degree, as they attempted to bring the people closer to the Torah and to proper observance of the commandments by means of these popular essays. Nonetheless, against the rabbinic literature arose a modern secular literature whose militant proponents were the principals and teachers of the Alliance Israélite Universelle.

The conservative reaction of the rabbis to the political and social changes taking place around them is expressed in their writings. For example, in Ḥayyim's responsa there is an interesting reference to the problems of observing religious precepts in the lifestyle of modern civilization, mainly in answer to the questions of Iraqi Jews who had migrated to India. But ideological and theoretical matters were also considered, in regard to social processes that developed following the grant of equal rights. For example, Rabbi Shimon Agasi of Baghdad (1852–1914), in his book *Imre Shimʿon,* severely censures those who chase after European education and the modern way of life while neglecting to uphold the religious commandments.[13]

Spiritual change also inspired interesting and significant developments in the rabbinic literature of this period, particularly the controversy over the Kabbalah in Yemen. Rationalist tendencies can be found as early as the writings of Rabbi Yiḥye Koraḥ (1840–81), although he too engaged in Kabbalah (for example, his commentaries on the poems of Rabbi Joseph ben Yisrael and Rabbi Shalom Shabazi). These tendencies grew ever stronger and became central in the thought of Rabbi Yiḥye Qāfiḥ and of his colleagues and pupils at the end of the nineteenth century and the first half of the twentieth. Torah study was deteriorating; pedagogy was in decay; superstition was widespread; and the later Kabbalah literature was all the rage. The books of the geonim and the medieval sages had fallen into disuse, whereas the works of the *maskilim* (Enlightenment Jews) exerted a powerful influence, as did the maskilim themselves who traveled to Yemen, especially Professor Joseph Halévy of Paris, who visited Ṣanʿā in 1870. In light of all this, Qāfiḥ concluded that no grounds existed for the attribution of the kabbalistic magnum opus, the *Zohar,* to the second-century rabbi Shimon bar Yoḥai, and that the doctrine of Kabbalah and its offshoots were foreign to the Jewish tradition. But this fierce attack on the Kabbalah, the like of which had not been seen elsewhere, was not intended to undermine the commandments or the Jewish tradition. Its aim was to elevate them to a higher intellectual level. In this, the dispute was entirely different from the controversy between the maskilim and the Orthodox in Eastern Europe. Note that also in Yemen, among the Muslim sages of the Zaydi sect, who were mainly under the pronounced influence of Muḥammad al-Shawkānī (who died in 1834), trends toward a return to the early Islamic sources and negation of the spread of mysticism and messianism were evident.[14]

The extreme views of Qāfiḥ found adherents among the young and the well-to-do of the community, especially those who were closely connected with the Turkish rulers and who had absorbed rationalist European ideas. But those views aroused sharp opposition among most of the community. As a result of this ideological-spiritual conflict, which was not free of socioeconomic and personal considerations, the community split into two separate sects, the *ʿiqqaeshis* (adherents of Kabbalah) and the *dardeʿis* (its opponents). The former in fact made the existence of the controversy known in 1914 to the Muslim ruler, the Imam Yaḥya, and his judicial court, claiming that the dardeʿis deviated from the accepted tradition. The charge of deviation was followed in 1917 by the accusation that the dardeʿis were the agents of foreign powers, the evidence being their links with the Alliance Israélite Universelle. The Muslim authorities always took such deviation as a politically dangerous manifestation that must be uprooted, lest the Jews cease to obey the laws of humiliation and Muslims themselves be tempted to rebel.[15] The Imam unconditionally supported the ʿiqqaeshis, as can be seen in the judge's opinion, to which was added the imam's ruling:

The wishes of both parties have been considered, and the chief matter on which they rest is the prevention of opposition to the Jews' usages in past generations, such as making the fringes [*tzitzit*] and the movements during worship, and what they do at the time of the circumcision and at the banquet of bridegrooms, and at table. Their customs should remain as they are, without any opposition and without blasphemy, without imprecation, and without scorn. . . . Whoever scorns another member of his faith or any of the known books accepted by them,[16] or whoever infringes the tradition when among other Jews, will be punished for that. . . . Now as for the book of the *Zohar:* the friends of Yitzḥak argue that it is one of the accepted books in their religion, and the friends of al-Qāfiḥ[17] argue that it contains things against the unity of the Name and His attributes; it has been agreed between them that condemnation of its readers, or opposition and scorn for it and its treatment of the heretics among the living and the dead, are to be avoided. . . .

We called whoever came here of the possessors of the protection [i.e., the Jews] . . . and we have been apprised of a little of what is said regarding the book of the *Zohar* to be contrary to the Torah, but this contradiction is not proven. . . . So there has been a clarification of what may prevent the division . . . with care to preserve what it is proper to do, and their differentiation from the Muslims, in keeping with the custom of yore. . . . No changes are possible on the part of any one of them if they wish to maintain the Mosaic religion. Anyone who objects is deserving of punishment, so as to prevent any move against the rule of Islam absolutely. Accordingly, let there be read at their synagogues and their study halls what Yiḥye Yitzḥak is accustomed to read from what is not an innovation.[18]

This fierce dispute stimulated the writing of several polemical books, intended to negate the Kabbalah or to prove its truth. The two foremost essays on this subject are Qāfiḥ's *Milḥamot Ha-Shem* (The Wars of God, 1931), and the Ṣanʿā sages' response, *Emunat Ha-Shem* (Belief in God, 1938). But no less important are the nonrabbbinic works produced by the colleagues and pupils of Qāfiḥ, to be discussed later in this chapter.

To sum up, political and social change was not a spur to creativity in the sphere of rabbinic literature among the Jews of the local communities. In places where a modern education system developed on the secular European model, such as Iraq, Persia, and Bukhara, a new form of writing displaced the traditional literature. But where the older education system persisted, as in Afghanistan and Kurdistan, no important religious centers for the development of rabbinic literature arose. Yemen was exceptional; the change there was not meant to undermine the importance of religion but to retain for it medieval features predating the influ-ence of the Kabbalah. Nevertheless, most literary creativity was directed there-after not to the rabbinic sphere but to others.

THE INFLUENCE OF EUROPEAN CULTURE AND WESTERN EDUCATION

The introduction of European culture and Western education in the latter half of the nineteenth century had relatively little influence on the way of life ei-ther of the Jews of the Middle East or of their Muslim neighbors. The effect was usually limited to the social elite, which maintained ties, usually economic, with Europe, and to the large cities. It was expressed in the forms of dress, religious observance, the acquisition of a secular education, and the position of women. European consumer goods, mainly foodstuffs, reached the Jewish community as a whole, but this did not change the patterns of family or communal organiza-tion. Yet as civil rights were extended to the Jews, the effect of European culture became more pronounced. As the social barriers between Jew and Muslim were lowered, the Jews became psychologically ready to absorb Western influences. Another important factor was the degree of openness of each country to West-ern culture, and this was contingent both on government policy and on the sta-tus of that country's international political and economic activity. In places that experienced far-reaching political change and were ruled by European powers, or were economically linked to Europe, the effect was naturally greater. This could be seen especially in capital cities such as Baghdad and Tehran, and in port cities such as Basra and Aden.

The discriminatory laws of Islam included restrictions on dress that were in-tended to humiliate the Jews and to differentiate them from the Muslims. When these laws were rescinded, the Jews tended to adopt the European forms of dress, or, more precisely, the costume of those Muslims who themselves dressed like Europeans. The change to European dress was not a protest by "progressive" groups against traditional Jewish customs but rather a reaction to the historic inferiority of the Jews to the Muslim majority. Thus, when Yemen was under Turkish rule (1872–1918), the Jews began to dress and act like Turks, smoking the nargila and cigarettes, listening to music, and above all wearing the tasseled Turkish tarboosh. The religious leaders objected: snipping off one's sidelocks and shaving one's beard were misdeeds bordering on sacrilege, and so was the change of dress (particularly by women). For example, in 1913, Agasi of Baghdad denounced the new styles in a sermon:

How much must we be embittered by the lack of modesty that is the latest thing among the women. It is an added impudence that they match their garments to the Christians' garments of licentiousness. This is contrary to what we are warned against, that is, not to be like the gentiles in their dress and their other deeds, as this is set forth in the *Shulḥan Arukh, Yoreh Deʿah,* para. 178. Instead, they squander their husbands' money on the trinkets and buttons that they place on those clothes until their cost exceeds that of the garment itself. They bring their husbands to bankruptcy and make them swallow alien influences. The dignity of Jewry dwindles in the eyes of the people, for most of the broken ones are Jews. . . . Still worse in casting off the duty of modesty is that they go bareheaded before all and know no shame. . . . All this is the evil imposed upon us in abundance by the schools of the Alliance, malignant "institutions" that have been established in our city.[19]

One interesting expression of European cultural influence was the adoption of foreign personal and even family names. In Iraq, many Jewish babies were given such names as George, Maurice, Edward, Charles, Marcel, and Laura; especially popular were the names of members of the British royal family. Likewise, a number of the Jews of Aden changed their family names to British ones, seeking names with a similar ring (ʿAwāḍ to Howard, for example). In Iran under the Pahlavi dynasty (1925–79), the Jews tended to change their names to Iranian ones with nationalist connotations.[20]

The economic and social status of women in traditional society everywhere was low. Women were not partners in religious life, nor did they participate in the spiritual or social leadership. Their almost exclusive occupation was with the household. They enjoyed no formal education at all, and virtually all women in the countries of the Middle East were illiterate. Until World War I, no real change occurred in this picture, except in Iraq, where Jewish girls' schools were established in Baghdad in 1890–93. The urban communities in Iraq, mainly Baghdad and Basra, were influenced by Jews who had migrated to India and elsewhere in the Far East but had retained strong ties with their homeland, though they copied the way of life of the British ruling class. A Jewish girls' school was opened in Tehran in 1893 by the Alliance. But this had no direct effect on women's status in Persia, because admission was limited to a tiny number of girls and because both unmarried and married women remained wholly dependent economically on their fathers or husbands. This situation began to change, principally in Iraq, under British rule after World War I. The network of girls' schools expanded, and women began to to work outside the home.

An important factor in the liberation of Jewish women in Iraq (from the

1920s), and somewhat even in Iran (from the 1940s), was the activity of the pioneering Zionist movements led by emissaries from Palestine. In Iran, Zionist influence on women was, however, very circumscribed, because after marriage even the "modern" women were subject to the absolute domination of their husbands. In the Jewish communities of central Asia, the process of women's liberation was faster, following the imposition of the secular, antitraditional Soviet regime. But in Yemen, Kurdistan, and Afghanistan, no change occurred in the status of women, because these countries were closed in varying degrees to external influences. It was the same in Aden, despite the exposure to European influences, owing to the community's determination to preserve its traditional way of life. Only when they migrated to Palestine were women truly liberated. Attempts to improve their status within the older communities usually encountered vigorous opposition from the rabbis.

When the countries in which they lived were opened to the economic and political interests of the Western powers, the Jews were also exposed to European notions of progress, education, and social equality. The local lifestyle became more European as the elite classes observed the diplomatic representatives, government and military personnel, military forces, merchants, journalists, academics, travelers, and tourists who flooded in. And, of course, many people of the Middle East visited Europe and thus became apprised of the way of life there.

One of the most influential results of this trend was the establishment of a modern education network with the help of the Alliance. Schools were established by the Alliance in the Middle Eastern communities after it was approached by local people who had learned of its activities in other countries. These petitioners were dissatisfied with the traditional system of schooling, with its small, dark schoolrooms and poor teacher training, inadequate teaching methods, and curricula consisting only of religious material. It was perfectly clear that the traditional school could not train a young Jew for integration into the modern way of life, precisely at a time of change in his legal and social status. During the nineteenth century, the traditional system had decayed on account of the upsurge in persecution and pressure on the Jews in that period, especially in Persia and Yemen. Only in Baghdad was there a noticeable revival in the traditional system, with the establishment in 1840 of the Abū Mnashshī Seminary by 'Abdallah Somekh. Its purpose was to offer young Torah scholars a high level of religious studies so as to provide religious leadership for the community, but this did nothing to promote the education of other children. Particularly grave was the condition of education in Persia, which did not go beyond the minimal level of teaching children to read the elementary holy texts, the siddur and the Pentateuch. In Yemen there was a move to improve traditional teaching methods and expand the curriculum, and the Alliance was contacted. The Turkish rulers objected, and that was the end of it; however, between 1909 and 1913 the intelligentsia succeeded in maintaining a local modern school under Turkish sponsorship. Friction within the community itself over the "spirit of liberty" circulating in the school eventually forced it to close down.

In Iraq and Persia, the religious leadership at first supported the creation of Alliance schools. Secular studies were not automatically rejected by the Jews of these countries. But once the rabbis became aware that the Alliance schools emphasized such studies and also taught foreign languages, rather than religious subjects, they displayed fierce opposition. As we have seen, in Iraq, Ḥayyim published an opinion in which he advocated a complete ban on the teaching of secular studies and foreign languages in traditional schools. In Persia it was argued that an Alliance education might weaken the Jewish family and cause young people to convert to Christianity, Baha'i, and even Islam. But despite opposition, the Alliance network continued to spread in Iraq and Persia, and in fact the traditional schools were obliged to adapt the methods and curriculum of the modern schools.

The Alliance and the other European Jewish organizations operating in the Middle Eastern communities brought forth a new type of Jew, one who aspired to blend into modern life and strove to develop the necessary skills. The Alliance combined the idea of progress with the French ideals of liberty, equality, and fraternity. But French education in the broader sense was almost wholly indifferent to the Jewish tradition as well as to local national traditions. Religious studies, to say nothing of religious observance or Jewish nationalist ideas, had no place in the Alliance curriculum. No wonder, then, that the Alliance students emerged from school detached from their community and its literary and spiritual roots; rather, they were imbued with ideas introduced from outside that community. Disconnected from Jewish sources, these students were also typically unsympathetic to the Zionist movement. This alienation from Jewish tradition is what lay behind the opposition to the Alliance in Iraq and Persia. It is doubtful that an Alliance education led many young people to assimilate or convert, but it certainly contributed to the loosening of their bonds with Jewish tradition.

In Iraq, after the Young Turk Revolution in 1908, the ideas of Turkish nationalism were taken up by some of the Jews. The Muslims were unwilling to embrace them, but, after the British conquest of Iraq in 1918, the gates of the civil service and higher education were opened to the Jews. Many Jewish intellectuals identified themselves as Iraqis of the Mosaic faith. Writers and artists worked as Iraqis, playing a significant role in the emerging Iraqi nationalism. Jewish writers wrote in literary Arabic on general themes—and not in Judeo-Arabic, certainly not in Hebrew, on Jewish themes. But it only took a short time for them to become disillusioned when Iraqi nationalism developed distinctly anti-Jewish tendencies.

The weakening of religion in the Jewish communities was certainly an outcome of modern education, but it was also affected by similar trends in the surrounding society. From the second half of the nineteenth century, nationalist elements had grown stronger throughout the region, and religion was rapidly enfeebled. After winning independence, all of these states ceased to be founded on Islamic law, even though Islam was recognized as the official religion. Thus, the Jewish communities were part of a society in which secularizing tendencies were growing ever stronger.

As for the Jews themselves, their desire to join the mainstream as equals, by exploiting the new opportunities created by changes in their legal status, naturally caused them to neglect the observances of their religion. Nonetheless, the Middle Eastern Jews, like their Muslim neighbors, never adopted antireligious ideas as one finds in Europe during this period.

The impetus toward secularization differed from country to country, depending on the local attitude toward religion, the spiritual strength of the Jewish community, and the degree of its integration into the mainstream. Yemen and Afghanistan did not experience any secularization. Prior to the Republican Revolution of 1962, Yemen was a theocracy, the head of state being the imam of the Zaydi sect. The life of the state was based on Islam in its Zaydi form. Not only were the Muslims enjoined by the regime to uphold the precepts of Islam, but the Jews were obliged to obey the precepts of Judaism. Only under Turkish rule could a faint tendency be distinguished in small groups in the Ṣanʿā community toward relaxation of the strict observance of Jewish customs. In Afghanistan, the status of religion in the life of state and society hardly changed, and the efforts of the ruler Amānullāh Khan (r. 1919–29), under the influence of Atatürk, to introduce liberal ways and even to enforce Western habits of dress, failed completely. Most surprisingly, it would appear, the Aden community also gave preference to religion even though it was an important international port, through which passed travelers from all over the world and in which lived a large population of British administrators and military personnel. The Jews actually declined the opportunity, offered to them by the British, of joining the civil service, because this would entail desecration of the Sabbath. The chief factor in this refusal was the power of the Jewish leadership, communal and spiritual, that was concentrated in the hands of a single family (the Moses/Messa family).

Real secularization processes, which effectuated economic and social change, were evident only in countries where the Jews did in fact enter the mainstream.

These were Iraq, Iran, and Bukhara, although the exact circumstances differed in each. In these countries the Jews were to a large extent integrated into the government education system or a modern Jewish system. In Iraq this began with the Young Turk Revolution; in Bukhara it came about after World War I, with the establishment of the Soviet regime; and in Iran it happened after the ascent of the Pahlavi dynasty in 1925. Once the Jews acquired a modern education and entered the economic system, whether through government and the civil service or through private business, they began to neglect Sabbath observance, *kashrut,* and worship. The hold of traditional values and the Hebrew language on the younger generation grew slack. In Iran, secularization was furthered by the weak spiritual condition of the Jewish communities, which at times involved ignorance of the most elementary religious commandments; in Bukhara, the extremely antireligious ideology of communism and the Soviet regime had its own effect.

An obvious difference existed between metropolises (such as Baghdad, Basra, and Tehran) and the provincial towns and villages. For example, in Kurdistan, but also in rural communities of Iraq and Iran, the status of religion was maintained. In these communities the Jews interacted less with the surrounding society, and their education system remained essentially traditional. The changes in economic life were very limited, and Jews were not obliged to work on the Sabbath in government and civil service or to open their businesses on the day of rest.

Naturally, secularization mainly affected those Jews who were already associated with the wider environment: members of the new upper class—with their European education, their wealth, and their connections with the rulers, particularly the colonial authorities—and middle-class merchants and professional men. By contrast, members of the lower class—the artisans and those supported by the community—usually continued fastidiously to preserve what tradition required. It is hard to estimate the fraction of the Jewish population that experienced secularization. The figure certainly varied from country to country. The process was accelerated in Iran from the 1960s, and it is thought to have encompassed at least 80 percent of the Jews of that country. The same proportion probably applied in Iraq, whereas in Kurdistan, as in Yemen and Afghanistan, the Jews remained for the greater part keepers of the tradition. As for the Jews of Bukhara, it is estimated that at least half of them ceased to observe the religious precepts.

Nevertheless, the ancient customs were maintained within the confines of the household and family. On Sabbaths and festivals, certainly the New Year and Day of Atonement, the "secular" Jews continued to attend the synagogue; they ate matzah on Passover, fasted on the Day of Atonement, and lit the Hanukkah candles. They certainly obeyed the basic Jewish practices around circumcision, marriage, divorce, and burial. Secularization never led to assimilation and conversion, even though an attitude of derision, at times even contempt, developed toward the commandments whose observance did not match modern life.

MODERN HEBREW EDUCATION AND ATTITUDES TOWARD ZIONISM

In 1926 Rabbi Joseph Gurjī, who had migrated from Afghanistan to Palestine, published his book *'Edut Bi-Yhosef,* a commentary on the book of Psalms that contains echoes of life there, particularly in Jerusalem, at the turn of the century.[21] Here is one of them:

> The Holy One, blessed be He, does not do miracles to liars. By mouth *Shalom* is spoken in Hebrew, but the deed will not be in Hebrew. They are Sabbath desecrators, and they engage in intercourse at the time of abstention. They swill libation wine. They have their beards and sidelocks and heads shaven. They do not don the phylacteries. They are sinners and they deflect others to free themselves of the commandments. The voice is Jacob's in Hebrew speech but the hands are Esau's in committing the acts.[22]

Who are these people to whom Gurjī refers—those whose national identity is difficult to define, who speak Hebrew but do not behave like Jews, the kind who are delaying redemption? Although he does not say it explicitly, he means the *ḥalutzim,* the pioneers, the people of the Second Aliyah who came to Jerusalem around 1910, especially to the Bukharan Quarter, the well-to-do and spacious neighborhood originally called Reḥovot. In and around this neighborhood lived most of the immigrants from the Iranian countries (Bukhara, Persia, and Afghanistan). These people were faithful to the Jewish tradition, and their idea of the Return to Zion was quite unconnected to the "official" Zionism of Herzl and his followers. They were wholly unacquainted with the phenomenon of secularization until they encountered it when ḥalutzim arrived in their neighborhoods in Jerusalem and Jaffa. The pioneers were suffused with powerful ideals that were not always congruent: on the one hand, the ancient national idea of the deliverance both of the people of Israel and of Palestine, on the other, the Marxist-communist-universalist notion of the abolition of social classes and religion.

The response of the Middle Eastern Jews to the ḥalutzim, as expressed by

Gurjī, was one of perplexity, but it was entirely different from the resolutely negative response of the European Jews in the Old Yishuv (except for a handful, headed by Rabbi Abraham Isaac Kook, who adopted a more positive attitude). The Hebrew speech of the ḥalutzim, and of course the fact that they had chosen to live in Jerusalem, were evidence that they should be regarded as members of the Jewish people. However, their infringement of the commandments was unacceptable to Gurjī. He was unwilling to exclude them from *klal yisrael,* the "entirety of Jewry," but hoped that they would repent and replace their anthropological definition of Judaism with one based on observance. Gurjī's perception of Judaism, which did not undermine the status of the Hebrew language or the centrality of the Land of Israel in their religious meaning, has characterized the communities of the Middle Eastern Jews in their lands of origin and in Israel to the present day.

Hebrew was part of the Middle Eastern cultural tradition, although it was not the spoken language of the Jews or their mother tongue in any country. It was taught in the traditional schools for study of the Bible, the liturgy, and other classical literature. As the forces of modernization, equal rights, and integration with outside society grew stronger, from the mid-nineteenth century on the knowledge of Hebrew declined among members of the younger generation who attended the Alliance schools. Although the graduates of the traditional system were fluent in Hebrew, it was far from being in daily use as a spoken language and certainly did not fall under the influence of the modern Hebrew of the maskilim.

The situation began to change after World War I. Under the rule of the British Mandate, the Jews in Palestine established ties with the Middle Eastern communities. Immigrants from Middle Eastern lands adapted to Hebrew far more quickly than those from European countries. In 1917–18, Hebrew-language schools had been founded in Samarkand by two Ashkenazic Jews, Y. Z. Amitin-Shapira and Shlomo Edelman, who did not know Tajik, the local dialect, and could communicate with their pupils only in Hebrew. The use of Hebrew expanded in the Jewish schools in other cities of central Asia until, in the 1922–23 school year, the Soviet regime withdrew its permission and Tajik was made the language of instruction.

In Iraq, the modern era of Jewish education began in 1921 with the coronation of King Faisal and his declaration of freedom of religion and education. Teachers and books were sent from Palestine to develop Hebrew instruction and to teach the history of Jewish settlement in Palestine, modern Hebrew literature, and the like. In fact, Hebrew education penetrated all the modern Jewish schools. In 1928, a young teacher of Afghani extraction even reached Afghanistan. For two years he worked at the Zionist school in Herat with great industry, despite the sharp opposition of the local conservatives. This was the time of the reformist king, Amānullāh Khan, who invited teachers from all over the world to come to Afghanistan and improve education there.

In Iran, however, where the non-Zionist Alliance controlled Jewish education until World War II, instruction in Hebrew was instituted only after the war and became still more widespread after the establishment of the State of Israel, with the change in the Alliance's position on Zionism. From 1942 on, emissaries of the Jewish Agency came to Iran and introduced the teaching of Hebrew and Zionist ideas into the modern schools. Naturally, this activity occurred mostly in Tehran and in a number of large provincial cities such as Isfahan, Hamadan, Ahvaz, and Kermanshah. There were no changes in the traditional schools or in the Otzar ha-Torah educational network, which was established in parallel with the development of Hebrew education.[23] The creation of the State of Israel and the good ties formed between it and the shah encouraged an expansion of Hebrew education in Iran.

Another active factor in the penetration of modern Hebrew education in the Middle East was the Brit 'Ivrit 'Olamit (World Hebrew Alliance). In the 1940s, this association sent emissaries to the Ṣan'ā and Aden communities to promote the teaching of Hebrew. The Yemenite Aharon Ben-David lived in Aden for several years, and in Ṣan'ā another Yemenite, Ḥayyim Tzadok, was active. In Ṣan'ā, a modern Hebrew school was founded at the initiative of young local intellectuals such as Rabbi Joseph Shemen and Rabbi Joseph Koraḥ, with the financial support of the World Hebrew Alliance. Noteworthy, too, is the activity of the emissaries of the Jewish Agency in the *Ge'ullah* camp in Aden, where thousands of refugees from Yemen were gathered. Men such as Shimon Avizemer and 'Ovadya Toviyyah prepared many of the young people in the transit camp to be the vanguard of immigration to the Land of Israel.

For several reasons, however, Hebrew education in these countries could not develop to the point of effecting a real change in the way of life and cultural perception of these communities. One factor was the opposition of the conservatives; another was the deterioration of relations between the local governments and the Jewish communities in the wake of the Jewish-Arab conflict in the Land of Israel. Jewish education was perceived, correctly, as part of the Zionist ideology, so it was prohibited in Iraq in 1932, when the country gained its independence. In central Asia, as we have seen, Hebrew education was banned from around 1922 because of the opposition of the Soviet regime to Jewish nationalist activity of any sort. In Iran, the Ayatollah Khomeini revolution severed the ties between the Jewish educational institutions and Israel. A third inhibiting factor was lack of interest. For example, in most of the communities in Kurdistan and Yemen, apart from Mosul and Ṣanʿā, traditional education continued to exist; such was the case also in most of the settlements in Iraq and Iran, apart from the capital cities and the large communities. Moreover, the increasing wealth of the Jews of Iran from the 1960s on reinforced their tendency to assimilate, which of course did nothing to enhance the status of Hebrew education.

MODERN LITERATURE

The Jewish communities of the Islamic Middle East sank into a deep spiritual decline after the marvelous flowering of the Middle Ages, and this decay grew worse after the Mongol invasion in the mid-thirteenth century. Only in Baghdad and Ṣanʿā was spiritual activity expressed, by reinforcement of Torah study and by literary creations of value beyond their time and place. Elsewhere, when recovery finally began, it was associated with the transition to modern life and with writing that lacked any affinity with traditional rabbinic literature. And even in Baghdad and Ṣanʿā, the new cultural activity overtook that literature in its importance and centrality. Modern literature in the Middle Eastern communities naturally developed from specific local needs and was usually written in the local languages. Nevertheless, this literature came under the influence of the Hebrew Enlightenment and was written in evident association with it. But this development came about 50 or 100 years after the burgeoning of Hebrew Enlightenment literature in Europe, and in certain places still later. The Enlightenment did not reach the members of some communities at all, until they left their homelands and went to the State of Israel.

Such writing as existed in the Middle Eastern countries did not arise from a spiritual crisis, like that of Europe in the nineteenth century. It was not concerned with problems of Jewish and human identity, the search for roots, or solutions to the existential problems posed by the transition to modern, secular life. In the Middle East, no real change occurred in social stratification or in the status of religion until the mid-twentieth century, and in certain places even later. There was no definitive, secular, ideological opposition to the life of tradition. Modern lifestyles were a copy, pale and unoriginal, at times ludicrous, of European ones, and likewise modern literature.

Finally, we may note the affinity of modern Jewish literature in the Middle Eastern countries with the writing of local non-Jews. Jewish spiritual life for centuries had been detached from Islamic spiritual life, an isolation that stemmed from the fear of each society of the influence of the other. This was particularly the case in regard to canonical writing by intellectuals and scholars. On the popular level there was fairly close contact, the common denominator being the shared spoken language. Only after World War I, when the illusion of equal rights spread among the Jews, did writers begin to work in the literary languages of the countries in which they lived. For the most part Jews did not write under the influence of European or Hebrew Enlightenment literature. The small quantity of belles-lettres written in the mid-nineteenth century and later was a continuation of the traditional literature in the medieval style, essentially liturgical or other religious Hebrew poetry. In Yemen, Jewish writers continued to write in medieval structures and meter, influenced by medieval Hebrew poetry, whereas in Iraq, Kurdistan, and Persia the influence was from the poetry of Najjārah. Nowhere did the poetry of the period reach new heights. Somewhat exceptional was the lyric poetry of Ḥayyim El'azar, which was collected in his book *Ḥayāt al-Ayyām*. These poems, written in Persian, not Hebrew, evince a clearly ethical, religious, and national leaning.

Jewish writers produced belletristic literature only in Iraq and central Asia in the first half of the twentieth century, and this too was not in Hebrew but in literary Arabic and in Tajik, respectively. Hebrew poetry was written in Iraq between the two world wars by a few intellectuals: Aharon Sasson, Ezra Haddad, and David Tzemaḥ. But, as we have seen, this period witnessed a slackening of the ties between the Jewish community and Hebrew culture because of political developments and, in central Asia, because of the ban on the use of Hebrew except for worship and Torah study. Moreover, in 1928 it became obligatory for the Jewish communities under Soviet rule to write in Latin script, as part of a sweeping reform aimed at choking off the Islamic legacy. And in 1938 the authorities decided not to transliterate the Tajik language into Cyrillic script, which in fact sounded the death-knell for Jewish literature in that language because Cyrillic was the only script taught in central Asia.

Writing by Jews in this region was sparse, although there were important achievements in certain genres, namely fiction and poetry, written in Tajik. Among the important storytellers were Ya'akov Ḥayyimov, the author of *Babajan* (1933), and Moshe Yehudayev, who became well known for his books *Small Farm Workers* (1934) and *Nasty Gossip* (1935). The most important poet was Muhib (Mordekhai Bichayev), author of the famous *Ghazālaiyyāt* (Love Poems).[24] There was much theatrical activity, both writing and performing, but it was of a fairly low artistic and literary level because of the tendency to melodrama.

This central Asian literature was largely socialistic, expressing the Jewish writers' desire to live within the spirit and society of the Soviet state, but it did not deny Jewish nationality; it was written in Tajik and in traditional literary forms, not in Russian, the lingua franca of the Soviet Union. By contrast, the modern literature of the Jews of Iraq was written in literary Arabic, which was isolated both linguistically and in content from the Jewish tradition. In fact, there was nothing Jewish in it; it sought to express patriotic Iraqi aspirations while suppressing any sign of Jewish feeling. Many of these writers went on to work in Hebrew once they had immigrated to Israel, or even in Arabic on Jewish subjects. But this happened after a rude awakening, when the illusion of Arab-Jewish amity had faded in Iraq.

The outstanding Iraqi Jewish writers are the poets Meir Basri (1935 on) and Jacob Bulbul-Lev (1941 on), who wrote in the sonnet form and other European structures, freeing themselves from the rigid forms of classical Arabic poetry; the short-story writers Anwar Sha'ul, author of the collection al-Ḥiṣād al-awwal (The First Harvest, 1930), and Shalom Darwish, author of the essays Wiswasāt Iblis (The Temptations of Satan, published in the periodical al-Ḥāṣid [1929–38]) and the collection Aḥrār wa-'abīd (Freemen and Slaves, 1948).[25] Although these writings are entirely devoid of Jewish motifs, the Iraqi intelligentsia did not accept these writers as legitimate, and the books surveying modern Iraqi literature ignore and deny their work. With good reason, Sasson Somekh called them the "lost voices."[26]

HISTORICAL LITERATURE

In addition to belles-lettres, the Jewish communities of the Middle East produced theoretical and historical literature. There is no more evident sign of the deep feeling of change passing in these communities in the mid-nineteenth century than the recording of local history. It is imbued with a feeling that a long and important era was about to end and that a new one was opening, different from what had gone before. Such narratives were composed in earlier centuries, too, sometimes out of a similar feeling and sometimes in consequence of a specific political or social crisis. For example, in the second half of the eighteenth century, Rabbi Yiḥye Ṣāliḥ wrote Megillat Teman (The Scroll of Yemen) to distinguish the traditions of the Yemenite Jews from the external influences and customs then entering the community.[27] In similar vein, Bābāi ibn Luṭf wrote Kitāb Anūsi (The Book of the Marrano), and his grandson Bābāi ben Farhād wrote Kitab-Sār Guzash-i Kāshān (The Book of the Events of Kāshān), in which they described the harsh decrees imposed on the communities of Persia in the seventeenth and early eighteenth centuries.

The first Middle Eastern Jewish historian in the modern era was Rabbi Ḥayyim Ḥibshūsh, a member of the circle of Yiḥye Qāfiḥ and a leading intellectual among the Jews of Yemen. He became known as the guide of Joseph Halévy on his travels in northeastern Yemen (1870). The influence of this European intellectual on his Yemenite escort was profound. Halévy instilled the rationalist concept in Ḥibshash, as the latter notes in the preface to his account of the journey, *Masse'ot Ḥibshūsh* (The Travels of Ḥibshūsh).[28] Rationalism is clearly evident between the lines of his essay "Korot Israel be-Teman" (The History of the Jews in Yemen), which takes us from the end of the ninth century (the start of the Zaydi imamate) to Ḥibshūsh's own times. He relies on historical documents of various kinds and on the oral tradition. He had no understanding of modern scholarly methods, so his account of events is not always entirely accurate.[29]

There are several essays in this vein. "Sa'arat Teman" (Yemen Tempest, 1954) by another pupil of Qāfiḥ, Rabbi 'Amram Koraḥ (who died in 1953), relates the history of the Jews of Ṣan'ā from the first Turkish occupation in the mid-sixteenth century to the immigration to Israel after the establishment of the state. "Divre Tzadikim ve-Zikhronam be-Teman" (The Words of Righteous Men and Their Memory in Yemen) by Yiḥye Qāfiḥ himself lists the writings of the Yemenite sages, many of whose manuscripts he and his pupils, especially his grandson Rabbi Joseph Qāfiḥ, rescued by purchase or by copying.[30] "Naḥalat Yosef" (The Bequest of Joseph, 1906) by Rabbi Shemu'el 'Adani is an encyclopedic composition containing, among other things, the history of the Jews of Aden, an account of the author's pilgrimage to Palestine, and a description of the customs of his community. The history of the Jews of Afghanistan from the events of 1839 to the immigration to Palestine at the end of the century are described by Mattityah Gurjī in his "Korot Zemannim" (Events of the Ages).[31]

These works were written in Hebrew. 'Azaryah Yusufof, a Bukharan intellectual, wrote his short essay "History and Customs of the Jews of Bukhara" in Tajik (unpublished). Habib Levy wrote in Persian, in Arabic script, his great three-volume *History of the Jews of Iran* (1960), a book for which its author depended mostly on oral traditions.[32]

There were many volumes written by immigrants from the Middle Eastern countries to Palestine, or by their children, dealing with the history of their communities, particularly of Yemen. Though more academic than those mentioned above, many of the works should be categorized as memoirs. Among the authors are Rabbi Shalom Alsheikh, Rabbi Abraham Naddāf, Rabbi Joseph Maḍmūnī, and Rabbi Joseph Ha-Levy (not to be confused with Professor Joseph Halévy).

Writing of a distinctly scholarly nature was produced in Iran and Iraq, where modern education, mainly provided by the Alliance, was available. In the years following World War I, several intellectuals composed works of a clearly Zionist leaning in Tehran. In 1920 the Society for the Dissemination of the Hebrew Language published 'Azīzullah Na'īm's book (in Persian, printed in Hebrew script),

History of the Zionist Movement. Eliyahu Ḥayyim, a teacher, published three stories in Judeo-Persian (1924–27) on Jewish tradition, history, and philosophy. An evident display of modernizing tendencies and of Jewish national awakening are the publications of this period in standard Persian, printed in Arabic script, including translations of Zionist classics such as Theodor Herzl's *The Jewish State* (1896) and original writing such as *A Short History of the Jews* (1946) by Farvaz Rahabar.

HEBREW PRINTING IN THE MIDDLE EASTERN COUNTRIES

As early as the sixteenth century, the Jews were the pioneers of printing in Islamic cities: in Constantinople, Fez, Safed, Cairo, and, later, Izmir. In the mid-nineteenth century, Hebrew printing houses were founded in several of these centers. Previously, the Jews in these communities had either imported printed books from Europe (chiefly Italy), Constantinople, and Izmir, or had continued the ancient practice of copying manuscripts, which were widely used, particularly in Iran and Yemen. There were no printers in these communities, which were remote from Europe; moreover, they had their own writing traditions, which did not find proper expression in printed books. In Iran, this applies mainly to Judeo-Persian literature and translations from Hebrew into that language, whereas in Yemen the reference is to its medieval gaonic school, which was pushed aside by the Kabbalah and the sages of Safed. Before the mid-nineteenth century, a few Baghdad scholars had sent their books to be printed in Constantinople and Livorno. The writings of the others remained in manuscript. Although at times desperate attempts were made (such as Ṣāliḥ's effort to have his books printed in India), many of these works were lost or remain entirely unknown to us.

Prior to World War I, a Hebrew press worthy of the name was to be found only in Baghdad, where it began to operate in 1866. Another, far less important press existed in Aden from 1891. Hebrew presses could also be found in several cities of India, where they were set up by Jewish immigrants from Yemen and Iraq or their descendants to serve both their own needs and those of the mother community.

Most of the books printed in Hebrew were intended for everyday use: prayer books, collections of piyyutim, tales, Bible books, *mishnayot,* homilies, and the like. Many of them were translations into the languages spoken by the Jews; most were not large, sometimes just pamphlets or a single page. The important, longer books continued to be sent abroad for printing, primarily to Jerusalem. This was especially so for the Yemenite and Iranian communities.

The local Hebrew presses of this period were far from adequate to satisfy the religious needs of the Middle Eastern communities. The presses in Jerusalem and Eastern Europe were still supremely important well into the twentieth century. At the end of World War I, printers set up shop in Tehran and Tashkent, a development linked to the spiritual revival and the spread of Zionism. In Yemen and Afghanistan, however, where the Islamic regimes survived the war, no Hebrew printing house was ever founded, nor in Kurdistan, though printers in Jerusalem who had emigrated from those countries filled the gap to some extent.[33]

JEWISH JOURNALISM

A Jewish press developed in this region only in Iraq, Iran, and central Asia—a clear sign of the modernization of education, and later of the growing commitment to Zionism in these countries. Journalistic endeavors were also closely connected to the establishment of local Jewish printing houses, which were supplemented by those in Calcutta and Bombay. The periodicals were mostly published in the languages spoken by the Jews in each place, except for two newspapers that appeared in Baghdad in Hebrew.

Journalism was a highly effective organizational and cultural tool, bringing the Middle Eastern communities closer to the world at large and introducing to them the ideas of the Jewish Enlightenment and the Zionist movement. Activity in this sphere in the second half of the nineteenth century was clearly inspired by the Jewish press in Europe and Palestine, whose publications were read in all the Middle Eastern lands, even faraway Yemen. In turn, the press was a powerful instrument by which Middle Eastern Jews made their coreligionists aware of their grave political condition, submitting letters and reports in order to draw the attention of their brothers and sisters in Europe and Palestine. The most important of these Middle Eastern writers was Rabbi Shelomo Bekhor Ḥūṣīn (1843–93), the leading figure in the first generation of intellectuals in Baghdad. His many articles were printed in almost all the Hebrew papers of the time in Europe as well as the Jewish papers in Baghdad and India.

Two main epochs can be discerned in the history of the Hebrew press in the Middle Eastern countries: from 1863 to World War I, and the postwar period. In the first period, journals were printed in Baghdad, Calcutta, and Bombay by Iraqi Jews, under the evident influence of the Jewish press in Palestine and Europe. Hebrew printing in the various Middle Eastern countries was in fact founded after the establishment of the journal *Ha-Levanon* in Jerusalem in 1863. That year, printers opened for business in Aleppo and Baghdad, and at the same time Moses Barukh Mizraḥi began to print by lithography the Hebrew periodical called *Ha-Dover* or *Dover Mesharim*. Seventeen issues of this journal appeared irregularly until 1871. But earlier still the first weekly in Judeo-Arabic—*Doresh Tov Le-'Ammo*—was published in Bombay, it too by lithography. This periodical appeared regularly from 1856 to 1866, after which several other Judeo-Arabic weeklies were published in Calcutta until the end of the nineteenth century: *Mevasser, Ha-Perah, Maggid Mesharim,* and *Ha-Shoshannah.*

The new national spirit was recognizable in the postwar Jewish press. In Iraq it had begun to flourish as early as 1908, but writing in Hebrew and Judeo-Arabic declined among Baghdad's Jewish intellectuals, who gravitated to the use of literary Arabic. A journal called *al-Zuhūr* (Flowers) was founded in 1909 by Nissim Joseph Somekh in partnership with a Turkish Muslim, but it did not last long. A Zionist awakening followed the Balfour Declaration of 1917, and in 1921 the short-lived Hebrew weekly *Yeshurun* was established in Baghdad by Aharon Sasson Nahum. After only five issues, it was replaced by a weekly written in Arabic called *al-Miṣbāḥ* (The Lantern), managed by Salmān Shīnah, who later became a member of the Iraqi parliament. Edited by one of the most important Jewish writers in Iraq, Anwar Sha'ul, this periodical appeared regularly from 1924 to 1928, and when it closed the highly experienced Sha'ul began another, called *al-Ḥāṣid* (The Harvester). *Al-Ḥāṣid* gathered to it the finest Jewish creative forces in Iraq throughout its existence (1929–39), and it acquired a place of honor in the press as a whole in that country. But *al-Ḥāṣid* deliberately and knowingly went beyond the Jewish framework in its content, though it was directed at Jewish readers. This policy, which reflected the outlook of the many Jews who considered themselves Iraqi citizens of the Jewish faith, was also seen in two other journals: *al-'Uṣba* (The Union), founded by the anti-Zionist Jewish Communist Union in 1946, and *al-Barīd al-Yawmyyi* (The Daily Post), established in 1948.

In Tehran in 1915, a periodical in Judeo-Persian called *Shalom* appeared and helped to strengthen ties between the community in the Iranian capital and those in the provincial towns, and it prepared the ground for Zionist activity. After the war, two important weeklies in Judeo-Persian were launched: *Ha-Ge'ullah* (Deliverance, 1920–23), the voice of the Zionist Organization in Iran, and *Ha-Hayyim* (Life, 1922–25). They were closed down because of the anti-Zionist policy of the Riza Shah, founder of the Pahlavi dynasty. After the shah was deposed during World War II, Jewish journals reappeared, all of a distinctly Zionist bent, in Judeo-Persian.

In central Asia, too, Jewish journals appeared after World War I in the Tajik dialect: *Roshnoy* (written in Hebrew script) in Samarkand in 1925, and at about the same time *Rahamim* (Compassion), in Bukhara. They did not last long, because of the Soviet ban on Hebrew script, but in 1929 a journal in Cyrillic and, subsequently, Latin characters made its appearance. This was *Bairuki Makhanat* (The Banner of Labor). All of these journals were intended not just to serve the Jewish people and their culture but also to promote communist indoctrination.

FOLK CULTURE

For centuries, elite Jewish culture of the Middle Eastern communities was almost entirely cut off from the Islamic environment. Religious and social barriers divided the Jews and their Muslim neighbors. In the folk culture, however, many elements were shared by the two populations.

Even in communities where Torah study was widespread, such as in Yemen and Iraq, Hebrew was not the spoken language in everyday use. Nor did the Jews avail themselves of the literary language wherever they lived, either for speech or writing. Instead, they adopted the lower level of the spoken language, and almost everywhere the Jews developed a dialect of the foreign tongue uniquely their own, so that Jewish languages were created other than Hebrew. Such were the various Arabic dialects of the Jews of Yemen, Aden, and Iraq as well as the diverse Persian dialects of Iranian Jewry. Furthermore, in a single country several dialects developed, by which one could determine the city from which someone hailed. So, despite the shared language of Jew and Muslim, there was not always a match in the development of the dialects spoken by each. One factor was the inclusion of many Hebrew (and sometimes Aramaic) words in the Jewish dialects; another factor—and this is a linguistic phenomenon of enormous interest—was that several of the Jewish dialects preserved earlier elements of the language that were not retained in the language of the Muslims.

The spoken language of the Jews of Kurdistan is of special interest. It is not Hebrew, or Arabic (the Muslim Kurds are not Arabs by race or language), or even Kurdish (Kurmanji), but an Aramaic dialect known as neo-Aramaic or, as the Jews call it, "the language of the *Targum*." This language, which was the tongue of Kurdistan from the time of the Talmud under Sassanian rule, was preserved in various dialects even among other minority religious groups apart from the Jews. Clearly, those local Jews who came into closer contact with the Islamic surroundings also acquired knowledge of Kurdish.

The different Jewish languages, then, were a means whereby popular culture was transported and transferred, particularly in that broad field called oral or folk literature. This includes popular genres such as stories, poems, sayings, riddles, and fables. In this domain, hardly any barrier existed between the Muslim and the Jewish carriers of folk culture. In fact it is hard to determine, except in relatively few cases, the provenance of a particular artifact in this or that genre. The "folk" characteristic of this literature is not only that it is not canonical, nor attributed to a given spiritual or social authority, but also, perhaps principally, that it is the legacy of all strata of Jewish society. Women, who in the Middle Eastern communities received no formal schooling and usually did not learn to read or write, were the main consumers of this literature.

Folk culture also gained a highly respected position in the sacred sphere and in canonical religious life. The lack of knowledge of Hebrew and the attraction of popular literature forced the religious authorities to allow it first a narrow opening, and ultimately a wide one, so as to bring all the people closer to knowledge of Torah and observance of the commandments. This process began as early as the fourteenth century in Persia, possibly even earlier, with the tafsīrs of the Bible and other Jewish classics into Judeo-Persian. The great epics of Shāhīn and 'Amrānī similarly served as educational tools for the extensive teaching of Jewish history and tradition. The poetry of the Jews of Kurdistan was similarly applied.[34] Moreover, elementary school teachers taught the Bible in the local dialect, not Hebrew. In certain places, such as Iraq and Kurdistan, these tafsīrs evolved into large-scale works, which were preserved in the oral tradition and only at times partially committed to writing. An exception to this was in Yemen, where such tafsīrs were not produced, perhaps because the Jews of Yemen continued to recite Saadiah Gaon's classic Arabic translation of books of the Bible. In Persia, Bukhara, and Kurdistan, where the social divide was great and the folk knew only the spoken language, a more comprehensive translation project was needed. Not only books of the Bible and the liturgy were translated but also primers in halakhah, and this was so even in more educated communities. In Yemen, for example, many sharḥs were composed in Arabic regarding the laws of ritual slaughter and the prohibitions, because many Jews worked as slaughterers. Thus Yiḥye Ṣāliḥ and Joseph Ḥayyim wrote special books on matters of purity (Sha'are Ṭahrah, Qānūn al-Nisā') for women, who knew no Hebrew.

The infiltration of popular culture into religious life was also evinced in the tendency of spiritual leaders to include folk tales, fables, and the like in their sermons and writings, to attract their listeners' attention. Ḥayyim was particularly notable in this respect, in his compositions *Imre Binah, Mashal Ve-Nimshal*, and *Nifla'im Ma'asekha*. Of course, these sermons were delivered in many communities in the spoken language, not Hebrew. Of particular interest is the place Arab-Muslim folk music won for itself in the liturgy of the Middle Eastern Jews. This process started in the second half of the sixteenth century in Safed, in the musical poetic work of Najjārah. The Jews adopted the melodies of Muslim love songs for prayers and piyyutim in the synagogue or in other para-liturgical assemblies; their sages even recommended it, to prevent or at least restrict the singing of actual love songs in Arabic, Turkish, Spanish, and Persian. Here is what Rabbi Barukh Shemu'el Mizraḥi wrote on his emigration from Kurdistan to Jerusalem in the preface to *The Book of Songs:*

> Since our people wandered from their land until the present day, a large part of them have learned and occupied themselves with those poems . . . [and praise is due to all the Jewish poets who] wrote poems in Hebrew, to the melody of the songs of the Arabs, whose purpose was solely to stop the people from singing love songs and songs of Arabs, but instead to engage in sacred songs, each at its appointed time.[35]

Although for centuries folk literature was transmitted orally, the process of writing it down seems to have begun in the eighteenth century, apart from the canonical tafsīrs of Persia, which were written down as early as the Middle Ages. We have a number of manuscripts from the eighteenth and nineteenth centuries of the literature of the Jews of Iraq, those who dwelt in Iraq itself or migrated to India, which form a treasury for learning about their popular culture. The favorable attitude of Rabbi Joseph Ḥayyim, the supreme spiritual authority in the Middle Eastern communities, especially to that part of the popular literature that could be enlisted for educational purposes, apparently was what induced the sages of Iraq even to have them printed. Indeed, a considerable number of the printed books of the Jews of Iraq, in Baghdad and the cities of India, are popular literature.

In Yemen, by contrast, the attitude of the Torah scholars to popular literature was mostly negative; essentially, it belonged to women. There was a single exception, which proves the rule—a composition entitled *Meshal Ha-Qadmoni* (The Ancient Proverb), whose moral purpose was a comparison of popular fables in Arabic and parallel fables from the rabbinic literature. This work was printed. Otherwise, the rich popular literature of the Jews of Yemen was not transcribed and certainly not printed. Only in the twentieth century, as a result of the interest of scholars, did the compilation of this literature begin, first by the researchers and then by members of the communities themselves, who meanwhile had immigrated to Israel. In this way folk tales, fables, and poems were saved by the thousands, just when the uprooting of this literature from its life source in the Diaspora put its continued existence in doubt. This initiative not only strengthened the tendency of the former Yemenite Jews to preserve their folk culture but also largely caused its resuscitation. For some time, these Jews had distanced themselves from this legacy for fear of a negative reaction by secular Israeli culture. But, thanks to cooperation between the researchers and the Yemenites, the popular culture of this community is represented in contemporary Israeli culture perhaps more than that of any other Middle Eastern community, certainly far beyond its demographic weight in the population as a whole.[36]

Everything one can say about popular literature generally applies as well to other aspects of folk culture, such as wedding customs, festivals, and children's games. These, too, lost the foundation of their existence with emigration. Moreover, prior to the emigration, a generation of intellectuals had already grown up in these countries who wished to copy Western ways. They neglected the Jewish tradition, which many perceived as primitive. Thus, the rescue of these popular customs occurred in Israel, though not so much in the form of active practice as in detailed written descriptions. It was the most exotic communities, Yemen and Kurdistan, that inspired the majority of these studies.

THE CULTURE OF MIDDLE EASTERN JEWRY
IN MODERN ISRAEL

Prior to the late nineteenth century, the contribution of the Jews of the Middle East to the culture of the Yishuv was very slight. The Yishuv had been built up principally by immigrants from North Africa, the Balkans, and Eastern Europe, though some individuals had come from the Middle Eastern lands, and some of these were quite distinguished spiritual leaders. For example, Shlomo 'Adani immigrated from Yemen in 1570 as a boy and later became head of the Hebron community; Shalom Shar'abi, also from Yemen, arrived in 1740 and became the leader of the kabbalist Beth El community in Jerusalem. But these, like other immigrants from the lands of the Middle East, were absorbed into the Yishuv without leaving any impression of the cultural heritage of their native communities. Not until the second half of the nineteenth century was there a desire on the part of these immigrants to preserve their communal identity. This began with the arrival in Hebron and Jerusalem of the eminent Mani and Yehuda families of Baghdad. Very rapidly, members of both families became notable in the spiritual and social leadership of the Yishuv, where they constituted an important component of the bridge between the Old Yishuv and the New. Their second generation, which was educated in Palestine, was connected by marriage to Ashkenazi families, and from these unions sprang Hebrew intellectuals and scholars who acquired their advanced education at European universities. Many became professional men: academics, lawyers, judges, and physicians. Their contribution was of the greatest importance for the formation of modern Hebrew culture in Palestine at the end of the century, especially in the attempt to connect this new culture with Arabic culture. This enhancement, though undoubtedly the fruit of Jewish education in Iraq, was achieved not by the efforts of a large group of Iraqi immigrants that preserved its communal identity but, rather, by just these two individual families.

Only after World War I did the number of Iraqi immigrants to Jerusalem reach several hundred, and these newcomers began to form a separate community maintaining its own institutions. These people, unlike the Mani and Yehuda families, did not embrace the education or culture of the West but reinforced, perhaps created, the trend toward seclusion of Middle Eastern Jews in Jerusalem. Furthermore, their rabbis very quickly assumed leadership positions in the community, almost totally detached from the Zionist movement and from the formal Yishuv leadership under the British Mandate. The influence of the Iraqi immigrants on the New Yishuv was accordingly minimal, except, as noted, for that of the Mani and Yehuda families. The members of this community in fact formed the backbone of that part of the Israeli population out of which, in the 1980s, arose the Shas movement under the leadership of Rabbi 'Ovadya Yosef, himself a native of Baghdad. Shas is critical of the mainstream Israeli culture, which was created essentially by European immigrants. Since the establishment of the state in 1948, the number of emigrants from Iraq has exceeded 120,000. Foremost among these were veterans of the He-Halutz movement and members of the Jewish underground in Iraq. They soon became involved in all aspects of life, including the professions and academic institutions, particularly in the private economic sector. They were almost entirely cut off from Jewish tradition and religious observance; nonetheless, they have contributed most significantly to the culture taking shape in Israel, chiefly as university professors, and still more through the work of important writers such as Sami Micha'el and Shim'on Balas. A special contribution of the Iraqi intellectuals, familiar with the Arab culture and language in their country of origin, has been the initiation of a dialogue with the intellectuals of the Arab minority in Israel.

The nucleus of pre-1948 emigrants from Iraq in Jerusalem was augmented by Persian Jews, who began to arrive as early as the 1880s, and their descendants. Owing to the frailty of their political and cultural condition, the Persians were economically and socially one of the weakest groups in the Old Yishuv, and they contributed the least to its culture. The circumstances of the arrivals from Afghanistan, and still more of those from Bukhara, were far better. The latter were deemed the well-to-do of the Yishuv at the turn of the twentieth century. They built the Reḥovot neighborhood, in its day considered the most luxurious in the city and later becoming known as the Bukharan Quarter. The Persians and Bukharans, and likewise the immigrants from Kurdistan, formed their own communal organizations for the purpose of conducting their religious life. The immigrants from Bukhara, supported by wealthy Bukharans in Palestine and abroad, produced liturgical books by and for the members of all the Iranian communities, but many were accessible only to speakers of Persian or Tajik, so no spiritual or cultural influence on anyone else was possible.

Matters were different for the immigrants from Yemen. They too began arriving in Palestine in large numbers from 1881, centering mainly on Jerusalem and Jaffa. This migration was organized after word spread through Yemen that the Ottoman rulers were encouraging Jews to move to Palestine and that land was being distributed to every newcomer. The reality of life in Jerusalem was a slap in the face: the Yemenites were coldly received by the city's Jewish community. Nevertheless, the influx from Yemen did not cease. In 1948, about half of all Yemenite Jews already lived in Israel, a percentage unequaled by any other Jewish community, Middle Eastern or Western. Unlike individuals who had come during earlier periods, the more recent arrivals were not assimilated into the Sephardic community, which formed the majority of the Yishuv and looked down on them. Instead, they began to consolidate as a self-contained group with its own institutions and tended to concentrate in certain neighborhoods. Their presence was highly visible, not only because of their relatively large number but also because of their distinctiveness in outward appearance and dress (see p. 932), in speech and Hebrew pronunciation, in the aspects of their religious observance—in fact in almost every area of life. True, this did not exercise any influence on the Sephardic and Ashkenazic majority, but these "odd" Yemenites attracted the attention of poets such as Naphtali Zvi Imber, the author of "Ha-Tikvah," and writers such as Ḥemda Ben-Yehuda, the wife of Eliezer Ben-Yehuda, the "father" of modern spoken Hebrew. The Yemenites' unique and ancient Jewish traditions particularly drew the attention of scholars such as David Yellin, the student of medieval Hebrew poetry; Abraham Idelsohn, whose subject was Jewish music and liturgy; and Eliezer Ha-Levi Gruenhut and Shlomo Wertheimer, who researched midrash and rabbinic literature. These and others like them, principally Shlomo Dov Goitein, created the romantic view of the Jews of Yemen, one that required, with some justification, that they and their heritage be seen as the image of ancient Jewry from the time of the ancient rabbis, the Second Temple, and even the days of the Bible.

The respected place of the Yemenites in the cultural mosaic of the land became more deeply rooted when they settled in the *moshavot* (agricultural villages) of the New Yishuv, from Gederah in the south to Yavne'el, Kinneret, and Zikhron Ya'aqov in the north. The "canonical" culture of Israel is based chiefly on the social and ideological tradition of the Labor movement since the time of the Second Aliyah in the early twentieth century, and the immigrants from Yemen participated in the fashioning of this heritage, something that cannot be stated with regard to the immigrants from other countries of the Middle East. And, in due course, the Yemenites played a role in the underground organizations during the Mandate: the Haganah, Etzel, and Leḥi.

Thus, without any deliberate act on the part of the Yemenite immigrants, their contribution to the culture of modern Israel has been greater than that of the members of the other Middle Eastern communities. Because the Ashkenazic leaders of the Labor movement, the cultural and social elite of the Yishuv, took a positive view of Yemenite culture, there was a readiness to absorb its values into the larger culture.

Appreciation of the culture of Middle Eastern Jewry was at first limited to two men, Eliyahu Eliachar and David Sitton, who represented the Ladino-speaking Sephardic majority that had dominated the Yishuv from the time of Naḥmanides in the thirteenth century to World War I. Following the creation of the State of Israel under the Labor movement and the influx of immigrants from Europe, the Sephardic communal organization began to voice criticism of the government's cultural policy, especially the notion of "the fusion of the exiles" (the melting pot) promoted by David Ben-Gurion. But this criticism was ineffectual. In the early 1960s, the "students' group for the fusion of the exiles" was active at the Hebrew University. Dozens of students participated, the majority being of Middle Eastern origin and the minority of European and American background, and much was heard from them about the need to integrate the history and traditions of the Jews from the countries of Islam into academic curricula and research programs. Among the most active members of this group were writers and poets such as Shelomo Avayo, Tuvya Sulami, and Eli 'Amir, and researchers such as the present writer.

But government and public institutions were not inclined to acquiesce to these demands until negative manifestations—such as the demonstrations of the Black Panthers—imperiled the orderly maintenance of the Israeli social fabric. Meanwhile, awareness was growing among the members of the Middle Eastern communities themselves, led by young people born and educated in Israel. Now began some fairly intensive documentation and preservation of the traditions of these communities, as well as attempts to transplant them into the new Israeli culture (see Eli Yassif's chapter on folk cultures in the State of Israel). This work was strongly encouraged by leading figures of the academic community such as Ḥayyim Ze'ev Hirschberg, Shlomo Morag, Dov Noy, Yehuda Ratzahbi, and Amnon Shiloaḥ. Publications of all sorts—books, periodicals, textbooks— were produced, in numbers previously unknown in the State of Israel. Without doubt, these publications massively enriched the public's knowledge of Middle Eastern Jewish culture and contributed to its integration into the larger culture of Israel. After public debates in the Knesset, at the initiative of Yitzḥak Navon (who was to become the first Sephardi to occupy the office of president of Israel), a special department was set up in the Ministry of Education and Culture charged to expedite such integration into the government education system and to assist in the development of research and teaching in academic institutions.

Of all the Middle Eastern immigrants to the State of Israel, those from Iraq are most noteworthy in this respect, beginning with Mordekhai Ben-Porat. He was the leader of the Jewish underground in Iraq in the year 1948, and he headed the great emigration operation. The Iraqi community has succeeded in establishing an important institution for the research and preservation of its heritage, a unique body, whose like no other community originating in the Islamic countries has been able to create in Israel. It is an active and vibrant center that conducts many activities both social and academic and applies modern means to bring the heritage of the Jews of Babylonia to the entire Israeli public.

However, the limited government activity and wide-ranging activity of the Middle Eastern immigrants was not enough, so long as a negative attitude toward their culture persisted in the Israeli public at large. Indeed, even in areas of popular culture such as singing and music, arguments have been made for more active integration of the Middle Eastern traditions. The composer Avihu Medina, whose parents immigrated from Yemen, has led this struggle. Moreover, the proportion of Israelis who are of Middle Eastern origin, and since the late 1950s who are from North Africa, particularly Morocco, has risen. Prior to the massive influx from the countries of the former Soviet Union, they constituted close to 60 percent of the population. The number of Middle Easterners in the academic institutions and in all spheres of culture and art has likewise risen. They have made notable economic strides, in contrast to their circumstances in the late 1940s and early 1950s, when their rapid immigration and their long stays in transit camps kept them in desperate economic straits for a fairly prolonged period. Together, all these factors, which may be seen as a tremendous achievement of education, have wrought a mighty change; to call it a genuine revolution in the role of the culture of Middle Eastern Jewry in the State of Israel would not be amiss.

Nevertheless, the physical separation of the immigrants from the places where their culture developed, the grave economic and social hardships they encountered in the early years in Israel, and the inimical attitude of the Sabras and the Jews of European origin have undoubtedly caused the loss of much of this cultural legacy. The younger generation, who have grown up in Israel, were educated at school and in the street to discard the "Diaspora heritage," although in recent years this delegitimation of Middle Eastern culture has almost entirely dissipated.

Unlike the Orthodox element in the Ashkenazic communities, anti-intellectual and anti-Zionist attitudes never developed among the Jews from the Middle East, nor did they after their migration to Israel.[37] These people joined the Zionist parties in large numbers and were ready to help realize the goals of Zionism by settling in development towns and remote villages. But after more than 30 years of life in Israel, large segments of the Middle Eastern and North African Jews have developed a sense of social deprivation as well as frustration with the attitude of the state toward the Jewish religious tradition. Their disappointment is reflected in the recent extraordinary upsurge of the Shas movement, which is now the third largest political party in Israel. This is not simply a clash between the Orthodox and the secular, or between anti-Zionists and Zionists. In fact, many Shas voters are Zionists, and many are quite distant from the religious way of life.

Still, even though all the members of Shas and its supporters, except perhaps for a handful, are of North African and Middle Eastern origin, there can be no doubt that this movement does not represent, politically or culturally, all the Middle Easterners in the State of Israel. They are fully integrated in diverse social and ideological frameworks. A clear-cut tenet in democratic Israel is that no ideological conformity is binding on one or another ethnic population group. The people of Middle Eastern origin and their descendants, a considerable proportion of whom are children of communally mixed couples and whose ethnic position is not clear, should certainly not be seen as a group that is ideologically uniform. This is perhaps one of the greatest achievements of the State of Israel at the end of its first half-century of existence.

NOTES

1. See, e.g., his response concerning a telegram that arrives on the Sabbath in his book *Rav Berakhot* (Jerusalem, 1962), 141–54.

2. On the tension between the Alliance and the religious Jewish leadership in the communities of Iraq and Persia, see Zvi Yehuda, "An Evaluation of the Educational Enterprise of the *Alliance Israélite Universelle* in Iraq Prior to World War I" (Hebrew), and Abraham Cohen, "Some Notes on the *Alliance* and the Jews of Persia" (Hebrew), both in Shim'on Schwarzfuchs, *Ha-Alliance bi-kehillot Aggan ha-Yam ha-Tikhon be-Sof ha-Me'ah ha-yod-tet ve-Hashpa'ato 'al ha-Matzav ha-Hevrati ve-ha-Tarbuti* (Jerusalem, 1987).

3. Hakīmān dīwān is still in manuscript. The only copy is preserved in the St. Petersburg Library. See Ḥayyim Schirmann, *Shirim Ḥadashim min ha-Genizah* (Jerusalem, 1966), 139–46.

4. See Abdallah Somekh, *Zivḥe Tzedeq (Responsa)* (Baghdad, 1904), no. 105, par. 70, 71, pp. 100–101. His pupil Ḥayyim also expands on this in his book of responsa, *Rav Pe'alim*, vol. 2 (Jerusalem, 1903), nos. 3–4, pp. 102a–103a. See also Yosef Tobi, "The Connection Between the Communities of the Middle East and Land of Israel" (Hebrew), in Avigdor Shin'an, *Hagirah ve-Hityashshvut be-Yisra'el uva-'ammim* (Jerusalem, 1984), 211–12.

5. The Jews of Kurdistan were mostly concentrated within the boundaries of modern Iraq; however, the territory called Kurdistan was divided among five modern political units: Iraq, Iran, Turkey, Syria, and the former Soviet Union. In each of these, apart from the Soviet Union, there were Jewish communities, and although their spoken neo-Aramaic differs in each, in social consciousness of the Jewish people in modern times they are considered members of a single community. Below we expand on what these communities had in common in social terms, apart from the language.

6. The Jewish community in Afghanistan is relatively new, having formed only after the imposition of Islam on the Jews of Mashhad in 1839. Many of the Jews of Mashhad fled to Herat in Afghanistan. The Sunni Islam there (of the Ḥanafi school) was easier for the Jews than the Shī'ite Islam in Persia. From a spiritual and cultural viewpoint, the Jews of Persia and of Afghanistan are indistinguishable, but the fact of living in a more comfortable political framework and under a different Islamic rule caused the latter to crystallize as a community with a different social awareness. We shall encounter a similar feature below, in respect to the Jews of Aden as compared with those of Yemen.

7. In modern Jewish discourse since the early nineteenth century, the Jewish dwellers of central Asia are called Bukharans, after their foremost community in its day, in Bukhara, the capital of an independent emirate. Today the region is divided among five republics of the former Soviet Union: Uzbekistan, Tajikistan, Turkmenistan, Kyrgyzstan, and Kazakhstan. Now Bukhara is in Uzbekistan.

8. A faithful reflection of the grave condition of the Jews of Persia in this period, and in other adjacent periods of persecution by the Shī'ite rule, is shown in the composition *Kitāb Anūsi* by Bābāi ibn Luṭf and in the essay *The Book of the Events of Kāshān* by his grandson Bābāi ben Farhād. Large excerpts from these works were translated into French by W. Bacher, "Les Juif de Perse au XVII et XVIII siècles," *Revue des Études Juives* 51 (1905): 121–36, 52 (1906): 77–97, and 53 (1906): 85–100. For a complete English translation of the second book, see Vera Basch Moreen, *Iranian Jewry During the Afghan Invasion: The Kitāb-I Sār Guzasht-i Kāshān of Bābāi b. Farhād; Text and Commentary* (Stuttgart, 1990). For a fine summary of the history of the Jews of Persia in that period, see Vera Basch Moreen, *Iranian Jewry's Hour of Peril and Heroism: A Study of Bābāi Ibn Luṭf's Chronicle (1617–1662)* (New York, 1987).

9. On commerce in printed books in Yemen, see Abraham Ya'ri, "The Sale of Books in

Yemen by Emissaries from the Land of Israel" (Hebrew), in his *Meḥkerei Sefer: Perakim be-Toldot Ha-Sefer ha-ʿIvri* (Jerusalem, 1958), 163–69.

10. Equal rights were granted to the Jews of the Ottoman Empire in a process lasting many years (1839–1908) in the framework of the general reforms known as the Tanzimat.

11. For a comprehensive introduction to the literature of the Jews of Persia, see Amnon Netser, *Otzar kitve ha-Yad shel Yehude Paras be-Makhon Ben-Tzvi* (Jerusalem, 1986), 11–69.

12. For an overview of the literature of the Jews of Kurdistan, see Yonah Sabar, "Various Genres of Literary Work of the Jews of Kurdistan" (Hebrew), *Peʿamim* 13 (1982): 57–70.

13. Shimon Agasi, *Imre Shimʿon* (Jerusalem, 1968), 243–44.

14. The possible affinity between the religious perceptions of the Jews of Yemen and those of the Muslims of Yemen in the Middle Ages and the modern period is a fascinating subject, which has not yet been researched, but I cannot expand on it here.

15. For a similar feature in the first half of the twelfth century in Egypt, see the complaint of Abraham, the son of Maimonides, before the Muslim ruler in Cairo in his day, that he was changing the accepted customs of worship. See M. A. Friedman, "A Cry of Despair at the Cancelation of the Recital of the Piyyutim: A Request to Approach the Sultan" (Hebrew), *Peʿamim* 78 (1999): 128–47.

16. This reference is chiefly to the *Zohar*.

17. The rabbi Yiḥye Yitzḥak, who served as the head of the community and the chief rabbi, was the leader of the ʿiqqeshis, whereas the rabbi Yiḥye Qāfiḥ, the foremost scholar of his generation, headed the dardeʿi faction.

18. A photocopy of the original ruling and its Hebrew translation are given by Yisrael Yeshaʿyahu and Aharon Ṣadoq, eds., *Shevut Teman* (Tel Aviv, 1945), 225–26.

19. Agasi, *Imre Shimʿon*, 244.

20. See Amnon Netser, "Problems of the Cultural, Social, and Political Integration of the Jews of Iran" (Hebrew), *Gesher* 25, nos. 96–97 (1979): 69–83.

21. Joseph Gurjī, *ʿEdut Bi-Yhosef* (Jerusalem, 1926). For details of this matter, see Ben-Zion Yehoshuaʿ, "Love of Zion and Zionism Among the Jews of Afghanistan" (Hebrew), *Kivvunim* 7 (1980): 43–57.

22. Gurjī, *ʿEdut Bi-Yhosef,* 3b–4a.

23. This educational network was established by R. Isaac Meʾir Levi, a member of Agudat Yisrael, who arrived in Iran in 1943 and stood for an extremist anti-Zionist ideology. The network did quite well, but it was inadequate to implant anti-Zionist ideas in the Jews of Iran.

24. On Muhib, see Jirzhi Bachka, "A Continuer of Judeo-Persian Literature" (Hebrew), *Peʿamim* 35 (1988): 198–203.

25. On the modern literature of the Jews of Iraq, see Sasson Somekh, "Lost Voices: Jewish Authors in Modern Arabic Literature," in Mark R. Cohen and Abraham L. Udovitch, eds., *Jews Among Arabs: Contacts and Boundaries* (Princeton, 1989), 9–20, and Reʾuven Snir, "A

Cultural Change in the Mirror of Literature: The Beginnings of the Arabic Short Story by the Jews of Iraq" (Hebrew), *Pe'amim* 36 (1988): 108–29.

26. *Somekh*, "Lost Voices," 18–19.

27. For a critical edition of this composition, see Yosef Tobi, *'Iyyunim bi-Megillat Teman* (Jerusalem, 1986), 31–55.

28. For a complete edition of the original Judeo-Arabic work with an abbreviated English translation, see S. D. Goitein, *Travels in Yemen: An Account of Joseph Halévy's Journey to Najran in the Year 1870 Written in San'ani Arabic by His Guide Ḥayyim Ḥibshūsh* (Jerusalem, 1941).

29. The essay was published by Yosef Qāfiḥ, " 'The History of the Jews in Yemen' by Ḥayyim Ḥibshūsh," *Sefunot* (1958): 246–86 (Hebrew).

30. The essay was published by Yosef Qāfiḥ, "The List of the Works of the Yemenite Scholars by Rabbi Yiḥye Qāfiḥ" *Tema* 1 (1990): 7–28 (Hebrew).

31. The essay was published by Re'uven Kashani, " *'Korot Zemanim'* by Rabbi Mattityah Garji of Afghanistan," *Shevet Va-'Am* 6 (1971): 136–59 (Hebrew).

32. Recently edited and abridged by Hooshang Ebrami and translated into English by George W. Maschke, as Habib Levy, *Comprehensive History of the Jews of Iran (the Outset of the Diaspora)* (Costa Mesa, Calif., 1999).

33. For a detailed list of the Hebrew printers in the Middle Eastern countries and the books they printed, see Abraham Ya'ri, *Ha-Defus ha-'Ivri be-Artzot ha-Mizraḥ,* 2 vols. (Jerusalem, 1936–40). Although over 60 years have passed since the publication of this book, it is still the only work on this subject.

34. See Yona Sabar, *The Folk Literature of the Kurdistani Jews: An Anthology* (New Haven, Conn., 1982).

35. Shemu'el Barukh, *Sefer ha-Shirim* (Jerusalem, 1924). See also Yehuda Ratzahbi, *Mi-Ginze Shirat ha-Kedem,* Jerusalem, 1991, 262–70.

36. For the domain of music, see, e.g., Marsha Bryan Edelman, "Middle East Meets West: The Impact of Yemenite Song on Popular and Art Music of Israel," in Ephraim Isaac and Yosef Tobi, eds., *Judaeo-Yemenite Studies: Proceedings of the Second International Congress* (Princeton, 1999), 135–41.

37. See Yosef Tobi, "Roots of the Attitude of the Jews of the Middle East to the Zionist movement" (Hebrew), in Joseph Hacker et al., eds., *Temurot ba-Historia ha-Yehudit ha-Ḥadashah* (Jerusalem, 1988), 169–92.

SELECTED BIBLIOGRAPHY

A. GENERAL

Moreh, Shemuel. *Jewish Contributions to Nineteenth-Century Arabic Literature.* Oxford, 1996.

Stillman, Norman. *Sephardi Religious Responses to Modernity.* Australia, 1995.

———. *The Jews in Arab Lands in Modern Times.* Philadelphia, 1991.

Tobi, Yosef. "The Jewish Centers in Asia," In Shemu'el Ettinger, ed., *Toldot Ha-Yehudim Be-Artsot Ha-Islam.*

B. IRAQ

Abbas, Shiblak. *The Lure of Zion: The Case of the Iraqi Jews.* London, 1986.

Ben Porat, Mordechai. *To Baghdad and Back: The Miraculous 2000 Homecoming of the Iraqi Jews.* Jerusalem, 1998.

Ganimah, Yusuf Risq Allah. *A Nostalgic Trip into the History of the Jews in Iraq.* Lanham, Md., 1998.

Gat, Moshe. *The Jewish Exodus from Iraq, 1948–1951.* Portland, Ore., 1997.

Hillel, Shlomo. *Operation Babylon.* London, 1989.

Rejwan, Nissim. *The Jews of Iraq: 3,000 Years of History and Culture.* London, 1985.

Sawdayee, Maurice. *The Impact of Western European Education on the Jewish Millet of Baghdad.* Microfilm. Ann Arbor, 1978.

Somekh, Sasson. "Lost Voices: Jewish Authors in Modern Arabic Literature." In Mark R. Cohen and Abraham L. Udovitch, eds., *Jews Among Arabs: Contacts and Boundaries.* Princeton, 1989.

C. KURDISTAN

Brauer, Erich. *The Jews of Kurdistan.* Detroit, 1993.

Rand, Barukh, and Barbarah Rush. *Jews of Kurdistan.* Toledo, Ohio, 1978.

Sabar, Yona. *The Folk Literature of the Kurdistani Jews: An Anthology.* New Haven, Conn., 1982.

D. IRAN (PERSIA)

Glanz, Iosef. *A Study on Jewish Education in Iran: Facts and Programmes.* Teheran, 1972.

Levi, Azaria. *The Jews of Mashad.* Jerusalem, 1998.

Levy, Habib, *Comprehensive History of the Jews of Iran.* Costa Mesa, Calif., 1999.

Loeb, Laurence. *Outcaste: Jewish Life in Southern Iran.* New York, 1977.

Moreen, Vera Basch. *Iranian Jewry During the Afghan Invasion: The Kitāb-I Sār Guzasht-i Kāshān of Bābāi b. Fārhād; Text and Commentary.* Stuttgart, 1990.

———. *Iranian Jewry's Hour of Peril and Heroism: A Study of Bābāi Ibn Lutf's Chronicle (1617–1662).* New York, 1987.

Spector, Daniel Earl. *A History of the Persian Jews.* Microfilm. Ann Arbor, 1975.

E. YEMEN

Ahroni, Reuben. *Yemenite Jewry: Origins, Culture, and Literature.* Leiden, 1986.

Goitein, S. D. *From the Land of Sheba: Tales of the Jews of Yemen.* New York, 1973.

YOSEF TOBI

————. *Travels in Yemen: An Account of Joseph Halévy's Journey to Najran in the Year 1870 Written in San'ani Arabic by His Guide Ḥayyim Ḥibshūsh.* Jerusalem, 1941.

Isaac, Ephraim, and Yosef Tobi, eds. *Judaeo-Yemenite Studies: Proceedings of the Second International Congress.* Princeton, 1999.

Nini, Yehoda. *The Jews of Yemen.* Chur, 1991.

Tobi, Yosef. *The Jews of Yemen: Studies in Their History and Culture.* Leiden, 1999.

Tudor, Parfitt. *The Road to Redemption: The Jews of Yemen, 1900–1950.* Leiden, 1996.

A Beta Israel potter in Ethiopia, 1980s.
(Photo: Galia Sabar)

RELIGIOUS INTERPLAY ON AN AFRICAN STAGE:

Ethiopian Jews in Christian Ethiopia

HAGAR SALAMON

Beyond their intrinsic interest as a group with an exotic and controversial identity, the Beta Israel (Falasha),[1] the Jews of Ethiopia, offer a unique example of a Jewish group in an ancient, non-Western, Christian society. Scattered across the vast reaches of northwestern Ethiopia, the Beta Israel constituted a religious and professional minority, living among a predominantly Christian population with which they shared both language and physical appearance. Moreover, they clearly saw themselves as a distinct group, maintaining a faith that the majority of Ethiopians had forsaken for the younger and now dominant creed of Christianity. Strongly identifying themselves with the Torah (*Orit,* the Old Testament written in Ge'ez),[2] which was the central focus of their beliefs, they meticulously observed its laws and dreamed of the coming of the Messiah and their return to the legendary Jerusalem.[3]

The enigma of Jewish life in Ethiopia, and the dramatic airlift of the entire community to the State of Israel in the early 1990s, aroused public debate both within and outside of the Jewish world. Implicitly assuming a dichotomous separation between Jews and non-Jews, the sole aim of these debates was a clear-cut answer to the question: are the Falasha *real* Jews? Previous studies dealing with this group were occupied with the same question. One school of thought characterizes their lives in terms of isolation from their surroundings and ongoing struggles, and it emphasizes their similarity to other, primarily historical Jewish groups.[4] A second school focuses on the cultural and religious similarity between them and their Ethiopian neighbors,[5] suggesting that the group originated from an apostate movement that broke off from Ethiopian Christianity in

This essay is based on my book *The Hyena People: Ethiopian Jews in Christian Ethiopia.* Copyright © 1999 The Regents of the University of California. I wish to thank the University of California Press for their kind permission to use this material.—H.S.

the fifteenth century around Gondar.[6] Without diminishing the inherent interest in the debate between these polar approaches, I believe that the explanations
engendered by both views are riddled with contradiction and ambiguity.

The ethnographic study of the relations between the Beta Israel and their
non-Jewish neighbors in Ethiopia at the level of daily interaction is as important
as the prevailing historical approach. This chapter, based on more than 100 in-
depth interviews I conducted with members of the Beta Israel now living in Israel, attempts to reconstruct the group's daily life in Ethiopia, focusing on the
individuals' own depictions of intergroup relations. My goal was to refract their
past through the special lens of their individual and collective memories and
thus to learn what it meant to them to be a Jew in Ethiopia.

Although the group's actual origins are pertinent to the question of their Jewish lineage, their self-identity as Jews in Ethiopia was defined solely in relation
to the dominant Christian society. Even in my initial interviews, it became clear
that, when people spoke of themselves, they were speaking of Christians as well,
though they lived among a mixed population of Muslims and others.[7] Even in
areas highly populated by Muslims, Christians dominated the Jews' lives. In the
memory of the Beta Israel, the Muslim presence merely allowed the spotlight to
fall on the conflict unfolding between the Jews and the Christians. The stories
told were a narrative reenactment of the Oedipal drama between Judaism and
Christianity—religion born of religion, and, in the ironic inversions of daily interaction, religion dominated by religion—acted out so powerfully in Ethiopia.
This situation did not change significantly until recent decades, when the awareness of a meaningful Jewish "other"—non-Ethiopian ("white") Jews—became
more fully present in the Beta Israel consciousness. The ethnography of Jewish
life in Ethiopia *is* the ethnography of the Jews' relations with their Christian
neighbors.

Recurring patterns of structure and content provide tools for understanding
the contingent relationship between a variety of themes that appear *prima facie*
unrelated. These include religious disputes, purity and impurity, the concept of
blood, conversion, supernatural powers, the image of the Ethiopian Jew as a
hyena, and the metaphors of clay vessels, water, and fire.[8] These themes constitute a conceptual system that stands for a reality often perceived by the Beta Israel as baffling and incoherent.

ATTRACTION AND REPULSION: EVERYDAY RELATIONS

The Jews in Ethiopia owned no land but worked as tenant farmers on Christian
land.[9] No less central was their work as craftspeople, the men specializing in

smithery and the women in pottery. Local Christian society treated these crafts with ambivalence. Though the products themselves were derided, and the practitioners despised, they were not only essential to that agricultural society but also highly valued for their quality. This ambivalence was expressed by attributing supernatural powers to the artisans, to account for the excellence of their products. To the Christians, the power to transform otherwise useless things into useful objects by means of fire was surely supernatural.[10] If the Jews could change the form and function of things, what might they do to people—including themselves? Rural communities needed the agricultural tools, knives, and clay vessels produced by the Beta Israel, and the eerie skills attributed to their makers endowed the products with a magical aura.

A complex system of daily contact existed between Jews and Christians, a framework of formalities of attraction and repulsion that permitted structured cooperation but set strict boundaries between the groups. These were most evident in the prohibition against physical contact. For the Jews, physical contact with any person who was not part of the Beta Israel (and thus considered impure) was prohibited. According to the official rhetoric, contamination resulted from even the slightest contact, whether accidental or out of some necessity, and the Jew was expected to undergo ritual purification.[11] In addition, the Beta Israel made an effort not to allow Christians into their homes. They especially avoided inviting Christian women, who did not live apart during their bleeding periods, as did their women, posing a risk of particularly virulent ritual contamination.

In more recent times, however, these rules of purity and impurity were less strictly observed. Even the practice of eating "Christian food" in the course of a shared meal was gaining acceptance, so long as the meal did not include meat. Still, many Jews, particularly among the older generation, were even stricter about avoiding physical contact with non-Jews.

In most regions where such avoidance was maintained, a variety of strategies was developed to permit regular and even intensive interactions. Among these was the use of freshly cut branches as a mat on which Christians could stand when entering Jewish homes and as a buffer-barrier that could be touched simultaneously by Jews and non-Jews working together in the fields.[12]

When a Christian wished to give a Jew money (as payment for handicrafts, for example) he or she might place the coin on animal droppings, and the Jew would take it from the dung. The droppings, they explained, canceled out the impurity. When a Christian woman came to speak with her Jewish neighbor, she would call from outside the home. The Jewish woman would step out to the yard and they would converse, the Christian remaining all the while on the other side of the fence. A Christian woman might be invited over for coffee, but she re-

Beta Israel women in the village of Walaqua, Gondar district, Ethiopia, 1984. (Photo: Galia Sabar)

mained outside the fence and was served her coffee in a special cup made of clay. After the visit, she would either take the cup away with her or break it.[13] Some Jewish families kept a second set of dishes for their Christian visitors, dishes that were stored in the yard on a tree or a bush. The neighbors were familiar with this practice and would take their own dishes whenever they came for a visit.

Many families maintained close ties with their Christian neighbors. In such cases, the neighbors would keep a special set of dishes for the Jews as well. When members of the two groups participated in joint celebrations and rituals, measures were taken to permit everyone to occupy the same site.

The practices of separation and avoidance of physical contact were rooted in the Beta Israel view that the Christians were unclean because they did not maintain the rules of purity practiced by the Jews. Nonetheless, we find a wide array of practices whose purpose was to permit proximate relations with the Christian neighbors.

One speaker narrated:

Except for us, there are no Jews in Matrawa. All around just *goyim* [meaning Christians]. Only our family moved there, because we had no land. I had a good friend, a Christian, and he invited me. They asked me to work and live with them and make things from steel and cloth, since I know how to do those things. We wanted a field. We got along with the *goyim*. They went with their religion and we went with ours. I would make things from steel and wood together, like knives and plows, because the Christians don't know how to make those things. Later they asked me to move to their place. When we arrived there, there was a house ready for us to go in, and in our last year [in Ethiopia], when our house was a little old, they fixed it for us. I would also make them rings not from gold and all sorts of things to wear not from gold. Also things to dig in the ground for agriculture and knives to cut the wheat. My second job was to make clothes and cloth. We grew our own food. We bought sugar, coffee, and salt. Except for those things, we didn't need to buy anything. I work and my Christian neighbors give me what I need. If I need help in the fields, planting or bringing down the crop or cleaning the weeds out, they would do it for me. We grew potatoes, and they planted tomatoes for me, because only I was there to make things [crafts], so they gave me much honor. Do you know how much they cried when we left [for Israel]?

This account describes a strong bond indeed.[14] Their specialization in specific branches of artisanship characterized the Beta Israel to such an extent that a number of researchers have suggested they be viewed more as a professional caste than as members of a different religion.[15]

The magical cunning of the Beta Israel was associated by Christians with the *Buda,* the mythical hyena, a central figure in the supernatural cosmology of Ethiopia.[16] This and other human/animal transformations connected with the supernatural were not exclusive to the Beta Israel, and similar associations are attached to other groups throughout Ethiopia and across Africa.[17] But the concrete accusations linking the Buda and the Beta Israel, according to the recollections of my interviewees, take on a unique dimension not found in other African contexts. The specific characteristics attributed to the Beta Israel Buda integrate accusations associated not only with their profession but also with their religious tradition and the conceptual differences between Judaism and Christianity in Ethiopia.

According to one widely held view, the Buda disguises itself as a human during the day but reverts to its natural state—a hyena—at night. (The appellations *Jib,* meaning "hyena," and *Jiratam,* meaning "tail," were used by neighbors of the Beta Israel to refer directly to this image.) This notion bespeaks a total dehumanization of the Jews. As hyena people, the Beta Israel were feared for their literal "eating" (that is, sucking the blood of living victims or of recently buried cadavers that they supposedly disinterred and used for their nutritional and ritual needs) and the more symbolic "eating" (casting an evil eye on the victim, who feels as though his blood has been sucked).[18]

The accusation that the Jews possessed magical powers had a strong influence on relations between the two groups. Fear of these powers moved the Christians to maintain their distance. The specific content of their charges against the Beta Israel combines the occupations typical of the group and their landless status with their religious belief. Religious-historical tales were cited as proof of the Jews' supernatural powers, and stories of the manner in which they were said to be employed against Christians were used to link these Jews with scriptural events. The Jewish smith was regarded as a descendant of the Jew who forged the nails for Jesus' crucifixion. Because it was set down in Holy Writ, the accusation was viewed as incontrovertible. In the same fashion, as we shall see, the Christians interpreted the sacrifice of sheep—a rite central to the Beta Israel celebration of Passover—as the annual reenactment of the crucifixion. Anti-Jewish accusations already familiar from other cultural contexts, in particular the killing of Jesus by the Jews on Passover and the ritual murder of Christian children by Jews,[19] joined with magical conceptions that flourished in Ethiopia, creating a multileveled system of confirmation. As the progeny of the Jews who crucified Jesus, the Beta Israel were accused of a continuing malevolent intent—an intent passed from generation to generation. It was "in their blood," even without their being aware of it.

FAMILIAL CEREMONIES, RELIGIOUS HOLIDAYS, AND GIFT GIVING

Strange as it may seem, the chaotic realm of accusation, dehumanization, and fear coexisted with another realm: the ritualistic, characterized by cooperation and conviviality. A man from the Gondar region recalled:

> If I have Christian friends I can invite them. If there's eating I give them a sheep for as many as are coming and they slaughter it alone, on the side. Each side sits alone, also the Muslims eat alone. Then when there's happiness and dancing, everyone joins together. . . . Now if, for instance, the Christians have a wedding, then I can't go in when they're eating. . . . If he gives a whole sheep and we're not that many people, then I take it home. After I take it home, maybe on Thursday or Friday I'll kill it. Then my whole family eats it.

Following the meal, everyone gathered in the central *das,* a special open hut built for ceremonies, and danced and sang for many hours. Hospitality customs were based on mutual acquaintance. Each group knew the other's rules and adhered to them scrupulously. With areas of cooperation and separation clearly defined, neighbors could indeed "enter" the social framework created by wedding rituals.

Weddings   Neighbors from different groups were usually invited to attend wedding ceremonies. The event was divided into two distinct parts: the religious ritual and the celebration. Generally, according to recollections of Beta Israel members, the religious part was not attended by the guests from the other group, and the festive meal was held separately but in physical proximity. Special huts were erected for each group so they could dine separately. Each group only ate meat that it had slaughtered. Consequently, when guests from a neighboring religious group were invited to a celebration, the hosts supplied the invited parties in advance with animals for slaughter as well as with the ingredients to prepare *injera* (bread) and *tella* (beer, usually made from barley)—the staples of every festive meal. When Christians were invited to a Jewish wedding, they received an animal that they slaughtered and cooked *during* the ceremony, using pots and cooking utensils they brought with them. When, however, Jews were invited to a Christian wedding, their representative was given the animal ahead of time, usually a few days prior to the celebration. The Beta Israel cooked the meat and divided it among the invited Jewish families, each taking its share to the party.

There were regions in which the guests' participation was more segregated. Joint dances were prohibited, and one could only watch the dancing. A Beta Israel woman from the Seqelt region told me:

> If we have a wedding we invite the Christian neighbors. Before the wedding I give them sheep, they have a *qes* [both Beta Israel and Christians use the same word for priest] and they perform the slaughtering on their own, far far away. And I [meaning the Jews] also slaughter far away. Then there's beer, and I give some to them. I also give them *injera* alone, that I had made. But if she invites me and she prepares the *injera*—I don't eat. If in a wedding I give them a sheep to slaughter and they eat it, we can't dance with them. Dancing is on the side [separately]; even [similarly], if I go to their wedding and they dance, I stand on the side and do like this [claps hand and sings], but don't dance with them.

When I asked her why it was so, she answered: "It's prohibited. It's blood in the house! It's prohibited to touch each other. If you dance, you might touch, so it's prohibited."

Although in some regions or among certain families there was more stringent avoidance of physical contact, this did not disrupt the mutual participation in celebrations that were so central to intergroup relations. Each group was aware of what the members of the other group were and were not permitted to do, and they tried to cooperate as much as possible with their rules. Thus, for instance, during fast periods for the Christians, and particularly when they had to give up meat for Lent, the Jews served other types of food.

The Christians, as construed in the memories of many of the people with whom I spoke, took care that the Beta Israel, in this particular ritual context, could maintain their rules governing slaughter and eating: "They were very re-

A Beta Israel woman preparing *injera* (Ethiopian bread), 1980s.
(Photo: Galia Sabar)

spectful from a religious point of view. They know what is permitted and prohibited. They would not try to force us. They gave us everything we needed in
advance."

Inviting members of the other religion was, then, common practice to promote
and encourage mutual familiarity and respect. Indeed, both groups made efforts
to facilitate their neighbors' inclusion in the ceremony. The steps of this "dance"
of inclusion and exclusion carried over into the rules governing gift giving.

Whereas members of the inviting group customarily brought only money,
guests from other groups brought both money and a gift. The money was given
to the celebrating family to help cover the great cost of organizing the event. It
functioned like a flexible "bank," raising a large amount of money in a short
time. The custom of bringing money to such rituals is deeply rooted in Ethiopian
tradition.[20] The amount of money given by each participant was scrupulously
recorded to ensure a reciprocal commitment, an agreement that transcended religious boundaries.

"The Gift of a Jew"   The gifts brought (in addition to money) by neighboring
groups were common to each of them and known in advance. These gifts carried
particular symbolic meanings charged with hidden messages.[21] Very often the
Beta Israel gave knives to their Christian hosts a few days before the wedding, to
enable their use at the ceremony. As it was explained to me: "If the Jew works

with iron he brings iron knives to the wedding. . . . He might bring three or four knives as a gift. That is the gift of a Jew."

The speakers drew a clear distinction between the different types of knives they made. There were curved knives (*kara*) used in daily agriculture; there were long, straight knives (*marejiya kara*) for animal slaughter; and there were smaller, more personal knives (*billawa*), rather like pocketknives, considered luxuries and used to cut meat, though not for slaughter. A Jew usually brought one of these to his Christian landowner when tenancy was established.

There were two kinds of billawa. One was double-edged; the other sharpened on one side only. A billawa that was given by a Jew to a Christian was invariably single-edged. The rationalization for this was: "If you bring a knife that is sharp on both sides, that is dangerous for him. A one-sided knife only he can use." The sharp side of the knife represented the receiver's domination, the dull side the Jew's subordination. The knife exchange struck me as odd: that the subordinate group should choose to pay tribute to the dominant group with a gift less powerful than that which they themselves used. But a further meaning was apparently embedded in this exchange: though the ostensible message was tribute and honor, the latent message was an exhibition of indispensability and strength, since it implied a reverse dependency. The dominant group relied on the Jews to provide their basic tools and perform the tribute ritual. The single-edged knife, then, had a double-edged meaning. Consider a widely told legend, much enjoyed by Ethiopian Jews:

A delegation of Christian notables came to Emperor Tewodros II—the "King of Kings," who ruled Ethiopia from 1855 to 1868—and asked him to annihilate all Ethiopian Jews. The ruler arranged a dispute at his palace, with both sides sending their representatives.[22] The emperor invited them to dine with him. Appetizing meats were laid before the guests, but there were no knives. Staring at the meat, unable to eat it, the Christians understood Tewodros's message and gave up their plan to destroy the Jews.

As a tool that can also be used as a weapon, a knife is a highly charged object.[23] When the Jews brought money to Christian weddings, they were establishing their unconditional support. But when they added the gift of a knife, they were simultaneously representing themselves, in a subtle but concrete ritualistic context, as a potential threat.

A wedding anticipates children and heirs. Inviting landless and politically powerless people to a fertility rite uniting masters of the earth honored the perpetuation of Christian dominance and highlighted the Jews' subordination. Their gifts, the knives that are indispensable to agriculture and animal husbandry, symbolized fertility. But the unstated fact that only the Jews made knives

A Beta Israel blacksmith in Ethiopia, 1980s.
(Photo: Galia Sabar)

carried a rather less submissive message. With it, the Jewish guest quietly reminded his host that he too was, in fact, indispensable, that theirs was a relationship of symbiosis—not merely subordination.

According to the hermeneutics of the Beta Israel, by bringing a live sheep to a Jewish wedding, the Christian landowners present themselves as providers. The Beta Israel portray themselves as the producers of the tools needed for agriculture or slaughter—to transform substance into sustenance. In this way, they emphasize the tremendous dependence of the Christians on the products they make and, on the symbolic level, on the Beta Israel themselves.

The knives represent their producers well: the act of production is thought to be lowly and, according to the Ethiopian belief, linked to the supernatural. Yet the object is necessary and—precisely because of its supernatural provenance—possesses a special quality. It is simultaneously despised and needed, threatening and protective. The choice of the type of knife, in conjunction with the ritualistic context in which it is given, emphasizes the cooperation and interdependence between the two groups.

Religious Holidays: Inclusion and Exclusion   Religious holidays are another arena for the interplay of approaching and distancing. The Beta Israel were thoroughly involved with the holidays of their Christian neighbors. They knew the names of the holidays, helped determine the precise day of the celebrations, and at times even participated in them. The cycles of the neighboring religions, the Christians in particular, were integrated into the Beta Israel division of the year into holy and profane periods. They employed the sacred days of other religious groups as markers around which the conception of time was arranged.[24] More-over, the neighboring religious groups consulted each other's calendars, the bet-ter to track the dates of their own holidays.

Clear rules governed participation in one another's holidays. Members of Christian and Muslim groups were not always free to attend Jewish festivals. Ex-clusions varied by region and occasion.

The holiday to which Christians were most typically invited was the Sigd. This festival was unique to the Beta Israel: it was celebrated neither by Jews in other parts of the world nor by non-Jews in Ethiopia.[25] It occurred once a year, on the morning of the twenty-ninth day of the eighth month (according to the Beta Is-rael reckoning). At that time, the Jews gathered in the main villages and towns and ascended a nearby mountain, where they fasted, read from the holy books, and prayed for mercy, forgiveness, and redemption. After the regional *qes,* ac-companied by fellow priests, delivered a sermon that included both preaching and blessing, a festive meal was consumed. The polythematic nature of the Sigd has not yet been fully investigated, nor have the ecumenical implications en-coded in it been explored.[26] For our purposes, it is noteworthy that a large num-ber of Christians attended the Sigd, and prayers were said in public areas in the presence of a large crowd that included Christians and converted Jews. Although most of the people I spoke to recalled that the non-Jewish guests usually joined the ceremony after the prayers—that is, during the celebration and feast—there were a few intriguing reports of Christians participating in the prayers. Accord-ing to the informants, their neighbors were familiar with the various stages of this holiday and knew the right times to join in.

The following detailed account from Ambober, a village in Gondar where a large Sigd ceremony was held, describes Christian participation:

They don't pray, just look. We give them something to eat, over there, on the side. If, for example, we slaughter bulls, we give each group according to their number. They stand on the side and listen to us during the prayers too. They listen from the beginning to the qesim [plural, as spoken in Hebrew] pray. They know Ge'ez and understand. Everyone listens: Jews, Christians, and Mus-lims. They listen and are very, very happy. They listen to everything from the Torah, from the Orit. . . . We translate it and they all stand and listen. The

Christian qesim can also attend, I invite them to come. Look, as far as the other holidays are concerned, they knew when Passover was held. They would ask us on what day we're beginning Passover but they didn't come over to us on Passover, nor on other holidays. Maybe they would come but they'd stay outside, they couldn't come in. The Jews don't go to the Christians during the holidays—each person stays in his own home. Sigd is *completely different*. A lot of people from all different places would come to us. We also invited a lot of people so that they would come and see our holiday.

The Christian holiday Meskel, in the region of Tigre, was described from a Jewish point of view:

The Christians celebrate Meskel, which falls a little before we celebrate Sukkot [Feast of Tabernacles]. This holiday is like Sigd is for us. First comes our Yom Kippur [Day of Atonement][27] and then their Meskel. They sing, take the wooden image of Mary to the river and dance there, and then they put her back in the church. We go to watch. We don't eat. They were glad if we had come to them. Each would give you his spot, it's a sign of respect and honor.

These examples illustrate the attempt to coordinate holiday schedules in Ethiopian culture. The festivals offered an opportunity for the expression of affinity between Jews and Christians while underscoring the concrete and symbolic differences between them, by giving occasion for the comparison of customs and origins.

The Beta Israel integrated animal sacrifice in their rites; Christians did not. Made aware by European missionaries[28] that mainstream Judaism had long ago abandoned the practice, the Christians, as the Jews recall, were highly critical of the survival of this discredited rite among their neighbors. Nevertheless, the Jews have a particularly vivid image of many Christians asking them to perform such a sacrifice on their behalf, which they understood as an acknowledgment of the special relationship between the Jews and God. The following dramatic account is from the Tigre region:

In 1950 there was a terrible bout of locusts in Ethiopia. At the time, qes Itzhak of Maharia was living by us in Godolo [a village in the Adiaro province of Tigre]. The Christians and the Muslims asked him to pray. They had a great Christian qes who was 80 years old and whose name was Gabrihat. He said that, if the locusts persisted, there would be a great famine, like when he was a child. He said to them: "Go to the Jews and convince them. Even give them money, buy a sheep, slaughter it and pray." Then Jews said that we don't want their money since the locusts are bad for us, too. We bought a goat ourselves and then everyone fasted for a day. We slaughtered the goat and didn't eat it. We put it on the fire, it was burnt, and everyone fasted. The locusts came in clouds and suddenly, all at once, the clouds turned away and went elsewhere.

The same event, recalled by a Jewish priest:

You know, a while back there suddenly came a terrible plague of locusts. It was approximately 30 years ago. At that time the Christians asked Abba Itzhak [the great Jewish priest of Tigre] that we pray. Abba Itzhak and all the qesim and all the elders of the tribe prayed. We slaughtered a goat and burnt it as well, and fasted until evening. After that the locusts didn't touch any place inhabited by Jews. I don't know, but the locusts performed a miracle and didn't eat our crops any more.

The sacrifice of a goat to God illustrates the commercial nexus that exists between man and deity. The animal—just like the gifts given toward the maintenance, care, and beautification of the Torah and houses of prayer—is the present a mortal offers to the Deity. The Beta Israel are perceived as fitting liaisons for this exchange—favored sons, as it were. This conception is expressed in the rhetoric of gift-giving during religious holidays. It is utterly contrary to the ordinary disputes and the disparagements that disfigured daily interaction between the groups.

Petitions for Prayer   As the Beta Israel choose to recall it, the practice of one group's petitioning the other to pray on its behalf added another dimension to the importance of holidays in the relations between the groups. The Sigd was particularly significant for the non-Jews, as an opportunity for Christians to ask the Jewish clergy to pray for them. These requests were not matched by similar requests by Jews of the Christian clergy. Personal petitions might include prayers to overcome infertility, to cure an illness, or even to harm one's enemy. Requests were also made on behalf of the entire community's agricultural needs: that rain either fall or cease, that neither hail nor locusts afflict the fields. Such petitions were made during other periods, as well, but the holidays in general and the Sigd in particular were viewed as most opportune. People whom I spoke with said that, during droughts, they themselves would turn to Muslim clergy, who were considered "experts" in rainfall, but Jews never made personal requests to the Muslim clergy.

When Christians enlisted the Jewish qesim, they proffered a preliminary gift. If the prayer were answered, the qes would receive an additional gift. Whereas the initial gifts were usually of a personal nature—an animal, grain, or even money—an answered prayer would customarily bring a parasol, which acknowledged the religious authority of the qes. Donations included money for construction and maintenance of the *masgid* (house of prayer), ceremonial objects such as fabric coverings for the Torah books or the Ark, or funds for purchasing Bibles or religious literature.[29]

A man from Ambober reports:

Once, for example, thieves were stealing a bull or a cow or money from a Christian. The victim would come to our Sigd. He would tell my grandfather that his possessions had been stolen and would ask him to pray for the death of the thief. He would say: "Pray for me, because God will hear your prayers." That's how the Christians would come to the Sigd. They used to bring us money and tell us that, if the thief died next year, they would bring more money. Muslims and Christians alike would come. It helps. I include it in the prayer in the Sigd and the Christian gives a garment for the Torah called *gerdo*. The Christian buys it if his thief dies, since that's a sign that the prayer reached God. He could also give us money or a garment for the Ark, which serves to conceal the Torah books. They also asked us to pray if it wasn't raining. In the morning we went to pray at this mountain we had and right away the clouds came. Quickly we ran home and say "Look, God listens to the Jews." The Christians said, "Please, you pray, it only rains if the Jews pray."

In recounting how Christians asked for their prayers, the Jews could not conceal a certain bitterness. Only Christians could own land, but it took a Jewish prayer to bring the rain that would make this land fruitful. Politically weak and economically deprived, the Beta Israel were granted an aura of power—particularly when that power could serve Christian advantage.[30] Moreover, this acknowledgment starkly challenged the notion that Christianity had replaced Judaism as the one true path to God. The historical priority of Judaism was acknowledged, but its legitimacy was contested. The Christians' need for the Jewish priests to pray for them blurred dogmatic lines of separation and complicated intergroup negotiations regarding the legitimacy of each religion.

THE TWICE-DISGUISED HYENA

Under the influence of their Christian neighbors, many Jews converted to Christianity. When I was doing my initial research, this fact was virtually unreported, but all of the people with whom I spoke knew either individuals or entire families that had converted. The conversion of Beta Israel members is characterized by a variety of processes and motives, including the appeal of the Christian faith in Ethiopia, the influence of the Protestant mission,[31] the policies of specific leaders, and the difficult material conditions and humiliation inherent in the lives of the Jews.

The motivating factor strongly emphasized by the interviewees was not the decision to *substitute one religious belief for another,* but the desire to *belong to another group.*[32] The gap between expectations and reality following the conversion—a gap discussed time and again in several variations—maintains this inherent liminality.[33] It was the pressure exerted on them by the Christians and the hope that such an action would improve their social and economic status that influenced the converts.

When people speak of their friends' conversions in Ethiopia, a number of themes recur. The converts are described as inhabiting a state of permanent liminality, somewhere between Judaism and Christianity. Their conversion is never completed; they are not "really changed" but are "stuck" in the passage from one group to the other. The relations between the Beta Israel, the converts, and Christian society, as positioned in the memory of the interviewees, are highly ambivalent, and the group's boundaries manifest tension between ethnic and religious criteria.

The passage from one religion to another involves, by definition, the departure from one status and the acceptance of a new one. Yet from the abundant data volunteered by the speakers, memory sketches a depiction of the converts remaining in a constant in-between state, even though they were baptized. The converts, it is said, remained Jews "within their hearts." The dominant Christian society continued to view them as a separate minority, even though they were no longer part of the Beta Israel group. They remained in a permanent intermediate category.

Said a man from Tigre who had studied for a while in Asmara:

The Christians wanted to convince us. When I was in Asmara they would say to me: "If you convert, we'll give you everything. If you enter Christianity, I'll be your *auligi* [godfather], I'll get you things, I'll give you my daughter, I'll do this

and that." Nobody in Tigre accepted. Nobody went. But in other places I know
that many went. But those that did convert suffered a great deal, since they
were lost in the eyes of the Jews but the Christians didn't really accept them either. Whoever knew them when they were Jews had a difficult time accepting
them as Christians. Inside, there was a sort of hate. Our parents separated us
from the Christians. The Christian wouldn't even give him [the Jewish con-
vert] their daughters. Then it became hard for us to touch their daughters. The
[converted] Jew might want the Christian's daughter, but the Christian didn't
agree. It is as if they put the converts in separate houses.[34]

Many informants emphasized that even converts who were putatively accepted into the Christian society while alive were barred from burial in Christian
cemeteries after death:

They [the Christians] try to convince us and we say no! . . . They told us that if
we come to them they'll give us money and there'll be land. They try to persuade us: "Believe in the *Wangel* (the New Testament)! It is the truth." So whoever wants money goes. He goes because he believes he'll have money and land,
and that's the way it is for a short while, but then they don't accept him. . . . Listen, in addition, if he dies, the Christians won't bury him in their grave. Just
like I'm telling you. In the end, they don't bury Jews in their cemeteries.

Cemeteries mark the boundaries separating groups, manifesting both the
ethnic and the religious affiliation of the dead. The cemetery is the place set on
earth where members of a religious group are gathered and from which their
souls ascend to heaven.[35] Thus, the informants see the exiling of the convert as
proof that they are not viewed as full Christians: even though they have undergone baptism, this cannot "change their heart."

Another aspect of this perception as portrayed by the Beta Israel was expressed in the suspicious and hostile attitude of the Christians, who continued to attribute supernatural powers to the converts.[36] In fact, the informants
claimed that these suspicions became even more severe after a Jew's conversion:

The Christians still suspect them of eating people's flesh. They think that
maybe the converts are worse than those who stayed in their own religion,
because those who remained in their own religion are known, so their destructive power doesn't work if you're careful and watch them. But those who are in
our midst still have that power and they're more dangerous. The Christians
claim this.

In the eyes of the Christians, as the Jews understand it, their supernatural powers do not disappear when they "disguise themselves" as Christians. Clearly, the conversion does not change the innate ethnic essence. Their "disguise" only makes it more difficult to identify them. A Jew is still a hyena, the Buda. His Christian identity is merely a better camouflage for his nocturnal operations. He is *doubly disguised,* and *doubly dangerous.*

BLOOD MATTERS: MENSTRUATION, SLAUGHTER, AND EATING

To further demonstrate the complexity of this multifaceted cultural system, let us pass from the descriptive to the symbolic level, tracing the motif of blood. Blood is articulated in three spheres—menstruation, ritual slaughter, and eating—all situated at the very core of the most primordial transformations of human existence. It is a highly charged symbol in many cultures.[37] Both Judaism and Christianity grant it great doctrinal significance. It symbolizes the covenant between the believer and God, and it is governed by many commandments and prohibitions.[38]

Ethiopian society brought the Beta Israel into daily contact with blood in a religiously significant way. Because the meanings attached to blood were central both for them and for Christians, blood became the major criterion for determining religious legitimacy, a battleground between different conceptions of the same symbol. In this battle, both sides used the same weapons. Although Beta Israel perceptions were deeply ingrained in Ethiopian culture, there was a constant process of negotiation over the parameters of their existence as a separate group within the Christian milieu.

As a key symbol for both groups, blood was an interface around which each struggled to define its distinct identity.[39] This primordial symbol was a focal point for communication and for the continual articulation of differences. When a member of the Beta Israel described modes of behavior and conceptions that pertained to blood, the description took cognizance of their neighbors' conceptions and praxes with regard to the same symbol. The two systems were understood to be opposed.

Menstruation   Menstrual blood was a central topic in the daily interaction. For the Jews, it determined the purity of the entire group. The authority was the Hebrew Bible verse, "And if a woman have an issue, and her issue in her flesh be blood, she shall be seven days in her menstrual separation: and whoever touches her shall be unclean until evening" (Leviticus 15:19). This was quoted to me during the interviews when we discussed the separation of Jewish women during their "unclean" periods. In accordance with the *Orit* (Leviticus 12:2–6), the Beta Israel also considered the postpartum period as impure (40 days if a boy was born, 80 for a girl). During their menstrual and postpartum periods, Beta Israel women were confined to a separate hut situated at the periphery of the Jewish dwellings. A stone fence set the area off from the rest of the village, and several women might occupy the hut simultaneously. Each month, a woman would retire for seven days to the "house of blood" ("*mergem gojo, mergem bet,* or *yedem bet*), and on the evening at the end of the seventh day she would purify herself in the river and return home. Although the women sometimes cooked for themselves in the "house of blood," they generally received food from outside, served to them over the stone fence. The existence of the "house of blood" and the customary separation were so conspicuous that at times it was described as the central sign that Jews lived in a village.

Unlike the Jews, Ethiopian Christian women did not maintain any special form of separation during their menstrual periods. Not considered impure at that time, they remained at home, cooked, and maintained contact with other

A Beta Israel woman in Beth Nida, the "Blood Hut." Walaqua village, Gondar district, Ethiopia, 1984. (Beth Hatefutsoth, Photo Archive, Tel Aviv; no. 5710. Photo: Doron Bacher)

people. The differences in menstrual customs between the Beta Israel and the Christians could, then, be known to all.

The privacy that characterized the Christian treatment of menstrual blood, as opposed to the openness of the Beta Israel treatment, was the subject of much debate. There were Christians who maintained that, although their wives remained at home during their monthly period, they refrained from sexual relations. In Jewish ritual, the female fertility cycle was given to public scrutiny, whereas for the Christians this was a private matter. The Beta Israel believed that, by making a woman's menstruation known to the community, they could control the time of conception and thus ensure the purity of the next generation. The Jews claimed that the Christians could never be sure who was the real father of a woman's children.

The attempt to control the purity of the next generation by following the monthly cycle was central to the way the Beta Israel perceived themselves. In intergroup debates about the customs of ritual impurity, they would provocatively argue against the Christians that "only when your mother is about to die will she reveal to you who your father is."[40] The deep concern with the menstrual blood of the other group indicated a unique convergence of categories for determining ritual purity, as each group portrayed the other's practices through its own religious terms of reference.

This sort of symbolic community between two competing religious groups is far from self-evident. For the Beta Israel, the two definitions of purity and impurity belong to the *same* symbolic and conceptual system.[41] The Christians' non-observance of the menstrual laws is cited by the Beta Israel as one of the main reasons for avoiding physical contact with them and for not eating food cooked by them. According to one woman:

> During their menstrual period, the Christian women stay at home [and don't move into the house of blood like the Jewish women]. Can I say something? They say to us, how come when you Jewish women bleed you leave the house? That's really disgusting! So we tell them that we got that from our Torah, we can't stay home during our period. That's how it is with our tribe. Everyone in Ethiopia is with his own tribe.[42]

And a man explained:

> Our women would spend seven days in the menstrual house, and on the seventh day they would immerse themselves. On that day they don't eat anything until evening. Christians don't care. They would say to us: Blood is a flower. What are you afraid of, it's flower blood. It's an *ababa* [flower].

This remark was accompanied by grimaces of revulsion. In another interview, a woman said:

> They would tell me, are you crazy to be in the house [the blood house] alone all day and all night? Maybe a wild animal will come to catch you. So I told her: All this time a wild animal has never come. They guard us when we are there.

Each group's interpretation of this event, as reincarnated through Beta Israel recollections, was accompanied by feelings of revulsion at the other side's practices, and it symbolically summarized the relations between the groups. Although they have different customs of purity and impurity, both groups are occupied with the purity and impurity of the "other." These categories served as a basis for disputations, comparisons, and evaluations. The different customs reinforce boundaries between the groups.[43] Yet this is done in a way that reveals the unspoken idea that the two groups are part of one system.[44] Intergroup conceptions about ritual slaughter and eating are also part of this understanding.

Slaughter Meat is a central ingredient in the Ethiopian diet, and both its slaughter and its preparation are governed by communal custom. Beta Israel slaughter was undertaken meticulously and with utmost attention to the relevant biblical prescriptions relating to the covenant between God and the believers (Exodus 29). Slaughter was described in vivid terms and accompanied by many demonstrations of emotion. Jewish slaughter was performed with a razor-sharp knife, so the passage from life to death was as quick and painless as possible: "Our qes slaughtered very well. The knife was not touched by the blood. It remained as it was, it was so clean afterwards. . . . With the Jews the knife is so sharp that the cow doesn't even hear that they are slaughtering it."

But the Beta Israel described the Christian slaughter as the very opposite of their own. It was "too slow" and therefore cruel; the Christians were depicted as people who ate meat from animals that were not slaughtered in accordance with careful and caring rules:[45] "The goyim don't care that it hurts the cow. . . . [T]he Christians will eat [meat] slaughtered by any one of them, even children and even slaves."

Although the Christians recited a blessing when slaughtering, the blessing was considered short and inappropriate in light of their "barbarian," "nonreligious" methods. The following description demonstrates the interviewee's meticulous acquaintance with Christian slaughter practices:

> But [giving] Jewish meat to a Christian, Christian to a Jew, Christian to a Muslim is forbidden. Because it's souls, right? The Muslims do *"bissimallah"* [in the

name of Allah], right? The Christians do *"basema ab wawald wamanfas qeddus ahadu amlak"* [in the name of the father, the son, and the holy spirit one God] and then slaughter. The Jews say *"Barukh yitbarek amlak yisrael"* [Blessed is the King (God) of Israel]. That is because the cow was in her life [alive], she had life, birds are the same, a hen was in its life so everyone does his own blessing. . . . In slaughtering there are differences; the Christians, even if they find a cow that is already dead, they would still eat her. If a cow fell down and died they would eat her. Even if she had died before. And also their knife isn't so good. We have a special knife just for slaughtering.

When asked how Christians felt about the Jews' slaughtering practices, the response was that the Christians likened them to the murder of Jesus. In Christianity, blood and the crucifixion of Jesus are intimately linked: Jesus' spilt blood is an indication that the Jews have transgressed the Old Testament prohibition against bloodshed. The blood of Christ is thus both a cause and a sign of the veracity of the new divine order.[46]

Jesus' blood is perceived as purifying, forgiving, and redeeming.[47] Being the progeny of Christ-killers, the Beta Israel carry "in their blood" inherited traits of the murderers of God.[48] The Beta Israel always slaughtered their animals outside, where all could see. The carcass was then hung on a tree in order to drain its blood. For the Christians, this act evoked Jesus' death on a cross of wood. The Christians also believed that the crucifixion was a Jewish paschal sacrifice, similar to the Beta Israel Passover sacrifice.[49] The conceptual circle revealed here is based upon a mutual projection between a doctrine (the crucifixion of Jesus by the Jews) and a reaction to praxis (the paschal offering). One speaker claimed: "[The Christians] always said to us: 'On Passover you take a lamb and hang it on a high tree and stab it, just like you Jews did to Jesus.'"

Each group is revolted by the slaughter customs of the other group, just as they are by the menstrual customs. The blood of the victim, which can, according to Judaism, strengthen the covenant between God and Jewish believers,[50] is viewed by the Christians as the blood on account of which the Jews were abandoned and a new covenant was established between God and the followers of Christ.

Eating The third theme involving blood is "eating" or, more specifically, the different practices governing the consumption of meat. The diet of the different groups in the area where the Jews lived was similar, and the Beta Israel spoke of a complete identity with regard to everything involving food.

The one exception was meat. As we have seen, animals were slaughtered and meat was handled differently by the two groups, each with its own rules governing cooking and eating. The Beta Israel repeatedly expressed their revulsion at the Christian custom of leaving blood in the slaughtered animal and even eating the animal "raw"—that is, still bloody.[51] The raw meat, they went on to say, carries many parasites that caused different kinds of diseases from which the Beta Israel were free. One man said:

> Christians will eat raw meat, like dogs. We say to them, you are eating like dogs, that's not good. We laugh with them. They say to us: You don't know, it's very tasty. . . . We tell them that if they don't cook the meat they will have worms in their bellies.

In the Hebrew Bible, eating bloody meat or consuming blood in any way is explicitly prohibited:

> Therefore I said to the children of Israel, None of you shall eat blood. . . . For the life of all flesh is its blood, on which its life depends: therefore I said to the children of Israel, you shall eat the blood of no manner of flesh: . . . whoever eats it shall be cut off. (Leviticus 17:12–14)

For the Christians, however, human and animal blood was perceived in the context of Jesus' purifying blood, and the symbolic consumption of that blood is one of the observances that grant the believer entry into heaven. One often-repeated allegation made by the Beta Israel is that, though they themselves had not witnessed it, the Christians drank the blood of Jesus and, in order to achieve eternal life, might even drink the blood of Christianized Jews after the converts had died. One interviewee explained:

> The Christians have a law that they call *"segaw wademu"* [His flesh and blood]. It is written in their *Wangel* that whoever eats the blood will go to heaven and there will be forgiveness for all his sins. So a little child or a man who wants to be a priest, they feed him blood. . . . [S]o we think that they take the converts,[52] they take their body and their limbs after they die.

It would seem that the Christians' consumption of raw meat was for the Jews concrete proof that there was truth in this story.

Thus the Christians are described by the Beta Israel as "blood eaters" who transgress one of the central edicts of the Torah, an edict linked in their understanding with culture and humanity in general. Yet the Christians' conception of the Beta Israel as Buda is also linked, as described earlier, to "eating."[53] The accusation that the Beta Israel were Buda, with all it implies in terms of invoking supernatural forces, was an accusation of "eating": "They would accuse us of eating a Christian" in their night guise as hyenas, creatures that show no respect for the critical boundary between life and death. In their night guise, the Christians believed, the Jews dug up children's graves and drank the babies' blood.

Jew and Christian thus accused each other of eating blood.[54] The Beta Israel abhorred the consumption of uncooked, bloody meat by Christians, whereas Christians claimed that the Beta Israel possessed magical "eating" abilities. In both groups the very humanity of the other group was placed in doubt. This symbolic reciprocity was forcibly expressed in both the content and the phonetics of the following account:

> The Christians would say to us that we are *jib*, a hyena, which eats people. So we would answer that they are *dib*—that is, a bear. Why? Because what does a bear eat? It eats raw meat, right? Maybe a mouse or something like that they [the bears] eat.

The boundaries between the groups were conceptually organized as a series of binary oppositions recurring on various levels. Blood was central to the relationship between the believer and God in both religions, but it was also a distinctive symbol of identity, standing at the center of the complex relations between them. Every time the Beta Israel described themselves, they gave a rich and detailed account of Christian behavior as well. These descriptions contained a surprising degree of emotional, symbolic, and conceptual similarity, organized symmetrically so that each group's customs were portrayed as the reflected shadow of the other's.

In another respect, the "choice" of blood as an identity symbol and group marker exemplifies the significance of separation for the Beta Israel. Their maintenance of menstrual customs (which are a condition for pure birth), of slaughter customs (which span the boundary between life and death), and of specific forms of "eating" (the activity that fortifies and maintains the body) distinguished them from their neighbors in a manner perceived as primordial, nonnegotiable, and impervious to persuasion. In these three realms was a "crossing of borders"[55] on the physical, tangible level with blood bursting forth, thereby trespassing its natural, set boundary within the body. Finally, there was a selective transferring of the symbolic to the social in the living relations between the two groups. On the social level, rules against trespassing were strictly enforced, but there was in fact much fluidity and actual passage between the groups. This tension between manifest declarations and actual practices turned the border crossing typical of blood into a highly charged focal point.

CHALLENGES TO IDENTITY

The fascination of Jews worldwide with the Beta Israel was more than mere appeal to an "exotic," isolated Jewish group in the heart of Africa. It resonated from far greater depths. The discovery of coreligionists perceived as racially "other" sparked fundamental questions of Jewish identity and aroused latent tensions between race and religion in Judaism. The discourse regarding the identity of the Ethiopian Jews, which took place across the entire Jewish world, therefore focused on origins, raising various speculations regarding the Beta Israel presence in Ethiopia.

It was therefore not surprising that, in 1973, the Sephardic chief rabbi of Israel issued a ruling, based on a rabbinic decision from four centuries earlier, that the group was descended from the lost tribe of Dan. This ruling, an outgrowth of the myth of shared origins, illuminates the paradox inherent when sensitivity over eugenic distinctions based on "race" mingle with the primacy of descent in Jewish identity. Significantly, the rabbinic proclamation linked the Beta Israel to the Jewish people in a way that did not challenge the underlying presumption of Jewish common descent.

For the Beta Israel, who were for a long period cut off from other Jewish communities, the question of Jewish identity was governed by the organizing dynamic of transformation and was profoundly related to Christianity. The drama of their position as a marginal group in Christian Ethiopia, however, was transformed to an internal drama when they encountered the Jewish world outside Ethiopia. The conceptual confrontation between the fixed boundaries of normative Judaism and the fluid Ethiopian model was central to this drama, and it assumed expression in the metaphor of skin color.[56]

Upon their arrival in Israel, the Ethiopian immigrants, with their undeniably different external appearance, were immediately seen as anomalous to the absorbing society. Whereas in Ethiopia they had regarded themselves as being light-skinned in relation to dark ("red" vs. "black"), in Israel another color scale was at work. A terminology of black and white came into play, and the Ethiopians found themselves being termed simply "black," without any distinction of shade. There were some who sought to assure themselves that, being Jews, they were not intrinsically black—a belief supported by a quaint article of faith that many generations of exposure to the African sun had burnished their original whiteness. "When we arrive in Israel," they told one another, "our dark color will fade away and the real Jews among us will finally be seen for what we really are: white."

Here, as with conversion, a transformation was expected. But the magic never happened, and the static Western model of constancy prevailed. Confronted with the embarrassing fact that the hoped-for transformation did not occur, the Beta Israel fell back on a variety of rationalizations. Some said that the change would take longer. Some claimed to have seen the coming of the change in the relatively lighter skin of their newborn in Israel. Others accepted their unchanged color as proof that Judaism was more than skin deep.

This chapter began with a general query: What does it mean to be a Jew in Christian Ethiopia? When Jewish religious authorities were debating the issue of admitting the "Falashas" to Israel, the question they had to answer was, "Are they real Jews?" But from the outset this was never a purely religious question, and in one guise—or disguise—or another, identity problems persisted, providing a challenging opportunity for reformulating the overall query. The question should not be "Are the Beta Israel real Jews?" but, rather, "What does it mean to be a Jew in the first place?"

The ethnography of Jewish life in Christian Ethiopia, and particularly the cultural manifestations and organizing principles governing the Beta Israel experience, allow for a more inclusive conception of Judaism as a cultural system. The racial "otherness" and "deviant" Judaism of the Beta Israel challenge simplistic assumptions about the physical and spiritual unity of the Jewish people and are a catalyst for the exploration of Judaism in a much wider cultural framework. Their very identity presents an opportunity to reconceive Judaism not through the imposition of external considerations of common origin or even religious practice but through an internal frame of reference. As Jewish identity is refracted through the prism of the Beta Israel experience, Judaism will continue to reveal itself in a dynamic and not always coherent fashion, joining competing voices and engaging in multiple and changing dialogues.

NOTES

1. Although usually designated as "Falasha" in most publications, this group refers to themselves as Beta (House) of Israel. Today they are popularly known as Ethiopian Jews.

2. Ancient Ethiopic, Ethiopia's Semitic liturgical tongue, used by Jews and Christians alike.

3. The Torah-centered, pre-rabbinic religious observance of the Beta Israel is a function of their existence as a Jewish community separated from other Jewish populations.

4. Among the early writers who treated the group as a clearly defined entity, the following traveler-scholars are prominent: J. Bruce, *Travels to Discover the Sources of the Nile,* 2d ed. (Edinburgh, 1805); J. Halévy, "Halévy's Travels in Abyssinia," in A. Lowry, ed., *Miscellany*

of Hebrew Literature, trans. James Pieciotto (London, 1877), 5–80; J. Halévy, "La guerre de Sarsa—Dengel contre les Falasha, extrait des Annales de Sarsa-Dengel," *Revue Sémitic* 14 (1906): 392–427 and 15 (1906): 119–63, 263–87; and J. Faitlovitch, *Notes d'un Voyage chez les Falachas (Juifs d'Abyssinie)* (Paris, 1905). The latter two, European Jews, were sent to Ethiopia in quest of traces of the "lost tribe," whose existence as a remote Jewish group sparked the imagination and emotions of many, especially of Jews, in the West. These travelers were instrumental in endowing Ethiopian Jews with their image of the "lost tribe." Their publications emphasized points of similarity between the Beta Israel and Jews elsewhere in the world and portrayed them as an isolated Jewish Diaspora living for long years as pariahs among hostile foreign surroundings. Protestant ministers who were sent to convert them to Christianity also emphasized the difference and uniqueness of their religion and customs compared to those of the Christians in Ethiopia, though their motivation in stressing the uniqueness was totally different. See J. M. Flad, *The Falashas (Jews) of Abissinia* (London, 1869); J. M. Flad, *60 Jahre in der Mission unter den Falachas in Abyssinien* (Giesen, 1922); H. A. Stern, *Wanderings Among the Falashas in Abyssinia,* 2d ed. (London, 1968); and S. Gobat, *Journal of a Three Years' Residence in Abyssinia,* 2d ed. (London, 1850). This emphasis continued to figure prominently in the studies by researchers who came later. See A. Z. Aešcoly, *Sefer ha-Falashim* (Tel Aviv, 1943); M. Wurmbrand, "Falashas," *Encyclopaedia Judaica,* vol. 6, (1971): cols. 1143–54; D. Kessler, *The Falashas—The Forgotten Jews of Ethiopia* (New York, 1982); S. D. Messing, *The Story of the Falashas—Black Jews of Ethiopia* (Brooklyn, N.Y., 1982); and, to a large degree, R. I. Hess, "Toward a History of the Falasha," in D. F. McCall, N. R. Bennett, and J. Butler, eds., *Eastern African History* (New York, 1969), 107–32. Despite the different sources they drew upon for their studies, all of these authors resorted to historical speculation regarding origins. They emphasized its social and religious uniqueness and presented the Jewish presence in Ethiopia as a product of intercommunal struggle. This presentation made the Beta Israel appear almost totally self-determined and isolated from their surroundings. To this stream may be added studies that implicitly strengthen this model by dealing with intergroup aspects and tend to ignore the existence of the group within the wider Ethiopian context, such as M. Schoenberger, "The Falashas of Ethiopia—An Ethnographic Study" (Master's thesis, Cambridge University, 1975); S. Ben-Dor, "Ha-Sigd shel Beta Israel: Ḥag Ḥidush ha-Brit" (Master's thesis, Hebrew University, Jerusalem, 1985); S. Ben-Dor, "The Religious Life of Ethiopian Jews" (Hebrew), in Y. Avner et al., eds., *Beta Israel: Sipuram Shel Yehudei Etiopia* (Tel Aviv, 1987), 58–63.

5. As contrasted with the "lost tribe" model, the "integrated group" model views the Beta Israel community as an integral part of wider Ethiopian history and culture. It emphasizes the many similarities between the Beta Israel and their Christian neighbors, and it cites their inclusion in the wider social setting. This is especially true for the historical studies by J. A. Quirin, *The Evolution of Ethiopian Jews: A History of the Beta Israel (Falasha) to 1920* (Philadelphia, 1992); K. K. Shelemay, *Music, Ritual and Falasha History* (East Lansing, Mich., 1989); and S. Kaplan, *The Beta-Israel (Falasha) in Ethiopia: From Earliest Times to the Twen-*

tieth Century (New York, 1992), who suggested that the Beta Israel emerged from a schism between Christian sects in the fifteenth century. This integral model has gained strength in scholarly circles. See, e.g., C. Conti-Rossini, *Storia d'Etiopia* (Bergamo, 1928); E. Ullendorff, *Ethiopia and the Bible: The Schweich Lectures* (London, 1968); E. Ullendorff, *The Ethiopians,* 3d ed. (London, 1973); V. Krempel, "Die Soziale—Eine Berufskaste in Nordwest Athiopien— die Kayla (Falascha)," *Sociologus* 24 (1974): 37–55; and, to a certain degree, W. Leslau, *Falasha Anthology* (New Haven, Conn., 1951). It is typical of this trend that even scholars who do not confine themselves to the historical conclusions reached by Quirin, Shelemay, and Kaplan could no longer ignore, as in the past, the wider Ethiopian context and its centrality for the study of the Beta Israel. Presenting them as one group in the conglomerate of religious collectivities in Ethiopia is also typical of literature pertaining to culture and society in general. See especially C. Rathjens, *Die Juden in Abessinien* (Hamburg, 1921); A. Pollera, *l'Abissinia di ieri* (Rome, 1940); E. Cerulli, *Storia della letteratura Etiopica* (Milano, 1956); F. J. Simoons, *Northwest Ethiopia: People and Economy* (Madison, Wisc., 1960); F. Gamst, *The Qemant: A Pagan-Hebraic Peasantry of Ethiopia* (New York, 1969), on the Qemant, who have certain customs similar to the Falasha; W. A. Shack, *The Central Ethiopians* (London, 1974); G. J. Abbink, "The Falasha in Ethiopia and Israel: The Problem of Ethnic Assimilation," *Social Anthropologische Cahiers* 15 (1984); G. J. Abbink, "A Socio-Structural Analysis of the Beta-Esra'el as an 'Infamous Group' in Traditional Ethiopia," *Sociologus* 39, no. 4 (1987): 140–54; G. J. Abbink, "L'enigme de l'ethnogenese des Beta Israel—Une approach anthropohistorique de leurs mytho-legends," *Cahiers d'études Africanes* 40 (1992); G. A. Lipsky, *Ethiopia: Its People, Its Society, Its Culture* (New Haven, Conn., 1962); and D. N. Levine, *Greater Ethiopia: The Evolution of a Multiethnic Society* (Chicago, 1974).

6. For other historical studies and speculations, see n. 9 below.

7. For example, the population included the Qemant. On this group, see Gamst, *The Qemant,* and Kaplan, *The Beta-Israel,* 160. For an ethnography of Amhara life in the highland plateau of Ethiopia, see S. D. Messing, "The Highland-Plateau of Ethiopia" (Ph.D. diss., University of Pennsylvania, 1957).

8. For a full study, see H. Salamon, *The Hyena People: Ethiopian Jews in Christian Ethiopia* (Berkeley, 1999).

9. Officially, the Ethiopian communist revolution of 1974 brought an end to the leasing of private lands, but the interviewees were adamant in their claims that they did not benefit from land redistribution. On the systems of land tenure in Ethiopia, see A. Hoben, "Social Stratification in Traditional Amhara Society," in A. Tuden and L. Plotnicov, eds., *Social Stratification in Africa* (London, 1970), 187–224; A. Hoben, *Land Tenure Among the Amhara of Ethiopia* (Chicago, 1973); D. Crummey, "Abyssinian Feudalism," *Past and Present* 89 (1980): 115–38; D. Donham and W. James, eds., *The Southern Marches of Imperial Ethiopia* (Cambridge, Engl., 1986).

10. Smithery has been linked with supernatural or magical powers as well as with Judaism in other cultures, some close to the Ethiopian (Africa) and others distant (Europe in

certain periods). In these cases, too, the craft of the smith was viewed with ambivalence and often involved social isolation. For a detailed discussion on smithery, pottery, and belief systems in Africa, see E. W. Herbert, *Iron, Gender and Power: Rituals of Transformation in African Societies* (Bloomington, Ind., 1993).

11. For a more detailed discussion, see Leslau, *Falasha Anthology; Aešcoly, Sefer ha-Falashim;* Schoenberger, "The Falashas." On the laws of purity and impurity, contact, and avoidance (also known as the Attinkugn laws) and their historical development, see Kaplan, *The Beta-Israel,* 132, 134–35. Historic testimonies from relatively late periods emphasize their strict adherence to the prohibition against physical contact with anyone who is not a part of their group. On this issue, see Aešcoly, *Sefer ha-Falashim,* 217, 219, 278; Halévy, "Halévy's Travels"; and Gobat, *Journal of a Three Years' Residence,* 10.

12. Green branches were viewed as a material that does not transmit impurity. They were used in various contexts to separate the impure from the pure. See Salamon, *The Hyena People,* 49–50, 119, 127, n. 5.

13. These clay cups, which were manufactured by the Jewish women, were cheaper than other cups made of bull or cow horns, and could be considered disposable.

14. A number of historical studies (e.g., Kaplan, *The Beta-Israel,* and Quirin, *Evolution*) point to the connection between the Jews' unlanded status and their work in handicrafts. Their distinct religious affiliation led to their being disenfranchised from ownership of agricultural land, which, in turn, forced them to work in artisanship, a very poorly regarded occupation in Ethiopia.

15. See, e.g., V. Krempel, "Die Soziale and wirtschaftliche Stellung der Falascha in der christlich-amharischen wirtschaftliche von Nordwest-Athiopien" (Ph.D. diss., Frein Universitat, Berlin, 1972), and Abbink, "A Socio-Structural Analysis."

16. See, for example, K. Honea, "Buda in Ethiopia," in *Wiener völkerkundliche Mitteilungen* (Wien, 1956), 20–22; S. D. Messing, "Health Care, Ethnic Outcasting, and the Problem of Overcoming the Syndrome of Encapsulation in a Peasant Society," *Human Organization* 34, no. 4 (1975): 396; and R. Pankhurst, *A Social History of Ethiopia* (Addis Ababa, 1990), 223–24.

17. On the hyena-man as a trans-African phenomenon, see, e.g., G. Calame-Griaule and Z. Ligers, "L'Homme-Hyena dans la tradition soudanais," *L'Homme* 1 (1961): 89–118; R. M. Dorson, "Africa and the Folklorist," in R. M. Dorson, ed., *African Folklore* (Bloomington, Ind., 1972), 3–67; and Herbert, *Iron, Gender and Power.*

18. See Messing, "Health Care"; Kaplan, *The Beta-Israel;* and Abbink, "A Socio-Structural Analysis." For a wider discussion on evil eye and the wet-dry categories, see A. Dundes, "Wet and Dry, the Evil Eye: An Essay in Indo-European and Semitic Worldview," in A. Dundes, ed., *Interpreting Folklore* (Bloomington, Ind., 1980), 93–133.

19. See, e.g., A. Dundes, "The Ritual Murder or Blood Libel Legend: A Study of Anti-Semitic Victimization Through Projective Inversion," *Temenos* 25 (1989): 7–32.

20. This network is characterized by a regional supragroup commitment, during which emerges a clear spatial definition of who belongs to this system. See H. Salamon, "Contacts

and Communication Among the Beta-Israel in Ethiopia: Regional Aspects" (Hebrew) (Master's thesis, Hebrew University, Jerusalem, 1986).

21. The importance of gift giving as a continuing process of exchange and commitment has been central to anthropology ever since the seminal works by B. Malinowski, *Argonauts of the Western Pacific* (New York, 1922), and M. Mauss, *The Gift* (London, 1969).

22. On the emperor's famous debate between Jewish and Christian religious leaders, see W. Leslau, "A Falasha Religious Dispute," *Proceedings of the American Academy for Jewish Research* 16 (1947): 71–95, and Salamon, *The Hyena People*, 83–85, 90.

23. See, e.g., *Funk and Wagnalls Standard Dictionary of Folklore Mythology and Legend* (New York, 1950), 584–85.

24. R. K. Molvaer, *Tradition and Change in Ethiopia* (Leiden, 1980), 64–65, states that the Ethiopians relied more on the "list" of holy days in establishing daily meetings than on the numerical dates. This was especially true in the more rural areas.

25. On Sigd as a unique holiday for Ethiopian Jewry, see G. J. Abbink, "Seged Celebrations in Ethiopia and Israel: Continuity and Change of a Falasha Religious Holiday," *Anthropos* 78 (1983): 789–810; Ben-Dor, "Ha-Sigd Shel Beta Israel"; Salamon, "Contacts and Communication," 62–68; and Shelemay, *Music, Ritual, and Falasha History*, 56, who remarks that "Sigd is . . . the most syncretist observance."

26. A good example of such analysis, in which the Jewish Mimuna in Morocco is examined in the context of symbolic intergroup relations, is H. Goldberg, "The Mimuna and the Minority Status of Moroccan Jews," *Ethnology* 17 (1978): 75–87.

27. For these holidays, see Leslau, *Falasha Anthology*, xxix–xxxv.

28. See, e.g., Kaplan, *The Beta-Israel*, 162–63.

29. Molvaer, *Tradition and Change*, 95, describes similar gifts given by Christians to the church in times of supplication or oaths.

30. These requests may be seen as another expression of the "power of the weak," in which the weaker group, politically, is perceived as representing a general, super-religious human morality, or as maintaining contact with the forces of nature in such a way as to allow for the fulfillment of wishes. The weaker group is often sought out if it is viewed as being more fundamentally or originally tied to the place. On power strategies of weaker groups, see also J. C. Scott, *Weapons of the Weak: Everyday Forms of Peasant Resistance* (New Haven, Conn., 1985), and J. C. Scott, *Domination and the Arts of Resistance: Hidden Transcripts* (New Haven, Conn., 1990). For an interesting comparison to the Jews in Muslim Morocco, see L. Rosen, "Moslem-Jewish Relationship in a Moroccan City," *International Journal of Middle Eastern Studies* 3 (1972): 435–49.

31. See also Kaplan, *The Beta-Israel*, 116–42.

32. An accepted typology in the literature of religious conversion distinguishes "recruitment" from "affiliation." This parallels the distinction the Beta Israel are trying to establish in claiming that the conversion of Ethiopian Jews is only "recruitment." On religious conversions in Africa from a cultural perspective, see J. D. Y. Peel, "Syncretism and Religious

Change," *Comparative Studies in Society and History* 10 (1968): 121–41; J. D. Y. Peel, "Conversion and Tradition in Two African Societies: Ijebu and Buganda," *Past and Present* 77 (1977): 108–41; E. Colson, "Converts and Tradition: The Impact of Christianity on Valley Tonga Religion," *Southwestern Journal of Anthropology* 26 (1970): 143–56; R. Horton, "African Conversion," *Africa* 41 (1971): 85–108; R. Horton, "On the Rationality of Conversion" (2 parts), *Africa* 45 (1975): 219–235, 373–99; and H. J. Fisher, "Conversion Reconsidered: Some Historical Aspects of Religious Conversion in Black Africa," *Africa* 43 (1973): 27–44.

33. The term "liminality" in this sense was developed by V. Turner, *The Ritual Process: Structure and Anti-Structure* (Chicago, 1969), and refers to the intermediary stage in transitional states.

34. On this issue, see also S. D. Messing, "50,000 Black Marranos," *Jewish Heritage* 13 (1971) : 22–24.

35. See, for example, E. Lord, *Queen of Sheba's Heirs* (Washington, D.C., 1970), and Salamon, "Contacts and Communication," 92–96. The "fixed site" (that is, the grave) emphasized the fixed liminality of the converts and the impossibility of a full intergroup transformation.

36. Messing, "50,000 Black Marranos," 23; Abbink, "The Falasha in Ethiopia and Israel," 65.

37. See, e.g., V. Turner, "Symbols in African Ritual," in J. Dolgin et al., eds., *Symbolic Anthropology* (New York, 1977), 183–94, and T. Buckley and A. Gottlieb, eds., *Blood Magic: The Anthropology of Menstruation* (Berkeley, 1988).

38. On the "covenant of blood" in rabbinic Judaism, see L. A. Hoffman, *Covenant of Blood: Circumcision and Gender in Rabbinic Judaism* (Chicago, 1996).

39. On blood as a "core symbol," see also R. Wagner, *Symbols That Stand for Themselves* (Chicago, 1986), 96–125. For discussion and elaboration of the term, see S. Ortner, "On Key Symbols," *American Anthropologist* 75 (1973): 1338–46.

40. Consider, in this context, their skepticism concerning the actual paternity of Jesus.

41. The level of overlapping between the symbolic systems is, in this case, greater than that found in many other examples. An additional point is of the dichotomy between pure and impure. Without going into too much detail, I will mention that, for the Beta Israel, purity is understood as the opposite of impurity, yet there are many subcategories of the two states that require concrete, contextual exploration.

42. Note the double nature of these statements, in which every description of a Jewish custom is accompanied by a description of a corresponding Christian one.

43. For this discussion, see also R. Rosen, "Le Symbolisme Feminin ou la Femme dans le Système de representation Judeo-Marocain, dans un Mochav en Israel" (Master's thesis, Hebrew University, Jerusalem, 1981), 46. In her reference to a different cultural context (North African Jewish women), the writer points at the strong element of Jewish identity inherent in going to the *mikveh* (ritual bath). She writes that "blood makes a woman out of a girl, and the mikveh makes a Jewess out of a woman."

44. On the usage of similar images and idioms between proximate Ethiopian groups,

the Amhara and the Dassenech, see U. Almagor, "Institutionalizing a Fringe Periphery: Dassenetch-Amhara Relations," in D. Donham and W. James, eds., *The Southern Marches of Imperial Ethiopia*, 108.

45. See also Leslau, *Falasha Anthology*, xx.

46. See, e.g., M. Eliade, ed., *The Encyclopedia of Religion* (New York, 1986), s. v. "Blood."

47. See A. Richardson, ed., *A Dictionary of Christian Theology* (London, 1977), 37–38.

48. Another example can be found in the Gojam region of Ethiopia, where the term "Damenenza" was a synonym for the Falasha, meaning "let His blood be on them" (S. Kaplan, *Les Falashas* [Turnhout, 1990], 154).

49. On sacrifice among the Beta Israel in Ethiopia, see D. Lifchitz, "Un Sacrifice chez les Falachas, Juifs d'Abyssinie," *La Terre et la Vie* 9 (1939): 116–23. For two extremely relevant and sophisticated discussions, see G. Feeley-Harnik, *The Lord's Table* (Philadelphia, 1981), esp. chap. 5, and Dundes, "The Ritual Murder," on blood libel legends and antisemitism in other cultural contexts.

50. For an elaborated discussion on the "covenant of blood" in Judaism, especially in the rabbinic period of the first two or three centuries C.E., see Hoffman, *Covenant of Blood*.

51. On the opposition cooked/raw as an expression of the boundaries between human and inhuman (civilized/uncivilized), see C. Lévi-Strauss, *The Raw and the Cooked* (London, 1969).

52. See also Abbink, "A Socio-Structural Analysis." There were those who spoke of the eating of the blood of dead Jewish children. When they were asked why only children, they explained that children were pure of sin. The same explanation was given to the eating of the blood of converts—i.e., Beta Israel members who became Christians. These people were considered clean of sin.

53. See the "Projective Inversion" argument in Dundes, "The Ritual Murder," 16–18.

54. Similar expressions at the end of the nineteenth century are cited in Halévy, "Halévy's Travels," 43. Other research, dealing with the relations between the Amhara and the Dassenech in Ethiopia, mentions a central image in which the Dassenetch describe the Amhara as "People who eat raw meat" (Almagor, "Institutionalizing," 108). Interestingly, this same image became central both for the Dassenetch and the Beta Israel in relation to the Christian Amhara. The perceptions that stand behind the two images are, nevertheless, very different, because the Beta Israel interpreted this image according to written biblical law.

55. On group borders, identity, and food taboos, see M. Douglas, *Purity and Danger: An Analysis of Concepts of Pollution and Taboo* (London, 1966).

56. See H. Salamon, "Racial Consciousness in Transition: From Ethiopia to the Promised Land" (Hebrew), *Jerusalem Studies in Jewish Folklore* 19–20 (1998) : 125–46, and H. Salamon, "Judaism Between Race and Religion: The Case of the Ethiopian Jews," in H. Goldberg, ed., *The Life of Judaism* (Berkeley, 2001).

SELECTED BIBLIOGRAPHY

Aešcoly, A. Z. *Sefer ha-Falashim.* Tel Aviv, 1943.

Faitlovitch, J. *Notes d'un Voyage chez les Falachas (Juifs d'Abyssinie).* Paris, 1905.

Flad, J. M. *The Falashas (Jews) of Abissinia.* London, 1869.

Halévy, J. "Halévy's Travels in Abyssinia," in A. Lowy, ed., *Miscellany of Hebrew Literature.* Trans. James Picciotto. London, 1877.

Kaplan, S. *The Beta-Israel (Falasha) in Ethiopia: From Earliest Times to the Twentieth Century.* New York, 1992.

Leslau, W. *Falasha Anthology.* New Haven, Conn., 1951.

Messing, S. D. *The Story of the Falashas—Black Jews of Ethiopia.* Brooklyn, N.Y., 1982.

Quirin, J. A. *The Evolution of Ethiopian Jews: A History of the Beta Israel (Falasha) to 1920.* Philadelphia, 1992.

Salamon, H. *The Hyena People: Ethiopian Jews in Christian Ethiopia.* Berkeley, 1999.

———. "Judaism Between Race and Religion: The Case of the Ethiopian Jews," in H. Goldberg, ed., *The Life of Judaism.* Berkeley, 2001.

Shelemay, K. K. *Music, Ritual and Falasha History.* East Lansing, Mich., 1989.

Ullendorff, E. *Ethiopia and the Bible: The Schweich Lectures.* London, 1968.

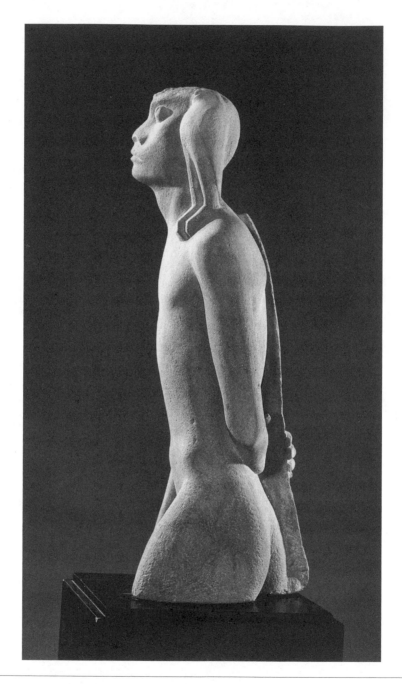

Yitzhak Danziger, *Nimrod*, 1939. Nubian sandstone.
(The Israel Museum, Jerusalem)

SEVEN

LOCUS AND LANGUAGE:

Hebrew Culture in Israel, 1890–1990

ARIEL HIRSCHFELD

As long as deep in the heart
The soul of a Jew yearns,
And towards the East
An eye looks to Zion,
Our hope is not yet lost,
The hope of two thousand years,
To be a free people in our land,
The Land of Zion and of Jerusalem.[1]

These lines from "Hatikvah" (1878), the poem by Naphtali Herz Imber that became Israel's national anthem, mention *mizrah,* the East, and its Hebrew synonym *kadimah,* eastward. This simple word, kadimah, touches upon the deepest
mythical roots of Hebrew culture. The word contains three distinct elements: it
is derived from *kadim,* which means East (Ezekiel 48:1, "for these are his sides
East [kadim] and West"), and from *kedem* in the sense of to proceed forward, to
make progress (Job 23:8, "Behold I go forward [kedem] but He is not there").
But kedem also has a temporal sense of a primordial era, an *Urzeit.* It is in this
third sense that it is analogous to mizrah—from the verb *zarah,* to shine—
because the rising sun appears in kedem not as an action and vision but as a
temporal concept: this is the primordial time, the basis of any historical thought.
The word kadimah in *Hatikvah* contains not one movement but a cluster of
movements, of vectors: the geographic movement eastward is also forward motion in the sense of progress and development—as opposed to regression and
decline—as well as a movement back in time to a primordial reality, but to a
time that is essentially new. The movement eastward is, then, at once historical
and antihistorical, a paradoxical movement with time and against it.

The romantic tension this word projects eastward is not the heritage of European Romanticism; it is one of its sources. Not only does the Bible contain
yearnings for a primordial purity, as in the verses "Renew our days as of old [*ke-*

kedem]" (Lamentations 5:21) and "Awaken as of old [*ki-yemei kedem*] eternal generations" (Isaiah 51:9), but it also expresses a sense of the distance and mystery that envelops the past, as in the verse "I will utter dark sayings [*ḥiddot*] concerning days of old [*kedem*]" (Psalms 78:2). Furthermore, the voice of God is heard from the East, from the "kadim": "An East wind shall come, the wind of the Lord coming up from the wilderness" (Hosea 13:15), and kedem is the site of the Garden of Eden: "And the Lord God planted a garden eastward [*mi-kedem*] in Eden" (Genesis 2:8).

There extends, then, from *Hatikvah*—composed on the brink of the twentieth century and borne by the Hebrew civilization that emerged in that century as its standard—an ancient umbilical cord that contains in its most archaic roots the Romantic movement toward mending the past (the *kadum*), which is mending the East (kadim), a movement that was reformulated throughout the history of Hebrew culture and became a definitive part of the eschatological end to the Jewish drama of exile. The concluding lines of the twelfth-century Spanish Jewish poet Judah Halevi's "Ode to Zion" present this motif in its purest, most distilled form:

> *Happy is he who waits and lives to see*
> *Your light rising, your dawn breaking forth over him!*
> *He shall see your chosen people prospering, he shall rejoice in your joy*
> *When you regain the days of your youth* [kadmat ne'urayikh].[2]

ZIONIST ORIENTALISM AND THE REVOLUTION AGAINST JUDAISM

The literary and plastic arts created by the first generation of the Zionist movement imported this ancient tension to the Land of Israel. This literary and visual expression, however, was drawn from sources that lay much closer to the cradle of the movement: from the nineteenth-century Europe, whose anxiety toward the East was a key element in its cultural identity. The chief formulators of the Romantic view of the Orient were Herder, Goethe, and Schiller, the leaders of the German neoclassicist revolution, who exercised a decisive—albeit, at times, indirect—influence on the artists and the writers of the Zionist "renaissance." Many important Romantic concepts found their way into Zionist ideology under the influence of these thinkers: the people understood as *Volk,* signifying not merely a human collective but an archaic essence that involves character, language, and connection to a land; naïveté as an existential integrity, untainted by the corrupting presence of sophistication; the primordial, the "classic," as indicating a moral purity and vitality; and the association of the "sublime" with the untamed forces of nature. These German "classicists" were the inventors of the new eastward gaze, which they combined with a yearning for a primordial era. Their primordial East was that of ancient Greece and the land of the Bible.

The contemporary Orient, however, was the Ottoman Empire, which had once been Europe's traditional enemy. The empire became, in the nineteenth century, a threatening symbol of all that is base and corrupt in culture as such, though this was in fact a reflection of Europe's own fears of itself. The Romantic gaze eastward was an attempt to bypass the present, to disregard the East in its present state and uncover its archaic form. The Orient became essentially bifurcated: a nearby civilization that was feared and derided (and yet mysterious and alluring), but was also the decrepit cover draped over the sublime body of Greek sculpture and biblical masterpieces. This conceptual structure mirrored, in a sense, the identity, the soul, of Europe: the East's threatening present served as a counterpart to the repressed subconscious of the European ethos, a violent and amoral world of passions, whereas the sublime, exemplary Oriental past corresponded to the conscious aspirations of European culture.

This cluster of attitudes regarding the East was taken over *in toto* by Zionist Hebrew culture, including the low estimation of the Ottoman Empire and the special link (in stark opposition to the traditional Jewish view) between classical Greece and the Bible. Only against this backdrop, which added to the yearning for a primordial and naïve purity a fascination with paganism (the child of "Greece"), can we understand the revolutionary consciousness of Zionism at its outset. The soul of Zionism contained more than a desire for revival and rehabilitation; it also contained an outright rejection of Judaism and the traditional way of life. The Romantic symbolism of Greece was used by Zionist writers to counteract the perceived decay of Jewish culture by means of an explicitly Jewish dynamic. "Athens," the traditional nemesis of "Jerusalem," was called upon to join the Hebrew culture of the East, not to bring about a European renaissance in Hebrew culture but to begin it anew, to re-found it differently. Saul Tchernikhovsky (1875–1943) became the chief spokesman of this "Hellenic revolution" with his poem "In Front of a Statue of Apollo" (1899):

> *I come to you, forgotten god of the ages,*
> *god of ancient times and other days,*
> *ruling the tempests of vigorous men,*
> *the breakers of their strength in youth's plenty!*
>
> .   .   .   .
>
> *I come to you—do you know me still?*
> *I am the Jew: your adversary of old!*
>
> .   .   .   .

I bow to all precious things—robbed now
by human corpses and the rotten seed of man,
who rebel against the life bestowed by God, the Almighty—
the God of mysterious wildernesses,
the God of men who conquered Canaan in a whirlwind—
then bound Him with the straps of their tefillin [*phylacteries*].³

The opening lines of the poem could have been written by Schiller or Hölderlin, but, as it continues, it presents a conflict that is no longer European but specifically Jewish. The poem is not spoken only from within a culture that has grown old and conflicted with the passing of the centuries; it is spoken at once from within a culture and *in opposition* to it. The poem situates the "renaissance" of Hebrew culture within a full awareness of its cultural singularity, seeking to replace the traditional Jewish dynamic in its entirety with another dynamic. "I am the first among those who return to you," says Tchernikhovsky, placing himself at the forefront of a movement that turns not against old age or "history" but against an ancient theology. Tchernikhovsky's poem reveals the radical revision that occurs when the Romantic view of the Orient is applied to Hebrew culture. From this point on, Hebrew culture must come to learn the elements of its own renaissance from outside sources.

The Zionist renaissance rejected the ancient theology of abstract monotheism, which must be destroyed, says Tchernikhovsky, by throwing off the tefillin that have bound the God of nature and vitality. If this culture is to be yoked to a place, a particular locus, where it is to construct for itself a concept of "the beautiful," this "beautiful" demands the constitution of an adequate concept of physical beauty—human and divine. Tchernikhovsky understood the far-reaching ramifications of the concepts "the folk" and "the beautiful"—both instrumental in the Romantic understanding of national renaissance—and revealed the conflict between the new Hebrew culture and the Jewish tradition, a conflict that led not only to abandoning tradition but also to actual abhorrence toward it.

"In Front of a Statue of Apollo" contains the origins of a dynamic that recurs in Israeli culture throughout the twentieth century: the imagery of renaissance is drawn from foreign sources that were—and still are—the traditional enemies of classical Jewish identity. Without this dynamic, we cannot understand the passionate interest of modern Hebrew culture in the cultures of Greece, Mesopotamia, and Arabia. The Oriental antiquities, the pagan force of "the God of men who conquered Canaan in a whirlwind," could only be learned anew through the non-Jewish East.

The tools with which modern Hebrew culture set out to "study" the East and to construct for itself a new-ancient Eastern identity were not forged in empirical experience but lifted, ready-made, from European culture. Even where the authors and painters, such as those of Boris Shatz's Bezalel School, sought to portray the "local" reality of the Land of Israel, it is evident that for many years they saw Palestine and its inhabitants through a thick, gaudy prism, produced by centuries of European culture and specifically by Orientalism, with its manifold expressions in the visual arts, literature, and music.

The myth of a "return to origins" was responsible for the dominance of the biblical Song of Songs and the Book of Ruth in holiday ceremonies and in dozens of songs written in Palestine between the 1920s and the 1940s. This myth further explains the dominance of the *pastoral* genre in poetry, prose, painting, and music, representing the golden age of humanity that was soon to be renewed.

Zionism revived another, much more complex myth: the Exodus from Egypt. As Richard I. Cohen discusses in his chapter in this volume, E. M. Lilien's graphic works—his illustrations of the Bible and the Passover Haggadah, which were very well known in the early twentieth century—portrayed Theodor Herzl as Moses, thus suggesting that the departure from the Diaspora was an Exodus from slavery to freedom. The myth of the Exodus became a powerful tool of propaganda in the first Zionist congresses but was also discussed in a very serious and complex manner by the Hebrew writers of the day. Their works often revealed another, nonpropagandistic aspect of the myth of national renaissance by confronting the very real tensions and traumatic breaks that are part of emigration. Most important, this literature called for practical criticism of the project of renewal.

Ḥayyim Naḥman Bialik, the dominant literary figure of the first-generation Zionists, wrote not only some of the most famous and most influential poems of the day but also the most problematic poem concerning the Zionist exodus, "The Dead of the Desert" (*Matei Midbar,* 1902). The poem tells the story of giants who crossed the boundaries fixed in the biblical Exodus and became desert rocks that arise from their frozen state after many years and begin to rebel. The rebellion fails, God forces them into another frozen state that lasts forever, and they become a legend told by a Bedouin nomad. In this work Bialik outlines a struggle between conflicting forces. The giants call out:

We are the brave!
Last of the Enslaved!
First to be free!
With our own strong hand,

Our hand alone,
We tore from our neck
The heavy yoke.
Raised our heads to the skies,
Narrowed them with our eyes.
Renegades of the waste,
We called barrenness mother.[4]

They are rebelling against God, seeking to set human bravery against the divine power. Moreover, the bravery is defined through the suffering and tragic struggle it entails: its connection to the desert that in turn becomes a "mother," an alternative to God. The pessimism of the work can be seen in its conclusion: "Here, as before, in the desert lie the six hundred thousand cadavers,"[5] which also marks it as part of the Exodus myth, six hundred thousand being the traditional midrashic number of Israelites who left Egypt. The victory of God and of the inhibiting forces allied to God is viewed as a tragic downfall and not as an alternative mode of existence.

This troubling picture of stagnation that takes hold of the people precisely at the time of their heroic passage to political independence was, it seems, the first major appearance of a voice that responded to the power of the "exilic" or "divine" past in Jewish culture. This voice grew stronger still in the works of the great prose masters of modern Hebrew literature, J. H. Brenner (1881–1921) and S. Y. Agnon (1888–1970). For Brenner, who immigrated to Palestine in 1909, it can be heard in his important novel *From Here and There* (*Mikan u-Mikan*, 1910), in the story "Nerves" ('*Atzabim*, 1911,)[6] and particularly in his last novel, *Breakdown and Bereavement* (*Shkhol ve-Khishalon*, 1918).[7] In *From Here and There*, Brenner reduces the forces at work in the Hebrew nation to three symbolically named figures: David Diasporin, who visits Palestine but returns to the United States; Aryeh Lapidot (a heroic name, literally "Lion Torches"), a learned Jew with his own private synthesis between Judaism and personal experience, who loses his son in the Land of Israel and struggles to inculcate in his followers an ethos of Jewish labor; and Oved Etzot (Hebrew for "Clueless"), the narrator, who unites the different forces. The final scene of the novel is a martyrological icon: Aryeh Lapidot and his little grandson arise from their mourning and gather thorns with which to bake bread. As they stand in a temporary clearing between thunderstorms, the narrator says, "the reality was one of thorns." Brenner counters the Zionist pastorale with the tense image of an eternal *via dolorosa*, without, however, denying the sanctity he attributes to his hero, whose life in the Land of Israel represents a successful struggle against the forces of exile. Brenner saw the reality of exile as more than a world of faith and tradition—it was a state of economic parasitism and indolence that had become the "anomaly of Judaism." Jerusalem is depicted not as the center of "Zion" but as the "holy butcher shop," the center of decrepitude that epitomizes exilic existence and resists change.

Agnon, the greatest modern Hebrew novelist, presents in *Only Yesterday* (*Tmol Shilshom*, 1945) a comprehensive reckoning of the first era of Zionism. Like Brenner, he deals with the second wave of Zionist immigration (during which time he was in Palestine). His hero, Yitzḥak Kummer, the grandson of Rabbi Yudil the Hasid, a man of tradition and steadfast faith, immigrates to the Land of Israel in order to raise it up from its state of destruction and be himself raised up by it. He tries to find work as a laborer in the Jewish agricultural settlements, but the farmers prefer cheap Arab labor. He becomes a painter and moves to Jerusalem, settling in the ultra-Orthodox neighborhood Me'ah She'arim, where he marries the daughter of Rabbi Feisch, a pillar of the community. The city itself is plagued with famine, drought, and disease. A "mad" dog bites Kummer, who dies, and his death precipitates the hoped-for rains. The grotesque resolution of the novel—the terrible death of the Zionist antihero—is a dark and enigmatic emblem that has challenged Agnon's interpreters for years. What is clear is that the author contrasts the Zionist space, exemplified in Tel Aviv and the agricultural settlements, with the powerful alternative space of Me'ah She'arim and of an ultra-Orthodox Judaism that is completely blind to the challenges and ideals of Zionism. This place "swallows" the protagonist, who is himself very different from the Zionist ideals of renewal. His name is an oxymoron: laughter (the Hebrew "Yitzḥak") and distress (Yiddish "Kummer"). To this one must add the other Yiddish meaning of "Kummer"—"the arriver"— and the symbolic dimension of "Yitzḥak" (Isaac) who exists, according to the midrash, in an eternal state of being bound (see the story in Genesis 22 of God's command to Abraham to sacrifice his son).

"Like all our brethren of the Second Aliyah, the bearers of our salvation, Isaac Kummer left his country and his homeland and his city and ascended to the Land of Israel to build it from its destruction and to be rebuilt by it."[8] Thus Agnon reworks the myths of the divine promise and of the journey to political realization (the Exodus) in a bitter, grotesque fashion. The pastoral myth of Zionism is pushed to the margins of *Only Yesterday*. At the very end of the novel, after Kummer's death, Agnon mentions the blooming of Judah and the Galilee—"And the Earth was like God's garden"—but excludes this imagery from the world he has constructed.

The Israeli literary critic Gershon Shaked speaks of "the Zionist meta-narrative" that stands "above" Hebrew culture, determining its values, its mores, and its ideals. Yet, despite the antireligious tendencies we have noted, the "Zionist meta-narrative" is really a variation of the "Jewish meta-narrative," that is, of the nation's movement toward redemption. Zionism activated within Jewish culture a store of eschatological tensions and provided even the most practical political acts much broader significance. The writers saw themselves as duty-bound to channel these forces and check the messianic side of the eschatological narrative. The tragic counterpoint that Bialik, Brenner, and Agnon added to the heroic optimism of the Zionist renaissance sought, among other things, to preserve the humanistic and very worldly dimension of the movement.

CONFLICT WITH THE ARABS AND THE CRISIS OF HEBREW ORIENTALISM

The contact with the East—both Jewish and Arab—continued to provide the regnant aesthetic model into the 1920s, but, particularly after the Arab riots of 1929, a rift appeared and widened between the subjects of this model, the Arabs, and their place in Hebrew culture. The riots marked the beginning of the violent conflict between the Yishuv and the Arabs, and they struck a mighty blow to the Israeli conception of place. The appearance of profound enmity toward the Jewish settlement quite suddenly disrupted the pastoral atmosphere Zionist propaganda ascribed to the Yishuv. That the riots began at the Wailing Wall was itself symbolic: the very site of "Zion" was also the site of the conflagration. This marked the end of the naïve, optimistic era in Israeli culture.

The local Arab populace no longer fit the window-dressing role forced upon it by the Zionist aesthetic. As a result, Hebrew culture began to erase the Arabs from the landscape, drawing aesthetic values from them while ignoring their concrete existence.

Brenner was the first to uncover the depths of this conflict. He rejected the Romantic-Orientalist view that viewed the Arab as a role model for the Jew wishing to renew his life "as of old." In his contact with the populace, Brenner developed a very critical, disenchanted view of the "Arab character" (he did not avoid such generalizations) and way of life. In his last essay—written a few weeks before he was murdered by Arabs in 1921—he describes his own role, as a Jew coming from the West, in relation to the Arab:[9]

> At darkness, I wandered in the dusty paths of the citrus groves at the end of the towns. All of them belong to those born in the country, to the Arabs. They are *theirs*.

Brenner passes by the house of a landlord, an *effendi*. He greets the effendi but receives no response whatsoever. Brenner writes:

> I pondered bitterly: if there is truth in the assumption that the people dwelling in Palestine are from our race, and the Palestinian *fellahim* are related to the remnant of Israel—I want no part of them! I have no other way, I must pass by them whether they want it or not, but it is better to meet with a Velikaja Russ [an authentic Russian] in Tambov—or with a Lithuanian around Kovno— than with these Polacks of the East.

Farther along the way, Brenner meets a poor, humiliated Arab boy who has been robbed of his wages by the effendi:

> At that time I chastised myself for not having learned Arabic. If only ... an orphan laboring! My young brother! Whatever the merits of erudite hypotheses, whether or not we are blood relatives, *I am responsible for you*. It is incumbent upon me to open your eyes and teach you the meaning of human relations! ... No, not a hasty revolution in the Middle East by the order of a certain well-known committee and through the emissaries of a certain well-known socialist politics—no, not politics! Perhaps this is precisely *not* our role, and perhaps we deal with it only out of necessity, in desperation, and when no other course of action is possible! No, no, not that! Rather soul-to-soul contact ... from this day on ... and for many generations ... for many days ... *and with no goal* ... *with no intention* ... save that of a brother, a friend and a companion.

Brenner was well aware, even in this essay, of the cultural distance and the potential enmity between the European immigrants and the indigenous Arabs. What is so fascinating about his position is its complete lack of romantic self-effacement in the face of the Arab East, a position that arises from a sense of the clear advantage of Jewish humanism: "It is incumbent upon me to open your eyes and teach you the meaning of human relations!" The pessimistic tone that is evident at the end of the essay stems from a profound recognition of the *excess power* inherent in the Western culture that was being brought to Palestine. The "hasty revolution" and "well-known socialist politics" suggest to Brenner a politics of mastery that forcibly effects changes in traditional ways of life. Such politics sound the death knell for what Brenner considers a role that is to be filled for many generations, namely, to be "a brother, a friend and a companion." The Westerner is to come to Palestine with *plenty* but not with *force*. Brenner's paradoxical formulation—the juxtaposition of a "role" to a deed that has "no goal" and "no purpose"—sets his views apart from the standard patronizing discourse of Zionist Orientalism. The "role" is coexistence that will be enriched by Western experience and thought, without establishing in advance its desired result.

Brenner's was a rare, solitary voice in Hebrew culture in two respects: first, in the total absence of sentimentality and complaisance toward elements of Arabic culture that appeared to Western eyes to be base and flawed; and second in his deep tolerance for the otherness of the stranger. Second, Brenner's position is one of the first statements of the conflict between Eastern and Western civilization that informs post-Orientalist Israeli culture to this day. Zionist Orientalism was bound up with the notion of a Jewish renaissance—the rebirth of the Jew into history—and of a return to a primordial past, which led to the emulation of Eastern images. The end result was nothing less than a surreal synthesis of a self-renewing Judaism and the Eastern experience, but the tension between the Jews and the Arabs excluded the possibility of an authentic assimilation between their two cultures. The life experience of the Palestinian populace, as well as that of Jewish immigrants from Arab lands, was not to be copied. The new, Zionist Jew was to be modern, urban, and urbane, an agent of progress; the Easterner was an innocent, naïve villager, still part of the natural world. The Old Yishuv uncovered a discordance between East and West that was deeper and more fundamental than that which existed in the "Orientalist" era of Zionism, whose surreal fantasies obscured the real problems. The break was precipitated by World War I and, more forcefully, by the Arab "riots" of the 1920s and 1930s. Equally, though, it was the product of the cultural makeup of the Third and Fourth Aliyot, the urban aliyot par excellence. These immigrants brought with them a vibrant European modernism that effectively did away with the shallow idealism of Zionist Orientalism.

The process, then, was twofold. The Arab was stripped of the aura of pristine originality and expelled from view altogether. Yet the landscape, the sky, and the air continued to bear the Arab's Eastern characteristics *even in his absence*. Abraham Shlonsky (1900–1973), perhaps the leading poet of the post-Bialik generation, demonstrated this cultural rift and the violence that flares up within it. Shlonsky's vision of the landscape is informed by his profound sense of its Eastern nature. In "Jezra'el," he repeatedly likens the landscape to camels:

> *Like a caravan of nursing camels with humps in the sky—*
> *God made the hills of Gilboa kneel,*
> *And the field of Jezrael like young she-camels*
> *Cling to the nipples of those breasts.*[10]

In "To This Point" (*Ad Halom*), the poet, who is well aware of his own foreign-ness, seeks to blend into this landscape:

> *Cause me to kneel, my God, like a camel disburdened.*
> *I will pause briefly here at your feet.*[11]

But in "Facing the Wasteland" (*Mul ha-Yeshimon*), when Shlonsky describes the work of the Jewish immigrants, the landscape loses its placid, pastoral quali-ties as well as its erotic dimension and becomes a scene of emptiness, desolation, and failure. When confronted with the Zionist enterprise, the East becomes *meaningless.*

> *Many, many, many generations*
> *The sands lay still like ivories,*
> *Latent, their rebellion quelled:*
> *None approach*
> *To disrupt them.*
>
> . . . . .
>
> *Suddenly the all-conquering shovel glimmered*
> *And the sand herds bleat*
>
> . . . .
>
> *I have vanquished you on this day*
> *Languishing camel:*
> *It is you who shall bring the mortar*
> *For the cement*
>
> . . . . .
>
> *Thus a road to a road—oh, bridle straps!*
> *Houses upon houses—like fists in the void!*

The same landscape metaphors—the camel and the herd—are used, but here they represent a hostility to be overcome, harnessed, domesticated, and placed in the service of the builders.

Shlonsky is quite aware of how intrusive this construction is, but he interprets it, reversing the pastoral scene above, as the intrusion of life into death:

> *With a psalm of victory I desecrated*
> *Your seed-hating desolation.*

Awaiting the revenge of the Eastern desert, he makes explicit its ethnic identity:

Now I know: the wasteland
Howls by night a prayer of vengeance.
And from afar,
Above the high domed roof of the mosque:
A crescent moon moves,
Like a scimitar.[12]

The terminology most suited to describe this conflict from a Western perspective is Schiller's distinction between the "naïve" and the "sentimental." The naïve individual opposes and "shames" culture, revealing it to be artificial and forced; he is blameless and unsullied, living in harmony and unconscious identification with nature. The sentimental person, by contrast, is an urbane sophisticate who has been exiled from the kingdom of the naïve but yearns to return and cleave to nature once again. Schiller's categories provide a fascinating key for understanding the cultural dialogue and dynamics between the two nations inhabiting Palestine and between the different Jewish ethnic groups. It is undoubtedly a dialogue between deaf interlocutors in which what is left unsaid undermines and even contradicts the explicit communications.

Both the Arabs and the Eastern Jews were perceived by the Zionists as "naïve"—at peace with their natural being, attentive to the cycles of nature and to the local landscape, driven by passions, oblivious to the "meaning" Western culture attributed to them. This naïveté, visible to the Western eye, is, of course, a Western notion that has nothing to do with how the East viewed itself. Primitivist Israeli painting that abstracted the landscape to brown arcs and turned the Arabs into simple, monumental, round-bodied feminine figures was, then, a sentimental gesture. But within Israeli culture the visual arts themselves acted as a sort of naïve voice opposed to the sentimental awareness of Hebrew literature.

One of the most penetrating instances of literary awareness of the gap between these cultures is S. Yizhar's description of a razed village in a story set during Israel's War of Independence:

The beds are still made, and the fire between the cooking stones still fuming, and chickens one minute peck through the rubbish as if nothing [is wrong] and the next flee squawking, slaughtered. . . . And the vessels in the yard are still in the very midst of their living concerns. . . . In one yard there stood a donkey with colorful linens and blankets heaped on its back, rolling off and fluttering to the ground . . . in the next yard were two sheep pressed, startled, into the corner, utterly bewildered (I later saw them bleating on our truck) and the large water jug was overturned on the threshold, dripping, astounded, the last of its waters into a puddle, half within the room, half without.[13]

Anna Ticho, *Jericho*, 1940. Brown chalk on paper.
(The Israel Museum, Jerusalem)

The precision and detail, the intimacy of Yizhar's description of the destruction of an Arab village, distinguish it from Orientalism: it is a faithful account, saturated with experience and empathy, not an idealized generalization but a sliver of reality, without a hint of biblical pastorality. Nonetheless, in situating the destructive encounter between two civilizations in a village, Yizhar is making a symbolic choice. The village, the center of Arab existence, is contrasted with the ravaging power of the Western Israeli, with his jeeps and hubris and derision. The water jug that is upset on the threshold of the household becomes a powerful symbol of trampled naïveté.

But Yizhar's was a singular voice, and much of Israeli culture continued to understand the East in terms of its naïveté. The Arab is attentive to nature and its rhythms; he is a beautiful, virile object of yearning; but he is also an innocent savage, a child in relation to culture and civilization. He possesses the simplicity of Eros and passions but lacks intellect and consciousness. In this, the conflict between the "naïve" and the "sentimental" involves an erasure of the Arab's otherness. He becomes an "emptiness" of sorts, against which Shlonsky waves his fist; the Arab is a vacuum into which the Westerner projects a part of his own personality. Israeli culture created through this conflict a powerful psychological symbiosis in which the East was transformed into the hidden, repressed aspect of its soul. The Arab twins who appear repeatedly in Chana Gonen's torrid dreams in Amos Oz's novel *My Michael*, exuding savagery and incest that are at once attractive and repulsive, are the other side of the sleeping Arabs in Naḥum Gutman's "Afternoon Rest" (*Menuḥat Tsohorayyim*). Oz's position is more critical and self-aware because he exposes the mindset that grasps the Arab as naïve, though he himself does not present them as such.

The visual artists who remained in the landscape tradition continued, up to the 1960s, to produce paintings of the "Arab village"—a detached, oblivious art, blind to the yawning chasm opening all around them. The establishment of Ein Hod, an artists' colony built in 1953 on the ruins of an Arab village, speaks for itself: the "naïveté" of Israeli painting led an entire community of artists to settle within the *subject* of the painting. They settled inside the "beautiful" of Israeli art, but here we are dealing with an instance of the beautiful that manifests in its actual history—unlike Safed and Jerusalem, two other cities that attracted these painters—the vacuity and destruction upon which this ideal is based.

Similarly, the paved roads of Judea and Samaria that "crisscross" and "bypass" the landscape harness it from without (much like Shlonsky's camel), leading the Jewish settlers to the mountaintops (their preferred site of settlement) where their mastery and dominance can be buttressed. From there they look down on the *pastoral landscape*, consuming it as "beautiful" and "innocent." In essence, they have turned the land into a painting.

Yehoshua Kenaz's first major work, *After the Holidays* (*Aḥarei ha-Ḥagim*, 1964) revealed a horrifying aspect of the psychological symbiosis with which the Jews characterized the Arabs: during the British Mandate, a Jewish man toils in the garden of a family in a settlement. One of the daughters watches him as he hoes, arousing his desire. He tries to channel his passion into the work, but it is too great, and he flees the settlement for the fields:

> It was still twilight. On the horizon red and green flames burned above the distant mountains. A little Arab girl stood in the middle of the field gathering her herd of black and brown goats together to take them home to her village. She spoke to them, scolded them, and hit them with a stick to goad them. There was no one in sight. The only sound was the melancholy chugging of the well engine in the distance.
>
> Baruch set upon her in the field and did a terrible thing to her.
>
> When he came to his senses he found himself lying in the field among the thorns and the dung, the panic-stricken goats running to and fro around him, bleating deafeningly. His eyes saw only death and blood and rags and black stains.[14]

Here we find the psychological-cultural paradigm in its purest form: civilization (the settlement), what lies beyond it, its "naïve" opposite—the fields and the herds—and the intractable anxiety of civilization that finds relief in the fields. However, the race to the fields, to the "naïve," is no longer the result of yearning but a flight, and the relief is not fecund; it is rape. The allusion to the story of Cain and Abel (Genesis 4:8, "And Cain set upon Abel in the field") reveals the complexity and the symbolic significance of the enmity: we are dealing with sibling rivalry, sibling hatred. The psychological structure is the same: the revenge of a person expelled from nature against a sibling whose sacrifice is lovingly accepted; the revenge of the farmer against the shepherd. That the Arab attacked is a young girl is no coincidence: the naïve is feminine and childlike, and she is ravaged and plundered by a man whose path to the feminine and the childlike has been blocked. The pastoral fantasy of Zionist Orientalism dissolves in the face of incestuous violence.

THE CREATION OF MODERN HEBREW

Modern Israelis speak Hebrew and write in Hebrew. Second-graders can open the Book of Genesis and read *"bereshit bar'a Elohim et ha-shamayim ve-et-ha'aretz"*—in the beginning God created the heaven and the earth—without translation or explanations. Ancient words are heard around the breakfast table and on the playground. Hebrew is the mother tongue. This phenomenon lies at the very heart of Israel's identity both as a culture and as a locus of Jewish political existence.

The revival of Hebrew was the most radical event of the Zionist revolution. It preceded the geographic movement toward Palestine and was essentially different from it. That movement, aliyah, involved a profound transvaluation of the notion of the individual Jew and of the Jewish people tantamount to a rejection of traditional Judaism and its fate in the Diaspora. The revival of Hebrew, however, created a very different dynamic, one that does not contradict the traditional definition of the Jews as a people and as a nation. On the contrary, the Hebrew revival wished to create an organic connection between the Zionist revolution and the ahistoric and nonterritorial loci of Jewish identity. The language of the Bible, the Mishnah, and Jewish liturgy, Hebrew was also for two millennia the medium of communication between Jewish communities. When the sages of Babylon wrote to those of Italy or the Rhineland, they did so in Hebrew. The language became a *place,* a locus, for a dispersed people, the earthly manifestation of Jewish faith. The revival of Hebrew constitutes, then, a connection both to the remains of ancient Jewish civilization and to the discourse of Diaspora Judaism.

The transformation of Hebrew into the language of daily speech, scientific inquiry, and literary production was not the result of alchemy. It was contingent, first and foremost, upon the unique place of Hebrew within Western culture. The "renaissance" metaphor is misleading, for Hebrew was never a dead language; it existed in an intermediate condition of "static life." In a 1913 essay titled "Language Pangs," Bialik characterized the condition of Hebrew as follows:

> A truly living language is produced by life and life's literature. It does not detain its offspring in the womb, rather is fruitful and multiplies constantly and of itself, releasing its creative power in its due season. . . . A truly dead language has nothing but the writing on the tombstones, work done by the stonecutter at a time of dire need. Not so our language, a "pseudo-living" language, that gives birth to very little and leaves much tucked in her womb; and it is our role to induce the birth.[15]

The "pseudo-living" language becomes a metaphor for the Jewish people, existing in a state of delayed fecundity, enduring a gestation period of eons. In this essay, as elsewhere, Bialik conceptualized language as the feminine manifestation of the spirit of the nation (he explicitly identified Hebrew as one of the manifestations of the *Shekhinah,* the feminine aspect of God), an eternal mother figure who requires the aid of her sons to return to her nurturing role. Clearly, the revival of Hebrew is not driven by revolutionary zeal but by Eros: a renewed bond with the maternal figure. It is an act of love.

The unique condition of Hebrew, which survived as a *written* language throughout the centuries of Jewish existence, illuminates the fascinating dynamic of its revival. The process began "from above," from literary and intellectual circles, and it took years for Hebrew to become the spoken language of the Jews in Palestine. The literature produced in Eastern Europe in the 1880s created a locus of living Hebrew long before there was a spoken, lived language. Bialik considered the Russian-Jewish writer Mendele Mokher Sforim (the pseudonym of Sh. Y. Abramowitsch [ca. 1836–1917]) as the starting point of this revival:

> Mendele is the first national artist of Hebrew literature. . . . He is the first to create a full, realistic Hebrew style. Up until Mendele we had language diversions, or language delusions, language gyrations and language patches; Mendele gave us a single, whole language, "human language." . . . He is almost the first in modern Hebrew literature who ceased mimicking books and began mimicking nature and life. He doesn't imitate the Bible or the Mishnah or the Midrash, rather [he] creates in the image and the likeness, according to the internal nature and the intrinsic spirit of Hebrew.[16]

The conclusion is critical: beyond the fact that Mendele was the first literary realist of the new Hebrew—his model is "nature and life"—he created a style that neither imitated earlier texts nor translated foreign ones. Mendele tapped forces that lay dormant within Hebrew.

In Bialik's terminology, a "national artist" is not one who deals with the concerns of the nation or writes of nationalist themes, but rather one who produces a literary corpus whose style and substance, whose very essence, is drawn from the linguistic reservoirs of the nation. His use of the phrase marks the heart of the process of revival. The national artist is able to renew the ancient language through the sheer force of his creative intuition while remaining *within* "the internal nature and the intrinsic spirit" of that language, drawing upon its existing grammar and vocabulary. The revival of Hebrew cannot be understood, and probably would not have been as effective, without the impressive literary corpus of Mendele, Bialik, Tchernikhovsky, Berdichevsky, Feierberg, Brenner, and Genessin, all of whom wrote in a cultural context that did not speak—and barely read—Hebrew. These authors founded a Hebrew "literary republic" that developed in the last decades of the nineteenth century and whose population never numbered more than a few thousand, but its influence was nonetheless profound (see David Biale's chapter in this volume).

Bialik was undoubtedly the father figure of modern Hebrew culture as a whole. This statement does not refer to his formal status as the "national poet," an epithet he acquired in his lifetime and that was further developed by the Israeli educational establishment; nor does it refer to his actual artistic accomplishments. It refers, rather, to the paradigm he established for the Hebrew artist. There was, of course, Hebrew literature prior to the works of Mendele and Bialik. But what is the difference between the poetry of Rabbi Moses Ḥayyim Luzzatto or Judah Leib Gordon and that of Bialik? It lies in something subtle, almost invisible—namely, the *myth of the poet.* Every culture has its own such myth. For Christian Europe it is the Orpheus story: a martyrological myth of one who enters into the divine realm (Hades) and pays for the journey with his life and love. The implicit perspective of European poetry is that of a chosen individual, blessed by the gods (the gift of the muses) but also cursed by them (the loss of love). This myth is erotic in its representation of poetry as a sublimation of carnal Eros. The poem, the "beautiful," is the divine substitute for the absent beloved. Bialik was well aware that the Hebrew poets who preceded him never considered either the myth of the poet or the origins of poetry; nor did they perceive the need to understand the European poetic model and replace it with a Hebrew model. A poet writing in Hebrew *without* breaking out of the European model is little more than a translator, working within a conceptual framework based on a pagan myth later adopted by Christians. Bialik knew, then, that without a new myth of poetic creation Hebrew culture would never become independent but would remain forever on the margins of the dominant Western culture.

Bialik set out to establish a poetic myth on parallel tracks: he created a "national persona" or a "national self" whose life-experience personifies the nation as a whole, and he yoked this national self to the figure of the biblical prophet. The first poem in which he makes this connection is "On the Threshold of the House of Study" (*Al Saf Beit ha-Midrash*, 1894). This poem is a manifesto of sorts of the new poetic myth: the opening lines announce that the personal experience of the speaker and the fate of the nation as a whole are identical:

> *Temple of my youth, my ancient house of study!*
> *Once again I come across your threshold that is now decayed,*
> *I see again your walls that are fading like smoke,*
> *The filth of your floor, the soot of your ceiling.*

Gradually, as the poem progresses, the voice of the speaker becomes increasingly forceful, alluding repeatedly to the language of biblical prophecy. The poem culminates in an explicitly prophetic statement as the poet, in the mode of classical biblical poetry, addresses the future:

> *You will not collapse in ruin, O tent of Shem!*
> *I will yet build you and myself be built.*
> *From your dust I will revive the walls;*
> *You will yet outlast palaces, as you outlasted*
> *On the day of great destruction, when fortified towers fell,*
> *And when I repair the destroyed temple of God—*
> *I will throw open the tent fly and tear open a window,*
> *And the light will push back its shadowy darkness,*
> *And with the ascent of the cloud will God's glory abide below;*
> *All creatures great and small will then know,*
> *Though the grass dries and the flower wilts—God endures forever!*[17]

What this early poem states in a blunt, perhaps even ponderous manner finds a more subtle and profound expression in Bialik's mature works. The poem "Alone" (*Levadi*, 1902) can serve as a model for his complex synthesis between personal fate, expressed in very intimate terms, and the national dimension of the speaker:

The wind carried all of them away,
The light swept all of them away.
A new song made the morning of their lives exult with song;
And I, a soft fledgling, was completely forgotten
Under the wings of the Shekhinah.

Solitary, solitary I remained, and the Shekhinah, too;
She fluttered her broken right wing over my head.
My heart knew her heart; she trembled with anxiety over me
Over her son, over her only son.

She has already been driven from every corner, only
One hidden nook, desolate and small, remained—
The House of Study—and she covered herself with the shadow, and I was
Together with her in her distress.

And when my heart yearned for the window, for the light,
And when the place under her wing was too narrow for me
She hid her head in my shoulder, and her tear dropped on my Talmud page.

Silently she wept over me and enfolded me
As though shielding me with her broken wing:
"The wind carried them all away, they have all flown off
And I was left alone, alone. . . ."

And something akin to the ending of a very ancient lamentation
And something akin to a prayer, a supplication-and-trembling:
My ear heard in that silent weeping
And in that tear, boiling—[18]

"Alone" clearly demonstrates Bialik's approach to the root symbols of traditional Judaism: the Shekhinah, the ancient personification of the nation's spirit, heir to the mourning *Ur*-mother in Jeremiah's vision, "Rachel weeping for her children, she refuses to be comforted" (Jeremiah 31:15); the bird in Psalm 84; and the dove in the liturgical poems (piyyutim) that descends from the symbolic heights and becomes a living creature, a close, even intimate presence. Under Bialik's guidance, the symbolic figure undergoes a transformation and takes on a psychological dimension. The Shekhinah is first depicted as an anxious mother hovering protectively over her son, but, by the poem's end, she is a dependent motherly figure, hindering her son from flying away and growing up. In Bialik's depiction of the relationship between mother and son, there is no abstract sense of awe. The relationship is a complex web of anxiety, compassion, grief, and subtle irony: the speaker is aware that his mother is repeating his own statement when she says, "The wind carried them all away."

As the "personal" and the "national" aspects are joined ever more daringly, so too the biblical-prophetic mode must pass through a new, personal prism. In his great poems "My Poetry" (*Shirati,* 1901) and "Splendor" (*Zohar,* 1901), Bialik transforms his childhood experiences into divine visions, presenting them as the anointing of a prophet. "My Poetry" addresses two questions: "Do you know whence I inherited my poetry?" and "Know you whence comes my sigh?" The "poetry" and the "sigh" are the two sides of Jewish poetry. The poetry comes from the father's domain, from the meager Sabbath feast, whereas the sigh is from the mother's, the financial difficulties and the shame of her widowhood, ultimately distilled in the image of the tear that falls into the dough she kneads for her children's bread. The poem's conclusion completes the connection to the image of the biblical prophet:

> *My heart knew well that tears fell in the dough;*
> *And when she gave her children warm new bread,*
> *Bread of her baking, bread of her pain, her woe,*
> *I swallowed sighs that seeped into my bones.*[19]

The mother's tears "seeped into" the bones of the speaker like the divine scroll the prophet Ezekiel consumes. This passage also indicates that the connection to the biblical source is not a one-way street. Not only does the human experience resemble the biblical paradigm but the opposite is true as well: the ancient figures of God, the *Shekhinah,* and the prophets resemble a father, a mother, and a son-poet. God, too, in all his vast glory undergoes psychologization in this poem. Bialik radicalizes the midrashic tradition in that he undermines the traditional textual hierarchy within Hebrew literature: the new text draws its religious authority and theological structure from the ancient work but also changes its meaning. For Bialik, this move has a chronological aspect as well, in which the late is no longer inferior to the early.

In this revolutionary move, Bialik draws daringly upon European Romantic philosophy—the idea that childhood is an era of purity and divine revelation—but he transforms these ideas, converting them, as it were, to Judaism, and associates them with the myth of Hebrew poetry, now understood as prophecy. The poet is anointed by God and maintains direct contact with the divine. This is not the hubris of the Greek hero who enters into the world of the divine (a motif later transformed in Christian martyrology) but a continuous *kabbalah* in the original sense of the word: tradition. The phrase "I inherited my poetry" is critical: the Hebrew poet continues an ancient genealogy of those chosen to receive God's word. The divine speech is found, through various metamorphoses, throughout the Jewish people and thus passes to the poet from Jewish daily life, from his parents' home.

Bialik's poetic language resonates richly (in a way that is inevitably lost in translation) throughout the different strata of Hebrew literature: his descriptions of personal, even mundane experiences recall a wealth of ancient texts—the Bible, midrash, the Hekhalot poetry, ancient piyyutim, and liturgy. The reference is not always a quote or explicit allusion—sometimes it is the morphological structure of the words, other times a matter of phonetic similarity. He always engages the ancient texts anew, endowing them with a different meaning, completely lyrical and psychological. Bialik himself says as much in "Should an Angel Ask" (*V-Im Yishal Malakh*, 1905):

> *From dead letters songs of life gushed forth,*
> *Shocking the famous dead upon the shelves.*
> *For they were different songs: of small bright clouds,*
> *Of golden beams of sun and shining tears.*[20]

It was the myth of the Hebrew poet that doubtless conferred upon Bialik's poetry its unprecedented authority. Bialik was the first of the moderns to deal with the meta-poetic issues that arise from the writing of specifically Hebrew poetry. From this point on, Hebrew literature had its own center; it was no longer dependent upon other literary corpora and could absorb outside influences with a clear sense of its particular identity, and not as passive imitation.

Bialik's influence extended far beyond the immediate circle of followers that formed around him in his lifetime. His use of the linguistic stores of Hebrew created a sense of freedom that is evident in Hebrew poetry to this day. His myth of the Hebrew poet continued after his death and was developed in the poetry of Shlonsky, Natan Alterman, Natan Zach, Meir Wieseltier, Yitzhak Laor, and Hezi Laskaly, and particularly in the writings of S. Y. Agnon and Uri Zvi Greenberg.

Not all the Zionists believed that Hebrew could function as the daily language of the Jewish state. Herzl, for one, imagined it would be German. Ahad Ha-Am did not think that Hebrew was suited for subjects outside the confines of "Judaism"; he intended it to be the language of Jewish scholarship but nothing more. Even literature appeared to him beyond the reach of Hebrew, because only a spoken language (such as Yiddish) could produce a Jewish literature. But the members of the Second Aliyah thought otherwise. Most came from the Jewish intelligentsia of Eastern Europe at the peak of their adolescent revolt and saw their immigration to Palestine as an act of rebellion against the world of their fathers, a world that prayed in Hebrew but spoke Yiddish. Hebrew became the language of the new Jewish locus in Israel. Eliezer Ben-Yehudah's great historical dictionary (composed by him in the first two decades of the twentieth century but not completed until 1957, thirty-seven years after his death) came to symbolize the renaissance of spoken Hebrew. And, indeed, Hebrew became a versatile modern language, well suited for scientific, literary, and daily life.

It was the shift of Hebrew literary activity from Eastern Europe during the Second Aliyah that established Palestine as the center of modern Hebrew culture, and the arrival of Brenner in 1909 symbolized this transition. From that point on Palestine, the new Jewish space, became the central and decisive subject of Hebrew literature; it became the Jewish topos both in the Greek sense of "place, region" and in the literary sense. That literature created its own historic dynamic, unlike the Hebrew literature prior to Mendele and Bialik, which developed through imitation of the ideas and styles of the surrounding Arab or European culture. Only after these ideas were recognized as exemplary by the host culture did Hebrew writers adopt them—usually after a generation or two (or more) had passed. This was still true of Bialik and Tchernikhovsky, who responded to European Romantic poetry written 60 and 70 years earlier. But once a firm stylistic center was established in Palestine—again, primarily through the work of Bialik and Mendele—an intra-Hebrew dynamic began to develop. Though doubtless still influenced by Western literature, the writers were driven by powerful internal arguments with each other, between the generations, and between them and the long history of the language and its literature.

Hebrew literature created for itself a sort of telescoped time, clearly apart from the European dynamic, not parallel to it and certainly not lagging behind it. From a European perspective (typical, perhaps, of the 1950s) it could be argued that in certain cases Hebrew prose was more avant-garde and "progressive" than European. (Genessin's "stream of consciousness" writing precedes Marcel Proust or Virginia Woolf, and so forth.) The "telescoping of time" had various causes: this was a distinctly new literature; that is, it found itself dealing with issues that had never been addressed in its culture. The novelty was thematic, first and foremost. Prior to Mendele, Bialik, and Tchernikhovsky, Hebrew writers had produced no detailed and realistic description of a forest or a field or a sunset. The fate of the individual, the human body, actual life circumstances, human relations and emotions—none of these had ever been described in Hebrew, and there were no terms for many of the key concepts. For Hebrew culture, the physical world was terra incognita. The problem was not simply one of vocabulary (the absence of words for flora, fauna, most human anatomy, and so on). The primary difficulty lay in the perception of reality: sensation, understanding, associations, the structure of human consciousness. The Hebrew idea of the "soul" was unchanged since the Middle Ages. Modern Hebrew needed, then, to constitute an entire *epistemology*, the goals of which were not philosophic but existential.

When Tchernikhovsky, on the threshold of the twentieth century, wrote his nature poems—"Facing the Sea" (*Le-Nokkah ha-Yam*), "From Within the Cloud" (*Mitokh Av he-Anan*, 1902), and particularly "Charms of the Forest" (*Kismei Ya'ar*, 1890)—he was quite aware that these descriptions (that is, these acts of perception, of seeing, and their translation into poetry) were almost without precedent in Hebrew. Unlike the poems of Wordsworth and Byron, who had the support of a rich poetic tradition involving observation of the world, Tchernikhovsky's poems are suffused with the awareness that these were the first such observations in Hebrew; an awareness that he, the poet, was a lantern lighting the way down an unfamiliar path. Thus the typical Romantic position so noticeable in his poetry—the sense of alienation and exile from nature and consequent yearning for nature's mysteries—is in fact unlike European Romanticism, and it arises from different sources. He writes in "Charms of the Forest":

And I, a mute person, will stand and listen: What is for me? Who is for me?
A foreigner, a stranger in their world, a foreigner, only narrowly plotting my
    path.[21]

Here he is writing *as a Jew* whose culture has a very well developed angelology but no names for trees or mushrooms. The deep romanticism that resonates throughout Hebrew literature until the beginning of the twentieth century is not a nostalgic yearning for a bygone aesthetic age but an attempt to deal with the natural world within the context of what, for the West, was a unique cultural consciousness. What had transpired in European culture since the Renaissance was for Hebrew literature compressed into a few generations.

The same sense of discovery, of a first formulation, that resonates in the works of Bialik and Tchernikhovsky fills the pages of Yizhar's masterpiece *Days of Ziklag* (*Yemei Ziklag*, 1957). The novel unfolds over the course of a few battle-filled days during Israel's War of Independence, but it deals primarily with the landscape, offering a detailed description of its space, light, soil, flora, and fauna. Yizhar, who constructed this grand narrative in a collective stream-of-consciousness, also analyzed the full spectrum of mental disturbances at work when the Jewish-Hebrew mind encounters expanses of nature. *Days of Ziklag* forms a direct link to Tchernikhovsky's questions in the poem cited above, or to Bialik's question in "In the Field" (*Ba-Sadeh*, 1894):

> *Tell me my mother, my earth, broad, plentiful, and great—*
> *Why do you not pull out your breast for me, a poor yearning soul?*

Let us conclude this discussion of the creation of modern Hebrew with Zach's poem "A Moment" (*Rega Eḥad*, 1962), which opens his collection *Different Poems* (*Shirim Shonim*) and demonstrates at once the newness of the language and its archaic resonances:

> *Quiet for a moment. Please. I'd like to*
> *say something. He went away and*
> *passed in front of me. I could have*
> *touched the hem of his cloak. I didn't.*
> *Who could have known what I didn't*
> *know.*
>
> *There was sand stuck to his clothes.*
> *Sprigs were tangled in his beard. He*
> *must have slept on straw the night*
> *before. Who could have known that in*
> *another night he would be hollow as a*
> *bird, hard as stone.*
>
> *I could not have known. I don't blame*
> *him. Sometimes I feel him getting up*
> *in his sleep, moonstruck like the sea,*
> *flitting by me, saying to me my son.*
> *My son. I didn't know that you are, to*
> *such an extent, with me.*[22]

The language of the poem is colloquial Israeli Hebrew. Not a single word is foreign to the active vocabulary of a modern Hebrew speaker. The tone is far from the declamatory style of ancient poetry. Still, the opening line—"ana ani ba"—is a pun in which the reader hears Reuven's words to his brothers in Genesis 37. Hebrew acts like a giant organ, producing echoes and the echoes of echoes at the slightest touch.

What is it that the narrator wishes to say? This is the tale of a missed contact: "I could have touched the hem of his cloak." And the Hebrew phrase *"shulei adarto"* (the hem of his cloak) evokes the Bible itself, though it never appears therein. Zach evokes all those who stand in the presence of God (or of God's messengers). The reader does not know the identity of the "he." Is it a father? Is it God? Undoubtedly both, but more than that: it is the absolute "other," the sublime. And yet this "other" is inextricably tied in the vocabulary and the living memory of ancient Hebrew to two words, "shulei adarto." Hebrew is felt as an immanent revelation, a medium of sorts for the sublime, transcendent presence. The "he" is, in a sense, language itself.

The second stanza describes the descent of the divine "he." He grows entangled in the lower reality. The Hebrew ear picks up the word play of *ḥol* (sand) and *ḥol* (profane). He descends from the heavens to the earth, touching the earth and the ḥol. His descent signals his end, his death. But the third stanza marks a reversal. The "I" feels him "getting up." This is not a miraculous resurrection, for "he" exists within the "I." The "I" senses him. The "he" (father, God, Hebrew) is part of the personality of the living person. Within the poet, within his soul, begins a new, different contact between the sublime "he" and himself. And the other says to the poet: "My son. My son. I did not know that you are, to such an extent, with me."

Again the Hebrew ear clearly discerns that the repetition of "My son" recalls David's lament on the death of Absalom. But the situation constructed in the poem is very different from the biblical father's mourning. Here it is the father who dies, and the speaker is his living son. The father figure (God, Hebrew) addresses the living son after its death, revealing the tragically missed opportunity that occurred in the individual and national past as well as the mutual obliviousness and rupture that characterize their covert relationship. But the very existence of this internalized other, the father-God, and the ability to communicate with him within one's own soul, creates a new sort of contact. The sublime presence of God, the Other, of language as a whole, becomes a living internal part of the poet.

The connection to Bialik's "Alone" is readily apparent. The mother figure, the Shekhinah, has been replaced with a sublime, divine father figure. The dependence, however, is much the same. More important, Zach repeats the psychological shift in which the impersonal God and tradition become an intimate, dear presence, equally dependent upon the living person. The poem contains in its narrative and its inherent power the tragic immanence of Hebrew speech. The living speaker of Hebrew is bound through it to the fallen God that is implicit in the language, and through God to the biography of God's nation. We recall the ancient source of the Hebrew word *davar* in the first line "Please, I'd like to say something [*davar*]." Davar is also the word of God, the logos, a principle that is enacted in each succeeding generation, secular and religious alike.

HEBREW MODERNISM AND THE CREATION OF THE NEW JEW

Modernism in Israel, which began with the generation after Bialik and Tchernikhovsky and of which Zach is a late representative, was unlike that of the West. The movement never actually broke with neo-Romanticism; only in the Israeli context does it become apparent that this was "modernism." It did not aim its arrows against an older world, nor was it interested in urban poetry with a tendency toward the abstract. It consisted, rather, in the search for an authentic Hebrew voice. The modernist movement in Israel focused on the spoken language and sought to reveal the "poetic" quality of the very mechanisms of speech. It was also bound up with the possibility of creating a new kind of Jew.

At the turn of the nineteenth century, Moshe Smilansky published a series of stories that extol handsome, virile, and eminently moral Eastern heroes. These figures, all constructed in the best Orientalist tradition, were intended as role models for Jewish readers. In his best-known story, "Hawaja Nazar" (1910), Smilansky's hero is a Russian-born convert to Judaism who immigrates to Palestine and becomes a powerful farmer with a heartfelt interest in the "Biblia." His handsome features and virility earn him the admiration of the local Arabs, who ask him to be a judge over them. The ultimate mark of his successful metamorphosis is the willingness of the Arab women to take him as a husband. Yet the story's conclusion points to a profound flaw in his Weltanschauung: wishing to see the Jordan, he sets out on a journey toward the river, but when he reaches it he is shocked by its modest dimensions. The pioneer, who swam in the great Volga as a child, leaps into the Jordan and drowns. The Jewish burial council refuses to bury him in the Land of Israel, because he is uncircumcised.

This conclusion reveals the full complexity of the notion of a "new person" or "new Jew": his beauty and virility stem from his gentile mother and mark him as an outsider to traditional Judaism. He is uncircumcised, which is to be understood by the reader as a physiological indication that he has not been "castrated" by Judaism (the symbolism is similar to the phylacteries at the end of Tchernikhovsky's poem "In Front of a Statue of Apollo"). However, his death in the Jordan reveals that he does not understand the local landscape: he becomes tangled in the shallow brush and cannot break free. In judging the Jordan, he makes use of foreign images (the Volga), but he runs up against the intractable local reality that proves too powerful for him. Finally, it should be noted that the Jordan symbolizes the entrance into the Land of Israel (in the Exodus narrative) and is the "holy river," a symbol of the sanctity of the land. In light of this, the pioneer's death may be an expression of the land's resistance to this bifurcated man, who is neither a native nor of the Jewish religion and nation. It is striking that Smilansky, the impassioned spokesman of early Hebrew literature in Palestine, rejects the one-dimensional ideal of the new man, revealing the European foreignness of this imagery of man and space. Smilansky is the first to demand of the Jew that he "know" the land in sexual terms as well, to consummate his love for it and take it for his bride.

The writers and artists of the Third Aliyah (beginning in 1919) sought to create precisely the same linkage between the Jewish religious tradition and both a new physiognomy and agricultural labor in Palestine. Shlonsky begins his poem "Toil" (*Amal*, 1927) as follows:

> We have a small hand with five fingers,
> Wax fingers thin to breaking.
> The pulse beats at their beginning and at their end—fingernails.
> Oh, what shall we do to the fingers on the day we labor with them?[23]

The hand, like the sister in the Song of Songs 8:8 ("We have a little sister and she has no breasts"), is immature. Its fingers are waxen, like those of scholars and merchants, and though it has a pulse and nails it is not yet ready for "the day we labor with them." Shlonsky's brilliant allusion to the Song of Songs hints that the laborer's day is analogous to the nuptial night when the sister will cease to be a girl and become a woman; the passage to the Land of Israel and to agricultural labor is a passage of maturation. He reveals the force that must drive the new Jew: "Pound mightily, human pulse! Grow wild, fingernails! We are going to toil!"[24]

The next poem in the cycle is an ode to sweat: "Oh, Sweat! Oh drops of blessing falling from my high forehead like dew from pure skies."[25] These poems create a broad network of concepts around the body—the hair, the skin, the physical power, and the sexuality that were to characterize the new Jew, the sensual, "wild" person who plows and nurses the land simultaneously. But the connection to Jewish tradition is not severed. In "Toil," Shlonsky links the imagery of the body and physical labor to the ceremonial reading of the Torah:

> Dress me, good mother, in a splendid coat of many colors
> And with dawn lead me to toil.
> My land wraps in light like a prayer shawl,

Houses stand like phylacteries.
And like bands of phylacteries glide hand-laid asphalt roads.

Thus a beautiful city offers her morning prayer to her creator.
And among the creators, your son Abraham,
Poet-roadbuilder in Israel.[26]

Once again, a poet evokes the tefillin, but now in a thoroughly secular context. The "good mother" is none other than Judaism personified, called upon to crown her son as he sets off for the religious ceremony of physical labor.

Uri Zvi Greenberg, the greatest modern Hebrew poet, presents in "Ascending Virility" (*Ha-Gavrut ha-Olah*, 1926)—his wonderful poem devoted to agricultural work in Israel—a complex synthesis between the ideal of labor and the prophetic-biblical image of the poet. The journey toward the Land of Israel is understood as an approach toward a "holiday of revelation," and the poet is God's chosen: "This is the body cast by God from a lodestone. Drawing to itself from a distance, it draws the one fleeing in the dead of night."[27] The sunrise, the stock symbol of the Zionist movement (heir to the Haskalah symbolism of light and dawn) is transformed in Greenberg's poetry and takes on a mystical quality; it becomes a divine fire that flows from man's body following circumcision. In the prose poem "Incision and Command" (*Ḥitukh ve-Tzivuyi*), he writes: "There is an inner sunrise that gnaws between the bones, wishing to break out as in the wide heavens and ignite upon me the fire stored in the soul. Its sunrise cries out from within to be revealed in my life."[28]

Greenberg's poetry further emphasizes the tendency—already visible in Shlonsky's poems—to link Aliyah and agricultural labor to the religious commandments. Greenberg describes immigration as compliance with a commandment spoken by previous generations:

Generations sunk in their pained flesh and blood in several soils throughout the
  world
Command the grandson:
Ascend to the Land of Israel and express us, living man!
Do not sing from the glory of the heavens, speak from the man who lives upon the
  soils:
The flesh, the blood, the nerves, the cartilage, the skin.
The garment, the bread, the water, the house, the vessels.
The woman, the cradle, the good baby in his infancy.
The soil, the iron, the lamp, the machine, the steering wheel.

Day and night: yearnings, distances, walkings.
The dream and waking reality are twins, there is almost no difference:
Each nourishes the other and each embraces the other
And both have rays in the midst of the days.[29]

The conclusion of this excerpt—"in the midst of the days"—situates the historic event in cosmic time, understood here as the conjunction of the midlife of the poet and the midlife of the nation. The modernist character of the poem, which draws on German expressionism and on Walt Whitman, connects it to twentieth-century events, including the rejection of the "old world" of declining empires and World War I. Within the dynamics of Israeli culture this modernist sensibility also rejects the poetics of the previous generation—the generation of Bialik. This ecstatic poetry, wild and unbridled by form, was modern Hebrew culture's Oedipal revolt against its founding fathers. Its significance is inextricably linked to the *place* the poetry dealt with; it was viewed as poetry of the Land of Israel.

The ecstatic sensuality of the 1920s was in no way limited to the poetry of Greenberg and Shlonsky. At this time visual art in Israel experienced its first "modernist" period, turning against the propagandist Orientalism of the first Bezalel School. Artists such as Reuven Rubin, Naḥum Gutman, Joseph Zaritzky, and Tziona Tajar created a stylistic language that joined the new person—muscular and tan—to the local landscape, the mountains, and the sky. In Ru-

Reuven Rubin, *First Fruits*, 1922–23. Triptych: oil on canvas.
(Rubin Museum Collection, Tel Aviv)

bin's great triptych "First Fruits" (*Bikurim*, 1923), a group of men and women, intermixed with donkeys, sheep, and fruit, are painted in earthen hues and arranged like saints in a Christian altarpiece.

This was the heroic period of Israeli culture. From the 1920s to the 1940s, Palestine was the center and dominant site of Hebrew artistic and literary creation. In the 1920s, the culture generated its own creative dynamic and began to establish a market for its works, in Europe and America as well as at home. (For its impact on Poland, see David Biale's chapter in this volume.) The leading writers of prose included Agnon, Ḥayyim Hazaz, Yizhar, Yehudah Burla, and Moshe Shamir; the preeminent poets included—in addition to Shlonsky and Greenberg—Alterman, Leah Goldberg, and Amir Gilboa. This was also the foundational period for Israeli music: classical by Isaac Edel, Alexander Boskowitz, Paul Ben-Ḥayyim, Oedoen Partos, and Mordechai Seter; popular or folk songs by David Zahavi, Mordekhai Zeira, Daniel Sambursky, and Nahum Nardi.

THE GENERATION OF 1948 AND
THE IMAGE OF THE SABRA

Wars are the clock ticking off the time of Israeli history: World War I; the "riots" of 1929 and 1936; World War II; the War of Independence, 1948; the Sinai Campaign, 1956; the Six Day War, 1967; the War of Attrition, 1969–71; the Yom Kippur War, 1973; the Lebanon War, 1982; the Gulf War, 1991. Not all these conflicts were equally significant in their cultural impact, and surely not in the same way, but together they create a ghastly rhythm in which every calm period is seen in Israel as a pause before future violence.

The War of Independence and the founding of the state were the most decisive cultural moments in Israeli culture. The Yishuv was certain that these were events of almost mythical proportions. The war was seen as the test of the new Jew. An entire generation was named for that war, "the generation of 1948," a designation that stood for a complete way of life and established a fixed image of bravery in Israeli culture. The absolute commitment of the Yishuv to the War of Independence left clear literary and artistic marks, particularly in the view that the individual is always a part of the "us," the collective. The war was, in the critic Dan Miron's phrase, "the anvil upon which Israeli culture was hammered out." It established a new center of identity and identification: whoever was not suited to the mores of the Sabras (the native-born Israelis), such as their Hebrew pronunciation, their rites of passage, and their existential challenges, found himself or herself excluded (see Eli Yassif's chapter in this volume). This new ideology became the basis for the most profound conflict in the post-1948 culture, between those who viewed themselves as heirs to the ideology and those who did not—the Jews of the East, the European survivors of the Holocaust, and the Orthodox community.

In the late 1940s, a prominent school of thought emerged that served as a catalyst in the development of the image of the Sabra, namely the Canaanite ideology, whose main spokesmen were the poet Yonatan Ratosh, the author and sculptor Binyamin Tammuz, and the important sculptor Yitzhak Danziger. The secularism that led the visual arts (from the 1930s on) toward abstract modernism had distanced itself from both Judaism and the East, electing instead a universalistic perspective in which Israeli art was seen as a branch of Western art. The "Canaanites," in contrast, loathed Judaism but embraced the East, though not the actual East—be it Jewish or Arab—but the one that preceded the monotheistic religions. They searched for national particularity in the soil itself—in its sand and stones, in the bowels of the earth, the deepest archaeological strata of Israeli space. In effect, they sought to bypass history, driven by a yearning for a lost state of archaic perfection.

Danziger's statue "Nimrod" (1939), though completed before the Canaanite group became active, was its harbinger and is to this day honored in the brief cultural memory of Israel as a masterpiece (see p. 1010). Nimrod is mentioned in Genesis 10:8 as a relative of the forefather of the Canaanites: "Cush also begot Nimrod, who was the first man of might on the earth." The statue is made of Nubian sandstone, which imparts a weighty symbolism: this is the desert stone representing the pure expanse, natural and untamed; it was taken from the red rock of Petra, a mysterious oracle of the ancient past. The statue is a curious, uncanny combination of a raised, pseudo-archaic head and a thin, sensual, and very realistic boyish body. Nimrod holds a bow in his left hand, part of it concealed behind his back; a bird is perched on his shoulder. The statue has been the subject of many interpretations and is one of the most famous subjects in the discourse of Israeli identity. Some see in it a rare, primordial beauty, others ravaging power, and others, in the 1990s, exilic weakness and sensual femininity. "Nimrod" remains an enigmatic emblem, tied to the feel of the local space, to the sandstone, to a primordial reality, and to the East; it is a work whose differing interpretations reveal the internal contradictions beneath the idealized façade of the Sabra.

The literary corpus of the generation of 1948 dealt primarily with the pre-state youth movements and the War of Independence, thus concentrating on the native hero and drawing away from any earlier Jewish context. The famous opening line of Shamir's novel *Stories of Eliq* (*Pirke Eliq*, 1951)—"Eliq was born of the sea"—locates the hero within nature itself, emerging like Aphrodite from the open space, resistant to any concrete genealogy. The Sabra, as he was portrayed in the works of Yizhar, Shamir, and Tammuz, was not only isolated from "Diaspora Jewry" but was forever frozen in a state of youth. The Hebrew words for young men, *ne'arim* and *baḥurim,* appear repeatedly in these contexts. It bears emphasizing—particularly against the backdrop of the Holocaust—that the physiognomy of the Sabra is blatantly Nordic: he is always tall, blue-eyed, and blond. The Sabra, the subject and the bearer of Israeli ideology, was built largely on hatred for the "old Jew" who was characterized using the imagery of European antisemitism. This literary representation evokes to no small degree the psychological markings of the "hostage syndrome," in which the captive begins to identify with his captors. Here, the Jew adopts the form of his tormentor. His eternal youth, meanwhile, keeps him from any serious moral conflict. The young soldiers of the War of Independence were killed before they could reach sexual or moral maturity, and they were likened by the poets to Adonis, who dies in the prime of his youth and is replaced by red flowers.

Ḥayyim Guri (b. 1923) was the outstanding poet of the generation of 1948 and one of the greatest Hebrew poets in the latter half of the twentieth century. In 1960, he published one of his best-known works, "Heritage" (*Yerushah*):

The ram came last of all. And Abraham
did not know that it came to answer the
boy's question—first of his strength
when his day was on the wane.

The old man raised his head. Seeing
that it was no dream and that the angel
stood there—the knife slipped from his
hand.

The boy, released from his bonds, saw
his father's back.

Isaac, as the story goes, was not
sacrificed. He lived for many years, saw
what pleasure had to offer, until his
eyesight dimmed.

But he bequeathed that hour to his
offspring. They are born with a knife in
their hearts.[30]

This poem, which deals with the fate of the Jews through the ages, is understood by most Israeli readers as an elegy for those who die to defend the Land of
Israel. It is often read at memorial services, along with Guri's equally famous war
poem of 1949, "Behold, Our Bodies Are Laid Out" (*Hinei Mutalot Gufotenu*).[31] It
is not political or religious leaders who link the binding of Isaac to fallen Israeli
warriors, but parents, students, and soldiers. Clearly the poem serves a human
need to make sense of death in battle by relating it to the sacrificial offering,
construing death in the wars of Israel as a direct continuation of Jewish fate
throughout history. However, on a less conscious level, this poem is a song of
protest. The last stanza—often quoted by people who do not know its source—
is the silent cry of a people whose very identity forces death upon them; for
whom belonging to the nation that inhabits the Land of Israel is like a knife in
their hearts. The heroic Sabra is also the victim Isaac.

The binding of Isaac is perhaps the most vigorous myth in Israeli culture,
having seized the place of the Exodus myth, which, as we have seen, was the clear
favorite in the early days of Zionism. It is recalled in innumerable texts besides
Guri's, most significantly in Agnon's *Only Yesterday*, discussed above, in which a
Zionist migrates to Israel and is "swallowed up" in Jerusalem, where he dies a
horrible death; and in Wieseltier's 1968 poem "Yitzhak's Story" (*Ma'aseh Yitzhak*), about an Israeli child who is sexually abused by the Zionist municipal
authority of Tel Aviv.[32] Wieseltier's Tel Aviv is like the shop of a corrupt and rapa-
cious Jewish bourgeois. Agnon and Wieseltier use the binding of Isaac in their
harsh critiques of Orthodox Judaism and the new secular materialism, respectively. Clearly, then, this myth is in no way limited only to war and death; it bears
on other aspects of Israeli life, as well.[33]

THE HOLOCAUST IN ISRAELI CULTURE

The image of Isaac bound for slaughter also conjures up the Holocaust, especially in the poem "Isaac" by Amir Gilboa (1917–1984), in which it is Abraham and not his son who dies in the forests of Europe. The terrible destruction
of the Jewish civilization in Europe, the Shoah in modern Hebrew discourse, did
not become part of Israeli culture until a generation later. Except for Gilboa's
poems and Greenberg's great poem "The Breadths of the River" (*Rehovot ha-
Nahar*, 1946), Israel did not produce a major work of art dealing with the Holo-

caust until the 1960s. Gilboa and Greenberg, the latter having literally prophesied the destruction of European Jewry in the 1930s, remained solitary—albeit powerful—voices. Otherwise, the Holocaust was repressed, relegated to the margins of Israel's cultural consciousness.

The Holocaust survivors who came to Israel found themselves in a society with which they could not communicate. In its early years, Israel's attitude contained more than an element of accusation: the victims of the Holocaust bore the responsibility for their tragedy because they had chosen to remain "exilic" Jews, that is, they were not Zionists and had not embraced the ethos of the new Jew. "Like lambs to the slaughter" was a phrase often used to describe the destruction of European Jewry. The physical appearance of the survivors ("so pallid, not the least bit tan") and their scarred, traumatized psyches set them apart from the Israelis, who viewed them with derision and condescension. They were known as *sabonim*, bars of soap, a slang reference to the cosmetic products the Nazis allegedly extracted from the bodies of dead Jews. For many years the term *sabon* designated a person who obeys unquestioningly. The survivors themselves said nothing; the callousness of the surrounding culture conspired, as it were, with their desperate need to repress their tragedy so as to continue living.

This began to change in the early 1950s with the reparations agreement between Germany and Israel. The subsequent public outcry provoked a furious debate in the Knesset, the press, and in the literary world. But the watershed event was the Eichmann trial in Jerusalem in 1961, when the State of Israel positioned itself, symbolically, as the prosecutor of the German nation. The trial was broadcast on the radio (television was not introduced in Israel until the late 1960s) and followed by the entire population. The court proceedings provided, for the first time, details of the Nazis' systematic extermination of the Jews. Only then did the enormity of the tragedy enter into the consciousness of the nation as a whole. From that point on, the Holocaust became one of the most important subjects of Israeli memory: survivors began to recount their stories, and their presence became a powerful, dominant voice in the collective self.

Aharon Appelfeld now began to publish a literary portrait of East European Jewry on the eve of World War II. He did not describe the horrors of the extermination, providing instead an anatomy of its genesis and development. His stories are sensitive and highly realistic portrayals of the Jewish bourgeoisie in progressively more hostile surroundings, up to the final collapse of that civilization.

Dan Pagis, who began publishing poetry in the late 1950s, did not address the Holocaust until the early 1970s. His poems, unquestionably among the most important artistic statements on the Holocaust, are treasures of modern Hebrew literature. They are included in school curricula and serve as an entrée to a broad and nuanced discussion of the theological and existential significance of the Shoah. His best-known poem, "Written in Pencil in the Sealed Freight Car," became an emblem of sorts for the Holocaust as a whole. Pagis's approach is daring and subversive. The relationship between the executioner and the victim is seen as a modern version of Cain and Abel:

> *Here, in this freight car,*
> *I, Eve,*
> *with my son Abel.*
> *If you see my older boy,*[34]
> *Cain, the son of Adam,*
> *tell him that I*

The sudden break that concludes the poem, a silence that announced an awful absence, is a profound poetic commentary on the philosopher Theodor Adorno's statement that there can be no poetry after Auschwitz.

THE CRISIS OF HEBREW CULTURE AFTER THE SIX DAY WAR

The Six Day War of 1967 marked the end of an era that spanned nearly 20 years in which Israel was governed by Socialist Zionism under the leadership of David Ben-Gurion and the Labor Party. This was the time of the "melting pot," when great waves of immigrants were absorbed into Israeli society, and also a period that witnessed the inchoate beginnings of a peace culture not committed to any political party. The Six Day War turned the little State of Israel into a much larger state of occupation. The victory aroused a sense of euphoria. The messianic forces in Israeli culture grew stronger, and the country became more like the "Promised Land" than ever. The Revisionist political groups were greatly strengthened, and the national consensus that had seemed to exist in the years following 1948 was shattered. The culture was divided, and the "doves," who produced most of the art, positioned themselves in opposition to the Occupation.

In 1973, the Yom Kippur War brought about the deepest crisis in Israel's self-image. The sense of security and power inculcated by the Six Day War was revealed as nothing more than hubris. For many, the shocking failure and the terrible toll of the war joined with its symbolic starting date to take on the appearance of a biblical plague. Israeli soldiers were exposed, for the first time, to the horrors of an extended modern war. The Arab enemy no longer seemed inferior. The very existence of the state was felt to be under constant threat. As a result, the image of the state as a large, protective mother hovering over the nation was utterly undermined, and the complete trust Zionism had previously enjoyed was replaced with a sober skepticism. The war set off, in a chain reaction of sorts, a series of cultural and political events: for the first time (1977) the leadership of the state moved from the socialist bloc to the political right (and it has been moving back and forth ever since), and the fabric of Israel's population—and its culture—began to disintegrate into ever smaller factions and fragments. The Lebanon War of the early 1980s further undermined the trust of the populace toward its political leaders, and it pushed the political and cultural schisms to the point of enmity.

The literary reflection of this crisis is exemplified in the poetry of Yonah Wallach (1944–85) and the novels of Yitzhak Laor (1948–). Almost 100 years after Tchernikhovsky's use of the tefillin as a symbol of Orthodox Judaism's imprisonment of the God of nature, Wallach returned to the symbol and gave it perhaps its most provocative expression in her famous poem "Tefillin" (1983):

Come to me
don't let me do anything
you do it for me
do everything for me
what I even start doing
you do instead of me
I'll put on tefillin
I'll pray
you put on the tefillin *for me too*
bind them on my hands
play them on me
move them with delight on my body
rub them hard against me
stimulate me everywhere
make me swoon with sensation
move them over my clitoris
tie my waist with them
so I'll come quickly
play them in me
tie my hands and feet
do things to me
against my will

turn me over on my belly
and put the tefillin *in my mouth*
bridle reins
ride me I'm a mare
pull my head back
till I scream with pain
and you're pleasured
then I'll move them onto your body
with unconcealed intention
oh how cruel my face will be
I'll move them slowly over your body
slowly slowly slowly
around your neck I'll move them
I'll wind them several times around your neck, on one side
and on the other I'll tie them to something solid
especially heavy maybe twisting
I'll pull and I'll pull
till your soul leaves you
till I choke you
completely with the tefillin
that stretch the length of the stage
and into the stunned crowd.[35]

Only against the backdrop of the "virginity" of Hebrew literature can this poem—and the provocative nature of Wallach's poetry of the 1960s and 1970s in general—be understood. The sexual ethos of Hebrew literature, at least up to the time of Wallach, Oz, and David Grossman, was similar to that of nineteenth-century European literature. Not only was it unable to credibly describe sexual relations, but it was equally inhibited in its expression of a wide array of feelings and actions that involve the body and the passions, such as desire, the naked body, or sexual behavior that does not fit the standard romantic notion, such as homosexuality. The narrow confines within which the human soul was treated, which excluded madness and violence as well, were breached only after the 1950s, after the second great modernist revolt of Hebrew literature (the first having been Shlonsky and Greenberg's against Bialik's generation in the 1920s). But even here there was a clear sense of restraint relative to European modernist writers of the 1920s and 1930s, and to their American counterparts in the 1950s and 1960s.

Wallach, who was deeply influenced by Allen Ginsberg, shook up the emotional and sexual concepts that had been acceptable in Hebrew poetry, and she undermined the idea of the typical poet. Instead of the wise poet, heir to a cultural and linguistic tradition (such as Zach and Yehuda Amichai), Wallach presents a fragile, tortured consciousness that can change sexual identity over the course of a single poem. She uncovers flashes of psychological trauma bordering on psychosis and constructs an active, frank, sexual persona. For Wallach as for Tchernikhovsky, the tefillin symbolize the body bound by the bridle of religious tradition. But Wallach breaks a number of taboos—the male monopoly on the ritual, the ritual context of the prayer—and turns the tefillin into a sex toy in a sadomasochistic encounter. It was no wonder that, shortly after its publication, the poem was quoted in the Knesset by a female representative of the National Religious Party who urged that it be denounced and censored. The conflict between free sexuality and Judaism is embedded in the poem, and through it Wallach exposes the great secular-religious tension that exists throughout Hebrew culture.

The People, Food Fit for a King (Am Ma'akhal Melakhim, 1993), a novel by Yitzhak Laor, is the most significant attempt yet to deal with the "bridle of tefillin." Laor presents a sweeping analysis of Israeli culture as based on the "silencing of the ugly." He charts something akin to an alternative history of the Six Day War in which a unit of neglected and marginal soldiers in the quartermaster corps finds a secret document that they conceal, and, as a result, the war and all its consequences are averted. It is as though this novel actualizes that which is implicit in Wallach's poetry and endows it with a moral and political force: the elevated Jewish tendency to glorify man while denying human passions and authentic feelings leads directly to Israel's militaristic war ethos. This impressive work is a sequel of sorts to Yizhar's Days of Ziklag in that, in each, a great writer offers his own penetrating analysis of Israeli culture at a time of crisis. Laor also continues Yizhar's complex discussion of the Jewish-Israeli body in the context of a particular locus, the landscape of Israel. At the same time, Laor reveals the profound break in Israel's consciousness in the post-1967 era. The sense of rebirth that accompanied Yizhar's rediscovery of the body and natural expanses, and which was tied to the sense of unity that characterized the War of Independence, was replaced with keen doubt as to the justness of the war and a dreadful realization that a Jew can be no less violent, cruel, and belligerent than other people.

The People, Food Fit for a King opposes Israeli reality to the traditional Jewish corpus: it contains many allusions to the Bible, ancient piyyutim, and modern Hebrew poetry, including some that borders on political propaganda. As against the "Apollonian" ethos of the tefillin, the sublimating Jewish ethos of restraint,

Laor introduces the ethos of martyrdom in the person of the medieval Rabbi Amnon of Mainz, whose famous piyyut "The Day of Judgment" (*Unetanne Tokef*) ends the novel: "Man comes from dust and to dust returns; he gets his food at the peril of his life; he is like broken earthenware; like withering grass and fading flowers; like a fleeting shadow and a driven cloud; like a puff of wind, like vanishing dust, like a dream that flies away."[36]

THE MIZRAHI JEWS IN HEBREW CULTURE

Like the survivors of the Shoah who came to the new State of Israel, so, too, the Jews from the Middle East and North Africa (the Mizrahim) did not fit into the image and ideology of the Sabra. It was not until the period of crisis after the Six Day War that they began to find their literary voice. Let us consider a highly pregnant passage from Yehoshua Kenaz's *Infiltration* (*Hitganvut Yehidim*, 1986):

Rahamim Ben-Hamo leapt from his bed, extending his arms to either side as though stretching after sleep. But he remained where he stood, swinging his arms up and down, and it was not yet clear what he intended to do. But the singers understood and Sammy called out to him:

"Come on, cutie!"

And Rahamim stepped toward them swaggering and mincing as he went, a teasing smile on his lips. For a moment he stood motionless, staring at the floor as though looking for the precise point on which to stand, then he closed his eyes and his face turned somber. . . . Rahamim opened his eyes and smiled and shook his plump body like a caricature of a belly dancer. His torso was bare and he wore only work pants with frayed hems that covered almost his entire feet, like the feet of a child.

Slowly the singers gathered round him and the circle grew thicker until no one remained sitting on his bed. Everyone came to see the spectacle. Some clapped their hand to the rhythm of the song, encouraging the dancer, others shouted insulting catcalls, and still others recoiled in stark revulsion. But everyone was drawn into the circle, as he shook his body and wiggled his neck and shoulders in a pampered, coquettish manner. He stood on his tip-toes, first opening his arms and shaking them in an inviting gesture, then pressing them to his chest as though in fear and protection, again and again daring and frightened, stepping forth and drawing back, charging into danger and imme- diately retreating into himself, startled, stroking his hips and thighs and wink- ing to those standing in front of him, then recoiling and covering his face with his hands as though ashamed of his behavior, as though he surmised what awaited him. He began to circle the crowd, skipping daintily, his hand outstretched to the audience as though pleading for his life, his head thrown back as if willing to accept the verdict, any verdict. . . .

He danced ceaselessly, and absent the Arabic song, all that could be heard were the drumming on the tin can and Raḥamim's labored breathing; he was covered with sweat—even his pants were wet at the waist and from time to time he would blow on his upper lip to clear a bead of sweat that had fallen from his nose. Suddenly he let out a stifled cry. A scream of pain or pleasure, then another, and his expression grew excited, and while his body was writhing in all directions he reached out his hand as though crying for help, as if the force of the pleasure or pain that caused the repeated moans was greater than he could bear. The ugliness of his bestial squirming and the groans accompanying it to the rhythm of the tin drumming—it was powerful, dark and fascinating, so much so that it almost ceased being ugly.[37]

I have cited this long passage because it contains, in a highly distilled form, what would otherwise require many volumes of documentation. *Infiltration,* like Pension Vauquer in Balzac's *Père Goriot,* gathers in one place—a basic-training army barrack in the mid-1950s—representatives of nearly all the sectors of Israeli society (except ultra-Orthodox Jews, who do not serve in the army). One soldier (the narrator) grew up on an established agricultural settlement, another comes from a Sephardic family that has been in Israel for many generations; among the others are a Holocaust survivor, a *kibbutznik,* a city dweller, and so forth. Raḥamim Ben-Ḥamo is "the Moroccan," and, like the others, Kenaz views him as a personification of the Mizraḥi populace. His dance is the Moroccan's "creation" in the wonderful symposium Kenaz depicts throughout the novel. The scene can be read as an allegorical representation of Israeli culture's approach to the Middle Eastern and North African immigrants who undertook the great aliyot of the 1950s. That a Moroccan fills this role is no accident: it is the choice made by Israeli culture itself. Kenaz here responds to a selection process that eludes numeric explanation, because the Moroccans have been designated the Mizraḥi Jews in the drama that pits East against West in Israeli culture.

The first key to understanding this passage lies in the choice of the belly dance as the Moroccan's "creation." This quintessentially Eastern dance form is an Orientalist choice par excellence from the perspective of the Ashkenazic narrator, but it is by no means unrealistic: music and dance, along with cuisine, are the aspects of Mizraḥi culture that remained most intact in the move to Israel. The material culture was severely damaged, and the literary tradition, mostly religious in nature, was terminated altogether. At the outset, Rahamim Ben-Hamo's belly dance looks somewhat ridiculous, a grotesque image that Kenaz creates through the very harsh juxtaposition of masculine and feminine elements. The "ugliness" and "bestial quality" that Kenaz attributes to the dancer in the eyes of the spectators are not balanced, initially, by Ben-Ḥamo's delicate charm and childishness. The Mizraḥi is ridiculous and repulsive, primitive in both his artistic language and his artistic medium (drumming on the empty can). Culturally, he is associated with Arab music and the "idea" of Arabness as embodied in the dance. In the novel, Arab music conflicts with the music of Telemann, Elizabethan poetry, and the songs of the Land of Israel, which represent a Western tradition: " 'We don't want Arab songs in the army!' cried Kippod, 'we don't want to hear that crap!'—'We don't like your Ashkenazi songs either,' said Sammy."[38]

It is fascinating to see how Kenaz shapes the dancer's behavior and its interpretation in the "Israeli" consciousness: it is unclear whether or not the dancer has himself internalized the gaze of the spectators and accepts their "verdict." Only his physical gestures are unambiguous, a universal language of body and expression. The ambiguous medium by which he reveals his particularity may ultimately be based on a grand misunderstanding, but a misunderstanding that concludes at a different point from where it started. Here lies the message encoded in the scene: the emotion and human force of the dancer ultimately break down the barrier of the "beautiful" and are accepted by the other spectators as beautiful ("almost ceased being ugly"), and thus as comprehensible and fascinating.

The process that unfolds in this scene is, in this reading, the extended one that has occurred within Israeli society over the past 50 years. Only in the past decade has the barrier between Mizraḥi and Ashkenazi been broken. Although the relationship between the two communities can be conceptualized in terms of the "naïve" vs. "sentimental" division that characterizes the conflict with the Arab East, the events and dynamics of this drama are very different. The Israeli concepts of "the ingathering of exiles" and "the melting pot" were much more violent and destructive for the culture of the Mizraḥi Jews than for that of the Arab populace, who, despite the political and social trauma of becoming a minority, nevertheless retained most of their culture. The concepts were predicated on the Mizraḥi communities breaking with their traditional way of life when they came to Israel. They encountered a more mature Israeli culture and thus were not the object of the love for the archaic East that so moved the early Zionists. (Only the first Yemenite immigrants had the "fortune" to be integrated into the Orientalist forefather-imagery.) The yearning anachronistically preserved in the portraits of the Arab village were absent from Israeli culture in the 1950s and the 1960s. The particularity and otherness of the Mizraḥi Jews elicited scorn and alienation, but nothing more.

The idea of the "melting pot" was a poetic fiction. The integration of Mizraḥi

Jews was in actuality a matter of rupture and erasure, made possible by their suppression from the dominant Western consciousness. Consequently, the first generation of immigrants was utterly destroyed, both as the bearer of a heritage and as a cultural authority for the next generation. Only the children of these immigrants—the generation of Raḥamim Ben-Ḥamo—could hope to build from the ruins a new cultural presence. Yet a second, "curatorial" approach toward this heritage developed, at once complementing and resisting the widespread derision and repudiation: manuscripts were preserved and cataloged, as were elements of the material culture, folktales, and traditional music. This scholarly approach, adopted by a small minority within the intelligentsia, preserved certain aspects of the razed heritage while keeping them outside the lifeblood of Israeli culture. The very presence of such artifacts in the state museums and the halls of academia demonstrates the violent break that occurred in the cultures of these communities upon their arrival in Israel.

Still, the idealized view that the Mizraḥi communities had preserved a cultural integrity that was suddenly destroyed when they got to Israel also fails to tell the full story of this complex drama. One fascinating interpretation of the encounter is Agnon's great story "Edo and Enam" (1951), which is, among other things, an allegorical critique of culture.[39] The story portrays the fate of songs that came to Israel from Enam—a Jewish mountain civilization in the East—with a woman named Gemulah. She had learned them from her father, a healer and a teacher of songs: "Gemulah his daughter aided him. She was accomplished in all their songs, those that they had once sung when they dwelt by the springs and also those of the mountains."[40] Gabriel Gamzu, a collector of ancient Hebrew manuscripts, comes to Enam from Israel and collects Gemulah as well, marrying her and then taking her to Israel. But Gemulah is a somnambulant. Her father gives Gamzu protective scrolls whose very presence in the house protects Gemulah during her nocturnal perambulations, lest she fall or fail to return home. And so Gemulah wanders moonstruck on the rooftops singing her father's songs. But Gamzu accidentally sells the protective scrolls to Dr. Ginat, a Jerusalem scholar who specializes in the grammar of Enam and Enamite hymns. The latter, for all his interest in Gemulah's songs, eventually causes her death. He falls in love with her and rushes to the rooftop to aid her while she sleepwalks. In his wakeful state he weighs heavily on the ledge, breaking it and toppling to the ground with Gemulah.

The moonstruck quality that surrounds Enam's poetry is a penetrating image for naïve ancient poetry, and spiritual traditions in general, in their encounter with modern civilization. The moonstruck daughter parts company with the earth at night, precisely at the time of sexual union; she cannot give birth because she is tied to the moon, and through it to her distant father, the healer and poet, who represents tradition. The force of Agnon's imagery lies not only in the aura of disembodied wholeness surrounding naïve poetry in the story but also in its lack of integrity, its neurosis. Gemulah's mother died giving birth to her, and the girl was raised by her father. His possessiveness becomes an oppressive force that prevents Gemulah from moving forward; the Eros within her faces "backward." Her virginal quality is linked to her father's androgyny (he is both father and mother), which Agnon ties to Enam's original sin—not immigrating to Jerusalem in the time of Ezra. Setting aside Agnon's view of remaining in exile as a moral flaw, it is clear he has managed to capture something that many cultural critics have failed to notice: the naïve folk tradition is not a perfect or whole force. It is inherently barren because its regenerative mechanism is defective (in Gemulah's case—her father's femininity). The traditional as such represents a state of dissociation, even isolation, a world in which the balance between "forward" and "backward" (masculine and feminine) has been disrupted. The traditional has no interest in the future; it can only look back.

Agnon's assessment of the Zionist "ingathering of exiles" is no less critical. He depicts the Zionist curators and collectors as aggregators of culture whose interest is purely intellectual, Western to the point of alienation from vital creativity. "Gamzu was of the opinion that this Ḥakham [sage] Gideon was no Jerusalem Ḥakham, but a European man of learning, an ethnologist or something of this kind."[41] Agnon draws the East-West conflict within Zionism to a tragic erotic climax that sounds the death knell of tradition. The West is symbolized by its materialism: the reduction of life to "texts" and medical conditions.

But Gemulah's fatal encounter with civilization represents not just the withering of a mysterious romantic integrity in the crude light of modernity. The inability of modern men (Gamzu and Ginat) to consummate their love for her is not a sign of the sexual and existential impotence of the Western intellectual who is drawn to a beautiful Eastern woman at peace with herself. On the contrary, these men harness the physical and rational tools at their disposal—yearning, care, intellect—in an attempt to revive, to make fecund, a spirit that has damaged its own fertility. But Zionism, as a modernist redemptive act, arrives too late and is thus an unsuitable tool. "Gamzu went on to relate how when he first came upon them they were dejected, with many sick at heart because of their long exile and long-deferred hope."[42] Agnon bases his interpretation of exile on the verse "Hope deferred makes the heart sick" (Proverbs 13:12). Hope, the attempt to postpone ad infinitum any connection to a concrete location, to a land of their own, created an irreparable rupture. Hope has its limits and, once they are exceeded, the heart itself grows ill. The profound romanticism of the story must not be understood as poetic obfuscation; it lies at the very heart of classical Zionism.

THE ISRAELI SONG

It is necessary to go beyond Agnon and emphasize the current cultural vitality of the Mizraḥi communities in Israel. Despite the terrible blow they suffered, they managed to rise from the ashes and initiate an insistent dialogue concerning their rightful place in contemporary culture. Note that the medium Agnon chose to represent the naïve—sung music—is in fact the very medium by which the Mizraḥi communities are establishing themselves at the forefront of contemporary Israeli culture, from the popular to the artistically sophisticated and sublime. (This development follows a by-now-complete victory in the kitchen.) The infusion of Mizraḥi music into culture is not a continuation of the Orientalist tradition but represents the slow development of a double connection: an external one between Israel and its neighbors—the Arab countries, Turkey, and Greece—and an internal one to the Jewish communities of Yemen, Kurdistan, Persia, and North Africa. This is a self-developing connection, not influenced by outside hands. Contemporary music contains Western elements (shows, concerts, records, instruments, amplification), Eastern ones (harmony, melody, instruments), and some that constitute a synthesis between the two, such as vocal technique, the tenor of the voice, and, most notably, lyrics. The creative tension that has been sparked between these two musical cultures is reminiscent of that which resonated in Egyptian music in the beginning of the twentieth century, when it encountered Western music.

The recent phenomenon of Mizraḥi music is the latest chapter in the saga of an indigenous element of modern Hebrew culture, the "Israeli song." This form of composition consists of melodic tunes sung by groups to the accompaniment of a guitar or an accordion; it is very different from Israeli artistic music. The outstanding Israeli composers—Mark Lavry, Paul Ben-Hayyim, Mordekhai Seter, and Oedoen Partos—synthesized the European modernist tradition and the musical symbols of the "East" (biblical tropes, the piyyut, and the Oriental maqāmat [harmony] tradition). Not so the Hebrew songwriters of twentieth-century Israel. Their songs were not "folk" songs, given that their intellectual intentions were equal to those of the classical composers. Nonetheless, they had a completely different approach to both European and non-European musical traditions. Most important, their songs preserved ties to Hebrew poetry and, through it, to the living language.

Until the 1970s, the Israeli songwriters belonged, musically speaking, to the nineteenth century; they were completely oblivious to later developments in "light" or popular music. The finest of these composers—Naḥum Nardi, David Zahavi, Mordekhai Zeira, Emanuel Zamir, Alexander Argov, Naomi Shemer, and Yoni Rechter—employed the musical language of Brahms and Tchaikovsky, and it is in this context that their works must be understood.

Their type of song is the "Israeli" art form par excellence and the only artistic medium that can be said to be uniquely Israeli. Again, it is neither a folksong nor an art song, nor, for that matter, a product of the mass entertainment industry. In its heroic era, the 1930s to the 1960s, it developed into a medium that combined musical, literary, and artistic creation, sometimes of very high quality, performed in a popular setting that is defined by a sense of community. This communality is distinct from the familial or tribal collectiveness of the traditional piyyutim and *zemirot* (holiday songs) as well as from the ensemble of the choir, typical of church music, that calls for obedience to musical rules that resemble (and at times are explicitly identified with) religious commandments. The Israeli song expresses a sense of belonging to the Zionist political structure, even before the founding of the State of Israel, and its central definition is not musical but political. As such, it knows no explicit aesthetic requirements. Unlike the traditional folksinger, the individual singer is not called upon to obey and preserve a tradition. The song expresses, rather, a particular type of interdependence. On the one hand, it depends upon singers in order to exist. On the other, as singers the individuals yield to the community, joining it rather than obeying it, emphasizing all the while their hoarseness and inability to sing on key—that is, the nonmusicality of their life. The individuals, then, are dependent upon the song that serves as a gathering point where they can be counted as members of the community, and in this manner they acquire an identity through the song.

The sense of community that permeates the Israeli song, and the identity of this community with the Zionist enterprise, is implicit in all aspects of this medium: language, lyrics, the manner in which it is sung, and the perspectives it represents. Sometimes it is a simple visual reference ("There lie the Golan mountains") or a formulaic shared biography ("When Mother arrived here, young and pretty"), but other songs introduce a complex expression of either a shared trauma or a traumatic disparity between the individual and the community or between the individual and life in Israel. This is the case with "Elifelet," Alterman's great dirge set to Argov's music, a fixture of Memorial Day services for more than half a century.

Through the unique combination of an artistic work and popular performance, the Israeli song creates a singular situation in which the singers do not "consume" a work as does the audience for a *chanson* or a musical play; rather, they perform it while they are themselves signified by it. This is an artistically open and dynamic state that is filled and closed only when the work is actualized in song. The establishment's support for the song composers, an outgrowth of the ideology of a revival of the "people," cannot explain the public's love of their music. Its broad acceptance is based on trust and a more primordial need. The song implicitly undermines the official Zionist position by providing a connection to the "exilic" mother figure, as Fania Bergstein wrote in her famous lyrics set to Zahavi's music, "thus I shall listen to my distant lullaby."

The archaic quality of the Israeli song is not so much a nostalgic retreat from the present as a vital and valid return to the musical past that provides a firm basis for the present ideal of musical beauty. Unlike twentieth-century art music, whose home could be either Vienna or New York, the Israeli song is committed to a particular place and to the lived experience within that place. The song is encountered empirically: it must be sung and heard and, as a result, has to accommodate itself to the spiritual world of its singers, a world firmly rooted in the nineteenth century. Therein lies its vitality. This is not the usual case of popular art marching two steps behind high art (another rule that came undone over the course of the twentieth century); it is, rather, the "time-capsule" that *is* the time of Israeli culture. The Israeli song is not an appendage to artistic music but an independent medium that admirably created for itself a tradition which is both stylistic and functional.

The Israeli song managed to link itself to the landscape, to the place of Israel. Its stylistic mixture—European classical, Russian popular, Hasidic, and, more recently, Mediterranean and Arabic—do not undermine this statement, because these styles were uprooted and replanted within the unique context of Israeli time and space. The music of the song, lacking even the thin tradition of Hebrew literature, reveals the true force of the bifurcation and foreignness that characterize Israel's cultural sources.

Another fascinating example of this time-capsule effect is Israeli rock music, precisely because it can be compared to the music of the Western youth culture that served as a model. Rock and roll has produced a number of impressive figures since the 1960s, among them Arik Einstein, Shalom Ḥanokh, Matti Caspi, Rami Fortis, and Yehudah Poliker. Nonetheless, this genre never "translated" to Hebrew. True, the composers adopted Anglo-American rhythms, harmonies, and orchestration, but the lyrics demonstrate that the Hebrew language never let them break free from the Israeli context. They simply could not embrace the rebellion and nihilism of Western youth. The person they portray is wholly committed to the common fate of Israeli youth, and when he does express anger it is never aimed at his parents or the establishment. Musically, Israeli rock is sad and melancholic; its lyrics are reminiscent of the classical Israeli song, often dealing with war and the experience of soldiers. Many rock songs are, in fact, songs of mourning and lamentation. They are the primary medium through which the young voice the trauma of their military baptism by fire, which has become the rite of passage of the Israeli adolescent.

The uniqueness of contemporary Israeli song is the heritage of the century-old cultural development that we have been tracing. As a final example of the singular dynamics of this culture, let us return to where we began, to perhaps the quintessential Israeli song, "Hatikvah." The melody of what was to become first the Zionist and then the Israeli national anthem was adapted to the lyrics of Naphtali Herz Imber by Shmuel Cohen, a native of Serbia, prior to his immigration to Palestine in 1888. Imber had written the lyrics in Romania, whence they wandered across Eastern Europe until they finally "stuck" to the melody Cohen knew as the Moldavian farm song "Carul cu Boi" (The Cart and the Oxen). From Serbia, the setting came to Rishon Le-Zion, one of the first Jewish settlements on the coast of Palestine, where it was given its final form. The melody was so widely accepted that all subsequent attempts to set the lyrics to other tunes were rejected. Abraham Isaac Kook, the chief rabbi of Palestine until his death in 1935, was both a mystic and a poet, and he wrote a poem, "Shir Ha-Emunah" (Song of Faith) and set it to the same melody, but it was rejected by the public. Imber's "Hatikvah" attained the status of an anthem long before it was declared the official song of the State of Israel and thereafter withstood all ideological attacks on it.

The words of "Hatikvah" have been criticized as too "exilic," foreign, and melancholy to serve as the hymn of the Zionist revolution. The Moldavian melody, known also from Bedrich Smetana's famous tone poem *Ma Vlast* (My Country), is, of course, foreign. In 1932, Y. Tzipin composed another melody, an optimistic march in a major key, a composition that is viewed as an original Jewish, Israeli work merely because its composer lived in Jerusalem. No one noticed, however, that Tzipin's composition was also foreign: a Viennese march, in the best Straussian tradition.

"Hatikvah" 's resilience is due precisely to its foreignness: it was its resistance to Zionism's optimism that made it attractive. The song is deeply subversive: we have not arrived at Zion and have never been a free nation in its own land. It expresses the *Tikvah*, the hope, in an ancient melody (which some claim is Spanish, not Moldavian). Its selection as the national anthem was not an ideological gesture so much as a response to the hosts of singers that identified so deeply with it and valued it so dearly. To this day, even in the most vacuous official ceremonies (and more so in ceremonies that are not pompous and empty), "Hatikvah" maintains an air of ambiguity: it is an official symbol that represents identification with the state, but its lyrics and melody bespeak suffering and wandering. In this it is unique among national anthems.

The story of "Hatikvah" reveals something about the forces at work not only in Israeli music but in modern Hebrew culture as a whole. The texts convey an impassioned commitment to the challenges and imagery of the Zionist movement, but emotionally, musically, they resist this ideology, preserving the "exilic" origins of the singers (including the Sabras) and giving voice to a powerful longing for a pre-Zionist—European or Mizraḥi—reality. To be sure, this ambiguity is rarely as plainly visible as in the case of "Hatikvah," the lyrics of which, as we have seen, speak of a movement forward and Eastward (kadimah) while the melody expresses a nostalgic gaze backward (kedem). Many other songs, particularly the more popular ones, contain a much more complex interplay between the music, the lyrics, and the contextual structures they create. But the rule holds true: the music resists the party's instructions, maintaining its ties to the past and deconstructing what the text seeks to join together. So, too, Israeli culture remains at once native and foreign, still in search of a home, even as it is firmly rooted in the new-old soil of that land of the East, the Land of Israel.

NOTES

1. Translated by Chaya Galai in *Remembrance Day, Independence Day* (Ramat Gan, Israel, 1999), 96.

2. T. Carmi, ed. and trans., *The Penguin Book of Hebrew Verse* (New York, 1981), 349.

3. Translated by Eisig Silberschlag in *Saul Tschernichowky: Poet of Revolt* (Ithaca, N.Y., 1968), 97–98.

4. Translated by Ruth Nevo in *Chaim Nachman Bialik: Selected Poems* (Jerusalem, 1981).

5. Nevo, *Bialik*, 114 (translation slightly altered).

6. Translated into English by Hillel Halkin in Alan Lelchuk and Gershon Shaked, eds., *Eight Great Hebrew Short Novels* (New York, 1983), 29–58.

7. Y. H. Brenner, *Breakdown and Bereavement,* trans. Hillel Halkin (Ithaca, N.Y., 1971).

8. S. Y. Agnon, *Only Yesterday,* trans. Barbara Harshav (Princeton, N.J., 2000), 3.

9. An entry from Brenner's notebook, dated Spring 1921. This quotation and the encounter is discussed in Ariel Hirschfeld, " 'My Peace Unto You, My Friend': On Reading a Text by Yosef Haim Brenner Concerning His Contacts with the Arabs," *Palestine Israel Journal* 2 (1992): 112–18.

10. Abraham Shlonsky, "Jezra'el," in Ruth Finer Mintz, ed. and trans., *Modern Hebrew Poetry: A Bilingual Anthology* (Berkeley, 1966), 170.

11. Shlonsky, "Ad Halom" in his *Shirim* (Tel Aviv, 1965), 196–98.

12. Shlonsky, "Mul ha-Yeshimon," ibid., 311–17.

13. S. Yizhar, "Hirbet Hiz'ah," in his *Arba'ah Sippurim* (Tel Aviv, 1959). The story was written in May 1949.

14. Yehoshua Kenaz, *After the Holidays,* trans. Dalya Bilu (New York, 1987).

15. H. N. Bialik, "Language Pains" (Hebrew), in *Kol Kitve H. N. Bialik* (Tel Aviv, 1971), 197–201.

16. Bialik, "Mendele and the Three Volumes" (Hebrew) in ibid., 242–45.

17. Ibid., 7–8.

18. Burnshaw, T. Carmi, and E. Spicehandler, eds., *The Modern Hebrew Poem Itself* (Cambridge, Mass., 1989), 25–27.

19. Nevo, *Bialik,* 20.

20. Ibid., 54.

21. *Isol Shirei Sha'ul Tchernichovsky* (Jerusalem, 1937), 75.

22. In Carmi, *Hebrew Verse,* 576.

23. In Finer Mintz, ed., *Modern Hebrew Poetry,* 179.

24. Ibid., 180.

25. Ibid.

26. Ibid., 185–86.

27. Uri Zvi Greenberg, *Kol Ketavav* (Jerusalem, 1990), 1:77.

28. Ibid., 78.

29. Ibid.

30. In Carmi, *Hebrew Verse,* 565.

31. The poem appears in Esther Raizen, ed. and trans., *No Rattling of Sabers: An Anthology of Israeli War Poetry* (Austin, Tex., 1995), 4–6.

32. Translated by Shirley Kaufman in *Modern Poetry in Translation* 14 (Winter 1998): 190–92.

33. See Ruth Kartun-Blum, "A Double Bind: The Sacrifice of Isaac as a Paradigm in Modern Hebrew Poetry," in her *Profane Scriptures* (Cincinnati, 1999), 15–62.

34. Carmi, *Hebrew Verse,* 575; I have slightly modified the translation. Two points should be clarified: the Hebrew "son of Adam" (*ben Adam*) also means "person" or "human being"; and the whole line "Cain, the son of Adam" (*Kayin ben Adam*) is a homonym to the Yiddish *keyn ben Adom* (not a person).

35. In *Wild Light: Selected Poems of Yona Wallach,* trans. Linda Zisquit (Riverdale-on-Hudson, N.Y., 1997).

36. Carmi, *Hebrew Verse,* 207–9.

37. Yehoshua Kenaz, *Hitganvut Yehidim* (Tel Aviv, 1986), 98.

38. Ibid., 93.

39. "Edo and Enam" appeared in English in *Two Tales by S. Y. Agnon,* trans. Walter Lever (New York, 1966), 141–233.

40. Ibid., 176. I have slightly altered the translation.

41. Ibid., 202.

42. Ibid., 175.

SELECTED BIBLIOGRAPHY

Alcalay, Ammiel. *After Jews and Arabs: Remaking Levantine Culture.* Minneapolis, 1993.

————, ed. *Keys to the Garden: New Israeli Writing.* San Francisco, 1996.

Almog, Oz. *Sabra: The Creation of the New Jew.* Berkeley, 2000.

Alter, Robert. *After the Tradition: Essays on Modern Jewish Writing.* New York, 1969.

————. *Hebrew and Modernity.* Bloomington, Ind. 1994.

————, ed. *Modern Hebrew Literature.* New York, 1975.

Band, Arnold. *Nostalgia and Nightmare: A Study in the Fiction of S. Y. Agnon.* Berkeley, 1968.

Diamond, James. *Homeland or Holy Land? The Canaanite Critique of Israel.* Bloomington, Ind. 1986.

Fuchs, Esther. *Encounters with Israeli Authors.* Marblehead, Mass., 1982.

————. *Israeli Mythogynies: Women in Contemporary Israeli Fiction.* Albany, N.Y., 1987.

Gluzman, Michael, and Naomi Seidman, eds. *Israel: A Traveler's Literary Companion.* San Francisco, 1996.

Harshav, Benjamin. *Language in Time of Revolution.* Berkeley, 1993.

Miron, Dan. *H. N. Bialik and the Prophetic Mode in Modern Hebrew Literature.* Syracuse, N.Y., 2000.

Ramras-Rauch, Gila. *The Arab in Israeli Literature.* Bloomington, Ind., 1989.

Segev, Tom. *1949: The First Israelis.* New York, 1998.

————. *One Palestine, Complete: Jews and Arabs Under the Mandate.* New York, 2000.

————. *The Seventh Million: The Israelis and the Holocaust.* New York, 1993.

Shaked, Gershon. *The Shadows Within: Essays on Modern Jewish Writers.* Philadelphia, 1987.

————. *Shmuel Yosef Agnon: A Revolutionary Traditionalist.* New York, 1989.

Sokoloff, Naomi B., Anne Lapidus Lerner, and Anita Norich, eds. *Gender and Text in Modern Hebrew and Yiddish Literature.* Cambridge, Mass., 1992.

Printed amulet with a magical square and formulas,
the portraits of Rabbi Israel Abuhatzeira (Baba Sali) and
Rabbi Shimon Bar Yohai and cloth flowers. (The Israel Museum,
Jerusalem; purchased in Netivot, 1988)

EIGHT

THE "OTHER" ISRAEL:

Folk Cultures in the Modern State of Israel

ELI YASSIF

In 1950, just after the founding of the State of Israel, the boy who was to become the Hebrew writer Eli Amir emigrated from Baghdad, the city of his birth, and was taken into one of the kibbutzim. He later wrote in his autobiography, *A Sacrificial Rooster*:

> For a long time, I lived on the margins of that society, lonely and isolated.... In order to quiet my fears and suppress my thoughts, I threw myself into work. The harder I worked with the hoe, the more carts I filled with manure, the more the affection of Dolek, a veteran member of the kibbutz, grew toward me. His stories would flow: about the Second and Third Aliyot [immigrations just before and after World War I], about dancing the *hora* until dawn, about the bitter ideological arguments, malaria, the wars with the Arabs, about God, hunger, backbreaking work, and also about the pride, ecstasy, and sensual intoxication.... These stories became like the fables of the "Thousand and One Arabian Nights," and had I not heard them with my own ears from Dolek, whose enthusiasm was as if the drama were taking place now, at this very instant, I wouldn't have believed that there was anything to them. But when I returned to my room from work, all of Dolek's stories would wilt like plants under the blazing sun.[1]

The 16-year-old boy from Baghdad could not see any fundamental difference between the folktales he had heard in his home country, such as the "Thousand and One Nights," and these stories of immigration, settlement, wars, and ideological struggles. Yet these stories, with all their vitality and belonging to the new place and time, did not take root within him; they still lacked the power to take their place next to the culture of his parental home.

DIALOGUE

Every process of immigration and resettlement creates a dialogue between the culture of the immigrants and the native culture. Let us therefore first examine the identity of the indigenous, folk culture of Israel that the waves of new immigrants encountered when they arrived.[2] The stories that they heard from representatives of the native culture were traditions passed on orally, written down in letters, memoirs, and kibbutz and youth movement journals, and repeated in the Hebrew press. At their center were events—both real and fictional—that were connected to the new Jewish community in Palestine, such as Tel Ḥai, where a group of pioneers, led by Joseph Trumpeldor, died fighting Arabs in 1920; the "tower and stockade" with which new kibbutzim were established overnight; and Masada and the *chizbat* (tall tale). Each of these stories or traditions deals with experiences, anxieties, and hopes that were integral to real life.

The first and foremost of these stories is the myth of Masada. The Jewish historian Josephus Flavius told in detail the story of the death of the Zealots on the great cliff next to the Dead Sea in 73 C.E., yet Jewish culture almost entirely ignored it for some 1,900 years. Only in the 1920s did groups of youth of various ideological factions begin to ascend Masada in an organized fashion and transform the place into a holy site dedicated to Jewish heroism.[3] The psychological and social consequences of the Holocaust, the creation of the State of Israel and the Israeli Army, with the values of heroism that accompanied it—all these turned the story of Masada into one of the foci of the new culture and transformed it from a historical tale into a myth.[4] As the story passed into collective national memory, not only did it undergo significant changes from Josephus's history but it also involved new rituals, as with every foundation myth. The youth movements, whose members began to climb the massif regularly and to perform ceremonial readings and dramatic enactments there, were the founders of this ritual process. But the rituals became institutionalized with the founding of the state when military units would climb Masada, swear their oaths of allegiance, and receive their personal weapons amid a dramatic staging, accompanied by displays of fire, of the events that had occurred there so long ago.[5] In this way, the soldiers of the Israeli Army would symbolically demonstrate their solidarity with the heroic deeds of the "defenders of Masada."

Integrating myth and ritual, Masada functions as a kind of "social charter" for the state. But the myth also constitutes an interesting combination of ancient Jewish traditions with the realities of the new Israel. The heroic stories of the watchmen of the first waves of immigration, the adventures of the Palmaḥ (the elite units of the Haganah), and the triumphant tales of the War of Independence all merged with the myth of ancient heroism at Masada; they forged a symbol that one could identify with (the soldiers pledging allegiance on Masada) and also a historical continuity in which the Israelis see themselves as replicating the deeds of their ancestors from antiquity (as in the rituals in which soldiers or members of youth movements dramatized with their own bodies the Masada story). When Amir encountered the myth of Masada among the heroic tales he was told on the kibbutz in the early 1950s, it had already become one of the pillars in the collective native consciousness. Yet it must have seemed strange and foreign to him, because the story is not part of the collective Jewish memory, and mass suicide, such as Josephus describes, has been in fundamental opposition to Jewish norms since the Middle Ages.[6] But two years later, when he was drafted into the Israeli Army, Amir too must have ascended the heights of Masada, sworn his oath of allegiance, and, through the myth and the ritual, officially joined the native society.

The episode of Tel Ḥai, in contrast, is a new and decidedly local tradition. The battle in the small Jewish settlement in the Upper Galilee in February 1920 between Arabs and a tiny group of Jewish settlers, which led to the fall of Tel Ḥai and the death of several of its defenders, became, almost paradoxically, a story of exemplary heroism and not of defeat.[7] The incident, which spread instantly through the press of the time, through oral tales, and, later, through folk songs, plays, memorial inscriptions, and children's stories, was reenacted ritually on the anniversary, a day of national memory on which a massive pilgrimage took place to Tel Ḥai, now reconstructed and sanctified. From the 1920s onward, additional ceremonies were held in educational and cultural institutions through the country. Here, too, the historical event, which had become myth, was not divorced from the major political debates of the day over the nature of "Zionist activism," the value of settlement of the land and how to establish its borders, relations with the Palestinian population, and other issues that engage public debate in Israel to this day.

The most interesting and original genre of folklore that developed before the founding of the state and had a strong impact on Israeli culture, and especially on spoken Hebrew, was the chizbat. This is a type of humorous story that is close to the genre of the tall tale or the confabulated story; in fact, the name itself is taken from the word for "lie" in Arabic. This kind of humorous tale developed among the members of the Palmaḥ, who trained and operated in secret during the British Mandate. They shared a common, special experience, a central element of which was storytelling carried on late into the night. The chizbat played a main role in this storytelling. Even though the Palmaḥ was dismantled after the creation of the state, the genre persisted for many years afterward, in different contexts of storytelling, both oral and written.

What made the chizbat so popular, especially in this period, and why did it disappear afterward? It has been pointed out that these humorous stories were based on a framework of binary oppositions: Levantine vs. European; traditional vs. secular; primitive vs. cultured; coarse vs. well-mannered; dirty vs. clean; sensitive vs. insensitive; shy vs. arrogant; speaker of proper Hebrew vs. speaker of slang; strong and violent vs. weak and compromising.[8] These oppositions can all be subsumed under the larger polarity of native (Sabra) vs. Diaspora Jew (immigrant), and, taken together, they suggest an identity conflict among the tellers of the chizbat and its listeners. Here is an example that includes some of these polarities: "Once the Hebrew teacher in Deganyah Alef was drowning in the Kinneret [the Sea of Galilee]. Precisely at the same time a bunch of the guys from the sports course of the Palmah were sitting there. But the teacher shouted, 'Hoshi'u! Hoshi'u!' [liturgical Hebrew for 'Help! Help!'] and no one understood what he wanted."[9] The joke is based on the dichotomies between learned Hebrew vs. Israeli Hebrew, between the Diaspora Jew and the Sabra-Palmahnik; religion (the language of the prayer) vs. secularity and ignorance of Jewish tradition; and culture (the Hebrew teacher) vs. the rude Palmah soldiers who take pride in their ignorance and are even indifferent to life (they hear someone shouting but continue to play their games).

The choice of this humorous genre as an expression by native-born Israelis of their ambivalence over identity derives not so much from the fact that the jokes solve the conflicts but rather that they formulate them very sharply: "The identity of the native-born must remain a paradox whose only solution is laughter."[10] This kind of search for identity also found expression in other popular genres, such as the folk song, folk dance, food, and typical dress. All of these expressed the stereotypes of a folk national culture in its formative period.

These identity struggles demonstrate that the native culture encountered by the youth from Baghdad in the beginning of the 1950s was far from a monolithic consensus. The native traditions were full of bitter polemics and ambivalences. The confrontation was therefore not between a fragile and collapsing immigrant culture and a mature and crystallized native culture but, rather, between two cultures, each searching for its own identity and, perhaps above all, for a path to the other. An actual meeting between these two branches of Israeli folk culture during this period seemed, however, almost impossible. The stories that the immigrants brought with them were based on ancient traditions, drawn from Jewish norms and values. Despite the great transformations that they underwent as they were transported to Israel, they remained fundamentally the same. The stories were basically supernatural, and the resolution of the plot was typically based on the intervention of a higher power.[11] The native traditions or myths, however, were totally new and, with the exception of Masada, appeared for the first time in Jewish culture. They were based on events in the history of the new settlement in Israel and were entirely naturalistic or realistic. The forces operating in them are political, social, and military, and they do not appear to reflect any Jewish values based on past traditions. Thus, the tales of the newer immigrants, based on ancient Jewish traditions, were entirely divorced from the stories of the veteran settlers.[12]

Yet, on closer examination, the question turns out to be much more complicated. As we have seen, the Masada myth, so widespread in the educational system, children's stories, theater, literature, and even historical and archaeological research, belongs, of course, to the Second Temple period. To be sure, it "disappeared" from collective consciousness until the modern period, but its roots go deep into Jewish culture, both positively and negatively. Even the myth of Tel Ḥai has traditional echoes, though it took place in a modern context. A few days after the fall of Tel Ḥai, the writer Moshe Smilansky wrote an article in the newspaper *Ha'aretz* in which he claimed that the youth of Israel had no holy places to which they might make pilgrimages. Now, after the eleventh of Adar, the date in the Hebrew calendar on which the settlement fell, Tel Ḥai would become a holy site, and site of pilgrimage. How could it be that in Palestine, in which every square kilometer contains a holy place, there were no places for young Jews to make pilgrimage? Smilansky was saying that the traditional sites lacked meaning for the young Jewish natives of the land, whereas Tel Ḥai possessed the qualities that these places lacked: settlement of the land, heroism, struggle with the Arabs, exemplary self-sacrifice, comradeship, and patriotism. Yet the very use of the loaded, traditional term "holy site" demonstrates that the new society was prepared to use old concepts from Jewish tradition in defining itself. The testimonies of the period turned Joseph Trumpeldor into a contemporary martyr by emphasizing how he sacrificed his life on the altar of an idea, a faith, a national goal—concepts that can be found in the traditional literature of martyrdom.

We can view the chizbat in a similar way. On the face of it, these stories were borrowed solely from the culture of the Palestinian Arabs and underwent a deep cultural transformation as they were adapted by the members of the Palmaḥ. But a deeper examination of the chizbat on the background of Jewish humor of the past reveals something different: the rich humoristic world of the Jews of Eastern Europe and, what is less known, of the Jews of the Middle East, both of which often have structural and thematic similarities to the chizbat. Here is one example from Russia:

A squad of Jewish soldiers [in the Russian Army] was sent out to reconnoiter
the path ahead. After a while, they returned and announced: "Artillery can pass
there, the cavalry can also pass, but infantry cannot pass." Their commander
challenged them: "Why can these pass and not those?" The leader of the squad
answered: "A black dog is there—and he is as big as a calf!"[13]

Compare this with the following chizbat from the War of Independence:

When the war broke out, they assembled all the Haganah officers in Tel Aviv
and evaluated new methods of warfare against the Arabs, dwelling especially
on psychological warfare. Everyone made suggestions, and arguments about
all of them ensued. Only Yeruḥam sat on the side and kept quiet. Finally, they
turned to him as an expert on Arab questions and asked what suggestions he
had. "First of all," said Yeruḥam, "we must know how many regiments the
Arabs have." "All right," they said. "Let's say that we know." "Afterward we have
to prepare cages appropriate to the number of regiments." "What cages?" they
asked. "What are the cages for?" "Regular cages with doors that one can open
by pulling a rope. Afterward you have to prepare smoke bombs." "Nu?" "When
an Arab regiment mounts an attack, we build a smoke screen behind which are
one or two cages. When the smoke disperses, you open the cage doors and let
the *dab* [Arabic for hyena] loose that was inside. For every regiment one or two
dabs, and we win the war."[14]

Both of these strikingly similar stories belong to the same tale type. In both
cases, the humorous story is based on the same situation: armies moving into
battle, dialogue between different members of the group, and the humorous way
a powerful army turns tail and runs when it confronts an animal that is not particularly dangerous, like a dog or hyena. Even the parody of a seemingly serious
military discussion over strategy is shared by the two stories, but it also resembles the give and take between Talmud students in an East European yeshivah,
or, alternatively, the idle chatter of those who frequent an Arab café. It is impossible, of course, to demonstrate a causal linkage between these two stories, and
there is no need to do so. The fact is that Jewish folklore from the Diaspora appears in that genre of folktale—the chizbat—so characteristic of the native Israeli culture.

If the encounter between that culture and the traditions of the immigrants
in the 1950s—the years of the great immigration—was supposed to bring about
the creation of a unified and monolithic Israeli culture, developments in the
1980s and 1990s demonstrated that this aspiration suffered a decisive defeat.

During this latter period, a confrontation occurred between secular, Western Israeli culture, and the ethnic and religious identity of large segments of Israeli society. This should be understood not as a confrontation between an "elite" and a "popular" culture but as a struggle over hegemony between different strands of folk culture within the state of Israel.

CONFRONTATION

On Ḥanukkah of 1996, as in the past, the Ḥabad (Lubavicher) Hasidim in Israel went to the Knesset to serve the members traditional Ḥanukkah jelly doughnuts. That year, however, a Knesset member from the Labor Party barred the door to one of the committee conference rooms, refusing to allow them in. The religious Knesset members, and those belonging to the conservative parties, were taken aback: the Hasidim were "only" performing a good deed, a religious precept! A compromise was reached only when a representative of these parties stepped out, took the package from the Hasidim, and brought the doughnuts in himself.

All this furor over a jelly doughnut can be understood only in the context of the 1996 elections. The Lubavicher movement was the most aggressive supporter of the right-wing candidate, contributing many millions of dollars, mobilizing thousands of activists, and chartering planes to bring Hasidim with Israeli citizenship to Israel to vote for Benjamin Netanyahu. As a result, the left in Israel no longer sees the Lubavicher movement as spiritual and religious, to be allowed as such to enter the Knesset, army camps, and secular schools, but as a political movement. It was clear to all that more than a bit of jelly lay within this traditional holiday treat. It had become the symbol of the great divide: the Lubavicher Hasidim sought to "feed" the Knesset—representative of the sovereignty of the State of Israel—with their "traditions." Labor Party members, representatives of the secular left, claimed that the sugar-dusted exterior of this seemingly innocent confection encompassed a clear political message: West Bank settlements, Israeli expansionism, and religious fundamentalism, as opposed to the classical, humanistic Jewish heritage.

But the context is even more complicated. The recipe for Ḥanukkah doughnuts calls for oil, as do the traditional lights, and both symbolize the miracle of Ḥanukkah: the entrance of the Maccabees into the holy temple after their victory over the Greeks, and the discovery of a tiny jug of olive oil that miraculously lasted eight days. The myth upon which the sanctity of Ḥanukkah was based is this miracle story, not the revolt against the great Greek empire, not the war and heroic victory, and not even the establishment of the last independent Jewish

state for 2,000 years.[15] An example of this difference of attitude toward the celebration of Ḥanukkah in the secular and the ultra-Orthodox communities could
be the explicit words of one of the spiritual leaders of the latter, Yitzḥak Breuer,
in 1982:

> The Hellenizers loved their people and their land in their own fashion. They
> loved the land but loathed the Land of Torah; loved the people but despised the
> People of the Torah; loved Greek licentiousness but hated the burden of
> Torah. . . . It is not for the Jewish State that the Hasmoneans fought but for the
> People of the Torah. They did battle against the kingdom of evil when it threat-
> ened the People of the Torah with destruction. . . . They also fought against the
> wicked among their own people. . . . This was a *kulturkampf.* . . . Greek culture
> triumphed over the whole world, and only the Torah culture was able to with-
> stand it.[16]

When the Lubavicher Hasidim bring these fried doughnuts to the Knesset,
they are saying that the essence of the State of Israel is not the political entity
represented by the Knesset, nor the army, nor any of the other institutions of
an independent nation. The essence of the State of Israel is, rather, this small
doughnut, the symbol of the heavenly miracle. Beyond the political conflict, this
debate represents the great kulturkampf played out every day in Israel: Are we "a
nation like all the other nations," or are we the bearers of the heavenly message
on earth?

The "doughnut incident" did not end here. That same day, the chief rabbi of
Israel was interviewed in the media. He lamented the fact that a doughnut, a
food product, had become the main symbol of Ḥanukkah. How, he asked, did
three-cornered pastries ("Haman's hats") come to be the essence of Purim, dairy
products the *sine qua non* of Shavuot (the "Festival of Weeks"), and an apple in
honey the sum and substance of Rosh Hashanah, the Jewish New Year? Where
are the spiritual messages of these holidays?—he cried. The rabbi deplored what
folklorists have known for a long time: that the concrete symbols of religious
ritual—the folkloric artifacts—are the main components of folk religion. When
stated, however, by the highest authority of the religious establishment, another
meaning comes to the fore. This is the classic clash between the learned, official
establishment and the folk religion. This establishment would undoubtedly prefer that Israeli society express its religious sentiments by studying the Torah, attending services, and accepting religious precepts as the guiding principles of
life, and not by eating doughnuts on Ḥanukkah or getting drunk on Purim.

The common denominator of both the political and the religious debates I have just described is the folkloric artifact. The concrete object at the heart of a local uproar reflects a much larger political debate over the elections, and beyond that lies yet another, even larger debate over the cultural meaning of the State of Israel and the ancient clash between the learned religious establishment and the folk religion.

However, the "doughnut controversy" is not the only example of a folkloric element looming large in public life. During recent elections many thousands of amulets were distributed to the voters, and blessings and charms were promised to those who would elect the "right" party. The Mimouna ritual—the traditional holiday of Moroccan Jews celebrated a day after Passover—is a favorite of politicians of almost all parties, who claim that this celebration expresses the special values that they personally hold in high esteem. The land of Israel may have the highest concentration of holy graves to be found anywhere. The discovery of such ancient graves, their restoration, the modification of municipal construction plans so as to avoid damaging them, and the organization of pilgrimages to these places, all cost huge amounts of the taxpayers' money. This raises endless political debates. Public radio and television stations in Israel play primarily Western music, both classical and popular. The communities of Eastern origin protest loudly about it: Why doesn't Eastern, Arabic music have equal play? The main argument of the Ashkenazim (Israelis of East European origin) is that Eastern music is not culture but folklore, thus its status and quality are, naturally, inferior.

These are some of the everyday debates, focusing on folkloric themes, that animate Israeli culture. The question as to why the folkloric artifact has such a central place in the political, economic, social, and religious debates is connected, it seems to me, to another question—namely, has it always been so? The answer to this question is categorically no.

By the 1950s and 1960s, the years of the mass immigrations, a distinct Israeli culture had taken shape. The descendants of the first great waves of immigration, which began at the end of the nineteenth century, aimed to shape a monolithic Hebrew culture with the use of the "ideal" tool—the melting pot. The confrontation of new immigrants of Eastern and Western origin with each other and, more traumatically, with the culture of the native-born caused the decline and eventual erasure of the original Diaspora cultures.[17] We have almost no evidence of saints' cults in the 1950s and 1960s; the deep hagiolatric beliefs and customs of the North African Jews are unknown for this period. So it was with the Mimouna festival: one of the most central and beloved celebrations of Moroccan Jews had vanished almost entirely. We know it was celebrated privately, within the confines of the family or small community. Such was also the case with Oriental and Yiddish music, which were almost officially banned from the national stations.

There can be no doubt that the heavy pressure of the official educational system, the radio and newspapers, the delegitimation of the "Diaspora culture" in Israeli society, and the hardships of finding jobs and eking out a living led the new immigrants to hide their cultural uniqueness and seek acculturation to the prevailing norms. The repression of folkloric themes meant an almost total erasure of ethnic identity. It was believed that the eradication of ethnic customs, food, music, beliefs, and traditions would hasten the transition from marginality to centrality. As is known from other immigrant areas, however, that could not happen: so long as the mobilization was external, built on repression, and not on internalization of the new political and cultural systems, the shift to the center of Israeli society could not be achieved.

The restoration of folk beliefs and rituals to the center of social life could take place only once it was acknowledged that the repression of ethnic identity, whose most salient characteristics are the folkloric themes, would not advance the ethnic group's status in society. On the contrary: only the accentuation of those characteristics could produce the ethnic unity and power that the dominant classes would have to acknowledge, and this acknowledgment was key to achieving the primary goal of advancement from margin to center.

A typical example is that of Mimouna. This ritualistic celebration of the beginning of spring brings North African Jews en masse to the public places, where they sit in Eastern-style tents wearing traditional clothes, preparing traditional foods, playing and dancing to special songs, and telling miracle stories of community saints.[18] Mimouna has become a pilgrimage site for prime ministers, ministers, and Knesset members of all political parties as well as military chiefs of staff and business leaders. All the movers and shakers of Israeli society, willingly or not, have embraced the ethnic group and its rituals as a legitimate part of Israeli culture. The main goal of moving from the margins to the center has here been achieved in full; the main vehicle of that transition was the folkloric theme.

THE SAINT

The core of folk culture in the State of Israel was imported over a period of more than a century by immigrants determined to preserve their folkloric traditions, their leaders, their foods and dress, and their native crafts. As with every migration, the Jewish folk cultures that developed for hundreds of years in the Diaspora went through a process of change and acculturation when they came to Israel. These developments did not happen overnight, and they are continuing even today, more than 50 years after the massive immigrations from North Africa and the Middle East. To distinguish sharply between folk culture imported from the Diaspora and that which crystallized in the State of Israel is therefore not always easy or even the right question. We need to understand each instance of Israeli folk culture as rooted in the pre-Israeli history of a particular community that adapted to the circumstances and needs of that community in the new Israeli reality.

The revival of the cult of the saints after its suppression in the 1950s and 1960s involved the miraculous transplantation of saints' graves from Morocco to various locations in Israel. In 1973, Rabbi David u-Moshe, a saint widely accepted among Jews of the Atlas Mountains, appeared in a dream to Abraham ben-Haim, a Moroccan immigrant living in a poor section of Safed. The saint instructed him to dedicate one room of his small apartment to the *tzadik* (saint). Ben-Haim followed these instructions. Since then, this shrine has become one of the most frequented pilgrimage sites in Israel. On the festival day in honor of this tzadik (the *hillulah*), many thousands of faithful visitors come to pay their respects. The same process of "immigration" to Israel of the long-dead saint is illustrated in another story:

> Two Jews lived in Kurdani [near Haifa]. On Purim night they sat and played cards. Both of them. The *Ḥacham* [the sage—Rabbi David u-Moshe] came to them at night and told them: Why did you forget me? They said to him: *Cidi* [our lord], we did not forget you. Did we forget you? How is it possible? Only the sea separates us. He said to them: No, I am not beyond the sea, I am in the old section of Ashkelon, house number so and so, at Waqnin's, at Shimon Waqnin's. They did not know him. On Purim I . . . sat with Rabbi Portal, and we ate *barkukes* [a kind of Moroccan doughnut]. I didn't sense their presence until they stood here with the car. They and their sons. They said Psalms, we ate together, and they left.[19]

A sociological analysis suggests a clear link between "the immigration" of the saints from Morocco to Israel and the establishment of the development towns. These settlements were founded artificially in locations set aside for new immigrants, in the absence of any comprehensible ecological or financial justification. Their nearly homogeneous populations (that is, new immigrants from a single given ethnic community) had no link whatsoever to the geographical location. For many years, population exchange in the development towns was a pronounced demographic phenomenon. Many of the original immigrants, lacking any firm connection to the towns—which tended to be ugly and bereft of ways to make a decent living—moved on, and others were brought in to replace them. Yet over some 20 years after the founding of the settlements, a firm nucleus of residents formed. These people developed a connection to the place by virtue of habit and the social ties created there over time—family, neighbors, friends. The most interesting manifestation of the sense of belonging to the place, and of a nascent patriotic sensibility, was the creation of "centers of the sacred." These, perhaps above all, illustrate that the link to their new home, initially imposed upon the residents, had become a natural and desired bond. In the case of David u-Moshe, there is direct testimony to support this explanation: in 1973, the Ben-Haim family planned to move out of the small apartment to which they had been brought upon immigrating to Israel in 1954. The appearance of the tzadik in Abraham ben-Haim's dream prevented, at the last minute, the family's move to a more spacious apartment in another part of town. Indeed, the consecration of the saint's room completely changed the face and image of the old neighborhood: thousands of visitors began to flock to it annually from all parts of Israel (and beyond). The consequent financial opportunities for the local populace sparked and augmented the bond between the town and its residents.[20]

The symbolic passage of the saints from Morocco to the development towns is the ultimate manifestation of the use of traditional ritual texts to express new content. Adoration of the saints, and the tales that bore and disseminated the rituals, were basic components of Jewish culture in Morocco. Arriving in Israel, Moroccan Jews encountered a new reality. The indoctrination of immigrants via the educational system contributed to the waning of the adoration and legends of the saints; there was nothing to link the Israeli reality to the culture they had brought with them. Only after putting down roots, over the span of a generation, could the community robustly restore the worship of the saints to Israelis of North African origin. One explanation of the phenomenon is that it gave religious legitimacy to the new semi-urban centers. Another derives from the community's self-image as peripheral to Israeli society. The desire to move from margin to the center is an obvious motive behind this revival of the veneration of saints in Israel.

Of utmost importance to our investigation are those tales of saints who were active primarily in Israel, as opposed to Morocco. There are many such examples, but here let us consider three personalities: Rabbi Israel Abuhatzeira, the "Baba Sali" of Netivot; Rabbi Mordekhai Sharabi of Jerusalem; and David u-Moshe, who, unlike the first two, died without having set foot in Israel (his faithful "brought him," as we have seen, to the country with the establishment of centers of homage in Ashkelon and Safed).

The Baba Sali's fame is not solely a function of his personality, since it is partly hereditary. He was a scion of a dynasty famed for its righteous miracle-workers and saints. Indeed, one of the family's patriarchs, Rabbi Jacob Abuhatzeira, underwent the same process of symbolic "passage" to the State of Israel. In one typical tale included in a collection of "praises" (hagiography) of the saint, the following is told:

> I heard a wondrous story, that in the city of Ashdod in our Holy Land, there lives a family by the name of Ben Gigi. The wife is a descendant of our Rabbi Jacob [Abuhatzeira] on her father's side, and the husband is a truly pious and God-fearing man. This couple had a daughter, born under a lucky star. They live on the top floor of a three-story apartment building. Now, when the girl was about three years old, she was playing on the balcony and she fell from the third floor, God spare us. The mother called to her daughter, Rachel! but she [did] not answer. She went outside and [saw] that the child had fallen. She ran down to see her daughter and saw that she was safe and sound. She asked her, "Who saved you?" The girl answered: "Rabbi Jacob Abuhatzeira came, and also Grandfather's father [that is, the father of Rabbi Isaac Shitrit, the mother's father], and they caught me before I reached the ground." And all who saw [that], rejoiced, and so did all the family. May the Merciful One perform miracles and wonders for us and may we be worthy to worship wholeheartedly by virtue of the tzadikim, may their virtue protect us, Amen.[21]

The realia here is that of modern Israel: urban life, apartment houses, and a set of unfamiliar perils with which the immigrants must learn to reckon. They mobilize the traditional apparatus for coping with the harsh circumstances in the Diaspora and apply it to the new setting: the saint skips across the voids of time and place to watch over and rescue the faithful. The geographical and spiritual distance does not stop him from departing the Diaspora for Israel. Significantly, the manifestation in this tale takes place before a representative of the new generation. The young daughter, born and educated in the new state, is the one to interpret correctly the significance of the miracle done for her. Therein lies an explicit assertion that faith in the righteous can pass to the next generation, notwithstanding its new circumstances that are almost diametrically opposed from those of its forebears. Life in Israel, for all its modern advances and vast sophistication, needs the power of the righteous no less than did life in the Diaspora.

There is no part of life in Israel around which legends of saints have not been created. Military service and Israel's wars are among the most salient characteristics of the new reality, with no precursor in Diaspora life. A typical tale in the hagiography of the Baba Sali begins as follows:

One day a family arrived at the home of our Rabbi. All the men had the long
hair and beards of mourning. You could see they were deep in grief. In reply to
the question of our Rabbi's servant, they explained that their brother had gone
to reserve duty, and many days had passed without their hearing a word from
him. The military authorities had thrown up their hands and gave notice
through the town major that they had no news.[22]

The saint demanded they leave off mourning, and he cited the verse "by no
means clearing the guilty" (Exodus 34, 7; Numbers 14, 18; Nahum 1, 3) for the
missing soldier to return whole and sound. Although they did not see the relevance of the verse cited (which can also mean, "the one who cleans will not be
destroyed"), the family accepted his instruction. The son did indeed return
home, no harm having come to him, and in the presence of the saint explained
that a miracle was done for him because "every Sabbath eve I clean our synagogue in Petaḥ Tikva. The *gabbai* [a synagogue official] is the only one who
knows about it." The tale includes such details of modern reality as army reserve
duty, soldiers missing in action, appealing to the town major, and the involvement of the military authorities. Alongside these is an impressive array of traditional motifs from Jewish sacred legends of the past: the narrative pattern of
appealing to the tzadik; his enigmatic response, whose prophetic power is revealed in the denouement; and reward and rescue by virtue of a single good deed
done by the hero, which is a widespread narrative motif in medieval Jewish
exempla.

In another tale, a father recounts that his son deserted the army because he
wanted to serve as a military driver rather than in a combat unit. The father
turns to Rabbi David ben Barukh for help after the son is caught and jailed. The
rest of his unit is killed in action on the Golan Heights, after which the deserter is
pardoned. The narrator adds: "I have three sons in Sinai. Each Monday and Friday I light a candle. First I ask for the children of Israel, and after that for my
sons." In the narrator's hierarchy of values, the saint's intervention is what has
saved the son from a prison term. Yet he is discomfited by his understanding that
this action defies the Israeli institutions of which he feels himself a part. This is
made clear in his apologetic conclusion to the tale, where the saint's action in
contravention of the military authorities is at odds with the narrator's own attitude. Other events connected to security are, for example, the saint Sharabi's
prescience regarding the outbreak of the Six Day War and consequent instructions to seal up the house with sandbags, or the foreknowledge of the rescue of a
pilot who had been captured by the Syrians in the Yom Kippur War, whose parents had appealed to the saint for help.[23]

Personal tales of salvation, in which the sacred power—the tzadik—takes action to save an individual in distress, are among the most widespread themes of past generations. War tales of the State of Israel do not differ from them in principle: the tzadik David u-Moshe informs his believers that the siren will soon begin and he must descend to the shelter; during the War of Attrition a shell falls on a military position, and a soldier who flies "seventy meters into the air" calls out the name of David u-Moshe and is saved; a Golani (infantry unit) soldier, lying in ambush, is surprised by enemy soldiers, but the saint, who appears suddenly, helps him dispatch the enemy and get a leave in reward. In another story, the saint saves a schoolgirl during the terrorist attack in Ma'alot after she appeals to him in prayer. The saint pushes her into a corner of the room and, when the shots begin, protects her with his body. When the children jump from the windows of the building, the saint holds her and brings her to the ground without injury.[24] The nature of the tales and their emotional charge do not differ fundamentally from tales of personal salvation in the folk literature of the past.[25] The main differences are in the details, such as the occupations of the active characters (soldiers instead of merchants or craftsmen) and the nature of the given danger (real battles). Israeli legends of saints typically merge active forces from traditional Jewish narratives with elements of the new reality: going off to reserve duty and the burden it places on the families, the disappearance of soldiers, the helplessness of the official security forces, and terrorist incidents.

Saints' legends whose theme is war offer a glimpse into the psychological and social background of their emergence. In one tale about David u-Moshe, the faithful Ben-Ḥaim of Safed relates the following:

[I]t all happened this year, before the festival of Rabbi Meir, three days before the festival [in Miron]. Some eight months now. [Rabbi David u-Moshe] came and said to me: "Not many people will come [to my festival] this year." I asked him: "Why?" "Because there will be cries like war. But my feast will be all right." After I told [the men of the synagogue] . . . what did I do, I bought a calf. From Rosh Hashanah I bought it, and I said, this will be for the festival. In a *moshav* [cooperative settlement] not far from here, we bought everything that he said, plates, forks, and the same week that the war was supposed to begin, Yom Kippur Eve [the war began the next day], [David u-Moshe] came to me and said: "Listen, today they will take half the synagogue and now I am going, because the war will begin at this time. But at the festival everything will be all right." I got up in the morning and I said: "What's going to happen? If I go to the police and tell them, they will not believe me, because the people are not believers. Now we will leave it at that."

[The interviewer:] Did you tell anyone else?

I told my wife, and some people in the synagogue. If there had been enough faith, they could have believed such a thing. Since the war started, since that night [the tzadik] has not appeared. I lit candles and everything.[26]

Ben-Haim tells his tale about eight months after the 1973 Yom Kippur War. During the war, and even more so during the interval between its outbreak and the telling of the tale, the country was consumed with the question of how it could have begun without warning, without advance knowledge. Answers to this burning question were offered in military, intelligence, political, social, and psychological terms. Ben-Haim translates the question into concepts borrowed from his frame of reference—veneration of saints. He holds that where the modern state's central institutions, such as the military and the political establishment, failed, the traditional world, considered marginal in the state, succeeded. The saint gave ample warning, but lack of faith precluded use of the information. The tale tries to turn a marginal group's set of beliefs into a legitimate active force in the state. Many weaknesses of the modern state could be cured, according to this conception, if only its citizens would wisely adopt the veneration of the saints as a central social norm.

It is noteworthy that, in the manifestation of the saint and in the storyteller's questions, the prime concern is not connected with the war and its aftermath but with the festival in honor of the saint; the war is liable to ruin the festival ceremony. The saint does not promise his believers that the war will end well, only that his festival will take place as usual. This is an excellent example of the manner in which military-political concepts circulating in the state undergo "translation" into concepts of belief. The results of the war and its significance for various areas of life in the country are not clear to the society of the faithful. The most important aspect, from their perspective, is the question of whether the basic structure of their lives, whose principal expression is the veneration of saints, is to be disrupted. The normative symbols that express the fears and hopes of the core society find expression in the peripheral society in the realm of faith in the saints.

Israeli saints' legends deal with other themes besides the military and security. These include the financial well-being of the faithful, as in the purchase and sale of businesses and tax matters (Sharabi); stock market investments and the buying of foreign currency on the black market (Sharabi); repair and sale of cars (the Baba Sali; Sharabi); the campaign waged against the establishment of public swimming pools allowing mixed bathing of men and women (Sharabi); and the wave of immigration from Russia (the Baba Sali). The effort to spotlight the saint's involvement in all areas of life in the modern state has a clear objective: to prove that the tzadik's power and influence have not waned. Despite Israeli society's distance from the Diaspora's traditional modes, the institution of the saints remains strong and vital enough to keep pace with modernization.

Still, the tales cannot ignore the frequent clash between scientific and traditional medicine. A sick girl from Ofakim had long been hospitalized in Beersheba when her father appealed to the saint, who instructed him to take her out of the hospital at once, against doctors' orders. On the way to Ofakim, the girl recovered. Another tale that expresses this kind of discord is transmitted as a tale of a personal experience:

On Friday, holy Sabbath eve, [Torah] portion "Ki Tisah" in the year 5742 [1982], I was summoned to the neighborhood clinic in Beersheba where my wife was in severe condition on account of hemorrhaging. From there we were rushed to Soroka Hospital. The doctors, three in number, who examined her determined unequivocally that an abortion was necessary. My wife was then three months pregnant. I hesitated, for one does not carry out an abortion so fast and a rabbi must be consulted. I asked the doctors to delay the abortion another hour and, after refusals and pleading, they consented. I set out in my car for the house of our Master and Teacher Rabbi Israel Abuhatzeira [the Baba Sali] of blessed and saintly memory. On Friday our Rabbi was not in the habit of receiving people, and at that hour in our Rabbi's room they were reading two [portions] Scripture and one [portion] Targum [Aramaic translation of the Torah]. After explanations to his servant, Rabbi Eliyahu Alfasi, may he be set apart for a long life, I entered, and took advantage of a short recess of the rabbis who sat with our holy Rabbi. I asked him if the abortion should be carried out. Our Rabbi blessed a bottle of water and ruled that it should not.

I left our Rabbi's house encouraged and rushed back to the hospital. I gave my wife the water to drink, and when the doctors came to continue preparations for the abortion, I suggested they reexamine her to see if it was still necessary. One of the three doctors said no further examination was required, but gave in to my wife's pleas. After the examination, all three were astounded, and one of the doctors murmured in wonder: "How is it possible? The fetus is back where it should be and the hemorrhaging stopped . . . ?" I was so happy, tears streamed out of my eyes, and I read Psalms in thanksgiving to God, may He be praised. Three days later, my wife was released from the hospital in excellent health, praise God. During the Passover holiday I was one of those who went up to our Rabbi's home, and I recall that he asked his visitors to bless him that he merit seeing the face of the Messiah. I did as he asked, and the others answered, "Amen." I reminded our Rabbi of the incident and said that my wife was again not feeling well. He reassured me and said: "You have nothing to worry about, on my responsibility" . . . and we had a healthy baby girl with God's help.[27]

The genre of legend, saints' tales included, draws its power mainly from the faith that the tale inspires among the listeners. To augment the force of the tale, the storyteller employs diverse rhetorical means, among which are a defined place and time familiar and close to the space of listeners, true-to-life details, and characters drawn from local reality. The tale above makes clear and bold use of all of these. The specific date on which the event takes place, the locale, and the active characters all operate to build up faith in what is being told. Tales of personal experience contain another dimension, that of first-hand knowledge. This places the story above argument; the storyteller himself attests that what happens in the tale is not something he heard from others or read in a book but that he lived through personally. Hence, this is the most life-like narrative model in the repertoire of saints' legends. Its narrative tension lies not only in the confrontation between the saint and the doctors; it stems also from the urgency of the moment. The husband has no time to dither; his wife's life depends on his decision. Indeed, the storyteller does a fine job of employing extremes to create narrative tension: the saint vs. the physicians, the necessity of immediate decision juxtaposed with the distance to the saint's home and the obstacles he must overcome before seeing him (the distance from Sorokah Hospital in Beersheba to the city of Netivot is about 45 minutes; the saint is busy learning; his servant delays the husband). These multiple tensions are meant to project to the audience the full weight of decision before the protagonist, in order to highlight its critical outcome (life or death). Each member of the audience is likely to face similar decisions, perhaps of less import. The tale is meant to serve as a model of appropriate conduct in the future.

Saints' legends on the theme of healing offer a glimpse into a significant current running below the surface in Israeli culture. They attest to a deep-rooted belief in supernatural forces, particularly where a sacred basis exists to support them—the supernatural power of charismatic, venerated personalities. This poses an interesting question: how can people living and educated in a Westernized, technological country believe in the same traditional supernatural forces as their forebears, whose structure of beliefs and ideas had more in common with the Middle Ages than with the modern world?[28] The question can be answered on various levels. First, belief in supernatural forces is hardly unique to Israeli society; it appears in various manifestations throughout both Eastern and Western cultures.[29] The main difference is that, in Israel, these beliefs are being restored to their former prominence. Among Moroccan Jews of the eighteenth and nineteenth centuries, they were a mainstay of religious faith, and now, in significant sectors of Israeli society (especially among those of North African descent), belief in the supernatural power of saints is accepted as normative and is supported by the religious establishment.

Another explanation has to do with the Israeli education system, which was intended primarily to strip immigrants from North African lands (and others as well) of their centuries-old folkways and to incorporate them, as quickly as possible, into Israeli culture. The resulting changes, however, were mostly superficial. More profound cultural and psychological shifts could not occur, either because the pedagogical concept was mistaken or because the time span was too short for such shifts to penetrate the deepest sociopsychological layers. It is thus no wonder that, approximately one generation after the great waves of immigration, a pronounced reaction has emerged against the alien values that Israeli society sought to implant. This reaction, for the most part, takes the form of a resolute return to values and beliefs of the past. (Expressions such as "restore the crown to its pristine splendor" are typical of this religio-ethnic process.)

The militancy of these tales comes across not only in their structure, such as the binary opposition of physician vs. saint, but also in their content. One representative tale of this sort describes an infant who suffered from severe vomiting. Doctors and medicines did not help; the parents were beside themselves:

> Then one day [the baby's mother] met a student of our Rabbi [Sharabi] and began to complain about her misfortune since she had to bring her son to the clinic every day for injections and treatments. The student asked her: "Have you appealed to one of the tzadikim of the generation to bless the child?" The mother answered in the negative. He said to her: "In that case, come and we will go to the tzadik, the man of God, Rabbi Mordechai Sharabi, and he will bless the child." At once the two directed their steps toward Shiloh Street [in Jerusalem], where our Rabbi lives. While walking, the student told the mother facts [*uvdot*] that took place with different people who came to our Rabbi and were saved on his account.[30]

The saint's students and followers seek to disseminate faith in him. In their efforts to reclaim souls, they grasp at opportunities provided by extreme personal distress and despair at the limitations of modern medicine. Tales (termed here as "facts" to avoid the fictional connotations of the word "stories" or "legends") of similar cases, showcasing the saint's success where medicine failed, constitute "proof" of his superiority over physicians in matters of health. The tales are thus one important weapon in the massive campaign waged by folk belief against modern science. In another tale, while a pregnant woman suffers heavy bleeding, her husband walks around grieving, his head bowed in concern. When his friend learns of the matter, he says to the husband: "Why haven't you gone to our Rabbi?" The husband replies, innocently: "For this purpose too one goes to the Rabbi?" Then the friend explains that "in *all matters* one should ask the advice of the great and wise ones of the Jewish people."[31]

This story implies that not only in matters of religion and faith should one turn to the saints but with any difficulty or obstacle one might encounter in the course of everyday life. Indeed, the examples above illustrate how these legends strive to apply the saint's authority to all spheres of life, including those identified with technology and modernity, like the army and security, cars and the stock exchange. This effort to prove the omnipresent validity and power of the faith should thus be seen as part of a larger campaign to encourage a mass return to it, in which the struggle against modern science (as in the tales of healing) is only one component.

Two large cycles of legends about David u-Moshe were told by Shimon Waqnin of Ashkelon and Abraham ben-Haim of Safed. Many of the legends revolve around the storytellers themselves and their proximity to the saint. These founders of centers of veneration do not regard the miracles performed by the saint as private events but as a vehicle to inspire belief in his power. Each of these hundreds of tales, spread by people near the centers of adoration—the founders, their families, or other functionaries connected to the saints' festival—serves as a means to attract more believers. In every tale at least one more person (the protagonist for whom the miracle is performed) joins the ranks of the believers.

Recruitment of the faithful is not motivated solely by spiritual altruism. Police, army officers, municipal employees, and the rest of the government authorities who become absolute believers in the saint give the center of adoration political clout as well. Indeed, in a characteristic tale of the establishment of the synagogue honoring David u-Moshe in Ashkelon, told by Waqnin, the authorities issued an injunction against its construction. The synagogue was built without a permit, in violation of the building code. A member of the committee sent to inspect the structure, a man who opposed its completion, was confined for three years in a psychiatric hospital in Beer-Yaakov until he acknowledged the saint's power and was cured. When permission was later requested to legalize the synagogue, the municipality dispatched a crew to tear it down because it had been built without a permit. Synagogue functionaries turned directly to the mayor, who dropped everything, accompanied them to the site, and gave the necessary authorization. Here, the legend has an explicit political function: it augments the power of the saint's court in the corridors of government in order to achieve social and economic goals. Indeed, the financial aspect is not absent from such tales either. For example, during the saint's festival, candles to honor him are sold at high prices. The purchase is considered praiseworthy indeed and confers a reward, such as a medical cure or economic prosperity. There is also considerable testimony regarding economic interests linked to the center for the adoration of the Baba Sali, and their aggressive advancement via the apparatus built by his son Barukh Abuhatzeira—the Baba Barukh. The commercial venues for the sale of sacred and profane objects in the vicinity of the burial site, the various permits, the generous donations, and so on, turn the saints' tales into a powerful economic engine.

Beyond their social or political functions, the legends of the saints fulfill a much more fundamental role: to give meaning to day-to-day events. The normative culture of modern Israel demands rational explanations for the myriad events for which no such explanation exists. The motorist who manages to stop at the last moment before crashing into an Arab's car; the young woman who successfully carries a child to term after a series of miscarriages; the soldier who is giving up hope of a lift when a mysterious vehicle appears suddenly out of nowhere and takes him home—these and thousands of other such miniature narratives all beg for rational explanations that cannot be furnished, except to say that they were the result of coincidence.

The legends provide a sense of order and meaning for their believers. When Waqnin wanted to build a synagogue in honor of David u-Moshe, he went ahead without permits or blueprints. When the injunction came to halt the construction, Waqnin did not understand: "Where we lived in Morocco, we also built without permits or engineers," he claimed. He acted not with intent to break the law but in order to go back and regain that same certainty and "order" he remembered from the Diaspora. There, any purpose for the sake of heaven, such as building a synagogue to honor a tzadik, could be carried out without the approval of the authorities.

Seeing all of life's events as a chain of miracles performed by a saint strengthens one's confidence and hopes, but it is above all an attempt to imbue life's events with meaning. Far from mitigating the need for such meaning, life in Israel has increased it. A comparison of the saints' legends told in Morocco and those created in Israel shows that the former deal primarily with miracles that take place in the vicinity of the graves of the saints and pilgrimage sites, or the web of relations between Jewish and Arab society, manifested primarily in tales of the type "the desecrator of the holy is punished" (Arabs injure the honor of the saint and are severely punished). The legends created in Israel are perhaps not more numerous, but they are certainly more diverse. They encompass all areas of life and society, and their purpose is to prove that there is no area, even in the modern industrialized state, where faith in saints cannot contribute. In this way, the immigrant culture expresses its hope that the new home of the community (the North African Jewish community, in this case) will maintain the set of meanings that was so essential a part of its life in the past.

RETURN TO RELIGION

The phenomenon of the "return to religion" or "born-again Jews" was among the most important social and cultural developments in Israel in the 1980s and 1990s.[32] I prefer the term "repentance movement," because it expresses more closely the religious and psychological meanings of the original Hebrew term, *hazarah bi-teshuvah.* The Hebrew concept is very old and the term heavily charged. The 10 days between the New Year and Yom Kippur are called the days of *teshuvah,* when a person is given the opportunity to think about the past year's sins, turn from them to the right path, and enter, purified, the great day of awe. Thus, the name of this movement was chosen carefully, and its impact is felt almost everywhere: in education, the arts, the army, and especially in the political system. Many analysts agree that the most important consequence of the 1988 elections was the spectacular growth of the religious parties, especially those that were aggressively engaged in bringing as many Jews as possible back to religion.[33] This movement, with its immense influence on Israeli social structure and politics, did not appear out of the blue. The return of hundreds of thousands of Jews "under the wings of religion" can be explained in several ways. Many of these "repenting" Jews are young men and women who, though educated in Israel within a modern, secular system, never really internalized secularist beliefs. The "repentance movement" legitimized their living according to their deep, tacit convictions and not according to what had been imposed on them by the educational system.[34]

Another important factor is socioeconomic. Most, but certainly not all, of the born-again Jews are of Middle Eastern origin and of low socioeconomic status. Their identification with neo-religious groups gives them a frame of reference that denies and rejects the modern society that has failed to afford equal status to them and meaning to their lives. The movement can be understood, then, in some respects, as a protest against and suppression of Middle Eastern or Sephardic Jews in Israel. Comparatively, the movement must be seen as part of the growing worldwide tendency toward fundamentalist and neo-religious ideologies, which is most perhaps evident in the Middle East.[35]

The success of the "repentance movement" can also be attributed to the intense activity of professional recruiters, rabbis, preachers, and political and social activists who use many means to reach thousands from all layers of society. Contacts between the recruiters and their public are developed on a variety of occasions. When people turn to a rabbi for advice or medical help, it is clear that they doubt the ability of modern counseling and health care to solve their problems. This initial act often becomes the first step in the full return to the traditional way of life.

However, the movement's success is less the outcome of these personal contacts, which have always been a part of the practice of Judaism, than of the novel use of the mass media, both direct and electronic. The direct media campaign consists mainly of mass performances in sport arenas or large auditoriums. These "revival" meetings (the Hebrew term used here is *hit'orerut*, "awakening") are a mixture of long sermons delivered by famous and charismatic preachers, performances of traditional songs, juggling acts, and other types of entertainment. On these occasions, thousands of men and women, seated separately, are exposed to extensive religious rhetoric. One of the most innovative of these techniques, but at the same time most traditional, is storytelling of the kind we have seen earlier.[36] The goal of these activities is to get as many in the audience as possible to attend the seminars and other meetings advertised during the performance.

THE MEDIA

The shift to communication in large groups, as in public events of the "return to religion" movement or in the political debates about folkloric themes discussed earlier, could not have taken place without the press and television. The media became one of the central vehicles for disseminating and discussing folk culture; it is impossible to understand the role and function of folk culture in the modern state in isolation from written and audiovisual journalism. The types of folk culture that interest the media and the ways they are presented and interpreted are among the most important factors defining the role of such culture in modern society.

Statistical surveys show that, in the 1960s and 1970s, only a few brief items describing folkloric events appeared in the Israeli press.[37] Most of these concerned holiday celebrations, religious rituals, or criminal cases in which the police brought witches or fraudulent healing-saints to trial. Since the 1980s, however, the press has published hundreds of articles related to folkloric events.

On January 8, 1984, Israel Abuhatzeira, the Baba Sali, died in Netivot. Every Israeli newspaper described his funeral in great detail. Mixed in with these reports were stories of the miracles and cures alleged to have been performed by the saint. The journalists heard them from his family and disciples, and repeated them with no attempt at interpretation or analysis. The death of the Baba Sali broke a dam. In the following years, hundreds of articles appeared, centering on folkloric material: tales of saints, demons and spirits, supernatural occurrences, folk medicine, magical rituals, prophecies, astrology, and other beliefs connected to supernatural forces. This flood of articles reached a peak 10 years later with the death of the rabbi of Lubavich in June 1994; stories of the miracles wrought by this Hasidic leader filled the newspapers that week.

In 1992, a 17-year-old boy named Itzik Balas was diagnosed with cancer, but he refused to be treated in a hospital. His mother turned to the judicial system, which ordered the boy to submit to treatment, but he escaped, his condition worsened, and he died.[38] An Israeli journalist attempted to reconstruct the last months of the boy's life. It turned out that, after Itzik escaped from the hospital, he had sought a cure from traditional folk medicine. From interviews with the boy's family, friends, doctors, and folk healers, it became evident to the reporter that a vast hidden network of popular folk medicine existed alongside conventional Western medicine in Israel. Folk healers, saints, amulets, traditional medicines, prayers, and rituals had been sought by the dying youth in place of the "scientific" medicine in which he had no faith. Tracing Itzik's last days, the reporter delved into a dark world in which the philosophical dilemma between faith and science turned into a question of life or death. Without imposing modern, rationalist Israeli culture on its subject, the story uncovered the painful conflicts, the despair and fear they fostered, and the temptation to run in many contradictory directions at once—in short, the complex and manifold world of folk religious faith.

Another typical example is the story of a girl named Efrat, from Dimona, who died of leukemia at the age of nine. On the first anniversary of her death, another daughter, resembling Efrat in appearance and character, was born to her parents, and they named her Efrat as well. According to her parents and the rabbi of Dimona, she was the resurrected soul of the girl who had died.[39] A journalist reported the story by means of interviews with family members, neighbors, and friends, starting from the birth of the first Efrat: the Oedipal relationship between the father and his only daughter, the diagnosis of the disease, the painful treatments, and the struggle by any means possible to save the girl's life. After her death, Efrat began to appear regularly in her parents' dreams, pleading with them to bring her back to the family. The local rabbi explained to them that only if the mother became pregnant would the girl be restored to them. And, in fact, when the mother was in her eighth month of pregnancy,

Efrat appeared in her father's dream and ordered him to stop mourning for her "because I am coming back home . . . I will return on the day that you mark the anniversary of my death at two in the morning, the same hour at which I departed." And so it transpired. The new baby resembled Efrat almost identically, she loved the same toys, and she made the same movements and facial expressions. Naturally, they also called her Efrat and her father was especially close to her, as he had been with her dead sister. Despite warnings by psychologists of the dangers of growing up with a "borrowed" identity, the family—and, indeed, the entire town—was convinced that they had witnessed a phenomenon well-known in traditional Jewish culture: the transmigration of a soul.

The conflict between old traditions and modernity operating here, as in the previous story, takes place within the souls of the people themselves: they are torn between pain over the loss of their daughter and the necessity for life to continue; between the rational, if cruel, knowledge that the dead Efrat cannot return to them and the illusion, founded upon ancient Jewish beliefs, that she can return in another body. The literary technique of quotations from the various participants in this case woven into a melodramatic plot brings the reader into the experience of the participants; these are precisely the techniques that pass for anthropological research.

Folkloristic reports typically originate in development towns such as Yeruham, Ashdod, Kiryat-Gat, Safed, Kiryat Shemona, and Bet Shean, places where journalists learn of pilgrimages to the graves of saints, the miracles wrought by faith healers, and other supernatural events. An example: "Eliahu Madmoni lives in the moshav of Hodaya next to Ashkelon, and he belongs to a select group of more than a dozen healers and producers of amulets operating in this region."[40] The reader is meant to form the impression that, out there in the hinterland, another culture is operating, foreign and strange compared to "ours." Some more examples: three Tel Aviv journalists "go down" to Beersheba to investigate a famous prophetess, and another reports on a new Christian saint in the Galilean village of Iblin or a miraculous chair in a store in Ashdod that causes infertile women to become pregnant.[41] Despite the fact that, in Iblin and Ashdod, people also read newspapers, the sense of geographical distance comes from the descriptions of these places: the Galilean village with its churches and eccentric characters, or the Ashdod "Mom and Pop" grocery store located in a bomb shelter (analogous, in a way, to caves in mystical literature), filled with sacred objects in every corner. These news reports thus seem to uncover for their readers foreign and exotic places within their own country.

At times, though, the journalists report from places that are truly distant, such as an account from Brazil about pagan magical ceremonies (which either pre-date the European conquest of Latin America or were brought from Africa) in which the spirits of gods or of the dead enter the bodies of the participants. In the course of these ceremonies, the participants sacrifice animals, use their blood, and enter into trances while dancing and bowing to the gods. Most interesting of all is that not a few Israelis participate in these rituals, and some are even among the organizers of them throughout Brazil.[42] Another news report describes the Ziara ritual in Egypt, which involves pilgrimage to the graves of saints. The reporter went to great lengths to travel to pilgrimage sites of both Muslim and Christians in Egypt, studied their historical sources and their social meaning, and described their processions, prayers, and dances as well as the commercial activities that accompanied them.[43] The reporter includes in his description of the Egyptian Ziaras the Jewish Ziara in Egypt—the pilgrimage to the grave of Rabbi Jacob Abuhatzeira in Damanhur—emphasizing the great similarities between the Jewish, Muslim, and Christian festivities. Another fascinating report describes rituals of exorcism of demons among the Ethiopian Jews and shows the similarity between these rituals in Ethiopia itself and among the Ethiopian immigrants to Israel. The reporter contrasts the sacred spaces in Ethiopia—the forest, steppe, or village—to the impoverished apartment where the ceremony takes place in Israel.

The exotic note in these reports stems from the sense of distance and not necessarily from the folkloric character of the practices. Brazil, remote villages in Egypt, and the steppes of Ethiopia are places at the very margins of the Israeli public's geographical consciousness. Yet, in the final analysis, all three of these cases deal with something Israeli: the pilgrimage to the grave of Jacob Abuhatzeira in Damanhur, for example, becomes the equal of the other Egyptian pilgrimages and thus puts the Israeli cult of saints in a new context, as an integral part of a Mediterranean culture and not only as an internal "Jewish" phenomenon. The newspaper stories suggest that these rituals need to be understood not according to "Israeli" concepts but rather as part of the Levant, a place in which most Israelis are not yet willing to admit that they belong. Even the pagan rituals in Brazil involve a phenomenon central to Israeli folk culture: the practice of young people to travel after their army service to the Far East or to South America and to take an active part in the local culture. Their involvement in these pagan practices thus reveals from a different angle one of the main cultural tendencies in Israel in recent years. These young men and women act in total opposition to the Jewish values with which they were educated and find spiritual meaning in other, completely foreign cultures. Even the exorcism of demons among the Ethiopian Jews is part of this phenomenon; the mass immigration of this community in the 1980s and 1990s changed almost overnight the meaning of the concept "Israeli." Virtually everyone believed that the Ethiopians would rapidly become "Israelis" in every way, but the revelation that their culture includes the belief in demons exposed this expectation as an illusion. When a reporter shows the great similarities between exorcisms practiced in distant Ethiopia and those that take place in Israel, the reader is forced to think about Israeli reality itself as alien. The Ethiopian becomes not just an immigrant in search of work and an apartment but rather the bearer of bizarre, foreign mysteries. We thought that we understood the reality of Israel, but, once we look at it through the prism of demons, it is not transparent anymore, but dark and obscure.

Perhaps the central point of tension in Israeli life that emerges from these "ethnographic" media stories concerns the Arabs living in Israel. Here is one example: a miracle that happened to Lubna, a girl from the village of Iblin.[44] When Lubna fell ill, Jesus revealed himself to her and healed her. Since then, he has continued to reveal himself to her on a regular basis and, through her, gives instruction to all the Christian communities in the Galilee. There is no fundamental difference between this story and the various journalistic accounts of Jewish saints: they report the same elements of a supernatural revelation, the similar social background of the saint, and the various statements made by believers as well as those representing the religious establishment. The "Baba-boy" from Bet Shean, whose revelation from Elijah turned him into a miracle-working saint, is a virtually identical Jewish version of the Arab girl's story.[45]

The search for eccentric characters among the Arabs of the Galilee has, however, another purpose. These news accounts describe village fortune-tellers, folk craftsmen, singers, and storytellers in order to reveal the romantic side of traditional Arab culture.[46] Miracle workers and basket weavers are equally integral parts of their geographic setting: they inherited their respective crafts from centuries-old traditions, passed from father to son. The healers and craftsmen make use of local materials, either from animals or from plants. They represent the "true" character of the Galilee no less than its rocky landscape. A comparison of articles written about Arab and Jewish folk customs suggests that the writers often see the Arab practices as "true" and "authentic" because they developed on the soil of Palestine, whereas the Jewish customs were imported from the Diaspora and planted artificially in the development towns. These picturesque descriptions of Arabic folklore are in fact attempts to reveal something about the Jews: they are proof of how alienated we are from nature, from the soil, from authentic beauty, and from simple faith.

Yet, according to another news report: "Lecturers in the university, doctors, lawyers, and actors all revert in difficult times to superstitious thinking."[47] In interviews with representatives of these prestigious professions—the pillars of "modernity" in Israel—the journalist reveals that even they hold beliefs in the supernatural and turn to faith healers, magical rites, and fortune tellers. There are, for example, doctors who refuse to perform operations on certain days they consider "unlucky," and actors who will not perform if they have to wear a costume from a play that failed. There are economists whose investments in the stock market are based on the advice of astrologers and fortune tellers, and university lecturers who ask a successful colleague to touch an article that they are sending off for publication "in order that his success may rub off on it." And there are politicians who carry with them at all times an amulet or written blessing that they received from a rabbi.

Even in the army, one finds widespread evidence of magical belief. The most striking example is that of the submarine *Dakkar*, which sank in 1968.[48] The submarine was originally British. When it was launched at the end of World War II, it was named *Totem* because a Native American chief in western Canada gave its crew a totem and promised that, so long as the totem was on board, no misfortune would befall the ship. The submarine was bought by the Israeli navy in 1967 and was emptied of all its contents in preparation for a complete refitting. The totem was also removed and was enshrined in the naval museum in Portsmouth, England. When work on the ship was completed in January 1968, the British offered to return the totem, but the military rabbinate, under the direction of the chief rabbi of the Israeli army, Shlomo Goren, strenuously objected on the grounds that the totem might be regarded as idolatry. So, the totem remained in Britain, and the *Dakkar* failed to complete its maiden voyage. The submarine disappeared in the Mediterranean and was found and recovered only in June 1999, nearly 32 years later. Many sailors, including high officers in the navy, who were involved with the purchase and renovation of the *Dakkar* are convinced that launching the ship without the totem was the real cause of its sinking. The article that reported this belief also uncovered dozens of similar superstitions among sailors and naval officers: days when one should not set out to sea; articles that should never be on a ship when it is launched; various magical rites to calm storms; and certain signs that a ship and its crew are in danger. The reporter interviewed the Israeli sailors, the British sailors who had sailed on the submarine during World War II, and even members of the Indian tribe that bestowed the totem, and from all of them emerged a common belief that the only explanation for the ship's disappearance was the absence of the magical object. In this story, we find representatives of a traditional culture—the Native Americans—and representatives of modern technology—the Israeli and British officers—in agreement about supernatural forces.

Journalistic reports like this one have uncovered a different Israel in both the geographical and cognitive senses. Two types of "otherness" have emerged: one of place, and one of consciousness. The different worlds of the development towns in the south, the Arab villages in the Galilee, and Israelis in far-flung corners of the earth are all geographically remote from the "center." But there is also an "other Israel" that can be found in the very heart of the cultural and economic establishment of the country. In opposition to everything one might expect in a modern society, rational norms shatter in the face of a widespread thirst for magical thinking. Here, the "otherness" is manifested in the search for archaic and ancient practices that the "first Israel," the Israel of the secular Zionist establishment, convinced itself had vanished from the world.

The many and varied folkloric news accounts teach us that Israeli society views its own inner tensions in two primary realms. The first is ethnic, and it is expressed in the division between center and periphery. Most of the reports about distant development towns deal with communities of Middle Eastern and North African Jews. The journalists who investigate and report on these folkloric phenomena typically imply, usually in camouflaged language, that this is a peripheral culture. The geographical gap between center and periphery is a cultural divide between "Israeliness" and "ethnicity." These news reports are important data not only because they describe this folkloric culture but even more because they actually create the consciousness of a periphery and its cultural difference.

The second tension is between rationality and magical thinking whose source is in the conflict between modern secularism and traditional religiosity. By revealing the existence of irrational thought in the very heart of secular Israel, the news articles create the sense that a struggle is being waged in which the secular education and the technology and science in which Israel excels cannot erase the desire for traditional ways of thought that can be found in any folk culture. Here, too, the journalists do not merely report on the phenomenon of magical thinking rooted in the midst of the modern world; they have also been the primary instigators of a public discourse that will surely preoccupy the culture of Israel in this next millennium.

NOTES

1. Eli Amir, *Tarnegol Kapparot* (Tel Aviv, 1983), 90. Unless otherwise noted, all translations are mine.

2. Such a description, from a historical point of view, was made by Anita Shapira, "The Native Generation" (Hebrew), *Alpayim* 2 (1990): 201–3.

3. Anita Shapira, *Herev ha-Yona* (Tel Aviv, 1994), 426–30.

4. Yael Zerubavel, *Recovered Roots: Collective Memory and the Making of Israeli National Tradition* (Chicago, 1995), 60–78, 114–37; Nachman Ben-Yehuda, *The Masada Myth: Collective Memory and Mythmaking in Israel* (Madison, Wisc., 1995).

5. Ben-Yehuda, *The Masada Myth*, 127–62.

6. Marc B. Shapiro, "Suicide and the World to Come," *AJS Review* 18 (1993): 245–64. On the halakhic attitude toward the mass suicide of the Masada people, see Abraham Grossman, "The Roots of Martyrology in Early Medieval Germany" (Hebrew), in Isaiah M. Gafni and Aviezer Ravitzky, eds., *K'dushat ha-Ḥayyim ve-Ḥeruf ha-Nefesh* (Jerusalem, 1992), esp. 116–17 n. 35.

7. Shapira, *Herev ha-Yona*, 141–56.

8. Elliott Oring, *Israeli Humor: The Content and Structure of the Chizbat of the Palmah* (Albany, N.Y., 1981).

9. Ibid., 149.

10. Ibid., 130.

11. Dov Noy, "Between Israel and the Nations in the Folk Legends of the Yemenite Jews" (Hebrew), in Shlomo Morag and Isachar Ben-Ami, eds., *Meḥkarei Edot u-Geniza* (Jerusalem, 1981), 229–95.

12. Eli Yassif, *The Hebrew Folktale: History, Genre, Meaning* (Jerusalem: Mosad Bialik, 1994), 437–479 [in Hebrew].

13. Alter Druyanow, *Sefer ha-Bdiḥa veha-Ḥidud* (Tel Aviv, 1963), 3: 195.

14. Oring, *Israeli Humor*, 178–79.

15. About the importance of this festival for the ideology of the Zionist movement, see Eliezer Don-Yehiya, "Hanukkah and the Myth of the Maccabees in Zionist Ideology and Israeli Society," *The Jewish Journal of Sociology* 34 (1992): 5–24.

16. Yitzhak Breuer, *Moriah* (Jerusalem, 1982), 89, quoted in Don-Yehiya, "Hanukkah," 13.

17. On these developments in the formative decades of Israeli culture, see the papers included in Shmuel N. Eisenstadt, *The Absorption of Immigrants: A Comparative Study Based Mainly on the Jewish Community in Palestine and the State of Israel* (London, 1954); see also Shmuel N. Eisenstadt, *Integration and Development in Israel* (New York, 1970).

18. H. Z. Hirschberg, "The 'Mimouna' and the Festivals of the End of the Passover Holyday" (Hebrew), *Zakhor Le-Avraham, Memorial of Avraham Elmaleh* (Jerusalem, 1972), 206–35; Harvey H. Goldberg, "The Mimuna and the Minority Status of Moroccan Jews," *Ethnology* 17 (1978): 75–87.

19. The text was told by Shimon Vaqnin, founder of the center of the rite in Ashkelon. See also Isachar Ben-Ami, "The Folk Veneration of Saints Among Moroccan Jews: Tradition, Continuity and Change," in S. Morag and I. Ben-Ami, eds., *Studies in Judaism and Islam* (Jerusalem, 1981), 311, no. 15. In late 1989, the daily press reported on actions taken to bring saints' remains to Israel: "In a secret operation, the bones of four saints were brought from a country in the Middle East . . . and interred in a cemetery of a municipality in the south. . . .

The chief rabbi of the municipality in the south, who yesterday confirmed the story, added that in question were the four rabbis held to be the most holy by descendants of the Sephardic communities in Israel, [rabbis] who died 250 years ago. According to the chief rabbi, if the names of the rabbis were made known, thousands of believers in Israel and the Diaspora would come to prostrate themselves on the graves. He noted that among those in question were miracle-workers, of whom legends were told even during their lifetimes" (*Yediot Aharonot*, Nov. 15, 1989). For further studies of the theme in Israeli folk culture, see Haya Bar-Itzhak, "Modes of Characterization in Religious Narrative: Jewish Folk Legends About Miracle Worker Rabbis," *Journal of Folklore Research* 27 (1990): 205–30; S. Sered Starr, "Rachel's Tomb: Societal Liminality and the Revitalization of a Shrine," *Religion* 19 (1989): 27–40; S. Sered Starr, "Rachel's Tomb: The Development of a Cult," *Jewish Studies Quarterly* 2 (1995): 103–49; and Yoram Bilu and Eyal Ben-Ari, "The Making of Modern Saints: Manufactured Charisma and the Abu-Hatseiras of Israel," *American Ethnologist* 19 (1992): 672–87.

20. Eyal Ben-Ari and Yoram Bilu, "Saints' Sanctuaries in Israeli Development Towns: On a Mechanism of Urban Transformation," *Urban Anthropology* 16 (1987): 243–72, develop the basis of these theses. Ruth Finnegan, *Tales of the City: A Study of Narrative and Urban Life* (Cambridge, Engl., 1998), studies similar phenomena in an English "developmental" town, Milton Keynes.

21. *Sefer Ma'aseh Nisim: The Chronicles and Wonders of Our Teacher and Rabbi . . . Jacob Abuhatzeira . . . the Almighty favored me and I collected and copied and wrote and edited what I have heard from preachers of truth, a summary of his life history, his deeds and wonders, by my insignificant and ignorant self, Abraham Mugrabi, may the Lord watch and keep me* (Jerusalem, 1968). Other hagiographical collections treated below are *Our Holy Rabbi the Baba Sali. His Holiness, Teaching, Leadership and Marvels . . . Rabbi Israel Abuhatzeira . . . by Rabbi Eliyahu Alfasi, former attendant to the holy man* (Jerusalem, n. d.).

22. *Our Holy Rabbi the Baba Sali*, 146.

23. On these army and war tales, see Isachar Ben-Ami, "On the Folklore of War, the Motif of the Saints" (Hebrew), in *Dov Sadan Festschrift* (Jerusalem, 1977), 95–96.

24. The tales mentioned appear in Ben-Ami, "On the Folklore of War," 92; tales of David u-Moshe are in Ben-Ami, "The Folk Veneration of Saints," nos. 41, 43.

25. Eliezer Marcus, "The Confrontation Between the Jewish People and the Nations in the Folktales of Jews from the Lands of Islam" (Hebrew), 2 vols. (Ph.D. diss., Hebrew University, Jerusalem, 1978); Dov Noy, "Between Israel and the Nations."

26. Ben-Ami, "On the Folklore of War," 89–90.

27. *Our Holy Rabbi the Baba Sali*, 132–33, told by Isaac Alush of Netivot.

28. In the Middle Ages and the dawn of the modern age, healing was among the most important subjects treated by tales of the Christian saints. See Stephen Wilson, ed., *Saints and Their Cults: Studies in Religious Sociology, Folklore and History* (Cambridge, Engl., 1983), 17–21, 150–52, and Keith Thomas, *Religion and the Decline of Magic: Studies in Popular Beliefs*

in Sixteenth- and Seventeenth-Century England (London, 1971), 209–51. Confirmed testimony attests to some three-quarters of the miracles in the hagiographical narrative being connected with the healing of illnesses. See J. M. H. Smith, "Oral and Written: Saints, Miracles and Relics in Brittany c. 850–1250," *Speculum* 65 (1990): 329.

29. On similar tales of healing in the fundamentalist movements in the United States, see W. Clements, "Ritual Expectation in Pentecostal Healing Experience," *Western Folklore* 40 (1981): 139–48; W. Clements, "Faith Healing Narratives from North-East Arkansas," *Indiana Folklore* 9 (1976): 15–39; V. Romano and I. Octavio, "Charismatic Medicine, Folk Healing, and Folk Sainthood," *American Anthropologist* 67 (1965): 1151–73; B. G. Alver, "The Bearing of Folk Belief on Cure and Healing," *Journal of Folklore Research* 32 (1995): 21–33; and T. Selberg, "Faith Healing and Miracles: Narrative About Folk Medicine," *Journal of Folklore Research* 32 (1995): 35–48.

30. *Rabbi Sharabi: Chronicles of His Life, Teaching, and Miracles . . . The Illustrious Rabbi Mordechai Sharabi, of Blessed and Saintly Memory,* comp. and ed. Yona Refaeli (Jerusalem, 1984), 222.

31. Ibid., 297.

32. The weekly *Politika* devoted its issue no. 42 (January 1989) to the political, social, and cultural aspects of the fundamentalist revival in Israel. The earliest comprehensive study of the movement is Janet Aviad, *Return to Judaism: Religious Renewal in Israel* (Chicago, 1983).

33. C. S. Liebman, "Jewish Fundamentalism and the Israeli Polity," in M. E. Marty and R. S. Appelby, eds., *The Fundamentalist Project*, vol. 3 (Chicago, 1993); 68–87.

34. S. Meislesh, *Ḥazarah be-Tesuvah: Tofa'ah ve-Anashim* (Givatayyim, 1984); M. J. Levin, *Journey to Tradition: The Odyssey of a Born-Again Jew* (Hoboken, N.J., 1986).

35. The comparative aspect of the phenomenon was studied by E. Sivan, "The Enclave Culture," in M. E. Marty and R. S. Appelby, eds., *Fundamentalisms Comprehended* (Chicago, 1995), 11–70, and B. Lawrence, *Defenders of the Book: The Fundamentalist Revolt in Islam, Judaism and Christianity* (San Francisco, 1990).

36. On using similar means in the United States, see L. Dégh, *American Folklore and the Mass Media* (Bloomington, Ind., 1994), 110–52, and W. C. Booth, "The Rhetoric of Fundamentalist Conversion Narrative," in Marty and Appelby, eds., *Fundamentalisms Comprehended*, 367–92. One such example is presented and analyzed in Yassif, *The Hebrew Folktale, History, Genre, Meaning* (Bloomington, 1999), 429–60.

37. Eli Abraham, *Ha-Tikshoret be-Yisrael: Merkaz u-Peripheria* (Tel Aviv, 1993).

38. Ayelet Negev, "Waiting for a Miracle" (Hebrew), *Yediot Aḥaronot,* Nov. 20, 1992.

39. Zvi Alush, "The Return of Efrat" (Hebrew), *Yediot Aḥaronot,* Dec. 31, 1993.

40. David Regev, "Amulets, Blessings and Holy Water, or: The Mystical Power of the Witch-Doctors (Hebrew), *Yediot Aḥaronot,* June 10, 1991.

41. Amos Nevo, "A Miracle in the Galilee" (Hebrew), *Yediot Aḥaronot,* Apr. 22, 1994; Amos Nevo, "The Miraculous Chair" (Hebrew), *Yediot Aḥaronot,* May 13, 1994.

42. Poula Zimerman, "Black Magic" (Hebrew), *Yediot Aḥaronot,* May 28, 1993.

43. Dan Arnon, "Not Even an Hour in the Pyramids" (Hebrew), *Ha'aretz*, May 14, 1993.

44. See Nevo, "A Miracle in the Galilee" (Hebrew), as well as two items about this story presented on the first and second channels of Israeli television on Dec. 13, 1993, and Dec. 14, 1993.

45. Neri Livneh, "A Miracle in the Village" (Hebrew), *Ḥadashot*, May 22, 1992.

46. Ayelet Negev, "I Saw Wonderful People" (Hebrew), *Yediot Aḥaronot*, Sept. 15, 1993; Idit Ben-Porat, "Beware of Zuba'a—The Demon of Friday" (Hebrew), *Ma'ariv*, Aug. 5, 1994.

47. Sigalit Shahor, "The Devils Are Coming" (Hebrew), *Yediot Aḥaronot*, July 1, 1994.

48. David Rathner, "The Curse of the Dakkar" (Hebrew), *Kolbo* (Haifa), Jan. 21, 1994.

SELECTED BIBLIOGRAPHY

Almog, O. *The Sabra: The Creation of the New Jew,* trans. H. Waizman, Berkeley, 2000.

Bar-Itzhak, H. *Israeli Narratives: Settlement, Immigration, Ethnicity.* Detroit, forthcoming.

Ben-Ari, E., and Y. Bilu. "Saints' Sanctuaries in Israeli Development Towns: On a Mechanism of Urban Transformation." *Urban Anthropology* 16 (1987): 243–72.

————, eds. *Grasping Land: Space and Place in Contemporary Israeli Discourse and Experience.* Albany, N.Y., 1997.

Ben-Yehuda, N. *The Masada Myth: Collective Memory and Mythmaking in Israel.* Madison, Wisc., 1995.

Deshen, S., and M. Shokeid. *The Predicament of Homecoming: Cultural and Social Life of North African Immigrants in Israel.* Ithaca, N.Y., 1974.

Doleve-Gandelman, T. "Symbolic Inscription of Zionist Ideology in the Space of Eretz-Israel: Why the Native Israeli Is Called Tsabar." In H. Goldberg, ed., *Judaism Viewed from Within and from Without.* Albany, N.Y., 1987.

Even-Zohar, I. "The Emergence of a Native-Hebrew Culture in Palestine, 1882–1948." *Studies in Zionism* 4 (1981): 167–84.

Gertz, N. "The Myth of Masculinity Reflected in Israeli Cinema." In G. Abramson, ed., *Modern Jewish Mythologies.* Cincinnati, 1999.

Katriel, T. *Communal Webs: Communication and Culture in Contemporary Israel.* Albany, N.Y., 1991.

————. *Performing the Past: A Study of Israeli Settlement Museums.* Mahwah, N.J., 1997.

————. *Talking Straight: "Dugri" Speech in Israeli Sabra Culture.* Cambridge, Engl., 1986.

Liebman C., and E. Don-Yehia. *Civil Religion in Israel: Traditional Judaism and Political Culture in the Jewish State.* Berkeley, 1983.

Muhawi, I., and Sh. Kanaana. *Speak Bird, Speak Again: Palestinian Arab Folktales.* Berkeley, 1989.

Oring, E., *Israeli Humor: The Content and Structure of the Chizbat of the Palmaḥ.* Albany, N.Y., 1981.

Patai, R. *Arab Folktales from Palestine and Israel.* Detroit, 1998.

Rabinowitz, D. *Overlooking Nazareth: The Ethnography of Exclusion in the Galilee.* Cambridge, Engl., 1997.

Salamon, H. *The Hyena People: Ethiopian Jews in Christian Ethiopia.* Berkeley, 1999.

Shapira, A. "Myth and Identity: The Case of Latrun, 1948." In G. Abramson, ed., *Modern Jewish Mythologies.* Cincinnati, 1999.

Shenhar, A., and H. Bar-Itzhak. *Jewish Moroccan Folk Narratives from Israel.* Detroit, 1993.

Shokeid, M. *The Dual Heritage: Immigrants from the Atlas Mountains in an Israeli Village.* Manchester, Engl., 1971.

Sobel, Z. *A Small Place in Galilee: Religion and Social Conflict in an Israeli Village.* New York, 1993.

Weingrod, A. *The Saint of Beersheba.* Albany, N.Y., 1990.

Yassif, E. *The Hebrew Folktale: History, Genre, Meaning.* Bloomington, Ind., 1999.

Zerubavel, Y. *Recovered Roots: Collective Memory and National Tradition.* Chicago, 1995.

Superman.

NINE

DECLARATIONS OF INDEPENDENCE:

American Jewish Culture in the Twentieth Century

STEPHEN J. WHITFIELD

"It is only by a study of Jewish institutions and literature that we shall begin to understand the puzzling character of the Jews," an essayist opined in Boston's *Andover Review* in 1888. He was not advancing a very early, disinterested rationale for Jewish Studies, nor was he optimistic that scholarship could succeed in fathoming the Jews: "Comprehend them we never shall. Their character and interests are too vitally opposed to our own to permit the existence of that intelligent sympathy between us and them which is necessary for comprehension."

This statement, splitting "us" off from "them," positing an extreme "alterity" that defeats the hope of any authentic communication, goes less directly against the grain of recent historiography than might be suspected. Indeed, the essay should be treasured by ironists, for its author was a 23-year-old legatee of the Lithuanian shtetl named Bernhard Valvrojenski, who transformed himself into Bernard Berenson—Harvard '87, Boston Brahmin, Episcopalian convert. His 1888 assertion is striking because he himself so brazenly contradicted it; the future master of artistic "authentication" was himself a poseur. In his final years as an expatriate in Italy, he retraced his origins by swapping Yiddish jokes with Zionists like Isaiah Berlin and Lewis Namier, and by admitting some pleasure in "drop[ping] the mask of being *goyim* and return[ing] to Yiddish reminiscences." Berenson called it "an effort . . . to act as if one were a mere Englishman or Frenchman or American,"[1] though that struggle did not stop him from letting the Roman Catholic Church administer last rites.

Such a life inverted the contemporary career of novelist Henry Harland

Grateful acknowledgment is made for permission to draw upon the following works, which I have previously published, for this essay: "Israel As Reel: The Depiction of Israel in Mainstream American Films," in *Envisioning Israel: The Changing Ideals and Images of North American Jews,* Allon Gal, editor (Detroit: Wayne State University Press, 1996); "Yentl" in *Jewish Social Studies,* 5, Fall 1998/Winter 1999; and *In Search of American Jewish Culture* (Hanover, N.H.: Brandeis University Press, 1999).—S.J.W.

(1861–1905), who inaugurated the themes of assimilation and intermarriage that would mark American Jewish fiction for the next century. His Jewish and gentile characters were not as mutually incomprehensible as Berenson claimed, and they showed themselves quite capable of falling in love with one another. Although Harland wrote *Mrs. Peixada* (1886) and *The Yoke of the Thorah* (1887) under the name of Sidney Luska, he was in fact a Protestant only pretending to be a Jew. He too expatriated himself, converted to Catholicism, and then lied to a reporter: "I never knew a Sidney Luska."[2] Shuffling cards of identity, switching and disguising names as declarations of independence in a society that might reward nobodies, putting on masks amid the fluidities of class and status, entertaining audiences by putting on blackface—this flair for adaptability made Jews at home in America, where any barrier dividing them from their neighbors eventually became so easy to surmount that it was sometimes difficult even to notice.

The instability of identity dooms the scholarly effort to separate with any finality what remains Jewish from what is American culture. Such distinctions can readily collapse because the national character has itself been altered under the influence of minorities like the Jews. Culture has been up for grabs in the United States, where English influence could itself be contested and where Alexis de Tocqueville was stunned in 1831 to find "a society formed of all the nations of the world . . . people having different languages, beliefs, opinions: in a word, a society without roots, without memories . . . without common ideas. . . . What makes all of this into one people?"[3] To this polyphony, Jews could add their own voices.

This chapter is an attempt to specify what that contribution has been and to suggest answers to the question of what is most noteworthy about Jewish culture in the United States, which became home to the largest, the richest, and probably the most secure Jewish community in the millennia since Abraham left Ur of the Chaldees. American cultural life is different because of what Jews have added to it, just as the nation changed Judaism and its adherents. The evidence can be found in the language they used, in the dreams of integration and democracy that nourished them, in the religious practices and beliefs they revised, and in the creative stimulus that resulted from the encounter with another minority group. Because the cinema is the only significant art to have been largely invented in the twentieth century, and because of the incalculable impact of films, two of them in particular can illustrate an American Jewish ethos in the process of redefinition.

WHAT IS JEWISH ABOUT THIS CULTURE?

The United States makes impossible the description of Jewish culture apart from its context. To ask of an artifact "Is it so authentic and distinctive that no gentile could have produced it?" is to impose too hermetic a standard. If *that* is the criterion, then a Jewish culture in the United States did not exist. Spiritual, aesthetic, and intellectual development could not be quarantined from the rest of society. At the Museum of the Diaspora in Tel Aviv, only one American *shul* is depicted among the celebrated synagogues of Jewish history, and yet the architect of Beth Sholom (1954) in Elkins Park, Pennsylvania, was Frank Lloyd Wright (see p. 1118). Nor did John Updike show any sign of strain in sending up the postwar Jewish novel by adopting—on three occasions—the voice of the blocked and beleaguered Henry Bech. Between what has been gentile and what has been Jewish, no firewall could be constructed. The larger culture has proved itself to be porous and hospitable, the smaller one often quite fragile and indistinct. No chasm divides the shape that Jews have given their experiences and the operations of the majority culture.

Jewish culture in the United States has not been endogenous, and an acute receptivity to outside forces makes it difficult to locate what is Jewish in American Jewish culture. But what makes that culture special is that values, symbols, and ideals have circulated in *both* directions—not merely from majority to minority, but in an interactive and reciprocal fashion. No historical moment can be discovered in which the Jewish minority was ever so insulated that its own culture could have been created apart from the play of centrifugal forces. Because that symbolic and expressive system was so permeable, because those who worked within it could not be cordoned off from an outside world that itself proved so open to Jewish influence, categorical rigidity is impossible to sustain.

The scope of this Jewish culture nevertheless needs to be specified. Any intellectual or artistic activity that Jews have initiated in the United States, whether or not such work bears traces of Judaism or of ethnicity, is an expression of American Jewish culture, even if that work does not bear directly or explicitly on the beliefs and experiences of the Jews. Whether representing them or not, these works are manifestations of the same intelligence, distillations of the same sensibility. For the historian of Jewish culture, books and plays and paintings depicting Jews may be especially revelatory. But to exclude from consideration whatever does not portray Jews blunts the effort to understand the Jews who created such works, and it would make the task of classification even more difficult than it already is.

Although the word "Jew" is unmentioned in the fiction of Franz Kafka, his status among Jewish writers of the twentieth century is as secure as anyone's (even if the canon itself no longer is). Written in Aramaic and Hebrew, the Book of Daniel is Jewish. Written in German, Martin Buber's *Daniel* (1913) is Jewish too. Written in English, E. L. Doctorow's *The Book of Daniel* (1971) should be similarly classified—and not only because this novel features Jewish dissidents but because Jewish culture ought to be deemed whatever Jews (or those whose conversion to a majority faith was insincere) have added to art and thought. Such a definition means that Jewish culture is not synonymous with Judaism. Because the Enlightenment and Emancipation dramatically shrank the sphere of religion, liturgical and spiritual topics should not exhaust the meaning of cultural expression.

"Content" cannot by itself distinguish what is Jewish from what is not, nor is the historian likely to discern any unifying principle in American Jewish culture. It is too diverse, too fragmented. Take 1934, for instance. Perhaps the most admired novel by any American Jew was published that year: Henry Roth's *Call It Sleep*. So was the most important book by probably the most creative thinker in the history of American Judaism: Mordecai M. Kaplan's *Judaism as a Civilization*. The novelist was then a Communist; the theorist taught homiletics at the Jewish Theological Seminary. Such dissimilarities ought to thwart any attempt to situate their books in the same historical context. (Both authors were New Yorkers. But no evidence has surfaced that either knew of the other's existence, much less that they read each other's books.) In the same year, Milton Steinberg contributed to Judaic thought with *The Making of the Modern Jew;* so did Harry A. Wolfson of Harvard with *The Philosophy of Spinoza*. Also in 1934, novelist Daniel Fuchs published *Summer in Williamsburg,* even as Lillian Hellman's *The Children's Hour* opened on Broadway. The retrospective discovery of a common pattern is improbable. Specimens that could be plucked from the following year—from *Awake and Sing!* and *Porgy and Bess* to *A Night at the Opera* and *Top Hat*—suggest that the Jewish imagination crystallized in many forms. Indeed, the critic Harold Rosenberg was right to deny the existence of a "Jewish art in the sense of a Jewish style in painting and sculpture." But inferences may be drawn from the existence of artists who are Jews. Although they may not have "been creating as Jews, they have not been working as non-Jews either. Their art has been the closest expression of themselves as they are, including the fact that they are Jews, each in his individual degree."[4]

That no single pattern is likely to emerge from scholarly investigation does not mean that certain emphases cannot be found, or that similar themes or ideas are impossible to consider. Clustering in particular fields, disproportionate expressions of certain interests are themselves signs of the animating power of a culture. The Nazis were wrong to believe in the existence of a "Jewish physics." But it is not an error to note the impact of Jews upon physics. Humor may be a universal phenomenon, yet a 1978 study calculated that four out of five professional comedians in the United States were Jewish;[5] the proportion should thus invite reflection on whether something like Jewish humor exists—and, if it does, why its place in Jewish culture is so secure. Mark Spitz ranks as one of the greatest swimmers who ever lived, and Kerri Strug is among the nation's most astonishing gymnasts. But no one would claim any special Jewish disposition toward aquatic or acrobatic skills or could account for the athletic gifts of these two Olympians in other than fortuitously individual terms. But when Jews are heavily drawn to certain fields, curiosity demands to be satisfied. Attentiveness to ethnicity in the formation of the nation's culture should not displace other readings, only complement them.

Few such contributions were excellent or influential—much less distinctive—until the late nineteenth century. Autonomy did not characterize the value system of the Sephardim, of the immigrants from German-speaking lands, or of their native-born progeny. Indeed, there would have been little if any American Jewish history had immigration from Germany in the mid-nineteenth century not dwarfed the sparse Sephardic community whose ancestors had come in the colonial era. There would have been little Jewish continuity had immigration from Eastern Europe not superseded the German Jews who created the primary institutions and dominated the community until the twentieth century.

In welcoming such immigrants, Emma Lazarus (1849–87) did more than typify an awakening of Jewish consciousness. "The New Colossus" (1883) remains perhaps the most famous poem an American Jew ever wrote, and its placement on the pedestal of the Statue of Liberty aptly suggests the importance of immigration in replenishing Jewish culture. Of Sephardic as well as Ashkenazic roots, Lazarus also happened to be the first Jew Ralph Waldo Emerson ever met, in 1876. His daughter Ellen expressed surprise in meeting "a real unconverted Jew (who had no objections to calling herself one)." How astonishing it was "to hear how [the] Old Testament sounds to her, and find she has been brought up to keep the Law, and the Feast of the Passover, and the Day of Atonement. The interior view was more interesting than I could have imagined." Although Lazarus's family was no longer observant, "Christian institutions don't interest her either."[6]

That visit to Concord, Massachusetts, coincided with the ceding of cultural authority from the Sephardim to the "second wave," which defined *Deutschtum* as the vehicle of civilization. "Racially, I am a Jew," the Reform rabbi Bernhard

Felsenthal acknowledged. "But spiritually I am a German, for my inner life has been profoundly influenced by Schiller, Goethe, Kant, and other intellectual giants." The cultural background that permeated Reform was indeed so Germanic that, in the movement's 1897 *Union Hymnal,* the melody for #95 was lifted directly from *"Deutschland über alles."* One German-American newspaper, *Der deutsche Pionier,* praised the immigrant Jews because, "without their patronage," German-language theater in the republic "would cease to exist."[7] Socially the families of German Jewish immigrants and their gentile counterparts sometimes operated in separate spheres, but the cultural institutions they created (such as singing clubs and reading clubs) were remarkably similar. In 1845, German Jews did create an early version of the Jewish Publication Society, but to discern a conspicuously Jewish culture of German provenance is especially frustrating.

They did transplant their religion, which they reformed (and then opted to reform further), and they did create permanent cultural institutions. But consider the plight of Mayer Sulzberger. As chairman of the publications committee of the Jewish Publication Society of America, he tried to recruit native-born authors. Unable to locate an American who could write a successful Jewish novel, he asked a London friend to find a British author instead. That is how Israel Zangwill (1864–1926) was recruited to write *Children of the Ghetto* (1892), a best-seller on both sides of the Atlantic. Yet, even then, the prospects for a viable Jewish culture did not become more secure. Zangwill feared narrowing his "appeal exclusively to a section" and told Sulzberger that "behind all the Jewish details, there must be a human interest which will raise it into that cosmopolitan thing, a work of art."[8]

Zangwill was at least willing to make literature out of Jewish subjects, however erratic his own consciousness of separateness. Paradoxically, he managed to combine an unflagging sense of allegiance to the Jewish people with the abandonment of Judaism and with marriage to a Christian. Emerson had expected "a new race" to emerge from the American "smelting-pot," and Zangwill dropped that first consonant to exalt the amalgamation of peoples in the New World. In promoting the hope of absorption, *The Melting-Pot* (1908) is a representative text, a melodramatic articulation of the dream of "Americanization" that was widely shared. Even the "imperial wizard and emperor" of the Ku Klux Klan was partly in Zangwill's corner. "When freed from persecution," Hiram Evans observed in 1926, West European "Jews have shown a tendency to disintegrate and amalgamate. We may hope that shortly, in the free atmosphere of America, Jews of this class will cease to be a problem." To be sure, Evans warned against "the Eastern Jews of recent immigration." Those particular "Ashkenasim . . . show a divergence from the American type so great that there seems little hope of their assimilation."[9] For them, the fires of the cauldron might not be hot enough. That is why the third wave of well over two million immigrants would determine the demographic and ideological possibilities of a vibrant Jewish culture; the United States would then harbor the largest Jewish population in the world, but also the one most free to determine its own destiny.

The philosopher who most vigorously challenged the pressures of "Americanization" was Horace M. Kallen (1882–1974). He called his alternative to conformism "cultural pluralism," and thus the most resonant defense of diversity could be credited to an immigrant rabbi's son. More eager to validate the Many than to envision the One, Kallen wanted the most irreversible of all human choices—the identity of one's grandparents—to become the foundation for the enlargement of freedom. An irrevocable fact could be converted into an opportunity for self-realization, a way to honor ancestry. The right to be equal, promised at the birth of the republic, also meant the right to be different. Cultural pluralism resembled an orchestra, and "each ethnic group may be the natural in-

As early as 1909, the Yiddish press satirized as well as exalted the possibilities
of an upwardly mobile assault on high culture.
(YIVO Institute for Jewish Research, Photo Archives, New York)

strument" contributing to the overall harmony and balance of the symphony. Each instrument realizes itself more fully in the society than it can by "segregation and isolation." Ethnicity need not be dismissed as parochial strutting or as an alibi for obscurantism but could instead promote national cohesiveness. "Plurality is a basic condition of existence," Kallen proclaimed.[10] An ardent secularist, he collapsed the ethical values of Judaism into Hebraism, a modernized variant of the religious civilization he believed had become outmoded. Kallen tried to reconcile the particularism of ethnicity with the general demands of democracy and to show that Hebraism was fully compatible with citizenship, because both, he believed, gave primacy to the ideal of freedom. That ideal would be tested and exercised—and "Hebraism" as well as other conceptions of Jewish culture applied—under conditions that in the twentieth century defied sharp boundaries.

THE LANGUAGE QUESTION

Nothing made authenticity more difficult to sustain than the decline of a separate vernacular. Indeed, the very word "Yiddish" did not become widespread until the end of the nineteenth century, when the threats that English posed were already noticeable. (Until then "Jewish" was the simple name for the language of the Ashkenazim.) As early as the 1870s, such American terms as "boss," "boy," "dinner" and "supper" had been introduced into ordinary immigrant speech, and within three decades at least a hundred other English words and phrases had been inserted—such as "never mind," "politzman," "alle right," and "that'll do." In *Yekl* (1896), a tale that Abraham Cahan (1860–1951) wrote in English, his eponymous protagonist renames himself Jake and rebukes the "backwardness" of his wife "in picking up American Yiddish." Although deeper causes shatter their marriage, Gitl's annoying error was to have used *fentzter* instead of *veenda*. Of course Cahan knew that Yiddish took on the coloration of wherever its speakers lived. When Mamie introduces herself, Gitl is confused, because Mamie "spoke with an overdone American accent in the dialect of the Polish Jews, affectedly Germanized and profusely interspersed with English, so that Gitl, whose mother tongue was Lithuanian Yiddish, could scarcely catch the meaning of one half of her flood of garrulity."[11]

The speed with which English insinuated itself should therefore occasion little surprise. To accelerate the prospects of socioeconomic advancement, an "English-Jewish" dictionary was published as early as 1891. Six years later, the *Tageblatt* began providing its readers with a full page in English. Before the outbreak of World War I, the *Complete English-Jewish Dictionary* had been published in 11 editions. No immigrant group was quicker to learn English. In that language Cahan wrote *The Rise of David Levinsky* (1917), a novel that calibrated the cost of personal success, even as he was editing the *Forverts* (from 1902 until his death). No wonder a journalistic rival accused Cahan's newspaper of conflating the two languages so badly that its subscribers knew neither Yiddish *nor* English. No wonder that Molly Picon, a star of the Yiddish theater, took an extended European tour beginning in 1911. She sensed a need to improve her Yiddish, which had become "completely bastardized."[12]

For a couple of generations, however, its cohesive if impure force could not be denied. In 1917 the collected works of the Yiddishist and publicist Chaim Zhitlowsky were published—not in Vilna or Warsaw or Kiev, but in New York City. There too Sholem Aleichem had resettled and died in the most populous Jewish city in the world, indeed in a metropolis so huge that its population in the 1930s exceeded that of any other state in the Union (including the rest of the Empire State). Jews loomed so large in the city that Temple Emanu-El seated more worshipers than Saint Patrick's Cathedral, and the tenacity of the tongue the new immigrants spoke is as noteworthy as its ultimate failure to resist the American Way of Life. An anarchist newspaper, *Di Fraye Arbayter Shtimme* (Free Voice of Labor), was founded in 1902 and lasted until 1977. *Der Tog* (The Day) held on from 1914 until 1971. Not until 1983 did the *Jewish Daily Forward* become a weekly, and about a decade later a visitor to its office on East 33rd Street noted that "circulation is sclerotic, fourteen thousand being the official, and highly generous, assessment." The youngest of the four full-time staffers was editor Mordecai Strigler (1921–98), who could enlist so few contributors that he often wrote half the newspaper himself, having used—over the previous four decades—about 30 pseudonyms.[13]

Each census recorded the decline of Yiddish. Its use probably peaked around 1930, when it had about 1,750,000 speakers. But that figure was failing to keep pace with demography. The absolute number of Jews was greater in 1940 than a decade earlier, but half a million fewer of them claimed Yiddish as their mother tongue. Henry Roth (1906–95) was nevertheless right to wonder, near the end of his literary career: "Who would have believed that I would have seen Yiddish disappear in one lifetime?" The trap that its writers could not elude dogged the career of Jacob Glatstein (1896–1971). Over half a year before Kristallnacht would expose the commitment of a nation-state to crush a vulnerable minority, he fathomed the terrible consequences of the loss of isolation. In "Good Night, World," the poet imagined a return to medieval corporatism, so that he might go

Back to my kerosene, my shadowed tallow candles,
Endless October and faint stars,
To my twisting streets and crooked lantern,

To my sacred scrolls and holy books,
To tough Talmudic riddles and lucid Yiddish speech,
To law, to duty, and to justice,
To what is deeply mine.

He told the "World, joyously I stride / Toward the quiet ghetto lights." Yet what did such a vow of renunciation mean? Glatstein's children were not enrolled in any Yiddish-language school, nor did he teach them the language. Each of his books—eleven volumes of poetry, three novels, six essay collections— revealed with deepening poignancy the reduced estate of Yiddish itself.[14]

Elsewhere in the Diaspora, Jews had not commonly been invited to enrich or to influence the host culture, freeing them to establish their own separate cultural space. But in the United States, which encouraged acculturation, the absence of genuine autonomy lengthened the odds of survival. Without a hermetic language, a threat to Jewish distinctiveness is posed, and a definable sensibility, anchored in idiom, runs the risk of disappearance. To command one's own language does not guarantee continuity and creativity, but it does at least communicate the sense of a peculiar destiny.

The vocabulary of Yiddish did not entirely die. Even Alex Portnoy admits to knowing 25 words—"half of them dirty, and the rest mispronounced!" The *mame loshn* was merely playing possum—in English. In an address at Bryn Mawr in 1905, Henry James feared for the integrity of his native tongue. The immigrants and their progeny were drawing "from the Yiddish even, strange to say," to "play, to their heart's content, with the English language, or, in other words, [to] dump their mountain of promiscuous material into the foundation of the American."[15] His concern was so overprotective that the novelist came across as a bit *meshuga*. But his anxieties were not unfounded. Even as *ganef* and *kibitzer* and *chutzpah* were enshrined in the dictionary, the vernacular was studded with phrases lifted from Yiddish like "Get lost" and "He knows from nothing" and "I should worry" and "Smart he isn't." One sign of the permeable and reciprocal features of this minority culture is Yinglish. Linguistic anthropologists have reached a consensus that "Gimme a bagel shmeer" is how New Yorkers order breakfast. The request can be translated as follows: "I wish you a very pleasant good morning. May I please have a bagel with a bit of cream cheese?" In Frank Loesser's *Guys and Dolls* (1950), Nathan Detroit declares his love to Adelaide in a daisy-chain of internal rhymes:

All right already, I'm just a no-goodnik.
All right already, it's true. So *nu*?

So sue me, sue me, what can you do me?
I love you.

Thus the momentum of the musical comedy was propelled giddily far away from the frippery of European operettas.

CROSSOVER DREAMS

When Jews could inject so much of themselves into the cultural life of an unfinished country, when crossover dreams could be realized so early and so quickly, the quandaries that were often posed to European Jewry seemed to dissipate. Take Max Nosseck's 1940 Yiddish-language film, *Der Vilner Shtot Khazn* (The Vilna Town Cantor). Later released as *Overture to Glory,* it recounts the career of a cantor who must choose whether to join the Warsaw Opera or remain in the Vilna Synagogue. The dilemma is serious; neither European high culture nor traditional Judaism allowed the protagonist to split the difference. Yoel David Strashunsky realizes too late that he has deserted his people. Emotionally spent, he dies in the shul after chanting *Kol Nidre.* His American counterpart is named Jack Robin and can realize the national ideal, which is to have it all. The "jazz singer" can knock over the Winter Garden audience by singing "Mammy" and honor his dying father by chanting *Kol Nidre* from a pulpit on the Lower East Side. Even as Nosseck was filming *Der Vilner Shtot Khazn,* the American-born cantors Jan Peerce and Richard Tucker were facing no such stark vocational choices; these tenors could please audiences at the Metropolitan Opera, too. They were free to cross cultural frontiers, with little sense that such barriers existed.

America meant autonomy, freedom, even power. Or so might be inferred from the enduring popularity of an icon that two Jews created. Jerry Siegel (1914–96), a thin, bespectacled high school student in Cleveland, was earning $4 a week as a delivery boy during the Great Depression, helping to support his family. Some of his savings, however, were spent on comic books. One night in the summer of 1934, he imagined Superman. A story came unbidden to the sleepless Siegel of the origins of a figure on a planet that would be destroyed, of the discovery of a child with exceptional strength near a Midwestern village named Smallville, of his assumption of a second identity: a "mild-mannered" reporter named Clark Kent. The next day Siegel raced to the home of his classmate Joe Shuster, the impoverished son of a tailor who had moved to Cleveland from Toronto; with Siegel doing the writing and Shuster doing the drawing, the pair was inspired to complete 12 newspaper strips that day. It took four years for *De-*

tective Comics to accept their work; within a decade or so, Superman had become one of the most familiar mythic characters on the planet.

He had special meaning for young Jews. Larry Gelbart, for example, would later write television shows, plays, and films. But he claimed that the greatest literary influence upon his Chicago childhood began—and virtually ended—with "Superman, *Action Comics,* first issue, June 1, 1938. Ten cents then, thousands now, but the memories are priceless." The only other text in Gelbart's home was the *Haggadah,* and he imagined as "the ideal book" one that had "Superman helping the Hebrews during the Exodus." Only slightly later, Jules Feiffer grew up in the Bronx, and the future cartoonist and playwright knew exactly what Siegel and Shuster were feeling: "We were aliens. We didn't choose to be mild-mannered, bespectacled and self-effacing. We chose to be bigger, stronger, blue-eyed and sought-after by blond cheerleaders. *Their* cheerleaders. We chose to be *them.*" Superman thus represented "the ultimate assimilationist fantasy," Feiffer realized. "The mild manners and glasses that signified a class of nerdy Clark Kents was, in no way, our real truth. Underneath that schmucky façade there lived Men of Steel!"[16] Snubbed by Lois Lane, unglamorous in his business suit, Clark Kent is a *schlemiel,* a weakling who does not fight back. Even as Arthur Miller's protagonist in the 1945 novel *Focus* puts on the eyeglasses that cause him to be mistaken for a Jew, the disguise of Clark Kent hints at the actual identity of his creators.

Superman is a foreigner in a country composed of foreigners; he is, in the phrase of one literary critic, a "Krypto-American immigrant."[17] On Krypton his name was Kal-El, the Hebrew phrase for a "god that is light" in weight—that is, a deity who does not oppress and is so light that he scoffs at the laws of gravity. Omnipotent and beneficent, Superman is like a god. In America the man of steel is an outsider who succeeds in a new world. He does so by applying his superhuman powers in a way that Jews typically wished others to behave—by helping the weak. Superman is an idealized gentile who honors his elderly foster parents' pleas to use his awesome, heroic potentiality "to assist humanity," to rescue the oppressed rather than dominate them (see p. 1098). He is episodically engaged in repair of the world. Superman is no Nietzschean *Übermensch;* instead, he is a sort of New Dealer. Conceived during the presidency of Franklin D. Roosevelt, to whom Jews showed deeper loyalty than did any other ethnic voting bloc, Superman signified the yearning to protect the vulnerable and to stimulate the confidence-building efforts at nationalist recovery. That is why he reliably fights for "truth, justice, and the American way." In his humanitarian acts, he is more effective than the golem who protects the Jews of Prague; the benefactor whom Siegel and Shuster fantasized into being is less parochial and thus more democratic as well.

The fulfillment of crossover dreams eluded other talented and creative Jews, however, such as Sholom Secunda. His career was paradigmatic. Born in Russia in 1894, Secunda was groomed to be a cantor. In 1906 his family immigrated to the United States, where the prodigy billed as the "Crown Prince of *Ḥazonim*" seemed destined for stardom. He exuded such promise that, in 1915, the Yiddish theater impresario Boris Thomashefsky introduced him to another kid who had demonstrated a flair for composition. But Secunda was shocked to learn that his potential collaborator had no formal classical training; he would be a drag. Later, George Gershwin would express his appreciation to Secunda for having made his own success possible: "If he had agreed to write with me, I, too, would now be writing music [only] for the Yiddish theater." In 1932, Secunda was inspired to write the music for "Bei Mir Bistu Shein" (To Me You Are Beautiful). Jacob (Joe) Jacobs wrote the lyrics, and in the Yiddish musical theater and at Catskills *simchas* (celebrations) the song was a hit. No one expected any wider national interest; in 1937, the team sold the rights to the song to a Yiddish music publisher and split the $30 proceeds.

The alluring vitality that a minority culture could nurture was not to be suppressed, however. The Catskills resort owner Jennie Grossinger claimed to have taught the song to two Negro entertainers whose stage names were Johnny and George. Maybe so, because songwriter Sammy Cahn insisted that he heard two black performers do the song in Yiddish, as early as 1935, in Harlem. Cahn was astonished to observe the crowd at the Apollo Theatre rocking with delight, so he asked himself: "Can you imagine what this song would do to an audience that understood the words?" He persuaded the three Andrews Sisters to record it for Decca. Its president, Jack Kapp, went along—but only if Cahn and his collaborator Saul Chaplin would translate "Bei Mir Bistu Shein," which they did. English was the precondition of popular interest. Cahn kept the title exotic by refusing to Anglicize it but elevating it into German: "Bei Mir Bist Du Schön."

It was released in late 1937, and, within a month, a quarter of a million records had been sold, along with about 200,000 copies of the sheet music. The Andrews Sisters' single became the number-one hit of 1938 and drove America wild. *Life* reported customers rushing into record stores asking for "Buy a Beer, Mr. Shane," and "My Mere Bits of Shame." Not until 1961 did Secunda regain copyright of his hit. Upon his death, 13 years later, he left behind a huge list of Yiddish and liturgical musical works. Perhaps because his oeuvre was "too Jewish," Secunda worked mostly in obscurity. Shortly before his death at 79, he had gone to Tokyo and, in the baths there, asked a masseuse to sing to him any American songs that she might know. She complied with a Japanese version of "Bei Mir Bist Du Schön."[18] The song had circumnavigated the globe.

Yet the ascent of Jewry in America was hardly frictionless, and the problems of adjustment confronting the uprooted were often searing. So quickly did Jewish immigrants and their progeny take to their new home, however, that the newcomers weakened, altered, and abandoned what had historically divided them from their neighbors—religion. Their piety would be tested in a society that was Christian (though the state was not), and, though American Jewish history cannot be satisfactorily recounted as a *Heilsgeschichte*, the holiness that was expressed in the United States merits analysis.

THE FATE OF JUDAISM

The scattered, tiny, and independent congregations formed prior to the Civil War were little more than burial societies that occupied buildings where prayers were uttered—though very rarely by rabbis (who, if they existed, were unaccredited and foreign-born). The first rabbi to brandish formal training, Abraham Rice, immigrated to Baltimore, where he was obliged to "dwell in complete darkness, without a teacher or a companion. . . . The religious life [of Jewry] in this land is on the lowest level, most people eat foul food and desecrate the Sabbath in public," he complained in 1849. "Under these circumstances . . . I wonder whether it is even permissible for a Jew to live in this land."[19] Coordination among Jewish institutions was limited, and the transmission of knowledge to the young was spasmodic and ineffectual. Less than a century later, Reform and Conservative synagogues were providing a diverse range of activities for adults and children alike; worship services were being conducted by rabbis who were professionally trained and attuned to the nuances of American culture; and religious schools were using curricula that were centrally developed and nationally propagated.

The historian ought to pause at that mid-century moment to suggest the conditions under which Judaism was then operating. In 1954, its adherents celebrated their tercentenary in the New World and injected their own upbeat mood into the triumphalist spirit of a moment in which national power and prosperity were at their peak. At the National Tercentenary Dinner that fall, the keynote address was delivered by President Dwight D. Eisenhower, whose most distant predecessor had pledged "to give bigotry no sanction, to persecution no assistance"; that promise to this religious minority had mostly been kept. There were innumerable blessings to be counted, and the path to full absorption into American society seemed unobstructed. A synoptic history of American Jews was published that year by Harvard's Oscar Handlin, who entitled his account of the experience of his coreligionists *Adventure in Freedom*. One year later, a self-trained theologian, Will Herberg, published a classic of religious sociology:

Protestant-Catholic-Jew elevated his fellow Jews to the status of equal partners in the piety that he claimed was the correlate of American citizenship. The claim amounted to the nifty feat of bestowing on the tiny Jewish population a role equivalent to the Taiwanese who occupied one of the five permanent seats in the United Nations Security Council.

In 1957, social scientist Nathan Glazer published what remains the most incisive analysis of the evolution of American Judaism. It did not disparage the feelings of satisfaction that permeated the Jewish community; there was much cause for contentment. But what lifted his volume out of the inevitable constrictions of its era was an awareness of the unacknowledged tensions, the unaddressed problems that were also integral to the communal condition. One dilemma could be said to dwarf—and perhaps even to determine—all the others, and Glazer expressed it with lapidary power: "There comes a time—and it is just about upon us—when American Jews become aware of a contradiction between the kind of society America wants to become—and indeed the kind of society most Jews want it to be—and the demands of the Jewish religion." He then mentioned three of those demands: the need to practice endogamy; the need to live as "a people apart"; and the need to consider the Diaspora as Exile—until the divine restoration to the Holy Land.[20] Jewish religious life could be recounted largely in terms of the difficulties its adherents faced in reconciling their lives in the United States with these "demands of the Jewish religion."

So soon after an anniversary drenched in collective pride, Glazer held up a mirror that was cracking. He revealed just over the horizon the troubles that would stem from success and from promises fulfilled. He specified the difficulty that the goal of an unmodulated integration would produce, which is that the American adjective would excessively modify the noun Judaism, leaving religion drastically reduced and distorted and risking obliteration. What might make the fate of American Jewry precarious was that the very ethos that permeated and inspired this minority group could not in any logically satisfactory way be reconciled with Judaism.

Would it become simply Reform Judaism? That had been the hope of Rabbi Isaac Mayer Wise (1819–1900), the master builder of the institutions of Reform in Cincinnati. His expectations were dashed. However, the impulse to modernize and to adapt to the New World would become commonplace. The proof of the triumph of Reform Judaism was not only that it had contrived to attract second-generation Americans, whose parents had come from Eastern Europe, but also that both the Orthodox and Conservative wings of Judaism felt compelled to imitate much of the institutional pattern that the rationalists of Reform had established. Beliefs and practices that had emerged in German principalities after Emancipation were transferred to the circumstances of a voluntaristic and rambunctious society. A *bet midrash* became a temple that sometimes became a center where secular activities were also conducted. A rabbi ceased to be (only) a legal scholar authorized to adjudicate disputes; he often became a pastor and a formally educated professional as well as an organization man, a fundraiser, and an emissary to the gentiles. (Such virtuosity was sometimes well compensated. The 1900 census revealed that the average Protestant minister was earning $731 annually. To cite an extreme case, Sinai Temple in Chicago was then paying Emil Hirsch over $12,000 a year.) The mandates of sisterhoods and brotherhoods were also altered, from social service in the slums to enhancements for participation in synagogue life itself. The "rule of thumb" that so often defined the pedagogy of the *melamed* (teacher) yielded to a bureaucracy that developed textbooks and other educational materials and devised and revised prayer books as well. All such adaptations were designed to satisfy particular needs, above all to retain the interest and membership of the young in a society in which all sects and denominations competed for souls.

To win—or at least to retain market share—meant accommodation to the nation's prevailing ideals. Freedom and happiness, Jefferson even boasted (prematurely), had been realized; America had therefore passed the test of civilization. When Freud later argued that freedom and happiness needed to be curtailed *for the sake of* civilization, his tragic view should be acknowledged as closer to the interdictions and commandments of traditional Judaism. Although the conflict between its obligations and American hedonism and individualism is hardly unique, no other religious group has been less pious than the Jews. Only a minority has been affiliated at any one time with a synagogue; by the end of the twentieth century, one in five Jews answered "none" to pollsters who asked them to specify their religion. By 1989, the Shoah ranked first as a marker of identity for American Jews. Second in shaping their sense of themselves were the two High Holidays, followed by domestic antisemitism. Chugging along in distant fourth place was God.[21]

How the Holocaust came to assume such importance is itself something that could not have been anticipated in 1945, or even 15 years later. Indeed, the more the murder of six million European Jews inevitably receded in time, the more overt did the claims to remember their extinction become. Consciousness of the Shoah did not become central to Jewish communal life any earlier than the 1960s; indifference and omission were far more characteristic of the community than the injunction: never again! In 1961, when *Commentary* conducted a symposium on the topic of "Jewishness and the Younger Intellectuals," only 2 of the 31 participants emphasized the imprint of the Holocaust on their lives. In his introduction to the symposium, the editor of the magazine, Norman Podhoretz, mentioned half a dozen factors impinging on the changed self-definition of the American Jew since World War II. He ignored the horror perpetrated by the Third Reich. Five years later, when the monthly conducted a symposium on "The Condition of Jewish Belief," very few theologians were willing to confront the implications of the Final Solution.

Several events and cultural moments were to make it decisive to the evolution of American Jewish culture. In 1961, Israel put Adolf Eichmann on trial for having organized the transportation of Jews to the extermination camps, and the judicial proceedings in Jerusalem tapped turbulent emotions that were presumed to have been buried. They were not. Then, in 1967, the Six Day War—especially as the noose seemed to be tightening around Israel prior to the conflict—raised fears that an entire Jewish community was once again imperiled. The very existence of the state seemed to be at stake; Israeli diplomat Abba Eban called it "politicide." Finally, the Holocaust shadowed the fate of the largest surviving Jewish community in Europe. The Soviet regime designed policies that promoted utter assimilation and also engaged in political and religious persecution, and a movement on behalf of this community was inaugurated in the United States, Western Europe, and Israel by the 1970s. That struggle was often animated by an awareness of what rescuers had failed to do in the 1930s and 1940s, and the movement slowed down the diplomacy of détente with the Soviet Union.

Two American films were especially influential in making the Nazi destruction of European Jewry central to the consciousness of Jews in the United States. The first was NBC's mini-series titled *Holocaust* (1978), which was produced by Herbert Brodkin and written by Gerald Green. No television program devoted to a Jewish subject had ever before registered such an impact; none has done so since. Director Steven Spielberg's Academy Award–winning *Schindler's List* (1993) probably occupies a similar niche in the history of the cinema, and his movie invited meditation on the rarity of rescue and on the mystery of goodness. Remembrance of the Shoah, observers of American Jewry have widely acknowledged, has helped to shore up faltering identity. With the decline of ethnic distinctiveness, with the gradual disappearance of cohesive working-class neighborhoods and kinship and friendship networks, with the failure of synagogues to extract membership dues from the majority of those who describe themselves to pollsters as Jews, nothing matched the Holocaust in entwining a fragmented and integrated community into one. Consider one contrast. The largest collection of Judaica in Washington, D. C., is assembled at the B'nai B'rith Klutznick National Jewish Museum. In 1998, it welcomed about 50,000 visitors while two million were flocking to the nearby United States Holocaust Memorial Museum.

In the tension between a historic faith and the temptations of liberal society, no extra credit should be awarded for guessing the outcome. Indeed, American Jews tended to entwine their religion with their politics, which was distinctly liberal. A progressive vision of social justice has been pivotal to their sense of what Judaism mandates; *tikun olam* (repair of the world) has been widely held up as an imperative. What is a "good Jew"? a team of sociologists asked along Chicago's North Shore in the late 1950s. Two-thirds of the suburbanites replied by claiming that they considered it essential to "support all humanitarian causes" and to "promote civic betterment and improvement in the community." Nearly a third considered such activities merely desirable. To be a "good Jew," nearly two-thirds claimed that it was at least desirable to be "a liberal on political and economic issues." A generation later, this proclivity was largely intact. A national survey disclosed that, when asked, "as a Jew, which of the following qualities do you consider most important to your Jewish identity . . . ?," half of the respondents answered: "a commitment to social equality." The other replies, two other sociologists reported, "were equally divided among religious observance, support for Israel, and miscellaneous other responses." Nearly half of those asked in one national survey agreed with the statement that "Jewish values . . . teach me to be politically liberal"; substitute the word "conservative" and 58 percent disagree. (Only 13 percent agreed.)[22] God is presumably still a supporter of the New Deal and its heritage of social reform.

Jews have been more likely than other American social groups to go to the polling booth but have been far less likely than their neighbors to attend houses of worship; synagogues have therefore been built accordingly. "Let them make me a sanctuary" is a divine request, "that I may dwell among them" (Exodus 25:8). But however exact some of the specifications, the Lord preferred to defer some decisions to architects, who concocted what historian Rachel Wischnitzer termed the "flexible plan." It was first used consciously on a large scale by the German-born and -trained Eric Mendelsohn (1887–1953), who arrived from Palestine in 1939. The layout that he devised for St. Louis's B'nai Amoona, completed in 1946, doubled the seating capacity for the High Holy Days, with folding walls joining the sanctuary, foyer, and auditorium. To be sure, Albert Kahn's Temple Beth El synagogue in Detroit had used folding walls four decades earlier, and in the 1920s the *American Hebrew* suggested an accordion shape to accommodate divergent seating requirements for the Sabbath and for the High Holy Days. In the year that B'nai Amoona was finished, architect Percival Goodman published a paper recommending the "flexible plan." But Mendelsohn pioneered in perfecting it, because suburbanization facilitated the use of horizontal space that dense ethnic neighborhoods had not allowed.[23]

Architectural history is an ideal demonstration of the difficulty—if not impossibility—of separating Jewish worship from osmotic influences. In Newport, Rhode Island, Peter Harrison's Touro Synagogue (1763) boasted a façade like the Congregational meeting houses of the colonial era, and the basilica and the high steeple of Congregation Beth Elohim made it resemble the Georgian churches of Charleston, South Carolina, where, after a destructive fire, the new synagogue (1841) was built in the Greek Revival style. In the same era, the Egyptian Revival that was popular for prisons and monuments led William Strickland to design Philadelphia's Mikveh Israel (1825) in that style. A little over a generation later, the Gothic Revival could be seen in the first two synagogues built in San Francisco, although the nation's first Jewish architect, Prague-born Leopold Eidlitz, used Romanesque for New York's Congregation Shaaray Tefila (1847). Having been commissioned to design showman P. T. Barnum's home (nicknamed "Iranistan"), Eidlitz put Moorish decoration atop a Gothic plan for New York's Temple Emanu-El (1868). When Kahn revised his Temple Beth El in Detroit in 1922, the resemblance to the Lincoln Memorial, which was dedicated that year, was undeniable.

Nor did modernism impose a distinctive style on synagogues. Some of the most brilliant modernist achievements were by non-Jews, like Wright's Beth Sholom. Minoru Yamasaki designed North Shore Congregation Israel in Glencoe, Illinois (1964), as well as Temple Beth El in Birmingham, Michigan (1974), and Paul Rudolph was responsible for Congregation Beth El in New London, Connecticut (1973). But the most popular architect of synagogues in American history was in fact a Jew. Percival Goodman designed more than 50 synagogues. Yet he rarely drew on historical references or symbolic preferences, and whether he found an apt and unique aesthetic for Jewish worship is dubious.

No wonder then that, after surveying synagogue designs in the first three postwar decades, one art historian tabulated such a multiplicity of styles that he despaired of locating anything "singularly expressive of a Jewish architecture." What revealed "the specifically Jewish activity within" was elusive. No clear answer emerged to the question posed by the critic Lewis Mumford in 1925: "Should a synagog be in harmony with the buildings around it, or should it stand out and proclaim the cultural individuality of the Jewish community?" That meant resolving a larger problem—"the general relation of Jewish culture to Western civilization."[24] Such categories may be too broad; that dichotomy obscures too many variations. What worked in Eastern Europe could not be duplicated in America, though both are part of "Western civilization." The house of prayer, study, and much else that brimmed with communal life could not be reconstituted where an innovation like the "flexible plan" represented perhaps the most American feature of synagogue architecture.

Interior of Beth Sholom Congregation, a synagogue in Elkins Park, Pennsylvania, designed by Frank Lloyd Wright. (Photo: David DeBalko)

Ideological pressures would enfeeble a distinctively Judaic notion; American democracy would affect the divine election of Israel. To believe in it could seem incongruent with egalitarian and pluralist ideals, and therefore what happened to chosenness reflects how an ancient faith confronted rationalism after the Enlightenment. The kiddush expresses gratitude to a deity "Who has chosen us from all peoples by giving us His Torah," and the *aleinu* (a prayer in praise of God's supremacy, recited at the conclusion of the service) acknowledges that God has granted Jews a unique destiny. Journalist Ḥayyim Greenberg (1889–1953) insisted that election "must not be taken to signify a superior *race* but a superior *faith,* destined to become the faith of the entire world. . . . The Jew, through his faith, is merely *advanced,* while the rest of the world is *retarded.*" Jews can see the divine light more sharply than Christians. But because they too have eyes, Christians will come around eventually. This argument is not taut, however. If all human souls are indeed spiritually worthy, then Greenberg's defense makes non-Jews look morally backward. It is difficult to affirm chosenness without offending against both liberalism and rationalism; a champion of both, publicist Leonard Fein, conceded that such "a declaration [is one that] almost none of us can take literally, and few of us can take seriously." Not that a counter-argument is inconceivable. "No people, race, or tribe is without ethnocentricity," Greenberg rebutted. "A certain degree of narcissism is requisite for the survival of an ethnic group." But election "never constituted a theoretical basis for Jewish domination over other, 'inferior,' races or peoples."[25]

After emancipation, election had to be reinterpreted as mission, or as Israel choosing God instead of the other way around. The notion nevertheless remained problematic, because it circulated in a society that endorsed the ideal of equality. Because rabbis were expected to vindicate Judaism among gentiles, public relations required that election be explained (or explained away). It "legitimated and even demanded an exclusivity" that most Jews "had repudiated," historian Arnold Eisen surmised. "It presumed a covenant with a personal God in whom they for the most part could not believe." Jews became understandably uneasy about a particularism based on holding a monopoly on truth. Although their destiny was prescribed directly from heaven, they wanted to be considered good citizens, which commonly meant repudiating whatever smacked of ethnocentrism. This dilemma Eisen phrased crisply: "Jews wanted to be part of America, and yet apart."[26]

Some of them were willing to abandon election if feelings of exclusivity and arrogance adhered so closely to it. Rabbi Mordecai M. Kaplan (1881–1983) added an objection that was pragmatic; so powerful an affront to democratic sensitivities could not be a worthy idea. "From an ethical standpoint, it is deemed inadvisable, to say the least, to keep alive ideas of race or national superiority, inasmuch as they are known to exercise a divisive influence, generating suspicion and hatred," he wrote in 1934. "The harm which results from upholding the doctrine of 'election' is not counterbalanced by the good it is supposed to do in inculcating a sense of self-respect."[27] The founder of the Reconstructionist movement thus wanted to drop chosenness from the liturgy. Such omissions represented one response to the communal quandary of choosing between separation and inclusion.

If any prayer became more problematic than the daily thankfulness for not being born a gentile, it was the expression of gratitude every morning for not being born a woman. Such a sentiment—and the rigidity of sex roles the prayer reflects—would inexorably yield by the late twentieth century to the claims of feminism. Female independence in the United States had struck Tocqueville as emblematic of egalitarianism. As *De la démocratie en Amérique* was being published, Rebecca Gratz was inventing the Jewish Sunday School movement in Philadelphia and, by making women responsible for educating the next generation, was enlarging their role. The Reform movement quickly asserted a goal of sexual equality insofar as it was feasible, and the indomitable Rabbi Wise interpreted the Torah as requiring the fulfillment of that goal. In the centennial year of the Declaration of Independence, he thundered in the *American Israelite* that, "according to Moses, God made man, male and female both in his own image, without any difference in regard to duties, rights, claims and hopes." Resenting the confinement of the Jewish woman to "a garret in the synagogue, isolated like an abomination, shunned like a dangerous demon, and declared unfit in all religious observances," Wise did much to honor such professions besides introducing the family pew.[28] In substituting confirmation for the bar mitzvah ceremony, he ensured that girls and boys would achieve parity.

The boundaries of the female within Judaism were stretched in other ways. Take the androgynously named Ray Frank (ca. 1861–1948). Born in San Francisco, she may have been (possibly in 1890) the first woman in history to preach from the pulpit on the High Holy Days. That event happened in Spokane, Washington, and launched the singular career of the "girl rabbi." The "female messiah" delivered sermons, primarily in the West, and published essays on Jewish women and on the Jewish family. Her commitment to female emancipation was qualified, however, because she opposed the suffrage and praised domesticity. Invited to deliver the invocation at the Jewish Women's Congress during the World's Columbian Exposition in 1893, Frank was closer to a revivalist than to a learned sage. But by 1910, feminism would become sufficiently implanted to be parodied in a musical that Thomashefsky wrote and staged, *Di Sheyne Amerikanerin* (The Beautiful American Girl): "*Vayber, makht mikh far prezident*" (Women, Make Me President) does not seek to attract the votes of men, who are dismissed as "*mamzeyrim*" (bastards) and "*ḥazeyrim*" (swine) who are fit for washing diapers ("*Zoln di mener daypers vashn*"). No wonder that Reb Smolinsky, the insufferable patriarch of Anzia Yezierska's *Bread Givers* (1925), laments: "Woe to America where women are let free like men." In such a democracy, his ambitious daughter Sara insists on pursuing happiness, despite the curses he inflicts upon her. Smolinsky "could never understand," she realizes. "He was the Old World. I was the New."[29]

So was Judith Kaplan Eisenstein (1909–96), who would marry a rabbi whose grandfather, Judah David Eisenstein, had translated the Declaration of Independence into both Hebrew and Yiddish. The milestone in her life occurred on the eighteenth of Adar, 5682 (three years before *Bread Givers* was published), when she became the first bat mitzvah in history. Her father was no Reb Smolinsky. Indeed, though Mordecai Kaplan and Yezierska's fictional patriarch were each granted four daughters, the Jewish Theological Seminary professor claimed that

Judith and her sisters were the four reasons for instituting the ceremony. The services on March 18, 1922, featured one small step for a woman. But one big step mankind was not quite ready to take; Judith stood below the pulpit and recited from her own printed copy of the Pentateuch, following the regular service in which men read from the Torah scrolls on the pulpit. The first girl in the Reform movement to imitate Judith Kaplan apparently did so in 1931. Another two decades would pass before the bat mitzvah ceremony became common.

Even then it mattered most to the Conservative movement, because Reform had depreciated the bar mitzvah ceremony and Orthodoxy discouraged gender equality. As late as the 1960s, many Conservative synagogues scheduled the celebration on Friday night to avoid reading the Torah, but by the 1980s few distinguished between bat and bar mitzvah ceremonies. The egalitarian logic of the bat mitzvah celebration could not be evaded; the claims of the Conservative movement to respect halakhah proved vulnerable to a democratic faith in the spiritual worthiness of women as well as men. What was the point of asking a 13-year-old to read from the Torah but then of denying her an *aliyah* (blessing the Torah) the rest of her life?

Consistency dictated only one answer. The right to equal treatment, Mordecai Kaplan believed, was accorded the female in American civilization. "There is no reason why the Jewish civilization should persist in treating her in this day and age as though she were an inferior type of human being."[30] Beginning in 1951, his Society for the Advancement of Judaism gave women aliyot as well as the right to be counted in the *minyan* (quorum); four years later, the Committee on Jewish Law and Standards of the Conservative movement's Rabbinical Assembly first confronted the issue of granting women aliyot. That gave impetus to the fuller equality of the 1970s and thereafter, as feminism swept through the nation itself. Some Orthodox congregations acknowledged the force of feminism with a special *seudat sh'lisht* (third meal) on Saturday afternoon, or on a Sunday morning, when a 13-year-old girl was expected to deliver a *d'var Torah,* a homiletic speech marking her maturation. By 1960, roughly 250 nominally Orthodox synagogues had reported instituting some sort of mixed seating, though a backlash was mounted against the feminization of Jewish culture. The momentum, however, could not be stopped.

The effect of the rising status of women was formidable. Because girls were widely expected to become bat mitzvah, the gender gap that had long marked Jewish education was largely closed. (Judith Kaplan Eisenstein would earn a doctorate and join the faculty of the Teachers' Institute as a specialist in Jewish music.) "Before the bat mitzvah became popular, one-third of American Jewish women used to receive no formal Jewish education whatsoever," sociologist

Sylvia Barack Fishman reported. But by the end of the century, "bat mitzvah preparations have brought Jewish girls into supplementary schools and day schools at nearly the same rates as their brothers."[31] By the end of the 1970s, the family pew and female participation in worship had become nearly universal features of the Reform and Conservative branches. The ease with which barriers fell cannot be explained without some reference to the incontestable authority of egalitarian ideals. In 1972, a group named Ezrat Nashim presented a series of demands at the annual meeting of the Rabbinical Assembly. The group sought female inclusion in the requirement to fulfill all ritual obligations; membership in synagogues; incorporation in the minyan; participation as equals in religious observances; eligibility to be witnesses in Jewish law; the right of women to initiate divorce proceedings; enrollment in rabbinical and cantorial schools; and encouragement to serve as leaders and professionals in synagogues and in Jewish communal organizations. Most of these goals were soon attained, and in 1973 the declaration that women had become eligible for the minyan was front-page news in the *New York Times*.

That inclusion was newsworthy because it meant an equal responsibility to pray. Historically exempt from the obligation to do so, women who had invoked a right to be counted in the quorum were dramatically shattering the rigidity of sex roles normative Judaism had prescribed. Because Reform required no minyan, and because Orthodoxy insisted on gender division, Conservatives again registered feminist struggles with greatest sensitivity, including the ineluctable challenge of female ordination. In 1903, Henrietta Szold (1860–1945) sought to enroll at the Jewish Theological Seminary, the rabbinical academy of the Conservative movement. As editor of the Jewish Publication Society and of the *American Jewish Year Book*, she exemplified a life of scholarship even before she had committed herself to a life of Zionist service. Nonetheless, Szold had to assure seminary president Solomon Schechter that she desired only to study and did not want to become what her father had been: a rabbi. With that understanding, admission to the seminary was assured.

In 1921, the prospect of female ordination was raised at the Reform movement's Hebrew Union College, which refused—though not in principle—to countenance so drastic a break with tradition; only the renaissance of feminism in the 1960s would reignite the demand to enter the professions. The intervening four decades were not barren of a sense of injustice, however. The president of the HUC-Jewish Institute of Religion was the archaeologist Nelson Glueck (1900–1971), who was married to hematologist Helen Glueck, a full professor at the Medical College of the University of Cincinnati. Her rank fueled conjecture that her husband's consciousness was fairly easy to raise. Shortly before his death, he expressed the hope of living long enough to ordain a woman. But he passed away shortly before Sally Priesand, who had been admitted to HUC-JIR in 1968, officially became the first female rabbi in history. Reconstructionist Sandy Eisenberg Sasso joined her two years later, and Amy Eilberg became the first Conservative rabbi in 1985. By 1992, about 280 women had become rabbis; the figured jumped to about 400 two years later.

What suggests the insinuating power of the national ambience is the plasticity even of Orthodoxy. A few of its rabbis even recognized the legitimacy of separate women's *tefilot* (prayer services). Increasingly, Orthodox women recited the kaddish in synagogues, and legal authorities found themselves devoting more attention to issues on which women were especially vocal, such as divorce rulings and reproductive rights. By the end of the century, so many girls were studying the Talmud in Modern Orthodox day schools that the chasm in formal education between the sexes became quite narrow. When the national propulsion toward greater equality reinforced a traditional reverence for learning, misogyny could gain little traction. Rabbi Joseph Soloveitchik of Boston was not alone in endorsing female study of the Talmud. So too did the Lubavicher Rebbe of Brooklyn, Menachem M. Schneerson, who turned out to be a pragmatist. Women who explored the Talmud, he argued, would be more effective in helping their own children learn and would be better able to resist the temptation of secular studies.

Within American Orthodoxy, the delivery of sermons in English and the appreciation of decorum in worship had once been innovations too, thanks to Joseph H. Lookstein of Manhattan's Congregation Kehilath Jeshurun in particular. He admired the tranquillity and tastefulness of Reform and Conservative worship, which he wanted Orthodoxy to emulate. According to his son, Lookstein "strove to combine warmth with dignity, the enthusiasm of Orthodoxy with the aesthetics of Reform, the tradition of four thousand years of Jewish practice with the modern active tempo."[32] In 1937 he founded the Ramaz School (and thus pioneered the day school movement) and scheduled no classes on Sundays or at Christmas—designated a winter break. Such redefinitions of sanctity helped to blur any sharp distinction between Judaism and American culture.

To claim that national values have somehow infiltrated a religion whose history can be autonomously traced is misleading. One of the strongest signs of how Jews have helped shape the larger culture—and one of the most convincing illustrations of reciprocity—is the rise of feminism itself. Since the 1960s, Jewry has disproportionately supplied the best-known activists, ideologues, and theorists in behalf of women's causes. Literary scholar Carolyn Heilbrun claimed that "to be a feminist[,] one had to have an experience of being an outsider more extreme than merely being a woman."[33] Indeed, the sense of marginality may have been something of an independent variable in the equation of activism. During the failed struggle for passage of the Equal Rights Amendment, pollsters learned that Jewish men were more likely to favor the Constitutional revision than were gentile women. The explanation may have been found in sociology more than in religious ideology. But the fate of feminism suggests that Judaism— far from constituting an impregnable barrier to the ideal of gender equality— could *become* consistent with it.

A DEMOCRACY OF TASTE

The democratic tendencies of American life, which promoted egalitarianism, were congenial to a minority that, though mostly urban in its geography, has not been typically urbane in its style. Gentility was for gentiles, and civility was an ordeal to which Jews were somewhat reluctant to submit.

For example, Julian Rose's vaudeville routine early in the century, "Lipinsky at the Wedding," poked fun at the standards of the well-heeled. Invited to "please come in evening dress," Ikey Blatt shows up in his pajamas. An item served to guests as "tomato surprise" is no surprise to Levinsky: "I ate 'em before lots of times." When his friend Lipinsky is scolded for having grabbed an entire roast chicken "all alone to eat," he reacts by rushing to grab some potatoes to put on the plate too. And so forth. The title of Richard Feynman's memoirs came from an incident on his first afternoon as a physics graduate student at Princeton, where the dean's wife asked him whether he took cream or lemon in his tea. The future Nobel laureate replied with a gauche "both," which startled her: "Surely you're joking, Mr. Feynman." He wasn't, though he delighted in puncturing pretense, in ignoring the rules of etiquette Emily Post had codified. (An earlier physicist, Albert Einstein, liked to read her famous manual of propriety—for laughs.) Attuned to the social conventions that he made a political point of repudiating, the impish radical Abbie Hoffman mocked "the notion of 'modesty' as something invented by WASPs to keep the Jews out of the banking industry."[34]

To believers in human uniformity and cultural homogeneity, an ingenuous document can also be cited: a letter to the editor of *Der Tog* in 1915. The English-language play that the writer had attended was deemed "passable, but the theater! It is not like our Jewish theater. First of all I found it so quiet there," this groundling reported. "There are no cries of 'Sha!' 'Shut up!' or 'Order!' and no babies cried—as if it were no theater at all!" Nor were fruits or sweets for sale. The formalities of the Anglophone theater reminded this kvetch of "a desert.

There are some Gentile girls who go around among the audience handing out glasses of water, but this I can get at home, too."[35] The *heimish* dimension of Jewish culture was also manifested in Allen Ginsberg, who was listed in the telephone book through the 1960s, after he had become perhaps the nation's most famous poet. Isaac Bashevis Singer (1904–91) also kept his name in the Manhattan directory for a while, even after winning the Nobel Prize for literature in 1978. Until the demands of fame grew exponentially, Singer often invited callers over for lunch, or at least for coffee. It is hard to imagine other eminent European-born novelists—even those who, like Thomas Mann or Vladimir Nabokov, were married to Jews—offering such unassuming hospitality.

Jews took so quickly to America because their culture was, if anything, an exaggeration of tendencies already evident in the society itself. Arriving en masse when the nation was moving from the countryside to the city, Jews were ahead of the curve. The Constitution required of new citizens the renunciation of aristocratic titles, which meant that nobility was less cherished than mobility, and an up-from-the-bottom scrappiness was so widely admired that the Jewish disregard of politesse did not appear peculiar. The apparent fluidity of the class structure, however, could not conceal what made America so different, which was that Jews occupied the advantageous side of the color line. Even as immigrants, they were elevated into the racially superior position. For blacks, equality was a cruelly distant, elusive ideal. Still systematically persecuted long after the Civil War, blacks nevertheless exerted an inescapable influence on the nation's culture, and their presence distinguished the culture of American Jews from other parts of the Diaspora. Sensitive to that impact, Jewish popular artists reworked it with such intensity that the entire culture was energized. Jews helped it to become mulatto.

When Irving Berlin (1888–1989) wrote "Alexander's Ragtime Band" in 1911, he was still such a greenhorn he was unaware that it wasn't in ragtime. Berlin's sensational international hit was a barely syncopated slow march that owes little to ragtime composers like Scott Joplin but does make explicit an indebtedness to a black style that was already pronounced on Tin Pan Alley. In any event, syncopation, or "ragging," may have been congenial to the remote descendants of the subjects of King David, the sweet singer of Israel. Rooted in and routed from the Mediterranean, their music exhibited the "complex rhythms and preference for the minor keys" that, according to one cultural historian, resembled what was considered the Negro sound.[36] Yet the Russian-born composer of "Alexander's Ragtime Band" remained oddly unsure of what he was adapting and unable to describe what he had been doing. "You know," Berlin later admitted, "I never did find out what ragtime was."[37] His excruciatingly limited formal training, and therefore his dependency upon an associate to make the notations, sparked the false suspicion that a black composer must have ghosted Berlin's hits. Such rumors paid tribute to his uncanny power to reproduce the frisson of black musicality.

He could satirize Jewish life and paint it black, too. In Berlin's "Sadie Salome Go Home" (1909), Mose strenuously objects to the decision of his girlfriend, Sadie Cohen, to become a strip-tease *artiste* instead of the dramatic actress she once wanted to be. So Yiddish-inflected is the song that Berlin rhymed "glasses" with "dresses," without abandoning a ragtime effect.[38] Versatile enough to write for both races (indeed for anyone), Berlin easily slipped the traces of his own ethnicity. He was closely associated with performers like Al Jolson and Fanny Brice, but also with others who were ineligible for a minyan, like Bing Crosby and Fred Astaire. Although a Jewish vaudevillian named Harry Richman intro-duced "Puttin' on the Ritz" as a "coon song," it was Ella Fitzgerald who made it famous when she advised strutting along "Park Avenue" as a remedy "if you're blue." For another black singer, Ethel Waters, Berlin wrote three songs in the musical *As Thousands Cheer* (1933): "Heat Wave," "Harlem on My Mind," and "Supper Time." The last one is sung by a woman whose husband has just been lynched by a white Southern mob; somehow she must tell her children that their father will not be returning home, ever. Though Berlin was no racial progressive, he insisted on an integrated cast of entertainers for *This Is the Army* (1942), which he organized and staged. The troupe was the only U.S. military unit to be desegregated during the war against the Axis.

Berlin's marriage in 1926 was reported by the *Times* with a headline identify-ing him as a "Jazz Composer." In fact he hated such music. The previous year, jazz had been linked exclusively with Jews like Berlin in Samson Raphaelson's preface to his play *The Jazz Singer,* which was based on his 1922 short story "Day of Atonement." Jazz is what the cantor's son is supposed to be singing in the film that broke the sound barrier. Blackface was featured, blacks themselves effaced. In following the rise of an American-born and -bred entertainer, *The Jazz Singer* (1927) made a point of excluding the minority that had created such music. "I have used a Jewish youth as my protagonist," Raphaelson explained, "because the Jews are determining the nature and scope of jazz more than any other race—more than the Negroes, from whom they have stolen jazz and given it a new color and meaning." Performers who exemplified "the rhythm of frenzy," like Jolson and Sophie Tucker, had "their roots in the synagogue. And these are expressing in evangelical terms the nature of our chaos today." Raphaelson thus promoted the transvaluation of values: "Jazz is prayer. It is too passionate to be anything else." And the fervor aroused in the nightclubs and dance halls could

The Jazz Singer, 1927. Patriarchal tradition stands between the mother and the son
who is going to assert his rights as a product of the New World.
Left to right: Eugenie Besserer, Al Jolson, Warner Oland.
(Wisconsin Center for Film and Theater Research; WCFTR-2672)

be compared only to the emotions tapped in evangelical churches or in shul
on the Day of Atonement.[39] Thus Henry Ford's *Dearborn Independent* reported
on the craze with the following headline: "Jewish Jazz Becomes Our National
Music."[40] Ford's weekly erred as obtusely as Raphaelson did; jazz was not only
Jews. But jazz was *also* Jews, who brought something to what blacks had invented.

A Jolson performance in 1917 had inspired Raphaelson to write "Day of
Atonement" and then *The Jazz Singer*. "My God, this isn't a jazz singer," he had
murmured. "This is a cantor!"—with his "tortured, imperial call." When the
movie opened, the reviewer for the *Forverts* saw no "incongruity in this Jewish
boy with his face painted like a Southern Negro singing in the Negro dialect." On
the contrary, what was obvious was "the minor key of Jewish music, the wail
of the ḥazan, the cry of anguish of a people who had suffered. The son of a line
of rabbis well knows how to sing the songs of the most cruelly wronged people in the world's history."[41] Al Jolson (1886–1950) was fluent in Yiddish but at-

tained renown as "the uncrowned king of minstrelsy." His coronation took place during his Broadway debut in 1910, when he applied burnt cork to belt out "Paris Is a Paradise for Coons." *The Singing Fool,* which Warner Brothers released a year after *The Jazz Singer,* earned more at the box office than any Hollywood film until *Gone with the Wind* 11 years later. Enough of the magic lingered after World War II to make *The Jolson Story,* starring Larry Parks, the biggest grossing film of 1946.

An assimilationist, Jolson was not assimilated, not quite house-broken. Indeed there was something demonic about him. The performer was unprecedented in his rawness and his lack of restraint. "The fury and the exultation of Jolson is a hundred times higher in voltage than that of [Theodore] Roosevelt," wrote an early critic of mass culture, amazed at "this galvanic little figure, leaping and shouting," eagerly responding to demands for his encores, happily returning to the stage. Having just "done more than any other ten men," Jolson would nevertheless announce, "You ain't heard nothing yet," and then do even more. Something about him could not be contained within the thin membranes of Victorian order, which is why it is fitting that he was so indelibly associated with blackface—even more so than was Fanny Brice or Sophie Tucker. Yet the cultural meaning of applying burnt cork remains somewhat mysterious. Perhaps blackface was a way of conveying emotions too deep to be expressed directly, too melancholy to be confronted in a promised land. Perhaps only when hidden behind a veil could the sadness that is endemic to life be weighed, which may be why critic Gilbert Seldes once observed that Jolson, despite his compulsive buoyancy, "created image after image of longing."[42]

By cavorting in blackface, he and other Jewish entertainers may have been taking out citizenship papers. By laying claim to the most enduring manifestation of nineteenth-century popular culture, perhaps these performers were invoking their right to be Americans. The allure of blackface was that, through its artifice, such performers could separate themselves from the Old World. By walking and talking like Negroes, Jolson and the others could transform themselves—and the masses they represented—from outcasts into Americans. Or something more sinister could have been operating. The Jews who inherited the conventions of minstrelsy were also blocking the entrances through which blacks might somehow have come and won a chance to speak for themselves. Their absence gave Jews a chance to ascend, by masquerading as a more despised minority. That was the price of national inclusion, through the avenue of upward mobility that show business provided. Blackface was a way of deepening the humiliation of blacks, because the mimicry that white performers cultivated injected painful reminders of enforced silence and civic inferiority. That other groups were also mocked in popular culture offered little consolation, because no other people was so victimized. On stage, the imitation was conscious, a projection of blackness so caricatured that these gestures of racial impersonation could be made fun of, as Jolson himself did with Yiddish inflections. If it was a joke, it was a cruel one.

Perhaps no other white composer showed a more intuitive appreciation of black music—especially the blues—than George Gershwin (1898–1937), whose indebtedness was deep. The first time he tried his hand at a major instrumental work, the result was a veritable evocation of the jaunty go-get-'em aura of the Jazz Age: *Rhapsody in Blue* (1924). His early idols were jazz pianists James P. Johnson and Luckey Roberts; his good friend was Fats Waller. As the ebullient composer of "I Got Rhythm," Gershwin did not seem out of place in Harlem's nightclubs and parties; nor did he have any trouble substituting himself for the leader "shouter" in a black church in South Carolina, while preparing for *Porgy and Bess.* For *George White's Scandals of 1922,* he inserted a Harlem operetta saturated with spirituals, ragtime, and the newly fashionable blues. So deeply had he turned black by plunging into Charleston's ghetto that the handful of white characters in *Porgy and Bess* (such as cops and lawyers) utter only a clipped speech that does not unfold into song. In the story of the cripple, Porgy, one critic has speculated, Gershwin discovered a moving "parable about oppression, alienation, corruption and the inviolability of a radical innocence of spirit." Whatever the psychic wound from which the composer suffered, this "folk opera" was difficult to categorize. The 1935 premiere provoked the music critic for the *New York Herald-Tribune* to call *Porgy and Bess* "a piquant but highly unsavory stirring-up together of Israel [and] Africa."[43]

But mixture did not mean equality, which musicians of African ancestry were denied for the most of the twentieth century. The systematic discrimination that penalized them required recourse to "cultural management." Talented and ambitious blacks could succeed in the music business only with the aid of Jews whose entrepreneurial skills made them indispensable intermediaries with the music publishers, the studio executives, the booking agents, and the operators of theater chains, who were usually *also* Jews. Six companies controlled 95 percent of the recording industry in the early 1940s: Columbia, Victor (later RCA), MGM, Decca, Mercury, and Capitol. In all, executives of Jewish origin were dominant. Until the civil rights victories of the 1960s, black musicians had precious few chances of controlling their own careers or working with black managers, and only Jews were willing to do for such jazz musicians what other whites would not stoop to accepting. These "cultural managers" did not work pro bono. But they too helped make the nation's arts mulatto.

Norman Granz performed that role for Ella Fitzgerald; so did Bob Weinstock for John Coltrane and Miles Davis. Louis Armstrong submitted his professional career to the business judgment of Joe Glaser, who was allowed to hire and fire members of the band, to decide which gigs to accept or reject, and even to pay the trumpeter whatever the cultural manager deemed appropriate. No witnesses ever came forth to insist that Glaser had taken a vow of poverty. But "Satchmo" is not buried in a potter's field, and his manager could share some credit for ensuring that Armstrong gained the international acclaim and earned the rewards to which his unmatched musical abilities entitled him. Could he have achieved as much fame and fortune without Glaser? Would Armstrong have wanted to make his own business decisions? The answers are not obvious. Other jazz greats, like King Oliver or Jelly Roll Morton, resented the exploitation that cultural management made possible, and they refused to pay the cost to their self-respect. Both of them died destitute and in oblivion.

The complicated relationship of the composer and bandleader Duke Ellington and Irving Mills suggests how the black-Jewish affiliation helped enlarge American culture. Mills had been born in such obscurity that 1894 represents only a guess, and he started out—like Berlin and Gershwin—as a song-plugger, trying to generate hits. In 1919 Mills founded, with his brother Jack, Mills Music, and they hit the jackpot with their second song, "Mr. Gallagher and Mr. Shean." When the blues became fashionable, Mills Music jumped in quickly, hiring such black songwriters as Shelton Brooks ("Darktown Strutters' Ball") and Henry Creamer ("Way Down Yonder in New Orleans"). Beginning in the 1920s (which F. Scott Fitzgerald named the Jazz Age), Irving Mills did for Ellington—and vice versa—what Glaser and Armstrong were doing for each other. Mills certainly cheated his client of his earnings and compounded such sins by giving himself credit as Ellington's collaborator, with both of their names attached to his songs.

Those celebrated ornaments of the nation's culture may have existed, however, because Mills Music was in the business of publishing songs. Stressing how much income could be derived from royalties, Irving Mills pushed his biggest client to *write* songs as well as play them. "Mood Indigo," "Creole Love Call," and "Solitude" were composed to meet the pressure of recording deadlines, and these works were sometimes finished in the studio. Because Ellington's manager was also the head of Mills Music, the incentives were weighted toward the composition of Ellington's own music over anyone else's, and this stimulated Ellington to keep writing and recording. (Because Glaser was not a music publisher, Armstrong had no such incentive.) Irving Mills had enough musical taste to advise Ellington on what kinds of work would become popular, to propose titles and themes, to hire lyricists to provide words, and to compensate for his tendency to over-arrange. The composer whose reputation may now exceed any other American's was gracious in praising his cultural manager for having "always preserved the dignity of my name . . . and that is the most anybody can do for anybody."[44]

The complications of musical appropriation and the mutual creativity of blacks and Jews can also be briefly traced in the career of Paul Robeson, whose rendition of "Ol' Man River," the show-stopper from Oscar Hammerstein II and Jerome Kern's *Show Boat* (1927), the baritone had made famous in London. "Musically it is a complete miracle," Robeson remarked, "the creation of a tone of the Negro spiritual by an alien to the Negro's traditions." He could prove such a claim by "sing[ing] it between two spirituals, and it is not a false note. There is no change in the emotional response of the audience." "Ol' Man River" proved how adroitly Jews could imitate the black sound and style, just as Robeson himself seemed to validate the Jewish faith that accidents of birth bore no relation to the aristocracy of talent. He also enjoyed a special status among Jews because his own emphatic leftism harmonized so smoothly with their political culture. In 1930, the social-democratic *Forverts* paid tribute to Robeson, who personified

> the cry of an oppressed people . . . the cry of an insulted and driven race. The cry of pain of a race through the mouth of an artist, through the musical lines of a performer. The cry was directed to the world, the appeal was made to all of mankind, but the first country that must listen should be—America.[45]

He reciprocated nearly two decades later—in Moscow. After World War II, Robeson could not help sensing the noose tightening around Jewish culture in the Soviet Union. When he performed the final concert of his 1949 tour, he said nothing about how Stalinism—to which he adhered, at the price of pariahdom at home—was extinguishing Yiddish literature. But in such an atmosphere, Robeson knew the political implications of Jewish music, and his single encore, he explained, was an expression of faith in the cultural relations between American and Soviet Jewry. After translating into Russian the lyrics of the Jewish partisans' song, "Zog Nit Kaynmal," he sang it in Yiddish:

> *Never say that you have reached the very end,*
> *When leaden skies a bitter future may portend.*
> *For sure the hour for which we yearn will yet arrive,*
> *And our marching steps will thunder: we survive!*[46]

The effect was electrifying, as Muscovites broke down, sobbed, and rushed the stage to touch and to hail "Pavel Vasilyevich."

LOVE AND MARRIAGE

So recurrent are the shadow and presence of blacks in the formation of American Jewish culture that the universalistic ideals so common to Western Jewry further reinforced a repudiation of whatever smacked of a particularist past. The cosmopolitan ideal, which was hardly unknown elsewhere in the Diaspora, was easily accommodated to a special consciousness of racial injustice and other forms of prejudice and to appeals to brotherhood that would transcend the artifices of birth. The injection of race as an impediment to romance, for example, suggests an enduring theme on Broadway, which is the yearning to overcome social barriers for the sake of love. This has been a topic of special interest to Jews.

One pivotal text is the musical version of a Shakespearean tragedy about star-crossed lovers who are Italian Catholics. Late in 1948, Jerome Robbins (1918–98) fielded a plea from an actor who was preparing to play Romeo and was having trouble getting into the role. When Robbins imagined updating the Elizabethan classic into the present, "that clicked in." He thought of "Romeo's passions" as "so extreme, so intense, so adolescent. It's all new and fresh." The choreographer telephoned Leonard Bernstein, whose diary early in 1949 noted:

> Jerry R. called today with a noble idea: a modern version of *Romeo and Juliet* set in slums at the coincidence of Easter-Passover celebrations. Feelings run high between Jews and Catholics. Former: Capulets, latter: Montagues. Juliet is Jewish. Friar Lawrence is the neighborhood druggist. Street brawls, double death—it all fits.[47]

From conception to opening night took another eight years. The Brooklyn-born Arthur Laurents, who wrote the book, changed the composition of the gangs. The Sharks were switched from Jews to Puerto Ricans, who are swarthy and speak with accents and are exotic strangers, in contrast to their lighter adversaries. But the "PRs" in *West Side Story* (1957) should not be taken for surrogate Jews, who historically tend to leave neighborhoods when trouble comes. The Sharks are different; with no suburbs to escape to, they fight (back). They are overtly resentful and cynical too.

What survived of Robbins's original conception was the hope that ancient rivalries and prejudices might be spurned for the sake of love. Such a theme has intrigued Jewish dramatists and librettists, who gave it a kick that consciousness of their own status might well have heightened. Nothing else raised more clearly the possibility of the Jews' absorption into the larger society, or testified more fully to the belief that the confinement imposed on their ancestors might be superseded. Intermarriage is probably the most sustained theme in cinematic images of Jews as well. Neither on Broadway nor in Hollywood was there concurrence with Bernard Berenson's view of "too vitally opposed" a set of "interests" between gentile and Jew to allow even for "intelligent sympathy." On the contrary, the nuptials uniting them would prove that America is different. The rejection of one's father has meant above all the freedom to choose one's spouse. The ultimate sign of accommodation has been the chance to marry outside the faith. The Hollywood happy ending requires that Jew and non-Jew be joined in matrimony, or at least in love, triumphing over the narrowness of particularism. Movies became so addicted to this theme that, even when Herman Wouk's 1955 best-seller concludes with Marjorie Morgenstern becoming Mrs. Milton Schwartz, her celluloid self (Natalie Wood) in *Marjorie Morningstar* (1958) manages to end up with the only gentile character in the picture.

But what if Jewish life cannot easily be understood in terms of overcoming prejudice and superstition through romantic love? What if Jewish destiny is imagined in nationalist rather than cosmopolitan terms? What if the framework is expanded beyond the Diaspora? Such questions were raised with "a novel of Israel" published in 1958 and with the film adaptation two years later. The answers revealed the ideological and artistic constraints of a vernacular culture.

AN IMAGINARY ISRAEL

The impact of Leon Uris's *Exodus* was extraordinary. For over a year it remained on the *New York Times* best-seller list, including 19 weeks perched at #1, and was a Book-of-the-Month Club alternate selection. For the rest of the century, the hard-cover edition did not go out of print. Although propaganda novels have a few times punctuated the history of mass taste, *Exodus* was unprecedented. It was not intended to arouse indignation over a domestic issue, such as the moral horror of slavery (*Uncle Tom's Cabin*), or the ugliness of urban conditions (*The Jungle*), or the plight of migrant farmers (*The Grapes of Wrath*). *Exodus* was published when interest in Israel was slight and when levels of philanthropy and tourism were—by later standards—low. Only a year earlier, Nathan Glazer had mentioned how slight was the effect of the new state on "the inner life of American Jewry." He argued that "the idea that Israel . . . could in any serious way affect Judaism in America" was "illusory."[48] When ethnicity was suppressed or disdained as a vestige of the immigrant past, no one could have suspected that Jewish identity might be susceptible to the Zionism *Exodus* promoted.

It was therefore astonishing that an American would write a Zionist epic that would become one of the publishing sensations of the era. The year that it was published, former prime minister David Ben-Gurion asserted: "As a piece of propaganda, it's the greatest thing ever written about Israel."[49] The popularity of *Exodus* was not just a tribute to the expanding hospitality of the majority culture; success in the bookstores was also evidence that Jewry was now permitted to view its own experience through American mythology, to think of itself not only as virtuous but as courageous, tough, and triumphant as well. Uris pulled off such a feat by outflanking or evading the customary concerns of the ethnic novel—the tension between Old World authority and tradition vs. New World promise and freedom. Ignoring such conventional literary issues as the peril posed to the family, or the crises of belief, he drew heavily on the exploits of Yehuda Arazi, a Mossad agent who operated "illegal" ships in the Mediterranean under the British Mandate and had drawn considerable press attention to the plight of Jewish refugees.

Uris thus transposed to the Middle East the adventure formulae that middle-brow American readers already expected. In making Jewish characters into heroes adept with guns, he knew how to keep the action flowing. One critic therefore was obliged to lodge a protest against the "stereotype-inversion" of *Exodus,* which "merely substitutes falsification for falsification, sentimentality for sentimentality." Uris's novel represented "a disguised form of assimilation, the attempt of certain Jews to be accepted by the bourgeois, philistine gentile community on the grounds that, though they are not Christians, they are even more bourgeois and philistine." This interpretation is mistaken. *Exodus* tapped a subterranean Jewish nationalism when the path toward full assimilation seemed unobstructed, and represented a detour for countless readers. "I have received thousands of letters in the last quarter of a century telling me that *Exodus* has substantially changed their lives," Uris noted, "particularly in regard to young people finding pride in their Jewishness. Older people find similar pride in the portrait of fighting Jews in contrast to the classical characterization as weak-spined, brilliant intellects and businessmen." One sociologist found it "virtually impossible" after the 1950s to visit a home of Reform Jews without seeing a copy of *Exodus.*[50] It undoubtedly awakened pride in the fulfillment of a dream that was democratic and humane as well as nationalist.

The romance between a Sabra and a gentile nurse from Indiana (the only important American character in the novel) was in the foreground of this saga of the genesis of Israel. The love story seemed to reiterate the staples of earlier popular works, in imagining how primordial hatreds might be abolished. But *Exodus* shattered that convention when the nurse, the incarnation of the majority culture, decides to join the Jewish independence fighters. That choice broke with the assimilationist impulses that previous American Jewish fiction had registered. Kitty Fremont, who is inducted or seduced into the turmoil of Middle Eastern politics and the Zionist cause, is a surrogate for American readers. She absorbs the shocks that wrench her out of a position of innocence and is led to understand the fundamental justice of Jewish claims for survival. As a woman, she comes to accept the masculine validation of the instruments of violence and realizes that words need not be the Jews' only weapon.

Producer-director Otto Preminger adapted the forthrightly Zionist novel into a film that fully shares that political perspective. *Exodus* therefore spikes the most durable theme in U.S. films (and fiction and plays) about Jews, which is their impulse toward intermarriage. At the center of *Exodus* is a short-circuited love affair between Ari and Kitty. Intermarriage has not been an especially pressing issue among Israelis, but it bedevils the assumption that minority survival meshes with the ideals of an open society like America. How *Exodus* resolved this dilemma became a breakthrough.

Overlooking the Jezreel Valley, Kitty proclaims that "all these differences between people are made up. People are the same, no matter what they're called." But Ari disagrees: "Don't ever believe it. People are different. They have a *right* to be different. They *like* to be different. It's no good pretending differences don't exist. They do. They have to be recognized and respected." Yet Kitty nourishes the hope that, if Ari can briefly forget that he is a Jew, she will no longer feel so much a Presbyterian. "There *are* no differences," she whispers as they kiss. She later realizes, however, that he is right and thus *isn't* Mr. Right: "We *are* different." After meeting his parents at Yad El, she sees something in "the way they looked at me, the way your sister talked to me." Ari meets her halfway: "I'd feel the same way in Indiana."

But what, after all, *is* so different about Ari, especially when the thrust of *Exodus* is to equate Zionism with Americanism? Earlier films and novels exalting intermarriage had minimized the contrast between Jew and gentile in the United States. When Ari tells Kitty "I'm a Jew," the meaning of that identity, however, is not elaborated. Ari's secular Jewishness seems limited, as though he were really a Canaanite, a man of the land more than a Jew of history. Yet both the film and the novel on which it was based helped to legitimate pluralism and to honor diversity. *Exodus* contributed mightily to the visibility of Israel on the American Jewish communal agenda and helped many of Uris's and Preminger's coreligionists to live vicariously in Israel, without the inconvenience of actually having to move there and have such heroes as neighbors. Indeed, one might argue that, by strengthening Jewish feelings and enhancing ethnic pride in America, *Exodus* helped to perpetuate the Diaspora.

Especially in the decade that began in the year of the film's release, a shift in American public culture could be detected. The respect paid to the ideal of diversity permitted not only an empathy with Jewish nationalism but also the right to champion the interests of Israel vigorously. Especially after the Six Day War of 1967, support for Israel became the *sine qua non* of Jewish communal affairs and leadership, so that an agnostic or even an atheist became more acceptable as an attribute of, say, a synagogue president than an anti-Zionist. Yet even the enormous popularity of films like *Exodus* among American Jews probably did little to narrow the cultural gap between them and the Jews of Israel. (The demographic gap has been rapidly shrinking, from 10:1 right after World War II to 3:2 in 1990.) Preminger's film had failed to depict state-making as a response not only to a legacy of hate but also as the fulfillment of a people's emerging sense of its own sovereignty. Zionism was designed not only as an antidote to antisemitism but as a realization of Jewish culture and destiny. The birth of *that* nation the film scarcely showed.

ADAPTATIONS

What Hollywood did more effectively was to reinforce what America itself promised, which was a happy ending. The tragic choices presented in the Middle East could be avoided; the grim closures characteristic of the Old World could be eluded. At the funeral rites for Jolson at Temple Israel in Los Angeles, comedian George Jessel eulogized him for "a gaiety that was militant, uninhibited and unafraid. [Jolson] told the world that the Jew in America did not have to sing in sorrow," and he should be credited for "the happiest portrait that can be painted about an American of the Jewish faith." His coreligionists could easily summon sentiments of gratitude, because America was supposed to put Jewish history out of its misery. When Sigmund Freud doubted that happiness was integral to "the plan of 'Creation,' "[51] this "godless Jew" had the weight of tradition behind him. Such stoicism might be contrasted with the New World, where Jews too felt entitled to stroll "On the Sunny Side of the Street" (lyrics by Dorothy Fields, the daughter of vaudevillian Lew Fields).

In measuring the distance from an Old World patrimony, in revealing how American Jews have adapted it, and in assessing the affiliations between high and popular culture, one index might be what Barbra Streisand did to and with Isaac Bashevis Singer's "Yentl the Yeshiva Boy" (1962). *Yentl* (1983) can serve as a parable of individual ambition, of ethnic assurance, and of the female yearning for emancipation. Just as the eponymous protagonist defies the rigidity of gender roles and denies that her cherished texts prohibit study for females like herself, Streisand challenged the ideal of fidelity to the text itself: her Yentl need not be only what Singer meant her to be. The cinema differs enough from books to honor its own aesthetic and historical imperatives.

In such differences might be noted not only a clash between the Old World and the New, or between the seriousness of the literary vocation and the prerogatives of box-office stardom. How a work of fiction was transformed into *Yentl* is an instance of Jewish culture manifesting itself. That transformation is exemplary because of the disorder—of something out of joint—that Singer's story itself recounts. Like any unsettling story or folktale, "Yentl the Yeshiva Boy" entails transgression; its protagonist is so fine a student that her father liked to say to her: "Yentl—you have the soul of a man." "So why was I born a woman?" "Even Heaven makes mistakes." She is portrayed in masculine terms, with her flat chest, her narrow hips, and her upper lip even betraying "a slight down."[52] This "yeshiva boy" is entangled in a web of duplicity so that she can satisfy an illicit passion for knowledge, and, to bring that story to the screen, Streisand risked charges of betrayal to Singer's original tale—and even to the distinctive ambience from which it had sprung. Indeed, the dangers of transgression against the authority of the Judaic past seem unavoidable in a culture that has propelled itself so far from the austerity of talmudic study. The refusal to be confined—either by the religious norms a deceitful Yentl violates or by the genre in which her fate was first imagined—is one way of summarizing the individualism and experimentalism of the national ethos that so affected Jewish immigrants and their descendants.

The conclusion that Singer gave his tale is suffused with entrapment and estrangement. At Avigdor's suggestion, Hadass learns, from a messenger bearing papers, of her divorce from Anshel, who has vanished. Now free to marry her, Avigdor divorces his own wife, Peshe, to marry Hadass, igniting much gossip among the townspeople. When a son is born, "those assembled at the circumcision could scarcely believe their ears when they heard the father name his son Anshel."[53] Though "he" is in effect reborn, the transvestite herself must wander. She needs to escape detection, but she cannot get rid of her disguise (and become merely Yentl) because she remains desperate to continue her talmudic studies. Singer's ending is so bleak as to foreclose any attractive options.

"Yentl the Yeshiva Boy" is set in a shtetl called Pechev, and *Yentl* was made in Hollywood, where heroines wriggle out of traps. Streisand's Yentl crosses an ocean in an effort to separate past from present, and on the ship is back to wearing female attire. She is herself again. But "was going to America Miss Streisand's idea of a happy ending for *Yentl*?" Singer asked. Why couldn't the protagonist have found numerous other yeshivas in Lithuania or in Poland that would have harbored "Anshel"? He inquired further: "What would Yentl have done in America? Worked in a sweatshop twelve hours a day when there was no time for learning? Would she try to marry a salesman in New York, move to the Bronx or Brooklyn and rent an apartment with an ice box and dumbwaiter?"[54] For an impoverished talmudist of any gender, he suggested, the United States was no promised land.

But because movies must at least *move* their characters forward (or backward), a logic to Yentl's trajectory can be traced: from a shtetl to a larger but still obscure town, then to Lublin, and finally across the Atlantic to another continent, where at its other end a new industry would master the techniques of retelling such stories. She would have immigrated just before the moguls, who had themselves come from Eastern Europe, were elevating their medium from "such non-literary amusements as travelogue and natural-history lectures, live musical entertainment, circus performances, [and] vaudeville acts," film historian Joel Rosenberg pointed out, and were adapting literary and dramatic works to privilege narrative.[55] Nor should Streisand's ending be read as unambiguously happy. By revealing herself to Avigdor, she has, after all, lost him. Her study partner is a conformist unwilling to challenge the rigidities of gender ("This is crazy: I'm arguing with a woman"), nor can he fathom why Yentl would still need to pore over the Talmud with the other alpha males of Jewish religious culture (though he offers her a furtive syllabus). Avigdor cannot foresee that he (or halakhah) might change, nor does he consider booking passage to America as well. Yet what better place to find individual fulfillment, "to see myself, to free myself, to be myself"? The choice of the United States was neither eccentric nor senseless for a woman who seeks a wider sphere for her own piety than what the Old Country appears to offer. It was, after all, where Singer himself found refuge as well.

What is exceptionally rare about *Yentl*, however, was its portrait of an internally complete Judaic cultural and religious life. So singular an ambience did not need to define itself under the pressure of a host society. That nowhere is the word "Jew" mentioned is a sign of the classiness of *Yentl*, which is so thoroughly Jewish in its subject matter and spirit that it barely hints at an external world that serves as a source of fear or of allure. In its indifference to the larger society, Streisand's film was thus something of a breakthrough in Hollywood. Another way of suggesting the singularity of *Yentl* is to note the utter absence of the theme of intermarriage. Several other films in which she starred (from *The Way We Were* to *A Star Is Born* to *The Prince of Tides*) highlight such relationships. In *Yentl* the impediments to true romance are not barriers between Jew and gentile but, rather, the tragicomic dilemma that both Avigdor and Hadass happen to "love" a study partner and a groom who is praised for having no secrets to hide. Such a triangle is entirely internal to the community.

Yet the very presence of Yentl implicitly defies the binarism so integral to Judaism, which divides sacred from profane, the Sabbath from the rest of the week, kosher from unfit, and—ineluctably—Jew from gentile. Yentl is ensnared in the mystery of what a category is and what function it serves, and as Anshel she challenges the viability of the distinctions upon which the Judaic system was founded. When Anshel exposes herself to Avigdor and becomes Yentl, she urges him to accept who she is. "There's no book with this in it," she pleads. Though no single artifact of the American Jewish imagination can be taken for an archetype, her monosyllabic plea is a credo, a declaration of independence. *Yentl* asks not to be joined at the hip with *Short Friday and Other Stories*, and demands that a film not be judged only by its deviations from a text. Indeed, despite the intense bookishness of the East European Jewish cultures Streisand celebrates, her movie aptly portrays the fate of Yentl, who doubts that the future is foreclosed in the book of life. The belief that history itself is something still to be written constitutes a supremely American contribution to Jewish culture.

THE NOVEL AS HISTORY

Although *Yentl* announces that novelties should not be sought only in novels and short stories, literature itself has been among the supreme expressions of American Jewish culture. The work of Singer, Saul Bellow, and Joseph Brodsky was recognized in Stockholm with Nobel Prizes; another American-based Jewish writer, Elie Wiesel, won a Nobel Peace Prize as well. Because all of them were born abroad (in Poland, Canada, the Soviet Union, and Romania, respectively), they embody the cosmopolitanism (or "extraterritoriality") that is characteristic of modern Jewish expression. Singer wrote in Yiddish, Brodsky wrote at first in Russian, and Wiesel has continued to write in French. No literary critic could discern in the tales and poems of these luminaries any common themes, preoccupations, or styles; on the spectrum of Jewish concerns and knowledge, these laureates diverged as well. Such variousness suggests that the literature of Jews in the United States resists easy summation.

Nevertheless, some generalizations can be offered in the form of a conclusion to this account of American Jewish culture. It was tilted noticeably to the left. That is why novelists of Jewish origin have been almost painfully aware of the price that material success has exacted in a land of opportunity. In novels ranging from Cahan's *The Rise of David Levinsky* to Nathanael West's *A Cool Million* (1934), from Budd Schulberg's *What Makes Sammy Run?* (1941) to the Canadian

Mordecai Richler's *The Apprenticeship of Duddy Kravitz* (1957), and down to Joseph Heller's *Good as Gold* (1979) and Philip Roth's *American Pastoral* (1997), the American dream of upward mobility is shown to be tarnished with disastrous moral and social consequences. The bigger the bank account, or the longer the résumé, or the more impressive the success, the more doomed the soul, the more poignant the pursuit of loneliness. Plays like Clifford Odets's *Golden Boy* (1937) and Arthur Miller's *Death of a Salesman* (1949) and *The Price* (1968) raise doubts about that dream as well. Cahan's protagonist, a wealthy cloak-manufacturer, can at least think back to the Old World of his pious childhood, to the austere intellectual standards (but limited economic horizons) of Judaic learning. Other characters have no such baseline against which to weigh their disquietude and unhappiness. But such literature represents a gesture of resistance, from within Jewish letters, to the celebratory individualism that has permeated American society.

A moralistic strain also pulsates through much of the fiction of American Jews, who have not only exhibited an interest in the waywardness of human conduct but also expressed the hope of correcting it. In Heller's *Catch-22* (1961), the military psychiatrist knows that something is terribly wrong with protagonist John Yossarian (an Assyrian-American who was Jewish in the original draft of the novel), because: "You don't like bigots, bullies, snobs or hypocrites.... You're antagonistic to the idea of being exploited, degraded, humiliated or deceived."[56] The senseless, endless cruelty of human existence is what faces the anonymous newspaper columnist, dispensing advice to the lovelorn, in West's *Miss Lonelyhearts* (1933), for which a classic remedy is proposed at the end of Bernard Malamud's *The Tenants* (1971): "mercy." The word is recorded 100 times on the page—in addition to the Yiddish *hab rachmones*. In *The Assistant* (1957), Malamud's brooding portrayal of an embattled grocer was inspired by memories of his own father. Here the remedy offered is stoic duty, of submission to social decay without yielding a sense of integrity.

The novelist's ethics of *menschlichkeit* do not derive explicitly from Judaism; there is nothing particularistic about the fortitude of the grocer. Indeed all human beings are Jews, Malamud believed, because our species is destined to suffer. Bellow's Arthur Sammler, a Holocaust survivor, "was aware that he must meet, and he did meet—through all the confusion and degraded clowning of this life through which we are speeding—he did meet the terms of his contract."[57] The desire to reduce injustice could have political ramifications, driving Cahan to democratic socialism, Henry Roth to communism, and other writers—from Samuel Ornitz, Michael Gold, and Daniel Fuchs to Allen Ginsberg and Grace Paley—to various versions of leftist dissidence and liberalism. Neither neutrality nor moral indifference is a hallmark of American Jewish fiction. But for most of the twentieth century, the ethical criticism of life upon which Jewish writers drew rarely stemmed directly from Judaism itself.

Only recently have the literary possibilities of religion been explored, and a heritage of faith may now be the only way of sustaining the American Jewish novel in any serious way. Because it is closing time for ethnicity and for the prospects of a viable secular identity, writers who have emerged from the varieties of orthodoxy or who are haunted by spiritual dilemmas may be the only plausible successors to the Nobel laureates and Pulitzer Prize winners of a previous generation. Only the observant—or those who were once observant—constitute the pool of talent from which the keenest observers of the Jewish experience might be drawn. Chaim Potok and Cynthia Ozick pioneered the fiction of faith. But the promise of the former, shown in *The Chosen* (1967) and *My Name Is Asher Lev* (1972), has not been realized. The latter is so powerful as an essayist and polemicist that critical appreciation of fiction such as *Trust* (1966) and *The Pagan Rabbi* (1971) may have been stymied. The future of American Jewish fiction may belong to younger writers like Rebecca Goldstein, Allegra Goodman, and Nathan Englander, who have confronted the intricacies of Judaism in a way that no earlier generation could match. Whether mysticism or ritual observance can be effectively cultivated as subjects of sophisticated fiction, and whether these and other younger writers can exercise the impact that earlier Jewish authors enjoyed, remains uncertain. But it is difficult to envision any other sensibility—besides religion—that might stimulate the imagination of the Jewish novelist in America.

For most of the twentieth century, however, the energies of such art were directed elsewhere and resembled the national yearning for autonomy. Indeed, a formidable list of major works could be compiled that have limned the struggles of sons and daughters for emancipation. Such books have been declarations of independence—from the intense pressure of the nuclear family, from the starched tyranny of patriarchy, from the suffocating ambitions of mothers, from the rigidities of religious tradition, and from the demands of duty, collective destiny, Jewish history itself. The ease with which the national ethos of liberation was internalized is recorded in Yezierska's *Bread Givers,* when Sara Smolinsky defiantly tells her authoritarian father: "I'm going to live my own life. Nobody can stop me. I'm not from the old country. I'm American!"[58] She is hardly unique. "I don't care for nobody," Jake declares in *Hester Street* (1975), director Joan Micklin Silver's cinematic adaptation of Cahan's *Yekl.* With an every-man-for-himself insouciance, Jake proclaims: "I'm an American fella."

Yet individualism does not fit snugly with *k'lal yisrael,* an ideal that subordinates the promotion of self-interest to communal claims. Radical freedom does not mesh smoothly with historical Judaism, which works out a covenant between a deity and a people. Nor is the goal of self-satisfaction consistent with acceptance of the yoke of the Torah. But the yearning to breathe free animates *Call It Sleep* and *Catch-22* as well as Bellow's *Henderson the Rain King* (1959), Norman Mailer's *An American Dream* (1965), Roth's *Portnoy's Complaint* (1969), Singer's *Enemies, a Love Story* (1972), and Erica Jong's *Fear of Flying* (1973). Written by Jews, these novels all explore the possibilities of casting off restraints, of achieving personal independence, of becoming an American Adam (or Eve) unbounded by the strictures of the past and the weight of institutions. Such books transcend whatever barrier might have distinguished the particular from the national, or what is Jewish from what is American. These works therefore testify to what is intriguing, inspiring, and problematic about the culture that a tiny but creative minority has forged—without feeling itself to be in exile.

NOTES

1. Quoted in Meryle Secrest, *Being Bernard Berenson: A Biography* (New York, 1979), 57, 358, 395.

2. Quoted in Leslie A. Fiedler, *To the Gentiles* (New York, 1972), 71.

3. Alexis de Tocqueville, *Selected Letters on Politics and Society,* ed. Roger Boesche, trans. James Toupin and Roger Boesche (Berkeley, 1985), 38.

4. Harold Rosenberg, *Discovering the Present: Three Decades in Art, Culture, and Politics* (Chicago, 1973), 227, 230.

5. "Analyzing Jewish Comics," *Time,* Oct. 2, 1978, p. 76.

6. Quoted in Alfred Kazin, "Introduction: The Jew as Modern American Writer," in Norman Podhoretz, ed., *The Commentary Reader* (New York, 1967), xv.

7. Quoted in Emma Felsenthal, *Bernhard Felsenthal: Teacher in Israel* (New York, 1924), 19, and in Rudolf Glanz, *Studies in Judaica Americana* (New York, 1970), 230, 232.

8. Quoted in Bryan Cheyette, "Englishness and Extraterritoriality: British-Jewish Writing and Diaspora Culture," in Ezra Mendelsohn, ed., *Studies in Contemporary Jewry* (New York, 1996), xii, 23.

9. Quoted in Werner Sollors, *Beyond Ethnicity: Consent and Descent in American Culture* (New York, 1986), 75, 95; see also Hiram Wesley Evans, "The Klan's Fight for Americanism," in Loren Baritz, ed., *The Culture of the Twenties* (Indianapolis, 1970), 106–7.

10. Horace M. Kallen, *Culture and Democracy in the United States* (1924; reprint, New Brunswick, N.J., 1998), 116–17.

11. Abraham Cahan, *Yekl and the Imported Bridegroom and Other Stories of the New York Ghetto* (1896; reprint, New York, 1970), 41, 49–50.

12. Quoted in J. Hoberman, *Bridge of Light: Yiddish Film Between Two Worlds* (New York, 1991), 65.

13. David Remnick, *The Devil Problem and Other True Stories* (New York, 1996), 358–61.

14. Quoted in Hana Wirth-Nesher, ed., "Introduction" to *New Essays on* Call It Sleep (New York: Cambridge University Press, 1996), 2; Richard J. Fein, ed. and trans., *Selected Poems of Yankev Glatshteyn* (Philadelphia, 1987), 101, 103.

15. Philip Roth, *Portnoy's Complaint* (New York, 1969), 224; Henry James, *The Question of Our Speech and the Lesson of Balzac* (Boston, 1905), 42, 43.

16. Larry Gelbart in "Books That Influenced Me," *New York Times Book Review,* Dec. 7, 1986, p. 46; Jules Feiffer, "The Minsk Theory of Krypton: Jerry Siegel (1914–1996)," *New York Times Magazine,* Dec. 29, 1996, pp. 14–15.

17. Sollors, *Beyond Ethnicity,* 100.

18. Quoted in Marvin Caplan, "The Curious History of 'Bei Mir Bist Du Schön,' " *American Jewish Congress Monthly* 62 (Jan.–Feb. 1995): 13–16; Sammy Cahn, *I Should Care: The Sammy Cahn Story* (New York, 1974), 63–71; " 'Bei Mir' Now Leads Best-Selling Songs," *Life,* Jan. 31, 1938, p. 39.

19. Quoted in Alan Silverstein, *Alternatives to Assimilation: The Response of Reform Judaism to American Culture, 1840–1930* (Hanover, N.H., 1994), 2.

20. Nathan Glazer, *American Judaism* (Chicago, 1957), 9.

21. Sidney Goldstein, "Profile of American Jewry: Insights from the 1990 National Jewish Population Survey," in David Singer, ed., *American Jewish Year Book* (Philadelphia, 1992), 89–90; Steven M. Cohen, "Jewish Continuity over Judaic Content: The Moderately Affiliated American Jew," in Robert M. Seltzer and Norman J. Cohen, eds., *The Americanization of the Jews* (New York, 1995), 397, 408.

22. Marshall Sklare and Joseph Greenblum, *Jewish Identity on the Suburban Frontier: A Study of Group Survival in the Open Society,* 2d ed. (Chicago, 1979), 322–24; Charles S. Liebman and Steven M. Cohen, *Two Worlds of Judaism: The Israeli and American Experiences* (New Haven, Conn., 1990), 97, 103, 112.

23. Rachel Wischnitzer, *Synagogue Architecture in the United States: History and Interpretation* (Philadelphia, 1955), 136–39, 148–52, 159.

24. Gary Tinterow, "Post World War II Synagogue Architecture," in *Two Hundred Years of American Synagogue Architecture* (Waltham, Mass., 1976), 34; Lewis Mumford, "Towards a Modern Synagog Architecture," *Menorah Journal* 11 (June 1925): 225.

25. Hayim Greenberg, *The Inner Eye: Selected Essays,* vol. 1 (New York, 1953), 5, 7, 17, and *The Inner Eye: Selected Essays,* vol. 2, ed. Shlomo Katz (New York, 1964), 56; Leonard Fein, "A Matter of Distinction," *Forward,* Oct. 10, 1997, p. 7.

26. Arnold M. Eisen, *The Chosen People in America: A Study in Jewish Religious Ideology* (Bloomington, Ind. 1983), 9, 13, 21, 62, 66, 97.

27. Mordecai M. Kaplan, *Judaism as a Civilization: Toward a Reconstruction of American-Jewish Life* (New York, 1934), 43.

28. Quoted in Pamela S. Nadell, " 'Top Down' or 'Bottom Up': Two Movements for Women's Rabbinic Ordination," in Jeffrey S. Gurock and Marc Lee Raphael, eds., *An Inventory of Promises: Essays on American Jewish History in Honor of Moses Rischin* (Brooklyn, 1995), 198.

29. Quoted in Mark Slobin, *Tenement Songs: The Popular Music of the Jewish Immigrants* (Urbana, Ill. 1982), 129, 131–32; Anzia Yezierska, *Bread Givers* (1925; reprint, New York, 1975), 205, 207.

30. Mordecai M. Kaplan, *The Future of the American Jew* (New York, 1948), 402.

31. Sylvia Barack Fishman, *A Breath of Life: Feminism in the American Jewish Community* (New York, 1993), 130, 131, 153.

32. Haskel Lookstein, "Joseph: The Master of His Dreams," in Leo Landman, ed., *Rabbi Joseph H. Lookstein Memorial Volume* (New York, 1980), 16–17.

33. Quoted in Susannah Heschel, ed., Introduction to *On Being a Jewish Feminist* (New York, 1995), 117–18.

34. Quoted in Mark Hodin, "Class, Consumption, and Ethnic Performance in Vaudeville," in Jack Salzman, ed., *Prospects*, vol. 22 (New York, 1997), 202, and in James Gleick, *Genius: The Life and Science of Richard Feynman* (New York, 1992), 97, 410, 411; Abbie Hoffman, *Soon To Be a Major Motion Picture* (New York, 1980), 166, 281.

35. "Letter to *The Day*," Nov. 11, 1915, in Irving Howe and Kenneth Libo, *How We Lived: A Documentary History of Immigrant Jews in America* (New York, 1979), 246.

36. Ann Douglas, *Terrible Honesty: Mongrel Manhattan in the 1920s* (New York, 1995), 358.

37. Quoted in Laurence Bergreen, *As Thousands Cheer: The Life of Irving Berlin* (New York, 1990), 69, 70.

38. Ronald Sanders, "The American Popular Song," in Douglas Villiers, ed., *Next Year in Jerusalem: Portraits of the Jew in the Twentieth Century* (New York, 1976), 202.

39. Samson Raphaelson, preface to *The Jazz Singer* (New York, 1925), 9–10.

40. Quoted in Albert Lee, *Henry Ford and the Jews* (New York, 1980), 29, and in Kenneth Aaron Kanter, *The Jews on Tin Pan Alley: The Jewish Contribution to American Popular Music, 1830–1940* (New York, 1982), 23.

41. Quoted in Robert L. Carringer, ed., introduction to *The Jazz Singer* (Madison, Wisc., 1979), 11, and in Hasia R. Diner, *In the Almost Promised Land: American Jews and Blacks, 1915–1935* (Westport, Conn., 1977), 68–69.

42. Gilbert Seldes, *The Seven Lively Arts*, rev. ed. (New York, 1957), 175–76, 178–79.

43. Wilfrid Mellers, "An American in New York," *New Republic*, June 14, 1993, pp. 44, 45, 46, 48, 49; Virgil Thomson, *A Virgil Thomson Reader* (Boston, 1981), 24, 27.

44. Quoted in James Lincoln Collier, *Duke Ellington* (New York, 1997), 68–69.

45. Quoted in Michael Kammen, *The Lively Arts: Gilbert Seldes and the Transformation of Cultural Criticism in the United States* (New York, 1996), 203, and in Diner, *In the Almost Promised Land*, 59.

46. Quoted in Martin Bauml Duberman, *Paul Robeson* (New York, 1988), 353.

47. Quoted in Martha Duffy, "West Side Glory," *Time,* May 29, 1995, pp. 64–65; Leonard Bernstein, *Findings* (New York, 1982), 144.

48. Glazer, *American Judaism,* 114, 115.

49. Quoted in Edwin McDowell, "*Exodus* in Samizdat: Still Popular and Still Subversive," *New York Times Book Review,* Apr. 26, 1987, p. 13.

50. Leslie A. Fiedler, *Waiting for the End* (New York, 1964), 91; Leon Uris to author, Apr. 16, 1985; Norman Mirsky, "Nathan Glazer's *American Judaism* After 30 Years: A Reform Opinion," *American Jewish History* 77 (Dec. 1987): 237.

51. Quoted in Herbert G. Goldman, *Jolson: The Legend Comes to Life* (New York, 1988), 301–2, and in Sigmund Freud, *Civilization and Its Discontents,* trans. and ed. James Strachey (New York, 1962), 23.

52. Isaac Bashevis Singer, "Yentl the Yeshiva Boy," trans. Marion Magid and Elizabeth Pollet, in *The Collected Stories of Isaac Bashevis Singer* (New York, 1982), 149.

53. Singer, "Yentl the Yeshiva Boy," 159–60, 169.

54. "I. B. Singer Talks to I. B. Singer About the Movie 'Yentl,' " *New York Times,* Jan. 29, 1984, sec. II, p. 1.

55. Joel Rosenberg, "Jewish Experience on Film: An American Overview," in David Singer, ed., *American Jewish Year Book* (Philadelphia, 1996), 11.

56. Joseph Heller, *Catch-22* (New York, 1961), 297.

57. Saul Bellow, *Mr. Sammler's Planet* (New York, 1970), 313.

58. Yezierska, *Bread Givers,* 138.

SELECTED BIBLIOGRAPHY

"American Jewish History and Culture in the Twentieth Century," *Jewish Social Studies* 5, nos. 1–2 (Fall 1998/Winter 1999).

Antler, Joyce. *The Journey Home: Jewish Women and the American Century.* New York, 1997.

Biale, David, Michael Galchinsky, and Susannah Heschel, eds. *Insider/Outsider: American Jews and Multiculturalism.* Berkeley, 1998.

Cassedy, Steven. *To the Other Shore: The Russian Jewish Intellectuals Who Came to America.* Princeton, N.J., 1997.

Cohen, Sarah Blacher, ed. *Jewish Wry: Essays on Jewish Humor.* Bloomington, Ind., 1987.

Diner, Hasia R. *Lower East Side Memories: A Jewish Place in America.* Princeton, N.J., 2000.

Doneson, Judith E. *The Holocaust in American Film.* Philadelphia, 1998.

Eisen, Arnold M. *The Chosen People in America: A Study in Jewish Religious Ideology.* Bloomington, Ind., 1983.

Erens, Patricia. *The Jew in American Cinema.* Bloomington, Ind., 1984.

Fischel, Jack, and Sanford Pinsker, eds. *Jewish-American History and Culture: An Encyclopedia.* New York, 1992.

Fishman, Sylvia Barack. *A Breath of Life: Feminism in the American Jewish Community.* New York, 1993.

Glazer, Nathan. *American Judaism.* Chicago, 1974.

Goren, Arthur A. *The Politics and Public Culture of American Jews.* Bloomington, Ind., 1999.

Gurock, Jeffrey S. *American Jewish Orthodoxy in Historical Perspective.* New York, 1996.

Hoberman, J. *Bridge of Light: Yiddish Film Between Two Worlds.* New York, 1991.

Howe, Irving, with Kenneth Libo. *World of Our Fathers.* New York, 1976.

Kessner, Carole S., ed. *The "Other" New York Jewish Intellectuals.* New York, 1994.

Klingenstein, Susanne. *Enlarging America: The Cultural Work of Jewish Literary Scholars, 1930–1990.* Syracuse, N.Y., 1998.

Linenthal, Edward T. *Preserving Memory: The Struggle to Create America's Holocaust Museum.* New York, 1995.

Novick, Peter. *The Holocaust in American Life.* New York, 1999.

Rosten, Leo. *The Joys of Yiddish.* New York, 1968.

Sarna, Jonathan D. *JPS: The Americanization of Jewish Culture, 1888–1988.* Philadelphia, 1989.

————, ed. *The American Jewish Experience.* New York, 1986.

Schwartz, Shuly Rubin. *The Emergence of Jewish Scholarship in America: The Publication of "The Jewish Encyclopedia."* Cincinnati, 1991.

Seltzer, Robert M., and Norman J. Cohen, eds. *The Americanization of the Jews.* New York, 1995.

Shechner, Mark. *After the Revolution: Studies in the Contemporary Jewish-American Imagination.* Bloomington, Ind., 1987.

Walden, Daniel, ed. *Twentieth-Century American-Jewish Fiction Writers.* Vol. 28 of *Dictionary of Literary Biography.* Detroit, 1984.

Whitfield, Stephen J. *In Search of American Jewish Culture.* Hanover, N.H., 1999.

CONCLUSION

DAVID BIALE

In the chapter on the Bible with which this cultural history began its first volume, Ilana Pardes portrayed the first Jews imagining their formative years as a collective biography:

> The nation—particularly in Exodus and Numbers—is not an abstract detached concept but rather a grand character with a distinct voice (represented at times in a singular mode), who moans and groans, is euphoric at times, complains frequently, and rebels against Moses and God time and again. Israel has a life story, a biography of sorts. It was conceived in the days of Abraham; its miraculous birth took place with the Exodus, the parting of the Red Sea; then came a long period of childhood and restless adolescence in the wilderness, and finally adulthood was approached with the conquest of Canaan.

How can this model help us conclude our journey through three millennia of Jewish cultures? At its very origins, the nation is not heroically united but rent with divisions and doubts. It moves from the primordial Exile in Egypt to the Promised Land, but the threat of future exiles hangs over it like an inescapable shadow. It wishes to establish its own individuated identity, but the fleshpots of Egypt beckon it back while the gods of Canaan lie in wait ahead.

So, too, in all the varieties of Jewish culture we have visited, diversity and interaction have been as much the rule as unity and isolation. At times, the narrative that the Jews tell about themselves speaks of "a nation dwelling alone and not counted among the other nations," as we remember from the prophecy of Balaam. But the story also contains fissures and factions, as well as bold crossings of borders.

The biblical narrative supplies all of the elements of later Jewish history—homeland and exile, fidelity and betrayal, divine revelation and the eclipse of God—but the one thing it does not provide is finality. To paraphrase the nineteenth-century philosopher of Jewish history, Nahman Krochmal, the nation goes through a natural cycle of birth, maturation, and old age—only to be born again and repeat the cycle. Every age of Jewish history may be seen as a collective biography.

Where, we might ask, is the present moment in the collective biography of the Jews in the cycle of life? Before attempting to answer this question, we must take note of how this volume has ended: with American Jewish culture. The contributors to this work debated long and hard about whether the final chapter should be on the State of Israel or the largest contemporary Diaspora community. Each suggests a certain goal, as if all that has preceded must point ideologically toward the final chapter. And, yet, we intend no such teleology, for we start with the assumption, as Stephen Whitfield says, that the future remains to be written. Rather than try to defend the particular way this history ends—and, of course, it had to end with one or the other—it may be more fruitful to think about these two largest communities as siblings in the collective family history of the Jews.

A century ago, the largest centers of Jewish culture lay in Europe, both East and West. Numerically, the Jewish communities of North Africa, of the Middle East, and of North America were relatively small and peripheral. Even farther to the periphery were the much smaller communities in South and Central America, Ethiopia, India, and China. Over the course of the past hundred years, the demography of the Jewish people has undergone a radical change and, with it, so has Jewish culture. The tiny community of Ottoman Palestine is now the State of Israel, which, demographers tell us, may soon contain the plurality of the world's Jews. The North American Jewish community, which had already begun to swell with immigrants in the year 1900, has probably reached its peak population, with demographers predicting a slow but steady decline, because of intermarriage and low fertility, in the decades ahead. Meanwhile, the great population centers in Europe, particularly in the East, were decimated by emigration and the Holocaust. A much reduced (though by no means dead) Jewish community exists in the former Soviet Union, as it does in other European countries, numbering altogether around one and a half million. Little is left of the Jewish communities in North Africa or the Middle East, with the exception of the State of Israel, just as little is left of the much smaller Indian or Ethiopian diasporas. Only in South Africa, Australia, Argentina, and Brazil do populations of 100,000 or more remain, but all are declining.

Our concern here is not with numbers, but with culture. After all, the tiny Ashkenazic communities of France and the Rhineland in the High Middle Ages rarely contained more than a few thousand souls and yet produced a powerful culture whose echoes still resonate today. The current demographic decline of the North American Jewish community comes at a time of cultural innovation and vitality, and we should be cautious about correlating one with the other. Is this community in its cultural adolescence or senescence? Its origins lie in the same mass migration out of Eastern Europe that also fed the Zionist settlement in the Land of Israel. In terms of the length of Jewish history, a century is culturally a very short time. Both Israel and the United States are young cultures that are still undergoing rapid changes. World-wide trends, such as feminism, and new media, such as film, have had enormous impacts on both cultures. The globalization of culture is likely to create both the greatest challenge and greatest stimulation to each of these communities.

Because the process of Jewish immigration is not yet complete for either Israel or America, cultural change may also come about from new immigrants. Although the dominant culture in Israel is in the Hebrew language, itself growing and changing with the rapidity of youth, there is now a flourishing Russian Jewish subculture there, with newspapers, books, theater, radio, and television all in the language of Israel's most recent immigrants. Whether this culture will have any more lasting power than did Yiddish culture in America (or, for that matter, in Israel itself) remains unknown. But even if it is ultimately translated into Hebrew, this immigrant culture will no doubt have an enormous impact on Israeli culture as a whole. Similarly, a vigorous Israeli subculture exists within—or beside—American Jewish culture, especially in New York, Los Angeles, and the Silicon Valley of the San Francisco Bay Area. Here, too, it remains to be seen what impact this subculture will have on American Jewish culture as a whole, which has always been a composite of many Jewish immigrations.

Indeed, from its earliest origins, the history of the Jews has been one of migrations, and Jewish culture has always been the product of the intense interactions with the new cultures in which the Jews found themselves. In this sense, Jewish culture has always evolved on a global stage, whether that of the empires of the ancient Near East, the Greco-Roman Mediterranean, or the later worlds of Islam and Christianity. Jewish culture itself frequently had a global reach as well: rabbis moved back and forth from Babylonia and Palestine; medieval legal authorities from France ventured into Spain; Polish rabbis wrote commentaries on Joseph Karo's Sephardic law code, written in Safed; and, on the level of popular religion, Jewish women and men shared similar customs in Yemen, Kurdistan, and Germany.

Jewish culture at the present moment has something of this global quality, but, with the transformations of modernity, it lacks the unifying force of rabbinic authority and a shared popular culture that characterized it for much of the past millennium and a half. Even if the authoritative Babylonian Talmud was modified by custom in many communities, or even rejected by a group like the Karaites, most Jews followed practices that were recognizable throughout most of the Jewish world. Today, Jewish culture bears a greater resemblance to the

Greco-Roman period of factionalism and competing claims of authority before the ascendancy of the rabbis. Then, too, a global culture called Hellenism laid claim as the "universal" culture against the "parochial" claims of ancestral Jewish custom. Then, too, Jerusalem was the religious and political center of a widely scattered Diaspora that recognized its centrality but also felt at home in foreign lands.

That world underwent a great crisis with the destruction of the Temple and, some centuries later, with the decline of the political and religious institutions of Palestine. Today, the situation is reversed in some ways, with the State of Israel ascendant as a center of Jewish culture. The great crises of this age are not the destruction of the Temple but the Holocaust that eradicated the cultures of Jewish Europe and, more broadly, the cultural pluralism ushered in by modernity. We stand at the threshold of an entirely new era, just as did the generations after the destruction of the Second Temple.

But one might go even further back for a historical analogy to the present moment: to the period of the Bible itself, not so much the Bible as it was finally edited and canonized but, rather, the many conflicting cultural threads from which it was woven. The formative years of ancient Israel were a period of extraordinary ferment in which those who would become Jews struggled to draw the ethnic and religious boundaries between themselves and their Canaanite, Egyptian, and Mesopotamian neighbors. A certain "orthodoxy" emerged at the end of this process and put its seal on the sources that recorded this struggle, but it is the cacophony of voices preserved in the Bible—the complaints of the people vs. the admonitions of Moses—that most resembles the state of Jewish culture today. There is, of course, a world of difference between the modern age and the ancient, but the problems of Jewish identity remain startlingly similar.

The Bible, like Homer's *Iliad* and Virgil's *Aeneid,* was an ancient attempt to imagine the origins of the nation. It is the foundational text on which all later Jewish culture—a culture quintessentially of commentary—was built. Jewish culture today is perhaps less closely tied to the biblical text as its source, but in one sense it is not entirely divorced from its predecessors. If the Bible is read not as one voice speaking but as many, so, too, all the cultures of the Jews described in these volumes represent many voices, responding, in myriad ways, to both text and context, each seeking to integrate a historical tradition with a specific cultural environment. Perhaps all these disparate voices from three millennia, assembled together under this literary roof, constitute the collective biography of Israel.

INDEX

Page numbers in *italics* refer to illustration captions.

ABOUT THE EDITOR

David Biale is the Emmanuel Ringelblum Professor of Jewish History at the University of California, Davis. He is the author of *Power and Powerlessness in Jewish History* and the editor of *Insider/Outsider: American Jews and Multiculturalism*. He lives in Berkeley, California.